THE *Wars* OF *Afghanistan*

MESSIANIC TERRORISM, TRIBAL CONFLICTS, AND THE FAILURES OF GREAT POWERS

Peter Tomsen

PUBLICAFFAIRS

New York

Text set in 11.5 point Arno Pro

The Library of Congress has cataloged the hardcover as follows:
Tomsen, Peter, 1940-
  The wars of Afghanistan : messianic terrorism, tribal conflicts, and the failures of
great powers / Peter Tomsen. — 1st ed.
    p. cm.
  Includes bibliographical references and index.
  ISBN 978-1-58648-763-8 (hardcover : alk. paper) — ISBN 978-1-58648-781-2
(e-book) 1. Afghanistan—Politics and government. 2. Afghanistan—History.
3. Afghanistan—History, Military. 4. Terrorism—Afghanistan. 5. Messianism—
Afghanistan. 6. Islam and politics—Afghanistan. 7. Tribes—Afghanistan. 8. Social
conflict—Afghanistan. 9. Great powers. 10. Afghanistan—Foreign relations.
I. Title.
  DS357.5.T66 2011
  958.1—dc22
                          2010053194

ISBN 978-1-61039-262-4 (paperback)
ISBN 978-1-61039-412-2 (paperback edition e-book)

LSC-H

10 9 8 7 6 5 4 3 2

Praise for *The Wars of Afghanistan*

"Accolades like 'magisterial,' 'definitive,' and 'vital' should be reserved for rare books like Peter Tomsen's *The Wars of Afghanistan*. Few Americans are as knowledgeable about that tormented land's past; none have been more savvy or prescient about its unrolling future. Tomsen's compelling narrative draws upon meticulous scholarship and virgin archives, personal frontline engagement, and close ties with major players. This multilayered volume melds sweeping history, cultural painting, political analysis, governmental battles, dramatic action, and provocative prescriptions. *The Wars of Afghanistan* is bound to have urgent impact and enduring resonance."

—Winston Lord, former U.S. ambassador to China and former president of the Council on Foreign Relations

"For those seeking to understand the origins of the west's entanglement in Afghanistan, Peter Tomsen's *The Wars of Afghanistan* offers deeper historical context. . . . [Tomsen focuses] presciently on the fast-deteriorating relationship between Washington and Islamabad. He argues plausibly that the U.S. has been hoodwinked by Pakistan, which has long used Afghanistan as a means of creating 'strategic depth' against India and fomenting jihad against the west."

—*Financial Times*

"[Tomsen] draws extensively on his own contemporary dispatches to show that, throughout his long association with the region, he repeatedly and vainly warned successive administrations about the follies of their policies—or lack of them."

—*Sunday Times*

"Excellent. . . . Tomsen knows the country, its culture, and the last thirty years of U.S. history there, inside and out."

Best Nonfiction of 2011

—*National Review Online*

"This weighty narrative . . . will be a major source for Afghan studies."

—*Library Journal*

"It is also difficult to imagine a more impeccably informed author than Peter Tomsen . . . now retired from the State Department (he has kept a close eye on the region ever since), and . . . [he] has produced a magnum opus. . . . The drug trade in Afghanistan is probably worth a billion or two billion dollars a year. . . . *The Wars of Afghanistan* is an important work and an urgent warning. Anyone with an interest [in] U.S. foreign policy in the region needs to read it, starting with our policymakers." —*Drug War Chronicle*

"Peter Tomsen, a former U.S. envoy to 'the Afghan resistance' from 1989 to 1992, reminds us in his sweeping history that the CIA has a miserable record in understanding the politics of the region. *The Wars of Afghanistan* is rich with details about his interactions with key players during this critical period. After the Soviet withdrawal, the United States continued to oppose compromise with the last Afghan communist ruler, Mohammad Najibullah, and to arm the mujahideen, including figures who are now fighting Americans. Drawing on these lessons, Tomsen persuasively calls for wresting policy-making away from the Pentagon and spy agencies, and advocates U.N. mediation of an Afghan peace process."

—*San Francisco Chronicle*, Best Books of 2011

"U.S. policy toward Afghanistan needs more careful calibration than the all-in/all-out policy schizophrenia of the last three decades. To be consistent and successful, our policy makers and practitioners in Afghanistan must be aware of the intense and often tragic history of our relations with that country. Ambassador Tomsen's book provides an admirable service toward that end."

—AmericanDiplomacy.org

"Through failure to understand past mistakes and a dangerous misreading of the nature of the tribal environment, Tomsen argues, American strategists have facilitated the Taliban's resurgence. *The Wars of Afghanistan* offers fresh, provocative solutions to shoring up the Afghan state, dealing with Pakistan's intrigue and duplicity, and returning a measure of stability and peace to this persistently chaotic region. This truly epic insider's account of modern Afghanistan is indispensable reading for anyone wanting to understand one of America's toughest foreign policy conundrums." —*The Foreign Service Journal*

"A fascinating tome." —*Philadelphia Inquirer*

"[A]dmirably sound." —*Times Literary Supplement*

"The reader will come away with a greater understanding of a land many of us knew little about, but in which we've had a military presence since 2002."

—Bookideas.com

Dedicated to my amazing wife, Kim

CONTENTS

PART I

TRIBAL INCUBATOR

PART II

FISSION

PART III

MISSION TO THE MUJAHIDIN

PART IV

AMERICA AND AFGHANISTAN

Photo insert is located between pages 420 and 421

To view online bibliography for this book,
  go to www.publicaffairsbooks.com/tomsen.pdf

MAPS

INTRODUCTION

America and its allies are mired in Afghanistan's endless war. It is still possible to achieve an acceptable outcome, but only if our policies respect Afghan history and culture and we heed the lessons of past foreign interventions.

That is why I wrote this book.

My motive sprang from concerns for our national interests and the desire of Afghans, Americans, and the broad international community to break the cycle of tragic wars in Afghanistan.

I have been personally involved in Afghan affairs for over two decades, including three years as U.S. special envoy to the Afghan resistance (1989–1992). This book reflects my firsthand experiences as well as my interviews of other eyewitnesses. It also draws upon the works of scholars, historians, journalists, and diplomats. It plows new ground in over six hundred newly declassified State Department, Pentagon, and CIA documents. It traces the sagas of the major actors since the 1979 Soviet invasion, many of whom I have known well. Where possible, I have presented documentary evidence and references to back up explanations and conclusions. The opinions and characterizations in this book, however, are my own and do not represent official positions of the United States government. Spaces marked "redacted" indicate the removal of words the United States government considers classified.

☙

There has been an explosion of documentaries and commentary on Afghanistan since 9/11. But a pervasive ignorance about this unique country and its history, culture, and tribal society persists in the West. Our misreading of the Afghan environment and Pakistan's intentions in Afghanistan are the main reasons why

America and the international coalition are today bogged down in the Afghan quagmire, wondering how this has happened despite the commitment of over 100,000 troops and $330 billion. If the United States does not change its policies, conditions in Afghanistan will look even worse in 2014 when the American-led combat troop drawdown is tentatively scheduled to end and the next constitutionally mandated Afghan presidential election is to take place.

U.S. policy during the 1980–1989 Soviet-Afghan war succeeded largely because it resonated with the mainstream aspirations of more than 20 million Afghans to expel the invader. After the Soviet pullout, the United States gradually shifted its attention away from Afghanistan and the region. Washington did not grasp the dangerous implications of Pakistani and Saudi strategy to transform Afghanistan into an extremist Islamic state. That Islamist vision, developed by Pakistani President Zia ul-Haq in the 1980s and carried on ever since by his military successors, contradicts fundamental U.S. interests. It has stymied efforts to end the wars of Afghanistan and combat global terrorism.

After 9/11 Pakistani President Pervez Musharraf formally joined President George W. Bush's war on terrorism. But on the ground, Pakistan clandestinely continued to provide sanctuary, training, and weapons to the Afghan Taliban and other Islamic militants to stage a counterattack into Afghanistan. The United States, after routing the Taliban, once again downplayed Afghanistan. Washington provided minimal assistance to war-devastated Kabul and redirected attention and resources to Iraq. The result was a Taliban resurgence.

Today bin Laden is gone, but al-Qaeda and its allies still view Afghanistan as the major arena—and the first step—in an epochal, twenty-first-century struggle between their extremist version of Islam and moderate Islam. Their strategy targets not only Afghanistan but also the West and pro-Western governments in the Muslim world. Their suicide bombers attack around the globe. Some indigenous Pakistani Muslim extremist groups tied to al-Qaeda have turned on the Pakistani state. Meanwhile, many Afghan leaders have failed to overcome their historical proclivity for infighting and placing personal aspirations above unity and stability in their country. Corruption pervades the government. President Hamid Karzai's regime is weak and unpopular.

We have suffered not only from poor policy but also from poor process and execution. Unwieldy, compartmentalized bureaucracies in Washington have failed successive Republican and Democratic presidents. As the 9/11 Commission noted in 2004, the current national security system was created after World War II to meet the challenges of a "different era" and to confront a "different enemy"—the Soviet Union. In the past decade it has been weighed down by vast numbers of employees and splintered by bureaucratic stovepipes. Giant military and intelligence institutions operate like mini-governments, administering their own budgets and sometimes contradictory policies.

The George W. Bush and Barack Obama administrations adopted some of the 9/11 Commission recommendations to improve interagency cooperation toward common goals. But they have not overcome debilitating interagency turf battles. The White House has yet to enforce disciplined implementation of a coherent Afghan policy, even while American men and women are fighting with valor and skill on the battlefield. The Pentagon and the CIA must function as policy-implementers, not policy-makers. They are indispensable to winning wars. They should participate in the deliberation process. But after decisions are made, their military and intelligence assets should concentrate on executing the policy.

ψ

The opening chapters of this book describe the historical forces that have forged contemporary Afghanistan, its tribal system, its traditions, and a moderate Islamic faith. They discuss the ethnic and tribal frictions that divide Afghans, and they explain the center-region equilibrium that mid-twentieth-century Afghan monarchs created to maintain stability and promote nation-building. During that half-century, the government in Kabul established a cooperative relationship with autonomous tribal and religious forces in the countryside. The center gradually extended its influence into the provinces and expanded the national army and police force. That structure holds the key to stabilizing the country today.

Part Two covers the wars of Afghanistan during the thirteen-year Afghan communist era, drawing on fresh material from the Soviet archives. The last chapter in this part describes Pakistani dictator Zia ul-Haq's vision to establish strategic depth against India by creating Pakistani hegemony in Afghanistan after the Soviet withdrawal. Since Zia's death in 1988, his successors have collaborated with Pakistani and Arab extremists to insert foreign versions of Islamic extremism into Afghanistan's fundamentally moderate tribal society. The Saudi government supported this futile venture during the 1980s and early 1990s, but then turned against the extremists when al-Qaeda began to threaten the Saudi kingdom in 1998.

Part Three shifts to a first-person narrative account of my three-year immersion in Afghanistan as President George H.W. Bush's special envoy to the Afghan resistance. I draw on declassified U.S. government documents to describe what happened during those pivotal years. There are firsthand accounts of my meetings with Mujahidin politicians and commanders, the former Afghan king Zahir Shah in Rome, Pakistani intelligence officers and other Pakistani officials in Islamabad, Saudi princes in Riyadh and Jeddah, and Soviet officials in Moscow.

Part Four examines the Pakistani Army's persisting strategy to mobilize radical Islamic fury against the Afghan government and the U.S.-led coalition inside Afghanistan. In its pursuit of this goal, Pakistan covertly fosters Islamic extremist groups that stage terrorist attacks against America and its friends and allies. The splendid American military-intelligence operation to kill bin Laden on May 1, 2011, in Abbottabad, yanked the veil from the Saudi terrorist's government-protected sanctuary in Pakistan. It exposed Islamabad's duplicitous denials that the world's most wanted terrorist was not in Pakistan. The killing of bin Laden reinforced important themes in this book—the epicenter of world terrorism is in Pakistan, not Afghanistan; the terrorist sanctuaries in Pakistan are breeding grounds for terrorists targeting many nations around the world, Muslim and non-Muslim; and Pakistan's genuine cooperation in the struggle against terrorism is essential to achieving success.

Bin Laden's death delivered a major blow to al-Qaeda's diverse terrorist network. It projected American power, competence, leadership, and determination. It lifted the morale of Americans and many others around the world. But it was not a decisive blow. The al-Qaeda ideology did not die with bin Laden, nor has it changed. Like the Cold War, the struggle against radical Islamist terrorism will be a multi-decade one.

At the end of Part Four, I propose a new direction, a way ahead, to end the wars of Afghanistan. The prescriptions will require great finesse and political will to succeed, especially in convincing Islamabad to change course. Will they need adjustments as developments unfold? Of course. Will they guarantee success in the next decade? No. But if we do not draw the appropriate conclusions from Afghan history and from the tragic consequences of foreign interventions in the Afghan cauldron, then we can guarantee failure.

The essence of this book is how history has shaped the current impasse. My hope is that the reader's journey through the wars of Afghanistan will inform the national debate on the way ahead. I believe that an enlightened path, over time, can yield the results we seek—to bolster our national security; to redeem the sacrifices of Americans, allies, and Afghans; and to lift the horizons of a region deeply scarred by conflict.

It is time to turn the page.

NOTE ABOUT TRANSLITERATION

Wherever possible, when there are different renditions of English, Afghan Dari, Pashto, Urdu, Arabic, Persian, and Russian names, I have used two rules to spell a word: (1) simplicity and (2) English phonetics. In instances where there are conflicts in the traditional spelling of names in the Latin alphabet— for example, between "Muslim" and "Muslem" or "Moslem"—I have chosen the more standard form, "Muslim." Where there are different versions of names of persons, I have attempted to use the spelling the individual uses, for example "Mahmoud" Baryalai rather than "Mahmud" or "Mahmood." The same applies to group names. For place names I have chosen the versions most often used in English—Yemen instead of Yaman, Medina instead of Medinah, Kabul instead of Kabool, and Panshir instead of Panjsheer. For simplification's sake, I have omitted the patronymic middle names commonly used by Russians and Ukrainians. When quoting statements, I have used a uniform transliteration of names, places, and organizations throughout this book.

CAST OF CHARACTERS

EARLY HISTORY

Alexander the Great: The fourth-century B.C. Macedonian conqueror who established an empire stretching from Greece to the Pamirs, introducing Hellenistic culture in the territory of present-day Afghanistan.

General Surena: The Parthian military leader whose 10,000 horse archers in 53 B.C. annihilated a 35,000-strong Roman army under Crassus at the Battle of Carrhae. Crassus was moving east through Mesopotamia, seeking to extend Rome's hegemony to the lands conquered by Alexander the Great two centuries earlier.

Abu Hanifa: The ninth-century founder of the first, most moderate, and most widespread (including in Afghanistan) of the four great orders of Islamic jurisprudence. Afghans believe Abu Hanifa's family originally came from Charikar.

Rumi: Afghans also claim the great thirteenth-century Sufi poet Jalaluddin Rumi, who was born in Balkh. He spent most of his life in Turkey preaching, writing, and meditating.

IN AFGHANISTAN

Ahmad Shah Durrani: Founder of the Afghan state in 1747. Pashtun. He built an Afghan empire encompassing parts of present-day India, Iran, and Central Asia.

Habibullah Kalakani: Better known as Bacha Seqao, the Tajik "son of the water carrier," he was the first to enter Kabul in 1929 after King Amanullah's hasty departure in his Rolls Royce. Bacha Seqao declared himself the new Afghan ruler but reigned only ten months before being driven from power.

Abdur Rahman Khan: Emir of Afghanistan (1881–1901). Pashtun. Ruthlessly suppressed internal revolts, launched wars of conquest in the Hazarajat and Nuristan, and fused together the modern Afghan state.

Amanullah Khan: Son of Habibullah. King Amanullah pushed modernization too fast in the 1920s. He did not possess a large standing army capable of putting down the tribal uprising that erupted against his reforms in 1928. Abdicated his throne in 1929 and fled into foreign exile.

Habibullah Khan: Son of Abdur Rahman Khan. Heeded his father's advice to implement social and economic reforms gradually. His network of European-style secular educational institutions became the foundation for Afghan modernization progress over the next seven decades.

Hashim Khan: Nadir Shah's half-brother and Zahir Shah's uncle. Directly ruled Afghanistan as prime minister from 1933 to 1946. Succeeded by his brother, Shah Mahmud.

Mohammad Daoud Khan: The older Musahiban dynasty brothers passed the prime ministership to Daoud Khan of the second Musahiban generation in 1953, bypassing Daoud's cousin King Zahir Shah. Daoud's advocacy of Pashtun irredentist claims on Pakistani territory backfired. He was forced to step down in 1963. Returned to power 1973–1978.

Mohammad Nadir Shah: Executed Bacha Seqao in December 1929 and created the Pashtun Musahiban dynasty that presided over nearly a half-century of modernization programs in constitutional, economic, and social areas. King Nadir Shah was assassinated in 1933. Succeeded by his oldest son, Zahir Shah.

Queen Soroya: Amanullah's wife, who promoted social, especially gender and educational, reforms in the 1920s.

Mahmud Tarzi: The foreign-educated Afghan intellectual who devised many of Habibullah's and Amanullah's reforms. He, too, was forced to flee abroad as furious rural tribes closed in on Kabul.

Abdul Wali: Zahir Shah's cousin and son-in-law. General Wali commanded the Central Army forces guarding Kabul. He failed to detect Daoud's 1973 coup. Daoud exiled Zahir Shah and Wali, abolished the monarchy, and made himself president of Afghanistan.

Dr. Mohammed Yousuf: A German-educated Afghan politician, Dr. Yousuf, a Tajik, served as prime minister from March 1963 to October 1965 when street demonstrations forced him to resign.

Mohammad Zahir Shah: King Zahir Shah was relegated to ceremonial functions until he took control of the Afghan government in 1963. In the ensuing "decade of democracy" he accelerated democratic reforms before being overthrown by his cousin Daoud Khan in a military coup in 1973. Died in 2007.

Communists

Hafizullah Amin: Pashtun. Member of Taraki's Khalq faction. He deposed President Taraki in September 1979. Was Afghan president for the four months leading up to the 1979 Soviet invasion.

Abdul Rashid Dostum: Powerful Uzbek warlord in northern Afghanistan. Famous for switching sides in accordance with prevailing winds, from the Soviets to the Mujahidin to the Taliban to the current Karzai regime.

Sayed Mohammad Gulabzoi: Khalqi air force officer and interior minister. Pashtun. In 2005 he contested and won a seat in the Afghan parliamentary elections.

Babrak ("Friend of Labor") Karmal: Purportedly Tajik. Leader of the *Parcham* (Flag) faction of the PDPA. Was president of Afghanistan for six years (1980–1986) after the December 1979 Soviet invasion.

Mohammad Najibullah: Pashtun. Known simply as Najib, he was a leading Parchami and secret police chief until the Kremlin installed him as Afghan president in 1986. Remained president until the Afghan communist regime collapsed in 1992. Executed by the Taliban in 1996.

Assadullah Sarwari: Dubbed "King Kong" for his ruthlessness when Khalqi secret police chief under Taraki. Pashtun. Soviets made him deputy PDPA leader after Moscow's 1979 invasion and later exiled him to Mongolia as ambassador.

Shahnawaz Tanai: Pashtun. Feisty Khalqi commando who rose to be defense minister in 1988. Staged an abortive coup against President Najibullah in 1990 and escaped to Pakistan. Under the tutelage of Pakistan's military intelligence, the ISI, Tanai joined forces with Mujahidin extremist leader Gulbuddin Hekmatyar and later the Taliban. He is active in contemporary Afghan politics.

Nur Mohammad Taraki: One of the founders of the Afghan communist party known by its acronym, PDPA. Pashtun. Was PDPA party leader and head of the Khalq (Peoples) faction of the party. Became Afghan president and prime minister after the April 1978 communist coup that ended Daoud's rule.

Mohammed Aslam Watanjar: Khalqi tank commander and minister in successive communist governments. Pashtun. Led the tank assaults that overthrew Zahir Shah in 1973 and Daoud in 1978.

Ghulam Farouk Yaqubi: A trusted ally of Najibullah and head of the Afghan secret police after Najibullah became president in 1986. Pashtun.

Mujahidin

Dr. Abdullah Abdullah: Born in Kabul. Received MD degree from Kabul University in ophthalmology in 1993. Joined Ahmed Shah Masood in the Panshir in 1986. Foreign minister of the Afghan government in exile (1998–2001). Foreign minister of Afghanistan (2001–2006). Runner-up presidential candidate in 2009.

Mohammad Fahim: Panshiri Tajik, one of Ahmed Shah Masood's generals. Succeeded Masood in September 2001, days after Masood's assassination. Coordinated with U.S. military to drive the Taliban from northern Afghanistan. Reputed to be very corrupt. Was defense minister (2002–2004). President Karzai's vice president (2009–present).

Sayyid Ahmad Gailani: Moderate. One of the seven Peshawar party leaders chosen by Pakistan to lead the Mujahidin. Titular head (pir) of the Qadiriya Sufi order. The ISI (Pakistan military's Interservices Intelligence Directorate) downgraded his once formidable Mujahidin military organization after the Soviet Army withdrew in 1989.

Abdul Haq: Moderate, nationalist, and popular Mujahidin Pashtun commander during the anti-Soviet jihad. Outspoken critic of ISI and CIA favoritism for the Afghan extremists, which precipitated an ISI-CIA cutoff of support. Organized the National Commanders' Shura in 1990. Opposed the introduction of American ground forces into Afghanistan after 9/11. Called for the United States to assist Afghans to chart their own destiny. Executed by the Taliban in October 2001 while attempting to rally anti-Taliban resistance in eastern Afghanistan.

Jalaluddin Haqqani: ISI-supported, Pakistan-based Pashtun warlord. Sunni extremist. Worked closely with Osama bin Laden in the 1980s. Taliban government minister and militia leader in the 1990s. His son, Sirajuddin Haqqani, today leads one of the three anti-Kabul and anti-U.S. coalition fronts operating from sanctuaries inside Pakistan.

Sirajuddin Haqqani: Afghan terrorist based in Pakistan. Son of Afghan warlord Jalaluddin Haqqani. Supported by the ISI. Leads the Haqqani terrorist network centered in North Waziristan, Pakistan. Works closely with al-Qaeda to mount attacks into Afghanistan.

Gulbuddin Hekmatyar: The warlord of choice of the Pakistani Army and of the Pakistani politico-religious party *Jamaat-i Islami.* Pashtun. Recruited by the ISI when a student at Kabul University in the early 1970s and has remained linked to the ISI. Was one of the seven Peshawar party leaders chosen by Pakistan. Support base remains mainly in Pakistan. Today, leads one of the ISI-organized anti-Kabul and anti-U.S. coalition fronts from sanctuaries in Pakistan.

Hamid Karzai: Moderate-nationalist Pashtun tribal leader from Kandahar. Political adviser to Sibghatullah Mojaddedi (1980–1992); deputy foreign minister of the Afghan government (1992–1996); in exile in Pakistan until October 2001, when, after American military intervention, he organized a

tribal uprising in southern Afghanistan with the assistance of U.S. Special
Forces. Afghan interim president and president (2001–present).

Abdul Karim Khalili: Moderate Hazara Shia cleric, succeeded Abdul Ali
Mazari as leader of the Hazara Hezb-i Wahdat (Party of Islamic Unity) after
the Taliban murdered Mazari in 1996. Has remained President Karzai's second vice president since 2002.

Masood Khalili: Personal friend and adviser to Ahmed Shah Masood. Ambassador to India (2001–2006), Turkey (2006–2010), Spain (2010–present).

Yunus Khalis: Conservative, virulently anti-Shia Pashtun religious cleric and
one of the seven Peshawar party leaders. Befriended Osama bin Laden during
the Soviet-Afghan war and facilitated his escape from Tora Bora into Pakistan
in December 2002.

Ismael Khan: Moderate, powerful Mujahidin Tajik commander in western Afghanistan during the Soviet-Afghan war. After the Soviets left, his military
position declined. Made a comeback in the West after the Najib regime collapsed in 1992. Captured Herat but lost it to the Taliban in 1995. Won Herat
again after the 2001 American intervention routed the Taliban, later moved
to Kabul to become energy minister in President Karzai's cabinet.

Ahmed Shah Masood: Successful Mujahidin Panshiri Tajik commander in
northern Afghanistan during the Soviet-Afghan war. Contended with Pakistani ISI and Gulbuddin Hekmatyar attacks during and after the Soviet-
Afghan war. Captured Kabul when Najib fell in April 1992. Fought the
ISI-backed Taliban and al-Qaeda (1995–2001). Killed by al-Qaeda two days
before the 9/11 attacks, on September 9, 2011.

Ahmed Zia Masood: Senior adviser to and brother of Ahmed Shah Masood.
Was President Hamid Karzai's first vice president (2004–2009), but broke
with Karzai and joined the opposition during that period.

Abdul Ali Mazari: Iran-supported Shia Hazara religious cleric, headed the Shia
Hezb-i Wahdat (Party of Islamic Unity) from 1989 to 1996. Taliban executed
him in 1996.

Sibghatullah Mojaddedi: A moderate, religious cleric and one of the seven Peshawar party leaders. President of the Afghan Interim Government (AIG) created in Pakistan by the ISI in 1989. Unelected interim Afghan president in Kabul from May to June 1992, after Najib's regime collapsed. Titular head (pir) of the Naqshbandiya Sufi order in Afghanistan. Chairman of the Afghan legislature's upper house after the 2005 parliamentary elections.

Anwar al-Haq Mujahid: Pakistan-based Afghan terrorist. Pashtun. Son of the late Peshawar party leader Yunus Khalis. Leads a small front launching cross-border attacks into Afghanistan. Supported by the ISI. Affiliated with al-Qaeda. Assisted Osama bin Laden's escape from Tora Bora into Pakistan in December 2001. Leads the Taliban Nangarhar Province Shura.

Mohammad Nabi Mohammadi: A moderate Pashtun, religious cleric, and one of the seven Peshawar party leaders. Continued to live in Pakistan after the communist regime fell in 1992. Died there in 2002.

Haji Abdul Qadir: Moderate-nationalist Pashtun Mujahidin commander, Abdul Haq's older brother. Head of the Jalalabad governing shura in the 1980s and up to 1996. Joined Commander Ahmed Shah Masood in the north to fight the Taliban that year. After the Taliban's ouster, became President Karzai's vice president, minister of public works, and governor of Nangarhar. Assassinated in July 1992.

Burhanuddin Rabbani: Badakhshani Tajik cleric, a graduate of Cairo's al-Azhar University, promoter of the Muslim Brotherhood and its causes. One of the seven Peshawar party leaders and part of the ISI-favored extremist wing of the Mujahidin (1980–1992). Unelected president of Afghanistan (July 1992–September 1996). Active in contemporary Afghan politics, held a seat in parliament, and chaired President Hamid Karzai's High Peace Council to reconcile with the Taliban, assassinated in 2011.

Abdul Razak: Pashtun rural mullah from Pakistan-Afghan border area. Taliban Interior Minister close to Pakistani military intelligence. Murdered Abdul Haq in October 2001. Thought to be one of the executioners of Afghan communist president, Mohammed Najib, in September 1996.

Abdul Rasoul Sayyaf: Former Afghan communist President Hafizullah Amin's cousin and a strong proponent of Islamism. Pashtun. Graduate of Cairo's al-Azhar University. From 1980 to 1996, was part of the ISI-sponsored and Saudi-patronized Muslim extremist wing of the Mujahidin and an active proponent of global jihad. He was a mentor of Khalid Sheikh Mohammed (9/11 Report).* One of the Peshawar seven party leaders, he was prime minister of the ISI-organized Afghan Interim Government (1989–1992). Later joined Masood's anti-Taliban Northern Alliance, and is today an influential member of the Afghan Parliament.

Gul Agha Sherzai: Powerful, considered to be very corrupt, Pashtun warlord from southern Afghanistan. Close to the ISI. Was governor of Kandahar Province (1992–1994) before the Taliban and after the Taliban defeat (2001–2003). He was a minister and a special adviser in President Karzai's government in Kabul (2003–2004) before becoming governor of Nangarhar Province in 2004.

Mullah Nooruddin Turabi: Rural Pashtun Mullah from Kandahar. Taliban minister of justice after 1996. Administered the rigid Taliban version of religious law, Sharia, during the Taliban period (1994–October 2001).

Jamil ur-Rahman: Afghan Wahhabi. Created a Wahhabi emirate in Konar Province in 1989 and declared independence in 1991. Murdered in 1991.

Abdul Rahim Wardak: Pashtun army officer who defected to the Mujahidin. Was military adviser to Pir Gailani during and after the Soviet-Afghan war. Worked closely with the ISI against the communist regime. Appointed defense minister of Afghanistan in 2004.

IN PAKISTAN

Qazi Hussain Ahmed: Islamic cleric, leader of the Jamaat-i Islami politico-religious party, the Pakistani branch of the Muslim Brotherhood. Mentor and strong supporter of Afghan extremist Gulbuddin Hekmatyar, later the Taliban.

---

* *The 9/11 Commission Report: Final Report of the National Commission on Terrorist Attacks upon the United States,* authorized ed. (New York: W. W. Norton, 2004).

Masood Azhar: Islamic cleric, graduate of Jamiat-i Ulema-i Islam madrassas, leader of the terrorist organizations Harakat ul-Ansar and Jaish-i Mohammad. Arrested in India for terrorist activities, freed when Pakistani terrorists hijacked an Air India airplane in December 1999. Periodically jailed and released by Pakistani authorities. Continues to organize international terrorist activities from bases in Pakistan.

Mirza Aslam Beg: Army chief of staff (1988–1991). Worked closely with Hamid Gul, the director general of the ISI, to maintain military domination of Pakistani politics and to install Afghan extremist Gulbuddin Hekmatyar in Kabul. Undermined elected Prime Minister Benazir Bhutto; later overthrew her. Pursued an anti-American foreign policy, including nuclear cooperation with Iran and support for Saddam Hussein in the first Gulf War.

Benazir Bhutto: Populist Pakistani politician and daughter of Zulfikar Ali Bhutto. Prime minister from 1988 to 1990 and from 1993 to 1996. On both occasions, forced to leave office before completing her term. Assassinated under mysterious circumstances at a December 27, 2007, election rally, a few weeks before a national election she was widely predicted to win.

Zulfikar Ali Bhutto: Pakistani politician. Prime minister (1971–1977). Deposed and executed by his army chief of staff, General Zia ul-Haq.

Asad Durrani: Lieutenant general and ally of Army Chief Mirza Aslam Beg and former ISI director Hamid Gul. ISI and MI (Military Intelligence) director (1990–1993). Following retirement, Durrani served as Pakistani ambassador to Germany and Saudi Arabia.

Hamid Gul: Lieutenant general and upholder of military control of the Pakistani state, patron of Afghan extremist Gulbuddin Hekmatyar and the Taliban and of global jihad. General Zia ul-Haq's ISI chief (1987–1989). Close to Osama bin Laden. Fired by Prime Minister Benazir Bhutto in 1989. Reassigned to prominent military positions by Army Chief Mirza Aslam Beg. Forced to retire by Beg's successor, General Asif Nawaz. After retirement, organized the "private-sector" virtual ISI of retired military intelligence officers. Presently coordinates closely with the ISI to promote Hekmatyar, the Taliban, and several Pakistani terrorist networks based in Pakistan.

Sultan Imam: ISI colonel, known as the "Father" of the Taliban. Played a leading role in organizing the Taliban in 1993 and 1994 and in assisting their conquest of most of Afghanistan in the mid-1990s. Kidnapped by a Pakistani Taliban splinter group in March 2010. Executed in captivity January 2011.

Asif Nawaz Janjua: Chief of the army staff (1991–1993), moderate, pro-West, Sandhurst graduate. Attempted but was prevented from withdrawing the army from Pakistani and Afghan internal politics. Died under mysterious circumstances in January 1993.

Mohammad Ali Jinnah: Founder of the Pakistani state. Shia. Advocated constitutional democracy blended with Islamic principles and civil liberties, including freedom of religion. Died in September 1948, a little over a year after Pakistani independence.

Shamsur Rahman Kallue: Lieutenant general. Voluntarily retired from the army when Pakistani military dictator Zia ul-Haq introduced his Islamization policy. Brought back by Prime Minister Benazir Bhutto to head the ISI in 1989, but effectively sidelined by Bhutto's rival, Army Chief Mirza Aslam Beg. Fired in 1990 after Bhutto was deposed.

Ashfaq Parvez Kayani: Chief of the army staff (2007–present). Head of the ISI (2004–2007) during the Taliban's comeback in Afghanistan. Promoted to army chief of staff in November 2007. Pulled army officers out of civilian government ministries in 2008. Pakistani Prime Minister Yousaf Raza Gilani gave General Kayani a new three-year term in July 2010. Under Kayani, the Pakistani military has continued to sustain the anti-Kabul, anti-U.S.-coalition Taliban offensives in Afghanistan from sanctuaries in Pakistan.

General Mohammad Ayub Khan: First Pakistani military dictator. Ruled from 1958 to 1969. Expanded the role of the powerful Pakistani military agencies (Inter-Services Intelligence Directorate, ISI, and Military Intelligence, MI) in domestic Pakistani politics and foreign policy.

Ghulam Ishak Khan: Pakistani president (1988–1993). Chairman of Pakistan's senate in 1988, constitutionally became Pakistani president when military dictator Zia ul-Haq died in a plane crash. Cooperated with the Pakistani

Army to limit the governing powers of elected prime ministers Benazir Bhutto and Nawaz Sharif. Deposed by the army in 1993.

Yaqub Khan: General and diplomat. Internationally respected Pakistani statesman. Moderate democrat. Foreign minister (1988–1991), former Pakistani ambassador to the United States, the Soviet Union, and France.

Pervez Musharraf: Chief of the army staff (1998–2007), overthrew, imprisoned, and then exiled Prime Minister Nawaz Sharif in 1999 when Sharif attempted to replace him. Ruled Pakistan for nine years before being forced into exile by popular uprisings and the threat of impeachment. Presided over the ISI's revamping of the Taliban inside Pakistan (2001–2005) and the Taliban's successful offensives from sanctuaries in Pakistan (2005–2008).

Javed Nasir: Lieutenant general, full-bearded Islamist, ISI chief (1992–1993). Promoted global jihad in the Balkans, the Middle East, Afghanistan, Central Asia, Kashmir, and Muslim Western China.

Fazlur Rahman: Islamic cleric, leads the arch-conservative Pakistani Islamist Jamiat-i Ulema-i Islam politico-religious party. Maintains strong ties to the Saudi Wahhabi religious establishment. Stalwart supporter of the Afghan Taliban, most of whose leading members studied at Jamiat madrassas in Pakistan.

Nawaz Sharif: Politician. Punjab-based leader of the Pakistani Muslim League Party and three-decade-long rival of the Bhutto family's Pakistan People's Party. Prime minister from 1990 to 1993 and from 1997 to 2000, but unseated by the army before completing either term. Close links to Saudi Arabia. Supporter of Afghan radical Gulbuddin Hekmatyar. Appeals to Pakistani jihadi constituencies during election campaigns. Javed Nasir, his 1992 appointee to lead the ISI, was a zealous supporter of global jihad.

Zia ul-Haq: General and military dictator of Pakistan from 1977 to 1988, when he died in a plane crash. Pursued Islamization programs in Pakistani domestic affairs and in Afghanistan. Suppressed democracy and civil liberties in Pakistan. Cooperated closely with the United States during the Soviet-Afghan war. He envisioned an Afghanistan led by Pakistan-supported

Afghan Muslim extremists after the Soviet withdrawal, thereby engendering Pakistani-Afghan strategic depth against India and an Afghan platform for Islamic holy war in Central Asia.

Akram Zaki: Diplomat and politician. Ambassador to China, the United States (briefly), Philippines, and Nigeria. Secretary general (equivalent to number two) of the Pakistani Foreign Ministry (1991–1993). Political ally of Muslim League leader Nawaz Sharif. Senator (1997–2002).

Asif Ali Zardari: Politician. Husband of Benazir Bhutto and a businessman. Inherited Bhutto's legacy and her Pakistan People's Party after her assassination in December 2007. The party won an overwhelming majority in January 2008 parliamentary elections. In September 2008, the parliament and provincial assemblies elected him president of Pakistan. Since his election, the Pakistani Army has continued to dominate ultimate decision making on major domestic and foreign policy issues.

IN SAUDI ARABIA

King Abdul Aziz al-Saud: Early twentieth-century founder of the modern Saudi state and current al-Saud dynasty. A succession of his sons in the second al-Saud generation have ruled Saudi Arabia since his death in 1953. The third generation is in the wings.

King Abdullah: Second generation al-Saud dynasty king of Saudi Arabia, 2005 to the present.

Bandar al-Sultan: Third-generation al-Saud prince, son of Defense Minister Sultan. Western-educated air force officer and pilot, accomplished diplomat, ambassador to the United States (1983–2005). From 2005 has headed the Saudi government's National Security Council.

King Fahd: King of Saudi Arabia (1982–2005). His half-brother, Crown Prince Abdullah al-Saud, served as de facto regent after King Fahd suffered a heart attack in 1995 and up to Fahd's death in 2005.

King Faisal: King of Saudi Arabia (1964–1975). Assassinated March 25, 1975.

Juhaiman al-Otaibi: Radical Wahhabi priest, led the November 20–December 5, 1979, Grand Mosque uprising in Mecca. Publicly beheaded in Mecca, January 1980.

Muhammad bin Abd al-Wahhab: Eighteenth-century founder of the Wahhabi variant of Islam. Preached return to the ways of the "pious predecessors," *Salaf as-Saaleh* (Muslims adhering to this interpretation of Islam are termed "Salafis"), living in the earliest centuries of Islam. He condemned subsequent accretions to the "pure" faith, including Shiism and Sufism.

Saud al-Faisal: Western-educated third-generation al-Saud prince, son of King Faisal. Experienced, multilingual diplomat. Foreign minister, 1975 to the present. Longest continuously serving foreign minister in the world.

Sheikh bin Baz: Blind theologian, member of prominent al-Sheikh religious family descended from founder of Wahhabi creed, Abd al-Wahhab. Ally of the al-Saud royal house. Chief Mufti of Saudi Arabia (1962–1999). Chairman of the Council of Senior Ulema at time of 1979 Mecca uprising.

Turki al-Faisal: Third-generation al-Saud prince, son of King Faisal. Western-educated, seasoned chief of Saudi external intelligence (1979–2001). Cooperated closely with Pakistan and the United States during Soviet-Afghan war, ambassador to Britain (2003–2005) and the United States (2005–2009).

TERRORISTS AND MILITANT ISLAMISTS

Abdullah Anas: Son-in-law and fervent loyalist of Abdullah Azzam. Befriended northern commander Ahmed Shah Masood. Living in Britain.

Abdullah Yusuf Azzam: Palestinian Islamic scholar, Muslim Brotherhood activist. Lived in Egypt and Saudi Arabia before moving to Pakistan, where he assisted foreign Muslims to participate in the anti-Soviet jihad. Initially close to but later fell out with Osama bin Laden. Supported northern commander Ahmed Shah Masood. Assassinated in Peshawar in November 1989.

Osama bin Laden: Saudi terrorist, founder of al-Qaeda in 1988. Perpetrator of the 9/11 attacks. Discovered hiding in Pakistan. He was killed by American commandos inside Pakistan on May 1, 2011.

Khalid Sheikh Mohammed: Kuwaiti-Pakistani terrorist. Senior al-Qaeda operative. Mastermind of the 9/11 attacks and many other international terrorist plots. Arrested in Pakistan in 2003. Held at Guantanamo Bay.

Omar Abdel Rahman: The "Blind Sheikh." Egyptian terrorist. Convicted of participation in the 1993 attack on the World Trade Center. Serving a life term in a U.S. prison.

Ahmed Omar Saeed Sheikh: British-born terrorist of Pakistani descent. Has committed multiple acts of terrorism in India and Pakistan. Arrested in Pakistan in 2003. Still in custody.

Ayman al-Zawahiri: Egyptian al-Qaeda terrorist, second in command to Osama bin Laden. Has headed al-Qaeda since bin Laden's 2011 death. Believed to be hiding in Pakistan.

IN THE SOVIET UNION, RUSSIA AFTER 1991

Sergei Akhromeyev: General. First deputy chief of the General Staff (1979–1984). Led the Soviet Defense Ministry's "Operational Group" that organized the Soviet invasion of Afghanistan. Later chief of the General Staff (1984–1988) and military adviser to Gorbachev (1988–1991). Participated in the August 1991 anti-Gorbachev coup and committed suicide after it failed.

Yuriy Andropov: KGB leader, Communist Party official. General secretary of the Communist Party (1982–1984). Previously KGB chairman (1967–1982), Politburo Afghan Commission member (1979–1982).

Leonid Brezhnev: Communist Party official. General secretary of the Communist Party (1964–1982).

Karen Brutents: Communist Party official. Deputy head of the Communist Party's International Department under Boris Ponomarev.

Konstantin Chernyenko: Communist Party official. General secretary of the Communist Party (1984–1985).

Anatoly Dobrynin: Diplomat. Ambassador to the United States (1962–1986), Politburo Afghan Commission member (1986–1989), head of the Communist Party's International Department (1986–1988).

Mikhail Gorbachev: Communist Party official. General secretary of the Communist Party (1985–1991). President of the Soviet Union (1990–1991).

Andrey Gromyko: Communist Party official. Diplomat. Soviet foreign minister (1953–1985). Politburo Afghan Commission member (1979–1985).

Alexey Kosygin: Communist Party official and Politburo member. Soviet prime minister (1964–1980).

Vladimir Kryuchkov: KGB official. KGB chairman (1988–1991) and Politburo member. Jailed in 1991 for organizing abortive coup against President Gorbachev, given amnesty in 1994.

Boris Ponomarev: Communist Party ideologue, Politburo Afghan Commission member (1979), chief of the Communist Party's International Department (1955–1986).

Alexander Puzanov: Soviet ambassador to Afghanistan (1972–1979).

Alexander Rutskoi: Air force pilot. Shot down twice during the Soviet-Afghan war. On the second occasion, captured by the Mujahidin, handed over to the United Nations, and returned to the Soviet Union. Russian vice president (1991–1993). Led delegation to Pakistan to meet with the Mujahidin in December 1991.

Eduard Shevardnadze: Communist Party official, diplomat. Foreign minister (1985–1990). Politburo Afghan Commission chairman (1986–1989).

Sergei Sokolov: General. The commander of the Soviet 40th Army, which invaded and occupied Afghanistan in 1979. Later Soviet defense minister (1984–1987).

Fikryat A. Tabeyev: Soviet ambassador to Afghanistan (1979–1986).

Dmitry Ustinov: Communist Party official. Politburo Afghan Commission member (1979–1984). Soviet defense minister (1976–1984).

Valentin Varennikov: General. Deputy commander of the Soviet 40th Army that invaded and occupied Afghanistan. Later headed the Soviet Defense Ministry's operational group managing the Afghan war. Was the defense minister's personal representative in Kabul (1984–1989). Supported the abortive 1991 coup against Gorbachev, was tried and acquitted.

Yuli Vorontsov: Diplomat. Ambassador to Afghanistan (1988–1989), concurrently Soviet deputy foreign minister. Also was ambassador to the United States, India, and the United Nations.

Boris Yeltsin: Communist Party official. Elected president of Russia in June 1991. Led popular opposition to the KGB-led aborted coup against Gorbachev in August 1991. Moved into the Kremlin after the USSR collapsed in December 1991.

IN THE UNITED STATES

Madeleine Albright: Secretary of state (1997–2001).

James A. Baker III: Secretary of state (1989–1993).

Milton Bearden: Station chief in Pakistan (1986–early 1989).

"Bill": Pseudonym for the U.S. station chief in Pakistan (1989–1992).

Richard Clarke: Coordinator on counterterrorism in the National Security Council during the Clinton administrations and in the early months of the George W. Bush administration. Resigned in 2003.

Karl Eikenberry: Ambassador to Afghanistan (2009–2011). Previously, chief of the Office of Military Cooperation in Afghanistan and commander of the Combined Forces Command in Afghanistan (2006–2007).

Tommy Franks: Commander of the U.S. Central Command (2000–2003). Led the American coalition that defeated the Taliban in Afghanistan (October 2001–December 2001) and Saddam Hussein in the second Gulf War in 1993.

Robert Gates: Secretary of defense (2006–2011). Previously deputy director of the CIA (1986–1989), deputy National Security Council adviser to President George H.W. Bush (1989–1991), and director of the CIA (1991–1993).

Richard Haass: Senior director for Near East and South Asian Affairs in the National Security Council during the George H.W. Bush administration (1989–1993). Director of policy planning, Department of State, and coordinator for policy toward the future of Afghanistan during the first George W. Bush administration (2001–2003).

Richard Holbrooke: United States presidential representative for Afghanistan and Pakistan (2009–2010). Previously, ambassador to Germany and the United Nations.

Karl Inderfurth: Assistant secretary of state for South Asian Affairs, Department of State (1996–2001).

Arnold Kanter: Under secretary of state for political affairs, Department of State (1991–1993).

John Kelly: Assistant secretary of state for Near East and South Asian Affairs, Department of State (1989–1991).

Zalmay Khalilzad: Special presidential envoy to Afghanistan in the National Security Council (2001–2002). Ambassador to Afghanistan (2003–2005). Later ambassador to Iraq and to the United Nations. Neoconservative.

Robert Kimmitt: Under secretary of state for political affairs, Department of State (1989–1991). Ambassador to Germany (1991–1993).

Stanley McChrystal: Commander of NATO, International Security Assistance Forces (ISAF), and American Forces in Afghanistan (2009–2010).

Edmund McWilliams: Special envoy to the Afghan resistance (1988–1989).

Robert Oakley: Ambassador to Pakistan (1988–1991). Previously ambassador to Zaire and Somalia, and senior director for the Middle East and South Asia, National Security Council.

David Petraeus: Commander of NATO, International Security Assistance Forces (ISAF), and American forces in Afghanistan (2010–2011).

Robin Raphel: Assistant secretary of state for South Asian Affairs (1993–1996). Senior advisor of Afghanistan-Pakistan, State Department (2009–present).

Christina Rocca: Assistant secretary of state for South Asian Affairs, Department of State (2001–2005).

Michael Scheuer: A senior CIA analyst and briefer on Afghanistan in the late 1980s and 1990s, head of the agency's Osama bin Laden Issue Station conducting covert operations to track bin Laden in the late 1990s. He left the Agency in 2004.

George Tenet: CIA director (1997–2004).

Thomas Twetten: Career member of the CIA clandestine service, the Directorate of Operations (DO). Heavily involved in DO Afghan affairs from about 1983 to 1991, first in the Afghan Mujahidin covert weapons program, then as a senior official in the Near East office, and from 1991 to 1993 as deputy chief of DO.

UNITED NATIONS

Lakhdar Brahimi: Foreign minister of Algeria (1991–1993), United Nations special envoy to Afghanistan (1997–1999), United Nations special representative to Afghanistan (2001–2004).

Benon Sevan: United Nations special envoy on Afghanistan (1988–1991).

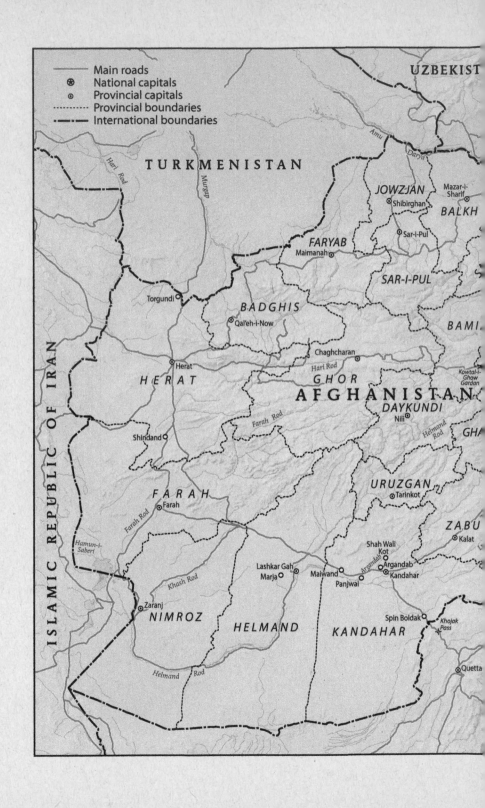

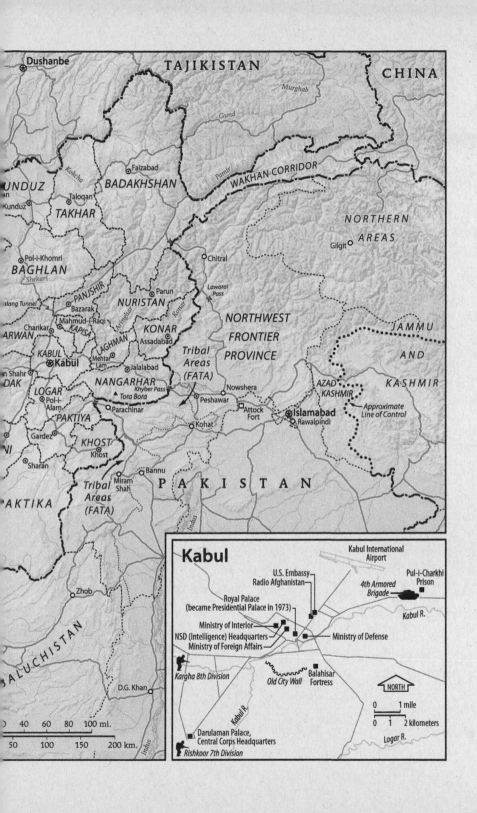

Dushanbe

TAJIKISTAN

CHINA

Murghab

Gund

Kokcha

Faizabad

BADAKHSHAN

Pamir

WAKHAN CORRIDOR

UNDUZ

Kunduz

Talogan

TAKHAR

NORTHERN

AREAS

Gilgit

Pol-i-Khomri

BAGHLAN

Shekari

Chitral

lang Tunnel

PANJSHIR

Bazarak

Parun

Lawarai
Pass

NURISTAN

Mahmud-i-Raqi

KAPISA

ARWAN

Charikar

LAGHMAN

KONAR

JAMMU

Assadabad

Kabul
Konar

NORTHWEST

AND

KABUL

Mehtar
Lam

Kabul

Jalalabad

Tribal
Areas
(FATA)

FRONTIER

PROVINCE

KASHMIR

n Shahr

DAK

NANGARHAR

Khyber Pass

Tora Bora

Nowshera

AZAD
KASHMIR

LOGAR

Pol-i-
Alam

Parachinar

Peshawar

Attock
Fort

Islamabad

Approximate
Line of Control

PAKTIYA

Kohat

Rawalpindi

Gardez

KHOST

NI

Sharan

Khost

Bannu

Miram
Shah

P A K I S T A N

AKTIKA

Tribal
Areas
(FATA)

Indus

Zhob

BALUCHISTAN

D.G. Khan

0   40   60   80   100 mi.

50   100   150   200 km.

Indus

Kabul

Kabul International
Airport

U.S. Embassy
Radio Afghanistan

Pul-i-Charkhi
Prison

4th Armored
Brigade

Royal Palace
(became Presidential Palace in 1973)

Kabul R.

Ministry of Interior

NSD (Intelligence) Headquarters

Ministry of Foreign Affairs

Ministry of Defense

Kargha 8th Division

Old City Wall

Balahisar
Fortress

NORTH

Kabul R.

0   1 mile

0   1   2 kilometers

Darulaman Palace,
Central Corps Headquarters

Rishkoor 7th Division

Logar R.

PART I

TRIBAL INCUBATOR

CHAPTER 1

Padshahgardi

Darkness shrouded Kabul. The narrow streets exuded an eerie silence. A chilly spring wind swept down from the nearby snowcapped mountain range dubbed Hindu Kush, "Killer of Hindus," centuries earlier.[1] These sentinels hovering over Afghanistan's capital had witnessed the violent rise and demise of numerous rulers during Afghanistan's history. Another round of Padshahgardi, *"ruler rotation," was about to begin. It would be no less bloody than its predecessors.*

Afghanistan's president, Mohammad Najib, nervously paced the empty halls of the cavernous presidential palace, the *Gul Khanna* (House of Flowers). It was shortly after midnight, Thursday, April 16, 1992. Fourteen years to the month had passed since gunmen from Najib's communist party had murdered another Afghan president and sixteen members of his family. Only seventeen months later, on October 8, 1979, the first Afghan communist president had been smothered to death with his own pillow as he lay in bed.

Najib knew he would be the country's last communist leader. He sensed dangers mounting all around him. He could no longer trust his generals. He had already evacuated his wife and children to India, where his brother-in-law was Afghan ambassador. They anxiously awaited his safe arrival in New Delhi, and Najib was determined to join them. He was getting out.

The disastrous Soviet-sponsored thirteen-year Afghan communist era was ending. Left behind was a ruined country. Of a population of fewer than 25 million, 1 million had died. Millions more had been wounded or disabled, 5 million exiled abroad, and another 5 million displaced internally. More than 15 million landmines remained buried in Afghan soil. The 1979 Soviet invasion had opened the way for Pakistani and Saudi-supported Muslim extremism to penetrate Afghanistan. Afghan, Pakistani, and Arab Islamic radicals, including Osama bin Laden, established footholds in the Pashtun areas straddling the Afghan-Pakistani border, and Pakistan and Afghanistan became the hub of global terrorism.

❦

Najib, as a Pashtun, belonged to Afghanistan's largest ethnic group, estimated to make up somewhat less than 50 percent of the country's population.[2] Two days previously, on April 14, he had convened a turbulent meeting at his presidential palace and accused two of his most senior generals of treason. They were, he said, secretly negotiating with elements in the Mujahidin, the anticommunist Afghan resistance. The two generals, Army Chief of Staff Mohammed Asif Delawar and Deputy Defense Minister and Kabul military commander Nabi Azimi, were indeed both cutting deals with the communist regime's enemies. They had secretly shifted their allegiance from Najib to Mujahidin commander Ahmed Shah Masood. Like Masood, Delawar and Azimi were members of Afghanistan's second-largest ethnic group, the Tajiks. Their abandonment of Najib was not unexpected. Forsaking a sure loser for a probable winner was a key survival mechanism in Afghan tribal warfare.

Najib's highest-ranking Pashtun generals were also betraying him. They had negotiated their own deliverance to Masood's brutal archrival, the Pakistani- and CIA-supported anti-American Pashtun extremist Gulbuddin Hekmatyar.

The Afghan tradition of changing sides—some would call it treachery— was also infecting Najib's civilian cabinet and communist party apparatus. Members of his cabinet frantically searched for new sinecures in the coming postcommunist dispensation of power. Foreign Minister Abdul Wakil, a Tajik, cast his lot with Tajiks Delawar, Azimi, and Masood. Najib's Tajik deputy in the Afghan communist party confidently told foreign visitors that Najib "must go." Najib's older brother, Sedigullah Rahi, defected to the United States. After surfacing in Washington, he described Najib as mentally deranged.

A fresh realignment of Afghan politics was in high gear, rising from the ashes of Najib's disintegrating regime. It cut across government and Mujahidin factions, following the contours of tribal, ethnic, and clan linkages. Most Afghans assumed a battle for Kabul was imminent. Violence, after all, was an accepted and expected option in Afghan tribal politics when consensus was out of reach. Loyalties beyond the family and clan were hardly ever secure. Today's ally could become an enemy tomorrow. Foreign-imported ideologies such as communism, democracy, and Islamism* were adopted and discarded depending on their usefulness in attracting outside patronage to wield against local rivals. The government was just one more arena in which numerous small tribal and ethnic factions constantly joined and abandoned unstable coalitions.[3]

Najib's position was increasingly precarious on that cold Thursday morning, April 16, 1992. Close supporters were shifting their allegiance to his enemies. He was cornered, surrounded by quislings. The Afghan president had once led KHAD, the regime's ruthless secret police modeled on the Soviet KGB. It was now headed by his hand-picked deputy and loyalist, Ghulam Farouk Yaqubi. But even that formidable lever of power was slipping from his grasp.

Just hours before Najib's face-off with Azimi and Delawar in the palace, the regime garrison at Bagram air base about 30 miles north of Kabul had defected to Masood without a fight. Najib assumed that his two Tajik generals had ordered the surrender. With Bagram under Masood's control, Azimi colluded with Masood and northern Uzbek warlord Abdul Rashid Dostum to airlift six planeloads of Dostum's fierce Uzbek militia from northern Afghanistan into Kabul Airport on government military aircraft. Dostum's forces had fought the Mujahidin under the communist banner for more than ten years. Now the Uzbek warlord had also switched sides. He was allied with Masood, Azimi, and Delawar, and they were coming for Najib.

While Najib's Tajik generals intrigued with Masood, Najib's Pashtun defense minister, Aslam Watanjar, conspired with Hekmatyar. Watanjar and the Pashtun interior minister, Raz Muhammad Paktin, facilitated the infiltration of Hekmatyar's Mujahidin into the capital. Pakistan's powerful military

---

* "Islamism" refers to the Islamic ideology championing the use of Sharia (The Path to the Watering Hole), or Islamic law, to order society. Interpretations of the language in the Koran form the foundation of Sharia. The interpretations vary widely, from the religious totalitarianism of al-Qaeda and the Taliban to the rigid conservatism of Saudi Arabia to the Muslim Brotherhood's stress on the politicization of Islam.

MAP 1.1   BATTLE FOR KABUL, APRIL 25–28, 1992

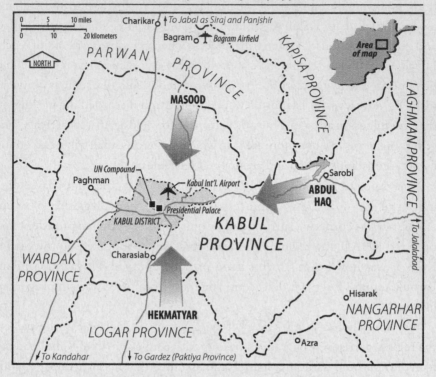

intelligence organization, the Inter-Services Intelligence Directorate (ISI), filled the ISI weapons pipeline from Pakistan to Hekmatyar's main base at Charasiab, 10 miles south of Kabul. Hekmatyar's rockets, made in China and supplied by the United States, began falling on the capital as Dostum's battle-hardened Uzbek soldiers dug in at Kabul Airport. Meanwhile, the famed Mujahidin commander Abdul Haq accepted the surrender of regime general Gul Rang at Sarobi, a corps headquarters on Kabul's eastern perimeter. Haq and Rang, both Pashtuns of the Ahmadzai tribe, hailed from the same Nangarhar village of Hisarak. They had been in secret communication for three years.

The race was on to see who would get to Kabul first—or, in the words of an American Civil War general, who would be "the firstest with the mostest."[4]

༄

For three years, from 1989 to 1992, I had encouraged hundreds of fractious Mujahidin leaders to avoid a battle for Kabul and reach a political consensus on a successor regime to Najib. As President George H.W. Bush's special envoy to the Afghan resistance (1989–1992), I shuttled between Pakistan, Saudi Arabia, the Soviet Union, and Western Europe to build international support for that Afghan consensus. U.S. policy backed a political settlement of the Afghan war led by the United Nations. American, Soviet, and UN diplomatic efforts had successfully guided warring factions to UN-supervised elections in Namibia in 1989 and Nicaragua in 1990. The Soviet Union's troop withdrawal in 1989 created conditions for a peaceful solution in Afghanistan as well. Agreement by Moscow and the other governments in the "outer circle" of nations around Afghanistan on a political solution to end the Afghan war was critical to a peaceful transfer of power from Najib to a successor government.[5] But Najib had to maintain control of Kabul until he transferred the reins of power.

For three years after the Soviet troop withdrawal, Najib's refusal to relinquish his grip on power to a noncommunist regime had impeded a political settlement. Now he was prepared to stand down to avert civil war and to save himself, but his situation was perilous. His army was disintegrating. Tajik generals were defecting to Masood, most Pashtun generals to Hekmatyar. A Masood-Hekmatyar battle for Kabul could plunge the country into an ethnic civil war between Pashtuns and Tajiks. Meanwhile, cooperation from Afghanistan's neighbors was not guaranteed. On April 15, Pakistan publicly reiterated its pledge to support the UN-led settlement process and end the war. Yet many doubted Islamabad's word. Pakistan's military and its ISI instrument had a long history of covertly reversing the Pakistani government's formal commitments to an Afghan peace agreement.

Inside the State Department in Washington, secret telegrams and CIA intelligence reports flew across the computer screens in my fifth-floor office overlooking the Potomac. My secretary's phone rang continually. She frantically recorded the names of journalists and foreign diplomats seeking information on the fast-moving events in Kabul. Abdul Haq contacted me from Sarobi to plead for food to sustain General Rang's 5,000 regime troops who had surrendered with him. Masood's brother, Wali Masood, called in battlefield situation reports to my deputy, Richard Hoagland, in the adjoining office. Thousands of Masood's Mujahidin marched unopposed down the two-lane road that meandered through the 90-mile-long Panshir Valley onto the broad Shomali Plain and past Bagram, stopping 10 miles north of Kabul.

Masood was now poised to enter the Afghan capital. "Nothing can save Najib now," Wali predicted.

Wali was right. Najib's control over events was rapidly deteriorating. He could only count on the loyalty of a few close advisers who were relatives, his palace guard force, and KHAD chief Yaqubi. But his enemies had also infiltrated KHAD. The Kabul Airport was Najib's only route of escape from Afghanistan, now that Bagram was in Masood's hands. But the regime general in charge of airport security had also gone over to Masood.[6]

For two years, United Nations Special Envoy Benon Sevan had promised Najib safe haven in India if he would step down as Afghanistan's president to facilitate a peace agreement. Sevan, at that moment, was in Pakistan attempting to persuade skeptical Mujahidin party leaders about the merits of his UN peace plan. In the early morning hours of April 15, 1992, Najib phoned a UN official in Kabul. He demanded that Sevan fly immediately to Kabul and extract him from Afghanistan.[7] He hoped Sevan's personal UN aircraft would spirit him to safety in India. Sevan agreed, intending to fly into Kabul with a fifteen-man neutral Afghan caretaker government, a "Council of Impartials," and fly Najib out to New Delhi.

At a little after one o'clock in the morning, April 16, 1992, five UN officials from Sevan's Kabul headquarters drove onto the sprawling grounds of the presidential palace. President Najib, dressed in a pinstriped suit, was waiting just inside the palace's grand portal. A thickset, mustached giant, known since his youth as "The Ox," he eagerly welcomed the five as they drove up. Najib gave a short speech, declaring his readiness to leave Afghanistan for the sake of peace. A UN team member responded that Najib was acting courageously. Najib embraced him. Najib's brother Ahmadzai; his senior adviser and chief of staff, General Mohammed Es Haq Toukhi, and Toukhi's wife and three children; a servant; and a bodyguard filed out of the palace into the vehicles. The UN officials informed Najib that Sevan would soon land at Kabul Airport in a UN aircraft. They briefly huddled to put the finishing touches on Najib's resignation statement, which Sevan had already prepared. It would be released to the press after Najib's arrival in New Delhi.[8]

Sevan's political settlement scenario initially seemed to be working. In a radio broadcast the previous month, on March 18, Najib had announced to the world his readiness to step down once the UN peace plan was in place. He was now vacating the presidency. But who would replace him? While

Najib and his UN escort were leaving the presidential palace, Sevan's UN airplane, piloted by an Australian, was landing at Kabul Airport. Seated next to him was his young assistant, British diplomat Andrew Gilmore. The "Council of Impartials" Sevan had planned to bring to Kabul was not with them.

The council, with UN help, was to have organized a *loya jirga*, or a "grand council." The loya jirga was a uniquely Afghan forum used to choose rulers during times of trouble. Hundreds of Afghan tribal leaders, politicians, and clerics gathered to reach major decisions, such as a consensus on the country's leadership. The loya jirga institution espoused fair representation and equality for all Afghan groups. A loya jirga, followed by elections, was at the heart of the U.S.-supported UN plan to extricate Afghanistan from over a decade of warfare and chaos.

The 1992 UN political settlement scenario needed strong support from the United States and the outer circle of nations surrounding Afghanistan to succeed. The United States, Russia, and all of Afghanistan's neighbors, including Pakistan, rhetorically backed the UN-led process. But Pakistan's generals and their powerful intelligence agency, the ISI, with support from the CIA and Saudi Arabia, had a contrasting, covert agenda. Pakistan's army was determined to impose a military solution to the Afghan conflict and not permit the Afghan population to determine its own destiny in a loya jirga or elections. It believed that any Afghan political settlement process would favor moderate-nationalist Afghans like Mohammed Zahir Shah, the exiled king in Rome; Hamid Karzai, the son of a prominent tribal leader; or moderate Afghan commanders such as Ahmed Shah Masood and Abdul Haq. They worried that a political solution could lead to close Indo-Afghan relations, catching Pakistan in a strategic vice between India and Afghanistan. An Afghan moderate-nationalist regime might also revive the "Pashtunistan" cause, implying unification of Pashtuns on both sides of the Afghan-Pakistani frontier. That outcome could precipitate Pakistan's disintegration.

Islamabad's generals intended to install the Islamist radical Hekmatyar in the power vacuum left by the communists. Their ultimate goal was to control Afghanistan, something no outsider could really do. The Saudi intelligence agency backed Hekmatyar and an Arabized Afghan Wahhabi radical, Abdul Rasoul Sayyaf. The two Afghan extremists would be dependable bulwarks against Iranian expansion into Afghanistan and Central Asia. Pakistan's army calculated that an Afghanistan ruled by pro-Pakistani Afghan religious extremists would create "strategic depth" against archfoe India, defuse the Pashtunistan issue, help keep Pakistan's secular democratic political parties at bay in Pakistan's domestic politics, and carry Islamic "holy war" into Muslim-populated Central Asia and to other world regions.

The CIA had grown accustomed to playing a subordinate role to the ISI during the twelve-year Soviet-Afghan conflict. The agency championed Hekmatyar as its favorite Mujahidin leader because he was the ISI's favorite. Rabidly anti-American, Hekmatyar had a reputation among Afghans for killing more Mujahidin than Soviets. In Washington briefings, the CIA parroted the ISI chant that "Islamic extremists fight the best." In fact, neither Hekmatyar nor Sayyaf ever won a battle against the Soviets or Najib. Masood won several, and Haq's Mujahidin regularly pierced the Soviet Army's three security rings around Kabul.

During interagency meetings on Afghan policy, CIA representatives endorsed interagency policy papers calling for a political solution to the Afghan war. Clandestinely, they pursued a contradictory policy, working with Pakistan's military intelligence for a military solution. While Najib and UN officials sped toward Kabul Airport to meet Benon Sevan on April 16, 1992, trucks weighted down by CIA weapons, ISI officers disguised as Mujahidin, ISI-trained Hekmatyar fighters, thousands of teenagers mobilized from Pakistani madrassas, and hundreds of Arab radicals stormed north toward Kabul from Pakistan's border areas.

American diplomatic pressure was badly needed to block a radical Islamic military hijacking of Afghanistan in the wake of Najib's departure. But the White House and the State Department's leadership had lost interest in Afghanistan as the Cold War wound down. On September 26, 1991, seven months before Najib bolted for Kabul Airport, I transmitted a secret telegram to Washington from the U.S. embassy in London. I warned that Pakistan's vision of an extremist outcome in Afghanistan would damage U.S. interests. The United States had to prevent a victory by the Islamic extremists Hekmatyar and Sayyaf. If they replaced Najib, I wrote, Arab terrorist groups in the Middle East would shift their bases to Afghanistan. In a follow-on December 16, 1991, cable, I urged that a political settlement must be put in place as rapidly as possible to forestall scenarios of continued instability and war in Afghanistan. If the UN plan failed, I wrote, "Najib may decide to get out while the getting is still good, leaving his rivals to fight over Kabul."[9]

The CIA's collaboration with the ISI to impose Hekmatyar on Afghanistan violated official White House and State Department Afghan policy statements supporting a UN-led political settlement of the Afghan war. Pakistani, CIA, and Saudi opposition to the UN plan posed a major threat to a peaceful transfer of power from Najib. The defection of Najib's most important generals to Masood, Hekmatyar, and Haq indicated that Najib's successor would be decided on the battlefield, not by the UN plan. Of the three, only Abdul Haq honored Sevan's request to hold back his forces. Masood's eyes remained fixed on Hekmatyar's rapid buildup along Kabul's southern approaches. Neither man trusted the other.

In February, another Masood brother, Ahmed Zia, had asked me to confer with him on the lawn adjacent to the American Consulate General in Peshawar, Pakistan, away from prying eavesdropping equipment. He told me that Masood supported the UN plan, but that he was also ready to defeat Hekmatyar if Hekmatyar attacked Kabul. By mid-April, Masood was poised to enter the capital first. He was not going to surrender the city to Hekmatyar and his Pakistani sponsors. Most of Najib's generals had defected to him. The ground units under his command were more numerous than Hekmatyar's. Masood also controlled the regime's combat aircraft captured at Bagram.

☙

Dim headlights guided the three-vehicle UN convoy as it quietly coasted out of Najib's sprawling palace compound at around 1:30 a.m. on April 16, 1992.[10] The vehicles turned left onto the darkened street and began the fifteen-minute drive to the Kabul Airport. The passengers leaned into each other to fight off the nighttime cold. Dan Quirke, an Irish national and UN official, drove the first vehicle, a Toyota Land Rover. UN political officer American Phillip Corwin was in the front passenger seat. Najib's bodyguard, clutching his AK-47, and Najib's servant were in the back. A second car, a sedan, was driven by Turkish diplomat Avni Botsali. Colonel Patrick Nowlan, an Irish army officer, rode shotgun. Najib and his brother were in the back seat. General Toukhi, with his wife and children, followed in a Toyota minivan.

The convoy's password, provided by KHAD, Najib's secret police, was accepted at two checkpoints on the airport road. Botsali radioed ahead to Sevan that the party was approaching the airport just as Sevan's aircraft was landing. At that moment, Najib's luck ran out. Afghan soldiers halted the convoy at the last checkpoint about 200 yards from the airport. A sergeant curtly informed the group that its password was incorrect. In fact, Kabul military commander General Nabi Azimi had just ordered the general commanding Kabul Airport to change it.

An infuriated General Toukhi leaped from the minivan to confront the sergeant. A lieutenant arrived and joined the heated discussion. One soldier pointed his weapon at Quirke. Toukhi persisted in demanding that the convoy be cleared to enter the airport. From the back of the sedan, Najib's booming voice reinforced Toukhi's protests. The lieutenant retorted that "a senior military level" had changed the password and that the president must return to Kabul. He told Toukhi that northern Uzbek commander Dostum and his militia had seized the airport terminal. Najib and his entourage would be killed if they drove into the airport.

President Najib was trapped. He could not go forward. It was not safe to retrace his steps to the presidential palace. Hostile generals were monitoring his every step. Around 2:00 a.m., the Afghan president instructed the convoy to turn around and proceed immediately to Sevan's UN office in downtown Kabul. He radioed his secret police chief, Yaqubi. Yaqubi assured Najib that he would investigate and be back in touch soon. A few hours later, Yaqubi was found dead at his desk, a pistol in his hand. Later in the day a KHAD spokesman announced that Yaqubi had killed himself. Nobody in Kabul believed it. Rumors flew through city bazaars at dawn that the fatal bullet had entered the back of Yaqubi's head while he was sitting at his desk looking away from an open window.[11] Teahouse chatter the following morning centered on a more likely version of who pulled the trigger—Yaqubi's Tajik deputy, who was another secret Masood ally in the regime.

Najib knew that his life was in great danger. He could not count on his own secret police. His two most powerful ministries had betrayed him. At that moment, Sevan, too, felt that his life was in jeopardy. He, his pilot, and his assistant, Andrew Gilmore, had landed at Kabul Airport at about the same time the UN convoy was leaving the palace. The airport was shrouded in darkness. As he looked out the window of his parked airplane Sevan experienced a strange feeling "that something had gone wrong." The utter silence was "spooky." Two shadowy figures, perhaps guards, stood on the tarmac outside. Once a solitary bicyclist circled the plane and pedaled away. There was no sign of the Afghan protocol officers who normally greeted him at planeside to accord VIP honors.

Sevan ordered his pilot to keep the doors locked. He called Botsali on his mobile radio. Botsali briefed him about the UN convoy's predicament. Sevan then phoned Afghan Foreign Minister Abdul Wakil and the Kabul military commander Major General Nabi Azimi. He protested that Najib had been blocked from leaving Afghanistan on his UN airplane. Preventing Najib's departure threatened to unhinge the UN peace plan, he warned. Azimi rushed to the airport.

UN diplomat Phillip Corwin later wrote that Afghanistan's spiral into chaos and civil war might have begun during those early morning hours of April 16, 1992, outside the Kabul Airport: "It was as if, at this very moment, on this very spot, a power vacuum replaced what little central authority still existed in Afghanistan; and that is why, I am convinced, this event must be given due significance in any history of the period. On this night, within a few hundred yards of Kabul airport, the sitting president of Afghanistan, Najibullah— a.k.a. Najib-e-Gao, or Najib the Bull—was deposed by anarchy."[12]

Around 4:00 a.m., Azimi informed Sevan that he could deplane. Sevan and Gilmore exited the aircraft. While walking with Sevan toward some waiting cars near the terminal, Gilmore glanced back and saw two lines of Dostum's heavily armed Uzbek militia emerging from the shadows around the airplane. Some were carrying antiaircraft-capable rocket-propelled grenades. On arriving at the UN compound, Sevan faced the incongruous situation of the president of Afghanistan seeking political asylum in his own country. Najib voiced alarm when Gilmore told of the heavily armed Uzbeks hidden in the airport darkness. "Andrey," the president exclaimed, employing the Russian-language's familiar version of "Andrew," "had I made it through the last checkpoint they would have shot us down as we were taking off and we would all have been dead."[13]

Kabul's muezzins were calling the faithful to prayers when Sevan asked the Indian chargé d'affaires if his embassy could grant political asylum to Najib.[14] Sevan gave the Indian chargé a formal diplomatic *note verbale* making the request. After checking with New Delhi, the chargé reported back that his government was unable to help, citing concerns about the safety of Indian citizens in Afghanistan. At 5:15 a.m., Sevan summoned sleepy-eyed

representatives from France, China, Iran, Pakistan, and India to the UN compound. He briefed them about the precarious state of the UN peace initiative
and Najib's aborted flight to India. Sevan limited a second meeting to the two
representatives from the Pakistani and Iranian embassies. In Najib's presence,
the Pakistani offered asylum to Najib in Pakistan. The Iranian assured Najib
that Iran would restrain Iranian-supported Mujahidin from creating instability in Kabul.

Struggling to contain his outrage, Najib brushed aside the fraudulent assurances of his long-standing enemies. He ridiculed their promises. He reminded them of the history of Pakistani and Iranian interference in
Afghanistan. Najib directed his most abusive comments at the Iranian. Corwin, who was present, feared that the huge Pashtun, "with his massive hands,"
would "simply walk over and pick the man up and throw him out the nearest
window." Najib's behavior reminded Corwin of the Incredible Hulk—he
seemed "to enlarge with each phrase, puff up like a venomous adder, as
though he were about to explode out of his skin."[15] Najib concluded his diatribe by lashing out at Sevan for breaking his commitments to him. Fore-
stalling further offers of foreign asylum, he announced his decision to remain
at the walled UN compound and abruptly left the room. Sevan announced
that the meeting was over, and the Pakistani and Iranian diplomats returned
to their fortified embassies.

Later that morning, Foreign Minister Abdul Wakil denounced Najib at a
hastily convened press conference. Previously considered by all to be one
of Najib's most senior officials, Wakil charged that Najib, the "ex-president"
of Afghanistan, had "resorted to fleeing the country irresponsibly." He revealed that "the armed forces of the Republic of Afghanistan . . . prevented
his flight and did not allow Najib to leave our country willfully and
thievishly." Wakil added, "with regret," that KHAD chief Yaqubi had "attempted suicide after receiving the news of Najib's escape."[16] Wakil told the
assembled journalists that he, Azimi, and other senior regime officials would
negotiate directly with Ahmed Shah Masood to arrange a transfer of power
to the northern commander.

Wakil's press conference erased any lingering hopes of a UN political settlement. Afghanistan's capital descended into chaos. Iranian-armed Shia Hazaras, constituting Afghanistan's third-largest ethnic group after the Pashtuns
and Tajiks, occupied western Kabul. Hekmatyar counted on predominantly

Pashtun neighborhoods in Kabul's southern suburbs to assist his assault from the south into the center of Kabul. Masood, Dostum, and the regime's Tajik generals who had defected to him controlled the center of Afghanistan's capital plus the northern and eastern sections of the city.

The Pashtun defense minister, Watanjar, converted Kabul's Bala Hissar Fort into a pro-Hekmatyar redoubt bristling with Pashtun fighters from the regime's and Hekmatyar's ranks. Iranian Revolutionary Guard officers enjoying diplomatic cover in Iran's Kabul embassy broke open regime armories in the city's overwhelmingly Hazara[17] western suburbs. They passed out weapons to thousands of Hazara youth anxious to defend their families against marauding Pashtun, Tajik, Uzbek, and Arab enemies. Hekmatyar's forces attacked Kabul's southern districts on April 25, and the battle raged for three days. Masood, Dostum, and regime generals who were allied with them launched a fierce counterattack. Afghan fighter planes loyal to Masood bombed the Bala Hissar Fort and strafed Hekmatyar's Afghan, Pakistani, and Arab fighters strung out on the Logar road south of Kabul. Street fighting spread into the western Hazara-populated suburbs.

The Afghan capital had not been sacked since rural Pashtun tribesmen had rampaged through the city in 1929. The April 1992 battle for Kabul ended that sixty-three-year respite from depredation. Fighters from all sides barged into homes, looting and killing. Women and young girls were savagely raped before the eyes of horrified family members. Several tons of gold were carted off from the Central Bank. Abdul Haq was disgusted to see "people shooting one another like wild dogs in the streets of Afghanistan's capital." He pulled his Mujahidin back to Jalalabad, located between Kabul and the Pakistani border. "I will not become part of the problem," he told me.[18] Masood pushed Hekmatyar's forces back to Charasiab. Hekmatyar rained ISI-supplied rockets onto Kabul, killing thousands in their homes and on the streets. Iran pumped weapons and money into Shia Hazara strongholds in the city.

The Mujahidin had never broken through Kabul's defenses during the twelve-year communist era. Now the Afghan capital was becoming a bloody battlefield. Day and night, the explosions of landing rocket shells shook residential areas. The staccato echo of machine-gun fire resonated through Kabul's streets and alleys. Saudi and Pakistani-supported Sunni Pashtun extremists with their Arab allies fought vicious battles with Iranian-supported Shia.

Refugees clogged the 150-mile road to Pakistan. In cars and buses, on donkeys, and on foot, regime civil servants and soldiers, high and low, joined ordinary Afghans moving out of the city toward their home villages. They assumed that the entire country was tumbling into anarchy. The living conditions in Afghanistan's thousands of rural microcommunities were bleak. But they offered a chance for survival. In the cocoon of the clan and tribe, they would keep their options open, their weapons handy, and wait for the latest round of Afghan Padshahgardi to play itself out in Afghanistan's lawless capital.

ψ

The curtain had come down on the disastrous communist era in Afghanistan. The Soviet Union's attempt to extend its sphere of influence over the Hindu Kush by subduing Afghan tribesmen had failed. Its communist ideology never found fertile soil in tribal Afghanistan, even under the heavy foot of the Soviet Red Army. The humiliating departure of Soviet forces from Afghanistan in February 1989 marked the beginning of the rapid demise of the Soviet Union, first as a superpower and soon as a nation.

But it was not only the Soviet Union that had disengaged, leaving Afghanistan to descend into extremism and anarchy. Much had changed in Washington's global strategy since 1986, when a glittering White House dinner hosted by President and Mrs. Ronald Reagan had honored Abdul Haq as a special guest. On that occasion the president had turned to the valiant Mujahidin commander, who had been wounded seventeen times fighting the Soviet Army, to offer a toast. "Abdul Haq, we are with you," Reagan declared above the din of thunderous applause from the guests in the ornate White House dining room.[19]

President George H.W. Bush was now in the White House with a fresh set of foreign policy advisers. They considered Afghanistan a third-tier issue left over from the Cold War. Other matters took priority over Reagan's earlier pledges to moderate-nationalist Afghan leaders like Abdul Haq. Just when a firm diplomatic push for a political settlement from the world's only remaining superpower was most needed, America was bowing out.

The Cold War ended on Christmas Eve 1991 when the Soviet Union collapsed. Soviet President Mikhail Gorbachev moved his belongings out of the Kremlin, and Russian President Boris Yeltsin moved in. Moscow's military and economic supply lines to the Afghan communist regime in Kabul evaporated. Five new struggling Central Asian states now separated Russia and Afghanistan. At its nearest point, the Russian border was more than 400 miles from Afghanistan.

"The president wants out," American diplomats told colleagues in the State Department's corridors. U.S. diplomats were instructed to adopt a low profile on Afghanistan. "Is that thing still going on?" President Bush asked a briefer who had informed him of renewed fighting under way in Kabul after Najib's ouster.[20]

The two Clinton administrations and the pre-9/11 Bush 43 administration outsourced American Afghan policy to Pakistan, which meant, in practice, to Pakistan's army and its intelligence arm, the ISI. From 1992 to 1994, the ISI had provided Hekmatyar with the rockets that turned the lovely mountain city of Kabul into an Afghan version of Dresden in World War II. In 1994, Pakistan would switch its support from Hekmatyar to the Taliban. An "unholy alliance" of the Taliban, al-Qaeda, and the ISI would dominate most of Afghanistan until al-Qaeda-piloted planes struck America itself.

๖

Ahmed Shah Masood controlled Kabul between 1992 and 1996. Najib remained cloistered in the walled UN compound during those four years before the Taliban arrived, virtually forgotten and forsaken. He and his small retinue were the sole occupants of the UN premises. The United Nations arranged for food and other daily essentials of life to be delivered to Najib and his three companions—his brother Ahmadzai, General Toukhi, and Najib's bodyguard, Jafter.[21] Najib's boredom was relieved by Indian Bollywood movies and occasional visits from American Alex Thier, a junior UN official. The United Nations tasked Thier with making monthly visits to the former Afghan president after the UN political mission's staff was evacuated from Afghanistan. The main purpose of each visit was to give Najib a UN satellite phone to converse with his wife in New Delhi. Thier recounted:

> The three of them were living for four years in this strange situation.
> It was very reminiscent of the scene in the movie *Goodfellas*, when
> they're in the prison together and cooking.... They were very much left
> alone inside in this house arrest situation. So, I took over this briefcase
> satellite phone to Najib to allow him to call his wife. In subsequent visits

I had the very difficult job—because the UN people claimed to have very little money for the telephone and it was far too expensive per minute to have him spending all of their budget—to warn him he had only a half hour a month and if he used more of that allotted time they were going to cut him off.[22]

Najib was too starved for news and outside contact to object. He warmly received the twenty-four-year-old American each time he visited, plying him with Afghan hospitality. Thier reported back that Najib's lavish attention, food, and conversation were interspersed with "tendencies of megalomania." Undeterred by living in ignominy not far from the presidential palace where he once reigned, Najib referred to himself in the third person—"Najib tried to do this . . . " and "Najib believes. . . . " Najib filled their many hours together with impassioned one-on-one speeches, intended, Thier felt, "to rehabilitate his image to me who wasn't much of an audience because I wasn't doing much at the time." His marathon presentations seemed to wear on his younger brother's nerves. Ahmadzai once took Thier aside and confided, "You know, my brother did some very, very bad things."[23]

In September 1996, Masood evacuated Kabul before Afghan Taliban, Pakistani, and Arab al-Qaeda fighters entered the city. Najib turned down Masood's offer of *nanawati*, the tribal tradition of sanctuary, to travel on his personal helicopter to the safety of the Panshir Valley. He decided to gamble that Taliban Pashtun leaders would also grant him nanawati, permitting him to fly to India to join his family. Pakistan had already assured UN Secretary General Boutros Boutros-Ghali that Najib's trip to India "would be facilitated." Boutros-Ghali sent his under secretary general, Marrack Goulding, to Kabul to elicit Najib's preference. Goulding reported back that Najib "had no fear of the Taliban" and that he insisted "his only enemy was Ahmed Shah Masood." Goulding also took his appeal to the Taliban in Kandahar. The Taliban leaders, he found, "had never heard of the United Nations." His statements to them "fell on deaf ears."[24]

At twilight on September 26, 1996, thousands of Taliban with their Pakistani and Arab allies began filtering into Kabul from the city's southern suburbs. Only hours earlier, Masood's last contingent had filed out of Kabul heading north, back to the Panshir Valley. An eerie silence gripped the city. Most of the arriving Taliban moved on foot—masses of shadowy figures shuffling through streets in the gathering darkness. Pickup trucks packed with bearded, black-turbaned Taliban moved among the throngs of foot soldiers gravitating toward the center of the capital. Kabul residents peered out through shuttered windows, wondering what the winner of this cycle of Padshahgardi would bring.

Four Taliban, including, by one Afghan account, a Pakistani ISI officer disguised as a Taliban, drove directly to the UN compound in a Japanese Datsun pickup. Their mission was to lure the former Afghan president out of the diplomatically protected UN premises.[25]

Najib, his brother Ahmadzai, General Toukhi, and Jafter, Najib's faithful Hazara guard, nervously awaited the Taliban's arrival in their basement living quarters in the UN building. They did not know whether Najib would be killed or honored. Najib's first cousin Hashim Paktianai, who had relocated to Peshawar after Masood seized Kabul, had traveled periodically to Kabul to deliver food and other items to Najib. A knowledgeable Afghan source recounted that Paktianai was in touch with Pakistani intelligence officers in Peshawar. They assured him that the Taliban would not harm Najib.[26] Paktianai conveyed the same deceptive "assurance" to Najib's wife in New Delhi, who regularly talked to Najib.

The trap was set.

Three Taliban entered the UN compound while their driver waited outside. Najib warmly greeted them.[27] He offered them tiny, elegantly wrapped packages of Swiss chocolate, joking that they were the only gifts he had on hand. The three Taliban lined up. One after another, they knelt down and kissed Najib's hand in a traditional Afghan gesture of respect. The Taliban invited Najib to come with them to the presidential palace. Najib enthusiastically accepted. Najib's natural megalomania played into their hands.

The Datsun pickup truck waited outside the UN compound's entrance, the driver at the wheel. Najib took the passenger seat. Toukhi, Jafter, and the three Taliban climbed into the truck's bed. Ahmadzai remained behind at the UN compound. Nearing the presidential palace, the driver slowed the vehicle to a crawl. He leaned his head out the window and suggested to Toukhi and Jafter that they return to the UN compound, as there would be no need for bodyguards at the palace. Toukhi responded, "Our President is with you. Without his permission we cannot leave the truck." Najib ordered the driver to stop the truck. He shouted back to Toukhi and Jafter that he would not need their protection inside the palace; they should return to the UN compound. Toukhi and the Hazara walked back to the UN building, where they found Ahmadzai in high spirits. He had put on a suit jacket in anticipation of joining Najib at the presidential palace.

Shortly after midnight, a second group of bearded Taliban arrived at the compound. They were less obsequious than the first. Snarling and cursing, they grabbed Ahmadzai and took him away. Toukhi and Jafter quickly left the UN premises, disappearing into the labyrinthine byways of Afghanistan's capital. By this time, the Datsun truck had driven Najib into the palace compound. He was taken to a room inside the palace, where he was brutally tortured, castrated, and shot. His body was then attached to a vehicle by a rope and dragged around the palace grounds. At first light on the morning of September 27, 1996, about seven hours after Toukhi and Jafter were dropped off near the palace, Najib's and Ahmadzai's bloodied bodies hung from a traffic pylon outside the palace walls, their cadavers mutilated. A wad of Soviet currency and cigarettes were stuffed into Najib's mouth and nostrils. Passing Taliban riddled the limp bodies with small-arms fire.

Najib's entrapment and execution carried the hallmarks of a classic intelligence operation. The Taliban, on their own, would not have taken such elaborate precautions to avoid violating the UN's diplomatic premises. Masood's intelligence reported that an ISI operation had disposed of Najib. This analysis is persuasive.[28] Once on the loose, the former Afghan president could have again become a dangerous Pakistani adversary, either inside Afghanistan or outside, in league with Pakistan's archfoe, India.

The reported ringleader of the three Taliban was the notorious Abdul Razak, a ruthless Taliban mullah from the porous Pakistani-Afghan borderland between Quetta and Kandahar. He was closely associated with the ISI and the ISI-aligned Pakistani politico-religious party Jamiat-i Ulema-i Islam (JUI, Society of Islamic Scholars). Many Afghans believed that Razak executed Najib inside the presidential palace.

ﺝ

After 9/11, American and allied forces entered Afghanistan. American and anti-Taliban Afghan militias drove the Taliban and al-Qaeda back to their original bases in Pakistan. Islamabad's generals could no longer prevent the Afghans from employing their ancient loya jirga institution, and Sevan's UN settlement blueprint was aggressively reactivated. A loya jirga in 2002 chose Hamid Karzai as interim Afghan leader; in 2004 he won the country's presidential election. Another loya jirga, held in 2004, endorsed a new democratic constitution. UN-assisted parliamentary elections were concluded in 2005.

Karzai invited Afghanistan's ex-king, Zahir Shah, to move back into the presidential palace. The seventy-seven-year-old former monarch reoccupied a wing of the mansion where he had spent his childhood and ruled for a decade (1963–1973) before his forced exile from Afghanistan; he lived there until his death of natural causes in 2007.

On March 17, 2005, Secretary of State Condoleezza Rice stood next to Karzai at a joint press conference in Kabul. Rice announced, "We have a long-term commitment to this country." She continued: "We learned the hard way what it meant to not have a long-term commitment. . . . After the Soviet Union left, I think it is well understood that we did not remain committed." In 2006, Secretary of Defense–designate Robert Gates told Congress that the United States had made a mistake in neglecting Afghanistan after the Soviet withdrawal.[29]

Prior to the Taliban, no religious cleric had ever ruled Afghanistan. After the Taliban's ouster in December 2001, most Afghans and foreign governments presumed that their five-year reign was an unfortunate aberration in Afghan history—one that would not be repeated. Pakistan's military dictator, General Pervez Musharraf, assured President George W. Bush that Pakistan had joined the United States in the war on terror. Pakistan, he claimed, would be a reliable partner in tracking down al-Qaeda and Taliban leaders who had fled Afghanistan into Pakistan.

But Musharraf was duping the Americans, playing a double game. The ISI concealed Taliban leader Mullah Omar in a Pakistani military cantonment near Quetta. Thousands of Taliban and al-Qaeda fighters escaped into the ISI-managed Islamist infrastructure of extremist madrassas, military training camps, mosques, and Saudi charity offices on Pakistan's Frontier,* and the ISI revamped and rearmed the Taliban for a comeback. Meanwhile, complacency paralyzed American Afghan policy. Once again the United States downgraded

---

* Pakistan's Frontier roughly covers the region between the Afghan-Pakistani border and the Indus River inside the Northwest Frontier Province. About a 100-mile extension of the Frontier continues along the Afghan border through Baluchistan to the Iranian border.

Afghanistan at a critical time. American attention and resources shifted to Iraq. The Pentagon leadership rejected a respected army major general's March 2002 proposal to begin immediately to rebuild the Afghan Army to defend the country. U.S. government civilian assistance to Afghanistan in the first year after the Taliban's overthrow fell below the assistance provided during the last year of Taliban rule. By 2005, the vital momentum that the United States had achieved by driving the Taliban from Afghanistan had been lost. Thousands of Taliban, Pakistani, and al-Qaeda fighters reentered Afghanistan from safe havens in Pakistan to attack U.S., coalition, and Afghan security forces. Rampant Afghan factionalism and corruption and skyrocketing opium production confounded international efforts to rebuild the Afghan state.

The George W. Bush administration reacted to the Taliban counterattack by devoting substantially more economic aid and troops to Afghanistan. For the first time in its history, NATO committed its military assets to assist a nation outside the European theater. More than fifty countries and the United Nations became involved in a common effort to block the return of the Taliban, al-Qaeda, and anarchy to war-wracked Afghanistan. But the troop buildup, and billions more in development aid, failed to quell the Taliban's resurgence.

The Obama administration has exhibited a better grasp of Afghanistan's internal dynamics than the Bush administration did during its time in office. Assisting Afghanistan to once again become a functioning state, as it was before the destructive communist and Taliban eras, however, would require much more than money and foreign troops. The ultimate success of the endeavor would depend on a more realistic assessment of Pakistan's motives in Afghanistan. Most of all, however, the United States and its friends and allies would need to gain a deeper understanding of the Afghan environment. To gain that understanding, one must begin with an examination of Afghan history, culture, and tribal society.

CHAPTER 2

Shatter Zone

In 53 B.C., marching through Syria toward Afghanistan, the Roman general Marcus Licinius Crassus found Parthian general Spahbodh Surena blocking in his way. Their armies clashed at the epic Battle of Carrhae east of the Euphrates. The Roman historian Plutarch wrote:

> They saw the enemy, contrary to their expectation, neither so many nor so magnificently armed as the Romans expected. For Surena had hid his main force behind the first ranks, and ordered them to hide the glittering of their armour with coats and skins. But when they approached and the general gave the signal, immediately all the field rung with a hideous noise and terrible clamour. . . .
>
> When they had sufficiently terrified the Romans with their noise, they threw off the covering of their armour, and shone like lightning in their breastplates and helmets of polished Margianian steel, and with their horses covered with brass and steel trappings. . . . They encompassed the Roman square before they were aware of it. Crassus commanded his light-armed soldiers to charge, but they had not gone far before they were received with such a shower of arrows that they were glad to retire. . . . The Parthians now placing themselves at distances began to shoot from all sides, not aiming at any particular mark (for, indeed, the order of the Romans was so close, that they could not miss if they would). . . .
>
> . . . They raised such a dust that the Romans could neither see nor speak to one another, and being driven in upon one another in one close body, they were thus hit and killed, dying, not by a quick

23

*and easy death, but with miserable pains and convulsions; for
writhing upon the darts in their bodies, they broke them in their
wounds.*[1]

Carrhae was one of the decisive battles of world history. The British historian
Olaf Caroe speculated that the soldiers on the winning side, Persian-speaking
Parthians, were the ancestors of today's Pashtuns. A branch of Surena's Suren
tribe once ruled the ancient Gandhara region surrounding modern-day Peshawar, capital of Pakistan's Pashtun-majority Northwest Frontier Province.[2]

Surena's decentralized tribal state humiliated the highly centralized Western superpower of the day by employing unconventional military tactics. His
Parthian army of 10,000 mounted archers annihilated the 35,000-man
Roman army. Carrhae was the worst Roman defeat since Hannibal had
crushed the Roman army at Cannae in 216 B.C. This time, the Romans would
not make a comeback. Sixty-seven years later, the great Roman emperor Augustus (27 B.C.–A.D. 14) negotiated the return of the seven legion standards
lost at Carrhae. But the West would not again appear at Afghanistan's door
until the nineteenth-century Western superpower, Britain, launched two invasions from British bases in its Indian Empire. In those intrusions, the
British would repeat the blunders of the Romans. And the Soviets would
make the same mistakes a century later.

The doomed Roman legionnaires at Carrhae squinting into the desert sun
toward the gathering Parthian cavalry were on a mission. The Roman Republic, soon to be an empire, had dispatched Crassus and his legions eastward to
reclaim the Hellenistic[3] lands between the Euphrates and the Pamirs that had
been conquered by the Macedonian King Alexander the Great three centuries
earlier. In 331 B.C., at the Battle of Gaugamela, Alexander had destroyed the
army of the Persian Achaemenian Empire. The Macedonian warrior-king
next captured Babylon, and then, after looting and burning down Persepolis,
the Achaemenian political and cultural capital, he continued east into Afghanistan, winning a string of battles and building new cities in or near contemporary Herat, Kandahar, Ghazni, Farah, and Jabal Saraj, north of Kabul.[4]

Alexander the Great carried Greek culture into Afghanistan. Greek
colonists arrived soon after, bringing with them the Greek language as well
as Greek art and literature. Alexander named most of the cities he built after
himself. Today, only modern-day "Kandahar," a corruption of "Alexander,"

retains the conqueror's name. The Hellenistic Empire left behind by Alexander lasted about three hundred years. After Alexander's death, his generals divided it into three parts. The Macedonian Seleucus and his Greek successors, Antiochus and Demetrus, ruled over Alexander's conquests in Afghanistan west to Palestine. In 239 B.C., the Bactrian Greeks in northern Afghanistan declared independence, establishing the Graeco-Bactrian Kingdom, which eventually expanded across the Indus deep into India. The flow of Greek colonists east continued, populating new cities and fostering Greek art and institutions. Greek coins carried the faces of local Greek rulers, and Greek became a common tongue of the ruling elites throughout the region.

A trove of folktales and legends about "the Great One," orally passed down throughout middle Eurasia, survives today. Alexander is known as "Iskandar." Afghan parents still occasionally choose Iskandar as the name for their sons—and Roxane, Alexander's wife's name, for daughters. Along the Afghan-Pakistani frontier, some Pashtun tribes—such as the Afridi, residing near the famed Khyber Pass—claim Greek ancestry. The Nuristanis, in Konar, who provided three hundred cavalry to Alexander's army,[5] explain that their race's light complexion and frequent blond hair and blue eyes originate from remnants of Alexander's army who stayed behind.

ψ

The Persian tribal migrations from Central Asia into present-day Afghanistan and Iran began after Alexander the Great's conquests and a century before the Parthians blocked Crassus's way east. From roughly 200 B.C. to A.D. 200, wave after wave of Persian-speaking Parthian, Saka, and Kushan nomads burst out of the Central Asian grasslands and attacked the Greek cities of Afghanistan. Ancient Balkh, the "Mother of all Cities" and the Bactrian Greek capital south of contemporary Mazar-i-Sharif in northern Afghanistan, was repeatedly sacked (see Appendix I).

Credible, comprehensive written records about the varied peoples inhabiting the vast Central Asian steppe in the centuries before and after the birth of Christ are lacking. None of these cultures possessed alphabets. It is clear, however, that this region became an incubator of nomadic tribal groups contesting one another for grazing land—the climate was too harsh to permit agricultural surpluses large enough to support the growth of cities.

A population explosion may have fueled the piecemeal nomadic migration out of Central Asia into the wealthier, more settled, and more organized ancient civilization of the time, which stretched from Rome through Persia and Afghanistan to China. In Europe, German barbarians under Arminius defeated a Roman army at the Battle of Teutoburg Forest south of the Elbe in A.D. 9, driving it back to the Rhine. Thereafter, Rome was consistently on the defensive against the endless chain of tribe driving tribe stretching back through the Central Asia steppe, west into Mongolia and the Takla Mekan,[6] a desert located in contemporary China's far western Xinjiang Province.

The nomadic invasions cast Afghanistan into a shatter zone for groups in search of booty and land. The Persian-speaking Parthian, Saka, and Kushan tribes, distant relatives of most contemporary Afghans, were the first to arrive. They attacked the Hellenistic cities established by Alexander the Great, pillaging, one by one, Balkh and then the Greek principalities at Kandahar, Ghazni, Jalalabad, Peshawar, and Badakhshan. Alexandria, near Kabul, was the last Greek city to fall in about 70 B.C., during the reign of the Greek king Hermaeus, but it was by no means the end of turmoil in the area. The Huns, and then the Turks and Mongols, continued to invade Afghanistan over the next 1,300 years.[7]

In the first century A.D. the Kushans overran Afghanistan and built an empire based near Peshawar in the region of Gandhara. Kushan kings adopted Buddhism.[8] Their empire profited from its location at the center of the Great Silk Road network of trade routes linking Han China to the Roman Empire. Caravans traversed Eurasia east to west, passing through the Afghan cities of Balkh, Kabul, Bamian, and Herat, and robust trade also moved along the north-south corridors linking Balkh, Kabul, Jalalabad, Peshawar, and Delhi. During the third to fifth centuries A.D., Buddhist missionaries traveling the Silk Road carved two giant Buddha statues into the soaring mountain cliffs of the Bamian Valley about 70 miles northwest of Kabul. The two standing Buddhas, 180 and 121 feet tall, survived invading armies for 1,500 years. In March 2001, the Taliban destroyed them for inciting idolatry and blasphemy and for violating their extremist "Islamic order."

The White Hun tribes, whom historians also identify as the Hephthaliti or Ephthalite Huns, burst out of the Takla Mekan into Central Asia and began flooding into Afghanistan in the fifth century A.D. As their name implies, the White Huns were Caucasians; according to the Byzantine historian Procopius, they had "white bodies and countenances that are not ugly."[9] The White Huns were unrelated to Attila's Black Huns rampaging through Europe at the same time.[10] They obliterated the Kushan Empire and everything else in their path as they proceeded into northern India.

The White Huns, like the Persian Parthians, Sakas, and Kushans, contributed to the bloodlines of most contemporary Afghans. Their empire, covering present-day Afghanistan, western Iran, and northern India, lasted into the second half of the sixth century. The current Pashtun tribal structure, customs, and language retain the imprint of the White Huns. They brought with them words that are prominent in today's Pashto vocabulary, including the word for "tribe," *ulus*, and *khan*, an honorific name for an important tribal elder or landowner.[11] The nineteenth-century British anthropologist H. W. Bellew listed White Hun and Pashtun shared attributes: "the rigid law of hospitality, the protection given to the refugee, the jealousy of female honour, the warlike spirit and insufferance of control, the pride of race, the jealousy of national honour and personal dignity, the spirit that loves to domineer."[12]

Instability and political anarchy shook Afghanistan and Central Asia after the White Huns marched through. Turkish tribes invaded in the tenth century, ransacking and pillaging down to the Indus Basin and through Persia into Anatolia. (In 1453, the Saljuk Turks overthrew the Byzantine Empire and established the Ottoman Dynasty, which lasted until World War I.) The great Arab expansion after Mohammed's death in 632 largely missed Afghanistan,[13] but it extended into Central Asia north of the Amu Darya, converting Turkish-speaking tribes to Islam; Arab and Turkish Muslim spiritual proselytes followed the Turkic sword into Afghanistan, conveying Islam's message. Arab Sayyids, whose name connotes ancestry extending back to the Prophet's daughter, Fatima, went to Afghanistan to spread Islam, married locally, and settled down. Most inhabitants of Afghanistan had embraced Islam by the mid-nineteenth century.

The Silk Road corridors through Eurasia were revived once more in the eighth and ninth centuries, but only north of the Amu Darya. Turkish and Mongolian invaders following the White Huns kept most of Afghanistan in the grip of anarchy. Genghis Khan's Mongol fury devastated middle Eurasia and East Asia in the thirteenth and fourteenth centuries. While stopping short of Western Europe and the scorching Indian plains, Mongol armies poured across the Amu Darya twice in the early thirteenth century. Genghis

Khan personally led the first assault in 1221, destroying the ancient Greek city of Balkh, then, with over 400,000 inhabitants, one of the largest population centers in the known world. The Mongols systematically massacred its population.[14] Herat surrendered to the advancing Mongol army but suffered Balkh's fate six months later when it revolted. Mongolian armies leveled Herat and went on to lay waste to Kabul and Ghazni. Moving west, the Mongols extinguished the Abbasidian caliphate in Baghdad, executing the caliph and the city's population of 200,000.

Afghanistan skidded deeper into the shatter zone. A fourteenth-century Arab traveler found Balkh uninhabited, the Panshir Valley deserted, and Kabul and Ghazni reduced to villages.[15] One hundred and sixty years after the Mongolians left Afghanistan, the Mongol-Turkic conqueror Tamerlane[16] tore through, killing, looting, and raping on his way to India. His armies massacred the inhabitants of towns and cities resisting his advance, piling their heads into giant pyramids.

The Mongolians, followed by Tamerlane's Turkic-Mongol hordes, depopulated cities, turned irrigated land into desert, and forced sedentary farming communities back into a nomadic existence. Afghanistan ceased to play its historic *entrepôt* role in Eurasian East-West trade. Instead, the population retreated into tiny, insular, tribal microcommunities in isolated mountain enclaves and valleys. Traveling through northern Afghanistan in 1272, the Italian Marco Polo observed that "the people have all taken refuge in fortresses among the mountains, on account of the Banditti and armies that harass them." In the early twentieth century, less than 8 percent of the population lived in towns with more than 10,000 people. Today, westerners traveling 20 miles outside of Afghanistan's major cities are startled to witness rural scenes of small, self-contained villages existing as they have for over a millennium.[17]

In contrast to Afghanistan, the clusters of civilization centers elsewhere in Eurasia gradually recovered from the Mongolian invasions. By the late seventeenth century, the Mughal Dynasty in India, the Chinese Manchus, and the Persian Safavid Empire had restored internal stability and economic growth. Expanding Russian and Chinese empires moved toward each other on the Central Asian steppe, absorbing the vast grasslands that had spawned the fierce nomadic invaders of their lands for 2,000 years.

The advance of European imperialism in the sixteenth to nineteenth centuries further intensified Afghanistan's isolation from broader regional and global currents. The European imperial expansion followed maritime trade routes around Africa into Asia, obviating the potential revival of the age-old land-centered Eurasian trade corridors through Afghanistan.

Instead of a crossroads of trans-Eurasian commerce, the Afghan highland became a battleground[18] for neighboring larger powers—a role that it has continued to play into contemporary times. The Indian Mughals and Persian Safavids fought to dominate the Afghan highland separating their empires. Neither was willing to commit the resources necessary to establish a lasting presence, or to restore the centuries-old international trade routes. Both recruited Afghan mercenaries, the Persians from the Durrani and Ghilzai tribes in southern Afghanistan, the Mughals from the eastern Ghilzai tribes. Kandahar changed hands repeatedly as Mughal and Persian armies, with their respective Afghan appendages, crisscrossed Afghanistan to attack one another.

The British gradually built their Indian Empire in the eighteenth and early nineteenth centuries. Afghanistan escaped colonization, a record that Afghans point to with understandable pride. But, while safeguarding their independence, they were also denied the modernizing benefits that India, Pakistan, and Iran received in their colonial—or, in the case of Iran, semi-colonial—association with the European imperial powers. In those countries, national unity and identity grew out of resistance movements to colonial control, such as the Indian Congress Party. While Western colonial influence led to the creation of disciplined armies and centralized administrative structures elsewhere in the region, Afghanistan remained fragmented. Tens of thousands of tiny rural tribal and ethnic groups did not look much beyond their isolated communities.

ψ

Fortuitous geostrategic circumstances in the eighteenth century opened a window for Afghans to throw off Mughal and Safavid control, establish an independent Afghan state, and briefly create an empire for themselves. The Safavid, Mughal, and Chinese Ching dynasties were all declining. The two European imperial giants, Great Britain and Russia, were still far from Afghanistan's periphery. Britain was preoccupied with wars in southern and eastern India. Russia was busy penetrating the Caucasus and northern Iran.

The Safavids had long capitalized on venomous Pashtun tribal rivalries to divide and conquer the Afghans. They ruled southern Afghanistan by sowing animosity between the two largest Pashtun confederations, the Ghilzai and Abdalis, later to be known as the Durranis. Safavid favoritism for the leading southern Ghilzai tribe, the Hotak, however, eventually culminated in the Iranian dynasty's own destruction. In 1709, Mirwais Hotak, the head of the Ghilzai Hotak tribe (the tribe of today's Taliban leader Mullah Mohammad Omar), invited the Safavid governor of Kandahar and the city's Safavid establishment to a banquet. There, he had them slaughtered to a man. Then Mirwais took over Kandahar city and convened a loya jirga that anointed him ruler. His kingdom was a small one. The majority of Ghilzai in southern Afghanistan were still nomads and difficult to organize, while the more numerous Abdalis were mostly sedentary, better organized, and fiercely resistant to Ghilzai hegemony.

When Mirwais died in 1715, his reach was still limited to Kandahar and the region immediately surrounding it. He was succeeded by his brother. Mirwais' son, Mahmud Mir, however, had other ideas: He assassinated his uncle and declared himself king. In 1722, Mahmud audaciously invaded Persia, leading a small army of Ghilzai horsemen. After defeating a Safavid army sent to halt his advance, he arrived at the walls surrounding Isfahan, the Persian capital. Preferring peaceful negotiation over armed resistance, the Safavid emperor opened the city gates and invited Mahmud in. Then, taking a cue from his father, Mahmud invited over one hundred Persian notables to a feast at the palace. He massacred them all and declared himself the new Persian emperor.

Persian dynastic histories prefer to downplay or ignore the sixteen-year interlude of Afghan Ghilzai rule in Persia. For their part, the Ghilzai still look back on Mirwais' and Mahmud's brief Hotak reign in Kandahar and Isfahan as crowning moments of Afghan history. But the Ghilzai's military capture of Isfahan proved to be their high point of empire building. They were fierce warriors but woefully unable to govern. Mahmud and his fellow tribesmen were relatively few in number and far from home, Sunni Afghans in a sea of Persian Shia.

Their sixteen years in power were tumultuous ones. The twenty-five-year-old Mahmud unleashed a reign of terror on Isfahan's population. When he cruelly turned on his Hotak kinsmen as well, his cousin, Ashraf, stopped the carnage by murdering him. In an unsuccessful effort to attract popular support, Ashraf paraded Mahmud's head through the streets of the Persian capital. That gesture could not save him. In 1736, Nadir "Slave of the Wonderful"

Quli, a camelman and part-time bandit of the Turkmen Afshar clan, raised a small force in northern Persia, expelled the detested Ghilzai from Isfahan in 1738, and established the Persian Afshar Dynasty. He gave himself the title of Nadir Shah. Ashraf Hotak fled into the Baluchistan desert toward Kandahar, only to be executed by a Baluch tribal chief who had switched his support to Nadir Shah.

Nadir Shah spent the first two years of his reign reestablishing Persian rule over most of Afghanistan. He reverted to the Persian practice of exploiting the deep-rooted rivalry between the Ghilzai and Abdali. The two tribes once again proved willing victims of foreign manipulation. Nadir Shah hired a sixteen-year-old Abdali aristocrat of the Abdali Popalzai tribe, Ahmad Khan, to join his personal staff. He elevated him to be commander of his army's largest cavalry contingent, composed mostly of Abdali tribesmen, all wearing pearl earrings.[19] Nadir's gifts of land to the Abdali were supplemented by lucrative opportunities to plunder during his foreign expeditions.

In 1738, with Ahmad Khan's assistance, Nadir Shah defeated the Ghilzai and captured their Kandahar stronghold. In retribution for Ghilzai depredations in Iran, Nadir expelled most of the Ghilzai tribes from Kandahar eastward to Zabul and Uruzgan. He transferred the confiscated Ghilzai lands to the Abdalis, emasculating Ghilzai power in southern Afghanistan until the late twentieth century, when Pakistan began to sponsor Ghilzai ascendancy over the Durranis in Afghanistan.

Using Ahmad Khan's cavalry force as his spearhead, Nadir Shah easily captured Delhi in 1739. There he cast covetous eyes on the Mughal emperor's splendid Peacock Throne and the giant Koh-i-Noor (Mountain of Light) diamond. According to legend, one of the women in the emperor's harem secretly informed Nadir Shah that he always kept the great stone wrapped up inside his turban. So, when Nadir invited the ruler, Mohammed Shah, to a victory banquet celebrating his capture of Delhi, the Mughal had to accept. When they were seated next to each other at the banquet, Mohammed Shah found himself in no position to reject Nadir's second invitation—that the two partake of the old custom of confirming their friendship by exchanging turbans. On returning to his chambers that evening, Nadir plucked the Koh-i-Noor from the Mughal emperor's turban and plotted his next move.[20]

The next day, he ordered a massacre of Delhi's population. The ensuing carnage is still referred to in India as Nadirshahi (Nadir's Scourge). The slaughter and looting continued for an entire day, culminating in Nadir Shah's pillage of the imperial treasury. The Persian conqueror sent home over a thousand elephants loaded down with the spoils of war, including the Peacock Throne,[21] as well as Indian masons, carpenters, and craftsmen.[22]

Nadir's seventeen-year reign ended in his tent. He had grown increasingly suspicious of those around him, including the members of his own royal family. Nadir relied more and more on Ahmad Khan's Abdali cavalry force, rather than his own Turkmen Qizilbash (Red Head) bodyguard force, for his personal safety. A French Catholic priest attached to Nadir's court noted that, "wherever he had halted, he had many people tortured and put to death, and had towers of their heads erected."[23] Nadir blinded his favorite son. He began to execute Qizilbash bodyguards whom he suspected of plotting against him. His suspicions about them were not misplaced.

One night in June 1747, Ahmad Khan, then twenty-five, was visited by an excited messenger sent from Nadir Shah's tent. The messenger transmitted orders from Nadir: Ahmad Khan was to mobilize his Abdali force and arrest all of the Qizilbash bodyguards the next morning. Unbeknownst to either Nadir or Ahmad Shah, however, a trusted agent of the Qizilbash commander had followed the messenger to Ahmad Khan's station and heard the exchange. He hurried back to warn his commander that the Afghans were planning to attack.

The conspirators decided to strike immediately. They entered Nadir Shah's tent. One of the Qizilbash guards severed Nadir's head from his body with his sword as the king rose from his bed. Pandemonium ensued. Ahmad Khan rushed to Nadir's tent only to find his head lying on the ground in a pool of blood. By this time, the Qizilbash bodyguards were plundering the encampment, including the women's quarters. Ahmad Khan and his Afghan mercenaries descended on Nadir's treasury and confiscated most of its contents, including the Koh-i-Noor. They rode back to Kandahar. A Persian scribe wrote at the time that Ahmad Khan took "advantage of the universal confusion which succeeded the murder of the tyrant (and) found means to carry off a great part of his wealth."[24]

Back in Kandahar, Ahmad Khan and eight other Abdali tribal chiefs convened a loya jirga to choose a new king. Ahmad Khan participated in the conclave as the leader of the small Popalzai tribe and his saddozai clan. Though he was much younger than the elders of the other tribes, his battle-tested

4,000-man mercenary force and the considerable war booty he had brought impressed the other chiefs. The participating tribal leaders debated their own kingly merits. Elders from the largest Abdali tribe, the Barakzai, pressed their claim to rule the new Afghan state. Ahmad Khan sat silently. After nine days of inconclusive discussions the selection process narrowed to two candidates: Ahmad Khan of the Popalzai tribe and Haji Ahmad Khan of the Barakzai tribe. A respected *darwish* (holy man) rose to break the deadlock, declaring: "Why all this verbose talk? God has created Ahmed Khan a much greater man than any of you; he is the most noble of all the Afghan families. Maintain, therefore, God's work, for his wrath will weigh heavily upon you if you destroy it."[25]

The other tribal chiefs unanimously accepted Ahmad Khan as Afghanistan's first king. The holy man plaited a circlet of wheat straw and placed it on Ahmad Khan's head. Ahmad Khan made himself *shah*, or king, of an independent Afghanistan. He added "Durrani" (Pearl of Pearls) to his title, becoming Ahmad Shah Durrani. His Durrani title became the name of the Durrani tribe.

Ahmad Shah founded the modern Afghan state. His tribal army annexed Kabul as well as present-day northern and western Afghanistan and Ghilzai eastern Afghanistan. During his twenty-five-year reign, to 1772, he conquered a short-lived Afghan empire. It encompassed Mashad in northern Iran, Bukhara in Central Asia, Peshawar, Kashmir, and much of northern India.

Ahmad Shah's personal charisma, bravery, and record of military successes attracted Pashtuns and non-Pashtuns to his side. It was, however, mainly the allure of booty rather than a sense of Afghan nationalism that fueled his empire building. He followed Nadir Shah's practice of rewarding his troops with the booty they captured and the women they defiled. His marriage alliances with important Durrani and Ghilzai families helped consolidate his empire.

The Afghan king managed his empire by following the feudal practice of ruling indirectly through indigenous power brokers. He stationed sons and other trusted representatives in conquered territories to collect tribute, leaving governing responsibilities in the hands of local leaders. The plunder he gathered in foreign raids, including eight to Delhi, filled his treasury and lubricated his tribal patronage network in Kandahar. Ahmad Shah did not create a government apparatus at the center. Rather, he ruled through the tribal jirga and allowed Pashtun tribal chiefs to keep their authority. In this way

MAP 2.1   AHMAD SHAH DURRANI'S AFGHAN EMPIRE, 1762

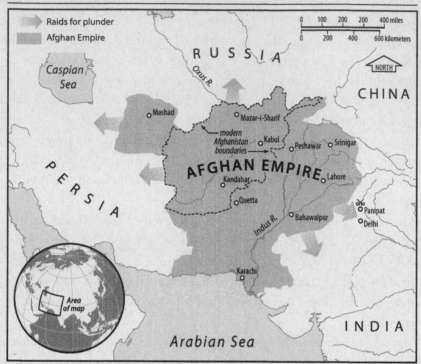

he did not follow the path of European and Russian monarchs, who subdued feudal barons and centralized military and administrative powers in their own hands. By maintaining the fractious, decentralized tribal system, Ahmad Shah ensured that the empire he had built would crumble after his death in 1772.

Ahmad Shah Durrani made immense contributions to the Afghan state and people. He led his country to independence and, briefly, to empire. He created a feeling of national unity and pride in the Afghan population. Today, he is respected as the father (*baba*) of the nation, the embodiment of Afghan nationalism. His disinclination to create national governing institutions, however, left another legacy that would outlive him: national disunity. His kingdom, in essence, was a confederation of independent tribal fiefdoms with minimal aspects of statehood.[26] He ruled through Pashtun tribal chiefs, not over them. The tribal chiefs who retained their autonomy under Ahmad Shah were less willing to cooperate with his sons and grandsons, and his aversion to establishing a strong central government thus hastened his empire's decline. The predatory outer-circle powers closing in on Afghanistan at his death all had what Ahmad Shah's successors lacked—a civil service, a functioning administrative machinery, and a central army instead of *ad hoc* tribal levies.

Ahmad Shah's strong military leadership qualities inspired his armies to victory after victory. But it was the patronage he distributed to his tribal followers and the loot they acquired during his campaigns that sustained their allegiance. The ancient Pashto adage, "There is no Khan without *Dostarkhwan* [tablecloth]," highlights the tribal leader's challenge to feed his followers. Each tribal chief needs to acquire recurring resources to sustain his position on the tribal summit. His ability to deliver resources becomes even more critical if he wishes to expand his domain beyond his kinship network. If he fails in this primary mission, he risks losing to tribal rivals and will be discarded.

ψ

External and internal pressures combined to pull down the Afghan empire and foment internal strife after Ahmad Shah Durrani died. The geopolitical environment in the outer circle of nations shifted substantially during the last three decades of the eighteenth century. The Sikhs in the Punjab rebelled, expelling local Durrani governors and eventually capturing Peshawar. The new Iranian Qajar Dynasty reclaimed Mashad and laid siege to Herat. Uzbeks recovered Bukhara. British power expanded into northern India, Sind, and Baluchistan in the first half of the nineteenth century. Quetta, 90 miles from Kandahar, became a British military outpost. Three Anglo-Sikh wars in the 1840s resulted in British absorption of the Sikh empire. Britain assumed control over Sikh possessions in Peshawar, Kashmir, and Pashtun-settled areas between the Indus River and the Suleiman Range. Russia approached from the north, annexing Tashkent, Bukhara, Khivo, Khokand, Turkmenistan, and the Afghan outpost of Kashk, only 40 miles north of Herat, between 1865 and 1879.

Bloody wars of succession tore Afghan unity. The Afghan tribal system does not recognize the principle of primogeniture. Dynastic succession from father to son helped stabilize emerging states in Europe, China, and Russia. Ahmad Shah did designate his second son, Timur Khan, to succeed him, but that did not deter some of his other sons from declaring themselves king.

Ahmad Shah's multiple wives each championed their child's right to the throne. Although Timur enjoyed the support of Ahmad Shah's *wazir* (prime minister or senior adviser), Paindah Khan, a powerful Barakzai chief of the Mohammadzai clan, his claim was challenged by his half-brother, Suleiman. After routing Suleiman's army, Timur agreed to grant him asylum, *nanawati*, in exchange for a pledge of loyalty. But when Suleiman returned to Kandahar, Timur violated his Pashtunwali commitment and executed him along with his older brother and two sons. To escape further coup attempts, Timur moved his capital to Kabul; thereafter, he rarely visited Kandahar. He chose Peshawar as his winter capital. There, his mother's membership in the powerful nearby Yusufzai tribe provided a security screen from Durrani intrigues in Kandahar.

Succession struggles resumed with a vengeance among Timur's twenty-three sons after his death in 1793. Timur's Yusufzai queen lobbied Paindah Khan, the Mohammadzai wazir, to support her son Zaman. Paindah Khan agreed, placing his Barakzai tribe, the largest within the Durrani confederation, behind Zaman's claim to the throne. With Paindah Khan's aid, Zaman assumed command of the Qizilbash force in Kabul that Timur had used for his personal security. Zaman also took over Timur's treasury, including the Koh-i-Noor diamond.

Feeling his position more secure, Zaman attempted to do what neither Ahmad Shah nor Timur had previously tried: build a central government and an army that were not dependent on unreliable tribal chiefs to provide him with manpower for his campaigns. This proved to be his undoing. As part of his reforms he dismissed his powerful wazir, Paindah Khan. In response, Paindah Khan's Mohammadzai clan convened a secret meeting in Kabul. Zaman heard about the meeting and arrested Paindah at his Kabul residence. Paindah's son, Fateh Khan, urged his father to resist, but the Mohammadzai leader proudly refused. He marched off under guard to the palace, head high, and Zaman immediately executed him on arrival at the palace.

The execution drew quick Barakzai retribution. Fateh Khan raised a large tribal army in the Durrani heartland, and it marched north with Mahmud, another son of Timur's, and put him on the throne. Zaman fled Kabul toward Peshawar but was betrayed by a Ghilzai tribal chief near Jalalabad, who held him in his stone fort until Fateh Khan's troops arrived. Once in Fateh Khan's hands, Zaman was blinded, his eyes pierced with a lancelet. With the help of relatives, Zaman was taken to Ludhiana in the Punjab, where he lived out the rest of his life on a British pension. Shuja, Zaman's full brother, managed to mobilize a Ghilzai force and eventually drive Mahmud from Kabul, reigning from 1803 to 1809. But with Fateh Khan's help, Mahmud counterattacked and defeated Shuja's forces. Shuja escaped to the Punjab, where he joined the blind Zaman as a guest-hostage of Sikh king Ranjit Singh.[27]

King Mahmud placed most affairs of state into Fateh Khan's hands and preoccupied himself with his harem and wine cellar. Fateh Khan's leverage was thus immense. Unfulfilled by serving Popalzai kings, he began to place his twenty-one Mohammadzai brothers into key posts in Kabul and the provinces. Then Fateh Khan slipped up: He led an expedition to Herat and arrested its Popalzai governor, one of Mahmud's half-brothers, on suspicions of colluding with Persia.

When he learned of the arrest, Mahmud's sadistic, half-deranged son, Kamran, imprisoned Fateh Khan and had him blinded with a dagger. He then took the Mohammadzai wazir back to Kabul, where his limbs were slowly cut off, one by one, in the presence of King Mahmud.[28] The Popalzai's torture and murder of the loyal Fateh Khan was the last straw for his Mohammadzai brothers. In 1818 they captured Kabul and established the Barakzai Mohammadzai Dynasty. Mahmud and Kamran fled to Herat. Ten years later, Kamran poisoned his father, then fell into a life of opium-driven debauchery. In 1842, his wazir murdered him.

With the Popalzais out of the way, the Mohammadzai brothers and half-brothers fought over the Afghan throne, unleashing a fresh round of Padshah-gardi within the clan that continued until 1881.

ψ

The nineteenth-century clash of the British Indian and Russian empires in Central Asia, known as "the Great Game," was often lethal for its players. The term was coined by a British army captain, Arthur Connolly, in the early nineteenth century and made famous by British novelist Rudyard Kipling. Connolly himself succumbed to the Great Game's violent vicissitudes on the emir of Bukhara's chopping block in 1842.[29]

The Russian imperial movement toward Afghanistan and India obsessed British strategic planners during the nineteenth century. Unlike the British, the Russians had the advantage of advancing from land, exploiting interior lines of troop movement, communication, and supply. Russian officers conducted secret visits to Afghanistan, and Britain's position on the Indian subcontinent appeared increasingly vulnerable.

In part to justify their strategic and economic-driven expansionism to domestic audiences back home, the British and Russian governments (not unlike twentieth-century Soviets) explained their motives in ideological terms. Rudyard Kipling elaborated on the "White Man's Burden," the responsibility to lift colonial populations out of ignorance and to civilize them. His writings became a rallying cry for proselytizing Christianity among subject peoples in the empires of the day. Russian leaders and the Russian media similarly heralded Russia's divine mission to civilize backward societies in the path of Russia's expansion across Central Asia and Siberia.

Britain adopted a "forward policy" in Afghanistan during the 1830s to prevent Russia from dominating Afghanistan. The British governor-general of India, Lord Auckland, was a fervent proponent of the forward policy. His political adviser, Sir William Macnaghten, soon also to lose out in the Great Game, confidently promised that a British invasion of Afghanistan would make the Hindu Kush the "insurmountable and I hope, lasting barrier to all encroachments from the Westward."[30] Auckland and Macnaghten assembled a 21,000-strong "Army of the Indus" to carry the exiled Afghan king, Shah Shuja, still exiled in the Punjab, to Kabul and place him on the throne. The British decision to replace the then Barakzai Mohammadzai ruler in Kabul, Dost Mohammad, with a member of the vanquished Popalzai line doomed their military expedition to defeat from the start. The Mohammadzai brothers had carved Afghanistan up into individual fiefdoms. They were continually at war with one another, but temporarily postponed their quarrels for the larger purpose of expelling the foreign invader.

The 1838 British invasion of Afghanistan established a pattern repeated during future invasions of Afghanistan: hubristic justifications, initial success, gradually widening Afghan resistance, stalemate, and withdrawal. Governor-General Lord Auckland's Simla Manifesto, issued on October 1, 1838, disclaimed any intention of invading Afghanistan. It announced that Britain was returning the legitimate Afghan ruler, Shah Shuja, to power "against foreign interference." Shuja, it argued, "had found an honorable asylum in the British dominions" and enjoyed "popularity throughout Afghanistan," in contrast to Dost Mohammad and "Barakzai chiefs," whose "disunion and unpopularity, were ill-fitted, under any circumstances, to be useful allies to the British Government." The manifesto gushed that Auckland "rejoices that, in the discharge of his duty, he will be enabled to assist in restoring the union and prosperity of the Afghan people."[31]

The Army of the Indus entered Kabul on August 7, 1839, and placed Shah Shuja in power. Deserted by all but a few, Dost Mohammad fled the city. He returned in 1840 to surrender to Macnaghten. Disregarding Shah Shuja's appeal that he be executed, the British exiled Dost Mohammad to India. Afghan opposition to the British occupation and the foreign-imposed Shah Shuja built steadily throughout 1840 and 1841. Occasional sniping at the British cantonment graduated into an outright siege. Dost Mohammad's twenty-seven-year-old son Mohammad Akbar Khan rallied Pashtun, Tajik, and Uzbek formations in the hills around Kabul to attack British patrols. In 1841, small groups of Afghans from the Ghilzai tribes between Kabul and India ambushed British supply convoys. On November 1, Macnaghten's political assistant, Lieutenant Colonel Alexander Burnes, was killed in his Kabul residence by an outraged Afghan mob. The mob cut to pieces two other British officers and Burnes's Indian bodyguard, and it looted the nearby British garrison's treasury, depriving Macnaghten of funds to pacify Afghan tribal chiefs and their followers.[32]

Macnaghten's weakening leverage led him to conclude a written commitment with Akbar Khan and other tribal chiefs to permit the British army's safe withdrawal back to India. In return, he agreed to restore Akbar Khan's father, Dost Mohammad, to the Afghan throne. At a later meeting, however, Akbar Khan skillfully exposed Macnaghten's earlier attempts to bribe some of the tribal chiefs present. Sensing danger, Macnaghten attempted to leave. Akbar Khan grabbed Macnaghten and stabbed him to death. His head was paraded through crowds of cheering Afghans in the Kabul bazaar.

British commander General Willian Elphinstone ordered a retreat to India in the dead of the bitter Afghan winter. Some 16,000 British, Indian, and Afghan troops, along with British dependents and camp followers, began a death march to India on January 6, 1842. Most perished in Ghilzai ambushes before reaching the first British outpost at Jalalabad. While the broken Army of the Indus was being decimated along the road to Jalalabad, Shah Shuja turned on the British, exhorting Afghans to expel the infidels from Afghanistan. But his bid to convert from Afghan turncoat to Afghan hero was

unsuccessful. He was lured outside of Kabul, betrayed, and murdered. The
British released Dost Mohammad and facilitated his return to Afghanistan.

The disastrous Afghan war discredited Britain's forward policy for three
decades. In 1878, the British tried again. This time, 33,000 British troops
crossed into Afghanistan, igniting the second Anglo-Afghan war. Again, the
British enjoyed early successes but eventual failure. Afghan ruler Sher Ali fled
to the Amu Darya. The Russians rejected his appeal for assistance. Isolated,
abandoned by Afghans, and in deteriorating health, Sher Ali died in February
1879. In May, the British forced his son, Yaqub Khan, to sign the Treaty of
Gandamak, surrendering to the British the Khyber Pass, the Pashtun tribal
areas east of the Khyber (in present-day Pakistan), plus the region north of
the Bolan Pass (also in present-day Pakistan) south of Kandahar province.
The Afghans agreed to British control of Afghan foreign policy and a permanent British residency in Kabul; the British, in return, promised an annual
stipend to Yaqub Khan and his successors. Prime Minister Benjamin Disraeli
publicly hailed Britain's success in pushing the empire's sphere of influence
to the Hindu Kush watershed.[33]

As is so often the case involving foreign invaders of Afghanistan, Disraeli's
declaration of victory was premature. The tempo of Afghan resistance to the
British occupation was proceeding according to Afghan time. On September
3, 1879, two months after the British representative moved into his new Residency in Kabul, a violent mob attacked and killed him along with his political
staff and military escort. In southern Afghanistan, on July 27, 1880, the
British army garrison at Kandahar marched out to confront a large Afghan
force descending from the north. The British were soundly defeated in the
resulting Battle of Maiwand, suffering some 1,000 casualties.[34] They retreated
to Kandahar and expelled the entire Afghan population from the city.[35]

Afterwords, the British commander, General Frederick Roberts, had every
reason to be pessimistic. He faced a growing insurgency in the countryside,
the likely prospect of an endless, expensive guerrilla war, and rising antiwar
sentiment back home. A new liberal government in London was calling for
terminating the expensive, unproductive Afghan war. Lord Roberts had deposed Yaqub Khan—there was no effective Afghan leader to pass responsibility to in Kabul.

At that depressing juncture, Afghanistan's inclination for the unpredictable
saved the day. A swashbuckler member of the royal Mohammadzai clan,

Abdur Rahman Khan, rode into Kabul on horseback. He was returning from twelve years of self-exile in Russia, where he had fled after attempting to overthrow his uncle, King Sher Ali.

Abdur Rahman wore a Russian military uniform. Fewer than one hundred men rode with him. Before arriving in Afghanistan's capital, he brashly proclaimed himself the new Afghan ruler. The British, sensing an opening to cut their losses and extricate their army from Afghanistan, and betting on Abdur Rahman's staying power, announced their recognition of his claim to be Afghanistan's next leader. In hastily organized negotiations with Abdur Rahman before leaving, the British agreed not to interfere in Afghan domestic affairs, not to station a representative in Kabul, and to provide Abdur Rahman with large subsidies. For his part, Abdur Rahman assured the British he would recognize the terms of the Gandamak Treaty and not establish foreign political ties with any nation other than Britain. Within two months, the entire British garrison in Kabul had been withdrawn from Afghanistan.

The British secretary of state for India, Lord Hartington, cogently summed up the bitter harvest of the two nineteenth-century Anglo-Afghan wars in an 1880 speech. His words, slightly amended, would resonate into the twentieth century: "As the result of two successful campaigns, of the employment of an enormous force, and of the expenditures of large sums of money, all that has yet been accomplished has been the disintegration of the State, . . . the assumption of fresh and unwelcome liabilities in regard to one of its provinces, and a condition of anarchy throughout the remainder of the country." Lord Roberts added, "I feel sure that I am right when I say that the less the Afghans see of us the less they will dislike us."[36]

☙

Abdur Rahman did not have much to start with in war-wracked Afghanistan. The royal palace had been so badly damaged that he had to live in a tent. The conflict had inflicted great economic damage in the Afghan Pashtun belt. In 1893, Abdur Rahman signed the Durand Line accord, formally giving Britain control of the Pashtun areas surrendered by Yaqub Khan in the Treaty of Gandamak. The 1,600-mile line, today's Afghan-Pakistan border, was drawn about 60 miles north of the Indus, through the Suleiman Mountains, then east to Chitral and west to Chaman, just north of Quetta. At the time, Britain interpreted the Durand Line as more of a demarcation of Britain's sphere of influence, the northern frontier for its empire, than an international border.

The Afghans, including Rahman Khan, resented the implication that the Pashtun lands originally taken by the Sikhs, including Peshawar, now lay further from their grasp. The Durand Line divided Pashtun tribes, clans, and even families. Some Afghan rulers denounced the treaty, and the Afghan government rejected its validity when the British transferred power to Pakistan in 1947.

Abdur Rahman's principal negotiating goal was not to reclaim lost territory but to expand the center's influence into the regions. He desperately needed British recurring resources, specifically money and arms to overpower his opponents inside Afghanistan. Britain sweetened his accession to the Durand Line agreement by raising his annual stipend by nearly 40 percent and allowing him to purchase arms and ammunitions in India.

The "Iron Emir" spent most of his twenty-one-year rule at war with Mohammadzai relatives seeking the throne and Ghilzai, Hazaras, Tajiks, and Nuristanis resisting his military operations to bludgeon them into submission. He relied on terror, brutality, and his army and secret police apparatus to suppress dissidence, and he executed influential tribal leaders who might one day pose a threat to his position. He exiled suspected conspirators, including many belonging to his Mohammadzai clan. Criminals were placed in cages atop wooden posts at roadsides, left to slowly starve to death.

Abdur Rahman fielded a 100,000-man army to ruthlessly suppress the great 1885–1886 Ghilzai rebellion. He uprooted troublesome Durrani and Ghilzai tribes and transported them to Uzbek- and Tajik-populated areas in the north, where they could balance local, non-Pashtun groups and act as a screen against further Russian encroachments on Afghan territory. Their dispersion among non-Pashtun groups made them dependent on the central government in Kabul. Rahman enrolled tens of thousands of Pashtun warriors in a Muslim jihad against Shia Hazaras in the Hazarajat and animist tribes in Kafiristan (Land of the Unbelievers). The Pashtun holy warriors were rewarded with plunder and land grants in the regions conquered by the emir's wars of internal imperialism. After subduing Kafiristan and forcibly converting most of its population to Islam, Abdur Rahman renamed it Nuristan (Land of Light).

Abdur Rahman did not follow Ahmad Shah's practice of basing his legitimacy on the tribal jirga. He assumed for himself the divine right to rule his Muslim subjects. He was an emir, the leader of a Muslim state, not a king. Opposition to his authority was portrayed as opposition to God, and Rahman did not hesitate to execute religious clerics who challenged him. For all Afghans, internal travel was restricted. Travel abroad was prohibited without government permission, a practice that was continued until the adoption of Zahir Shah's 1964 democratic constitution.

Rahman carefully prepared his oldest son, Habibullah, to succeed him. Habibullah's many brothers and half-brothers were kept on a tight leash, pre-empting wars of succession among the princes. When, unique among the Afghan rulers gaining the throne in the twentieth century, the Iron Emir died in his bed in 1901, he passed a rudimentary central government on to his son.

Britain's defeats in the two Anglo-Afghan wars and the relative stability in Afghanistan during Abdur Rahman's reign dampened Russo-British imperial aspirations in Afghanistan. The rising power of Germany in Central Europe at the end of the nineteenth century also worked to Afghanistan's advantage. The two empires along Afghanistan's periphery suspended their Great Game rivalry in Afghanistan in order to confront Germany and its allies. Russia and France concluded a defensive alliance in 1894 to counter the 1882 Triple Alliance of Germany, Austria, and Italy, which Turkey joined on the eve of World War I. In 1904, Britain and France signed the Triple Entente, which Russia joined in 1907, basically rounding out the network of two interlocking alliance systems that inexorably drifted toward the outbreak of World War I in 1914.

A series of diplomatic conferences beginning in 1885 and culminating in the 1907 Russo-British St. Petersburg convention consigned Afghanistan to a buffer role between the British and Russian empires. The Russians acknowledged Britain's role in guiding Afghan foreign policy, agreeing to deal with Afghanistan on political matters only through the British government. Britain agreed not to annex any more Afghan territories. Without reference to Afghans, British and Russian negotiators established Afghanistan's northern boundaries with Russia, China, and Iran. By 1873, the two countries had reached agreement on the Amu Darya as the boundary between Russia and

Afghanistan in the northern middle sector of the Russo-Afghan frontier. Anglo-Russian boundary commissions demarcated the border on the ground in the western sector between the Amu Darya and Iran. In 1895, another Anglo-Russian boundary commission extended Afghanistan's eastern boundaries by means of a 50-mile-wide sliver of land to the Chinese border. Known as the Wakhan Corridor, this particular piece of colonial map-making reinforced the Afghan buffer by ensuring that the British Indian and Russian Central Asian empires did not touch each other.

Britain and Russia showed restraint in Afghanistan long after the 1907 convention became defunct. Common opposition to Germany continued to buttress their mutual restraint in Afghanistan during the twenty-year hiatus between the two world wars. Stalin's focus on internal consolidation of power in the 1920s and 1930s helped to prolong Afghanistan's respite from outer-circle military threats, as did British-Soviet cooperation during World War II.

The 1979 Soviet invasion of Afghanistan dramatically ended Afghanistan's role as a buffer between Great Powers. Over three decades of warfare fueled by outside powers followed. Afghanistan fell back into the shatter zone, suffering bloodshed and destruction not witnessed since the Mongolian invasions in the thirteenth century.

CHAPTER 3

Tribe and Mosque

The very name Pashtun spells honor and glory
Lacking that honor what is the Afghan story?
In the sword alone lies our deliverance
The sword is our predominance.

—KHUSHAL KHAN KHATAK,
SIXTEENTH-CENTURY AFGHAN
TRIBAL CHIEF AND POET[1]

There are two types on the Path.
Those who come against their will,
the blindly religious people,
and those who obey out of love.
The former have ulterior motives. . . .
The former memorize their proof-texts
of conformity and repeat them.
The latter disappear into whatever draws them to God.

—JALALUDDIN RUMI,
THIRTEENTH-CENTURY
AFGHAN SUFI POET[2]

Why have foreign governments repeatedly ended up in the Afghan quagmire? The answer lies principally in their misunderstanding of the complicated mosaic of Afghan tribes and the influence of religious leaders. Foreign powers have failed to appreciate the way these Afghan groups interact with one another and with the central government in Kabul.

No central government in Afghan history has ever directly governed the regions, mainly because of the tribal and religious resistance to central government authority. The tensions in this power triangle of government, tribal, and religious forces have marked Afghanistan's history. The central government reached its apogee of influence during Abdur Rahman Khan's rule (1880–1901) when the Iron Emir superseded the clergy, declaring himself God's representative and the supreme religious power in Afghanistan. He assumed the authority to apply Sharia and declare jihad, and his army ruthlessly crushed tribal opposition. Abdur Rahman's Mohammadzai successors lost some ground in the first three-quarters of the twentieth century but still held the upper hand over tribal leaders and clergy up to the 1978 communist coup. The subsequent more than three decades of continuous war, down to the present, have weakened the center and strengthened the tribal and religious sides of the triangle. The emergence of warlords, criminals, and narcotics traffickers (sometimes rolled into one) and Pakistan's sponsorship of extremist proxy warfare in Afghanistan have disrupted and in some areas destroyed the traditional government, tribal, and religious balances at the local and national levels.

Tribalism and Islam have been living with one another in Afghanistan since the arrival of Islam in the ninth century. Islam in most of Afghanistan became absorbed inside the tribal cocoon, grafted onto centuries of pre-Islamic Hindu, Buddhist, and animist customs. The ancient Pashtun tribal code, *Pashtunwali* (the way of the Pashtun), predominated. Tension between tribe and mosque, however, was never absent. A Pashtun saying, "Pashtuns accept half of the Koran," depicts the age-old struggle for influence between khan and mullah, or the mosque and *hujra*, the tribal chief's guesthouse.

While cast in various forms, the competition between tribe and mosque is, at its core, a contest for raw power, locally and nationally. The religious leader espouses Sharia, which accepts no boundary between the religious and the temporal. Mullah Omar claims to interpret God's will as revealed to the Prophet in the Koran. Omar insists that religious and political legitimacy is consigned by God to religious clerics like himself who can interpret Koranic law. President Hamid Karzai bases his legitimacy on elections, deferring to a constitution drafted by men and approved by a loya jirga; the Afghan Constitution cites the loya jirga as "the highest manifestation of the people of Afghanistan."[3] A tribal community leader bases his legitimacy on the Pashtunwali code passed down within Pashtun tribes from generation to generation from pre-Islamic times. He is a devout Muslim, but his personal influence is rooted in Pashtunwali.

Differences between Pashtunwali and Sharia abound in the villages and rural areas where more than 80 percent of Afghans live. Sharia permits women to keep their dowry after marriage or following a divorce and to inherit property. In Pashtunwali, the girl's bride price goes to her family, not to the girl herself. *Zan, zar, zamin*—women, gold, and land—add up to a triad of tribal property that a tribesman must defend at all costs. One Pashtun told me that an Afghan Mujahidin willing to achieve martyrdom in the name of Islam would, at the same time, "not accept Islam when asked to give a share of his land to his daughter."[4] Pashtunwali permits the killing of boys and girls who elope and of women who commit adultery. The Koran prescribes other punishments and does not stipulate execution for adultery.

The independent-minded streak in the Afghan character resists clerical dictation. Indeed, the tribesman rejects attempts by any outsiders, including religious figures, to limit his freedom. Community jirgas and *qazis* (Muslim judges) administering the law in most rural areas generally defer to tribal codes and traditions, not to Sharia, in meting out justice. Since there are no jails, justice is swift and decisive. A murder case can result in the victim's family executing the culprit on the spot. More often, however, Pashtunwali seeks to avoid punitive family-on-family measures because they can heighten the level of violence between families in the tribe. Promoting tribal harmony and reconciliation takes precedence over punishment. Serious crimes can be resolved by handing over one or more unmarried women from the offender's family along with a cash payment. This Pashtunwali resolution, not found in Sharia, staves off future vendettas by uniting the bloodlines and preserving the honor of both families.

☙

Afghanistan is sometimes described as a museum of nationalities. The incessant invasions over many centuries created the present ethnic and racial mosaic

MAP 3.1   ETHNIC GROUPS IN AFGHANISTAN

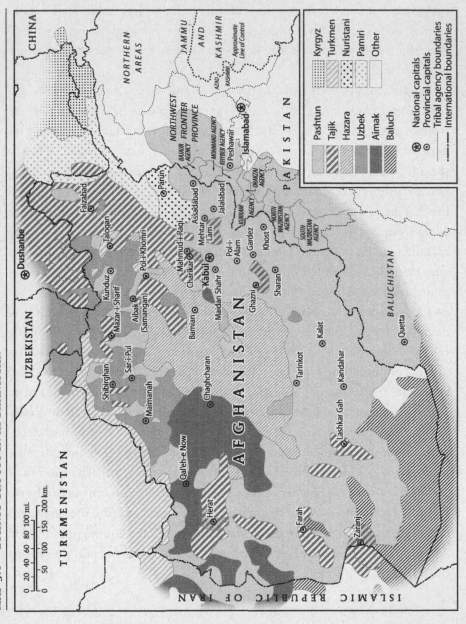

depicted on Map 3.1. Each group brought with it different characteristics that have affected Afghanistan in their own way.

Persian, Arabic, and British writers gave greater attention to the Pashtun tribes than to other ethnicities, in part because the Pashtun tribes make up the largest ethnic group in Afghanistan.[5] Pashtuns have dominated the contemporary Afghan state since it was created in the eighteenth century. The British Empire's conflicts with the warlike Pashtun tribes on both sides of the Durand Line also explain this emphasis. Pashtun resistance to the British became a part of British lore about their Indian Empire. British scholars and frontier officials studied the Pashtun tribes, learned Pashto, and translated Pashto literature and poetry into English.

In rural southern and eastern Afghanistan, the great majority of Pashtuns remain sedentary agriculturalists. They are raised to adhere proudly to their Pashtun tribal and clan identities. About 300,000 Pashtun *kuchis* (nomads) continue the age-old practice of herding their flocks and pitching their tents in the Afghan highlands during the summer, then moving back to homes in the Pashtun belt during the winter.

The Nuristanis in the high mountains of the eastern Hindu Kush arrived before the invasions by Persian-speaking nomads began in about the second century B.C. Although remnants of Alexander the Great's army are said to have contributed to their European features, the Nuristanis are more likely descendents of the earliest Aryan migrations from Central Asia, which occurred during the second millennium B.C. One wing of this migration went west into Europe, while the other swept south into Afghanistan, Persia, and the Indian subcontinent.

The Nuristanis appear to have remained bottled up in remote enclaves in the towering eastern Hindu Kush, while the Aryan tribes and future invaders from the steppe intermingled with the darker inhabitants of the subcontinent and with each other. Today, the approximately 230,000 Nuristanis live in tiny villages carved into the sides of soaring mountains rising to 21,000 feet above sea level. The narrow valleys and steep mountains are also home to tall deodar cedars that local Nuristani lumber barons cut down and illegally smuggle into Pakistan.

The inaccessibility of Nuristani communities and their isolation from one another as well as the outside world help to explain why this ethnic group is divided into six major tribes with five different languages. Each language is derived from the Sanskritic Indic (in contrast to the Persian) branch of the Aryan linguistic tree, and some of the tribes, most notably the Kalasha,[6] the second largest, bear Sanskrit names.

The Nuristanis and the Dards, a smaller group, also of Aryan descent,[7] scattered in northeastern Afghanistan, exhibit European characteristics, including fair skin, often blue eyes, and red or blond hair.[8] The British, Germans, and other Europeans developed romantic notions of these remote tribes during the nineteenth and early twentieth centuries, with British authors connecting the Dards to the Dardans, a people recorded in Hellenic times as assisting the Trojans in their wars with the Greeks. Rudyard Kipling's short story "The Man Who Would Be King," written in the 1880s, seemed set in wild, remote Nuristan and adjacent Konar province.

The Nazis in the late 1920s and 1930s investigated reports of blue-eyed, blond Afghans, and particularly Nuristanis and their similarity to German Nordics. In 1927, a German racial theorist wrote, "But it is especially among the Afghans that a Nordic strain seems to have been preserved . . . in the mountains," preventing the "dilution of Nordic bloods." Another German writer observed that the Afghans "could just as well have been born on a farm in north Germany as in the huts of their mountain slopes," isolated enough from other peoples to have retained their "pure" Aryan ancestry.[9] Two Nazi racial expeditions toured Nuristani villages in the 1930s and returned to Germany with photos and head measurements.

The Nuristanis are known for their uncompromising opposition to armed outsiders. Mostly nonliterate, and brave fighters, they became archconservative Muslims after their forced conversion by Abdur Rahman Khan in the 1890s. Ahmed Shah Masood established his first resistance base against the Afghan communist regime in Nuristan in 1978 before moving on to the Panshir.

The Tajiks, the second-largest Afghan ethnic group, are mainly settled in northern and western Afghanistan. Like the Pashtuns, however, they can be encountered in every section of the country, including inside the Pashtun belt. They follow the basic precepts of the Pashtunwali code. *Taj* in Arabic means "ornament," and Tajik mythology traces Tajik origins to the ornaments once worn by the Prophet. Although Tajiks are generally referred to as a distinct ethnolinguistic group, they usually identify themselves by their families' original geographic location. The numerous Tajik communities near Herat in western Afghanistan thus call themselves "Heratis." The Tajiks in the Panshir Valley are "Panshiris."

The Panshiri Tajiks and Tajiks living in adjacent Kohistan on the Shomali plain, between Kabul and the Panshir Valley, have a Pashtun-like reputation for military prowess of the kind demonstrated so well by Ahmed Shah Masood and his Mujahidin during the Soviet-Afghan war and the Taliban period. But their warlike reputation goes back to at least the early nineteenth century, when British officer Alexander Burnes, traveling through the region, contrasted the local Tajik inhabitants and the Tajiks elsewhere in Afghanistan:

> It is a source of deep regret that this beautiful country should be inhabited by a race of men so turbulent and vindictive as the Tajiks have here proved themselves to be, and yet, throughout Afghanistan generally, the same Tajiks form the most peaceable classes of the population. Here, however, their blood feuds are endless, a week never passes without strife or assassination. . . . "Blood for blood" is their motto and their rule; and as they still rigidly follow it up, every fresh act of violence increases the number of feuds, and extends the misery resulting from them still more widely.[10]

Today's basic Tajik social units are generally small and limited to family and clan, not large tribes. Tajiks make up a large portion of Kabul's population; they are active in commerce and frequently fill the roles of artisans, shopkeepers, teachers, and government bureaucrats. Many held down important ministerial portfolios under Pashtun rulers. One Tajik, Dr. Mohammed Yousuf, was appointed prime minister following Afghanistan's first democratic election in 1965. Tajiks Burhanuddin Rabbani and Ahmed Shah Masood controlled the Afghan government in Kabul for four years, 1992–1996, after Najib fell.

The Baluch are divided along kinship lines into tribes and have a more rigid hierarchical structure than Pashtuns and Nuristanis. Having arrived in the early Persian migrations, they are located in the southwestern corner of Afghanistan adjacent to other Baluch tribes living in southeastern Iran and northwestern Pakistan's Baluchistan Province.

The Hazara are Afghanistan's third-largest group after the Pashtuns and Tajiks. Their numbers are estimated at between 10 and 20 percent of the population, depending on whether a Hazara or non-Hazara is counting. The overwhelmingly Shia Hazara seem to have always occupied the bottom rung of Afghanistan's socioeconomic ladder. Their minority Shia faith, along with their Mongoloid racial stock, has contributed to their low social status in the eyes of Afghanistan's other ethnic groups.

A widely accepted, if unproven, theory is that Hazaras are descendants of garrisons left behind by Genghis Khan's Mongolian invasions. Their Mongoloid features appear to bear this out. The name Hazara comes from *Hazar*, which translates as "one thousand" in most Central and South Asian languages. Mongolian military formations were divided into units of tens, hundreds, and thousands. The Hazaras speak Hazaragi, a dialect of Dari, or Afghan Persian. The rugged topography of the Hazarajat has afforded some form of protection against outsiders.

The Hazaras and the Nuristanis were the first to revolt against the Afghan regime in Kabul after the April 1978 communist coup. Except for the town of Bamian, neither the Afghan communists nor the Soviet Army managed to recover the Hazarajat for the remainder of the Soviet-Afghan war. Today the Hazarajat and the Panshir Valley stand out as two regions where the mostly Pashtun Taliban have been unable to acquire a firm foothold.

The Uzbek, Turkmen, Aimak, and Kyrgyz Turkish minorities in northern Afghanistan are descendants of the Turkic peoples who immigrated into Afghanistan from Central Asia during the first millennium. Except for the Aimaks, all are related to larger ethnic communities of the same names across the border in Central Asia. The 1917 Bolshevik Revolution, Stalin's collectivization policies in the 1930s, and the resulting Muslim *Basmuchi* (Soviet-labeled "bandits") uprising in Soviet Central Asia provoked fresh waves of Uzbek, Turkmen, and Kirghiz refugee movements across the Amu Darya into northern Afghanistan. Descendants of these more recent Turkish-speaking arrivals provided some of the most dedicated Mujahidin fighters of Afghanistan when the Soviet Union invaded in 1979. Those whose families came centuries earlier, such as Uzbek Abdul Rashid Dostum, tended to side with the Soviet invaders.

Despite these tribal and ethnic divides, the great majority of educated Afghans of all ethnicities still refer to themselves as Afghans. In meetings that I had with Ahmed Shah Masood, he alluded to himself as an Afghan, never a Tajik. Tajiks have no interest in joining Tajikistan; for that matter, Uzbeks have no desire to join Uzbekistan, Pashtuns do not wish to become Pakistani, and Turkmen are not interested in joining Turkmenistan.[11]

At the same time, three decades of war and the Taliban's Pashtun chauvinism and Saudi-influenced Sunni extremism have dampened the sense of Afghan nationalism among the Tajiks, Hazaras, and Turkic minorities north of the Hindu Kush watershed. They retain bitter memories of their loss of land to Pashtuns sent north during Abdur Rahman Khan's brutal military expeditions in the 1890s and again in the twentieth century. Most of the northern non-Pashtun groups joined the Mujahidin in the anti-Soviet war (1979–1989). They emerged from that bloody decade well armed and ready to resist imposition of the Taliban's religious extremism and Pashtun nationalism.

During Taliban rule (1996–2001), the Pashtun northern enclaves were favored over non-Pashtuns in the settlement of land and water disputes. The non-Pashtuns retaliated after the Taliban were overthrown in October 2001, sometimes forcing Pashtun families to flee to refugee camps in Pakistan. The cycle began again when Taliban expanded from their ISI-managed bases in Pakistan into the northern provinces in 2007. Today, the see-saw conflict is intensifying, and it is disrupting Afghanistan's unity as a nation-state.

The Pashtuns remain the single most influential ethnic group in Afghanistan. Taken together, the Pashtuns in Afghanistan (about 14 million) and Pakistan (about 24 million) also constitute the largest tribal group in the world. Every Pashtun is aware that the term "Afghan" originally referred only to the Pashtun tribes. With the appending of the ancient Indo-European word *stan* (place of) to "Afghan," the state created by the Durrani Pashtuns in the eighteenth century became known as Afghanistan. With the exception of Kohistani Tajik Bacha Seqao's brief occupation of Kabul in 1929, and the Rabbani-Masood regime (1992–1996), all the twentieth-century governments of Afghanistan, including the monarchies, the communist regimes between 1978 and 1992, the Taliban, and the post-9/11 government, have been led by Pashtuns.[12] Understanding the Pashtun tribal system is therefore crucial to understanding contemporary Afghanistan.

The great majority of Pashtuns—like most other Afghans—live as they have for centuries in small, agrarian, kinship-bound communities. Authority rests in the hands of a male elder in the family. The average Pashtun boy grows up in a village on a mountainside or an isolated valley where land is controlled by his solidarity group, known as *quam* ("community" or "identity," connoting both tribal and territorial inclusiveness). Being raised as a pious Muslim, the young Pashtun is taught early that Allah decides, to a great extent, where he will be on his journey through life. The village mullah may teach him to read some Arabic script in the Koran and recite the words with little or no comprehension of the meaning, and the boy will be essentially nonliterate during his lifetime.[13]

The young Pashtun's only consistent means of support and protection are his family and his broader kinship network. The concentric circles of influence on his life move outward from family, clan, and tribe to nation.[14] Clan and tribal elders in his broader kinship group may exercise some influence over his family—but not real authority. The family patriarch will jealously guard his autonomy, negotiate with outsiders, and make the political, economic, and other decisions. He will decide how to respond to appeals from clan, tribe, and the government to mobilize his family's men and resources.

The youngster will learn about life from his parents, grandparents, and other older relatives in his extended family, which can have up to five hundred members. He will be instructed, through oral lessons and experience, about preservation of honor; survival of self, family, and clan; and respect for elders.[15] He will acquire a mistrust of adversarial tribes, particularly if a vendetta is ongoing. He will grow up somewhat suspicious of non-Pashtun ethnicities as well as foreigners and government representatives. His parents will attempt to marry him at an early age to a first cousin on his father's side to keep the family's bloodline and property ownership intact. At the same time, he will probably confront his male cousins during his lifetime, contesting marriage partners in the family and the inheritance of property.[16]

Gradually, the Pashtun boy imbibes the traditions, practices, and values embedded in the pre-Islamic Pashtunwali code of conduct. He learns how to practice the self-defense necessary to survive in Afghanistan's Hobbesian conditions. He is taught the most important Pashtunwali commandment of *badal*, or retribution.[17] A price must be extracted for a perceived wrong or insult, even at the risk of death. Disputes arising from the defense of individual or family honor and family property—women, gold, and land—can lead to blood feuds lasting for years or decades.[18]

The Pashtunwali code bestows honor and prestige on Pashtuns who offer hospitality. Be they friend or foe, priest or bandit, food and shelter must be accorded to the guest. Further, nanawati (asylum) must be granted to an enemy or stranger who lays down his weapons and surrenders. The young Pashtun will internalize these and scores of other Pashtunwali tenets, chief among them the importance of avoiding shame, defending his tribe, practicing Islam, and projecting dignity and strength. Defending the honor of family women, *namus*, is especially obligatory. If a wife, daughter, or mother is insulted, the clan and the entire tribe are insulted and will expect the immediate family to retaliate.

The Pashtun boy will also learn about the jirga (council) tradition. A jirga of village elders can be convened to mediate and sometimes resolve disputes between individuals within an extended family. It can be utilized to discuss the village's reaction to overtures from the government, North Atlantic Treaty Organization (NATO) forces, or the Taliban. It also addresses intratribal, economic, social, and criminal issues. The members of the jirga, generally family or clan leaders, have an equal say. The emphasis is on decision making by consensus, and disputants who commit their case to the jirga are bound by the outcome.

A Pashtun boy is taught to be proud of his Pashtun heritage and to embrace a love of individual liberty as well as a respect for both *nikat* (family or ancestral line) and tribe. The first question Pashtuns often ask each other is "Who is your father?" Tribal members whose ancestors achieved fame in battle or made valuable contributions to the tribe and nation are held in high esteem. Bravery, a Spartan-like fearlessness in combat, defiance of intimidation, and confidence in victory are all highly esteemed Pashtun attributes.

Pashtuns believe that they share a common ancestor, Qais, who lived in Afghanistan at the time of the Prophet in the seventh century A.D. Each Pashtun tribe and clan is named after an eponymous ancestor descended from Qais. The names of Pashtun tribes end with wording that links the tribe to its progenitor, such as *i* (of), *zai* (sons of), or *khel* (clan of).[19] Many Pashtuns trace their family trees back through multiple generations to Qais (Appendix II depicts the two largest tribal confederations, Durrani and Ghilzai).

In the early seventeenth century, Persian scribes at the Mughal court in Delhi carefully recorded the Afghan chronicles—oral accounts of detailed Pashtun genealogies enmeshed in mythology that had been passed on by word of mouth from father to son for centuries.[20] According to the chronicles, Qais was personally converted to Islam by Mohammad in Medina, and he

MAP 3.2   PRINCIPAL PASHTUN TRIBES

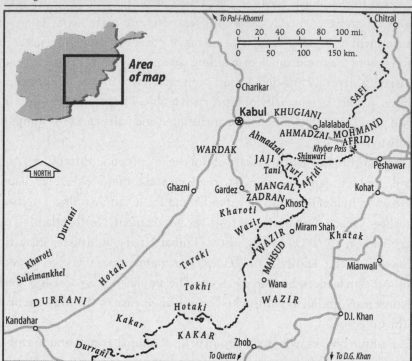

Reprinted from Leon B. Poullada, *Reform and Rebellion in Afghanistan,*
1919–1929: King Amanullah's Failure to Modernize a Tribal Society.
Copyright © 1973 by Cornell University.
Used by permission of the publisher, Cornell University Press.

and his fellow Afghans valiantly fought by the Prophet's side in the battles
leading up to his victorious march on Mecca in 630.

Qais is said to have married a daughter of the Prophet's own Quresh tribe.
There are many conflicting versions in the mythology about which tribes are
linked to which sons born of this union. Qais had at least three sons, maybe
four (the chronicles differ on the exact number). The eldest, Saraban, and
his son Sharkbun are the ancestors of the Durrani tribe. Qais' granddaughter
Matto is believed to be the ancestor of the Ghilzai Hotak, Ahmadzai, Tokhi,
Suleiman Khel, Taraki, and Kharoti. Saraban's second son, Kharshbun, is the
forefather of Pashtuns centered in Pakistan's Northwest Frontier Province,
notably the large Yusufzai tribe, the Mohmands, and the Shinwaris.

The Karlanis, or "hill tribes," are found on both sides of the Suleiman
mountain slopes near the Durand Line separating Pakistan and Afghanistan

northwest of Peshawar. The Karlanis include the Zadrans, Mangals, Khugiani, Jaji, Tanai, Afridis, Waziri, Orakzai, and Khattacks. The fifth and last major Pashtun tribal group is the Ghurghusht, which contains the large Safi tribe, spread in an arc from the Afghan-Pakistani Konar border area to northeast of Kabul, and the Kakar, which straddle Pakistan's Baluchistan border with southern Afghanistan.

The American military has found that a thorough knowledge of the Pashtun tribes and of their tribal adversaries and allies is critical to success in Afghanistan. Hundreds of NATO civilian and military "Human Terrain" specialists stationed in the provinces pore over tribal genealogy charts identifying local kinship links of friends and rivals along with the characteristics, political orientations, and geographic locations of the ethnic and tribal groups.

Cataloging and analyzing the innumerable Pashtun tribal rivalries in the countryside is a major objective. American commanders have learned the hard way that favoring one individual or group over others inside the ever swirling Afghan political cauldron can destroy centuries-old local tribal balances. The favored tribe uses the resources to establish its ascendancy over other tribes, which together are more numerous; the latter, in turn, combine their efforts to reduce the former's newfound leverage. Instead of unity and stability, the wholly unintended result can be intertribal violence or worse. The offended tribes may turn toward the Taliban for resources to oppose the favored tribe, its American patron, and the Afghan government.[21]

In his 1973 biography on Amanullah Khan, the king of Afghanistan from 1919 to 1929, the late U.S. diplomat and Afghan specialist Leon Poullada masterfully described the bewildering multiplicity of distinct "conflict situations." First, there are conflicts between individuals within the same tribe, cousin versus cousin being the most prevalent. Intratribal conflicts, such as the nineteenth-century struggle between the Durrani Popalzai and the Durrani Barakzai for the Afghan throne, form the second category. Third and fourth are two types of intertribal conflict. One type is intertribal conflict between tribes of the same ethnicity. The Durrani versus Ghilzai competition within the broader Pashtun tribe is an example. The other intertribal conflict category involves conflict between two tribes of different ethnicities—for example, Hazara versus Pashtun. The fifth category concerns conflict between one or more tribes and the rulers in Kabul. Each of these conflict situations repeatedly arise in Afghanistan and appear in the chapters of this book.[22]

Attempts by foreign states and nonstate entities, such as al-Qaeda, to manipulate Pashtun tribal differences to deepen their influence in Afghanistan have sometimes succeeded for a time but more often backfire. Usually, the Afghan beneficiaries pledge allegiance to the ideology of their outside patron while avoiding any commitments that might limit their freedom of maneuver against local rivals. At an opportune time, they switch to other patrons, always with an eye to increasing their personal power and wealth and weakening their local rivals.

☙

Islam is an indelible part of the Afghan identity. Afghans are proud of the great Islamic jurist, Abu Hanifa, whose family emigrated from Charikar north of Kabul to Baghdad in the eighth century. In Baghdad, Hanifa founded the moderate school of Islamic jurisprudence named after him. The Hanafi School, the most popular of the four leading Sunni legal orders in the Islamic world, predominates in Afghanistan, Pakistan, Bangladesh, Muslims in India, Turkey, and some parts of the Arab world. Afghans also lay claim to the internationally renowned Sufi mystic poet Jalaluddin Mohammad Balkhi, universally known as Rumi. Rumi was born in ancient Balkh in 1207, and when he was a teenager, he and his family were forced by the approaching Mongolian army to flee to the region of present-day Turkey, where he lived out the rest of his life.[23]

The departure of Abu Hanifa and Rumi for more stable regions of the Muslim world demonstrated the decline of intellectual and cultural vigor in Afghanistan resulting from the nomadic invasions from Central Asia. The Afghan shatter zone through subsequent centuries was unable to sustain the great Islamic cultural, religious, and educational institutions that flourished in Baghdad and elsewhere in the Middle East. After the Mongol invasions, Herat, Mazar-i-Sharif, and Jalalabad did make some important contributions in art, poetry, and literature before falling victim to the next invading army or domestic civil wars. Usually, however, Sunni Afghans seeking a religious education in the nineteenth and early twentieth centuries traveled to *madrassas* (religious schools) in Bukhara, Central Asia, and British India. Shia students studied at universities in Kufa and Karbala in present-day Iraq.

Though most nonliterate Afghans have minimal knowledge of the details of Islam, they display a fervent commitment to their religion. Rich or poor,

Afghans express their religion at the tombs of holy men, poets, and martyrs. Pilgrims visit piles of rock thought to hold spirits and ghosts or the grave of a local divine. Thousands of such shrines across the countryside offer opportunities for worshippers to seek cures for the sick, increased fertility, or rainfall, though the mosque is the place of worship for communal prayer, religious rituals, and holiday festivities. On Fridays, the imam (prayer leader) delivers a religious sermon, the *khutbah*, which mentions the current ruler in Kabul by name. Imams regularly use the khutbah to reflect on political issues of the day.

Generally, the village mullah is chosen by the khan or a jirga from among local tribesmen. He performs religious functions on a part-time basis, serves as the village notary public, presides over marriages and funerals, and conducts religious classes for boys in the mosque. Girls receive instruction from their mothers at home. Senior clerics, or *ulema*, in towns and cities are generally more literate and knowledgeable than their village counterparts. They are full-time religious leaders and wield considerable influence in their communities. Their families probably have married into the local tribal elite. They dispense guidance to men and women on moral, legal, and medical matters; lead Friday prayers at the larger mosques; and teach advanced classes in Islamic studies in colleges and at prestigious madrassas.

Universal adherence to Islam has not translated into Afghan political unity. Religious polarization among Afghans can be as divisive as tribal and ethnic differences. The tensions between Afghan Sunni and Shia Muslims damage unity in Afghanistan as they do in most other parts of the Muslim world. The Shia-Sunni divide dates back to the seventh-century selection of a successor, or "caliph," to the Prophet Mohammad when he died in 632. Uthman, the third caliph chosen, was not from Mohammad's clan. In choosing Uthman, the *shura* (council) of Muslim religious leaders at the time bypassed Ali, the Prophet's cousin and the husband of Fatima, Mohammad's only surviving child. That decision inaugurated the great Sunni-Shia schism forty-eight years following Muhammad's death.

After Uthman's assassination in 656, Ali was selected to be the fourth caliph. Uthman's tribe challenged Ali's ascendency. Uthman's nephew, Muawiyah, defeated Ali's army and established a competing new dynasty, the Umayyad caliphate, at Damascus. In 661, Ali was assassinated in a mosque in Kufa, Iraq, by a murderer wielding a poisoned sword. Ali's followers took up the "Shiat al-Ali" (Partisans of Ali) banner and became known as "Shia."

Shias still contend today that the first three caliphs, Abu Bakr, Omar, and Uthman, were legitimate political and military leaders but illegitimate spiritual leaders. Mohammad's religious authority, they believe, can only be passed down to imams who are direct descendents of the Prophet. The Shia therefore revere Ali as the first imam, the only caliph after Mohammad who could legitimately exercise both temporal and religious authority. Muslims upholding the validity of the first three caliphs became known as Sunni, from the Arabic word *sunnah* (tradition).

Shias hold that the Prophet's spiritual authority was embodied in twelve divinely inspired, infallible imams directly descended from Ali. The line of living imams continued until the ninth century, when the twelfth imam disappeared, becoming the "Hidden Imam." The "Twelvers" believe that, at a chosen time, the Hidden Imam will emerge from seclusion as a messianic deliverer, the *Mahdi,* who will relieve the oppression and suffering of the Shia. "Twelver" Shia in Afghanistan include the Hazara, the Qizilbash, and small Pashtun and Tajik Shia enclaves in the Pashtun belt. A smaller Shia sect—the Ismailis, or "Seveners"—are led by the European-based Aga Khan. They number less than a million in Afghanistan and believe that the Aga Khan is a direct descendent of Ismael, a son of the sixth imam.

Afghanistan was fertile ground for the Arab and Persian Sufi[24] missionaries spreading Sufism's reform message in the Muslim world from the eleventh century onward. Like Protestants dissenting against Catholic clergy during the European Reformation, Sufis sought to remove the encrustation of clergy, sterile dogma, politics, and worldly goods which they preached had come to separate individual believers from God. Religious *pirs* (religious guides) taught their students, *murids,* how to circumvent the clergy and connect directly with God.

The Sufi paths to God are numerous, depending on the teaching of individual pirs. Some have drawn on Buddhist, Hindu, and monastic Christian practices designed to reach God through ascending phases of meditation. Others have emphasized achieving union with God through tantric-style magic, mysticism, frenzied levels of ecstasy, and the use of drugs.

Sufism settled naturally into Afghanistan's moderate tribal culture. Itinerant Arab pirs married into local communities. Their Sufi orders spread to other towns, villages, and nomad camps, and their students headed madrassas and established their own religious platforms around Afghanistan. The renowned sixteenth-century Pashtun Sufi mystic Rahman Baba attracted a huge following. Other Sufis wandered the countryside as darvishes or *faqirs* (wandering pir mendicants living by alms). Sufi pirs in the tribal areas occasionally succumbed to the more violent instincts of tribalism, however, inciting uprisings against the local tribal aristocracy or the government in Kabul.[25]

The most popular Sufi orders in Afghanistan today are the Qadiriya and Naqshbandiya. The Qadiriya line of pirs, founded by Abdul Qadir Gailani in Baghdad, multiplied and spread through Ghilzai areas in the east and west into southern Afghanistan. The Naqshbandiya Sufi order is also well established in the Pashtun belt. Mojaddedi pirs, known as *hazrats* (saints), have crowned Afghan kings, married into royal families, and served as government ministers.

CHAPTER 4

Modernizing Monarchs

Abdur Rahman Khan, the "Iron Emir," united Afghanistan during his twenty-one-year reign. On his deathbed in 1901, he urged his successors to proceed slowly:

> *My sons and successors should not try to introduce reforms of any kind in such a hurry as to set the people against their ruler, and they must bear in mind that in establishing a Constitutional Government, introducing more lenient laws, and modeling education upon the system of Western universities, they must adopt all these gradually as the people become accustomed to the idea of modern innovations.*[1]

The leaders of three Muslim countries, Afghanistan, Iran, and Turkey, began to modernize their countries during the first three decades of the twentieth century. Turkey and Iran followed a more linear, European-style progression to become centralized states.[2]

The Turkish leader Mustafa Kemal was a highly popular and successful general who instituted a revolution from above to build a modern, secular Turkey. Declaring that Turkey "cannot be the land of Sheikhs, dervishes and disciples of certain sects,"[3] he introduced European civil and criminal codes, abolished the Ottoman caliphate, established a constitutional republic, and put down two large-scale religious rebellions, publicly executing the clerics who led them. Turkish women were granted the right to vote and to hold office. The state outlawed *purdah*, the seclusion of women, including the wearing of the veil, and the Turkish hat (the *fez*) worn by men.[4] Universal education was enforced by the Ministry of Education. Kemal introduced a Western-style judicial system and launched a series of five-year economic modernization plans. He was later named Ataturk, "Father of the Turks," by the elected Turkish National Assembly.

Reza Shah in Iran, the founder of the Pahlavi Dynasty, faced formidable tribal opposition when he deposed the Qajar Dynasty in 1925. Reza Shah was a strong-willed, secular military officer. Before seizing power, he commanded the "Cossack Brigade," a well-organized, well-trained, and well-equipped military force.[5] As Iran's new shah, he modernized the army and used it to mount a series of military expeditions to force tribal allegiance to the central government. Tribal chiefs who resisted were executed or imprisoned. The state confiscated their land. Some rebellious tribes were forcibly removed from their tribal territories and settled near urban areas. Reza Shah also embarked on an ambitious reform program. He created a civil service and modernized the military; introduced a system of secular education financed by a land tax; built a north-south railway; instituted new commercial laws eliminating clerical involvement in the economy; and relegated the Sharia courts, dominated by clerics administering Koranic law, to marriage and divorce affairs, later dismantling them completely. His Western-style legal system included laws requiring men to wear Western clothing. Tribalism as a way of life declined, and by the 1970s it had virtually disappeared in most of Iran.

It took decades for the Pahlavi Dynasty of Iran and the Turkish republic led by Ataturk to overcome tribal and religious opposition to central control. Abdur Rahman Khan started that process in Afghanistan at the end of the nineteenth century. His large army ruthlessly suppressed tribal uprisings. The Iron Emir successfully unified Afghanistan within its present borders, but he possessed neither the resources nor the military power to directly govern the regions. Recalcitrant tribes and clans in the hinterland continued to administer their internal affairs, using centuries-old tribal codes and traditions. The centralization of authority in Afghanistan was therefore still far from complete when the Iron Emir died in 1901.

For twentieth-century Afghan rulers, building a national infrastructure of roads and communications to knit the country together was more difficult in mountainous, landlocked Afghanistan than in Turkey or Iran. Turkey's and Iran's relatively more urban and literate populations made the center's establishment of a monopoly of coercive power in the regions easier. So did Ataturk's and Reza Shah's greater access to internal economic resources and their military backgrounds.

In contrast to Ataturk and Reza Shah, the Afghan modernizing monarchs succeeding Abdur Rahman Khan were not able to develop a critical mass of military and political power sufficient to overcome tribal and religious resistance in the regions. Each of them had to contend with tribal leadership rivalries within their own Mohammadzai clan (the first of Poullada's five "conflict situations"), a problem Ataturk and Reza Shah did not face.

The tribal leaders' curse of recurring resources frustrated the cash-strapped twentieth-century Afghan monarchs. Autonomous tribes in the countryside resisted taxation, and there was little commercial activity from which to draw revenue. The inhabitants of the thousands of rural microcommunities where most Afghans lived were nearly all nonliterate. Then as now, most Afghans eked out their livings on small subsistence farms yielding minimal surpluses, far from the government's reach. Afghans in the countryside generally did not much care about the world outside their tribal territory. Their support for a national Afghan "corporate will" was weak,[6] and appeals by modernizing monarchs to "catch up" with other modernizing nations held little allure.

During his reign (1901–1919), Habibullah followed his father's advice to proceed cautiously in carrying out reforms. He avoided modernization programs likely to threaten the privileged positions of tribal and religious leaders. He cultivated good relations with the British colonial government in India to maintain the flow of the British subsidies granted to his father, and they continued to the end of his reign. The British were happy to comply, having concluded that the annual payments worked better than invasions.[7] In return, Habibullah had to accept British control of Afghan foreign policy and the Durand Line.

Only one tribal uprising (by the Mangals in Paktiya in 1915) occurred during Habibullah's nineteen-year reign. Early on, he organized a State Council to liaise with tribal leaders and to provide a means by which they could report their views to him. He freed tribal leaders imprisoned by Abdur Rahman and invited pro-reform Mohammadzai families that had been forced into exile by his father to return to Afghanistan. One of these exiles, Mahmud

Tarzi, the son of a prominent Mohammadzai, returned from Syria determined to reform Afghanistan. Two of Tarzi's daughters married sons of Habibullah; one married Amanullah, the future king. In addition, the five Musahiban "equerry" brothers, who were also Mohammadzai—including Nadir Khan, another future king—were permitted to return from India.[8] Habibullah appointed Nadir Khan commander-in-chief of the army, and he made his older half-brother, Hashim Khan, military governor of Herat.

Habibullah also sought close relations with the two top Sufi clerics in Afghanistan: the Mojaddedi hazrat, head of the Naqshbandi Order, and the senior-most Gailani pir of the Qadiriya Order. With Habibullah's helping hand, by the early twentieth century the Mojaddedis and Gailanis were among the largest landowning families in Afghanistan. Their extensive properties enhanced their susceptibility to Habibullah's influence, as did each family's marital alliances with Habibullah's multitudinous offspring.

Habibullah took other steps to defuse religious opposition. One of his fathers-in-law, the chief religious qazi of Afghanistan, frequently reminded religious audiences that violating the emir's will was violating Allah's will. Habibullah preserved government control of the madrassas and examinations to qualify for religious positions, and he continued Abdur Rahman Khan's control of waqfs (religious endowments collected from land revenues and donations). He also kept senior clerics on the government payroll to ensure their loyalty; personally composed a manual on religious rituals to be practiced during worship (it remains in use in many Afghan mosques today); and divorced his fifth wife to stay within the Muslim parameters for marriage (only four wives are allowed).

His tribal and religious flanks reasonably secure, Habibullah cautiously turned to reforming Afghan society. Mahmud Tarzi was an enthusiastic adviser on the path to follow. He organized a group of reformers calling themselves the "Young Afghans." The group included the future King Amanullah and the Musahiban brothers as well as young civil servants, writers, intellectuals, and "detribalized" sons of tribal chiefs who had settled in Kabul. They subscribed to the modernization and nationalistic ideas popular among Muslim reformers in Turkey and Iran.

From 1911 to 1918, Tarzi expounded on two main themes in his new bimonthly journal The Torch of News: "Muslims must modernize or perish," and "Colonialism and imperialism must go."[9] Tarzi called for the equality and unveiling of women, universal education, and the building of roads in Afghanistan to connect the country to the outside world. Habibullah agreed with Tarzi's reform direction, but he disagreed on the pace. The ruler's gradualism frustrated Tarzi and the Young Afghans, but they had little choice. Habibullah was their only ally capable of resisting tribal and religious opposition to their ideas.

Habibullah advanced slowly but steadily. He founded the first secular high school in Afghanistan, naming it after himself—Habibya. The Kabul humor mill joked that Habibullah created Habibya to educate his many children; he had over one hundred from his four wives and numerous concubines. Muslim Indians and Turks were imported to manage and staff Habibya, which taught math, geography, and foreign languages as well as religious subjects. Some courses at the all-male institution were taught in English. Graduates of Habibya went on to occupy influential positions inside and outside of government in the coming decades, and alumni included the sons of Afghan kings, generals, prominent tribal leaders, and wealthy businessmen.

Habibullah established a Ministry of Education and a teacher-training center to provide instructors to the growing number of elementary and high schools in the country where secular subjects were taught. He created the first officers' training school, the Afghan Military Academy, which was administered by a Turkish colonel. He founded Afghanistan's first hospital in 1913. Habibullah also inaugurated the country's first public works program, building roads to connect the capital to nearby towns.

Habibullah personally imported the first automobile into Afghanistan in 1905. He drove it himself. An American engineer was hired to build Afghanistan's first hydroelectric plant; the two General Electric generators the American installed at Jabal Es Saraj, northeast of Kabul, provided power to Habibullah's palace in downtown Kabul and several government buildings. Habibullah introduced the telephone and telegraph to Afghanistan, and he encouraged entrepreneurs to open factories. His innovations extended to sports as well: Two golf courses were constructed near Jalalabad and Kabul. When out on the links, Habibullah occasionally found petitions from local tribal groups requesting assistance stuffed into the holes on the putting greens.[10]

Habibullah's army was still benefiting from British subsidies when World War I broke out in 1914. He supported the British, hoping that in exchange Britain would restore Afghanistan's control of Afghan foreign policy, which had been lost in the hated 1879 Gandamak Treaty. When the British demurred, Tarzi, Amanullah, and Nadir Khan pressed Habibullah to side with Germany and Muslim Turkey and declare independence. A German-Turkish delegation arrived in 1915 and spent ten months in Afghanistan. The delegation's leaders, Captain Oskar von Neidermayer and Turkish official Kasim Beg, urged Habibullah and his cabinet members to capitalize on British weakness, declare full Afghan independence, and attack India. In return, the German and Turkish negotiators promised to restore the Indian portion of Ahmad Shah Durrani's empire to Afghanistan.

Habibullah drew out the negotiations while secretly assuring the British he would stay neutral. In May 1916, the frustrated delegation returned to Europe empty-handed. The Young Afghans resented Habibullah's missed opportunity to reclaim Afghanistan's full independence from the British. In 1918, a Habibya student attempted to assassinate him as he drove through Kabul's narrow streets. Executions and numerous arrests of Young Afghans followed. Habibullah closed Tarzi's journal and imprisoned two of his correspondents. Tarzi isolated himself in his family compound.

The victory of the Allies in World War I only increased Young Afghan resentment. In the eyes of the Young Afghans, Habibullah had failed to exploit Britain's preoccupation with the war in Europe to declare full Afghan independence and regain control of Afghan foreign policy. Habibullah responded to the rising indignation against him by delegating more and more official responsibilities to others and occupying himself with his favorite pastimes, hunting and enjoying his harem. His retreat from personally overseeing matters of state would not have been approved by his father, the Iron Emir, who during his life had always kept the reins of power firmly in his own hands.

At age fifty, Habibullah was assassinated by a pistol shot fired into his head as he lay asleep in the early morning hours of February 19, 1919, while on a hunting trip in Laghman. Rumors of the assassin's identity proliferated. The British press mentioned Amanullah, while the Bolsheviks blamed the British. Others accused Tarzi and Afghan Army commander Nadir Khan. Although no conclusive evidence has ever been uncovered, most indicators pointed to Habibullah's Mohammadzai clan as being responsible for the murder. Habibullah's personal security at the hunting camp was handled by a Mohammadzai officer. His son Inayatullah and his brother Nasrullah had been positioned in tents just outside the inner circle of Habibullah's bodyguards when the king was shot. Nadir Khan was not far away.

Habibullah's older brother, Nasrullah, and Habibullah's son Amanullah each laid claim to the Afghan throne after the assassination. Amanullah won the power struggle. He sentenced his uncle to life in prison in the palace dungeon, where Nasrullah died two years later. Amanullah executed the Mohammadzai colonel and a sergeant who had been assigned to guard Habibullah in the hunting camp. He then boldly set out to modernize Afghanistan at a pace his grandfather, Abdur Rahman Khan, had advised against.

Amanullah's long-term vision, encouraged by his mentor and father-in-law, Mahmud Tarzi, centered on transforming Afghanistan into a centralized, secular state. His decade-long reign (1919–1929) flouted the Iron Emir's wise counsel to gradually reform Afghanistan's conservative, atomized tribal society. Amanullah assumed the title of king, closed his harem, and announced he would have only one wife, Tarzi's daughter, Queen Soroya. In one of his early speeches, he forecast his intention to create a modern Afghanistan that would "take its proper place among the civilized powers of the world."[11] He envisioned a unitary state structure with a modern civil service circumventing local tribal leaders. The central bureaucracy would directly govern the countryside, administering security, justice, taxation, and social programs based on laws passed by a national Afghan parliament and approved by himself as a constitutional monarch. Women would enjoy equality, escape purdah, and be able to marry men of their own choice.

The first item on Amanullah's agenda was reclaiming control of Afghanistan's foreign policy from Britain. He sent a letter to the British viceroy that assumed that Afghanistan was *already* independent: "Our independent and free Government of Afghanistan considers itself ready and prepared at any time and season to conclude, with due regard to every consideration of the requirement of friendship and the like, such arrangements and treaties with this mighty Government of England as may be useful and serviceable in the way of commercial gains and advantages to our Government and yours."[12]

Driving his message home, Amanullah grabbed the handle of his sword while announcing at a public gathering: "I have declared myself and my country entirely free, autonomous and independent both internally and externally. My country will hereafter be as independent a state as the other states and powers of the world are. No foreign power will be allowed to have a hairs-breadth of right to interfere internally or externally with the affairs of Afghanistan, and if any ever does I am ready and prepared to cut its throat with this sword." Ensuring that the British, too, would hear his message, Amanullah turned to the viceroy's Indian representative seated nearby and asked if he had understood his statement. The envoy tersely responded, "Yes, I have."[13]

In his response to Amanullah, the British viceroy ceded no ground. In an April 1919 letter he ignored Amanullah's declarations of independence and reaffirmed previous Anglo-Afghan treaties that gave Britain control of Afghan foreign policy. Less than three weeks after receiving the British response, Amanullah ordered Afghan forces under his army commander, Nadir Khan, to cross the Durand Line and attack India.

Neither the Afghans nor the British were prepared for the third and last Anglo-Afghan war. The best British combat units and nearly a million native Indian troops were still in Europe, North Africa, and the Middle East. In India, the British were coping with a rising tide of Indian nationalism and calls for independence that had surfaced after World War I. British forces held major advantages over the Afghans, particularly a small air force, and weapons superiority in the form of machine guns and armored vehicles. Amanullah could count on the experienced General Nadir Khan and thousands of tough, well-armed, motivated Pashtun tribal fighters on both sides of the Durand Line.

Shinwari, Zadran, Mangal, and Mohmand volunteers kicked off the war by storming over the Durand Line on May 3. The British declared war on May 6 and ordered eight British divisions, reinforced by three cavalry brigades, up to the Pashtun tribal agencies in the Northwest Frontier Province (NWFP) bordering Afghanistan.[14] Before they arrived, the British-commanded Pashtun militia stationed on the Frontier began to disintegrate. The Khyber Rifles, the Zhob militia, and the Tochi, Wana, and Chitral scouts each fielded about 1,000 tribal infantry commanded by British officers. The militia manned small forts and conducted mobile patrols in the six tribal agencies facing the Durand Line. They were in charge of keeping the peace and guarding the border with Afghanistan. One after another, the British-officered Pashtun militia units broke up and defected to the Afghans. The famous Khyber Rifles unit, raised from the Afridi tribe, was the first to go, its deserters joining hundreds of Pashtuns on both sides of the border attempting to capture the Khyber Pass. Further west, Waziri and Mahsud tribal militia in the Kurram and North and South Waziristan tribal agencies went over to the invading Afghans.

The British struck back from the air, surprising the Afghans, who had never experienced an attack from that quarter. Three British bombers battered the invading tribal forces at the strategic Khyber gateway to Afghanistan. British infantry advanced from Peshawar intending to clear the Khyber Pass and move on to Jalalabad. Nadir Khan, meanwhile, crossed the border to the west with fourteen regiments and assorted Afghan tribal allies. Thousands of fierce Wazir and Mahsud tribesmen in North and South Waziristan rushed to join him as he fought through the Tochi River Valley in North Waziristan and attacked the British garrison at Thal. The Afghan general's unexpected transport of artillery over the mountainous border area stunned the British. Unlimbering their artillery pieces from the backs of camels, the Afghans commenced a bombardment of the Thal military cantonment.

The British nightmare of the entire Frontier going up in flames seemed to be coming true. The Waziri and Mahsud population in North and South Waziristan were in full revolt. Further south, the Zhob Kakar tribal militia decamped with their arms and supported Nadir Khan's invasion. Abandoning plans to attack Jalalabad, the British diverted troops intended for that mission to the relief of Thal. British forward posts in the combat areas were evacuated. Local tribesmen inflicted heavy casualties as the defenders made their way back down to the Indus Plain. Mutinous Waziri tribals pursuing fleeing British troops looted the treasury and military arsenal at Wana, the South Waziristan administrative center.

The British ordered urgent reinforcements to the Frontier from bases deeper inside India. British warplanes attacked Kabul, bombing Amanullah's palace and military installations in the Afghan capital. A large British force relieved Thal. At that point—June 3, only a month into the fighting—a ceasefire was declared. Both sides were ready for an armistice. Amanullah was shaken by the British bombing of his palace. Britain was deep in postwar debt and not eager to engage in another expensive guerrilla war with Afghanistan. Further inconclusive fighting could also incite more Pashtun tribes in the tribal agencies to support the Afghan invasion, possibly infecting other parts of already restless India with revolutionary fervor.

Both sides made concessions at the peace talks held in Rawalpindi in early August 1919. The British agreed to give up control of Afghan foreign policy. They rejected Amanullah's demand to hand over North and South Waziristan and informed the Afghan negotiators that Britain's annual subsidy to Amanullah would be terminated. While this threatened to damage the Afghan Army, Amanullah's spirits were high. His popularity at home soared, as did Nadir's. August 19, the date that the Rawalpindi Treaty was signed, became, and remains, Afghan Independence Day. Amanullah built a victory monument in Kabul, portraying a British lion enveloped in chains and surrounded by broken pieces of a British cannon captured by Nadir Khan near Thal.

Amanullah dispatched Afghan diplomatic envoys to the Soviet Union, Iran, Turkey, France, and Italy to establish Afghan diplomatic relations with states other than Britain. Major world capitals announced recognition of Afghan independence, and President Warren Harding received Mohammed Wali Khan, Amanullah's Afghan emissary, in Washington.[15]

In 1922, Amanullah launched an ambitious domestic reform program. He established a European-style Council of Ministers, and with the help of French and Turkish advisers he prepared Afghanistan's first constitution. The document officially called for the equality of women. Amanullah relied on military conscription to expand the national army. Conscription reduced the center's dependence on tribal chiefs to provide forces for government military offensives against rebelling tribes. In another step certain to raise tribal resentment, Amanullah lowered subsidies to tribal chiefs.

Building on Habibullah's educational reforms, Amanullah established a new Ministry of Education that presided over all government schools. He opened more secular high schools to provide the future managers and technocrats for Afghan modernization, including an English high school, Ghazi, staffed by Indian Muslims; a high school where instruction was offered primarily in French, Istiqlal; and a German-language high school, Nejat.[16]

By 1928, to the discomfit of many mullahs, 40,000 students were enrolled in the government's secular schools.[17] Scores of Afghan graduates began to flow to European countries, India, and the United States for advanced studies. The king started an adult education program. He built a police training academy and supported Queen Soroya's establishment of an intermediate school for girls in Kabul. Some female high-school graduates from elite families in the capital were sent abroad for higher education at government expense. Amanullah built a new Turkish-style compound, which he called Darulaman (Abode of Peace), for himself in Kabul's southern suburbs. It included a racetrack, a movie theater, and a garage, where Amanullah parked his Rolls Royce.

The accelerating tempo of Amanullah's reforms and the danger of a tribal and religious backlash worried Nadir Khan. The head of the British mission in Kabul cited Nadir as complaining to him that Amanullah was moving too fast with his reforms. According to the British envoy, Nadir added that "Afghans as a race were fanatical, bigoted, and conservative, and it was unsafe to ride roughshod over their cherished customs and attempt to dragoon them into civilization on the European standard."[18] In 1924, Amanullah's gender reforms sparked another Mangal revolt near Khost at a time when the cessation of British subsidies had weakened the army. As the revolt simmered, Nadir Khan left for Paris, depriving Amanullah of his commander-in-chief and best general.

The army units that Amanullah sent to suppress the Mangals were beaten back. Amanullah resorted to bribing local Mangal enemies, the Shinwari, Mohmand, and Afghan Waziris, to quell the uprising. He bought two warplanes from the British and hired German and Russian pilots to fly them. The aircrafts bombed Mangal tribal forces and villages. The uprising lost steam and collapsed. Discouraged tribesmen left rebel ranks and returned to their villages. In a spectacle reminiscent of ancient Roman parades celebrating victories over the barbarians, long lines of sullen Mangal prisoners were forced to file past Amanullah during a victory celebration in the capital. Amanullah executed the religious leader of the revolt along with fifty-three of his followers. He built another victory pillar in the capital to commemorate his vanquishing of the Mangals. The new obelisk proclaimed the "triumph of knowledge over ignorance."[19]

Afghanistan's idealistic and naïve young king and his father-in-law Mahmud Tarzi, his foreign minister, pressed their reform agenda even harder after the Mangal revolt. New power plants electrified parts of Kabul; Amanullah personally taught adult education classes; and trucks, buses, and cars navigated Kabul's narrow streets. The Afghan king conducted a seven-month "Grand Tour" of Europe to signal his country's emergence on the world stage. He was feted by kings, presidents, a pope, and the Bolsheviks during visits to Egypt, Italy, France, Germany, Britain, Poland, the Soviet Union, Turkey, and Iran. The secular reforms implemented by Ataturk in Muslim Turkey and by Reza Shah in Muslim Iran especially impressed him. From Tehran, Amanullah personally drove his new Rolls Royce, Queen Soroya at his side, back to Kabul, "bursting," according to a biographer, "with plans for bold new moves and revolutionary undertakings."[20]

An overconfident Amanullah summoned a jirga of around a thousand tribal chiefs, clerics, and government officials soon after his return. He ordered the attendees to come in European suits and homburg hats—and without beards. Kabul barbers and tailors were thrilled; tribal and religious leaders were not. Their irritation escalated to anger after listening to their king's four-day oration on the new reforms he intended to implement: a more secular constitution separating church and state; a movement of the Friday Sabbath to Saturday; an increase in the land tax; a new civil service bypassing tribal leadership to deal directly with the people; a Western-style judiciary; a change in conscription from two years to three; and government certification of mullahs already teaching in educational establishments. Amanullah lectured that the superior vigor of the British and German races was due to late marriages and suggested that minimum marriage ages be set for women at eighteen, men at twenty-two. Addressing a smaller meeting of six hundred tribals and clerics, he announced his intention to abolish the burka. As he spoke, Queen Soroya slowly arose from her seat and removed her veil. Gasps and a low roar of disapproving murmurs rolled through the meeting hall.

The tribal uprisings after Amanullah's jirga were ferocious and transregional. In desperation, Amanullah renounced his reforms, but this did not prevent uncoordinated tribal attacks on Kabul from the south and the north. Amanullah's desperate straits whetted the appetite of his Mohammadzai relatives and trusted advisers to side with the rebellion and seize the throne. The nephew of former emir Yaqub Khan entered Afghanistan from India and declared himself the country's new ruler; Ali Ahmed Jan, Amanullah's Mohammadzai cousin and brother-in-law, also proclaimed himself king and rallied Shinwari rebels to attack Kabul. Tajik rebel Habibullah Kalakani, known as "Bacha Seqao" (son of a water carrier), moved on Kabul from the north.[21] Bacha Seqao took advantage of Amanullah's weakening position and captured an army garrison at Jabul Seraj on December 10, 1928, threatening the capital. Meanwhile, the senior Mojaddedi hazrat slipped out of Kabul and joined Shinwari rebels in eastern Afghanistan. The chief qazi of Kabul attempted to flee to India. The king, hearing of his plans, captured him and had him executed in the palace dungeon.

The Pashtun tribes were infuriated that a Tajik would contest the Afghan throne, but Bacha Seqao got to the capital first. Amanullah fled Kabul on January 16, 1929, driving his Rolls Royce. Bacha Seqao sent cavalry to run him down. Amanullah's luxury car got stuck in a snowdrift, but frantic pushing by the king and his brother dislodged it just in time. Amanullah roared off toward Kandahar as the horsemen rode up. He continued on to Bombay and sailed for exile in Italy, where he died in 1960.

After moving into the Gul Khanna Palace, the nonliterate Bacha Seqao had a proclamation released announcing his elevation to the Afghan throne as Habibullah II. The Mojaddedi hazrat supported his accession. Pashtun Ghilzai tribesmen south of Kabul captured Amanullah's cousin and pretender to the throne, Ali Ahmed Jan, and handed him over to Bacha Seqao. Afghanistan's new ruler allowed Ali to kiss the cannon before being tied to it and blown to bits.

Tajiks were happy to see one of their own on the Afghan summit, but resentment smoldered in the Pashtun belt. For nine months, Ghilzai disunity and unwillingness to assist the restoration of the Durrani Mohammadzai dynasty helped to sustain Bacha Seqao's tenuous hold on the capital. Meanwhile, the brigand-turned-Afghan-ruler proved unable to provide good governance to Kabul or the country. Only two of his cabinet members could read. His Kohistani followers marauded through the streets of Kabul, plundering homes and raping women. His appointment of a Tajik as governor of Jalalabad angered the Ghilzai tribes. The Durranis were outraged by his appointment of a Ghilzai as governor of Durrani Kandahar. Foreign governments viewed Bacha Seqao as a passing phase likely to be replaced soon. No government recognized his regime. London and Moscow worried that unless a Durrani king was restored to the Afghan throne, an extended state of chaos could result and spread beyond Afghan's borders.

Nadir Khan and his Musahiban brothers traveled to India from France. The British allowed Nadir to recruit Waziri and Mahsud tribesmen in the tribal agencies to capture Kabul. Zadran, Jaji, and Shinwari tribesmen jumped on the Musahiban bandwagon as it crossed the Durand Line and paraded north toward the Afghan capital. With fierce Waziris in the lead, Nadir's tribal force brashly bypassed Gardez and Ghazni and attacked Kabul on October

12, 1929. Bacha Seqao escaped into Kohistan. Later, lured by Nadir's promise of clemency, he returned to Kabul. According to Tajik folklore, Bacha Seqao's followers urged him not to trust Nadir. Bacha Seqao responded: "Come, let us go to Kabul because I have been King, and am not afraid to die, for if we go to Kabul, the treacherous Durrani will surely kill us. So do not be afraid, it will be as Allah desires. I return to Kabul either to be king or to be a corpse."[22]

Prior to Bacha Seqao's surrender, a jirga of the Pashtun tribal chiefs participating in the attack on Kabul had chosen Nadir Khan to become Nadir Shah, the new king of Afghanistan. The jirga insisted that he cancel his clemency to Bacha Seqao and execute him, a clear violation of Pashtunwali. Nadir summoned Bacha Seqao to a royal audience and informed him that, while he had personally forgiven him, the jirga had sentenced him to death. Kohistani legend describes Bacha Seqao as laughing while being escorted from the palace dungeon to the west wall of the building. There, on November 1, 1929, Bacha Seqao, his brother, and ten of his followers were shot down by a firing squad.

ॐ

Despite its violent origins, Nadir Shah's Musahiban Dynasty ushered in a half century of peace and nation building in Afghanistan. It has been termed the "Era of Tranquility" in recent Afghan history. State authority and tribal and religious power brokers reached an accommodation: The Musahibans occupied the pinnacle of the triangle but respected the domain of tribal and religious leaders.

Beginning in 1929 the dynasty embarked on a nation-building drive unprecedented in Afghan history. It lasted forty-nine years, until the April 27, 1978, Afghan communist coup. Nadir and his four brothers shared Amanullah's modernizing goals, but their tactics resembled Habibullah's gradualism. They maintained a degree of family solidarity rarely seen in Afghan royal families. Nadir functioned as chairman of a family board of directors, with the brothers discussing affairs of state during weekly family dinners at the royal palace. Their sons later joined the deliberations as they came of age.

The 1931 Afghan Constitution promulgated by Nadir placed all executive, legislative, and judicial power in the hands of the dynastic rulers, laying the foundation for a multidecade period of economic growth and political stability. As in Ahmad Shah Durrani's time, receding pressures from Afghanistan's periphery created a favorable international environment for the country's development. The buffer zone between empires still held. Stalin, concentrating on internal consolidation of his power through the 1930s, walled off the USSR, established state control of the Soviet Union's economy, and systematically annihilated all internal opposition to his rule. Britain considered the Musahiban rule over the Afghan buffer essential to blocking Soviet expansionism toward its Indian Empire.

Nadir's authoritative character and emphasis on co-opting rather than confronting tribal power centers set the tone for stable Musahiban rule. His reputation as a strong commander-in-chief and a military hero in the Afghan War of Independence tightened his grip on the throne. He spoke English and French in addition to Pashto and Dari, which enabled him to communicate easily with representatives of foreign powers.

The five Musahiban brothers and their sons were the first Afghan rulers to spend their formative years abroad. Nadir, Hashim Khan, Mohammad Aziz, Shah Mahmud, and Shah Wali had grown up together in India. They were educated at the exclusive English-language Dehra Dun Hill Station School northeast of New Delhi. Nadir and his son Zahir had learned French during their five-year self-exile in France at the end of Amanullah's reign.

The Musahiban brothers carefully groomed their sons for future leadership positions. After returning to Afghanistan, Zahir and his cousin Daoud attended Habibya and the Afghan Military College in Kabul. A third cousin, Abdul Wali, Shah Wali's son, graduated from the Military Academy two years after Zahir. He was sent off to the prestigious Sandhurst Military Academy in England. Zahir became minister of defense in 1932 at the age of only eighteen and was named minister of education a year later. Abdul Wali was made a general in the Afghan Army after his graduation from Sandhurst; Daoud also became a general and later succeeded Zahir as minister of defense. During his two decades of service in the Afghan Army, Daoud supervised promotions within the officer corps and oversaw the army's slow modernization.

It was during this period that familiar rivalries between Pashtun cousins appeared in the royal family's second generation. Abdul Wali and Daoud competed with one another for marriage alliances with their first cousins. Daoud was at a disadvantage. Abdul Wali was Nadir's full nephew, whereas Daoud was only a half-nephew. Daoud proposed a marriage between his younger

FIGURE 4.1   SEEDS OF THE MUSAHIBAN ROYAL RIFT

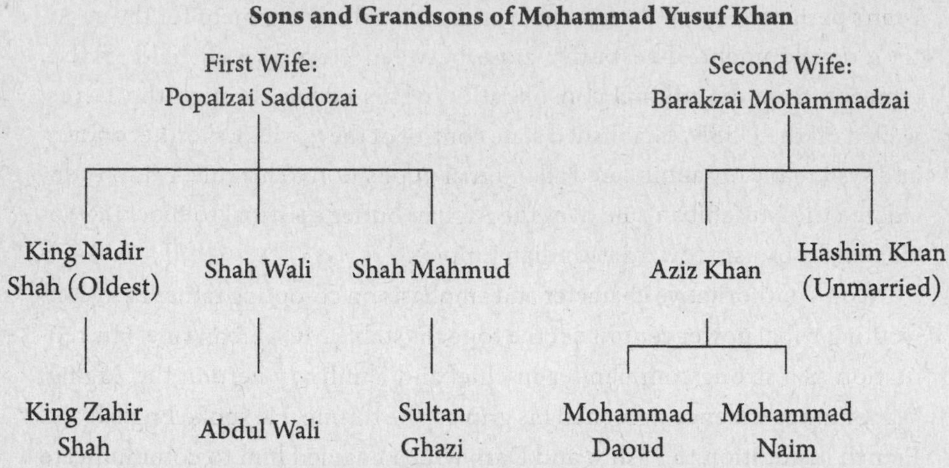

Sons and Grandsons of Mohammad Yusuf Khan

First Wife:
Popalzai Saddozai

Second Wife:
Barakzai Mohammadzai

| King Nadir Shah (Oldest) | Shah Wali | Shah Mahmud | | Aziz Khan | Hashim Khan (Unmarried) |

| King Zahir Shah | Abdul Wali | Sultan Ghazi | Mohammad Daoud | Mohammad Naim |

brother, Mohammad Naim, and their half-cousin, Zahir's sister, Bilkis, but Nadir Shah and Zahir betrothed her to Abdul Wali instead. Abdul Wali's marriage into Nadir's direct line strengthened his position in the line of succession to the throne. Daoud's branch of the family lost out, and the resulting rivalry between the Pashtun cousins would contribute to the tumult that befell Afghanistan in the late 1970s.

King Nadir Shah and his brothers knew that establishing a strong army and acquiring financial solvency were critical to their dynasty's long-term survival and successful Afghan modernization. The search for recurring resources was the first challenge they faced after gaining power. The central government's authority and administrative capacity were still too weak to extract taxes from Afghanistan's well-armed population. Abdur Rahman Khan and Habibullah had received British subsidies to create strong armies capable of subduing tribal rebellions against the center. Amanullah's neglected army, deprived of British subsidies, had crumbled when the tribes rose in 1928. Nadir desperately needed to establish a Kabul military garrison to remain in power. The tribal militias that had brought him to Kabul had departed, satiated with loot. They could quickly return. Having overthrown one king, they could overthrow another. Nadir also had to "sweeten the mouth" of religious clerics whose loyalty was ephemeral.

The British, determined to maintain a stable Afghan buffer, were the first to help, providing an initial grant of 10,000 rifles, ammunition, and a large grant of approximately £175,000[23] to organize a new army. Wary of too much dependence on Britain and especially the Soviet Union, Nadir turned to Germany, Italy, and Japan for loans and technical advisers to strengthen the central government and spur economic growth. German military advisers joined Turkish officers to train Nadir's army, and some German military equipment was provided. Mainly, German foreign aid financed roads, dams, and power plants. The regime sponsored laissez-faire economics. Exports of Afghan fruits and textiles steadily rose during the 1930s.

Factories built by an emerging business class sprouted in Kabul and other urban areas. The German-built Mahipur power plant, drawing on the waters of the Kabul River, significantly upgraded the supply of electricity to the capital's homes, businesses, and government offices. More and more cars and trucks mingled with donkey-drawn carts on Kabul's streets. Wealthy businessmen, doctors, and other professionals built homes in the exclusive Wazir Akbar Khan section of Kabul, also populated by members of the Mohammadzai elite, the foreign diplomatic corps, foreign businessmen, aid workers, teachers, and their dependents. They sent their children to India and the West for higher education. A growing middle class of educated Afghans staffed the swelling ranks of the government bureaucracy and the military. By 1950, the multiethnic "Kabuli" population of a half-million was in its third generation of detribalized city dwellers.

With German and Italian advice and resources, the regime developed an interlocking system of state-controlled banks, holding companies, and factories based on the Italian fascist economic model. A central bank, Bank-i-Milli (Bank of the People), invested public and private deposits in both private and state-controlled enterprises. Most of the funds went to large, government-favored monopolies producing foreign exchange earning exports, such as lambskins and textiles. The government controlled the majority of shares in the central bank.

In the countryside, King Nadir Shah replaced Amanullah's hopeless quest to transform Afghanistan's tribal society with an "encapsulation" strategy to co-opt the tribes, while not directly challenging their local control. Mutual respect and productive communication were at the core of the center-region partnership. The center accepted decentralized community authority. Tribal and clan leader chiefs continued to govern on the basis of their local tribal codes and customs, appointing tribal leaders known as *maliks* in the Pashtun belt and *arbabs* in the north to liaise with the government. In return for financial assistance and development projects from the center, rural leaders were expected to maintain stability in their areas. Nadir invited tribal khans to Kabul to participate in loya jirgas, government development conferences, and the annual meetings of Parliament. Local tribal chiefs participated partly because it increased their prestige in an honor-bound society.

The Musahiban brothers promoted the Pashtun language, establishing a Pashtun academy in Kabul. The government transported thousands of landless Ghilzai families to fertile plains and valleys in the north and west, as had been done during Abdur Rahman Khan's reign. This second wave of forced migration of Pashtuns into settled Tajik, Uzbek, and Hazara areas deprived the northern minorities of valuable agricultural and pasture land that they had occupied for centuries. The Ghilzai Kharoti family of Gulbuddin Hekmatyar was among the migrants resettled in Kunduz.

Developing an army and a small air force was a key part of Nadir's strategy to contain tribal threats. It steadily grew in size and capability, reaching 60,000 troops deployed in three corps around the country. The Central Corps was headquartered at Amanullah's Darulaman Palace. Three military units also guarded the capital: the 8th Division at Kargha west of Kabul, the 7th Division at Rishkor south of the city, and the 4th and 9th armored regiments at Pul-i-Charkhi on the road to Jalalabad. The Musahiban brothers dealt severely with political dissidence. An article in Nadir's 1931 constitution warned that the government would suppress "signs of unrest and rebellion, tending to the disturbance of public peace."[24] After two early Shinwari and Suleiman Khel flare-ups in eastern Afghanistan, only two tribal revolts occurred during the next four decades: a Safi revolt in 1947 and another Mangal uprising in 1959. Both were suppressed.

The Musahibans took a number of steps to placate prominent national religious leaders. The constitution noted the importance of Islam and Sharia. Nadir revived Habibullah's council of clerics, which advised the king on religious and legal matters. He made the head of the Mojaddedi family minister of justice in his first cabinet and his son-in-law the deputy minister. He appointed senior clerics from around the country as members of the new parliament.

The Musahibans' careful handling of religious leaders gradually brought them and their offspring into the country's power structure. They and their children and grandchildren entered the growing Kabuli upper and middle class.[25] Their sons and daughters studied side by side at Kabul's prestigious high schools with children from the royal family and business and military leaders of the day. At the same time, the constitution was crafted to ensure the cohabitation of secular civil law administered by civil officials; customary law based on local tribal codes and Pashtunwali; and religious law as applied by qazis. These three streams of law were later recognized in the 1964 constitution, adopted during Zahir Shah's rule, and in the 2004 post-Taliban constitution.

The most serious early threat to Nadir's consolidation of power came not from rural-based tribal or religious leaders, but from a powerful Yusufzai Pashtun family long settled in Kabul: the Charkhis. Three Charkhi brothers, Ghulam Siddiq, Ghulam Nabi, and Ghulam Jilani, had supported Amanullah during the 1928–1929 Afghan Civil War. They enjoyed close ties with Ghilzai tribal leaders in eastern Afghanistan. Privately, they condemned Nadir's "usurpation" of Amanullah's throne, charging that he should have restored the ousted king to power after defeating Bacha Seqao. The Charkhi criticisms were reported back to the Musahiban brothers by Nadir's spies, setting the stage for a classic Afghan tribal vendetta featuring a downward spiral of *badal*—retribution for retribution, blood for blood.

In November 1932, Nadir summoned Ghulam Nabi Charkhi to the palace and accused him of provoking the Zadrans in Paktiya to rise against the government. Ghulam Nabi responded by questioning Nadir's legitimacy as king. Enraged, Nadir had Nabi executed. Other members of the Charkhi family suspected of being connected to the plot were immediately arrested, including Ghulam Jilani. Nadir dismissed Ghulam Siddiq, Afghan ambassador in Berlin, and replaced him with his older half-brother, Mohammad Aziz, Daoud's father. Then, on June 6, 1933, an Afghan student in Berlin walked into the Afghan embassy and assassinated Mohammad Aziz. A few months later, an attempt on Hashim Khan's life failed. Believing Britain to be colluding with Nadir Shah, an Afghan student entered the compound of the British diplomatic mission in Kabul on September 7. He shot and killed a British diplomat, an Indian clerk, and an Afghan servant. Nadir responded decisively. In addition to executing the assassin, he executed all male Charkhi family members over the age of fourteen. But the Musahiban's ruthless massacre of the Charkhis did not completely erase the lust for *badal*, at least for one young Charkhi family member who survived.

On November 8, 1933, the one-year anniversary of Ghulam Nabi's execution, Nadir was shot in the mouth at point-blank range by a student attending an afternoon award ceremony in the palace garden. He died instantly. The seventeen-year-old assassin was one of Ghulam Nabi's adopted sons.

Shah Mahmud, the only Musahiban brother then in Kabul, invited a group of prominent officials and Kabul citizens to the palace that evening to declare their allegiance to Zahir Shah, Nadir's nineteen-year-old son. The notables present quickly approved. Only hours after Nadir's assassination, a cannon was fired on the palace grounds to signal that Nadir's vacant throne had been occupied by Zahir Shah. The destruction of the Charkhi family removed the last major obstacle to the consolidation of Musahiban rule, which continued for another forty-five years. The young Zahir Shah reigned as a ceremonial king from Nadir's assassination in 1933 until 1963. His uncles, Hashim Khan and Shah Mahmud and his cousin Daoud ruled Afghanistan during these three decades.

Prime Minister Hashim Khan skillfully maneuvered Afghanistan away from the vortex of Great Power confrontations before and during World War II, as Habibullah had done during World War I. The Germans tried again to exploit Afghanistan's long-standing antipathy toward Britain. Germany counted on its record as Afghanistan's leading aid donor for over two decades to elicit Afghan cooperation, ideally another Afghan invasion of India's predominately Pashtun northwest province. Such an invasion, or even the threat of one, would draw British military manpower and resources away from German armies in the West. If the Afghans resisted placing direct military pressure on India, the Nazis hoped that they would at least permit Germany to activate the thorns of the "prickly hedge," the trans-Durand Waziri, Mahsud, Mohmand, and Afridi tribes, against British India. But German strategists in Berlin failed to appreciate that the prickly hedge's thorns faced Kabul as well as New Delhi. Arming these unpredictable tribes endangered the Musahiban Dynasty as well as the British.

The British were vulnerable. The periodic emergence of "mad mullahs" instigating tribal uprisings in the quasi-independent Pashtun tribal agencies had been a constant menace to the British in the early twentieth century. In 1936, a potential German ally, Waziri religious leader Mirza Ali Khan, known as the Faqir of Ipi, declared jihad against the British. His debut on the Frontier was a Waziri rout of a three-regiment British force north of the main British military base at Razmak, South Waziristan, in November 1936. The Mahsuds joined the uprising in 1937. The viceroy responded by increasing British force strength in North and South Waziristan to twenty-eight battalions, more than half the troops in British India.[26]

Despite the heavy British military presence in the Pashtun tribal agencies, an area less than the size of Massachusetts, British control never extended much beyond military cantonments and the few roads built into the tribal agencies.[27] British authorities increasingly responded to tribal raids with punitive air strikes, bombing villages, crops, and livestock as well as military targets. Aircraft-enforced free-fire zones impeded the movement of people and goods between villages occupied by dissident tribes. During the 1930s, King Nadir Shah and his brothers were happy to keep the prickly hedge's thorns pointed at the British. They received and bestowed honors on "wanted" Pashtun tribal leaders in British India who had fled to Afghanistan. Afghan subsidies were quietly sent to Pashtun chiefs resisting British control. Afghan government radio broadcasts demanded that Britain respect tribal autonomy.[28]

Ultimately, Nazi attempts to manipulate the Afghans to serve German objectives during World War II backfired. German *Abwehr* military intelligence officers and diplomats made the same mistakes that the British had committed, which subsequently were repeated by the Soviets, Pakistanis, and Americans over the course of the rest of the century and into the present one. Fundamental ignorance of Afghanistan undermined every German initiative.

While Germans in Berlin calculated how to leverage their generous aid to the Afghans, the Musahiban brothers, led by Prime Minister Hashim Khan, examined their options. They decided to distance Afghanistan from the World War II belligerents. King Zahir Shah issued a neutrality proclamation on August 17, 1940. Undaunted, the Germans reiterated their World War I offer to return the Indian regions that had been conquered by Ahmad Shah

Durrani. Hashim Khan turned down the offer and secretly kept the British informed. In 1941, the German invasion of the Soviet Union made any Afghan collaboration with Germany hazardous, given Afghanistan's geographic location between British India and the USSR, now allies in the war against the Axis. German military setbacks in 1943 at Stalingrad and in North Africa stiffened Afghanistan's posture of overt neutrality.

German officials in Berlin attempted to organize anti-British activities from Afghan territory with or without the approval of Afghan authorities. They ordered German agents in Kabul to equip Indian revolutionaries operating there to launch sabotage attacks against British targets in India and incite an Indian uprising. German and Italian intelligence agents in Kabul established clandestine contacts with the Faqir of Ipi in South Waziristan. The Afghan government warned the Germans about the misfortune suffered by all those who attempted to manipulate the Frontier tribes. German ignorance about Frontier tribal dynamics, the Afghans pointed out, guaranteed that their covert activities would fail.[29]

Afghan bluntness did not deter the Germans. In 1941, an Italian intelligence agent traveled to South Waziristan and opened contacts with the Faqir of Ipi with a view to furnishing arms, ammunition, and communications equipment for raids against British troops. The Italian provided the Faqir with a substantial amount of Afghan currency and £12,000. The Faqir agreed to receive a radio operator to train his men in operating a German shortwave radio transmitter; he returned the British pound notes, stating his preference for American dollars or gold.[30]

The Abwehr took over the Faqir of Ipi's portfolio from the Italians. German intelligence gave the Faqir of Ipi the code name *Feuerfresser* (Fire-eater). When two Abwehr agents with Waziri escorts left Kabul for South Waziristan, dressed as Afghans, they were carrying money, weapons, maps, and radio equipment. On July 19, 1941, a fifty-man Afghan Army unit surrounded the German encampment. During the ensuing firefight, the Waziris ran away. One of the Germans was killed, the other captured. Back in Kabul, the German minister told Afghan officials the mission was merely "exploratory" and a "tragic mistake."[31] The Afghans believed that the operation had probably been penetrated by the British from the beginning.[32]

The German position in Afghanistan deteriorated as Allied victories in Europe mounted. When the Italians abandoned the Axis cause in 1943, the chief of Italian intelligence in Kabul briefed American and British diplomats on German intelligence operations and handed over Axis codebooks. Hashim Khan jailed pro-German Afghan sympathizers in Kabul, a move the British minister in Kabul appreciated. He reported in 1945 that the Afghan prime minister's policy was "of the greatest advantage to us."

The crowning blow to Germany's toehold in Afghanistan was the Afghan government's submission to a joint British-Soviet ultimatum to expel all nondiplomatic Axis nationals from Afghanistan. Reza Shah in Iran rejected a parallel British-Soviet ultimatum. The Afghans watched as British and Soviet armies rolled into Iran and deposed him. Having sent Reza Shah into exile in South Africa for the remainder of his life, they placed his son, Mohammad Reza, on the throne.[33]

Some Afghans urged Afghan resistance to the ultimatum, which supremely violated Afghan sovereignty and the Pashtunwali imperative of providing protective hospitality to guests. Hashim Khan, choosing a more prudent course, convened a tame loya jirga in order to distribute the blame for Afghan capitulation to the entire country. The loya jirga's approval of Afghanistan's written acceptance of the ultimatum was balanced by a shrill government declaration that Afghanistan would allow no additional limitations on its sovereignty and independence. One hundred and eighty Germans and their dependents were trucked to Peshawar, leaving only a skeletal staff at the German legation in Kabul. As Allied armies closed in on Germany from east and west, the Afghan government ordered the Germans to downsize their mission in Kabul to a handful of diplomats, who departed at the end of the war.

The Musahiban Dynasty avoided the fate of Reza Shah by ending Afghan neutrality and siding with the Allies as World War II wound down. In domestic affairs, the family's older generation masterfully balanced the center-region equilibrium, prolonging national stability into the postwar years. In 1953, they passed the torch to the second generation. Under Daoud Khan and Zahir Shah, the drive for modernization continued throughout the 1960s and into the 1970s. But it was during these two decades that the tribal scourge of cousin-on-cousin rivalry ripped the royal family apart, with disastrous results for the dynasty and for Afghanistan.

CHAPTER 5

Red Sunrise

The wife of the U.S. embassy administrative counselor, Annette Woodward, sat in the bleachers with other parents, half-watching their children
play a baseball game. A dance party the previous evening had been a late
one, and the parents were sleepy. It was a mild spring morning in Kabul,
April 27, 1978.

"We were just thinking that after another couple of hours we could go
home and go to bed," Annette recalled twenty-five years later. "We were
not really paying attention to the game, to be honest":

> Then something seemed to be out of the ordinary. All the kids were
> shouting. They dropped bats, balls, and gloves and raced across the
> field toward the main street leading to the presidential palace two
> blocks away and the Ministry of Defense one block away. I looked up
> the road and saw a line of tanks noisily moving at high speeds, past
> the embassy and toward the presidential palace and the Ministry of
> Defense. I noticed they were churning up and destroying the tarmac.
> I thought something was wrong. Afghan ministries had just worked
> hard to spruce up the city in preparation for the Non-Aligned Con-
> ference Afghanistan was to host next week—painting, sweeping, and
> cleaning. A few minutes later, tank firing filled the air. We scooped
> up the kids and raced home.[1]

Annette's husband, Don Woodward, then nearby at the embassy, recalled
that an embassy Marine Guard ran outside of the chancery just in time
to see a tank fire a round directly into the Ministry of Defense. Embassy

*officers and military attachés scrambled to the roof to observe the situa-
tion, and a helicopter gunship fired a rocket. It missed them by just 20
feet.[2]*

*Soviet-trained Afghan military officers were at the controls of the tanks
and warplanes. It was the opening salvo of the Afghan communist coup,
an event that ushered in more than three decades of continuous warfare.
By the time the last Soviet troops left Afghanistan in 1989, nearly all of
the progress Afghanistan had made in the previous half-century, its impressive gains in modernization, were obliterated.*

Two post–World War II geopolitical developments in the region damaged
Afghanistan's buffer status between the Great Powers. The first was Britain's
withdrawal from the subcontinent in 1947. The British departure from the
region removed the main deterrent to Soviet penetration of Afghanistan. The
vacuum left by one unified state in South Asia blocking Soviet expansion was
filled by two bickering states set against each other, India and Pakistan. Many
thousands of Hindus and Muslims perished during the 1947 partition of the
subcontinent. Preoccupied with their mutual hostility, neither India nor Pakistan devoted attention to sustaining the Afghan buffer—the main focus of
Britain's military doctrine for over a century. This meant that the Afghan government needed to act wisely in bending the new regional balance of power
to preserve Afghan independence—or fall victim to the vicissitudes of geopolitical rivalry among its more powerful neighbors.

The advent of the Cold War was the second major change in Afghanistan's
external environment. Stalin had neglected the Third World, but after the
Soviet dictator died in 1953, U.S.-Soviet global competition expanded from
Europe into Asia, Africa, and Latin America. Nikita Khrushchev resumed
Russia's nineteenth-century "pause and push" southern advance. Afghanistan was the first country in the Third World to accept large-scale Soviet
economic and military assistance. The Soviet Union became Afghanistan's
principal outside patron. Soviet intelligence agencies clandestinely exploited
burgeoning Soviet-Afghan ties to expand Moscow's network of agents inside
Afghanistan.

Britain's provision of arms and funds to the Musahiban regime had reinforced internal Afghan stability, propping up the Afghan buffer. When Britain

left the subcontinent, the new Indian and Pakistani governments went to war in Kashmir. The Indo-Pakistan military confrontation closed down British military shipments to the Musahiban rulers in Afghanistan. The new Indian government confiscated military equipment the British had earmarked for the Afghan government in Kabul, and informed Britain that the paperwork documenting the transfers had been lost. When the British supplied copies, the Indian authorities declared they had no legal obligation to implement Britain's commitment.[3] The Pakistani government was particularly reluctant to fulfill colonial-era military agreements with Afghanistan, since the arms transferred to the Kabul regime could be turned against Pakistan.

The Afghan regime watched helplessly as the British weapons larder closed. America was a potential source of arms, but Washington was a tough sell. The United States was rapidly becoming a close ally of Pakistan. Pakistan signed the American-sponsored Southeast Asian Treaty Organization (SEATO) and the Central Treaty Organization (CENTO) treaties. It was a valuable link in the chain of alliances the United States was building to contain Soviet expansionism.[4]

Winds of change were also blowing within Afghanistan after World War II. Hashim Khan passed the prime ministership to Shah Mahmud in 1946. Shah Mahmud tried but failed to steer increasing demands for political liberalization into democratic channels. On September 20, 1953, a Musahiban family meeting of the senior brothers and their children assembled to decide which of the two second-generation sons, Zahir Shah or Daoud Khan, should receive the mantle of leadership from Shah Mahmud. The elder Musahiban brothers and half-brothers had buried their differences and closed ranks during the twenty-four years since taking power in 1929. Zahir Shah and Daoud Khan were cousins as well as brothers-in-law. But the cousin-on-cousin rivalry so common in Afghan society would fuel their rivalry for the next twenty-five years. Daoud Khan felt it most. Abdul Wali was another second-generation cousin, the son of Musahiban elder Shah Wali. Like Daoud, an army general, he would throw his weight behind his full-cousin, Zahir Shah, in the coming struggle for power.

The meeting handed the reins of authority to Daoud; Zahir Shah would remain a ceremonial monarch. At forty-three, Daoud was older than Zahir Shah, who was then thirty-nine. Daoud's style was authoritarian. He had spent most of his career in the armed forces and was commander of the Central Corps when he became prime minister in 1953. Mid-level and senior officers had benefited from his patronage. Daoud's autocratic style and aloofness followed in the tradition of Nadir Shah and Hashim Khan. He shared Amanullah's supreme self-confidence, rooted in his belief that he knew Afghanistan and its people well. Proud, tough, and cunning, he was determined to quicken economic and social reforms and to postpone political liberalization. He was committed to the creation of Pashtunistan, an ambiguous Afghan irredentist claim to primarily Pashtun-settled areas in Pakistan's Northwest Province and in Baluchistan. Daoud's championing of Pashtunistan was a direct challenge to the new state of Pakistan's territorial integrity.

Daoud was restless. He sought to modernize Afghanistan quickly. He intended to finance a modern military to stand up to Pakistan, launch an ambitious economic development program, and construct a strong government at the center. Daoud was suspicious by nature. He tended to act unilaterally, occasionally ruthlessly. His hard-headed approach was the antithesis of Amanullah's quixotic idealism and naïveté. He had once served as minister of interior, where he managed the Afghan secret police. As prime minister, he expanded this feared body. It monitored his critics, suppressed opposition to his rule, and kept tabs on foreign missions in Afghanistan.

Daoud needed a foreign patron to accomplish his ambitious goals. The United States was his first choice. America was far away and nonthreatening. Daoud's appeal for arms and assistance was delivered confidentially in Washington by Prince Naim, his foreign minister, younger brother, and closest adviser. But the Eisenhower administration did not wish to equip Daoud's army because it did not want to challenge Washington's Pakistani treaty partner on the matter of Pashtunistan. In a humiliating diplomatic note delivered to the Afghan ambassador in Washington on December 28, 1954, Secretary of State John Foster Dulles rejected Daoud's request, advising that, "instead of asking for arms, Afghanistan should settle the Pashtunistan dispute with Pakistan." Daoud was outraged. Dulles added insult to injury by breaking the confidentiality of the bilateral diplomatic exchange with Naim, revealing the contents of his response to the Pakistani ambassador in Washington.[5]

One month later, in January 1955, Daoud formally accepted a Soviet offer of military assistance. He convened a loya jirga in Kabul to endorse Afghan acceptance of Soviet arms. In December 1955, Daoud rolled out the red carpet for the high-profile Khrushchev visit to Afghanistan, the first stop by the Soviet leader on his first trip abroad to inaugurate Moscow's outreach to the Third World.

On his deathbed in 1901, Abdur Rahman Khan had warned future Afghan ruler Habibullah: "My last words to you, my son and successor, are: Never trust the Russians."[6] Daoud's Musahiban uncles had conducted normal state-to-state relations with the Soviet Union while suppressing the Soviet presence in Afghanistan. Soon after overthrowing Bacha Seqao, Nadir dismissed all of the Soviet military advisers, technicians, and economic officials that Amanullah had invited into Afghanistan. His secret police closely monitored the movement of Soviet diplomats in Afghanistan, and he prohibited Soviet officials from distributing propaganda in Afghan languages. His regime outlawed the communist party and allowed Afghan religious figures to denounce the anti-Islamic policies of the Soviet Union.

Daoud believed he could benefit from Soviet aid and limit Soviet espionage. His decision to accept Soviet advisers, along with Soviet economic and military support, was a radical departure from the policies of the older Musahiban generation. His Pashtunistan policy corresponded with the Soviet strategy to weaken America's containment of the USSR, and Khrushchev publicly backed Daoud's Pashtunistan cause.

Daoud's tilt toward the Soviet Union earned lucrative returns for the underdeveloped Afghan economy and the poorly equipped Afghan Army. The 1955 Khrushchev visit was crowned with the signing of a $100 million Soviet loan agreement. More accords followed—on air communications in 1956; on border controls in 1958; on telecommunications, road building, bridge construction, and hydroelectric power in 1959; on cultural exchanges in 1960; and on housing construction in 1962. Cheap long-term Soviet credits financed the 425-mile hard surface road from Kandahar to Herat and on to Turgundi on the Soviet border. The Soviets constructed another highway connecting Kabul with northern Afghanistan and the Soviet border at Termez. The project required digging the 1.7-mile-long, 11,100-foot-high Salang Tunnel. Both Soviet-built roads would sustain the weight of the heavy vehicles, including Soviet tanks, that were later to sprint south from Termez and Turgundi during Moscow's 1979 invasion of Afghanistan.

Soviet aid workers built dozens of factories. Soviet funds financed construction of airports at Kabul and Mazar-i-Sharif, which Afghanistan's national airline, Ariana Air, used for international as well as domestic flights. Soviet engineers supervised the establishment of a military airport at Bagram for Daoud's air force of Soviet-provided and -maintained bombers and MIG fighters. Soviet machinery paved Kabul's streets and erected two huge Soviet-style bakeries in Kabul. Soviet planners worked collaboratively with Afghan ministries to develop Daoud's Soviet-style five-year plans, begun in 1956. Foreign aid, most of it Soviet, provided over 60 percent of the five-year-plan project funding.[7]

Soviet KGB and military intelligence agents from the GRU (the Russian acronym for Soviet military intelligence) tunneled deeply into Afghan government and society.[8] The KGB made Afghanistan one of its primary focuses. Moscow's intelligence structure in Afghanistan steadily grew in size, sophistication, and capabilities. The KGB's network of agents penetrated the prime minister's office, government ministries, the Afghan secret police, universities, and commercial establishments. GRU recruitment in the Afghan Army was facilitated by hundreds of Soviet military advisers stationed at Afghan Army bases, who sifted out officers for training in the Soviet Union. A section of the KGB's Second Chief Directorate dealing with foreigners in the USSR picked up the Afghan civilian and military trainees after they arrived, recruiting hundreds.[9]

The KGB "Residency" at the large Soviet embassy in Kabul was the nerve center of Soviet spy operations in Afghanistan. Undercover KGB officers worked in diplomatic, advisory, journalist, teaching, and other capacities around the country. The TASS news correspondent in Kabul, as in many other cities around the world, was a KGB agent.

Nur Mohammad Taraki, who later became the first Afghan communist leader, was recruited by the KGB in 1951 and given the code name "Nur." In 1953—while still a Soviet agent—he worked as the press and cultural attaché at the Afghan embassy in Washington. After leaving Washington he stayed abroad for three years, traveling in India, Pakistan, and reportedly the Soviet Union and Eastern Europe. When he returned to Afghanistan, the KGB provided him with regular payments to carry out communist underground operations and to finance his newspaper *Khalq* (Masses) and personal expenses. Taraki met with KGB officers in cars and at the TASS correspondent's house.

He passed information to the KGB on the domestic Afghan situation, the Pashtunistan issue, and the Afghan Army. He provided names of Afghans he believed were ripe for recruitment. On Soviet instructions, Taraki applied for and gained a position as a translator at the American embassy's U.S. aid mission (1956–1958) and later in the U.S. embassy itself (1962–1963). One of his functions was to translate the embassy's daily Afghan press summary for transmission to Washington.[10]

The huge Soviet aid program provided a cushion for the KGB to foster an Afghan communist movement, with Taraki as its main vehicle. He organized the first Marxist study group in Kabul in 1956, giving it the same name as his newspaper, *Khalq*. Most of the leftist students, teachers, and government workers participating were, like Taraki, Pashtuns from undistinguished rural backgrounds. Two other future communist leaders of Afghanistan, Babrak Karmal ("Friend of Labor") and Hafizullah Amin, became KGB agents in the 1950s. A former KGB major who defected to Britain reported in 1982 that Karmal had worked as a KGB agent for many years and "could be relied on to accept our advice."[11] Karmal was jailed for his left-wing student activism at Kabul University in 1953. He befriended a Marxist revolutionary and theoretician, Mir Akbar Khyber, in prison. After their release, Karmal and Khyber launched a separate Marxist study group in 1960. They named it Parcham (Flag), and it attracted mostly Dari-speaking Tajiks from middle- and upper-class Kabul families. Mohammad Najib, a medical student and a Ghilzai Pashtun from Paktiya, was an eager participant.

Hafizullah Amin, a young Kharoti Ghilzai educator from Paghman in the mountainous terrain northwest of Kabul, joined Taraki's study group. Amin exploited his native charisma and boundless energy to attract followers from among the boarding students at high schools where he taught. After obtaining his master's degree in education from Columbia University, he was elevated to a high-school principal and director of a teachers' college. The appointments gave him access to hundreds of potential recruits, both teachers and students.

The KGB Residency in Kabul and the Politburo in Moscow must have been delighted by the KGB's harvest of Afghan spies. In fact, the numerous Afghan agents in the KGB net and the KGB's later fathering of an Afghan communist party were mirages. Instead of steadily nudging Afghanistan toward the Soviet "socialist community," KGB agents and their GRU counterparts were

lowering the Soviet Union deeper and deeper into the chaotic Afghan political cauldron, where ideologies cannot survive and loyalties are forever tran-
sient. On two occasions the KGB tried to fuse Taraki's mainly Pashtun
communists and Karmal's predominantly Tajik communists into a united
communist party, only to see their artificial creation implode a short time
later. The Soviets never succeeded in using the Afghan communists to impose
their vision on Afghanistan's many other factions. It would take three decades,
many billions of rubles, and tens of thousands of Soviet lives for Soviet leaders to come to this realization.

ψ

Daoud's pro-Soviet direction and the growing Soviet influence in Afghanistan
worried the new Kennedy administration when it took office in 1961. President Dwight D. Eisenhower's secretary of state, John Foster Dulles, had considered neutrality "immoral and shortsighted."[12] President John F. Kennedy
adopted a more nuanced foreign policy toward Third World countries, such
as Afghanistan, that were leaning toward the USSR. His administration
sought to weaken their ties to Moscow while encouraging their neutrality in
the Cold War. A 1961 U.S. National Security Council memorandum noted
that "the United States should try to resolve the Afghan dispute with Pakistan
and encourage Afghanistan to minimize its reliance on the Communist bloc
for military training and equipment."[13] From 1958 to 1978, several hundred
Afghan military officers participated in the U.S. military's International Military Education and Training Programs (IMET) in the United States.

   The limited U.S. military training program for Afghanistan could do little
to offset Daoud's dependence on Soviet military training and equipment.
The Kennedy administration was better able to balance Soviet influence in
Afghanistan through economic assistance, education, road building, and energy projects. Afghanistan became one of the largest recipients of Peace
Corps programs worldwide. Western aid projects, including those sponsored
by the United States, were mostly located south of the Hindu Kush. The Soviets concentrated their projects in the north. Though well below Soviet aid
levels, the assistance from the United States and its allies was sufficient to expose Afghanistan to Western ideas and practices.

   Educational initiatives were among the more successful programs sponsored by America and the West. Several American universities—the Uni-

versity of Nebraska at Omaha, Columbia University, the University of Wyoming, Southern Illinois University, and Indiana University—signed contracts to revamp Afghanistan's entire education system from elementary school through college. Over 2,000 Afghan students and educators were given scholarships to study in the West. American professors taught at Kabul University and Afghan teacher-training institutions in Kabul and Afghan provinces. In addition, British, French, and German aid programs upgraded the elite Habibya, Istiqlal, and Nejat high schools, which had been founded by Habibullah and Amanulláh. Over a hundred foreign professors, most from the West, taught at Kabul University's campuses. In response, the Soviets opened a large Polytechnic Institute in Kabul, staffing it with Soviet administrators and faculty.

Supervised by the U.S. Army Corps of Engineers, the American Morrison-Knudson Company constructed the 312-mile-long Kabul-to-Kandahar highway. The Federal Aviation Administration (FAA) funded a 49 percent Pan American Airline stake in Afghanistan's Ariana Airlines, with Pan American training Ariana staff and providing modern equipment for Ariana air operations. Ariana used American-built aircraft to expand its air service domestically and to points in Europe, the Middle East, and South Asia. The United States also financed the construction of the Kandahar Airport. More than $50 million in U.S. assistance was pumped into the Helmand River project, also supervised by Morrison-Knudson. The project was designed to resuscitate the once-fertile lower Helmand River Valley, which had been destroyed during the twelfth-century Mongolian invasions.[14]

The Soviet Union considered the left-leaning Daoud a Soviet asset in highly conservative Afghanistan and endeavored to keep him in power. Soviet intelligence instructed the small but growing Afghan communist movement not to oppose Daoud. They wanted him to survive. A pro-Soviet Afghanistan would keep the American system of alliances away from Soviet borders in Central Asia, and Daoud's Pashtunistan policy usefully irritated an American ally, Pakistan. Nevertheless, it was Daoud's adamant insistence on Pashtunistan that ultimately led to his fall from power in 1963. His concept of Pashtunistan was not precisely defined, and it never gained traction inside Pakistan. Baluch tribes in Pakistan wondered why Daoud had included Baluchistan within Pashtunistan without their approval.[15] The trans-Durand hill tribes had their own interpretation of Pashtunistan—continuity in their state of splendid isolation from both Afghanistan and Pakistan. Uniting Pakistani and Afghan Pashtuns did not appeal to Afghan Tajiks, Uzbeks, and Hazaras.

In 1960, Daoud sent Afghan troops disguised as tribesmen across the border into Pakistan's Bajaur tribal agency northwest of Peshawar. The intrusion, into an area where the Durand Line was not well defined, was driven back by local Bajaur Pashtun tribes who opposed any interference in their affairs from Afghanistan or Pakistan. In 1961, Daoud organized a larger, more determined Afghan incursion into Bajaur. This time Pakistan employed American-supplied F-86 Sabre jets against the Afghans, inflicting heavy casualties on Afghan army units and tribesmen from Konar accompanying them. To Daoud's embarrassment, several Afghan regulars captured inside Pakistan were paraded before the international media.

Pakistan's military dictator, General Ayub Khan, closed Pakistan's consulates at Kandahar and Jalalabad and insisted that Afghanistan shut down its consulates in Peshawar and Quetta. Not backing down, Daoud gave Ayub Khan one week to cancel his actions. Ayub Khan let Daoud's deadline expire. He then escalated tensions by blocking all trade routes across the Durand Line. The restriction cut off the centuries-old annual winter migration of over a million Afghan Pashtun nomads into Pakistan. More important, the Pakistani blockade severed Afghanistan's main economic and trade corridors to the outside world.

Daoud looked to Moscow for help. Soviet planes airlifted Afghanistan's entire 1961 fruit crop to markets in the USSR and Eastern Europe. Afghanistan and the Soviet Union signed new transportation agreements to offset closed Afghan-Pakistani trade routes by constructing roads to the northern Soviet-Afghan border. But these stopgap measures could not compensate for the devastating economic consequences that the Pakistani blockade inflicted on Afghanistan. Long-standing resentment of Daoud's autocratic rule and close Soviet ties combined with the economic downturn resulting from the blockade led to calls for him to retire. Daoud chose this moment to request Zahir Shah's approval for a new one-party constitution that would expand his already considerable powers. When Zahir Shah rejected his proposal, Daoud angrily submitted his resignation to the king. For the first time since ascending to the throne in 1933, Afghanistan's mild-mannered monarch now had the mandate to rule as well as to reign.

৺

Older Afghans who experienced Zahir Shah's "new democracy" (*demokrasi-i-naw*)[16] period (1963–1973) consider it the high point of the half-century era of tranquility existing before the 1978 communist coup. Kabul's liberal educated elite and rural tribal khans came together under his leadership to form a constitutional coalition. They charted a democratic trail without the kind of direct encouragement the United States gave to Germany, Japan, and South Korea in the 1940s and 1950s. Zahir Shah promoted liberalization of Afghan politics. In contrast to Daoud, he was open and receptive to advice. While his uncles and his cousin, Daoud, ruled Afghanistan, the king had traveled throughout the country engaging Afghans at all levels. He was personally acquainted with thousands of community leaders, clerics, and farmers. A steady stream of Afghans representing diverse ethnic groups called on him at his palace.

During his decade of democracy, the king strove to include non-Pashtun minorities in the political process. He appointed a Tajik, Dr. Mohammed Yousuf, to be his first prime minister and made Abdul Sattar Sirat, an Uzbek, deputy prime minister. Yousuf was a respected and popular Tajik Kabuli. He held a PhD from the University of Göttingen and was fluent in English. Early on, Zahir Shah also increased the number of provinces from ten to twenty-nine in order to give more provincial regional administrative units to both non-Pashtun and Pashtun groups.

Zahir Shah's 1964 constitution was drafted by a team of highly respected Pashtun and Tajik intellectuals. Whereas Daoud had centralized power in his hands, the constitution dispersed it among executive, legislative, and judicial branches. The framers hoped the constitution would strengthen the growing sense of nationalism and unity in the country. The document established a bicameral legislature. It featured a 216-member lower house, the Wolesi (Peoples) Jirga, elected by universal adult suffrage to a four-year term, and an 84-member upper house, the Meshrano (Notables) Jirga. One-third of the latter body was to be appointed by the king, one-third by elected provincial jirgas, and one-third directly elected by provincial voters. The constitution delegated unspecified authority to elected provincial and district councils, leaving details of the councils' responsibilities to be decided by parliament. A Supreme Court was established to oversee the judicial branch of government.

The cabinet system adopted in the 1964 constitution was based on the French constitutional model.[17] The prime minister and his cabinet were appointed by the king and made accountable to parliament. The constitution enumerated a series of individual liberties, including equality before the law for all Afghan citizens, freedom of speech, freedom of the press, freedom of assembly, and due process. It maintained the balance between Islam and the state, secular law, Pashtunwali, and Sharia. Islam was declared the "sacred religion of Afghanistan." A formulation on the supremacy of the Hanafi School of Sharia in the 1931 constitution was adjusted to permit the Shia and non-Muslim religious groups to follow their own religious orders. Implicit authorization of secular law was indicated in the constitution's statement that no law "repugnant to the basic principles of the sacred religion of Islam" could be adopted, a formula drawn on by the team that later drafted Afghanistan's 2004 constitution.[18]

One provision of the 1964 constitution, known as the "Daoud Clause," appeared to have been specifically inserted to prevent Daoud's return to power. Article 24 stipulated that: "Members of the Royal House shall not participate in political parties, and shall not hold the following offices: Prime Minister or Minister; Member of Parliament; Justice of the Supreme Court."[19] The king's appointment of Mohammad Yousuf following the 1965 parliamentary elections exhibited his intent to end the Musahiban domination of Afghan politics. No Musahiban family members were included in his first cabinet, which was drawn mostly from Kabul's educated elite. Twelve cabinet members held PhDs.

A feeling of positive momentum and optimism prevailed during the loya jirga debate approving the constitution. Only about 15 percent of the population voted in the 1965 elections, due to budgetary and administrative obstacles. The great majority of the ballots were cast in Kabul and provincial towns. Not surprisingly, members of the traditional elites in rural areas, local tribal and ethnic khans, and prestigious religious figures dominated the parliaments elected in 1965 and 1969.

Zahir Shah reinstated balance in Afghan relations between the West and the Soviet Union. His new government ceased disseminating anti-Pakistani propaganda. Iranian Shah Mohammad Reza hosted a Pakistani-Afghan-Iranian tripartite meeting in Tehran, which restored Afghanistan's trade corridors into and through Pakistan. The consulates were reopened. During the 1965 Indo-Pakistani War, Afghanistan quietly assisted Pakistan by permitting Iranian arms and ammunition to transit Kandahar en route to Pakistan. Afghanistan also provided a safe haven for Pakistani civilian airplanes at Afghan airports. Afghanistan's partiality for Pakistan during the 1971 Indo-Pakistani War was carefully muted. It contradicted Moscow's warming ties with India.[20]

Zahir Shah's visits to Moscow in 1965 and 1971 were counterbalanced by meetings with President Kennedy in Washington in September 1963 and visits to Western European and Arab capitals. The king discontinued Daoud's practice of siding with Moscow in the Sino-Soviet dispute. Zahir Shah and the Chinese president exchanged visits and signed a border demarcation agreement. China became one of Afghanistan's larger aid donors.

Zahir Shah's democratization program and his restoration of Afghan neutrality between the superpowers raised concerns in Moscow that the Soviet Union was losing its investment in Afghanistan. Soviet leaders decided to create an Afghan communist party, a step not taken when Daoud was in office. In 1965, Soviet KGB intelligence agents combined Taraki's Khalq study group with Karmal's Parcham study group to become the Peoples' Democratic Party of Afghanistan (PDPA). About thirty Afghan communists gathered in Taraki's living room on January 1, 1965, to hold the PDPA's first party congress. They selected Taraki as the party's general secretary, with Karmal as his deputy. A five-member Politburo and a Central Committee were established.

Taraki's stage-managed selection as general secretary earned him an invitation to visit Boris Ponomarev, head of the influential International Affairs Department of the Soviet Communist Party's Central Committee in Moscow, later in 1965. Taraki was told to inform Afghan authorities that he was making the trip as a guest of Soviet writers and the Society of Afghan-Soviet Friendship. According to KGB defector Vasili Mitrokhin, Ponomarev instructed Taraki in Moscow on how to organize the PDPA's party offices, publish his *Khalq* newspaper, and set the financing rules and strategy of the PDPA.[21]

After Taraki's visit, one of Ponomarev's deputies, Ivan Milovanov, told Taraki's Soviet handlers in Kabul that their "work with the party leaders of the PDPA must be done in such a way that the authorities knew only a few of the leaders of the party, such as Taraki and Babrak." Milovanov issued orders for the two PDPA leaders to "train senior members secretly in case those known to the authorities were arrested" and should "use legal possibilities, in particular the setting up of student and youth organizations, trade unions and so on."[22] Coached by the KGB, the PDPA turned its attention to building a large party membership. The recruiting emphasis was on Afghan military officers, government bureaucrats, and students, from both Kabul University and high schools in the capital.[23]

The growing Soviet-nurtured Afghan communist movement created a backlash within Afghanistan's conservative Muslim population. At Kabul University, violent clashes between observant Muslim and communist students became commonplace. An Islamist group of professors in the university's Theology Department looked to Pakistan and Saudi Arabia to offset Soviet backing for the Afghan communist movement. One of these professors, Ghulam Mohammad Niazi, had returned from Cairo's al-Azhar University with a degree in Islamic studies in the 1950s. Al-Azhar was the most prestigious Islamic center of learning in the Muslim world. It was at the time also a bustling center of Muslim Brotherhood activity. The Brotherhood propagated its version of a "pure" Muslim state based on Sharia. Its message was virulently anti-Western, anticommunist, and anti-Zionist and firmly against tribal, ethnic, and nationalistic affiliations that watered down unity within the worldwide community of believers (umma).

The Jamaat-i Islami (Society of Islam), a Pakistani politico-religious party, was the Pakistani branch of the Muslim Brotherhood. It regularly sent the Jamaat deputy party leader, Qazi Hussain Ahmed, to Kabul to help establish an Afghan Muslim Brotherhood branch. Ahmed, a Pakistani Pashtun based in Peshawar, worked closely with Pakistani military intelligence, the ISI. He assisted Niazi to organize the Afghan offshoot of the Muslim Brotherhood, the semi-clandestine Jamiat Islami Party.[24] Two other Theology Department professors who followed Niazi to al-Azhar, Burhanuddin Rabbani and Abdul Rasoul Sayyaf, helped Niazi launch the Afghan Jamiat Islami. Rabbani became Niazi's deputy in the new Islamic party.

The traditional Afghan clergy was suspicious of the extremist agenda propounded by the Islamist professors. They were comfortable with the equilibrium between Islam and Western-based reforms grounded in the 1964 Afghan Constitution. Muslim Brotherhood doctrine, like the communist propaganda seeping into Afghanistan, condemned the Sufism practiced by most Afghans as a feudal anachronism and tool of the ruling elite. The Ikhwanis (Muslim Brothers) considered the Mojaddedi and Gailani families societal "parasites," and the Sufi orders "a misrepresentation of Islam."[25]

Many traditional clerics won election to parliament and spoke out against communist infiltration of Afghanistan. In an emotional parliamentary debate broadcast by Kabul radio, Mohammad Nabi Mohammadi, a traditional Ghilzai Mawlawi and future Mujahidin leader, read aloud from the atheistic writings of Marx, Engel, Lenin, and Stalin to refute Afghan communist claims of Islam's compatibility with communism.[26] When Babrak Karmal mocked Nabi on the floor of parliament, the huge Pashtun cleric physically attacked Karmal, sending him to the hospital.

From Kabul University, Niazi, Rabbani, and Sayyaf introduced Afghan students to the Muslim Brotherhood philosophy. The professors organized a student wing of the Jamiat Islami party, Sazman-i Jawanan-i Mosalman (Organization of Young Muslims) or Muslim Youth. The Muslim Youth competed with the communists for recruits, scouring Kabul's high school and college campuses.[27] The two fought each other both on and off campus and organized frequent student strikes, immobilizing university academic activity.[28] Many of the Muslim Youth activists were more interested in combating the spread of atheistic communism into Afghanistan than in proselytizing the Muslim Brotherhood's creed. One was Ahmed Shah Masood, a Panshiri Tajik whose father, Dost Mohammad, was then a colonel in the Afghan army. The family owned a home in the lovely Panshir Valley north of Kabul. Dost Mohammad was a man of strong faith, and Ahmed, his third son, a student at the Russian Politechnik, often accompanied him to the mosque. Like his father, Ahmed was an Afghan patriot and an avid reader of the great Sufi poets. He would later become one of the most famous Mujahidin commanders in the Soviet-Afghan war.

Gulbuddin Hekmatyar was a leading instigator of Islamist violence on campus. A charismatic orator, he was also uncompromising, intelligent, and ruthless. All of these traits would characterize his next fifty years in Afghan politics, from campus agitator to present-day guerrilla leader operating from Pakistani sanctuaries against the government in Kabul and the U.S.-led coalition supporting it.

Hekmatyar was a Kharoti Pashtun from a small landowning peasant family living near the town of Imam Sahib in Kunduz Province. His family had been part of the second wave of immigration organized by the monarchy to resettle landless Ghilzai Pashtuns in Tajik-, Uzbek-, and Hazara-populated northern Afghanistan in the 1930s. He and his siblings grew up speaking Dari as well as Pashto and had lost touch with their tribal roots south of the Hindu Kush. The lack of a strong tribal identity probably buttressed his commitment to the radical Islamist cause.

Hekmatyar's first academic stop had been the Afghan Military Academy, where he ran afoul of the administration and was expelled for misbehavior. He then gained admission to the American-assisted Engineering College at Kabul University. After joining the Muslim Youth, he abandoned his studies to devote full-time to political activism. While Taraki and Amin made regular visits to the Soviet embassy and the TASS news correspondent's home, Hekmatyar was periodically dropping by the Pakistani embassy. In November 1989, the Pakistani ambassador-designate to Australia, Bashir Babar, revealed that Hekmatyar had been a paid Pakistani agent in the early 1970s.[29]

༅

Internal and external pressures undermined Zahir Shah's democratic reforms. The communist and Islamist student movements actively opposed his democratic order. The communists proved far more disruptive. Four Parchamis, led by Babrak Karmal, won seats in Afghanistan's first parliamentary election, which was held in September 1965. On the opening day of parliament in October, Karmal was at the forefront of a violent student demonstration that forced Zahir Shah's newly chosen prime minister, Yousuf, to dissolve his caretaker government. Two students were shot and killed when General Abdul Wali, the new commander of the Central Corps, sent in troops to restore order.

Yousuf tendered his resignation to the king. The unrest, coupled with the appearance of covertly organized communist and Islamist cells in the army, alarmed General Abdul Wali, who was Zahir Shah's closest adviser. As a result, Wali and the aging Mohammadzai military leadership resisted loosening controls on the freedom of expression, assembly, and the media promised in the 1964 constitution.

Zahir Shah's natural timidity further obstructed the growth of democratic processes and institutions. After much delay, both houses of parliament passed bills to legalize political parties and hold provincial and district council elections—important steps in the democratization process—but the king did not sign them. The first bill would have permitted moderate and liberal parties to organize. These groups could have rallied public support to counter the communist and Islamist opposition parties, which were already operating illegally. The second bill would have allowed local elected community leaders to grow grassroots democratic institutions.

After Yousuf's departure in October 1965, four modernizing prime ministers rose and fell in short order: Mohammad Hashim Maiwandwal (1966–1967), Nur Ahmad Etemadi (1967–1969, 1969–1971), Abdul Zahir (1971–1972), and Mohammad Musa Shafiq (1972–1973). Demonstrating his routine passivity, the king failed to use his extensive constitutional powers and prestige to support them. Nor did he back the anticommunist Maiwandwal's attempt in the 1960s to launch an informal democratic movement to draw intellectuals, civil servants, students, and parliamentarians into a liberal coalition. Maiwandwal's effort collapsed.

Despite the mounting difficulties thwarting democratic progress, the two decades spanning Daoud's first regime and Zahir Shah's period in power witnessed steady progress in social, educational, and economic reforms. The changes were most apparent in Kabul. The capital's educated elite, royal family members, government workers, military officers, and businessmen lived much like their counterparts in Muslim Islamabad, Tehran, and Ankara. A comfortable home; a car; children attending elite, foreign-language schools; weekends in Jalalabad; and picnics in the Pagman hills became the norm among Kabul's growing middle- and upper-class families. Interethnic marriages were common. Expatriates and wealthy Afghans played golf at the Kabul Golf Club. Afghanistan's growing ties with the outside world introduced a dose of internationalism to life in the capital. The foreign community of diplomats, aid workers, teachers, and their families ballooned into several thousand. Hippies considered Afghanistan a must stop on their travels through Asia.

Daoud and Zahir Shah's gender reforms in the workforce and in education were bold and effective. By the early 1960s, Kabul University and secular primary schools had become coeducational. By 1978, women were well represented among the 40,000 teachers in more than 3,800 schools in Afghanistan. They also worked in government offices and hospitals. There was one woman minister in each of the first three cabinets formed during Zahir

Shah's constitutional period, and four Afghan women were elected to parliament. The royal family, Gailani Qadiriya pirs, and the Mojaddedi hazrat enrolled their daughters and granddaughters in the prestigious French-sponsored Malalai Girls High School, where French was the primary medium of instruction. In sports, the girls at Malalai carried on a friendly rivalry with the girls at Zarguna, a girls' high school where instruction was primarily in English. Other girls' high schools were established in Herat, Kandahar, Mazar-i-Sharif, and Ghazni. The total number of Afghan females in educational facilities climbed from about 3,000 in 1949 to 96,585 (13.4 percent of the student population) in 1970.[30] Girls and boys conversed together in Kabul University study halls, jukeboxes played American rock-and-roll songs in downtown coffee shops, and a disco opened on the top floor of the Spenzar Hotel. Miniskirts appeared on the streets of Kabul in the late 1960s.

Zahir Shah failed to act decisively when a devastating three-year drought scorched the countryside from 1969 to 1972. A Soviet reduction in economic aid during this period exacerbated economic problems. The demands of the Vietnam War lowered American aid levels. The government found it difficult to meet government payrolls and to maintain the large infrastructure projects funded by foreign aid over the previous two decades.

On September 7, 1972, the pro-Islamist, anticommunist editor of the *Gahiz*, a religious weekly, was assassinated in broad daylight. The government and Kabul's citizenry were shocked. Investigators discovered that the bullets that killed him were of Soviet origin. Soviet Ambassador Sergei Petrovich Kiktev, previously identified in the Western press as a KGB Middle East specialist, abruptly departed Afghanistan. Two months later he resurfaced in Morocco as the new Soviet ambassador.[31]

Zahir Shah responded to the mounting challenges in 1972 with his characteristic passivity, delegating authority to General Abdul Wali. Wali and the security services increased repressive measures. By late 1972 Kabul was ripe for another round of Padshahgardi. Only a small number within the liberalizing elite remained committed to pressing forward on the democratic path. In 1972, U.S. Ambassador Robert G. Neumann predicted that Zahir Shah's democratic system would not last another year.[32] Teahouse gossip speculated about which one of Zahir Shah's cousins would overthrow him—Abdul Wali or Mohammad Daoud.

୰

Mohammad Daoud had spent his decade out of power preparing his come-back against his cousin. That dovetailed with Moscow's discontent with Zahir Shah's foreign and domestic policies. Daoud had proven his usefulness to the Soviet Union during his decade as prime minister. The Afghan strongman stood out as the one member of the ruling elite with a pro-Soviet orientation. In 1967, only two years after its forced marriage, the small PDPA, with about three hundred members, had split into squabbling Parcham and Khalq fac-tions. Soviet intelligence maneuvered the Parchamis into an alliance with Daoud to put Daoud back in power by means of a military coup.[33] At the same time, the KGB kept the more militant Khalqi leaders, Taraki and Amin, in re-serve in case Daoud turned against the Parchamis.

Soviet KGB officers coordinated with Daoud,[34] Parcham leader Babrak Karmal, and communist Afghan military officers who carried out the coup on July 17, 1973. Soviet-trained Afghan armor officers at the 4th Armored Brigade base near Pul-i-Charkhi prison were assigned to lead the military at-tack on Zahir Shah's palace. Zahir Shah's minister of interior, Dr. Nematullah Pazhwak, a secret Parchami, marshaled his ministry's security forces, includ-ing the secret police, to support the operation. On the night of the coup, Zahir Shah was in Europe for an eye operation.[35]

The nighttime coup was successful. The U.S. embassy reported explosions in Kabul beginning at 2:30 a.m., Kabul time, coming from the direction of the royal palace.[36] Abdul Wali and the palace guard were caught completely by surprise. A tank column led by Parchami Major Faiz Mohammad and Khalqi Captain Aslam Watanjar occupied the grounds of the palace and sur-rounded other key government buildings. Abdul Wali surrendered after a tank blasted a hole in the wall of his house. Defense Minister Khan Moham-mad and Prime Minister Musa Shafiq were arrested and jailed. Daoud put Wali and his father, Shah Wali, Daoud's uncle, in the ancient Bala Hisar Fortress. Daoud broadcast a statement on Radio Kabul criticizing Zahir Shah's "pseudo-democracy." He announced the abolition of the monarchy and creation of a republic. Later the same day, Radio Kabul informed its lis-teners that Daoud was Afghanistan's new president, head of state, prime min-ister, minister of foreign affairs, and minister of defense.

The 226-year-old Afghan Durrani monarchy slipped into the pages of history without a whimper. Zahir Shah followed Amanullah's path to Italy, moving into Saudi-financed retirement in a comfortable home in Rome's suburbs. Abdul Wali and Shah Wali joined him in 1975.

The full extent of Daoud's plotting with the pro-Soviet Parchamis was indicated by the composition of his post-coup regime. A classified U.S. embassy airgram transmitted to Washington reported that Daoud had established a Soviet-style Central Committee in which Parchami Babrak Karmal and party theoretician Mir Akbar Khyber played leading roles. Parchamis were appointed to most of the key cabinet slots that Daoud personally had not taken. Daoud designated Parchami ideologue Hassan Sharq to be his first deputy prime minister, Major Faiz Mohammad to be his minister of interior, and Nematullah Pazhwak to be minister of education. Other Parchamis took over cabinet portfolios for finance, agriculture, communications, and border affairs.[37]

The Parchamis rapidly used their newfound power to eliminate potential political opponents. On October 20, 1973, a group of Parchami Interior Ministry police officers strangled former Prime Minister Maiwandwal in his jail cell. Few believed the regime's statement describing Maiwandwal's death as a suicide. The sixty-one-year-old Mohammadzai former defense minister, General Khan Mohammad, was also executed. Daoud and his Parchami allies next turned on the Islamists. Niazi and Sayyaf were arrested; and fifty Islamist activists, including Hekmatyar, Masood, and Rabbani, fled to Pakistan.

Daoud's post-coup domestic and foreign policy adjustments gave Soviet leaders every reason to conclude that their United Front venture with Daoud had succeeded. Parcham leaders were now heavily represented in the Afghan government. They were poised to replace Daoud when he passed from the scene. The Afghan dictator, at sixty-four, had only one functioning lung and suffered from respiratory disorders. But as always, things in Afghanistan rarely turn out as planned.

Daoud's first two years in office went smoothly for the Soviets. His only foreign visit during 1974 was to Moscow, where he was warmly welcomed by Soviet party leader Brezhnev, Prime Minister Alexey Kosygin, and other Soviet leaders. Through top-secret messages delivered by the KGB Resident in Kabul, Taraki and Amin were instructed "to stop internecine fights"[38] and move forward "on the basis of cooperation with the Republican regime and the Government of the Republic under the leadership of Muhammad Daoud."[39] The Parchamis were happy to comply.

A spate of new economic aid agreements followed Daoud's visit to Moscow. Soviet aid in agriculture, energy, industrial projects, and other areas increased. Daoud changed the Afghan planning cycle from five to seven years to better meld with the Soviet seven-year planning cycle. In late 1974, the two sides established a joint economic commission. Initially, Daoud's pro-Soviet gamble appeared to benefit him. He had used Moscow to return to power, just as Moscow was using him to spin its self-serving web inside Afghanistan. The Soviets, no doubt, retained painful memories of Anwar el-Sadat's unexpected expulsion of thousands of Soviet advisers from Egypt in 1972. Daoud must have been aware of instances where Moscow had swiftly abandoned allies, as it did in 1977 by halting arms shipments to Somalia during the Ogaden War.

Daoud slowly concentrated more and more executive, legislative, and judicial authority in his own hands—authority he could use against the Parchamis as well as other political opponents. In 1975, he established his own party, the National Revolutionary Party, and outlawed all other parties. He then began to purge Parchamis from the government, dismissing Parcham cabinet ministers one by one. He removed Interior Minister Faiz Mohammad. Air force officer and known KGB contact Abdul Qadir, who had also supported Daoud's coup, was transferred to the humiliating position of chief of the slaughterhouse in the capital. Babrak Karmal was put under surveillance. By 1977, all Parchamis in Daoud's post-coup cabinet had been replaced by familiar faces from Kabul's traditional governing elite, many of them Mohammadzai. Daoud's purge missed two key communists still embedded in the Interior Ministry. They were Najib's future KHAD chief, Farouk Yaqubi, and the vicious Sayed Daoud Tarun, who would later head the Interior Ministry's secret police.

Daoud proceeded to lower Afghanistan's dependence on the Soviet Union, shifting Afghan foreign policy back to Zahir Shah's genuine neutrality. Once again, Afghanistan's senior khan traveled abroad in search of recurring resources. During a visit to Tehran, the shah of Iran announced a $2 billion aid package with the implied condition that Daoud must abandon the Pashtunistan issue and normalize ties with Pakistan. Daoud sent his brother, Mohammad Naim, to meet Zhou Enlai in Beijing. Naim assured the Chinese that Afghanistan would remain a good friend. American Secretary of State Henry Kissinger visited Daoud in 1974 and 1975, urging him to reconcile with Pakistan. President Jimmy Carter invited Daoud to visit him in September 1978. Daoud increased the number of Afghan military trainees sent to the United States. He also traveled to oil-rich Saudi Arabia, Kuwait, Egypt, and Turkey, all solidly anti-Soviet states. He publicly questioned Soviet ally Cuba's hosting of the next nonaligned summit, charging that "Cuba only pretends to be non-aligned." He promised that Afghanistan would encourage "true non-alignment" when it hosted the next Non-Aligned Foreign Ministers Conference scheduled to be held in Kabul in May 1978. By the end of 1976, Daoud had lowered the number of Soviet military advisers in Afghanistan from 1,000 to 200.[40]

Pakistani prime minister Zulfikar Ali Bhutto, meanwhile, decided to pressure Daoud into loosening his ties with Moscow and ending confrontation with Pakistan. Many of the Young Muslims had fled to Pakistan in the wake of Daoud's July 1973 coup. The thoroughly secular Bhutto decided to capitalize on their anti-Daoud Islamic fervor by giving them military training and arms to attack Afghan provincial towns and military outposts inside Afghanistan. The Young Muslims were told their attacks would spark a general uprising to overthrow Daoud. Pakistan would support the rebellion. On his part, Bhutto knew the scattered, small-scale military operations would fail. But they would accomplish his and Pakistan's foreign policy objective of enticing Daoud to seek Pakistani assistance to clamp down on the Young Muslims inside Pakistan and to improve Afghan-Pakistani relations. Bhutto's manipulation of the Afghan exiles in Pakistan to serve Islamabad's geopolitical interests was remarkably successful. Future Pakistani military and civilian leaders would perfect the strategy during the coming decades. Bhutto ordered the ISI and the head of the Northwest Frontier Province tribal Frontier Constabulary police force, Nasrullah Babur, to begin military training of about a hundred Young Afghan refugees at Attock Fort on the Indus River north of Islamabad. The ISI and Babur assigned Hekmatyar to be their liaison with the group.[41] In July 1975, the ISI infiltrated small bands of the armed Afghans back into Afghanistan. Ahmed Shah Masood was sent to the Panshir Valley. Other detachments went to Laghman, Nangarhar, and Badakshan. Hekmatyar remained in Pakistan.

All of the attacks failed; most did not even get off the ground. Ninety-three of the combatants were rounded up, and three were executed.[42] Bhutto reaped the benefits of the futile Young Muslim attacks. Daoud subsequently widened his strategic opening to the United States and its allies to include Pakistan. Afghan and Pakistani foreign ministers met in Kabul later in 1975, and Daoud and Bhutto exchanged visits in 1976. Hostile propaganda ceased. Trade increased. In June 1977, Bhutto returned to Kabul. After Zia ul-Haq overthrew Bhutto in July 1977, the normalization process accelerated. In September that same year, Zia traveled to Kabul, and in March 1978 Daoud went to Islamabad for more meetings with Zia. A joint economic commission was established, and the two leaders agreed to meet in Kabul during the summer of 1978.

Daoud spoke with emotion at a large gathering arranged by Zia at the beautiful Shalimar Gardens in Lahore.[43] "Your strength is our strength, your welfare is our welfare and your stability is our stability," he said. "Let's walk hand in hand in the warm glow of brotherhood and sincerity to cover the distance lying ahead of us. . . . I hope the friendship between Pakistan and Afghanistan will be permanent and everlasting." He concluded by reciting lines written by Mohammad Iqbal, Pakistan's poet laureate:

> *The continent of Asia made of water and clay is but one body*
> *In that body the heart is the Afghan nation*
> *The destruction of that nation will result in the destruction of Asia*
> *The prosperity of that nation will bring about the prosperity of Asia*
> *As long as the heart remains free, the body will be free*
> *Otherwise, it will become like a straw on the path of the wind.*[44]

Soviet displeasure at Daoud's foreign policy adjustment and his purging of the Parchamis prompted a fresh KGB attempt in 1976 to force the squabbling Khalq and Parcham wings to reunite.[45] The KGB operation angered Daoud, who learned of it through his secret police. Daoud resolved to raise the issue in a one-on-one meeting with Soviet leader Brezhnev during his planned April 1977 visit to Moscow. His acting foreign minister, Waheed Abdullah, requested the meeting on the Afghan delegation's arrival in Moscow.

The first day of Daoud's talks with Brezhnev, Premier Kosygin, and other senior Soviet officials featured standard expressions of friendly relations, but an undercurrent of tension flowed beneath the surface. Brezhnev complained about the shah's military buildup; Daoud defended the shah and stressed Afghanistan's intention to be genuinely nonaligned. The tension in the air escalated to acrimony on the second day. Brezhnev harbored the typical Soviet penchant to be suspicious of those outside of Soviet control. He entertained unrealistic expectations of how the Afghan president should respond to the enormous patronage of the powerful Soviet Union. These tendencies collided with Daoud's Afghan values, which prioritized independence, honor, equality, hospitality, and, not least, the imperative of retribution for perceived wrongs.

According to Afghan Deputy Foreign Minister Abdul Samad Ghaus, who was present, Brezhnev, staring directly at Daoud, recalled that in the past Afghanistan had not permitted economic aid experts from NATO countries to work in northern Afghanistan near Soviet borders. Brezhnev complained that "this practice was no longer strictly followed." The Soviet Union "took a grim view of these developments and wanted the Afghan government to get rid of these experts, who were nothing more than spies bent on promoting the cause of imperialism."[46]

Ghaus later wrote in his memoirs that, at this moment, "a chill filled the room." Daoud's face became "hard and dark." Then, "in a cold, unemotional voice," the Afghan president rebuked Brezhnev in front of the other Soviet leaders present, declaring that his comments "could never be accepted by the Afghans, who viewed his statement as a flagrant interference in the internal affairs of Afghanistan." Daoud said that Afghanistan "greatly appreciated its ties with the Soviet Union, but this partnership must remain the partnership of equals." Then, according to Ghaus, he firmly announced: "We will never allow you to dictate to us how to run our country and whom to employ in Afghanistan. How and where we employ the foreign experts will remain the exclusive prerogative of the Afghan state. Afghanistan shall remain poor, if necessary, but free in its acts and decisions."[47]

Daoud then stood up, turned, and headed for the distant door of the glimmering Kremlin hall. Brezhnev, President Nikolai Podgorny, Premier Kosygin, and the Russian interpreter followed in pursuit. Daoud's aides, walking at his side, implored him to engage the Soviet leaders trailing the Afghan entourage. Daoud turned and shook hands with Brezhnev, who announced his readiness for a private meeting with Daoud at Daoud's convenience. Daoud loudly responded that there was "no longer any need for that meeting," shook hands with Podgorny and Kosygin, and walked out.[48]

Brezhnev and Daoud did not meet for a third day of talks. More aid agreements were signed, but each side knew a Rubicon had been crossed. Within three months of the Brezhnev-Daoud *contretemps* in Moscow, Soviet intelligence had consummated reunification of the Khalq and Parcham factions. Daoud's closest adviser and brother, Mohammad Naim, correctly interpreted the KGB's resurrection of the PDPA as the initial step toward a communist coup. "You know the gamble is lost," he told Daoud's acting foreign minister, Waheed Abdullah. "We played our hand and lost. . . . Sooner or later a small minority will seize power and, by the force of arms, will rule the entire people."[49]

Taraki was again selected PDPA secretary general with Karmal as his deputy. Taraki's assistant, Hafizullah Amin, was put in charge of planning the coup to oust Daoud. Amin chose Khalqis to conduct military operations. Aslam Watanjar, a Klalqi tank commander in Daoud's 1973 coup, was assigned to lead the tank assault on the palace. Khalqi air force officers Mohammad Gulabzoi, Daoud Tarun, and Assadullah Sarwari were to seize Bagram air base and organize air attacks on Daoud's palace.

Taraki later claimed the coup was originally planned for August 1978.[50] The April 17 murder of Babrak Karmal's close Parcham confidant, Mir Akbar Khyber, by unidentified assassins moved that time frame up by four months. Speculation that the regime, the CIA, the KGB, or Amin was behind Khyber's assassination energized Kabul's rumor mill. The assassins were never caught, although Karmal later accused Amin and executed two Khalqis for the murder.[51]

A funeral procession of over 10,000 marched past the American embassy shouting anti-U.S. and anti-regime slogans. During the burial ceremony, Taraki, Karmal, and other PDPA leaders lambasted the government for killing Khyber and called for the overthrow of Daoud. On April 26, the government arrested those who had spoken at the funeral, charging them with inciting rebellion. Amin was not on the list of those detained, since, probably according to plan, he had not attended the burial ceremony.[52] Frantic activity by known PDPA members at Amin's home, with many arrivals and departures, precipitated his arrest the following day, but not before he had activated the coup.

A Western diplomat theorized that even at this point, Daoud could have saved himself and his regime by employing Abdur Rahman Khan's merciless methods, such as shooting the PDPA leaders in their jail cells.[53] The great majority of army officers, including top commanders, remained loyal to Daoud. Regular army units could have been immediately deployed into Kabul to protect the palace and other installations until the fighting subsided. Instead, premature celebrations over the PDPA arrests were held at 7th Division headquarters at Rishkor on Kabul's southern outskirts and 8th Division headquarters at Kargha northwest of the capital. Daoud lost more time by calling a cabinet meeting to discuss the disposition of the arrested PDPA leadership. By then it was too late.

The few hundred communist junior officers who mounted the coup made up for their lack of numbers by focused, disciplined application of armor and air against the presidential palace, the Ministry of Defense, and other key government offices. At 9:00 a.m. on April 27, 1978, Major Watanjar left the Pul-i-Charkhi barracks leading a column of about sixty tanks from the 4th Armored Brigade.[54] The Khalqi air force officers seized control of Bagram air base. Major Tarun personally executed thirty air force officers who had surrendered. Seven MIG-21s, accompanied by helicopters, flew toward Kabul to support Watanjar's tanks, and the Ministry of Defense was quickly occupied. Army communications links between the presidential palace, government security ministries, and the 7th and 8th Divisions on Kabul's outskirts were cut, inhibiting counterattacks by loyal troops. Two fighters launched from Shindand air base in western Afghanistan were too low on fuel to be effective when they reached Kabul airspace. Watanjar's tanks, Khalqi-piloted aircraft, and Khalqi-led commandos mounted a fierce attack on the 1,300-man Presidential Guard at the palace compound. Daoud ended his cabinet meeting and ordered participants to try to save their lives.

Defense Minister Haidar Rasouli managed to get to Rishkor and the 7th Division to raise a force and advance toward the presidential palace from the south. Khalqi-piloted aircraft flying out of Bagram bombed Rasouli's line of advance, blocking its further progress. Rasouli was captured the next day and shot. At around 2:00 a.m. on the morning of April 28, the Afghan communists launched a massive armor and air assault on Presidential Guard elements still stubbornly holding out on the palace grounds. By 4:00 a.m., the last remnant of some two hundred Presidential Guards laid down their arms. Inside the palace, Daoud placed his twenty-four family members who chose to remain with him, in the living room on the ground floor. They were unarmed. Daoud hoped they would be spared. He occupied a protocol room next door to the living room, unholstered his pistol, and waited for the Khalqis to come. When Khalqi troops rushed into the palace, Daoud confronted them in the hallway outside the two rooms. They immediately gunned down Daoud and most of the people in the living room. Only seven survived the massacre.

In the early-morning darkness of April 29, 1978, army captain Pacha Mir Khan and his squad of soldiers stood a lonely vigil around the rim of a ditch on the Pol-i-gon plain near the 4th Armored Brigade headquarters.[55] Pol-i-gon stretches from the massive walls of the Pul-i-Charkhi prison down to and along the Tangi Gorge, a high canyon southeast of Kabul overlooking the Kabul-Jalalabad Road. Captain Khan, a Tanai Pashtun from Paktiya, was the 4th Armored Brigade's chief logistics officer. Although a devout Muslim, he was on friendly terms with Khalqi major Aslam Watanjar and other communist officers in the brigade. When reporting for duty on April 28, he found that communist officers now commanded the brigade. They had ordered him to take his men and a bulldozer to this desolate spot on the plain.

At 5:00 in the morning a truck drove up, turned, and backed up to the ditch. Its fine design and beautiful canopy identified it as belonging to the Royal Palace. The truck was followed by a shiny yellow Chevrolet. Khan noted four lights mounted in front, not the customary two. Perhaps it had also belonged to the royal family.

Watanjar stepped out of the Chevrolet. With him was an imposing figure in a black coat. The two men peered down into the ditch while communist soldiers opened the back of the truck to reveal a pile of bodies. These were the fully clothed victims of the massacre at the palace. One by one, the soldiers tossed them into the ditch. Khan did not recognize the first two bodies, but he recognized the third as President Daoud. The fourth was Daoud's youngest daughter, Zarlasht, "Golden Branch," age twenty-three. Her green pants and youth caught Khan's attention. More bodies, including those of children, were thrown into the ditch. Khan noted that the coterie of communist officers and soldiers was larger now. They and their leader stood in a ring circling the ditch, looking down at the grotesque sight below. Khan's men occupied empty spaces around the ditch and also looked down.

Captain Khan broke the eerie silence by asking permission to turn the heads of the dead bodies toward Mecca, per Muslim tradition. Hearing no reply, Khan climbed into the ditch and gently straightened out the bodies, pointing each head toward the holy city.

Climbing out of the ditch, Khan approached the elderly driver from the palace, who was still at the wheel of the truck. He asked if he could cover the bodies with the truck's canopy. The driver whispered back, "I have eaten these people's salt for thirty years. How can I be afraid of my life, if you are not afraid of yours? Take it." Khan ordered his troops to place the canopy on the pile of bodies. Instead of objecting, Watanjar and the communist cadre, seemingly in shame, maintained their positions around the ditch, their heads locked in a downward gaze. They held this posture until Khan's bulldozers began to dump huge mounds of dirt into the ditch. After their work was completed, the group dispersed. The palace truck and the shiny Chevrolet drove off. Khan's bulldozer and tractor made their way back to the 4th Brigade's headquarters.

A few nights later, Khan and his family were hiding in the back of a large commercial truck on the road to Paktiya. They stopped overnight at his wife's village. Khan's father-in-law assured them that Gulabzoi, a distant Zadran cousin (and future communist interior minister), would protect Khan if he remained in the Zadran tribal region. Khan declined. He knew he was already marked for death. After a brief stop in his own village in the Tanai area, Khan took his family across the Durand Line into North Waziristan in a truck transporting wood. The Pakistani political agent stationed in North Waziristan provided a small house to Khan and his family. As an officer from the notorious 4th Armored Brigade, Khan was an important defector.

A week later, ISI officers arrived with Gulbuddin Hekmatyar in tow. Their questions lasted a full day. Hekmatyar's detailed inquiries about the whereabouts of individual military officers, government officials, and teachers showed a thorough understanding of the situation in the capital. To Khan, the debrief near the Afghan-Pakistani border displayed an incestuous relationship between Hekmatyar and the ISI.

The next day Khan and his family were taken to the North Waziristan tribal agency's capital, Miram Shah. Later, he moved his family to Peshawar, where he became a Mujahidin commander.[56]

The catastrophic thirteen-year communist era in Afghanistan had begun.

PART II
FISSION

CHAPTER 6

Commissar Meets Tribesman

Top-secret Soviet Communist Party Central Committee postmortem analysis on Soviet failures in Afghanistan, dated May 10, 1988:

> *Exactly ten years ago, in April 1978, a revolutionary coup occurred in Afghanistan, one of the most backward countries of Asia.*
>
> *It was carried out by a relatively small number of military men, members of the PDPA advocating Marxist-Leninist slogans. The Afghan revolutionaries honestly were trying to reform their country. But having taken power in their hands they pursued matters along an unsustainable maximalist path in a feudal society with deep vestiges of tribal foundations and the predominance of the Muslim religion in all spheres of public life. They promoted a mission of radical socialist reforms for which there was neither a social nor an economic basis nor was there support from the masses. . . .*
>
> *From the very beginning the situation was still further complicated by the sharp differences between the two factions in the PDPA who were still feuding with one another in the period preceding the Revolution and during another time fighting one another more than with the forces opposing the Revolution. . . .*
>
> *. . . The most glaring mistakes and leftist deviations were committed in the socioeconomic sphere with regard to religion, alienating the people from the revolution.*
>
> *. . . Above all [was] the fact that the appearance of armed foreigners in Afghanistan was always met with arms in the hands [of the population]. This is how it was in the past, and this is how it happened*

> *when our troops entered [Afghanistan], even though they came there*
> *with honest and noble goals.*
> *... Moreover, the intensity of the internal Afghan conflict contin-*
> *ued to grow, and our military presence was associated with the force-*
> *ful imposition of customs alien to the national characteristics and*
> *feelings of the Afghan people, which did not take into account the*
> *multiple forms of economic life, and other characteristics, such [as]*
> *tribal and religious ones.*
> *... However, often our people, acting out of their best intentions,*
> *tried to transplant the approaches we are accustomed to onto the*
> *Afghan soil, encouraging the Afghans to copy our ways. All this did*
> *not help our cause.*[1]

The Soviet Union plunged into Afghanistan with little heed to the disasters suffered by previous invaders. Kremlin strategists shared the core misconceptions that had guided British, German, and Mughal intrusions into the Afghan briar patch: ignorance of Afghan society, overconfidence in the ability of a mighty empire to impose its will on Afghanistan, and failure to appreciate the cost of capturing the strategic center square on the Eurasian chessboard. Soviet military power had compelled other neighbors in Eastern Europe and Mongolia to do Moscow's bidding. Certainly Afghanistan would not be a bigger challenge.

The first step in Soviet empire-building was to mold a compliant surrogate regime. That process had already been perfected a century earlier during the tsarist expansion into the Muslim lands of Central Asia, and after World War II, Bulgarian, Czech, East German, and Mongolian communist lackeys had faithfully executed the Kremlin's instructions in their respective countries. Finding equivalent sycophants in tribal Afghanistan would prove more difficult.

The Afghan communists' unilateral decision to spring the April 27, 1978, coup against the Daoud regime had been the first indication that Afghanistan would not become the Soviet Union's latest manageable satellite. Alexander Morozov, the deputy KGB Resident in Kabul, later wrote that, through its own agents within the PDPA, the KGB had discovered in the days before the coup that Nur Mohammad Taraki and Hafizullah Amin were about to go into action. Alarmed, the Residency relayed the information to KGB chief Yuriy Andropov's deputy, First Department Director Vladimir Kryuchkov. Soviet

Ambassador Alexander Puzanov, who had led the Soviet diplomatic mission in Kabul for six years, reported to Soviet leaders in Moscow. "In our view," he advised, "such extreme action in the present situation could lead to the defeat of the progressive forces in the country." After Politburo-level clearance, Kryuchkov instructed the KGB Resident to tell Taraki and Amin that a coup would result in "disaster" for the PDPA and should be called off.[2]

An emergency KGB meeting with Taraki took place at the villa of a TASS Soviet news agency official in Kabul. Taraki was told the following: "We have learned that some members and supporters of the Khalq faction of the PDPA are rather erratically disposed and irresponsibly calling for an uprising against the regime of President Daoud. The Communist Party of the Soviet Union (CPSU) Central Committee believes that this would not only destabilize the situation in Afghanistan but would also be fraught with dire consequences for the PDPA and all other left-wing forces in the country."[3]

The next day, Ambassador Puzanov was as surprised as other foreign diplomats in Kabul to hear that communist tanks had assaulted Mohammad Daoud's presidential palace. According to a Soviet journalist, Puzanov "simply slept through the April coup."[4] Puzanov frantically cabled Moscow, warning that the West and Daoud may have lured the PDPA leaders into a fatal trap. The PDPA was on the verge of destruction, he warned.[5] When the coup succeeded, Puzanov conducted a joyful meeting with Taraki in the presidential palace. The Soviet ambassador playfully showed him the Kremlin's talking points for delivery to Daoud. The message to the now-deceased Afghan president requested leniency for Taraki and his comrades.

Puzanov's exuberance would be short-lived. The PDPA had seized power in the capital, but most of Afghanistan had never been directly ruled from Kabul. The first in-depth analysis of the coup that Puzanov sent to Moscow, in May, overlooked this fundamental lesson of Afghan history. He assured the Soviet leadership that the PDPA had assumed control of all regions of Afghanistan. Even more optimistically, Puzanov anticipated progress in ending the Khalq-Parcham feuding within the PDPA, informing Moscow that his embassy was taking steps "to overcome the differences in the Afghan leadership."[6] Puzanov was a member of the Soviet Communist Party's Central Committee. He enjoyed close personal relations with Afghans of all political persuasions. His views were respected in Moscow, and his messages were widely read in the Kremlin.

The Soviet leadership was elated. The successful coup and Puzanov's assessment demonstrated that the Soviet-led global "socialist community" was gaining ground. The Soviet side in the Cold War had just taken in a new member. Only a decade previously, Afghanistan had been a fulcrum of Cold War regional competition. Soviet influence had now crossed the rim of the Hindu Kush into South Asia. The United States had been pushed back to the Pakistani-Afghan border. Soviet policymakers believed that, over time, the same strategies that had consolidated communist victories in other countries would also prevail in Afghanistan.

Soviet media commentary reported that Afghanistan had voluntarily joined the socialist community. Soviet diplomats around the world urged their Western counterparts to recognize the "new realities" in Afghanistan. "The clock cannot be turned back," they insisted. The Brezhnev doctrine, enunciated at the time of the 1968 Soviet invasion of Czechoslovakia, posited that the Soviet Union was obligated to intervene in other communist countries should their communist system be endangered. Now that Afghanistan had joined the pro-Soviet socialist community, it would not be allowed to leave it.[7]

That Afghanistan was not Mongolia or an Eastern European satellite was lost in a cloud of Soviet hubris. The Brezhnev doctrine would face insurmountable obstacles there. Outside of a relatively small group of communists in Kabul and some other Afghan cities, relatively few Afghans had been won over to Moscow's socialist camp. Naturally, what the Soviet Union had not really gained could not be lost.

✤

Taraki wasted little time in requesting massive Soviet resources to preserve "the Great Saur Revolution" (Saur is the Afghan lunar calendar month during which the Afghan communist coup took place). He informed Puzanov that "Afghanistan, following Marxism-Leninism, will set off on the path of building socialism and will belong to the socialist camp." At the same time, Taraki recognized that immediate identification of Afghanistan as communist could provoke a domestic and foreign backlash. He assured Puzanov that he would proceed "carefully" and inform the people "later" of the PDPA's true goals.[8]

The Kremlin, too, wished to hide the communist nature of the regime until it consolidated its grip on power. Three days after the coup, on April 30, 1978, Moscow instructed Puzanov to extend diplomatic recognition to Afghanistan's communist government. He did so privately to Taraki. A public announcement was delayed for three days until the first batch of countries, led by India and several pro-Soviet governments, conveyed diplomatic recognition. In a parallel April 30 meeting, the KGB Resident sent guidance to Amin from the Soviet Politburo: Taraki should be announced as president of the government to be established as soon as possible, "but it should not be mentioned that he was general secretary of the PDPA."[9]

The chief of the KGB's First Directorate, Vladimir Kryuchkov, was the first high-level Kremlin official to travel to Kabul after the coup.[10] Taraki boasted to him that the Great Saur Revolution heralded the same global significance as the 1917 Bolshevik Revolution. Most of his comments in the meeting addressed his desperate need for Soviet aid. A KGB officer in the Kabul Residency at the time Kryuchkov visited later reported that Taraki had told Kryuchkov: "We have the power but we don't know what to do with it. Please dispatch here as many advisers as possible for our armed forces, the PDPA in each of our ministries. Teach us to manage the state, and we will do everything we are taught."[11]

Thousands of Soviet advisers poured into the country. Daoud had cut the number of Soviet military advisers down to 200 before the communist coup; barely five months after it, there were 2,500 in-country.[12] East Germans replaced West Germans advising the Afghan national police. Soviet advisers were assigned to Afghan intelligence agencies, communist party headquarters, party front organizations, and positions in the government bureaucracy, both in Kabul and in the provinces. Khoshal Peroz, a communist general who participated in the 1973 and 1978 coups, observed that "the Soviets were everywhere—we joked that even a cook had to have a Soviet adviser."[13]

KGB officers collaborated with PDPA intelligence officials to seize Daoud's secret police archives, including lists of Daoud's intelligence agents.[14] The PDPA, with KGB assistance, established a substantially enlarged Afghan secret police institution. Modeled on the KGB, it was given the lofty title of "Department of Defense of the Interests of Afghanistan." Known and feared by its Pashto acronym, AGSA, the new Afghan communist spy agency would grow into a huge Soviet-Afghan organization controlling domestic and foreign intelligence, counterintelligence, border security, covert action, several elite combat units, and disinformation capabilities.[15]

Soviet Communist Party advisers were tasked with guiding the PDPA in its transition from a political party out of power to one exercising a monopoly of power in Afghanistan. This required PDPA solidarity. Soviet advice to maintain Khalq-Parcham unity appeared to be honored in the immediate aftermath of the coup. The Khalq-Parcham balance in the PDPA Central Committee that had been created under Soviet pressure in 1977 was reinstated.[16] Taraki continued as PDPA general secretary, and Parchami leader Babrak Karmal became his deputy.

Taraki was named president of Afghanistan on May 1. The PDPA Politburo met that day to divide cabinet portfolios between Khalqis and Parchamis, giving an advantage to the Khalqis. Taraki also became prime minister. Amin was designated first deputy prime minister and foreign minister. Karmal, who was Parchami, and Aslam Watanjar, a Khalqi, were appointed deputy prime ministers. The important Defense Ministry post went to Abdul Qadir, a nominal Parchami but in fact more loyal to Moscow than to either PDPA faction. Assadullah Sarwari, who, like Watanjar, was both a Khalqi and a longtime KGB agent, was put in charge of AGSA, the secret police. Others with long-standing KGB ties predating Zahir Shah's rule were also given important appointments in the party and government.

Publicly, Taraki and Soviet spokesmen continued to deny that Afghanistan had become another Soviet satellite. During a May 4 press conference, Taraki told skeptical Western journalists that he was neither a communist nor a Marxist. He declared that Afghanistan would remain nonaligned between East and West. Soviet attempts to mask the communist identity of the PDPA were facilitated by the Carter administration's intensive focus on Iran at that time. Soviet diplomats in Kabul and Washington ridiculed the idea that the PDPA was communist. The Carter administration did not react to Pakistani warnings about Soviet imperial intentions in Afghanistan. Meanwhile, Taraki prayed at the mosques on Fridays. He requested that the United States and other Western donor countries maintain their assistance programs in Afghanistan. Astonishingly, eleven days after the coup, the U.S. embassy in Kabul reported to Washington that it could not judge whether or not the 1961 Foreign Assistance Act's prohibitions against aid to communist countries applied to the PDPA regime. The United States decided to continue economic and military aid, and other Western countries followed suit.

The rapid conclusion of Soviet-Afghan agreements belied Taraki's preposterous claim that his government was nonaligned. From the Political Section in the American embassy in Moscow, I reported to Washington on a flurry of agreements between the PDPA and the USSR. Twenty of them were concluded in quick succession, culminating in an umbrella friendship and cooperation treaty that was personally signed by Taraki and Brezhnev in the Kremlin on December 5, 1978. The security clause in the treaty was more open-ended than those Moscow had concluded with other countries. It called for the USSR and Afghanistan to "consult with each other and take by agreement appropriate measures to ensure the security, independence and territorial integrity of the two countries."[17] This wording would later be used by the Soviets to justify their invasion of Afghanistan.

❧

The 1978 Afghan communist coup contributed to an image of ascending Soviet power and declining American influence in the world. The Soviet Union had seized the global initiative. American power was waning. Watergate, the 1973 Arab oil embargo, and America's humiliating departure from Vietnam had sapped American self-confidence.

Vietnam, Laos, Cambodia, and Angola had joined the Soviet-led anti-West socialist community three years before the PDPA coup. All signed their own friendship treaties with Moscow. Thousands of Cuban troops along with Soviet and Cuban military advisers propped up the Marxist regime in Angola. A huge Soviet arms airlift to Ethiopia initiated in 1977 enabled the Moscow-aligned Mengistu regime to ruthlessly crush its opponents in a fury of Red Terror. In June 1978, two months after the Khalqi coup, Soviet aircraft transported 5,000 Cuban troops to South Yemen to help Cuban-trained Yemeni militia overthrow the government. The president was replaced by a pro-Soviet Yemeni communist and executed.[18]

A sustained, multidecade expansion of Soviet strategic and conventional arms threatened to alter the balance of power between the United States and the Soviet Union. The Soviet buildup had eroded America's postwar superiority in nuclear weapons. Parity between the two superpowers was formally announced during the 1972 Nixon-Brezhnev summit in Moscow. By the late

1970s the Soviet Union had gained advantage in numbers of strategic delivery systems, nuclear warheads, and conventional ground and naval forces.

Within the Soviet Union, the well-lubricated Soviet propaganda machine enjoined Russians to believe that the USSR was spearheading the "global march of socialism."[19] In tsarist times, the Kremlin's "civilizing" vision abroad had diverted the eyes of the Russian population from their leaders' lack of legitimacy and their country's poverty. Now the Soviet Union told its citizens that it was spreading communism to the oppressed peoples of the world trapped in economic misery by the chains of international capitalism. Afghanistan's "Saur Revolution" was the latest step in that long journey.

President Jimmy Carter had earned a reputation of weakness and inconsistency in his dealings with the Soviet Union. While Moscow's military buildup proceeded apace, Carter canceled the neutron bomb and B-1 bomber programs and scaled back production of long-range missiles. His response to Soviet advances in the Third World was muted. Secretary of State Cyrus Vance argued for negotiations with Moscow, while National Security Adviser Zbigniew Brzezinski advocated a hard line. Vance's and Brzezinski's contradictory foreign-policy speeches exhibited a zigzag U.S. approach to Soviet expansionism that lasted until Vance's resignation in 1980.

American equivocation was painfully acute in Iran, where America was losing an ally while the USSR was gaining one in next-door Afghanistan. Carter publicly praised the shah in a 1977 state dinner in Tehran, noting the "admiration and love which your people give to you."[20] Less than two years later, on January 16, 1979, revolutionaries led by Ayatollah Khomeini drove the shah into exile. Khomeini-supported students conducted the first (one-day) seizure of the American embassy and its staff, including Ambassador William Sullivan, on February 14. That same day, four gunmen from a small Marxist Shia group snatched the American ambassador to Afghanistan, Adolph Dubs, from his vehicle on a Kabul street, then barricaded themselves with their captive in a room at the downtown Kabul Hotel. They demanded the release of their leader, a Shia cleric who had already been executed by Sarwari's secret police. Secretary Vance described the "surreal scene" in the State Department's Operations Center the following day: "In one corner, one group sought to coordinate negotiations in Kabul to secure Dubs's release; in another corner, a second group struggled to keep in touch with Sullivan in Teheran."[21]

The Tehran embassy staff was freed the next day, only to be kidnapped again nine months later, on November 4, 1979, after Sullivan was recalled. Ambassador Dubs, a State Department specialist on the Soviet Union, was not so fortunate. He was killed when a volley of bullets was fired into the hotel room by Afghan security forces under the supervision of KGB officers and, from his office, Khalqi Sayed Daoud Tarun, the brutal Interior Ministry police chief. The fusillade was ordered despite the frantic objections of American embassy political counselor Bruce Flatin and American consul Michael Malinowski, who had rushed to the hotel. The United States vigorously protested to Soviet authorities in Washington and Moscow. Two months later, over lunch at the Berlin Restaurant in Moscow, a vexing, inadequate Soviet response was orally delivered to me by a Soviet contact with KGB ties, Oriental Institute professor Yuriy Gankowskiy. His explanation merely rehashed the Soviet propaganda line about the murder: The assault on the hotel room, he said, was necessary to prevent Dubs's execution by the kidnappers. The kidnappers alone were responsible for his death.

Well-grounded suspicions of Soviet involvement in Dubs's death remain unresolved to this day. American attempts to investigate the ambassador's murder were stonewalled by Foreign Minister Amin and by Soviet officials in Kabul and Moscow. A detailed assessment of the tragedy prepared by the State Department's Office of Security Assessment concluded that the Afghan government's explanations were "incomplete, misleading and inaccurate."[22] This official assessment and interviews with Flatin and Malinowski indicated that the attacking force may have deliberately killed Dubs.[23] One of the Soviets, a KGB officer, according to U.S. records, initiated the assault with a wave of his hand. After some forty seconds of continuous firing into the room by the attacking Afghan security forces, they entered the room and several more gunshots from small-caliber weapons were heard. Flatin, Malinowski, and the embassy doctor waiting 30 feet down the corridor with a gurney were not allowed to enter the room until the second round of firing ended. The lack of any injuries to the Afghan security forces indicated that the kidnappers had offered little resistance.[24]

When the two embassy officers and the embassy doctor ran into the room, Ambassador Dubs was barely alive. The two kidnappers lay dead on the floor. The doctor pronounced Dubs dead minutes later. Subsequent U.S. government forensics tests showed that nine of the twenty bullets in his body had been fired by a .22-caliber weapon, but only a machine gun and two pistols of higher caliber were found in the room—presumably belonging to the kidnappers. None of them had fired the .22-caliber rounds.[25] Nevertheless, powder burns next to the points of entry of the .22-caliber rounds, including the four to the head, revealed that they had been fired into Dubs at point-blank range—within three inches of his body.[26]

The embassy officers' visit the next day to the morgue, where the alleged bodies of the four kidnappers were laid out, raised further suspicion that the attacking force had killed Dubs. The officers recognized the two kidnappers who had been killed in the room. A third, whom they had seen detained in the hotel lobby when they arrived from the embassy, lay next to them. The Afghan government officials present claimed that he had later died in an Afghan hospital. It was more likely that the Soviets or regime security forces had killed the third kidnapper to prevent him from being interrogated by the embassy. The embassy officers speculated that another body present at the morgue was a "filler" for the fourth kidnapper, who had probably escaped before his accomplices entered the hotel with Dubs.

KGB defector Vasili Mitrokhin's revelations in a February 2002 publication strengthened the case for KGB complicity in Ambassador Dubs's murder. Mitrokhin wrote that the Soviets viewed Dubs's long involvement in Soviet affairs and his "deep knowledge of the situation in the USSR and Soviet foreign policy" as "dangerous"; he would attempt to prevent Afghanistan from becoming "too close to the USSR." Mitrokhin stated that "a gun of unknown origin similar to a Kalashnikov was planted in the room and registered as taken from the terrorists." One of the kidnappers was captured but then executed "to frustrate requests from the Americans to question him."[27]

The regime's suspicious handling of Dubs's murder angered Washington and precipitated a drawdown in U.S. embassy personnel stationed in Kabul. The United States reduced its aid to low levels of humanitarian support, then, following the Soviet invasion, cut off all assistance. Washington did not send another American ambassador to Afghanistan until 2002, twenty-three years later.

ψ

Soviet Ambassador Puzanov's promise to his Kremlin bosses that he would attempt to close the Khalq-Parcham rift came to grief. No one, Afghan or foreigner, could have fulfilled such a commitment. The Khalq-Parcham feud was as deadly and irresolvable as the Musahiban-Charkhi blood-for-blood vendetta had been a quarter-century earlier.

Each faction was important to Moscow in different ways; they complemented one another. The Khalqi leaders were mostly Ghilzai Pashtuns. They recruited followers mainly from Ghilzai clans in eastern Afghanistan of lower socioeconomic status. The Parchami leaders were generally well-educated urbanites from middle- and upper-class families, and the majority were Kabulis—overwhelmingly Tajik, plus some detribalized Pashtuns like Najib whose forebears had transcended the tribal way of life. Most Khalqis spoke Pashto, whereas most Parcham members spoke only Dari. Khalqi roots were firmly planted in eastern Afghanistan, where the Pashtunistan cause enjoyed the greatest popularity; the majority non-Pashtuns in Parcham were not interested in the Pashtunistan issue. The Khalqis recruited frequently from the middle and lower ranks of the officer corps where eastern Pashtuns, such as Watanjar, Sarwari, and Gulabzoi, were heavily represented. They resented the Durrani glass ceiling Daoud had imposed that blocked their advancement to the top of the military establishment. Daoud had not promoted any officers trained in the Soviet Union to general officer rank. The Parchamis predominated in the civil bureaucracy. Khalqi women and girls stayed at home; Parchami women and girls were often educated and in the workforce. Both factions had one thing in common. They assumed that their powerful Soviet patron would not fail to provide the necessary recurring resources to sustain the gains of their successful Saur Revolution.

Puzanov could no more bring Taraki and Karmal together than he could bring the Khalqis and Parchamis together. The enmity between the two men was personal, tribal, and unbridgeable. It flowed downward through the ranks of their respective factions. Taraki claimed that the PDPA was better united without the Parchamis: The Khalqis, he said, did not need them. "We will run over those who oppose unity with a steamroller,"[28] he told Soviets urging reconciliation. They counted on Soviet recognition of Khalqi predominance over Parcham in the military. Taraki and Amin flaunted their devotion to the Soviet Union and Marxism-Leninism. Karmal complained to his Soviet advisers that Puzanov favored the Khalqis. He passionately argued that only Parchamis were capable of attracting the "progressive" noncommunist constituencies necessary to broaden the base of the regime.

Khalq-Parcham infighting turned lethal after the Khalqis consolidated their control of AGSA and the Defense Ministry. The KGB Residency reported that Taraki and Amin had unleashed "a real terror" against the Parchamis. Parchami leaders appealed to the Soviets for protection, charging that Taraki was a CIA agent and Amin was "an American agent under deep cover." Karmal's half-brother, Mahmoud Baryalai, carried the Parcham case to Soviet Communist Party headquarters in Moscow, where he accused Puzanov of lying about the true state of affairs in Afghanistan and sacrificing the lives of Parchamis "to Khalqi brutality."²⁹

Frustrated, Puzanov appealed to Boris Ponomarev, the powerful Soviet Communist Party International Department chief and alternate Politburo member, to come to Kabul to persuade Taraki to restore Khalq-Parcham unity. Ponomarev and his deputy, Karen Brutents, flew to Kabul, but their arguments failed to impress Taraki. Ponomarev sarcastically reported back to Moscow that Taraki "agreed that my displeasure was justified (and) thanked me for my advice. And everything continued as before." A KGB report alerted Moscow that the Soviet pressures for Khalq-Parcham unity had annoyed Taraki and Amin. Khalq cabinet members nicknamed Puzanov "the little tsar"; the finance minister asked his Soviet adviser not to take the place of ministers.³⁰

Taraki and Amin intensified their offensive against the PDPA's Parcham wing. During the second half of 1978, they exiled Parchami leaders Karmal, Baryalai, and Najib abroad to be ambassadors to Prague, Islamabad, and Tehran, respectively. In November 1978 they charged the exiled Parchami ambassadors with complicity in a coup against Taraki. Summoned home by Foreign Minister Amin for possible execution, they instead abandoned their posts, but not before cleaning out their embassies' bank accounts.

Taraki and Amin used the pretext of the alleged Parcham coup to conduct a violent, sustained purge of their implacable Parchami enemies. Taraki dismissed the Parchami ministers remaining in the cabinet and arrested many senior Parchami military officers and more than four hundred Parchami mid- and senior-level cadres. The Khalqi head of counterintelligence informed his KGB counterpart that "investigations were only held in cases where the accused were prepared to give evidence. The rest of those arrested were shot."³¹ Army Chief of Staff General Shahpur Ahmadzai was among the top military officers executed. AGSA secret police arrested Minister of Defense Abdul Qadir and Planning Minister Sultan Ali Keshtmand, one of the original founders of the PDPA in 1965, the only Shia in the cabinet, and a close associate of Babrak Karmal. Both were sentenced to death; their forced confessions were read on Radio Kabul. Meanwhile, AGSA chief Sarwari, known as "King Kong" and the "Butcher" among the prisoners at Pul-i-Charkhi prison, personally supervised the torture of Qadir and Keshtmand, his former colleagues in the PDPA Politburo and in the government cabinet. By early December 1978, the Khalqi domination of the PDPA was complete.

The Khalqi decapitation of the Parchami wing of the PDPA shocked the Soviets. Puzanov and the KGB Resident visited Taraki and Amin to request that the ministers' lives be spared. They pointed out that both had participated in Daoud's overthrow and were friends of the Soviet Union. Taraki lessened the death sentences to fifteen-year imprisonments. Taraki's reprieves for Qadir and Keshtmand provided little solace to the Soviets. They could not compensate for the Khalqi's sweeping purge of the Parcham leadership. Prospects for PDPA unity and base broadening to bring noncommunist groups into the PDPA tent were now more remote than ever.

KGB messages to Moscow reported that the Khalqis had narrowed the PDPA base to "a sect of people chosen and devoted to their leader and connected to each other through family relationships and their interests to retain power for their own personal aggrandizement."[32] A top-secret Soviet Politburo document lamented: "The Soviet leadership has many times given its recommendations and advice to the leaders of the Democratic Republic of Afghanistan on a high level. They have pointed to their mistakes and excesses. But the Afghan leaders, displaying their political inexperience, rarely heeded such advice."[33]

How did Soviet policymakers so greatly underestimate the challenge of transforming Afghanistan from a tribal to a communist society ruled by a well-disciplined communist party? There were world-class Afghan scholars in Soviet think tanks, notably the prestigious Oriental Institute's Yuriy Gankowskiy, who had spent his academic career studying, visiting, and writing about Afghanistan. But the Soviet leaders cocooned at the top did not consult him or other Soviet scholars knowledgeable about Afghanistan. Gankowskiy bitterly confided to a Soviet journalist: "They don't know what they're doing. They are provoking a conflict, which could go on for centuries."[34]

One explanation for the Soviet leadership's misinterpretation can be found in the vastly different historical, cultural, and religious legacies that separated Russians and Afghans. Russian history exhibited an unremitting pattern of central rule over an acquiescent population, whereas Afghan history was marked by determined opposition to central rule by well-armed tribal communities in the countryside. Marxist-Leninist practices of democratic centralism (whereby once a decision is made at the top it is obeyed at all lower echelons of the party) and Soviet Communist Party unity may have been transferable to communist parties in Eastern Europe, but they would not gain traction in fragmented, tribal Afghanistan.

The Soviet Union's ideology focused on the horizontally layered class makeup of European countries and China, which Karl Marx and many non-communist writers had analyzed. Class conflict between small wealthy elites at the top and poverty-stricken masses below had driven the French Revolution. In Russia, the Bolsheviks—and later Stalin—had exploited class-warfare stratagems to mobilize large numbers of have-nots against haves, poor urban workers against plutocrats, and peasants against Kulaks. In China, Mao Tse-tung had mobilized the rural poor against the wealthy in both city and the countryside. But base broadening along class lines did not fit the vertical patterns in Afghanistan's tribal society. Afghanistan's tribal population is not divided horizontally; instead, loyalties move upward and downward within thousands of tribal and ethnic clusters. Brezhnev missed this point when he triumphantly announced, in December 1978, that Soviet-Afghan relations were "now based on class belonging."[35]

The great majority of the approximately 15,000[36] PDPA members at the time of the communist coup had little grasp of Marxism-Leninism or the history of the world communist movement. The bulk of rank-and-file members were semiliterate at best. Most of the Khalqis were of rural origin or only one generation removed from their rural roots. At the time, Afghanistan's tiny proletariat amounted to fewer than 20,000 workers scattered in some fifteen different factories—a stark contrast to the approximately 320,000 mullahs in the country.[37]

The Soviets constantly demanded that Taraki and Amin broaden the PDPA base to include Afghan factions outside the communist party. Building such communist-led united fronts was a standard Soviet tactic in other Third World countries. Daoud's demise was a good illustration of the dangers inherent in a narrow base of support in Afghanistan's factionalized society. Daoud's recapture of power in 1973 was initially welcomed by Afghans tired of the economic malaise and growing internal instability under Zahir Shah. But, one by one, Daoud alienated elements that had previously supported him. By the time of the 1978 communist coup, he was opposed by liberal democrats and intellectuals championing democracy as well as by Soviet-supported Parchamis and Khalqis, Pakistani-supported Islamists, and many moderate tribal leaders resentful of their exclusion from the political process. His backers were reduced to his immediate family and the small, privileged elite at the top of the long ruling Mohammadzai clan.

Taraki and Amin's main agenda was to eliminate their potential rivals in the party blocking their way forward. Both Pashtun Ghilzais interpreted their overthrow of Daoud as ending the long era of Durrani tribal subjugation of the Ghilzais dating back to the eighteenth century. For the two Khalqi leaders, Karmal might have been a communist, but they also considered him a Tajik. They viewed "Afghan" as synonymous with "Pashtun." Their long vendetta brooked no possibility of compromise; Tajiks like Karmal had no right to the Afghan throne. Any advance by Karmal necessarily meant their own retreat.

A tribal leader in Afghanistan is chosen to protect and increase tribal assets, not to surrender them to rivals. If he gives ground, he puts his own leadership position at risk. Competitors within the tribe may question his image of courage, personal honor, and tribal pride. It would be better for the tribal leader to die fighting for his tribe's possessions than to bargain them away. This aversion to compromise also demands that, once on top, a tribal leader and his supporters must prevent rivals from reaching the summit. If a competitor should occupy the commanding heights, it would be his turn to push down.

Moscow's initial euphoria about the PDPA coup progressively gave way to dismay during the second half of 1978. Warring Khalqi and Parchami factions gave a uniquely Afghan twist to Voltaire's observation that revolutions devour their own children. Soviet objections behind closed doors could not dissuade Taraki from creating a personality cult around himself. All government offices sported photographs of the "Great Leader," often posted side by side with his "Great Disciple," Hafizullah Amin. Embarrassed Soviet delegations toured Taraki's Kabul home, which had been converted into a museum containing Lenin-like displays of Taraki's furniture, pens, and writings. During their Kabul visit, Ponomarev and his deputy, Karen Brutents, witnessed festive celebrations surrounding Taraki's sixty-second birthday celebration in the capital. Brutents noted that Taraki's birthday cake was sixty-two layers high.[38]

The radical reforms introduced by the Taraki regime in the summer and fall of 1978 broke the four-decade equilibrium between center and countryside. The Khalqi edicts were patterned after the Bolshevik decrees that had been issued in the wake of the overthrow of the Russian government in 1917. A detailed Soviet record of Taraki's early December 1978 discussions with Brezhnev in Moscow cited Taraki as boasting: "In its domestic policy the PDPA has adopted a program of radical revolutionary socio-economic reforms to the benefit of the working class; these reforms will help abolish any remains of feudalism and semi-feudal social relations; they will provide for the . . . building up of a society free from exploitation, based upon the progressive ideology of the working class and scientifically-grounded socialism."[39]

Taraki's decrees caused great consternation throughout the country, especially in the rural areas. The two on gender equality and land reform provoked the most outrage. Using communist jargon, the regime announced its intention to eliminate "the unjust patriarchal and feudalistic relations which exist between husband and wife." The gender decree prohibited the tradition of gift-giving from the groom and his family to the bride's family to formalize marriages. It placed a small monetary limit on dowries given by the bride's family and introduced a rule requiring the bride's consent for marriage. Sixteen became the minimum age of marriage for females, eighteen for males.

The decree on land reform ignited another wave of indignation in the countryside. Article I proclaimed that PDPA land reforms would eliminate "feudal and pre-feudal relations," ushering in a society "without hostile classes and free of exploitation of man by man." To achieve this transcendent goal, it limited single-family holdings to 15 acres. Extra land would be seized and divided among the landless and among cooperatives established by farmers with fewer than 12.5 acres.[40] The unenforceable land-reform decree generated hostility from tenant and landlord alike. In most of Afghanistan, the two were bound together by tribal and clan ties. Both viewed the government's attempts to seize land as *haram*, or forbidden in Islam. Young PDPA cadres with military escorts sent to the countryside to implement the PDPA reforms were expelled from villages, kidnapped, and sometimes murdered.

Marxist-Leninist sloganeering on Kabul radio broadcasts, and the introduction of a new flag—red with a yellow seal—that was similar to those in the Soviet Central Asian Republics, stirred popular resentment that the Afghan communists were attempting to foist Soviet atheism on the country. The Taraki regime's omission of the standard Islamic invocation—"In the name of God, the merciful and compassionate"—from radio broadcasts intensified the regime's anti-Islamic image. Mullahs fulminated against the PDPA decrees in their Friday sermons. Taraki ceased attempting to appease the Afghan religious establishment. He publicly called Afghanistan's mullah population "Satan's brothers." Amin hurled threats, announcing that "those who under the sacred name of Islam plot against the April revolution and are in the service of the enemies of the people, will be construed as traitors." He warned that the party would "crush them to the extent that they forget the bellows of Daoud."[41]

ψ

The regime met the mounting opposition to its radical reform agenda with more repression and terror campaigns. Pul-i-Charkhi prison east of Kabul became a combined jailhouse, torture chamber, and execution ground for arrested Parchamis, liberal politicians, intelligentsia, professionals, teachers, and military officers. On June 9, 1979, the regime executed all of the Islamists who had been held by Daoud at Pul-i-Charkhi except for Amin's cousin, Kabul University professor Abdul Rasoul Sayyaf. Tahir Badakhshi, a Tajik and also another founder of the PDPA, was shot. By the fall of 1979, a Russian general estimated that the regime had executed more than 50,000 Afghans.[42]

In private meetings, Soviet officials warned PDPA leaders that the regime's extreme brutality would swell the ranks of the Mujahidin (Holy Warriors). When Puzanov urged moderation, Taraki rejoined that, "Lenin taught us to be merciless towards the enemies of the revolution and millions of people had to be eliminated in order to secure the victory of the October Revolution."[43]

Soviet Premier Alexey Kosygin advised Taraki to stop executing professional military officers. "In Stalin's time," he explained, "many of our officers were put in jail. And when the war broke out, Stalin was forced to send them to the front. These people showed themselves to be true heroes. Many of them rose to high rank."[44] Taraki countered by reminding Kosygin of the USSR's own bloody past.

Amin regularly identified himself with Stalin and his methods. During meetings with Soviet visitors, he proudly pointed to *The Collected Works of Stalin*, which was prominently displayed near his desk. The executions and torture at Pul-i-Charkhi prison, built with Soviet aid in the late 1970s, did, in significant ways, recall the carnage carried out by Stalin's secret police in Lubyanka cellars in downtown Moscow.[45] Pul-i-Charkhi's giant walls and watchtowers surrounded eight stories of cell blocks. It was built to accommodate 5,000 prisoners. More than twice that number, including whole families with children, were crammed into its rooms. Overcrowding and the lack of toilets at the prison created a stench of human feces that spread for miles. After the nighttime burial of Daoud and his family, the regime continued to use the treeless Pol-i-gon expanse around the massive facility as a site for mass executions and a graveyard.

The regime's relentless violence was not confined to Pul-i-Charkhi. AGSA gunmen with lists of regime enemies spread through Kabul and into the provinces, hunting down and executing religious and tribal leaders. Tribal chiefs and their male relatives disappeared in a "Red Terror" campaign to weaken Afghanistan's most prominent tribes.

PDPA terror eliminated or forced into exile key managers, technicians, and bureaucrats who had previously run Afghanistan's civilian and military bureaucracies. The regime's executions of Daoud-era senior military officers virtually eliminated the senior ranks of the PDPA army. Fearful for their lives, many officers fled to Pakistan, Europe, and the United States. Soviet military advisers assigned to the Afghan Army struggled to fill huge gaps in Afghan military leadership and technical expertise; they reported mass desertions, defections, poor motivation, lack of competence, and chronic indiscipline. In 1986, eight years after the Saur Revolution, Soviet Foreign Minister Andrey Gromyko grumbled, "In the Afghan army, the number of conscripts equals the number of deserters."[46]

President Taraki's and Foreign Minister Amin's belligerent policies toward Afghanistan's three non-Soviet neighbors exacerbated the regime's beleaguered condition. More than 2,000 miles of Afghanistan's porous borders abutted China, Iran, and Pakistan. Yet, the potential for Afghanistan's larger neighbors to assist the growing anti-PDPA insurgency inside Afghanistan did not impress Taraki and Amin. Early on, Taraki announced Afghanistan's unqualified support for Moscow's anti-Chinese Asian Collective Security Plan. Taraki rebuffed Puzanov's advice to elevate the damaged Afghan-Pakistani dialogue and to take a "friendly step" in relations with Iran.[47] Instead, Amin publicly disassociated Afghanistan from the Afghan-Iranian Helmand River Treaty signed by Zahir Shah and strengthened during Daoud's last full year in power.

The regime's precarious position inside Afghanistan made good relations with Pakistan especially important. Pakistan had announced diplomatic recognition of the Afghan communist government. Soviet advisers stressed that alienating Pakistan would damage the PDPA's ability to establish control over the provinces on the Afghan-Pakistan border. Nevertheless, for several months Taraki ignored President Zia ul-Haq's request to visit Afghanistan. When the visit occurred and Zia finally arrived at his presidential palace, Taraki lectured the Pakistani president on the finer points of communism and badgered his guest about Pakistan's close ties to the United States. In a well-publicized speech, Amin reopened the Pashtunistan wound, declaring that the Northwest Frontier Province and Baluchistan were part of Afghanistan. Diplomatic protests generated by Amin's bluster were delivered in Moscow as well as Kabul. How could the Soviet Union's Afghan client make such provocative statements unless they had been blessed beforehand by the Kremlin?

In April 1979, the Soviet Politburo took a major initiative to reverse the PDPA's suicidal course. It dispatched a senior KGB officer, Vasily Safronchuk, to Kabul to work on broadening the PDPA's base. Installed in an office next to Taraki's presidential suite, Safronchuk appeared to enjoy some initial success. His advice to stop alienating conservative tribal and religious interests led to Taraki's abrupt announcement on July 15, 1979, that land reform could be wrapped up, since it had been successfully implemented. Taraki and Amin were less amenable to Safronchuk's appeals on base broadening. "We are among enemies," Amin bluntly responded.[48]

Safronchuk became increasingly pessimistic about his ability to influence the PDPA. Khalqi leaders rejected his advice to establish "a national front, like other countries have done." Safronchuk complained to the American embassy's chargé d'affairs, Bruce Amstutz, that Taraki and Amin were "very sensitive about any suggestion of sharing power. They are stubborn people."[49]

❦

Armed uprisings against the PDPA regime began to break out around the country two months after the Afghan communist coup. Initially, they were led by local tribal khans, traditional ulema, Sufi pirs, and army deserters like Captain Khan—not the Islamist parties of Gulbuddin Hekmatyar and Burhanuddin Rabbani then being assembled and armed by the ISI in Pakistan. Spontaneous, uncoordinated insurgencies had already liberated all of Nuristan,[50] most of Konar Province in eastern Afghanistan, and the Hazarajat region west of Kabul when Taraki signed the PDPA friendship treaty with Brezhnev in Moscow on December 5, 1978. The habitually restive hill tribes in eastern Afghanistan, however, had remained largely quiescent until the appearance of the regime's gender and land reforms, which threatened their tribal customs. They were stirred to take action. Their anti-PDPA protests quickly spread through the Pashtun belt and into adjoining provinces in central and western Afghanistan.

Tribal groups began harassing regime outposts in the eastern Pashtun-populated provinces bordering Pakistan during the winter of 1978–1979. In the spring, Naqshbandi Sufi pir Sibghatullah Mojaddedi proclaimed an anti-communist jihad from Miram Shah in North Waziristan, calling for Afghan Mujahidin to take up arms and overthrow the PDPA regime. Mujahidin attacks across the border into Paktiya, Ghazni, and Nangarhar multiplied. Mujahidin fighters captured two district capitals in Paktiya. The regime responded by assaulting the Mojaddedi family compound in Kabul. Seventy male family members, including the senior Naqshbandi hazrat, Ibrahim Mojaddedi, were arrested, taken to Pul-i-Charkhi, and executed.

The rapidly deteriorating internal situation in Afghanistan inspired the creation of a four-man Special Commission within the Soviet Politburo to focus on Afghanistan. Although heavy in seniority, the commission's membership was ill suited to understand the Afghan realities. The members, Yuriy Andropov, Dmitry Ustinov, Andrey Gromyko, and Boris Ponomarev, were

FIGURE 6.1   MAJOR SOVIET INSTITUTIONS MAKING AFGHAN POLICY

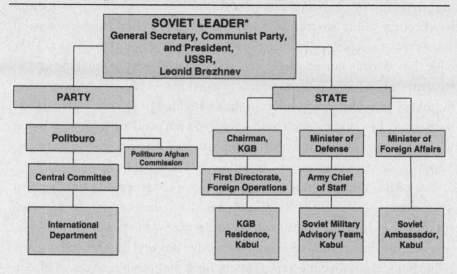

all taken from the Politburo's conservative wing. Each had climbed up the CPSU rungs during the doctrinaire Stalinist era; creativity, flexibility, and dynamism were not their strong suits. In microcosm, the body reflected the deep domestic paralysis gripping the Soviet Union during the late 1970s and early 1980s.

The Soviet system's Achilles' heel was its atrophying leadership—a curse not uncommon to dictatorial systems. Ossification of Soviet leaders—physical and mental—had already begun when Stalin died in 1953 at age seventy-three. A Central Committee member wryly observed that those remaining in the supreme policymaking body, the Politburo, "had what amounted to life tenure as long as they could more or less stand upright."[51] In Moscow, several of us in the American embassy Political Section charged with monitoring Soviet news programs periodically saw Brezhnev's Politburo associate Konstantin Chernyenko propping up Brezhnev from behind as the Soviet Union leader read statements in front of TV cameras.

At seventy-two, General Secretary Brezhnev was the oldest and most infirm Politburo member at the time of the communist coup in Afghanistan, and poor health had sapped his leadership capabilities. After Brezhnev's death in 1982, his personal physician revealed that only the regular infusion of drugs had kept the ailing Soviet leader active after 1975.[52] Brezhnev was a serial consumer of sleeping pills during both daytime and nighttime hours. They contributed to his slurred speech and occasional disorientation during high-level meetings. To the embarrassment of other Soviet officials, he sometimes mumbled when discussing affairs of state with foreign visitors. Mikhail Gorbachev recalled one meeting with a foreign communist delegation during which Brezhnev suddenly forgot the topic he was discussing. The conversation, Gorbachev remembered, "carried on as if nothing had happened."[53]

Yuriy Andropov, the head of the KGB from 1967 to 1982—and the most influential member of the Politburo's Afghan Commission—largely controlled the channeling of information to Brezhnev. At sixty-five, Andropov was also the only commission member under seventy. Aloof, cautious, and polite but at the same time imposing, cunning, ambitious, and reserved, Andropov eschewed the lavish lifestyle enjoyed by most Politburo members. In his memoirs, Gorbachev described him as "a brilliant and large personality."[54] The KGB grew in size and power during Andropov's fifteen years at the helm of the huge spy agency.

Though Andropov's KGB did not repeat the kind of mass executions that Stalin's NKVD had carried out during the 1930s, the KGB director did not hesitate to use force. As Soviet ambassador to Hungary in 1956, he helped stamp out the Hungarian Revolution and dispose of its leaders, including the ninety-year-old Hungarian party chief Imre Nagy, who was shot. As a reward, Andropov was brought back to Moscow and made a party secretary in the vast Central Committee bureaucracy. His next promotion, in 1967, took him to KGB Lubyanka headquarters on Dzerzhinsky Square. The following year, he played a major role in suppressing the Czech uprising. In 1973, he became the first Soviet secret police chief since Lavrenti Beria to gain a Politburo seat. In 1982 he was moved back to the Central Committee to become one of two second secretaries and Brezhnev's heir-apparent. Though no longer running KGB headquarters, Andropov was still considered, both inside the USSR and abroad, to be the Soviet Union's chief spymaster.

Under Andropov, the KGB remained the Soviet Union's most important instrument for regime survival. Its cloak of secrecy, bureaucratic compartmentalization, deception, and emphasis on short-term, clandestine operations over long-term political strategy contributed to Soviet failures in Afghanistan.

Andropov relied on his KGB operatives in Afghanistan for information, analysis, and policy proposals.[55] KGB Resident Boris Ivanov, not Ambassador Puzanov, was seen by the feuding PDPA faction leaders as the most powerful Soviet official in Afghanistan. Ivanov was not subject to Puzanov's control, and he frequently bypassed the Soviet ambassador, transmitting his reports through secret KGB channels directly back to Andropov and his protégé, Vladimir Kryuchkov. Ivanov's case officers passed wads of cash and advice to Afghan communist party and government officials and simultaneously spied on them. As in all Soviet embassies, KGB agents were hidden in every section. Others operated undercover as military and civilian advisers, businessmen, and journalists.

Andropov's closest ally on the Politburo commission was Dmitry Ustinov, who was seventy-one when the commission was created. Ustinov presided over the second most important Soviet power ministry, the Ministry of Defense. He rose to the Politburo through the vast military-industrial complex, not the uniformed services. Soviet military officers viewed their minister as more political than military. Ustinov followed Andropov's lead in Politburo discussions, even when his generals advocated other courses.

Andrey Gromyko, seventy at the time, was third in the Afghan commission's pecking order. Gromyko had been Soviet foreign minister for twenty-six years. Known as "Mr. Nyet" in foreign capitals, "he was always 'comrade yes' to his superiors," according to a Central Committee member and the leading Soviet specialist on the United States, Georgy Arbatov. Gromyko deferred to Andropov during leadership meetings, and he "practically cowered before Ustinov."[56]

Party bureaucrat Boris Ponomarev, then seventy-four, was the four-man commission's junior member. A perennial "candidate" but never full Politburo member, he had headed the Communist Party's influential International Department for twenty-nine years. Ponomarev, a staunch Marxist-Leninist, propagated the orthodox line of the senior party ideologue, seventy-seven-year-old Politburo member Mikhail Suslov.

The immobility in the Soviet leadership bred inertia in Soviet domestic and foreign policies, including on Afghanistan. There was no twenty-fifth amendment to remove incapacitated Soviet rulers. For their part, the aging Politburo members were comfortable in their geriatric leadership ward and preferred not to risk their personal positions by advocating change. Gorbachev later wrote in his memoirs that this permitted each to run his own "diocese" with minimal demand for change from the outside.[57] When Brezhnev died in 1982, his successor, Andropov, reigned as Soviet leader for only two years before dying. Chernyenko replaced Andropov, but he, too, soon died, having served only fourteen months as general secretary. Each passed his last months on earth in the same hospital that Brezhnev had patronized during his closing years, plagued, like him, by multiple infirmities.[58]

As general secretary, neither Brezhnev, nor Andropov, nor Chernyenko could adjust to the rapidly deteriorating situation in Afghanistan. Their reaction to incompetent PDPA leaders and unending problems in Afghanistan was confusion, anger, more advisers, and more weapons. They plied communist concepts on the Afghan communists, who remained mired in Afghan tribal politics and infighting. Soviet leaders vilified Taraki and Amin during Soviet Politburo meetings. Taraki's KGB handlers in Kabul gave him a new code name, "Cockroach" (*Tarakan*), in their secret communications with Moscow.[59]

ψ

On March 17, 1979, a public uprising and mutiny of the 17th Army Division stationed in Herat took control of Afghanistan's western capital, murdering hundreds of regime officials and scores of Soviet advisers and their dependents. A panic-stricken Taraki appealed to Lieutenant General Lev N. Gorelov, the senior Soviet military adviser in Kabul, for Soviet "ground and air support" in addition to more weapons and military equipment to take back the city. The Politburo had a lively debate. Gromyko argued, "Under no circumstances, may we lose Afghanistan." Prime Minister Kosygin and Politburo Secretary Andrey Kirilenko questioned the wisdom of sending Soviet troops into Afghanistan, asking: "Whom will our troops be fighting against if we send them there? . . . We will be required to wage war in significant part against the people." Kosygin supported Kirilenko, opposing direct Soviet intervention: "Let them create their own special units which could be redeployed to the more difficult regions in order to quell the insurgents," he stated. Andropov, the *eminence grise* at the table, straddled the debate divide. He advised that the Politburo decision should "bear . . . in mind that we will be labeled as an aggressor, but that in spite of that, under no circumstances can we lose Afghanistan."[60]

The Politburo reconvened the following day, March 18, 1979, to hear the results of two urgent Kosygin-Taraki telephone conversations the previous evening. Kosygin reported that Taraki had emotionally rejected the Soviet proposal to speed up Soviet arms assistance, military training, and humanitarian aid instead of sending troops. "If Herat falls," he warned, "then the revolution is doomed." Soviet soldiers of Tajik, Uzbek, and Turkmen origin, serving "as crews for tanks and armored cars, dressed in Afghan uniforms," he suggested, could be dispatched immediately to Herat.[61] Taraki recommended that the Soviet troops advance from Soviet Turkmenistan and Kabul to recapture Herat.

Kosygin repeated the Politburo decision not to send Soviet troops to put down the uprising. He asked Taraki why the regime was not sending military units stationed elsewhere to Herat, or mobilizing workers to take back the city. Kosygin relayed Taraki's frenzied answer to his stunned Politburo colleagues: "Almost without realizing it, Comrade Taraki responded that almost nobody does support the government. In Kabul, we have no workers, only craftsmen. . . . Uprisings have emerged throughout the entire country, and the army is too small to be able to pacify the insurgents everywhere."[62]

Andropov told the Politburo meeting that Soviet intervention was "entirely inadmissible."[63] His comment prompted Gromyko to abandon his interventionalist position: "I fully support Comrade Andropov's proposal to rule out such a measure as the deployment of our troops into Afghanistan," Gromyko said. "Our army, when it arrives in Afghanistan, will be the aggressor. Against whom will it fight? Against the Afghan people, first of all, and it will have to shoot at them. . . . And all that we have done in recent years with such effort in terms of détente in international tensions, arms reductions, and much more—all that would be thrown back. Of course, this will be a nice gift for China."[64]

The Politburo decided to accelerate weapons transfers and food aid to the PDPA regime and to increase training of Afghan military officers, but not to deploy troops to Afghanistan. Taraki was summoned to Moscow, where Brezhnev bluntly informed him that intervening militarily "would only play into the hands of the enemies—yours and ours." Brezhnev exhorted Taraki to unite the PDPA and "achieve ideological-political solidarity throughout its ranks from top to bottom." He unrealistically counseled Taraki to emulate the early Bolshevik practice of creating "committees" of the poor in rural areas "to repel feudalists and capitalist landowners" and to close the Afghan-Pakistani border. Ponomarev's deputy, Karen Brutents, later described Brezhnev's recommendations to Taraki as "worthless."[65]

Pressure for PDPA unity from the highest level of the Soviet leadership, the dispatch of thousands of Soviet military advisers, plus the acceleration of economic and military aid, including combat jets and helicopters, did not reduce the steady flow of bad news from Afghanistan. The KGB Resident in Kabul observed that the failed PDPA reforms had "turned the majority of the country's population into their enemies."[66] Resistance to communist rule spread from the countryside up to the gates of the heavily guarded Afghan capital.

By the spring of 1979, the PDPA's unrestrained violence against "class enemies" had alienated Kabul's educated urban population. Radio and TV stations trumpeted communist slogans. High-school textbook chapters on religion were replaced with paeans to Taraki, Lenin, and Stalin. To the chagrin of Kabuli movie fans, Soviet propaganda movies shut out Hollywood and Indian films at movie houses and on TV. Afghan farms and factories exporting to the West were closed down for "assisting capitalist economies."[67] Thousands of frightened refugees were fleeing Kabul, heading to Jalalabad and into Pakistan. The regime's extension of military conscription from one to three years accelerated the exodus.

Meanwhile, local bands of Mujahidin periodically cut Kabul's lines of communication, isolating the capital and other urban areas from each other and interrupting access to food, energy, and other essential commodities. From the Pakistan side of the Afghan border, tens of thousands of Pashtuns joined the jihad. The ISI established scores of military training camps in the Pakistani tribal agencies. At the time of the March Herat uprising, the KGB estimated the number of antiregime fighters entering from Pakistan at 3,000 a month and rising.[68] Hazara and Qizilbash Shia staged a violent uprising in western Kabul in July. Sarwari's AGSA security police savagely repressed it, rounding up hundreds of Shia off the streets, from homes and shops. They were transported under guard to Pul-i-Charkhi and summarily executed.

The deteriorating Soviet position in Afghanistan increased the influence of the hard-liners in President Carter's inner circle led by his national security adviser, Zbigniew Brzezinski. The Soviet and Afghan regime's callous handling of Ambassador Dubs's murder in February, the March mutiny of an entire Afghan division in Herat, the spreading anti-PDPA insurgency, and aggressive Soviet advances in Africa with the help of thousands of Cuban troops enhanced their leverage on Afghan policy over Secretary of State Cyrus Vance's conciliatory approach. They saw an opportunity to damage and possibly reverse Moscow's Third World offensive in Afghanistan and to draw the Soviet Union into a "Vietnamese quagmire."[69] On July 3, 1979, Brzezinski convinced President Carter to begin a $500,000 nonlethal covert aid program to the Afghan rebels. The modest aid package, calibrated to avoid provoking the Soviet Union, was limited to medicines, radio equipment, and propaganda materials. It would grow into a program costing billions during the 1980s.

A brand new headache for Soviet strategists unexpectedly erupted in the early summer months of 1978: A deadly power struggle within Khalq between the "Great Teacher" Taraki and his "Great Disciple" Amin further shrank the already narrow PDPA base of support. Their fight for the party's summit quickly evolved into a typical Afghan vendetta. Personal will to power superseded ideology, party solidarity, and the unending Soviet pleas to broaden the regime's base. Each focused on placing his personal supporters in key government positions. The American embassy in Kabul reported to Washington: "We have been observing for 18 months how this Marxist party (the PDPA) has been destroying itself. . . . By way of illustration: if you take the list of nineteen ministers who were confirmed in April 1978, there have been 25 changes among them. The number of changes among deputies is even greater—34. One purge follows another and it is difficult to imagine how the regime manages to survive."[70]

In July Amin grumbled to Puzanov that Taraki was "concentrating the leadership in his own hands."[71] Puzanov heard identical charges from Taraki about Amin. In a confidential message to East German leader Erich Honecker, Brezhnev fumed: "Despite our persistent calls for both sides to act in concord with the interest of defending and strengthening the Revolution's achievements and not to exacerbate the situation, neither side took any appropriate measures to reinstate unity."[72]

The behavior of Moscow's unmanageable Afghan clients became too much for some Soviet leaders. At one Politburo meeting, Kirilenko blurted out that "the government of Afghanistan itself has done nothing to secure the situation. . . . We gave it everything. And what has come of it? It has come to nothing of any value. . . . So you see what kind of Marxists we have found!"[73]

In fact, no outsider, including the Soviet Politburo, could divert the two Khalqi leaders from their chosen path. Like two scorpions in a bottle, Taraki and Amin were embarked on a fight to the death.

CHAPTER 7

Big Fox Catches Little Fox

There is evidence that Moscow's position in the actions of some of its representatives fanned the mutual distrust between Taraki and Amin. . . . In addition to the embassy, Moscow used KGB officers as liaisons with Taraki and MOD [Soviet Ministry of Defense] officers with Amin. The competition between the two agencies, which I witnessed in person in Kabul in July 1979, played a role in the relations between the two leaders and increased their confrontation. At the same time, the KGB, an organization with political objectives as well, was unsympathetic toward Amin's policies. Then they began to distrust him. Naturally, this increasingly influenced the disposition of the Soviet leadership and could not fail to influence Taraki's conduct. Finally, the opponents' coteries—as always in situations with two centers of power—worked to promote the confrontation between their bosses.

As confrontation increased, Moscow, including Soviet leaders, increasingly intervened on Taraki's side. . . . In my opinion, the participation in and promotion of the confrontation between Taraki and Amin was a serious blunder by Moscow. . . . Now, a person who was distrusted by Moscow came to power, and relations with him were compromised by the Soviet position on his confrontation with Taraki. . . . [The Soviet leadership] was using insufficient and incorrect intelligence, and unclear or even erroneous perceptions, about the specifics of the Afghan situation. . . . In many ways, the tactics selected by Moscow were based on these perceptions; the tactics were doomed to failure.

—KAREN BRUTENTS, FORMER DEPUTY CHIEF
OF THE INTERNATIONAL DEPARTMENT,
COMMUNIST PARTY OF THE SOVIET UNION, 1998[1]

❧

All Soviet attempts to export the Brezhnevian model to Third World countries eventually failed. The Egyptian breakaway was the most painful: After foiling a Soviet coup attempt in Egypt in 1972, Egyptian President Anwar el-Sadat sent 20,000 Soviet military and civilian advisers home and a few years later cast his lot with the United States.[2] Soviet leaders constantly worried that the unpredictable Afghans would follow Sadat's example, ask the Soviets to leave, and seek U.S. friendship and assistance.[3]

Moscow never found an Afghan political leader who, once in power, continued to be a faithful subordinate. In the summer and autumn of 1979, Afghan President Nur Mohammad Taraki and Prime Minister Hafizullah Amin concentrated on eliminating one another rather than defeating the Mujahidin insurgency. Their worsening blood feud presented Moscow with a Hobson's choice. Taraki had managed to develop a warm personal relationship with Leonid Brezhnev during his three visits to Moscow, and he spoke fluent Russian. But the elderly Afghan president was indecisive and inept. Amin did not enjoy Taraki's personal ties to Brezhnev, and his facility in English rather than Russian stoked suspicion in Moscow. So did his time as a student in the United States at Columbia University. A Soviet official described Amin as "volatile, opportunist and very cruel." Amin's advice to Soviet leaders to remember that "Afghans thought one thing, said another, and did an altogether different thing,"[4] may have sounded familiar to Amin's Soviet advisers, but the comment must also have enhanced their doubts about his trustworthiness.

The rivalry between Soviet bureaucratic officials in Kabul and Moscow severely undermined Soviet policy effectiveness in Afghanistan. Similar interagency "stovepipe" battles would also subvert American success in Afghanistan in the years after the Soviet withdrawal and following America's intervention in Afghanistan in the wake of 9/11. In early 1979, the Soviet government attempted to address the problem by requiring that all intelligence sent from the Soviet mission in Kabul be countersigned by the ambassador, the KGB Resident, the senior military intelligence officer, and the chief Soviet military adviser in country.[5] The procedure failed to end interagency competition, most notably between the KGB, which supported Taraki, and Soviet military advisers and military intelligence officers from the GRU, who backed Amin.

❧

Startling remarks by the East German ambassador, Hermann Schwiesau, to American chargé d'affaires Bruce Amstutz on July 17, 1979, were the first clear indication to Washington that Moscow intended to back a Taraki coup to oust Amin. Though he acknowledged Taraki's shortcomings, Schwiesau identified Amin as the main culprit behind the PDPA's many failings. He told Amstutz that President Taraki was weak and indecisive, a "kindly teacher, philosopher and writer" who was ill informed about what was happening inside Afghanistan. The East German envoy thought "the Parchamis could work with Taraki but not Amin." In the conversation with Amstutz, Schwiesau repeated three times that the "closing chapter of this government" was at hand. He confidently signaled that "August is going to be hot, and I don't mean the weather."[6]

It is possible that Schwiesau took it upon himself to say more than he was instructed to when talking to Amstutz. Or he may have been sent on a fishing expedition by the Soviets—perhaps senior KGB official Vasily Safronchuk—looking for a positive sign of American receptivity to discarding the brutal Amin. Whatever the case, it would have been unusual for the representative of the USSR's most loyal Eastern European satellite to speak so directly about Soviet intentions unless his remarks had been approved beforehand by the Soviets. Two days later, American embassy political counselor Bruce Flatin found Schwiesau still focused on Amin at a diplomatic reception in Kabul. Schwiesau commented that Amin was very alert to developments but probably not aware of everything that had occurred during the past week. He indicated that the Soviet effort to get rid of Amin had moved into a more active phase. When asked whether Amin would accept his fate quietly or fight, Schwiesau replied that he did not know.[7]

Perhaps sensing Soviet favoritism for Taraki, Amin methodically began to gather the reins of power. The elderly Taraki did not resist. Amin took over the prime minister portfolio in March. In July, he used it to remove well-known KGB collaborators and Taraki allies Aslam Watanjar, Sher Jan Mazdooryar, and Sayed Mohammad Gulabzoi from the ministries of defense, interior, and communications, respectively. Amin assigned the three to lesser cabinet positions and personally took command of the powerful Defense Ministry. He appointed his brother-in-law, Major Mohammad Yaqub, as military chief of staff. The cabinet reshuffle was done without consulting Taraki. It positioned Amin for a future showdown with the Afghan president.

After Amin's power grab, the American embassy reported to Washington that Ambassador Schwiesau was suddenly taken ill. He was whisked to the Kabul Airport in an ambulance and placed on an Aeroflot flight to Moscow.[8] Schwiesau's deputy, widely assumed to be an operative of Stasi, the East German intelligence agency closely tied to the Soviet KGB, complained to an American diplomat that he was unable to catch his ambassador at the airport for a final handshake before Schwiesau was airborne. An American embassy cable to Washington regretted that Schwiesau's "diplomatic colleagues were denied an opportunity to bid him farewell."[9]

By early July 1979, if not before, the KGB had consolidated its control of Soviet Afghan policy, marginalizing the pro-Amin GRU and the uniformed Soviet advisory team in Kabul. In late July, the Pakistani deputy chief of mission (DCM) in Moscow informed me that the Soviets were preparing to move Babrak Karmal from his KGB safehouse in Prague to Moscow. This was another indication that the KGB was gaining the upper hand over the Soviet military. This direction of events was not surprising. Yuriy Andropov dominated the Politburo's Afghan Commission. Defense Minister Dmitry Ustinov deferred to Andropov; so did Andrey Gromyko and Boris Ponomarev. The two senior KGB officers in Kabul, Vasily Safronchuk, stationed in the office next to Taraki's at the presidential palace, and KGB Resident Boris Ivanov, managed implementation of Soviet Afghan policy in Afghanistan.

On September 1, 1979, Andropov and his deputy, Kryuchkov, presented a KGB memorandum to the Soviet Politburo. The document laid out the KGB blueprint for ousting Amin and forcing Taraki to reconcile with the Parchami leader, Karmal: "A way should be found to remove Amin from the leadership of the country, as he is guilty of pursuing a flawed internal policy," it pronounced. "Taraki should be persuaded that it is essential to establish a democratic coalition government, the leading role in which must be given to members of the PDPA, including Parchamis. . . . A 'fallback' leadership of the DRA [Democratic Republic of Afghanistan] should be prepared."[10] The KGB memorandum became the foundation for Soviet policy for the next four tumultuous months.

Implementation of the KGB's anti-Amin strategy began on September 10 during a meeting between Brezhnev and Taraki in the Kremlin. Taraki was returning to Afghanistan through Moscow after a summit meeting of non-aligned countries in Havana. Brezhnev's comments to him, according to a KGB defector, amounted to a "direct and open instruction to Taraki to get rid of Amin."[11] Brezhnev warned Taraki that Amin was intriguing against him. He also advised the Afghan president to include "prominent Parchamis in his Cabinet." Taraki's remarks to a group of Moscow-based Afghan students at the airport just prior to his departure for Kabul indicated that he had gotten the message: "In order to ensure the good health of the Party, it will be necessary to get rid of the mosquito, which made it impossible for the Party to sleep at night."[12] Taraki's scarcely veiled reference to purging Amin demonstrated his confidence. He believed that Brezhnev's favor made Amin's removal inevitable. A TASS news agency photo of Brezhnev hugging a smiling Taraki during the departure ceremonies projected to the world strong Soviet support for the Afghan president.

While Brezhnev and Taraki plotted in Moscow, Amin schemed in Kabul. Unknown to Taraki, Major Sayed Daoud Tarun, a member of his delegation and the Afghan Interior Ministry's secret police chief, was providing Amin with detailed accounts of Taraki's conversations in Moscow.[13] Although the Soviets excluded Afghan Foreign Minister Shah Wali, a member of Amin's faction, from Taraki's most sensitive discussions with Brezhnev, Wali, too, was picking up tidbits from pro-Amin Soviet military contacts in Moscow and passing them on to Amin in Kabul.

As Taraki's presidential aircraft approached the Kabul Airport, the KGB Residence in the Soviet embassy claimed that it had foiled an Amin attempt to shoot down Taraki's plane.[14] Meanwhile, KGB collaborators Watanjar, Mazdooryar, and Gulabzoi were planning to assassinate Amin on his way to the airport to meet Taraki.[15] Their point man in the government was the AGSA chief, Assadullah Sarwari. Two AGSA sharpshooters were posted near the Kabul Radio-Television Center, next to the American embassy on the road to the airport. If not a coconspirator, the KGB Residency was at least aware of the plan to ambush Amin. But so was the wily Amin. Sarwari's trusted deputy and cousin, Aziz Ahmed Akbari, knew of the assassination plot. Unbeknownst to Sarwari, he was keeping Amin fully informed.[16]

A large crowd of PDPA ministers and workers dutifully gathered at the Kabul Airport on September 11 to welcome their "Great Teacher" home. The crowd collectively gasped when Taraki's approaching plane suddenly veered sharply upward and away from the airport, "barely missing the top of a mountain ridge." An hour later, the presidential aircraft was still listlessly circling the airport, unable to land. The first concrete sign that the plan to ambush Amin on the airport road had failed occurred when Amin personally drove onto the tarmac in a small white Volkswagen bug rather than his chauffeured car. As a reminder to all about who was in charge, Amin signaled to the airport control tower to permit Taraki's plane to land. He was the first to greet Taraki as the Afghan president stepped down from the aircraft.[17] Watanjar was second in the receiving line. Upon arrival at his presidential palace, Taraki briefed the cabinet on his visit to Moscow. Amin and the four demoted ministers who had just attempted to kill him were in attendance. It was Taraki's last cabinet meeting.

The next few days were wild even by Afghan standards. Unpredictable events unfolded at a rapid clip. "We do not know what tomorrow will bring," a shell-shocked Soviet diplomat confided to an American embassy official in the middle of the week.[18] Brezhnev, speaking to East German leader Erich Honecker, said, "It is difficult to say in which direction events will lead."[19]

On the morning of September 12, Tarun secretly contacted Amin to inform him that Taraki was planning to invite him to dinner at the presidential palace. Taraki, Tarun said, was going to offer Amin an overseas ambassadorial post. The presidential dinner invitation was delivered and accepted. Amin told Taraki of the attempt by the four Khalqi ministers to assassinate him on the way to the airport and demanded that all four be punished. Taraki refused. He instead proposed that Amin serve "briefly" as an Afghan ambassador abroad.[20] Taraki mentioned Brezhnev's suggestion to induct Parchamis into the cabinet. Amin angrily declined the ambassadorial appointment and the idea of reconciliation with the Parchamis. He insisted that Taraki resign all of his party and state positions. Taraki refused, and Amin stalked out of the palace. From his home, he phoned Taraki to reiterate his demand that the four Khalqi ministers be immediately arrested.

The Taraki-Amin power struggle reached a climax on September 13. A Soviet Politburo document later recounted: "Taraki evidently was about to remove Amin from the leadership, but he displayed indecisiveness and hesitation, and it is possible that he lacked sufficient forces to carry out his intention."[21] At this critical juncture in the crisis, the Soviet Politburo took the unprecedented step of assembling a powerful four-man delegation in Kabul representing the diplomatic, intelligence, and military power of the USSR to transmit united Politburo positions directly to Taraki and Amin. Led by Ambassador Alexander Puzanov, the delegation included KGB Resident Lieutenant General Boris Ivanov; General Ivan G. Pavlovskiy, who was the commander of Soviet ground forces and deputy defense minister (and visiting Kabul at the time); and the chief of Soviet military advisers in Afghanistan, Lieutenant General Lev Gorelov.

The Politburo commission ordered the highly authoritative Soviet delegation to demand that Taraki and Amin "come together" and "act in concord from a position of unanimity." The message was to be delivered in the name of Brezhnev and the Soviet Politburo. In the event that Taraki requested Soviet military assistance to oust Amin, the delegation was instructed to inform the Afghan president that "we cannot take it upon ourselves to arrest Amin."[22]

During the late morning of September 13, Taraki consulted with Gulabzoi, Watanjar, Mazdooryar, and Sarwari at the palace. After their deliberations, he phoned Amin and invited him to lunch to discuss "normalization of the leadership."[23] From inside the palace, Tarun advised Amin that his safety would be in danger if he accepted the invitation. Amin declined the invitation.[24] He instead put in motion an intra-Khalqi coup against Taraki— exactly the opposite outcome the KGB had in mind. Amin told his brother-in-law, Defense Ministry Chief of Staff Yaqub, to stop taking orders from Taraki. In addition, he instructed Yaqub to replace pro-Taraki military army commanders in Kabul and the provinces with Amin supporters.

Later in the afternoon, an enraged Taraki phoned Amin. Taraki insisted that Amin rescind the new military appointments. Amin refused. The Soviet quartet, having rushed back to the palace to defuse the escalating crisis, reminded Taraki about the Soviet leadership's message to reconcile with Amin. Taraki protested that Amin was "defying his orders" as presidential commander in chief.[25] The Soviet delegation next sought out Amin. They found him at the Defense Ministry issuing instructions to military units around the country. Amin curtly informed the Soviet delegation that it was he and not Taraki who now directly controlled all Afghan Army divisions in Afghanistan. A Soviet Politburo report laconically noted that "Amin continued actively preparing to achieve his ends and Taraki, as before, was indecisive and clearly unable to put an end to Amin's activities."[26]

Watanjar, Gulabzoi, and Sarwari feared for their lives. At 7:30 p.m. on September 13, KGB guards at the Soviet embassy in Kabul were astounded by

the sudden appearance of the three Taraki allies at the embassy gates, armed
bodyguards in tow. The three men requested an immediate meeting with
Ivanov. After a long wait, they were told that the KGB Resident wished them
to prepare a written report of their concerns. The following morning, Gulabzoi, who was decked out in full Zadran tribal turban, vest, and trousers, accompanied by the two other Afghan ministers, arrived unannounced in an
unmarked Toyota sedan at the home of Gulabzoi's KGB case officer. Once
inside, Gulabzoi handed the KGB official a ten-page indictment of Amin for
delivery to Ivanov. The charge sheet listed a series of Amin's purported meetings with American CIA agents and diplomats.[27] The KGB spy drove the
three former ministers in his personal vehicle to the Soviet embassy. They
were housed in a KGB-guarded villa inside the embassy compound. Their
mustaches were shaved off, and they were given KGB uniforms to wear. KGB
officials took Watanjar to a communications room in the Soviet embassy,
where they told him to mobilize anti-Amin Khalqi military officers. He began
to do so, but the effort was called off when one ranking officer he contacted
refused to move his units unless he was ordered to do so by the PDPA Politburo.[28] Watanjar's KGB handlers assumed that Amin would soon know about
the phone call and have even more reason to suspect that the Soviets opposed
him.

ψ

The events of the next day, September 14, showed that nothing could stop
Taraki and Amin from carrying on their personal vendetta. Despite the
PDPA's utter dependence on Soviet patronage for its survival, they ignored
Soviet demands to reconcile. Broader communist ideals and sharing power
were secondary considerations compared to upholding honor, avoiding
shame, and dominating the summit.

During an acrimonious conversation in Taraki's second-floor office at the
presidential palace on the morning of the 14th, Amin repeated his demand
that the ministers who tried to assassinate him be arrested. Taraki agreed to
replace Gulabzoi and Sarwari, but he insisted that Watanjar become defense
minister. Amin rejected the compromise. Shortly after Amin left the palace,
the Soviet delegation returned. They warned Taraki that the "situation had
again deteriorated" and advised him to invite Amin back for a meeting in their
presence.[29] Taraki phoned Amin and requested that he return. Amin agreed,

but only on the condition that Puzanov guarantee his safety. Puzanov personally gave him the guarantee, speaking over the phone. Puzanov's assistant later recounted what happened next:

> As we were waiting for Amin, Comrade B. S. Ivanov said that there were persistent rumors that the order had been given to kill Amin as soon as he appeared at the House of the People. Taraki said this was not true. A few minutes later, sub-machine gun fire was heard on the other side of the door to Taraki's office. Comrade L. N. Gorelov went to the window and saw Amin running along the walls of the grounds of the residence.[30]

Amin had gotten as far as the wide staircase ascending to Taraki's second-floor palace office where Taraki and the Soviet delegation awaited him. Major Tarun and Nawab Ali, a senior AGSA agent, preceded him up the stairs. Taraki's guards stationed at the top of the stairs opened fire, killing Tarun instantly and wounding Ali. Amin dashed from the building back to his car. He shrewdly told his driver to use a side exit to leave the palace grounds. Bullets fired by a rooftop sniper missed their mark as Amin's vehicle roared out of the palace toward the Defense Ministry across the street. Ali was taken to a nearby Kabul hospital for treatment of his wounds. That night he was strangled to death in his hospital bed.[31]

Taraki contacted Amin by phone as soon as Amin returned to his office. While the Soviet delegation listened, Taraki told Amin that the staircase shooting had been an unfortunate "misunderstanding." Ignoring the fact that Amin had visited him without incident only a few hours earlier, Taraki explained that the guards' instructions had been "to keep everyone out."[32] He had forgotten to alert them that Amin was coming. Taking the phone, Puzanov requested an immediate meeting with Amin. Amin consented. As they descended the stairs outside Taraki's office, the four Soviets stepped over Tarun's lifeless body, pockmarked with bullet holes to the head and chest. After arriving at the Defense Ministry, the delegation restated the Soviet leadership's talking points to an agitated Amin, urging him to step back from confrontation and close ranks with Taraki. Puzanov cynically expressed condolences over the death of the merciless Tarun, "a true friend of the Soviet Union."[33] The incessant ringing of Amin's phone, the bustle of activity inside and outside of his office, and a tank round loudly fired on the street just under his window forced postponement of the discussion. Amin proposed that the delegation return at 7:30 p.m. that same evening.

The delegation's departure freed up Amin to put the finishing touches on his coup. Within minutes, the sound of machine-gun fire erupting from the presidential palace grounds signaled to Kabul residents that the Taraki-Amin feud was being resolved in the usual Afghan way. Amin had returned to the palace compound, this time with a large military contingent. Members of Taraki's Presidential Guard force, who were secretly allied with Amin, seized Taraki and placed him under guard in a small guesthouse near the palace. The presidential bodyguards who resisted were transported to 4th Armored Brigade headquarters and executed.

Two "Flash" precedence American embassy telegrams sent to Washington caught the high tension in the air created by this latest round of Afghan Pad-shahgardi in Kabul. The first message reported a loud explosion and small-arms firing coming from the presidential palace at 5:30 p.m., adding, "The streets near the embassy are filled with tanks, troops and armored personnel carriers." Employing standard State Department bureaucratic jargon, the second cable commented, tongue-in-cheek, that Watanjar had been replaced and his "onward assignment is not known." It characterized Sarwari's replacement as "a man named Aziz." In fact, Aziz was Aziz Ahmed Akbari, Sarwari's turncoat cousin.[34]

By the time the Soviet delegation returned to the Defense Ministry at 7:30 p.m., Amin was in complete control of the PDPA and the Afghan government. The change in Afghan leaders did not distract the high-powered Soviet delegation from conveying to Amin their outdated talking points on reconciliation with Taraki. In response, Amin passionately denounced Taraki for twice attempting to kill him, once on the way to the airport, and again on the presidential palace stairs. He excoriated Taraki for "his egoism, authoritarianism and despotism"[35]—a set of adjectives perfectly applicable to Amin as well. Amin claimed that he now was under great pressure from Afghans to seek revenge for the killing of Tarun and Nawab Ali. He explained to his Soviet guests that PDPA unity could now be strengthened by Taraki's absence—the rationale Taraki had earlier used to resist Soviet objections to Karmal's ouster. Closing the unproductive meeting, Amin stunned his Soviet visitors by informing them that the PDPA Central Committee would soon meet to relieve Taraki of his state and party positions.

The next day, September 15, the Soviet delegation was back in Amin's office with a fresh set of instructions from Moscow. The Soviet Politburo's talking points now contained a much more urgent request—sparing Taraki's life. Taraki's close personal ties to Brezhnev made saving him a high priority. Amin was told that the Soviet Politburo wished to see Taraki remain in a purely ceremonial position of president to ensure unity and continuity in the PDPA leadership. Amin responded that he would consider the Soviet suggestion.

Amin did not consider it for long. A few hours later, a Central Committee meeting of the PDPA, chaired by Foreign Minister Shah Wali, "accepted" Taraki's "wish" to resign from all of his government and party posts for "health reasons and physical incapacity." On September 16, Afghan state-controlled TV and newspapers carried prominent images of smiling Central Committee members raising their hands in unanimous support of the resolution. Guards at the government's Radio-Television Center next to the American embassy tore down the photos of Taraki that were hanging on the building's external walls and replaced them with a huge "Long Live Amin" poster. Amin took over the Afghan presidency and all of Taraki's other positions. He ordered flags to be flown at half-mast to honor the slain Tarun and Ali. The Afghan media praised Tarun and Ali as national heroes and religious *shahids* (martyrs). Tarun's hometown of Jalalabad was renamed Tarunshar (Tarun city). The American embassy reported that, in fact, Tarun would be remembered by most Afghans as a "brutal, psychopathic killer second only to Amin in the amount of blood on his hands."[36]

Amin had bagged Taraki, but he still wanted the three ministers hiding in the Soviet embassy. Afghanistan's new president launched a media blitz charging Gulabzoi, Watanjar, and Sarwari with treason. The KGB Residence was instructed to reject any Afghan assertions that the three former ministers were at the Soviet compound. During one of his discussions with the Soviet delegation, Amin noted that, although Mazdooryar had gone home, Watanjar, Sarwari, and Gulabzoi seemed to be at the Soviet embassy. Puzanov categorically denied that this was true.[37]

Soviet strategists in Moscow and Kabul now faced an irreconcilable dilemma. Through Soviet propaganda and diplomacy they had conducted a

worldwide offensive praising the accomplishments and unity of the PDPA's
revolutionary government in Afghanistan—but the anti-PDPA rebellion was
surging in the provinces and PDPA internal struggles were receiving worldwide publicity. Worse still, Amin seemed impervious to Soviet requests even
though his new government and his security forces were completely dependent on Soviet patronage. Time-tested Soviet methods to engineer the internal political dynamics of other communist governments were not succeeding
in Afghanistan. On the contrary, instead of influencing Afghans to conform
to Soviet ways, the Afghans were enlisting different Soviets to support them
in their rivalries with each other. In effect, Soviets representing contending
military and intelligence bureaucracies in Moscow and Kabul transmuted
themselves into typical Afghan factions—or joined one of the competing
Afghan factions—flailing around inside the rambunctious Afghan political
cauldron. Like Pakistanis and Americans in future decades, the Soviets would
discover that once inside the cauldron, it would be difficult to get out. Ponomarev's deputy, Karen Brutents, captured the Soviet predicament well in his
memoir: "The Soviet Union's support for the new regime made it a hostage
to factionalist, immature and imbalanced forces, which it would be unable to
control. Moscow fell into a trap and was drawn into a game with increasingly
higher stakes, a game it could neither control, nor win."[38]

The Afghan communists' destruction of the indigenous political apparatus
that had maintained stability in Afghanistan for a half century made the game
impossible to win. The center was now at war with the regions; a foreign
ideology was at war with Afghan history, culture, and society. The Soviets
and the Afghan communists could not win these wars. Only restoration of
the center-region balance by an Afghan government seen as legitimate by
most Afghans could end the bloody turmoil unleashed by the Great Saur
Revolution.

ψ

The grim situation in Afghanistan spurred Brezhnev and Andropov to reduce
the number of Soviet decisionmakers on Afghan policy to a "troika" of three:
Andropov, Ustinov, and the pusillanimous Gromyko. Their first challenge,
smuggling Watanjar, Sarwari, and Gulabzoi out of Afghanistan to Soviet territory, would be code-named "Rainbow." The exfiltration operation began

on September 18 when a clandestine KGB team arrived at Bagram Airport on an IL-76.[39] Onboard were ten KGB embassy guards, some KGB specialists in making disguises, and two medium-sized containers. One carried wigs, hair dyes, military uniforms, and other materials designed to disguise Gulabzoi and Watanjar as Soviet KGB embassy guards rotating out of the country. The other was for Sarwari, whose bloodthirsty infamy made him the most recognizable of the three. He would be placed inside this second container, which was equipped with oxygen tanks, for the trip to the airport.

The following morning, in a secure area at the Soviet embassy, Sarwari was placed in the second container and hooked up to the oxygen tanks. The container was sealed and lifted onto a truck loaded with diplomatic bags. Watanjar and Gulabzoi, dressed as KGB guards, climbed into the back of a truck crowded with KGB embassy guards returning to the Soviet Union. The two vehicles traveled in a Soviet diplomatic convoy to Bagram Airport. There, the disguised Watanjar and Gulabzoi boarded the IL-76 along with the Soviet embassy guards, and the container carrying Sarwari was moved onto the aircraft along with diplomatic baggage. The plane flew to Tashkent in Uzbekistan, where the three ministers were taken to a fenced-in Communist Party compound. Their rooms were equipped with KGB eavesdropping machinery. After KGB technicians filled up ninety-two tapes of conversation, the three were taken to a KGB safehouse in Moscow to await instructions on their role in the next round of Padshahgardi in Kabul.

Disposal of the ministers' Toyota, which had been parked in Gulabzoi's KGB case officer's garage, wrapped up Operation Rainbow. The methods chosen for this final task would have been at home in a Peter Sellers spy comedy. Deputy KGB Resident Morozov later wrote that "four KGB operatives," who were "specifically chosen for their physical resemblance to the four Afghans" smuggled to Moscow, drove the Toyota from the case officer's villa to the Soviet embassy. As Morozov described it, the "stupid" decision to do this was made "high up in the KGB to destroy the material evidence—The car was dismantled, sawn apart and buried in a place not far from the embassy." Morozov speculated that, "if the Afghans ever dig it up, they will surely rack their brains about the motives behind the act."[40]

Amin's heavy reliance on Soviet military and economic assistance did not stop him from retaliating against Moscow for supporting his enemies in the

PDPA. On October 6, Foreign Minister Shah Wali summoned the ambassadors of "friendly" communist countries to the Foreign Ministry for a comprehensive briefing on Taraki's failed "conspiracy" and Amin's ascendancy. Safronchuk represented the Soviet embassy. The Chinese ambassador was not invited. The Yugoslav ambassador was. He relayed to the American embassy a detailed readout of Shah Wali's condemnation of Ambassador Puzanov. Wali informed the ambassador that, before the September 14 attempted assassination of Amin at the palace, Puzanov had guaranteed his safety. He stated that, contrary to Puzanov's denials, three of the four former ministers had been given sanctuary at the Soviet embassy, and had later moved elsewhere. The implications of Wali's message were clear: The Afghan government was accusing the Soviets of having colluded with Taraki against Afghanistan's new president.[41]

Three days later, on October 9 at 6 p.m., Puzanov, Gorelov, Ivanov's deputy, and Pavlovskiy trooped back to Amin's office to convey another authoritative message from the Soviet leadership. Speaking formally to Amin on behalf of the Soviet Politburo, Puzanov protested Wali's accusations of Soviet collusion in the attack on Amin. He also refuted Wali's statement that he, Puzanov, had personally given Amin assurances about his safety in a phone conversation from Taraki's office. He demanded that Wali publicly retract his allegations. Amin refused. If the Soviets really believed in their positions, he said, they could make a unilateral refutation of Wali's statements. The Afghan government would not publicly respond to the Soviet position.[42] The meeting ended in deadlock.

A stream of appeals to spare Taraki's life were conveyed to the wayward Amin directly and indirectly through multiple channels. They came from Brezhnev, from the Politburo collectively, from Puzanov, from the KGB Residency, and from Soviet military advisers in Afghanistan. Initially, Amin's feedback appeared promising. He assured the Soviets that Taraki's guesthouse near the palace's main gate was well guarded to prevent an attack on his life.[43] But then a string of events indicated that Amin had no intention of letting Taraki live. On October 6, Taraki's wife was taken from the guesthouse and transported to Pul-i-Charkhi prison. Taraki was cut off from all outside visitors, and the phone line to the guesthouse was severed. During the evening of October 8, on Amin's orders, two brothers who were charged with guarding him, former members of his personal security force, entered his bedroom. Fearing the worst, Taraki promised to resign from all of his party positions. He handed over his party membership card and offered to return to his pre-revolution house in Kabul, where the party had been founded in 1965. The assassins were not swayed. They smothered Taraki with his own pillow.[44]

Amin embargoed the news of Taraki's death until just after a late-afternoon meeting with the Soviet delegation on October 9. At 8 p.m. that evening, after the Soviet delegation's departure from Amin's office, Radio Kabul announced that Taraki had "died yesterday morning of a serious illness, which he had been suffering for some time." Brezhnev was furious, as were other Soviet leaders. In his memoirs, Gromyko linked Amin's double-cross to the Soviet decision to invade Afghanistan.[45]

Amin's execution of Taraki after receiving Brezhnev's personal appeal that he be spared incensed Soviet leaders. His insolence must have ranked with Daoud's unruly reaction to Brezhnev's offensive remarks during their April 1977 meeting in the Kremlin. Amin, however, was not through. He skipped the November 7 reception celebrating the Bolshevik Revolution held at the Soviet Embassy. He formally asked for Puzanov's recall.[46] The troika had no alternative but to comply. Puzanov returned to the Soviet Union and was hurriedly retired.[47] At Amin's request, the senior Soviet adviser to the minister of interior was also replaced. In his demands that Moscow recall high-ranking Soviets in Kabul, however, Amin did not net his most dangerous adversary in the Soviet mission: KGB Resident Ivanov.[48]

Taraki and Amin had long ignored Soviet advice to improve ties to Pakistan and Iran. After executing Taraki, Amin initiated a spate of diplomatic gestures to Tehran and Islamabad, presumably to balance Afghanistan's dependence on Moscow. His sudden enthusiasm to improve relations with Pakistan was closely monitored by the Soviets. Their fears were confirmed by reliable reports that Amin's representatives had secretly met with Gulbuddin Hekmatyar in Konar Province.[49]

Amin's attempts to reduce his dependence on the Soviet Union came to naught. The Afghan despot's untrustworthiness and his widespread unpopularity among Afghans undermined his search for new foreign patrons. Memories of Amin's complicity in Ambassador Dubs's murder were still fresh in Washington. Amin gave interviews to American correspondents and met with the American chargé three times. After the third meeting, Amstutz advised Washington that the best response to his olive branches was "a low profile, trying to avoid issues, and waiting to see what happens."[50]

In early December, Amin's Foreign Ministry proposed a summit with Pakistani President Zia ul-Haq. Amin sweetened the proposal by turning off Afghan media attacks on Zia. In a Pakistani newspaper interview, he explained away his previous Pashtunistan rhetoric as mere references to Afghan nomads on seasonal excursions with their flocks into Pakistan. Zia subtly finessed Amin's proposal for a meeting but permitted the Pakistani Foreign Ministry to begin planning for a visit by Pakistan's foreign minister to Kabul. Meanwhile, Zia's ISI continued to covertly train and arm Mujahidin groups attempting to overthrow Amin's shaky regime.

ψ

The independent-minded Amin may have longed for a Tito-type nationalistic break from the Soviet Union. His failure to locate new foreign benefactors, however, tempered his previous disregard for Soviet sensitivities. By early November, it was clear that Moscow remained his only option. He was not a tribal chief holed up in a mountainous redoubt deep in tribal territory, protected by kith and kin; he was in a densely populated, multiethnic city surrounded by Afghans who hated and feared him. Taraki's overthrow had narrowed Amin's base to family, clan, and a relatively small group of pro-Amin Pashtun PDPA military officers.

Mujahidin bands roamed freely in the countryside, gobbling up more and more territory. Purges, desertions, and army mutinies had reduced the army's size from 100,000 at the time of the communist coup to between 50,000 and 70,000.[51] An August mutiny by the 26th Paratroop Regiment stationed inside the old Bala Hisar Fort in Kabul was squashed by helicopter gunships and MIG aircraft firing directly into the fort. Later that month, an entire army brigade mutinied in Konar, killing their officers and Soviet advisers before fleeing across the border into Pakistan. Amin's position was perilous. He knew that the KGB had penetrated his security services, the PDPA, the military, and the government bureaucracy. He also knew that his enemy Karmal and other exiled Parcham leaders were in Eastern Europe, presenting themselves to Soviets as more reliable allies than himself. Khalqis Watanjar, Gulabzoi, and Sarwari were in the Soviet Union thirsting for revenge. They would be eager accomplices in his destruction. In October, American chargé d'affaires Amstutz, describing Amin's position in a cable to the State Department, wrote: "Clearly, he is aware of the mortality rate of Afghan leaders." Amstutz reported that during their meetings, Amin several times prefaced his comments by noting, "Even if I am killed tomorrow. . . . "[52]

In October, in a macabre attempt to discredit Taraki, Amin had the Interior Ministry publicize the names of 12,000 Afghans who had been executed at Pul-i-Charkhi while Taraki was president.[53] Amin, of course, was as responsible as Taraki for the reign of Red Terror. Amin followed up the public outcry against the regime with another bloody purge. This one seemed directed at depriving Moscow of potential candidates to replace him. His victims ranged from senior PDPA political and military leaders to prominent Afghans who had served in the administrations of Daoud and Zahir Shah. He ordered the execution of jailed former prime minister Nur Ahmad Etemadi. A flurry of arrests and executions of military officers cascaded through the Defense Ministry and the provinces.

In speeches and media interviews, Amin struggled to persuade Soviet leaders to tolerate him. He hoped Moscow did not really care which Afghan faction leader ruled in Kabul as long as Afghanistan remained in the pro-Soviet camp. Rhetorically (but not in practice), Amin indulged long-standing Soviet advice to create a constitution and conciliate rather than confront Islam. Speaking to a group of Soviet, East German, and British journalists after new Soviet economic aid agreements were signed in October and November, he said, "We are convinced that if there were no vast economic and military aid from the Soviet Union, we could not resist the aggression and conspiracy of imperialism."[54]

But it was too late for a reconciliation. "Everything aside, the person who assumed the helm of power in Afghanistan on September 14, 1979, did not have the trust of the Soviet leadership," Brutents later wrote.[55] The Soviets worried that the unpredictable Amin would lurch to the West as Sadat had done in 1972. The crumbling of the U.S.-Soviet détente in the closing months of 1979 enhanced Afghanistan's global geostrategic importance to Moscow. In October, the U.S. Congress had refused to vote on the SALT II strategic arms–control treaty signed by Carter and Brezhnev the previous June. The

American decision to counter Moscow's midrange SS-20 missile threat to its European allies by stationing Pershing and cruise missiles in Western Europe exacerbated U.S.-Soviet tensions. So did the American military buildup in the Indian Ocean in response to the November 4, 1979, seizure of American hostages in Tehran. The December 15 announcement that the United States and China would establish diplomatic relations increased Soviet apprehensions of a coalescing anti-Soviet American, Chinese, Japanese, Western European condominium aimed at isolating the Soviet Union. Meanwhile, deteriorating Soviet-Iranian relations during 1979 left Afghanistan as the only friendly country along the USSR's long southern frontier.

The specter of rising Islamic radicalism was an additional concern to Soviet policymakers. The Iranian hostage crisis and the attack on the Grand Mosque in Mecca by Islamic dissidents on November 20, 1979, demonstrated the rising threat of militant Islamism in the broader region. Soviet decisionmakers suspected that the United States was behind clandestine arms shipments going to the Mujahidin. Fallacious KGB reports announced the arrival of U.S. troops in Jalalabad and spoke of American plans to move signals-intelligence facilities used to monitor Soviet missile launches from Iran to Afghanistan.

Andropov's prominence in the Soviet Politburo did not bode well for Amin. The KGB boss had compiled an imposing record of crushing disobedient clients in Hungary and Czechoslovakia. Amin was now in Andropov's crosshairs. Ivanov's KGB team in Kabul began bombarding Kremlin policymakers with doomsday scenarios about Afghanistan's direction under Amin. More realistic advice from pro-Amin Soviet military officers in Afghanistan was suppressed or ignored. KGB anti-Amin reporting was not shown to Puzanov's successor, Ambassador Fikryat A. Tabeyev, or to senior Soviet military advisers in Kabul.

Soon after Taraki's murder, a Politburo report cited "the necessity of doing everything possible not to allow the victory of counterrevolution in Afghanistan or the political reorientation of Amin towards the West." On October 29, 1979, a highly classified Politburo assessment, accompanied by a decree, castigated Amin as "a power-hungry leader who is distinguished by brutality and treachery." The document enumerated a litany of Amin's many sins: practicing "insincerity and duplicity" in dealing with the Soviet Union; devising "fictitious accusations" against other PDPA members; packing the PDPA leadership with "people who are devoted to him, including a number of his relatives"; and intending "to conduct a more 'balanced policy' in relation to the Western powers." A KGB message from Kabul accused Amin of conspiring with the "extreme Muslim opposition" to expel all Soviets from Afghanistan.[56]

Amin's top priority was survival; Moscow's top priority was to liquidate him. The Soviets mounted a two-pronged strategy. The first, orchestrated by Andropov's KGB, focused on deceiving Amin into believing that the Soviet leadership had decided to forgive his previous disobedience. Amin's KGB advisers feigned reconciliation, convincing him that Taraki's murder was forgotten and that they trusted him as the only viable PDPA leader left in Kabul capable of delivering the fruits of the April Revolution. The second prong began with a Soviet military buildup of combat units north of the Amu Darya and at the exclusively Soviet-controlled sector of Bagram air base near Kabul.

Moscow's first move to lure Amin into a false sense of security was a hypocritical visit by Puzanov, Ivanov, Gorelov, and Pavlovskiy to Amin's residence. They conveyed the Soviet leadership's congratulations on his "election" as PDPA general secretary. Brezhnev and Kosygin followed this up with a highly publicized message to Amin congratulating him on his selection as president of Afghanistan. An avalanche of congratulatory messages from pro-Soviet communist governments and communist parties around the world immediately followed. Soviet agencies responded favorably to Amin's request for additional military supplies. Soviet logistical support was provided to deploy two Afghan divisions from northern Afghanistan to insurgency-plagued eastern Afghanistan and Kabul's southern defense perimeter. Additional regime radio stations were established with Soviet assistance.[57]

The Soviets had turned down Taraki's request for Soviet ground forces during the March Herat uprising, but that position changed once the decision was made to assasinate Amin. Now Amin's appeals for more Soviet assistance played into Andropov's hands. At Amin's request, a Soviet doctor arrived to attend to his health. A Russian nanny helped oversee his children, and two Soviet chefs were assigned to Amin's kitchen staff. Both of the chefs were KGB agents. One of them, Mutalin Talybov, was a Farsi-speaking native from the Soviet Republic of Azerbaijan who had previously operated in Iran as a KGB illegal.[58]

Amin requested a full battalion of Soviet troops, disguised as Afghan soldiers, to bolster his personal security detail. He may also have hoped that his request would underscore his loyalty to Moscow. In any case, his willingness to appear a hostage to Soviet control fit nicely into the Soviet strategy to eliminate him. A 520-man GRU "Muslim Battalion," made up of Soviet military personnel recruited from the Muslim populations of Central Asia, took over the middle perimeter of security around Amin's residence in Kabul. Amin's personal security contingent, comprising some 150 relatives and tribal militia recruited from his tribal network in Paghman, filled out the inner ring in and immediately around his residence and office. Two thousand Afghan infantry and armored troops manned the outer perimeter. In mid-December, elite KGB Zenith commandos were attached to the Muslim Battalion.

The growing insurgency in previously stable northern Afghanistan inspired a fresh set of requests from Amin for Soviet troops. He solicited two full Soviet divisions to be stationed north of the Hindu Kush, away from Kabul, and appointed his brother Abdullah Amin as the senior Afghan government official in northern Afghanistan.[59]

The Soviet military buildup on both sides of the Amu Darya did not escape the notice of American diplomats in Moscow and Kabul. U.S. embassy officers in Moscow traveling through Central Asia reported the call-up of Soviet reservists. In October, a secret assessment transmitted to Washington by the American embassy in Kabul called attention to the "growing Soviet military presence in Afghanistan," which it characterized as "ominous." The message reported that a six-hundred-man battalion from the 103rd Airborne Division had arrived at Bagram and was converting one section of the airport into a Soviet-controlled enclave. The cable estimated that 3,600 Soviet combat troops and 3,000 Soviet military advisers were present in Afghanistan.[60]

Concurrently, KGB military units, mainly additional KGB Zenith commando companies and border guard troops, were flown to Afghanistan to secretly infiltrate the capital area. Two undercover KGB communications specialists were sent to inspect the vulnerability of Afghan communication facilities in Kabul. North of the Afghan border in Central Asia, a total of 55,000 troops, including the 108th Motorized Rifle Division in Uzbekistan and the 5th Motorized Rifle Division in Turkmenistan, were mobilized. In late November, the size of the 103rd Paratroop Regiment at Bagram was expanded to 2,500 troops. A Soviet armored battalion based at Bagram took over security responsibility for the highway from the Salang Tunnel to the

Amu Darya. Another battalion of the 103rd Airborne Division was positioned at Kabul Airport.[61]

The American embassies in Moscow and Kabul and Defense Department and State Department analysts in Washington debated whether or not the Soviet Union would invade Afghanistan. The United States issued its first warning to Moscow in March 1979.[62] Private American admonitions continued through diplomatic channels during the summer and fall. The Soviets forcefully denied any intention of invading Afghanistan. On December 4, a State Department memorandum stated that "the Soviets appeared to have concluded that the advantages of more direct intervention in Afghanistan now outweighed the inevitable price the Soviets would pay in terms of regional and US reaction." On December 5, a State Department spokesman publicly questioned Soviet intentions. Also in early December, the CIA identified the establishment of a Soviet command post at Termez, on the Soviet side of the Amu Darya, opposite the Soviet-built Afghan highway leading to Mazar-i-Sharif and Kabul. The United States briefed its allies on Soviet preparations, and Deputy Secretary of State Warren Christopher summoned the Soviet chargé d'affaires to the State Department to express concern. On December 17, the Soviet deputy foreign minister, Viktor Maltsev, told American ambassador Thomas Watson in Moscow that he was "surprised and puzzled" by the ambassador's request for an explanation of the Soviet buildup. Maltsev indignantly noted that "Soviet-Afghan relations are between two sovereign states and the business only of those two states, not subject to interference from third states."[63]

✵

The gradual Soviet military buildup to overthrow Amin moved steadily forward. Fashioning a new PDPA unity government to replace Amin was the final piece of Moscow's invasion plan. On October 25, 1979, a KGB lieutenant colonel was sent to Prague to work with Babrak Karmal on forming a new PDPA regime to replace Amin. With KGB assistance, Karmal wrote a "personal letter" to Brezhnev on October 30 to inform him that "the leading members of the Afghan Communist Party are prepared to organize and unite communists, patriots and all the progressive and democratic forces in Afghanistan."[64] During the first few days of November, the KGB transferred Karmal and Najib to Moscow for secret meetings with anti-Amin Khalqis Sarwari, Watanjar, and Gulabzoi.

With the KGB's helping hand, the PDPA exiles agreed to set aside their differences and form a government. Karmal was named president, prime minister, and party general secretary. Sarwari's appointment as Karmal's deputy gave the necessary Khalqi balance at the top, and Najib was designated head of intelligence. A new, broad-based PDPA platform, crafted with KGB guidance, jubilantly promised "to end forever the split in the ranks of Afghan communists and to unite in a new Party, friendship with the USSR and the struggle against imperialism" in post-Amin Afghanistan.[65] The pledge, of course, was worth no more than the paper it was printed on.

Andropov coyly attached the PDPA's government-in-exile party platform to a personal memorandum that he gave to Brezhnev. The memorandum was deceptively written to assure other readers that the general secretary had approved a Soviet military invasion of Afghanistan. It falsely portrayed Babrak Karmal, instead of the KGB, as devising the operational plans to overthrow Amin. Andropov led off the memorandum by charging that Amin had secretly contacted an American agent, thereby indicating his intention to shift toward the West.[66] He continued:

> Recently, we were contacted by a group of Afghan communists abroad. In the course of our contact with Babrak (Karmal) and Asadullah Sarwari, it became clear (and they informed us of this) that they have worked out a plan for opposing Amin and creating new Party and state organs. But Amin, as a preventive measure, has begun mass arrests of "suspect persons" (300 people have been shot). In these conditions Babrak and Sarwari, without changing their plans of opposition, have raised the question of possible assistance, in case of need, including military. We have two battalions stationed in Kabul, and there is a capability of rendering such assistance. . . . But, as a precautionary measure in the event of unforeseen complications, it would be wise to have a military group close to the border. . . . The implementation of the given operation would allow us to decide the question of defending the gains of the April revolution, establishing Leninist principles in the Party and state leadership of Afghanistan, and securing our position in this country.[67]

A formal Politburo decision to invade Afghanistan was still required.[68] By securing Brezhnev's formal approval, the troika calculated, it could achieve a fait accompli over the objections certain to be raised by Kosygin and others in a larger Politburo meeting. A Politburo debate such as occurred during the March Herat crisis would certainly spark protests from members opposed to sending troops to Afghanistan; uniformed military officers participating might also argue against an invasion.

The Andropov-led troika circumvented these obstacles by organizing an extraordinary meeting in Brezhnev's Kremlin office, nicknamed the "Walnut Room," on the afternoon of December 12. Before seeing Brezhnev, they privately elicited the endorsement of the second-ranking Politburo member, top party ideologue Mikhail Suslov.[69] In Brezhnev's presence, the general secretary's close confidant Konstantin Chernyenko, a Politburo member, wrote four sentences in longhand on a sheet of paper authorizing Andropov, Ustinov, and Gromyko to "introduce amendments of a non-essential character" in order to carry out "measures" in country "A." One of the four sentences Chernyenko scrawled entrusted "the execution of all of these measures" to the troika.

The meeting affixed a number identifying the paper's contents as a formal decree of the Party Central Committee. Brezhnev's faltering signature appears at the bottom of the paper; at the top of the document, Andropov, Ustinov, and Gromyko, in that order, penned their names. The paper was hand-carried to other full Politburo members. All signed except for Kosygin.[70]

Andropov's powerful position in the Politburo gave the KGB the lead in managing Amin's overthrow and Karmal's installation as Afghanistan's next leader. That helped sow the seeds of the Soviet debacle in Afghanistan. The mammoth Soviet spy agency was highly insular, compartmentalized, and secretive, and it was resistant to cooperation with other Soviet agencies better equipped to understand Afghanistan. KGB political assessments praised KGB operations. KGB analysts skewed events to "prove" a preferred outcome, which invariably was hard-line conservative and geared to preserve a KGB monopoly over Soviet Afghan policy formulation and execution. KGB recommendations flowed freely to the Afghan Commission troika while others, including the Soviet ambassador in Kabul and pro-Amin Soviet generals in the Soviet military advisory mission in Kabul, were left out of the loop.

Officers in the KGB's Kabul Residence were ill equipped, by background and training, to understand the unique Afghan tribal environment. KGB methods might allow them to successfully assassinate a disobedient Afghan president, but they could not help them to deliver a dependable Afghan leader or a stable, pro-Soviet Afghanistan. Amin was not a CIA agent; Karmal was not a puppet. The two-decade record of KGB failures in Afghanistan became a classic case of intelligence agencies operating in self-imposed cocoons, screening out policymaking agencies more familiar with the complexities of the indigenous environment. Covert-action policy became national policy. Under KGB control, Soviet Afghan policy produced the same counterproductive results that American overreliance on the CIA would generate in Afghanistan a decade later.

KGB preparations for regime change in Afghanistan were already in high gear before the Politburo's endorsement of the Soviet invasion on December 12. By this date, the KGB had already cobbled together Karmal Parchamis and anti-Amin Khalqis into the shadow PDPA government set to replace Amin's regime. On December 4, KGB Major General Vadim Kirpichenko, Kryuchkov's deputy, was given a false name and passport and flown by Soviet military aircraft into Afghanistan "to prepare the operation in Kabul to remove Amin from power." Kirpichenko and Ivanov inside Afghanistan, and Andropov and Kryuchkov in Moscow, became the lead Soviet players organizing and carrying out Amin's overthrow. They communicated with each other through KGB coded communication channels not accessible to other officials at the Soviet embassy. The KGB coordinated its elite Zenith commando units, the GRU Muslim Battalion, Soviet paratroopers, and Soviet ground forces to eliminate Amin's regime and replace it with Karmal's government.[71]

Major General Vasiliy Zaplatin, head of the Soviet military training mission in Afghanistan, traveled to Moscow in early December to argue against the invasion. In a meeting with Defense Minister Ustinov, he took issue with a KGB analysis of the Afghan situation, prepared by Ivanov's Kabul Residency, which had not been shown to him in Kabul. Zaplatin told Ustinov that he would not have trusted the Afghan sources cited in the KGB analysis; nor would he have signed the document if he had seen it in Kabul. Ustinov responded curtly, dismissing Zaplatin's advice.

ॐ

Several KGB attempts to assassinate Amin during mid-December miscarried. On December 7, the KGB secretly flew Karmal, Sarwari, Watanjar, and

Gulabzoi to the Soviet-controlled cantonment at Bagram to stand by in case KGB operations to kill Amin succeeded. But Amin remained an elusive quarry. On December 14, an operation by Zenith sharpshooters to assassinate him on a Kabul road was aborted when his vehicle suddenly accelerated to a high speed. A KGB plan to storm the presidential palace using KGB commandos and the Muslim Battalion was shelved at the last minute as too risky. On December 16, the two KGB cooks in the presidential palace's kitchen bungled a poisoning attempt on President Amin's life, although Amin's nephew and secret police chief, Assadullah Amin, was seriously injured and collapsed. Amin's Soviet doctor fraudulently diagnosed him with hepatitis and recommended that he be evacuated to the Soviet Union. Amin's nephew, his Afghan doctor, and an Afghan bodyguard were taken to Moscow, where the nephew was placed in the tender care of a Soviet hospital.[72]

After the aborted poisoning operation, Karmal and the four Afghans at Bagram were flown back to the Soviet Union on Soviet military aircraft. They would return to Bagram on the eve of the Soviet invasion. On December 17, as tension mounted, Amin shifted his residence to the Tajbeg Palace near Afghan Central Command headquarters at the Darulaman complex in Kabul's southwest suburbs. The Muslim Battalion, KGB commandos, and the Soviet members of Amin's household staff followed him to the new location, away from crowded Kabul, on top of a hill covered with trees.

On December 4, the same day General Kirpichenko had flown into Bagram, the Soviet leadership had sent an exuberant message to Amin hailing the first anniversary of the Soviet-Afghan friendship treaty. In a meeting with Ambassador Tabeyev on December 6, Amin stressed the importance of a Moscow visit to meet Brezhnev, already agreed to in principle. Amin repeated his request for deployment of Soviet combat units north of the Hindu Kush to help quell the spreading Mujahidin insurgency. The Afghan president was pleased to hear from Safronchuk during the latter's mid-December farewell call that Moscow had accepted this recommendation. Nikolai Tauzin, the Soviet minister of communications, arrived in Kabul on December 24 for consultations with the Afghan government. He paid a courtesy call on Amin just hours before KGB commandos attacked his Tajbeg Palace residence.[73]

Amin dismissed suspicions voiced by some of his generals about the large number of Soviet combat troops arriving in Afghanistan and occupying strategic points in and around the capital. Soviet signals intelligence taped

Chief of Staff Yaqub, on December 26, "alarmingly reporting" to Amin "that the Soviet troops were arriving in quantities that exceeded the agreement." Amin interrupted, asserting, "So what, the more they come, the better for us."[74] The Soviet buildup also worried the Afghan commander at Bagram. In an unprecedented move, he ordered Afghan helicopters to fly over the cantonment where Soviet paratroopers were stationed.[75] His concerns were not far-fetched. The KGB had just reinserted Karmal and the other members of his Soviet-created government-in-waiting into the Soviet-controlled section of the base.

☙

Moscow's invasion strategy was calibrated to preempt military countermoves by the United States and its allies. An immediate reaction by the U.S. military to the Soviet invasion of Afghanistan was, in any case, unlikely. During the previous three years, President Carter had not compiled a record of firmness in dealing with Soviet provocations. Washington's concentration on the Tehran hostage crisis also rendered prospects for an American military countermove remote. Western nations were absorbed in Christmas festivities when the airlift of 7,200 more Soviet paratroopers into the Bagram base and Kabul Airport commenced on December 25, 1979. American embassy military attachés cabled Washington on December 26 that a massive Soviet airlift into Kabul Airport was under way. By 4:00 p.m. that afternoon, they had counted about two hundred flights landing in groups of three and dropping off armored vehicles and "troops dressed in both combat fatigues and the winter-hat overcoat."[76]

To mask the large size of the invasion from U.S. signals intelligence, all orders for troop movements were issued orally from Ustinov and orally sent down the chain of command.[77] General Sergei Sokolov, who was also first deputy defense minister, did not fly to his 40th Army headquarters at Termez to take charge of the invasion until December 24. At twilight on Christmas Day, the 108th Motorized Rifle Division began crossing military pontoon bridges constructed over the Amu Darya. The division's tanks, armored personnel carriers (APCs), and trucks drove south into Afghanistan on asphalt roads and over bridges built years previously by Soviet engineers to withstand the weight of heavy armor.[78] Ustinov delayed the release of the 5th Motorized Rifle Division into western Afghanistan until midnight, December 27, after Soviet forces had occupied Kabul.

Carefully prepared ruses were deployed to mislead the Afghans. On December 25, Solokov flew from Termez to Kunduz to meet with Amin's older brother, Abdullah Amin, who supervised northern Afghanistan. The two discussed the counterinsurgency role of the 108th Division north of the Hindu Kush. They agreed to station the division's units at Kunduz, Taloqan, and other Afghan cities, all in northern Afghanistan, far from Kabul, as Amin had requested.

The Soviets had no intention of keeping the agreement. The following day, December 26, Solokov ordered the division to cross the Hindu Kush on the Soviet-built Salang Highway and rapidly move to Kabul.[79] On arrival, the division's regiments were deployed to predetermined blocking positions to prevent the Afghan 7th Division at Rishkor and the 8th Division at Kargha from reinforcing Afghan units in the capital. By this time, the main body of the 103rd Airborne Division had landed at Kabul Airport. The airlift of units from three other paratrooper regiments increased the number of Soviet airborne troops in the Afghan capital to over 10,000 men. During the late afternoon and evening of December 26 and in the daytime hours of December 27, the paratroopers occupied high ground in and around the center of the city. Soviet air assault troops landed in Kunduz and seized Abdullah Amin. KGB technicians attached explosive charges to the communications box under Pashtunistan Square in central Kabul that contained the cables for Kabul's civilian and military telephone system.

⚜

By the late afternoon of December 27, Soviet troops had secured most of Kabul. The moment had come to deliver the *coup de main* to Amin's regime. Two core members of Amin's quam, Abdullah Amin and Assadullah Amin, his brother and nephew, respectively, had already been picked off. From Moscow, Andropov and Kryuchkov closely monitored the closing of the ring around Amin. They may have worried that the bold, unpredictable Pashtun might once more slip through the KGB trap. Much depended on Amin's continuing assumption of Soviet friendship.

Two days before their December 27 assault on Amin's hilltop palace, the Soviet Zenith commandos hosted a "pilaf reception" for Afghan officers in the Afghan president's personal security force. During the function, the commandos probed for weaknesses in the Tajbeg Palace defenses. One Zenith officer recalled: "During the reception, [we] tried to get the Afghans to talk. Toasts were raised to Soviet-Afghan friendship [and] combat cooperation.... Sometimes Soviets serving the reception served Soviet officers water instead of vodka."[80]

Soviet Minister of Communications Tauzin had just departed after his courtesy call on Amin on the afternoon of December 27 when Amin, his family, and their guests sat down for lunch at the Tajbeg Palace. Earlier that morning, Amin had delivered a rousing speech praising Soviet-Afghan friendship to a large group of PDPA members celebrating the anniversary of the PDPA's founding. A sham birthday party, organized by the Muslim Battalion for one of their own officers, allowed the Soviet military advisers to Amin's personal security detail to depart the palace.

During lunch the KGB activated a second and final attempt to poison Amin. Many at the table, including Amin, passed out. The members of an Afghan television crew in an adjoining room were also poisoned. A quick search of the kitchen to inquire how the food had been prepared revealed that the two Russian cooks had absconded.[81] Afghan doctors stationed at Darulaman military headquarters rushed to the palace and pumped the stomachs of Amin and others who had fallen ill. Amin was slowly regaining consciousness when two Soviet doctors arrived. They insisted that he be taken to a Soviet military clinic for immediate treatment, but by this time, Amin's chief bodyguard and the Afghan doctors were thoroughly suspicious of Soviet intentions. They angrily rejected the Soviet doctors' proposal.

At 6:45 p.m. on December 27, when the KGB-led assault on the palace began, Amin was still not fully conscious. The attack, carried out by a force of seven hundred, was timed to start a few minutes before the charges in downtown Kabul destroyed the capital's telephone system. The blast cut all telephone links between Afghan military units and destroyed the ability of anyone in the capital to phone for reinforcements. In addition, the explosion was a prearranged signal to other KGB Zenith units around Kabul: Once they heard it, with the support of Soviet paratroopers, they were to carry out simultaneous attacks on Chief of Staff Yaqub's office at the Ministry of Defense, the Ministry of Interior, secret police headquarters, the Radio-Television Center, and other important government installations. The customary closure of all government offices at 2:30 p.m. on Thursday afternoon in anticipation of Friday prayers had already emptied most government buildings.[82]

Soviet military advisers stationed at Afghan military bases in the capital area, taking advantage of the exodus, had already removed firing pins from tanks, taken batteries from Afghan military vehicles, and placed locks on ammunition depots. When the attacks on the Tajbeg Palace and government buildings in Kabul began, the advisers urged their Afghan counterparts to stand down until the clamor in the city ended. Out of communication with each other and with the Ministry of Defense headquarters, the great majority took their advice.

Soviet Ambassador Tabeyev was surprised by the outbreak of gunfire in the city during the early evening of December 27. He had not been told that Soviet forces would go into action that night. When the lights at his residence suddenly went out, and probably with no pun intended, his wife angrily shouted at him: "They are even keeping you in the dark." The incensed Soviet ambassador phoned Kirpichenko to demand an explanation. Kirpichenko replied that he was too busy at the moment to brief the ambassador but would do so on the following morning.[83]

Sarwari and Gulabzoi, members of the future Karmal-led government, accompanied the KGB commandos assaulting Tajbeg Palace. They wore the uniforms of the KGB Zenith unit. Watanjar was integrated with Zenith commandos assigned to attack the Radio-Television Center next door to the American embassy on the airport road. Abdul Wakil was attached to the Zenith unit attacking the Defense Ministry, where Chief of Staff Yaqub was that day. Meanwhile, Karmal remained under Soviet protection at Bagram.

Only at the Tajbeg Palace and the radio-television building did the Soviets face strong resistance. As part of the strategy to quickly disable Amin's military potential, the Soviet commander of the 103rd Airborne Division, Major General Ivan Ryabchenko, was scheduled to meet with General Yaqub. The meeting was under way when the Pashtunistan Square explosion loudly resonated through Kabul. A radio linking Yaqub to his division commanders was nearby. Immediately rising from his chair, Yaqub reached for a machine gun on a nearby table. But a KGB commando, disguised as a paratrooper in Ryabchenko's delegation, tackled Yaqub before he could grab his weapon.

Soviet and Afghan military officers who had been engaged in pleasant conversation seconds earlier fell on each other in a fight to the death. The Soviets enjoyed a clear numerical advantage over the Afghans. In addition to Ryabchenko's delegation, Yaqub's Soviet military advisers were in the room, and they assaulted their former advisees. KGB Zenith troops already moving through the lightly guarded building burst into the room and joined the hand-to-hand combat. Yaqub was wrestled to the ground, shot, and wounded. A large man, well over 200 pounds and over 6 feet tall, he was able to fight his way to a nearby lounge, where he was finally subdued by a swarm of Soviet officers and Zenith commandos. Soviet accounts claim that Yaqub was taken to another room to meet with Abdul Wakil, who shot and killed him with a pistol.[84] It is more likely that Zenith officers finished him off.

KGB commandos participating in the attack on Amin's Tajbeg Palace were under orders not to take Amin alive.[85] The assault, code-named "Operation Storm 333," was initiated by a deafening barrage from heavy "Shilka" machine guns firing 23-mm shells from all directions at the surprised defenders, who were still recovering from the poison attack. The commandos, wearing white armbands to prevent fratricide, ran uphill toward the palace's main gate and a side window of the palace. It was a dark, cold winter night. The wooded terrain surrounding the palace and knee-deep snow slowed the assault. Members of Amin's Paghman tribal militia scattered among the trees caught the attacking Soviets in a deadly crossfire.

Soviet accounts tend to glorify the Tajbeg battle, though they differ on important details. Most set the number of Soviet attackers killed at ten or fewer, including KGB colonel Grigoriy Boyarinev, who led the assault. KGB defector Vasili Mitrokhin, who had direct access to KGB after-action reports, however, wrote that over 100 of the 700 KGB commandos in the attack were killed. The high casualty count, Mitrokhin noted, compelled Andropov to forgo the usual practice of placing the photos of the fallen at KGB headquarters in Moscow.[86] There are no reliable estimates of how many Afghans were killed, but the numbers probably range into the hundreds. Some Soviet versions described the battle as lasting only forty minutes, others for two hours. A Western military attaché reported that stiff resistance at the Tajbeg Palace did not cease until "the middle of the night,"[87] more than five hours after it began.

Early on, the 2,000-man outer perimeter of regular Afghan troops seem to have surrendered to Muslim Battalion units. Amin's tribal security guard, inside and immediately surrounding the palace, fiercely resisted. The first Soviet armored personnel carrier moving up the narrow path to the palace was knocked out by an antitank round; the disabled APC blocked the path of other armored vehicles, which in turn were pinned down by a hail of gunfire from the woods and the palace.

The element of surprise, superior numbers, the effects of the poison attack, and the continuous barrage of heavy machine-gun fire cascading onto the palace gradually took their toll on the defenders. The palace's generator-powered lights were turned off after KGB commandos fought their way into the building. By then, a continuous roar of exploding grenades and the sharp cackle of machine guns mixed with shouts from men, women, and children inside the palace. KGB commandos moved from floor to floor, tossing live grenades into pitch-black rooms, following them up by bursts of machine-gun fire.

Contradictory versions of Amin's death abound. One fable related by a KGB commando described Amin as calmly downing a cocktail at the bar on the second floor of the palace when he was killed. Weeks after Amin's death, the new Karmal government's propaganda machine claimed that pro-Karmal Afghan troops led by Sarwari and Gulabzoi had captured Amin and carted him away to be officially tried and executed by the PDPA. A third version held that Amin was found dead on the floor of his office, a victim of grenade fragments. Yet another account maintained that a KGB commando discovered Amin lying on the floor unconscious. He checked the photo of Amin each member of the assault units carried, confirmed his identity, and shot the prostrate Afghan president point blank in the head.[88]

During the KGB assault, Sarwari and Gulabzoi remained hidden in a Soviet APC at a safe distance from the fighting. One KGB commando, Nikolai Berlev, recounted that after the battle, a "frightened and completely broken" Sarwari was escorted from the APC to identify Amin's body. Berlev wrote that Sarwari "cheered up almost at once" when he saw that Amin was dead.[89] Berlev's own account depicted Amin as fighting back from his second-floor study, dressed in an Adidas T-shirt and blue boxing shorts. According to Berlev, Amin, still armed, had bolted from the study when a grenade was tossed into the room and was instantly shot dead.

However Amin was finally killed by his supposed Soviet allies, he probably went down fighting, much like Daoud had the previous year. Amin was no stranger to violence. As long as he could stand, it is safe to assume he was firing back, expecting to die by the gun as he had lived by the gun.

Amin's immediate family was not subjected to the kind of gruesome mass executions that the PDPA had mercilessly administered to Daoud's family during the April 1978 coup. They did not, however, emerge unscathed from the Tajbeg battle. Two of Amin's sons were killed during the fighting. One, an eight-year-old boy, was shot in the chest. Amin's youngest daughter was wounded in the leg, and his wife, two older daughters, and a daughter-in-law were imprisoned at Pul-i-Charkhi. Foreign Minister Shah Wali's wife, one of the Afghan guests at the dinner, was reportedly killed while lying in a bed still unconscious from the poison attack.[90] In Moscow on December 27, the day of the attack on the Tajbeg Palace, Assadullah Amin, Amin's nephew, was taken from his hospital bed and incarcerated in the infamous Lafortova Prison.[91] Andropov later informed the Politburo that, at Karmal's request, he had been sent back to Afghanistan for trial. Karmal had both Abdullah (Amin's brother) and Assadullah executed at Pul-i-Charkhi.

One after the other, downtown Kabul government ministries were seized by Soviet forces without a fight. The government's Radio-Television Center, located next door to the American embassy, was an exception. The KGB operation to capture the facility had been meticulously planned by a Zenith commander, senior lieutenant Anatoly Ryabin, a trained engineer. Ryabin had made two visits to the center before the assault to reconnoiter. He then led the attack. Two platoons of Soviet paratroopers, accompanied by Watanjar, were to advance on the center from Kabul Airport and neutralize the eleven Afghan tanks and four APCs parked at the main entrance. Watanjar's task was to entice the Afghan tank crews and door guards to surrender without a fight, enter the building with a prerecorded speech by Karmal, and arrange for its broadcast from the radio station's studio.

Afghan employees inside the building saw Ryabin and a small fleet of Soviet vehicles arriving at the front door precisely at the moment the KGB explosion took out the Afghan telephone system. The commander of the Afghan guards radioed his superior at the 4th Armored Brigade at Pul-i-Charkhi for permission to allow Ryabin and those with him to enter the building, and permission was given. Several minutes later, the 4th Armored Brigade headquarters radioed back and ordered the commander to resist. Heavy fighting immediately broke out inside, on the street, and on the roof of the building. The Afghan tanks fired their machine guns at approaching Soviet paratroopers. Screaming in Pashto, Watanjar told the Afghan soldiers to cease fire, reminding them that he was a Pashtun from Paktiya. The tanks manned by Paktiya tribals obliged, while those occupied by soldiers from Kandahar, Nangarhar, Konar, and Balkh continued firing away.

Haji Sayed Daoud, a senior producer at Kabul Radio, was in the television station's soundproof cubicle with earphones on when the KGB commandos broke into the room, spraying it with bullets.[92] There were no Afghan guards or weapons in the room, only broadcasters and technicians. Several were immediately shot and killed standing or sitting at their desks. An Afghan engineer who had just returned that day from his honeymoon was shot in the back of the head, dying instantly. Daoud and others still alive hurriedly crawled under their desks. The commandos took all the center's employees into an empty, unheated room and forced them to lie face down on the floor. Outside the building, fighting still raged. Barrages of Soviet rockets fired from the Bala Hisar fortress destroyed the Afghan tanks and APCs defending the building.

At 8:00 p.m., while Soviet commandos and Afghan defenders battled for control of the Radio-Television Center, a prerecorded Karmal message broadcast from a transmitter at Soviet 40th Army headquarters in Termez began crowding into Radio Kabul frequencies. Karmal lauded Taraki, his longtime nemesis, as a religious shahid. He announced the destruction of the "bloody apparatus of Hafizulla Amin and his minions, these agents of American imperialism." Blending communism and Islamism, he called for an Islamic jihad to advance "the glorious April Revolution."[93] Meanwhile, the center's radio equipment continued to transmit prerecorded pro-Amin programs. Listeners contacted Afghan government officials to complain that they were hearing two different broadcasts over the same Radio Kabul frequency. They asked which version was accurate. The dueling Amin-Karmal radio broadcasts, Karmal's from Soviet soil, Amin's from Radio Kabul in the Afghan capital, continued until 9:00 p.m.

KGB commandos finally established control of the Radio-Television Center at about 10:30 p.m. At 2 a.m. on December 28, Watanjar forced a Radio Kabul broadcaster to read a prepared transcript proclaiming that Karmal was the new Afghan president, prime minister, and PDPA general secretary. Another prerecorded tape of Karmal speaking was then played. Karmal announced the names of the Parcham and Khalq members of Afghanistan's new government agreed to in Moscow: Sarwari as first vice president and deputy PDPA chief;

Keshtmand as second vice president; and Watanjar, Qadir, and Gulabzoi as members of the Revolutionary Council's "presidium."

After a pause of fifteen minutes, Radio Kabul declared that the government of Afghanistan "earnestly demands that the USSR render urgently, political, moral, and economic assistance, including military aid, to Afghanistan. The government of the USSR has accepted." Following yet another pause, Radio Kabul reported at 3:15 a.m. that "the revolutionary tribunal has sentenced to death Hafizulla Amin for the crimes he has committed against the noble people of Afghanistan." It informed its listeners that the sentence "has been carried out."[94]

At 9 a.m. on December 28, Watanjar assembled the Radio-Television Center's staff and their Japanese adviser in a conference room of the bullet-scarred building. He told them that they were allowed to go home and should not return until further notice. Senior Producer Haji Daoud and most other employees did not wait for the return-to-work notice. They packed up what belongings they could and fled down the Jalalabad road to Pakistan.

᪾

Soviet military and KGB forces had captured Kabul. Karmal would soon move into the presidential palace with his Soviet advisers and guards. But neither the Soviets nor Karmal controlled the countryside. More important, the Soviet leadership's assumption that the Karmal government supported by the 40th Army and the KGB would pacify Afghanistan was a fantasy. Amin was dead, but the Khalq-Parcham feud was not. As the Soviet Union would discover, Karmal sought foreign favor for personal reasons. His motives were devoid of ideology or sincere friendship with the Soviet Union.

In a 1991 press conference after the Soviet withdrawal from Afghanistan, Karmal announced: "I was against the Soviet presence here. I did not invite them here and eighty percent of my actions were against the Soviet invasion."[95]

CHAPTER 8

Green Dawn

A faint glow along the distant African rim of the Red Sea pierced the darkness. It was a little after five o'clock on the morning of November 20, 1979, at Mecca's Grand Mosque, Islam's holiest site. Mohammad Ibn Subeil, the elderly, white-bearded Saudi imam of the holy shrine—the muezzin[1]— was about to give morning prayers from one of seven towering minarets. Thousands of pilgrims clad in white robes began to stir in the courtyard below as the imam, honoring a tradition dating to the time of the Prophet, stared in the direction of the Kaaba[2] at the center of the sacred sanctuary. He began to chant aloud the ancient, sonorous melody of the Adhan[3] verses: "Allah is Great, I bear witness that there is no deity except Allah." His words drifted through the still morning air, above the mosque complex and over the nearby city of Mecca.

Suddenly, in the middle of the call to prayer, a frenzied young Saudi cleric wrested the microphone from Subeil's hand and pushed him aside. The man's wild, piercing eyes warned the imam away. Shouting into the microphone, the trespasser announced his name, Juhaiman bin Muhammad bin Sayyaf al-Otaibi. He called on Muslims to overthrow the ruling al-Saud royal family. He screamed that it was corrupt, polluted by westernization. The al-Sauds, he declared, had aligned themselves with Christians and Jews. They had left the path of Islam and lost their religious legitimacy to rule. The mosque's powerful loudspeaker carried Juhaiman al-Otaibi's condemnation of the Saud royal house for many miles in all directions. It rang in the ears of the thousands of pilgrims fleeing the Holy Sanctuary and the battle surely to come. The people of Mecca heard it. So, shortly, would the world.

Atop the mosque's minarets, Juhaiman al-Otaibi's followers fired down on army units attempting to scale the walls. Army tanks lunged against the mosque's thick wooden gates. But the tanks could not break the gates down. The army retreated. A highly embarrassed king, Khalid al-Saud, secretly contacted the French for advice on how to retake the holy sanctuary, one he had sworn to protect.

The Abdul Aziz al-Saud dynasty faced its biggest crisis since it established the modern Saudi state early in the twentieth century.

The Grand Mosque uprising took place only five weeks before Soviet KGB commandos and Afghan President Hafizullah Amin's Kharoti tribesmen fought to the death on the wooded slopes below Amin's palace. The two bloody contests, although separated by geography[4] and the composition of opposing forces, had much in common. The outcome of both battles was decided in the month of December 1979. In both cases the attackers espoused ideological justifications for their warfare. The Soviet commandos hastened the march of communism in the world. The Saudi religious extremist Juhaiman al-Otaibi was out to reclaim Islam from the al-Saud infidels ruling Saudi Arabia.

Ultimately, neither battle was about ideology. The KGB commandos attempting to kill Afghanistan's president were destroying an obstacle in the way of Soviet expansionism. Juhaiman and his accomplices[5] mobilized religious fanaticism to overthrow the Saudi government. They fought for power in the name of Islam.

Both battles influenced the course of world history. The Soviet assault on Amin's Tajbeg Palace unleashed a chain of events that weakened a mighty superpower and sped the end of the Cold War. The uprising in Mecca inspired a militant Islamic "awakening" in Saudi Arabia. It radicalized a generation of young Saudi devotees of the ultraconservative Saudi Wahhabi sect. An American writer later observed: "It is painfully clear: the countdown to September 11, to the terrorist bombings in London and Madrid, and to the grisly Islamist violence ravaging Afghanistan . . . all began on that warm November morning, in the shade of the Kaaba." In 2006, a retired Saudi military officer seemed to concur. Surveying the damage from an al-Qaeda terrorist strike in Riyadh, he dryly commented, "All the terrorists we see now are leftovers of Juhaiman."[6]

These separate comments by an American and a Saudi refer to the blending in the 1980s and 1990s of Juhaiman's radical Wahhabism and the inter-

MAP 8.1   THE KINGDOM OF SAUDI ARABIA

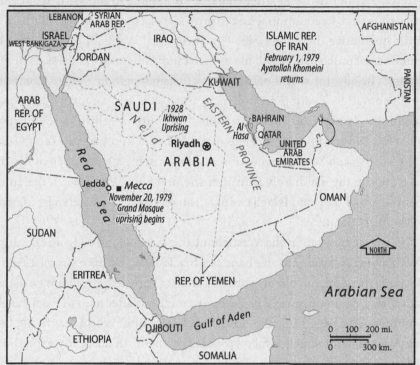

national militancy of the Muslim Brotherhood. After the Mecca uprising and the Soviet invasion of Afghanistan in December 1979, Saudi preachers and (mostly Egyptian) Muslim Brotherhood zealots carried this violent ideological hybrid to the Pakistani Frontier, where Pakistani military dictator Zia ul-Haq worked with Arabs and with Pakistani and Afghan extremists to inject the doctrine into the ranks of the Afghan Mujahidin movement.

Zia's military successors, with Saudi money, continued to fan the messianic ideology and operate the extremist training network on the Pakistani Frontier after the dictator's death in 1988. They created the Taliban in 1993 and assisted it to conquer most of Afghanistan. Today, the ISI, the Afghan Taliban, al-Qaeda, and Pakistani and Afghan fanatics still promote the ideology first brought to the Frontier in the early 1980s. Its natural offshoot of global terrorism poses an existential threat to the West, to moderate Islamic countries, and to the Saudi kingdom itself.

From the time of the Soviet withdrawal, bin Laden's main goals had been to overthrow the al-Saud dynasty, gain control of the Saudi state, and create a totalitarian political order stretching from Indonesia to southern Spain. His tactics had much in common with those used by Lenin and Stalin. Obfuscating the qualitative divide between the puritanical Wahhabi creed followed by millions of pious Saudis and his terrorist movement was at the core of his strategy. The absolutist Wahhabi branch of Islam taught in Saudi Arabia and carried abroad by Saudi petrodollars in the 1980s and 1990s made young Muslim minds especially susceptible to his political call to defend Islam against Muslim and non-Muslim enemies. Bin Laden's propaganda capitalized on the 1980–1989 Soviet occupation of Afghanistan, the presence of American troops in the Saudi holy land after the first Gulf War (1991), the 2003 U.S. invasion of Iraq, and Israeli confiscation of Palestinian land in Jerusalem and the West Bank.

The knowledge gap in the West about the cultural and religious context of Wahhabism played into the hands of bin Laden and his extremist Arab, Pakistani, and Afghan collaborators.[7] A similar knowledge gap long existed about Soviet communism and its deceptive methods after the 1917 Bolshevik Revolution. The West gradually closed that breach after World War II. In contrast, American intelligence failed to identify the birth and early expansion of Islamist militancy during the Soviet occupation of Afghanistan and in the decade that followed it.

In 1996, former CIA director and future defense secretary Robert Gates wrote that the CIA examined ways to increase fundamentalist Arab participation in the anti-Soviet Afghan war, "perhaps in the form of some sort of 'international brigade.' . . . We expected post-Soviet Afghanistan to be ugly, but never considered that it would become a haven for terrorists operating worldwide."[8] The surprise is that almost a decade after 9/11 the knowledge gap about the nature and strategy of radical Islamic groups and their creeds in the Muslim world persists.

Juhaiman al-Otaibi's 1979 Mecca uprising inflamed a sensitive rift in Islam between cleric and ruler as old as religion itself. Religious legitimacy to rule had been an eagerly sought commodity by kings and potentates in medieval Europe. It was granted or withheld by popes who claimed the ability to interpret the divine will of God as revealed in the Bible. Popes fielded their own army in the Italian Papal States and promised life in Paradise to Christian soldiers marching off to the anti-Muslim Crusades.[9] They excommunicated dissident emperors, kings, nobles, and wayward priests. During the sixteenth century, Protestant sects prospered and multiplied. In God's name, they fought Catholic rulers and each other. From 1559 to 1715 Europe remained in a nearly perpetual state of religious warfare.[10] In 1541, under John Calvin's leadership, the Calvinist city-state of Geneva rewrote its constitution and laws to conform to Calvin's literal interpretation of the Bible and theory of church domination of the state. The pope, kings, Calvinist firebrands, Anabaptists, and Anglicans wielded Christianity to expand their power, wealth, and territory.

The Renaissance and, above all, the anticlerical Enlightenment philosophers of the seventeenth and eighteenth centuries, stressing reason and science over dogma, delivered a fatal blow to institutionalized religion's control over European rulers and their organization of society. The spread of modern education, and the Western emphasis on Roman law, not religion, as the source of legal systems, led the trend in the West toward contemporary secular nationalism. Religion largely settled into the realm of personal faith, virtually separated from the functions of government. Christian extremists attempting to assert divine authority to enforce their will over others fell to the level of religious cults.

The popes and Protestant clergy had largely lost their claim to political prominence by the end of the sixteenth century. Islamic religious leaders in the Middle East did not. They stood for the Islamist integration of the temporal and the religious. On the one hand, they accepted that Islamic tradition prohibited rebellion against religiously observant rulers implementing Sharia, God's law; on the other, they held that only senior Islamic jurists trained in Koranic law could authoritatively interpret the Koran's divine text, issue the legal judgments known as *fatwas*, and determine whether or not a ruler was abiding by Sharia. In Islamic religious states such as present-day Saudi Arabia, this is still the case. Each Saudi monarch acceding to the throne reiterates the pledge "to adhere to the Koran, the Muslim holy book, as the country's constitution."[11] Thousands of senior clergy and laymen then line up to perform the ancient "Obedience" (Abaya) ritual, pledging loyalty to the ruler, "except in what would disobey God." After a Saudi king ascends to the throne, the jurists, the "Guardians of the Sharia," theoretically can decide whether or not he is truly implementing God's law. They contend that only learned ulema, not the ruler, have the authority of "binding and loosing" (*ab alhaq*) the community of believers by approving new rulers and removing them when they abandon Islam.[12]

The ability of senior clergy to deny Saudi kings religious legitimacy to rule ostensibly provides the Saudi religious establishment considerably more political influence than is held by clergy in the West—or, indeed, by clergy in any Muslim-populated state governed by civil law rather than Sharia. Accordingly, Saudi kings have found it necessary to guard their religious flanks. Juhaiman's call for the overthrow of the al-Saud dynasty, however, was vitiated by his low level of religious training. He was merely one of 50,000 preachers in the Saudi Kingdom, not a jurist entitled to issue fatwas. During the uprising, the chief mufti, the preeminent religious jurist in Saudi Arabia, held ultimate authority to question the al-Saud dynasty's legitimacy, and he sided with the government against Juhaiman, as we shall see.

Juhaiman al-Otaibi, Osama bin Laden, and a host of other contemporary Islamic revolutionaries with little or no religious training have often relied on the militant thirteenth-century jurist Taqi al-Din ibn Taymiyyah (1263–1328) to justify their violence. Ibn Taymiyyah stressed the obligation of all ulema to pronounce takfir* on rulers who abandoned the faith, a religious transgression punishable by death. He pronounced takfir against the thirteenth-century Mongolian invaders who had captured Baghdad and Damascus and converted to Islam, issuing fatwas to charge that they were religious imposters incapable of administering Sharia, and he declared jihad, "holy war," against the Mongolian armies unjustly occupying Muslim lands. The rebellion he inspired was demolished, but his militant doctrines were not. They provided a religious model for bin Laden and other radical Islamists calling for jihad against Western political, military, and cultural "invasions" of Muslim countries.

Ibn Taymiyyah was probably the most famous theologian in the ultraconservative Hanbali school of jurisprudence. He said Muslims must follow the traditions and practices of the Salaf-as-Saaleh, the "pious ancestors," the initial three generations of Islamic leaders who guided Islam through its first century of existence. The Hanbali school, founded by Ahmad ibn Hanbal of the ninth century, is one of four Sunni legal orders developed during the early

---

* In Sunni Islamic law, takfir is the act of excommunicating someone who professes Islam but has become an apostate. The maximum penalty is death.

centuries of Islam (the others are the Hanafi, Shafi'i, and Maliki schools). The different interpretations of Sharia among these four schools of law are as varied as interpretations of the Bible in Christianity, and similarly contextual.[13] The further Islam spread from the Arabian Peninsula, the more it accommodated Greek, Persian, and other influences. The Hanafi legal code became the most liberal and flexible. Important Hanafi jurists were from Persian-speaking backgrounds.

The differences between the Hanafi and Hanbali doctrines are key to understanding current tensions between moderate and conservative Islam in the Muslim world today. The more flexible Hanafi doctrine has far more adherents. It is tolerant of parliamentary lawmaking and politics expressed in elected bodies and tribal councils. Its founder, the scholar Abu Hanifa of the eighth century, preached the importance of *ijtihad* (independent reasoning) in order to adjust Islamic law to modern circumstances and advocated "the freedom to make new laws" to conform to changing times.[14] Rulers like the Ottoman caliphs[15] (1453–1924) preferred Abu Hanifa's less threatening, more pluralistic legal system in managing their multiethnic Muslim populations. In modern times, the Hanafi doctrine has dominated in the Muslim democracies of South Asia, where civil and Islamic law occasionally cohabitate in democratic constitutions.[16] Hanbali clergy, in contrast to those in the Hanafi tradition, believe that lawmaking should be done by religious jurists trained in Sharia, and that politics should be conducted in the mosques, not by elected legislators or presidents.[17]

☙

The first Saudi religious state emerged in 1744 in the desert heartland of Nejd, part of the vast, conservative bedouin center of the Arabian Peninsula. Mohammad bin Saud, who ruled the petty Kingdom of Diriyah, near present-day Riyadh, formed an alliance with a local Hanbali preacher, Sheikh Abd al-Wahhab. Saud controlled the state, the administrative machinery, and the army, Abd al-Wahhab the religious establishment. Their children intermarried, and the descendants of the two families continue to rule Saudi Arabia today.

Born in 1703, Abd al-Wahhab had studied at Hanbali schools in Mecca and Medina. He was heavily influenced by the militant jihadi writings of ibn Taymiyyah, and like ibn Taymiyyah he called for a return to Islam in its "pure" form, as it existed during the time of the Prophet and his companions. The doctrine of *tawhid* (the "oneness" of God) permeated every aspect of Abd al-Wahhab's version of Islam. His preaching reflected the bedouin culture's austere ways, and he taught separation from non-Muslims. Severe bedouin restrictions on women that were not mandated in the Koran or Sunnah became deeply entrenched in Wahhabism. Today, Wahhabism continues to undergird the religious and political legitimacy of the Saudi state.

Abd al-Wahhab insisted that superstition and the layers of foreign influence from Greek, Persian, and pagan sources be peeled away from Islam. He taught that all traces of rationality, science, art, and music not in the Koran and Sunnah were corrupt overlays on the original faith. All Muslims who did not practice the true faith were infidels or worse—apostates subject to takfir. He harshly criticized Sufi pantheism[18] and Shia visits to the tombs of saints as violations of God's oneness. There could be no co-eternals. Abd al-Wahhab ordered the Saudi kingdom's bedouin warriors to destroy all idolatrous tombs and shrines, including the tombs built for the Prophet and his wives and companions. Only God could be worshipped, not even his Messenger. Shia mosques in Mecca and Medina were also considered idolatrous and razed.[19]

Juhaiman al-Otaibi's religious revolt was the third major religious uprising against the al-Saud dynasty during Saudi Arabia's history. The first occurred after Abd al-Wahhab's death in 1792, when the al-Sheikh family used its religious leverage to reduce the Saud ruler's authority. Wahhabi fanatics destabilized the annual Haj pilgrimage to Mecca. They murdered Shia and Sufi pilgrims. They whipped or turned back pilgrims who were not appropriately clothed[20] or who conducted non-Wahhabi religious rituals. The violent interruption of the Haj reverberated through the Muslim world. The Ottoman caliph in Istanbul, himself sworn to protect the Muslim holy places, sent an army to destroy the Saudi state. It obliterated the Saud kingdom's base at Diriyah in 1818. Members of the al-Sheikh family fled or were executed. The reigning Saud monarch, Abdullah bin Saud, was taken to Istanbul and publicly beheaded.

In 1905, the alliance of the Saud and Sheikh clans was resuscitated by Abdul Aziz al-Saud. Wahhabism resumed its role as the official ideology and unifying bond of the Saudi state. Abdul Aziz's bedouin armies reconquered the Nejd. They went on to take the Hijaz, where the two holy cities of Mecca and Medina and Islam's two most sacred mosques are located, and nearly all of the rest of present-day Saudi Arabia. During the 1920s, Wahhabi zealotry again arose to endanger the al-Saud dynasty. This time, the religious threat to the monarchy came from the Ikhwan (Brotherhood), the most fanatical part of Abdul Aziz's bedouin army recruited from the deserts of Nejd. Abdul Aziz's priority of preserving his kingdom's stability clashed with the Ikhwan's Wahhabi vehemence. One of the most prominent Ikhwan tribal leaders was Juhaiman's grandfather.

During the 1920s, the Ikhwan bedouin communities constructed a "martial-pietistic"[21] infrastructure from which to wage holy war against Sunni Muslim infidels and Shia communities. It was a forerunner of the Islamist network built by Pakistan's ISI with Saudi and CIA funding along Pakistan's border with Afghanistan in the 1980s. The Ikhwan complex of madrassas and military training camps produced thousands of fighters eager to purify the Saudi state's newly conquered territories. The Ikhwan conducted raids against the Shia minority in the eastern Saudi province of Hasa bordering the Persian Gulf. They attacked and destroyed Shia tombs in the Shia holy city of Karbala, Iraq, including the venerated Shia shrine of the third Shia imam, the Prophet Mohammad's grandson Hussein.

In 1928, King Abdul Aziz's relations with the Ikhwan reached a breaking point when an Ikhwan fatwa openly accused him of refusing "to fulfill his duty . . . to spread and impose the Wahhabi faith and to restore Muslims to 'the correct path.'"[22] In 1929, the Ikhwan openly revolted. With the help of British warplanes, Abdul Aziz attacked and completely destroyed the Ikhwan movement.

The crushing of the Ikhwan gave the al-Saud royal house fifty years of respite from threats to its religious legitimacy—until the 1979 Mecca uprising. In 1932, Abdul Aziz formally proclaimed the establishment of the Kingdom of Saudi Arabia. He preserved the al-Saud partnership with the al-Sheikh clan but took steps to prevent future threats from the religious right. Concentrating absolute power in his own hands, Abdul Aziz made himself head of state and prime minister. He appointed all cabinet ministers as well as governors; the Saudi Grand Mufti;[23] members of the Senior Ulema Council, which the Grand Mufti chairs; the clerics on the Supreme Court; and the judges presiding over the lower religious courts of the kingdom. The king permitted no political parties or elections. He placed his sons and grandsons in the most influential government positions, including all of the power ministries, Defense, Interior, the National Guard, Intelligence, and Foreign Affairs. On his deathbed, he instructed that the succession proceed horizontally through his sons. Since then, the Saudi throne has been passed down through brothers and half-brothers. The succession process has operated well, with one exception,[24] through the reigns of five monarchs: Saud (1953–1964), Faisal (1964–1975), Khalid (1975–1982), Fahd (1982–2005), and Abdullah (2005–present).

ψ

The discovery of vast oil deposits in Saudi Arabia in the 1930s permitted Saudis, in the words of a future Saudi king, to go "from riding camels to driving Cadillacs" in one generation.[25] King Abdul Aziz and President Franklin D. Roosevelt's meeting on an American warship in the Red Sea in 1945 created an unwritten U.S.-Saudi alliance that continues today. The partnership basically exchanges American protection of the kingdom for Saudi oil exports to the United States and its allies.[26] Both sides benefit. The Saudis receive American security guarantees against external enemies as well as massive amounts of investment, technology, and expertise from the United States. The United States benefits from Saudi control over one-fourth of the world's known oil reserves, 13 percent of world oil production, and two-thirds of its spare production capacity.

Since Abdul Aziz's death in 1953, his sons have assiduously cultivated their relations with the Wahhabi ulema, the biggest potential challenge to their survival. The royal family grants the ulema lavish funding and a quasi-monopoly over the kingdom's sprawling religious network of 17,000 mosques[27] and educational institutions. Cabinet ministers chosen from senior ulema ranks supervise the ministries of education, religious, and *dawa* (preaching) affairs; the Haj; and higher education. The Saudi religious establishment trains judges to apply Sharia. It manages TV, radio, and Internet websites that propagate religion at home and abroad, and Saudi courts mete out punishments that conform to a literal interpretation of the Koran. Those guilty of blasphemy are fined, lashed, and imprisoned. Thievery is punished by amputation of a hand. Murderers and perpetrators of *fitna* (anarchy) are beheaded. Segregation of women is rigorously enforced: They cannot drive, they cannot leave home without wearing a *chador* (head-to-toe black cloak), and they must be attended by a male relative. Bearded *muttawa*, quasi-vigilantes, roam cities and towns looking for offenders of the strict Wahhabi legal code. They report to the Commission on the Promotion of Virtue and Suppression of Vice, a government-funded arm of the official religious establishment, which draws its mandate from a Koranic verse:

> And from among you there should be a party who invite to good and enjoin what is right and forbid the wrong.

The religious police, which operated in essentially the same way under the Afghan Taliban from 1996 until October 2001, enforced restrictions on women,[28] located and destroyed alcohol, and prohibited "un-Islamic" behavior.

Abd al-Wahhab's al-Sheikh clan has remained loyal to the al-Saud dynasty since Abdul Aziz's reign. In a 2004 speech delivered as 2 million Muslims were gathering for the Haj pilgrimage, Grand Mufti Abdullah al-Sheikh, the supreme religious leader in the kingdom, announced that "seeking to overthrow existing legitimate regimes is forbidden." He went on to "praise the leaders of the Kingdom of Saudi Arabia," warning that "God says the penalty of those that fight God and his prophet and spread violence and terror is to be killed, crucified or have their hands and legs chopped off."[29]

Juhaiman al-Otaibi's 1979 Mecca uprising exploited growing resentment in the kingdom to the Western presence in the Muslim holy land. The Wahhabi clergy and the large, pious, Saudi middle class detested the influx of tens of thousands of Western oil specialists and their families brought into Saudi Arabia to develop and operate the oil industry. Non-Muslim Western families shopped in urban malls and the covered *souks* (bazaars). Hundreds of unveiled Western women drove and walked unaccompanied on city streets and in airports. The conspicuous presence of westerners violated a Koran-based injunction to "expel the Jews and the Christians from the Arabian Peninsulas, until only Muslims remain there,"[30] one that Juhaiman al-Otaibi and later Osama bin Laden would often repeat.

The opulent lifestyles of the royal descendants of Abdul Aziz also stirred religious and popular scorn. King Abdul Aziz had sired forty-seven sons by twenty-two different mothers, and by 1980, the size of the royal family exceeded 7,000.[31] To maintain harmony among royal family members, the thousands of princes enjoying the "Royal Highness" mantle were granted handsome allowances, high government positions, and palaces. The princes' affluence provoked ridicule among ordinary Saudis and clerics living in communities outside the posh suburbs in Riyadh and Jeddah where most princes reside, and criticism was especially rife in the lower and middle ranks of the Wahhabi ulema.

Juhaiman's revolt shocked the Saudi monarchy. It also threatened the position of the senior Wahhabi "court clergy." Younger ulema began openly criticizing Chief Mufti bin Baz, a direct descendant of Abd al-Wahhab, and the Council of Senior Ulema that he chaired. They questioned whether bin Baz and the Council of Senior Ulema were truly fulfilling their responsibility to ensure that the government was ruling in accordance with Sharia and resisting a Western cultural offensive under way in the Saudi holy land.[32]

Three days after the occupation of the Grand Mosque, Grand Mufti bin Baz's council closed ranks with the monarchy against the rebels. It issued a fatwa giving the government religious legitimacy to enter the Grand Mosque in Mecca and crush Juhaiman's revolt. The two texts it referenced were:

> But fight them not at the Holy Mosque unless they first fight you there. But if they fight you, slay them. Such is the reward of those who suppress the faith.
>
> He who comes to you while you are unanimous in your opinion and wants to divide you and disperse you, strike off his neck.[33]

The first is from the Koran; the second is a hadith. The fatwa lashed out at Juhaiman and his followers for violating the holiest site in Islam and urged the government to take effective measures, including military ones, if necessary, to reclaim the mosque.[34]

Armed with this religious sanction against the insurgents, the Saudi military attacked the stadium-sized holy sanctuary on November 24. American-made M-113 personnel carriers thundered through a hole blasted in the mosque wall, their .50-caliber machine guns blazing. Hundreds of Saudi soldiers followed the armored vehicles into the sacred compound. Juhaiman and his men fought back with automatic weapons, pistols, grenades, and daggers. After inflicting heavy casualties, they retreated into the ancient underground maze of dark tunnels, tiny passages, and cisterns beneath the Grand Mosque. The government's offensive stalled for a week amid man-to-man combat conducted in complete darkness beneath the holy sanctuary. Juhaiman and his fighters ambushed Saudi troops from hidden passageways and wall niches. The dead lay where they fell; the wounded cried out for water and food. CIA-provided tear gas worsened their plight,[35] but the rebels pressed wet cloths against their faces and descended further underground. The gas followed the air currents upward.

Responding to King Khalid's request for advice, the French government sent a three-man unit of the elite antiterrorist Groupe d'Intervention de la Gendarmerie Nationale (GIGN) to Saudi Arabia. The Saudi military positioned the unit at a military base near Mecca. There, the French commandos trained Saudi security forces in the use of the gas dichlorobenzylidene-malononitrile, the same chemical later used by Russian forces during the 2002 Chechen hostage incident in Moscow. The Saudi gas attack surprised, debilitated, and demoralized the rebels, and on December 4, the last remnant, including Juhaiman, surrendered.[36] In early January 1980, after the Council of Senior Ulema issued another fatwa supporting the government, Juhaiman and sixty-two of his followers were condemned to death by an Islamic court. They were taken to eight different cities (Juhaiman to Mecca) around the country and publicly beheaded.[37]

Juhaiman was dead, but his radical Wahhabi ideology advocating total Islamization through violence was spreading. Two momentous developments during the chaotic month of December 1979, however, gave the al-Saud dynasty valuable opportunities to divert the rising discontent against the monarchy into other channels.

One was the Soviet invasion of Afghanistan. The Soviet Union's attack on its small Muslim neighbor offered the royal family space to project itself as the defender of Islam against a non-Muslim aggressor. The second was Ayatollah Khomeini's Iranian Revolution. Khomeini charged that the al-Sauds were no less an American implant in the Islamic religious cosmos than the shah he had just overthrown. Shrill Iranian radio broadcasts to Saudi Arabia in Arabic enjoined the "revolutionary masses" in the kingdom to "resist the government" and announced that "the ruling regime in Saudi Arabia wears Muslim clothing, but it actually represents a luxurious, frivolous, shameless way of life, robbing funds from the people and squandering them."[38]

Khomeini's propaganda blitz excoriating the American "Great Satan," the Soviet "Lesser Satan," and Israel appealed to many Muslims in Saudi Arabia and the broader Muslim world. But it was Khomeini's pan-Islamic reach across the ancient Shia-Sunni chasm that most alarmed the Saudi monarch, the Wahhabi clergy, and Saudi Arabia's conservative Sunni population.

The Wahhabi establishment considered Shia to be infidels. Shiism was recognized as Iran's official religion in Khomeini's new constitution. The Shia devotion of ayatollahs as quasi-deities and the Shia worship of saints and the shrines of holy men violated the Wahhabi tawhid emphasis on the oneness of God. The Saudi government and the Wahhabi ulema interpreted Khomeini's promise to "export Islam everywhere"—"the same version of Islam which is currently in power in our country"[39]—as a dangerous Shia assault on Sunni Islam. Iranian Shia pilgrims in Mecca attempting to distribute photos of Ayatollah Khomeini and pamphlets praising the Iranian Revolution fought pitched battles with Saudi security forces.

On November 28, 1979, in the midst of the Grand Mosque crisis in Mecca, violent pro-Khomeini demonstrations erupted in the oil-rich, Shia-minority eastern province of Hasa in Saudi Arabia. The demonstrators carried posters of Khomeini and called for more government aid to the province. The Saudi government rushed 20,000 troops to Hasa to restore order. Afterward, Saudi engineers constructed a causeway connecting the kingdom with the small island nation of Bahrain to facilitate its ability to deploy troops there if the Sunni ruling house on the atoll was threatened by the Shia-majority population. Meanwhile, Saudi propaganda trumpeted the dangers of Iranian and Shia expansion into Sunni lands and highlighted Sunni-Shia religious differences. When the bloody Iran-Iraq conflict broke out in September 1980, Saudi Arabia rushed to fund Saddam Hussein's war machine with tens of billions of dollars. Saudi rhetoric characterized the conflict as a war between all Arabs and Iran, Shia and Sunni. Meanwhile, American naval vessels based at the Saudi port of Bahrain kept Iran's military force contained above the Straits of Hormuz.

☙

From the time Abd al-Wahhab preached two centuries ago, Wahhabism had exhibited an insular nature rooted in the bedouin tribal communities of the Nejd. During the 1970s, hundreds of Arab Muslim Brotherhood activists from the Middle East and North Africa, fleeing police dragnets in their own countries, were given sanctuary in Saudi Arabia. They infused a militant internationalist current into the Juhaiman-sparked "awakening." The Ikhwanis, also known as Muslim brothers, were mainly Arabs from educated, middle-class backgrounds. Some, such as the rotund, bespectacled Egyptian physician Ayman al-Zawahiri, came from privileged families. Zawahiri and Abdullah Yusuf Azzam, a Palestinian Islamic scholar, were two of the better-known Ikhwani exiles who sought refuge in Saudi Arabia. They were both destined to play important roles in radicalizing the Afghan jihad. Zawahiri would eventually team up with Osama bin Laden to launch terrorist attacks against the United States and other countries around the world.

Azzam was born in the Palestinian town of Jenin in 1941. He fled to Jordan during the 1967 Arab-Israeli War and then moved on to Cairo. He received master's and doctoral degrees in Islamic studies at Cairo's ancient and prestigious al-Azhar University in the early 1970s. In Cairo Azzam also joined the Muslim Brotherhood and mixed with other Ikhwanis, notably Zawahiri, who had obtained a degree in pharmacology in 1974 and a master's in surgery in 1978 from Cairo University.

Zawahiri was a hard-core Ikhwani from an early age. He joined the Brotherhood at fourteen and became active in the violent fringe of the organization. While in Egypt, Azzam and Zawahiri interacted with the blind Egyptian sheikh Omar Abdel Rahman, the organizer of the first attack on the Twin Towers in 1993. Future Afghan Mujahidin leaders Rabbani and Sayyaf attended al-Azhar roughly at the same time as Azzam. They, too, became enthusiastic Afghan proponents of the Brotherhood's doctrine. Rabbani, Sayyaf, Azzam, and the blind sheikh would come together again, along with bin Laden, in Peshawar during the 1980s.

The Saudi government and Wahhabi clergy gave the Muslim Brothers a warm welcome in the kingdom. The government's one condition was that the Muslim Brotherhood avoid involvement in Saudi domestic politics. Political parties were not allowed in the kingdom. The Brotherhood honored that condition, concentrating instead on proselytizing Saudi youth. Some went into business and the Saudi media. Many, including Abdullah Azzam, obtained positions in Saudi religious universities and high schools. Thousands of Saudi students became their pupils. In classrooms and in the textbooks they wrote, the Muslim Brotherhood exiles melded rigid Wahhabism with the Muslim Brotherhood philosophy of Sayyid Qutb, the Brotherhood's most prominent theorist. The two doctrines—Wahhabism and Qutbism—strategically reinforced each other.

In his writings, Qutb advocated obligatory armed jihad against nonobservant Muslims as well as non-Muslims. His concept of offensive jihad went beyond the defensive war justified in the Koran.[40] Qutb maintained that the West's imperialism, and its espousal of nationalism, secularism, and democracy, were designed to prevent the unity of the Islamic *umma*. He championed the revival of the Muslim caliphate stretching from Spanish-occupied Andalusia to Indonesia.[41]

Azzam, Zawahiri, and Rahman settled in the Jeddah area and coordinated their proselytizing with Mohammad Qutb, Sayyid Qutb's brother, who taught at Mecca's Umm al-Qura University,[42] a breeding ground of radical Wahhabi and Ikhwani activity. Zawahiri worked as a pharmacist in a local medical clinic and spent time at the Jeddah headquarters of the World Assembly of Muslim Youth, a quasi-governmental missionary organization established to propagate Wahhabism around the world.

Azzam lectured at Jeddah's prestigious Abdulaziz University. He taught his students that jihad should be considered the sixth pillar of Islam. Participating in legitimate jihads in defense of the faith, he insisted, was a moral requirement for Muslims.[43] Azzam also linked the Palestinian jihad against Israeli occupation of Palestine and the Soviet invasion of Afghanistan in a fatwa he issued after the Soviet Army attacked Afghanistan. His fatwa's promotion of an Afghan Islamist state ruled by Sharia did not conform to Afghanistan's pre-communist political order, the moderate Hanafi religious code prevailing in Afghanistan at that time, or to the tolerant Sufi Islam historically practiced by most Afghans.

Azzam's fatwa gave near-term priority to the Afghan over the Palestinian jihad. He envisioned an Islamist victory in the Afghan jihad as a stepping stone to an Islamist victory in the Palestinian jihad: "Whoever can, from among the Arabs, fight jihad in Palestine, then he must start there," he wrote. "And, if he is not capable, then he must set out for Afghanistan. For the rest of the Muslims, I believe they should start their jihad in Afghanistan. It is our opinion that we should begin with Afghanistan before Palestine."[44]

During his stay in Saudi Arabia, Azzam attracted the respect and friendship of many senior Wahhabi clerics, including Chief Mufti bin Baz. One of

Azzam's students at Abdulaziz University was Osama bin Laden, then, reportedly, a shy, impressionable, thoroughly observant Wahhabi. Bin Laden's father, Mohammad bin Laden, was a fabulously wealthy owner of a construction firm in Saudi Arabia who ultimately sired at least fifty-four children.[45] His mother was a teenage Syrian, one of the wives whom Mohammad bin Laden married and divorced in order to remain within the four-wife limit imposed by Islamic law. When Azzam and bin Laden met, the latter had already been inducted into the Brotherhood by a Syrian Ikhwani, one of his high-school teachers in Jeddah.[46] Like other Saudi students drawn to the Brotherhood, he read deeply into Qutbism and the writings of ibn Taymiyyah and other militant Muslim theologians. He attended lectures in Jeddah given by Mohammad Qutb. Azzam and bin Laden forged a close teacher-student, mentor-apprentice bond in Saudi Arabia that would later flourish and then fall apart in Pakistan.

The December 25–28, 1979, Soviet attack on Afghanistan could not have come at a better time for the beleaguered Saudi King Khalid and his brothers. Juhaiman and his group were still holding out in the Grand Mosque cellars, and Shia riots rocked the province of Hasa, when the Soviet Army crossed the Afghan border. The Saud monarchy moved quickly to burnish its image of defending Islam, to contain Iran, to repair relations with the large Saudi religious establishment beyond the court clergy, and to strengthen Saudi-American cooperation.

Soothing the religious clergy was the most urgent requirement after the Grand Mosque was recaptured. To accomplish this task, the al-Sauds mobilized the most potent weapon at their disposal—money. Since the discovery of oil in the kingdom, the family had become skilled at distributing revenue from oil sales to ward off threats and to gain support.

To co-opt dissidents in the religious establishment, the government funded programs that further tightened the Wahhabi clergy's grip on education. Saudi rulers initiated a lavishly funded Wahhabi missionary offensive that reached more than eighty countries around the world, including Pakistan and Afghanistan. The vehicles were Saudi "charities." A number of these, notably the Muslim World League (MWL), had been established earlier by royal decree. King Khalid and his brothers personally supported the creation of new charities run by the Wahhabi ulema. The MWL, with an executive committee chaired by Chief Mufti bin Baz and including government ministers, remained the largest. Operating in some sixty countries, the organization built hundreds of overseas mosques, financed Islamic universities and madrassas, sponsored scholarships for study in the kingdom's religious institutions, and distributed books and literature propagating ultraconservative Wahhabism.

New royal decrees created affiliates of the MWL: the International Islamic Relief Organization (IIRO), the World Assembly of Muslim Youth (WAMY), and the al Haramain Islamic Foundation. Aside from charities linked to the Saudi government,[47] thousands of private Saudi charities, mosques, and individual Saudi citizens added to the massive increase in the flow of Saudi wealth abroad.[48]

By radio, television, and word of mouth, Mujahidin shouts of *Allah Akbar*, reports of Soviet atrocities against Afghans, and tales of Mujahidin heroism while fighting the Soviet Army resonated through Saudi mosques, palaces, and homes. Supporting Afghan holy warriors to defeat the Soviet Union was the main engine driving the massive flow of Saudi cash into Pakistan and many other countries around the world. The royal family and the Wahhabi establishment gave liberally to the four radical Sunni party leaders in the resistance, all of whom were in Pakistan and had been favored by Zia ul-Haq. The two extremist Ghilzai Pashtuns, Gulbuddin Hekmatyar and Abdul Rasoul Sayyaf, received most of the funds. Burhanuddin Rabbani and Mawlawi Yunus Khalis, another extremist leader chosen by Zia, were also supported.

No Saudi money went to Afghan Shia, and only token amounts went to the three main Sufi party leaders in Peshawar—Sibghatullah Mojaddedi, Sayyid Ahmad Gailani, and Mawlawi Mohammad Nabi Mohammadi. The distribution of resources conformed to the Saudi strategy to build a hostile Sunni wall around Shia Iran. Saudi-supported Iraqi armies pressed Iran from the west; the American fleet stood watch from the south; and the Afghan Sunni Mujahidin extremists and Zia's Pakistan formed a pro-Saudi radical Sunni barrier against Iranian eastward expansion.

Saudi funding for the anti-Soviet Afghan jihad moved through two pipelines. One was managed by Prince Turki al-Faisal, the nephew of the king and head of the kingdom's external intelligence agency, the General Intelligence Directorate (GID). Most of the aid Turki managed was integrated into the CIA's covert weapons program. The Saudi government matched the American contribution dollar for dollar. The CIA purchased the weapons and handled the transportation logistics until the cargo was transferred to the ISI in Pakistan. Turki and Yusef Motabbakani, the Saudi ambassador in Islamabad, distributed millions more in cash to radical Sunni Mujahidin politicians, ulema, and commanders in Pakistan who advocated a future Afghanistan ruled by Sharia.

The second "private" Saudi pipeline splintered into innumerable public and private charities and individual donors. It was much larger, though no one ever knew how large, given the complete lack of oversight by any government entity. The Muslim Brotherhood's infiltration of all of the major charitable bodies gave the Ikhwani operatives access to both ends of this pipeline. With their hand on the spigot at the receiving end in Peshawar, they funneled a large percentage of Saudi wealth to extremist Mujahidin groups on the Pakistani Frontier.

Many of the Saudi charities' offices in Pakistan and around the world were directly under Ikhwani control. An investigation by an American with the support of the Saudi government after 9/11 concluded the following:

> Very senior Saudis privately admit that the Saudi Ministry of the Interior, Saudi Foreign Ministry, and Saudi intelligence failed to properly characterize many of the "Islamic" causes that have received Saudi money. Even funds transferred to very reputable causes like the Saudi Red Crescent seem to have been misused in some cases. The Muslim World League is a heavily funded group whose missionary efforts are reported to have moved money to elements of Al Qaida and different extremists groups like [Sheikh Omar's] Gamiat Islamiya and the [Zawahiri-led] Islamic Jihad in Egypt, and Abu Sayyaf in the Philippines. Money also went to causes with hardline or extremist elements like the Muslim brotherhood in Egypt and Jordan or Hamas in the Gaza.[49]

Saudi control over the recipients of Saudi funds inside Pakistan ranged between weak and nonexistent. Nor did private Saudi donors have a say in where the money went. Pakistani President Zia and the ISI made those decisions, and they devoted a major portion of both Saudi and American aid to the construction of a sprawling complex of madrassas, military bases, training camps, mosques, Saudi charities, and weapons warehouses in northern Pakistan along the Afghan border. At the heart of this complex were thousands of madrassas educating Afghan children—some of the 3 million refugees in camps near the Afghan border. The madrassas gave one to two years of madrassa indoctrination to thousands of young Afghans, followed by military training. At that point, they were sent across the Afghan border to confront the Soviet Army.

Azzam, Zawahiri, and Rahman joined the parade of Saudi Wahhabi radicals, ordinary Saudi citizens, and Ikhwanis traveling to Pakistan to join the Afghan jihad in the 1980s. The Saudi government encouraged the outflow. Saudi Airlines granted 75 percent discounts on air travel to Pakistan, and at one point the Pakistani embassy in Riyadh reported issuing two hundred visas a day.[50] The rush of Saudi religious zealots to Pakistan and Afghanistan relaxed the pressure on the royal family from domestic religious radicals. Saudi religious extremists instead pursued martyrdom in Afghanistan. Indeed, the royal family probably shared their aspirations.

In Peshawar, Muslim Brothers staffing Saudi charities coordinated with the ISI, the Pakistani Muslim Brotherhood affiliate Jamaat-i Islami, and radical Mujahidin personalities, especially Gulbuddin Hekmatyar. Abdullah Azzam moved to Islamabad in 1981 to join the faculty of the Saudi-funded Islamic University there. In 1984, he relocated to Peshawar and opened a "Services Bureau." Bin Laden made frequent trips to Peshawar to assist with the bureau, which received Arab jihadis arriving from abroad, provided orientation, and sent the newcomers on to extremist Mujahidin and independent Arab military groups inside Afghanistan. Azzam and bin Laden coordinated closely with Zia ul-Haq's ISI office in Peshawar. Zia himself kept in touch with influential Saudis in the kingdom, including Chief Mufti bin Baz.[51]

Bin Laden's brother-in-law, Mohammad Jamal Khalifa, headed the Muslim World League office in Peshawar during the mid-1980s. In 1988, he moved to Manila and opened a branch office of the World Assembly of Muslim Youth. He made the charity a front for bin Laden's terrorist operations in the Philippines and Asia. Al-Qaeda operatives, including Khalid Sheikh Mohammed, mastermind of the 9/11 attacks, and his nephew Ramzi Yusuf, traveled to Manila in the early 1990s to help Khalifa strengthen al-Qaeda networks in Southeast Asia and plan terrorist attacks in the region.

A Western correspondent wrote a month after 9/11 that the export of Wahhabi radicals to Afghanistan "may have bought the Saudi royal family an extra

25 years in avoiding its own home-grown Muslim extremists." The breathing spell could not continue indefinitely. On May 13, 2003, three al-Qaeda suicide bombers, driving vehicles packed with explosives and backed up by gunmen, some wearing Saudi National Guard uniforms, simultaneously attacked three residential areas in the Saudi capital. The attack killed thirty-five people, including eight Americans. Many more were injured. Saudi authorities subsequently seized more than two hundred suspected al-Qaeda members and over twenty tons of weapons and explosives. "This was an attack on the royal family. . . . That is the harsh reality," a Saudi official lamented.[52]

The 2003 attack was followed by a crackdown on religious dissidents in the kingdom. The government arrested hundreds of imams, including three who spoke out in support of the suicide bombers.[53] Al-Qaeda continued its offensive against the Saudi monarchy after the 2003 bombing, targeting Saudi government buildings, U.S. military facilities, and royal family members. Some attacks have succeeded; others have been preempted by Saudi intelligence. In 2009, an al-Qaeda group based in Yemen launched cross-border raids into Saudi Arabia. That same year, in August, an al-Qaeda suicide bomber attempted to assassinate a senior prince in the royal family, one of King Abdullah's nephews.

Thus, thirty-one years after Juhaiman's beheading, the al-Saud dynasty finds itself confronting yet another militant religious challenge to its ruling legitimacy—one that it helped to foster at birth, one that it must quell to survive.

CHAPTER 9

Insubordinate Puppets

An Afghan magazine editor's comment to a Soviet KGB officer, after the Soviet invasion:

> *Amin was hated, but the arrival of foreign troops in Kabul and other parts of the country brings no joy to Afghans. . . . The inhabitants of Afghanistan consider that it would be a good thing for the Soviet troops, having done their job, to return to the USSR before their presence begins to make Afghans feel hostile.*[1]

Afghan energy minister and anti-Taliban Mujahidin commander Ismael Khan, speaking to an Afghan audience in Herat Province on October 2, 2008:

> *Foreign forces must not remain for long in Afghanistan, and they must not think they are permanent guests in our country.*[2]

"They've already repeated all of our mistakes," Russian ambassador Zamir Kabulov explained to a Western journalist in Kabul in October 2008. He added, "Now they're making mistakes of their own, ones for which we do not own the copyright."[3] Kabulov was right in some important respects. From 1980 to 1986, the Soviets pressed a policy best described as Sovietization of Afghan institutions and governing processes. After that approach failed and the Soviet Politburo decided in 1986 to withdraw from Afghanistan, Moscow shifted to a policy of "Afghanization." That term is familiar to Americans today as NATO moves toward troop drawdowns in the second half of 2011. Other buzzwords associated with the Soviet Afghanization strategy in the late 1980s also generate ominous echoes today: "capacity building" to enable a weak, unpopular Afghan government to take direct control of Afghan civil and military institutions and prosecute the war to a successful conclusion; a "reconciliation" strategy to split the insurgency and attract insurgent moderates into a power-sharing arrangement; and frantic diplomacy to convince foreign supporters of the insurgency, particularly Pakistan, to cease interference in Afghan internal affairs. Albeit to a far lesser degree and severity, the Soviet interagency disputes have been repeated by U.S. military, intelligence, and diplomatic agencies in Afghanistan; so has the pattern of Afghan faction leaders exploiting the interagency differences to strengthen their own positions against rivals. The Soviets were never able to subordinate the conflictive agency strategies on the ground into one integrated policy.[4]

There are, of course, valid comparisons that can be made between the nine-year occupation of Afghanistan by the Soviet Union in the 1980s and the decade-plus heavy involvement in Afghanistan by the United States and its coalition partners after September 11, 2001. Yet, in fundamental ways, the comparison is misleading.

The Brezhnevian Politburo, in the words of one of its members at the time, "envisioned Afghanistan as a 'second Mongolia' which would leap from feudalism to socialism" in one bound with the help of the Soviet Army and Communist Party.[5] There was no basis for this fantastical assumption in Afghan history and culture. The Afghan communists before and after the Soviet invasion were always a tiny fringe element on the extreme edge of the Afghan political spectrum.

The Soviet invasion of Afghanistan, moreover, was a blatant imperialistic act. The American military intervention was prompted by al-Qaeda's attack on the American homeland from Afghanistan. If 9/11 had not occurred, the United States would not have attacked al-Qaeda and the Taliban. Virtually the entire world opposed the Soviet invasion and the Soviet attempt to install a communist regime in Afghanistan. The overwhelming majority of the international community, including Russia, has supported the U.S.-led overthrow of the Taliban and the American-led coalition's attempt to assist Afghan stabilization and reconstruction.

ψ

On December 27, 1979, as the fighting in Kabul was winding down, the Soviet government sent a top-secret cable to all Soviet ambassadors abroad. The instructions ordered the ambassadors to immediately visit the head of state or the official acting for him in the countries where they were posted to explain why the Soviet Union had sent "a limited military contingent to Afghanistan to carry out missions requested by the Afghan government." The ambassadors' awesome task was to persuade their host governments that the Afghan leadership had requested Soviet assistance and that the change in Afghan leaders was done by Afghans alone. The Soviet envoys were told to assure that "the leaders of the government of Afghanistan have turned to the Soviet Union for aid and assistance in the struggle against foreign aggression." The USSR had "responded to this request . . . with approval." The message cited the 1978 Treaty of Friendship with Afghanistan and the UN Charter's allowance for individual and collective self-defense to legitimize the dispatch of Soviet troops.[6]

A more detailed top-secret telegram was simultaneously sent to "friendly" communist parties abroad from the Soviet Communist Party. It condemned slain Afghan president Hafizullah Amin for "violations of elementary norms of legality," "widespread repression," "impermissible acts," and "terror against honest persons devoted to the cause of the revolution." The document railed against "foreign reactionary forces," including the CIA and the "Beijing leadership." Without mentioning the KGB's control of Amin's overthrow from start to finish, the telegram elliptically declared, "There have been found forces which have risen decisively against the regime of H. [Hafizullah] Amin, removed him from power, and created new governing bodies for the Party and the country." The message gave unearned praise to Babrak Karmal's leadership qualities, predicting that "such a leadership will facilitate the strengthening of the People's Democratic Party of Afghanistan."[7]

The Soviet invasion triggered withering criticism from governments and media around the world. Foreign leaders and news outlets ridiculed Soviet propaganda and diplomatic explanations of the invasion. At an emergency United Nations General Assembly Special Session convened in January 1980 to debate the Soviet invasion, speaker after speaker mocked Soviet justifications for marching into Afghanistan. The Soviet delegation was repeatedly asked why the legitimate, internationally recognized president of Afghanistan would invite Soviet forces into the country in order to kill himself, murder the head of the Afghan Army, and shoot or arrest most of the Afghan cabinet members. Media commentators called attention to the overlapping December 27 broadcasts by Radio Kabul, one from a clandestine transmitter in the Soviet Union relaying Karmal's taped announcements, and one from Amin's government. A State Department release to the media scorned Soviet accusations that Amin was a secret CIA agent, asking "why a CIA agent would have sought to impose a Marxist regime upon his country as Amin did." The release sarcastically recalled that it was Brezhnev and Kosygin, not President Carter, who had congratulated Amin on his "election" as Afghanistan's president after Amin had killed Taraki.[8]

In a United Nations General Assembly vote on January 14, 104 countries approved a resolution condemning the intervention in Afghanistan. The resolution called for the "immediate, unconditional, and total withdrawal of the foreign troops from Afghanistan."[9] India was among the delegations that abstained. Eighteen voted against the resolution, including the Soviet Union, Afghanistan, the three Soviet republics, and Soviet client states in Eastern Europe and the Third World.[10]

The Soviet invasion of Afghanistan strengthened an evolving coalition of anti-Soviet major world power centers. The strategic grouping, consisting of the United States, China, Western Europe, and Japan, rejected Soviet claims that its vault over the Hindu Kush was defensive, aimed at protecting the USSR's southern border. The United States interpreted the movement of Soviet power toward Indian Ocean sea lanes and Persian Gulf oil as offensive. President Carter told a group of congressmen that if the Soviets were not deterred in Afghanistan, they would "move again and again until they reached warm water ports or until they acquired control over a major portion of the world's oil supplies." A week after the Soviet invasion, U.S. Defense Secretary Harold Brown traveled to China to strengthen Sino-American defense cooperation. After his visit, Brown announced that the two countries had "taken big steps in strategic relations."[11]

In Muslim countries, Friday sermons at mosques appealed for support to Afghan Mujahidin warriors defending the faith against godless communism.

A meeting of the thirty-five-member Organization of the Islamic Countries (OIC), scheduled for January 28, 1980, was shifted from Singapore to Islamabad to project Islamic solidarity behind Pakistan and Afghanistan. The conference declared that Muslim governments would not recognize the Karmal regime and demanded a Soviet withdrawal.

Two days after the Soviet invasion, Khomeini's new Islamic government of Iran announced: "Because Afghanistan is a Moslim country and a neighbor of Iran, the military intervention of the government of the Soviet Union . . . is considered a hostile measure not only against the people of the country but against all Moslims of the world." In a blunt letter to Gromyko, the Iranian foreign minister asserted, "Your utterances are socialistic while your deeds are imperialistic."[12]

Meanwhile, Saudi Arabia's King Khalid ordered the establishment of a "private" committee under his brother, Prince Salman, governor of Riyadh Province, to raise funds for the Mujahidin. The U.S. embassy in Saudi Arabia reported that a fatwa issued by Chief Mufti bin Baz authorized the payment of zakat to the Afghan "freedom fighters."[13] The Saudi government agreed to match the American covert funding for the Mujahidin begun by the Carter administration in July 1979 and substantially increased by President Ronald Reagan after he took office in January 1981.

In the months after the Soviet invasion, the American and British governments attempted to convince the Soviet Union to revive Afghanistan's buffer status in Central Asia. The State Department and National Security Council staff members proposed offering Moscow Western guarantees of Afghanistan's neutrality if the Soviets withdrew their army. On February 9, 1980, the European Community foreign ministers, led by British Foreign Secretary Lord Carrington, proposed a "bloc-free" neutral Afghanistan, provided the Soviet military left.[14] President Carter wrote to Yugoslav President Broz Tito, a cochairman of the nonaligned group of nations, saying the United States would "guarantee" Afghanistan's "true neutrality" if Soviet troops promptly withdrew.[15] The Soviet ambassador in Washington, Anatoly Dobrynin, carried a private assurance to Moscow from Carter's national security adviser, Zbigniew Brzezinski, saying that "the United States was for a neutral Afghanistan, friendly to the Soviet Union like Finland, but not another vassal like Mongolia."[16]

The Western proposals to resurrect the Afghan buffer were supported by some at a Soviet Politburo session in early April 1980. Dobrynin later wrote that he believed "Brzezinski's suggestions could have provided a basis for negotiations." Deputy foreign minister and Politburo member Georgy Korniyenko argued that Brzezinski's suggestion to turn Afghanistan into an Asiatic Finland was an arrangement the Soviet Union could agree to. According to Communist Party official Karen Brutents, party ideologue Boris Ponomarev shot back: "How can one compare Afghanistan and Finland? Finland is a capitalist country." Korniyenko feigned surprise that Afghanistan had suddenly "matured into a socialist country." One of Ponomarev's deputies, Rostislav Ulyanovski, sermonized: "There is no country in the world today that is not ripe for socialism."[17]

A secret Soviet Politburo decree issued on April 10, 1980, buried the American and British initiatives to re-create the Afghan buffer. Postulating that Afghanistan was now "a part of the zone of the Soviet special interests," the decree registered the Politburo's "decisively negative reaction to the absolutely hopeless plan for 'neutralization' of Afghanistan."[18] Dobrynin later wrote that the Soviet rejection of the Anglo-American proposals was a missed opportunity that would prove costly to the Soviet Union. The Brezhnev Politburo was determined to stick with Karmal, he lamented, adding: "By the time Gorbachev at last abandoned him, it was too late to negotiate."[19]

Three months after the Soviet invasion, American intelligence had already concluded that the Soviets were not going to accept the Afghan buffer idea. A secret Department of State analysis forwarded to Secretary of State Cyrus Vance on March 4, 1980, noted that the Soviet media was giving "little public play" to the Western proposal. "Moscow," it surmised, "probably believes that it can eventually stabilize the situation in Afghanistan, and that, as it does, international pressure will decrease, much as it did in 1968 with Czechoslovakia."[20]

The Soviet Union's invasion and its rejection of Western initiatives to revive the Afghan buffer in Central Asia sapped what little energy remained in détente. President Carter faced a tough challenge from Ronald Reagan in the November 1980 presidential elections. Many Americans considered Carter too weak to handle Soviet aggression. Days after the invasion, his naïveté inadvertently surfaced in an unusual acknowledgment to the press that would return to haunt him on the campaign trail: "My opinion of the Russians has changed most dramatically in the last week, more than even in the previous two and a half years before that."[21] Presidential candidate Reagan's declaration in a New York speech, "I don't agree that our nation must resign itself to inevitable decline, yielding its proud position to other hands,"[22] suggested to voters that he would be more resolute in standing up to the Soviets.

Carter levied twenty-six sanctions against the Soviet Union. They included an Olympics boycott, a grain embargo, withdrawal of the SALT II treaty from the Senate, cessation of dual-use technology sales, fishing restrictions in American waters, and closure of the Soviet consulate in New York and the American consulate in Kiev. The administration's new "Carter Doctrine" warned the Soviet Union that any attempt to control the Persian Gulf would be repelled "by any means necessary, including military force."[23] Carter's harder line did not affect Soviet behavior. In a letter to Carter, Brezhnev showed no flexibility: "I must with all certainty stress that the change in the Afghanistani government was the result of the Afghanistanis themselves and only by them. Ask the Afghanistani Government itself."[24]

Reagan handily won the 1980 election, carrying forty-four out of fifty states. He gave minimal attention to the U.S.-Soviet negotiating track during his first term in office. Instead, he concentrated on a $1.6 trillion military buildup to achieve a position of military superiority over the Soviets and bargaining from a position of strength. "Defense is not a budget item, spend what you need,"[25] Reagan told the Defense Department. The buildup included development of the Trident III submarine, the MX intercontinental missile, the mobile Midgetman missile, the B-1 and Stealth bombers, and an expanded navy. Reagan also produced and stockpiled the neutron bomb, which Carter had shelved.

A new "Reagan Doctrine" provided support to states and Third World movements resisting Soviet expansionism, such as Pakistan, the Mujahidin in Afghanistan, the Contras in Nicaragua, guerrillas fighting pro-Soviet governments in Ethiopia and Angola, and Cambodian insurgents battling Vietnamese invaders. In 1981, the Reagan administration gifted Zia ul-Haq with a $3.2 billion aid package spread over a six-year period, equally divided between military and economic assistance. A follow-up grant to Pakistan in 1986 provided another $4.2 billion.[26]

ψ

On December 31, 1979, the Politburo's Afghan Commission praised Babrak Karmal's government in a secret post-invasion assessment:

The situation in the country is normalizing. . . . Babrak can be described as one of the more theoretically equipped leaders of PDPA,
who soberly and objectively evaluates the situation in Afghanistan; he
was always distinguished by his sincere sympathies for the Soviet
Union, and commanded respect within party masses and the country
at large. In this regard, the conviction can be expressed that the new
leadership of DRA will find effective ways to stabilize completely the
country's situation.[27]

The report prematurely concluded that the Parcham-Khalq schism had
been "liquidated."[28] It complimented the Karmal regime's vow to fight for the
"complete victory" of the "revolution" and "to strengthen in every possible
way the friendship and cooperation with the USSR."[29]

The Soviet military was ubiquitous in Kabul and other Afghan cities in
the months after the invasion. Soviet troops in the country outnumbered the
Afghan Army by four to one. Soviet soldiers directed traffic in the capital and
guarded important government buildings. The Soviet 40th Army headquarters were colocated with the Afghan Army's Central Corps headquarters at
Darulaman. An Afghan military officer, who defected, reported that Soviet
military officers countersigned all orders issued to Afghan units.[30]

By 1984, the number of Soviet civilian advisers helping the PDPA to build
Soviet-style socialism in tribal Afghanistan climbed above 10,000.[31] President
Babrak Karmal later said that the Afghans "stopped working" and decided to
"lay all the burden and responsibility for practical work on the shoulders of
the advisors."[32] Soviet advisers prepared speeches and resolutions for PDPA
meetings, formulated Afghan development plans, wrote the talking points
for Afghan press conferences, and issued lists to Afghan ministries stipulating
who was to be promoted. Articles appearing in the Afghan press were written
in Russian in Moscow, then forwarded to Kabul for translation into Afghan
languages and publication in Afghan government media outlets.

A visiting Soviet journalist marveled at the Sovietization of Afghan institutions:

Not a single undertaking[,] be it political or economic—was carried
out by the Afghans themselves. Only with the direct participation of
the Soviet representatives. The information of the party and govern-

ment apparatus was assisted by Soviet advisors. The same applied to the development of the armed forces, ... the state security service, the militia, social organizations, newspapers, and so forth. There was nothing innovative about such participation: merely, one state model (and not the best version at that) was forced onto another country. The [Afghan] First Secretary ... couldn't take a single step without permission from the Soviet Central Committee advisor. The [Afghan] Republic's Minister of Defense could not issue a single order without prior approval from the Soviet Ministry of Defense Advisor.[33]

Yuriy Andropov's KGB continued to overshadow Soviet diplomats and military and civilian advisers in giving direction to the Afghan government and its security forces. KGB officers occupied commanding positions in key Afghan ministries.[34] Vasily Safronchuk returned to Afghanistan to lead the Soviet advisory team at the Afghan Foreign Ministry. KGB commandos guarded the presidential palace and Karmal himself. A KGB chauffeur drove his limousine. Once again, Soviet KGB chefs prepared the Afghan president's food. Soviet doctors administered to his health needs.

The KGB chose Parchami Mohammad Najib to head its Afghan secret police counterpart, the KHAD "Government Information Agency."[35] KGB officers of ethnic Uzbek, Tajik, and Turkmen origin were transferred to Kabul to work as Afghan KHAD operatives. Najib described KHAD meetings as beginning with the KGB advisers seated away from the table. "As the conference goes on," he said, "the debate gets higher and the advisors move closer to the table, while the Afghans move away, and finally the Soviets are left to quarrel among themselves."[36]

Three weeks after the invasion, Andropov reiterated his satisfaction that "Babrak's doing great work regarding the strengthening of unity."[37] The new Afghan president may have been less aggressive than Taraki or Amin, but tribal values of *badal*, score settling, personality politics, and beating down rivals contesting the summit guided his actions. Additionally, Karmal was no longer in Moscow. He now sat in the presidential palace. Although utterly dependent on recurring Soviet resources, he could exercise reverse leverage. Despite the promises about forging party solidarity in his letter to Brezhnev before the invasion, the Parchami Afghan president set out to exact revenge from his Khalqi enemies.

Karmal's first move after the invasion was to assign Parchamis to fill senior military and administration positions occupied by Khalqis. The Khalqis resisted. The Khalqi governor of Kandahar refused to turn over his office to Karmal's Parchami appointees when he arrived. The Khalqi commander of the 14th Division at Ghazni led a mutiny against the new Parchami general Karmal sent to relieve him.[38] Karmal's appointee backtracked to Kabul. Soviet advisers blocked several Karmal attempts to purge Sayed Mohammad Gulabzoi, Aslam Watanjar, and Sher Jan Mazdooryar, the Khalqi ministers of interior, communications, and transportation, respectively, in Karmal's made-in-Moscow cabinet.

Khalqi faction leaders spurned Soviet attempts to force Parcham-Khalq collaboration. They told their Soviet handlers that subordination to Parchamis was unworkable given the Khalqi two-thirds majority in party membership and four-fifths predominance among PDPA military officers.[39] The Indian ambassador in Kabul recorded in his diary that firefights between Parcham and Khalqi gunmen periodically interrupted his sleep. He wrote, "It is only the Russian presence and Russian advice which is keeping the power structure and the Party intact and functional."[40]

Soviet leaders adopted the practice of shuttling divisive PDPA members to Moscow for counseling sessions. Some stayed for months, some for years. Some never returned to Afghanistan. The first to go was Assadullah Sarwari, Karmal's deputy in the PDPA leadership and the titular leader of the Khalqi faction. On Soviet Ambassador Fikryat Tabeyev's recommendations, Sarwari was transported to Moscow for "medical treatment." The treatment evidently failed. Sarwari was made Afghan ambassador to Mongolia and sent to Ulan Bator.

Over the next several years, Soviet advisers tried out and dropped dozens of ministers for displaying factionalism, corruption, secret ties to the Mujahidin, or simple indolence. KGB reports inculpated Parchami Vice President Nur Ahmed Nur for "drinking tea every day, from 8:00 a.m. to 10:00 p.m., chatting by the samovar."[41] Nur was transported to Moscow. He did not return. The Afghan defense minister, Major General Mohammad Rafi, accused of ignoring the advice of his Soviet advisers and of incompetence, was also taken to the Soviet capital. He stayed there for two years. Rafi was replaced in the Defense Ministry slot by Abdul Qadir, who was more responsive to Soviet direction than most other PDPA military officers. But Qadir was also incompetent and ineffective. Khalqi military officers refused to report to a non-Khalqi: Qadir lasted two years before the Soviets threw up their hands and appointed a Khalqi to the Defense Ministry position.

During this period, Najib's KHAD became a Parchami bastion in the government, and Gulabzoi's Ministry of the Interior grew into an opposing Khalqi fortress. Gulabzoi was the top Khalqi in Afghanistan after Sarwari's exile. Stocky, five foot three, mustached and sideburned, he treated Najib like a dangerous foe and Karmal like a powerless figurehead. "Babrak," he once quipped to a KGB officer, "is the president of the court rather than the country," adding, "I am not the Minister of Internal Affairs of Kabul[,] as most of the country is controlled by the rebels."[42]

Najib and Gulabzoi were both tough Pashtuns from Paktiya Province, and they followed the standard Afghan practice of staffing their ministries with family members and personal loyalists. Their feuding with one another elicited more Soviet invitations to Moscow for therapy. In 1983, Gulabzoi was summoned with a group of fellow Khalqis to attend two months of Soviet lectures on the need for party unity and base broadening. Najib was also flown to Moscow and ordered to end factionalism.

Karmal, too, became a frequent flier to Moscow, where Andropov, Gromyko, and Ustinov coached him on leadership. The training did not improve his job performance. A KGB analyst branded the Afghan president "a passive leader of the Party and country." "His only concern was how to compromise the leaders of the Khalq faction," he wrote.[43] In 1984, challenges to Karmal's inept stewardship of the country arose within his own Parcham faction. Karmal's cousin, Finance Minister Abdul Wakil, led an underground movement to drive him from office. Wakil was sporadically joined by Najib, who wished to succeed Karmal. Mahmoud Baryalai, Sultan Ali Keshtmand, and Abdul Qadir supported Karmal and opposed Najib and Wakil.

The absence of a viable Afghan government in Kabul capable of attracting popular support remained a major problem for Soviet policymakers during Moscow's eight-year occupation. The insurgency in the countryside steadily grew in size and firepower. The urban population resented the Soviet occupation. Events on the ground belied the Soviet Politburo's conclusion that a "wave of patriotic sentiments" had greeted "the deployment of Soviet forces."[44]

When Soviet invading columns approached Herat and Kandahar, pro-Amin Khalqi troops joined with local Mujahidin commanders to defend both cities.

A huge popular demonstration against the Soviet invasion shook Kabul for three days starting February 21, 1980. It became known as the "Hoot uprising," named after the Afghan calendar month coinciding with February. The event began after dark when a continuous roar of *Allahu Akbar* (God is great) soared through the night air from the throats of an estimated 400,000 men, women, and children standing on rooftops or in the streets. Afghan security personnel abandoned their posts. Many joined belligerent mobs gathering in the streets near Soviet-occupied hotels and government buildings. A Soviet journalist trapped that evening in the Kabul Hotel vividly captured the mood of popular rage:

> Darkness came quickly. A dull, strange sound swelled outside. Only a very large crowd could generate such a noise. . . . I went over to the dark blue drapes and opened them a chink. . . . The sight that met my eyes was truly dreadful. The neighboring "Pak" hotel was already ablaze like a haystack. Two overturned Chavdar buses—a gift from fraternal Bulgaria to the people of revolutionary Afghanistan—smoldered in the middle of the road. The flames cast an eerie glow over a multitude of turbaned men and veiled women. . . . I feared the knives in the hands of my medieval contemporaries.[45]

On February 22, General Sokolov, commander of the 40th Army, declared martial law and a curfew. He ordered Soviet tanks and infantry to patrol the capital, to block all roads leading into the city, and to shoot Afghans challenging the curfew. More than three hundred demonstrators were killed;[46] many more were wounded and arrested.

The Soviet military's use of force to kill demonstrators, including girls, sparked popular outrage and more demonstrations in other Afghan cities. Soviet brutality against civilians in urban areas helped fuel a general uprising in the countryside. From about mid-1980 through the end of the Soviet occupation in early 1989, over 80 percent of the country and 85 percent of the population were outside the control of the Soviet Army and the Afghan communist regime.

The invasion and the ensuing turmoil sparked a wave of desertions from the Afghan Army and the departure of senior Afghan civil servants to Pakistan and the West. The Afghan Army shrank to 30,000,[47] and Western intelligence sources estimated that only one-third to one-half of those who remained in their army posts were trustworthy and effective. In military as well as civilian areas, the Soviet Union made itself the "supported" government and the Karmal regime the "supporting" government. The Sovietization of the escalating Afghan war was a strategic blunder, guaranteed to fail in the long run.

ψ

General Sokolov had fought wars in the tradition of World War II Russian generals: with decisive frontal offensives that attacked armed combatants and civilians alike. An Afghan uprising in Kandahar three days after the Soviet invasion had been ruthlessly suppressed by Soviet tanks and aircraft. Whole neighborhoods of Kandahar were reduced to rubble. A massive Soviet offensive up the Konar Valley preceded by carpet-bombing killed few Mujahidin but produced numerous civilian casualties, depopulated villages, and sent thousands of Afghan families streaming across the border into Pakistan. The refugee population in Pakistan and Iran increased from 750,000 and 100,000, respectively, in 1980 to 3.5 million and 1.7 million in 1984.[48]

The Soviet Army was trained to fight large land battles on European plains, not guerrilla warfare against tribes in Afghanistan's rugged terrain. General Sokolov's tactics repeatedly miscarried. In early 1981, he erroneously reported to Moscow that he had trapped Mujahidin forces in the mountains along the Pakistani border. "The large amount of snow which has fallen in February will not allow the adversaries to take cover in the mountains," he predicted, noting that the Mujahidin's "exit routes to the south, west and east are cut off. To the north are mountains which are inaccessible in winter."[49] Nevertheless, the Mujahidin escaped.

Sokolov accelerated his scorched-earth policy. Large areas of the countryside became free-fire zones. Soviet aircraft and helicopter gunships leveled mountainside villages and mercilessly decimated nomad caravans and encampments. They seeded rural areas with millions of tiny butterfly mines, some designed to look like children's toys. Villages located near Mujahidin ambush sites were routinely destroyed, their inhabitants killed or driven away.

MAP 9.1   THE SOVIET INVASION AND OCCUPATION OF AFGHANISTAN

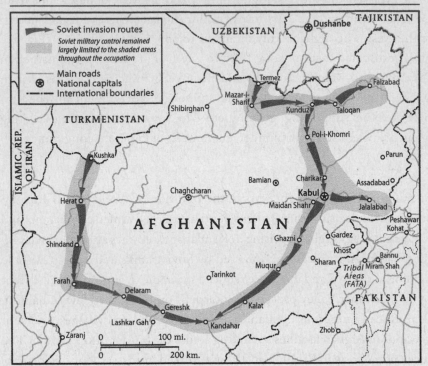

Reprinted with permission from, *The Soviet-Afghan War:
How a Superpower Fought and Lost*, trans. and ed. Lester W. Grau and
Michael A. Gress (Lawrence, KS: University of Kansas Press, 2002), p. 16.

Karmal told the KGB that he feared "Afghanistan would end up without a
work force."[50]

The Soviet Army's strategy of terrorizing the Afghan population was counterproductive in the land of the blood feud. The carpet-bombing and other
atrocities only increased the Afghan lust for *badal*, and Soviet barbarity was
met with Afghan barbarity. Few prisoners were taken by either side, but those
captured, wounded, or left behind faced a gruesome end. The carcasses of
destroyed Soviet trucks, tanks, and APCs littered roadsides. Demoralized Soviet soldiers resorted to consumption of widely available narcotics and sold
their weapons to Afghans. Known as "Afghantsi," Soviet soldiers rotating back
to Soviet civilian life carried tales of the brutalization of a resentful population, fueling antiwar sentiment in Soviet society.

The number of Soviet troops in Afghanistan was inadequate to gain sustained control in any one region, much less the country as a whole. Soviet control of Afghan territory was never firmly established outside the ring road, the cities bordering it, the provincial capitals, and some district capitals. Forty percent of Soviet manpower was tied up in guarding lines of communications, bridges, airfields, military bases, and urban areas strung along the ring road. Another 35 percent secured convoy traffic. Logistics demands absorbed other Soviet units, leaving relatively few Soviet forces available for combat operations.[51]

Soviet troops encountered determined opposition in the countryside. Courageous, highly motivated resistance fighters were familiar with every hill, ravine, cave, and escape route in their local areas. The insurgents benefited from unlimited manpower, high morale, a civilian population ready to provide safe havens and food—and time to spare. "They have the clock, we have the time," was a popular Mujahidin proverb during the Soviet occupation.

The Soviets received little help from the Afghan regime's army. PDPA politicians left the mighty Soviet military to defeat the Mujahidin while they concentrated on factional infighting. General Sokolov described Afghan troops as "illiterate, ill-trained, unready for combat, and without military training or discipline."[52] Most Afghan conscripts had no loyalty for the Afghan regime. Advance leakage of Soviet operational plans from pro-Mujahidin Afghan military officers was a major problem.

Soviet estimates placed the number of Mujahidin combatants at around 130,000, scattered in over 3,000 separate "detachments." American intelligence gauged the number of active Mujahidin fighters at 150,000, although this number of insurgents was never in the field at any one time. Less than a dozen Mujahidin personalities received significant international attention. The Pakistani media lionized Ghilzai Pashtun extremists Gulbuddin Hekmatyar and Jalaluddin Haqqani based in Pakistan. The Western press gave more coverage to moderate commanders such as pro–Zahir Shah Durrani Pashtun Haji Latif in the south, Tajik Ismael Khan in the west, Panshiri Tajik Ahmed Shah Masood in the north, and Ghilzai Pashtun Abdul Haq in the east.

Ahmed Shah Masood and Abdul Haq were two of the most effective commanders in the field. Strong-willed moderate nationalists, they demonstrated strong organizational and analytical skills rarely found within the fragmented Mujahidin. Whereas Afghan radicals based in Pakistan exploited ISI-distributed weapons and money to recruit fighters, Haq and Masood relied on their charisma, military successes, inclusiveness of all Afghan groups, and fierce independence from Pakistani influence to attract followers. They employed the jirga tradition of deliberation, equality, and voluntary consensus to build their forces. Haq's Mujahidin were mainly Pashtuns, Masood's Tajik. But Afghans from all major ethnic groups rallied to their side. Their fame spread into the PDPA bureaucracy and army. Haq developed an impressive intelligence network among Khalqis in the regime. Masood's spies were mostly Parchami military officers and politicians. Both Haq and Masood stubbornly rejected ISI and CIA plans for a military end to the war involving direct assaults on Kabul and other major cities mainly led by Hekmatyar. Their strategy emphasized the establishment of deep roots in the population, low civilian casualties, interethnic unity, prosecution of the war in a political-military manner through small-unit actions to wear down the enemy, and patient negotiations to attract mass defections, all leading to a relatively bloodless transfer of power.

Abdul Haq's Arsala clan had a history of service to the Afghan state. One of his ancestors, Arsala Khan, was Afghan foreign minister before the second Anglo-Soviet war (1878–1881). Another was one of the Afghan generals who defeated the British at the Battle of Maiwand. Abdul Haq's father, a deputy governor of Helmand, died when Haq was seven, and Haq grew up in the Arsala family's Jabbar Khel clan's Ahmadzai strongholds of Hisarak and Sorkh Rud near Jalalabad in Nangarhar Province. His Mujahidin career began early, at age sixteen. After Daoud's coup he was imprisoned for antiregime underground activity. His family bribed regime officials to gain his release, and he fled to Pakistan. When the Soviets invaded Afghanistan, Haq organized his Kabul front of more than 1,000 Mujahidin. They carried out ambushes and sabotage operations along the capital's eastern, southern, and western flanks. Haq personally led nighttime raids into the city, attacking military targets and kidnapping Soviets.

In August 1986, Haq and a few of his men successfully fired an incendiary round from a 107-mm rocket launcher into an ammunition warehouse at the 9th Division Kargha garrison west of Kabul. The seven-story Soviet ammunition dump, the largest in the country, exploded in a giant fireball. The operation lifted Mujahidin pride and morale countrywide. Haq's military career ended fourteen months later, on October 11, 1987, when he stepped on an antipersonnel mine hidden in a drainage ditch. He lost his right foot.[53] Even before his foot wound took him off the battlefield, Haq had earned the ire of the CIA and the ISI by his outspoken criticism of their favoritism for the Afghan extremists in the Mujahidin. The ISI cut him off. The CIA rebuffed him. He was "yesterday's man."[54] Milt Bearden, the CIA station chief in Pakistan during the mid-1980s, brought ridicule on Haq by calling him "Hollywood Haq"—hardly befitting a brave Mujahidin commander who had been personally honored by President Ronald Reagan in 1985 and by British Prime Minister Margaret Thatcher in 1986.[55]

Ahmed Shah Masood began his career as a guerrilla leader in Nuristan after the Soviet invasion. From there he moved to his native Panshir Valley to organize a Mujahidin front, which he designated the Shura Nazar (Council of the North). Masood's father and brothers supported his activities from Peshawar.[56] His oldest brother, Deen Mohammad, a former Afghan military officer, was assassinated on a Peshawar street as he was about to travel to the United States. Two other brothers, Yahya and Ahmed Zia, represented him to the Pakistani government and the American embassy.

Masood created the most effective Mujahidin military organization of the anti-Soviet war. He read deeply into the writings of experienced guerrilla leaders, such as China's Mao Tse-tung and Vietnam's Vo Nguyen Giap. Masood was a brilliant tactician. He made maximum use of deception to draw large Soviet formations into ambush sites where his firepower could be concentrated. When Soviet pressure on his Panshir redoubt lessened, Masood struck Soviet convoys on the nearby Salang Highway and rocketed the huge Soviet air base at Bagram. Masood's hit-and-run attacks frustrated Soviet generals up to the last days of the occupation. Former Soviet commander in Afghanistan Boris Gromov once complained that Masood's Mujahidin "could convert the [Salang Pass] area into a graveyard for the Russian troops by only throwing rocks."[57]

The Soviets launched two major offensives into the Panshir in 1980. Two more followed in 1981, and two in 1982. The multiweek campaigns devastated villages and destroyed crops. Combat aircraft and helicopter gunships ripped through the valley, supporting Soviet infantry and armor columns. Each time, Masood's forces would occupy the high ground above the single

Panshir Valley road where it passed through narrow canyons, pouring rocket and small-arms fire on the advancing Soviet troops, forcing them to retreat after suffering heavy casualties.

By 1983, the two sides were ready for a respite from combat. The six offensives had resulted in heavy Soviet casualties but had failed to subdue Masood. Masood's counterattacks on Salang Highway traffic had reduced food and fuel supplies in Kabul to dangerously low levels. The Soviets calculated that a cease-fire would allow them to rebuild stockpiles of essential commodities in Kabul. Masood, meanwhile, needed time to regroup his forces, repair damage to the Panshir Valley's infrastructure, and expand his front outside the Panshir.

Masood demanded that the cease-fire negotiations exclude the PDPA: He would only negotiate with the Soviets. In exchanges of letters with Soviet 40th Army generals, he rejected Soviet suggestions to meet at a neutral site. The Soviet delegations would need to drive into the Panshir. Masood's Mujahidin would guarantee their security. Masood met the Soviets in his uniform at his Panshir headquarters. The negotiations lasted three days. The two sides agreed to a cease-fire agreement of six months. Masood interpreted it as applying only to the Panshir.[58]

Masood used the cessation of hostilities to bring Mujahidin commanders from eight northern provinces into his Council of the North. He spent weeks trekking to small Mujahidin bases in Takhar, Badakhshan, Baghlan, and Parwan to meet with commanders in jirga settings, ascertain their views, and coordinate with them on plans for future operations in northern Afghanistan. His organizing successes in northern Afghanistan, later to extend into the Hazarajat and Nuristan, rested on his reputation as a successful commander, his inclusive approach, the military training programs he offered at his training sites in the Panshir, and his distribution of captured Soviet weapons.

Back in the Panshir, Masood divided his forces into three categories: village militia trained to fight locally; well-armed light infantry units of about eighty fighters each, capable of moving rapidly within the Panshir and to adjacent areas; and a "central" force of heavily armed thirty- to forty-man commando units able to strike targets two or more days' march from the Panshir. Masood established Council of the North committees to deal with political, military, economic, and social issues and developed a rudimentary structure of schools, health clinics, and social services funded by USAID, Arab donations, and his own budget.

MAP 9.2   MASOOD'S EXPANSION IN NORTHERN AFGHANISTAN, 1985–1989

In April 1984, after the expiration of the cease-fire and cold weather, the Soviets resumed large-scale attacks on the Panshir. A devastating ground and air offensive lasted through the summer months. Fully briefed beforehand by his agents in the Afghan regime and army, Masood evacuated the civilian population from the valley. After the Soviets withdrew, he pushed outside the Panshir and captured the Fakhar Valley in southern Takhar Province. He also overran the regime's 20th Division base at Nahrin in Baghlan. A final Soviet attempt to crush Masood in June 1985 was repelled.

Soviet failures to eliminate Masood on the battlefield were interspersed with many attempts to assassinate him. One of the most notorious plots occurred in 1984, when the KGB and KHAD trained a former high-school classmate of Masood's to kill him with a KGB-designed pistol firing poison darts. The potential assassin's family discovered the plot and pleaded with him not to carry it out. Their son went to the Panshir and defected to Masood. Masood arranged for him and his family to emigrate to Germany.

Masood's challenges did not start or end with the Soviets. Pakistan's military dictator, Zia ul-Haq, and Gulbuddin Hekmatyar, Zia's choice to rule Afghanistan after the Soviets left, were alarmed by his territorial expansion through the northern provinces and into Nuristan.

Hekmatyar was thirty-seven years old and Masood thirty-one when Masood's cease-fire with the Soviets ended. Hekmatyar collaborated with the ISI, Jamaat-i Islami's Qazi Hussain Ahmed, and radical Arabs, including Osama bin Laden, to build his military, political, and financial infrastructure inside Pakistan. He utilized his great advantage in weapons and money to recruit Mujahidin commanders and establish his own intelligence network in Kabul, primarily among Khalqi military officers. Meanwhile, Masood, despite leading the largest and most successful combat command in the Afghan resistance, received relatively few of the American- and Saudi-donated supplies distributed by the ISI. ISI weapons shipments dipped further as Masood's Council of the North expanded its territorial control in the north. Masood's stubborn streak of independence, his suspicions about ISI intentions, and the ISI's demand that he perform assigned roles in its overall war strategy increased tensions between him and both the ISI and CIA. The ISI told the Americans that Masood was not a team player. Masood's view was that he would not support a military strategy designed by foreigners.

Masood tried to enlist the help of Mujahidin leader Burhanuddin Rabbani to gain access to ISI-controlled American and Saudi weapons. Rabbani was also a northern Tajik. His ideological and political ties, however, were with the Muslim Brotherhood and the three Afghan Ghilzai Pashtun extremists nurtured by the ISI: Gulbuddin Hekmatyar, Abdul Rasoul Sayyaf, and Yunus Khalis. Rabbani did make some efforts to respond to Masood's appeals for help. At the same time, he knew that Zia and the ISI were hostile to Masood's growing military power inside Afghanistan. Rabbani's political survival and ability to supply his other commanders depended on access to ISI cash and weapons. He could not alienate the ISI.

In a series of letters to Rabbani between 1981 and 1984, Masood kept up a steady drumbeat of appeals for assistance. At first, the tone of his letters was optimistic. They contained detailed analyses of his plans and lists of the military arms, money, and equipment needed to achieve them. Rabbani did not respond. In 1983 Masood's letters demonstrated growing frustrations with Rabbani's failure to meet his requests. One letter upbraided Rabbani for sacrificing the "biggest interests of the country." "Nothing has reached us," he protested. In another letter, Masood remonstrated that Rabbani had made "repeated promises" to send supplies, but the supplies "never materialized." It was a "source of worry" to him and his followers and had "discouraged us from taking further steps."[59]

Masood lashed out at Rabbani's Tajik military committee chairman, Ayub, a close associate of Hekmatyar: "I know my efforts were blown by the wind because you listened to a few individuals like Ayub," he wrote.[60] By late 1984, Masood's letters to Rabbani had become very brief; he had given up hope that Rabbani would honor his requests for supplies.[61] Masood continued to survive and expand by capturing Soviet and regime weapons, ammunition, and supplies.

The ISI and Hekmatyar organized deadly attacks on Mujahidin loyal to Masood to contain his territorial expansion. As early as August 1981, Masood wrote to Rabbani that "Hekmatyar, unfortunately, is trying to escalate the war against us." By 1984, three Hekmatyar commanders, well supplied by the ISI, were attempting to tie Masood down: Ustad Farid in Parwan Province on Masood's western flank; Mohammed Bashir in Badakhshan from the east; and Sayed Jaglan, who occupied a strategic ridge in the Fakhar Valley near Masood's headquarters. In a letter to Supervisory Council commanders, Masood explained that "some Pakistanis" did not wish to see a strong Mujahidin "center" in the north. They considered "the creation of such a center not in their interest" and had "joined hands with the internal opposition to sabotage our good work."[62]

ψ

The eighteen-year Brezhnevian era, characterized by preservation of the status quo—and leaders in wheelchairs—did not die with Brezhnev on November 10, 1982. Although second-ranking Politburo member Mikhail Suslov also died in 1982, hard-line ideologues averse to change continued to dominate the Soviet leadership. The doctrinaire Nikolai Tikhanov, seventy-five, became prime minister when Kosygin died in 1980 at age seventy-six. Yuriy Andropov was sixty-eight and already suffering from liver failure and emphysema when he replaced Brezhnev in 1982.

Mikhail Gorbachev and other young reformers hoped that Andropov would revitalize the sagging Soviet system when he succeeded Brezhnev in

1982. If Andropov ever had such intentions, his failing health erased that possibility.[63] During Andropov's limited time as general secretary, the Soviet propaganda machine continued to mouth Brezhnev-era formulations on the Afghan war. Andropov escalated Soviet military operations against the Mujahidin. He mentioned Afghanistan only once in the nineteen key speeches he delivered when party general secretary. Andropov's successor, Konstantin Chernyenko, best remembered as Brezhnev's personal aide and shadow, had an even shorter tenure. He died after thirteen months as general secretary and proved even more resistant to change. Chernyenko never mentioned Afghanistan at all in the thirty-five major speeches he delivered as Soviet party leader.[64] Soviet Afghan policy remained on automatic pilot.

Chernyenko passed away on March 10, 1985, at the age of seventy-four. Gorbachev organized an emergency Politburo meeting to designate the head of Chernyenko's Funeral Committee and thus Chernyenko's de facto replacement as party general secretary. Fortunately for Gorbachev, two conservative members were unable to get to Moscow in time to cast their votes.[65] Gorbachev ordered the doors of the meeting room closed and insisted that no participant leave before the vote took place. The tactic worked. Only a few hours after Chernyenko's death, Gorbachev became the Funeral Committee chairman and the next Soviet leader. The following morning, Soviet newspapers featured Gorbachev's selection as party leader on page one. That same day, a quickly arranged meeting of the party's Central Committee rubber-stamped Gorbachev's victory.

Gorbachev's rise to the pinnacle of the Soviet power structure on March 11, 1985, inaugurated momentous new directions in Soviet foreign and domestic policies, including on Afghanistan. His opposition to the Soviet military occupation was not only ideological. Ending the war was essential to achieving his two overarching goals—improving relations with the United States and implementing far-reaching reforms at home. During his first months in office, he concentrated on clearing away Brezhnev-era holdovers in the leadership. He appointed reformer Nikolai I. Ryzhkov, age fifty-six, to replace hardliner Nikolai Tikhanov as prime minister. Tikhanov was retired. Gorbachev made another prominent reformer, Eduard Shevardnadze, fifty-seven, foreign minister and a full Politburo member. Andrey Gromyko, seventy-six, was sent upstairs to become chairman of the Supreme Soviet, though he kept his Politburo seat for two more years. Ideologue Boris Ponomarev lost his job at the party's International Department as well as his Politburo seat. He was replaced by Anatoly Dobrynin, sixty-six, an American specialist and former Soviet ambassador to the United States.

Gorbachev revamped the Politburo Commission on Afghanistan, appointing Shevardnadze as its chairman to balance the influence of the KGB chief and minister of defense. Dobrynin filled the commission's fourth seat. With Ryzhkov's support, Gorbachev, Shevardnadze, and Dobrynin maneuvered within the Politburo to lay the groundwork to remove Soviet combat troops from Afghanistan. "We need to pursue a firm policy of getting out of there in two years," Ryzhkov told a 1986 Politburo session. "It is better for us to hand out weapons and ammunition. And have them fight themselves if they want to."[66]

Ryzhkov expressed the sentiment of a great number of Soviet officials, soldiers, and ordinary citizens frustrated by the military stalemate and unwinnable war in Afghanistan. At formal Politburo sessions, Gorbachev read aloud heart-wrenching letters he had received from the parents of soldiers who had died: 1,280 Soviet soldiers lost their lives in 1986 alone.[67] The Soviet military controlled less territory and population in Afghanistan in 1985 than it had when the Soviet Union invaded in 1979.[68] The high morale and fighting skills of the Mujahidin contrasted with the military ineffectiveness of Afghan regime units. A 1986 Soviet military report criticized the Afghan Army's "carelessness, a lack of conscientiousness in organizing combat operations, the low quality of missions carried out and the senseless death of [our] people."[69] Desertions remained at a high level—30,000 a year.[70]

In 1986, the Reagan administration shifted to a more aggressive "victory" strategy in Afghanistan, exacerbating Soviet problems. President Reagan signed National Security Defense Directive (NSDD) 166, which directed the U.S. government, "by all means available," to remove the Soviet Army from the country. NSDD 166 led to a sharp upswing in covert military assistance to the Mujahidin, including provision of sophisticated American Stinger anti-aircraft missiles.[71] American covert aid and Saudi matching funds totaled $250 million in 1984, rose to $470 million in 1986, and to $610 million in 1987.[72] The CIA station chief in Pakistan, Milt Bearden, wrote that more than 60,000 tons' worth of weapons and supplies were transported to Afghan commanders in the field every year at the time.[73] The increase in U.S. assistance took its toll on Soviet troops. "The military situation has recently become worse. The shelling of our garrisons has doubled," Sokolov told a Politburo meeting in 1987.[74]

Prospects for Soviet military progress in Afghanistan were grim. Soviet force levels in the country reached 130,000 in 1982 and remained at that level until the 1988 Soviet withdrawal began. An additional 40,000 Soviet troops were staged from Soviet territory into Afghanistan during the war. Postwar casualty figures released by the Soviet government of 13,310 killed were understated. In 2002, a retired Soviet lieutenant colonel placed Soviet soldiers killed in Afghanistan at over 26,000, nearly twice the official figure.[75] The initiative on the battlefield after 1984 clearly lay with the Mujahidin.

A huge Soviet-Afghan regime offensive overran Jalaluddin Haqqani's base at Zhawar Kili in Paktiya Province in April 1986, but the Soviets could not hold it. Soviet military intelligence reported that Masood's forces were on the move in northern Afghanistan, "expanding their territory." The assessment advised that launching attacks on Masood's bases "would not give practical results either from a military, or moreover, from the political point of view."[76] In April 1987, Masood's Mujahidin captured the large Kara Munjan Afghan regime base, opening the way to the Pakistan border 25 miles away.

About six months after assuming power, in October 1985, Gorbachev called a Politburo meeting to muster a consensus behind withdrawal from Afghanistan. A Politburo member later recalled that "by that time nobody dared openly oppose it."[77] Defense Minister Sokolov approved the decision by announcing he was prepared to "wrap things up."[78] Gorbachev pocketed the meeting's agreement in principle to end the war. That was a major accomplishment, one that would have been impossible during the Brezhnev era. Four months later at a major party conference, describing the Afghan war as a "bleeding wound," Gorbachev signaled that the Soviet Union would withdraw from Afghanistan. He instructed the Soviet delegation at the UN-sponsored Afghan settlement talks in Geneva to speed up negotiations to end the war, and he ordered six Soviet regiments back to the Soviet Union in 1986.

In June 1986, Gorbachev presided over the last major round of musical chairs in the PDPA's leadership. That month he deposed Babrak Karmal, who was forced to resign as party general secretary for the usual reason of "bad health." Karmal's "penchant for alcohol abuse" was tacked on as an additional justification for removal.[79] Gorbachev made KGB protégé and KHAD chief

Mohammad Najib Afghanistan's new president and party leader. Najib was dynamic, charismatic, tough, and intelligent. He was Kabuli-educated at the elite Habibya high school, held a medical decree, and spoke fluent Dari, Urdu, Russian, and English. An Ahmadzai Pashtun from Paktiya, he was married to a Mohammedzai.

A November 13, 1986, Politburo meeting discussion dramatically underscored the Soviet decision to pull out of Afghanistan. The chief of general staff, Marshal Sergei Akhromeyev, soberly announced that "We control Kabul and the population centers but on occupied territory we cannot establish authority," adding, "We have lost the battle for the Afghan people." Comments at the meeting reflected the continued losses the Soviet Union would inevitably suffer by remaining in Afghanistan—international isolation, higher battlefield casualties, expenditure of between $4 billion and $8 billion a year to continue to fight an unwinnable war, and growing antiwar sentiment within the Soviet population, but no military progress.[80]

The Politburo's decision to withdraw Soviet troops from Afghanistan was far easier than determining *how* to withdraw and actually implementing that withdrawal on the ground. Over the next two years, three Politburo factions emerged during contentious Politburo debates on the Soviet exit strategy. Premier Ryzhkov, Deputy Foreign Minister Korniyenko, and Soviet Chief of Staff Sergei Akhromeyev, later military adviser to Gorbachev, espoused a liberal and rapid disengagement course. They insisted that it was "absolutely unrealistic to think that the PDPA would stay in power after the Soviet troop withdrawal." For the PDPA to survive, it would need "to forgo the major share of power" and agree to a coalition government representing "the various sections of Afghan society."[81] The liberal faction argued that quick disposal of the Afghan albatross would accelerate the Soviet Union's strategic engagement with the West and benefit Gorbachev's domestic economic reforms.

The KGB chief, Anatoly Chebrikov, backed by Defense Minister Sokolov, countered that the Soviet Union could not endure the humiliation of a defeat in Afghanistan by abandoning Najib and the PDPA. They argued that the Reagan administration's bid for victory required the Soviet Union to keep Afghanistan in the Soviet sphere of influence. A decision by the Reagan administration to continue covert weapons supplies to the Mujahidin as long as the Soviets armed the regime in Kabul—even *after* a Soviet withdrawal—strengthened the conservatives' position. (The administration's decision to continue U.S. arms shipments as long as the Soviets did so became known as "positive symmetry." A simultaneous arms cutoff by both sides was termed "negative symmetry.")

Gorbachev and Shevardnadze made up the third, and most influential, Politburo faction in the debates on the exit strategy. They accommodated the conservatives' demand to continue supporting the regime after the Soviet withdrawal. More than his liberal reform allies, Gorbachev knew the dangers inherent in provoking the type of conservative backlash that had overthrown Nikita Khrushchev. He postponed the Soviet withdrawal until 1988–1989 to allow time to build up Najib's security forces. Gorbachev may also have calculated that he could use the delay to increase his influence within the military and KGB through more dismissals and appointments.[82]

At the November 13, 1986, Politburo session, Gorbachev revived the Afghan buffer zone concept rejected by the Brezhnev Politburo in 1980. Gromyko, once again backtracking from previously espoused positions, declared: "Our strategic goal is to make Afghanistan neutral." Gorbachev added, "We have set a clear goal: help speed up the process so we have a friendly, neutral country and get out of there."[83] After taking over from Karmal, Najib obligingly announced that Afghanistan had become a neutral, nonaligned state.

The Politburo approved an Afghanization strategy committed to rapidly turning over full military and political responsibility to the weak Afghan government. Afghan Commission Chairman Shevardnadze announced, "We must regard Afghanistan as an independent country and entrust Najib to make decisions himself."[84] Pleased with KGB protégé Najib's promotion, Deputy KGB chief Kryuchkov agreed at a later meeting, suggesting that the Soviets "shift everything onto Afghanistan and have them learn to manage to act independently."[85] The Soviet military initiated a massive transfer of arms, equipment, and food to Afghanistan to sustain Najib's regime after the Soviet departure. The weaponry, brought by land and by air, included hundreds of SCUD surface-to-surface missiles, with Soviet teams to fire them, and MIG-27s.

Gorbachev made "national reconciliation" part of the Soviet exit strategy. He assigned Najib to carry it out. The policy's objective was to bring Afghans together under a repackaged PDPA regime. Najib would retain the leading role while giving some ministerial positions to moderate Mujahidin leaders who were ready to cooperate. In 1987, Najib publicly invited the Mujahidin to participate in a national dialogue to end the war, proclaiming a general amnesty for all who had opposed the regime. He renounced communism. Party and government media outlets identified Afghanistan as an Islamic state. Najib added the spiritual suffix "ullah" to his name, becoming Najibullah. He initiated a massive name-changing exercise to disassociate the party and the government from their past. KHAD became WAD (in English, Ministry of State Security); the PDPA morphed into the Watan (Homeland) Party. The new names did not alter the nature and functions of these repressive Soviet-modeled state organs. Eleven of the thirteen members of the Homeland Party's new "Executive Committee" were carried over from the PDPA Politburo.

Najib appointed some trusted non-PDPA leftists as prime minister and members of the cabinet. He boasted to Gorbachev that the Homeland Party's first Congress "was held in an atmosphere of unity, glasnost and democracy and confirmed that the overwhelming majority of Party members favor deepening the policy of reconciliation and dialogue and collaboration with other political forces of society."[86]

Gorbachev personally took it upon himself to tutor Najib on how to operate inside the Afghan political cauldron. He conducted four meetings with Najib in the Soviet Union during 1987 and 1988 to spell out strategems to make the Afghan government more acceptable to Afghans and the international community. Repeating previous Soviet advice that had gone unheeded by every PDPA leader since the 1978 coup, Gorbachev told Najib to include all "ethnic groups, sectors and population groups in the country" in his national reconciliation dialogue. Testing Najib's Marxist expertise, he reminded the burly Pashtun that "it's important to look for such ways to solve the problem which would dialectically consider their interests and organically integrate the ethnic groups in the process of consolidating society." He further (and futilely) exhorted: "It is especially important not to permit debates between the former Khalq and Parcham wings. Send this [message] to the comrades from us."[87]

The implementation of the Soviet exit strategy from Afghanistan did not go well. In a May 22, 1987, Politburo meeting, Commander of Soviet Ground Forces Valentin Varennikov grumbled, "There is no sense of homeland there.

There's kin, the tribe and the clan. . . . We are agitating for socialism and imposing the idea of a national democratic revolution . . . but they don't understand any of that there."[88] A June 1987 analysis by "Soviet military experts" in Afghanistan said "the policy of national reconciliation has not yet yielded the expected results."[89] The two-page analysis was filled with evidence that Mujahidin leaders were vehemently opposed to the policy. "The leadership of the Afghan counterrevolutionaries has unleashed a broad propaganda campaign to discredit and distort its substance and goals," the report stated.[90] "As a result of threats and acts of terrorism many Afghan members of national reconciliation commissions have ceased work or even display obvious passivity." The analysis indicated that the Mujahidin interpreted the policy as a sign of weakness and they only needed to press on to final victory.[91]

ψ

In the final analysis, neither the liberal nor the conservative Politburo exit strategies had any prospect for success in Afghanistan. Sooner or later, on Afghan time, the Afghan population would put an end to the communist era. PDPA leaders were despised by the overwhelming majority of Afghans. They were contemporary Shah Shujas, installed by a foreign army. To many Afghans, the Afghan communists had brought dishonor and shame on their country by inviting in the Soviet Army. The Soviets had destroyed much of Afghanistan's infrastructure, killed over a million Afghans, and driven a third of the population out of the country.

The United States and other foreign governments supporting the Mujahidin rejected Soviet recommendations to restore Afghanistan's buffer status. Washington was no longer interested in neutrality for Afghanistan. Neither were Pakistan and Saudi Arabia, since a neutral Afghanistan would likely mean a moderate Afghanistan intent on returning the country to its traditional tribal moorings. They sought a Muslim extremist outcome.

By late 1987, Soviet commanders had turned the great majority of offensive operations over to Afghan regime forces. In February 1988, Gorbachev stated publicly that all Soviet troops would be withdrawn from Afghanistan over a ten-month period starting on May 15. The Geneva Accords were signed on April 14 by the foreign ministers of Afghanistan and Pakistan, with the United States and the Soviet Union as guarantors. Like the 1954 Geneva

Agreement ending France's failure to reestablish its Indochina Empire, the Geneva treaty merely certified the military realities on the ground and provided a face-saving cover for Great Power retreat.

In Kabul, Soviet diplomats and intelligence officers watched a new eruption of Parcham-Khalq infighting with dismay as Soviet forces prepared to depart. Babrak Karmal and his half-brother Baryalai attempted to overthrow Najib. Khalqi Interior Minister Gulabzoi also plotted against Najib. Najib imprisoned Baryalai, and the Soviets evacuated Karmal to Moscow for the usual Soviet "medical treatment." Gulabzoi was also taken to Moscow. When Soviet reeducation programs failed to overcome Gulabzoi's enmity against Najib, the Soviets ended his long tenure as interior minister by making him Afghan ambassador in Moscow.[92]

The Geneva Accords specified that the Soviet withdrawal would be "frontloaded." Soviet negotiators agreed to bring home half the Soviet troops during the first three months of the withdrawal, from May through July 1988. The rest would leave by February 15, 1989. The United States and Pakistan urged the Mujahidin not to attack the departing Soviet troops. This enjoinder was only partly successful. Moderate commander Ismael Khan allowed the peaceful withdrawal of thousands of Soviet troops from southern and western Afghanistan through the border-crossing point at Turgundi above Herat. Hekmatyar and other Afghan radicals in Pakistan, however, vowed to continue fighting during the Soviet pullout.

Masood did not reveal his intentions. Nor did he respond to Soviet invitations to reopen negotiations on exercising restraint during the Soviet pullout. This concerned the Soviets. Ever since the first Soviet convoys had been attacked on the Salang Highway during the 1979 invasion, the Salang Pass and its tunnel complex had remained the single most vulnerable strategic transportation chokepoint in Afghanistan. Keeping the Salang Highway open was vital to a successful withdrawal of the last Soviet troops remaining in Afghanistan from the capital area back to the USSR.

In October 1988, then Soviet chief of staff Varennikov wrote to Masood but received no reply. In November, Moscow ordered the Soviet military to deliver a list of talking points to Masood designed to elicit his cooperation. They proposed the creation of a Tajik autonomous region in the north and offered Soviet aid to "support the population of Panshir and the areas adjoining the above sector of the highway."[93] Masood still did not answer. A Soviet military report in the fall of 1988 urged continuing the Soviet outreach to the northern commander:

> In our view . . . [we] ought to step up efforts to establish contacts with A. Shah to assure [our] prospects. It is inadvisable to get involved in combat operations with him. Our troops could end up in an extremely serious situation if they suffer large losses, are forced to stay for a long period, or are evacuated by air from regions located to the south of the Salang [Pass] since ground communications will be cut off. Moreover, to conduct a large-scale operation against A. Shah would require an additional introduction of troops from the Soviet Union; one cannot be conducted with the forces which remain. But this would lead to an escalation of combat operations with all ensuing consequences.[94]

On December 18, the Soviets sent another letter to Masood. Authorized by General Varennikov and Deputy Foreign Minister Yuli Vorontsov, who was also serving as Soviet ambassador in Kabul, the letter exhibited a harsher tone than earlier ones. It reprimanded Masood for his unresponsiveness and stressed the urgency of discussions. The "stabilization" of Masood's territories and the Salang Highway was necessary, it said, especially to permit the "continuous supply of food and essential goods" to Kabul. The letter offered assistance to "the residents of South Salang and Panshir." An answer was requested by December 25.[95] On December 26, a day after the Soviet deadline, Masood sent a defiant response, warning: "If you begin combat operations then we will give you a fitting reply."[96]

On January 23, 1989, Politburo Afghan Commission chairman Shevardnadze and five other Politburo members authored an authoritative—and pessimistic—memorandum on the situation. The document exhibited the anger and frustration prevailing in the Soviet leadership three weeks before the final Soviet troop drawdown was scheduled to end:

> The current situation raises for us a number of complicated issues. On one hand, if we renege on our decision to withdraw troops by February 15, there would be extremely undesirable consequences on the international front. On the other hand, there is no certainty that after our

withdrawal there will not be an extremely serious threat to a regime which the entire world associates with us. Moreover, the opposition can at any time begin to coordinate its activities, which is what American and Pakistan military circles are pushing for. There is also a danger in that there is no true unity in the Afghanistan party, which is split into factions and clans.[97]

Gorbachev and his advisers decided to answer Masood's defiance with a massive display of Soviet power. On January 24, the day after the memo was transmitted, the Soviets commenced a huge air bombardment along both sides of the southern Salang Highway and in Masood-controlled territories near the road. Strategic backfire bombers flying from bases in the Soviet Union leveled villages along the road and killed thousands of civilians. Two days later, Masood wrote to Vorontsov: "I received your warning. The bombings which followed it and those crimes which your people committed . . . will change nothing."[98] The Soviets "have understood the psychology of the Afghan people" and "it is impossible to drive them to their knees."[99]

The remainder of Soviet land forces in the Kabul area departed Afghanistan on the Salang Highway during the first two weeks of February. On February 15, representatives of the world media were invited to record the triumphant return of the last Soviet soldier over the Termez Bridge linking Afghanistan and the Soviet Union. Scores of cameras clicked as a bemedalled General Boris Gromov, the last Soviet commander in Afghanistan, saluted the Soviet flag from the Afghan side of the bridge. Prearranged wild cheering erupted from Afghan soldiers and Soviet troops stationed on opposite sides of the 50-yard-long span. After the salute was rendered, Gromov began his theatrical walk to Soviet soil.

Bands played. Gromov's fourteen-year-old son ran toward his father from the Soviet side. The boy thrust a bouquet of flowers into the general's hand exactly at the midway point of the bridge. The cheering gradually died down as, hand in hand, Gromov and his son walked into the crowd of Soviet well-wishers. The former Soviet commander in Afghanistan did not look back at his Afghan comrades watching from the other bank of the Amu Darya.

The primary legacy of the Soviet invasion and nine-year occupation was Afghanistan's descent back into the shatter zone. The horrendous carpet-bombing

of heavily populated areas along the Salang Highway in the closing days of
the occupation did not demonstrate Soviet power; instead, it symbolized the
Soviet military's failure in Afghanistan. The bombardment was the last gasp
of the Soviet war machine's nine-year visitation of death and destruction in
Afghanistan.[100]

The Mujahidin victory erased the image of the Soviet Army's invincibility
dating from the 1943 Battle of Stalingrad. Inside the Soviet Union, anguished
memories of the war, lingering popular bitterness about wasted Soviet lives,
and war-related social ills brought back by a half-million disillusioned Soviet
veterans hindered Gorbachev's domestic reform programs. Huge amounts
of additional Soviet aid financed a "decent interval" between the Soviet withdrawal and Najib's inevitable collapse three years later. In July 1994, two years
after Najib's regime crumbled, former Soviet Politburo member Georgy Korniyenko wrote:

> In the beginning of 1989 Shevardnadze and his associates were tri-
> umphantly stating that they "turned out to be right," when the imme-
> diate collapse of the former regime did not take place, especially after
> the Soviet troops' withdrawal from Afghanistan. They only hushed up
> about the billions that our country had to pay to continue the massive
> military and economic support of this regime. This kept it in power
> for some more time.[101]

Keeping the PDPA on life support for another three years permitted Pakistan and Saudi Arabia additional opportunity to position their Afghan extremist protégés to penetrate the vacuum left behind by Najib's regime.
Meanwhile, American intelligence and diplomatic analyses, imprisoned in
Cold War constructs, remained oblivious to the radical Islamic menace gathering on the Pakistani Frontier.

At the moment Gromov and his son were walking off the Termez Bridge
into a throng of Soviet soldiers, another celebration began 400 miles away in
Islamabad deep inside the American embassy. CIA Station Chief Milt Bear-
den later wrote that, on his instruction, a clerk sent an immediate cable to
Langley with two words, etched out of Xs covering the whole page, stating
"We Won!"[102]

Both the Americans and Soviets were exaggerating their successes. The difference was that the Soviets at the time knew this. The Americans did not. In the coming decades, the United States would be locked in a global struggle against the violent Islamic extremism spawned on the Pakistani Frontier during the Soviet-Afghan war.

CHAPTER 10

The General's Vision

Excerpts from a 1992 State Department intelligence analysis of Gulbud-
din Hekmatyar, transmitted by secret State Department telegram to
American embassies in Pakistan, Saudi Arabia, India, and Europe, de-
classified on April 6, 2000:

> *Gulbuddin Hekmatyar is a radical Muslim fundamentalist who be-*
> *lieves his divinely-ordained destiny is to rule Afghanistan. However,*
> *his single-minded and ruthless pursuit of power has alienated him*
> *from the overwhelming majority of his countrymen. Hekmatyar is*
> *the most divisive element in current attempts to hammer out a suc-*
> *cessor government in Kabul. His accession to power would be resisted*
> *by force by many of the commanders on the ground. Hekmatyar's al-*
> *liance with the most hard-line elements of the former Kabul regime*
> *and his willingness to assassinate other resistance figures who stand*
> *in his way have repelled most Afghans. Hekmatyar is virulently anti-*
> *Western. He has frequently targeted U.S. and Western interests in Pa-*
> *kistan. He supported Iraq in the Gulf War despite having long been*
> *a beneficiary of Saudi largesse.*
>
> *Hekmatyar's espousal of militant Islam was probably a manifes-*
> *tation of his strong opposition to the king, Zahir Shah, which appears*
> *rooted in tribal rivalry. Hekmatyar belongs to the Ghilzai Pushtun*
> *tribal confederation which traditionally has opposed the Durrani*
> *Pushtuns. Hekmatyar's antipathy to the former king is well known.*
> *As is his contempt for traditional Pushtun institutions such as the*
> *Loya Jirga. Hekmatyar's ideas and his organization reflect the strong*

influence of the Muslim brotherhood (with which he is in contact, ac-
cording to a subordinate) and the Jamaat-i Islami party of Pakistan,
whose leader, Qazi Hussein Ahmed, remains his staunchest sup-
porter. Hekmatyar also supports other international Islamic causes.
His training camps reportedly have hosted Kashmiris, Algerians, and
other Islamic radicals from around the world, who, after a stint with
the resistance in Afghanistan, return home with their newly-acquired
military and political skills.[1]

It is sometimes debated whether historical trends create leaders or leaders create historical trends. Pakistan's military dictator Zia ul-Haq's eleven-year dictatorship in Pakistan fell into the latter category. Previous Pakistani military rulers had dismissed civilian governments and seized power before Zia overthrew Prime Minister Zulfikar Ali Bhutto in 1977. But Zia was different from the secular, military despots who preceded him. He was personally deeply religious, the son of a Mawlawi. He was determined to redirect Pakistan's mainstream Islam in a rigidly Sunni Islamist direction, away from the moderate foundation where it had rested for centuries. In Afghanistan, Zia's empowerment of minority Afghan extremist leaders such as Gulbuddin Hekmatyar and collaboration with Arab militants, including Osama bin Laden, led inexorably to the Taliban, the continuing warfare in Afghanistan, and the messianic Muslim terrorism plaguing the world today. Zia's military successors have maintained the alliance he forged with radical Islamism, suppressing Pakistan's secular political parties and overthrowing elected governments. In 2007, a leading American specialist on Pakistan voiced concern that it may be "too late for civil society in Pakistan to withstand growing pressures from radical Islamists and too late for the army to come up with a strategy" to withdraw from Pakistani politics.[2]

The movement for a homeland for Muslims in the subcontinent picked up momentum in the 1930s when it became clear that the British were leaving. The movement's leader and Pakistan's later founder, Mohammad Ali Jinnah, did not differentiate between Islam's many currents. The crucial question of "which Islam" should prevail was not decided. After independence, that question became a controversial issue in Pakistan's internal politics. The Pakistani Muslim Brotherhood offshoot, Jamaat-i Islami, insisted that the new nation should develop into an Islamic state governed by Sharia. Democratic-minded Pakistanis, Pakistanis of the Shia minority (about 20 percent of Pakistan's population), and the moderate Sunni-majority, Sufi-influenced Barelvi sect disagreed. And Pakistan's secular, westernized elite supported a moderate, modernizing Pakistan based on the Western model, rooted in civil society and tolerant of different religions. This latter group included Jinnah and Pakistan's first prime minister, Liaquat Ali Khan. After Pakistan's birth, Jinnah eloquently declared, "You are free; you are free to go to your temples, you are free to go to your mosques or to any other place of worship."[3]

The loss of Pakistan's two most authoritative leaders not long after Independence dealt a major blow to Pakistan's prospects for democratic growth and political stability.[4] Jinnah, the country's first civilian leader, died only thirteen months after Pakistani independence. Prime Minister Liaquat Ali Khan was assassinated in October 1951. The constant turnover of unelected prime ministers after Liaquat Ali Khan's death—six during the next seven years—further undermined stability. So did the influx of millions of refugees after partition, economic problems, and Pakistan's defeat in three wars with India. The last, in 1971, ended with the traumatic succession of Bangladesh from Pakistan.

On Pakistan's northwestern flank, Mohammad Daoud, Afghanistan's strongman in Kabul, pressed his irredentist Pashtunistan claim on Pakistan's Northwest Frontier Province and Baluchistan during his first period in power (1953–1963) and for nearly three years after his 1973 coup. The Soviet Union's opportunistic support for Pashtunistan and Moscow's alliance with India raised the specter of a geostrategic vice on Pakistan. Indian Prime Minister Indira Gandhi's acceptance of the 1979 Soviet invasion of Afghanistan and India's provision of military and economic aid to the PDPA regime only increased Pakistan's apprehensions about Indo-Soviet collusion.

Indo-Pakistani discord has remained South Asia's most persistent strategic feature since the British departure in 1947. The bitter Indo-Pakistani enmity is fed by memories of millions of Hindu and Muslim lives lost during the bloody 1947–1948 partition riots as well as by religious differences and unresolved territorial disputes, especially the dispute over Kashmir. The mutual hostility extends beyond the level of governments, permeating the general population of both countries. In Pakistan and India politicians can often gain or lose votes based on how tough they are perceived to be against the other side.

"Liberating" the Indian-occupied area of Muslim-majority Kashmir remains a popular issue in Pakistan. Each country makes credible claims to
Kashmir. In 1947, the princely state's Hindu maharaja's accession to India
met the agreed criteria set before partition that the Indian princes would determine whether to join India or Pakistan.[5] India's position, however, has been
damaged by its refusal to allow Kashmiris to make their own preferences
known in an act of self-determination. In 1948, the Indian ambassador to the
United Nations, on instructions from his government, assured the UN Security Council that a plebiscite would be conducted to ascertain the wishes of
the Kashmiri people. India later reneged on its plebiscite commitment and
virtually annexed the larger portion of Kashmir it occupied during the first
Indo-Pakistani war in 1947–1948.

Military intervention in Pakistan's domestic affairs began when religious
riots erupted in the early 1950s. Islamist groups led by Jamaat-i Islami activists demanded that the Ahmadi sect be declared non-Muslim.[6] In February
1953, the police were unable to cope with Jamaat-engineered violent demonstrations in the Punjab. The government turned to the army to restore order.
That intervention set an unhealthy precedent. A new wave of Jamaat demonstrations in the fall of 1958 prompted General Iskander Mirza, Pakistan's president, to declare martial law in Pakistan on October 7, 1958. Three weeks
later, Pakistan's chief of army staff, General Muhammad Ayub Khan, arrested
Mirza and sent him into exile in Britain. Ayub Khan, a thoroughly secular
general opposed to Jamaat's Islamization agenda, appointed himself "martial
law administrator" and "field marshal." He ruled Pakistan until March 1969.
When he stepped down, Pakistan was already beginning to look like an army
with a state rather than a state with an army.

Ayub Khan and Zia ul-Haq held opposite views on the role of religion in
domestic politics. Nonetheless, their dictatorships had much in common.
Both followed a hard line toward India, kept military spending over 60 percent of the federal budget, ridiculed democracy, centralized power, enlarged
internal security and intelligence organs, and suppressed domestic political
dissent. Ayub Khan often said that Pakistan was not ready for Western-style
parliamentary rule; Zia proclaimed Pakistan's political parties "defunct."

Ayub, like Zia a decade later, benefited from Cold War geopolitical trends
motivating Washington toward alliance relations with Pakistan. Ayub Khan
and Zia utilized the American economic and military assistance that Wash-

ington provided (intended to help contain the USSR) to balance India's ever-increasing military might and to keep the inefficient Pakistani economy afloat. The Eisenhower and Kennedy administrations handsomely rewarded Ayub Khan for Pakistan's membership in the Southeast Asian Treaty Organization and the Central Treaty Organization. The Johnson administration terminated aid to India and Pakistan when a new Indo-Pakistan war broke out in 1965, but the Reagan administration resumed large-scale aid to Pakistan in 1981.

The Pakistani Army's main instruments of internal political control since Ayub Khan's dictatorship have been the Inter-Services Intelligence Directorate, or ISI, and Military Intelligence, or MI. Under Ayub, the clandestine responsibilities of the two military intelligence agencies ballooned in domestic as well as foreign policy arenas. This was certainly not the intention of British Major General William Cawthorne when he founded the ISI in 1948. Cawthorne was a member of the British team that pieced together the Pakistani Army from Muslim regiments drawn from prepartition British India. After independence, he was the Pakistani Army's first deputy chief of staff and first director of military intelligence. Outside Pakistan-occupied parts of Kashmir, Cawthorne limited the ISI's role to collecting military intelligence and coordinating intelligence operations among the three military services (army, navy, and air force). The Pakistani prime minister appointed the ISI's director general, an officer of lieutenant general rank, on the advice of the commander of Pakistan's armed forces.

Military dictator Ayub Khan gave the ISI more responsibilities after his 1958 coup: sustaining military rule in Pakistan, monitoring domestic political opposition, and advancing Pakistan's interests abroad. The ISI began to function like intelligence organizations in other dictatorships, tapping the phones of opposition figures, harassing critics of the military regime, conducting media campaigns, intimidating influential citizens, and carrying out occasional assassinations.

Pakistan's defeat in the second Indo-Pakistan war in 1965 and popular demonstrations against Ayub Khan's military dictatorship forced him to hand power to a military successor in 1969. The country's humiliating defeat in the 1971 third Indo-Pakistani war and the resulting loss of East Pakistan (which became Bangladesh), including over half of the population, compelled then military ruler Yahya Khan to resign. Pakistan's People's Party politician Zulfikar Ali Bhutto stepped into the power vacuum. A cabinet minister at age thirty and prime minister at forty-five, Bhutto's meteoric rise and promises of a return to democracy after fifteen years of military rule raised hopes within Pakistan's educated elite and the media that he would move the country back to the democratic path it was on during its early years of independence. Bhutto instead became an authoritarian ruler, jailing his political opponents and catering to the religious right. In foreign policy, Bhutto improved Pakistan's relations with China and Saudi Arabia to balance Islamabad's ties to the United States.

Pakistan's covert training and arming of Muslim proxies to help fight its foreign enemies date back to the 1947–1948 and 1965 wars with India. The recruits, mainly Pashtuns from the tribal agencies motivated by religious fervor, partially offset India's advantage over Pakistan in military manpower. The proxy strategy, however, failed to turn the tide of battle. The first Indo-Pakistani war ended with India occupying three-fifths of Kashmir, including the capital, Srinagar.[7] Pakistan named the smaller portion of the former princely state it occupied Azad (Free) Kashmir.

During the 1965 war, Ayub Khan made a second unsuccessful attempt to conduct proxy war in Kashmir. The operation was named "Operation Gibraltar." ISI-trained Pashtun tribals attacked Kashmir but were driven back. Before the 1971 Bangladesh War, the ISI coordinated with Jamaat-i Islami to train two brigades of religious students studying at Jamaat madrassas in West Pakistan. One brigade was named al-Badr ("the moon" in Arabic) and the other al-Shams ("the sun"). The world press documented numerous atrocities, massacres, beheadings, and rapes committed by the two groups. Their brutal treatment of civilians rallied more Bengalis to the side of those calling for independence from Pakistan.

Bhutto's initiation of a clandestine proxy war in Afghanistan in 1975 differed from the three earlier precedents in an important way: This time, Pakistan would be organizing foreign nationals—young Afghan exiles—to overthrow a foreign government. Bhutto insisted on the utmost secrecy. He established and chaired an interagency "Afghan cell" to set strategy. The army chief, the ISI director, Foreign Ministry officials, and the chief of the NWFP constabulary participated in the meetings. The Afghan Young Muslim exiles were rounded up and sent to the Pakistani military base at Attock Fort on the

Indus. Attock's towering walls shielded their military training from Daoud's spies. Bhutto's one-week proxy war in Afghanistan failed militarily, but it achieved his political objective of drawing Daoud into negotiations with Pakistan. That was, in fact, how Bhutto had planned it. The Afghan survivors straggling back to Pakistan had been duped.

❦

By March 1976, after three years in power, Bhutto had tightened his grip on domestic politics, but had not established his authority over Pakistan's army. That month, he reached outside the cohort of anglicized, scotch-guzzling, secular Pakistani generals trained during the colonial period to choose another army chief: Lieutenant General Zia ul-Haq. Zia's modest socioeconomic background and strong religious values, Bhutto probably calculated, set him apart from other generals, reducing the risk of a military coup. Bhutto passed over six of Zia's superiors to make him Pakistan's next chief of army staff, or COAS.

Zia ul-Haq was an Indian-born Muslim from a very religious middle-class family. He was neither charismatic nor personally engaging. Of medium height, he wore his black hair slicked back and parted in the middle and waxed his mustache. Zia was very polite and exuded humility. He demonstrated no interest in politics. He once told an interviewer: "Drinking, gambling, dancing and music were the way the officers spent their free time. I said prayers instead. Initially, I was treated with some amusement—but my seniors and my peers decided to leave me alone after some time."[8]

Bhutto's choice of Zia to command Pakistan's military forces was a dangerous one. So was his selection of Lieutenant General Gulam Jilani Khan as ISI chief. General Khan conspired with Zia to overthrow Bhutto in 1977. Zia imprisoned the deposed prime minister for a year before sending him to the gallows.[9] He retained Khan as ISI chief after hanging Bhutto.

Zia proved adept at realpolitick during his eleven-year dictatorship, skillfully managing relations with the Soviet Union, the United States, India, China, and other countries important to Pakistan. His approach was discerning, bold, and deceptive. He pursued a constant dialogue with Moscow during the Soviet occupation of Afghanistan while keeping the water boiling in Afghanistan—cool enough to prevent Soviet military provocations against Pakistan, but hot enough to keep Soviet casualties at a painful level. Zia's proxy war strategy in Afghanistan relied on the maxim, "If the guerrilla is not losing, he wins." The Mujahidin safe havens in Pakistan and the ISI's provision of training, arms, and guidance guaranteed a continuous battlefield stalemate in Afghanistan.

In the process, Zia reached agreements with Moscow that he did not intend to honor. In his memoirs, President Reagan's secretary of state, George Shultz, recalled Zia's explanation to President Reagan about how Pakistan would be able to violate the commitments it had made to the Soviets in the April 1988 Geneva Accords. In a telephone conversation with Reagan, Zia had said the Pakistanis "would just lie about it," Shultz wrote. "Zia told him that Muslims have the right to lie in a good cause."[10]

Zia lied to the Americans as well. In a May 1984 conversation with Vice President George H.W. Bush, he declared that Pakistan's nuclear program was entirely peaceful, a comment belied by reliable U.S. intelligence reports. "You have my personal assurance," Zia told the vice president. The month before Zia's pledge to Bush, Pakistani nuclear scientist A. Q. Khan had boasted to a Pakistani newspaper that Pakistan had already successfully enriched uranium to a weapons-grade level. Two months later, in July 1984, several Pakistani nationals attempting to purchase nuclear-weapons-making items were apprehended in Texas and Canada. Bipartisan congressional critics of the Reagan administration's forbearing approach to Zia's lies passed the Pressler Amendment in 1986. The country-specific legislation conditioned U.S. aid to Pakistan on annual certification by the executive branch that Pakistan neither possessed nor was developing a nuclear weapon.[11]

Zia substantially enlarged the ISI during his eleven-year rule and increased its responsibilities. Ultimately more than 12,000 military officers[12] were deployed down to the district level in Pakistan and at diplomatic posts overseas. Thousands more civilian informants and agents served as the ISI's eyes and ears in government offices, at mosques, in the media, and within political parties. Zia relied on the ISI to collaborate with Pakistan's religious parties, liaise with Arab extremists, implement his domestic Islamization programs, suppress pro-democracy groups, and manage Pakistan's proxy war in Afghanistan. The ISI's control of the Afghan war and Afghan Mujahidin operating from bases in Pakistan was captured in the memoirs of the ISI brigadier in charge of the ISI's Afghan Bureau, who wrote that when starting his assignment, he "was now cast in the role of overall guerrilla leader." The brigadier revealed that 67 to 73 percent of all CIA- and Saudi-funded weapons were delivered by the ISI to the main Afghan extremist party leaders whom Zia favored: Gulbuddin Hekmatyar, Burhanuddin Rabbani, Yunus Khalis, and Abdul Rasoul Sayyaf.[13]

☙

Pakistani dictator Zia ul-Haq's vision for Afghanistan's future was sweeping, audacious—and unrealizable. In the midterm, it sought to install a radical Islamist Afghan regime in Kabul led by Gulbuddin Hekmatyar after the Soviet withdrawal. In the longer term, Zia imagined the formation of an Islamist confederation of Pakistan and Afghanistan.[14] Saudi Arabia's oil wealth would reinforce this powerful geostrategic bloc, pointed like a cocked pistol at India. Zia envisioned that, eventually, the five Muslim-populated Soviet Central Asian Republics would join the Pakistani-Afghan confederation.

Zia enjoyed elaborating on his vision with the help of a large map he pulled out for like-minded visitors and trusted ISI members in his inner circle. The map depicted his Islamist grouping projecting "strategic depth" against India. When combined, Pakistan's military forces, Mujahidin and Pakistan religious militia fighters, Muslim holy warriors from the Middle East, Saudi oil money, and Pakistan's nuclear weapons would neutralize India's large military and demographic advantages over Pakistan. The weight and religious zealotry of Zia's Islamist coalition would erase the stain left by three lost wars with Hindu India and provide the manpower to pry India out of Kashmir. The offensive thrust of Zia's vision was not limited to India. The Islamist coalition would also carry the holy war banner into the Middle East and beyond.

The Islamization of Pakistan's society was the foundation of Zia's vision. He once commented, "Pakistan is like Israel, an ideological state. Take out the Judaism from Israel and it will fall like a house of cards. Take Islam out of Pakistan and make it a secular state, it would collapse."[15] Zia's presidential and martial law decrees aspired to create a "new Islamic order" in Pakistan. His 1979 "Hudood Ordinances" ordered extreme penalties for crimes, ranging from the severing of hands for theft to execution for women convicted of adultery. (A victim of rape was required to produce four male witnesses or face an adultery charge.) Other decrees established Sharia courts to administer Islamic justice in specific areas and to annul any law in Pakistan that did not conform to Sharia.

Pakistan's two major politico-religious parties, Jamaat-i Islami and Jamiat-i Ulema-i Islam, played important roles in Zia's Afghan strategy. Jamaat forged close ties with radical Afghan Ghilzai Pashtuns operating against Soviet troops in eastern Afghanistan—Hekmatyar, Sayyaf, Khalis, and Jalaluddin Haqqani. Jamiat worked closely with the ISI to organize Afghan Pashtuns in southern Afghanistan, mainly extremist Pashtun Ghilzais such as future Taliban leader Mullah Mohammad Omar. Zia appointed politicians and clergy from the religious parties to his cabinet and gave them judicial positions in his newly created network of Sharia courts. Zia directed that the Islamic tax, or zakat, required of all Muslims be collected by government offices staffed by clerics. Zia's allies in the two Pakistani Islamist parties were the principal beneficiaries.

Zia's decrees favoring Sunni Islamist groups in Pakistan drove wedges into the existing religious and ethnic chasms in Pakistani society that democracy might have bridged. His favoritism for extremist Sunnis inspired Sunni sectarian militia to attack Shia mosques, unleashing Shia counterattacks. Armed Sunni fanatics took over "un-Islamic" Barelvi mosques and Sufi meeting halls. The resulting religious violence continues to the present, claiming thousands of lives each year.

Zia made the Pakistani Army a focus of his Islamization campaign. He introduced "holy war" doctrine as a subject to be taught at Pakistani military institutes and instituted a "beard allowance" to encourage soldiers to grow beards. Loyalists who retired from the military were rewarded with lucrative executive positions in five huge military "welfare foundations." The foundations controlled hundreds of businesses, banks, and educational institutions financed by the federal budget.

Zia named himself president and martial law administrator of Pakistan. But his real source of power was the army. He retained his military command title as COAS throughout his dictatorship. When he passed over secular British- and American-trained officers for promotion, scores of generals and colonels from the Ayub Khan era voluntarily retired. Meanwhile, army recruiters concentrated on inducting more officers from lower-middle-class Pakistani society, where the religious right had deep roots.

To accomplish his goals, Zia fashioned three potent strategies. First was proxy warfare in Afghanistan to drive out the Soviet Army. Second, the development of an Islamist infrastructure on the Pakistan Frontier to train Muslims from Afghanistan, Pakistan, and other countries to wage jihad in Afghanistan, Central Asia, and other world regions. Finally, he pursued close ties with the Reagan administration and Saudi Arabia to fund the Afghan war and to modernize Pakistan's military.

Zia relied heavily on his ISI and MI chiefs to pursue these goals, in particular Lieutenant General Mohammad Akhtar Khan, a relative of Zia's, who led the ISI from 1983 to 1988. During this period Zia also worked directly with Akhtar Khan's peppery and brutal deputy, Major General Hamid Gul. In 1988, he promoted Gul to replace Akhtar Khan. Jamaat's Qazi Hussain Ahmed and Gulbuddin Hekmatyar played key subordinate roles in implementing parts of Zia's strategies. Nawaz Sharif, a Punjabi businessman, occasional Zia cabinet minister, and future Pakistani prime minister, was also part of the Zia team. U.S. and Saudi resources financed Zia's proxy war in Afghanistan, while the 3 million Afghan refugees in Pakistan offered the ISI a huge military recruiting pool. A Pakistani scholar summed up the modus operandi:

> The [ISI] Afghan Bureau, in short, undertook to provide for the refugees and to train and equip the Mujahidin forces, churning out over 80,000 warriors between 1982 and 1987, and even taking on the risky task of selecting "volunteers," often Pashtuns from the regular Pakistani Army who were fluent in Pashto or Dari (Afghan Farsi) and were infiltrated into Afghanistan to guide the Mujahidin and help them use unfamiliar weapons systems effectively. Such soldiers were under strict instructions not to reveal their identity. If they were captured, Pakistan would deny that they were from the Pakistani Army.[16]

Thousands more Mujahidin fighters inside Afghanistan slipped through Soviet lines to solicit weapons and ammunition in Pakistan, then returned to their communities to resume fighting.

Zia's ISI-managed religious-military complex along the Pakistan Frontier functioned much like the Ikhwan complex of madrassas, mosques, and military training camps built by Wahhabi zealots in the Nejd desert in the 1920s. The ISI administered the Islamist network. It was made up of hundreds of Saudi-financed madrassas, military training facilities staffed by Pakistani ISI and regular military officers, Saudi charities dispensing funds, Pakistani Jamaat and Jamiat mosques, and small Muslim Brotherhood and Wahhabi bases on the Frontier.

The promotion of madrassas over the secular school system was a key ingredient in Zia's Islamization programs and the ISI's proxy war in Afghanistan. Pakistan's state education system steadily deteriorated during his dictatorship, and the number of madrassas in the country greatly increased. By 1988, according to one source, there were 2,891 madrassas in Pakistan, including more than 1,800 that were affiliated with Jamaat and Jamiat or their splinter parties. Jamaat's madrassas were mostly located in the tribal agencies around Peshawar and in the Punjab; Jamiat's were concentrated in Baluchistan and the Karachi area. The moderate Barelvi and Shia madrassas, numbering 717 and 47, respectively, hardly grew at all.[17] The ISI located numerous madrassas inside the Islamist war-making infrastructure near UN-supported Afghan refugee camps on the Afghan-Pakistani border.

Most taught the rigid Deobandi doctrine of the Jamiat-i Ulema-i Islam religious party.[18] The madrassas enrolled tens of thousands of young Afghan refugee children and Pakistani Pashtun boys from nearby villages. According to a Pakistani scholar, "these soldiers of God were crafted for one function alone—to kill the infidel communists or die trying, and view either outcome as the ultimate victory."[19] Under the influence of Saudi money and Saudi preachers on the Frontier during the 1980s and 1990s, the Frontier madrassas adopted an increasingly militant anti-Shia, anti-Sufi, and anti-West line, manufacturing armed fanatics for the Mujahidin extremist parties and later the Taliban to fight in Afghanistan and also Kashmir.

ꙮ

The Soviet occupation of Afghanistan made Pakistan a leading candidate for President Reagan's support for Third World insurgencies targeting Soviet-aligned governments.[20] Reagan and his top advisers forged a close working relationship with Zia, and U.S. military, economic, and covert assistance to Pakistan skyrocketed during the 1980s. Pakistan became the fourth-largest recipient of American aid after Israel, Egypt, and Turkey.

As part of the anticommunist Reagan Doctrine, the administration initiated what expanded into a multidecade policy of outsourcing U.S. Afghan policy to Pakistan. A 1983 cable to Washington from the American embassy in Islamabad was an early manifestation of this course: "Since the Soviet invasion of Afghanistan," it said, "we have largely been content to follow Pakistan's lead . . . in dealing with the Afghan resistance."[21] The Reagan administration terminated previous U.S. economic sanctions and restrictions on military assistance to Pakistan, looking the other way regarding Zia's active nuclear weapons development program. The Pentagon delivered more than forty F-16 combat jets and advanced radar systems to Pakistan as part of Washington's $3.2 billion military-economic aid package for Pakistan assembled in July 1981, the first of two six-year plans. In 1986, the administration prepared another, larger package, giving Pakistan $4.2 billion for the next six-year period, 1988–1994. Zia received Pakistan's share of antiaircraft Stinger missiles before they went to the Mujahidin, secretly passing some on to China for reverse engineering.

The CIA transferred billions more to the ISI to manage the Afghan war. The huge flow of covert arms and money kept the Soviet Army bogged down in Afghanistan. The Reagan administration accepted Zia's condition that the United States largely bankroll the costs of the Afghan war but let Pakistan decide how the money should be spent. CIA offices in Pakistan for the most part adhered to Zia's demand that American arms and money be provided directly to the ISI, that there be no CIA contact with Afghans unless overseen by ISI officers, and that Americans train Pakistani military officers to train Mujahidin on new weapons rather than directly training the Mujahidin. Zia prohibited CIA officers from crossing into Afghanistan or entering the tribal agencies.[22]

The Pakistani restrictions on CIA direct engagement with the Mujahidin did not apply to American diplomats. A young American press and cultural officer with broad contacts among the Mujahidin at the time wrote years later that Pakistan was using American aid to support "totalitarian despots" like Gulbuddin Hekmatyar in the resistance, rather than pro-Western, pro-democracy Afghan forces. The officer thought that, "in a very profound respect we had no policy—we followed Pakistan's." After months of hearing complaints from Afghans, he began to submit reports to his superiors on what he was hearing without appending a comment. One evening, the ambassador, "chomping on a cigar," told the officer, "I don't agree with what your peacenik friends tell you." After a few drinks, the ambassador whispered to the young officer that "he ran the embassy for the CIA and State Department be damned."[23]

☙

Private Saudi money proved vital to building, equipping, and maintaining Zia's war-making infrastructure on the Frontier before covert funds began to arrive in the mid-1980s from the CIA and its Saudi equivalent, the General Intelligence Directorate (GID). Brigadier Mohammed Yousuf, chief of the ISI's Afghan Bureau, wrote of this early period: "It was largely Arab money that saved the system. By this I mean cash from rich individuals or private organizations in the Arab world, not Saudi government funds. Without these extra millions the flow of arms actually getting to the Mujahideen would have been cut to a trickle."[24] A CIA officer stationed in Islamabad in the late 1980s estimated private Saudi donations for military and humanitarian purposes at $20 million to $25 million every month.[25]

Tactically, the ISI attempted to keep Americans and Arabs apart, even while comingling their resources at the operational level. They did their job well. In 2000, a former CIA official reportedly recalled that "the Agency's officers in Pakistan seldom left the embassy in Islamabad and rarely ever met with the leaders of the Afghan Resistance, let alone with Arab militants."[26] Saudi intelligence officers, under GID Director General Prince Turki, were allowed more leeway than the Americans to contact Afghans and Arabs. But they, too, were expected to subordinate their actions to Zia's strategy. The GID coordinated with the ISI and with Abdullah Azzam's Services Bureau in Peshawar during the 1980s. Turki's chief of staff, Ahmed Badeeb, couriered money from Saudi Arabia to Zia personally and to ISI generals.[27]

Throughout the 1980s, the common anti-Soviet cause kept radical Arab groups together, submerging their internecine religious and political differences. The revered Abdullah Azzam, known in the Muslim world as the "Father of the Afghan Jihad," encouraged this solidarity. In speeches and meetings, he called the Afghan jihad a "gift from God" to unite the umma in defense of Islam. He continued to sound his theme that it was the religious duty of all Muslims to support the Afghan jihad. He praised the multinational character of Arab assistance, proudly noting that "the first Arab martyrs of the jihad were from Palestine and Kuwait."[28]

Azzam's Services Bureau became the main base of the Muslim Brotherhood in Pakistan. Azzam personally helped hundreds of foreign Muslims arriving on the Pakistan Frontier during the 1980s. Like other Arab charities in Pakistan, Azzam's Services Bureau was functionally divided into offices dealing with military and humanitarian matters. It published an Arabic-language magazine, *al Jihad*, extolling the Brotherhood's ideology and glorifying the exploits of Arabs in the anti-Soviet war. It "worked closely with Pakistan, especially the Inter-Services Intelligence (ISI), the Saudi government and Egyptian governments, and the vast Muslim Brotherhood network."[29]

Azzam traveled often to the Saudi Kingdom, to cities in the Middle East, and to Europe and America during the 1980s, raising funds and recruiting young Muslims to participate in the Afghan jihad. In Peshawar, he created an umbrella Islamic Coordination Council. Representatives of Saudi charities in Pakistan attended the council's regular meetings in Peshawar, meant to synchronize the huge flow of money coming in from Saudi Arabia and the Gulf Emirates.

Azzam was aided by his former student Osama bin Laden, who periodically traveled to Peshawar before moving there in 1984. Then only twenty-six, bin Laden was a major fundraiser for Azzam. He created an "Islamic Salvation Council" with offices in Riyadh and Jeddah to raise money to finance the Services Bureau, tapping his large clan and other respected families in Saudi Arabia for donations. Azzam liberally distributed funds to ISI-favored Ghilzai Pashtuns, especially Hekmatyar and Sayyaf. Azzam and bin Laden were closest to Hekmatyar. They provided him with Arab doctors, medicine, and food as well as foreign fighters. With their help, Hekmatyar's son-in-law and closest adviser, Ghariat Baheer, spent five years in Saudi Arabia raising money and falsely portraying Hekmatyar as the overarching leader of the Afghan jihad.

Bin Laden began to operate beyond Azzam's purview in 1985. He independently transported construction machinery from the bin Laden family's depots in Saudi Arabia to Peshawar. He used it to build bases, training camps, and madrassas for Afghan extremist factions. Prince Turki was pleased with bin Laden's performance. His assistant, Ahmed Badeeb, later recalled that bin Laden "was responsive to specific direction from both the Saudis and Pakistani intelligence agencies during the early and mid-1980s": "We were happy with him. He was our man. He was doing all what we ask him."[30]

In late 1987, bin Laden's bulldozers were working both sides of the border. He built a "military academy" for Sayyaf at Sada in the Khurram Tribal Agency,

FIGURE 10.1   ARAB GROUPS COOPERATING WITH THE ISI ON THE
               PAKISTANI FRONTIER, 1980–1989

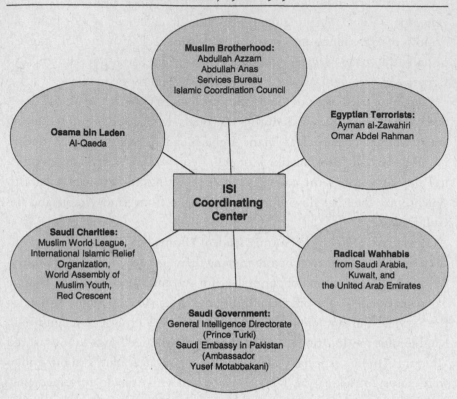

called the "Parrot's Beak" because of its geographic protrusion into Afghanistan, east of Tora Bora in Nangarhar and west of Khost. He befriended Jalaluddin Haqqani, the wiry Ghilzai Zadran commander and mullah from Paktiya, and expanded Haqqani's bases in North Waziristan and at Zhawar Kili across the border in Paktiya. He strengthened Khalis's Tora Bora cave complex south of Jalalabad and built roads to assist poverty-stricken Pashtun mountain villages on both sides of the Durand Line in the Tora Bora area. The local popularity he reaped from these projects later facilitated his escape from Tora Bora and disappearance into Pakistan's tribal agencies after 9/11. Bin Laden also enlarged an existing Hekmatyar base near Khost, built a second base for Sayyaf near Jaji in Paktiya, and established one for himself nearby, calling it "The Lion's Den." In late 1987, a combined Soviet-PDPA attack on bin Laden's base forced him and his men to pull back into Pakistan.

The first phase of the Soviet withdrawal, beginning in May 1988, allowed freer movement of Afghan Mujahidin and Arab militants into eastern Afghanistan. There, Egyptian terrorists Ayman al-Zawahiri and Omar Abdel Rahman coordinated with the ISI, bin Laden, and Hekmatyar to establish small operating bases for Arab militants in Nangarhar, Paktiya, and Konar. A white-robed Afghan Wahhabi, Jamil al-Rahman, began to build a Wahhabi emirate with Saudi money in Konar Province. About this time, bin Laden stepped up efforts to bring non-Arab Islamic militants to Pakistan. Bin Laden's brother-in-law Mohammad Khalifa, head of the Saudi Islamic Relief Charity office in Manila, sent Filipino members of the radical al-Sayyaf group to Pakistan for training.[31] Over one hundred Burmese Muslim separatists of the Rohinga Solidarity Group were trained at camps run by Hekmatyar and Haqqani in the tribal agencies.

❧

Pakistan descended deeper and deeper into the Afghan political cauldron after the 1979 Soviet invasion. Although Islamabad, too, would ultimately fail to fashion a viable Afghan leadership, it has proved better than either the Soviets or the Americans at manipulating Afghan tribal politics. During the Soviet occupation, Pakistani Pashtuns working in the ISI's Afghan cell were thoroughly familiar with the Pashtun tribal mosaic on both sides of the Durand Line.[32] Indeed, many among them came from Pashtun tribes straddling the border—Durrani Achakzai, Kakar, Shinwari, Waziri, Momand, and Safis. Speaking Pashto, growing beards, and wearing Afghan clothes, they easily melded into Mujahidin and, after 1994, Taliban formations operating inside Afghanistan. They were ideal recruiters of Pakistani tribal agents on the Frontier to serve as intelligence sources and even influential Mujahidin (later Taliban) leaders inside Afghanistan.

By repeatedly failing to fabricate an Afghan leadership in the 1980s, Zia, Akhtar, and Hamid Gul demonstrated the wisdom of a metaphor the moderate Afghan resistance leader Abdul Haq told me and others many times. The tale portrays a foreigner balancing two connected trays attached to a handheld weighing device used in South Asian bazaars. The foreigner carefully loads one tray, and then the other, with frogs. Just as he puts the last few frogs on the second tray, some frogs on the first tray hop off. As the foreigner returns those frogs to their original position, frogs on the second tray leap to the ground, or attempt to jump to the other tray. Before long, all of the frogs are in motion, moving in one direction or another. The foreigner gives up.

Zia's first sally into the cauldron stymied attempts by over a thousand Afghans to convene a loya jirga in Quetta in 1980 and then in Peshawar in 1981.[33] He wanted his favored Afghan Islamists, not the moderate nationalists chosen by a loya jirga, to lead Afghanistan after the anti-Soviet war. Denied the ability to form a genuine Afghan consensus, the atomized Afghan refugee population in Pakistan disintegrated into hundreds of political groups based on tribal, ethnic, and religious affiliations. Fifty-four different political parties registered with Pakistani officials. Few amounted to more than the leader's personal quam. Their feuds and competition for scarce resources stifled any chance for solidarity against the common enemy occupying Afghanistan— or to organize an Afghan political entity to negotiate with Zia and the ISI.

In 1976, with help from the ISI and Jamaat-i Islami, Hekmatyar's Hezb-i Islami (Party of God, hereafter referred to as Hezb) became the first self-described Afghan political party to emerge inside Pakistan. ISI financial and administrative support sustained his large party infrastructure, propaganda outlets, and commanders' network. Hekmatyar organized Hezb along Leninist lines, led by himself, the all-powerful emir. Strict discipline was imposed on party officials and members. Following the usual Afghan practice, Hekmatyar made his close relatives, in his case three sons-in-law and a nephew, his most trusted advisers. New members were carefully vetted before induction into Hezb, and Hekmatyar centered all military, religious, and political authority in his own hands at the top of the party's pyramidal structure.

Hekmatyar's party manifestos imitated the PDPA's shrill calls for transforming Afghanistan's tribal society. But his propaganda promised a Muslim utopia instead of a communist paradise. The Pashtun firebrand advocated a centralized, revolutionary, Islamic state ruled by Sharia; his militant Islamist foreign policy parroted Muslim Brotherhood themes. Hekmatyar frequently appeared at the side of Qazi Hussain Ahmed, the Jamaat leader, before Pakistani audiences to call for more jihads after the Afghan jihad was won. In one May 1987 rally in Pakistan, he promised, "If the Mujahidin continue to fight persistently, the day is not far when the occupied areas of Soviet Central Asia will also be liberated."[34]

The ISI steered the majority of American-Saudi combined covert and private aid to Hekmatyar. He was the ISI's favorite Mujahid and therefore the

CIA's favorite Mujahid. A photograph of the sour-eyed, thin-faced man wearing his signature black turban was the only picture in the living room of the Saudi ambassador in Islamabad, Yusef Motabbakani. The Saudi government and Saudi religious leaders permitted Hekmatyar to maintain collection boxes at mosques in the Kingdom. Libyan leader Muammar Qaddafi also provided substantial funds to Hekmatyar.

After the Soviet Union began its withdrawal in May 1988, Hekmatyar began to equate the United States with the Soviet Union as an enemy of Afghanistan in his public statements. During this period, his commanders in southern Afghanistan fought pitched battles with Mullah Akunzada, a powerful Alizai commander, to control Helmand's opium fields. Hekmatyar's radio station and newspapers falsely touted him as the most popular of the Mujahidin leaders and the primary spokesman for the entire resistance movement. In reality, the great majority of Mujahidin commanders and party leaders feared and hated him for his refusal to cooperate with other Mujahidin and for attacking non-Hezb Mujahidin groups and personalities in Pakistan and Afghanistan.[35]

Burhanuddin Rabbani led the second-largest Mujahidin organization, Jamiat Islami (Islamic Unity), adopting the party label that had originally been used by the theology faculty at Kabul University. Rabbani faced an uphill battle in competing with Hekmatyar. His Tajik origins placed him at a disadvantage. Zia's strategy favored Ghilzai Pashtuns, most notably Hekmatyar. The great majority of Rabbani followers were Tajiks. Jamiat and Hezb remained the largest parties in the Mujahidin until Pakistan created the Taliban in 1994.

The efforts of Zia and the ISI to bring Hekmatyar, Rabbani, and other Mujahidin politicians together in Peshawar were no more successful than Soviet attempts to force Parcham-Khalqi unity in Kabul. The Pakistanis disregarded abundant historic evidence that any Afghan political entity established by foreigners is artificial and doomed to ultimate failure. The ISI's first endeavor at Afghan coalition-building occurred in September 1978, when it made a former member of the Afghan Parliament, Mawlawi Mohammad Nabi Mohammadi—a moderate Ghilzai Ahmadzai from Logar Province—head of a high-sounding Mujahidin coalition, Harakat-i-Inqilab-i-Islami (Revolutionary Islamic Movement). The ISI forced Hekmatyar to sign up. Mawlawi Yunus Khalis, one of Hekmatyar's more important faction leaders from Nangarhar, refused to join. He instead formed his own Hezb party, Hezb-i Islami Khalis. Afghan bickering and infighting overwhelmed Nabi's Harakat Mujahidin front from its inception. When it collapsed in a chaotic flutter three months later, Nabi made the lofty Harakat masthead the title of his own political party.

The four parties—Hezb, Jamiat, Harakat, and Hezb-Khalis—became five when Naqshbandi pir Sibghatullah Mojaddedi formed his Jebha-i-Milli Najat (National Liberation Front) in early 1979. Soon after, Sayyid Ahmad Gailani, the Qadiriya pir, announced the establishment of his own Mahaz-i-Milli Islami-yi Afghanistan (National Islamic Front of Afghanistan).

After the December 1979 Soviet invasion, the ISI made another attempt to organize the resistance leaders into a loose coalition. It anointed Abdul Rasoul Sayyaf as the leader of a new united front, the ambitiously named Islamic Union for the Freedom of Afghanistan (Ittehad-i-Islami Bara-yi-Azadi Afghanistan). Ittehad could not long survive the infighting among the seven Mujahidin leaders, whose only goals were to aggrandize their personal power and keep the other six down. Hekmatyar adamantly rejected Ittehad, arguing that none of the other party leaders equaled his stature and strength. Moderate party leaders Gailani and Mojaddedi protested that they could not abide Sayyaf's Wahhabi extremism.

The ISI temporarily gave up coalition building after Ittehad collapsed in 1981. It pieced together a very loose "Alliance" of the seven parties. Since none of the seven leaders would accept the leadership claim of any other, the ISI established a rotating Alliance spokesman position. Each leader performed as spokesman for a four-month cycle. This allowed all seven parties to keep their complete autonomy, separate ISI-funded party offices, warehouses, prisons, and field commanders who benefited from their personal patronage.

The rotating Alliance system survived until the Soviet pullout commenced in May 1988, after the Geneva Accords. Zia decided at this point to try again to bring the seven together under one roof. The ISI assembled an "interim government" to replace Najib's regime. It was led by Wahhabi zealot Ahmed Shah Ahmadzai, Sayyaf's deputy, and did not last long. "We shall take up our Kalashnikovs if they try to impose this man on us," Gailani told Iqbal Akhund, Pakistan's national security adviser.[36] When Mujahidin radicals Rabbani and Khalis also objected, the ISI discreetly nudged the Ahmed Shah Ahmadzai interim government into its dustbin of stillborn Mujahidin coalitions.

☙

Zia's sudden death in a plane crash on August 17, 1988, shortly after takeoff from a Pakistani military base suspended the ISI's Afghan leadership-making projects. Investigations into the cause of the crash were inconclusive, and conspiracy theories abounded.

The Pakistani rumor mills ruled out the government's conclusion that mechanical failure caused the military C-130 to go down. American ambassador Arnold L. Raphel and the U.S. embassy's military attaché perished with Zia in the crash. Speculation about who may have killed Zia focused mainly on the Soviet KGB, Najib's KHAD, and the Indian intelligence agency RAW (Research and Intelligence Wing of the Cabinet Secretariat). Soviet and Indian leaders, and Najib in Kabul, viewed Zia as a dangerous adversary. Soon after Zia's death, ISI colonel Faizan, head of the ISI's Quetta office, privately voiced another opinion on who killed Zia to an Afghan acquaintance. "We will not reach Zia's vision now," he moaned. "The Americans have killed him."[37]

After Zia's death, the dictator's deputy chief of army staff, Mirza Aslam Beg, and ISI chief Hamid Gul held the control levels of the army, and therefore Pakistan. Zia had appointed them to their positions in March 1987, and in the seventeen months before the plane crash, they had obediently implemented his instructions. As the new COAS, Beg enjoyed much greater formal authority than Gul did. But Gul, the dynamic ISI ringmaster of the Afghan holy war, wielded great power. After Zia's death, Beg deferred to Gul, defending him when he drew domestic and foreign criticism for his ruthlessness.[38]

Beg and Gul complemented one another. The silver-haired COAS was soft-spoken and passive to the point of being dull. Gul, privately dubbed the "Plucky Little General" by the American ambassador, was short in stature, dynamic, and devious.[39] He spoke in passionate bursts, sometimes hurling Islamist slogans, and sent his children to Christian convent schools. The two shared Zia's visceral hatred for India. After the Soviet departure, they also adopted an intense anti-American attitude that later matured into active, unapologetic promotion of al-Qaeda and the Taliban. Zia's military intelligence director, Major General Asad Durrani, became a junior partner to Beg and Gul. The threesome was determined to preserve the army's dominant position in Pakistani politics.

The decades-old competition for Pakistan's soul stirred slightly after Zia's death. Pakistan's educated upper and middle classes hoped that the new military leaders would allow the long-delayed parliamentary elections in November 1988. Beg's agreement to go ahead with the elections was widely hailed in Pakistan and abroad. But the democratic dawn after Zia's eleven years of military rule turned out to be a false one. Beg and Gul did not intend to risk a resounding victory by Benazir Bhutto, the daughter of former premier Zulfikar Ali Bhutto, at the polls. The parliamentary majority many thought she would win would make her a dangerous enemy—one determined to avenge the military's overthrow and execution of her father. They decided to let the electorate vote but make sure it would not make a mistake.

Gul brazenly rigged the election, denying Bhutto's Pakistan People's Party (PPP) a clear majority. His ISI pieced together an anti-PPP coalition, the Islami Jamhori Ittehad (IJI), that gave a leading role to Qazi Hussain Ahmed's Jamaat Party.[40] Nawaz Sharif attached his Muslim League Party, the second-largest after Bhutto's PPP, to the ISI-manufactured coalition. Military Intelligence Director Durrani later admitted in a public affidavit to Pakistan's Supreme Court that Beg ordered him to provide "logistical support" to the IJI. He testified that large sums, well over $2 million, were placed in IJI bank accounts in Karachi and other cities for Bhutto's opponents.[41] Asked later for clarification at a Supreme Court hearing, Beg bluntly stated: "It would be in the fitness of things that further proceedings on this matter be dropped."[42] And they were.

Bhutto was forced into governing from a fragile parliamentary base, hemmed in by the military nemesis that had hanged her father. Asked later to justify his actions, Gul replied: "Where the security concerns are overwhelming—and right from the beginning, Pakistan has been in the eye of the storm—these concerns become uppermost both in the minds of the establishment and the nation. And that is why, again and again, the nation veers to the support of the army—even if the army acts against the political institutions."[43]

After Zia's death, the Beg-Gul union organized late-night foreign-policy brainstorming sessions with like-minded generals. The discussions dwelled on Pakistan's geostrategic direction in the world. A Pakistani brigadier attending the discussions described the participants as "pseudo-intellectuals"[44] with romantic notions of global geopolitics.

The deliberations spun three strategic "doctrines" to lay on top of Zia's "Strategic Depth" concept. One postulated building a "Strategic Consensus" among Muslim Pakistan, Afghanistan, Iran, and Turkey. Saudi Arabia was left out of the strategic grouping. Although a non-state entity, the Muslim Brotherhood was included. The Strategic Consensus was aimed at giving Islamic muscle to "Strategic Defiance" of the United States and the Saudi royal family. Pakistan's provision of nuclear weapons technology to Iran would shore up Islamic "Strategic Deterrence" against American, Israeli, and Indian anti-Islamic "tyranny"[45] in the world. A "regional defense production cooperation" body would integrate the armed forces of the four "consensus countries."

The strategies concocted at General Beg's after-hours salon were plainly unrealistic. Neither Turkey nor Iran was interested in building strategic depth against India. These two countries at the time were attempting to improve political and economic relations with New Delhi. Secular Turkey was pro-American and a member of NATO. Iqbal Akhund, Prime Minister Bhutto's national security adviser, said the "more immediate purpose" of Beg and Gul's doctrines "was to keep a handle on Benazir's foreign policy, in particular with regard to Afghanistan and India."[46]

ॐ

ISI Director General Gul's final attempt to mold the seven Mujahidin party leaders into a coalition occurred as the last Soviet troops were leaving Afghanistan in January and the first two weeks of February 1989. Bhutto's foreign minister, Yaqub Khan, and her national security adviser, Iqbal Akhund, cochaired her government's first Afghan cell meeting, convoked to hear Gul's plans to organize an Afghan Interim Government (AIG) to take over in Kabul. No Afghans were invited. Khan and Akhund told Gul that once the ISI formed the AIG, the Pakistani government would not recognize it until the Mujahidin captured a major city in Afghanistan.[47] Gul informed that a Mujahidin *shura* ("council" in Arabic) would meet in February to choose the AIG. The AIG would conduct elections for a permanent government on July 31. The new government would be functioning by September 1989, and ready to assume power in Kabul after an offensive that the ISI was organizing toppled the Najib regime.

The ISI staged the shura in Rawalpindi, near Pakistani military headquarters. A prominent Afghan delegate complained that the heavy Pakistani presence was "conspicuous, overpowering, and grotesque."[48] Gul's plans for the shura required that the top seven AIG positions be distributed among the seven Mujahidin party leaders. Each of the seven was allowed to handpick sixty delegates to fill the 420 seats at the shura. The procedure guaranteed that the four extremist Mujahidin leaders—Hekmatyar, Sayyaf, Rabbani, and Khalis—would appoint a majority of the delegates.

Since four of the seven party leaders were Ghilzai Pashtuns, the shura's membership ended up mainly Ghilzai, though the Ghilzai represent less than 20 percent of Afghanistan's population. Geographically, northern, western, and southern Afghanistan were underrepresented. Altogether, only 38 of the 420 delegates came from southern and western Afghanistan, the Durrani Pashtun heartland. Gul's rules for the shura also grossly underrepresented the Hazara Shia, who made up about 15 percent of Afghanistan's population, along with Tajiks, Uzbeks, and members of Afghanistan's other ethnic minorities— well over half of Afghanistan's population. Except for Yunus Khalis, the party leaders invited few field commanders to participate in the shura. They packed their delegations with family members, other relatives and clan members, paid workers manning desks in their Peshawar offices, and loyalists certain to vote for them. A majority of the delegates espoused anti-Shia, anti-Sufi, anti-royalist, and anti-traditionalist positions.

From its opening on February 10, the shura resembled a chaotic circus. The seven Mujahidin leaders spent most of the time arguing with one another. The ISI's schedule had called for a three-day gathering. It lasted for over two tumultuous weeks. Prince Turki arrived from Saudi Arabia to help Gul contain the anarchy. On the first day, Gailani lashed back when Hekmatyar harshly challenged the legitimacy of some of his delegates. Rising from his chair, Gailani shouted back that he would retaliate by rejecting Hekmatyar's delegates. The uproar was finally squashed by a vote in which everyone agreed to accept everyone else's delegates.

On February 14, Mojaddedi led his contingent out of the shura for four days to protest Pakistani interference. In a confidential cable to Washington, the American embassy reported that "every faction in the shura is putting out its own version of, and disinformation about, all the backroom maneuvering that is going on. There are no neutral sources of information. Even the official press outlet for the shura, Afghan News Agency, is in fact controlled by one of the parties—Hezb Islami-Gulbuddin, and is distorting the news accordingly."[49]

Rancorous debate over the lack of fair representation in the shura destabilized proceedings for several days. ISI organizers finally agreed to sit 20 more delegates representing some small parties, raising the shura's attendance to 440. Gul permitted Mojaddedi to travel to Iran in order to entice 8 Shia parties headquartered in Tehran to join the gathering; Mojaddedi was told to offer 80 seats, which was 20 more than each party leader was allowed. He returned with a list of 100 Shia names. In protest, Hekmatyar boycotted the shura for 3 days. He returned after Sayyaf and Khalis furiously torpedoed Mojaddedi's deal.

The Mujahidin leaders passed the next 13 days denouncing each other and the shura. No more votes were taken, and no progress was made toward choosing a government. Each of the seven delegations insisted that their party leader be AIG president. Abdul Haq ceased attending; Zahir Shah–era moderates walked out. Finally, probably under ISI's tutelage, Zadran commander Jalaluddin Haqqani intervened to break the deadlock. The delegates were aware of Haqqani's record as a fierce Mujahidin commander, his close ties to the ISI, and the large amount of Saudi patronage sustaining his madrassas in North Waziristan.

Guided by Gul and Prince Turki behind the scenes, Haqqani broached a formula to break the stalemate. The bandolier of bullets crossing his chest and the holster housing an Enfield pistol indicated he meant business. Haqqani suggested that two delegates from each party, not including the seven leaders, accompany him to his house in Islamabad. He proposed sequestering them there until they came up with a mechanism to distribute the AIG cabinet portfolios among the seven leaders. Haqqani insisted that the leaders agree on the spot to accept his formula.

After another bout of mutual recrimination, the seven agreed. At this point, Haqqani unexpectedly reached into his pocket and pulled out a sheet of paper describing his procedure. He asked the leaders to sign. Six did. Hekmatyar refused, arguing that the process violated Islamic law. Haqqani grabbed the handle of his revolver and thrust the paper into Hekmatyar's hand, thundering that Hekmatyar either sign or go into Afghanistan and see how much popular support he really had among Afghans. Hekmatyar signed the agreement, writing out an objection next to his signature.

Haqqani locked the group in a boiler room at his home. He allowed no phone or other contact with the outside world. It took two full days for the committee to agree that the election would be conducted by secret ballot. They accepted Haqqani's procedure for the balloting the next day.

When the shura reconvened, the 440 delegates were given a ballot with the names and photos of the seven leaders who would fill out the interim government cabinet. Each delegate was instructed to circle only two photos on his ballot—one for his party leader, the other for one of the six outside his party. The party leader who received the most votes would be president; the second-largest vote winner would be prime minister. The remaining five leaders, in order of the votes received, would choose from four key cabinet positions (defense, interior, foreign affairs, and reconstruction) and chief justice of the Supreme Court.

The ballots were counted on February 24, 1989. The 456 votes cast by 440 delegates[50] suggested at least some ballot-box stuffing. Mojaddedi edged out Sayyaf by 1 vote, 174–173, to become president. Sayyaf won the prime ministership. Nabi came in third, Khalis fourth. The ISI favorite, Hekmatyar, was a poor fifth, with only 126 votes. Rabbani came in sixth and Gailani seventh. Gailani's low tally was influenced by his announcement before the voting that he did not want his delegates to vote for him. Rabbani's poor showing reflected the unwillingness of the overwhelming Pashtun majority at Gul's shura to vote for a Tajik.

Loud protests erupted among the delegates when Hekmatyar's ANA news service announced that he had become defense minister before Nabi and Khalis, who received more votes, could choose their ministry. Nabi, the third-highest vote-getter, immediately announced, through his spokesman, that he would claim the Defense Ministry. Khalis chose interior. Thoroughly embarrassed by his junior rank, Hekmatyar countered that he would not accept the Foreign Ministry. Prince Turki personally lobbied him to accept the post, no doubt with considerable financial inducements. Hekmatyar finally agreed. Relieved, Turki returned to the Saudi embassy in Islamabad only to be told, on arriving, that Hekmatyar, in a radio broadcast, had just repeated his decision to reject the Foreign Ministry position.[51]

Hekmatyar, Rabbani, and Gailani sulked in their tents after the elections but were compelled to move into their new offices, Hekmatyar the AIG Foreign Ministry, Rabbani the Reconstruction Ministry, and Gailani the Supreme Court. Hekmatyar pulled out of the AIG six months later; Rabbani and Gailani continued but publicly denounced both the shura and the AIG. Gailani attended few AIG meetings and threatened to resign from the AIG if new elections were not held within six months. (He did not honor that pledge.) AIG Interior Minister Khalis pronounced his view that the shura elections had been un-Islamic.

The new AIG president, Mojaddedi, appreciated the outcome. Prime Minister Sayyaf was equally satisfied. The two new AIG leaders fielded numerous media interviews (although Sayyaf banned women journalists from his). Prince Turki was pleased that the Rawalpindi Shura results excluded Shia based in Tehran from the AIG. The Saudi government quickly recognized the AIG. Tehran did not.

The ISI's manipulation of the shura discredited the AIG in the eyes of the great majority of Afghans. Criticism of the AIG was especially strong from Afghans who had been denied the opportunity to participate. Together, they represented most of the Afghan population. Aside from Saudi Arabia, only the United Arab Emirates and Malaysia recognized the AIG. The Rawalpindi Shura limited the AIG's governing mandate to one year. As the deadline approached, the six AIG leaders (minus Hekmatyar) unilaterally extended their tenure indefinitely. Over the next three years, until Najib fell, they shrewdly parried all outside pressures to hold another shura, a loya jirga, or elections that could send them into political oblivion.

Unfazed by the interim government's lack of Afghan or international support, Hamid Gul passionately appealed for diplomatic recognition of his handiwork at a March 6, 1989, Afghan cell meeting chaired by Prime Minister Bhutto. American Ambassador Robert Oakley attended. Once more, no Afghans were present. Bhutto reminded Gul that the AIG must control a major city inside Afghanistan before Pakistan could recognize it, and Oakley concurred, adding that the United States would follow Pakistan's lead regarding recognition of the AIG. Gul responded that Bhutto's conditions would be met. He said that preparations for a Mujahidin attack on Jalalabad were well under way.[52]

Gul's choice of Jalalabad, Afghanistan's fourth-largest city, seemed a logical one. Jalalabad was readily accessible from Mujahidin bases in Pakistan approximately 30 miles away. It was situated on a major road artery connecting Peshawar through the Khyber Pass to Kabul and was closer to Pakistan than to Kabul. It lay in the heart of mainly Ghilzai-populated eastern Afghanistan, surrounded by commanders affiliated with Hekmatyar, Sayyaf, Khalis, and

Haqqani and their knots of Arab fighters. With a Napoleonic flourish, Gul declared that the battle would last less than a week, "if the government was prepared to allow for a certain degree of bloodshed."[53]

There was plenty of bloodshed. Most of it was suffered by 15,000 ill-prepared, disorganized, and divided Mujahidin guerrillas attempting a conventional assault on a well-fortified city.

PART III

MISSION TO THE MUJAHIDIN

CHAPTER 11

Mission Impossible[1]

Bowing to congressional pressure, the Bush administration has named a special presidential envoy with the rank of ambassador to the Afghanistan resistance but the diplomat will be stationed here rather than in the field, according to administration officials.

They said Secretary of State James A. Baker III has chosen Peter Tomsen, deputy chief of the U.S. Embassy in Beijing, as a compromise candidate to resolve disputes over the appointment in the State Department and between it and Congress.

There was no indication yesterday that the administration might recognize the resistance's recently established "interim government," but it was understood that Tomsen will be the envoy to Afghanistan if and when the rebels oust the current Soviet-backed regime.

Tomsen will report to senior department officials rather than Robert Oakley, the U.S. ambassador in Pakistan, who had sought to maintain responsibility for Afghan as well as Pakistani affairs....

Sen. Gordon J. Humphrey (R-NH), the leading congressional advocate of naming such an envoy, said he was generally pleased with the decision even though his own candidate for the job—Zalmy Khalizad, an Afghan-born scholar now with the Rand Corp.—lost out.

"Anything is better than nothing. Time is of the essence now," Humphrey said. "All the bold [diplomatic] strokes are coming from the Kabul government. We've got to gain the initiative."

—DAVID B. OTTAWAY, *WASHINGTON POST,* 1989[2]

✼

Winter Siberian winds still blew from the north on the morning of March 12, 1989, casting the Chinese capital of Beijing into a deep freeze. Less than a month had passed since General Boris Gromov had theatrically followed the last Soviet soldier over the Termez Bridge back onto Soviet territory. "The deputy secretary of state is calling you," my secretary whispered into the embassy intercom. I was in my third and last year as deputy chief of mission to Winston Lord, the American ambassador to China. I wondered why Lawrence Eagleburger, the Department of State's second-highest official, was phoning. Larry's friendly, calm voice came through as I picked up the phone. "The secretary wants you to be the president's 'special envoy to the Afghan resistance' with the rank of ambassador," he began, referring to President George H.W. Bush's secretary of state, James A. Baker III. "The Soviets withdrew last month. We expect the resistance will soon be in Kabul and you will have the inside track to be our next ambassador."

Delighted, I accepted the appointment. I would be returning to the region where I had lived for seven years—two as a Peace Corps volunteer in a Nepali village, five as a political officer at the American embassy in New Delhi and the American consulate in Bombay. I had worked in three State Department geographic bureaus since entering the Foreign Service twenty-two years earlier—Near Eastern and South Asian Affairs (NEA), East Asian and Pacific Affairs (EAP), and European and Canadian Affairs (EUR). I had led the India, Nepal, Sri Lanka office, one of NEA's two South Asian directorates, in the early 1980s. I considered the South Asian wing of NEA my career "home" bureau.

I later discovered that senior NEA managers with whom I had worked closely in past assignments had placed my name on Eagleburger's list of candidates for the Afghan special envoy position. My tours as a political officer in the Soviet Union and (twice) in China may have strengthened my candidacy. The Soviets had just withdrawn their army from Afghanistan, but Soviet aid and diplomatic leverage sustained the Najib regime. I would be involved in negotiations with the Soviets to end the continuing war in Afghanistan. China was a neighbor of Afghanistan and an emerging colossus on the world stage. It would also play a role in the Afghan endgame.

Chinese and American policies on Afghanistan dovetailed in early 1989. Both countries wanted the Soviets out of Afghanistan. During my three-year appointment as deputy chief of mission in Beijing (1985–1989), I had participated in secret CIA weapons-buying meetings with Chinese People's Liberation Army generals. Whole factories owned and run by the Chinese military were switched over to producing Soviet-style AK-47s, RPGs, and 122-mm and 144-mm rocket launchers to be shipped to Karachi. Chinese generals happily pocketed the fat CIA checks, approximately $100 million a year, to spend on their own weapons programs.[3]

Soviet diplomats in Beijing were visibly worried when the Soviet Union began its ten-month withdrawal from Afghanistan in May 1988. Vladimir Fedotov, my amiable counterpart at the Soviet embassy, took me by the arm during a diplomatic reception and appealed, "Help us get out!" The mood was different in the Chinese Foreign Ministry. Foreign Ministry officials I met urged the American government to increase, not lessen, pressure on Moscow while its position inside Afghanistan was weak. "More Soviet concessions are yet to come," a Chinese Russian-speaking diplomat I had known in Moscow happily predicted.

After the deputy secretary's phone call, the State Department instructed me to stay on in Beijing as chargé d'affaires after Ambassador Winston Lord's April departure, in order to cover Mikhail Gorbachev's historic May 15–19 visit to China. While not triumphant, the visit did seal long-postponed normalization of relations between the two communist giants. Gorbachev largely accomplished his main goal—restoring more balance in the American-Chinese-Soviet strategic triangle. The 1979 Soviet invasion of Afghanistan had driven the United States and China together. The February 1989 Soviet withdrawal from Afghanistan removed a major obstacle in the way of Moscow's ties with the United States and China.[4] It provided Gorbachev diplomatic flexibility to engage with America and China. After Gorbachev's visit to Beijing, the United States could no longer assume Chinese hostility toward the Soviet Union. Nor could China assume continued American-Soviet estrangement. Both the United States and China would now allow for improved bilateral relations with the Soviet Union, even while preserving Sino-American relations as the strongest side of the great power triangle.

The improvement of U.S.-Soviet and Sino-Soviet relations did not work to the advantage of the Mujahidin. Now that U.S.-Soviet relations were improving, American enthusiasm for Afghan "Freedom Fighters" could dim. China ceased viewing Afghanistan as an obstacle in Sino-Soviet relations after the Soviet Union withdrew its troops from Afghanistan. American interest in Afghanistan began a long, downward slide after the Soviet pullout. The pendulum of superpower concentration swung toward Eastern Europe. The once large Western media presence in Peshawar, Islamabad, and Kabul moved on to Berlin, Prague, Budapest, and Warsaw where the next inning of history was unfolding. The Gorbachev Doctrine, permitting Eastern bloc nations control over their internal affairs, ruled out further Soviet military intervention to preserve the Soviet empire. During 1989, the "Year of Miracles," one after another of the Soviet Union's Warsaw Pact allies broke with Moscow, replacing their ruling communist parties with pro-Western regimes. The November 9, 1989, opening of the Berlin Wall marked the end of the Cold War and dramatically confirmed the demise of the Brezhnev Doctrine. Two months later, the Warsaw Pact was dismantled. East Germany folded into West Germany. Anticommunist shockwaves rippled eastward, gradually seeping into the Soviet Union itself.

American diplomatic and intelligence reports on Afghanistan, copied to me in our Beijing embassy, bristled with optimistic projections about a Mujahidin victory after the Soviet withdrawal. A March briefing memo prepared for President George H.W. Bush stated: "The intelligence community continues to argue that the Kabul regime will fall within 6–12 months following the completion of the Soviet troop withdrawal." The Chinese government shared American optimism about an imminent Mujahidin victory. In April an article in a Chinese government magazine said the PDPA was "unable to recover the momentum" and "marking time until defeat."[5]

Ominous signs that my special envoy appointment would not be a bed of roses began appearing before I left China. Washington's "where I sit determines where I stand" turf-war mentality, energized by outsized egos, made it natural that the idea of a special envoy to the Afghan resistance would provoke bureaucratic resistance to my appointment.

The pressure for a special envoy on Afghanistan came from conservative champions of the Mujahidin in Congress, not from within the executive branch. The State Department's NEA Bureau, which handled Afghan affairs, argued that a special envoy was not necessary; the Afghan portfolio was already being ably managed by the bureau's Directorate of Pakistan, Afghanistan and Bangladesh (PAB) within NEA.

The Reagan administration had earlier attempted to fend off congressional demands for an Afghan special envoy. Conservatives in Congress, led by Republican senator Gordon Humphrey of New Hampshire and Democrat Charlie Wilson of Texas in the House of Representatives, pushed harder. Unable to resist any longer, the White House compromised by appointing Edmund McWilliams, a midlevel Foreign Service officer, to fill the slot in 1988 while Soviet troops were leaving Afghanistan. Congress got its special envoy. The subambassadorial level of the appointment placated State's NEA Bureau.

Ed McWilliams was an excellent choice. Although not bearing an ambassadorial cachet, he had developed impressive experience in Afghan affairs. McWilliams had served in Kabul during the Soviet occupation. He knew Afghans in Najib's regime and many Afghans in the resistance. He spoke Afghan Dari. But the bureaucratic cards were stacked against him: The NEA Bureau's decision to place McWilliams in Ambassador Robert Oakley's Islamabad embassy guaranteed friction. McWilliams was a specialist on Afghanistan, not Pakistan. He relied more heavily on Afghan than Pakistani perceptions of the ongoing Afghan conflict. His analyses diverged from those propounded by Ambassador Oakley and CIA Station Chief Milton Bearden, who had grown used to managing the Afghan as well as the Pakistani portfolio. Oakley; his deputy chief of mission (DCM), Beth Jones; and political counselor Edward Abington all outranked McWilliams.

From the embassy in Islamabad, McWilliams traveled frequently to meet Mujahidin along the Afghan-Pakistani frontier. The congressional legislation required that he have independent reporting authority. His reports to Washington described the outrage of Durrani tribal royalists in southern Afghanistan, Ahmed Shah Masood's followers in the north, moderate tribal and party leaders, and Afghan intellectuals about ISI preparations to install Gulbuddin Hekmatyar in Kabul after Najib's defeat.

The stage was set for a bureaucratic collision. In October 1988, two months after arriving in Islamabad and only a few weeks after Ambassador Oakley arrived, McWilliams drew on his meetings with Mujahidin sources to pen a major policy message to Washington. The twenty-eight-paragraph message challenged long-standing U.S. support for the ISI's promotion of Hekmatyar. Circulated in the White House and in the State and Defense departments, the telegram spoke of "a growing frustration, bordering on hostility among Afghans across the ideological spectrum and from a broad range of backgrounds toward the government of Pakistan and toward the U.S." McWilliams reported that "most of these observers claim that this effort (by Hekmatyar and ISI) has the backing of the radical Pakistani political party Jamaat Islami and of radical Arabs."[6]

The cable infuriated Ambassador Oakley as well as Jones, Abington, and Bearden. When McWilliams gave no quarter, they decided that if he could not be silenced, he would need to be hamstrung. Bearden branded McWilliams "that little shit."[7] The CIA cut McWilliams off from sensitive agency reporting.

Oakley's penalties were harsher. The ambassador ridiculed McWilliams in embassy meetings and to his face. McWilliams's classified reports to Washington on the Afghan situation, "slugged" for me in Beijing, became separated into two sections. The first contained McWilliams's analysis as the special envoy, and the second presented Oakley's criticism of McWilliams's judgments. McWilliams proposed fresh initiatives to end the Afghan conflict. Oakley appended objections, saying that McWilliams's suggested policy changes would be counterproductive. During an Afghanistan briefing for a senate staff delegation in his ambassadorial residence, Oakley ordered McWilliams to leave the room. The shocked members of the delegation reported back to Senator Gordon Humphrey in Washington that McWilliams had been "cut out of CIA channels" and that Oakley had "openly reprimanded him in our presence, telling him to 'shut up,' and saying that he wouldn't take any more of McWilliams' 'bullshit.'"[8]

Senator Humphrey and other angry congressional conservatives believed that the executive branch was losing interest in Afghanistan and was moving toward abandoning the Mujahidin. They lobbied the White House to elevate the Afghan special envoy to the ambassadorial level on a par with Oakley. Humphrey insisted that the special envoy be given interagency authority to manage U.S. Afghan policy inside the administration. After George H.W. Bush won the November 1988 presidential election, the bipartisan congressional pressures only mounted, with Senators Humphrey, Robert Byrd (D-WV), and Robert Dole (R-KS) leading the campaign in the Senate. Congressmen Charlie Wilson (D-TX), Don Ritter (R-PA), and Dana Rohrabacher (R-CA) did the same in the House. The closure of the American embassy in Kabul on the eve of the Soviet troop withdrawal, they insisted, made an ambassadorial-level designation for the special envoy urgent. They attached an amendment to the 1989 State Department appropriations bill establishing the position with ambassadorial rank.[9]

Congress got its way during secretary of state–designate Baker's Senate Foreign Relations Committee confirmation hearing. Senator Humphrey especially pressed for a positive response to the demand for appointment of a high-level Afghan special envoy. Baker agreed to grant the ambassadorial rank, assuring the committee that the ambassador would report directly to him. But Secretary Baker's statements did not guarantee that the Afghan special envoy chosen by President Bush would enjoy the authority that bipartisan congressional conservatives were demanding. Baker specified that the special envoy would only "*participate* in Washington considerations of all aspects of policy towards Afghanistan." He would travel frequently to the region to meet resistance leaders and engage the new Afghan Interim Government (AIG).[10]

Through my friends in the NEA Bureau, I learned that Senator Humphrey and NEA had competed to fill the special envoy position with their own candidates. Baker and Eagleburger settled the dispute by turning to me, a South Asian area specialist with Soviet and Chinese experience. The decision to select me instead of an experienced ambassador indicated the administration's reluctance to give the position substantiated authority. The posting was my first ambassadorial assignment. My relatively junior standing in the national security pecking order would limit my influence in status-conscious Washington.

It was common knowledge in the administration and media that my position had been thrust on a reluctant administration by congressional conservatives. I was a compromise candidate, as the media was reporting.[11] I would be an ambassador, a newly minted one, outside NEA but reporting to the deputy secretary or an under secretary. My eight years in NEA and South Asia positions did give me some leverage. So did my two years in Moscow and six years in China.

My future effectiveness as special envoy, however, would heavily depend on developing good working relationships with NEA and the European Bureau in the State Department, which managed relations with the Soviet Union. I would need to coordinate with NEA's Office of Pakistan, Afghanistan and Bangladesh (PAB). The U.S.-Pakistani relationship, not Afghanistan, was PAB's major preoccupation. There were 130 million Pakistanis. Nobody knew how many Afghans there were, but the number did not exceed 25 million. Pakistan was a functioning state; Afghanistan was not. Pakistan had allied itself with the United States during the Cold War. There was, of course, considerable sympathy for Pakistan in Washington in recognition of its "frontline" role in the defeat of the Soviet Army in Afghanistan. Good relations with Pakistani government officials would be essential to my success.

Unhelpful press leaks regarding my appointment began before I left China in late May 1989. Some obviously came from the White House, senior levels of the State Department, and the CIA. Others could have come from anywhere else in the executive branch, Congress, or the American embassy in Islamabad. They made the difficult special envoy assignment even harder. Before my appointment was announced, a March 18, 1989, front-page *Washington Post* article, citing "diplomatic and Congressional sources," described my special envoy position as a rebuff to Pakistan. My selection was described as "an effort to limit Pakistan's political influence among the guerrillas." The article reported that "some State Department officials in Pakistan and many in Washington argue that the United States should tighten its control of the aid pipelines and press the ISI to stop what they see as interference in Afghan politics."[12] It quoted an unnamed "U.S. diplomat" as accusing the ISI of building up Hekmatyar and "keeping the Resistance divided to preserve its own influence," thus risking a "civil war" between Mujahidin groups if Najib collapses. The article speculated that "Afghanistan is a deeply traditional country whose popular interpretations of Islam are at odds with fundamentalism— a fact that leads many analysts to believe that an Islamic revolutionary such as Hekmatyar would be unable to win power even with Pakistani support." Another source in the article, "a U.S. official," added some ambiguity about Pakistan's intentions, stating, "We don't know how far ISI is going to go in trying to boost Hekmatyar into power."[13]

Foreign correspondents from other countries who were stationed in Washington cabled home stories characterizing my appointment in anti-Pakistani terms. A Chinese journalist reported to Beijing that official sources in Washington linked my appointment to "increasing concerns in the United States that Afghan Moslem fundamentalists would become a dominant political force in post–civil war Afghanistan and drive the guerrilla government in an anti-West direction."[14]

The Indian media happily embraced the anti-Pakistan interpretation of the new special envoy position and took it to new heights. The *Times of India* viewed the appointment "as a step by the U.S. to assume a more direct role in the current phase of the Afghan conflict, instead of relying on Pakistan." The article cited Senator Humphrey as telling reporters that "the Pakistani filter was fine during the Soviet occupation but it's not necessarily helpful to exclusively rely on Pakistan in this new phase of the war."[15]

The media typecast me as anti-Pakistani, clouding my prospects for forging a productive working relationship with the Pakistani government, State's NEA Bureau, the CIA, and Ambassador Robert Oakley. The Pakistani government informed Washington that it did not want me based in Pakistan. I assumed that Ambassador Oakley was pleased with that. It would be hard to find a resident ambassador in any embassy welcoming a second ambassador resident in-country. My home port would be Washington, which was also to my liking. It would give me immediate personal access to top decision-makers on Afghan policy in the executive branch and Congress when I wanted it. I would shuttle out to Pakistan to meet with the Afghan resistance, consult with the Pakistan government, and travel to Saudi Arabia and other countries involved in Afghanistan as necessary. The mobility would permit me to participate in U.S.-Soviet negotiations on Afghanistan in Washington and in other capitals.

I was still in Beijing on April 4, 1989, when the Department of State spokeswoman, Margaret Tutweiler, announced my appointment as special envoy to the Afghan resistance with the personal rank of ambassador.[16] Friends and colleagues in the large Beijing diplomatic corps phoned to congratulate me. Soviet Deputy Chief of Mission Vladimir Fedotov visited me at the U.S. embassy. He graciously extended his best wishes for my success. On leaving, he paused to say he regretted that, given the nature of my new appointment, he would be unable to host a farewell social function in my honor. Ambassador Oakley unexpectedly phoned from Islamabad on an unclassified open line. "I don't know whether to congratulate you or commiserate with you," he quipped. I joked that he would play a role in deciding how that would play out. We exchanged commitments to cooperate closely with each other.

Members of the Beijing diplomatic corps and Western reporters plied me for information on Afghan developments. The battle for Jalalabad was still under way in April 1989. Each week the Swedish ambassador asked me when the city would fall into Mujahidin hands. Relying on CIA and Embassy Islamabad reporting, I confidently—and incorrectly—predicted an early Mujahidin victory.

In our meetings in the Beijing diplomatic circuit, Soviet Deputy Chief of Mission Fedotov grew more confident each passing week about the Najib regime's prospects for survival. "Your assessment about Afghanistan is wrong," he volunteered. In many conversations during our three-year association in Beijing, Fedotov had proven to be well informed and straightforward. His rejection of the conventional wisdom that Najib was losing and the Afghan Mujahidin were winning troubled me. Was he spreading disinformation or was U.S. intelligence reporting behind the curve?

The Pakistani ambassador to China, Akram Zaki, invited me to a reception honoring a visiting delegation of the recently formed Afghan Interim Government. It was headed by the AIG foreign minister, Gulbuddin Hekmatyar. The reception took place in Zaki's spacious living room. Hekmatyar, then forty-one, was slight, grim faced, and reserved. His dark, fish-like, hooded eyes were his most distinguishing feature. Toward the end of the reception, Ambassador Zaki asked me to stand next to Hekmatyar for a group photo. Our forced small talk was not pleasant. He glared at my necktie. After a few seconds' pause, he muttered: "Afghans don't like red." It was one of my best ties. I looked down at him and curtly responded, "The Chinese do." We had no further exchange through the reception and the dinner, nor, for that matter, ever again.

I left China at a time when Chinese leaders faced the biggest challenge to their rule since they defeated Chiang Kai-shek's Nationalists on the battlefield in 1949. The huge antigovernment protests in downtown Tiananmen Square, with smaller echoes in 250 other Chinese cities, were humiliating. Millions of Chinese demonstrators ringed downtown Tiananmen on the evening of May 18, forcing Chinese officials to shift Gorbachev's farewell banquet from the Great Hall of the People next to Tiananmen to another location. The banquet fiasco magnified the Chinese leadership's loss of face before the world and the Chinese population.

On the morning of May 20, 1989, my wife and I were waiting at the airport to depart China when a somber-faced Li Peng, China's hard-line prime minister, appeared on a nearby television screen wearing a Mao suit. Li announced the imposition of martial law, abruptly terminating China's tentative ten-year-old movement toward political liberalization. On June 4, a long column of tanks from Inner Mongolia roared onto Tiananmen Square, guns blazing. The carnage prolonged Chinese Communist rule in China. It also delivered a severe blow to the Communist dynasty's mandate from heaven.

❦

The United States and the West were fortunate to have President George H.W. Bush and Secretary of State James A. Baker III managing foreign policy as the world lurched from the Cold War into the next epoch. The transition was fraught with peril. Since the mid-eighteenth century, no fundamental shift in the world's balance of power had occurred without a major war. The arsenals of the superpowers contained tens of thousands of nuclear weapons. President Bush, Secretary Baker, Soviet President Gorbachev, and Soviet Foreign Minister Eduard Shevardnadze adroitly steered their countries through this very dangerous period of world history.

President Bush and Secretary Baker were moderate Republicans who needed to retain the support of Republican conservatives in Congress to govern. Bush chose Dan Quayle as his presidential running mate partly to maintain a link with the conservative wing of the party. Quayle and William Kristol, his neoconservative chief of staff and spokesperson, espoused a more conservative foreign policy agenda that included "staying the course" in Afghanistan. Foreign Service Officer Jon Glassman, the American chargé d'affaires who closed the U.S. embassy in Kabul when the Soviets withdrew, was on Quayle's staff.

The vice president and his team, Senator Gordon Humphrey, and Charlie Wilson in the House of Representatives looked to me to generate Mujahidin success and prevent the national security bureaucracy from backsliding into passivity on Afghanistan. So did the Saudi ambassador to the United States, Prince Bandar al-Sultan, a regular presidential guest at the White House with his able deputy, Rihab Masood. The Saudis were justifiably pleased that their joint effort with the Americans and Pakistanis had helped expel the Soviet Army from Afghanistan. But the Soviet-supported Najib regime remained in Kabul, and the Saudi government was committed to continuing the war until Najib was overthrown.

The conservatives in Congress watched closely for evidence that Bush; his national security adviser, Brent Scowcroft; and Secretary Baker were abandoning Afghanistan and sacrificing the Mujahidin for the greater good of U.S.-Soviet relations. I kept this in mind during briefings of conservative congressmen and their staffers. Any misstep with Congress could send me to a next assignment in the State Department's Geographer's Office.

Secretary of State Baker was well versed in Washington's backroom politics. When chief of staff to the president during Reagan's first term and treasury secretary in his second term, he had learned how to deal with bureaucratic opponents. Baker brought trusted subordinates from the Reagan administration over to State and placed them near his office on the department's seventh floor. Deputy Secretary Eagleburger, State Department Spokeswoman Margaret Tutweiler, Under Secretary for Political Affairs Robert Kimmitt, Policy Planning Director Dennis Ross, and Congressional Affairs Assistant Secretary Janet Mullins had all worked with Baker in the two Reagan administrations. The heavy influx of political appointees provoked grumbling in the corridors of the State Department, where little is left unsaid. Foreign Service officers ruefully christened Baker's inner circle "the Star Chamber." Baker publicly fired back, saying he would not permit the Foreign Service to capture him.[17]

The State Department bureaucracy gradually adjusted to playing by Baker's rules. Corridor griping died away. The world was quickly changing. There was important work to be done. Baker was the president's most important foreign policy adviser. He transcended other agency heads in the national security apparatus. Foreign policy proposals accepted by Baker and his Star Chamber would be put on a fast track to implementation.

My aspirations for proximity to the secretary or to Deputy Secretary Eagleburger were dashed a week after returning to Washington. "The Eagle" summoned me to a meeting with Bob Kimmitt and the assistant secretary for NEA, John Kelly. Eagleburger's large seventh-floor office was half dark. The under secretary sat behind his desk, one hand holding a cigarette, the other a respirator. The respirator's tiny hose end went into his mouth after

FIGURE 11.1   MAJOR BUREAUCRATIC ACTORS ON AFGHAN POLICY

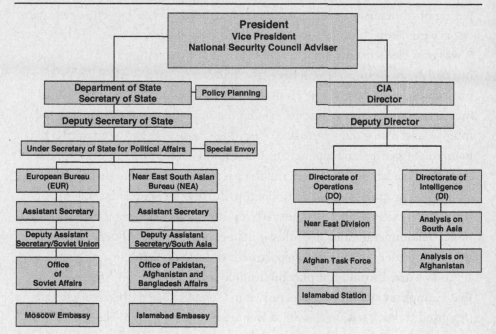

each puff. The permanent twinkle in Eagleburger's eye indicated to me that he reveled in this incongruity.

The time had come to decide where I would land in the bureaucracy. It was already clear to me that the administration had decided to ignore the congressional legislation's lofty requirement that the ambassadorial-level special envoy "shall coordinate United States policies and programs with the Afghan Resistance." It was yet to be clarified where I would fit into the State Department's hierarchy. NEA Assistant Secretary John Kelly had inherited Afghanistan as part of his NEA portfolio. Eagleburger, however, had made a personal commitment to Senator Humphrey that I would be "adequately staffed" and that I would be "a policy player in Washington" on Afghan matters.[18]

"I want you to support Peter," Eagleburger told Kimmitt and Kelly through the undulating cloud of cigarette smoke drifting above his desk. Kimmitt and Kelly were silent. So was I. After the meeting, one of Kimmitt's assistants, a former NEA colleague, phoned to tell me that "Bob did not like that meeting." The meaning of this message was quite obvious. On the seventh floor, Kimmitt considered Afghanistan to be in his domain, not Eagleburger's.

I was reminded of something a respected scholar had once written, comparing bureaucrats to fish in a giant coral reef: To survive jagged edges and hungry predators, the bureaucrats must "find a supportive ecological niche."[19] It was now clear that my niche would be inside Kimmitt's coral reef. This was not bad news. Kimmitt was in the Star Chamber; he had worked with Baker previously, both at the White House and in the Treasury Department. A former army paratrooper, Kimmitt exuded a command presence. He was tall, intense, and demanding, but also collegial and witty. He had a reputation for being disorganized and a penchant for running late. More important, however, his friendships with Baker and the president assured me that his policy advice and proposals would go to the top. Further, in State Department corridor conversations, he had a positive reputation for eliciting the views and policy recommendations of professional Foreign Service officers. Many political appointees in the State Department did not do that.

To be sure, I would not play the lead coordinator role on Afghan policy that Humphrey and other conservatives in Congress had wished for. Kimmitt intended to lead, within the State Department and with other agencies. I would, however, be a semi-independent player on Afghan affairs and enjoy a direct channel for oral and written communications to the under secretary. That relationship was all I could expect. And it worked out very well.

Collegiality reigned at my June 20 swearing-in ceremony in the lovely Jefferson Room on the seventh floor of the State Department. Deputy Secretary Eagleburger presided. I reiterated the core premise of U.S. Afghan policy in my formal remarks: a political settlement in Afghanistan that would end in an act of self-determination for the Afghan people to choose their own leadership. Noting that "the great majority of Afghans" saw no role for the discredited Najib regime in a political solution to the war, I urged support for "Afghans themselves" to set "the future political course for their nation," without outside interference. In his comments, Eagleburger offered the full support of the State Department. He remarked: "Peter has a greater personal stake in success than is usual in our business, for only if our policy objectives are achieved will he be able to take up a coveted assignment—the United States Ambassador to free Afghanistan."[20]

The oratory at the ceremony was well received by the Mujahidin, Pakistanis, and Saudis, who hoped that the United States would not walk away from Afghanistan. Our ambitions to oust Najib, however, overlooked the changing situation on the ground in Afghanistan. Events had taken a turn for the worse. The great majority of the Mujahidin inside and outside Afghanistan rejected the AIG formed by Hamid Gul at the Rawalpindi Shura. The Mujahidin were losing at Jalalabad. These twin disasters strengthened Najib's military position in Afghanistan. They reduced U.S. and Pakistani negotiating leverage to insist on his departure in the context of a political solution. Prior to the Soviet pullout, the United States had been negotiating from a position of strength. After the unrepresentative Rawalpindi Shura and imminent Mujahidin defeat at Jalalabad, the Soviets would claim this advantage.

Inside the beltway, Kimmitt created an informal Afghan Policy Group, called the "Kimmitt Group," to guide Afghan policy. It operated at the sub-cabinet level. I obtained Kimmitt's permission to lead a new interagency Afghan Coordinating Committee (ACC) to forward policy options to the Kimmitt Group and prepared an "Action Memorandum" to Secretary Baker establishing the ACC.[21] It stated that the special envoy would coordinate policy on Afghan-related issues at the working level. I would spend a good deal of my time dealing with Congress and the media on Afghan matters. The CIA, the Defense Department, and the National Security Council cleared the memorandum. Baker and Kimmitt signed it, formally establishing the ACC. NEA Assistant Secretary Kelly and his South Asia deputy assistant secretary, Teresita Schaffer, declined to clear the document but sent NEA representatives to ACC meetings.

I convened my first ACC meeting a week before departing Washington on my first trip to Britain, Pakistan, and Saudi Arabia on June 24, 1989. The spirited discussion revealed a deep chasm between the optimists and the pessimists on whether U.S. strategy was succeeding in Afghanistan. State Department NEA Bureau, Department of Defense, and CIA participants exuded optimism that the Mujahidin would soon overthrow Najib. They urged that the United States continue to arm the Mujahidin until Najib collapsed. The National Security Council's Richard Haass and the State Department's Policy Planning and Intelligence and Research Office (INR) representatives were pessimists. They expressed skepticism that continuing support to the Mujahidin was still in U.S. interests.

The optimists stressed Najib's unpopularity and weakness. The Soviet economy was deteriorating, weakening Moscow's ability to keep Najib's regime afloat. The pessimists contended that the Soviet departure took away the only unifying stimulus within the fractured resistance. Najib had survived. Major world powers were disassociating themselves from the Afghan resistance. China had dropped Afghanistan as an obstacle to Sino-Soviet normalization; Western European sympathy for the Mujahidin was diminishing. The French had already announced their intention to reopen their embassy in Kabul, thus giving some legitimacy to Najib's regime. Italy planned to follow France's precedent.

Three influential offices at the meeting, the NSC, the State Department Policy Planning office, and State's Soviet Desk, argued that persistence in overthrowing Najib could harm the warming trend in U.S.-Soviet relations. The Cold War was over. Gorbachev sought cooperative relations with the United States. Conservatives in the KGB and military were resisting. The West should "help Gorbachev out." Arming the Mujahidin to overthrow Najib was giving ammunition to the Soviet hard-liners who opposed him.

These same themes were gaining currency in important think tanks and in the American media. Scholars and news commentators contended that the United States must facilitate Gorbachev's historic initiatives to release Moscow's grip on Eastern Europe and jettison expensive Soviet Third World "outposts" far from Soviet borders: Angola and Ethiopia in Africa, Cuba and Nicaragua in Central America, and Vietnam and Laos in Southeast Asia. Afghanistan was an exception. Astride the USSR's vulnerable southern flank, it was more important to Moscow than to Washington.

The optimist-versus-pessimist divide permeated my consultations in Congress, the White House, the CIA, and the DOD during my last two weeks of interagency meetings before leaving Washington. Just a few weeks into my new job, I was in a listening mode. I would defer engaging in policy debates until I was able to form my own impressions after direct engagement with the Afghans, Pakistanis, and Saudis.

The Senate was my initial stop, followed by the House of Representatives. During the next three years, I would need to secure congressional support for the CIA's annual covert budget and the $80 million cross-border aid projects operated by the United States Agency for International Development in resistance-controlled areas. USAID contractors operating out of Pakistan fielded more than 1,400 Afghan health workers inside Afghanistan. They operated 110 clinics and 7 hospitals in the Afghan provinces. The cross-border program sponsored over 1,000 primary schools. USAID's Afghan Constructions and Logistics Unit (ACLU) built roads in Mujahidin-controlled areas and transported American-donated food aid to poverty-stricken villages. Non-USAID projects included U.S. military mine-removal training courses for Afghans. The "McCullum program," named after a Republican congressman from Florida, airlifted wounded Mujahidin to the United States and Europe for treatment at American hospitals. Radio Free Afghanistan, created by Congress and attached to Radio Free Europe in Munich, transmitted pro-Mujahidin broadcasts into Afghanistan. Finally, the United States Information Agency had established the Afghan Media Resource Center (AMRC). Haji Daoud, previously an announcer on Radio Kabul before the Soviet invasion, was the AMRC manager. AMRC produced battlefield reporting and images of the war for audiences around the world.[22]

During two lengthy conversations in his cozy hideaway office under the Capitol Dome, Senator Humphrey[23] laid out what he expected of me. More than any other lawmaker, Humphrey had been responsible for creating my position. He wanted results. Humphrey challenged me to create a coordinated Afghan strategy within the executive branch. "Nobody is in charge of Afghan policy," he said. "The CIA alliance with ISI is out of control." He alleged that the closing of the CIA pipeline in December 1988, while the Soviet Union's massive airlift of arms to Najib's regime was under way, had destroyed the Mujahidin's battlefield momentum. Three weeks after our conversation, Senator Humphrey took to the Senate floor, declaring: "Let us not permit the Soviets to win through clever political maneuvering what they failed to win by force of arms. . . . Self-determination (for the Afghan people) is not forced power-sharing with a Nazi-like regime."[24]

His marching orders delivered, the senator escorted me downstairs to the entrance of the cloistered Senate Chamber. Inviting me to wait outside, he entered and returned with the Senate's Democratic majority leader, Robert Byrd, and Republican minority leader, Robert Dole, in tow. After introductions, Dole told me, "We will support you." Byrd added: "We created your position and support you from the heart."

The ride on Congress's underground rail line from the Senate to the House takes less than a minute. I would make that trip often during the next three years. My first call in the House was on Congressman Charlie Wilson, a conservative Democrat. He was a tall, lanky Texan, and exceedingly friendly. Huge ceiling-to-floor framed photographs of Mujahidin warriors hung in the

flamboyant congressman's office. Beautiful women manned the desks outside. A calico cat wandered through their offices, occasionally sauntering out
the door and down the House corridor outside.

Charlie Wilson and I had first met when he visited China in 1988. He was
Humphrey's pro-Mujahidin counterpart in the House of Representatives. His
zeal mirrored Humphrey's, but their styles differed. Charlie's warm Texas in-
formality contrasted with Humphrey's formality, which may have reflected
his New England background. Charlie's tendency was to discuss rather than
to instruct. During our first meeting, he observed that the Mujahidin were
not as "fired up" as they used to be. He mused that the CIA had lost some of
its edge after the Soviet withdrawal. Charlie stated his support for me and
wished me luck.

For the next three years, Charlie was critically important to maintaining
assistance levels to the Mujahidin. He occupied seats on the House Permanent Select Committee on Intelligence (HPSCI), the House Appropriations
Committee, and the latter's Defense Appropriations Subcommittee. He could
influence funding for both the large CIA-run Afghan covert program and
USAID's economic projects. He constantly worked his friends in Congress
to get funding for the Mujahidin. In secret House Intelligence Committee
hearings, Charlie helped me win approval for Afghan appropriations. He followed up my oral testimony with blazing sermons on why the administration's
funding for Afghan programs should be approved. HPSCI committee members from both parties were aware that acceding to Charlie's eloquent appeals
guaranteed his vote for funding their own pet projects.

My meetings with a dozen liberal and conservative members of Congress
outside the network of vocal Mujahidin supporters in late June 1989 revealed
significant wavering in pro-Mujahidin sentiment. Some congressmen expressed the general opinion, "We helped them to defeat the Soviets. They
helped us. We no longer have an obligation to the Mujahidin." Staunch supporters of Israel voiced fears that ISI- and CIA-backed Afghan Muslim extremists might take over Afghanistan.

The full-day CIA briefing I received at the agency's Langley Headquarters
hewed closely to the CIA optimist line that a Mujahidin military victory was
near. That heady prognosis had not changed since 1988, when a National Intelligence Estimate (NIE) predicted: "We judge that the Najibullah regime will

not long survive the completion of the Soviet withdrawal even with continued Soviet assistance.... The regime may fall before withdrawal is complete."[25]

The agency's analytical wing, the Directorate of Intelligence (DI), was at one with the clandestine Directorate of Operations (DO) in predicting an early Mujahidin victory. CIA Afghan analyst Michael Scheuer straddled both directorates. This amalgamation of covert operations and intelligence analysis violated an important axiom generally respected by Western intelligence agencies. The axiom requires that intelligence analysis not comingle with clandestine operations. When it does, the analysis can lapse into justifying the operations rather than presenting an objective appraisal of their performance. That error had already damaged American interests in Iran during the Iran-Contra affair. It would be repeated in Afghanistan.

I asked Directorate of Operations briefers about Senator Humphrey's assertion that CIA weapons shipments to the Mujahidin had slowed drastically in late 1988, despite congressional appropriations meant to keep the arms pipeline open. I assumed the agency's belief that Najib would quickly collapse when the Soviets withdrew had contributed to this decision. The briefers acknowledged Humphrey's accusation that weapons transfers to Pakistan had slowed. Their explanation, which had already surfaced in the media, cited the urgent need to cover important financial shortfalls in satellite programs— a higher priority than Afghanistan now that the Soviets were withdrawing. CIA briefers assured me that the hiatus in shipments had ended. Ships were on the way to Karachi, they said. Fresh arms would be in Mujahidin hands by July. Najib's demise was not a question of whether, but of when.

I found strong support for the Mujahidin in the Department of Defense. Under Secretary Paul D. Wolfowitz and Assistant Secretaries of Defense Henry Rowen and Richard Armitage stressed the importance of defeating Najib and maintaining close relations with Pakistan.

My final round of consultations took place at the National Security Council in the ornate Executive Office Building attached to the West Wing. Richard Haass, senior director for Near East and South Asian Affairs and special assistant to the president, was a major actor on Afghan policy in Washington. He saw President Bush's national security adviser, Brent Scowcroft, and Scowcroft's deputy, Robert Gates, on a daily basis and personally briefed the president on Afghan issues. He would be a good sounding board of their views on Afghan policy. Haass got straight to the point. He told me that the Mujahidin glass was half empty, not half full—and the remaining water in the glass was draining out the bottom. He doubted the Mujahidin would succeed in overthrowing Najib. The administration and Congress had finite patience: Haass stated that the administration would support covert weapons appropriations for just one more fighting season—that is, until December 1989. His message was clear. The Mujahidin had limited time to claim their victory. That time was running out.

Haass turned out to be wrong on the time line, but he accurately portrayed the National Security Council's desire to remove the Afghan stumbling block standing in the way of improved U.S.-Soviet relations. Haass's warning diverged from eight years of American presidential statements committing the United States to standing by the resistance until Afghans achieved self-determination. Only four months previously, on the day after General Gromov and the last Soviet soldiers to leave Afghanistan stepped back onto Soviet soil, President Bush had issued a formal White House "Statement by the President" that reaffirmed what U.S. officials had been saying throughout two Reagan administrations: "As long as the Resistance struggle for self-determination continues, so too will American support."[26] The president repeated this same formulation in a letter to Gorbachev.

I would spend a good deal of my time during the next three years maintaining assistance flows to the Mujahidin until the Soviets ceased theirs. The State Department's policy planning director, Dennis Ross, and the National Security Council's Scowcroft and Haass would increasingly press for a unilateral U.S. cessation of arms to the Mujahidin without a reciprocal Soviet arms cutoff. For me, the abandonment of negative symmetry, whereby both sides would simultaneously end arms shipments to the Afghan belligerents, carried significance far beyond Afghanistan. An image of U.S. resolve in the world was vital to maintaining a successful foreign policy. A unilateral U.S. cutoff reversing years of steadfast U.S. support for the Mujahidin would badly damage that image.

❦

My wife, Kim, and I were thrilled to receive a dinner invitation from President Bush before I left Washington. I hoped that the invitation demonstrated his personal interest in Afghanistan. Perhaps I might find an occasion to directly elicit his views on the American way ahead in Afghanistan.

Instead, the tranquil evening turned out to be an entirely social one, and most delightful. A small group of government officials from the State Department, the Pentagon, and the CIA attended with their spouses. We gathered for drinks and dinner in the flower garden just below the East Wing on a warm summer night. Mrs. Bush was in Kennebunkport. The president informally moved from table to table, chatting with his guests. After dinner, he took us on a tour of the first and second floors of the historic East Wing of the White House. We then descended to the movie theater, where ushers offered us popcorn and soft drinks. The president personally introduced the 1950s-era black and white Western film before the show started. When the movie ended, he graciously escorted us to a side door of the East Wing and wished us goodnight. As we drove home, Kim commented that the evening seemed to animate the president as much as his guests.

※

My three years of shuttle diplomacy began when I left Washington in late June destined for London, Islamabad, Peshawar, Chitral, Quetta, and Riyadh. For four busy weeks, I had absorbed an immense amount of information about Afghanistan, encompassing bureaucratic conflicts over Afghan policy, doubts about Mujahidin prospects for victory, declining American interest in Afghanistan, and a growing assumption that a continuing stalemate in Afghanistan would undercut the administration's major goal of improving U.S.-Soviet relations. None of my briefings touched on the ISI-nourished, transnational, radical Islamic network rising on Pakistan's Frontier. Before boarding the Pan American flight to London, I swung by the State Department's Operations Center to pick up a letter from Secretary Baker introducing me to AIG President Sibghatullah Mojaddedi.

In London, I walked to the British Foreign Office for consultations with Lord David Gillmore, deputy under secretary covering the Americas and Asia. During my career, I had learned that it was well worth the extra effort expended to stop by London and hear the British Foreign Office's interpretation of world events. The British experience in dealing with the rest of the world is deeper than our own. The Anglo-American special relationship is one of our most valuable partnerships. And, of course, the British have had their own painful history in Afghanistan.

Lord Gillmore was a warm host, immaculately attired, and anxious to discuss Afghanistan. After opening pleasantries, he embarked on a lucid overview of the situation in Afghanistan. His frame of reference seemed to hark back to Russo-British rivalries when Britain's core goal was to protect its Indian Empire, defend the Durand Line, and shape Afghanistan into a buffer state between the two imperial giants of the day. Gillmore suggested that the concept of an Afghan buffer be resurrected. He informed me that Soviet Vice Foreign Minister Igor Rogachev was visiting the next day. He planned to seek Rogachev's reaction to the idea.

Gillmore recommended that the principal focus be to strengthen Pakistan's stability. Afghanistan was the means to an end, not the prize. Pakistan was the prize. He called for Pakistan to be sealed off from the Pashtunistan issue, adding that Afghanistan could stay in its usual chaotic state. It had always been like that anyway.

Continuing, Gillmore proposed that Afghanistan be allowed to return to its "normal" condition: a weak central government with strong regions, a neutral state in Central Asia that does not draw outsiders to interfere. His analysis of the Afghan situation struck me as excellent if Pakistan-centric. Pakistan was the larger country and strategically more important. But recent history had shown that the two countries were each crucial to achieving the regional peace and stability that Britain and the United States sought.

During the next three years I would come to believe there was an underlying contradiction in Britain's Afghan policy. On one hand, the policy condemned the ISI's destructive support for Hekmatyar and the Afghan extremists. On the other, it tended to advocate a Pakistani sphere of influence in Afghanistan. That was an unrealizable goal, as the Soviets had just experienced. The large Pakistani emigrant population living in several British cities may have influenced British authorities to maintain good working relations with the Pakistani government, including its intelligence agencies. I wondered if Britain's receptivity to a Pakistani sphere of influence in Afghanistan was a holdover from Britain's imperial period, when British diplomacy attempted to draw Afghanistan into its Indian Empire's sphere of influence.

Gillmore suggested that the Russians be persuaded to remove Najib and one or two of his senior advisers. The most powerful Mujahidin commanders outside Kabul, he said, would need to be involved in the coalition regime succeeding Najib. The middle class in Afghanistan, he remarked, was anti-Soviet and would reject any Soviet attempt to reassert Moscow's influence in post-Najib Afghanistan.

Then he handed over a scathing Foreign Office indictment of Hekmatyar's divisive role in Afghan politics. The document cataloged Hekmatyar's numerous assassinations of Afghans and foreigners, including the British journalist Andy Skrzypkowiak in 1986.[27] Two of Gillmore's South Asian Office staff members participating in the meeting sharply criticized the ISI and the AIG. Any Afghan Resistance political organization organized by the ISI, they warned, would be terminal and counterproductive. Najib, not the resistance, was now winning the propaganda war. There was an urgent need to move the resistance center of gravity inside Afghanistan before Najib permanently established himself in Kabul.

Gillmore's analysis, in particular his observation that the Soviets would need to be convinced to remove Najib, coincided with what I had heard in Washington. His two assistants' assessment that the correlation of forces in Afghanistan was now moving in a direction favorable to Najib would undercut that objective. Gorbachev had overcome conservative pressures when he removed Karmal in 1986. Since late 1988, however, the conservative forces in the Politburo had capitalized on his domestic economic setbacks and the "loss" of Eastern Europe to stage a comeback. Gorbachev and his reformist allies were now on the defensive. The conservatives were well positioned to sustain the flow of money and weapons to Najib.

In London I also met Gordon Adams, the highly regarded chief of the BBC's Afghan service. Adams's pessimism matched that of the Foreign Office. He said that, for the first time, the BBC was seeing a questioning of the jihad in letters from Afghan listeners. He thought that commanders inside Afghanistan held the key to success.

My consultations in London were instructive but also depressing. They reinforced the gloomy assessments of the Afghan situation sounded by the pessimists in Washington. That situation was about to get worse.

CHAPTER 12

Potemkin Government

*Reincarnating the Alliance Seven as an interim government did nothing
to overcome the differences that had prevented them from developing a
common policy and leadership.... Throughout its brief, barren and ineffectual existence, the members of the so-called Interim Government remained at sixes and sevens among themselves, their internecine bickering
and feuds as bitter as their hatred of the Kabul regime.*
—IQBAL AKHUND, NATIONAL SECURITY ADVISER
TO PRIME MINISTER BENAZIR BHUTTO, PAKISTAN, 2000[1]

When my British Airways flight from London landed at Islamabad airport
on June 29, 1989, I was not yet aware of the monopoly Pakistan's army still
exercised over Afghan policy following Prime Minister Benazir Bhutto's election victory. A March 1989 intelligence briefing paper I had read in Washington reached the opposite conclusion: "The intelligence community's
assessment is that PM Bhutto faces no major threat to her rule from GOP
[Government of Pakistan] policy on Afghanistan."[2] That same month, the
State Department NEA Bureau's deputy assistant secretary responsible for
South Asia assured Congress that Pakistan's status as the fourth-largest recipient of American aid was justified by its return to democratic governance:

The United States cannot turn its back on the exciting new democratic
government of Pakistan after supporting its military dictatorship....

Gen. Beg argues publicly that the best interests of the military are served by helping to maintain conditions of civil order necessary for stable, civilian rule and dedicating itself to the primary duty of national affairs.[3]

Prime Minister Bhutto had toured Western capitals announcing her new government's support for a political solution to the Afghan war, one ending in an act of self-determination by Afghans choosing their own leadership. Her official pronouncements exactly overlapped with American goals in Afghanistan. In sharp contrast, the ISI was exploiting CIA and Saudi weapons and money to insert the virulently anti-American extremist Gulbuddin Hekmatyar into Kabul by military force. The Pakistani Army's strategy countermanded U.S. interests. But the American intelligence and diplomatic communities did not report, much less propose countering, Pakistani Army Chief Mirza Aslam Beg's and ISI Director Hamid Gul's preparations to transform Afghanistan into a revolutionary Islamist state.

Beg and Gul manipulated alliances with Bhutto's Pakistani political enemies, Muslim League chief Nawaz Sharif, and the Pakistani politico-religious parties to hamstring her authority and maintain the military's control of the Pakistani state. The Zia-era constitution's Eighth Amendment allowed the Pakistani president to dismiss prime ministers, their governments, and the National Assembly and call for elections within ninety days. Beg could ask President Ghulam Ishak Khan to pull that lanyard at any moment.

The 1977 coup by Zia ul-Haq against her father must have never been far from Bhutto's mind. Vindicating her father's legacy had been her principal preoccupation since Zia ul-Haq had executed him a decade before her December 1988 election. Bhutto's victory accomplished that goal. But the price for remaining in office was to stay out of the army's way on Afghanistan, Pakistan's nuclear program, and other areas key to sustaining the army's paramountcy over the Pakistani state.

Prime Minister Bhutto paid that price, but only after making a brief, spirited attempt to loosen the military's grip on power in the months leading up to my late June arrival in Pakistan. She began her confrontation with Beg by attempting to cut off his budding nuclear dialogue with Iran. The army chief had visited Tehran and informed Iranian President Akbar Hashemi Rafsanjani that he was ready to assist Iran with nuclear technology. During her subsequent visit to Iran, Bhutto told Rafsanjani she did not approve of Beg's initiative. Bhutto next fired Hamid Gul on May 31, 1989, on the eve of her departure for a visit to Washington. She did not follow the standard practice of requesting the chief of army staff, in this case General Beg, to propose candidates to succeed Gul. She made the appointment herself, without consulting Beg, choosing a retired lieutenant general, Shamsur Kallue. A former corps commander, Kallue was associated with the group of senior retired officers who had opposed Zia's dictatorship and Islamization programs in Pakistan's army.

Bhutto's offensive threatened to reverse the Pakistani Army's twelve-year-old control of Pakistan's politics. The ISI was critical to the military's ability to sustain its preeminence in Pakistan established by Zia in 1977. Pakistan's generals used the ISI to suppress domestic political opponents. The military spy agency was the army's most important instrument in implementing Islamization programs, maintaining the jihadi infrastructure along the Frontier, conducting proxy warfare in Afghanistan (and soon Kashmir as well), and managing Pakistan's secret development of nuclear weapons. Now, Pakistan's new prime minister was brazenly attempting to wrench it from military control.

Beg struck back. Prime Minister Bhutto had won the elections, but he had the guns. He emasculated Kallue's authority by ordering his military subordinates in the ISI to report to him, not to Kallue. Beg excluded Kallue from his strategy sessions with the corps commanders, a privilege extended to previous ISI chiefs. He appointed Gul as his special adviser on Afghanistan and gave him a corps command in the Punjab. From those positions, Gul continued to dictate Afghan war strategy. Beg also shifted some of the ISI's Afghan responsibilities to the director of military intelligence, Lieutenant General Asad Durrani, who responded to Gul's instructions. Beg created and assumed leadership of a new Afghan policy coordination cell within the government as well. The chief of army staff crowned his triumph over the prime minister by personally calling on her. During their meeting, he informed Bhutto that the army's nine corps commanders opposed her.[4]

Bhutto backed down. In public appearances at home and abroad, she gave cover to the Pakistani military's covert attempt to force a military solution to the Afghan war, develop nuclear weapons, and provide Iran with nuclear weapons technology. Later, after her dismissal from office, she revealed that in 1989 she had wished to pursue a peaceful political solution of Afghanistan following the Soviet withdrawal, but the ISI "did not agree, wanting to give the Mujahaideen the taste of victory by marching into Kabul as conquerors."[5] During her June 1989 visit to Washington, Bhutto lied to a joint session of Congress: "Speaking for Pakistan, I can declare that we do not possess, nor do we intend to make, a nuclear device."[6] The transfer of sensitive centrifuge technology and bomb-making blueprints to Iran through Pakistani nuclear scientist A. Q. Khan advanced Beg and Gul's anti-American "strategic consensus" (with Iran) and "strategic defiance" doctrines, even while large-scale military and economic assistance from Washington's second six-year aid package, approved in 1987, continued to flow to Pakistan.[7]

꿀

My trips to Pakistan always began with briefings at the American embassy in Islamabad. Ambassador Robert Oakley was a polite host during my stopovers on the way to and from the Afghan-Pakistani Frontier to meet with the Mujahidin. The sprawling, well-guarded, walled embassy compound in Pakistan's capital city occupied dozens of acres. Ambassador Oakley's opulent residence, manicured lawn, flower gardens, and swimming pool offered a pleasant moorage after my long flights from the United States, or when I returned from weeks of meetings with Mujahidin near the Afghan border. At the same time, the resplendent embassy building seemed like an American cocoon, separated from the daily life and bustle of the Pakistani world outside.

The embassy briefings during my three-week visit to Pakistan in June and July 1989 clung to the optimist line I would later hear from Pakistan's ISI director generals at ISI headquarters and Saudi intelligence chief Prince Turki al-Faisal in Riyadh. The briefers acknowledged that the Mujahidin defeat at Jalalabad was a setback but said the United States should not give up now. The countrywide offensives that the ISI was planning for the fall would restore Mujahidin military momentum. The AIG was stretching its governing tentacles into Afghanistan, appointing Mujahidin provincial governors. A new, more credible Mujahidin shura to select a broad-based interim resistance government would be held within the one-year deadline the AIG had set in February. They continued to see Hekmatyar as the most organized and aggressive Afghan resistance leader. I regularly heard the erroneous refrain: He may not be very likeable, but his commanders killed more of the enemy than those of any other Mujahidin group.

Once alone, I told Ambassador Oakley of the contrast between the embassy's assessment and the views of some in Washington as well as the British Foreign Office. Oakley reiterated the majority optimist perspective, which in Washington had been emblazoned into my talking points for delivery to the Pakistanis, Afghans, and Saudis: The United States should continue to move forward with its Pakistani and Saudi allies. Oakley believed that downgrading the AIG would create "unnecessary friction with the AIG, commanders and shuras, anger the ISI and make the Saudis nervous."[8] In a separate meeting, Station Chief "Bill"* concurred with the imperative to stay the course on Afghan policy. He described the ISI plans for an aggressive fall offensive against regime-held cities. ISI briefers told me that their strategy to besiege Jalalabad, Khost, and Kandahar before the 1989 Afghan "fighting season" ended in December would make significant progress. Khost, they said, was likely to fall to the Mujahidin in 1989.

My discussions with Ed McWilliams revealed a different assessment of events in Afghanistan. I met him in his tiny embassy office. He seemed lonely, isolated, but unbowed. He stated that most of his Afghan contacts considered Hekmatyar and the AIG to be Pakistani-created puppets. He believed that the AIG's unpopularity was blocking Mujahidin military and political progress. And without such progress, the Soviets would not force Najib to step down in favor of a political settlement. The war would continue, and Najib would hold on in Kabul. Some lower-level American diplomats in Pakistan sought me out to make the same points.

Coordinating with Benazir Bhutto's foreign policy advisers was an important objective during each of my visits to Pakistan. After the embassy and ISI briefings, I called on Foreign Minister Yaqub Khan and Bhutto's national security adviser, Iqbal Akhund. They appeared to view me as a vehicle to press Pakistani military leaders and the ISI toward a political solution of the Afghan war, which they emphatically supported. I was an independent American

---

* "Bill" is a pseudonym. This station chief and some other officers in the CIA's clandestine service are given fictitious first names in this book to protect their true identities. The use of pseudonyms is a common practice among foreign intelligence agencies around the world.

channel back to Washington, a diplomat like them, capable of forcing generals Beg and Gul to make fundamental changes in Pakistan's Afghan policy, which they were unable to do.

Yaqub Khan, a retired general, was the most successful diplomat in Pakistan's postindependence history. Born a prince, the son of the last maharaja of Rampur in India, he looked and acted like a Chief Wazir at the Mogul emperor's court and the world-class statesman he was. He was tall, graceful, and elegantly dressed, his thin face finely accented by soft, intelligent eyes, silver hair, and a razor-edged aquiline nose. Pakistan's multilingual foreign minister had played a major role in guiding the meandering Geneva negotiations to their successful conclusion in 1988. His strategic approach to foreign policy issues impressed his American and Soviet counterparts. He later served as Pakistan's ambassador in Washington and Moscow, and, after retirement, as the United Nations' special envoy to mediate the Western Sahara dispute.

Once we were alone, Yaqub Khan was stunningly open about his disdain for Hekmatyar, the Pakistani military's favoritism for the AIG, and its sabotaging of his Foreign Ministry's attempt, with the United States and the Soviet Union, to negotiate a political solution to the Afghan war. Pakistan's elder statesman vigorously pronounced that a political settlement was desperately needed after the Soviet pullout and was now possible. The Soviet Union was not irretrievably wedded to Najib. The exiled king, Zahir Shah, could play a unifying role. The problem, he said, was that Beg and Gul were emotionally committed to Hekmatyar. Hekmatyar was their flawed engine to achieve a military victory in Afghanistan. Hekmatyar's triumph in Afghanistan would avenge the humiliation of the 1971 defeat by India in the Bangladesh War. Yaqub Khan hoped that Beg's Hekmatyar policy line would not be prolonged for another two years—until Beg retired in August 1991. Then it could be too late to achieve a political settlement.

National Security Adviser Akhund voiced similar frustrations over the ISI's control of Pakistan's Afghan policy when we met. He told me that the United Nations should convene a large representative Afghan gathering to choose a new Afghan leadership if the AIG failed to do so before its term expired on March 25, 1990. Yaqub Khan's and Akhund's sentiments were passionately reiterated by one of their subordinates, a future Pakistani ambassador and experienced Afghan specialist. The ambassador arranged a one-on-one meeting with me at a secure location. His main point was that the United States needed to pressure Beg to support a political resolution of the Afghan war. Bhutto and the Foreign Ministry, he said, believed that the AIG could never function as a government. But the United States could not count on Bhutto or the Foreign Ministry for assistance on an Afghan political settlement. The official divulged that Hamid Gul carried great influence with General Beg, who had a "lax style." Beg tended to let "matters drift." Gul and the ISI erroneously believed Hekmatyar would "deliver the goods for Pakistan." The ironic thing, he asserted, was that Hekmatyar could never rule Afghanistan. Afghans hated him. He would be overthrown even if the ISI managed to put him in power.[9]

Yaqub Khan's and Iqbal Akhund's remarkably blunt comments about the civilian-military divide in the Pakistani government on Afghan policy startled me—and significantly influenced my own evolving thoughts on why U.S. strategy was not working inside Afghanistan. The Pakistani ambassador's more detailed presentation made behind closed doors also surprised me. And so did the hostile media treatment I encountered in Pakistan. A headline for Hekmatyar's daily, *Shahadat* (Martyrdom), read, "Tomsen's Model of Islamic Government in Afghanistan." The article derided me as "an uninvited guest with cheekiness, stubbornness," and carrying a "satanic plan."[10] The Pakistani *Muslim* ran a cartoon of me looking down at three wretched Mujahidin stuck at the bottom of a well, sarcastically noting, "I am a well-wisher of Mujahidin." *Al Jihad* (The Holy War), the Muslim Brotherhood's newspaper published in Peshawar, charged that I "was responsible for the failure of the Jalalabad battle."[11]

The Soviet and Afghan communist media joined the chorus. A commentary by Najib's news agency, *Bakhtar*, declared: "The White House Administration has sent Peter Thomsen [sic] as its Special Envoy to the Afghan armed opposition groups stationed in Peshawar. Thomsen [sic], on the one hand, supervises the activities of the armed opposition groups and, on the other, continues the U.S. all-sided military assistance to the war-mongers at the demand of P. Thomsen's [sic] much destructive power."[12]

A Soviet TASS news agency article distributed worldwide alleged that I, along with Oakley, was preparing a "lightning offensive involving 10–15,000 men" to seize Jalalabad.[13] The Soviet ambassador in Kabul, Yuli Vorontsov, accused the United States of helping Pakistan launch military offensives against Afghanistan. A U.S. official backgrounder in Washington responded that I was in Pakistan but "not planning war strategy."[14]

ψ

I was relieved to leave the acrimony on Afghan policy behind in Islamabad and finally set out for the storied Frontier on July 5, 1989. The conflicting views of the AIG in Washington and Islamabad did not change the chant guiding U.S. strategy: "Give the AIG a chance." American Afghan policy, in practice, was tethered to Pakistan's official policy, which remained the "front-line" state in the war against the Soviet puppet regime in Kabul. The AIG was the only resistance political entity allowed by Pakistan to function on Pakistani soil. Foreign diplomats and journalists had no choice but to make the rounds of AIG offices in Peshawar if they wished to meet with a Mujahidin political organization in Pakistan. My instructions were to engage the AIG leaders and press for the broad-based shura they had announced would be organized within a year. I would encourage them to honor that pledge; to overcome their differences; to bring the Shia and other important Afghan groups into the AIG; and to make the AIG a credible political alternative to Najib's PDPA regime in Kabul. In President George H.W. Bush's words, the challenge was to persuade the AIG leaders to "fashion a stable, broadly based government responsive to the needs of the Afghan people."[15]

That was a tall order.

My encounters with Mujahidin politicians, commanders, religious clerics, and tribal chiefs along the 1,500-mile-long Afghan-Pakistani Frontier of flinty mountains and deep valleys would become the most enjoyable—and instructive—part of my job. I decided to seek out representatives of all the Mujahidin groups, not just the AIG and the extremist Afghans favored by the ISI and the CIA. The hundreds of Afghans I met during twenty trips to the Frontier over the next three years were faithful to the famous tradition of lavish Afghan hospitality, even when they could not afford it. Nearly all volunteered their thanks to the United States for assisting in their jihad against the Soviet Union. Many advocated mullahocracy. Many more wanted Afghanistan to return to the precommunist Zahir Shah era of relative tranquility. I met fearsome-looking rogues, young Talibs (Islamic students), and Western-educated professors. Long-bearded, tall, and proud Afghan tribal elders came outfitted in colorful turbans and shawls denoting their tribal identification.

I made a special effort to engage Afghans left out of the AIG: commanders based inside Afghanistan, southern Durranis clamoring for the return of Zahir Shah, Shia, Tajiks, Afghan intellectuals, commander-turned-political organizer Abdul Haq, and Ahmed Shah Masood's brothers, Ahmed Zia and Yahya. This varied group repeated the same complaints about ISI and CIA favoritism for Hekmatyar that they had made to McWilliams during his visits. All expressed supreme confidence that Najib and the communists in Kabul would sooner or later be overthrown. Allah would decide when.

I used the embassy's aircraft, Pakistani airline flights, Pakistani military helicopters, and ground transportation to get to small Mujahidin bases tucked into mountainsides in the tribal agencies along the Afghan-Pakistani border. I traveled through North and South Waziristan and westward to the remote district capital of Zhob. In Peshawar, I met AIG party leaders, ministers, and commanders. Quetta was my window on the war in southern and western Afghanistan. There I spoke with the famous southern Durrani commanders Haji Latif and Mullah Naqib as well as Allaudin Khan, the deputy to western Tajik commander Ismael Khan. My visits to Chitral in Pakistan's far northeast permitted me to monitor developments in Masood's occupied areas in northern Afghanistan.[16]

The American consul in Peshawar, Mike Malinowski, arranged my schedule for meeting Mujahidin politicians and commanders in the city.[17] Mike and his consulate staff were most helpful during each of my visits. Dick Hoagland, the consulate's branch public affairs officer, later served as my deputy.[18] I coordinated closely with Hank Cushing, who managed USAID's $80 million cross-border Afghan assistance program inside Afghanistan as well as its road-building organization, the Afghan Construction and Logistics Unit (ACLU). In Quetta, Afghan-American Ziauddin (Zia) Mojadedi, the local USAID representative and VOA stringer, helped with scheduling and interpreting.[19] Zia was a storehouse of knowledge about Afghanistan.

On leaving Islamabad, we drove north on the legendary Grand Trunk Road. The British Raj used this strategic artery to connect the northern provinces of the Indian Empire to New Delhi and Calcutta. The highway permitted rapid movement of military reinforcements north of the Indus to confront tribal uprisings led by mad mullahs and phantom Russian armies closing in on the Khyber Pass. The journey to Peshawar covered 120 miles. Outside Islamabad, we found the roadway thoroughly cluttered with people and animals. There were not many women to be seen—they stayed inside— but multitudes of men walked, rode bicycles, drove cars, and mingled at road-side bazaars around tables laden with fruits, vegetables, and plastic household items. The outside walls of buildings were festooned with Urdu-sketched ad-vertisements of Western products like Coca Cola and Pepsi.

The highway became more crowded as we moved through Punjab Province toward the Indus River border with the Northwest Frontier Province (NWFP). Men and boys pulled donkeys. Tongas—wooden, two-wheeled ve-hicles drawn by horses—plodded along ahead, slowing traffic to a crawl, while camels, their heads high above men and machines, strode forward, heedless of the mix of humanity, animals, and smoke-belching vehicles around them. "Flying coaches," inter-province buses, roared by. So did the large multicolored "jingle" transport-trucks that ply the roads of the subcon-tinent. In Hindu India, paintings of Hindu gods Ram, Vishnu, or Ganesha— or Indian movie actresses—adorn their sides. In the Islamic state of Pakistan, the trucks were covered with flowers, geometric designs, graceful Arabic let-tering, and American F-16s. Further from Islamabad and closer to the Indus River, the terrain gave way to rolling hills and a harsher, brown-streaked coun-tryside. The snowcapped Suleiman range rose ahead of us, crowned by the 15,600-foot-high Safed Koh (White Mountains), home to the Tora Bora cave complex just across the border in Afghanistan.

Suddenly, the highway sloped down to the rushing waters of the mighty Indus. The spectacular Attock Fortress, built by the great Mughal emperor Akbar to fend off marauding bands of Pashtun tribesmen, guarded the Punjab side of the river. The Afghan Young Muslims had trained inside its walls in 1975. The massive fort hovers over a yawning, 200-yard-wide gap where the Indus dramatically narrows into a deep canyon. Far below, giant heads of white foam leap skyward as the river angrily plunges southwest toward the shores of the Arabian Sea. Giant battlements bulge from the corners of the dark colossus. Whoever controlled this fortress controlled the strategic gate-way separating South and Central Asia. Just upstream from Attock, the Kabul River's muddy discharge from the Hindu Kush merged with the larger, blue-tinted Indus current, drawn from Himalayan glaciers a thousand miles distant, near Tibet.

The refreshing Frontier wind welcomed us as we crossed the thick highway bridge over the Indus next to Attock Fort into the Pashtun-majority NWFP. The great Eurasian conquerors Alexander the Great, Tamerlane, and Babur had passed this way. So had Sikh and British armies marching north, expecting to tame the Afghans. We continued on the road to Peshawar along the Kabul River's bank past Nowshera, home of a Pakistani Army division. We passed the battleground where fanatic Muslim and Sikh holy warriors had slaughtered one another in 1823. The Afghans lost that battle and with it the Durrani dynasty's winter capital of Peshawar.

One hour later, we entered Peshawar, home to over 2 million people. It lies in a valley of the same name that is pierced by three major passes. One is the Kohat Pass, which opens to the tribal agencies to the west, including wild and woolly North and South Waziristan. The most famous is the Khyber Pass, only 10 miles northwest of Peshawar on the Grand Trunk Road, a few miles from the Durand Line and 35 miles from Jalalabad. The Malakand Pass, where Winston Churchill's unit once skirmished with the Mohmand tribes, is located northwest of Peshawar city. Beyond it lies the Mohmand and Bajaur tribal agencies and the beautiful Dir and Swat valleys. Further east along the Durand Line is fabled Chitral and the Chinese border.

It took 150 years and the Soviet-Afghan war for Peshawar to recoup its Afghan character. The city's proportion of Afghan residents rose sharply after the savage Soviet bombing campaigns forced more than 3 million Afghan refugees to flee into the NWFP. By the time I arrived, the streets of the city overflowed with thousands of Afghan merchants, turbaned Mujahidin, mullahs, and tribesmen.

After a day of briefings at the American consulate in Peshawar, America's Afghan-watching post on the Frontier, we set out for Miram Shah in North Waziristan to meet Afghan commander Jalaluddin Haqqani. The three-hour journey took us through the Kohat Pass into Pashtun hill-tribe territory. The bare, nearly treeless rock-strewn hills of North Waziristan were criss-crossed by countless goat trails. Little wonder that the Waziri tribes inhabiting this wasteland turned to plundering in the fertile valleys of the Indus basin below. We stopped for lunch with a district political officer at his cozy colonial-era bungalow. He described the recent application of Pashtunwali to two young adulterers in his district. The boy and girl were thrown into a hole and stoned to death by angry Waziri tribesmen.

Bidding farewell to our host, we climbed steadily upward through more brush-covered hillsides toward the snowcapped Suleiman range pinpointing the Afghan-Pakistani border. The house-fortresses fencing in reclusive Pashtun families dotted the mountainsides, ridges, and valleys—a common sight on both sides of the Durand Line. Their high stone walls surrounded brownish-white rectangular homes made of stone and hardened mud. A tower rose at one of the corners, irregularly punctured by holes so that the inhabitants could monitor the approach of tribal foes—or fire down on them. We saw few people during our early afternoon drive, even though North and South Waziristan are the most populated of the seven tribal agencies.

Haqqani received us in his family compound outside Miram Shah. Wiry, long-haired, and wild-eyed, he fit the colonial-era image of the charismatic mullah on the Frontier. Our discussion took place in his tiny living room over green tea. The furniture was spartan. Outside, about a dozen Mujahidin cradling shiny AK-47s loitered about. Haqqani wore a secondhand U.S. Army camouflage shirt over his baggy pants. His turban was spun abnormally high for a man of below medium height. Originally white, it had faded into a dirty gray. Haqqani's black, stringy beard—uncut, per strict Wahhabi tradition—hung down from the lower reaches of his coarse, thin face.

The meeting with Haqqani lasted an hour. He spent most of the time complaining that the CIA's reductions of arms shipments beginning in late 1988 had weakened his military capability. He opened a notebook and showed me his weapons inventory. His voice rising, he asked how he could fight if he had not received any arms or ammunition for eight months. Haqqani protested that the cut-off had compelled him to purchase ammunition and arms at the Pakistani arms bazaar at Teri Mangal near Parchinar, in the nearby Khurram tribal agency. He was down to 2 Stingers and only 400 heavy Spanish 120-mm mortar rounds. He was also out of mine-clearing belts. I responded that 5,000 were stored in an ISI warehouse in Islamabad. "They are probably the Pakistanis'," he announced. I told Haqqani that I would look into his complaints.

Haqqani's demands for more weapons, ammunition, and money would become a constant refrain that I would hear from both moderate nationalists and radical Islamist Mujahidin for the next three years. The moderates invariably levied an additional demand on me—to force the ISI to evenly distribute American aid between them and the extremists. This was beyond my authority. Aside from ISI, the Saudi charities on the Frontier and the Saudi government also transferred millions in cash to Haqqani and other Afghan Islamists. Haqqani's collection boxes were stuffed at Friday mosque services in the Saudi Kingdom. Scores of young Arabs signed up to fight alongside his Mujahidin bands.

While we spoke, Haqqani's CIA-purchased Chinese rockets were landing on Khost. The regime-controlled capital of Paktiya Province, less than 10 miles away and about 80 miles from Kabul, still held out. Afghan Army units and pro-regime tribal militias drove each of Haqqani's ground attacks off the Khost plain and back across the Afghan-Pakistani border, their resolve stiffened by Haqqani's well-known cruelties against captured prisoners. Urban youth unwillingly impressed into the Afghan Army off Kabul streets hoped they would be sent to garrisons in the north facing Masood rather than to Khost, where capture meant certain death. A VOA reporter on assignment in Paktiya was once asked by Haqqani to interview some captured regime soldiers. One of the trembling young POWs, desperately reaching out for any lifeline, told the reporter, "I'm not guilty. So if they kill me, you're going to become guilty." When the interview ended, Haqqani tossed the reporter an AK-47 and invited him to execute some of the prisoners. The reporter declined. The prisoners were each given a last meal of a banana, taken behind a large rock, and shot.[20]

The ISI prediction that Khost would fall proved overly optimistic. Haqqani lacked local Mujahidin allies from other tribes, and his ISI, CIA, and Saudi sponsors could not spend enough to shift the complicated tribal landscape in Paktiya to his side. The province's confusing patchwork of hundreds of small, independent tribal quams contending for position against one another defied management from outsiders. The constant infighting among the seven party leaders in Peshawar added fuel to the incessant local tribal rivalry. If one tribal group affiliated itself with one of the Peshawar seven, its tribal competitors joined a competing party.

Influential Ahmadzai commanders to the north and east of Khost might have made the difference between victory and defeat for Haqqani. But they were not interested in delivering the isolated communist outpost to the Zadran fanatic. The moderate Ahmadzai khans disliked Haqqani's religious extremism. ISI payments occasionally bought their temporary coordination with his attacks on Khost, but never for long. Naim Kuchi, one of Sibghatullah Mojaddedi's commanders in Paktiya, considered Haqqani a bigger threat to his Ahmadzai tribe than Najib, also an Ahmadzai from northern Paktiya.

Najib's skillful manipulation of tribal divisions among the Mujahidin helped keep the isolated Khost outpost on the Pakistani border in the regime column. The Afghan president's Ahmadzai clan was in Paktiya. He was well versed in the crosscurrents of tribal animosities in his native province. His bribes turned tribal chiefs against Haqqani or bought their neutrality. Important cabinet ministers in the PDPA were also from Paktiya. Defense Minister Shahnawaz Tanai and Interior Minister Aslam Watanjar used their tribal connections in the province to throw back Haqqani offensives. The stray parachute drops of food and ammunition from PDPA aircraft falling outside of Khost's defensive perimeter, purposeful or not, offered an additional inducement for local tribes not to capture the city.

ψ

After returning to Peshawar from Miram Shah, I dove into a week of back-to-back meetings with scores of Mujahidin from all major tribal, ethnic, and religious groups and regions of Afghanistan. Abdul Haq stood out. He was articulate, strong-willed, passionate, and, above all, tenaciously independent. His politics were traditional, moderate, and inclusive, in the mold of the Afghan jirga. His prominent Arsala family tribal pedigree and widely respected war record gave him a national reputation among Afghans. The ISI opposed him for all of these reasons. CIA officers in Pakistan and Washington parroted ISI disinformation that Haq had only a limited following inside Afghanistan. His leg disability made him militarily irrelevant. Haq's self-promoting interviews with Western reporters, they contended, painted a false portrait of a former "middle-level" commander[21] whose time had passed.

During our first meeting, Haq gave me a tour of a war room adjoining his office. A huge map of Kabul and the provinces surrounding it was laid out on a table. It showed the location of regime military garrisons and police checkpoints. Haq said a successful political settlement process would generate massive defections of regime troops to the Mujahidin. When I asked him if he would join the AIG to strengthen it from the inside and push for a political solution, he initially refused, correctly calling it unrepresentative of most Afghan groups. Mujahidin, he argued, would not fight for a government created by the ISI. He accused Pakistan of seeking a military solution to the war when only a political solution could end it. After our second meeting Haq reluctantly agreed to enter the AIG, groaning that it was beyond repair.

I made the same request to Ahmed Zia, Ahmed Shah Masood's younger brother and his liaison with the ISI and CIA in Pakistan. He answered that Masood was ready to work with the AIG, but believed it was unrepresentative and formed by Pakistan. He complained that Masood had only heard of the attack on Jalalabad on the BBC. Since he was not involved in the ISI's war planning, he refused to support it. In any case, Zia stated with a smile, the ISI's intention was to install Hekmatyar in Kabul after Jalalabad fell. Ahmed Zia asked that the United States provide assistance directly to Masood. To assist the northern commander, I arranged for USAID's Afghan Construction and Logistics Unit to construct a road from Masood's warehouse at Gharm Chesma above Chitral into the areas he controlled in the north. The road would strengthen Masood's military position in northern Afghanistan by facilitating the transportation of supplies from Pakistan.

I learned a great deal in my first encounters with Mujahidin in Peshawar, Quetta, and Chitral during my July trip to the Frontier. Nothing, however, had prepared me for my meetings with the AIG party leaders in Peshawar, whom, aside from Hekmatyar, I had not met before—neither classified biographical notes produced by intelligence agencies in Washington, nor briefings at the U.S. embassy in Islamabad and the consulate in Peshawar, nor a Durrani tribal elder's warning that "all of the wealth in America cannot convince the seven to unite." Hekmatyar, the AIG foreign minister, turned down the American consulate's proposal to meet with me. Our terse 1989 exchange in Beijing must have convinced him that I would not be willing to indulge his anti-Americanism and tyrannical methods. This suited me fine. By the time of my first visit to Pakistan, his murderous politics and Pakistan's sponsorship had turned most Afghans against him.

THE MULLAH WARRIOR

My calls on AIG party leaders in Peshawar began with Interior Minister Yunus Khalis. We met inside a dimly lit room in his two-story cement house. Khalis's aide interpreted. Flies circled us as teenage boys served green tea and biscuits.

FIGURE 12.1   THE SEVEN PESHAWAR PARTY LEADERS

NAME	ETHNICITY	RELIGION	PARTY	POLITICAL AFFILIATION
Gulbuddin Hekmatyar	Ghilzai Pashtun	Sunni extremist Islamist	Hezb-i Islami Gulbuddin	Muslim Brotherhood
Mawlawi Yunus Khalis	Ghilzai Pashtun	Sunni extremist Islamist	Hezb-i Islami Khalis	Muslim Brotherhood
Abdul Rasoul Sayyaf	Ghilzai Pashtun	Sunni extremist Islamist	Ittehad	Muslim Brotherhood
Burhanuddin Rabbani	Tajik	Sunni extremist Islamist	Jamiat Islami	Muslim Brotherhood
Sayyid Ahmad Gailani	Qadiriya Sayyid*	Sufi Pir	Mahaz	Moderate-Nationalist
Sibghatullah Mojaddedi	Naqshbandi Sayyid*	Sufi Pir	Jebha	Moderate-Nationalist
Mawlawi Mohammad Nabi Mohammadi	Ghilzai Pashtun	Sunni traditional cleric	Harakat	Moderate-Nationalist

* Denotes Arab ancestry

At age sixty-nine, Khalis was the oldest of the Peshawar seven. Red henna coursed through his hair, eyebrows, and beard. The beard was long but not as long as Sayyaf's. Khalis had huge, rough hands. A loose *shalwar kamiz* sloped over his bulging stomach.

Khalis had a well-earned reputation for marrying young women. He took full advantage of Islam's allowance of four wives. In 1990, at age seventy, he married a teenager. Sixteen years later, an American correspondent who interviewed Khalis noticed a young girl and boy in the room. He was told that both youngsters were products of yet another marriage to a seventeen-year-old.[22]

Khalis was a Khugiani (Khugiani is the name of a district in central Nangarhar as well as a tribe). He was the closest of the Peshawar seven to his Afghan tribal roots, an earthy Pashtun mullah and ardent Afghan nationalist. He considered the Geneva Accords an interference in Afghan affairs. Khalis was an anti-Shia extremist who maintained close ties to Osama bin Laden. The ISI gave him the "third-largest share of the more than $3 billion of weapons and funds that the CIA invested in the Jihad."[23] Khalis did not let his extremist Sunni ideology interfere with his respect for the tribal Pashtunwali code. He could abide a loya jirga to choose an Afghan leadership, but he did not approve of democratic elections. Sovereignty rested with Allah, not the people. One of his followers explained that "Maulawi Sahib believes not in counting heads, but in weighing them."[24]

Khalis's unadorned outward appearance was misleading. Drawn to the Muslim Brotherhood in the 1960s, he was the first Afghan to translate Sayyid Qutb's writings into Pashto. His articles and poems appeared in Kabul and Jalalabad newspapers during Zahir Shah's reign. Khalis was deputy editor of the Ministry of Justice's magazine, and he periodically gave religious lectures on Kabul radio. Local officials and prominent families sought him out for counsel in religious matters. By night, he was active in Rabbani and Sayyaf's semi-clandestine Jamiat party based in Kabul University's Theology Department.

Khalis's party, Hezb-i Islami Khalis, was the strongest of the seven parties in the strategic province of Nangarhar through which the Peshawar-Jalalabad-Kabul road passed. The large aristocratic Arsala clan rallied behind Khalis and formed the backbone of his party. The clan's support for him was in the khan-mullah tradition. Before the communist coup, Khalis had lived with the Arsala family in Nangarhar, providing religious instructions to the children, including three brothers destined for Mujahidin leadership roles. Two of the brothers, Haji Qadir and Abdul Haq, became prominent Mujahidin commanders. Qadir was the most effective Mujahidin commander in Nangarhar during the Soviet-Afghan war. Adept at coaxing consensus from fractious commanders of different tribes, he was the elected leader of the Jalalabad Shura of some twenty commanders representing the seven Mujahidin parties. Qadir was quartermaster for Khalis's commanders in Nangarhar, supervising a large arms depot in Landi Kotal, located in Afridi territory just below the Khyber Pass in the Khyber Agency.

The oldest Arsala brother, Deen Mohammad, Khalis's deputy, shared Khalis's Islamist outlook. He ran the party office in Peshawar and was Khalis's liaison with the ISI and the other three AIG extremist parties. A senior officer in the ISI's large Afghan Bureau was a distant cousin. Like many ISI officers, he grew a beard and adjusted his clothing and ideology to conform to the militant extremism the ISI promoted among the Mujahidin.

Khalis opposed Hekmatyar's messianic quest to rule Afghanistan, which helped his relationship with moderate party leaders Mojaddedi, Nabi, and Gailani. But he was inflexible on religious doctrine. Turkish Prime Minister Turgut Ozal once stormed out of Khalis's house when the Afghan mullah observed that

Turkey's secular democracy was not sufficiently Islamic. Khalis schemed with Sayyaf to fill AIG offices with hundreds of orthodox Sunni mullahs, ban Shia participation in the AIG, and decorate the AIG as a "pure" Islamic regime governed by qualified clerics administering a conservative Sunni version of Sharia. The rigid anti-Shia rules that Khalis and Sayyaf enforced inside the AIG delighted Saudi Arabia's religious hierarchy. Prince Turki, the Saudi intelligence chief, made periodic grants to the AIG, supplementing the regular CIA payments.

Khalis's famous sense of humor occasionally lightened the atmosphere of our otherwise sterile meetings. I once proposed to him that the AIG broaden its base by incorporating Shia leaders. He smiled and replied, "They must first become Sunnis." Khalis liked to recount a White House meeting during which he attempted to convert President Reagan to Islam. He handed Reagan a Koran, asking the president to accept Islam so that the two could enter Paradise together. The president politely declined.

Khalis's fondness for leaving the comforts of Peshawar to wage jihad inside Afghanistan helped draw other Pashtun mullah-warriors to his party. They shared his Pashtun ethnocentrism and inflexible Islamist ideology— characteristics that would later define the Taliban. Two future Taliban leaders, commanders Mullah Mohammad Omar, a Ghilzai Hotak from southern Afghanistan, and Jalaluddin Haqqani, signed on with Khalis.[25] Khalis's preference for the war zone distinguished him from the other Peshawar party leaders. Gailani, Rabbani, Nabi, and Mojaddedi rarely entered Afghanistan. Sayyaf's and Hekmatyar's trips into Afghanistan were brief, heavily guarded, well photographed, and usually just over the border to ISI-supplied base camps. Khalis was different. He buckled on his pistol and joined operations against the enemy in the Tora Bora area of southern Nangarhar, sleeping under the stars and firing at regime outposts.

Khalis's commanders hosted Arab revolutionaries. One commander, Engineer Mahmood[26] in the Shinwari country east of the Khyber Pass, turned about twenty regime defectors over to his Arab allies for execution during the Battle of Jalalabad. Afghans in the area reported that Mahmood had charged the Arabs $10,000 per head. The Arabs showed no mercy. They sat the bound prisoners in a row and, one after another, beheaded them with knives. One of Sayyaf's commanders near Jalalabad also turned defectors over to Arab extremists who tortured and executed them.[27]

Not surprisingly, my talking points on AIG unity and the need for a broad-based AIG loya jirga or shura made little impression on Khalis. During our meeting in July 1989, I criticized his party and commanders for executing regime defectors. The killings, I told him, violated human rights and strengthened the regime. I sent Khalis a follow-up letter asking that his followers protect prisoners and turn them over to the Red Cross. A few weeks later, Khalis presided over a prisoner release ceremony. In a press conference he organized for the occasion, he repeated some of the points I had made to him.

Khalis's response to my advice on handling prisoners did not carry over to other issues, most importantly a political settlement of the Afghan war. During the next three years he sat stoically as I presented the case for new AIG elections and a negotiated transfer of power from the Najib regime to the Mujahidin. I made no headway. For Khalis, the Afghan war would be decided through the barrel of a gun.

THE IKHWANI

I called on Jamiat leader Burhanuddin Rabbani directly after Khalis. Rabbani collaborated with Sayyaf and Khalis to make the AIG a "pure" Islamic government, enforcing a rigid brand of Sharia. He sought an Islamist outcome in Afghanistan, as they did. Among the seven, he was the most active participant in the Muslim Brotherhood's international network.

Rabbani's surroundings during our many meetings were as affluent as Khalis's were plain. The Jamiat leader maintained large homes in Dubai and Ottawa in addition to Peshawar and Islamabad. He always dressed neatly. An ultraclean, flawlessly wrapped white or black turban and finely trimmed white beard framed his small, light-skinned face, typical of descendents of the White Huns who had made mountainous Badakhshan Province their home centuries ago. He often wore a pastel shawl over one of his crisp white shirts and light brown tunics. He spoke fluent English and Arabic. Rabbani was mild mannered and cagey. In his memoirs, Iqbal Akhund, Benazir Bhutto's national security adviser, wrote that he "looked (misleadingly, as it later turned out) meek and self-effacing."[28]

Rabbani married only once, and two of his ten children settled in the United States and Canada. One daughter married Masood's younger brother, Ahmed Zia. Rabbani's Islamist politics did not discourage his independent-minded wife and daughters from mixing with men and women at cocktail parties in Islamabad and in Western capitals. They wore only headscarves, in contrast to the wives of Sayyaf, Hekmatyar, Khalis, and commanders Abdul Haq and Masood, whose womenfolk were virtually invisible to outsiders.

Rabbani came to our first meeting primed to lay out a list of grievances. He complained that his personal subsidies had been cut and that his commanders no longer received CIA-supplied ordnance. Jamiat was the only party that projected a countrywide presence; it boasted Pashtun as well as Tajik and other non-Pashtun commanders. Why was he being discriminated against in weapons supplies and funding? He chafed at the Reconstruction Ministry booby prize he was left with at the Pashtun-dominated Rawalpindi Shura, arguing that continuing warfare inside Afghanistan ruled out reconstruction for the foreseeable future. He accurately pointed out that American-supplied construction assets were deployed to Khalis-, Hekmatyar-, and Haqqani-controlled areas in eastern Afghanistan, not to his mostly Tajik commanders concentrated in the northern and western regions of the country.

Rabbani was right. The ISI's (and therefore the CIA's) priority was to strengthen the military position of the extremist eastern Ghilzai Pashtun leaders in the AIG—Hekmatyar, Sayyaf, and Khalis—plus Haqqani. They refused to transfer construction machinery, equipment, and cement to Rabbani's Reconstruction Ministry, which was an empty vessel. Western aid programs providing education, health, agriculture, and humanitarian assistance inside Afghanistan were managed by Western nongovernmental organizations resistant to sharing their resources with Rabbani and the other AIG party leaders.

During our meeting, I urged Rabbani to help forge unity in the AIG. He was the only Tajik party leader, and although his party was Tajik centered, it included Mujahidin from all ethnic groups. I commented that the ACLU road project I had initiated to reach Masood's bases in the north would balance the road projects under way in eastern Afghanistan.

Islamist ideologues in the Muslim Brotherhood and the Saudi religious establishment insist that Islam disregards tribal, ethnic, and racial divisions within the umma. All Muslims are equal. In Peshawar politics, however, the majority Pashtuns did not accept Rabbani's leadership and religious credentials. He was a Tajik. Neither Pakistan's top generals nor the ISI trusted Rabbani. Rabbani compensated for his minority status by deftly positioning himself between Hekmatyar, Sayyaf, and Khalis, on one side, and the three AIG moderates—Gailani, Mojaddedi, and Nabi—on the other. When the

ISI needed someone to symbolically break AIG deadlocks or to lead an AIG delegation abroad, they often turned to him. Since he was the sole Tajik among the seven, Western reporters and diplomats erroneously considered him to be a moderate. In fact, he was a hardened anti-American Ikhwani extremist.[29] During the first Gulf War, Rabbani joined Hekmatyar and Sayyaf and the Muslim Brotherhood's international network to support Saddam Hussein and oppose Saudi Arabia and the U.S.-led coalition.

Rabbani's closeness to the ISI strained his relations with Masood and Ismael Khan, his two largest commanders. His duplicitous political style was exhibited in the schizoid manner in which he received guests. One face, presented to me at our first meeting, cultivated a moderate image articulated in well-spoken English. He brought westernized, English-speaking members of his party to join our conversation. His other face, the more genuine Rabbani of the Muslim Brotherhood, was presented during visits of Arab benefactors, Afghan and Pakistani Islamists, and the ISI. On those occasions Rabbani was often joined by his senior adviser, Nurullah Emad, a hard-line Islamist who cooperated closely with Hekmatyar and Sayyaf. Internationally, the Tajik alim projected moderation in Washington and European capitals and aggressive anti-Western Afghan positions at international Ikhwani conferences.[30]

THE WAHHABI

"You will join us in our victory," the tall, gaunt, bulky Abdul Rasoul Sayyaf said as he smiled through his huge beard, inaugurating our first encounter. We shook hands at his headquarters in the teeming Jalozai refugee camp south of Peshawar off the Grand Trunk Road. In our meetings, Sayyaf was gregarious and ingratiating. In smooth-spoken English, he thanked America for its support for the Afghan jihad. Behind the charade, the beefy Kharoti's politics were anti-Western, anti-Sufi, and, when it came to Afghan Shia, homicidal. In public speeches to Afghan, Pakistani, and Saudi audiences, he lashed out at the "pagan hands of the West." In 1990, he would join Rabbani and Hekmatyar in virulently opposing the United States, Saudi Arabia, and Kuwait in the first Gulf War.

Sayyaf's style matched that of Amin's, his first cousin and Paghmani neighbor. Amin became an opportunistic missionary of communism, Sayyaf of international Islamic revolution. He expounded the global militancy of the Muslim Brotherhood, telling visitors that he would move on to other jihads after the Afghan jihad ended in victory. In speeches, he extolled the su-premacy of Islam and the unity of the Muslim umma. He declared that "the struggle of Kashmiri Muslims from oppressive Hindu domination is a true Islamic jihad." The Palestinian issue could only be settled through armed jihad.[31] Sayyaf also routinely pronounced King Zahir Shah an infidel.[32]

Sayyaf's path to Wahhabism and the Muslim Brotherhood began in his na-tive Paghman, where he had attended a public high school and the government-supported Abu Hanifa Madrassa. He studied under Rabbani at Kabul University's Faculty of Theology, did graduate studies in Koranic law at al-Azhar University in Cairo, and became an assistant professor at Kabul Uni-versity. During Sayyaf's four-year teaching career in Kabul, he published a magazine, *Shariyat*, explicating the practice of Koranic law in an Islamic state.

Daoud's secret police were tracking Sayyaf's antiregime activities with Rabbani, Hekmatyar, and Masood on Kabul University's campus in the early 1970s. In 1974, he attempted to escape arrest by obtaining an American stu-dent visa. Sayyaf had already cleared immigration at the airport in Kabul and was walking toward an airplane, bound for a one-year law program in the United States, when he was detained by plainclothes policemen and jailed. He languished in prison for six years, through the 1978 communist coup and the Soviet invasion. His cousin Amin[33] protected him from the communist firing squads that annihilated scores of other Islamists imprisoned by Daoud and, afterward, the PDPA. His Paghmani relatives delivered food and other amenities to him in jail.

Released amid the confusion of Karmal's amnesty announcement after the Soviet invasion, Sayyaf fled to Pakistan, where he propagated the Wahhabi dogma. Previously, Wahhabism had been almost nonexistent in Afghanistan and Pakistan. Sayyaf coordinated with the Saudi clergy to bring Saudi pro-fessors and preachers to Pakistan. His Saudi-financed madrassas, military bases, and training camps became a haven for violent Muslim militants from around the world.

Prince Turki and Saudi religious charities in Peshawar and Quetta bestowed their favor on Sayyaf after his arrival in Pakistan. Wearing his signature flowing brown Saudi robe, the long-bearded alim traveled frequently to Saudi Arabia. He enthralled King Fahd and Saudi religious leaders with his passionate calls, delivered in flawless Arabic, for Dawa—spreading the Wahhabi doctrine. In 1985, Saudi Arabia presented Sayyaf with the King Faisal International Prize.

Back in Peshawar, Saudi funding powered the building of his party, Ittehad. The Afghan rumor mill at the February 1989 Rawalpindi Shura pronounced that Saudi bribes distributed to delegates had bought him the AIG prime ministership.

Sayyaf's arabized name, Abd Rab al-Rasul Sayyaf, "Servant of the Lord of the Prophet," could have been translated as "Servant of the Saudi Religious Establishment." Saudi cash funded his Wahhabi University in the Jalozai refugee camp where he established his headquarters. Sayyaf named it *Dawawal Ishad*, "Disseminator of Islamic Knowledge" in Arabic. Clergy from Islamic universities in Saudi Arabia taught there. They sent promising Afghan students to higher religious studies in Saudi Arabia. Arab Ikhwanis worked at Sayyaf's *al Banyan* (The Foundation), a Mujahidin newspaper in Peshawar that published a separate Arabic edition.

Sayyaf collaborated with Abdullah Azzam, Prince Turki, and the Saudi religious establishment to sponsor the travel of thousands of foreign fighters to Pakistan and into Afghanistan. Many were teenagers on holiday from their schools or youths who had already graduated but hoped to conduct a brief jihad before returning to their classes or jobs in the kingdom. Others were violent jihadis eager for combat and martyrdom.

Sayyaf and his followers worked with Abdullah Azzam's and Osama bin Laden's Services Bureau in Peshawar to arrange accommodations for those seeking exposure to the anti-Soviet jihad. Sayyaf's Saudi-financed *Saada* (Echo) military training facility was a half-day's drive away. ISI officers attended Saada graduation ceremonies. During the 1980s and 1990s, the numerous foreign jihadis trained at Sayyaf's Saada complex included the Egyptian extremist who assassinated the speaker of the Egyptian parliament in 1989 and the founders of the Abu Sayyaf terrorist group (named after Sayyaf) operating in the southern Philippines. Ramzi Yousef, the notorious mastermind of the first al-Qaeda attempt to blow up the World Trade Center in 1993, was another Saada trainee.[34] So was Khalid Sheikh Mohammed, future al-Qaeda mastermind of the 9/11 attacks. According to *The 9/11 Commission Report*, Sayyaf was Mohammad's "mentor" and employer between 1988 and 1992 in Peshawar.[35]

Sayyaf's Wahhabi proselytizing, his opportunism, and Saudi sponsorship alienated Afghan nationalists, moderates, westernized intellectuals and royalists, Shia, and traditional Hanafi clergy. At the same time, his aggressive "buying out" of commanders and political supporters from other parties angered

Hekmatyar and the AIG party leaders and displeased the ISI. The defection of fully one-half of the Hezb executive committee to Sayyaf in July 1989 riled ISI strategists. Saudi funds were, however, an important ISI resource. The Saudi government and clergy were hefty donors to Zia's vision. As a consequence, Sayyaf's Saudi-filled treasure chest made him less vulnerable than the other six leaders to direct ISI control. Prince Turki's generous parallel donations to Hekmatyar did not dispel the ISI's annoyance. Nor did it quell Hekmatyar's resentment that Sayyaf was Riyadh's favorite Mujahidin leader.

As AIG prime minister, Sayyaf exercised more authority than Mojaddedi enjoyed in the largely ceremonial post of AIG president. Sayyaf had the last say on the AIG budget, which was mainly financed by the American taxpayer. He loyally served his Saudi benefactors by blocking Shia entry into the AIG. With the other AIG leaders and the ISI, he derailed attempts by the United States, the Pakistani Foreign Ministry, the United Nations, and moderate Afghans to convene a broad-based Afghan gathering to choose the legitimate Afghan leadership that the AIG had promised in the wake of the flawed Rawalpindi Shura.

THE PRESIDENT

AIG President Sibghatullah Mojaddedi looked the part of a grand medieval caliph when he warmly greeted me at the entrance to his well-furnished reception room in July 1989. Our conversation was a welcome break from Sayyaf's phony camaraderie, Rabbani's insincerity, and Khalis' obduracy. His bright white turban blended perfectly with a Colonel Sanders'–style white spade beard. His elegant white robe symbolized his saintly status as the supreme hazrat of the Naqshbandi Sufi Order. A slight man of sixty-four when we first met, he projected dignity, energy, pride, and amiability. His narrow face framed intelligent, friendly eyes and a narrow nose. He carried within him genuine compassion for his country, his religion, and people. He had a razor-sharp wit, capable of sending those around him into great peals of laughter.

Mojaddedi's spacious villa seemed like a small palace. A huge, uniformed, black-bearded bodyguard in sandals, "General" Khan Mohammad, loomed behind Mojaddedi wherever he went. Courtiers scrambled about. Mojaddedi's chief courtier was a future Afghan president, Hamid Karzai, then thirty-two. Affable, sincere, and cordial, Karzai was Mojaddedi's closest political adviser as well as his press spokesman and speechwriter. Karzai's father was chief of the influential Durrani Popalzai tribe, a former deputy speaker of parliament, and a leading Afghan reformer during Zahir Shah's decade of democracy. The Karzai family's pro–Zahir Shah tribal following in southern Afghanistan was one of Mojaddedi's important constituencies. It was also a source of ISI disfavor and one reason why Mojaddedi's party received only 3 to 5 percent of ISI funding.[36] True to Afghan practice, Mojaddedi's sons populated his inner circle. One, Zabibullah Mojaddedi, was his party's treasurer and the AIG minister of health.

Mojaddedi's authority in the AIG ended at his front portal. During our many meetings in his presidential office and dinners at his residence, I never saw the AIG prime minister or any of the AIG ministers in the AIG cabinet. "They would not sit in the same room with each other," an ISI brigadier general wrote when forced to waste his time in independent meetings with each of the seven.[37] Cabinet sessions were rare and an arena for bitter arguments when they took place. The three AIG moderates fought the four Islamists. Mirroring intra-Parchami and intra-Khalqi conflicts in Kabul, ceaseless conflicts raged within the moderate and extremist AIG wings.

The Naqshbandi pir could be remarkably straightforward in expressing his views. During our first meeting, Mojaddedi invited me outside to give a joint press conference to Western, Pakistani, and Afghan reporters. Most questions dwelled on whether the American commitment to the Mujahidin remained strong after the Soviet withdrawal. One reporter asked about Yasser Arafat's recent offer to mediate between Najib and the AIG. After I dismissed the offer, Mojaddedi vehemently castigated the PLO for supporting the Soviet Union and PDPA during the Soviet occupation. His slashing comments made front-page news the next day in the Pakistani media. I could not but reflect, however, that Hekmatyar, Rabbani, and Sayyaf would have given different answers if they, instead of Mojaddedi, had been leading the press conference, and their party newspapers would have reported accordingly.

Mojaddedi was equally candid two months later during a discussion at the White House with CIA Director William Webster. While we were waiting to see President Bush, the white-bearded Sufi pir astonished Webster by asking him to donate a radio station to the AIG. Webster countered by asking Mojaddedi to establish a more efficient accounting system for the CIA funds disappearing inside the AIG's maw. Mojaddedi, who was known to pocket his share of the leaky AIG budget, chose not to respond to the request.

Many observers deduced that Mojaddedi had won the AIG presidency because his party was the weakest. Afghans resist surrendering their autonomy to strong leaders. While it is true that he had the smallest number of commanders and he was the least threatening of the AIG leaders, other factors also pushed his vote count higher. At sixty-four, Mojaddedi was older than all but one of the other party leaders, Khalis. Afghans respect age. Furthermore, as the spiritual leader of the Naqshbandi Sufi Order, Mojaddedi was an important religious figure. He was also an al-Azhar University graduate. That made him both a learned alim entitled to issue religious fatwas and a living Sufi saint with a network of *murids* (religious followers).

Mojaddedi was one of the earliest high-ranking Afghan clerics to issue a fatwa declaring holy war against the PDPA regime. After distributing his fatwa in Peshawar in January 1979, he moved to Miram Shah, North Waziristan, to encourage cross-border attacks against PDPA installations inside Afghanistan. During our conversation, I could see that Hafizullah Amin's retaliation in Kabul—the execution of the revered hazrat of the Naqshbandi Order, Ibrahim Mojaddedi, and Ismael Mojaddedi, his son and heir apparent, and more than forty other males in the Mojaddedi family—still weighed on his mind.[38] He occasionally asked me to ascertain the whereabouts of any possible survivors of the massacre.

Mojaddedi's grief at the PDPA's destruction of his clan was sincere. At the same time, he benefited from the tragedy. He was the nephew of Ibrahim Mojaddedi and the grandson of Ibrahim's father and predecessor. Although not in the direct line of succession before the massacre, the carnage made him the next hazrat, the most senior Mojaddedi in the long line of Naqshbandi pirs going back to the Prophet himself.

Several factors limited Mojaddedi's political influence. Mojaddedi's proneness to emotional outbursts lowered his credibility among Afghans, who value self-control in social relations. In public remarks he periodically lashed out at the ISI for interfering in Afghan politics, at Hekmatyar for killing Afghan rivals, and at Washington for abandoning the Mujahidin. Pakistan's generals and the ISI distrusted his pro–Zahir Shah politics. Like Gailani, Mojaddedi was a Sayyid, the descendant of Arab Sufis, not a Pashtun. His small party budget motivated him to sell a large portion of the weapons he received, thus magnifying his party's image of corruption. The ISI made Sayyaf's radical deputy, Ahmed Shah Ahmadzai, and Rabbani's extremist minister of information, Najibullah Lafraie, members of Mojaddedi's delegation when he traveled abroad as AIG president. The two English-speaking Islamists monitored Mojaddedi's behavior in high-level negotiations. During the September 27, 1989, meeting with President Bush in the White House, they intervened to recast Mojaddedi's comments to the president.

Saudi funds did not flow to Mojaddedi. Saudi clergy and their Afghan allies scorned the Sufi branch of Islam. Saudi princes and religious clerics resented Mojaddedi's trips to Tehran to negotiate integration of the eight Shia Wahdat parties into the AIG. The Iranian ayatollahs, too, frowned on Mojaddedi's Sufi lineage and his pro-Western, democratic leanings. They welcomed and honored him when he visited Tehran but gave him negligible material support.

THE RELUCTANT PIR

Sayyid Ahmad Gailani was the most westernized of the Peshawar seven. Mojaddedi emitted exuberance; Rabbani cunning; Hekmatyar, Sayyaf, Khalis, and Nabi Pashtun muscle. Gailani projected geniality. He exhibited a lively sense of humor at our first meeting. When I suggested that he and the other AIG leaders sweep their differences under the rug, Gailani responded that this would require an extraordinarily large rug.

Gailani also displayed insecurity during our meetings. The ISI grouped him with Mojaddedi as a committed supporter of the Durrani-led, precommunist Afghan establishment. After the Soviet pullout, the Pakistani military intelligence agency had drastically cut back his budget to facilitate ascendancy of the three Ghilzai Pashtun Islamists in the AIG. Gailani's last-place showing at the ISI's Rawalpindi Shura increased his anxieties about the ISI's intention to marginalize him and his party after the Soviets withdrew. In our first conversation, Gailani stated his hope that the United States would reward his pro-Western orientation. He repeatedly pressed me for resources to stave off disintegration of his party.

Gailani required more resources than the other AIG leaders in order to maintain the opulent, secular lifestyle to which he was accustomed. During his childhood, he had been second in line to become the next pir in the hereditary Qadiriya line going back to the great twelfth-century "Saint of Saints" Abd al-Qadir, the Sufi pir of Baghdad. His brother's descent into alcoholism and subsequent death led to Gailani's inheritance of the Qadiriya mantle when his father died. Religious instructors tutored Gailani at home during his early years. He later briefly studied religion at the government's Abu Hanifa madrassas in Paghman and attended some classes with Rabbani at Kabul University's College of Theology. But the new educational opportunities offered to Afghan youth during the 1960s and 1970s and the Western ideologies blowing into Afghanistan reduced his desire to attend to his spiritual duties. He chose a mainly secular, westernized direction in life. By early adulthood, Gailani was happily assimilated in the diplomatic-business-political circle of Kabuli nightlife. His marriage to one of King Habibullah's granddaughters further cemented his elite connections. During the mid-1970s, his home in Kabul became known for the lively, hard-drinking parties he hosted attended by foreigners and westernized Afghans. The royal family's control over licensing of imported luxury cars allowed Gailani to establish his Peugeot dealership, the largest automobile firm in the capital.

The brutal PDPA massacre of the Mojaddedi clan in January 1979 frightened Gailani. Leaving everything behind, he and his family members had fled to Pakistan. Gailani commanders during the Soviet-Afghan war outnumbered those of Mojaddedi, Khalis, or Sayyaf. Typical of the other Afghan parties, the top echelon of his party was filled with family members. Gailani appointed his eldest son, Hamed, an able, diminutive politician, as his deputy. Muhammad, a second son, and Gailani's twenty-five-year-old daughter Fatima were close advisers.[39]

The party's second tier was made up of former middle- and senior-grade officers in the precommunist Afghan Army, high-ranking Afghan civilian bureaucrats and royalty from that period, and Afghan intellectuals. General Rahmatullah Safi, who received commando training in the United States, Britain, and the USSR before the communist coup, was a close military adviser. Rahim Wardak, a former colonel in the Afghan Army, headed Gailani's military committee. Gailani's smartly dressed English-speaking commanders, dubbed the "Gucci Muj" by reporters, shared his pro-Western sentiments. They arranged trips into Afghanistan for Western politicians, including Congressman Charlie Wilson, and foreign journalists.

Gailani maintained residences in Kabul and Europe before the Soviet invasion. The ISI financed his homes in Islamabad and Peshawar after he arrived in Pakistan: The Saudis furnished him with a luxurious flat in London near the Marble Arch overlooking Hyde Park. It accommodated his periodic sojourns in Europe.

Gailani's position of AIG Supreme Court chief justice gave him the responsibility to organize the follow-on AIG shura to elect a new leadership. He delivered speeches and produced a series of election blueprints that he gave to me under his party's formal letterhead. In practice, however, he honored the preference of the ISI and the other AIG leaders to avoid the promised broad-based shura to choose a more representative Mujahidin leadership to challenge Najib.

Gailani's personal differences with Mojaddedi, driven by jealousy and personal ambition on both sides, extinguished any potential for joint action by the two. Nabi would have been a willing ally in a triangular alliance of the three moderate parties. Their solidarity could have weakened the influence that the four AIG Islamists enjoyed. But neither Gailani nor Mojaddedi were willing to imperil their limited popular support by aligning with the other. Each was addicted to hoarding power and unwilling to share it.

Starved of ISI resources after the Soviet withdrawal, Gailani needed to follow ISI guidance to remain a player in Mujahidin politics in Pakistan. His ISI case officers skillfully exploited his insecurity and penchant for an affluent living style. They correctly assessed that the nervous pir would be more pliable than the mercurial Mojaddedi in conducting ISI-controlled negotiations with the Soviets and the PDPA regime. From the Soviet withdrawal up to Najib's collapse in April 1992, Gailani held a series of "secret" meetings with Soviet and PDPA diplomats in European capitals, including one with Najib in Geneva in November 1990.

Gailani's Saudi-financed apartment in London was the main base for his regular trysts with Soviet officials. Those meetings, like others with PDPA leaders, including Najib, were dramatically covered by the Pakistan and Mujahidin media. Soviet policymakers must have viewed their not-so-classified dialogue with Gailani as helpful in exacerbating divisions within the resistance. The ISI probably hoped that Gailani's meetings would sow suspicion between Najib and his hard-line Khalqi opponents in Kabul.

Neither the Soviets nor the ISI took Gailani's private negotiations seriously. Nor did I. My evenings with Gailani in his homes in Peshawar and Islamabad usually took place over dinner, featuring delicious Afghan pilaf and mutton topped with raisins and nuts. Gailani would begin by staging emotional paroxysms about the ISI's reduction in weapons and money to his party. Having no direct authority over ISI and CIA arms distribution, I could only await the end of his protests. During these conversations, Gailani would update me on his (not so) confidential meetings with Soviet diplomats and PDPA leaders in Europe. In response to his briefings, I ritualistically described the damage his unilateral attempts to negotiate a deal with the Soviets and Najib caused for Mujahidin solidarity. Both of us, of course, were aware that his outreach to the avowed enemies of the Mujahidin in Kabul was being separately paralleled by all of the other six Peshawar party leaders to their own contacts inside Najib's regime.

A GENTLE RASPUTIN

Mawlawi Nabi was the last AIG leader I called on during my July 1989 visit to Peshawar. In some ways Nabi looked like Rasputin, the Russian monk who perished serving the ill-fated Romanovs. The Ghilzai alim wore a dark, drooping cloak over his wide shoulders. His large beard was jet black, and his eyes looked tired and somber. The former member of parliament from Logar periodically stuffed pinches of snuff into his large nose as we talked.

In conversation with Nabi, I quickly concluded that he was not a Rasputin, but rather a gentle giant, polite and caring. He was a traditional Sufi cleric who supported modern democratic institutions that the Koran did not mention as well as education for both girls and boys. Nabi's proudest moment was punching out Babrak Karmal on the floor of parliament in 1965. His next proudest moment was denying Hekmatyar the AIG Defense Ministry after the Rawalpindi Shura voting ended.

Nabi was a widely respected, moderate, pro-royalist cleric in precommunist Afghanistan and a member of the large Ahmadzai tribe in eastern Afghanistan. He had been a popular teacher at two large madrassas, one in Logar and the other in Ghazni. In the early 1980s, Nabi's Harakat commanders outnumbered those from other parties. The majority were conservative rural mullahs who were the first to take up arms against the communist regime. Many had studied under Nabi.

The sharp upswing in CIA covert funds and Saudi cash into the coffers of the four radical Islamist parties from 1985 onward thinned out Harakat ranks. Numerous field commanders left Nabi for the better-financed extremist parties. The defections were not driven by religious ideology. The commanders inside Afghanistan sought recurring resources to fight the Soviet Army and compete with local Afghan rivals. Many commanders returned home from visits to Peshawar with multiple party cards. After the Soviet pullout, an ever-increasing number of commanders accepted Najib's bounty, even if this entailed periodic trips to Kabul to be photographed at communist party meetings.

By the time we first met in July, Nabi's natural passivity and lack of leadership skills had cut him off from most of his remaining commanders. He gave responsibility for managing day-to-day party affairs to his two corrupt sons. Major Harakat commanders, such as Mullah Akunzada in Helmand, paid respect to their party leader in Peshawar. Meanwhile, they chartered their own course—in Akunzada's case, that course was opium production. Nabi's AIG Defense Ministry in Peshawar was inactive: Around a hundred village mullahs from his party sat idly in empty offices drawing CIA-provided salaries. The ISI planned and directed military operations against Najib's government directly from its Islamabad headquarters and the ISI branch offices in Peshawar and Quetta.

During my three years as special envoy, I could count on Nabi's formal backing for each step the United States took to generate a peaceful settlement of the Afghan war. In practice, this support meant almost nothing. The ISI maintained ultimate control over him. That was fine with the unambitious Logar cleric. He was content to take his monthly ISI payment, follow ISI guidance, and undertake periodic Saudi-funded pilgrimages to the holy cities of Mecca and Medina.

ψ

Tragically, the seven party leaders whom Hamid Gul had designated to lead the AIG—the men who were supposed to help bring peace, stability, and self-determination to Afghanistan—filled much of their time maneuvering against each other. Their personal lust for power overshadowed all other objectives, such as Afghan unity and a political resolution of the Afghan war. Each relied on the ISI as their lifeline for political survival. This vulnerability heightened their venomous rivalry. When sent abroad to represent the Mujahidin, they passed their time squabbling over hotel room assignments, airplane seating, and other minutiae.[40] The ISI, of course, was fully aware of their many foibles and the AIG's utter inability to function. The hopelessly fragmented Peshawar seven occupied the Mujahidin political vacuum in Pakistan and kept the resistance divided. The AIG was, in fact, a façade for the ISI's covert strategy to put Hekmatyar in Kabul through military force. The fictional Mujahidin government would then be discarded like an old mop.

CHAPTER 13

Pakistan Pivots

Loud knocking at the front door interrupted nighttime slumber at American consul Mike Malinowski's residence in Peshawar, Pakistan, near the Afghan-Pakistan border. It was 2:00 a.m., well past curfew, on July 14, 1989. Mike and I stumbled down the stairs and opened the door. Ahmed Shah Masood's two brothers, Ahmed Zia Masood and Yahya Masood, with American reporter Richard Mackenzie, burst into the living room. Ahmed Zia shouted that a massacre had taken place in the Fakhar Valley in Takhar Province. Hekmatyar commander Sayed Jamal had executed thirty Masood Mujahidin several days previously, on July 9–10.

The slain Mujahidin had been returning from a six-day Council of the North conference convened by Masood at his headquarters at the center of the valley during the first week of July. Before the meeting, representatives of the council had visited Jamal specifically to discuss safe passage for the council's commanders and their men as they traveled through a mountain pass at the end of a valley he controlled. In front of the emissaries Jamal had sworn on the Koran that he would not harm Masood's Mujahidin transiting his area.

Jamal did not keep his commitment.

Hours after Ahmed Zia's alert, U.S. national security officials in Washington were poring over the shocking description of the carnage reported in a confidential cable, "Major Mujahidin Internecine Massacre," from the Peshawar consulate:

> *After the Council's coordinating meeting ended on or about July 9, a group of Jamiat Mujahedin bound for their bases in Takhar and*

Baghlan Provinces moved down the valley for home. The first group
included a jeep carrying noted Jamiat Takhar Province commander
Mullah Abdul Wadud and four of his men. All five were captured
and executed by Sayed Jamal. The next day Sayed Jamal captured
another twenty-five homeward-bound Jamiat Mujahedin. Sayed
Jamal held these men for a day and then executed them all.

Ahmed Zia placed the blame for the killing squarely on Hezb-e-
Islami leader Gulbuddin Hekmatyar. He said that Sayed Jamal long
had been in conflict with Jamiat forces in Takhar Province. He said
that the fact that Sayed Jamal took a full day to kill the second group
of Mujahedin that he captured indicated that the killings were done
on orders from Hezb-Hekmatyar headquarters in Peshawar.[1]

The incestuous ISI-Hezb relationship raised suspicions that the insti-
gators of the Takhar massacre could be found at the ISI as well as at Hezb
headquarters in Pakistan.

The Soviet withdrawal from Afghanistan stretched out over a nearly ten-
month period ending February 15, 1989. Moscow's phased departure coincided with a fundamental shift in Pakistan's Afghan policy from a defensive
to an offensive strategy. Instead of resisting Moscow's attempt to extend the
Soviet sphere of influence into Afghanistan, Pakistan now sought to expand
its own sphere of influence northward over the Hindu Kush to the Amu
Darya. Although cloaked in the veil of a covert proxy war and messianic Islamic ideology, the strategy amounted to an invasion of one sovereign country by a larger one.

With its switch to a forward policy in Afghanistan on the heels of the Soviet withdrawal, Pakistan inaugurated its own long, agonizing, costly, and ultimately unsuccessful journey into the Afghan quagmire. Zulfikar Ali Bhutto's
first Pakistan proxy war in Afghanistan using the exiled Young Muslims as
cannon fodder began and ended in 1975. Islamabad's second proxy war lasted
from 1978 to 1988. The third started in the summer of 1988. It continued
with rising intensity until al-Qaeda-piloted airplanes smashed into the Twin
Towers and the Pentagon on 9/11. By that time, thirteen years later, hundreds
of Pakistani regular army and ISI officers, thousands of Pakistani troops, tens
of thousands of Pakistani religious fighters, and Osama bin Laden's two al-
Qaeda brigades were fighting in Afghanistan with no end in sight.

American diplomats and intelligence officers in Pakistan and Washington did not report, much less analyze, Pakistan's strategic pivot into Afghanistan or its scheme to install the anti-American Hekmatyar in Kabul. The resulting information vacuum deprived American policymakers of facts and assessments vital to U.S. interests in the region. The best opportunity to resist the pivot and end the wars of Afghanistan arose in late 1988 and 1989 as the Pakistani Army was shifting to an offensive posture. The United States not only missed that opportunity, it actually supported the shift by continuing to transfer hundreds of millions of dollars of covert military and economic aid to Pakistan. The covert funds were delivered directly to the ISI, whose pro-extremist military strategy inside Afghanistan violated the American and Pakistani governments' formal commitment to a negotiated end to the Afghan war.

ψ

ISI strategists in 1988 and early 1989 did not consider Najib's Soviet-backed regime to be the main obstacle to Pakistan's plans to dominate Afghanistan after the Soviets withdrew. Moderate-nationalist Pashtun Durrani commanders near Kandahar, Ismael Khan in western Afghanistan, and Ahmed Shah Masood in northern Afghanistan were greater obstacles to realizing Zia's vision for Afghanistan than Najib's 100,000-man military force and 100,000-man paid militia.

Masood and Khan were the most powerful commanders inside Afghanistan. Both prickly Afghan nationalists with a long record of resisting Pakistani and Iranian dictation, they did not operate from Pakistani territory. Nor had they traveled to Pakistan during the anti-Soviet war. Nominally they were members of Burhanuddin Rabbani's Jamiat party. In reality they were autonomous power centers in Afghanistan. They were suspicious of Rabbani and his top adviser, Nurullah Emad.

Masood's Supervisory Council of the North and Ismael Khan's four-province Houza-i Junogharb (Emirate of the Southwest) were located far from ISI control levers. Masood was the more dangerous of the two. The entrance to his fortified Panshir redoubt lay only 60 miles north of Kabul. His 10,000-man Council of the North force was a hammer poised to fall on the capital.

The ISI moved against Ismael Khan first. The short, white-bearded Tajik had fought the Soviets to a standstill in western Afghanistan during the Soviet occupation. Directly or indirectly, about 7,000 fighters from all ethnic groups

were under his umbrella when Soviet convoys rumbled north toward the Soviet border in August 1988. Khan had secretly negotiated the peaceful withdrawal of the 22,000 Soviet troops in western Afghanistan through direct and
indirect communications with Soviet generals. The huge movement of Soviet
troops took place—in reverse—four months shy of the ninth anniversary of
Moscow's invasion of Afghanistan. Soviet journalists embedded with the last
10-mile-long line of trucks, APCs, tanks, and jeeps reported their unimpeded
movement past Mujahidin groups gazing down from nearby hills. There were
no casualties.

At the time, Khan was simultaneously negotiating surrender terms with the
commander of Najib's 17th Division in Herat. He was also in contact with
regime tribal militia on the western outskirts of the city. A pro-Khan underground city council was poised to administer Herat after it went over to Khan.[2]

The ISI methodically began to emasculate Ismael Khan's power base in
late 1988, after it was clear the Soviet Army was really leaving Afghanistan. It
terminated Khan's $500,000 annual payment[3] and drastically curtailed its
shipments of weapons and ammunition to him. In February 1989, Khan sent
his deputy, Allaudin Khan, to Pakistan to plea for arms. Allaudin later told
me in Peshawar that, in his presence, ISI chief Hamid Gul had personally examined Ismael Khan's letter and operational plan to capture Herat. Gul ordered his deputy, the chief of the ISI's Peshawar office Brigadier Mohammad
Afzal Janjua, to meet Ismael Khan's request for assistance. But the ISI had
subsequently forwarded only one package of 200,000 rounds of AK-47 ammunition, a tiny amount, Allaudin Khan complained. It was inadequate to
defend Ismael Khan's bases, much less capture Herat. In fact, Gul did not
want Ismael Khan to capture Herat. Pakistan's pivot into Afghanistan demanded dismantling, not strengthening, his military infrastructure.

Ismael Khan's position was weakening, but more setbacks lay ahead. He
asked Iran for arms to capture Herat, but negotiations broke down when he
rejected Iranian conditions that he felt violated Afghan sovereignty. Najib's
division commander in Herat severed contacts with Khan after the Mujahidin
pullback from Jalalabad in May 1989. The ISI transferred money and fresh
arms to a Hekmatyar commander in Herat Province, Amanullah Khan, with
instructions to attack Ismael Khan's Mujahidin. Rabbani collaborated with
Gul to undercut Ismael Khan. His extremist deputy, Nurullah Emad, a Herati,

provided funds to the pro-regime Herati militia guarding Herat's western approaches to remain loyal to Najib and oppose Khan. One of Khan's commanders later complained to me that Khan "fell for the promises of Rabbani even though he knew Rabbani was lying and working with ISI."[4]

Facing opposition from Pakistan and Iran as well as from Hekmatyar and Rabbani, Ismael Khan abandoned his plans to capture Herat. Through 1989 and 1990, his dwindling resources cost him the loyalty of more and more commanders. Many succumbed to the pressures and accepted patronage from Najib and local Hekmatyar commanders.

Ismael Khan's personal failings facilitated the ISI's reduction of his once formidable Mujahidin front. He was a fighter, not a politician, and lacked Masood's political skills and charisma. During the anti-Soviet war, he encouraged a personality cult around himself and was depicted as the "emir" of the southwestern "emirate." His pretensions, however, alienated commanders, tribal leaders, and sophisticated Herati urban dwellers. By 1991, Allaudin was desperately appealing to me for food to sustain Ismael Khan's diminished position in western Afghanistan.

ψ

The ISI had completed the piecemeal demolition of Ismael Khan's once robust military force by the time I arrived in Pakistan in late June 1989. Two weeks later, Sayed Jamal massacred one-third of Masood's top commanders at the mouth of the Fakhar Valley in Takhar Province. It was the deadliest manifestation yet of the hostility of the ISI—and Hekmatyar—toward Masood's northern front, and far more effective than anything Hekmatyar had attempted during the Soviet occupation. Masood had immediately alerted his commanders in the northern provinces when word reached him about the massacre at his headquarters in the middle of the Fakhar Valley. He worried that Sayed Jamal's ambush presaged a general Hekmatyar offensive against him throughout the north. From his Fakhar headquarters, he used his British-supplied encrypted Jaguar radios to order his top commanders to adopt a defensive stance. He also activated a sophisticated British-donated "scanner" to monitor radio transmissions from Hekmatyar's command post in Peshawar to Jamal. The scanner intercepted a Jamal conversation. As Masood listened in horror, Jamal was told to execute the second group of prisoners.

Rabbani may not have been aware of the well-prepared plot to assassinate many of Masood's most able commanders. Whether he was or not, he did not forewarn Masood.

The slow demolition of Ismael Khan's power base in western Afghanistan went unnoticed by the media in Pakistan and internationally. The Fakhar massacre did not. The Pakistani press portrayed the massacre as just another bloody example of Mujahidin disunity. The ISI pressed this line. In contrast, the massacre shocked supporters of the Mujahidin in the West. Masood's legions of enthusiasts in the United States and Europe generated a firestorm of criticism against Hekmatyar, who was widely identified by the Western media and diplomatic circles as the culprit behind the murders. Don Ritter, the Republican congressman from Pennsylvania who headed the congressional task force on Afghanistan at the time, joined British journalist Sandy Gall in calling for an investigation. AIG President Mojaddedi charged Hekmatyar with responsibility for the attack and promised an AIG inquiry. The American embassy in Islamabad and I urged the Pakistani Foreign Ministry, ISI Director Kallue, and President Mojaddedi to launch it quickly and make it credible. Rapid action was imperative if the AIG was to be taken seriously by the international community.

Weeks, then months, passed while the AIG extremists and moderates argued over the composition of an investigating committee. The Pakistani Ministry of Foreign Affairs attempted unsuccessfully to galvanize the AIG to action. But the Afghan account was in the ISI's domain, and the ISI was not interested in discovering who was responsible for the killing of Masood's commanders. AIG party leaders could do little without ISI direction. Neither Western diplomats nor Western intelligence eyes and ears were able to identify the ISI's complicity in the massacre.

Masood decided to act on his own. Sayed Jamal's ambush left him with only one possible response: *badal*, or retribution. In Afghanistan's Hobbesian state of chaos, brute force was respected, and survival depended on an image of strength. Millions of Afghans in regime- and Mujahidin-controlled areas, and in refugee camps in Pakistan and Iran, were closely watching for his response to the massacre.

The Fakhar Valley's entrance was firmly under the control of Jamal's Mujahidin. But Masood's advantage was greater, as his forces outnumbered Jamal's. Hekmatyar's base was in Pakistan, not Afghanistan. The loyalty of

Hekmatyar's commanders in the region was not personal; Hekmatyar's party was simply the most lucrative source of recurring resources. Declaring war on Masood after the massacre would deliver no payback to them except painful casualties among their Mujahidin. The most powerful commander in northern Afghanistan had been provoked. They decided that their best approach to Masood's vendetta against Hekmatyar and Jamal was Sufi aloofness. They would not waste their own Mujahidin in a futile attempt to rescue Jamal.

In his usual meticulous way, Masood undertook political and military preparations to dispose of Jamal. He sent delegations to other regional commanders affiliated with Hekmatyar's Hezb to assure them that his enmity was directed only against Jamal. He organized a committee of religious clerics to meet at his headquarters to examine the Fakhar massacre. The group issued a fatwa declaring Jamal's killing of other Mujahidin anti-Islamic. The religious decree called for Jamal's arrest and punishment. Masood then brought his most effective commander, Panshiri Pena Khan, from the Shomali Plain to lead the assault on Jamal's mountain bastion above the Fakhar gorge overlooking the entrance to the valley. Armored with the religious legitimacy the fatwa gave him and possessing overwhelming force, Pena quickly routed Jamal's demoralized fighters. Jamal himself conducted a brief defense in a rocky canyon nestled in the upper reaches of the Fakhar gorge before surrendering on August 18.

Sayed Jamal was taken to Masood's Fakhar headquarters immediately after his capture. According to Masood's political adviser, Daoud Mir, who was present, the northern commander was engrossed in a meeting with some of his commanders when Jamal was brought before him. Mir described the bearded Hezb commander as thin, bony-faced, and covered with filth from turban to sandals.[5] His baggy pants were sprinkled with blood from a leg wound. Masood slowly rose from a table ringed by several of his commanders when Jamal, unbound, was pushed to the floor 10 feet in front of where he stood. Mir recalled that Masood's entire face narrowed. His eyes receded and darkened with hatred as he stared in silence at the cowering, "animal-like"[6] figure beneath him. In disgust, Masood momentarily turned away from the man who had killed thirty of his Mujahidin. Suddenly turning back toward Jamal, he ordered the two guards standing behind the prisoner to give him fresh clothes and have a doctor dress his wound.

Jamal chose that moment to justify his actions. In a high-pitched voice, he accused Masood of never showing kindness to him, never training his Mujahidin, and giving him no choice but to associate with Hekmatyar. Masood angrily ordered Jamal taken away. Turning back to his meeting, he looked upward and exclaimed, "My God, how can our country cope with such men."[7]

Hekmatyar's radio stations in Pakistan broadcast that it was Najib's communist forces that had seized Jamal and handed him over to Masood. Masood's media countered: "Contrary to the claims of the Hezb, the operation which led to the arrest of Jamal had few casualties among the Mujahidin on both sides and the civilian population suffered no casualties."[8]

In an interview given to Western journalists in Taloqan, the capital of Takhar Province, that same day, Masood blamed Hekmatyar for the massacre of his Mujahidin: "Hezb has a history of these types of actions. Engineer Hekmatyar cannot tolerate his rivals. Hezb does not have any program for the defeat of the Kabul regime. He [Hekmatyar] opposes those people who do have a program, and creates problems for them. Hezb was fully aware of the purpose of our meeting in Fakhar and that it would end the present stalemate on the battlefield. This was the reason for setting the ambush."[9]

Abdullah Anas, the Algerian son-in-law of Abdullah Azzam, head of the Muslim Brotherhood–managed Services Bureau in Peshawar, knew and admired Masood.[10] He believed a Masood-Hekmatyar reconciliation would accelerate the triumph of the Afghan jihad. Anas trekked to Masood's base in Fakhar to request mercy for Jamal. He urged Masood to close ranks with Hekmatyar to fight the common foe—the communist regime in Kabul.

Masood warmly welcomed and feted Anas, but he disregarded his appeal to pardon Jamal. He instead reconvened the group of Afghan clerics to decide the prisoner's fate. The meeting produced a second written fatwa condemning Jamal to death. While AIG extremists and moderates in Peshawar continued to haggle over the composition of an AIG investigating commission, Jamal, his brother, and two of his accomplices in the Fakhar massacre were executed at a public hanging in Taloqan on December 24, 1989.

It was easier for ISI strategists to destroy Ismael Khan's loose Mujahidin network in the West than to undo Masood's virtual ministate in the north. Khan gave little attention to political and economic matters. Masood's strength in northern Afghanistan ultimately rested on the Supervisory Council's well-laid political and economic foundation and popular support. A majority of the north's Tajik population was loyal to him. In the Panshir Valley, the loyalty was fierce. Pashtun communities in the north respected Masood for his military achievements. Some were active members of Masood's Council of the North.

Masood's intelligence capabilities exceeded those of Ismael Khan—and of all other Afghan commanders active at that time. His network of spies had been a vital part of his military successes against the Soviets and would continue to aid him against the ISI, Hekmatyar, and the Taliban in the future. Masood's Jaguar radios, provided by British intelligence, gave him secure, instantaneous communications with his key commanders and political advisers.[11] His sophisticated scanners intercepted messages transmitted by the regime and by Hekmatyar. Masood personally transmitted coded messages to spies and informants inside Najib's regime as well as in Pakistan. His young cousin Mujibur Rahman and another trusted Panshiri, working in a room near his office, recorded conversations from intercepts and provided protection for the code books. They wrote down every message Masood sent and received and guarded the code room around the clock.

The ISI's and Hekmatyar's escalating military pressures on Masood compelled him to call off his planned assaults on several regime-held northern cities, approved at the early July Shura Nazar conference attended by over one hundred commanders. Masood went on the defensive, protecting the territory he held against threats from the regime and the ISI. He prepared his Mujahidin forces for the inevitable showdown with Hekmatyar and his Pakistani backers.

ψ

While the ISI's new forward policy marginalized Ismael Khan in the west, Masood absorbed the Fakhar massacre damage and repelled Hekmatyar's follow-on attacks. In the east, chaos reigned. The near universal ideological solidarity within the resistance to drive the Soviet invader out of Afghanistan during the Soviet-Afghan war had buckled after the Soviet withdrawal. Pakistan's narrowing of its patronage stream to Hekmatyar and its favored Ghilzai extremists alienated the great majority of tribal leaders and commanders in eastern Afghanistan who were left out.

The ISI still enjoyed a plentiful flow of American- and Saudi-supplied weapons and cash to build up Hekmatyar's military power. But by choosing sides among Afghan rivals, it further undermined the ideological singleness of purpose existing during the anti-Soviet jihad and ruled out the prospects for the necessary political foundation needed to pursue its strategy inside Afghanistan. Its promotion of Hekmatyar generated widespread opposition and precipitated anarchy in the countryside. Hundreds of small tribal factions turned their full attention to resource acquisition and factional infighting. Commanders in Nangarhar fought each other for control of poppy fields and trafficking routes into Pakistan.[12] Acute shortages of foodstuffs in war-ravaged eastern Afghanistan exacerbated growing chaos.

For eight months after the Soviet Army evacuated eastern Afghanistan in late 1988, a steady stream of U.S. Agency for International Development (USAID) and United Nations World Food Program (WFP) humanitarian-aid convoys crossed into the eastern provinces. They drove to isolated rural areas bordering Pakistan to deliver wheat, medicine, and agricultural implements to community jirga and shura councils for distribution to poverty-stricken villages. The system worked well until May 1989, when one of Hekmatyar's commanders in Paktiya confiscated a convoy carrying 88 metric tons of wheat. A rash of incidents involving food convoys followed in Konar—aside from Takhar, the only province the regime had abandoned to the Mujahidin after the Soviet pullout. At the end of May, Jamil ur-Rahman, a Saudi-financed Afghan Wahhabi cleric in Konar, hijacked a thirteen-truck USAID food convoy.

Najib skillfully exploited the unpopularity of Hekmatyar and the AIG in the eastern provinces to diminish opposition to his regime. He announced he had asked the Soviets to leave and touted his Islamic credentials in radio broadcasts from Kabul. With no credible Afghan political center of gravity in either Kabul or Peshawar and the Soviet invader gone, thousands of Mujahidin returned home to their villages to support their families. "Commanders are losing their Mujahidin day by day," Hamid Karzai told an American journalist. "They're moving on to other things, slipping into private life. The enthusiasm isn't there anymore."[13] Veteran Afghan commander Mullah Malang told me in Quetta on July 10, 1989, that "the spirit of jihad is dying out": "Before the Mujahidin were spiritually motivated; now they are seeking material goods."[14]

In Konar, Jamil ur-Rahman and Hekmatyar refused to recognize a new Konar governor appointed by the AIG. They barred his entry into the province. After backing their own governor for a brief period, they fought each other for control of the province. "Liberated" Konar tumbled into chaos.

A June 5, 1990, statement issued by Hekmatyar's media outlets called on all Mujahidin groups to put a halt to Afghan assistance programs financed by the United States, other Western nations, and the United Nations. The incendiary announcement, carried widely by the Pakistani and Western press, created consternation in Western diplomatic circles and fear among Western and Afghan nongovernmental organizations that administered the programs. USAID required deliveries of cross-border assistance to be monitored by USAID-approved Afghans. When that effort faltered, USAID suspended food shipments into eastern and southern Afghanistan. Najib's regime turned the resulting food shortages into a political weapon. His garrisons at isolated locations spread along the Pakistani border gave food packages to local communities. The communities took the free food and cooperated with rather than attacking the regime enclaves.

The Soviet departure, Najib's astute manipulation of tribal politics, and the ISI's support for the AIG extremists produced a paralyzing stalemate in southern Afghanistan. The Soviet withdrawal had raised hopes among the southern Durrani tribal elite that the precommunist Afghan traditional tribal order would be revived. The vehicle would be a loya jirga presided over by Zahir Shah. It would choose an Afghan government to replace Najib's regime. But a loya jirga and its certain selection of a moderate-nationalist Afghan government were not objectives of Pakistan's new forward policy in Afghanistan.

The optimist camps in Washington and Islamabad portrayed Kandahar as about to fall to the resistance. This made sense. Kandahar's main supply lines stretched 500 miles through Mujahidin-infested areas to Kabul. The countryside around Kandahar swarmed with Mujahidin fighters from all tribes and ethnic groups. Najib's regime could only resupply its Kandahar garrison by air.

The two most powerful Mujahidin commanders in Kandahar Province were anticommunist, pro–Zahir Shah Durranis. Barakzai Durrani Haji Latif, known locally and in the foreign press as the "Lion of Kandahar," was eighty years old when the Soviet military pulled out of southern Afghanistan. Commander Mullah Naqib,[15] an Alokazai Durrani, was a traditional Afghan mullah and pro–Zahir Shah Afghan nationalist. He initially joined Mojaddedi's royalist Afghanistan National Liberation Front (ANLF) but later associated himself with Rabbani's better-endowed Jamiat. Naqib was a hardened fighter who was averse to taking prisoners. He controlled the heavily populated, fertile, strategically located Argandab district north of Kandahar on the road to Herat.

Durrani tribal elders in Kandahar, in Quetta, and in the refugee camps near Quetta defiantly rejected the Ghilzai-centered AIG when it was created by the ISI at the Rawalpindi Shura. They launched another attempt to organize a loya jirga after the Soviet withdrawal—this one inside Afghanistan. Mawlawi Mohammad Sabir, a Kandahari religious teacher in his mid-eighties, performed the same role the legendary Mawlawi had played at the historic 1847 loya jirga that selected Ahmad Shah Durrani as Afghan king.[16] Sabir and Mawlawi Jinabi, another respected religious figure—who was from Naqib's Argandab district and was over one hundred years old—toured the province calling for Mujahidin unity, a negotiated takeover of Kandahar, and the rejection of both Najib's regime in Kabul and the AIG in Peshawar. A large jirga in the Panjwai district outside of Kandahar appealed for Zahir Shah to return to Afghanistan and preside over a national loya jirga to choose a new Afghan leadership.

The ISI's first reaction to the jirga movement came in early June 1989. It flew Hekmatyar and a contingent of his eastern Ghilzai Mujahidin to Quetta, Pakistan, in Pakistani aircraft. Hekmatyar toured refugee camps near Quetta. He clamored for a military offensive against regime-held Kandahar. His appeals to rekindle holy war drew derision and flying stones from angry refugees. Hekmatyar encountered more hostility when he traveled by vehicle across the border into Kandahar Province, the Durrani heartland. Haji Latif ambushed his convoy, lacing it with small arms and rocket fire. Hekmatyar's SUV came under attack, and he hurriedly returned to Quetta, vowing revenge.

The Najib regime, the ISI, and the AIG extremists had a shared interest in blocking the revival of the traditional Durrani power structure in Afghanistan. Najib's short-term objective in regime-held Kandahar, as elsewhere in Afghanistan, was to divide the Mujahidin and keep them out of regime-held areas. He played on the many tribal rivalries in Kandahar Province to disrupt the campaign for a loya jirga. Mujahidin tribes fought over the debris at the abandoned Soviet military base at Rabat, 80 miles east of Kandahar. At a site further east near the Kandahar-Zabul border, another horrendous human rights incident occurred. One hundred and fifty regime soldiers, mostly Ghilzai Nurzai, defected to a Durrani Popalzai commander and were shot. The mass execution stoked the flames of ancient Durrani-Ghilzai hatred lying just below the surface in Kandahar Province.

Colonel Faizan, the seven-year chief of the ISI's Quetta office, conspired with anti-Durrani AIG Ghilzai mullahs to destroy the loya jirga campaign. Faizan and his deputy, Major Sultan Imam,* staffed the AIG office in Quetta with representatives of the extremist parties headed by Gulbuddin Hekmatyar, Abdul Rasoul Sayyaf, and Yunus Khalis. Faizan then organized an anti-Durrani Islamist Argestan Shura, named after a district southeast of Kandahar bordering Pakistan. The leaders of the Argestan Shura, all mullahs, would later become Taliban leaders.[17] Faizan told a visiting American that his shura had decisively reversed three hundred years of Durrani rule in Afghanistan.

In the spring of 1989, Argestan Shura Mujahidin began firing ISI-supplied rockets into Kandahar city, killing civilians and destroying property. The bombardments strengthened the regime's hold on Kandahar. A Hekmatyar commander in the Argestan Shura attacked Mullah Naqib's base in Argandab Province. Both sides used artillery and surface-to-surface rockets against each other. Twenty-eight combatants and numerous civilians died in the four-day battle.[18]

On August 8, 1989, Haji Latif was poisoned at his base west of Kandahar. Many Afghans pinned the blame on the ISI and Hekmatyar. The assassination of the Barakzai commander proved catastrophic for the moderate Durrani cause. Latif's oldest son, Gul Agha, seized two Afghans near the scene of the tragedy, declared them KHAD agents, and ordered their immediate execution. Few believed that Gul Agha, who was known locally as an ISI contact and drug trafficker, had caught the real culprits. Whoever the guilty party was, Latif, a bitter opponent of Pakistani interference, was replaced by Gul

---

* Major Sultan Imam, later to be promoted to colonel, was one of the most active ISI operatives in Pakistan's Afghan proxy wars. A Punjabi, his true name was Amir Sultan Tarar. He was assigned to a Special Forces training course at Fort Bragg early in his career. His choice of "Imam" as a nom de guerre, like his long white beard, were probably inspired by a case officer's desire to appeal to the Afghan extremists that ISI favored.

Agha. The burly Gul Agha had grown close to Faizan and his deputy Imam while working as his father's liaison with the ISI Quetta office during the Soviet-Afghan war.

After Latif's death, Najib picked apart what remained of the Durrani loya jirga initiative. Governor Nural Haq Ulumi, a general of royal Mohammadzai Barakzai descent and a graduate of Afghan, U.S., and Russian military training courses, had played an important role in defeating the Mujahidin at Jalalabad. Najib sent him to Kandahar to maintain regime control of the province.

Ulumi did his job well. The new regime governor of Kandahar persuaded Najib to pull Dostum's hated Jouzjani Uzbek militia back to Kabul. He stopped forced conscription into the Afghan Army; encouraged unemployed youth to join his paid militia to defend Kandahar; and released prisoners when requested by moderate Durrani commanders. He did not interfere with the Mujahidin narcotics-trafficking corridors to Pakistan.

Ulumi was related to Peshawar party leader Sayyid Ahmad Gailani's wife, a member of the royal Mohammadzai clan. He cordially received Gailani's son, Hasan, in Kandahar for negotiations, escorting him through the peaceful streets, now filled with former Mujahidin fighters. Foreign correspondents also wandered through Kandahar in July 1989. The reporters filed stories about Mujahidin shopping in city bazaars, congregating with locals in tea shops, and watching colorful Indian films in the city's movie theaters. *Washington Post* correspondent James Rupert quoted one saying, "We don't like the government, and we don't like Najibullah. . . . But we also don't like the people in Peshawar."[19]

Ulumi's astute handling of Gul Agha was one of his more notable political successes in Kandahar. The new Kandahar governor exploited their common Barakzai tribal heritage and Gul Agha's greed, collaborating with him to stage fake "attacks" by Gul Agha on the American-built Kandahar Airport southeast of the city. At the appointed time, for the benefit of ISI agents observing the operation, Gul Agha's Mujahidin harmlessly fired off rockets and light weapons near the airport. Along the airport runway, Ulumi's troops set oil drums on fire and made loud noises. In return, Ulumi allowed Gul Agha to sell ISI-provided American wheat inside Kandahar city in return for keeping the peace. Gul Agha pocketed the profits. He submitted voucher requests to the ISI for more money and additional ammunition to replenish that expended during the farcical airport operations.[20]

꙰

Pakistan's new forward policy in Afghanistan was carefully prepared and well executed. It was also two-faced. Pakistan's generals assured American visitors they were staunch allies committed to a negotiated Afghan political settlement. Instead they sought a military solution. Ironically, the chasm between the ISI and the Pakistani Foreign Ministry on Afghan policy mirrored the rift in Washington between the CIA and the State Department. The CIA indulged the ISI's quest for a military solution, while the State Department pursued the political settlement option endorsed by the Bush administration and offered to Gorbachev and Shevardnadze at U.S.-Soviet summit meetings.

If American intelligence agents in Pakistan ever did discover Pakistan's 1988–1989 policy pivot into Afghanistan, this momentous shift important to U.S. interests never appeared in the hundreds of classified documents on Afghanistan produced annually in Washington and at the American embassy in Islamabad. Willful ignorance, incompetence, and the CIA's focus on tactical rather than strategic "taskings" overseas may have contributed to this failure. The CIA's dependence on ISI reporting on the Afghan war certainly was also part of the problem. With rare exceptions, CIA reports on military and political developments inside Afghanistan came from the ISI, since the CIA lacked human intelligence sources inside Afghanistan.

Two separate U.S. government "stovepipes" emerged after the Soviet withdrawal, each marching to a different drummer on U.S. Afghan policy. The State Department stuck to the formal policy line: helping the Afghans to organize a political settlement, a broad-based loya jirga, or elections without the participation of Najib and other important PDPA leaders. The CIA stayed on automatic pilot from the nine-year Soviet-Afghan war, supporting the ISI's doomed attempt to achieve a Hekmatyar-led military victory in Afghanistan. Ambassador Oakley fluctuated between these two poles while working from the premise that Afghanistan belonged in Pakistan's sphere of influence. Years later, he defended that position, asking an interviewer, "Whose sphere of influence was it supposed to be under—the United States?"[21]

In the longer run, American acceptance of a Pakistani sphere of influence in Afghanistan guaranteed that the Afghan war would continue. Historically, one regional power attempting to bring the Afghan highland into its orbit invariably triggered resistance from other regional powers, leading to endless conflict. After the Soviet exit, only a common agreement among all of Afghanistan's neighbors to respect its neutrality and independence—to, in effect, restore Afghanistan's late-nineteenth- and early-twentieth-century buffer role in Central Asia—could have ended the Afghan war and stabilized Afghanistan and the region.

The 9/11 Commission's investigations extensively documented how the CIA's compartmentalization and institutional resistance to sharing information with other agencies contributed to the 9/11 disaster. After the Soviet withdrawal from Afghanistan, the CIA's insular mentality and its self-imposed wall between what it knew and was doing—and what policymakers needed to know, including about what it was doing—delivered a severe blow to American national security interests at a crucial juncture of the Afghan war.

The wall also blocked my own hopes for a meaningful dialogue with the agency's covert operations wing, the Directorate of Operations, in Washington and Pakistan. During my first visit to the Frontier in July 1989, Mujahidin in Peshawar informed me that the ISI were training Hekmatyar's *Lashkar-i Issar* (Army of Sacrifice), conventional battalions totaling 3,000 men armed with heavy weapons, to attack Kabul. I raised the issue with Islamabad Station Chief "Bill," asking why the CIA was investing so much in building Hekmatyar's combat power while moderate Mujahidin commanders like Masood, Ismael Khan, and the southern Durranis had been cut off. Bill's answer was purposefully vague and unsatisfactory. I worried there was no prospect to dissuade him from moving in lockstep with ISI and its favoritism for Hekmatyar. And he knew that on my return to Washington I would oppose the ISI-CIA buildup of Hekmatyar's military capacity.

U.S. policy called for military pressure on Najib to force the Soviets to accept a political solution. The CIA had refilled ISI warehouses with weapons and ammunitions by September 1989. But the ISI was not distributing this ordnance to field commanders in sufficient quantities countrywide to apply the necessary military pressure to produce a political settlement. Most Mujahidin did not wish to fight for the Pashtun-sponsored AIG. Nor did they support Najib. The CIA persisted in predicting military progress, but there was no progress. Meanwhile, Mujahidin clashes with other Mujahidin were causing far more casualties than those inflicted by Najib's security forces. The relatively minor confrontations between resistance groups during the Soviet occupation escalated into pitched battles after the Soviet departure. From his embassy in Kabul, Soviet Ambassador Vorontsov gleefully reported to the Soviet Politburo that the resistance was "fighting both against the Kabul regime and among itself." "They hate each other more than they hate Najibullah and the Kabul politicians," he wrote.[22]

Bill and his CIA team in Islamabad were best situated to notice and monitor the Pakistani policy shift, as they were the closest to the ISI. The station's officers coordinated with their ISI counterparts on a daily basis. The ISI depended on CIA funds and weapons to execute Pakistan's pivot into Afghanistan. The CIA's Islamabad Station officers knew that the ISI was using American covert funds to place Hekmatyar in Kabul. They must have kept CIA headquarters in Langley informed. Arguably, the ISI's favoritism for Hekmatyar during the Soviet occupation could have been justified as serving the strategic Cold War objective of forcing the Soviet Union out of Afghanistan. But once the Soviets had left Afghanistan, the CIA should have fallen behind the consistent American policy through four administrations of both political parties to support a political settlement restoring Afghanistan's independence and ending in self-determination of the Afghan people. On the contrary, in the words of respected American Afghan specialist Steve Coll, a journalist during this period, the CIA continued its "close collaboration with Pakistan and Saudi intelligence." It "remained deeply committed to a military solution in Afghanistan. They were going to finish the job," Coll wrote.[23] That job was to assist the ISI to mount an attack on Kabul, overthrow Najib, and replace him with Hekmatyar. The CIA not only went along with Pakistan's forward strategy into Afghanistan, it actively supported the strategy.

During press conferences and meetings in Pakistan with Afghan Mujahidin, I continued to present the official American policy line. In classified messages to Washington, however, I wrote that, under current circumstances, a protracted stalemate, not a Mujahidin victory, could lie ahead. In a July 22, 1989, cable to Washington, I stated the possibility that the war would continue: "Most of the three million refugees will remain in Pakistan. The fighting will drag on for years."[24]

By my third trip to the Frontier in September 1989, I had determined that staying the course meant staying a failing course. The Mujahidin were in disarray, while Najib was surviving. His speeches and propaganda against the Afghan extremists in Pakistan struck a responsive chord among many Afghans. The Mujahidin no longer held the battlefield momentum they had enjoyed during the Soviet occupation. Two-thirds of the field commanders had stopped fighting the Kabul regime.

An axiom of foreign policy–making posits that if the assessment of the policy environment is flawed, the policy springing from that assessment will be flawed. I could see that the conventional wisdom in Washington that the Mujahidin were winning was incorrect, but did not know why. I decided to make my own personal, firsthand assessment of why U.S. policy was drifting. This meant sacrificing attention to pressing congressional, media, and bureaucratic demands in Washington in order to spend more time listening to Afghans along the Frontier. Over the next ten months, I made eight visits to Pakistan to meet Pakistanis and Afghans, and one to Europe to meet ex-king Zahir Shah. I also traveled six times to Saudi Arabia to confer with Saudi intelligence chief Prince Turki al-Faisal.

The conclusions I reached were alarming. Far from a vehicle for Mujahidin political unity, the AIG was fomenting Mujahidin disunity. There was a huge gap between the official American-Pakistani military strategy and its execution on the ground by the ISI and the CIA. After the Jalalabad debacle, American and Pakistani officials had agreed on the importance of convening a more representative Afghan gathering than the shura the ISI had organized at Rawalpindi. The new leadership that emerged from a second, more broad-based Afghan gathering would be better positioned to mobilize opposition to the Najib regime from all groups and regions in Afghanistan. Najib's stretched forces, unable to defend multiple fronts, would be compelled to surrender more and more territory. Faced with the inevitable collapse of the regime, the Soviet Union would agree to drop him and accept a negotiated settlement of the Afghan conflict.[25]

But the ISI was not implementing the political settlement strategy that U.S. and Pakistani policymakers had agreed upon. Pakistan and Saudi Arabia were satisfied with the AIG; Saudi Arabia recognized the AIG as the legitimate government of Afghanistan; and American covert funds and Saudi cash funded its operations. The AIG leaders were not taking any steps to convene a new, broad-based shura, knowing that it would almost certainly deselect them. The ISI continued to build up Hekmatyar's conventional capabilities while denying fresh arms to moderate commanders, and this clearly clashed with Pakistan's stated commitment to a political solution of the war.

✤

The three Afghan political entities that Pakistan and the Soviet Union sponsored—Najib, Hekmatyar, and the AIG—were artificial creations placed on Afghanistan's political terrain by foreign powers. Each bore the stigma of a foreign puppet. They could survive, but only as long as their foreign patrons were willing to provide recurring resources. All were opposed by the great majority of Afghans.

The attempts by the Pakistani Army and Mikhail Gorbachev's Politburo to decide which Afghan faction would rule Afghanistan after the Soviet pullout were destined for certain failure. Only a credible political process inclusive of Afghanistan's major ethnic and tribal groups could have resulted in a leadership acceptable to the majority of Afghans and ended the war. Pakistan's hopeless venture to place Hekmatyar and later the Taliban in Kabul would inflict many more years of inconclusive, bloody warfare on Afghanistan. The continuing Afghan war would also harm Pakistan. An ongoing refugee burden; the blowback of Islamic terrorism, violence, and lawlessness; "the Kalashnikov culture" of guns and violence; narcotics; and international estrangement would push Pakistan lower and lower on the Failed States Index, a list compiled by the Fund for Peace based on twelve indicators of risk.[26] In June 2009, Pakistan ranked tenth from the bottom, between Guinea and Ivory Coast.

The Soviet Union's decision to continue propping up the Najib regime after its withdrawal was also a poor investment. The resources wasted in Afghanistan by the USSR between 1989 and the end of 1991, when the Soviet Union finally collapsed, were desperately needed at home. Najib tried to refurbish his image, but he could not erase what a Pentagon intelligence report called his "intolerance for opposition and a readiness to eliminate political opponents."[27] The Soviet commitment to the brutal ex-KHAD chief fueled Khalq-Parcham infighting, chronic instability within the PDPA power structure, and rejection of the Kabul regime by most Afghans.

During 1989 and 1990, Najib received relatively more outside patronage than his Afghan adversaries in Pakistan. At a time when the ISI was cutting off commanders not associated with the Afghan radicals, he was flush with Soviet cash. U.S. funding for the covert weapons program leveled off in 1989 and thereafter steadily diminished, while Soviet assistance to Najib's regime in 1989 soared to $300 million a month, in addition to the $1 billion in armaments left behind by the departing Soviet Army. By mid-1990, total Soviet aid to Najib's embattled regime reached $5 billion a year. In 1989, Najib told Gorbachev that, of 270,000 counterrevolutionaries, "a third of them are talking to us; 50,000 are irreconcilable; and the rest are taking a wait-and-see position." Najib offered to recognize the right of Mujahidin commanders to govern the areas they controlled and stated his readiness to conduct peace negotiations with any resistance leader ready to end the bloodshed in the country.[28] All was to no avail. He was marking time. The only question remaining was not whether he would go but when he would go.

A fascinating *Komsomolskaya Pravda* article published in Moscow in 1991 explained why: "The tribal and field commanders fight[,] if not for themselves[,] then for whomever will give them the greatest advantage: either the Najibullah regime or the opposition," it said. "Najibullah gives them money, agricultural equipment, and automatic weapons and says: Use them[,] but you must not fight against my government but protect this road from here to here which is strategically important to me. They agree." Soon, however, "a bearded peasant 'from the other side' comes along, reproaches them for cooperating with 'nonbelievers,' and offers them more. And they leave—taking with them the money, agricultural equipment, and automatic weapons." And yet, "they may return" to Najibullah "if Najibullah offers them more." The result is a neverending cycle, and "the prices get higher because the demand exceeds the supply."[29]

In reality, Najib's shaky regime, the AIG, and Hekmatyar's Hezb party in 1989 were each makeshift foreign-shaped sandcastles, vulnerable to the incoming tide or the next strong wind. The ISI and Hekmatyar had burrowed deep into Najib's army. They secretly intrigued with Khalqi Defense Minister Shahnawaz Tanai to overthrow Najib. Ambassador Yuli Vorontsov and the KGB Resident decided not to intervene when Najib arrested more than one hundred Khalqi military officers implicated in two attempted coups against him in September and October 1989. But when KHAD agents loyal to Najib tried to jail Tanai, the most senior military officer in the regime, Vorontsov rushed to the presidential palace to demand his release. Soviet Foreign Minister Eduard Shevardnadze secretly flew to Kabul to go through the timeless

Soviet lecture themes about the virtues of party unity. He warned Najib and Tanai that Soviet aid would be terminated if Parcham-Khalq rivalry did not cease. For the Parcham and Khalq leaders, however, the impulse to continue their vendetta and annihilate the other was stronger than the attraction of Soviet aid.

Masood built up his spy network in Najib's regime without foreign assistance. He monitored the ISI's and Hekmatyar's plotting with Defense Minister Tanai to attack Kabul. In a 1993 interview with British journalist Sandy Gall, he recalled that, after the Soviet withdrawal, "we had penetrated the regime very deeply." His agents included the 10th Division commander near Bagram, the Kabul garrison commander, and the security chief of Kabul Airport. Farid Mazdak, Najib's Tajik deputy in the party, and Mazdak's brother, General Yar Mohammad, second in command of KHAD, were also secretly allied with Masood.[30]

From the time of the Soviet withdrawal until the 1992 disintegration of Najib's regime, the Soviets and Pakistanis competed to see which side could push over the other side's Afghan sandcastle first. In 1989, the Soviet Politburo's hopes were rising that pervasive Mujahidin disunity and infighting would allow Najib's regime to survive. Pakistan's generals believed they were on a winning course. Unknown to me, ISI plans for a Khalqi-Hekmatyar coup were in an advanced stage. Ismael Khan struggled to survive in the west. Masood was preoccupied with defending his northern base areas from the ISI and Hekmatyar's attacks. Eastern and southern Afghanistan were in disarray. The AIG leaders were engrossed in quarrels with one another.

By the end of 1989, preparations were well advanced for an ISI-engineered Hekmatyar-Khalqi seizure of Kabul, top-down. But Afghanistan is an unpredictable place. Things almost never turn out as planned, especially when the planning is done by foreigners.

CHAPTER 14

Tilting at Windmills

An Associated Press correspondent has reported from Washington that the United States is changing tactics vis-à-vis Afghanistan.

The White House knows that it can no longer rely on Afghan opposition leaders in Peshawar. Who then can it rely upon? Only on rebel field commanders? Is this what it means by "new tactics"? The U.S. Ambassador to the Mujahidin headquarters Peter Tomsen spent all the summer of last year trying to win their favour by supplying U.S. arms to military formations within Afghanistan first and foremost. But he was not much of a success, because the CIA, which implemented these plans, had to rely on Pakistani intelligence in smuggling arms over the border. But the Islamabad establishment has a liking for fundamentalists of the Gulbuddin Hekmatyar–type and not for nationalist-minded "resistance" forces within Afghanistan, for which Pakistan's "patronage" is unacceptable.

—TASS SOVIET NEWS AGENCY, 1990[1]

For nine months, from August 1989 to April 1990, I broke many lances charging Don Quixote's mythological windmill. I and others in the State Department were not aware of the Pakistani Army's hegemonic objectives in Afghanistan. One after another, U.S. initiatives to partner with Pakistan to break the stalemate in Afghanistan and end the war through a political process stumbled and collapsed. American policymakers did not see through the Pakistani Army's two-faced Afghan policy. The CIA officers closest to the ISI may also have misunderstood Pakistan's motives—or been blinded by willful ignorance and Langley's institutional determination to "win" the Afghan war militarily.

Official briefings in Washington and Islamabad were of little use in explaining the paralyzing stalemate in Afghanistan. During the fall months of 1989, I directly engaged hundreds of Mujahidin on the Frontier to uncover the reasons for the lack of progress. I had concluded that Najib's longevity had more to do with Mujahidin disunity than with the enormous amounts of military and economic aid he was receiving from the Soviet Union. But I did not know why the Mujahidin were not undertaking political and military steps to replace him.

U.S. policymakers believed that Pakistan's cooperation was essential to achieving a negotiated settlement of the Afghan war—and by late 1989, it was obvious that Pakistan's supreme military leader, Army Chief of Staff Mirza Aslam Beg, controlled Pakistan's Afghan policy. What was not obvious to me and other policymakers in Washington was that Pakistan's clandestine pivot into Afghanistan was already well under way. Beg and former ISI chief Hamid Gul had no intention of coordinating with the United States and ending the war with a negotiated settlement. Their pivot into Afghanistan erased any prospect for a political solution of the Afghan war—the centerpiece of U.S. policy and my principal goal as special envoy. And Beg's ISI was covertly using CIA-provided American weapons and money to transform Afghanistan into a radical Islamist bastion ruled by Hekmatyar, the most anti-American faction leader in the Afghan resistance.

In late 1989, General Beg, Prime Minister Benazir Bhutto, and the U.S. government propagated identical messages, highlighting that Najib's departure would be followed by an Afghan act of self-determination, a loya jirga or elections to choose the postcommunist Afghan leadership. Meetings on Afghan strategy in Washington assumed the United States would "stay the course" with Pakistan and Saudi Arabia in Afghanistan. A common refrain was, "We don't want to have a gap between ourselves and the Paks. We need to bring them along"—an illusory formulation that would be repeated often in the decade following 9/11. In negotiations with the Soviets, President George H.W. Bush and Secretary of State James A. Baker III grouped Afghanistan with other former Cold War battleground states—Nicaragua, Cambodia, Namibia, and Ethiopia—where political settlements under UN auspices were going forward. American policymakers believed Pakistan supported the Afghan peace negotiations. During each of my trips to Pakistan, I briefed the Foreign Ministry and the ISI director general on the latest round of U.S.-Soviet negotiations.

Beneath the positive rhetoric, the U.S. and Pakistani governments were traveling in separate ships in opposite directions. Beg and Gul were implementing Zia ul-Haq's Islamist vision for Afghanistan. They may have calculated that America would one day move into opposition when the vision moved closer to reality. Until then, however, they would sustain Washington's misconception of a common U.S.-Pakistani purpose in Afghanistan. Washington's great diplomatic weight pressed down on the Soviets to remove Najib. In addition to the covert assistance delivered to the ISI, America's annual economic and military aid to Pakistan totaled more than $500 million in both 1989 and 1990, making Pakistan the third-largest recipient of U.S. aid after Israel and Egypt.[2]

Although it was nominally America's ally, the truth was that Pakistan was implementing a policy in Afghanistan that contradicted U.S. policy and U.S. interests. And Washington was subsidizing that policy.

In late 1989 and 1990 Beg continued to promote what a reporter later characterized as "an alliance between Pakistan, Iran and Afghanistan" that would grow into "the core of the Muslim world."[3] Beg proposed that the ISI and Iran's spy agency, the Revolutionary Guards, work together inside Afghanistan.[4] He reportedly returned from an early 1990 visit to Tehran assured that Iran would support Pakistan in another war with India.[5]

Prime Minister Benazir Bhutto and Foreign Minister Yaqub Khan were the only Pakistani leaders who could have resisted Beg and Gul's ill-fated pivot into Afghanistan. Bhutto's defeat in her power struggle with Beg in mid-1989 closed off that alternative. President Ghulam Ishak Khan and Bhutto's political opponent Nawaz Sharif supported Beg's pivot into Afghanistan. Hekmatyar's mentor, Jamaat leader Qazi Hussain Ahmed, was part of Sharif's election coalition.

Army Chief Beg and President Khan permitted Bhutto and Sharif to contest parliamentary elections but limited their ability to govern.[6] Pakistani journalist and scholar Ahmed Rashid aptly described the oscillation between military rule and degenerate civilian government in Pakistan during the 1990s: "No

FIGURE 14.1   PAKISTANI PRIME MINISTERS DISMISSED, 1990–1999

Prime Minister	Tenure
Benazir Bhutto	December 1988 to August 1990, one year, nine months
Nawaz Sharif	November 1990 to April 1993, two years, five months
Benazir Bhutto	October 1993 to November 1996, three years, one month
Nawaz Sharif	February 1997 to October 1999, two years, eight months

genuinely elected political government in Pakistan has ever been allowed to finish a full term in office and then—if disliked by the people—be voted out of office. Democracy has failed to take root largely because the army has never allowed it to take root, but also because the politicians have never practiced democratic norms of behaviour and tried to build institutions rather than personal power bases."[7] The army repeatedly cited corruption and abuse of power as the main reason for overturning civilian governments even though both ailments resurfaced during periods of direct military rule.

The Pakistani Army's self-appointed role as custodian of real power in Pakistan, its monopoly on national security decisions, and its repeated dismissals of elected governments crippled prospects for democratic institutions. Concurrently, many Pakistanis believed that the Bhutto and Sharif dynasties had to share the blame for Pakistan's enduring economic problems and political instability during the 1990s. Bhutto and Sharif both campaigned on promises to end corruption, implement effective economic and political reforms, improve law and order, and alleviate poverty. But neither produced any lasting accomplishments in any of these areas while in office. They instead devoted their energies to enriching themselves, delivering patronage and jobs to loyal party members, and granting favors to the moneyed status-quo forces supporting them. Their cabinets usually contained more than fifty ministers, mostly party loyalists who used their position to provide employment to family and clan members and to rake in graft.

My meetings with numerous Afghans in August 1989 along the Frontier confirmed what I had heard in July: The overwhelming majority of Afghans opposed the AIG, the Afghan radicals that Pakistan championed, and Najib. The urban-educated and Pashtun tribal leaders in the south and east insisted that Zahir Shah play a catalytic role in restoring the internal Afghan political consensus necessary to unite the country after Najib was gone. In most of rural Afghanistan, village elders and jirgas still presided over local clans and communities administering ancient tribal codes and customs. They, too, rejected the Pakistan-supported Afghan extremists.

At the same time, the nine-year war had thrown up independent militia leaders paid by the Soviets and Najib, on one side, and Pakistan's ISI, on the other. Commanders were generally rooted in tribal communities in one way or another. The militia leaders, later called "warlords," wielded influence based on the number of men and heavy weapons they controlled. Aggrandizing their personal power and greed motivated them, not ideology. Uzbek Abdul Rashid Dostum was the most powerful warlord financed by Najib's regime. Gulbuddin Hekmatyar held that dubious distinction among the Mujahidin groups based in Pakistan. They and hundreds of other petty warlords in the countryside, many just criminals, fomented instability in Afghanistan. They were answerable to no one, their paymasters included.

During a series of Washington interagency sessions that August, I recommended that the United States, Pakistan, and Saudi Arabia mobilize the Afghan moderate mainstream. Afghanistan's problems demanded political, not military, solutions. I reported that my meetings with Afghans revealed a popular desire to return to the precommunist era of tranquility in Afghanistan. Most Afghans were overwhelmingly conservative in their religion, but moderate and traditional in their politics.

I also recommended that I make a stop in Rome in early September to open a dialogue with Afghanistan's most prominent moderate, ex-king Zahir Shah. To many war-weary Afghans, he symbolized the traditional Afghan state, a state that had existed in relative peace for a half-century before the communist coup. Zahir Shah enjoyed a unique national stature. He remained much more popular than any of the Peshawar seven or Najib. The United States and Pakistan, I said, had failed to exploit his political potential to bring Afghans together. The time had come to encourage the ex-king to promote a political settlement that would remove Najib and end the war. Zahir Shah opposed the Najib regime. He could play a bridging role among all major Afghan groups, including the Shia, in the political settlement process. In high-level U.S.-Soviet negotiations, President Mikhail Gorbachev and his foreign minister, Eduard Shevardnadze, might see an advantage in Zahir Shah symbolically leading his country back to the peace it had enjoyed during his reign.

My recommendation was approved by the Kimmitt Group, which also endorsed my proposal to send weapons and money directly to moderate Mujahidin commanders inside Afghanistan who backed a political solution to the war. The meeting agreed that Hekmatyar and other extremists calling for military victory in Afghanistan should be marginalized.

I traveled back to Pakistan in late August to present the new U.S. strategy for breaking the impasse in the Afghan war. Foreign Minister Yaqub Khan avidly supported it. He asked that I formally present the proposal at a meeting in the Foreign Ministry. ISI representatives, at my request, were present for my briefing in the Foreign Ministry's conference room. Ambassador Robert Oakley and Station Chief Bill accompanied me. An ISI Afghan specialist, Brigadier Batcha,* and another ISI officer sat at the end of the long conference table separating the U.S. and Pakistani delegations. Batcha gazed at me with a quizzical look but said nothing when I read my talking points, including the rationale for a dialogue with Zahir Shah.

Yaqub Khan complimented the proposed American initiatives to break the stalemate in Afghanistan. He praised the idea of starting a dialogue with Zahir Shah, something he had proposed to me during our meetings. The foreign minister suggested that he could "drop in" on Abdul Wali, Zahir Shah's closest adviser—as well as his cousin and son-in-law—to pave the way for my meeting with the former monarch. He would do it on his way to a September 5 meeting of nonaligned nations in Belgrade; I would follow up and hold talks with Zahir Shah on September 6, after seeing the Mujahidin in Peshawar and briefing Prince Turki in Riyadh. At ISI headquarters in Islamabad, General Shamsur Kallue did not object to my Rome visit. In Peshawar, the six AIG party leaders (Hekmatyar was the seventh, but he had abandoned the AIG in August) split along expected lines. Gailani, Mojaddedi, and Nabi, the three moderates, supported the opening to Zahir Shah. Sayyaf and Khalis vociferously objected, and Rabbani adopted his usual noncommittal posture.

---

* "Batcha" was not the brigadier's real name. The ISI officers working with the Mujahidin used pseudonyms.

The apparent concord over my trip to Rome among those who had attended the Foreign Ministry meeting ended abruptly as I prepared to depart Islamabad on September 1 for Riyadh and Rome. Station Chief Bill unexpectedly appeared at the door of Oakley's office suite at the American embassy. Oakley was busy at his desk. I was drafting cables. "Peter can't go to Rome," Bill declared. "It's going to upset the offensive we have planned with ISI."[8] I found his comment strange. We had just had lunch together. He had raised no objection then. Oakley demanded an explanation. Bill explained that it would ruin the offensive that the ISI was planning to launch in Afghanistan before the snow closed the passes. My Rome visit would "demoralize" the Mujahidin, and the offensive would fail. I hurriedly phoned the State Department only to learn that the agency's chief of Near East clandestine operations, Tom Twetten, had just visited Under Secretary for Political Affairs Robert Kimmitt in the State Department to deliver the same objection to my visit. Twetten insisted that the Zahir Shah initiative be canceled, though he had personally endorsed it during the meeting in Kimmitt's office.

Kimmitt was faced with no choice but to call off the visit to Rome. It was obvious to him, as it was to me and to Ambassador Oakley, that the ISI offensive would be no more successful than the Jalalabad attack. If I went to Rome, the State Department would be blamed for the failure; if I did not go, the offensive would fail anyway.

I speculated that the reversal in the CIA's position could be traced to Brigadier Batcha's report from the Foreign Ministry meeting back to the military's high command. The military must have insisted that the visit be canceled; the agency's delayed turnaround was done at the behest of Beg and Gul. It was irrelevant that ISI director Kallue had not objected to the trip, because Kallue was Bhutto's, not Beg's, nominee to run the ISI. A few moments later, a secret State Department cable with "Immediate" precedence arrived.[9] The cable, addressed to Islamabad, Riyadh, Moscow, Rome, and Peshawar, reflected the department's annoyance. It stated that the Kimmitt Group would be convened for another policy session the day after I returned—and that the Zahir Shah option remained very much on the table.

ψ

I flew on to Saudi Arabia on September 1. I decided to place my recommendation on Afghan policy in a cabled analysis from American Ambassador

Charles Freeman's embassy in Riyadh. It would be a primer for the Kimmitt Group when it met after my return to Washington. My seven-page message recommended less reliance on the AIG and more support for moderate Afghans who would back a political settlement. I identified Hekmatyar as the biggest threat to achieving a political settlement: "Hekmatyar can be counted on to act unpredictably," I wrote, "and in ways that further alienate him from other Afghans, who fear and deeply mistrust him. The events of recent months have severely undercut any possibility that he will come out on top: we should promote this trend carefully through implementing our strategy."[10]

The cable reiterated my arguments that arms supplies be sent directly to individual field commanders inside Afghanistan who supported a negotiated settlement. It emphasized the importance of the U.S.-Soviet dialogue to achieve a political settlement, acknowledging that the extremes on the Afghan political spectrum—namely, Najib and Hekmatyar—might have to be excluded: "Our main interlocutor on the outline of a political solution should continue to be Moscow, which controls Najibullah and will make the concessions. We should keep the UN engaged, utilize them, but hammer out the essential settlement points with the Soviets themselves in bilateral talks. These points should include a genuine Najib transfer (not sharing) of power."

I recommended that the transitional regime should take over the levers of power from Najib. The bureaucracy could stay in place: "An act of self-determination would be the final step of the transitional arrangement. As in pervious Afghan elections, moderates would almost certainly obtain a large majority."

I knew my recommendations would not find favor with the CIA. But the time had come to implement one American policy, not two. The agency's covert program was an important tool in U.S. Afghan policy. But it should be used to achieve strategic policy goals established in Washington and not to counter them.

Congress, like the administration, supported a political outcome of the Afghan war. In appearances before congressional committees, I regularly testified with William H. Webster, director of the CIA from 1987 to 1991; his deputy, Richard Kerr; and Tom Twetten, the CIA's deputy director of the Directorate of Operations, the agency's clandestine service. We jointly assured the committees that U.S. policy centered on a political settlement of the war. We informed the committee members that the Mujahidin military pressure generated by the congressionally funded covert program was a means to achieving this political outcome, not an end in itself. Inside the executive branch, I participated in writing the presidential "Findings" laying out the policy guidelines for the CIA's covert program.[11] The Findings, signed by President Bush, clearly stated that a political settlement of the continuing Afghan war was the goal of U.S. policy.

My recommendations to shape the covert program to meet overall U.S. foreign policy goals precipitated resentment at Langley. CIA clandestine service officers had long considered the Afghan war "their" war.[12] "Martin,"* the head of the CIA Afghan Task Force at CIA headquarters, called on me at my State Department office to deliver a warning. We had served together amicably at previous posts. Nonetheless, he was blunt: "Stay out of our affairs," he told me. Just as bluntly, I responded that the agency could not make the Afghan covert program its self-declared monopoly. It was one part of U.S. policy on Afghanistan to end the war by a negotiated political settlement.

The agency's objections did not stop me from pressing my views. I still received formal agency briefings and testified with CIA executives at my elbow in Congress. But for the remainder of my appointment as special envoy, my relations with the CIA were tense and sometimes hostile. On one occasion, the Turkish government complained that the agency's Afghan briefer, Michael Scheuer, had given an interpretation of U.S. Afghan policy during his visit to Ankara that clashed with the presentations I had just made during a stopover to brief the Turks.

On another occasion, after a session with the House Intelligence Committee during which I explained the U.S. strategy, Congressman Charlie Wilson of Texas took me aside. With a broad grin, he said, "Peter, the agency thinks you and Oakley are full of shit." During my trips to Peshawar, Mujahidin such as Ahmed Zia Masood and Gailani military adviser General Rahmatullah Safi informed me that CIA and ISI officers had asked for readouts of my meetings with them.

ψ

The Riyadh policy telegram helped to inform the new two-track Afghan strategy that had emerged from interagency discussions in September. The first

---

* "Martin" is a pseudonym.

track was political. The United States, Pakistan, and Saudi Arabia were to pressure the AIG to fulfill its commitment to hold a genuinely broad-based shura by February 1990, the election deadline it had established for itself at Rawalpindi. If the AIG was unwilling to sponsor a new shura, the United Nations would be asked to help the Mujahidin organize one. Meanwhile, the United States would continue its high-level diplomatic efforts to persuade the Soviet Union to drop Najib. My trip to Rome would take place in early 1990. At that time, I would encourage Zahir Shah to support the new AIG shura and to publicly demand that Najib transfer power to the Mujahidin. The second track was military and called for transporting weapons to moderate commanders and tribal shuras inside Afghanistan. The new strategy called for diplomatic representations to Pakistan and Saudi Arabia describing the damage Hekmatyar was causing to Mujahidin unity and asking that the ISI cease supplying him with U.S.-provided arms, money, and equipment.

I returned to Pakistan in October and November to promote the two-track Afghan policy to the Pakistanis and Mujahidin. Ambassador Oakley separately lobbied Pakistani leaders to accept it. Pakistani reactions to the proposed strategy mirrored Islamabad's military-diplomatic reaction in August to the aborted Zahir Shah visit. Foreign Minister Yaqub Khan welcomed it. He was pleased that the Zahir Shah option was still alive. At a dinner and a meeting at ISI headquarters, ISI Director Kallue agreed with the two-track policy.

AIG party leaders in Peshawar continued to fend off demands for a new shura. Mojaddedi coyly suggested that any new gathering merely pass a vote of confidence on the current AIG. Sayyaf repeated his position that the AIG already constituted a pure Islamic form of government. It was sufficiently broad based, he said, and there was no need to change it.

The ISI continued to deny weapons support to northern commander Ahmed Shah Masood, indicating that the Pakistani Army still opposed him. As the single most powerful commander inside Afghanistan, his support would be important to applying military pressure on Najib and essential to reaching a successful political settlement of the war. When I visited Masood's weapons warehouse at Gharm Chesma, 20 miles north of Chitral, in November, I saw bare shelves. About 2,000 donkeys Masood had sent to bring arms to the Panshir were milling around. Masood's warehouse manager told me he would need to send them back to the Panshir without loads, since winter snows would soon block the passes in the Hindu Kush. He sighed that the unproductive donkey expedition had cost Masood a lot of money.

At a November Kimmitt Group meeting in Washington, I proposed that a committee composed of Department of Defense officials, CIA representatives, and me be formed to study the reasons for the deteriorating Mujahidin military situation in Afghanistan. The CIA objected but agreed to a compromise: A U.S. military officer, to be selected by the Pentagon, would conduct the assessment. In late November, a U.S. Army lieutenant colonel made a nine-day visit to Pakistan to carry out the assessment. His report implicitly criticized the ISI's management of the war and predicted there would be no military progress.[13]

"The most glaring problems are the obvious lack of comprehensive campaign planning and accompanying coordinated military action on the part of the resistance," he wrote. He described the "supply system" as "inefficient at best and divisive at worst." It hindered "the effective implementation of the operative military strategy" and stopped "proven resistance forces from realizing their full potential." "If the problems noted above are not corrected," he warned, "it is doubtful that the resistance will be able to generate enough military pressure to force a political settlement, and—under the present conditions—a military victory is out of the question."[14]

While waiting to testify at a November secret hearing of the Senate Intelligence Committee, I complained to CIA Director Webster that CIA ordnance was still not going to Masood. Webster pulled an agency memo on the subject from his briefcase and handed it to me with an air of satisfaction. It informed Webster that Masood was receiving ISI weapons. Pointing to the memo, I said: "That is not correct." I explained to Webster that I had just visited Masood's weapons warehouse in the foothills of the Hindu Kush, and it was empty. I also said I did not believe the ISI had any plans to fill it up. Webster looked startled. His reaction and the memo indicated to me that the agency did not have a good grasp of what the ISI was actually doing with weapons the United States was supplying.

ψ

On December 14, 1989, General Beg invited me to fly down to a Pakistani military base in Sargodha in the Punjab for talks with him on Afghanistan.

Beg and several of his corps commanders, including Hamid Gul, were supervising a large Pakistani military exercise near the Indian border.

Beg was still personally leading the Afghan policy coordination cell that
he had created within the Pakistani government. The chairman of the policy
cell, Major General Khalid Moghul, was present at our meeting, along with
Ambassador Oakley, Hamid Gul, and the director of military intelligence,
General Asad Durrani. General Kallue's absence underscored his lack of influence on Pakistan's Afghan policy. The Pakistani Foreign Ministry was not
represented at the meeting.

I was pleased to have an opportunity to personally brief Beg on the two-
track policy. My optimism, however, was checked by a conversation I'd had
with Abdul Haq only a few days previously in Peshawar. According to Haq,
Beg had recently made several anti-American remarks to AIG leaders in Peshawar. He had criticized the United States for sacrificing Afghanistan in
order to improve relations with the Soviet Union. If accurate, Beg's comment
suggested that he opposed the American effort to convince the Soviets to
drop Najib in favor of a political settlement. Haq's description of Beg's remarks to the AIG leaders was troubling. But I had little choice but to present
U.S. views to Pakistan's army chief and to clear up misunderstandings.

Major General Moghul began the meeting with a slide presentation in
which Pakistan and the United States were portrayed as moving forward together toward a political settlement of the Afghan war. His support for a new
AIG shura and for strengthening the commanders' shuras inside Afghanistan
coincided with the two-track policy.

Settled deep inside a huge easy chair, Beg next passed out a document entitled "Points for Discussion with Ambassador Tomsen." A quick glance
through the paper told me that it advocated a massive buildup of the current
AIG, a step that the United States would be sure to reject until the new AIG
shura was held. Beg described the document as his new "action plan" to
strengthen the AIG. He asked Moghul to explain it. Moghul described creation of an AIG general secretariat to improve efficiency; "twelve to fifteen"
new AIG-commanded regional headquarters inside Afghanistan; a joint operations planning cell within the AIG Ministry of Defense to plan military
campaigns; and an operations center to conduct them inside Afghanistan.
Moghul announced that a new AIG "information secretariat" would absorb
the separate media offices of the AIG leaders. He unrealistically foresaw that

the new secretariat would end the confusing practice of AIG leaders issuing conflicting versions of AIG positions. Moghul then confidentially announced that the AIG cabinet had decided to submit its plans for the new broad-based shura on January 1, 1990.

After Moghul's briefing, Beg read through a list of items in the final section of his action plan, which was entitled "Cooperation Required from the U.S." It contained a list of complaints that he claimed reflected AIG views. The first protested outside interference in AIG matters. This was followed by demands for the cessation of "intrusion" into AIG shura planning, the return of Afghan children from the United States, formal American recognition of the AIG, and the channeling of all American and other Afghan foreign aid through AIG ministries. When Beg put down the paper, Hamid Gul declared that "anything" going into Afghanistan should be coordinated through the AIG.

Then it was my turn. Moving forward in unison with Pakistan to wrap up the final phase of the Afghan war was an important plank in U.S. policy. But the Pakistani emphasis on building up the dysfunctional AIG diverged from the two-track American policy. I quickly decided that picking up where Gul left off would sour the atmosphere of the meeting. So I began by outlining the opportunities U.S. summit diplomacy with the Soviet Union offered to force Najib to step down. The Soviets had eliminated Amin in 1979 and removed Karmal in 1986. They would remove Najib under the right conditions. The Soviets had already agreed in principle to a transition period in U.S.-Soviet talks. That implied their readiness to drop Najib. The new AIG shura could be the first step in a political process to create a broad-based Afghan body to receive the transfer of power from Najib. To gain credibility among Afghans, the next AIG shura to select a leadership had to be more representative of all major Afghan groups. I expressed hope that the AIG would meet its January 1 deadline to announce convening of a new shura.

I handed a paper to Beg detailing the critical comments I had heard about the AIG from commanders, tribal leaders, and refugees along the Frontier. One commander predicted that another shura monopolized by the seven party leaders would be "useless." Another ridiculed AIG comments supportive of an Afghan state ruled by Sharia. Several others suggested involving Zahir Shah in the settlement process. Drawing on interagency-cleared talking points, I noted that associating Zahir Shah with the AIG would rally important tribal groups behind the Mujahidin banner and further isolate Najib. I noted that the Afghan war could not be won without Masood. I described Hekmatyar as a major obstacle to Mujahidin political and military unity; his divisiveness was helping Najib to stay in power.

Hamid Gul, unable to restrain himself any longer, interrupted me before I could wrap up my briefing. He protested that the AIG had been created by a representative shura at Rawalpindi. I replied that my travels and conversations with hundreds of Afghans along the Frontier showed that the AIG was not supported by any of the major tribal or religious groups. Gul shot back that it was impossible in the Afghan context to get more representative than the AIG. He gruffly ruled out Zahir Shah's involvement and recited the standard ISI critique of moderates: They had no following inside Afghanistan. Ambassador Oakley swept into the conversation at this point, supporting Gul. He incorrectly asserted that Zahir Shah had no support inside Afghanistan.

Oakley's unexpected intervention caught me offguard. He was well aware that initiating a dialogue with Zahir Shah in Rome was already an approved element of the two-track policy. His statement unhelpfully exhibited U.S. divisions on Afghan policy in front of Beg and his generals. It implicitly gave credibility to Gul's defense of the AIG and his erroneous claim that Zahir Shah had no support inside Afghanistan.

The Beg meeting rapidly wound down after the contentious discussion of Zahir Shah. On the way to the door, I took Beg aside to underline the need for concrete evidence of Mujahidin military progress to generate pressure on the regime and the Soviets—even the fall of a small provincial capital, such as Kalat, the capital of Zabul, or Uruzgan's capital, Tarinkot, would help. Beg immediately turned to Moghul standing at his side and ordered him to see that one of these small towns was captured (each with a population of less than 4,000). The notable aspect of this brief exchange was not that Beg's order was successfully executed—an ISI operation was accordingly mounted, and it easily snatched Tarinkot away from the Najib regime. Rather, it was that the ISI was purposefully *not* using one of the Mujahidin's greatest strengths: the ability to easily capture small, vulnerable provincial capitals near Pakistan. The ISI's strategic goal was to install Hekmatyar in Kabul, top down, by means of a Hekmatyar-Khalqi attack on the Afghan capital. Capturing multiple regime-held enclaves could set off an unstoppable chain reaction ending in Najib's replacement by moderate commanders inside Afghanistan rather than by Hekmatyar.

꒜

Pakistan's disinclination to break the Afghan stalemate prompted the Bush administration to send Under Secretary Kimmitt to Saudi Arabia and Pakistan to sell the two-track strategy at a higher level. He took along a proposal to organize elections in Mujahidin and regime-held areas, the latter supervised by the United Nations and not the Najib regime. Those elected would come together in a large gathering to select a transition entity. Najib, under Soviet pressure, would transfer power to the transition entity, which in turn would organize an act of Afghan self-determination, a loya jirga or national elections.

Under Secretary Kimmitt's discussions in Riyadh, Islamabad, and Peshawar were no more successful than mine. The Saudis were not interested in another AIG shura that could change the AIG's Sunni extremist center. The Saudis feared that Sayyaf, a sure veto of Shia inclusion in an Afghan government, might not retain his influential position in a new AIG. Saudi officials signaled their disagreement with Kimmitt's ideas in their usual subtle way. Only one lower-ranking Saudi official came to Ambassador Freeman's dinner honoring Kimmitt. The minister of commerce and two Foreign Ministry officials accepted the invitation but did not show up.

Army Chief Beg boycotted the January 16 Kimmitt negotiating session at the Foreign Ministry in Islamabad. Foreign Minister Yaqub Khan again found considerable overlap in the U.S. and Pakistani positions. General Moghul and Brigadier Batcha provided a briefing on the military situation in Afghanistan, predicting Mujahidin military victories and a new AIG shura later. Kimmitt stated that it was important for the AIG to announce its election plan before Secretary of State Baker's February 6–7, 1990, meeting with Shevardnadze in Moscow, which would precede the next Bush-Gorbachev summit, scheduled for April. He reiterated American warnings about Hekmatyar's divisive activities within the Mujahidin and repeated the U.S. request that he be cut off from U.S. arms. Following Kimmitt's remarks, I stated that in order to conduct a credible shura, the AIG Election Committee needed to be inclusive of all major Afghan groups.

Concluding the meeting, Yaqub Khan pronounced Pakistan's general agreement with the American approach. He concurred that the AIG Election Committee should be flawless in its image and unbiased in the election process. The foreign minister promised to reassemble the American and Pakistani

delegations in Islamabad to resolve a few "minor issues" after Kimmitt returned from meeting with the AIG in Peshawar. The following day, however,
Pakistan unceremoniously canceled the meeting. Once more, Beg must have
disapproved of Yaqub Khan's favorable reception to an American proposal.

The under secretary fared no better in his January 17 meeting with the
AIG in Peshawar. The AIG ministers sat sullenly as Kimmitt urged them to
honor their pledge to hold a new leadership shura. Mojaddedi made a few
cautiously positive comments in response. Then, probably as prearranged,
Rabbani broke into the dialogue. I was astonished at how quickly Rabbani's
voice climbed to a shrill level, reminiscent of Chinese propaganda broadcasts
during Mao's Cultural Revolution. He looked very nervous. For about a
minute, Rabbani loudly rebuked the United States for providing inadequate
levels of aid to the Mujahidin. He then recoiled back into his seat. An embarrassed Mojaddedi abruptly ended the meeting, telling Kimmitt that the AIG
cabinet would discuss his proposals and inform me of the results. He predicted that the new AIG shura would take place before May 31, 1990. In fact,
it was never held.

My consultations in Riyadh, Islamabad, and Peshawar on the heels of Kimmitt's departure from Pakistan confirmed that Saudi Arabia, Pakistan, and
the AIG disapproved of the American strategy for an Afghan political settlement. In Riyadh, Prince Turki restated his preposterous position that the AIG
was performing well. He said he would soon place another $10 million into
the AIG's bank account. In Islamabad, Pakistani Foreign Ministry officials restated the ministry's support but seemed embarrassed that they lacked influence to back it up. The equally powerless Kallue said he had little to offer on
the Kimmitt proposal. When I raised the subject of Masood, Kallue said he
had just sent sixty truckloads of arms to Masood's Gharm Chesma warehouse. I later discovered that Kallue had been true to his word: The trucks
had been sent, but the ISI and Rabbani had diverted nearly all of them to
other commanders. In Peshawar, Sayyaf repeated his line that the AIG represented a pure Islamic government and that it should not be changed. Mojaddedi railed against AIG "fanatics" for holding up the shura, even though
he also would oppose an election that might unseat him.

☙

I spent three more weeks on the Frontier in January and February 1990 listening to Afghan views and gathering firsthand accounts of developments inside Afghanistan. Everything I heard was negative; some accounts were ominous. I learned that the ISI was building training facilities in eastern Konar Province for Kashmiri, Afghan, and Pakistani extremists fighting in Kashmir. By chance, I encountered Brigadier Batcha in Islamabad. He informed me that he was being transferred to the ISI's Kashmir cell. I took that as another indication that the Kashmir insurgency was about to heat up, which it did later in 1990.

A wave of assassinations, many in broad daylight, erupted in 1990.[15] The victims were any Afghans who might stand in the way of Hekmatyar's path to power. They included intellectuals, tribal leaders, and politicians as well as Afghan aid workers employed by Western humanitarian organizations. Afghans universally blamed Hekmatyar, and Mojaddedi once publicly named Hekmatyar as the culprit.[16]

In the early months of 1990, threatening letters written in Pashto, and printed in Hekmatyar's and Sayyaf's refugee camp office facilities, were distributed in cities and refugee camps in the Northwest Frontier Province. They warned of revenge against Afghans opposing jihad as well as against Parchami (but not Khalqi) agents. One Peshawar newspaper article quoted a night letter ordering "Afghan women employed in hospitals, schools and western relief organizations to give up their jobs as it was immoral and against Islamic injunctions or face consequences." A thirty-six-year-old nurse working at the Mother and Child Clinic in Peshawar had been abducted from her home on May 15, 1990, just a few weeks before her wedding date. The article reported that she "was allegedly taken to [Hekmatyar's] Shamshatoo Refugee Camp, . . . raped and killed."[17] Rahim Chenzaie, the publisher of a local Dari-language newspaper with pro–Zahir Shah views, was kidnapped in broad daylight in Peshawar after having a heated argument with one of Hekmatyar's press spokesmen, an American citizen. Chenzaie was taken to Hekmatyar's prison in the refugee camp, then transported to Hekmatyar's Sergai Shaga military base near the Afghan border, where he was reportedly killed.[18]

Little or no publicity attended the political assassinations. For two years I appealed to the Pakistani Foreign Ministry and ISI director generals to seriously investigate the assassinations and prosecute the guilty. I received many promises in response, but there was no follow-up and no arrests, much less trials and convictions. Ambassador Oakley told the Pakistani foreign secretary that the killings "risked disrupting progress towards a political settlement" and threatened the continued operation of humanitarian assistance to Afghanistan and Afghan refugees. An embassy cable to Washington reported that Oakley "noted the involvement of Hekmatyar and Sayyaf in such acts."[19]

The sudden cessation of construction of the northern road into Masood's base areas inside Afghanistan in 1990 raised my suspicions. I learned that the USAID road-building NGO, the Afghan Construction and Logistics Unit (ACLU), had ordered the construction crew building the road back to Peshawar. Upon investigation, I discovered that ISI officers were stationed inside ACLU offices. Hekmatyar's brother occupied a midlevel ACLU position. The investigation concluded that the order that had recalled the ACLU road crew back to Peshawar had been fraudulent.[20]

In the course of the ACLU investigation, I also discovered that Hekmatyar's cadres were ensconced in scores of American and other foreign NGOs along the Frontier. Two Hezb party members were employed at Radio Afghanistan, the American-funded Afghan radio station attached to Radio Liberty in Munich. Later in 1990, during the buildup to the first Gulf War, they broadcast support for Saddam Hussein and condemned the U.S.-led Gulf coalition. At my request, USAID began to weed out the Hezb networks embedded in the American NGO community. I also asked the head of Radio Liberty to investigate the Hezb moles at Radio Afghanistan. On my return to Washington, an NEA colleague passed me an Embassy Islamabad informal back-channel message to NEA disapproving of my "purge" of ACLU and Radio Free Afghanistan.[21]

A three-hour meeting with an ISI brigadier, Mohammad Afzal Janjua, and ISI colonel, Sultan Imam, at the ISI Peshawar branch office on February 11, 1990, yielded no results.[22] They showed no interest in carrying out Pakistan's professed policy of promoting an Afghan peace settlement. I asked them to reestablish an ISI dialogue with Masood, to resume sending supplies to Masood, and to engage him in the planning of military operations against Najib. Recalling General Kallue's decision to send sixty truckloads of weapons to Masood in December, I expressed disappointment that only four ultimately reached Masood's Gharm Chesma warehouse. I noted that the rest had been diverted to other commanders elsewhere in Afghanistan. Even the small quantity of weapons delivered to Gharm Chesma had been destroyed in a mysterious explosion. I requested that the ISI investigate the underground network responsible for the growing number of assassinations of Afghans on Pakistani soil and arrest the guilty parties.

Janjua said the ISI was aware of the kidnappings and was following up on them, but he seemed indifferent. Imam stated that Masood's refusal to cooperate with ISI military strategies disqualified him from receiving aid. Janjua described a recent ISI meeting of Kabul area commanders meant to "squeeze" Kabul. But his anodyne briefing did not foresee the military progress that ISI officials had earlier predicted in their briefings of Kimmitt in Islamabad in January.

At the end of his briefing, Janjua made a casual remark that caught my attention. He said that over sixty families from PDPA Defense Minister Shahnawaz Tanai's tribe had "emigrated" to Pakistan on February 9. Leaving the ISI office, I pondered what this might mean. Tanai was now the head of the Khalqi faction in the regime, and he was, like Hekmatyar, a Ghilzai Pashtun. Tough, wiry, and fearless, he was also a Soviet-trained commando. Tanai had personally led the commando unit that had breached the walls of Haqqani's Zhawar Kili bastion in 1986. His special forces had helped squash the Mujahidin attack on Jalalabad in the spring of 1989.

Open-source and classified reporting during February disclosed that Tanai was locked in a showdown with Najib in Kabul. Najib was planning to put 124 Khalqi officers accused of coup-plotting against him on trial on March 6. Kabul was extremely tense. Did the sudden "emigration" of Tanai's clan to Pakistan indicate that another round of Khalq-Parcham violence was in the offing?

Three weeks later, the connection between the "emigration" of Tanai's clan to sanctuary in Pakistan and the tense scene in Kabul became obvious when the PDPA defense minister hurled his Khalqi armor, infantry, and war planes against Najib's presidential palace in a bold bid to overthrow his Parcham rival. In the best Afghan tradition of changing sides, Tanai had secretly thrown in his lot with Pakistan against the Soviet Union and President Najib. The ISI was counting on Tanai's Khalqi regiments and Hekmatyar's *Lashkar-i Issar* battalions to deliver a quick knockout blow against Parcham strongholds in Kabul and topple Najib's regime. Tanai had timed his coup to take place on the day that the arrested Khalqi officers were to go on trial. One-third of Najib's Politburo—all Khalqis—supported the coup.

Najib's decision to put the Khalqis on trial quicker than expected appeared to have triggered the Tanai coup before the ISI could move Hekmatyar's battalions into place south of Kabul in Logar Province. When Tanai struck on the day the trial was to begin, March 6, Soviet intelligence was also caught off-guard. So was Pakistan's foreign secretary in Islamabad, who wrongly claimed at a hastily called press conference that the Mujahidin had entered the city and were fighting alongside Tanai's forces.

Tanai's tanks and troops charged downhill into Kabul from Darulaman Central Corps headquarters in the city's southwest suburbs. Bloody chaos raged in Kabul during the fighting. Pashtun-officered Khalqi army units fought hand-to-hand with Tajik-led Parcham KHAD units loyal to Najib. Khalqi pilots based at Bagram flew more than forty combat sorties over Kabul, bombing and strafing Najib's presidential palace and government buildings. Twelve bombs struck the presidential palace. The first landed only 50 feet from the office where Najib was working, obliterating a one-story building. Najib, with several aides and servants running behind him, rushed to a palace bunker. There he lifted a secret trapdoor opening to an underground tunnel, which took him to an isolated spot next to the Kabul River to rendezvous with friendly KHAD troops.[23]

The fate of Najib and his PDPA regime hung in the balance until March 7, the second day of the coup. That day, in Washington, NEA Assistant Secretary of State John Kelly and I testified at a hearing of the House Foreign Affairs Committee on Capitol Hill. Not having been forewarned by either the CIA or the ISI that a coup was in the offing, we had little information to offer in response to questions posed by members of the committee. In Pakistan, the American embassy publicly described the anti-Najib Khalqi-Hekmatyar alliance as "a step towards peace in Afghanistan."[24] Some American embassy officials joined ISI officers in urging Mujahidin commanders in Pakistan to rush to Kabul and join the attack on Najib's regime. Meanwhile, the ISI frantically radioed Masood to strike Kabul from the north.

Masood declined. It was too late, he radioed back: Tanai's army units were already retreating. Masood was right. Khalqi Interior Minister Aslam Watanjar had decided to support Najib, not Tanai, and thus saved Najib and his tottering government. Watanjar was a Pashtun Khalqi on the outside but a controlled Soviet asset on the inside,[25] and the Soviets wanted Najib to survive. Watanjar ordered Interior Ministry paramilitary police battalions to attack the rebellious Khalqi flanks. After a day of ferocious combat and hundreds of casualties, pro-Najib forces drove Tanai's army units from the capital. Frustrated Soviet officers looked on while KHAD rockets pummeled Tanai's Central Army headquarters at Darulaman and destroyed Soviet-made combat jets parked at Bagram air base. Entire neighborhoods in Kabul were destroyed. Extensive damage at Bagram caused flight operations to be shut down for several days.

In a press interview three years later, Masood claimed that his secret allies in Najib's army had defeated Tanai: "In one sentence I am saying to you—and it is not an exaggeration, it is reality—that the Tanai coup d'état was not defeated by Najib but by our people in the army."[26]

Tanai and his family fled by helicopter to the outskirts of Peshawar, where they were personally welcomed on arrival by ISI officers and Hekmatyar. Tanai continued to wear his Afghan army uniform in Pakistan. He told a press conference that he remained Afghan defense minister. Najib was the renegade, he claimed. Tanai and his wife and children were housed at a Pakistani military housing area near Islamabad. One of Hekmatyar's assistants became Tanai's interpreter at press interviews. Tanai used those occasions to sarcastically voice his regret that Hekmatyar's Mujahidin battalions had not shown up as promised during the coup fighting. Hekmatyar, who convened his own heavily attended press conferences to defend his Tanai alliance, pointed out that the AIG had offered amnesty to communists in the regime if they defected. Tanai was therefore entitled to that offer.

An explosion of outrage cutting across all resistance factions denounced Hekmatyar's unilateral grab for power in league with communist Khalqis. Sayyaf publicly warned against cooperation with communist infidels. AIG president Mojaddedi went further. He issued an emotional fatwa declaring Hekmatyar an infidel. The defection of eight Hezb executive committee members to Sayyaf's party embarrassed Hekmatyar. The Shia Hezb-i Wahdat leader, Karim Khalili, announced that if the coup had succeeded, Afghanistan "would be in . . . worse shape than before since, in our view, Tanai is worse than Najib."[27]

Just two months after the failed March 6 coup, I heard from reliable Mujahidin sources that the ISI was planning a second Tanai-Hekmatyar coup for the fall of 1990. In May, Janjua, Imam, Tanai, and Hekmatyar met with select Nangarhar and Konar commanders at a secret location in Konar, just across the Pakistani border. Janjua told the commanders to prepare for a Mujahidin assault on Jalalabad. He stated that the attack would be timed to coincide with two other ISI-planned military operations—against Khost and Gardez—and another Khalqi coup in Kabul. Hekmatyar's ISI-trained "Army of Sacrifice" would attack Kabul from the south and east.

Nangarhar commanders who were at the meeting later informed me that they were about to raise objections to another risky ISI attack on Jalalabad when a bombing run by Kabul regime aircraft preempted further discussion. The participants scattered in different directions, and the ISI officers fled back over the border to Pakistan.

During the Soviet-Afghan war and before the Tanai coup, Pakistan had accumulated enormous gratitude and goodwill among Afghans everywhere. Afghanistan's Muslim neighbor did not do the fighting and dying to drive the Soviet Army from Afghanistan. Afghans did that. But Pakistan had resolutely supported Afghanistan during a perilous period of its history. Pakistan was the frontline state, the safe haven, the Mujahidin armory, the Mujahidin base from which it became possible to force the Soviet Union to leave Afghanistan. India, in contrast, demeaned itself in Afghan eyes during the Soviet-Afghan war. It continued its economic, diplomatic, and military assistance to the Najib regime throughout the Soviet occupation and even after the Soviet withdrawal.

The March 6, 1990, Tanai coup marked a watershed in the Afghan war that had begun in 1978. The coup dramatically showed that the most publicized Afghan jihadi in the resistance was not fighting for Islam. He was fighting for power. The coup was the opening round of a string of failed ISI attempts over the next two decades to implant a compliant Afghan regime in Kabul. But extending Pakistan's sphere of influence into Afghanistan would run up against violent resistance by the majority of Afghans, as the Soviets and the British before them had found. In the end, Pakistan would not achieve Zia's Islamist vision: Islamabad's hegemony in Afghanistan; strategic depth against

India; and an Islamic extremist platform from which to export militant Islam to other world regions.

The Pakistani Army's 1988–1989 pivot into Afghanistan as the Soviets were withdrawing and the March 6, 1990, Tanai coup plunged the Afghan war into a new phase in which one outside power—Pakistan—replaced another—the Soviet Union—seeking to dominate the unruly Afghans. As a consequence, Pakistan surrendered the opportunity to terminate the Afghan conflict with a political settlement in which Afghans chose their own leadership. By following this course in partnership with Afghans, Pakistan could have enjoyed strategic depth against India simply by virtue of the huge reservoir of Afghan gratitude following the Soviet withdrawal. Afghan appreciation for Pakistan's help might have lasted for generations. In addition, Pakistan could have made itself the foundation for a trans-Eurasian network of north-south roads, pipelines, and electricity grids transiting Afghanistan to energy-rich Central Asia. Pakistan's generals instead recklessly squandered this opportunity in a quixotic attempt to dominate Afghanistan. Afghan commander Ahmed Shah Masood was right when he told a European audience in 2000 that "the best way for Pakistan would have been to restore peace in Afghanistan. And it would have been in the interest of all, Afghanistan, Pakistan and Central Asia. But Pakistanis have greater plans, motives and expectations. I will tell you about their motives in one sentence. As I said earlier, Pakistan wants to become the axis of all Islamic countries in the region. But that is something which is beyond the capacity of Pakistan."[28]

The Tanai coup also illuminated the appalling American intelligence misunderstanding about Pakistan's covert strategy in Afghanistan. I assumed that Station Chief Bill must have known about the coup. I did not know whether Ambassador Oakley or his deputy, Beth Jones, had had prior knowledge. In a March 17, 1990, *Washington Post* article, journalists Steve Coll and James Rupert favored the view that they had probably been alerted. Their article, citing "sources in Pakistan and Washington," reported that the U.S. embassy in Islamabad had "tried unsuccessfully . . . to press the Afghan Mujahidin rebels to launch a major military offensive against Kabul" to support the attempted coup. Coll and Rupert deduced that U.S. policy "continued to be influenced by the goals and methods of Pakistan's military intelligence agency." In response to the article, the embassy sent a nimbly worded confidential cable to

Washington denying that it had "played a significant supporting role" in assisting "GOP (Government of Pakistan) efforts to press the Mujahidin to launch military operations in parallel with the coup."[29]

The daily fare of U.S. intelligence spot reports on Afghanistan failed to cover another distressing trendline—the activities of "Wahhabis" and Arab terrorists living in Peshawar. I saw no U.S. intelligence reporting on Osama bin Laden (whom I first heard about from newspaper reports in 1998, along with many Americans), although he remained in Peshawar well into 1989, or on the Egyptian terrorists Ayman al-Zawahiri and Abdel Rahman, who lived in Peshawar.

The intelligence shortfall at the time was noted by White House counterterrorism specialist Richard Clarke during his March 2004 testimony to the 9/11 Commission. Clarke commented that "no one in the White House was ever informed by the intelligence community that there was an al Qaeda until probably 1995." According to Clarke, "Had we a more robust intelligence capability in the late 1980s and early 1990s, we might have recognized the existence of al Qaeda relatively sooner" and been able to "nip it in the bud."[30]

CHAPTER 15

Wahhabi Emirate

Mawlawi Jamil ur-Rahman ruled an independent emirate in Konar Province on the Pakistani border in 1990. He called his dominion Salafi; he and his followers adhered to the strict Wahhabi variant of Islam. Rahman was a Muslim cleric from the large Safi tribe in Konar.

Rahman had many enemies. Gulbuddin Hekmatyar, Abdul Rasoul Sayyaf, Yunus Khalis, Muslim Brotherhood extremists, and the ISI opposed his independent emirate. One listless, hot, summer afternoon, Rahman was by himself, offering midday prayers in a family residence on the Pakistani side of the border. Armed guards at the front door waved by a lone Egyptian Arab clad in the white robes of a Muslim holy man and carrying a Koran. They did not know the visitor's Koran had been hollowed out enough to allow room for a small .32 caliber pistol.

The guards immediately rushed to the sound of three pistol shots. Rahman lay crumpled on the ground. Meanwhile, Hekmatyar's fighters were rampaging through Rahman's emirate, killing and looting.

Rahman's remarkable Wahhabi ministate, a foreign religious transplant from the placid deserts of Saudi Arabia to the rugged mountains of Konar,[1] faded away. Its emir lay dead, felled by bullets fired by an Egyptian Muslim Brotherhood fanatic. The Wahhabi emirate slipped into Afghan history—one more failure by outsiders attempting to transform Afghanistan's tribal society into their own image.

Even before my swearing-in as special envoy, I resolved to visit Saudi Arabia as often as possible to coordinate with the Saudi government on Afghan policy.

I did so on my first visit to the region in June and July 1989 and fourteen more times over the next three years. The U.S. ambassador to Saudi Arabia, Charles "Chas" W. Freeman, encouraged these stopovers.

Afghanistan's Muslim population reveres the Islamic holy land where the Prophet Muhammad lived and taught. The Saudis had proven a valuable partner in the nine-year effort to drive the Soviet Army from Afghanistan. They were still providing half of the funding for the CIA's covert program. The royal family, private Saudi donors, the Saudi clergy, and quasi-governmental charities raised billions more for the Afghan jihad. Every year, the Saudi government covered all expenses for hundreds of Mujahidin clerics, commanders, refugees, and politicians to travel to Mecca to perform the Haj, the annual pilgrimage and one of the five pillars of Islam.[2]

These were not the only reasons that Chas had advised me to engage the Saudis on Afghanistan. It was also because Saudi-American bilateral relations were important. The kingdom's uncompromising anticommunism was a boon to the United States during the Cold War. Saudi Arabia had lined up with the United States against the pro-Soviet leftist regimes of Gamal Abdel Nasser in Egypt in the 1950s and 1960s and Hafez al-Assad in Syria in the 1970s and 1980s. Saudi oil production was vital to sustaining economic growth in America and around the world.[3] Saudi diplomacy and cash had periodically played behind-the-scene roles in U.S.-brokered agreements in the volatile Middle East, such as the 1975 Sinai Accord. Saudi Arabia's decision to ignore its Organization of Petroleum Exporting Countries (OPEC) production quotas in the 1980s and to substantially increase its oil output helped to lift America and the rest of the Western world out of an economic slump.[4]

Flying into Riyadh's Bechtel-constructed King Khalid International Airport, located just 20 miles north of the capital, was always an experience. On one occasion, a corpulent, middle-aged, and very drunk Saudi passenger caused a scene in the British Airways first-class cabin. Two flight attendants had to wrestle him back to his seat and strap him down. The Englishman sitting next to me volunteered that such incidents were not uncommon on flights into Saudi Arabia, where alcohol is forbidden.

The Saudi government's cordial reception on my arrivals from Europe and sometimes from Pakistan followed a standard procedure. Saudi protocol officers rolled up to planeside in stretch limousines to pick me up after my flight landed. A brief drive to the Riyadh airport's Royal Pavilion VIP lounge was next on the schedule. There, a spacious room was furnished with Egyptian-style Louis XIV gilded furniture. A South Asian waiter in a crisp white uniform and gloves served dates and cardamom coffee. Outside, a giant fountain sent water 100 feet into the air.

The city of Riyadh is located in the central heartland of Saudi Arabia on the immense desert plateau of the Nejd ("Upland"). The Nejd covers more than half of the Arabian Peninsula. Riyadh's population of 2 million in 1990 made it the largest urban center in the kingdom. Numerous skyscrapers—including the 992-foot-high Kingdom Tower—rise into the sky. Government offices operate in Riyadh for most of the year, but during the scorching summer months, most ministries follow the king's shift to the breezy Red Sea city of Jeddah, over 500 miles away by air. Some fifty embassies in Riyadh, or at least the ambassadors and their senior staffs, must travel to Jeddah if they want to conduct official business. Most of my fifteen trips to Saudi Arabia required me to travel to both cities to meet with Saudi and U.S. embassy officials.

The large number of princes is one of the unique features of the Saudi kingdom. Many of the princes are entitled to be addressed as "Your Royal Highness." Others, not directly descended from Abdul Aziz al-Saud, the current al-Saud dynasty's founder, but still in the family, are addressed simply as "Your Highness." The state budget's subsidies to the numerous princes cause some resentment within the Saudi population. So do other unwritten princely perquisites—lateral entry at high levels into the government and easy personal access into business and academic posts. Hundreds of palaces purchased by the princes from their state subsidies are located in posh Riyadh and Jeddah suburbs. In Jeddah, the palaces lining the Red Sea coastline include imposing castles topped with battlements and a copy of a Chinese Ming Dynasty palace.

The army of foreign workers in Saudi Arabia is another unique facet of the desert kingdom. The demands of the ever-expanding oil industry and of building a new transportation network at the time required the importation of Western specialists and foreign workers. Much of the labor force came from Arabic-speaking Muslim countries. In 1990, the Saudi government officially estimated the Saudi population at 14.8 million, and the number of foreigners working in the kingdom at around 5.3 million.[5] The huge expatriate community was overwhelmingly from Muslim-populated Asian and Arabic-speaking

African countries—Egyptians, Yemenis, Sudanese, Syrians, Kuwaitis, Pakistanis, Filipinos, Bangladeshis, and Afghans toiling in both the cities and the countryside. They sent most of their earnings back to families in their home countries. Western technicians and their dependents numbered almost 300,000, including around 180,000 Europeans and 92,000 North Americans.[6]

The most striking aspect of the Saudi state is the austere religious curtain that envelops it. According to American scholar David Long, while some Saudis resent the rigid application of Islamic law, the great majority of the population accepts it: "Virtually no one, even the most modernized Saudi, advocates abandoning the Shari'a as the basis of the Saudi Arabian constitutional system or the Wahhabi doctrine of Tawhid (strict monotheism) as the basis of Saudi foreign and domestic policies. Separation of church and state, the basis of Western secularism, would be viewed as not only ludicrous by most Saudis but heretical as well."[7]

Contemporary Saudi Arabia is the only Arab country that has organized itself in the mold of the Islamic states of the Middle East during the classical or traditional Islamic era, dating roughly from the seventh to the nineteenth centuries.[8] The al-Saud family monarchy and al-Sheikh high clergy have delivered fundamental stability and gradual economic modernization to Saudi Arabia since the 1930s without parliaments or other democratic institutions. The Koran is the Saudi constitution. In judicial organs, the puritanical religious establishment interprets "God's law" as it is drawn from the Koran, the Sunnah, and authoritative hadiths.[9] The Saudi religious establishment oversees the approximately 50,000 preachers in the country, manages thousands of mosques, and staffs the Ministry of Education, the Ministry of Dawa (Missionary) and Islamic Affairs, and the Ministry of Haj. During his reign, King Fahd adopted the title of "Custodian of the Two Holy Mosques"—the mosques at Mecca and Medina—to emphasize the linkage of Saudi Arabia's religious and secular identity in his person.

Chas Freeman and I spent many hours talking about how to continue the U.S.-Saudi partnership on Afghanistan beyond the Soviet pullout. We debated many questions: How could the United States encourage Saudi Arabia to contribute constructively to a political settlement of the Afghan war? Could the Saudi government be convinced to direct the huge flow of money from Saudi Arabia to the Afghan Mujahidin who support an Afghan political settlement? Nearly all of the millions of dollars in private and religious Saudi donations was going to the most radical Mujahidin who opposed a negotiated settlement. With whom should I meet in the Saudi government to explain the need to shift from the mainly military approach that had been pursued since the Soviet invasion to one prioritizing a political settlement?

The answer to this last question was straightforward. Saudi Arabia's King Fahd and his brothers controlling the key power ministries and the kingdom's senior ulema were rarely accessible. I needed to concentrate on three third-generation princes who had been educated in the West and seemed more likely to understand, and hopefully support, negotiations to force Najib to transfer power to the Mujahidin. These princes were Foreign Minister Saud al-Faisal; his brother, Turki al-Faisal, who was chief of the General Intelligence Directorate (GID), the nation's powerful foreign intelligence agency; and Bandar al-Sultan, the Saudi ambassador in Washington. In the event they agreed with U.S. policy, Saud, Turki, and Bandar were well placed to encourage their elders in the royal family and the al-Sheikh high clergy that a military victory by the Afghan extremists was not possible, and furthermore, that empowering the minority radical fringe of the resistance and their radical Arab allies posed a long-term danger to the Saudi kingdom itself.

I repeated these points to Saudi officials on countless occasions but made little headway. Saudi goals in the Afghan holy war left little room for a broad-based Afghan political settlement process. A political accord involving all Afghan groups would open the way for Afghan moderates and Shia to influence the government in Kabul. They would call their government Islamic. But it would not be a "pure" Islamic government following the conservative Saudi interpretation of Sharia and enforced by the clerical establishment. A moderate Afghan government would re-create the democratic institutions that had existed during Zahir Shah's rule. The constitution would likely be modeled on the precommunist 1964 westernized constitution, which specifically identified Afghanistan's Islam with the moderate Hanafi order. Democratic institutions would give a voice to the Afghan Shia, between 15 and 20 percent of the Afghan population. A representative Afghan government in Kabul would seek positive ties with Shia Iran.

This general direction was anathema to the Saudi clergy. Hard-line religious ideologues in Saudi Arabia believed that the Afghan war must be fought to the end, until *Dar al-Harb* (Land of the Infidel) became *Dar al-Islam* (Land of Islam). Saudi Arabia favored the Afghan radicals who called for a military resolution of the Afghan war and the creation of an Islamic state governed by Sharia: Hekmatyar, Sayyaf, and Khalis. Prince Turki had personally helped to create the Islamist-centered AIG. The Saudi government formally recognized the AIG.

My first meeting with Prince Saud was basically a courtesy call. The Saudi foreign minister and his deputy, Abd Al Rahman al-Mansouri, hinted that the Afghan portfolio was entirely in Prince Turki's hands. In Washington, I found Prince Bandar and his deputy, Rihab Masood, engaging and helpful in passing messages and requests to Turki in Saudi Arabia, or, as the need arose, to Yusef Motabbakani, the Saudi ambassador in Islamabad. I continued to make the obligatory protocol stop at the Foreign Ministry during each stop in Saudi Arabia. But my main interlocutor for the next three years became Prince Turki. We held over thirty rounds of talks at his offices and homes in Riyadh and Jeddah, in the State Department, in London, and in Islamabad.

Chas was right to advise me to seek Prince Turki's support for an Afghan political settlement. This was, however, a daunting challenge, made more so by Prince Turki's tenacious practice of following the ISI's lead. Like the CIA, Turki's GID had supported the ISI's strategic pivot into Afghanistan after the Soviet pullout. Pakistani and Saudi relations were excellent. The two Muslim states regularly exchanged high-level visits. Saudi oil was shipped to Pakistan at concessional rates. Since Zia's accession, Pakistan had stationed a full brigade of the Pakistani Army in Saudi Arabia.[10]

Diplomacy is sometimes called the art of the possible. But delivering Saudi Arabia's support for an Afghan political solution to end the Afghan war seemed impossible. I made negligible progress in negotiations with Prince Turki during my first seven visits to Saudi Arabia, up to August 1990. When Saddam Hussein invaded Kuwait that month, menacing Saudi Arabia itself, persistent diplomacy began to pay off—at least for a while.

ψ

Prince Turki was the eighth and youngest son of the late King Faisal, the nephew of King Fahd, and the grandson of Abdul Aziz, the founder of the present al-Saud dynasty. His paternal grandmother was a member of the influential al-Sheikh family, direct descendants of Abd al-Wahhab, creator of the Wahhabi religious order in the eighteenth century. Turki was only thirty-four years old when King Fahd gave him the "Afghanistan file" during a 1980 meeting with Zbigniew Brzezinski, President Carter's national security adviser.[11] He was in his second year as chief of Saudi external intelligence, and the Soviet Union had just invaded Afghanistan. Turki became the Saudi government's point man in dealing with the Afghan war.

Turki's exposure to America had begun in his formative years. In 1964, when he was fourteen, King Faisal had sent him from the gilded royal palace in Riyadh to the exclusive Lawrenceville School in New Jersey. He enrolled at Georgetown University in 1967 but left before graduating to continue his studies at Cambridge University and the University of London, where he received a degree in 1971. In 1973, back in Saudi Arabia, he joined the Foreign Liaison Office, then an intelligence arm of the Saudi government headed by his half-brother. Four years later King Fahd elevated him to be GID director general with the rank of minister.

By the time of our first meeting in July 1989, Turki had already amassed a large reservoir of knowledge about Afghanistan. He had experienced the many foibles of the seven Mujahidin party leaders. Like others, he had discovered that attempts to mediate their differences always failed, that paying them to cooperate with each other was a waste of money, and that the ISI was sensitive to direct Saudi or American initiatives with the Mujahidin.

Turki's knowledge of Afghanistan and the Mujahidin was kaleidoscopic, and it was clear that his GID agents and Ambassador Yusef Motabbakani's embassy in Islamabad kept him well informed. The ISI and the CIA also briefed him on Afghan events. My views and accounts of Afghan developments offered him a separate channel of information. It came directly from Mujahidin sources, and at times it must have differed from what he was hearing from the CIA and the ISI about the situation on the ground inside Afghanistan. Turki gave as much as he received during our many hours together.

From our first conversations, I sensed that Turki did not welcome my comments about the futility of a military solution to the Afghan conflict and the widespread unpopularity of the AIG among Afghans. He questioned whether U.S. policy was changing course. I responded that American policy remained the same: to replace the communist government in Kabul with a Mujahidin government. The Soviet withdrawal, however, had created a different set of political and military conditions that the United States, Pakistan, and Saudi Arabia could exploit. The United States was urging Soviet leaders to drop Najib as part of a political settlement to end the Afghan war. The Mujahidin needed to directly engage the Soviets toward this end and not allow Najib to monopolize Moscow's attention. Mujahidin military pressure to force the Soviets to remove Najib was important. But it should be viewed as tactical, serving the strategic goal of a transfer of power from Najib to the Mujahidin and a peaceful conclusion to the war consummated by an act of Afghan self-determination. Afghans should be allowed to choose their own leadership during the settlement process. History had repeatedly demonstrated that attempts by outside governments to put their favored Afghans in Kabul always failed.

The wide gap separating Turki's position and mine never spoiled the atmosphere of our negotiations. We shared a mutual interest in Afghanistan and admiration for the Afghan Mujahidin. Turki's personal warmth, soft-spoken style, unfailing courtesy, sense of humor, and deep familiarity with America allowed our conversations to proceed in a comfortable, candid atmosphere.

Our many meetings, however, were inconclusive. We would start by repeating our mutual intention to carry forward American and Saudi cooperation on Afghanistan. Working with Pakistan, our two countries had helped the Mujahidin roll back Soviet expansionism in Afghanistan. We shared a common interest in installing a Mujahidin government in Kabul. The United States and Saudi Arabia would assist with Afghanistan's reconstruction after the war.

When the exchanges turned to what should be done to realize these common goals, they lapsed into reiteration of our two conflicting official positions. I articulated the U.S. policy to support the Afghans in choosing their own leaders. I pointed out that most Saudi private cash to Afghans was going to the divisive extremist elements of the resistance—those opposing a negotiated conclusion of the war. I warned him that isolating the Afghan Shia and strengthening the minority, virulently anti-Shia Sunnis like Sayyaf only drove the Shia into Iran's arms. I recalled that failed Saudi attempts to isolate the Shia in Lebanon had produced just such a result. Iran had radicalized the large Shia minority in southern Lebanon, creating Hezbollah and a dangerous pro-Iranian Shia stronghold on Lebanese territory. During one meeting, I gave Turki a petition that Afghan Hazara Shias had presented to me. It criticized Iran and appealed for inclusion of their representatives in the AIG. He politely accepted the document but did not pursue the topic.

Turki showed no flexibility on Iran. To him, Mujahidin unity translated into Mujahidin Sunni unity against Shia. He warned that Iran was attempting to gain control of the Afghan jihad. It sought to eliminate American and Saudi influence in Afghanistan and place an Afghan Shia regime in Kabul with Soviet assistance. He urged that the United States join Saudi Arabia in recognizing the AIG.

Turki did not accept my suggestion that the AIG be encouraged to reach out to Zahir Shah in Rome. He listened carefully but did not react when I suggested that Saudi Arabia engage Ahmed Shah Masood instead of isolating him. Nor did he respond when I said that radical Mujahidin beneficiaries of Saudi aid considered themselves enemies of the Saudi government as well as of the United States. Turki sat silently as his notetaker scribbled down my cautionary points. Once, he alluded to "internal" difficulties he might face by attempting to influence donations going to Afghan extremists from Saudis outside the government. Most often, he simply observed that the Afghan jihad was immensely popular among Saudis from all walks of life. The government could not control the actions of private Saudi citizens donating money to the Afghan jihad.

I sensed that Turki probably accepted some of my arguments. Even if he agreed, however, he probably would not have been able to persuade important elders in the royal family and the Saudi clergy to accept them. The Saudi commitment to continuing the Afghan war helped to preserve good relations between the royal family and the religious establishment. It defused the threat of Juhaiman al-Otaibi's radical Wahhabism. The Saudi public and wealthy private donors were happy with the status quo. In general, it appeared to me at the time that the Saudi government did not worry very much about what was happening in Afghanistan as long as these internal Saudi audiences were satisfied that their government was defending Islam.

‿

After my meetings with Prince Turki in Riyadh or Jeddah, I often took the late-night flight to Karachi. The composition of passengers on the shiny green and white Saudi Airlines Boeing 747 never varied much. The economy section was always crammed with Pakistanis from the half-million complement of Pakistanis working in the Saudi kingdom. Red-and-white-checkered headdresses blanketed the first-class and business-class sections. My deputy and I usually sat alone in the upstairs compartment. Saudi male and Pakistani female flight attendants walked the aisles. Most passengers slept.

A fascinating contrast between the departure terminal in Jeddah and the arrival terminal in Karachi illuminated the striking differences between the Saudi and South Asian environments. The terminal left behind in Jeddah was as silent as a church on Monday morning. Every square foot of the ultra-modern building had been immaculately cleaned by foreign workers from East and Southeast Asia. The Karachi airport on the other side of the Arabian Sea was a different world altogether. Clamorous, and undisciplined, it was packed with the colorful sea of humanity encountered throughout the sub-continent. People from all of Pakistan's ethnic groups; Sindis, Pashtuns, and Muslim Bihari immigrants from India; Baluch and Punjabis; men in turbans and men in suits; women, veiled and unveiled; and children pushed against one another. Tall, thin porters balancing huge white bundles on their heads made their way through the crowd. Cab drivers trolled for fares, grabbing the suitcases of well-dressed passengers and gesturing toward the exit.

Upon landing in Karachi, the passengers on my flight dispersed. The Pakistani workers traveled back to their rural villages or to lower- and middle-class suburbs in Pakistani cities to reunite with their families. The Saudi and other Arab travelers pursued diverse programs. Most older Saudis, ulema, and religious laymen were committed to Dawa. They planned to spread the tenets of the Wahhabi creed among the more than 3 million Afghan refugees in Pakistan, Pakistani tribesmen in the tribal agencies, and young Arabs on the Frontier who had deviated from the true faith originally preached by Muhammad Ibn Abd al-Wahhab in the eighteenth century.[12]

In some respects, these Saudis resembled the British missionaries of the colonial period. Those earlier proselytizers had built Christian schools, hospitals, and churches. They spread the Christian gospel among the Hindu and Muslim populations of the subcontinent. Their quest to save souls reaped its richest harvest among the poorer rungs of society, the non-literate and un-employed, and the untouchables among Hindus. The Wahhabi missionaries who came to the Frontier in the 1980s and 1990s employed similar methods. Distinguished Saudi professors taught Islamic studies at Sayyaf's Dawa and Jihad University located in the Jalozai refugee camp outside Peshawar. A village in the camp commemorating the Prophet's seventh-century migration from Mecca to Medina housed the Saudi teaching staff and Arab students. One section of Arab charities along the Frontier built hospitals, dispensaries, and orphanages for Afghan refugees. Most operated another section that trained and armed Arab militants to fight in Afghanistan or other countries in the world.

The Wahhabi missionaries and the Christian missionaries who came before them differed in important ways. The latter sought to transform the religious beliefs of the local population to Christianity. The Wahhabi missionaries had a wider agenda. Their ambitions stretched beyond religion to social behavior, politics, and military issues. The Wahhabi curriculum taught enmity toward Christians, Jews, and Muslims, such as Shia and Sufis, not subscribing to the Wahhabi variant of Islam. The most radical among them justified pronunciations of *takfir* (similar to excommunication; see Chapter 8) against *kafirs* ("unbelievers," people claiming to be Muslims but who had left the faith). The educational practices in the thousands of Saudi-financed madrassas located near and inside the 344[13] UN refugee camps along the Frontier emphasized religious indoctrination.[14] Many hundreds of these madrassas turned young Afghan refugees and local Pashtun boys* into fanatics trained to kill Muslims and non-Muslims alike on command. Their methods were no different from those used by American cult leaders David Koresh and James Jones to brainwash their followers; medieval Christian priests motivating non-literate European peasants to war against other Christian sects; or extremist Ikhwan leaders in Saudi Arabia's Nejd in the 1920s to indoctrinate their fighters.

Young radical Wahhabis also took the air bridge from Saudi Arabia to Karachi. They were the heirs of Juhaiman al-Otaibi and his messianic zeal. Some intended to fight, while others came to teach in the madrassas, which played a critical role in the ISI-managed holy war infrastructure on the Frontier. They believed in militant jihad against Islam's foes: Iran, the West, the Saudi royal family, and bin Baz's court ulema. The Wahhabi zealots disseminated Juhaiman's violent doctrine in the madrassas, which, ironically, were financed by the Saudi royal family and Saudi charities.

---

* In the absence of government schools, Pashtun families along the Frontier sent their sons to the religious madrassas, which offered a free education and lunch.

Arab terrorists fleeing from the secret police in their home countries made the terrorist passage to Pakistan unannounced, in small groups or by themselves. They included the Egyptian Ayman al-Zawahiri, his brother Mohammad, and Abdel Rahman, the Blind Sheikh. The Egyptian revolutionaries moved into rented houses in Peshawar's western and northern suburbs, living without passports and without interference from Pakistani authorities. They mixed with ISI officers, Hekmatyar, Sayyaf, and Osama bin Laden. From Peshawar, they sent instructions to their gunmen in Cairo to assassinate Egyptian leaders, security personnel, Coptic Christians, and visiting Western tourists.

Saudi money and Arab manpower played important roles in the functioning of the ISI's holy-war infrastructure of madrassas, military training sites, mosques, and arms depots that were spread out along the Frontier. Author and journalist Peter Bergen estimated the total number of Arabs entering Pakistan during the ten-year Soviet occupation in the "low tens of thousands."[15] A Saudi professor who spent five years teaching at Sayyaf's university during the late 1980s told an interviewer in 2006 that "the majority of Arabs who came to join Jihad did not like military organization and discipline. They were chaotic. Some of them would come in for a week, go on an operation, shoot, fight, invade then return. Some others would come in for a month or two only, and so on."[16]

Most of the jihadis were Saudis, followed by Yemenis, Algerians, and Egyptians. The number of them who actually trained in Hekmatyar, Sayyaf, Haqqani, or Arab camps and crossed into Afghanistan to fight or do humanitarian work during the 1980s likely did not exceed a few thousand. Bergen wrote that the Arab fighters were essentially extras on the battlefield.[17] Abdul Haq and other Mujahidin commanders complained to me that the Arabs were highly motivated but did not have the endurance skills to move rapidly across the mountainous terrain with Afghan Mujahidin to conduct hit-and-run attacks against the enemy and quickly withdraw to fortified bases. They were valuable magnets for Saudi lines of cash, but they endangered the lives of the Mujahidin who felt compelled to protect them during combat.

There were also religious tensions between the Arab fighters and the Afghan Mujahidin. Demands by orthodox Wahhabis that moderate Afghan Sunni Hanafis follow the Wahhabi method of praying angered Mujahidin commanders and fighters.[18] Some Saudis lectured Afghans to discard their Sufi practices, such as worshipping at the graves of saints. In 1989, an Islamic court in Kandahar declared that Wahhabis were unbelievers (*kafir*). One of the leading Arabs on the Frontier, Services Bureau founder Abdullah Azzam, counseled Arab jihadis that no Arab could "find his way into the eyes and hearts of Afghans" by insulting the Hanafi Islam practiced by Afghans. "We cannot," he said, "correct their jihad and their way of thinking."[19]

The Soviet withdrawal from Afghanistan ended the period of active cooperation among the Arab groups in Pakistan. The unifying cause of waging an Afghan holy war against the invader of a Muslim country was gone. Long submerged sectarian, political, national, and personal chasms dividing the Arabs along the Frontier sprang to the surface. The underlying reason for their internecine conflicts was a struggle for power and dominance, not theology. The finer theological divergences only made the resulting clashes between the Arab Islamist factions more deadly.

The deterioration in inter-Arab relations paralleled the upswing in infighting within the Mujahidin after the Soviet withdrawal. A power vacuum now loomed in Kabul. The question of who would fill it after the tottering Najib regime collapsed created cross-cutting coalitions of Arabs and Mujahidin. Some Arabs opposed Pakistan's favorite Mujahidin, Gulbuddin Hekmatyar. Most supported him. Traditional Wahhabi clergy opposed the radical Wahhabi militants. Wahhabi ulema criticized the political Islam of the Muslim Brotherhood. The Muslim Brothers themselves were split between violent revolutionaries led by Zawahiri and Rahman and those urging unity among all the Arab factions to finish the Afghan holy war, led by Abdullah Azzam.

The Arab disputes played out in passionate arguments, intrigues, betrayals, and violence in Peshawar neighborhoods populated by Arabs. They wielded takfir against one another. The "Group of Immigration Against Unbelievers," headed by Algerian Akman al-Jazaeri operated from a house in Peshawar. Al-Jazaeri's self-appointed mission was to identify and kill Arab unbelievers. That meant any Muslim who disagreed with him.[20] A prominent Arab Ikhwani visiting Peshawar in 1989 moaned that Peshawar had "become a horrible place . . . Arabs don't like each other. Takfirs, tensions . . . splinters, fanatic groups."[21]

MAP 15.1   ISLAMIC EXTREMIST FOOTHOLDS IN BORDER AREAS, 1988–1989

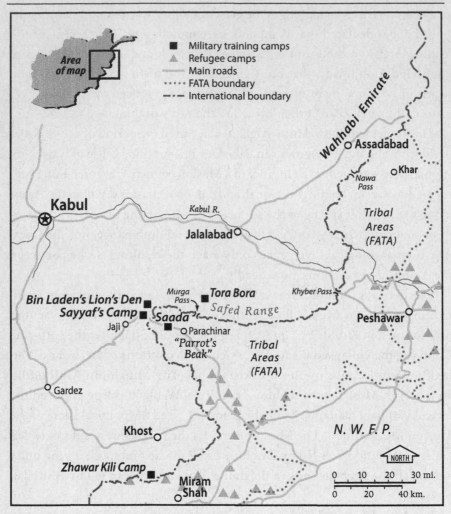

Rivalry between Abdullah Azzam—a Palestinian—and his Algerian son-in-law Abdullah Anas, on one side, and the two Egyptian terrorists Ayman al-Zawahiri and Abdel Rahman, on the other, escalated when the Soviet withdrawal moved into high gear in the middle of 1988. Azzam urged Arab unity behind finishing the Afghan jihad before moving on to other jihads. He exhorted Arabs in Pakistan to meld with Afghan resistance groups and not to create separate Arab combat units, which Zawahiri and Rahman were doing. He disputed the Egyptians' violent terrorist tactics in Egypt, which endangered innocent civilians, and opposed their demand to overthrow the al-Saud monarchy. Zawahiri and Rahman at the time were already busy organizing terrorist attacks in Egypt and other countries. They were also establishing small, exclusively Arab training bases in Khost, Paktiya, and Nangarhar in order to prepare Arab fighters primarily for overthrowing the Egyptian government, but also for global jihad. A Wahhabi alim close to Azzam at Sayyaf's university accused Zawahiri's Egyptian jihad of having "no roots in the jihad battlefield."[22] The two feuding Arab factions each vied for Osama bin Laden's personal attention, support, and money. Beginning in about 1986, the year Zawahiri moved permanently to Peshawar, bin Laden had already begun to shift away from his old mentor, Azzam, toward Zawahiri and Rahman.

Bin Laden constructed a small military base, "the Lion's Den," for about a dozen Arab fighters near Sayyaf's camp in Paktiya in late 1986. The small encampment, which he named after himself (Osama means "lion"), signaled his rejection of Azzam's Afghanistan-focused strategy. Some journalists and scholars have speculated that Zawahiri's ability as a doctor to attend to bin Laden's serious liver ailment may have helped him pull bin Laden to his side. It is more likely that the strong-willed bin Laden made the decision to opt for global jihad on his own. After the Soviets left Afghanistan in 1989, Rahman and Zawahiri engaged in fierce debates with each other over their share of bin Laden's money and tactical issues. Rahman abandoned Peshawar later that year. He traveled to Sudan and onward to the United States, where he was arrested for involvement in the 1993 World Trade Center bombing. Bin Laden and Zawahiri strengthened their alliance of sanctified terrorism on a global scale "to unite all Muslims and establish a government which follows the rule of the caliphs."[23]

Despite their political and ideological estrangement, Azzam and bin Laden avoided the appearance of a formal split. Abdullah Anas later recalled that "the disagreements among Abdullah Azzam and bin Laden were very confidential and secretive and except for three or four people, no one else knew about it." Bin Laden could not disregard Azzam's reputation in the Arab world as the foremost promoter of the Afghan jihad. Azzam's personal contacts reached high into the Saudi royal family and the kingdom's Wahhabi clergy. Azzam, on his part, must have valued bin Laden's continuing donations to his Services Bureau.[24]

In August 1988 bin Laden and Zawahiri established al-Qaeda al-Askariya (The Military Base) across the border in Paktiya near the Lion's Den and Sayyaf's Jaji camp. Bin Laden's al-Qaeda terrorist movement took its name from the base and became the organizational springboard for his and Za-wahiri's global terrorist operations.

The ISI's high regard for bin Laden was indicated by its approval for him to organize and train his Arab militia force of about three hundred Arab militants at his new base. Bin Laden reciprocated the ISI's favors by helping to fund the Pakistani intelligence agency's and Nawaz Sharif's manipulation of the December 1988 parliamentary elections to deny Benazir Bhutto a parliamentary majority. In October 1989, Bhutto accused bin Laden of pay-ing members of Pakistan's parliament to overthrow her in a no-confidence vote. Bin Laden left Pakistan for Saudi Arabia after the vote failed and Bhutto continued as prime minister. The Saudi government confiscated his passport.[25]

҂

While bin Laden and Zawahiri were organizing al-Qaeda, Azzam was trekking through Afghanistan's Hindu Kush mountain passes to the Panshir Valley for a rendezvous with northern commander Ahmed Shah Masood. Abdullah Anas had spent the three previous summers with Masood. He told Azzam that ISI and Hekmatyar's anti-Masood propaganda was false.[26] Ma-sood was a conservative and observant Muslim. He was also the single most successful Afghan commander in Afghanistan. Azzam sent an Iraqi Ikhwani, Abu Abbas, to confirm Anas's opinion of Masood. Abbas returned with an even more enthusiastic appraisal of the Tajik commander than the one Anas had delivered.[27]

Azzam's trip to visit Masood stretched from August into September 1989 and lasted six weeks. Jamiat party leader Burhanuddin Rabbani accompanied him to the Panshir before returning to Pakistan. Azzam brought along his two sons, Muhammad, then twenty-three, and Ibrahim, fourteen. He recorded lengthy diary notes about his long conversations with Masood, Masood's commanders, and Arabs he encountered on his trip and the history, landscape, and people of the north. He constantly worried about the effects of the cold and the trip's arduous conditions on his sons' health.

Azzam spent many hours with Masood and his commanders. He came to extol Masood as the perfect combination of a holy warrior, an inspiring leader of Muslim soldiers and people, and an adherent to the faith. Azzam hailed Masood's military successes against Soviet forces, victories that no other Afghan commander had achieved. In his diary he noted Masood's polite, humble style and the admiration accorded him by commanders from all ethnic groups and ordinary Afghans. He wrote: "From the five heavy folds on his forehead, which were the sign of a difficult life, I could read his tale of pain and misery and the heavy responsibility of a jihad placed on him since he was very young; the heavy scars in his soul and body have taken away his youth."[28]

Azzam expressed amazement at how much Masood was able to accomplish with so little assistance from Pakistan. In one conversation with Masood, he quoted the lines of an Arab poet, Yusuf Abu Halala, to explain his feelings about the commander:

> *I want to kiss your sword*
> *I want to serve you if you want me*
> *I want to clean the dust from your boots*

Before leaving the Panshir, Azzam was moved to compose his own poem about Masood's valor:

> *I have been targeted and wounded by arrows from all directions*
> *My chest was covered with blood*
> *Each time I moved, I was pushed back by spears*
> *Finally, I wasn't afraid*
> *And the fear itself was sacrificed*[29]

The more Azzam engaged Masood, the more he became committed to supporting him. On returning to Peshawar from the Panshir Valley, Azzam defended Masood at an in absentia "trial" conducted by twenty-three Arabs accusing Masood of "servitude to the West and being an infidel." The charge sheet also claimed he was a Shia posing as a Sunni.[30] Azzam, bin Laden, and a Yemeni cleric presided. Bin Laden, the Yemeni, and nearly all of the Arabs at the trial spoke against Masood. Azzam, Anas, and another Arab who fought with Masood defended him. Azzam proclaimed during the proceedings: "I will praise Masood until the last day of my life." The "court" deadlocked. No decision was issued for or against Masood. After the trial, Azzam wrote a book about his trip to the north and his meetings with Masood.[31] He planned to publish the book, entitled *A Month with Heroes*, at his Services Bureau's printing facility.

In October 1989, Azzam flew to Saudi Arabia determined to create a positive image of Masood in the Saudi kingdom and to raise money for him. His public speeches and interviews in Saudi cities coined fresh variations of praise for Masood. He was the "warrior-saint" of Islam. Masood's military genius was greater than Napoleon's. Masood had defeated the Russians; Napoleon could not. In one speech, Azzam criticized Pakistan's treatment of Masood as a "disobedient person." He remarked that "most propaganda against Masood is spread by Pakistani generals" and observed that "Masood did not trust Pakistanis and always feared that they might assassinate him."[32]

The Pakistani embassy in Riyadh and Hekmatyar's representatives in Saudi Arabia undoubtedly reported Azzam's glorification of Masood and his criticism of Pakistan's attempts to discredit him back to Pakistan. Azzam's public statements and the news that he was about to publish his book on Masood set the stage for a confrontation with Hekmatyar after he returned to Peshawar.

Azzam remained highly respected in Arab and Afghan Mujahidin circles, despite his estrangement from bin Laden and Zawahiri. His one-man drive to assist Masood, however, was undermining the ISI's forward strategy in Afghanistan. Azzam was based in Pakistan. He was therefore treading on dangerous ground.

Soon after Azzam returned to Peshawar, Hekmatyar requested that he come alone to his office. Abu Talha, Azzam's Kuwaiti assistant, accompanied him to the meeting. Hekmatyar personally barred Talha from entering his office. When Azzam emerged from Hekmatyar's office, Talha noted he had an angry look on his face. When Talha asked him what happened in the meeting, Azzam curtly responded: "I received a warning. If this book is published, I will receive a bullet." Azzam decided to set the Masood book aside to be published at a later date.

On November 24, 1989, Azzam and his two sons were driving to Friday prayers at Sab'al Layl Mosque on Jamrud Road in Peshawar. Many Arabs of different nationalities regularly attended prayers there. Azzam's oldest son, Muhammad, had arrived home from Jordan the previous day with his new wife. He and Ibrahim were in the car with Azzam. Azzam was scheduled to deliver the Friday sermon at the mosque.

As the car approached the mosque, a huge bomb that had been placed inside a small water canal adjacent to the road was detonated. A Saudi friend of Azzam's recalled: "Upon hearing the news, we each ran to the mosque and saw the scattered bodies.... His sons had been blown to pieces, some of their remaining limbs were found fifty meters away, or hanging from trees. The Sheikh's body was kept intact though, and there were no visible wounds on it."[33] As with the dozens of political assassinations in Peshawar during the 1980s and 1990s, no culprits were ever detained. No trials were held, and no one was ever convicted or jailed. Probably no serious attempt was made to find the guilty.

Osama bin Laden had moved back to Saudi Arabia two weeks before Azzam's assassination, but his absence from Peshawar did not prevent some from suspecting that he was complicit in Azzam's murder. During a 1998 interview with al-Jazeera, bin Laden brushed aside an accusation by an Arab, Muhammad Sadiq Howayda, who had trained in one of his camps, that he commissioned Azzam's assassination. Bin Laden blamed the American government for the accusation, "for which it has no evidence."[34]

Azzam's son-in-law, Abdullah Anas, later accused bin Laden of organizing Abdullah Azzam's murder. A prominent Saudi cleric living in Peshawar implicated Zawahiri's Egyptian Jihad group: "They hated Sheikh Abdullah Azzam, possibly seeing him as an obstacle to the execution of their own agenda in Afghanistan."[35]

Circumstantial evidence on Azzam's assassination also points to Hekmatyar and ISI. Azzam joined the long line of victims assassinated in Pakistan who posed an obstacle to Hekmatyar's path to power. It is noteworthy that Azzam's book was not published until 1996, the year the ISI abandoned Hekmatyar, the Taliban captured Kabul, and Hekmatyar fled to Iran.

꙰

Jamil ur-Rahman, an Afghan cleric who embraced Wahhabism, established his independent emirate in the Konar Valley in 1990.[36] His headquarters were in Assadabad, the provincial capital. Saudi King Fahd and Chief Mufti bin Baz donated generously to Rahman's emirate. Saudi mosques and private Saudi businessmen pumped many millions more into his 5,000-man army, his mosques, his religious madrassas, and his network of social services. Hundreds of Saudi fighters, clerics, and teachers fought for Rahman and staffed the emirate's offices. Rahman gave his emirate the Arabic name *Jamiat al-Dawat al-Koran w-al Sunnah* (Society to Preach the Koran and Sunnah). He advocated living in the way of the Prophet and his companions in the first century of Islam. Along with his Afghan and Arab followers, he propagated the Dawa in Konar and adjoining provinces.

Rahman had earned a reputation as a brave resistance leader during the Soviet occupation. His local popularity and membership in the Safi tribe, Konar's largest, helped him win an election as Konar's provincial governor in 1989. But Konar was a dangerous place. Rahman's patron, the Saudi kingdom, lay 1,000 miles from his emirate. Pakistan was in between. As Rahman's emirate grew, Hekmatyar, Khalis, and the AIG refused to recognize his election. They appointed their own Konar governors. Rahman's superior ability to attract Saudi cash angered AIG Prime Minister Sayyaf. The Peshawar-based Arab Muslim Brotherhood and Zawahiri detested him. Most ominously, the ISI was growing suspicious of Rahman's expanding kingdom, one that it did not control, especially after he declared that his emirate was an independent country on January 30, 1991.

In December 1990 Jamil ur-Rahman sent me a two-page letter responding to my request that he release twelve USAID trucks he had seized as they were delivering wheat to villages in Konar. His letter informed me that the wheat was safely stored in one of his warehouses "as a trust." Rahman went on to claim that his emirate's control of Konar Province was complete. He wrote that he had captured a nearby Nangarhar district from the Najib regime and was in the process of driving regime troops from a Laghman district also bordering Konar. He requested that U.S. assistance to villages located in his emirate be sent directly to his government for distribution. Unable to recognize his Islamic emirate's independence and concerned about Rahman's proclivity to hijack wheat, USAID halted shipments to areas under Rahman's control.

Rahman's expanding Islamic emirate became the second-largest Wahhabi state in the world. Footage of bearded emirate soldiers marching in unison carrying shiny Kalashnikov rifles, and of beautiful Saudi-style mosques and newly constructed madrassas and hospitals was broadcast to TV audiences in Saudi Arabia. Rahman's border police allowed only bearded men and fully veiled women into the emirate. He banned tobacco and the display of flags. His security forces sought out and destroyed the tombs of venerated Sufi saints in the territory he controlled. Rahman asked the International Committee of the Red Cross (ICRC) to cease using its Red Cross emblem in the area. When ICRC representatives demurred, he politely informed them that he no longer needed ICRC assistance.[37] Rahman's forces stopped convoys belonging to Hekmatyar and other commanders passing through his emirate and confiscated the arms, ammunition, and food they were transporting. Some professors at Sayyaf's Dawa and Jihad University shifted to Rahman's better-endowed madrassas. Rahman began to eclipse Sayyaf's fund-raising in Saudi Arabia.

Pakistan's generals and ISI officials worried about Rahman's burgeoning emirate. Rahman, like Azzam earlier, had grown too independent of ISI influence. He had declared independence. He was humiliating Hekmatyar. His security forces were blocking Hekmatyar's military supply corridor through the Nawa Pass into Konar and onward to the provinces in the north and around Kabul. His emirate now abutted Masood-controlled areas. An alliance between the two anti-Hekmatyar Mujahidin would threaten Pakistan's pivot into Afghanistan. Rahman had to be eliminated and his emirate destroyed.

Rahman's capital, Assadabad, was located 30 miles north of the Pakistani border at the Nawa Pass entrance to Konar; his forces occupied a checkpoint on the Afghan side of the border. In July 1991, Hekmatyar mounted an attack from Pakistan through the Nawa Pass and up the Konar road toward Assadabad. A simultaneous assault was launched from Hekmatyar's bases in Nangarhar. The fighting was intense. Saudi ulema in the emirate frantically contacted Saudi ambassador Motabbakani in Islamabad. Motabbakani appealed to the ISI to halt Hekmatyar's military operation. Rahman offered a cease-fire and suggested outside mediation. Hekmatyar rejected the cease-fire and pressed his assault, only to suffer defeats on both fronts. Rahman's army of Arabs and Afghans reoccupied their checkpoint at the Nawa Pass.

After his defeat, Hekmatyar agreed to mediate his differences with Rahman—but it was a tactical ruse. The Hezb firebrand and the ISI prepared another attack, this one backed up by Pakistani troops and artillery.[38] On August 27, 1991, the second offensive commenced with a Pakistani artillery bombardment of emirate forces clustered on the Afghan side of the border before the Nawa Pass. High-caliber Pakistani machine-gun fire rained down on the Afghan and Arab defenders from the mountain ridge above the pass. A column of Hekmatyar fighters and Pakistani soldiers, disguised as Mujahidin, fought their way through the pass and attacked Assadabad. Ambassador Motabbakani rushed to Peshawar to stop the fighting, arriving just before midnight on August 29. He asked the AIG president, Sibghatullah Mojaddedi, to intervene with Hekmatyar. Mojaddedi agreed. But the AIG president exercised no influence over the ISI or Hekmatyar.

That same day, Jamil ur-Rahman fled to a family residence in Khar, across the border in Pakistan's Bajaur tribal agency. The next day, Friday, August 30, during the noon prayer hour, an Egyptian dressed in the long white robes of a Wahhabi preacher made an unannounced call on Rahman while he prayed on a carpet laid out on the ground inside the compound. The visitor was Sharif Ali, a twenty-four-year-old journalist who had lived in Peshawar under the alias Abdullah Roomi. He had previously worked for the Muslim Brotherhood's Arabic-language newspaper, *al Jihad*. More recently, he had been employed by Sayyaf's Arabic-language *al Bunyan*.

Around the same time, families living about half a mile away noticed a Hezb vehicle parked near their homes with three men inside. At about 12:30 p.m., three sharp pistol shots reverberated off nearby mountains, and the vehicle slowly pulled away. It moved in a southwesterly direction, on the road back to Peshawar.[39] The families later concluded that the Hezb occupants were there to confirm that Ali had carried out the assassination.

Rahman died instantly. The guards posted outside the house seized Ali and placed him in a locked room in the house. Rahman's relatives wrapped Rahman's body in white cloth to prepare it for burial.

Pakistani police soon appeared at the front door and asked to question the assassin. This stimulated an intensive but hushed debate among Rahman's relatives inside the house. They believed that Rahman's bitter foes, the ISI and Hekmatyar, were behind his assassination. The perpetrators of dozens of political assassinations of Afghans in Pakistan who opposed Hekmatyar had never been arrested and brought to justice. Handing the assassin over to the Pakistani police meant delivering him to those ultimately guilty of Rahman's murder. On the order of the family elder present, the guards unlocked the room holding Ali and gunned him down.[40]

Rahman's murder shocked the Saudi royal family, Chief Mufti bin Baz, and the broader Saudi religious establishment. On September 4, King Fahd dispatched a six-person delegation, headed by his personal special envoy, Abdullah al-Muhsin al-Turki, to Islamabad. Turki, dean of the renowned Mohammad al-Saud University in Riyadh, asked the Pakistani president, Ghulam Ishak Khan; Army Chief Mirza Beg; and the ISI to spare Rahman's Wahhabi state. His appeal was ignored. Hekmatyar would not have attacked without Pakistani guidance and assistance.

At a formal luncheon held in honor of the visiting Saudi delegation covered by the media, the secretary general of Pakistan's Foreign Ministry attempted to put Rahman's assassination to rest. "Saudi Arabia and Pakistan," he announced, "had agreed to work together for promotion of unity among Afghan Mujahidin."[41]

A Pakistani helicopter took al-Turki to the Pakistani border to meet with Hekmatyar. He asked the Hezb leader to resolve his differences with Rahman's successor, Maulawi Samiullah. (In Peshawar, rumors circulated that al-Turki sweetened his request by handing over a package containing over $1 million.) But only a husk of Rahman's domain was allowed to remain. The emirate, shorn of independent military and political capabilities, would not rise again. The ISI resumed sending weapons through Konar to Hezb commanders around Kabul and in northern Afghanistan. It coordinated with extremist Arabs to create bases in eastern Konar Province to train and equip the Lashkar-i Taiba Pakistani religious militia to attack targets in Indian-occupied Kashmir and in the Indian heartland. Foreign graduates of the Lashkar-i Taiba camps were also sent to the Balkans and the Middle East to conduct holy war.

The destruction of Jamil ur-Rahman and his kingdom sent a message to the Saudi government and clerical establishment that Pakistan would not tolerate independent, Saudi-supported footholds inside Afghanistan. Saudi funding for the ISI's holy-war infrastructure on the Frontier was welcome. So was Saudi money to finance mosques and Islamic education centers inside Pakistan. But the Saudi cash register would not be permitted to disrupt the Pakistani Army's plans to install Hekmatyar in Kabul.

The assassinations of Abdullah Azzam and Jamil ur-Rahman were painful setbacks for Riyadh and precursors of more to come. Azzam and Rahman were highly esteemed in the kingdom. Rahman's emirate was a source of pride, a venerated manifestation of Saudi ideology and Dawa advancing across Afghanistan's mountains and valleys.

Pakistan's generals correctly assumed that they could still count on the continued flow of Saudi funds. That calculation outlasted Azzam's and Rahman's demise. There would, however, be limits to Saudi forbearance. Saudi Arabia's returns from its investments in Afghanistan would steadily shrink during the 1990s. After 9/11, Pakistan would find it increasingly difficult to bridge the chasm between al-Qaeda intrigues to overthrow the al-Saud dynasty and the dynasty's will to stay in power.

CHAPTER 16

Desperately Seeking Moderates

Our main difficulty is with ourselves. I am not pessimistic we can find a solution. No Afghan regime or political party will ever be very much different from the Afghan society to which they belong.
—ZAHIR SHAH, 1990[1]

The failed Hekmatyar-Tanai coup attempt of March 6 and 7, 1990, exposed the utter dependence of the Najib regime and the seven Mujahidin party leaders on their respective foreign sponsors. Only pressure from Soviet advisers on Interior Minister Aslam Watanjar saved Najib during the ferocious fighting in Kabul. Watanjar could have betrayed Najib and his own Khalqi faction, but he would not cross the KGB. Hekmatyar's ISI-trained Army of Sacrifice never penetrated the capital's outer defenses. Najib survived. Tanai escaped to the ISI and to Hekmatyar's open arms in Pakistan. The ISI integrated five Khalqi generals and hundreds of Soviet-trained Khalqi armor, artillery, and communications specialists defecting with Tanai into Hekmatyar's conventional battalions.

Najib temporarily strengthened his position in the aftermath of the coup attempt. In terms of leadership skills, dynamism, and charisma, he was superior to any of the seven Mujahidin party leaders in Peshawar. The Afghan dictator's KHAD bastion of power, led by Ghulam Farouk Yaqubi, his former deputy, proved its loyalty during the fighting. Najib purged over 3,000 Khalqi officers and soldiers in the Afghan Army and Air Force. But the Afghan president was unable to change the basic structure of dispersed military power among government security agencies left over from the Soviet occupation. Moscow's legs were out of Afghanistan, but its hands remained. The five hundred Soviet KGB and military advisers still in Afghanistan continued to perform Moscow's balancing act with Parchamis and Khalqis. Soviet economic and military aid sustained Najib's regime.

Soviet "divide-and-rule" tactics after the occupation deterred Najib from completely eliminating the Khalqi foothold in the military and the Interior Ministry police forces. No one PDPA entity—the presidency, the army, air force, KHAD, or the Ministry of the Interior—was able to accumulate overwhelming power and independence. The KGB manipulated the chronic contention among Afghan tribal and ethnic factions inside the regime to stay in control, just as the ISI was doing with the seven divided leaders in Peshawar—and just as the Mughals and Iranian Safavids had done three centuries earlier.

The KGB and ISI tactics were effective in the short run, but in the long run both spy agencies were destined for strategic failure. Najib's and Hekmatyar's dependence on Soviet and Pakistani patronage, respectively, rendered them illegitimate in the eyes of the Afghan population. Tanai's switch to Hekmatyar and the ISI demonstrated the KGB's inability to contain the Khalq-Parcham vendetta. The coup shattered the false veneer of PDPA unity that Soviet negotiators were peddling in U.S.-Soviet negotiations.

Najib's appointment of Watanjar to replace Tanai as defense minister did not stop Khalqis from plotting against him. Najib knew that Watanjar's primary loyalty lay with the Soviets, and that his secondary loyalty was to the Khalqis who still dominated the army, not to him personally or to the party. Watanjar had led the tank assaults that ousted King Zahir Shah in 1973 and Daoud in 1978. He remained a dangerous foe.

Anti-Najib intrigues within Najib's own Parcham faction proliferated after the Khalqi coup collapse. His Parchami opponents worried that the Afghan dictator would next turn on them to further consolidate his power. Babrak Karmal's brother, Mahmoud Baryalai, led one of the three Parcham groups in the PDPA seeking to oust Najib. KHAD reported to Najib that Baryalai loyalists in the presidential palace were conspiring against him. Najib fired his food taster and dismissed several colonels and lieutenant colonels in his Presidential Guard.[2]

Outside the palace, some of Najib's senior Parchami generals began to engage in more frequent dialogue with Ahmed Shah Masood. General Azimi, commander of the Kabul garrison, and General Asif Delawar, chief of staff, concluded an informal cease-fire agreement with the northern commander. General Abdul Rashid Dostum, commander of 40,000 mostly Uzbek fighters, monitored the anti-Najib intrigues in Kabul. Dostum's military commitment to Najib was financial rather than personal or ideological. In the Afghan environment, it was therefore fungible. Dostum was a warlord, essentially a paid mercenary. He constantly measured the direction of the prevailing political winds and estimated Najib's ability to pay. Any wavering of Soviet assistance to Najib would prompt him to reevaluate his options.

On the other side of the Durand Line, the Tanai coup attempt threw Pakistan's divide-and-rule strategy into disarray. The ISI's undisguised attempt to insert Hekmatyar into Kabul over the heads of the other six party leaders left the Mujahidin even more fractured than Najib's shaky regime. Although completely financed by the Soviet Union, Najib's government functioned as well as many others in the Third World. The AIG did not function at all, and the coup only magnified the AIG's irrelevance.

The majority of Afghans scorned the ISI-created AIG. The four extremists— Gulbuddin Hekmatyar, Abdul Rasoul Sayyaf, Yunus Khalis, and Burhanuddin Rabbani—constantly conspired against one another. So did the three AIG moderates. Sayyid Ahmad Gailani aggressively exhibited his rejection of AIG President Sibghatullah Mojaddedi's leadership pretensions during a call by Mojaddedi, Gailani, and Mohammad Nabi Mohammadi on Saudi King Fahd in his royal palace. In a gesture of personal respect, the king gifted his personal band of prayer beads to Mojaddedi, the titular head of the AIG. Gailani quickly objected, observing, "There are three of us here." Caught in an awkward situation, the Saudi monarch ordered a courtier to bring two more prayer bead sets for Gailani and Nabi.

The Tanai coup's exposure of the Hekmatyar-Tanai alliance escalated squabbling among the seven leaders about their individual dialogues with the regime, the Soviets, and Iran. Hekmatyar shrugged off Mojaddedi's pronouncement of *takfir* against him for aligning with Tanai.[3] Khalis criticized Mojaddedi's and Gailani's visits to Tehran to meet with the Iranian Hezb-i Wahdat group of eight Afghan Shia parties. In November 1990, Gailani traveled to Geneva for his much-publicized "secret" meeting with Najib. The other leaders scoffed at Gailani's claim that he had squeezed "concessions" from Najib. Mojaddedi maintained his own back channel to his relative, Suleeman Laik, a high regime official and one of the founders of the PDPA.

❦

The stalemate in Afghanistan enlivened discussions in interagency meetings in Washington. I began to question basic assumptions underlying U.S. Afghan policy and advocated change. Before the Tanai coup, I had grown increasingly convinced that Pakistan was implementing a two-faced Afghan policy. The Pakistani Foreign Ministry's criticism of Beg and Gul's support for an Afghan extremist military victory in Afghanistan, echoed by Edmund McWilliams and other disgruntled U.S. embassy diplomats, was the first sign of fundamental differences on Afghan policy. During the next eight months up to the Tanai coup, the ISI's blatant favoritism for the anti-American Hekmatyar, the assassinations of moderate Afghans in Peshawar, and the ineffective, irremediable AIG also indicated that our Pakistani ally was playing a double game. I thought that the Tanai coup attempt could not have been a rogue operation. The ISI was firmly inside the Pakistani military hierarchy and General Beg was Pakistan's military commander.

CIA officers objected to my assessment that a battlefield stalemate existed in Afghanistan. They claimed the Mujahidin were winning. Others advocated acceptance of the Mikhail Gorbachev and Eduard Shevardnadze proposal for a Najib-Mujahidin power-sharing coalition government. The National Security Council's Richard Haass told participants in a Kimmitt Group meeting that the time had come for the Mujahidin to negotiate a peace agreement directly with Najib. I felt that this was not possible. There was no legitimate interlocutor in the resistance capable of talking to Najib. During interagency discussions I injected some Mujahidin realities that had to be factored into U.S.-Soviet negotiations on an Afghan political settlement. Despite their chronic disunity, there was unanimity among moderate and extremist Afghans on one issue: that Najib and his closest associates could neither participate in a political settlement process nor share power in postwar Afghanistan. The United States must proceed on the assumption that any U.S.-Soviet agreement that involved resistance acceptance of Najib and his associates would be rejected in strong and violent terms by a broad spectrum of the resistance. This was not a value judgment; it was a fact I had learned after hundreds of meetings with Afghans.

In Congress, I faced rising opposition to the administration's unproductive Afghan policy. Congressmen and their aides read media reports about clashes between "the CIA, which seeks an outright guerrilla victory, and the State Department."[4] Congressional staffers forwarded papers to members of Congress documenting the absence of resistance military activity and the fatal flaws of the AIG. Senator Gordon Humphrey (R-NH) and representatives Don Ritter (R-PA) and Dana Rohrabacher (R-CA) criticized Pakistan for cutting off assistance to Masood and Ismael Khan. Anthony Beilenson (D-CA), chairman of the House Intelligence Committee, demanded an explanation of why American aid was going to the Afghan extremists. House hearings on Afghanistan ended in spirited debates between Beilenson and Steve Solarz (D-NY), on one side, and Charlie Wilson (D-TX) and Henry Hyde (R-IL), on the other. Charlie would pound the table and vociferously demand that America not abandon the Mujahidin.

The Democrats held majorities in both houses. Charlie Wilson utilized his considerable legislative skills to round up enough fellow House Democrats to join the Republican minority in approving appropriations for the Afghan covert and USAID programs. In the Senate, I devoted considerable time and effort to private meetings with moderate Democrats David L. Boren (Oklahoma), John Glenn (Ohio), and Sam Nunn (Georgia) and Republican William Cohen (Maine) and their staffs to gain their votes. Boren's staffer, future CIA director George Tenet, gave me good advice on points to make with the senators.

The congressional strategy worked, but just barely. In early 1990, Congress voted to continue supplying covert aid to the resistance but reduced the level from $300 million in 1989 to $250 million.[5] Congressmen and senators supportive of Afghanistan privately warned me after the votes were cast that time was running out for Mujahidin appropriations.

Congress's continued (although somewhat reduced) appropriations for Afghanistan, the shock of the Tanai coup, and the AIG's impotence and the long lapse in Mujahidin military momentum created an opening for new ideas to achieve an Afghan political settlement. In interagency meetings, I proposed three policy initiatives. The first two, establishing a U.S. diplomatic opening to Zahir Shah and strengthening contact with Masood, dated back to the fall of 1989. The third was encouraging a National Commanders' Shura.

I recommended that the United States work with Pakistan, Saudi Arabia, and the Mujahidin to help the Afghans create a national shura of commanders to coordinate military operations inside Afghanistan.[6] If the shura was broadly representative of all Afghan groups, it would increase military pressure on the regime and force a political settlement. The ISI would need to properly supply the shura with weapons and encryption-capable communications equipment. Most important, it would have to give the commanders leeway to make their own decisions on military strategy and tactics. I predicted that Hekmatyar and the minority Mujahidin radicals in Peshawar would become progressively isolated if the commanders' shura got off the ground and expanded.

To increase political and psychological pressure on Najib's regime, I proposed that the United States initiate a dialogue with Zahir Shah, an idea that had been postponed by the CIA the previous September. The CIA's dire warnings that my visit to Rome would undercut the ISI's fall offensive had proved to be wrong. The ISI-led offensive had failed anyway. Zahir Shah was a symbol of tolerance, nationalism, and political moderation among Afghans. A majority of the Afghan population retained favorable memories of his reign. His decade of democracy had been a time of relative peace and stability, and he remained a potential force for peace in Afghanistan.

Resistance radicals, especially Hekmatyar and Sayyaf, viewed the former monarch as a threat to their ambitions, and they would oppose his association with resistance politics. The ISI would probably oppose a U.S. opening to Zahir Shah. Prime Minister Benazir Bhutto and Foreign Minister Yaqub Khan, however, would support one. I proposed that the Zahir Shah dialogue not be limited to the United States. He should conduct separate negotiations with Pakistan, Saudi Arabia, and the AIG.

My final recommendation was to reach out to Masood in the north. I was in communication with Masood through letters. I had met with his brother, Ahmed Zia, on each of my trips to Pakistan. The USAID road into his area had been a gesture of American support. I believed that his involvement in the commanders' initiative was vital to giving it a nationwide character. I could communicate directly with Masood and with Pashtun commanders to encourage Masood's participation in a commanders' shura. I could also ask the Pakistani foreign minister and Prince Turki to receive emissaries from Masood. The Pakistani and Saudi dialogues with Zahir Shah and Masood

would benefit the political settlement process by opening up long-closed political space for moderate-nationalist Mujahidin.

Perhaps owing to the absence of any other ideas to break the depressing
Afghan deadlock, Under Secretary Kimmitt and most of the other participants in the policy review group accepted my recommendations. The CIA
reiterated its objection to the Zahir Shah initiative but approved the commanders' shura concept and the outreach to Masood. The agency's support
for the commanders' shura was essential to selling the idea to the ISI and to
Prince Turki. Under Secretary Kimmitt overruled the CIA regarding my
Rome visit to meet with Zahir Shah.

Kimmitt added two more initiatives to the new Afghan policy package.
The first was to renew negotiations with the Soviet Union on a U.S.-Soviet
cessation of arms to the Afghan belligerents, or "negative symmetry." The
second was to pass the lead on an Afghan political settlement to the UN secretary general and his special envoy, Benon Sevan. Sevan could now try his
hand at piecing together an Afghan political settlement. The United States
would step back and support his efforts.

I shuttled back to Riyadh, Islamabad, and the Pakistani Frontier in April and
May 1990. The Saudi, Pakistani, and Mujahidin response to opening a dialogue with Zahir Shah and supporting a countrywide shura of Afghan commanders was largely positive. Prince Turki agreed to provide funds to the
commanders' initiative and to receive Zahir Shah's envoys. Noting that Saudi
Arabia recognized the AIG, Turki suggested that I ask Zahir Shah to support
the AIG shura process. In Islamabad, Foreign Minister Yaqub Khan and Foreign Secretary Ahmad Khan Tanvir strongly supported both initiatives. ISI
Director Shamsur Kallue gave his backing. The Foreign Ministry and Kallue,
like Turki, asked me to urge Zahir Shah to endorse the AIG's sponsorship of
a new shura. That would, I knew, be a bitter pill for the king to swallow, but
one that might dissuade Pakistan's generals from again derailing a U.S. dialogue with the king. Foreign Secretary Tanvir informed me that Pakistan was
ready to receive Zahir Shah's representatives.

In Peshawar, I explained the rationale for my visit to Rome to the extremists
and moderates in the AIG. Sayyaf predictably opposed the idea; Khalis was
distressed by it; Rabbani noncommittal; and the three moderates supportive.

I spent many hours with a group of important moderate commanders Abdul Haq brought together to help him organize the commanders' shura: Amin Wardak (Pashtun, Wardak), Mullah Malang (Pashtun, Badghis), Taj Mohammad, known as Qari Baba (Pashtun, Ghazni), and Mullah Sayed Hasan Jaglan (Hazara, Ghazni).* I counseled them to confine their planning activity to military matters and to stay out of politics. I suggested they engage Masood and Ismael Khan and bring Shia commanders into the shura. I also sent a letter to Masood recommending that he join the commanders' shura.

I asked Hank Cushing, the USAID representative in Peshawar, to keep the construction equipment for Masood's road on the other side of the Hindu Kush during the winter months of 1990–1991. Work to extend Masood's road from Topkana on the Pakistan border to Zebak near the Soviet border should not be postponed until the snow melted in the mountains; it could commence in the spring of 1991 so that the road would reach Zebak by the end of the year. From Zebak, the Russian-built road network to other northern areas would give Masood vehicular access throughout the north and down to the Shomali Plain bordering Kabul.

For the United States, the road would serve four purposes. First, it would demonstrate direct American support for Masood. Second, it would strengthen his ties to the Peshawar-based National Commanders' Shura. Third, it would give him access to weapons, ammunition, and food supplies available on the open market in Pakistan. Most important, in the event of Najib's unexpected collapse, it would substantially strengthen his ability to move on Kabul from the north before Hekmatyar and Tanai could attack from the south. If a political solution could not be obtained before Najib's regime disintegrated, the cause of peace in Afghanistan would be better served if Masood captured Kabul before Hekmatyar could. Masood supported a broad-based, inclusive outcome of the Afghan war. Hekmatyar did not. His declared goal was violent international jihad.

ψ

Unfortunately, in 1990, Zahir Shah was the only truly national figure in the bleak, fragmented Afghan landscape. There was no other resistance entity,

---

* *Jaglan* means "major." Some Afghans, on reaching that rank, keep it as part of their name.

political or military, that enjoyed even a sliver of national leadership legitimacy among the Afghan people. My principal objective in our meetings was to urge him to lend his stature to a political settlement of the Afghan war.

At Pakistan and Saudi insistence, his backing of the AIG shura process was a price he had to pay to begin a political dialogue with the United States. My negotiating partner, the intermediary who had to present this condition to Zahir Shah, was Abdul Sattar Sirat, Zahir Shah's former deputy prime minister and justice minister. A trained Islamic jurist, Sirat, sixty-five, lived in Saudi Arabia and taught Islamic studies at King Abdulaziz University in Jeddah. He was short, balding, pleasant, and polite, a moderate Muslim who was extremely well informed about the Mujahidin as well as about Saudi Arabia and Pakistan. He was related to Masood's senior political adviser, Yunis Qanuni.

I came to trust and respect Sirat. He spent considerable time at Zahir Shah's villa outside Rome, but we held talks in Riyadh and Jeddah. I candidly explained to him the U.S. concerns about Zahir Shah's reputation for passivity, procrastination, and nonaction. Washington wanted my visits to Rome to produce concrete results. In addition to a statement of support for the AIG shura, I presented a second precondition for starting my dialogue with Zahir Shah: an announcement by the king clarifying his rejection of Najib and his regime.

Zahir Shah and his advisers labored hard to meet the first condition, a statement supporting the AIG shura. Sirat and I exchanged several drafts of a public statement to be issued by the king. The final version, which was ultimately read over Voice of America (VOA) airwaves, declared: "We are hopeful that the AIG of the six organizations working with other organizations based in Iran, as well as valiant commanders, prominent Afghan personalities, intelligentsia, religious personalities and local leaders, will find a formula resulting in the convening of such a loya jirga that would lead to fulfilling the aspirations of our heroic people."[7]

Zahir Shah made two public statements condemning Najib and his regime before our July 9–10, 1990, meetings in Rome. The first, carried by the Italian news agency ANSA to an international audience, stressed the illegitimacy of the Najib regime, opposed communist participation in a coalition, and called the removal of Najib a prerequisite for peace. A May 11 "Proclamation" given to the VOA and the BBC reiterated some of the same themes.[8]

There was another step I thought would be necessary in order for the Zahir Shah meetings to take place: preventing a repeat of the CIA's last-minute intervention the previous September, which had forced the postponement of my visit. Kimmitt and I knew it would occur—and it did. In June, the agency renewed its efforts to call off the trip to Rome. After confirming the National Security Council's approval, Under Secretary Kimmitt signed an action memorandum authorizing the visit.[9]

On July 9, 1990, I arrived in Rome to inaugurate the first of five rounds of talks with Zahir Shah over the next twenty months, the last on March 2, 1992, the month preceding Najib's collapse. All five meetings took place in his villa in a comfortable Rome suburb. At the beginning of each session, in a gesture toward regality, the king would walk across the dining room into the living room and hold out his hand to me and my deputy and the political counselor of the U.S. embassy in Rome, John Brims. The former monarch was seventy-five years old at our first meeting. He was tall and alert, pensive, and self-confident. He was a gracious host, and he seemed to be in robust health, surrounded by his large family, which spanned several generations.

Once the king was seated, General Abdul Wali, Zahir Shah's first cousin and son-in-law, took over as translator. He sometimes went beyond translating to interpreting the king's views.[10] Many Afghans believed General Wali was still the power behind the throne, as he had been during the king's period in power, 1963–1973.

Our discussions opened with formalities. The king expressed his wish that our two days of talks would produce "further steps" and "coordinated action" to end the Afghan conflict. I complimented him on his recent public rejection of the Najib regime and his support for a broad-based AIG shura. He reiterated his opposition to any power-sharing formula involving Najib, then criticized elements in Pakistan that undermined Mujahidin unity and opposed an independent Afghanistan. I briefed him on the U.S.-Soviet negotiations aimed at an Afghan political settlement. The Soviets claimed they wanted peace in Afghanistan with Najib playing an important role in a coalition government. The two objectives contradicted each other. Zahir Shah interjected that the Soviets must completely remove Najib and the PDPA. They could not share power. I said that external powers could help set the framework for an Afghan political settlement, but only Afghans could create a new leadership conducive to lasting stability. Zahir Shah agreed. The superpowers, he felt, could contribute only so much to a political solution. He added: "Our main difficulty is with ourselves. I am not pessimistic we can find a solution."

On the second day, our talks became more candid. I told Zahir Shah that, notwithstanding his recent public comments, many Afghans perceived him to be fence-sitting—attempting to establish a neutral position between two sides, to become a "third force." Zahir Shah smiled and repeated a Dari proverb about a person sitting on a dike between two fields, reluctant to step down in either direction. I also smiled in urging him to leave the dike behind, make more announcements opposing Najib, and become more active in the peace process. I suggested he begin a dialogue with Pakistan and Saudi Arabia. The Pakistani and Saudi governments, I informed him, were ready to receive his envoys.

Zahir Shah immediately stated his readiness to send envoys to Pakistan and Saudi Arabia. He then noted that Najib's regime was severely fragmented. There was a "nucleus" of ideologically dedicated Afghan communists in the regime, but the great majority were opportunists. Identifying themselves as Khalqis or Parchamis did not change their tribal way of responding to events. His next comment was marvelously perspicacious: "No Afghan regime or political party will ever be very much different from the Afghan society to which they belong."

Summarizing our discussions at the end of the second day, the king agreed to make more statements against Najib, to begin a dialogue with Pakistan and Saudi Arabia, and not to criticize the AIG. He expressed hope that Pakistan would grant the necessary visas to his representatives. He recalled that Pakistani president Zia ul-Haq had been very receptive of a dialogue during their two meetings in Rome in the 1980s, but once back in Pakistan, Zia had not followed up on the idea. The king stated that the American positions and his views were identical on almost all issues. Hinting that his opinion on the AIG differed from Washington's, he remarked that "it was time to go beyond the AIG." Before ending the meeting, he registered his strong opposition to rocket attacks on Kabul and Kandahar that inflicted civilian casualties. The bombardments, he warned, were creating anti-Mujahidin sentiment and support for Najib.

Seeing me off outside the entrance to the king's residence, General Wali paused a moment. He told me he still felt responsible for not detecting Daoud's 1973 coup in time to stop it. He longed for the day when Zahir Shah could return to the palace in Kabul. Wali said his only wish was to be army chief of staff.

The July 9–10 initiation of the U.S.–Zahir Shah dialogue, hopefully to widen and include Pakistan and Saudi Arabia, opened one small door to a political settlement that had been closed for over a decade. The Rome talks put an end to high-level Soviet visits to Zahir Shah. Najib's public offers to pass power to Zahir Shah continued but no longer with the implication that the king was swinging to the regime's side.

A Zahir Shah dialogue with Saudi Arabia and Pakistan could finally begin. In October, Zahir Shah dispatched Professor Sirat and a high-ranking member of the royal family, his first cousin Sultan Mahmoud Ghazi, to Islamabad and Riyadh as his personal emissaries. In Islamabad they met with President Ghulam Ishak Khan, Additional Foreign Secretary Riaz Mohammad Khan, and ISI officers. In Riyadh they held cordial meetings with King Fahd and Prince Turki.

❧

During my visits to Peshawar in May, June, and August, I was pleased to note that Pakistan was assisting Abdul Haq's efforts to organize a National Commanders' Shura. Numerous Afghan commanders along the Frontier and inside Afghanistan eagerly seized the opportunity to break out of the constraints imposed by the ISI's fifteen-year suppression of independent Mujahidin initiatives in Pakistan.

Abdul Haq became the commanders' shura's de facto Afghan founder, fundraiser, and administrator as well as the main point of contact between the commanders and the Pakistani, American, and Saudi officials. He and his cohort made spectacular progress in launching the commanders' shura. Hamid Karzai and his father, Popalzai leader Abdul Ahad Karzai, encouraged Durrani commanders in the south to participate. Ismael Khan sent his deputy, Allaudin Khan, from western Afghanistan, to take part in the proceedings. Jalaluddin Haqqani joined as well and offered his Zhawar Kili bastion across the border from his Miram Shah headquarters in Paktiya for gatherings of the shura inside Afghanistan.

In May 1990, Haq and his associates held an organizational meeting of forty commanders at Zhawar Kili. Later in the month, about a hundred commanders attended the shura's first conference at Zhawar Kili. The second commanders' shura meeting took place there on June 22–24 with more than three hundred commanders from around Afghanistan in attendance.[11] Three

SCUD missiles fired by regime gunners at the Zhawar Kili cave complex did not interrupt the discussions.

To avoid alienating the AIG, the commanders decided not to establish a political committee. They barred five AIG representatives sent as "observers" from attending the second meeting. Rabbani, Sayyaf, and Hekmatyar told their commanders not to join the shura, but several commanders from their parties came anyway. Mojaddedi, in contrast, asked his (relatively few) commanders to actively participate. The large Shia representation at the second meeting (15 percent) bridged the Sunni-Shia gap, which was still afflicting the AIG. Uzbek and Turkman commanders from the north also attended. The American consulate in Peshawar reported that commanders from southern and western Afghanistan "revealed a strong enthusiasm for participating in the commanders' shura process. . . . They were mostly from the tribal groups in the south who felt isolated and disenchanted with the AIG/ISI."[12]

Ahmed Shah Masood did not send representative to the first or second meeting. Following the second meeting, Haq sent two commanders to Masood's headquarters in the Fakhar Valley. They formally invited Masood to attend the third meeting and to select the site where it would be held. In September, Masood sat down with a second commanders' shura delegation at his Fakhar headquarters near Taloqan to plan the third meeting. They decided to hold it October 9–14 in southern Badakhshan at Shah Selim, across the border from Pakistan north of Chitral. Masood assigned Daoud Mir, one of his political advisers, to work at the shura's Peshawar headquarters.

Masood's involvement in the shura was a breakthrough. It confirmed the national character and moderate-nationalist center of the shura. After he joined, Rabbani, Nabi, and Gailani muted their criticism. Khalis did not relent in opposing it. Sayyaf asked Hekmatyar to collaborate in creating a rival commanders' shura of Islamist commanders. Sayyaf announced that an Islamic "cleansing" committee of representatives from his and Hekmatyar's parties would study the Islamic credentials of all applicants.

The burgeoning membership of the commanders' shura seemed to catch the ISI off guard. ISI chief Kallue was a strong supporter, but the second-tier ISI colonels along the Frontier answering to Beg and Gul raised objections. Colonel Faizan, head of the ISI's Quetta office, warned Mujahidin transiting Quetta on their way to attend the commanders' meeting in Peshawar to turn back. He called the shura an "American plan."[13]

The ISI's tolerance of the commanders' shura was important to its further development. The participation of Haqqani and other commanders close to the ISI provided insurance that the shura would not grow hostile to Pakistan. So was ISI's control of weapons supplies to most Mujahidin commanders. The lack of a central political-military control mechanism inside the shura exposed it to ISI manipulation. There was no command post from which to plan and manage military operations. There was no discipline except self-discipline. There were no membership qualifications to attend meetings, other than claiming to be a commander. One of the shura organizers, Hazara Sayed Jaglan, told me, "You have to let everyone walk through the gates of the city, bad with the good."[14] The nonexistent membership criteria made it easy for the ISI to infiltrate the shura and to "pluck" commanders out of it through intimidation tactics or offers of material support.

On August 6, 1990, General Beg and President Ghulam Ishak Khan removed Prime Minister Benazir Bhutto from office, accusing her of corruption, mismanagement, nepotism, and abuse of powers. The coming Gulf War may have influenced the timing. The growing independence of the commanders' shura and the opening of the U.S. dialogue with Zahir Shah might also have contributed to Beg's decision to dismiss Bhutto.

ISI director Kallue had been supportive of the commanders' shura and the opening to Zahir Shah. Beg moved immediately to fire Kallue and replace him with Lieutenant General Asad Durrani. Durrani was director of military intelligence and continued in that post even after taking the helm of the ISI.[15] He had worked closely with Gul during Zia's dictatorship. Foreign Minister Yaqub Khan retired from his post at around the same time.

Durrani's first task was to rally Mujahidin support behind the second Hekmatyar-Tanai assault on Kabul planned for September. That required inserting Hekmatyar back into the AIG. Durrani summoned the seven leaders to inform them of the ISI's decision. Once all seven were together—a rare occasion—he announced that an attack on Kabul would be led by the new AIG defense minister, Gulbuddin Hekmatyar. This, he said, necessitated some AIG cabinet changes. Anyone who disagreed should resign from the AIG. Durrani then dictated that Nabi would move up to the AIG presidency. Mojaddedi would move down to become foreign minister. The new ISI chief's instructions to the AIG neatly coincided with the KGB's periodic games of musical chairs played in Kabul during the Soviet occupation.

Durrani's meeting with the AIG leaders ended in disaster. He may have underestimated the deep enmity that the other six leaders felt toward Hekmatyar. More important, he underestimated their determination to hold onto their seats. Losing them could mean the political wilderness, possibly poverty.

After the meeting, Mojaddedi wasted no time in complaining to Western journalists that he was being removed from the AIG presidency. The six AIG leaders falsely alleged in a written statement, which was published in the local *Frontier Post*, that "the AIG and its president had been elected unanimously by a nationwide advisory shura." Its "dissolution" was therefore "beyond the capability of others."[16] Faced with this unusual example of AIG solidarity, the ISI decided to bypass the AIG as the Mujahidin front for the second Hekmatyar-Tanai attack on Kabul. Hekmatyar would not be wearing the AIG defense minister cap when he marched into Kabul. But the show of defiance by the six AIG leaders could not be overlooked. The ISI drastically reduced the AIG's $5 million monthly budget—financed by the CIA-Saudi covert program—sending hundreds of AIG employees, mostly family and clan members of the AIG leaders, back to the refugee camps.

ψ

While the ISI was organizing the second Hekmatyar-Tanai attack on Kabul, I was tied up in Washington with an extended series of congressional hearings on Afghan policy and appropriations. They lasted from the end of August through September 1990. At the time, Ambassador Oakley was on a month-long vacation, and his deputy chief of mission, Beth Jones, was chargé d'affaires at the American embassy in Pakistan. During this time, I received no indication from the CIA that a second ISI attempt to place Hekmatyar in Kabul was under way, although I testified side by side with CIA executives in several classified hearings in Congress, arguing for the continuation of the CIA's covert arms program. It was obvious why the agency kept me in the dark: I would have insisted that the attack be canceled.

Ambassador Oakley and I flew into Islamabad on Monday, October 3, 1990. It was my ninth and most action-packed trip to Pakistan. I had only a few hours to spend that evening with Oakley and Station Chief Bill. Early the next morning, I was scheduled to fly to Chitral to meet with Mujahidin commanders in the north, including commanders who were preparing for the third commanders' shura at Shah Selim over the border in Afghanistan. I also planned to meet Masood's brother, Ahmed Zia. Masood and his delegation of Council of the North commanders were then trekking through Nuristan's mountains toward Shah Selim to attend the third commanders' conference, scheduled to begin October 9.

At his residence, Oakley and I discussed the talking points I was planning to present to the Pakistani government and the Mujahidin. U.S. relations with Pakistan had just suffered a major blow that was certain to decrease America's influence with the Pakistani government. On October 1, President Bush had declined to certify that Pakistan did not possess a nuclear weapons device.[17] The resulting termination of U.S. military and economic aid generated cries of betrayal from a broad range of Pakistani politicians.[18]

My next stop was the home of CIA Station Chief Bill.[19] The conversation that evening was the lowest point of my three-year special envoy appointment. Bill must have been aware of interagency decisions in Washington, cleared by CIA headquarters, to break the Mujahidin political-military stalemate, reach out to Zahir Shah and Masood, assist in the development of a commanders' shura in order to increase military pressure on the regime, and pursue an Afghan political settlement. In June, with Bill at my side, I had called on ISI Director Kallue in his office to reiterate the U.S. decision to cut Hekmatyar off from U.S. arms and assistance. Kallue assured me that Pakistan was no longer supplying arms or money to Hekmatyar, and indeed had terminated rent payments for his home in Islamabad. Now Kallue was gone. But the U.S. policy position opposing American arms and money to Hekmatyar still stood.

Bill told me that ISI chief Durrani had recently brought him and Hekmatyar together to discuss the next Kabul offensive. Bill said that Hekmatyar had assured him that he could capture Kabul if given the weapons. Bill asked Hekmatyar if he would cooperate with other commanders in the operation. Hekmatyar answered that he would.[20] The results of the exchange were clear: Bill had given the CIA's, and thus the American government's, green light to the ISI for another Hekmatyar-Tanai attempt to overthrow Najib by military force. I was stunned. I told Bill that by endorsing Hekmatyar's attack on Kabul, he was violating fundamental U.S. policy precepts agreed to in Washington by his own agency. American policy was to cut Hekmatyar off, not to build him up. Bill looked at me impassively as I spoke. I assumed his superiors in Langley had approved the offensive. The U.S. government was conducting two diametrically opposed Afghan policies.

I arrived in Chitral the next morning. My first meeting was with Ahmed Zia Masood. After welcoming me, he castigated the United States for helping Pakistan organize the planned Hekmatyar-Tanai attack on Kabul. I responded that I spoke for all U.S. government agencies. U.S. policy supported a political solution to the Afghan war inclusive of all Afghan groups. The United States opposed the ISI's Kabul offensive favoring Hekmatyar. If launched, it would fail and produce massive civilian casualties. Normally unemotional by nature, Ahmed Zia shouted back that his brother and the commanders' shura opposed the Pakistani plan. He asserted that Masood was fully capable of stopping Hekmatyar's advance on Kabul. His forces were within striking distance of the capital—only 60 miles away. He threatened that if Pakistani troops reinforced Hekmatyar and Tanai on the road to Kabul, Masood and other Afghan commanders would "confront" them.

My second meeting in Chitral was with a group of commanders preparing for the October 9 opening of the commanders' conference at Shah Selim. Their protests about the planned Hekmatyar-Tanai attack on Kabul were as strident as Ahmed Zia's. After I repeated U.S. opposition to the ISI offensive, the commanders described their arrangements for the meeting. They said Shah Selim was out of SCUD range but vulnerable to air attack. They had placed antiaircraft weapons around the meeting site. No AIG personnel would be allowed to participate. The thirty most important Mujahidin commanders who would participate represented all of Afghanistan regions and principal ethnic and religious groups. The conference would create a coordinated nationwide military strategy for 1991.

Ahmed Zia and the Afghan commanders' remonstrations against the Hekmatyar-Tanai plan in Chitral paled in comparison to the firestorm I encountered after arriving in Peshawar late on October 5. The Mujahidin protests hit me like a blast of cold mountain wind. Tribal leaders, Islamists, royalists—all vied for attention to vent their objections. Red in the face, Abdul Haq scolded me, charging that I had one policy, but the CIA had another. Nabi Mohammadi complained that Kabul's 2 million people could not escape Hekmatyar's rocket bombardment—there would be a massacre. I explained that the United States opposed the attack. Nabi expressed surprise, volunteering that he had heard the United States was behind the plan. After a pause he told me he was relieved to hear that the United States opposed it.

On October 6, ten leading commanders in the commanders' shura sharply questioned me about the Hekmatyar-led offensive on Kabul. Abdul Haq, Amin Wardak, Sayed Jaglan, and Masood's adviser, Yunis Qanuni, told me that since so many other Mujahidin factions opposed Hekmatyar, his coup against Najib would collapse. Hekmatyar's rocketing of Kabul, however, would produce a civilian bloodbath.

That same day, I called on Sayyaf and Khalis. They also denounced the ISI's plan. Sayyaf invited me outside to his garden for a private conversation. In our previous meetings I had written off his insincere statements about Afghan-U.S. friendship. Behind his camaraderie was a closed mind. America was not an ally. It was an adversary. I therefore was surprised when the tall, corpulent alim leaned over the table between us with a frightened look in his eyes, his long beard skidding across a pile of fruit in a bowl. Speaking in whispers to prevent his words from being picked up by eavesdropping equipment, he appealed to me to stop the Hekmatyar attack on Kabul. I felt that, at least at this moment in time, Sayyaf actually meant what he said. Only the United States, not his patrons in Saudi Arabia, or his radical Wahhabi and Muslim Brotherhood confederates, could force Pakistan to call off the second attempt by Hekmatyar and Tanai to capture Kabul. If they succeeded with the ISI's assistance, Sayyaf, of course, would be left behind. Hekmatyar would not share power with him—or with any of the other party leaders.

Khalis told me that the Pakistani plan was a "conspiracy" calling for "Hekmatyar's forces to rocket Kabul and then to join with defecting Khalqi commanders to seize power." According to Khalis, "the plan was formulated by Pakistan without consulting resistance leaders": "All other resistance elements rejected the plan." He notified me that non-Hezb commanders would soon begin to attack Hekmatyar's convoys passing through Nangarhar and Paktiya on their way to Hekmatyar's bases south of Kabul.[21]

During further meetings in Peshawar, I learned more details about the Kabul attack from other Mujahidin contacts. Some were probably exaggerated, but others were not. Mujahidin observers at the Torkham border post counted over four hundred trucks with rockets moving through the Khyber Pass toward Kabul. General Tanai now commanded *Hekmatyar's Lashkar-i Issar* battalions. My Mujahidin sources told me that ISI colonel Afzal Janjua had predicted that 30,000 Mujahidin in the Kabul area would support the Hekmatyar-Tanai assault on Kabul. They estimated that fewer than 5,000 Hezb fighters would actually show up.

On October 6 and 7 I phoned and sent classified telegrams to Washington and the embassy in Islamabad detailing the potential disaster that lay ahead should the ISI offensive go forward. I reported that, apart from Hekmatyar's faction, moderate and extremist Mujahidin groups were unanimous in opposing the ISI-planned offensive. I cited Mujahidin comments to me that the United States backed the planned attacks on Kabul.[22] I emphasized there was no possibility that Hekmatyar and Tanai would be able to break through the 100,000-man regime cordon around the capital. The only result would be tens of thousands of civilian deaths from massive rocket bombardments. In one cable, I wrote that the planned ISI offensive "evoked the worst suspicions within Mujahidin circles that Pakistan intended to replace Najib with Hekmatyar." In a separate note to Oakley, I recommended that Washington demand that Pakistan call off the attack, and I suggested wording for a presidential letter to deliver that message to Pakistan's leadership. I asked my deputy Tom Greene to make the four-hour trip by road to Islamabad to personally carry the note to the embassy.

The embassy responded as it had after the first Hekmatyar-Tanai coup attempt in March 1990, with a mixture of unanswered questions about the ISI plan, steps it was taking to clarify the situation, and opposition to the attack. A secret embassy message sent to Washington on October 8 stated that the embassy and the CIA station were attempting to understand why the Mujahidin were so concerned about the ISI plan. The "COS met Durrani's deputy of OPS chief Janjua for almost three hours October 8 going over situation at greater length," the cable stated. It reported:

> At present it is not repeat not at all clear that the plans actually call for
> stepped-up rocketing of civilian targets in Kabul or that it is to put Gul-
> buddin into position of dominance over other Resistance leaders or
> even that plan is aimed at direct assault upon Kabul. There are wide-
> spread rumors and press reports to that effect which we are checking
> carefully.

The cable assured Washington that "further sessions here are being scheduled so we are fully informed of details of the plan." It suggested wording for a presidential letter to be sent to the Pakistani government.[23]

A second cable placed on the wires to Washington six minutes earlier strained to rationalize the ISI's planned attack. The embassy, it said, had learned from a variety of sources that the offensive's "objective is not the capture of Kabul," but "the improvement of Resistance positions around the city so that rocket attacks may be launched against regime targets more effectively." The telegram then made room for the success of the Hekmatyar-Tanai coup, defined as "a secondary component of the plan." It anticipated the possibility that there would be "an internal upheaval within Kabul by disenchanted Khalqi officers and a call for the Mujahidin to support such a coup attempt."[24]

In contrast to Ahmed Zia Masood's warning that his brother's forces would resist the Hekmatyar-Tanai offensive, the cable stated, "We have heard that Masood supports the plan, which his people repeatedly denied." It went on to say that "the U.S. has not had an opportunity to review the scope of the alleged plan for a new assault on Kabul and is not certain what the plan actually is"; that the United States was "strongly and unalterably opposed to any plan which includes as a major component the large scale rocketing of urban areas and the consequent risk of inflicting heavy casualties among civilian populations"; that "we do not favor efforts to give Gulbuddin a position of dominance"; and that "we are making our views known to the GOP [Government of Pakistan]."[25]

Within days, the White House brushed aside the ambiguities and conveyed strong U.S. opposition to the offensive. The Pakistani government called off the attack. The ISI-Hekmatyar truck convoys—loaded down with rockets—returned to Pakistan. The following week, a displeased Durrani confirmed to me in Islamabad that the Kabul offensive had been postponed.

ψ

The Shah Selim commanders' meeting began on October 9. Photos of the prominent commanders sitting on a carpet in a circle, jirga fashion, were sent around the world. For the first time in twelve years, a broad-based Afghan resistance institution was functioning by and for Afghans.

A Mujahidin victory symbolizing progress, the one I requested from Beg in our November 1989 meeting, occurred only four days before the Shah

Selim commanders' meeting commenced. The fall of Tarinkot, Uruzgan's capital, raised the morale of the shura participants. It was the first major Mujahidin success since the Soviets had left Afghanistan more than a year and a half earlier. Hamid Karzai used his Popalzai Durrani connections to rally Popalzai tribals around Tarinkot. He secretly negotiated the defection of the regime's governor and most of the five-hundred-man defending force. The rest surrendered after some initial resistance.[26]

Ahmed Shah Masood walked or rode on horseback for five days to reach Shah Selim. To avoid assassination, he disguised himself with a scarf over his face and wore dark glasses. He chose four senior commanders representing different ethnic groups in the Council of the North to accompany him. Some forty large tents were struck 100 yards from the meeting site where the commanders could talk, become acquainted with one another, and sleep at night. Mojaddedi, Rabbani, Gailani's son (Hamed), Abdullah Anas, and Abul Hassan, the Saudi chief of the World Muslim League in Peshawar,[27] were permitted to camp out at the tent site but not to enter the conference area. A double ring of armed guards circling the meeting site were told to permit only commanders and their immediate aides to enter the shura area.

Following Afghan tradition, the most influential commanders, Haqqani and Masood, spoke last. Masood listened attentively to other speakers and took notes. The commanders vowed to support national unity. They agreed that Afghans needed to formulate their own military plans or endure more defeats like Jalalabad. Speaking last at the end of the second day, Masood began his presentation by saying, "I am an Afghan, not a Tajik." Speaking for over two hours, Masood summed up and elaborated on what other commanders had said. He recommended that the shura adopt an "out-in" military strategy during 1991, capturing cities and regime garrisons far from Kabul, then slowly closing in on the capital.

Masood advised against an early offensive against Kabul. It would cause unnecessary civilian casualties and might not succeed. He endorsed the shura's planning for creation of nine "zones" around the country. Commanders' shura subheadquarters in each zone would develop and execute attacks aimed at seizing targets in their areas. The multiple attacks would be coordinated to occur simultaneously, preventing the regime from utilizing its air force and mobile units to defeat them one by one. Masood expressed confidence that by the fall of 1991 a number of regime strong points would have fallen. The momentum lost in 1988 and 1989 would shift back to the Mujahidin. He suggested the establishment of four fronts in the Kabul region. Representatives of the four fronts could form a joint shura to devise a plan to capture the city. The final assault on Kabul would not begin until the commanders' shura and the AIG had reached a consensus on an overall "political plan" for postwar Afghanistan.

The commanders concurred with Masood's summation of the shura's battle plan for 1991. They agreed to establish a communications network among themselves and with the commanders' shura office in Peshawar. The "Final Communiqué of the Third National Commanders' Shura," issued on October 14, stated that the meeting had produced "complete agreement." The communiqué announced the nine administrative zones. It demanded that the Kabul regime transfer power and promised amnesty to regime "soldiers."[28]

Unexpectedly, the ISI director, General Durrani, arrived at Shah Selim on a Pakistani military helicopter two days before the shura was to end. He delivered a message from General Beg inviting Masood to Islamabad. Masood's immediate inclination was not to go. He had not left Afghanistan for thirteen years, a record that enhanced his reputation among Afghans inside and outside the resistance. The ISI had treated him as an enemy. He may have worried about becoming another name on the long list of Afghans assassinated inside Pakistan if he accepted Beg's invitation.

Masood delayed his response to the invitation. He tended to ponder important issues, discussing them with his advisers before making decisions. Masood's aide, Daoud Mir, stayed with Durrani through the day, away from the commanders' meeting area. Durrani, Mir later recalled, grew irritated. He pointed to Mujahidin antiaircraft guns on a nearby hill and asked Mir why they were pointing toward Pakistan and not Najib's regime.[29] Late that afternoon, Durrani flew back to Islamabad without Masood's reply to Beg's invitation.

Durrani was due back the next day to get Masood's answer. Masood knew his decision would have profound implications for the future of the commanders' shura and the war against Najib. Haqqani and other commanders long favored by the ISI urged Masood to accept Beg's invitation. Rabbani, Abdullah Anas, and Abul Hassan also encouraged Masood to go to Islamabad and meet Beg. They pointed out that Masood could use his meetings with Beg to mend fences with the ISI and with Hekmatyar. Beg's support would be crucial to obtaining the heavy weapons, ammunition, and cash necessary to carry out the shura's 1991 military campaign. Moderate commanders, Abdul Haq among them, were suspicious of Beg's intentions. The commanders' shura was an expression of Afghan independence from foreign control. Was Beg's invitation part of a Pakistani scheme to somehow induce the shura to advance Pakistan's goal of supporting Hekmatyar and the Afghan extremists? The moderate commanders wanted to widen the distance between Pakistan's ISI and the Afghan resistance, not close it.

After the formal closing of the commanders' shura on October 14, Masood informed the commanders that he would have an answer for Beg the next morning. He told his closest advisers that he intended to invoke the Muslim religious practice of *istikhara*. He would pray for God's guidance. The answer would come down to him by the waking hour. The next morning, Masood informed the commanders that he would go with Durrani to Islamabad to meet with Beg.[30]

Masood was more politically astute than most of the other Afghan commanders and politicians. At age thirty-two, however, he had no experience dealing with governments. He was not at home in the Machiavellian world of international politics. He thrived in small group settings with Afghans, like the Shah Selim meeting. Rabbani, Masood's erstwhile Jamiat party leader, viewed Masood's meeting with Beg as an opportunity to boost his personal influence with the Pakistani army chief of staff and inside the resistance. One proposal Beg planned to offer Masood was a grand Jamiat-Hezb, Rabbani-Hekmatyar political alliance to overthrow Najib. Masood would be Rabbani's main spear carrier.

☙

The commanders' shura meeting with Beg took place at his headquarters inside the army's Rawalpindi garrison. Masood, Haqqani, Haq, and other shura commanders attended. Hekmatyar was also present.[31] When the sound of Beg's footsteps in the corridor leading to the army chief's large conference room triggered a rush to the door, Masood alone remained in his seat. He stood to shake hands with Beg only when the Pakistani general approached his side of the table.

In the face of American pressure and near universal Mujahidin hostility to the Hekmatyar-Tanai attack, Beg had already called off the assault on Kabul by the time of the meeting. Nevertheless, he started his presentation by counseling the commanders to support a Hekmatyar attack on Kabul. He twice requested that Masood close the Salang road. Masood refused. When Beg raised his voice to repeat his request, Masood defiantly stood up as if to leave. The other commanders in the room grabbed him by the shoulders, urging him to sit down and hear out Beg.

Beg made his private lunch for Masood after his session with the commanders the centerpiece of Masood's visit to Islamabad. According to Masood, Beg laid out his geostrategic vision for Pakistan and Afghanistan, urging that the two Muslim countries combine forces after Afghanistan's liberation. Beg called for Pakistan and Afghanistan together to foster Islamic revolutions in the Muslim world. There was, Beg claimed, a leadership vacuum in Islamic countries. He claimed that Pakistan's assistance to the Afghan jihad placed it in a unique position to fill that vacuum.

Saudi Arabia could not fill it. It was too closely associated with the Untied States. Iran was unable to provide leadership because of Sunni-Shia differences in Sunni majority Muslim countries. Utilizing a map, the general pointed to the five Soviet Central Asian Republics. A different color distinguished them from the rest of the USSR. He remarked that following Najib's defeat, Pakistan and Afghanistan could start a new jihad to free the Muslim populations of Soviet Central Asia. Afterward, the two countries could assist other Islamic revolutions in Muslim regions of the world where jihads were already under way, such as in Kashmir, or where they had not yet begun. He predicted that India would disintegrate when the Islamic revolutionary wave reached an advanced stage.

During the lunch, Beg told Masood that he had suspended the Kabul offensive. He promised weapons and money to support the commanders' shura strategy. He asked Masood to accept his concept of a Hekmatyar-Rabbani "high command" combining the military capabilities of the two largest Mujahidin parties. Masood's combat power would form the backbone of Rabbani's military contribution to the alliance. He stated that the ISI would provide Masood with ample assistance if he agreed with his suggestion, even if Pakistan had to reach into its own stocks of armaments to supply him.

Masood accepted Beg's proposal for a Hekmatyar-Rabbani high command. Turning it down would have closed the door to ISI supplies that the commanders required for their 1991 offensive. He may have believed in the sincerity of Beg's promise to deal collectively with the commanders' shura and to support its strategy. A separate commanders' shura meeting hosted by ISI chief Durrani reinforced that impression. Durrani told Masood, Haq, and other commanders that the Pakistani government's Afghan cell had formally ratified Beg's decision to back the Afghan commanders' shura.

It is highly likely that Hekmatyar and Masood considered their alliance unworkable from the outset. Their postwar plans for Afghanistan were irreconcilable. So were their personal agendas. The Hekmatyar-Masood vendetta could not be papered over by foreign-crafted reconciliation formulas. Like the intra-PDPA feuds, it would only end with the death of one of the protagonists. Masood, a Tajik, would insist on full equality with the Pashtun Hekmatyar. The megalomaniac Hekmatyar could never accept equality with Masood or any other Mujahidin leader.

At Beg's suggestion, Masood and Hekmatyar signed an accord to ease tensions between them by holding elections in the north. Hekmatyar issued a public statement calling off his attack on Kabul. But it did not take long for the agreement to fall apart in the implementation stage. Four months after the signing ceremony in Pakistan, the U.S. consulate in Peshawar cabled Washington that Hekmatyar was again "working to install himself in power by means of a coup . . . cooperating with Khalqi elements in the military." "Both sides," the consulate said, "report that there has been little progress in implementing the Hekmatyar/Masood accord, or a wider Hezb/Jamiat reconciliation. There have been scattered reports of confrontations both south and north of the Hindu Kush."[32] In January 1991, Masood's intelligence agents arrested six Hezb members in Taloqan who were preparing to assassinate him.

If wresting cash and weaponry from ISI reserves was Masood's main goal in his talks with Beg, he succeeded. During his stopover in Peshawar on his way back to Afghanistan, ISI trucks carrying weapons and equipment were already on the roads to his Gharm Chesma warehouses above Chitral. Beg kept his word on financial assistance as well. Ahmed Zia and Daoud Mir unloaded three ISI pickup trucks carrying 70 million Pakistani rupees in newly printed, crisp bills at Ahmed Zia's residence in Peshawar.[33] They piled the stacks of notes in Mir's guest bedroom. Mir recalled that the mountain of money emitted a horribly bad smell. It was impossible to sleep. He could not open the windows that night for fear of hands reaching in to steal the cash.[34]

The strategy Beg wanted Masood to support was not a new one. It coincided with the Muslim Brotherhood's long-term goals, with Zia's vision, and with Beg and Gul's doctrines of strategic consensus, strategic defiance, and strategic deterrence.[35] After his return to the north, Masood convened his senior advisers to discuss Beg's geostrategic presentation at Pakistani Army headquarters in Rawalpindi. He explained his concern that Beg's ideas went beyond assisting Afghanistan and ridding it of Najib's communist regime. He told his advisers that Beg's vision of fostering international Islamic revolutions helped to explain why Pakistan had supported Hekmatyar from the beginning.[36]

۝

The leaders of the commanders' shura returned to Peshawar from their Islamabad meetings with Beg and Durrani in high spirits. Abdul Haq later boasted to me that he had conducted ten meetings with the ISI's Brigadier Janjua in two weeks. Janjua had personally written down the money, weapons, and supplies the shura was requesting to capture territory in each of the nine combat zones during 1991. Haq stated that simultaneous attacks would begin in the early spring at Khost and gradually expand around the country. The final attack on Kabul would occur only after the Afghans reached agreement on a broad-based political entity to replace Najib's regime. Haq sketched three initiatives he was preparing to speed formation of an Afghan body to take power from Najib in a political transition: creation of tribal and ulema shuras inside Afghanistan; their linkage with the commanders' shura; and enlistment of Zahir Shah to preside over a loya jirga bringing together all these groups. Haq's ideas were in the tradition of Afghan consensus politics. They overlapped with the jirga proposals earlier offered by the United States. I urged Haq to proceed cautiously, enlist UN support, and, especially, to retain Pakistani cooperation.

Before traveling back to the north, Masood expressed optimism to journalists in Peshawar about the commanders' implementation of a "new unified battle plan" for 1991 agreed to at Shah Selim.[37] From Peshawar, he phoned me in Saudi Arabia to describe the success of the Shah Selim meeting. At his request, I reiterated that the United States had not supported the Hekmatyar attack on Kabul. I congratulated him on the progress of the commanders' shura movement. He thanked me for the support of the United States. He predicted that 1991 would finally bring battlefield successes to the Mujahidin. I suggested that he encourage Zahir Shah to play a constructive role in a political settlement. Masood asked me to send word to the king that he wished to meet Sirat inside Afghanistan to discuss political coordination.

I passed on Masood's comment to Zahir Shah during my second meeting with him on December 16 in Rome. The king stated his readiness for a dialogue with Masood and remarked that the commanders' shura should play a role in the political settlement process. He told me that Abdul Haq had asked him to lend his support to the political settlement process. He placed a positive gloss on Sirat's and Sultan Ghazi's negotiations with Prince Turki in Riyadh and President Ghulam Ishak Khan, General Durrani, and the Pakistani Foreign Ministry in Islamabad. Sirat, who was present, explained that he and Ghazi had asked the Pakistanis and Prince Turki to consider Zahir Shah another resistance voice adamantly opposed to Najib. They invited a Pakistani delegation to visit the king in Rome. The Pakistanis so far had not responded.

Pakistani officials never did take up Zahir Shah's invitation to continue their dialogue in Rome. In fact, the actions of General Beg and the ISI at the end of 1990 and the beginning of 1991 indicated they had concluded that both the commanders' shura and the U.S. dialogue with Zahir Shah were moving Afghan trends in the wrong direction. On November 21, 1990, an article written by retired ISI brigadier Mohammed Yousuf, chief of ISI's Afghan Bureau in the mid-1980s, showed that General Beg's fanciful and unrealizable strategic ambitions in Afghanistan and the Muslim world had not changed. The article, printed in the Pakistani daily *The Muslim,* sounded the alarm that the United States was implementing "a deliberate and well-thought-out covert plan" meant to "deny the victory of the 'fundamentalists' to establish an Islamic state in Afghanistan." Yousuf accused the United States of sabotaging the Mujahidin attack on Jalalabad to prevent Najib from falling. He hallucinated that the victory America denied in 1989

> would have created a politico-religious base and momentum for the
> beginning of Islamic revolutionary warfare against the USSR by most

of her Muslim populations adjacent to Afghanistan. The psyche and natural follow-up of this movement would have led to an Islamic bloc comprising Afghanistan, Pakistan, Iran, Turkey and the Islamic Soviet Republics. With friendly China, this Islamic bloc would have stood against the expansionist designs and aspirations of the superpowers and regional powers like India . . . [and] helped to solve the outstanding disputes of the Palestinians and Kashmiris. The whole superpower structure and political scenario of South Asia and the Middle East could have changed.[38]

Except for sending the initial arms shipment to Masood, and, later, weapons for the March 1991 attack on Khost, the ISI did not honor Beg's pledge to provide supplies to carry out the commanders' operational plans for attacks inside Afghanistan in 1991. Instead, rumors of a third Hekmatyar-Tanai assault on Kabul began to circulate in Pakistan. In February 1991, the American consulate in Peshawar reported that another Hekmatyar-Tanai attempt to overthrow Najib had collapsed before it could be activated. Najib's KHAD rolled up an entire network of more than five hundred underground agents preparing the coup, executing the leaders and jailing the rest. Too late, Hekmatyar's Hezb apparatus discovered and "arrested one of its radiomen who had passed all party communications to Kabul for years."[39] The debacle delayed the third Hekmatyar-Tanai coup attempt for nine months.

ψ

The Yousuf article's strategic posturing corresponded to the Beg doctrine's antipathy to the U.S. and Saudi Arabia. It also paralleled the Pakistani army chief's condemnation of the tough U.S. reaction to Saddam Hussein's August 1990 invasion of Kuwait and military buildup on the Saudi border. Beg blocked the departure of a contingent of 2,000 Mujahidin preparing to go to Saudi Arabia to join the U.S.-led coalition defending the Saudi kingdom. The ISI's favorite Mujahidin, Hekmatyar, Rabbani, and Sayyaf, declared their support for Saddam Hussein. Their opposition and Beg's position distressed the Saudi royal family, which had supported Pakistan and the Mujahidin during the long anticommunist Afghan jihad. Saddam Hussein's Iraq was among the few Arab regimes that still maintained friendly relations with Najib's regime.

The ISI continued to prevent the departure of the symbolic Mujahidin contingent to Saudi Arabia even after U.S. Secretary of State James A. Baker III told a congressional committee that it had already arrived in the kingdom.

In December, Hekmatyar traveled to Baghdad and met with Saddam Hussein. He offered to send his Mujahidin to help fight alongside the Iraqi Army. In a press conference, he conflated the Soviet Army in Afghanistan with the American-led coalition in Saudi Arabia: "We have fought against alien troops in Afghanistan for more than ten years and how can we now support alien forces in the Gulf?" Rabbani publicly announced: "This is an unjust war imposed on Iraq. We are not a party to it."[40]

Speaking to Pakistani journalists on January 20, Beg described Saddam Hussein's invasion of Kuwait as "a trap to find justification for pulverizing Iraq." He forecast that the United States "could face the same fate as the Soviet Union did in Afghanistan."[41] That same day, AIG President Mojaddedi took issue with Beg's defense of Saddam Hussein. He told a VOA interviewer, "I think Saddam considers Kuwait as one of its colonies. . . . Even Afghan refugees who have come from Kuwait talk about the horrible stories and atrocities that Iraq has committed in Kuwait."[42]

Rabbani, Hekmatyar, and Sayyaf participated in a pro–Saddam Hussein international Muslim Brotherhood conference in Lahore on February 15–17, 1991. The conference ended a week before the outbreak of the ground war on February 24. Qazi Hussain Ahmed's Jamaat sponsored the event. A "Who's Who" list of Brotherhood notables, from the vice president of Necmettin Erbakan's Turkish Welfare Party to Sudan's Hassan Turabi, attended. The conference's twenty-point communiqué denounced "the war the West has unleashed against Islam and its civilization." It went on to say that "this alliance of the Crusaders and Zionists headed by the USA is striking at the Muslim lands to impose their absolute sovereignty and control."

Prince Turki broke away from urgent, war-related matters in early February, before the ground attack on Saddam Hussein's forces began, to fly to Islamabad and persuade Beg to release the Mujahidin force. By that time, the air campaign had made it clear that Saddam Hussein's army would be expelled from Kuwait. On February 11, the ISI permitted only 308 Mujahidin from the parties of Khalis, Mojaddedi, and Gailani to travel to Saudi Arabia and join the coalition. Soon, photographs of Afghan fighters conversing with U.S.

troops appeared in local American newspapers.[43] Beg quieted down after the American-led coalition's decisive defeat of Saddam Hussein.

Pakistani military commander Mirza Aslam Beg's and the ISI's support for Saddam Hussein in the months leading up to the first Gulf War became a forgotten story after the U.S.-led coalition's victory. Both inside and outside of the policymaking community in Washington, Americans still viewed Pakistan as a close ally. But the cold reality was that Pakistan's army chief, his eminence grise Hamid Gul, and the ISI considered the United States an adversary, not an ally. Their attempts to influence the outcome of the Gulf War had not succeeded. They could, however, decide whether or not the Afghan war would continue. And they did, drawing on hundreds of millions of dollars in American covert aid to organize yet another Hekmatyar-Tanai attack on Kabul.

Afghan ruler Abdur Rahman Khan with the foreign secretary of India during a visit to Rawalpindi, 1885.

Credit: © Hulton-Deutsch Collection/CORBIS

King Amanullah Khan, with Queen Soroya, reviewing French troops in Paris during Amanullah's visit to European capitals, January 26, 1928.

Credit: © Getty Images

President Mohammad Daoud Khan presides over a meeting of his new Central Committee after his July 17, 1973, coup overthrowing his cousin, King Zadir Shah.

Afghan President Nur Mohammad Taraki speaks at a May 6, 1978, press conference in Kabul.

Afghan President Hafizullah Amin addresses a press conference in Kabul after his September 14, 1979, coup against Taraki.

Credit: © Bettmann/CORBIS

Afghan President Babrak Karmal in January 1980, just after the Soviet invasion installed him in power.

Credit: © Henri Bureau/Sygma/CORBIS

Afghan President Mohammad
Najib gestures while answering a
question during a press
conference in Kabul, 1988.
Credit: © Reuters/CORBIS

Pakistan President Zia ul-Haq speaking outside
the White House on October 3, 1980, after
meeting with President Jimmy Carter. National
Security Adviser Zbigniew Brzezinski stands
behind them.
Credit: © Wally McNamee/CORBIS

Commander Abdul Haq and Prime Minister Margaret Thatcher at No. 10 Downing Street in London, March 11, 1985.

Credit: © AP Photo/Press Association

Soviet POW under village arrest in northern Afghanistan, circa 1986.

Credit: Courtesy of Haji Mohammad Daoud collection

Ahmed Shah Masood briefing his commanders before a military operation in 1987.

Credit: Courtesy of Daoud Mir collection

Opposition leader Benazir Bhutto speaks to about 80,000 supporters during a campaign rally in downtown Rawalpindi, Pakistan, April 1986.

Credit: © Reuters/CORBIS

A reception in Beijing honoring visiting Afghan Interim Government Foreign Minister Gulbuddin Hekmatyar, hosted by Pakistani Ambassador Akram Zaki. Hekmatyar is on the author's right and Ambassador Zaki is on his left, April 20, 1989.

Credit: Author's photo archive

Ahmed Shah Masood and Palestinian Muslim Brotherhood activist Abdullah Yusuf Azzam in the Panshir Valley, September 1989. One of Azzam's sons walks behind him.

Credit: Courtesy of Daoud Mir collection

A press conference outside AIG President Mojaddedi's residence, July 6, 1989. From left: Ambassador Robert Oakley; the author; Afghan Interim Government President Sibghatullah Mojaddedi; American consul in Peshawar Michael Malinowski; and (partially visible) Mojaddedi adviser Hamid Karzai.

Credit: Courtesy of Haji Mohammad Daoud collection

Abdul Haq meeting with several leading commanders of the National Commanders' Shura, summer of 1990.

Credit: Courtesy of Haji Deen Mohammad collection

Author with Prince Turki al-Faisal, chief of the Saudi government's General Intelligence Directorate, in Riyadh, January 1990.

Credit: Author's photo archive

Afghan Interim Government Prime Minister Abdul Rasoul Sayyaf in his office, February 1990.

Credit: Author's photo archive

Afghan Interim Government
Interior Minister Yunus Khalis,
Peshawar, February 1990.
Credit: Author's photo archive

Third National
Commanders' Shura
meeting, Shah Selim,
Badakhshan Province,
October 9–14, 1990. Ahmed
Shah Masood is pointing.
Jalaluddin Haqqani and
Sayed Hasan Jaglan are on
his right. Abdul Haq is at the
far left.
        *Credit: Haji Deen
        Mohammad collection*

Former Afghan monarch Zahir Shah troubled over next steps in the Afghan peace process at his residence in Rome, December 16, 1990.

Credit: Author's photo archive

TOMSEN ASKS AIG TO BROADEN BASE — (NEWS)

Author attempting to convince Afghan Interim Government cabinet minister Burhanuddin Rabbani to negotiate with ex-king Zahir Shah, December 13, 1989.

Credit: Frontier Post

Deputy Foreign Minister Hamid Karzai greets American delegation headed by author at the Kabul Airport, June 14, 1992. A State Department security officer is on author's left.

Credit: Author's photo archive

Meeting with Defense Minister Ahmed Shah Masood at the Ministry of Defense, Kabul, June 14, 1992.

Credit: Author's photo archive

Prayers offered at the signing of the Islamabad Accords, March 7, 1993. Sitting from left: Peshawar party leaders Gulbuddin Hekmatyar; Burhanuddin Rabbani; Sibghatullah Mojaddedi; and Mohammad Nabi Mohammadi. Standing from left: Pakistani Minister of State for Foreign Affairs Siddiq Khan Kanju; Iranian Deputy Foreign Minister Alleaddin Brojerdi; Pakistani prime minister Nawaz Sharif; and Saudi prince Turki al-Faisal.

Credit: © Saeed Khan/AFP/Getty Images

Masood with Daoud Mir, his envoy to France, north of Kabul, April 1996.

Credit: Courtesy of Daoud Mir collection

Osama bin Laden and Ayman al-Zawahiri during a November 2001 interview with a Pakistani journalist at a secret location in Afghanistan.

Credit: © STR/PAKISTAN/Reuters/CORBIS

Pakistani general Pervez Musharraf, Prime Minister Nawaz Sharif, and Saudi Defense Minister Prince Sultan attend a military briefing in Taxila, Pakistan, on May 6, 1999, six months before Musharraf ousted Sharif in a military coup.

Credit: © Saeed Khan/AFP/Getty Images

Former Pakistani ISI chief Hamid Gul and Jamaat-i Islami party leader Qazi Hussain Ahmed at a September 3, 2007, meeting in Islamabad.

Pakistani Army Chief of Staff General Ashfaq Parvez Kayani greets CentCom Commander General David Petraeus before their meeting in Islamabad on November 3, 2008.

Presidential candidate Dr. Abdullah Abdullah campaigning for votes in Afghanistan's 2009 presidential elections.

Credit: Courtesy of Dr. Abdullah Abdullah

President Barack Obama, Secretary of State Hillary Clinton, and Special Presidential Representative to Afghanistan and Pakistan Richard Holbrooke at the State Department in Washington, DC, January 22, 2009.

Credit: © AP Photo/ Charles Dharapak

CHAPTER 17

Irreconcilable Policies

Excerpts from the author's policy message, classified secret, cabled from the American embassy in London to Washington, dated June 21, 1991:

The USG* should follow a unified line in insisting to the GOP† that the ISI disengage from resistance politics.

The overwhelming majority of Afghans inside and outside Afghanistan strongly want peace, without either extreme,‡ neither of which stands any chance of prevailing in an act of self-determination. . . . The main challenge of the settlement process is to prevent the two Afghan extremists promoted by hard-liners in Moscow and Islamabad from co-opting or destroying the process. . . .

A U.S.-Soviet agreement on bilateral negative symmetry or a separate multilateral arms cutoff with the SAG§ included should remain our first priority objective in Afghanistan. We should continue to press the Soviets to agree to a date certain, as they did on Angola.

It is important that all USG agencies should maintain maximum pressure on the GOP political leadership to prevent [redacted] from undermining the settlement process through support for the Islamic radicals.[1]

---

* United States Government.
† Government of Pakistan.
‡ The two extremes in the cable referred to Soviet-supported Najib and Pakistan-backed Hekmatyar.
§ Saudi Arabian Government.

ψ

Operation Desert Storm was an American military triumph, a watershed in global politics. The decisive victory coincided with the decline of the Soviet Union. The massive 675,000-strong U.S.-led coalition suffered only 240 dead, including 148 Americans. In a stunningly successful 100-hour ground campaign, Saddam Hussein's army was driven out of Kuwait, suffering more than 25,000 casualties. The small 308-man Afghan Mujahidin contingent was among the first coalition units to enter Kuwait City.

The quick victory in the first Gulf War contrasted with the seemingly endless Afghan war. Top American foreign-policy makers, President George H.W. Bush, Secretary of State James A. Baker III, and National Security Adviser Brent Scowcroft still viewed distant Afghanistan as a conflict left over from the Cold War. The Cold War was over. The United States had won. Cooperating with the Soviet Union to defuse regional conflicts was now a U.S. foreign-policy priority. Gorbachev was recalling Soviet troops from Cuba near America's southern borders, while American support, through the ISI, for Gulbuddin Hekmatyar's offensives against Najib threatened the USSR's southern borders.

Under Secretary for Political Affairs Robert Kimmitt and I tried to close the gap between the State Department and the CIA's Directorate of Operations on Afghan policy. I met twice with Deputy CIA Director Richard Kerr to resolve differences. But the agency persisted in backing the ISI's military attacks on Kabul aimed at replacing Najib with Hekmatyar. A unitary U.S. Afghan policy would have maximized Washington's leverage to end the Afghan war. Instead, the United States was still implementing two contradictory policies. Pakistan was doing the same thing. The difference was that Pakistan's army was coordinating Pakistan's two-faced policy at the top—as it would do after 9/11. The U.S. policy was not coordinated from the top. Separately, the State Department and the CIA were operating at cross purposes. That was a certain recipe for paralysis and ultimate policy failure.

On January 3, 1991, Under Secretary of State Kimmitt made the State Department's frustration with the CIA public. In his interview with *New York Times* reporter Clifford Krass, he accused the CIA of contravening U.S. Afghan policy. "In recent weeks," Krass wrote, "Mr. Kimmitt has battled with Central Intelligence Agency officials who would like to unleash the guerrillas in Afghanistan in one last effort." He quoted Kimmitt as saying: "If they have a problem at the agency it is with me carrying out a policy that has been set down by the Secretary and reaffirmed by the President during the June summit. . . . So I have no hesitation in saying that their problem is not with me but with the senior leadership of this department and this Government. I think they are just bucking policy."[2] The CIA's unilateralism on Afghanistan would remain an irresolvable problem for Kimmitt—and for me—until we moved on to our next assignments.

ॐ

It is conceivable that, after the failed ISI-Hekmatyar-Tanai March 6, 1990, coup, General Beg and his nine corps commanders seriously considered the American advice to leave the Afghans—with UN help—free to determine the way ahead for their country. Many Afghans from all groups, grasping what seemed to be an unprecedented opportunity, in a few short months during the summer of 1990, used their newfound political and military space to put together the commanders' shura, create a Mujahidin military strategy for 1991, and start to build a political transition process to replace Najib based on the Afghan jirga tradition of community consensus. The October Shah Selim commanders' meeting inside Afghanistan laid the foundation for the long-delayed military pressure on Najib to transfer power to an interim government chosen by Afghans. Zahir Shah was pleased to see the political logjam break. He and Ahmed Shah Masood engaged the governments of Pakistan and Saudi Arabia. Prince Turki provided funds to the commanders' shura. Saudi Arabia considered retaliating against the betrayals of Gulbuddin Hekmatyar and Abdul Rasoul Sayyaf during the Gulf War.

It is, however, far more likely that the Pakistani Army and the ISI had decided to loosen ISI controls on the Mujahidin in Pakistan during the summer of 1990 in order to see how the Afghans would use their newfound freedom, then attempt to channel those actions toward achieving Zia's vision. Beg tried that with Masood during their meeting in Rawalpindi. When Beg's idea of a Masood-Hekmatyar alliance quickly evaporated, he shifted back to sponsoring only the extremists in the Mujahidin. The ISI sharply reduced weapons and money going to Masood. By April 1991, he was no longer receiving any help. Contrary to ISI Brigadier Afzal Janjua's commitments to Abdul Haq, the ISI did not provide arms to the moderate Pashtun commanders in the commanders' shura to attack regime-held towns in eastern and southern Afghanistan. Pakistan's generals made an exception for the March 31, 1991, attack on Khost, since Jalaluddin Haqqani, who led the attack, was a long-standing collaborator.

In December 1990, ISI Director General Asad Durrani created another "made-in-Pakistan" Afghan government, this one called the "Leadership Council." The organization of the Leadership Council canceled out the six AIG leaders' refusal to accept Hekmatyar back into the AIG fold. The ISI pieced together the original seven Peshawar leaders or their representatives, and a few other Afghan splinter groups, to establish an interim government to replace Najib. The AIG would continue to exist, but the Leadership Council would be the political platform for the ISI's next Hekmatyar-Tanai coup attempt in Kabul. Pakistan's new prime minister, Nawaz Sharif, supported the strategy. Jamaat-i Islami, Hekmatyar's biggest cheerleader in Pakistan, was part of Sharif's governing coalition. Sharif actively cooperated with the ISI's buildup of the religious paramilitary group, Lashkar-i Taiba (Army of the Pure), which recruited most of its fighters from Sharif's home province, Punjab, where his brother was chief minister. After Yaqub Khan's retirement, Sharif took the foreign minister portfolio himself and appointed Ambassador Akram Zaki, whom I had known in China, to be secretary general of the ministry.

During 1991 the ISI organized several more Pakistani religious paramilitary groups tied to Pakistan's two major religious parties, Jamaat-i Islami and Jamiat-i Ulema-i Islam. These militia organizations mass-produced thousands more Islamic militants available for holy wars in Afghanistan, Kashmir, and around the world during the 1990s. The ISI worked with Jamaat, Jamiat, and Arab radicals on the Frontier to establish scores of new training camps in Pakistan and Konar, Paktiya, and Nangarhar provinces in Afghanistan. ISI chief Durrani and Pakistani Foreign Ministry officials gave evasive answers when I raised the subject of the paramilitary groups. U.S. government internal intelligence reporting did not go much beyond simply identifying them.

While in Pakistan, my deputy, Richard Hoagland, and I stepped up efforts to gather information on the rising danger of foreign extremist groups on the Frontier. To avoid clearance problems at the U.S. embassy in Islamabad, I waited until I got to Europe before reporting to Washington our findings about ISI's support to radicals.

ψ

Through 1991 and up to the fall of Najib in April 1992, U.S. strategy continued on the uphill climb of convincing Pakistan and Saudi Arabia to back a
UN-brokered political settlement. Pakistan pocketed over $100 million in
annual U.S. covert aid to the Mujahidin plus millions more in the form of
weapons the United States captured in the Gulf War, transported to Pakistan,
and passed to the ISI. Pakistan utilized this mountain of weaponry, including
Iraqi tanks and artillery, to pursue a Hekmatyar-Tanai spearheaded military
strategy that contradicted U.S. interests and policies.

The administration and Congress reacted to the two-year stalemate in Afghanistan by slowly distancing the United States from the Afghan conflict.
The Kimmitt Group's decision to toss the political-settlement ball to the
United Nations and UN Special Envoy Benon Sevan was the right one. Pakistan and Saudi Arabia had turned down three U.S. proposals to break the
political-settlement impasse, the last by Under Secretary of State Kimmitt.
My main task now was to support Sevan to sell his political settlement proposal to Islamabad, Riyadh, and the Mujahidin. There was little reason to expect that Sevan would be more successful than the United States. Pakistan's
army was still determined to implant Hekmatyar in Kabul.

The second principal prong of U.S. policy in late 1990 into 1991 carried
more potential for success: concluding a negative symmetry agreement with
the Soviet Union. Under Secretary Kimmitt took the lead in negotiating the
simultaneous and mutual U.S.-Soviet arms cutoff in highly secretive talks
with Soviet Ambassador Alexander Bessmertnykh in Washington. I assisted
him by analyzing the Russian-language drafts, comparing them to the U.S.
drafts, anticipating Soviet negotiating positions, and suggesting U.S. negotiating tactics.

Secretary Baker's and Kimmitt's emphasis on concluding a negative symmetry agreement with Moscow advanced the administration's objective of
an Afghan political settlement in three ways. First, the termination of arms
shipments to Najib and the Mujahidin would reduce the influence the KGB
and the CIA were having on the political-settlement process. Second, negative symmetry would speed Najib's downfall. And third, the declining patience of U.S. members of Congress with the Afghan war would eventually

lead to a unilateral U.S. arms cutoff: Without a negative symmetry agreement, the Soviets would continue to arm Najib, who would reject a political settlement, and the Afghan war would continue.

Within the national security bureaucracy at that time, only the CIA's clandestine wing, the Directorate of Operations, opposed a U.S.-Soviet negative symmetry accord. The CIA's analysis arm, the Directorate of Intelligence, and the State Department's Bureau of Intelligence and Research (INR) felt that negative symmetry would hurt Najib more than the resistance in the long run, given the regime's dependence on superior firepower.[3] State Department and CIA analysts—I thought correctly—judged that Mujahidin morale would initially dip, but that the Mujahidin's much larger manpower base would eventually shift the balance to a resistance victory.

Kimmitt adroitly guided the negative symmetry negotiations to a conclusion in his secret one-on-one meetings with Ambassador Bessmertnykh in Washington. At the beginning of 1991, only one small blank remained in the draft accord: It was for a specific "date certain" when the U.S.-Soviet cutoff would occur. The United States was ready to insert the date and sign the accord, but the Soviet KGB and military leaders in Moscow refused to agree to a date. Their domestic position was strengthening; Gorbachev's was weakening.

ψ

I made two trips to Saudi Arabia and Pakistan in February and March 1991 in the aftermath of the Gulf War. My briefings of Prince Turki and Pakistani officials covered the current status of the U.S.-Soviet dialogue, including negative symmetry, as well as military, political, economic, refugee, and narcotics issues. My main priorities were to assist Benon Sevan's peace efforts and to encourage the moderate momentum under way in the resistance since mid-1990. The latter objective involved maintaining Pakistan's tolerance, if not support, for the commanders' shura; encouraging Masood and Zahir Shah's engagement with Pakistan and Saudi Arabia; promoting Saudi support for the commanders' shura; and monitoring the gradual development of tribal and ulema shuras inside Afghanistan. Collectively, these trends had already broken the monopoly the seven party leaders had exercised over resistance politics since Zia ul-Haq's time.

During our talks in Riyadh, Prince Turki expressed Saudi outrage at Hekmatyar and Sayyaf's betrayal during the Gulf crisis. The two Mujahidin extremists had supported Saddam Hussein and delayed the arrival of the Mujahidin contingent to help defend the kingdom against the Iraqi dictator— despite the fact that they had long been the biggest beneficiaries of Saudi aid. Turki informed me that the Saudi government had cut them off. At my request, he invited Masood to send a delegation to Riyadh. Masood's political advisers, Daoud Mir and Ahmed Zia, flew to Riyadh and spent several hours at Turki's home appealing for a more positive Saudi attitude toward Masood. After their meeting, Turki remarked to me that the commanders' shura could mark a turning point in the war: The Saudi government, he said, would support it. He stated his readiness to continue the Saudi dialogue with Zahir Shah.

In Islamabad on March 14 at 2:30 p.m. Saudi Ambassador Yusef Motabbakani, Ambassador Oakley, and I filed into General Durrani's ISI conference room for a meeting. Station Chief Bill attended, as did Riaz Khan, the Pakistani Foreign Ministry's senior Afghan specialist and a future Pakistani foreign secretary; Brigadier Afzal Janjua; and other ISI officers. The three ambassadors represented the two countries that had stood by Pakistan and Afghanistan during the past twelve years of the Afghan conflict. After all were seated, General Durrani began his presentation. He announced that the goal of the meeting was to "clear the air," to wipe away the mistrust that had emerged during the Gulf War. He pointed out that the leaders of the ISI's Afghan team were in the room and asked for frank talk to resolve differences.

Ambassador Motabbakani spoke first. He furiously censured Hekmatyar, denouncing his abandonment of the AIG, his failure to fulfill promises he had made to Prince Turki; and his divisive activities within the Mujahidin. Without pausing, but leaning forward toward Durrani, Motabbakani said that he was speaking under instruction. He advised Durrani that his government was displeased with Hekmatyar's and Sayyaf's betrayal during the Gulf War and with the ISI initiative to establish the "Leadership Council." He told Durrani that the creation of the Leadership Council threatened the close U.S.-Saudi-Pakistani cooperation in Afghanistan that had existed previously. It was created without consulting with the Saudi or the American governments. His government would not cooperate with the Leadership Council or any organization that included Hekmatyar and Sayyaf.

The Saudi government, Motabbakani continued, had cut off assistance to Hekmatyar and Sayyaf and was studying whether Rabbani belonged in the same category. "They betrayed us and they will betray you," he declared. The Saudi government was impressed with the National Commanders' Shura, he explained, and was directly providing funds to it. "Let's go in the direction of Abdul Haq," he proposed. Durrani did not respond. He simply stared at the Saudi envoy. Oakley interjected that the Americans had first heard of the Leadership Council from the Mujahidin, not the ISI. He agreed with Motabbakani's opposition to the Leadership Council, which seemed designed to bring Hekmatyar back together with the six other leaders of the AIG.

Invited to speak, I noted that the U.S. government, like the Saudi government, did not want any of its resources going to Hekmatyar and Sayyaf. I suggested that the time had come to dispense with the failed Mujahidin structures created by outsiders in the past. The Pakistani, Saudi, and U.S. governments had long sought to end the Afghan war with a political settlement. A military solution was not possible. The three governments should assist UN efforts to help the Mujahidin themselves, in the Afghan jirga tradition, to develop a consensus process leading to a large Afghan gathering, perhaps a loya jirga, to replace Najib with a new leadership chosen by Afghans. Only an Afghan government seen to be selected by Afghans could stabilize the country and end the war.

After politely hearing the three ambassadors out, Durrani spoke for forty minutes. He offered no indication that the ISI would be changing course. What happened in Afghanistan was in Pakistan's vital interest, he said. That was not true for the United States and Saudi Arabia. They could leave the field; Pakistan did not have that option. Pakistan welcomed advice from friends, but in the end it must be the main actor. Durrani claimed that the Leadership Council idea was still being considered. It was worth trying. Implying that Hekmatyar remained the ISI's favorite, he said that the three governments should worry less about personalities and more about defeating Najib. He repeated the ISI line used in the past, saying that U.S.—and now Saudi—demands that the ISI not provide their resources to Hekmatyar and Sayyaf would not apply to their commanders in the field who were fighting well. That condition effectively negated the cutoff, given Hekmatyar's and Sayyaf's influence over their commanders.

Janjua intervened to speak against the idea of the commanders' shura assuming a political role. Somewhat unexpectedly, Foreign Ministry official Riaz Khan then spoke up. Taking the American and Saudi side, he cautioned the ISI against launching the Leadership Council. He stated that it would risk hurting the commanders' shura and Pakistan's good relations with the Mujahidin's other foreign supporters.

The meeting ended with handshakes and smiles but little agreement on any of the issues discussed. General Durrani had been a generous listener but had, in essence, spurned all of the recommendations put forward by the three ambassadors and the Pakistani Foreign Ministry's senior specialist on Afghanistan. The meeting was depressing but exactly synchronized with my experience in dealing with the ISI for the past two years. I held out scant hope that its favoritism toward the extremist minority in the resistance would change.

Eventually, the Pakistani military's reach for hegemony in Afghanistan would suffer the same fate as the Soviet and British interventions, notwithstanding the Islamic cloak that Pakistan's army was casting over its proxy war. The only result would be Islamic extremist propelled death, destruction, and anarchy inside Afghanistan—and blowback into Pakistan.

The March 14 Durrani meeting demonstrated that General Beg and his corps commanders were not going to make the basic change in Pakistan's Afghan policy requested by the United States, Saudi Arabia, the United Nations, the Soviet Union, and the Afghans. Washington was not inclined to press the issue after the heady U.S. victory in the Gulf War. It was losing interest in Afghanistan. In the time remaining in my special envoy appointment, I was determined to exert what influence I could to advance a peaceful, negotiated conclusion to the Afghan war. But I knew that I would be struggling against an unyielding tide in the region and inside the U.S. national security apparatus.

Moving to Peshawar after the Durrani meeting, I advised commanders along with tribal and religious leaders to keep up the political and military momentum against Najib, cooperate with Benon Sevan, and support a political settlement. I stuck to generalities and refused to advise the commanders on tactics in organizing their shuras or carrying out military operations. I had learned that while Afghans often sought foreign help in bridging their personal, tribal, and ethnic divisions, they viscerally opposed foreign-sponsored initiatives to pressure them. Zahir Shah's observation, that in the end Afghans had to resolve their differences, was exactly right. The commanders needed to unite their own ranks, reject external interference in the shura's activities, and move forward.

I knew that Hekmatyar would attempt to twist the U.S. decision to cut him off to his political advantage. Leaks to the U.S. media from Washington bureaucrats had already announced cessation of U.S. aid to him and Sayyaf (and erroneously to Rabbani) before my February arrival in Pakistan. Qutbuddin Helal, Hekmatyar's close adviser and son-in-law, told foreign journalists in Peshawar that termination of American aid was a "blessing in disguise" for Hekmatyar.[4]

At my request, USAID laid off all known Hezb party members still employed by its road-building organization, the Afghan Construction and Logistics Unit (ACLU), and sent more road construction equipment to Masood's road project in the north. The road from Chitral to Zebak was completed in November 1991, ahead of schedule and two months after Masood captured that city, strengthening his military position in the north and weakening Hekmatyar's. To further illustrate the American break with Hekmatyar, I asked that USAID deny Hekmatyar's party its normal quota of scholarships to study in the United States. Several members of the Hezb executive committee angrily trooped into USAID's regional office in Peshawar, indignantly protesting to office director Hank Cushing. Hank, a rugged, straightforward veteran of USAID operations in Vietnam, gruffly responded in kind: "Let's face it, you hate us and we hate you."[5]

Before leaving Pakistan I accepted an invitation to dine with Rabbani at his Islamabad residence. I assumed that the U.S. media reports grouping Rabbani with Hekmatyar and Sayyaf in the U.S. aid cutoff had alarmed him and that he would be anxious to confirm his pro-U.S. credentials. Rabbani's criticism of the United States and Saudi Arabia had been egregious, but his rhetoric was less strident than Hekmatyar's and Sayyaf's. As usual, he had allowed some flexibility to reverse himself, depending on future events. I tried to exploit his predicament and push him out of his cherished middle ground between Mujahidin radicals and moderates. Rabbani would be hardline Islamist if he was sure of his footing, but I wanted him to move toward the moderates. He always retreated when threats loomed. Nominally tied to Masood, he had much to lose if Hekmatyar managed to seize Kabul. I felt the conditions were ripe for another Rabbani political shift, this one embracing the political settlement process.

Rabbani performed exactly according to stereotype during our two-hour discussion and then during dinner. He chose a known moderate-nationalist, Masood's friend and adviser Masood Khalili, to join him and interpret. As we sat down, I had just begun to present my talking points when Rabbani interrupted me. Reading from prepared notes, he embarked on a long monologue that started with noting his happiness about the U.S. victory in the Gulf War. His voice mounted to a nervous shriek as he lambasted the ISI, Hekmatyar, and Sayyaf for opposing Saudi Arabia and the United States. Rabbani claimed that he was facing many Najibs in the form of ISI officers telling him what to do. He explained that at the Muslim Brotherhood–organized Lahore conference, he had spoken out in favor of Kuwait but was in the minority and was forced to sign the final communiqué. This was a lie, as was his next claim—that he tried to send his Mujahidin to Saudi Arabia.

Turning to Mujahidin politics, Rabbani explained that he was making every effort to neutralize Hekmatyar and Sayyaf by drawing closer to them. This struck me as another lie. Rabbani warned that the ISI would try to destroy all the progress that had been made in a broad-based direction during 1990. He stated his support for the commanders' shura and offered to form a joint "front" with Mojaddedi, Gailani, Nabi, Khalis, and Shia representatives to achieve a political settlement. That was good news.

During the remainder of the evening, I pressed Rabbani to put his pledge to work with the moderates into practice. He promised he would. I left his dinner that night convinced that he would move in that direction, but I wondered how long it would be before he doubled back to Hekmatyar and Sayyaf.

The March 31 attack on Khost, billed as the kickoff of the commanders' shura 1991 military campaign, was neither planned nor organized by Afghan commanders. It was an ISI operation from start to finish, geared to enhance the position of the Afghan Islamists in the aftermath of the battle. The leading moderate Ahmadzai tribal chief in Paktiya, Haji Naim, was a prominent member of the commanders' shura and the head of the Ahmadzai tribal shura. The ISI armed his tribals but assigned them a combat role subservient to Jalaluddin Haqqani's and Gulbuddin Hekmatyar's forces.

Khost was defended by more than 3,000 men from the regime's regular army and militia. An equal number of Mujahidin were in the attacking force. Before the attack, I wrote to six party leaders asking that they treat prisoners humanely. The Afghan population would turn against the Mujahidin if the massacres at Jalalabad were reenacted at Khost.

Pakistani Special Services Group (SSG) commandos, and artillery and communications specialists attached to the Mujahidin assault groups positioned around Khost, coordinated the command and control, artillery, and communications functions during the fighting. On the morning of March 31, 1991, the Mujahidin attacked Khost from multiple directions. When Hekmatyar's fighters failed to take the main Khost airport, Haji Naim's Ahmadzai tribals stormed and seized it, taking heavy casualties. Mujahidin attacking forces west of the city were thrown back by the regime's tough 59th Commando Group and Khost tribal militia. By mid-afternoon, however, the Ahmadzai tribals were fighting their way into the city. Haqqani's Mujahidin followed them, capturing the garrison's command post. Soon after, more than 2,500 regime troops in the city surrendered. Hundreds more escaped to Gardez, 40 miles away on the road to Kabul. About 500 regime troops were killed and 400 wounded during the fierce fighting. In addition, 160 Mujahidin died, 121 of them Ahmadzai. A regime deputy defense minister and two KHAD generals were among the captives. The ISI took control of the heavy weapons captured: 25 tanks, 12 of them working, and more than 50 artillery pieces.

The fall of Khost was a major defeat for the regime. Najib, regime defense minister Aslam Watanjar, and numerous army officers had tribal ties to the province. In the past, Mujahidin disunity and Najib's bribes of tribal chiefs in Paktiya had protected the remote regime outpost on the Pakistani border. Haqqani told me at the U.S. consulate in Peshawar that he believed that Mujahidin unity was the reason for the victory and that the commanders' shura had created that unity. He proudly informed me that regime prisoners had been turned over to the Swiss International Committee of the Red Cross (ICRC).[6]

Under Secretary Kimmitt publicly described the Khost victory as part of the U.S. emphasis on a political—not military—solution to the Afghan war. During a United States Information Agency WorldNet broadcast, he stated:

> I think that the fact that the struggle inside Afghanistan continues indicates the fragility of the regime of Najibullah and the PDPA. The U.S. and the Soviet Union, as early as October and September of 1989, made clear that we supported a transition period leading to a political process that would culminate in an act of self-determination by the Afghan people; that is, for the Afghan people to choose their own leadership rather than to have one imposed upon them. I would hope that

the fact the fighting has continued, and perhaps a city like Khost [has fallen,] will make it clear to Najib and the PDPA regime that the time has come to move beyond the current phase, to get to a point where there can be a legitimate act of self-determination by the Afghan people themselves. We certainly support the brave struggle of the Afghan resistance and will continue to support that struggle.[7]

In June, while the snows were still melting in northern Afghanistan, Masood began the northern offensives he had promised at the Shah Selim commanders' meeting.[8] His campaign was characteristically well planned and decisive. It lasted a little over a month, from June 20 to the end of July. Most of the regime strong points that he captured were defended by paid militias whose loyalties were fluid. The first and most intense battle was at Khwaja Ghar, seized in late June. In his next offensive, beginning on July 7, Masood captured the large town of Khanabad near Kunduz. In a quick-fire manner, his offensive next rolled up Zeebak on the Pakistani border on July 16, the strategic Badakhshan town (and ancient Greek colony) of Eshkashim on the Amu Darya border with the USSR on July 20, Rostaq on July 24, Chah-i-bad on July 26, Dasht-e-Qaleh on July 28, and Wakhan on July 29.

Masood now controlled more than 300 miles of Afghanistan's border with the Soviet Union. His new conquests prompted a Soviet request for border negotiations. Masood agreed, but insisted that the talks take place on the Afghan side of the Amu Darya at Eshkashem. He told the Soviets the talks should be bilateral, following the pattern of those conducted during the Soviet-Afghan war—without the presence of regime representatives. The Soviets accepted his conditions. The American consulate in Peshawar reported to Washington that Moscow's acceptance of direct talks at Eshkashem "implied its acceptance of Masood's virtual sovereignty in the northern border areas where he controlled forces." The consulate cable further informed Washington that "the Soviets, who initiated the contact, pledged not to intervene in Masood's campaign to liberate the northeast portion of Afghanistan. . . . In acquiescing to Masood's domination of the north, the Soviets thus trade the ineffective border control achieved by the Kabul regime with the presumably tighter control to be exercised by Masood's forces."[9] During the negotiations, the Soviets accepted Masood's request that the Soviet border-control post in Eshkashem, established after the 1978 communist coup, be moved back across the Amu Darya to Soviet territory.

MAP 17.1 MUJAHIDIN 1991 VICTORIES

The Soviet border concessions to Masood were grounded in Moscow's re-
alpolitik. Masood was a moderate-nationalist who publicly backed a political
settlement of the Afghan war if Najib and the PDPA gave up power. He was
an obstacle to the ISI's campaign to install Hekmatyar in Kabul.

The Khost victory, Masood's victories in the north, the May capture of the
far southwestern city of Ziranj, the capital of Nimroz Province, and Zahir
Shah's outspoken public rejection of Najib all increased military and political
pressure on the Soviets to drop Najib. Rabbani's decision to swing over to
the Mujahidin moderate camp and support a political solution was also important and timely, even if fungible. It was made as the United Nations was
finishing a year-long round of consultations with the United States, the Soviet
Union, Pakistan, Saudi Arabia, and Iran as well as the Mujahidin and Najib
on the way forward to a negotiated end to the war. Washington had handed
the Afghan political settlement hot potato over to UN Secretary General

Javier Pérez de Cuéllar. The UN special envoy, Cypriot national and veteran UN diplomat Benon Sevan, was dynamic and hard working, a skilled negotiator, and thoroughly familiar with the Afghan issue. On May 21, 1991, Pérez de Cuéllar announced a five-point Afghan political settlement framework that Sevan had prepared. The UN gave Sevan the mandate to achieve two interrelated levels of consensus on the modalities of a political settlement—an intra-Afghan consensus and an "international consensus," particularly among regional powers involved in the Afghan war. The external powers would cease supplying arms once the transition mechanism was in place, and Afghans would observe a cease-fire. "Free and fair elections in accordance with Afghan traditions" to select a "broad-based government" would follow. The language in the statement left open the option of a loya jirga instead of, or in conjunction with, elections—a procedure later implemented by the United Nations with U.S. backing after the Taliban's ouster in 2001. UN success would, to a great extent, depend on the willingness of outside powers to support Benon Sevan's efforts and not create competing Afghan settlement initiatives.

In mid-1991, the stars were not aligned enough to produce a breakthrough in peace negotiations. Najib was losing territory and population to the Mujahidin, but Soviet KGB and military constituencies in the Kremlin's leadership were blocking negative symmetry. Despite horrendous economic problems at home, they were transporting more than $3 billion in aid to Najib annually. In addition, Pakistan's army was not going to cease implementing its own Afghan settlement plans. Pakistan's prime minister, Nawaz Sharif, had a history of working with the ISI. He had collaborated with Hamid Gul and Asad Durrani to fix the 1988 elections in order to prevent Benazir Bhutto from winning a parliamentary majority. He brought Qazi Hussain Ahmed, a vocal supporter of a radical Islamic military conclusion to the Afghan war, into his government. Sharif personally sympathized with the Pakistani Army's preference for Hekmatyar. He shored up Pakistan's plausible denials of ISI sponsorship of Hekmatyar's serial military offensives to overthrow Najib while disingenuously endorsing the UN political settlement process.[10]

Sharif's new secretary general of the Pakistani Foreign Ministry, Akram Zaki, briefed me and other diplomats about an April 3 Afghan cell meeting that he said had formally approved the UN-led Afghan political settlement.

Under his leadership, the Foreign Ministry created a tripartite "Consultative Committee" made up of Pakistanis, Iranians, and Mujahidin representatives. The Pakistani and Iranian governments, however, not Afghans, selected the Afghan participants exiled in their countries to fill out the Afghan delegation. In the view of ordinary Afghans, this discredited the tripartite initiative from the outset.

Sevan told me he did not approve of the tripartite initiative because it was designed to choose an interim regime that answered to Islamabad and Tehran, not to the Afghan people. Sevan's goal was to create a framework that Afghans could use to choose an interim government, which in turn could hold elections or a loya jirga to select a new Afghan leadership untainted by foreign hands. In effect, Zaki and the Iranians were circumventing the UN's May 21, 1991, settlement plan that they had both accepted.

Pakistan and Iran were key players on Afghanistan. Sevan had no choice but to wait for their tripartite scheme to collapse under the weight of Afghan objections. In my meetings with Mujahidin, all resistance commanders as well as tribal and religious leaders rejected the trilateral project.

Pakistan chose four of its seven party leaders—Rabbani, Mojaddedi, Gailani, and Nabi—to head up the Mujahidin contingent. Iran put forward leaders from the Mujahidin group it had created in 1990, the Hezb-i Wahdat. The first tripartite conference was held in Islamabad July 29–30. Zaki led the Pakistani delegation, while Iranian foreign minister Abbas Magnum Velayati headed the Iranian delegation. The concluding "Joint Declaration" stressed "the pursuit of a just peaceful settlement of the Afghanistan problem, . . . which should lead to the replacement of the present illegal government in Kabul and the establishment of an elected government."[11]

In meetings with Pakistani officials, Ambassador Oakley and I continued to register our objections to the ISI's resuscitation of the Leadership Council, but with no effect. The ISI organized a signing ceremony establishing the "Afghan Resistance Leadership Council," including Hekmatyar, Rabbani, Sayyaf's deputy Ahmed Shah Ahmadzai, and the three AIG moderates. The Peshawar seven dominated the Leadership Council's ten-member executive body.[12] The council and a "commission" of "60 or 100" persons chosen by these seven were tapped to select the "Provisional Government" of Afghanistan when Najib was removed.[13] The formal establishment of the Leadership Council was another clear indication that Pakistan did not intend to honor its commitment to work within the UN framework. Yunis Qanuni, Masood's adviser working in the commanders' shura office in Peshawar, told me that the Leadership Council was formed to destroy the commanders' shura. Haji Deen Mohammad, Khalis' deputy and Abdul Haq's brother, predicted that the Leadership Council would fail because it was not formed by Afghans.

The ISI stopped supporting the commanders' shura after the victory at Khost. It began to lay the groundwork for Hekmatyar-Tanai-led attacks on Jalalabad and Gardez, Paktiya's capital. Gardez lay only 35 miles from Kabul. Its capture would open the road to the Afghan capital. The Agency followed the ISI's lead in drawing down its assistance to the commanders' shura after Khost fell. A meeting I suggested between the deputy station chief and Abdul Haq broke up following an angry exchange between the two.

The ISI's cutoff of support to Haji Naim and the Ahmadzai tribes that had done most of the fighting at Khost underscored the Pakistani Army's return to degrading Afghan moderates in the resistance and exclusively backing the extremists. Haqqani removed Ahmadzai representatives from the Khost shura set up under his leadership after the battle. In a May 27 meeting in Peshawar, an Ahmadzai tribal leader told me that the ISI, Haqqani, and Hekmatyar were prohibiting moderate members of the commanders' shura, including Haji Naim, from entering Khost. He accused Hekmatyar's Mujahidin of raising Hezb party flags in Khost neighborhoods, looting the Khost weapons armory, and occupying key government buildings.[14] The pillaging of Khost and the regime's Scud attacks on the city drove 20,000 more refugees into Pakistan.

Additional hurdles to a UN-led political settlement arose in mid-1991. During the summer, I began to hear from Saudi Ambassador Motabbakani and Mujahidin sources that the Saudi government had decided to mend fences with Hekmatyar and Sayyaf. Speaking to representatives of the media after returning from a meeting with senior Saudi officials in Riyadh, Sayyaf adviser Mohammad Yasir—who was rabidly anti-American—noted that both sides had "agreed to open a new chapter."[15] I heard later that Chief Mufti Bin Baz had convinced King Fahd to veto recommendations to close Hekmatyar's and Sayyaf's offices in the kingdom. The al-Saud royal family was, once again, allowing the Saudi clergy to determine the kingdom's Afghan policy. On August 22, the director of Arabian Peninsula affairs at the U.S. State Department told an Afghan Coordinating Committee meeting that he "doubted" the Saudis would "be moved towards promoting a political settlement[,] because the royal family appears to be vulnerable to fundamentalists and may be willing to allow more conservative forces to set the agenda on certain issues, including aid to the Afghan Resistance Islamic radicals."[16]

In talks with Prince Turki in Riyadh in May, I reminded him of the strong objections he and Motabbakani had expressed about the ISI's Leadership Council and its promotion of Hekmatyar and Sayyaf. Turki merely replied that Khost had gone well, and Jalalabad and Gardez were next. I sensed that he was comfortable with the Saudi government's decision to reverse its position; he may even have helped engineer the reversal. In October, Turki traveled back to Pakistan to personally reopen the Saudi dialogue with Hekmatyar.

New Afghan peace plans sprouting in Europe outside the UN framework also impeded Benon Sevan's efforts. Two separate proposals sponsored by a Swiss institute in cooperation with the Swiss Foreign Ministry and the German Socialist Party (SPD) envisioned Najib sharing power with the Mujahidin under the titular leadership of former king Zahir Shah. Zahir Shah informed me he had refused to associate himself with these peace plans. Sevan told the Swiss government that Zahir Shah could "neither come on a white horse nor on Swiss Air." I made two trips to Europe in the fall of 1991 to discourage the two initiatives. The Swiss foundation and the SPD agreed to drop their settlement projects and support the UN process.

Quelling the proliferation of Afghan peace proposals also drew me to the Vatican's Foreign Ministry in Rome. Monsignor Claudio Celoi, a Foreign Ministry officer in charge of Asia at the Holy See, asked me to stop by to discuss a peace initiative that Najib had sent to Pope John Paul II.[17] During our meeting in his Vatican office, lined with lovely biblical scenes, Celoi informed me that Najib had requested that the pope mediate the differences between his regime and the Mujahidin. Celoi was rightly skeptical that Muslims would accept the pope as a mediator. I agreed, recommending that the Vatican instead issue a low-key papal statement wishing peace for Afghanistan. Celoi accepted the suggestion.

ψ

While Pakistani, Saudi, Soviet, and even European support for the UN plan was faltering in mid-1991, American attention to Afghanistan was plummeting. The adjustments in U.S. policy on negative symmetry and the passing of responsibility for an Afghan political settlement to the United Nations were necessary and well executed. But both steps unavoidably indicated to the Mujahidin, to the Pakistanis, Saudis, Soviets, and Iranians, and to Najib that the United States was disengaging from Afghanistan. Moreover, Under Secretary Kimmitt, the administration's experienced and able leader on Afghan policy, was preparing to take up his next appointment as U.S. ambassador to Germany in early September.

In the spring of 1991, the National Security Council escalated its pressure for a unilateral arms cutoff by the United States. Some in Congress echoed that demand. During executive branch meetings and secret hearings in Congress, I drove home the point that American credibility in Afghanistan and elsewhere around the world dictated that we take the Soviets out of the war with us. A unilateral American arms cutoff would destroy American diplomatic leverage with Pakistan, Saudi Arabia, and the Soviets. Without America's active engagement, a political settlement and a negotiated outcome of the Afghan war would be impossible. I argued that the United States must continue to pressure the Soviet Union to agree to a specific "date certain" for a mutual arms cutoff.

A startling phone call to me from *New York Times* correspondent Elaine Sciolino on May 9, 1991, threatened to throw the secret U.S.-Soviet discussions about negative symmetry into the public domain. She phoned to get my reaction to a "very high level National Security Council source" who had told her that the administration was requesting no funds for the Afghan resistance in the 1992 budget. The source had asserted that the Afghan conflict was now a "civil war." I declined to comment even off the record. I did note, however, that I would not accept the information provided by her source.[18]

Sciolino phoned back later that day to probe further. She claimed to have talked to "absolutely the highest levels of the administration," but she added that they were below the president. I suspected that her sources were White House National Security Adviser Brent Scowcroft and his assistant, Richard Haass. She claimed that two very senior White House officials had now confirmed that the decision had been made to give no assistance to the Afghan resistance in the 1992 fiscal year. One of the officials, she said, had remarked that the administration had decided to make a fundamental shift in Afghan policy. According to Sciolino, they were planning to reverse the course of the last eleven years and cease all support to the resistance. She added that "someone just below Bush had briefed some foreign officials in even stronger terms." Sciolino asked for my reaction.

I said that I could not comment on such highly classified budget matters, even off the record, but I refused to accept the information her sources had provided. She would have to talk to someone more senior than me in the State Department to get a more detailed answer. I added that 1992 was the third appropriation cycle on Afghanistan in which I had been involved. In both 1990 and 1991, the same reports about fundamental changes in administration policy and an end to funding for the resistance had circulated, and they had turned out to be wrong. I suggested that Sciolino not repeat the miscalculation. Sciolino acknowledged that she had also been told "the funding situation could be changed," and she would "play" with the story some more. Her long May 12 article in the *New York Times* gave coverage to both of the opposing views in the administration, noting that the budget process still had two more months to go.[19]

During the summer months, the Bush administration grew more frustrated over the impasse in the negative symmetry negotiations. In June, a four-word phrase, "The president wants out," began to be heard in State Department corridor conversations about Afghanistan. During a meeting with Pakistan's Senate chairman in the State Department on June 14, 1991, Secretary of State Baker expected "that we could not sustain our present Afghan program in Congress beyond the end of this fiscal year" ending on September 30. The Soviets were willing to stop arms shipments, he stated, but we still needed to agree to a deadline. The secretary stressed that "both he and the President felt it was now time to get a political solution."[20]

Boris Yeltsin, the popularly elected president of the Russian Federation, also wanted to disengage from Afghanistan. He called for the Soviet Union to terminate all assistance to the country.[21] His influence was increasing in Moscow while Gorbachev's and that of his hardline opposition was decreasing.

The factional maneuvering inside the Kremlin over Soviet Afghan policy may have been behind a reckless attempt by the Soviet embassy in Washington to strengthen the proponents of unilateral negative symmetry in the administration. In July, Al Kamen, the *Washington Post* correspondent assigned to the State Department, stopped by my office to ask why the United States was not agreeing to Soviet desires to conclude the negative symmetry agreement. He handed me the entire text of the secret negative symmetry draft agreement, which, in Washington, was known to only a handful of State Department diplomats and Soviet embassy officials. I tried not to show my amazement. Smiling, Al asked for my comment before he finished his article, which he pointed out would be printed the next day.

I quickly flipped through Al's copy of the top-secret agreement. I saw immediately that it was a true copy, except for two telltale signs. The signature lines of the last page placed "The Government of the Union of Soviet Socialist Republics" before "The Government of the United States." It is international diplomatic practice for governments to put their country's name first on the signature line of their copy of an agreement. I surmised that he had received it from a Soviet embassy official, but the official forgot to reverse the sequence of the signature lines. Furthermore, the bracketed space reserved for the "date certain" had been doctored.

I explained to Al that the Soviet embassy was attempting to influence him to serve Soviet propaganda purposes to project the United States as the unreasonable party in the U.S.-Soviet negotiations and Moscow as the aggrieved party. Specifically the Soviets were using him to press the administration toward a unilateral negative symmetry agreement. Al indicated that the Soviet embassy was his source. The next day, he ran his story with limited reference to the negative symmetry agreement. I phoned the political officer at the Soviet embassy responsible for Afghanistan and protested his embassy's leakage of a secret U.S.-Soviet document.[22] The Soviet diplomat promised to "investigate" and get back to me. I never saw him again in Washington.

ψ

On August 18, 1991, the Washington debate about unilateral negative symmetry became an academic one as the Soviet chapter of the Afghan Great Game began to close. On that day, the three main power ministers in the Soviet government, led by KGB chief and old Soviet Afghan hand Vladimir Kryuchkov,[23] staged a sensational coup to overthrow Soviet President Gorbachev.[24] Kryuchkov, Minister of Defense Dmitri Yazov, and Minister of Interior Boris Pugo, together with Soviet Prime Minister Valentin Pavlov and Vice President Gennady Yanaev, created a State Committee on the State of Emergency to execute the coup. Gorbachev's own trusted chief of staff, Valery

Boldin, was allied with the plotters. He accompanied the head of the KGB's Ninth Directorate in charge of Gorbachev's personal security to place the Soviet president under house arrest in the Crimea where Gorbachev was vacationing. Two Soviet-Afghan war veterans—Gorbachev's personal military adviser, Marshal Sergei Akhromeyev, and the Soviet ground forces commander, General Valentin Varennikov—also betrayed Gorbachev.

The coup lasted for three eventful days during which time the seventy-four-year-old Soviet state wobbled on a precipice. Watching from Washington, those of us who had served in Moscow wondered if a familiar pattern in Russian history was repeating itself. Was it to be another brief period of reform—Gorbachev was in his sixth year—situated between long periods of autocracy? Would the Soviet Union relapse, becoming once again a state ruled by terror and unrelenting repression of its population?

Boris Yeltsin, the president of the Russian Republic, climbed into a tank parked in downtown Moscow. He vehemently condemned the coup before foreign television cameras. His defiant speech and the popular uprising he inspired were beamed worldwide and back into the Soviet Union by foreign broadcasts. The Soviet citizenry in Moscow had had enough of the Communist Party. Military and KGB officers disobeyed Kryuchkov's and Yazov's orders to arrest Yeltsin. Troops began to defect and join the protesters. Slowly, applauded by thousands of men and women, with people of all ages lining Moscow's wide boulevards, the tanks turned around and rumbled back to their bases outside the city. The coup collapsed. The key organizers were arrested. Interior Minister Pugo and his wife committed suicide; so did Marshal Akhromeyev, but not before leaving behind fifty rubles (about one dollar at the time) to pay his bill at the staff cafeteria.[25]

On August 21, the day the coup collapsed, Gorbachev flew back to Moscow and a power struggle with Yeltsin. Gorbachev's authority emanated from the dying Soviet Union, Yeltsin's from his June 12, 1991, election by voters in the Russian Republic.[26] The Soviet Union began to break apart. Ukraine declared its independence on August 24. It was followed the next day by Belarus and then by Moldova on August 27, and Azerbaijan on August 30. Over the next three weeks, five other former republics declared their independence. The Soviet cabinet voted to dissolve the KGB and change its name. Yeltsin banned the Soviet and Russian communist parties. A referendum in Leningrad changed the name of the city back to St. Petersburg.

Washington's national security agencies worked overtime to assess the significance of the USSR's disintegration. Secretary Baker was already scheduled to conduct a high-level American visit to Moscow in September. Afghanistan was high on the list of subjects he would discuss with Boris Yeltsin and the new Soviet foreign minister, Boris Pankin.[27] One of Baker's main objectives during his visit would be to fill in the "date certain" blank in the negative symmetry draft and finally sign the agreement. His briefing papers judged that Gorbachev, Yeltsin, and Pankin were ready to accept the date certain now that the Kremlin conservatives were in decline.

I left Washington on August 29 for Islamabad. I wanted to be in Pakistan to explain the agreement to the Pakistani government and the Mujahidin before it was signed and to follow up after it was concluded. I planned to urge Pakistani military and civilian officials to cancel offensives inside Afghanistan and support a negotiated end to the Afghan war.

During three days of talks in Islamabad in early September, Akram Zaki and General Durrani gave me the standard Pakistani professions of support for an Afghan political settlement. On September 4, Zaki assured me there would be no more military offensives. In a newspaper interview after I left his office, he confirmed publicly what he had just pledged to me moments previously in our private meeting. His interview appeared on the front page of *The News* in Pakistan on September 5. It reported:

> Zaki said he discussed Pakistan's concept of a political settlement with Peter Tomsen, US envoy for the Afghan Resistance, when Tomsen called on him here Wednesday. . . . On April 3, this year the Afghan cell, Pakistan's highest decision making body on Afghanistan, decided to back diplomatic option for restoring peace to that war ravaged country. But the collapse of the communist system in the Soviet Union has once again encouraged radicals among the Mujahideen and their supporters. They want to try the military option again.
>
> Akram Zaki described all these as "mere rumors" and said: "Since April 3 Pakistan has been supporting the political option systematically, genuinely and sincerely."[28]

Zaki's categorical public confirmation of his private assurance to me that Pakistan was no longer pursuing the military option was unprecedented. But it perplexed me. I had come to know him in Beijing and Islamabad. I thought he would not deliberately lie to me as General Durrani did so smoothly. Was Zaki being sincere? Did his emphatic statements that Pakistan had abandoned the ISI's covert offensives to overthrow Najib militarily and place Hekmatyar in power reflect the true intentions of Prime Minister Sharif and Army Chief Beg? Or was he merely another role player in the Pakistani Army's strategy to dupe the Americans, keep U.S. covert weapons flowing into the ISI's hands, and continue on to the next Hekmatyar-Tanai assault on Kabul? I did not know, but I considered that the weight of evidence still suggested Pakistan was again deliberately misleading the Americans. Perhaps Zia's comment to President Reagan that lying to Soviet officials was justified since they were non-Muslims applied also to American officials.

I met with ISI Director Durrani twice on September 4 and 5, the second time at a lunch he was hosting. Benon Sevan also attended. During the lunch Durrani reiterated that the ISI now backed an Afghan political solution. Sevan informed us that he had met with Najib the day before in Kabul and he was now "one thousand percent" sure that Najib would surrender power to a transition mechanism once it was established. Durrani remarked that if Najib relinquished power, the transition should go well.

On the morning of September 6, I flew to Peshawar. I had sent Richard Hoagland ahead to Peshawar two days previously to meet as many Mujahidin as possible. His briefing on my arrival was uniformly negative and ominous. The ISI was again sending hundreds of trucks filled with weapons and rockets across the border.

A torrent of Mujahidin protests against the ISI-organized offensives superseded my talking points on all other issues. Ahmed Zia Masood started off my first meeting, held at the U.S. consulate in Peshawar, on a low key. He thanked the United States for building the road to Zebak. The Mujahidin could now drive from Chitral to northern Afghanistan in six hours, a trip that had previously taken two weeks on foot. He then shifted to a more aggressive tone. He excoriated the ISI for violating General Beg's promise to support the commanders' shura. The ISI had stopped sending assistance to Ahmed Shah Masood in the spring, but Masood was now heavily armed: He had captured all the weapons he needed during his 1991 offensive. Ahmed Zia told me that Masood had next planned to seize Faizabad, Badakhshan's capital and the regime's last foothold in the north. He intended to suggest holding the next commanders' shura meeting there. After hearing of the ISI's offensive against Jalalabad and Gardez, his brother had turned his army around and was moving it toward Kabul to defend it against Hekmatyar.

When I escorted Ahmed Zia from the consulate to the front gate, he stopped me in the driveway. We were alone, away from listening devices. He looked me in the eye and asked: "What are you doing? A Gulbuddin-Khalqi coup? . . . We have our allies in the regime. We are ready. We can capture Kabul in the name of the commanders' shura." I answered that U.S. policy supported a UN-assisted Afghan political settlement. A military solution attempted by any Afghan faction would fail. Once again Ahmed Zia's assumption that the United States was supporting the latest Hekmatyar-Tanai offensive troubled me. It was clear that preparations for another ISI-organized offensive were well advanced. The CIA had to be aware of the attack. Once again agency officials had chosen not to inform Under Secretary Kimmitt or me of their plans.

Over the next three days in Peshawar I heard more angry Mujahidin complaints about the ISI offensive. Hamid Karzai exhibited the flashes of outrage that American officials would experience after 9/11. He asked me why heavy weapons captured from Iraq that the Americans had transported to Pakistan for Mujahidin use were being given to the extremists who had supported Saddam Hussein. Why had the moderate commanders who had sent their Mujahidin to join the allied coalition in the Gulf War not received any of the Iraqi war booty? If the ISI and Hekmatyar captured Kabul, he asserted, the moderate Mujahidin would revolt.

I asked for a meeting with Rahmatullah Safi, who had been an Afghan Army general during Zahir Shah's rule. Safi was a friend of Congressman Charlie Wilson and of America. He was well connected to Mujahidin commanders, a supporter of the commanders' shura, and a graduate of the American Special Forces training program at Fort Bragg, North Carolina. He had been one of Gailani's military advisers but was now on his own. General Safi was a huge man, well over six feet tall. He genuinely cared about others. He was thoroughly honest and fielded a marvelous wit. From him I could get a good picture of the potential disaster brewing across the border in Afghanistan.

Safi invited me to his home in Peshawar for dinner. We talked for hours. His readout confirmed that a worst-case scenario was developing. He told me that the ISI was moving weapons and equipment across the border to support two synchronized attacks, one on Jalalabad and the other on Gardez. The fall of these two cities would presage an assault on Kabul. Safi said that the ISI had planned to begin the offensive on September 15 but would not be able to complete the buildup by that time. He said that panic would erupt in Kabul if Jalalabad and Gardez fell. Najib could collapse. Rocket barrages would precipitate anarchy in Kabul, clearing the way for Hekmatyar and Tanai to capture the city.

Safi continued that the ISI was concentrating Hekmatyar's and Sayyaf's forces in northern Paktiya. Hekmatyar would be positioned to enter Kabul first. I asked why the commanders' shura could not disrupt the offensive. "It's too late," Safi responded. He commented that Hamid Gul was in charge of the buildup. Brigadiers Janjua and Batcha and Colonel Imam were assisting Gul. "It's the old team: Beg, Gul, Durrani, and Nawaz Sharif," Safi moaned. At this point, he mitigated his anguish with a bit of gallows humor. With a slight smirk just visible under his thick white moustache, Safi quipped, "First we were invaded by our enemies, now we are invaded by our friends."

I quickly cabled all I had heard to Washington and the embassy in Islamabad. On September 9, the State Department instructed me to return immediately to Islamabad and deliver a tough message to General Durrani. In most countries, such an important diplomatic presentation would be made first to the president, prime minister, or foreign minister; in Pakistan, bitter experience had demonstrated that their influence on Pakistan's Afghan strategy was negligible. The message from the United States needed to be presented promptly, directly, and precisely to the Pakistani official in charge of the military offensive, ISI Director General Asad Durrani.

On September 12, accompanied by Elizabeth Jones, the chargé d'affaires of the American embassy in Islamabad, I called on Durrani in his office to present the formal talking points cabled from Washington demanding that Pakistan cancel the ISI-planned attacks. Reading from the document, I cited reports that the ISI was assisting Mujahidin groups to carry out offensives against Jalalabad and Gardez. I stated that Secretary Baker was in Moscow about to discuss Afghanistan with Soviet officials. The recent changes in the Soviet leadership presented an opportunity for a breakthrough in the U.S.-Soviet political settlement talks. It would be a serious mistake to escalate the fighting now by launching major attacks on cities or by rocketing Kabul.

I read on: Pakistan had frequently reaffirmed to the U.S. government its commitment to a political settlement of the Afghan conflict. The Soviets had often stated their skepticism about whether this was Pakistan's real intention. The fact that the ISI was preparing another offensive had led the United States to wonder what Pakistan's agenda for Afghanistan truly was. The document concluded that, if there was truth to the reports the United States had been hearing about the offensive, Pakistan must take the actions necessary to call off these attacks. Having finished reading the American talking points, I handed over the document to General Durrani.

Durrani was clearly confounded by the official U.S. demand that he cancel the offensive. A long pause ensued while he slowly read and reread the talking points. He seemed to be at a loss for words. I broke the silence by explaining that the United States and Pakistan should together adjust to the new and final phase of the Afghan war—a negotiated settlement leading to Najib's exit and Afghan self-determination. Secretary Baker would shortly sign the negative symmetry accord with Foreign Minister Pankin in Moscow. Communist rule in the Soviet Union was ending, just as it was in Afghanistan. I asked that Pakistan join the United States and the Soviet Union in the arms cutoff and assist with the UN plan to achieve a peaceful conclusion of the war.

Durrani listened to my words but hesitated to give a substantive response. He seemed cornered. The Pakistani decision on whether to cancel the offensive would be made above his pay grade, by General Beg. I saw from his demeanor that he resented the American demand that he call off the attack but could not say so. Instead he prevaricated. After emitting a nervous chuckle, he sarcastically asked me if the United States wanted him to cancel the attack the next day. Yes, it did, I answered. The attack was a classic example of a military policy defeating an overarching political objective. It would produce the opposite of what the United States and Pakistan wished to achieve in Afghanistan. Evading my reply and the Washington talking points, Durrani wondered aloud if someone could give him a list of targets to attack. I was tempted to tell him that the answer was obvious, in the lines of the document he had just read. I instead replied that our main focus should be on a peaceful political transition from Najib to an interim regime organized by the United Nations and chosen by Afghans.

Chargé Jones remarked that the Soviets interpreted Khost as a signal that the military option was superseding the political option. Durrani retorted that there would have been no political progress if Khost had not fallen. He requested that I suggest a postponement date for the offensive. I answered that American and Pakistani support for the political settlement meant the offensive was not necessary. As the meeting ended, Durrani asked me what kind of formulation on Afghanistan might emerge from the American-Soviet talks. I said that it would fall within the framework of the UN proposal.

After the meeting with Durrani, Richard Hoagland and I went to the Soviet embassy in Islamabad. Soviet Ambassador Victor Yakunin had asked me to give him an update on Soviet POWs and MIAs in Afghanistan. I briefed him on the latest information on Soviet POWs and MIAs that we had acquired from Mujahidin along the Frontier. After thanking us, Yakunin and his political counselor questioned Pakistan's commitment to a negotiated outcome in Afghanistan. Yakunin asked for my opinion. I answered by reciting a Russian proverb, *Pozhivyom-uvidem*, the equivalent of the English "Time will tell."

The next day, September 13, 1991, Secretary Baker and Soviet Foreign Minister Pankin signed the negative symmetry agreement in Moscow. Later, Baker wrote in his memoirs that a quick agreement on negative symmetry had become possible primarily because the KGB and the hard-liners who had staged the failed Soviet coup were now discredited.[29] That same day, Chargé Jones delivered a letter, dated September 13, 1991, from Secretary Baker to Pakistan's new minister of state for foreign affairs, Siddiq Khan Kanju, reiterating many of the talking points I had presented to Durrani.

The secretary wrote that the negative symmetry accord had opened the way for a political settlement resulting in "the establishment in Afghanistan of a government acceptable to the majority of the Afghan people." The letter stated the readiness of the United States to work with Pakistan and others to implement the UN-led Afghan political settlement. It complimented the "skill and discretion" that UN Special Envoy Benon Sevan had exercised in negotiating a peaceful outcome of the war. The secretary informed that negative symmetry was timed to go into effect on January 1, 1992. The American embassy also hand-carried a copy of the secretary's letter to ISI Director Durrani personally on September 13.[30]

I flew back to Peshawar on September 14. It was important to explain the implications of negative symmetry to the Mujahidin. The end of Soviet lethal aid to Najib would accelerate his departure. I also had another purpose for returning to Peshawar. I considered it almost certain that General Beg would not cancel the ISI's planned offensive. I intended to ask Mujahidin commanders and tribal chiefs not to carry it out.

My suspicions proved accurate. Weapons and ammunitions were still pouring across the border. Most of the Mujahidin I met during my four-day return to Peshawar did not need convincing to subvert the planned attack. The Ahmadzai tribal chiefs in the commanders' shura led more fighters in Paktiya than Hekmatyar, Sayyaf, and Haqqani combined. They assured me that the attack on Gardez would not succeed. They had already convinced most of the paid tribal militias brought to Paktiya by the ISI and Hekmatyar from other provinces to return to their villages. The military fronts that the ISI was building around Gardez fell apart.

Haji Qadir, the head of the Mujahidin Jalalabad Shura of commanders, was the key to scuttling the Jalalabad assault. Qadir was a moderate nationalist like his brother, Abdul Haq. He spoke fluent English and German. He was bedridden with a bad case of jaundice in a Peshawar hospital when I went to see him. I walked part of the way to the hospital on foot to evade surveillance. The hospital was in a heavily populated area of Peshawar, crowded with tiny shops, blaring taxis, crying children, and shouting hawkers. Its white-washed walls had long since receded into various shades of dark gray. Climbing up stairs and negotiating corridors jammed with sick and bandaged patients, I reached Qadir's second-floor room. He lay in a small bed overhung by a mosquito net. The only other furnishing was a small wooden chair near the bed. The famed commander looked frail and tired. He was dressed in a white gown, cut off above the knees. He had black circles under his eyes.

We talked for only fifteen minutes. I explained the reason for my visit. I said that the United States firmly opposed the ISI strategy to attack Jalalabad. The Gardez buildup was unraveling. The United States hoped that Qadir and the Jalalabad Shura would decide not to cooperate with the ISI's planned attack on Jalalabad.

I could see that Qadir was already in agreement before I concluded. "We were concerned about this at the time of the Jalalabad battle in 1989," he whispered, recalling Hamid Gul's failed Jalalabad attack, which had cost thousands of Mujahidin casualties. He stated his fear that the attacks on Jalalabad, Gardez, and ultimately Kabul would precipitate a Pashtun-Tajik conflict in Afghanistan. He told me that I need not worry. "The planning is all in my head," he said. I walked out of the hospital knowing that the attack on Jalalabad would not take place.

Over the next three weeks the offensive against Jalalabad fizzled out. Only extremist Mujahidin moved on Gardez when the orders to advance were issued in late September, not enough for a victory. Military briefers in Washington told me in November that the Mujahidin around Gardez and Jalalabad dispersed in early October. Infuriated, Pakistani officers gathered up all the heavy weapons brought from the Gulf and took them back to Pakistan.

Before leaving Pakistan for Saudi Arabia, I stopped by Station Chief Bill's embassy office on September 19. I inquired if he also had asked the ISI to abandon its military offensive on Kabul. Bill answered that clearance problems in Washington had delayed his own representation to Durrani for six days after the chargé and I had met with the ISI chief. He had just personally delivered it to Durrani. I hoped—but could not be sure—that Bill's meeting with Durrani marked the end of nearly three years of two U.S. agencies implementing two contradictory Afghan policies.

The September 13, 1991, signing of the U.S.-Soviet negative symmetry agreement was a historic event. It was comforting to know that American weapons and money would no longer be funneled to the ISI to empower Hekmatyar and the extremist fringe of the resistance. Despite doubts, the administration and Congress had held out for a date certain on which both superpowers would simultaneously terminate arms transfers. We had taken the Soviets out with us and weakened Najib and Hekmatyar. The negative symmetry accord signaled the beginning of the end of the destructive thirteen-year communist era in Afghan history. Unfortunately, it did not end the wars of Afghanistan.

CHAPTER 18

From Marx to Mullahs

Secret telegram, London 17650, "Afghan Strategy–U.S. Policy," from Special Envoy Tomsen, EXDIS KHYBER, September 26, 1991:

> *We have achieved a number of remarkable successes in Afghanistan over the past decade, ones that previously had been deemed as unobtainable: the full Soviet troop withdrawal in an acceptable timeframe, and most recently, Soviet agreement on a date certain for negative symmetry. A political settlement is also attainable, provided the U.S. continues actively to use its considerable influence and prestige to reach it.*
>
> *We should not exaggerate our ability to influence events, nor should we underestimate it. While Afghanistan is a receding issue in U.S. global interests, how the conflict ends ought to be important to the U.S. because of our heavy involvement and investment over the years, and also because our handling of the end-game will be of considerable significance to the Soviets, the Saudis, and the Pakistanis. Our perseverance will have an influence on how we are viewed in the Muslim world generally—a point King Fahd's son, Saud bin Fahd, made to us in Jeddah a few days ago. It will be a major factor in preventing the minority Islamic extremists from seizing power militarily, an outcome which would be a blow to U.S. objectives in regional stability, U.S.-Soviet ties, and combating terrorism and narcotics.*
>
> *... Our strategy ... should be principally aimed at preventing a victory by the minority but well-organized and -funded Islamic extremists Hekmatyar and Sayyaf:*

- *An extremist seizure of Kabul would plunge Afghanistan into a fresh round of warfare, which could affect areas adjoining Afghanistan.*
- *Should Hekmatyar or Sayyaf get to Kabul, extremists in the Arab world would support them in stoking Islamic radicalism in the region, including the Soviet Central Asian Republics, but also in Saudi Arabia and elsewhere in the Arab world.*
- *As Iran, Syria, and Lebanon become less hospitable havens for Arab terrorist organizations, they could shift their bases to Afghanistan. We have noted reports that Arab terrorists trained in Sayyaf's training camps were involved in the assassination of the Egyptian speaker of Parliament and in the attempted Algerian coup. Other reports indicate that, among others, Kashmiri and Burmese rebels also train with Islamic extremists in Afghanistan.*

A non-extremist-centered alternative to Najib would

- *Be an outcome the Soviets would wish to cooperate with us on reaching, strengthening U.S.-Soviet relations.*
- *Provide the best hope for continuity and stability in Afghanistan, since the overwhelming majority of Afghans oppose the Islamic extremists.*
- *Vastly improve our ability to deal with the Afghan narcotics problem. Afghanistan is the second largest exporter of illicit narcotics products in the world.*

In sum, the U.S. remains the most influential outside party involved in Afghanistan. It is in the U.S. interest to remain actively engaged in the final phase of the conflict, in close cooperation with the UN, Soviets, GOP,* SAG† and the resistance, guiding it toward a non-extremist outcome which most Afghans and outsiders support.[1]

U.S. President George H.W. Bush, Secretary of State James A. Baker III, and Soviet President Mikhail Gorbachev skillfully guided the world's two superpowers past the shoals of a potential cataclysmic war into the post–Cold War era. That was an extraordinary accomplishment. The process lasted about three years, from 1989 to 1991. During that period Afghanistan dropped

---

* Government of Pakistan.
† Saudi Arabian Government.

down to a second-tier priority for the Bush administration. The September 13, 1991, negative symmetry agreement pushed Afghanistan down to the third tier. After negative symmetry went into effect on January 1, 1992, Afghanistan was largely forgotten by high-level policymakers in Washington. National Security Adviser Brent Scowcroft's deputy, Robert Gates, recalled in his memoirs, after the Soviets were gone, that "now Afghans could resume fighting among themselves—and hardly anyone cared." A CIA analyst seconded to the White House later wrote that he could not recall "a single senior-level meeting" on Afghanistan during 1991 and 1992.[2]

History abounds with examples of foreign-policy failures committed by Great Powers during transformational periods in international politics. The mistakes often follow foreign-policy triumphs. The temptation to cling to the status quo, to resist change, to remain locked in familiar, time-tested positions, is seductive. Generals plan for fighting the last war, not the next one. Political leaders succumb to the attraction of what has worked well in the past without addressing the emerging challenges of the future. These costly miscalculations are usually the result of Great Powers confusing their national *interests* with earlier foreign-policy *positions*, ones which seemingly have met the test of time. But history is always chasing time. And time is always in forward motion.

After World War II, the Truman administration perceived the grave danger that Soviet expansionism posed to the United States and its allies. America faced a new world with a new threat that was different from the old ones but just as menacing. Truman and his advisers crafted the North Atlantic Treaty Organization (NATO) and the Marshall Plan to meet this new threat, and over the next forty years America and its allies successfully contained the Soviet Union.

When the Soviet Union finally imploded in 1991, President Bush proclaimed his U.S.-led "New World Order" to replace the Cold War standoff that had lasted almost fifty years. But Bush and his team did not see—much less attempt to counter—the next danger to the United States and its friends and allies that was emerging in Afghanistan and Pakistan: virulently anti-American militant Islamic extremism. Scowcroft's statement, "We prefer what is as opposed to the alternative,"[3] demonstrated the same complacent mentality that paralyzed U.S. foreign policy in the 1930s during the rise of Nazi Germany and militarized Japan.

In a 2009 letter to me, a respected Australian-Pakistani author and specialist on Pakistan and Afghanistan, Dr. Rizwan Hussain, wrote that "the period
1991/92 was the most crucial period of the Afghan conflict and it was the
most opportune time when the U.S. could have compelled Pakistan to cease
its interference in Afghanistan."[4] Dr. Hussain was right. The United States
had reached a high point in its influence in global affairs after the first Gulf
War. It was the only remaining superpower. It had persuaded the Soviet
Union to stop its assistance to Najib and halted its own arms shipments. But,
contrary to comments by some commentators after 9/11, the United States
did not "leave" Afghanistan after the Soviet pullout. From 1989 to 1992, it
invested substantial diplomatic, military, and economic aid to help the
Afghans achieve self-determination. After negative symmetry, it should have
continued to wield its great influence to end the Afghan war and prevent the
rise of Islamic extremism in Afghanistan. Instead, it tuned out Afghanistan,
effectively outsourced its Afghan policy to Pakistan, which meant the Pakistani Army and the ISI, and walked away.

Pakistani-supported Islamic extremism moved into the vacuum left in Af-
ghanistan. The long-term repercussions foreseen in the September 26, 1991,
London cable were severe. They inexorably led to the rise of the Taliban, al-
Qaeda's training camps in Afghanistan—and 9/11.

For a very brief period when the negative symmetry accord was finalized,
the United States exerted its diplomatic muscle in high-level, firm communications to Pakistan's leadership. The tough talking points I presented to ISI
chief Asad Durrani on September 12, 1991, the day before negative symmetry
was announced, laid down an American marker. The secretary's letter to Pakistani Minister of State for foreign affairs Siddiq Khan Kanju the next day
delivered a message from the top of the U.S. government, which neither the
American embassy in Islamabad nor I could match in terms of firepower:

> The search for a solution to the Afghan problem will now enter its
> most crucial phase, and I ask your full support as we move ahead. First
> and foremost, I ask that you join with the U.S. and the Soviet Union
> in cutting off new supply of weapons to Afghanistan.... Second, I urge
> that you join in giving full support to the UN Secretary General and
> his representative as they work with the Afghans to define the structure
> of a transition mechanism and to move toward implementing a polit-

ical settlement. We have all supported his statement of principles on Afghanistan. This is the time to start putting them into practice.[5]

"Finally," the secretary concluded, "I would like to reinforce our earlier request that your Government discourage any thought of a major military offensive at this time. We have a real opportunity to bring about a peaceful settlement of the sort both our Governments have long sought. It would be tragic to miss this chance and risk further inconclusive and bloody conflict."[6]

Secretary Baker's message to Pakistan's leaders was the last gasp in U.S. efforts to exert high-level pressure on Pakistan to support an Afghan political settlement. Within a few months, Pakistani Prime Minister Nawaz Sharif and the ISI had correctly judged that President Bush and Secretary of State Baker would not back up their words with actions. Confident that Bush's foreign policy team would not push back, Sharif and the ISI ignored all three of Baker's demands: Pakistan did not join U.S.-Soviet negative symmetry; the ISI continued its military offensives to install Gulbuddin Hekmatyar in Kabul; and it scuttled rather than assisted the UN political settlement process.

Within the Bush administration, senior officials dismissed the continuing Afghan conflict as a civil war. That assessment was misleading. It was a civil war, but not in the classic definition of the term. In fact, the Afghan civil war was more comparable to the Spanish Civil War of the 1930s than to the American Civil War of the 1860s. The American Civil War was a domestic conflict; the Spanish Civil War was a domestic *and* an international conflict. Spain became a battleground for competing foreign ideologies and the foreign states and nonstate entities promoting them. During the early 1990s, Afghanistan too became a cockpit for international ideological and power rivalries as well as a country ripped by civil war. The Spanish Civil War lasted three years and ended in 1938. As of 2011, the Afghan war has lasted thirty-three years and no end is in sight.

All of Afghanistan's larger neighbors, including Pakistan, had agreed to the UN plan's call to exercise mutual restraint and to support Benon Sevan's peace initiative. On the ground, Pakistan flagrantly violated its commitment, guaranteeing that the wars of Afghanistan would continue. Over the next two decades, the more Pakistan attempted to impose its Pashtun extremists on Afghanistan, the more Iran, India, and the Soviet Union, and later Russia, supported the northern non-Pashtuns.

✤

I wrote the September 26, 1991, policy message quoted at the beginning of this chapter to persuade American policymakers that Afghanistan was a post–Cold War issue still important to U.S. interests. The Pakistan-stoked fanatical Islamist militancy visibly rising from the embers of the ongoing Afghan war blocked the way to peace in Afghanistan. I believed that the United Nations and Benon Sevan would be unable to persuade external powers and the Mujahidin to implement a political settlement without heavy and continuous high-level U.S. diplomatic pressure. ISI-supported Afghan and Arab radicals were making Afghanistan a base for world terrorism. Islamic terrorists from other world regions were moving into Afghanistan, and they espoused a millenarian religious ideology harmful to the United States, to the West, and to the world.

I earmarked my cable for wide distribution inside the White House and national security agencies in Washington. The message warned against American passivity in handling the end game of the Afghan war. Negative symmetry was a positive step, but it was not the finish line. The telegram presented a way ahead for U.S. policy. It urged Washington policymakers to stay actively engaged in the final phase of the Afghan war and to aggressively steer the settlement process toward a nonextremist outcome. An extremist victory would be disastrous for U.S. interests.

During the first three weeks of October 1991 I made the rounds in Washington, driving home the same arguments I had made in the September 26 cable. I pointed out that the retirement of Mirza Aslam Beg, Pakistan's chief of army staff, on August 17, 1991, and the appointment of his successor, General Asif Nawaz Janjua,* offered an opening to shift Pakistan's army away from a military solution to the Afghan war favoring the Afghan radicals. Beg was the first Pakistani army chief who had been aggressively anti-American. The Sandhurst-trained Nawaz wished to improve relations with the United States. He was as forthright as Beg was wily. On assuming command, Nawaz had vowed to reverse the fourteen-year era of military domination of Pakistan's in-

---

* General Asif Nawaz and Prime Minister Nawaz Sharif shared a common name but were not related.

ternal politics. In his first public statement after being sworn in, Nawaz announced: "As the democratic process has now taken hold, I would like it to be clearly understood that the Army must have nothing to do with politics."[7]

The new army commander deprived Beg's main ally, Hamid Gul, of his corps command in the Punjab, assigning him to manage an ordnance factory. Stung by ignominy, Gul retired. Except for the heavily bearded ISI colonel Sultan Imam, the entire second tier of Zia-era, pro-Hekmatyar ISI officers along the Frontier were rotated back to regular army positions.[8]

Colleagues in the Department of State and officials in the Department of Defense, the Central Intelligence Agency and the National Security Council gave me a polite hearing after I returned to Washington in late September. No one, however, was interested in following up my recommendations cabled from London or my suggestion to pursue the opportunity on Afghanistan that Asif Nawaz's appointment offered. Under Secretary Kimmitt had already left Washington, arriving in Bonn on September 5 to take up his new responsibilities as American ambassador to Germany. Arnold Kanter was now the under secretary of state for political affairs. He was an experienced diplomat but lacked Kimmitt's extensive knowledge of Afghan external and internal dynamics.

The administration's shift in Afghan policy after the September 13 negative symmetry agreement went beyond changes in personnel. For the first time since the Soviet 1979 invasion of Afghanistan, the locus of the State Department's policymaking on Afghanistan was removed from the "seventh floor" occupied by the secretary of state, deputy secretaries, and under secretaries and pushed downward in the bureaucracy to the regional Near Eastern and South Asian (NEA) Bureau. Under Secretary Kanter dissolved the interagency Kimmitt Group and delegated Afghan policy to NEA Assistant Secretary Edward Djerejian. Overwhelmed with domestically charged Middle East problems, Djerejian in turn delegated the Afghan portfolio to his South Asia Deputy Assistant Secretary Teresita Schaffer, and the director of Pakistan, Afghanistan, and Bangladesh, Edward Abington.[9] The bureaucratic readjustment in the State Department further reduced high-level attention to Afghanistan. Schaffer and Abington, the former political counselor in the American embassy in Islamabad, worked closely with Ambassador Oakley's replacement, Ambassador Nicholas Platt, and his deputy Elizabeth Jones. With no

American embassy in Kabul, the embassy in Islamabad and the U.S. consulate
in Peshawar continued to report on and interpret back to Washington Pakistan's Afghan policy and developments in Afghanistan.

The department's decision to downgrade attention to the Afghan war
flowed from the White House and Secretary Baker's resolve to disengage from
Afghanistan after the September 13 negative symmetry agreement. That fundamental policy shift did not have in mind—but rapidly led to—intensified
outsourcing of America's Afghan policy to Pakistan. The resulting policy
mindset would continue in a counterproductive bureaucratic rut through the
Clinton and George W. Bush administrations until 9/11, when al-Qaeda
attacks staged from Afghanistan resuscitated Afghanistan as an important
foreign policy priority.

At our first meeting in his office, Under Secretary Kanter absorbed my
presentation and asked questions, but I could see that he had little interest
in Afghanistan. He had worked under Brent Scowcroft on U.S.-Soviet arms
control issues at the National Security Council from 1989 to 1991, and I
sensed that he shared Scowcroft's belief that Afghanistan was a civil war, an
unnecessary irritant in U.S.-Soviet relations. During our second meeting,
Kanter told me that Secretary of State Baker wanted out of Afghanistan and
that the United States would now become like all other players on the Afghan
issue. He asked me to concentrate on promoting the UN peace initiative to
the Mujahidin, Pakistan, and Saudi Arabia; urge Pakistan and Saudi Arabia
to join the U.S.-Soviet negative symmetry accord; gather information on Soviet POWs; and report on events.

Apart from analysts in the State Department's Bureau of Intelligence and
Research, I found no bureaucratic ally in the government to support placing
my warnings about Islamic extremism in key interagency policy documents
that were under preparation after negative symmetry. They essentially ratified
American disengagement from Afghanistan. An important NEA Afghan policy
paper bound for the White House listed only four priorities for Afghanistan,
the last three largely out of reach unless the war ended: retrieving Stinger missiles in Mujahidin hands, promoting regional stability, refugee return, and
combating narcotics. I attempted to add a fifth—preventing a Muslim extremist victory in Afghanistan—but NEA refused to clear it. In the end, I was only
able to insert a watered-down statement (not a policy goal) on the potential
Islamist threat from Afghanistan. The language was taken from my London

cable: "A radical Islamic fundamentalist regime in Kabul would set back our objectives of regional stability; cooperation between it and other extremist parties could fuel further instability."[10] The CIA vetoed my suggestions to utilize covert funds to assist moderate Afghans to implement the UN plan. Instead, the agency was given a modest sum to promote the political settlement process in cooperation with the ISI, a decision certain to undercut rather than advance the UN effort. The White House approved the paper.

୰

The door was already beginning to close on a political settlement of the Afghan war when I left Washington on October 24, 1991, for Saudi Arabia and Pakistan. It was my fifteenth trip to the region and one of the most unproductive. The administration's decision to disengage from Afghanistan considerably narrowed my terms of reference. I was discouraged but determined to do my utmost to advance U.S. goals within the abbreviated framework of my new instructions. After almost three years, I had come to know well the key Pakistani and Saudi officials dealing with Afghanistan. I was also well acquainted with most of the Mujahidin faction leaders. Per Under Secretary Kanter's instructions, my main objective would be to advance a political settlement and work closely with Benon Sevan. I also was determined to continue my reporting on the activities of Islamic extremists on the Frontier while gathering information on Soviet POWs from my Mujahidin contacts. I coordinated with USAID, NEA, and the refugee office in State to maintain aid flows to Afghan refugees in Pakistan and begin anti-narcotics projects inside Afghanistan.

In Riyadh and Islamabad, Prince Turki and General Durrani were clearly aware of Washington's growing disinterest in Afghanistan. The American covert weapons program was ending. U.S. arms shipments to Pakistan had terminated on October 15. American humanitarian assistance for Afghanistan was $60 million in 1991 and declining.[11] It would be phased out within two years. Pakistan and Saudi Arabia no longer needed the United States to balance Soviet intimidation.

In Pakistan, I tried to reassure Benon Sevan and the Mujahidin that the United States was committed to the UN process. Benon Sevan told me that the majority of Afghans "sincerely regret that you have no interest in settling the Afghan war." In Peshawar, Abdul Haq's angry comments reflected the general sentiments of moderate Afghans I met. I included their views in my reporting to Washington, knowing they would be read with disinterest or not at all:

> During most of your involvement in Afghanistan, you gave military resources only to kill communists. You spent billions of dollars to crush the Soviets. That helped us—we know that and we are thankful for your help. But it also helped you, too. It is not responsible to back off now and say we are on our own. Now that you have won, you are turning your back and leaving us with our problems. Your withdrawal is leaving us, while we are still weak, at the mercy of the Pakistanis and other outsiders. You are not proving that you care about democracy here. Some people here in Afghanistan do want peace and security and democracy. But they are the ones you are abandoning. Your withdrawal is strengthening the radicals. Most of us already are cut off from resources, but Hekmatyar and Sayyaf are getting more than ever from their Pakistani and Arab sources. . . . These monsters are turning on the Afghan people, but they will turn on you, too. If they come to power, the extremists will use terrorism and opium to damage the U.S.[12]

Benon Sevan's settlement process was the only solution capable of ending the long Afghan war and preventing a new one. The United Nations was the least tainted by foreign hands. Its plans to organize a broad-based Afghan assembly to choose the next Afghan government capitalized on the consensus tradition embedded in the Afghan jirga system. UN Secretary General Javier Pérez de Cuéllar envisioned a meeting of 150 Afghans in Europe by the end of October 1991. The gathering would select a working group of midlevel Afghans who, with UN help, would organize a larger conclave of more than 1,000 Afghans to choose the interim government. The interim government would receive the transfer of power from Najib and organize general elections to choose an Afghan leadership.

Over the next five months, I supported Sevan's efforts to organize the transition. In private meetings, I encouraged Afghans, Pakistanis, and Saudis to cooperate with him. I briefed Sevan fully on everything I had learned that might be helpful to him. At Sevan's request, my deputy, Richard Hoagland,

and I advised Sevan on the wording of UN statements. We gave him Afghan maps, drew up lists of commanders and politicians likely to accept the UN plan, and suggested Afghans from Kabul who would be acceptable to the Mujahidin in the transition process.

Sevan explained to Afghans that the UN approach was a process for them to choose their own leaders; it was not a vehicle for foreign powers to make that choice. His pleasant personality, sincerity, and boundless energy gained him the respect and admiration, if not always the cooperation, of Afghans, Americans, Pakistanis, Russians, Iranians, Saudis, and Europeans. Sevan's ingrained optimism enhanced his effectiveness.

Sometimes Sevan and I disagreed. I advised him not to ignore Ahmed Shah Masood—or to rely on the untrustworthy Burhanuddin Rabbani to speak for Masood. Sevan instead called Masood a Muslim Brotherhood fundamentalist. He did not reciprocate Masood's attempts from inside Afghanistan to establish a direct dialogue—a miscalculation that later proved detrimental to Sevan's mediation efforts. Sevan also believed that Najib would be able to remain in power for another year or more. He would smile when challenging my view that Najib must soon announce his resignation to accelerate the settlement process, jesting that the Afghan dictator had outlasted the Soviet withdrawal, negative symmetry, Gorbachev, and the USSR, and would probably outlast Yeltsin as well.

I advised Sevan that Najib should be convinced to relinquish control while he still had a power base in Afghanistan. Pakistan's generals and most Mujahidin groups would allow the UN political settlement process to go forward only as long as they calculated Najib could not be overthrown militarily. Once Najib began to lose control—and it was only a question of when he would lose control, not whether he would—his transfer of power from a sinking ship would have little meaning. The UN initiative would no longer be needed to get rid of him. Mujahidin groups would rush to Kabul from all directions. The result would be continuing warfare, anarchy, and, possibly, a radical Islamic takeover of Kabul.

UN Secretary General Pérez de Cuéllar lightly hinted that Najib should eventually step down in an October 17, 1991, statement on Afghanistan: "I have been given assurances that some of the controversial personalities concerned would not insist on their personal participation, either in the intra-Afghan dialogue or in the transition mechanism" and would "relinquish their posts." Pérez de Cuéllar's pronouncement did not faze Najib. An enormous ego fed his reluctance to transfer power. A Soviet diplomat in Kabul remarked, "He has the type of personality that could go to the end." Najib told Western reporters that "the demand for my resignation is coming from men who do not represent the people." He even sent a letter to President Bush in December requesting a presidential-level dialogue.[13]

Najib's position in Kabul gradually weakened. The withering away of the USSR in December 1991 deprived him of his Soviet patron. He may have outlived the onset of negative symmetry on January 1, 1992, but he would not be able to outlive its effects. The clock was ticking. Russian arms shipments to the regime ceased by late December, as did shipments of aviation fuel. President Boris Yeltsin recalled military and KGB advisers back to Russia. The Russian government informed Najib that after March 1, 1992, food shipments would need to be paid for in cash.

Najib still faced deadly Khalqi opposition inside his regime. Groups within his Parcham faction also looked for ways to overthrow him. Some of his senior generals were secretly negotiating with different Mujahidin factions. Abdul Rashid Dostum, the Uzbek commander of Najib's largest mercenary force, was in touch with a new paymaster, Uzbekistan President Islam Karimov. In early December 1991, Karimov agreed to assist Dostum. The first Uzbek shipments of humanitarian and lethal aid to Dostum arrived at Dostum's Shibargan headquarters in the north on December 26, 1991.

Najib's stocks of arms and food were dwindling, while his Mujahidin enemies remained well supplied. The ISI could still draw on $600 million in weapons and cash left from the U.S.-Saudi covert program, 17,000 tons of Gulf War booty, and the unending flow of cash from private Saudi benefactors. Najib would face new Mujahidin offensives when the snows melted in the spring of 1992. Masood's victories in the north had filled his arms depots. Most of his army was now positioned in the Panshir Valley, just 90 miles from Kabul. But Najib showed no sign that he was leaving.

The majority of commanders and tribal leaders in the Mujahidin supported the UN process. Many hoped the United Nations would give former king Zahir Shah a ceremonial role in that process. The seven Peshawar party leaders knew that the UN gathering, or, indeed, any open settlement process, would expose their unpopularity, sending them into political oblivion. The ISI was their sole political lifeline. They jockeyed against one another to attract endorsements from Pakistan, the United States, Saudi Arabia, Iran, Russia, and the United Nations.

Sibghatullah Mojaddedi, Sayyid Ahmad Gailani, and Burhanuddin Rabbani gave lip service to the UN proposal, but privately they lobbied with outside powers to arrange for the transfer of power to themselves. Mojaddedi insisted that his election as AIG president at the (discredited) Rawalpindi Shura entitled him to lead the transition after Najib stepped down. Rabbani attempted to leverage his carefully cultivated neutral stance between the three moderates and three radicals to elicit Pakistani, Iranian, U.S., and Russian sponsorship as the compromise candidate. Meanwhile, Gulbuddin Hekmatyar, Abdul Rasoul Sayyaf, and Yunus Khalis relied on ISI support and Saudi money to bypass the UN process entirely. The three Ghilzai extremists continued to work with the ISI to seize Kabul militarily.

In November, Mojaddedi led a delegation of the Tripartite Council to the annual gathering of the UN General Assembly in New York. After meeting Soviet Foreign Minister Boris Pankin, he claimed that Pankin had given him his support to replace Najib. Rabbani promoted his own leadership virtues to Pankin when chairing a Mujahidin Tripartite Council delegation arriving in Moscow on November 11 for four days of talks. An ISI officer, Brigadier Tariq, was at Rabbani's elbow during the negotiations.

Tariq and Rabbani outnegotiated Pankin. The Soviet foreign minister's primary goal was to gain Rabbani's agreement to return Soviet POWs before a Russian delegation traveled to Islamabad on December 19, and at least before the end of the year. Rabbani and Tariq agreed to include wording in the joint communiqué, issued on November 15, "to do everything possible to release all POWs." They committed to return the first group of Soviet POWs before the end of 1991. Pankin, from the Russian side, agreed to endorse the creation of an Afghan "Interim Islamic Government"[14] in the joint communiqué. The phrase "Islamic Government" was regularly used by Rabbani, Hekmatyar, Sayyaf, Khalis, and their radical Arab and Pakistani backers to describe the extremist pan-Islamist regime they intended to establish in Afghanistan after Najib's ouster. Tariq and Rabbani considered the use of the term to signify Soviet approval for the Afghan resistance extremist faction to staff the interim government taking power from Najib.

Back in Pakistan, Rabbani and Tariq touted Pankin's concession as evidence that the Soviets, outside the UN framework, were ready to transfer power directly to the Leadership Council. The ISI made preparations to close the deal during Russian Vice President Alexander Rutskoi's December 19 to 21 visit to Islamabad.

ψ

My talks in Riyadh from November 19 to 24 confirmed that Saudi Arabia had forgiven Hekmatyar and Sayyaf for supporting Saddam Hussein during the Gulf War. The Saudi monarchy was facing a fresh wave of religious dissidence within the Wahhabi establishment over the lingering presence of 5,000 American troops in Saudi Arabia. The royal family's decision to resume Saudi aid to Hekmatyar and Sayyaf placated the religious establishment. The two most outspoken anti-American Mujahidin leaders had been the leading recipients of Saudi funding before the Gulf War. Their return to this favored status undermined the UN peace process. Hekmatyar used the renewed flow of Saudi funding to purchase several Pakistani factories producing small arms and ammunition, antiaircraft, and antitank missiles. Sayyaf built a huge military base for his Afghan and Arab fighters just over the Afghan border at Torkham.

The Saudi government's appeasement of the Wahhabi establishment coincided with the arrival in Pakistan of several hundred additional Arab militants from the Gulf and the Middle East. They came to finish off the communist regime in Kabul. During this same period, insurgencies against pro-Western Arab regimes, led by "Afghan-Arabs" returning to their countries, intensified in Algeria, Egypt, and Tunisia. Radical Arab and Pakistani extremists embedded in Saudi charities moved into the Caucasus, Bosnia, and Somalia.

Against this backdrop, Prince Turki cordially received me and Richard Hoagland in his Riyadh office on November 23. The pungent aroma of incense wafted through the air. Turki wore a lovely yellow robe and a white-and-red-checkered Saudi headscarf. We sat down in a dimly lit corner of his office around a coffee table. Turki, as always, accentuated the positive. Speaking without notes, he eloquently described the successful Saudi-American cooperation in the Gulf War as the latest demonstration of the enduring strategic partnership between our two countries. He praised the U.S.-Saudi-Pakistani collaboration, which had forced the Soviet Army out of Afghanistan and would soon end the Afghan war.

I responded that I could not share his optimism. The Afghan war would only end when the Afghans themselves believed they had gotten back their country and outside interference stopped. Reading from official talking points, I asked that the Saudi government coordinate with the United States in supporting the UN process and refrain from backing other settlement options; that it join the U.S.-Soviet negative symmetry accord; and that it halt the flow of Saudi money going to extremist Mujahidin who opposed the UN process.

Speaking softly, Turki stated the reasons why the Saudis could not accept the American requests. On negative symmetry, he said that Iran would supply weapons to their Mujahidin clients if Saudi Arabia cut off its aid. Iran would exploit the UN process to increase its role in Afghanistan. The Saudi government could not restrict private donations going abroad. Turki added he had no objection to Pakistani plans to convert the seven party leaders into the interim government.

Beginning on November 24, I spent seventeen days in Pakistan encouraging Pakistanis and Afghans to back the UN plan and assist Benon Sevan. Prime Minister Nawaz Sharif and his government continued to proclaim their support for the UN process. At the Pakistani Foreign Ministry, Akram Zaki and Riaz Khan restated Pakistan's commitment to the UN mediation effort.

At ISI headquarters, General Durrani confirmed to me that the ISI had established the Leadership Council. He said the deputies of the seven leaders would become cabinet ministers in the interim government, and the Leadership Council would supervise them. Durrani expected to present this interim government concept to Russian Vice President Rutskoi when he arrived on December 19. If Rutskoi agreed with his plan, it would be submitted to the United Nations for approval.

I responded that the ISI's unilateral attempt to decide the composition of the Afghan transition entity violated the Pakistani government's commitment to support Benon Sevan and the UN process. Imposing the seven party leaders on Afghanistan had never worked in the past. It would fail again. Durrani disagreed. I reported his unworkable scheme back to Washington. Ironically, later in the day at the Foreign Ministry, Afghan specialist Riaz Khan repeated to me the same arguments for assisting Sevan's efforts that I had just made to Durrani. He stressed Pakistan's firm adherence to the UN process. I answered that I had just heard the opposite from Durrani.

In Peshawar, Afghan tribal leaders and moderate commanders repeated their support for the UN process. Masood's political advisers, Yunis Qanuni and Daoud Mir, conveyed Masood's approval, provided that Najib would step down and the PDPA would not participate in the peace process. Peshawar party leaders Mojaddedi, Gailani, Nabi, and Rabbani were pleased that the ISI had resurrected the Leadership Council. It was their only path to continued relevancy. As usual, none of them mentioned the continued suffering of the Afghan people inside Afghanistan and in the crowded, dusty refugee camps in Pakistan. Their focus was solely on how to climb up to the Afghan summit after Najib left. Behind closed doors, their political vendettas against one another were as bitter as ever. At lunch in his presidential office in Peshawar on December 1, Mojaddedi beamed as he told me that Sevan had assured him that he would be head of the interim government. After a slight pause, he asked that I not tell the other leaders.

When I met with Gailani, he explained that he had agreed to the Leadership Council's transformation into the interim government in order to reform it. He boasted that he knew more Afghans than Zahir Shah did. The people loved him, he remarked, because he was a *pir*. In a half-gesture toward the UN process, Gailani offered to cooperate with me and Benon Sevan and asked that we tell him what to do. Gailani accused Rabbani of having twenty-five faces and said he did not want Mojaddedi to be president. Rabbani was less effusive in propounding his leadership capabilities. He had an aide do that. One of his advisers broke into our conversation to suggest that the other six party leaders should defer to Rabbani because he had led the Mujahidin delegation in the negotiations with Foreign Minister Pankin in Moscow.

On December 3, General Durrani convened a nighttime meeting to inform the Leadership Council members about their future positions in the interim government. Sayyaf was represented by his deputy, Ahmed Shah Ahmadzai; Khalis did not attend, nor did he send a representative. Hekmatyar's presence gave the meeting the air of a reunion. Before Durrani spoke, Mojaddedi humorously asked Hekmatyar to promise not to assassinate him and the other leaders. Hekmatyar smiled and agreed, provided the other leaders did not assassinate him. Mojaddedi and Hekmatyar shook hands. Then the leaders dutifully listened while Durrani explained that the Leadership Council's interim government would assume power from Najib. One of them would be designated as president, but none of the remaining six could occupy ministerial posts. They would be assigned ministries and appoint their party members to those positions. Durrani disclosed that the ISI had already dissolved the Pakistani Foreign Ministry's Trilateral Council. That was a blow to Rabbani, the sole Tajik present. He had led the Trilateral delegation talks in Moscow and was looking forward to performing the same function when the Rutskoi delegation arrived later in December. At a stroke, Durrani had just dashed his hopes to lead the transition.

I called on Durrani accompanied by Richard Hoagland on December 9 before flying to Bonn, then London, and back to Washington. I predicted that his plans to revive the seven would fail. They would also delay the UN peace process and damage Benon Sevan's effectiveness.

"Don't worry about Benon Sevan," he said. "He told us to create something from the seven. Hopefully, we can make the Leadership Council stick. There is a very short time before Rutskoi comes."

"Benon Sevan should be in from the beginning," I said.

"If Benon Sevan thinks he's going to decide, then he's mistaken," Durrani rejoined.

"Benon Sevan is the catalyst," I countered. "If an important government like Pakistan has started an initiative, then he will need to talk to you."

"What does he want?" Durrani asked. "What is he looking for? Has he spelled out the support he needs but hasn't gotten it?"

"Yes," I replied. "But we need to maintain dialogue with him as we proceed, not after the fact. For example, you took an important step, which is a formula for the transition. Did you discuss it with him?"

"I'll consult with Benon Sevan if he's around," Durrani asserted. "But if Benon Sevan does not do anything, do you expect us to sit around and wait?"

Durrani rejected my suggestion that Pakistan join the U.S-Soviet negative symmetry agreement. Pakistan's arms shipments, he said, would stop when the interim government assumed power in Kabul.

Before leaving his office, I questioned Durrani about whether his strategy was taking Pakistan deeper and deeper into the Afghan briar patch. The British and Russians had encountered its thorns. Would Pakistan be next? Durrani reflected for a moment before acknowledging that Pakistan did blame Russia and Britain for meddling in Afghanistan. He observed that sometimes Pakistan gets in too deeply.

Durrani escorted me to the embassy car parked outside. Shaking my hand, he wished me a safe flight to Europe and turned away. Then he turned back and muttered to me, "With the Afghans, everybody loses."

Richard Hoagland and I returned to the embassy to cable Washington about the day's disappointing events. Durrani had not budged on making the ISI-created Leadership Council the interim government. Not chosen by Afghans, it would be rejected by the Afghan population and prolong the Afghan war.

On December 9, the day I met with Durrani, an event of great significance in world affairs was under way at the Belovezhskaya Forest resort near the Soviet-Polish border near Brest. There, in the only European game preserve protecting the European bison, Russian President Yeltsin and the presidents of Ukraine and Belarus dissolved the seventy-four-year-old Soviet state. Those among the fifteen republics of the former Soviet Union that had not yet proclaimed their independence (including Russia) were now independent countries.[15]

On December 11 and 12 in Bonn, I briefed Ambassador Kimmitt and the German Foreign Ministry on Afghan developments. On December 13, Richard Hoagland and I flew to London for consultations with the British Foreign Office. My stopover in London before flying to Washington fortuitously coincided with Pakistani Army Chief Asif Nawaz's visit to Britain. The most powerful man in Pakistan was on a nostalgic trip, consulting with his British military counterparts and visiting Sandhurst, his alma mater, where he had excelled on the boxing team. I continued to believe that Pakistan's new chief of army staff might differ from his predecessor, General Beg, on Afghanistan, as he did on other issues.

I called on Sir John Coles, deputy under secretary of Britain's Foreign Office, on December 13 to brief him on Pakistan's strategy to remodel the seven party leaders into the interim government, bypassing the United Nations. The ISI, I stated, was hacking away at the time Benon Sevan desperately needed to convene a truly representative gathering aimed at choosing the interim government. The ISI's Leadership Council option was unacceptable to most Afghans. It would not work. The 1992 fighting season was only three months away. Warlordism and chaos would envelop the country if the UN process did not get under way soon.

Coles was furious. He stated that General Nawaz had been very critical of the seven during talks on Afghanistan in Britain. Nawaz, he said, was adamantly against the seven playing a role in the transition. Coles agreed with my suggestion that he discuss Afghanistan with Nawaz before he returned to Pakistan. Nawaz was the only one capable of ending ISI machinations and putting Pakistan back on the UN track. And that was exactly what Pakistan's new chief of army staff would attempt to do when he returned to Islamabad.

On December 19, Soviet Vice President Rutskoi arrived in Pakistan for the second session of negotiations with Pakistan and the Mujahidin. His visit was an embarrassing fiasco for both sides. Rutskoi rejected the Pakistani Leadership Council option for the Afghan transition. He insisted that Pakistan live up to its obligations to facilitate the UN peace process. A former POW himself,[16] Rutskoi came hoping to personally escort some freed prisoners back to Moscow. He asked that the Mujahidin honor the commitment in the Moscow joint communiqué to do everything possible to release all POWs. Ignoring the communiqué, Hekmatyar defiantly announced at the meetings that no POWs would be returned to Russia until after Najib transferred power. During a pause in the negotiations, Hekmatyar attempted to slink away. To the delight of the Russians and Mujahidin present, General Durrani grabbed him by the neck and threw him back into the room with Rutskoi.

The frenzy characterizing Rutskoi's negotiations with the Mujahidin and the ISI continued right up to his departure from Pakistan. The Mujahidin had not met his request to take at least one POW home. While the Russian delegation was boarding its aircraft at the Islamabad airport, a panicked Mojaddedi rushed to planeside and handed over an alleged Soviet POW of Turkmen origin to Rutskoi. Rutskoi took the Turkman on board the plane but later returned him to Mojaddedi's care through the International Committee of the Red Cross. On December 25, a Rutskoi aide told the BBC that "the freed man had never served in the Soviet army and was, in fact, an Afghan."[17]

ψ

Generals Asif Nawaz and Zia ul-Haq differed in many ways. They did, however, share one thing in common: Both could act boldly and swiftly. After returning from Britain, Nawaz apologized to the Soviets for the Rutskoi visit debacle. He then moved to end the ISI's favoritism for the Peshawar seven, join the United States and Russia in backing the UN peace process, and commit Pakistan to the negative symmetry agreement. He made ISI chief Durrani commandant of Pakistan's National Defense College, effective on March 3, 1992. Brigadier Yusub Ali Dogar became the new head of the ISI's Peshawar office, replacing Janjua.

Dogar informed the seven party leaders and Afghan commanders that there would be no more weapons, ammunition, or military equipment crossing the Afghan border after January 1, 1992. The ISI cleaned out arms warehouses in the tribal agencies bordering Afghanistan and transported the ordnance south for storage in the Rawalpindi area. On January 2, General Asif Nawaz stopped in Rome on his way to the United States to meet with Abdul Wali and discuss a possible role for Zahir Shah in the transition process. Wali told the BBC afterward that he hoped Nawaz could meet with Zahir Shah soon.[18]

The reaction from the Afghan hard-liners and Pakistani Jamaat-i Islami leader Qazi Hussain Ahmed to Nawaz's dramatic changes in Pakistan's Afghan policy was immediate and scathing. Ahmed described Nawaz's Rome visit and his firing of Hamid Gul as a major shift in Pakistan's Afghan strategy intended to please the United States. Hekmatyar charged that Nawaz had met with Abdul Wali because "America wanted to impose Zahir Shah on Afghans." Sayyaf told reporters that the Rome meeting was part of an "international conspiracy" against "establishing an Islamic order" in Afghanistan. Meanwhile, a jirga of over 150 Afghan tribal elders and moderate commanders in Peshawar declared support for the UN plan. An Ahmadzai tribal chief used the jirga platform to thank General Nawaz for meeting with Abdul Wali. The jirga passed a resolution condemning Ahmed for interfering in Afghan affairs.[19]

A Pakistani government Afghan cell meeting chaired by Nawaz on January 25 consummated Pakistan's policy shift. Two days later, simultaneous statements by UN Secretary General Boutros Boutros-Ghali in New York and Pakistan's Foreign Ministry in Islamabad reaffirmed the UN peace process and Pakistan's commitment to it. The Pakistani statement, issued in the name of the minister of state for foreign affairs Kanju, announced: "The Government of Pakistan has decided to support the UN Secretary General's efforts for the convening of an Afghan Assembly to decide an interim government acceptable to the Afghans. . . . We will facilitate the convening of a representative assembly and respect its outcome."[20]

The authoritative Pakistani statement triggered a rush of enthusiastic press releases from foreign governments. The State Department spokesman welcomed the Kanju statement and reaffirmed U.S. support for the UN secretary general and his representative, Benon Sevan. A Russian official observed that the "Russian government appreciates [the] recent statement of Pakistan in support of the United Nations formula." It was "no exaggeration," a Moscow Radio commentary gushed, to state that Pakistan's "major shift" on Afghanistan would "pave the way for peace."[21]

Mainstream Pakistani media commentaries praised Kanju's statement for ending Pakistan's previous "foot dragging" and "wishy-washy approach" on Afghanistan.[22] Mujahidin reaction split along familiar lines. Hekmatyar and other hard-liners vilified the Pakistani shift. Masood's representative announced his readiness to support the UN assembly. Moderate Afghan tribal leaders and commanders rejoiced. Ismael Khan sent word to me through his representative in Pakistan that he supported the UN political solution.

ψ

My sixteenth and final trip to the region began in January 1992 and ended in early March. In late January, I found an exceptionally hopeful atmosphere in Islamabad and along the Frontier, so hopeful that I found it hard to believe what I was hearing. For the first time since Zia's 1977 coup, a Pakistani chief of army staff was throwing his weight behind Pakistan's official Afghan policy and a political settlement organized by the United Nations. There was no longer a covert ISI policy directly contradicting the Pakistan government's formal policy—there was just one Pakistani policy. Since the CIA invariably followed its Pakistani sister intelligence agency's lead, this meant there could finally be one U.S. policy too.

I met with General Durrani on February 22. This time, there was no daylight between our positions. He staunchly supported the UN process and its inclusion of all Afghan groups. He acknowledged his past reservations about tribal participation. Now, he said, the Afghan tribes were the one big hope. Benon Sevan should take the lead; Pakistan would support him. Durrani recommended that serious planning begin on Afghan reconstruction.

In Peshawar, Mujahidin told me about a remarkable February 7 Durrani meeting with the seven parties in which he forcefully advocated Mujahidin cooperation with Benon Sevan.[23] In his completely unexpected lecture opening the meeting, Durrani recalled that the ISI had given the seven many opportunities to achieve a victory in Afghanistan. First, the AIG was tried. It failed. Then the commanders' shura and Trilateral Council failed.

Durrani stated that the UN political process was now the only option left. Pakistan, he informed them, had now chosen that option. He predicted that the UN assembly would bring all Afghan groups together and create conditions for the Afghan people to choose, by majority, their government. He advised the parties to support the United Nations and provide Benon Sevan with their lists of candidates for the UN assembly.

A long silence followed Durrani's virtual disassociation from Pakistan's decade-long policy of patronizing the seven. Speaking first, Rabbani asked Durrani to confirm that the military option was over. Yes, Durrani said, it was. He encouraged Rabbani to back the UN process and to provide Benon Sevan with his list of nominees for the UN assembly. Mojaddedi expressed his agreement with Durrani but asked for money and resources to prepare for the UN assembly. Durrani responded that the ISI would attempt to help. Khalis, speaking next, complained that Pakistan was no longer helping to bring an Islamic government to Afghanistan. Durrani noted that Afghans were Muslims and could decide this issue themselves. Khalis walked out the door, forgoing Durrani's luncheon invitation to the party leaders after the meeting.

Wahhabi zealot Mohammad Yasir, head of Sayyaf's political committee, then took the floor. He declared that Pakistan had abandoned the jihad but the Mujahidin had not. His voice rising, Yasir emitted an Islamic battle cry and declared war against the United Nations, Zahir Shah, and the United States.

Mojaddedi stood up. He protested Yasir's remarks, then followed Khalis out of the room. Durrani sarcastically thanked Yasir for his recommendation. He advised him that the military option was not a wise one. Only Najib would benefit. The Afghan people, he stated, supported a political solution under the United Nations. This prompted another moment of silence. Then Nabi Mohammadi got up. Without speaking a word, he left, with Yasir trailing behind him out the door. Only Rabbani and Gailani's son Hamed stayed for Durrani's luncheon.

᭙

I called on Akram Zaki, director general of Pakistan's Foreign Ministry, on the afternoon of February 20. With great satisfaction, Zaki declared that Pakistan had now moved from the legacy of General Beg to the realistic views of General Nawaz. Zaki spoke confidently, like an official finally in charge of his brief. He proudly predicted that Pakistan would now participate with the United States, Russia, and the United Nations to support the UN peace process.

I had heard many such optimistic forecasts from Pakistani diplomats, including from Zaki himself. They had always turned out to be wrong. Was this time really different? More than Pakistan's Afghan policy was at stake. The dispute in Pakistan over whether to pursue an Islamist military victory in Afghanistan or to support the UN political process was part of the long-running Pakistani debate between proponents of a Pakistani Islamic state and a democracy, between Pakistani military dictators and civilian prime ministers. It revolved around the very nature of Pakistan and began at Pakistan's founding.

Moderates visualized a modernizing Pakistan on the Western model, a Muslim nation but also a democratic one based on secular law rather than Sharia. Islamists favored Islamization of Pakistan's society and state. Zia, Beg, and Gul were in the latter category. They attempted to Islamicize Pakistan's domestic, political, social, and religious life and to Islamicize Afghanistan as well. General Nawaz, the scion of generations of army officers, was in the tradition of the British-educated secular Pakistani generals Zia had forced to retire. He wished to take the army out of Pakistan's domestic politics and religion and to improve relations with the United States. Beg and Gul considered the United States a long-term strategic adversary. They enforced the military's domination of Pakistani politics.

Zaki's optimism that Nawaz's realism had superseded Zia's legacy was heartening but yet to be confirmed. Zia's and Beg's Islamization programs in the Pakistani military had been under way for fourteen years. There were now many sympathizers and outright members of Pakistan's politico-religious par-ties in the Pakistani military. The American suspension of military and eco-nomic aid to Pakistan and India in 1965, and to Pakistan only in 1990 under the Pressler Amendment, remained a source of bitter resentment among mili-tary officers. Dating back to 1975, numerous ISI officers and NCOs had been directly involved in training and operational aspects of the Afghan jihad. They worked alongside Hekmatyar, Sayyaf, and Khalis, the Pakistani religious par-ties, and Arab extremists, including Osama bin Laden and Ayman al-Zawahiri. Hamid Gul and hundreds of other retired ISI officers and NCOs helped the ISI carry out its proxy wars in Afghanistan and Kashmir. This cohort was loyal to Zia's legacy. They amounted to a virtual ISI, supposedly in the private sector, but working closely with the ISI's ultra-secret "S" Department.[24]

General Nawaz, therefore, could not personally turn around Pakistan's Afghan policy by merely reassigning or retiring several generals and expect the army to follow his new direction. A February 26, 1992, Pakistani editorial incisively summed up the challenges he faced. Nawaz, it stated, had "much going for him" and was "exactly what Pakistan needed at this juncture." "But," the editorial continued, "his task will not be an easy one":

> When Gen Beg articulated an anti-West, pro-Iraq position during the Gulf War, reflecting public hysteria in much of the Muslim world, he found considerable support within the army. When Gen Gul was abruptly transferred, eyebrows were raised again. It is also no secret that several senior officers in critical positions who were promoted during the last two years, share many of the concerns of soldiers like Beg and Gul. Therefore, unless the new COAS [chief of army staff] is able to persuade his senior colleagues of the compelling wisdom of these times and institutionalize extensive reforms and re-education within the army, he will not be able to make his political initiatives stick.[25]

ψ

General Nawaz gave a desperately needed Pakistani lift to the UN settlement option, but it did not last long. Unfortunately for the United Nations and for peace in Afghanistan, Prime Minister Sharif sabotaged the process. In the end, General Nawaz did not resist. He had publicly announced his intention to take the army out of politics; consequently, he could not later engage in a political showdown with the prime minister on Pakistan's Afghan policy.

After his Foreign Ministry's January 27 proclamation, Sharif told the press that an "Islamic government of Mujahidin" would replace Najib. The watchful Pakistani press correctly interpreted Sharif's remark "to be a clear break from the position taken by his minister for foreign affairs, Siddique Kanju, not long ago that Pakistan would support the UN framework . . . with or without Mujahidins."[26]

There were other signs demonstrating that Sharif would oppose the UN option. The prime minister did not honor the standard procedure of consulting Chief of Army Staff Nawaz Sharif when he appointed a family friend and outspoken Islamist, retired Major General Javed Nasir, to be the next ISI director general.[27] Nasir was rumored to be a member of Jamaat-i Islami. By appointing Nasir ISI chief, Sharif ensured that the commander of Pakistan's powerful military intelligence organization would mainly answer to himself, not Nawaz. In addition, after Pakistan's January 27 commitment to the United Nation's Afghan framework, Sharif made no effort to compel pro-Islamist members of his ruling coalition to accept the government's official Afghan policy. Ijaz ul-Haq, Zia's son and the minister of labor, manpower, and overseas Pakistanis, openly criticized Pakistan's policy shift in speeches and press interviews. He vowed that Pakistan's government would have to cross over his dead body if it tried to impose its decision. Sharif's religious affairs minister joined the condemnation of the UN process.[28]

After the Kanju statement, Hekmatyar told a press conference that he and Sharif "shared the same ideas on Afghanistan." He vilified the UN plan. The Mujahidin, Hekmatyar declared, "would not mount a train which will be driven by Mr. Sevan." He continued: "Western countries do not want an end to the Afghan war. They fear the emergence of an Islamic bloc of countries." In an interview with his ANA news agency the next day, Hekmatyar lashed out at moderate Mujahidin criticism of his Pakistani mentor, Qazi Hussain Ahmed, stating, "This must have been issued by the government of Peter Tomsen because that government is against the unity of the Mujahidin."[29]

I conducted forty-four meetings with Mujahidin on the Frontier during three weeks in February. Commanders, tribal leaders, and politicians were all closely monitoring Pakistan's two-faced Afghan policy, guessing at where it would finally end up. The Mujahidin radicals were a small minority, but they still enjoyed resources and enthusiastic backing from Saudi, Pakistani, and Muslim Brotherhood extremists based in Saudi charities inside Pakistan. In the meantime, the number of Arab militants and other foreign radicals on the Frontier continued to increase. They were taken to training camps run by the ISI, Hekmatyar, Sayyaf, and extremist Arabs in Pakistan and across the border inside Afghanistan. Extremist banners in Arabic waved over Peshawar streets. Burmese, Uzbek, and Filipino Muslims along with numerous Arabs wandered through city bazaars. Egyptian fighters affiliated with Zawahiri and Abdel Rahman trained at Hekmatyar's bases in Paktiya and Nangarhar, while Saudis flocked to Sayyaf's camps at Sada, Torkham, and Jaji. The Arab al-Jihad encampment near Jalalabad, operated by Abu Ayub, a Kurdish Iraqi, ballooned to more than three hundred well-armed fighters. Foreign Islamic militants trained at ISI-organized Lashkar-i Taiba camps in eastern Konar and near Muzzafarabad in Pakistani-controlled northern Kashmir. During our meetings in Peshawar, Abdul Haq and Hamid Karzai called attention to the expanding foreign Islamist threat on the Frontier. Haq asked me why the United States did not pay attention to terrorism. He compared America to a huge elephant: "One hundred people push on it and it doesn't blink, but when it decides to move, it lumbers forward and crushes everything."

The thrilling but brief period following Pakistan's January 27 announced policy shift to the UN plan ignited a burst of moderate tribal activity. Provincial district and local tribal shuras sprang into existence, with Abdul Haq in the east and Popalzai Hamid Karzai in the south actively pushing the tribal unity trend. Karzai concentrated on the Kandahar region. The Ahmadzai shuras centered in Paktiya spread into adjoining provinces. Popalzai, Barakzai, and Nurzai tribal shuras emerged in the south, all declaring support for the UN process.

Benon Sevan's optimism remained steady despite the evidence of Sharif's opposition to the UN option. He told journalists on February 23 that he "had been convinced by Pakistani Prime Minister Nawaz Sharif that he was genuinely committed to the UN peace plan."[30] Sevan flew with me to Riyadh on February 24. We conducted separate meetings with Prince Turki. Turki was more positive on the UN process than previously but carefully hedged his comments. Moving on to Rome, we found former Afghan king Zahir Shah and his advisers unwilling to back up their verbal support of Sevan's peace initiative. In his meeting with Sevan on March 1, the king refused to turn over his list of nominees for the UN assembly to choose the next Afghan government. Sevan playfully chided him, telling the ex-king, "You should have a little bit of Sihanouk in you."[31]

I called on Zahir Shah the next day to urge him to provide the list to Sevan and throw his weight behind the UN process as he had long promised he would do during our Rome meetings. I was no more successful than Sevan. The former Afghan monarch complained about his financial problems. He and Abdul Wali demanded to know the names of the Afghans whom Sevan was considering for the UN assembly before Zahir Shah gave his list to Sevan. I told them that Sevan could not do that for any of the Afghan factions. Abdul Wali and Abdul Sattar Sirat grumbled about the UN's choice of language for the name of the UN-organized assembly.

After three hours of discussion, it was clear that Zahir Shah's legendary passivity had overwhelmed any previous inclination he might have harbored to support the UN gathering. Afghanistan's last monarch, the only real symbol of Afghan nationhood, chose to return to the sidelines and not use his influence to support the UN peace process. At this critical juncture, he thereby verified his own critique of Afghan leaders: "Our main difficulty is with ourselves."

At the Rome airport on March 2, Sevan informed me that he would fly to Geneva, consult with UN Secretary General Boutros-Ghali, and prepare the UN announcement on convening the first Afghan gathering in Geneva. It would be scheduled for mid-April. On my long flight back across the Atlantic to Washington I worried that the foundation of the UN plan was fractured beyond repair. The paucity of lists in Sevan's hands was one of the many difficulties he faced. Only Mojaddedi and Gailani had given him their suggestions. And, of course, every passing day meant the loss of more precious time.

☙

During my next trip to the region from January to March 1992, Najib's military position continued to deteriorate. General Abdul Momen, the commander of the regime's 70th Division at Heyratan on the Amu Darya, defied Najib's order to transfer his command to a Pashtun general appointed by Najib. Rashid Dostum, commander of the predominantly Uzbek 53rd Division, and Sayyed Kayan, commander of the Ismaili 80th Division stationed north of the Salang tunnel, declared their support for Momen, a Tajik. The three generals accused Najib of plotting with Hekmatyar to replace non-Pashtun commanders in the north with Pashtuns. Ahmed Shah Masood quickly established a dialogue with the rebellious generals, advising them to hold their areas and coordinate with his local Mujahidin commander, Atta Mohammad.[32]

The northern mutiny by Najib's non-Pashtun generals raised the specter of ethnic partition of Afghanistan, which Jalalabad Shura leader Haji Qadir had mentioned to me five months previously, in September 1991. The Pashtun versus non-Pashtun split reflected in the bitter feud between Hekmatyar and Masood now polarized Najib's regime. Najib sent his Tajik chief of staff, General Asif Delawar, to negotiate with Dostum and calm tensions. Delawar was already secretly colluding with Masood, and he returned to Kabul empty handed. Najib's next emissary, Major General Nabi Azimi, the Tajik commander of the Kabul garrison, was also in clandestine contact with Masood. Azimi was in Mazar-i-Sharif on March 17, when the forces of Dostum, Momen, Kayan, and Atta Mohammad occupied the city, Afghanistan's second largest and the capital of Balkh Province. They declared their independence from Najib.

From the darkest days of the Soviet occupation, Masood had talked with his advisers about a postwar moderate-nationalist Afghan government defended by commanders who had conducted the jihad from inside Afghanistan. A British journalist who often visited Masood believed the powerful northern commander was determined to "resist any transition body in which the Pakistanis have influence."[33] Masood desired to capitalize on the nationalism that the commanders' shura had displayed at Shah Selim. He was concerned, however, that the ISI had infiltrated the shura, emasculating it after the Khost victory. While his military grip closed around Kabul during the first week of March, Masood sent out feelers to sound out Pashtun commanders, tribal leaders, and ulema about his proposal.

Several times during late 1991 and early 1992, Masood had sent word to Benon Sevan and me through his advisers Daoud Mir, Yunis Qanuni, and his brother, Ahmed Zia, that he supported the UN-brokered transition as long as it did not include Najib and PDPA members.[34] Sevan had not accepted Masood's invitation to travel to northern Afghanistan for direct talks on a political settlement. While Sevan's busy schedule and the complicated logistics of such a trip may have ruled it out, Sevan's absence "annoyed Masood."[35] During a 1993 interview with a British correspondent, he recalled:

> Everybody thought that if there was a military solution it would be through Hekmatyar and the Pakistanis, and if there was a political set-tlement, it would be through the Benon Sevan peace plan. I can give an example. When Benon Sevan started his work in Afghanistan, I sent him a message through Daoud. . . . We told him: on the whole we are not against your programme. But I want to make it clear that you should neither forget, nor ignore the role of the internal commanders. You shouldn't be kept busy in Peshawar, you should think about Af-ghanistan. We made it clear that we would advance as far as the out-skirts of Kabul and halt there. We said we would give him the opportunity to work with Afghan parties and come to a conclusion with them about Afghanistan. . . . I asked him for a meeting. He said "yes," but later he didn't come. When he was prepared to meet me, the fighting had started.[36]

After Dostum's declaration of independence on March 17, Najib con-cluded that his position was hopeless. The next day, reading a statement that Sevan had drafted, he stated his intention to "transfer all executive power and authority to the transitional government from the first day of the transition period."[37] Najib's announcement cut short Masood's attempt to organize a "third force" transition option excluding the Kabul regime and the seven ISI-linked leaders in Peshawar.[38] It also set off frantic military activity by Mu-jahidin in Pakistan and around Kabul to fill the emerging power vacuum in Afghanistan.

In Peshawar, the ISI's Javed Nasir, Qazi Hussain Ahmed, and Abul Hassan, the Ikhwan who headed the Saudi World Muslim League office in Pakistan, intensified their pressure on the seven to agree on a power-sharing arrange-ment for the interim government.[39] On March 22, Benon Sevan asked Prime Minister Sharif not to reconstitute the seven into the transition entity. By that time, Nasir was already negotiating with the seven on the distribution of cab-inet portfolios. The bickering among the seven about cabinet positions leaked into the Pakistani press. Prime Minister Sharif and ISI chief Nasir's efforts to transform the Leadership Council into the interim government burst into the headlines.⁴⁰

Sevan hurried to counter the revival of the Leadership Council and salvage the UN initiative before a battle for Kabul overtook his settlement initiative. He proposed that a UN-organized pretransition Council of Impartials of only fifteen members be formed immediately. Sevan planned to take the council to Kabul on his UN aircraft and to fly Najib to India. After Najib's exit, the council and Sevan would organize an Afghan assembly in Europe to choose the interim government at the end of April. The interim government would replace the council and organize elections for a legitimate Afghan leadership, ending the Afghan war.

Moving with extraordinary speed, Sevan flew to Tehran on March 29 where he obtained Iranian consent for his proposal. He went to Islamabad on April 1 and secured Nawaz Sharif's disingenuous approval. On April 2 Sevan met with Najib in Kabul. Najib agreed and gave Sevan his list of nominees for the Council of Impartials. That afternoon, Sevan returned to Pakistan to brief Prime Minister Sharif, ISI's Nasir, and Foreign Affairs Minister of State Kanju on his progress. On April 4, Sevan collected lists for the Council of Impartials from Mojaddedi, Gailani, and Nabi. Hekmatyar, Sayyaf, and Khalis rejected Sevan's overtures. Still playing brinksmanship, Rabbani withheld his list.

Sevan hurried back to Tehran on April 6 to update the Iranians. There, Hezb-i Wahdat gave him their list for the council. On April 8, Sevan flew back to Peshawar in a last-ditch attempt to get Rabbani's list, but the cunning Ikhwani refused to hand it over. For Rabbani, the ISI's Leadership Council, not the UN process, was now his more dependable path to power. The same day, Sevan went to Geneva to brief UN Secretary General Boutros-Ghali. On April 10, Boutros-Ghali overoptimistically announced that "all the governments concerned" had "expressed their full support" for Sevan's proposal, as had "the vast majority of Afghans Sevan had consulted."⁴¹ The secretary general made an appeal for all involved to assist Sevan's efforts.

Sevan was exhausted. In ten days, he had done everything possible to gain international, regional, and Afghan backing for his peace plan, culminating in the UN secretary general's announcement. But it was not enough. Nawaz Sharif's commitments of cooperation were not sincere. He and ISI Director General Nasir planned to make the Leadership Council the interim government. They intended to present the seven Peshawar leaders to Sevan as the Afghan transition regime when he returned to Pakistan.

On April 13, Sevan flew to Islamabad. Some of the members of the council he had chosen had already arrived in Pakistan from Europe and the United States, and they were prepared to continue on to Kabul and take over from Najib. Pakistan's embassies abroad were issuing expedited visas, covering the travel costs and urging Sevan's selected council members to fly to Islamabad immediately.[42]

At ten in the morning on April 14, Nawaz Sharif received Sevan at his Islamabad residence.[43] Javed Nasir was present along with about thirty Mujahidin. Except for Hekmatyar, all of the Peshawar party leaders were in the room. Qutbuddin Hilal represented Hekmatyar, his father-in-law. The leaders vehemently rejected Sevan's Council of Impartials. Sevan defended the council and asked for their amendments. His request thrust the six party leaders into their normal pastime of nonstop quarreling. In the late afternoon, in what seemed to be a prearranged ploy, the seven leaders turned on Sevan and demanded that they form the interim government. Sevan challenged the seven to agree among themselves on the makeup of the transition entity. The invitation ignited a fresh round of loud arguments, this one between the leaders over who would lead the interim entity.

Earlier on April 15, Najib had requested that Sevan fly to Kabul immediately and evacuate him to New Delhi. Sometime before midnight on April 15, Sevan told Sharif that the seven leaders were not going to reach agreement. He broke away from the meeting, rushed home, then to the airport, and took off in his UN plane for Kabul. By the time he landed at the Kabul airport, Najib had retreated to the UN compound.

After Sevan's departure, Rabbani chose to repudiate his eight-month flirtation with the political settlement option in a VOA broadcast. In the broadcast and in an April 15 press release, he fiercely denounced the UN peace initiative. The invective in Rabbani's press release foreshadowed the aggressive face of a Muslim Brother he would later project as president of Afghanistan: "We will not allow foreigners from anywhere to implement their dirty plans and goals which will divide the country or incite the Afghans. We are waiting for the last strongholds of atheism and infidelity to fall."[44]

The next day, April 16, Mojaddedi phoned VOA to declare that the UN plan to send the Council of Impartials to Kabul had collapsed. That same day, Masood announced that events in Afghanistan had moved beyond the UN plan. At an April 24 press conference, a frustrated Sevan summed up: "No one is prepared to make a compromise." He joked: "Agreements signed in the morning disappeared in the evening. They are written in invisible ink."[45]

CHAPTER 19

From One War
to the Next

The extremist/non-extremist post-Najib struggle for power around Kabul could continue for months or years. Alternatively, it could end up with the Afghans getting rid of the externally supported extremists.

U.S. Policy: U.S. perseverance in maintaining our already established position in Afghanistan—at little cost—could significantly contribute to the favorable moderate outcome:

- Sideline the extremists,
- Maintain a friendship with a strategically located friendly country,
- Help us accomplish our other objectives in Afghanistan and the broader Central Asian region, e.g., narcotics, stinger recovery, anti-terrorism, Soviet POWs.

We are in danger of throwing away the assets we have built up in Afghanistan over the last 10 years, at great expense. The fallacious attitudinal underpinning of this approach is (a) Afghanistan was a Cold War, 1980s issue, not an issue today, (b) the U.S. cannot influence the direction of events in Afghanistan and, (c) we have no resources to invest there and should not get sucked in.

The danger is that we will lose interest and abandon our investment/assets in Afghanistan, which straddles a region where we have precious few levers. We need to proceed in a pragmatic, hard headed manner. We should

begin by establishing a policy overlay for the region integrated with our
broader policy in the Eurasian region.
                    —AUTHOR, CONFIDENTIAL MEMORANDUM, 1993[1]

The Great Game takes place in the Afghan highland, the strategic nexus between contending power centers in Eurasia. The outside players come and
go, attempting without success to control Afghanistan or to deny it to their
adversaries. Afghanistan's regional neighbors, Pakistan, Iran, and Uzbekistan,
moved to the forefront of the Great Game following Najib's April 15, 1992,
overthrow. The United States and Russia temporarily left the field.

Najib's collapse also marked the end of the era of Western imperialism in
South Asia dating back to the eighteenth century. The European armies and
civilian and intelligence bureaucrats who had once dominated the region
were now gone. The Soviet Union had vanished. The ideological contest between communism and Islam was no longer relevant. Inside Afghanistan, the
extremist versions of Islam exported to Afghanistan from Pakistan, Saudi Arabia, and Iran now competed with each other and with the mild, indigenous
Afghan Hanafi order.

The Islamist sects gaining beachheads in war-wracked Afghanistan during
the 1980s and 1990s were in agreement that the country should be trans-
formed from a tribal to an Islamic state governed by an ultraconservative version of Sharia, not constitutions and elections. They, however, profoundly
disagreed with each other on the nature of the Islamic state that would succeed Najib. The two extremist Sunni factions, the Deobandis and Wahhabis,
considered the Shia to be infidels who needed to be marginalized, if not annihilated. The Afghan Shia lobbied Iran for arms to prepare to battle the extremist Sunnis. Iran used its religious links to Afghanistan's large Shia
minority to propagate Khomeini's aggressive Shia revivalism and expand Iranian influence in Afghanistan. Al-Qaeda and Muslim Brotherhood operatives
sought to transform Afghanistan into a holy-war bastion, an unassailable base
from which terrorists could strike the West and pro-Western Arab governments in the Gulf and the Middle East.

The volatile mix of rival Islamist sects threatened stability in Afghanistan
and Pakistan and, in the long run, the entire South-Central Asian region of
over a billion inhabitants. Afghanistan after Najib's collapse was already a
trembling linchpin of diverse tribes, ethnic and religious groups connected

to Pakistan, Iran, the predominantly Muslim Xinjiang Province in western China, and the new Central Asian Republics. If the linchpin disintegrated into sectarian conflict, the ripples could activate these centrifugal forces prevailing in the region prior to the colonial period. Pakistan, more than any other bordering state, would suffer from the fallout. Shia comprised roughly a fifth of the population in Pakistan as well as Afghanistan. Pashtuns made up over 20 percent of Pakistan's population and about 40 percent of Afghanistan's population. Baluch tribes straddled both sides of the Afghan-Pakistani border.

Pakistan's ability to project its power and influence into Afghanistan was superior to that of Afghanistan's other neighbors and to India when Najib's regime crumbled in April 1992. The steady flow of Saudi petrodollars undergirded the Pakistani Army's pursuit of Zia's vision in Afghanistan. The ISI's Saudi-financed Islamist infrastructure on the Pakistani Frontier and across the border in the Afghan Pashtun belt mass-produced Pakistani, Afghan, and Arab holy warriors for combat inside Afghanistan and Kashmir. The ISI's Leadership Council and Gulbuddin Hekmatyar were poised to fill the leadership vacuum left by Najib in Kabul. Al-Qaeda, Muslim Brotherhood extremists, and Prince Turki's General Intelligence Directorate supported the ISI's extremist-centered Afghan strategy.

Iran in 1992 was the main player in the post-Najib Great Game inning blocking Pakistan's hegemonic aspirations. Tehran was a formidable challenge. Since Islam's great Shia-Sunni schism in the seventh century, Iran had grown proficient at neutralizing threats from its majority Sunni neighbors. Iranian strategists guided the eight-party Hezb-i Wahdat Shia alliance it had created in 1990 to balance Pakistan's seven-party Sunni alliance. Scores of Iranian intelligence officers operated inside Afghanistan, some under diplomatic cover in Kabul, Herat, and Mazar. They bought off Sunni as well as Shia commanders. Iran transported its arms and Iranian influence through the Shia-majority Hazarajat to Shia-populated communities in western Kabul and Mazar-i-Sharif.

It was against this contentious geostrategic backdrop that another phase of warfare descended on Afghanistan after Najib's collapse. It lasted for nine years, ending with the October 7, 2001, American intervention in Afghanistan after the 9/11 attacks. During this period, Afghanistan was consumed by ethnic and sectarian conflict fanned from the outside by Pakistan, Iran, and Saudi Arabia. India and Russia coordinated with Iran in the late 1990s to prevent Pakistan's Taliban proxy and its al-Qaeda ally from controlling Afghanistan.

Pakistan's strategy of mobilizing Sunni extremism and Pashtun nationalism to dominate Afghanistan could not succeed. Arming some Afghan factions to dominate other Afghan factions is not a wise tactic to use in the Great Game. There are always many factions left out who will resist and foreign patrons who will support them. Furthermore, the Afghans favored by Pakistanis were as undependable as the Afghans sponsored earlier by the Soviets and British. Pakistan's seven party leaders' compliance with ISI instructions was relatively assured as long as they were inside Pakistan. Once in Kabul, they marched to their own drummers.

ψ

Ahmed Shah Masood, never in Pakistan's or Iran's net, took his army out of the Panshir onto the Shomali Plain above Kabul in the weeks before Najib collapsed. We were in regular contact through his younger brother Wali Masood in London. I relayed U.S. messages through Wali to Masood in Jabal Saraj and Charikar advising him not to move unilaterally against Kabul and to cooperate with the United Nations and other Afghan groups to achieve a political solution to the Afghan war. Masood at the time was in frequent touch with members of the commanders' shura, notably Abdul Haq and other commanders opposed to Pakistan's Leadership Council. He conveyed to me, through Wali Masood, his intention to protect Kabul from Gulbuddin Hekmatyar and to support a broad-based transition.

Najib's collapse, however, forced Masood to change his mind. A major battle with Hekmatyar loomed. Hekmatyar was playing on Pashtun worries that a Tajik, another Bacha Seqao, intended to occupy Kabul and set up his own regime.[2] Masood desperately needed Pashtun allies—especially Pashtuns opposed to Hekmatyar—and he needed them quickly. Kabul was vulnerable to Hekmatyar's forces, which were gathering in Logar Province. The northern commander decided that military exigencies took priority over his preference for a broad-based transition delinked from Pakistani influence. Within days after Najib fled to the UN compound on April 15, 1992, Masood invited the Leadership Council to Kabul to accept the transfer of power from the regime. Masood's decision paid off in the short term because it allowed him to draw Hekmatyar's Pashtun adversaries in the Leadership Council to his side. In the long run, his overture to the Leadership Council based in Pakistan to form the interim government proved disastrous. The seven leaders would bring their personal vendettas against one another, their unpopularity among ordinary Afghans, and ISI intrigues with them to Kabul.

Masood's invitation to the Leadership Council to form a government painted Hekmatyar into a corner. The other six leaders opposed him. They were not going to choose Hekmatyar to lead the transition. His only alternative was to attack Kabul and seize power. On April 17, 1992, Hekmatyar and his ISI advisers entered Afghanistan to organize his offensive. They moved his conventional battalions, now numbering six, from Pakistan to his base at Charasiab in southern Kabul Province near the Logar border. Former Khalqi generals, artillery and infantry units, 1,000 Pakistani Jamaat volunteers, 2,000 madrassa students, and a few hundred Arabs augmented his buildup.

On April 21, while Masood remained outside Kabul, Hekmatyar issued an ultimatum to the regime to hand over power directly to his council of Kabul commanders (which meant to him) by April 23. When that deadline expired, he extended his ultimatum to April 26.

Hekmatyar was isolated, but he enjoyed a major political advantage. The remaining six Peshawar leaders were still arguing among themselves in Pakistan over who would lead the transition. King Fahd sent a personal message to them brandishing a Koranic passage to encourage consensus: "Hold fast all together by the rope ... and be not divided. And obey God and his apostle and fall into no dispute lest you lose heart and your power depart."[3] Prince Turki returned to Peshawar to assist the negotiations.

On April 24, in the presence of three Pakistani leaders (Prime Minister Nawaz Sharif, Chief of Army Staff General Asif Nawaz Janjua, and ISI Director General Javed Nasir), Prince Turki, Jamaat-i Islami's Qazi Hussain Ahmed, and Muslim Brotherhood Arab activists, the six party leaders signed the "Peshawar Accords."[4] The agreement resolved a dispute between Sibghatullah Mojaddedi and Burhanuddin Rabbani over the interim presidency by making them both president, *ad seriatim*. Mojaddedi was allowed to occupy the post for the first two months. (He wasted little time in issuing "Decree Number One" in his name.) Rabbani was named to succeed Mojaddedi and serve for four months. The Peshawar Accords specified that during their combined six months in office, the two interim presidents, together with the Leadership Council, would organize a large jirga to choose a new interim government.

The agreement stipulated that the interim government selected by the jirga would organize elections within eighteen months.

While Mojaddedi and Rabbani would successively fill the position of interim president, and Hekmatyar, in abstentia, was assigned the prime minister's portfolio, the remaining leaders had to be satisfied with assigning their party loyalists to ministerial portfolios. The Pakistani creators of the Peshawar Accords may have hoped this arrangement would prevent the breakdown suffered by the AIG. Of course, they failed to achieve that goal. Sayyid Ahmad Gailani was given the Foreign Ministry; Abdul Rasoul Sayyaf the Interior Ministry; Mohammad Nabi Mohammadi the Justice Ministry; Yunus Khalis the Education Ministry; and Burhanuddin Rabbani the Defense Ministry. Rabbani immediately appointed Masood as defense minister. Hamid Karzai became deputy foreign minister.

The agreement made Rabbani chairman of the Leadership Council. It required that the party leaders in the council remain behind in Peshawar until Mojaddedi's term expired in late June. Rabbani and Sayyaf quickly violated this rule. They were on the road to Kabul within days of Mojaddedi's arrival in the capital. Hekmatyar, meanwhile, was already inside Afghanistan preparing to attack Kabul. Such infractions were not surprising. The leaders had broken every Pakistani-engineered compact they had signed dating back to the first Nabi-led National Front agreement in 1983. In fact, the Peshawar agreement began to fall apart even as the six leaders were sitting down to sign it in the presence of their Pakistani, Saudi, and Muslim Brotherhood patrons. A group of Shia present protested and walked out. Hekmatyar's representative and son-in-law, Qutbuddin Hilal, rejected the agreement and left before the signing. Gailani signed but rescinded his approval four days later.

The signing of the Peshawar Accords forced Hekmatyar's hand: His zeal to rule Afghanistan could only be realized by the gun. He correctly anticipated that Mojaddedi would rush to the capital to preside over a rapid transfer of power to himself. Therefore, Hekmatyar needed to strike first, before Mojaddedi entered Kabul and presided over the transfer-of-power ceremony.

On the evening of April 24, Masood contacted Hekmatyar at his Charasiab base south of the capital to discuss the Peshawar Accords signed earlier that day. Hekmatyar told Masood he was going into the city. Masood responded, "Fine, but come with the other leaders. If you come by yourself, others will stand in your way."[5] The next morning, Hekmatyar ordered a full-scale air and land attack on Kabul. It was the day before his April 26 ultimatum expired. Forty tanks under a Hezb commander charged into the city from the south.[6] Abdul Rashid Dostum's tanks and artillery along Kabul's southern perimeter raked the armored column with canon fire, instantly killing the Hezb commander.[7] Masood dispatched more than thirty aircraft from the Bagram and Kabul airports to strafe the attacking force, stalling its advance.

Masood's brother Wali phoned me in the State Department from London to announce the start of Hekmatyar's attack. He predicted a Masood victory. Abdul Haq's brother forwarded a message to me from Haq informing that his Mujahidin at Sarobi would block any Hekmatyar attempt to enter Kabul from the west.

A spate of reports from multiple sources described ISI's active support for Hekmatyar's attack. They charged that the ISI's Afzal Janjua, Sultan Imam, and Hamid Gul were inside Afghanistan. Gianni Picco, a senior political officer at the UN's New York headquarters, phoned me in the State Department to say that the ISI was "going all-out in support of Hekmatyar." The Russian embassy counselor in Washington rushed to the U.S. State Department to complain about ISI interference on behalf of Hekmatyar. He proposed a joint U.S.-Russian demarche to Pakistan objecting to the ISI's assistance to Hekmatyar's offensive.

I sent an immediate cable to the American embassy in Islamabad requesting its response to these reports. The embassy replied that it had found no evidence that the ISI was arming Hekmatyar or encouraging him to attack Kabul. To describe this response as perplexing would be a gross understatement. Four days later, after the embassy telegram arrived, Pakistani journalist Ahmed Rashid said he personally witnessed and reported on "fifty trucks of arms and ammunition" destined for Hekmatyar's forces in Logar traveling from Pakistan into Afghanistan.[8]

Following up the Islamabad embassy's cable, and on instructions from the State Department, a U.S. diplomat in Moscow informed the Russian Foreign Ministry that "the U.S. sees no need to proceed with a joint approach to Pakistan concerning [the] Russian claim that Islamabad is assisting Hekmatyar."[9] Deputy Assistant Secretary on South Asia Teresita Schaffer assured the Russian embassy political counselor in Washington: "We have guessed wrong before and may be wrong again. Nonetheless, it seems that Hekmatyar wille [sic] brought into the process in some fashion, but there will not be a smooth relationship."[10] The embassy's validation of Pakistan's denials that the ISI was assisting Hekmatyar's offensive may have related to the State Department warnings to Pakistan that the ISI's involvement in the Kashmir insurgency was putting Pakistan at risk of being placed on the State Department list of states supporting terrorism.[11]

In an interview with retired U.S. Ambassador Dennis Kux years later, a former Pakistani ambassador in Washington recalled that Under Secretary Arnold Kanter warned her in late 1991 that Pakistan's placement on the U.S. list of states sponsoring terrorism "will end the U.S.-Pakistani relationship."[12] In a separate interview with Kux, Nicholas Platt, U.S. ambassador to Pakistan in 1991 and 1992, stated that, at the time, he raised the terrorism issue "at every level from the Prime Minister on down." Kux wrote: "The Pakistan government, the response went—much as it had in the case of the Afghan war—was offering only political and moral support for the Kashmiri insurgency."[13] The embassy's handling of Pakistan's fraudulent explanations seemed to reflect concern that the widely reported ISI assistance to Hekmatyar's attacks on the new regime in Kabul—in addition to the Kashmir insurgency—could tip the balance and lead to Pakistan's inclusion on the U.S. list of states sponsoring terrorism.

The first phase of the battle for Kabul went in Hekmatyar's favor. Masood and his Parchami allies had not detected hundreds of Hekmatyar's Mujahidin slipping quietly and unarmed into Kabul over the previous weeks. Khalqis in the regime had given them weapons once they were inside the city. As a result, fighting in the capital's southern and central districts was intense on April 25 and 26. Late on the afternoon of April 26, those monitoring the battle for Kabul were surprised to hear a radio announcement from Hekmatyar. He claimed victory, triumphantly declaring that, with the sole exception of the Radio-Television Center, his forces controlled the city. An Islamabad embassy cable reported that Hekmatyar had publicly boasted that Dostum was in his custody. The cable quoted Hekmatyar as announcing that there was "no longer any need to transfer power as a Mujahidin government (i.e., his own) [was] now in control."[14]

Hekmatyar's assertions were exaggerated. He had managed to seize some key government buildings and military bases in Kabul, but not most of Afghanistan's capital. Masood initiated a blistering counterattack. His troops ripped through the city late on April 26 and into April 27, driving Hekmatyar back into Logar. Except for some Hekmatyar fighters holding out in the Interior Ministry, the battle for Kabul was over by the morning of April 28. Masood's forces controlled the city. They awaited Interim President Mojaddedi's afternoon arrival. Mojaddedi's 150-person convoy drove into Afghanistan's capital with much fanfare. Arriving from Peshawar, it carried many of his relatives and followers, security personnel, and journalists, including a BBC crew. Celebratory gunfire and shouts of "Allah Akbar" arose as he entered Kabul. Regime Prime Minister Fazle Haq Khalyikar and Foreign Minister Abdul Wakil formally transferred power to Mojaddedi in a ceremony at the Foreign Ministry. Mojaddedi wore a flowing gray robe and his signature white turban atop a gold headband. Less than an hour after the ceremony, Hekmatyar defiantly fired a barrage of rockets into the city. In a press conference called to hail the transfer of authority, Mojaddedi accused Hekmatyar of violating Islamic law and Afghan tradition.[15]

In the evening hours later on April 28, in a lead convoy of ten jeeps trailed by over one hundred tanks, Masood entered Afghanistan's capital. In his standard low-key style, he quietly settled into the Defense Ministry.[16] From his new office in the presidential palace late on April 28, Mojaddedi delivered an eloquent radio and TV address commemorating the transfer of power. He granted Masood a private audience, declaring him the "Protector" of Afghanistan. That night, under the glare of TV lights, Mojaddedi chaired the first meeting of the Interim Council.

A stream of congratulatory messages from foreign governments addressed to Interim President Mojaddedi was read over Kabul radio. Nawaz Sharif, Asif Nawaz, Javed Nasir, and Prince Turki flew to Kabul for a three-hour visit on April 29, the first of a parade of foreign well-wishers coming from abroad. Passengers on Sharif's Pakistani C-130 were startled when the heavily bearded Nasir shouted an Islamic battle cry as the plane crossed into Afghan air space.[17] Once on the ground, Sharif promised Pakistan's full political support to the interim government, handing Mojaddedi a check for 250 million rupees (about $10 million).[18] At that moment, ISI trucks bearing arms and ammunition were rumbling through Torkham toward Hekmatyar bases in Logar to stock his warehouses for his next attack on Kabul.

ψ

Mojaddedi waited only a week after arriving in Kabul to make his own grab for power. In the words of American consul Jerry Feierstein in Peshawar, Mojaddedi became the "Avignon Caliph," sweeping aside the rules of the Peshawar Accords limiting his authority as interim president. He was now in the presidential palace in Kabul, not in Peshawar boxed in by ISI handlers. He could finally prevail over the other six leaders.

In a spirited monologue to correspondents at the presidential palace, the seventy-year-old Mojaddedi dramatically declared that he planned to retain the presidency for two years instead of two months. He unveiled a thirty-six-ministry "caretaker" cabinet that had not been mentioned in the Peshawar Accords and was, in effect, a new government—his government. The Peshawar agreement had given Hekmatyar the prime ministership. Mojaddedi left that slot empty. There was minimal overlap with the cabinet Rabbani was to lead.

At his press conference, Mojaddedi ebulliently branded Hekmatyar an "outlaw." He boasted that, "if we give the order, Hekmatyar will be dust." Alluding to the recent Watts riots in California (April 29–May 1, 1992), he demanded that Dostum, whom he had promoted to a four-star general, keep his Uzbek militia units in Kabul to prevent looting "like in Los Angeles." Exulting in his self-proclaimed promotion, Mojaddedi described himself as "the only one who could bridge the deep ethnic and religious divisions" in Afghanistan. The people, he claimed, were insisting that he stay in office for two years until national elections could be held.[19]

Mojaddedi's lurch for power set off another familiar cycle of recrimination among the Peshawar leaders. From a base south of Kabul, Hekmatyar accused Mojaddedi of "fanning the fire" by creating another Mujahidin government. Sayyaf thundered, "As long as we carry guns on our shoulders we will not let anyone stay a day more than his tenure." Rabbani muted his anger against Mojaddedi but retaliated by issuing his own decrees directly from his Leadership Council office in Kabul, several of which contradicted Mojaddedi's decree promulgated from the nearby presidential palace. Mojaddedi castigated Rabbani for introducing a "dualism in the administration of the country's affairs."[20]

Pressing his case to rule Afghanistan, Mojaddedi organized a stage-managed jirga of selected commanders and tribal and religious notables in the palace. He invited foreign journalists to witness the acclaim he received from his followers. To the assembled reporters, he repeated his claim that the country wanted him to remain president and to organize a loya jirga.

Sayyaf angrily left Kabul to establish a new Saudi-financed Wahhabi military bastion in the hills next to his native town of Paghman. From there, he dispatched hundreds of Afghan and Arab zealots into nearby West Kabul to kill, kidnap, capture, and behead Hazara Shia. Sayyaf's holy war against the Shia widened the spectrum of violence and chaos in the city provoked by Hekmatyar's attack the previous week.

ﺀ

The ISI's support for Hekmatyar's failed April 25–28 offensive against Kabul delivered a major blow to prospects for a stable post-Najib transition. Mojaddedi's brazen attempt to prolong his reign further disrupted chances for a smooth transition process. Sayyaf's launch of a holy war against Kabul's Shia population was perhaps the final act that closed the door to peace in Afghanistan. The sectarian and ethnic fighting he and Hekmatyar unleashed along with their Pakistani and Arab allies precipitated internal upheavals that destroyed most of what had not been ruined during the previous fourteen years of warfare.

Beginning in May and through the summer and fall of 1992, tough Iranian-armed Wahdat Shia based in Kabul's western suburbs fought Sayyaf's Wahhabis with small arms, grenades, and mortars. Ferocious hand-to-hand combat swirled only a half-mile from Mojaddedi's presidential palace. In a broadcast from his new Paghman fortress, Sayyaf blasted the Wahdat Shia for being "armed, equipped, and provoked by a foreign country." Mojaddedi indirectly blamed Saudi Arabia, chastising Sayyaf for "collaboration with foreign enemies of religious unity" and provoking "a destructive war against the Wahdat party." Mojaddedi lacked Sayyaf's military power. But he possessed presidential appointment power. Afghanistan's interim president took the National Security Ministry from Sayyaf and gave it to his Hezb-i Wahdat ally, along with seven other ministries.[21]

In May and June, the death toll from the Sayyaf-Wahdat street fighting climbed into hundreds of combatants and civilians. Over 4,000 were wounded, and some 800 were being held hostage.[22] A senior Wahdat leader, Ustad Khalili,[23] accused Sayyaf's Afghan and Arab Wahhabis of beheading over 100 Shia.[24] Ethnic and sectarian factions carved Kabul's neighborhoods into heavily guarded enclaves. Large posters of Ayatollah Khomeini were posted in Wahdat-controlled West Kabul. The seven Peshawar parties occupied separate sections of the city. Small, unsupervised bands of armed Mujahidin wandered the streets conducting home invasions, robberies, murders, and rapes against Kabul's terrified citizenry.

Hekmatyar's sporadic shelling of the open city added to the mayhem. By August, his bombardments had killed more than 1,800 civilians, wounded thousands more, destroyed whole residential áreas, and sent some 500,000 people fleeing from the capital in all directions.[25] Meanwhile, a May 18, 1992, Islamabad embassy cable to Washington expressed unwarranted optimism that Pakistan had cut ties with Hekmatyar and Sayyaf and was backing the UN peace effort: "The GOP's [Government of Pakistan's] vow to respect the outcome of the UN settlement and leave behind those who did not wish to participate signaled the end of Pakistani patronage of certain Mujahidin groups, notably radicals Gulbuddin Hekmatyar and Abdul Rasoul Sayyaf."[26]

Mojaddedi's interpretation of his commander-in-chief authority created friction with Defense Minister Masood. Masood objected to Mojaddedi's promotion of Dostum to a four-star general and bestowing the rank of lieutenant general on three other military officers without consulting him. Masood also refused to recognize Mojaddedi's appointment of Gailani's Pashtun military adviser, Rahim Wardak, as his chief of staff in the Defense Ministry. Like Gailani, Wardak had a reputation for having close ties to the ISI.

On June 20, Masood's troops guarding the radio station intercepted Mojaddedi's son, Zabibullah, carrying a presidential proclamation inviting provincial officials to Kabul, ostensibly to witness Mojaddedi's transfer of authority to Rabbani. The proclamation aroused the radio announcer's suspicion that Mojaddedi was planning to make another attempt to extend his presidential term, this time backed by an audience of personal loyalists flooding in from the provinces. When the announcer resisted reading the document, Zabibullah threatened him. Masood, alerted by his guards, phoned Zabibullah and told him Mojaddedi was only interim president and could not speak for all of the Mujahidin. When Zabibullah persisted, Masood curtly warned him that if he did not leave the Radio-Television Center, he would see to it that he was expelled from the country.

Mojaddedi struck back by harshly denouncing Masood when giving Friday prayers at Kabul's main mosque. Masood was in the crowd outside the mosque listening to Mojaddedi's angry rebuke carried over the mosque's loudspeaker. He remained seated on the ground during the public reprimand, then walked back to his office in the Defense Ministry.

࿘

After Najib's fall, Masood possessed greater combat power than Hekmatyar in the Kabul region. Hekmatyar, however, could count on support from Pakistan. His April attack on Kabul was only the first round of a three-year campaign to capture the city with Pakistani assistance. Besides Nawaz Sharif and the ISI, he was supported by Jamaat's Qazi Hussain Ahmed, wealthy Saudi contributors, and hundreds of fanatical Arabs.

Masood underestimated the opposition he faced. He told a May 5 press conference that, "from the military point of view[,] Hekmatyar is no longer in a position to threaten the Islamic government that has been established in Afghanistan."[27] Looking back a year later, Masood acknowledged his misjudgment:

> So when the regime was defeated and we were pushed into the fighting, what happened? Pakistan interfered very powerfully, giving [Hekmatyar] money, ammunition and weapons, sending advisers to commanders, to the leaders, and provoking [certain] commanders.... From a military point of view, we wanted to limit the war, and keep it from spreading. We took defensive positions ... but our strategy of limited fighting did not work.[28]

The ISI was following a classic "fight and negotiate" strategy to wear Masood down. The strategy alternately swung back and forth between periods of military offensives and periods of diplomatic, propaganda, and psychological pressures. The main objectives were to drive wedges between the faction leaders in Masood's loose coalition and to confuse and demoralize his forces defending Kabul. The ISI could be patient. Incremental progress, not a quick victory, was the goal.

The ISI and Hekmatyar's "fight and negotiate" strategy was shrewdly calibrated to achieve maximum effect. Hekmatyar's media outlets in Pakistan
fanned Pashtun nationalism against Masood. He cast himself as the champion
of Pashtuns, determined to liberate Kabul from the Tajik Masood and Uzbek
Dostum who occupied it. A Hezb spokesman accused Masood of signing a
secret agreement with Dostum and the Iranian-backed Wahdat to establish
a pro-Iranian government in which Masood would be president and Dostum
defense minister. The Peshawar agreement's designation of Rabbani to be
Mojaddedi's successor sharpened suspicions in the Pashtun belt that non-
Pashtuns were plotting to take over Afghanistan's capital. Pashtun commanders in the Nangarhar Shura switched to a neutral stance between Hekmatyar
and Masood[29] and closely watched Rabbani's actions and statements. Would
he organize the loya jirga envisioned in the Peshawar Accords after replacing
Mojaddedi on June 20? Or would he attempt to monopolize power?

On May 25, the ISI lured Masood into cease-fire negotiations. On that day,
Hamid Gul and the Saudi deputy minister of the interior, Prince Naef, persuaded him to meet with Hekmatyar in a gully 12 miles southeast of Kabul.
Without reference to Interim President Mojaddedi, Masood and Hekmatyar
signed a cease-fire pact. It mandated the unreachable goal of elections in six
months and called for Mojaddedi to leave office after finishing his two-month
term, and for Hekmatyar's Hezb party to join the government.

Soon after the signing, Hekmatyar began a propaganda campaign, picked
up by the Pakistani and international media, claiming that he and Masood
had agreed to send Dostum's troops back to the north. Masood denied this.
But the damage was done. Dostum's commander in the capital protested to
reporters that only Dostum, not Masood, could order his Uzbek militia to
stay or leave Kabul. From his presidential palace, Interim President Mojaddedi blasted the cease-fire agreement. He told a May 27 press conference
that Masood and Hekmatyar had "no authority" to agree to the removal of
the militias from Kabul or to set a timetable for elections.[30]

Hekmatyar violated the cease-fire agreement soon after he signed it. He
did not join the Interim Government; he disparaged it. On June 4, his gunners resumed their bombardment of Kabul, blasting downtown office buildings and residential areas into rubble. When a reporter asked him who was
in charge in Kabul, Hekmatyar smiled. "Whoever possesses tanks, planes,
helicopters—he rules."[31]

⚜

State Department planning for the reopening of the American embassy in Kabul began in October 1991, following the September 13, 1991, signing of the U.S.-Soviet negative symmetry agreement. On April 23, 1992, a week after Najib's ouster, the department recommended that President Bush appoint me to be the next American ambassador to Afghanistan. The statutory rationale for my position, special envoy to the Afghan resistance, no longer existed. Najib was gone. The Mujahidin—or, better, some factions of the Mujahidin— were in Kabul.

The American embassy in New Delhi had continued to pay the salaries of the Afghan foreign service nationals (the official State Department term for foreign national hired staff working at American overseas embassies and consulates) still employed by the embassy after American chargé Jon Glassman lowered the American flag on January 31, 1989.* By May 1992, department staffing and budget arrangements to reopen the embassy were well-advanced. An enterprising *Washington Times* American journalist dropped by the ambassador's residence that month. He found twelve Mujahidin guards from Masood's Council of the North camped inside. "There are AK-47 assault rifles stacked in the living room and a jungle-green hand grenade rests on a delicate rosewood table next to a cup of tea," he reported. Abdul Rasoul, the embassy's loyal Afghan maintenance supervisor, briefed the reporter on the recent theft of "'dishes, glasses, plates, ice cream machines, . . .' and other items" by bandits who climbed over the wall surrounding the ambassador's home. "Thanks God the thieves were detected and we got back our stuffs," Rasoul proudly informed the reporter.[32]

Reopening the American embassy would be an essential first step toward refocusing Washington's attention on important U.S. interests in Afghanistan and the region surrounding it. The Afghan linchpin was lodged in the middle

---

* At great risk to themselves and their families, the Afghan foreign service nationals in Kabul maintained and protected the U.S. embassy chancery and other official American properties during the tumultuous 1990s up to late 2001. During the formal reopening of the embassy on December 17, 2001, about sixty of the foreign service nationals were recognized for their bravery and perseverance in fulfilling their responsibilities despite bombardments, street fighting, and the constant threat of arrest or death.

of what former National Security Adviser Zbigniew Brzezinski described as the "arc of crisis" stretching from the Middle East through Iran to Pakistan. The country could become a future stabilizer or destabilizer in Eurasia. Violent Islamist extremism had struck roots along the Afghan-Pakistani border, and it was seeping deeper into Afghanistan.

The moderate, tribal impulse of Afghanistan was a barrier to the spread of radical Islam. An American embassy in Kabul could shore up moderate and traditional forces in the country, work with the Afghan government to assist Afghanistan's return to the democratic path, combat narcotics production, facilitate the return of the largest refugee population on earth, and oversee the American contribution to UN-led international reconstruction programs in Afghanistan. It would give Washington not only a geostrategic view of South Asia but a wider Eurasian perspective ranging to the important powers of China, Russia, and Iran as well as the new Central Asian Republics. An American embassy in Afghanistan would also offer Washington recommendations on Afghan policy to balance the perspective on Afghanistan proposed by the American embassy and CIA office in Islamabad. Such turf battles between embassies overseas were not unusual. American ambassadors in Tel Aviv and Cairo, New Delhi and Islamabad, Ankara and Athens regularly lay out their contending arguments for Washington's attention. Policymakers in the White House, State Department, and other agencies are best placed to weigh the options and make the hard decisions.

A recommendation that I call on the new Afghan government in Kabul was sent upstairs for Secretary James A. Baker III's signature on May 8. Fortuitously, the approaching June 16–17 Bush-Yeltsin summit in Washington overcame for a few weeks the monumental disinterest in Afghanistan that now seemed to prevail in the White House. The subject of Soviet prisoners of war* in Afghanistan would be at the top of Boris Yeltsin's agenda. President Bush and Secretary Baker would need to respond. The importance of the Soviet POW topic[33]—not the growing threat of Muslim extremism in Afghanistan, not soaring narcotics production in Afghanistan, or any other Afghan-related subject—had raised the urgency of sending a delegation to

---

* The Soviet government was interested in learning as much as possible about Soviet POWs and Soviets who were declared Missing in Action (MIA). Hereafter, Soviet POWs and MIAs will be collectively referred to as "Soviet POWs."

Kabul. The NEA memo advised Secretary of State Baker that an envoy to Kabul would "show the flag, renew contact with Mujahidin leaders, assess first hand our policy options, and address the POW issue before the summit . . . The most logical envoy will be Peter Tomsen." Secretary Baker approved the memo, and the trip was scheduled to begin May 31.[34]

A confidential telegram from the Islamabad embassy on May 17, however, cited serious security concerns regarding sending a U.S. delegation to Kabul. The State Department's Bureau of Diplomatic Security drew on the dire warnings in the cable to oppose the visit altogether. The cable stated:

> The control tower operates only intermittently. The supply of power to the airport is erratic and the landing lights do not always work. From dusk to curfew (roughly 7:00 P.M. to 9:00 P.M. local time) the sky is full of "happy fire," including flares, tracer rounds, and automatic weapons fire. The airport is subject to artillery shelling. There are Mujahedin groups with anti-aircraft capability in and outside the city. Both regime forces and the Mujahedin had access to sophisticated missiles that can shoot down aircraft; those missiles are still out there. [Unconfirmed] press reports May 17 say that anti-aircraft fire was directed at Russian Foreign Minister [Andrei] Kozyrev's aircraft when it departed Kabul.[35]

The embassy's message did not mention that the string of foreign delegations protected by Masood's security forces safely arrived in and departed from Kabul every week. No aircraft using the Kabul Airport, civilian, military, or foreign, including regular UN flights, had been harmed.[36] Flights from New Delhi on Afghan Ariana and Indian Airlines brought hundreds of passengers to the airport weekly.

The planning process for the trip to Kabul showed Washington at its bureaucratic worst. The visit became a vehicle for endless interagency meetings. The White House and Defense Department recommended that the delegation travel to Kabul on a U.S. military aircraft.[37] This idea energized interagency debates on how to protect the airplane on the ground at Kabul Airport and organize living arrangements for its U.S. Air Force crew.

The interagency wrangling peaked during a May 15 meeting with representatives of the Joint Chiefs of Staff and International Security offices in the Pentagon. With the best of intentions, Defense Department representatives suggested I take along a Delta commando squad on a military aircraft.[38] I feared that this proposal was certain to ignite another round of memos and meetings in the bureaucracy. Time, however, was now of the essence. Decisions needed to be made. I believed that in the final analysis, Masood would need to handle my delegation's security in Kabul. He had conveyed to me through his brother Wali in London that the delegation would be well protected.

Meanwhile the delay in sending an American delegation to Kabul was undermining the nascent authority of the Afghan government and magnifying American disinterest in Afghanistan. Deputy Foreign Minister Hamid Karzai told a news conference at the Afghan Foreign Ministry that Pakistani, Saudi, Russian, Swiss, French, and Iranian delegations had flown into Kabul to meet the new Afghan Interim Government. A reporter for Agence France-Presse in attendance wrote, "He hoped that a delegation from the United States would also visit Afghanistan soon."[39]

To circumvent the bureaucratic logjams in Washington, I proposed that the delegation be small. In addition to Richard Hoagland and myself, I arranged for only a State Department diplomatic security officer and a State Department communications specialist to accompany me. We would travel without a U.S. security contingent, using the daily Afghan Ariana commercial flight between New Delhi and Kabul.* I accepted the Italian government's invitation to stay at the Italian embassy in Kabul.

The National Security Council, State Department—except for the Diplomatic Security Bureau—and the Defense Department quickly concurred. In coordination with the State Department's Near East and South Asia Bureau and the Russian office in the department, I prepared a two-week schedule to begin with a commercial flight to New Delhi arriving June 4. After a final assessment of security conditions in Kabul, we planned to fly there on June 7 for a day and a half of meetings with President Mojaddedi, the Foreign Ministry, Defense Minister Masood, and other Afghan officials. After returning

---

* Afghan and Pakistani flights between Kabul and Islamabad were some six months away, Pakistani diplomat Riaz Mohammad Khan informed us. The Kabul–New Delhi Ariana flight had begun to operate during the Soviet occupation and had continued uninterrupted since then.

to New Delhi June 8, Richard Hoagland and I would take an Aeroflot flight to Moscow to conduct three days of meetings with Russian officials on the Soviet POW issue. Over the previous two years, I had gathered information from Mujahidin sources on Soviet POWs for President Bush and Secretary Baker to pass on to President Gorbachev and Foreign Minister Shevardnadze at their summit meetings. By May 1992, I had extensive new information on Soviet POWs to provide to Russian officials in Moscow and to Ukrainian officials in Kiev, our last stop on the trip. The Russian and Ukrainian public's interest in the fate of their soldiers left behind in Afghanistan was as intense as American interest in American POWs imprisoned in North Vietnam during and after the Vietnam War.[40]

In Washington I cleared the talking points we would use in Kabul, New Delhi, Moscow, and Kiev with the appropriate agencies. The only problem we encountered was at the CIA—and it was a familiar one. A CIA officer objected to me discussing the topic of Stinger missile recovery with Defense Minister Masood. I informed him that in Kabul I would be speaking for the entire U.S. government. Stinger recovery was not only a CIA issue; it was a U.S. government priority. I insisted on raising the issue with Masood. The CIA sent me a one-sentence talking point. It informed Masood that a CIA delegation would shortly visit Kabul for direct talks with him on Stinger recovery.

Our four-person delegation flew to New Delhi on June 4 to await Under Secretary Arnold Kanter's final decision about the trip to Kabul. On June 6, the day before the delegation was to fly to Kabul, the embassy in Islamabad, citing security problems, recommended to Washington that the visit not go forward. The embassy's telegram said that Benon Sevan's Turkish UN deputy, Avni Botsali, then stationed in the Afghan capital, had urged that the trip be canceled. The embassy proposed that the American consul in Peshawar go instead. An urgent State Department meeting chaired by Under Secretary Kanter was convened to reassess the visit. The Diplomatic Security Bureau and a representative of the under secretary of state for management vigorously opposed the visit on security grounds. Under Secretary Kanter decided to delay the trip. The State Department sent an urgent, secret cable to Islamabad explaining the decision. The cable ignored the Islamabad embassy's proposal that the consul in Peshawar make the trip.[41]

The Afghan government reacted bitterly. Avni Botsali was summoned to the Foreign Ministry to receive a stern protest from Deputy Foreign Minister

Karzai for misconstruing the security situation in Kabul. The Foreign Ministry sent a diplomatic note to the State Department assuring that there were no security obstacles and that all preparations for our delegation's visit had been made.

The visit to Kabul postponed, the State Department instructed me to proceed immediately to Moscow and Kiev and make presentations on Soviet POWs before the U.S.-Russian summit. It directed me to be back in New Delhi on June 12 for a second attempt to go to Kabul, "if security improves."[42]

The Soviet Aeroflot flight to Moscow on a low-slung, web-like fabric seat lacking a seatbelt, in an ancient, rattling Soviet aircraft, was somewhat unnerving. The panoramic view of the beautiful snow-capped mountains of Afghanistan and the broad, green sweep of the Central Asian steppe en route more than made up for the cramped ride. Moscow was very hot. The people on the street seemed more animated and better dressed than I remembered from the late 1970s during the Brezhnev period. On the way to the American embassy in Moscow I asked the Russian driver about a curious throng of men in well-tailored suits standing together under a bridge overhang near the large Kiev Railway Station. "They're former KGB employees out of work," he nonchalantly answered in Russian.

Our first and most important meeting was with Lieutenant General Ruslan Aushev,[43] whose lengthy title was "Chairman of the Committee on Military-Internationalists under the Council of the Heads of Government of the Commonwealth."* While serving as a paratrooper in Afghanistan, he had earned the Hero of the Soviet Union medal, the highest award for bravery given by the Soviet state, equivalent in prestige to the American Congressional Medal of Honor. General Aushev could have easily played the handsome Colonel Vronsky, Anna Karenina's lover in Leo Tolstoy's famous novel. He was tall, barrel-chested, alert, friendly, and eager to talk about Soviet POWs. Russian officials publicly stated that more than three hundred POWs remained unaccounted for inside Afghanistan. They estimated the number still living at below one hundred. I presented extensive documentation to him describing fifty-two Soviet POWs, some deceased and others living, including photos, which Richard Hoagland and I had collected from Mujahidin sources. Over

---

* The "Military-Internationalists" were Soviet soldiers who had done their "internationalist-socialist duty" but were left behind in Afghanistan.

half of the POWs were from the Muslim-populated Central Asian Republics. The Mujahidin had accepted them as fellow Muslims. Most of the Soviet POWs had married Afghans and melded into local communities. All had converted to Islam.

Each Soviet POW case was fascinating in its own way. Masood had been so impressed by one Ukrainian POW, who was named Leonid Khudovskiy, and renamed Nasradullah by the Mujahidin, that he made him one of his bodyguards. Some cases were very sad. A Mujahidin commander gave me a video, filmed by another commander in Helmand, that showed an emaciated, delirious young Ukrainian man in Afghan clothing. He was chanting in Ukrainian while seated crosslegged on a rope bed. Before leaving Washington, I had learned that he had died. Richard and I worried that it might devastate his parents to see the video, but we decided to give it to the Ukrainian government's POW specialists when we were in Kiev. They would decide whether or not to pass it on to the family.

In Moscow, I also called on the chairman of the Russian Supreme Soviet's POW subcommittee, Russian Foreign Ministry officials, and private Russian POW activists. All were clearly moved by the information and photographs of Soviet POWs that we gave to the Russian government. They asked me to convey their gratitude to President Bush and Secretary Baker for their sincere assistance in accounting for Soviet POWs still in Afghanistan. The Ukrainian authorities and legislators in Kiev were equally enthusiastic and grateful for the POW information we provided to them. In both Moscow and Kiev, I asked that Russia make a greater effort to locate the estimated 1,000 Afghan children who had been taken to the Soviet Union during the Afghan war.* After Richard Hoagland and I departed from Moscow on June 12, a *New York Times* article, headlined "U.S. Helps Russians Search for Missing in Afghanistan," reported our POW briefings in Moscow and Kiev and the transfer of photos from the Mujahidin. That same day President Yeltsin wrote to the U.S. Senate Select Committee on POW/MIA Affairs offering to help the United States account for American prisoners held in the Soviet Union during the Cold War.[44]

---

* The Russian and Ukrainian governments and the other newly independent states that emerged from the Soviet Union did not seriously follow up my requests to return Afghan children who had been taken to the USSR during the Soviet-Afghan war.

When Hoagland and I returned to New Delhi, we learned that Kabul was calm. Hekmatyar and the ISI were in a "negotiation" phase. But the American embassy in Islamabad cautioned Washington that the trip now coincided with the Muslim holiday of Eid, which marks the end of Ramadan, the holy month of fasting. I informed the State Department that, since Afghan officials in Kabul were anxious for the visit to take place, that did not pose a problem. The Italian Ambassador to India, Gabriele Menegatti, and the Italian chargé d'affaires in Kabul insisted that Kabul was quiet and the visit must go ahead. On June 13, the day of decision in Washington on whether the Kabul visit should proceed, Masood's Defense Ministry ordered a "full security alert" in the Afghan capital. An Associated Press story wired from Kabul the next day reported that "a day before the American delegation's unannounced arrival" security forces were attempting to "round up members of rebellious guerrilla bands" and "tanks and armored vehicles rolled through the streets."[45] Back in Washington, Under Secretary Kanter overruled opposition from the Diplomatic Security Bureau and the under secretary for management and approved our Kabul trip. The Afghan government agreed to keep the visit confidential until we departed Kabul.

The Ariana flight took off on time at 7:30 a.m. on June 14. A middle-aged blonde woman from Canada walked up and down the isle proselytizing the Afghan passengers on board. She stopped near our seat and asked if we were an American delegation going to Kabul, and then if we were Christians. I tried to encourage her to go to other passengers. She did, but not before giving me a small gold-colored cross and informing me that a Cuban delegation was seated a couple of rows back. While landing, we saw rusty, dilapidated tanks, some with turrets blown off, lying scattered in fields adjacent to the runway. One rested on its back, as if in a deep sleep, its tracks and cannon pointed skyward.

Our first meeting was a call on Minister of State for Foreign Affairs Mohammad Saljooki and Deputy Foreign Minister Hamid Karzai at the Foreign Ministry, our formal hosts for the visit. In delivering my talking points, I stressed that the Afghan people had not chosen any of the seven leaders in the Leadership Council. Instability and chaos would continue to torment Afghanistan until a large Afghan gathering fairly representing all of the country's major groups met to select leaders. I said there was little chance that the American embassy would reopen if the current violence in the streets of

Kabul continued. Saljooki and Karzai appealed for American reengagement and U.S. economic assistance.

From the Foreign Ministry we moved on to the nearby presidential palace to meet Interim President Mojaddedi. He was the only one of the seven leaders in Kabul at the time. Hekmatyar was in Logar, preparing for his next bombardment of Kabul. Sayyaf was in his Paghman hills cave complex, dispatching groups of Arab and Afghan jihadis down into nearby West Kabul to attack Hazara Shia infidels. Rabbani, chairman of the Leadership Council, was visiting Pakistan. Nabi, Gailani, and Khalis preferred their comfortable homes in Peshawar and Islamabad to the uncertainties of living in Kabul.

A crowd of Afghan and international media representatives greeted us at the main entrance to the presidential palace. Najib had left from here for the airport only two months before, expecting to fly to India. A disorderly jumble of Mojaddedi's aides and dozens of journalists and photographers swarmed into the palace with us. We were carried by the crowd past several enormous bare rooms, which appeared to have been looted, before entering an ornate hall where Mojaddedi stood with arms outstretched. He wore his usual bright white turban and the robe of a Sufi saint. Smiling broadly, he gestured for us to sit on beautiful gold brocade chairs surrounding a magnificent glass table.

Members of the press were led away after a few minutes. I handed a personal letter from President Bush to President Mojaddedi. It reiterated American encouragement to Afghans to establish "a broadly based government through a political process" and pledged reconstruction assistance.[46]

After I made my presentation, Mojaddedi invited me into a small reception room off the main hall for a private conversation. Once we were alone, he told me that the Afghan people wanted him to remain in office. So did the Russians. He promised that he would hold a loya jirga. He warned that if he transferred power to Rabbani, as called for in the Peshawar Accords, the center of power in the government would shift from moderates to the extremists. He asked for American support.

Mojaddedi was politically inclusive, tolerant, and pro-West, a senior religious cleric and Sufi leader. His Islam was firmly in the traditional Hanafi camp, the opposite of the raging extremism of Hekmatyar and Sayyaf. Among all the leaders, he was the most moderate and, relatively speaking, the most likely to lead Afghanistan back to its moderate-nationalist moorings. I felt

Mojaddedi was right about Rabbani. He would probably hold on to power and steer Afghanistan in an extremist, anti-Western direction.

But I could not give him an endorsement. The U.S. government, like the British government, the United Nations, and the international community generally, could not support a claim by any single Afghan to lead Afghanistan. I turned down Mojaddedi's appeal for American backing as gently as I could. I explained that Afghan history and the Afghan people would judge him badly if he were seen as pursuing personal power. His departure after two months need not end his political career. He could make a political comeback. Mojaddedi looked down. I sensed he had expected this answer. After a few jabs at Masood—he was disappointed that Masood had not established security in the capital—we slowly walked back to the larger group.

Over lunch with Saljooki and Karzai at the Foreign Ministry, Karzai noted that the entire ministry staff and 99 percent of the Afghan civil service had remained to serve the new government. About two hundred PDPA leaders had fled Kabul. Babrak Karmal and Abdul Wakil were at Hayratan, attempting to enter Uzbekistan. Karzai lamented the violence between Iranian-armed Wahdat and Saudi-supported Wahhabi Sunnis. He said the Foreign Ministry's written diplomatic protests to the Pakistanis, Saudis, and Iranians to stop interfering in Afghanistan had produced no results. Pakistan was deeply involved in Hekmatyar's attacks on Kabul. The Iranians had opened a consulate in Mazar-i-Sharif without requesting approval from the Afghan government.

Foreign Minister Salman Gailani, a relative of Pir Sayyid Ahmad Gailani, focused on Pakistani support for Hekmatyar's shelling of Kabul during our afternoon meeting and at the breakfast he hosted the next morning. He read aloud from Afghan intelligence reports, detailing deliveries of ISI weapons and ammunition to specific Hekmatyar bases at specific times in Logar, Ghazni, and Nangarhar provinces. I said that the United States would raise the issue with Pakistan. I urged that the Afghan government also continue to do so, directly to the government of Pakistan, in both Kabul and Islamabad.

Our session with Masood on June 14 was the most important meeting of the delegation's visit to Kabul. The street in front of the Defense Ministry was cordoned off and thick with army troops and tanks. Masood's political adviser, Yunis Qanuni, welcomed us at the door of the Defense Ministry. His armed Council of the North Mujahidin lounged in the first-floor corridors. We threaded our way up a railed staircase past elderly Afghan petitioners and entered Masood's large office. Red, yellow, and black telephones from Soviet-occupation days rested on his desk and in sitting areas around the room. Television lights came on, cameras whirled and snapped. Two Masood advisers, Dr. Abdullah and Daoud Mir, greeted us.

At precisely 4:00 p.m., Masood walked into the room, weaving through the throng of photographers, journalists, and Afghan military officers and civilians. A large smile broke across his face, and we exchanged jokes. After the media departed, I repeated the forty-minute presentation that I had made earlier to Mojaddedi and the Foreign Ministry. I again stressed that none of the seven leaders or any other Afghan had been chosen by the Afghan people to lead the country. Many Afghans and foreign supporters of Afghanistan hoped that Masood would use his influence to see that a representative loya jirga inclusive of all of Afghanistan's groups was held. The United States believed that only a broad-based political settlement could end the long Afghan war.

Masood was a good listener, his head bowed downward. I had the impression that he was agreeing to what I said. He had previously made these same points to me and the media. The crowded room fell silent for a minute while he gathered his thoughts. He began his response by making it clear that he wanted the Americans back and the American embassy reopened. He praised the United States at length for assisting the Mujahidin and for winning the Cold War against the Soviet Union. None of our Afghan interlocutors during the visit had spoken so openly about American help to Afghanistan.

Masood shifted to the current situation in Afghanistan and the way ahead. He spoke nonstop for over an hour, concurring with the importance of returning stability to Afghanistan through a political settlement. He stated in a determined voice that a loya jirga would be held within four months and that it would fairly represent all Afghan groups. In a factual, methodical manner, he described Pakistan's and Iran's interference in Afghanistan after Najib's overthrow. He passed an order in Dari to Daoud Mir to follow up on a request I had made on narcotics. He looked forward to the arrival of the CIA delegation to discuss Stingers.

Masood's description of the security situation in Kabul and Hekmatyar's threat to the city was excessively optimistic. He stated that law and order in the city was improving, when in fact it was not. Though Masood commanded the single largest military force in Afghanistan—and had outmaneuvered the

ISI and Hekmatyar to win the first prize, Afghanistan's capital—the sands were already beginning to shift beneath his feet. The ISI's and Hekmatyar's "fight and negotiate" strategy was slowly pulling elements in his fragile military coalition toward Hekmatyar and persuading individual Pashtun commanders in eastern Afghanistan to oppose him. There was no functioning government in Kabul—or, indeed, a cohesive Afghan state. Most of the countryside and major cities were managed by independent shuras, and the capital was sinking into anarchy.

Dostum was unhappy. His militia dominated the northern tier provinces near Mazar-i-Sharif. He could recall his troops from Kabul at any time, or even turn them against Masood. Dostum and Wahdat together controlled about half of the Afghan capital. There was absolutely no chance that the three extremist Pashtun Islamists in the Leadership Council—Hekmatyar, Sayyaf, and Khalis—would accede to Dostum's demand for seats in the interim cabinet. Hekmatyar clamored for the expulsion of Dostum and Wahdat from Kabul. Moderates Gailani and Nabi resided in Pakistan. They were vulnerable to ISI pressures and threats from Hekmatyar's assassination squads. The pusillanimous Rabbani had a history of obeying the ISI and ignoring Masood.

Despite all these concerns, I took away from the long discussion with Masood a feeling that the discredited Hekmatyar would not dislodge him from Kabul. Masood could hold out but it was unlikely that he would be able to attract major Pashtun allies. Only a fair, inclusive Afghan gathering attracting Pashtun representation could do that. The ISI had leveraged its Ghilzai extremist proxies to block that option for twelve years. They were well positioned to continue to do so.

After more meetings at the Foreign Ministry on June 15, Deputy Foreign Minister Hamid Karzai escorted us back to the airport. He handed over President Mojaddedi's response to President Bush's letter, thanking America for assisting the Afghan Mujahidin, requesting continued American aid, and asking that the United States reopen its embassy. After we had a cup of tea in the airport lounge and said our farewells at planeside, the Ariana flight lifted off around 5:00 p.m.

Our visit to Kabul to meet Mujahidin leaders had shown the flag. The feedback from Washington was positive on the cables we transmitted reporting our meetings. U.S. and regional media coverage was also favorable, barring some disinformation from Hekmatyar's ANA wire service.[47]

But the visit did not reverse America's disengagement from Afghanistan. More high-level visits than mine by Pakistan's prime minister and the Russian and Iranian foreign ministers exhibited to Afghans and the world that their countries intended to remain seriously engaged with Afghanistan. My rank projected American disinterest. I had advised the Afghan government that it needed to establish stability, but America's disengagement was one of the reasons for the rising instability.

Back in New Delhi, I learned that the CIA Stinger retrieval team would soon visit Kabul. The trip was to be mounted from Islamabad and would include ISI as well as agency officers. This, to me, was a bad idea. It would project to the new Afghan government that the operational CIA-ISI collaboration for a pro-Hekmatyar military conclusion to the Afghan war was continuing into the post-Najib period. This would not be in U.S. interests. Using a secure phone inside the American embassy in New Delhi, I asked the State Department to demand that the CIA conduct the trip without ISI officers. After returning to Washington, I was told that the CIA visit was adjusted to involve only Americans, but was not able to confirm that the agency actually carried out the visit on its own.

⚘

During the second half of June and throughout July 1992, I phased out the special envoy's office and worked on restaffing the American embassy in Kabul. In August, my wife Kim and I began Dari language training at the State Department's language school in Arlington, Virginia. But the ambassadorial appointment process was prolonged by Washington politics and depressing events in Afghanistan.

On August 10, Hekmatyar unilaterally broke the latest cease-fire with Masood by unleashing a massive three-week bombardment of Kabul. Twice during the fall of 1990 and 1991, I had coordinated with other U.S. officials to force the Pakistani government to cancel similar Hekmatyar offensives involving plans for the bombardment of Kabul. This time, the United States did not pressure Pakistan to call off the rocket attacks. The special envoy position had been abolished. There was no American embassy in Kabul to request Washington's intervention with Pakistan to halt the shelling. The embassy in Islamabad chose not to intervene.

Hekmatyar's rockets massacred hundreds of Kabulis, wounded many more, and destroyed whole neighborhoods and city landmarks, including the Foreign Ministry. Foreign embassies and the homes of diplomats came under fire, the Bulgarian ambassador was wounded, and two Russians were killed. A rocket damaged the U.S. embassy. Several foreign embassies, including those of Russia, France, and Italy, closed their doors and evacuated their citizens. This was, of course, one of the purposes of the terrible shelling of the crowded city—to drive out the foreign presence and isolate the fledgling Afghan government from the international community.

Prime Minister Sharif and his Foreign Ministry continued to tell American diplomats, visiting U.S. officials, and the media that Pakistan would not allow its territory to be used by elements attacking the new Afghan government.[48] Meanwhile, ISI trucks carrying rockets, ammunition, and other armaments ferried supplies to Hekmatyar's base camps south and east of Kabul. Hekmatyar's ISI-assisted ANA news agency in Islamabad and his newspaper in Peshawar, *Shahadat*, published articles glorifying his murderous rocket barrages against Kabul's 2 million inhabitants.

Another cease-fire went into effect on August 29. Fifteen minutes before the deadline, Hekmatyar's artillery fired dozens of rockets into West Kabul Shia neighborhoods, killing twenty-five more civilians and wounding fifty.[49] Hekmatyar and the ISI used the next month to refill his ammunition depots. In late September, they flaunted the cease-fire and resumed launching rockets into Kabul. On October 3, lobbying by John Malott, the first interim head of the State Department's new Bureau of South Asian Affairs,[50] and I generated an unprecedented State Department press statement condemning Hekmatyar's latest bombardment of Afghanistan's capital. The statement was rhetorical, and from the State Department only. It had no effect on America's disengagement policy. But for the first time in the twelve-year Afghan conflict, the United States publicly criticized the Hezb tyrant who had once been extolled by ambassadors and CIA officers:

> The recent savage bombardment of Kabul by forces under the command of Gulbuddin Hekmatyar caused tremendous suffering. These actions, taken in pursuit of personal ambitions, were responsible for

the deaths of hundreds of innocent people in Kabul. We condemn these ruthless actions and will continue to oppose anyone who uses violence to subvert the political process which we believe is central to resolving the Afghan conflict.[51]

A senior CIA Directorate of Operations officer who had long worked with the ISI and knew Hekmatyar well was the first to protest the statement. He phoned the Department of State's Near East Bureau to demand an explanation (readily available in the statement) as to why Gulbuddin Hekmatyar had been singled out from other Afghans for criticism.[52]

The angry phone call from the DO executive, a former head of the agency's Afghan Task Force and still involved in Afghan affairs, underscored that Washington would still be conducting two contradictory Afghan policies after I moved on to my next assignment in the East Asian and Pacific Bureau. The CIA's approach melded intelligence gathering and intelligence operations, whereby selective intelligence reporting could justify the results of intelligence operations. More harmfully, it also melded intelligence and broader American political policy. During my three years as special envoy, the agency and the ISI had decided who in the Mujahidin would receive hundreds of millions of dollars in U.S. assistance.

As a consequence, U.S. weapons and cash directly and indirectly empowered America's worst enemies, Hekmatyar and his radical Arab and Pakistani allies. Those attempting to implement the formal American policy backing a political settlement of the war—embedded in the CIA findings authorizing the covert program—did not have the resources to support their efforts. The agency's unilateralism and preoccupation with short-term tactical operations over strategic, long-term outcomes ruined prospects for ending the wars of Afghanistan.

Washington had tumbled into a similar conundrum during the Iran-Contra affair, which was first publicized by a Lebanese newspaper in 1986. It ended a few years later with fourteen indictments of Reagan administration officials. The Iran-Contra scandal involved many of the same actors and demonstrated most of the hallmarks of the conflicting State-CIA Afghan policies after the 1990 Soviet pullout.

At the CIA, Director William Casey, Deputy Director Robert Gates, and DO officer Thomas Twetten, along with NSC staffers, were conducting an

Iran policy without the knowledge of Secretary of State George Shultz. When Shultz found out, he persuaded President Reagan to restore the single chain of command on Iran policy from the president on down through the foreign affairs bureaucracy. Reagan agreed. With some opposition from Vice President George H.W. Bush[53] and Deputy CIA Director Gates (Director William Casey had died), Shultz managed to take Iran policy away from the CIA, restore the separation of intelligence and policy on Iran, and insist that future intelligence reporting on Iran not be permitted to rationalize intelligence operations.[54]

During my time as Afghan special envoy, I felt that Under Secretary Robert Kimmitt understood the damage the CIA's unilateral Afghan policy was causing. I sensed from my personal briefings of other subcabinet officials in Washington, including at the agency and White House, that many others were aware of the problem. I did not have enough access to President Bush or Secretary Baker to plumb the reasons why they were letting this crippling situation continue to fester, and not acting to enforce one unified American policy as Shultz had done on Iran. In 2004, during an interview with journalist and author Roy Gutman on policy clashes between State and CIA on Afghanistan, former Ambassador Robert Oakley speculated that State was just not willing to mount a major challenge against the CIA—perhaps Secretary Baker did not want to take on Langley.[55] I left for my next assignment in the East Asian Bureau not knowing the reasons for this top-level reticence to end the dueling Afghan policies.

Four days after the State Department's condemnation of Hekmatyar's rocket attacks, on October 7, a Pakistan-based Hezb spokesman and American citizen, Nawab Saleem, issued Hekmatyar's strident rejoinder:

> Afghanistan is the graveyard of the British and the Russians and insha'allah it will also become the graveyard of the arrogant Americans. The Afghans will rub the American pigs' snout in the ground in Afghanistan if they continued [sic] to poke anti-Islamic fire in Afghanistan.... We call upon all Muslim nations and communities to rise up to the challenge of the world arrogance, the number one enemy of Islam.[56]

☙

On October 22, 1992, the director general of the Foreign Service and the director of State Department personnel sent me a formal letter congratulating me on my selection to be the next U.S. ambassador to Afghanistan. However, because of security concerns, in November the State Department decided not to reopen the U.S. embassy in Kabul. Though disappointed, I felt it was the right decision. Hekmatyar's rocket attacks, later to be continued by the Taliban, made a U.S. diplomatic presence in Afghanistan's capital, like those of other Western countries, untenable. The embassy did not reopen its doors until after al-Qaeda struck the U.S. homeland from Afghanistan on 9/11, almost a decade later.

Following President Clinton's victory in the November 1992 elections, I was appointed principal deputy assistant secretary of state for East Asian and Pacific Affairs. For the next three years, I worked on East and Southeast Asian issues in the department. From 1995 to 1998, I served as U.S. ambassador to the Republic of Armenia before retiring in 1998, after a thirty-two year career in the Foreign Service.

A U.S. Afghan-Pakistani policy better attuned to American national interests during the months after Najib fell could have forced Pakistan to end its proxy war in Afghanistan. Eleven days before President Clinton took the presidential oath of office on January 20, 1993, Secretary of State Baker wrote to Prime Minister Sharif to repeat American warnings to Pakistan that its sponsorship of terrorism could land it on the U.S. terrorist list. Although the same ISI training camps were sending violent jihadis into both Afghanistan and Kashmir, Baker's January 9, 1993, letter only mentioned Pakistan-supported terrorist activities in Kashmir and the Indian Punjab. It informed Sharif that Pakistan was on a U.S. watch list and the subject of "active continuing review for possible inclusion on the State Department's list of terrorist states." The Clinton administration did not pick up that cudgel. It further outsourced U.S. Afghan policy to Pakistan, guaranteeing that the wars of Afghanistan would continue through the 1990s.

As a result, during that decade the country that had been a key Cold War battleground, where a valiant people had helped bring down the last great political totalitarian state of the twentieth century, became a major post–Cold War battleground, forced to suffer the messianic fanaticism of the first religious totalitarian movement of the twenty-first century. The Afghan conflict became one of the longest-running wars in human history.[57]

PART IV

AMERICA AND AFGHANISTAN

CHAPTER 20

Unholy Alliance

In the early morning darkness of Christmas Day, December 25, 1999, Colonel Gul,* the head of the ISI's Kandahar office, knocked on the door of Mawlawi Akhtar Mohammad Mansoor's home in the city of Kandahar. Mansoor was the Taliban's minister of civil aviation and future deputy head of the Taliban under Mullah Mohammad Omar. When he opened the door, Gul alerted him that a plane would soon land at Kandahar's airport. Mansoor hurried to the airport. Only later did he ask another Taliban official how Gul had heard before he did that an unannounced airplane was in the air and about to arrive. The answer was that the ISI's unholy alliance partners had hijacked it.

The plane was Indian Airlines Flight 814. There were 149 passengers on board, including one American. The flight had originated in Kathmandu, Nepal, bound for New Delhi. Five Pakistani Islamic militants armed with knives had seized control of the airplane in Indian airspace at 4:30 p.m. on December 24, the previous day. It landed briefly at Amritsar in the Indian Punjab and flew on to Lahore, Pakistan. The Pakistani government ordered the plane refueled, refusing the Indian request to block the plane from departing. Flight 814 flew on to the United Arab Emirates (UAE), where it landed at a military airport during the hours of darkness. By then, the hijackers had stabbed one Indian male passenger to death and wounded two others. One, while tied up, was stabbed seven times. He miraculously survived by playing dead.

---

* "Gul" is a pseudonym, not the ISI colonel's real name. He was not related to former ISI Director General Hamid Gul.

The plane was now approaching Kandahar. Gul drove up in a two-vehicle ISI convoy just before it landed. The colonel ordered Afghan airport workers to roll a stair ladder to the airplane's side. Gul ascended the stairs and conferred with the hijackers. He seemed to know them. He shouted down to the small crowd watching from below, "They need water and food." The Afghans and Pakistani soldiers who were with Gul pulled boxes from his vehicles and carried them up the stairs and into the airplane.

Afterward, the Afghans reported to Mansoor that weapons and ammunition were concealed below old newspapers covering the boxes.

The hijackers demanded the release of three Pakistani terrorists who were being held in Indian jails. One was Maulana Masood Azhar. He was general secretary of the Pakistani terrorist group Harakat ul-Mujahidin, which had been placed on the State Department's list of Foreign Terrorist Organizations (FTOs)[1] in October 1997. Azhar was a bin Laden ally and graduate of a large Jamiat-i Ulema-i Islam madrassa in Karachi. He had reportedly helped al-Qaeda train some of the Somalis who had killed eighteen Americans in Somalia in 1993.[2] A second Indian prisoner, Ahmed Omar Sheikh, was a notorious British terrorist of Pakistani descent who would later be sentenced to death for his involvement in the kidnapping and murder of American journalist Daniel Pearl. The third prisoner was a Kashmiri.

The negotiations lasted a week and ended on New Year's Day. An Indian aircraft flew the three prisoners from India to Kandahar. They were released into the Taliban's custody. Indian Airlines Flight 814 took off for New Delhi. Osama bin Laden that night hosted a party in Kandahar for the three released prisoners and the hijackers. During the next three weeks, the CIA failed to uncover the ISI's orchestration of the plane hijacking. The American government accepted Pakistan's insistence that it was not involved. "We do not have reason to believe that the government of Pakistan had foreknowledge, supported or helped carry out this terrorist hijacking," State Department spokesman James Rubin announced to the media.[3] Meanwhile, the short, bulky, black-bearded Azhar made a triumphal tour of Pakistani cities and army bases. He delivered passionate speeches extolling global holy war. And he formed a new Pakistani religious paramilitary organization, Jaish-i Mohammad (Army of Mohammad).[4]

The Pakistani ISI strengthened its unholy alliance on Pakistan's Frontier after Najib fell. It was composed of ISI personnel; Afghan extremists, most notably Gulbuddin Hekmatyar and later the Taliban; al-Qaeda; the two Pakistani religio-political parties, Jamaat-i Islami (JI) and Jamiat-i Ulema-i Islam (JUI); and thousands of international jihadis from Arab countries, Uzbekistan, China's Xinjiang Province, Burma, the Philippines, and the West. The ISI coordinated with JI and JUI and their paramilitary militias to manage dozens of jihadi military training camps inside Pakistan and just across the Afghan border in Konar, Nangarhar, and Paktiya provinces.

Pakistan's generals considered the unholy alliance a strategic asset. It was the military's vehicle for achieving former Pakistani president Zia ul-Haq's vision: strategic depth against India, Pakistani hegemony in Afghanistan, and promotion of Islamic holy war in Kashmir and elsewhere. The alliance reinforced the army's emphasis on Islamization at home and helped maintain its domination of the Pakistan state.

The unholy alliance was not an alliance in the literal meaning of the term, including after it spread its tentacles into Afghanistan from Pakistan's Frontier later in the 1990s. Rather, by the middle of the decade it had evolved into a loose network of autonomous and semi-autonomous parts. In varying degrees, each part pursued the twin goals of converting Afghanistan into a radical Islamist state and making it a base for exporting militant Sunni extremism to other world regions. The Taliban emphasized the former. Al-Qaeda, foreign jihadi intending to organize Islamist revolutions in their countries of origin, and Pakistani religious militias stressed international jihad. The ISI emphasized both. The inevitable byproduct of this volatile mixture of Afghan, Pakistani, and international holy warriors was terrorism on a global scale.

During the 1990s and down to the present, Pakistan's military and civilian leaders became highly skilled at denying Pakistan's covert empowerment of its unholy alliance partners inside Afghanistan and in Pakistan—in other words, lying. Their repudiations of foreign charges that Pakistan was interfering in Afghanistan have followed a standard pattern, with adjustments to fit changing circumstances and audiences. Islamabad's transcendent talking point on Afghanistan has remained consistent: "Our policy is one of non-interference in the internal affairs of Afghanistan." In 1999, parliamentary leader Raja Mohammad Zafarat Haq claimed that Pakistan "would not allow anyone from its soil to interference [sic] in Afghanistan."[5] In 2006, while NATO forces fought back Taliban incursions into Afghanistan from Pakistan, Pakistani Army spokesman Major General Shaukat Sultan Khan called allegations that

Pakistan was harboring training camps for cross-border networks "absurd." In 2008, Pakistani military spokesman Major General Athar Abbas was asked to respond to a well-documented Rand Corporation study that found "active and former officials in Pakistan's intelligence service and the Frontier Corps" providing the Taliban "with training at camps in Pakistan, as well as intelligence, financial assistance and help crossing the border." Abbas responded, "We reject this claim of sanctuaries being aided by Pakistan's army or intelligence agencies."[6]

ॐ

The ISI-created and -sustained Pakistani paramilitary militias tied to JI and JUI and their offshoots were a vital part of the unholy alliance (Appendix VI). The militias recruited and indoctrinated their fighters in JI and JUI madrassas. Osama bin Laden and some of his senior lieutenants had worked with the ISI in the late 1980s to create the first—and still the largest— paramilitary group, Lashkar-i Taiba. Since its founding, Lashkar-i Taiba has maintained close ties with al-Qaeda.[7] The ISI also organized Harakat ul-Ansar (Front of the Companions of the Prophet) in the late 1980s. Lashkar-i Taiba's training facilities were established in eastern Konar and Pakistan. Harakat ul-Ansar, which later melded into the U.S.-designated FTO Harakat ul-Mujahidin, set up training camps in Pakistan's portion of Kashmir. The two religious militias sent thousands of mostly Pakistani and Afghan fighters into Kashmir to battle Indian security forces.

By 1993, Lashkar-i Taiba and Harakat ul-Mujahidin fanatics were operating in Afghanistan, Bosnia, the Caucasus, western China's mainly Muslim Xinjiang Province, North Africa, and other parts of the Muslim world, often in concert with al-Qaeda's operatives. Lashkar-i Taiba and Harakat ul-Mujahidin were tied to Fazlur Rahman's JUI and JUI splinters. Rahman himself and his party were part of Benazir Bhutto's political coalition. JUI leaders served in her governments in the 1990s. Jamaat's Qazi Hussain Ahmed participated in Nawaz Sharif's governing coalitions during the same decade. Jamaat leaders collaborated with the ISI in managing Jamaat's paramilitary religious group, Hezb ul-Mujahidin (Party of the Mujahidin).

Many thousands of international jihadis poured into Pakistan during the 1990s to obtain military training and indoctrination at the ISI-managed religious parties' paramilitary camps in Pakistan. By 1995, Pakistan's Frontier region had become the hub of global terrorism. The Muslim Brotherhood and radical Wahhabi-managed charities headquartered in Peshawar worked through their branches in Asia and Europe to finance and coordinate terrorist cells. Saudi Wael Hamza Julaidan, one of the original founders of al-Qaeda in 1988, worked out of the Ikhwani Services Bureau in Peshawar. He forwarded money to the Brooklyn branch of the Services Bureau to help fund the first World Trade Center bombing in 1993. Khalid Sheikh Mohammed, a Pakistani-Kuwaiti Arabic-speaking al-Qaeda terrorist organizer moving between the Persian Gulf, Pakistan, Afghanistan, the Balkans, and the Philippines at the time—and the future architect of the 9/11 attacks and one of the murderers of American journalist Daniel Pearl—wired money to his nephew Ramzi Yousef in New York City to mount the attack.[8] While the Egyptian terrorist Omar Abdel Rahman's participation in the operation led to his arrest and incarceration for life, Yusuf flew out of New York on an Air Pakistan flight and returned to Peshawar. For most of the next three years, until his arrest in 2005 in Pakistan, Yusuf resided openly in a bin Laden guesthouse in Peshawar.[9] Over the next seven years Khalid Sheikh Mohammed drifted among safehouses in Peshawar, Karachi, Manila, and the Balkans, organizing more terrorist strikes against American targets. His last hiding place, the site of his 2003 capture, was the home of Pakistani Army Major Adel Qudoos, located in the garrison city of Rawalpindi where the army is headquartered.

During 1993 and 1994, Abu Hassan, the hardline Ikhwani head of the Saudi World Muslim League branch office in Peshawar, sent cash to his predecessor (and bin Laden's brother-in-law), Jamal Khalifa, in Manila. Khalifa registered his Islamic charity as a humanitarian organization but spent its budget on anti-Western terrorist operations. He and Khalid Sheikh Mohammed plotted to assassinate the pope and President Clinton during their 1994 and 1995 visits, respectively, to the Philippines. They laid plans to bomb the U.S. embassy and Philippine Airlines flights departing from Manila.[10]

ISI Director General Javed Nasir and retired ISI chief Hamid Gul were the main coordinating points for unholy alliance operations in 1992 and 1993. Former ISI Director General Asad Durrani and Afzal Janjua, also retired generals long associated with Gul and Hekmatyar, were active in Gul's "private-sector" cohort. Known as the "Jihadi Generals," they helped connect the unholy alliance's Pakistani, Afghan, and foreign components operating in Pakistan, Afghanistan, Kashmir, the Middle East, and Europe. Gul was at the forefront. He often went into Afghanistan. He traveled to Sudan in 1993 to confer with bin Laden and met him again in 1994.[11] While pretending to exist outside the government, Gul's "virtual ISI" in reality operated as part of the ISI. It grew in size as more and more ISI officers and NCOs retired and joined its ranks.

During the 1990s, huge transfers of Saudi cash continued to fortify the ISI's holy-war infrastructure on the Frontier and, after the Taliban's victories in Afghanistan, the unholy alliance's massive training networks in Afghanistan. The Saudi royal family tolerated and patronized the outpouring of unregulated contributions to Saudi charities exporting the Wahhabi creed and promoting holy war worldwide.

The upswing in Arab militants traveling to Pakistan and Afghanistan just before and following Najib's collapse in April 1992 added to the unholy alliance's international character. The number of Egyptian combatants alone in Pakistan rose to more than 1,200 by 1994. Unholy alliance training camps multiplied inside eastern Afghanistan. An Arab captured by Ahmed Shah Masood in 1993 told a Western reporter that Afghanistan was "the only place to train" for those "wishing to fight in Bosnia, Kashmir, Israel and Tajikistan."[12] Omar Abdel Rahman's son opened a new military training facility 8 miles north of Jalalabad at Durunta near an al-Qaeda facility experimenting with chemical warfare material.[13]

A Pakistani newspaper exposé on Javed Nasir in 2002 provoked the former ISI chief into a public defense of his personal covert involvement in Pakistan's global holy war during his notorious 1992–1993 tenure. The Koran-quoting, self-adoring Nasir[14] gave himself the credit for victory in the Bosnian War during a court room hearing. Referring to himself in the third person, Nasir declared: "A true practicing Muslim[,] he could not compromise the interests of Islam and Pakistan. Despite a UN ban . . . we successfully airlifted sophisticated anti-tank guided missiles, which turned the tide in favor of Bosnian Muslims[,] . . . much to the annoyance of the U.S. government."[15]

Nasir's zeal for global jihad went beyond the Balkans. According to former senior Pakistani police officer, author, and scholar Hassan Abbas, he sent arms to "Chinese Uighur in Xingjian Province, rebel Muslim groups in the Philippines, and some religious groups in Central Asia." In 1993, Nasir and Hekmatyar transported 1,000 Afghan Hezb fighters to assist Muslim Azerbaijan in its war against Christian Armenia.[16] The thousands of Pakistani, Afghan, and foreign graduates of ISI-managed military training camps turned much of Kashmir into a combat zone. India responded by flooding its part of the former princely state with some 400,000 army and paramilitary troops. New Delhi's large-scale deployments suppressed the insurgency, but casualties were high on both sides, and especially high among Kashmiri civilians. During the 1990s, Kashmiri-born rebels gradually became an ever smaller minority of the jihadis fighting in Kashmir. While the great majority of Kashmiris hated the Indian occupying force, they did not subscribe to the foreign jihadis' intention to make Kashmir a Wahhabi-style emirate governed by an intolerant Sunni version of Sharia.

During the last year of the George H.W. Bush administration and through the first Clinton administration, Pakistan's army and the ISI steadily enlarged the unholy alliance. Osama bin Laden's return to Afghanistan in 1996 escalated the global terrorist activity emanating from Pakistan and Afghanistan in the Middle East, the Persian Gulf, and the Caucasus. Pakistan's smokescreen of plausible denials—and its use of proxies—lured the United States into a false sense of complacency. U.S. diplomats and intelligence officers in Islamabad and the sprawling intelligence community in Washington did not recognize the dangers posed to the United States by the terrorism threat rising along the Afghan-Pakistani Frontier, even after the 1993 World Trade Center bombing. They were the first line of defense in assessing the dangers and recommending policies to meet them. These individuals, all well meaning and dedicated, heavily influenced their superiors, who were juggling many more problems. Ultimately, of course, the responsibility for success or failure in American foreign policy must lie with top policymakers, including those at the cabinet level and the president himself, especially when American national security is endangered.

Richard Clarke, President Clinton's White House counterintelligence adviser in the late 1990s, told the 9/11 Commission that, in the early 1990s, "there was no capability . . . to know that al Qaeda existed, let alone to destroy it." The intelligence community's human intelligence capacity was weak or nonexistent in Afghanistan, bin Laden's base of operations. It was not until early 1997 that the U.S. government acquired reliable information

on al-Qaeda.[17] Al-Qaeda was not placed in the State Department list of Foreign Terrorist Organizations until October 1997.

Secretary of State Baker's January 9, 1993, letter to Pakistani Prime Minister Nawaz Sharif warning that Pakistan could be designated as a state sponsoring terrorism was the only forceful action taken by the United States to
compel Islamabad to cease supporting terrorism up to 9/11.[18]

In focusing on the ISI's insurgencies in Kashmir and India, however, Baker
and those under him missed the unholy alliance's broader terrorist operations
inside Afghanistan and globally. Sharif took some steps to show that Pakistan
was complying. He replaced ISI head Javed Nasir with General Javed Ashraf
Qazi. He dispatched Foreign Ministry Secretary General Akram Zaki to
Washington to assure the new Clinton administration that he was cracking
down on terrorism.[19] Pakistani authorities sent several hundred Arab radicals
in Pakistan across the border into Afghanistan, a trend under way in any case
since Najib's fall. Insurgent attacks in Kashmir dipped for a year, then shot
up to a new high after the Clinton administration took over.

The Baker letter did elicit a limited Pakistani response in Nasir's departure.
It should have been the precedent for more U.S. counterterrorism pressure.
Instead, six months after Clinton took office, on July 14, 1993, State Department spokesman Michael McCurry told journalists that Pakistan had taken
"a number of steps that appear to have responded to our concerns."[20]

The U.S. government did not mount an independent American policy on Afghanistan during the 1990s to accomplish its national interests in Afghanistan. Those interests included: a peaceful end to the Afghan war brokered
by the United Nations to stabilize the region; suppression of terrorism and
narcotics trafficking; the return of 3 million Afghan refugees to Afghanistan;
and strengthening human and gender rights. In 1996, the American ambassador in Islamabad, Thomas Simons, candidly acknowledged to a visitor that
a separate U.S. Afghan policy did not exist.[21] By outsourcing Washington's
Afghan policy to Pakistan, the United States was in practice accepting Islamabad's claim to a sphere of influence in Afghanistan, which in turn meant subscribing to the Pakistani Army's unrealizable drive to make the country a
bastion for Islamic extremism.

To fill the policy vacuum, the Clinton administration formulated an Afghan strategy that remained tenaciously in place over the next eight years leading up to the September 11, 2001, al-Qaeda attacks on the United States. It was not a policy, only a strategy that marginally adjusted in reaction to events, such as the al-Qaeda bombings of two U.S. embassies in Africa in 1998. Four cardinal features characterized the strategy. The first feature was a grand delusion about Islamabad's hegemonic intentions in Afghanistan. In 2009, Pakistani-Australian scholar Dr. Rizwan Hussain diagnosed this delusion, explaining, "The Pakistani leadership was (and still is) duplicitous and expert in dissimulation. Its tactics were aimed to dupe the U.S. and the West into believing that Pakistan was inclined towards a negotiated settlement, but in practice there was a convergence of opinion amongst the civil and military leadership that Pakistan should impose its clients in Kabul."[22]

Outsourcing America's Afghan policy to Pakistan was the second feature of U.S. Afghan strategy pursued in lieu of a policy. The CIA continued its outsourcing of U.S. policy to ISI; the Clinton State Department adopted the same approach in 1993. In the absence of a U.S. embassy in Kabul or a special envoy on Afghanistan, the American embassy in Islamabad reported on and interpreted Afghan issues from its perspective in Pakistan. In practice, the combination of outsourcing U.S. Afghan policy to Pakistan and the grand delusion reinforced Pakistan's promotion of Islamist extremist proxies to control Afghanistan.

The third policy feature was the Clinton administration's periodic rhetorical affirmation of U.S. goals in Afghanistan without an effective policy to implement them. American leaders and diplomats eloquently voiced strong U.S. support for UN mediation to end the Afghan war. But Washington did not vigorously back up the UN special envoys' attempts to break through Pakistan's barriers to a peaceful settlement.[23] The UN secretary general indirectly gave vent to UN frustrations with U.S. policy in 1997 when he declared in a written statement: "Sadly, it could be argued that in these circumstances the role of the United Nations in Afghanistan is little more than that of an alibi to provide cover for inaction."[24]

The fourth feature of America's Afghan strategy was the United States' disengaged neutrality toward all Afghan groups, moderates and extremists alike. The Afghan extremist groups were empowered by Pakistani and Saudi money and weapons. Moderate-nationalists such as Ahmed Shah Masood, Abdul Haq, Haji Qadir, and Hamid Karzai; Wahdat leader Ustad Khalili; and Durrani tribal and religious leaders were natural U.S. allies. They desperately sought American attention and support to compete with the extremists. They made the rounds in Washington, visiting the State Department, the CIA, and Congress. They frequently called on the American embassy in Islamabad to request American assistance. During the 1990s and up to 9/11, U.S. officials responded with the same disengaged-neutrality talking point, followed by the reminder that the United States supported UN mediation among the Afghan parties. President Clinton's assistant secretary for South Asian Affairs, Robin Raphel, testified in Congress that "the U.S. does not favor one faction or another nor does it give any group or individual support," adding, "The United Nations is the best place to broker a negotiated peace." In 1993, Hamid Karzai, who at that time was Afghan deputy foreign minister in Kabul, called on the acting deputy chief of mission at the American embassy in Islamabad to request assistance for Afghan moderates. He was told that "the U.S. does not favor any individual or faction and has no desire to play in the Afghan arena."[25]

As part of its new posture of disengaged neutrality between moderates and radicals, the Clinton administration acted quickly to restore political contact with ISI favorite Gulbuddin Hekmatyar, thus retracting the previous American condemnation of the anti-American demagogue. The American consul in Peshawar was directed to meet Hekmatyar at his Charasiab base in Logar, the launching pad for his devastating rocket barrages into Kabul. Carrying out absolutely futile instructions, the consul requested that Hekmatyar stop shelling Kabul and let the UN peace process go forward.[26]

The American strategy of disengaged neutrality, like outsourcing U.S. Afghan policy to Pakistan and rhetorical diplomacy, including on UN mediation, strengthened the Afghan Islamic extremists, weakened the majority moderate-nationalists opposed to the extremists, and bolstered Pakistan's destructive course in Afghanistan. The U.S. approach was counterproductive to U.S. interests and publicly declared goals in Afghanistan.

֍

The ISI's and Hekmatyar's fight-and-negotiate strategy continued uninterrupted past Burhanuddin Rabbani's assumption of the presidency from Sibghatullah Mojaddedi on June 28, 1992. On June 29, Hekmatyar, in a radio broadcast, demanded national elections within four months. Five days later, without waiting for his impossible deadline to expire, he resumed his bombardment of Kabul, killing an estimated 100 and wounding 300 on the first day.[27] Meanwhile, Mojaddedi moved to his brother's home in Florida where he calculated his next move—which was joining Hekmatyar in Charasiab to oppose Rabbani and Masood.

After taking over the basically powerless position of interim president, Rabbani rapidly verified moderate Afghan predictions that he would attempt to put the Muslim Brotherhood stamp on Afghanistan. His Ikhwani lectures broadcast by Radio Kabul dismayed the moderate shuras that now controlled nearly all of the newly liberated cities in the regions. Drawing on Koranic nomenclature used by the earliest caliphs, Rabbani announced that the long-awaited jirga mandated by the Peshawar Accords would be an Islamic *ahl al-hal wa qud* (council of solution and pact). Most Mujahidin politicians, commanders, and regional shuras correctly assumed that Rabbani was wielding religious slogans to camouflage a grab for power. They boycotted the council when it met on December 30, 1992, in Kabul. Rabbani was the sole candidate for president—delegates were forced to vote for him before taking the podium to speak. On December 29, the 1,335-man staged gathering gave Rabbani an eighteen-month term, after which national elections were to take place.[28]

Rabbani followed up his bogus election by laying claim to the religious mandate exercised by a ruler of a medieval Islamic state. He informed his radio and TV audience: "Dear brothers, after your decision to elect a President, you know what the Sharia instructs. Sharia will be declared through your ulema as well. Thus, from now on anyone opposing Islam, opposing our Islamic state, is a rebel. This is the instruction of God."[29] But Rabbani did not possess the military power to back up his declaration of divine authority. Nor did Masood. Hekmatyar responded by unleashing another bombardment of Kabul. Hezb-i Wahdat Shia leader Abdul Ali Mazari publicly rebuffed Rabbani's Islamic government.

In January, after Rabbani's religious council ended, Masood ordered an offensive into West Kabul to bring the Shia population there under government control. Mazari's Wahdat fighters held their ground. In February, Masood's artillery and infantry allied with Abdul Rasoul Sayyaf's Wahhabi zealots to launch a second assault. This one targeted the crammed Hazara-populated

THE WARS OF AFGHANISTAN

Afshar section of western Kabul and killed hundreds of Wahdat fighters and civilians. An estimated 70 or 80 of those killed during the attack were non-combatants. Another 700–750 men and young boys were reportedly seized and taken away, and later died in captivity.[30] Mazari reacted by shifting to Hekmatyar's side. Uzbek leader Rashid Dostum also threw his weight to Hekmatyar after Rabbani rejected his demand for ministerial positions in the government.

At the end of February, Pakistan decided that the time was ripe for another negotiating round in its fight-and-negotiate strategy. Prime Minister Sharif invited the seven party leaders plus Dostum and Wahdat leaders to his residence in Islamabad. Masood cautioned Rabbani not to trust Pakistani mediation, but Rabbani went anyway. Prince Turki flew in from Riyadh to lend Saudi support to the latest Pakistani attempt to mold an Afghan government. Sharif presided.

The first five days of discussions were marked by bitter arguments. Several Peshawar party leaders insisted that Sharif bar Dostum's delegates from participating in the negotiations. Some Afghans in the room refused to talk to one another. Rabbani stubbornly rejected ultimatums that he step down. Hekmatyar had turned down the prime minister position allotted to him in the Peshawar Accords. This time, he accepted it, pointing out that his prime minister responsibilities allowed him to dismiss Defense Minister Masood. Rabbani argued that his commander-in-chief authority overrode Prime Minister Hekmatyar's authority to fire Masood. Hekmatyar stalked out and went to Peshawar. An ISI helicopter brought him back to Islamabad. On the sixth day, Turki stood up and recited several Koranic verses calling for Islamic unity. That had no effect.

Finally, at 4:30 in the morning on Sunday, March 7, Nawaz Sharif grabbed a sheet of paper and wrote down the configuration of the next Afghan government. His piece of paper became known as the Islamabad Accords. It allowed Rabbani to remain as president for another eighteen months and specified that elections would be held when his term expired. Attempting to further chip away at Masood's military substructure, Sharif's peace plan created a Defense Commission to take over responsibilities for military affairs. The paper gave Prime Minister Hekmatyar authority to appoint and fire cabinet ministers, but only after consultations with President Rabbani. Dostum's

Russian- and Uzbekistan-financed army far outmatched Hekmatyar's and rivaled Masood's. The Islamabad Accords drawn up for the Afghan leaders to sign, however, ignored that reality. The final wording did not even mention Dostum's name.

Masood formally resigned as defense minister after Rabbani accepted Sharif's formula for his government. He continued, however, to act like the defense minister and appointed his adviser, Yunis Qanuni, to be acting defense minister. Several members of the new Defense Commission, including Sayyid Ahmad Gailani adviser Rahim Wardak, arrived from Pakistan to take up their responsibilities, but were given none. Masood's loyalists complained that Wardak always managed to be in Pakistan when the ISI and Hekmatyar resumed shelling Kabul.

The Islamabad Accords fell apart not long after the leaders signed the agreement. Pakistan's foreign authorship of the new Afghan regime immediately delegitimized it in the eyes of Afghans, including most of the signatories. At least four who signed it believed that Sharif had maneuvered Hekmatyar into a domineering position in Kabul.[31] To expiate these shortcomings, Prince Turki arranged for the Afghan signatories, including Shia Wahdat representatives, to fly on a special aircraft to the Grand Mosque in Mecca. In the Kaaba, Islam's holiest sanctuary, they signed an Arabic version of the Islamabad Accords in the presence of King Fahd and promised to close ranks. After the Saudi trip, the Iranian government hosted a third signing ceremony in Tehran. That one was written in Persian.

The Islamabad Accords suffered the same fate as all the other agreements the seven leaders had signed in the past. It disintegrated in a bizarre series of events soon after the leaders crossed the border into Afghanistan. Haji Qadir, the moderate Nangarhar governor, head of the Jalalabad Shura, and brother of Abdul Haq, detained their convoy. He put them under guard inside the aging winter palace of former king Amanullah in Jalalabad. Qadir demanded that the leaders reaffirm their intention to share power and cooperate. More bickering over power-sharing arrangements raged for several days. Claiming illness, Sayyaf was allowed to leave the palace and seek a doctor. With the help of some local followers, he absconded to his Paghman fortifications in the hills just northwest of Kabul. Qadir conceded defeat and released the others. Hekmatyar and Mojaddedi went to Charasiab, and Rabbani returned to Kabul.

In June 1993, Rabbani and twelve members of his cabinet drove to Hekmatyar's Charasiab base to watch the Afghan chief justice swear Hekmatyar in as prime minister. Rabbani solemnly told the new cabinet, "I hope we will in an honest way fulfill our obligations."[32] An assassination attempt on Rabbani's life during his presidential motorcade's return to Kabul immediately punctured that hope. The Islamabad Accords lapsed into obscurity.

In September 1993, the Pakistani Army and Hekmatyar shifted back to direct military action against Masood. On September 8, Hekmatyar inaugurated a four-month round of fighting with another ultimatum. He demanded that Rabbani and the entire Afghan cabinet collectively resign to facilitate "a free general election" to be held within one month. Wahdat Shia leader Mazari proclaimed that he "wholeheartedly welcomed brother Hekmatyar's proposals,"[33] which would have set a record for organizing and holding a national election.

In December 1993, the ISI convinced Dostum to team up with Hekmatyar.[34] Dostum obliged. On New Year's Day 1994, after extensive preparations, he and Hekmatyar initiated a major offensive against the capital. Dostum's aircraft, based in Mazar-i-Sharif, bombed Kabul while Hezb artillery contingents poured rockets and mortar rounds into the city. Forewarned of the attack by his intelligence network, Masood decimated Dostum's front lines and drove the combined Hekmatyar-Dostum attacking force back to Charasiab.

Against all odds, Masood had beaten off another Pakistan-supported Hekmatyar attack on Kabul. The Tajik commander was nevertheless aware that he was losing ground and was cornered politically.[35] Instead of expanding the Kabul government's narrow support base, Rabbani's lust for power had united all the main Afghan factions against his beleaguered regime. Pakistan's negotiate-and-fight strategy was maneuvering Masood's coalition partners towards Hekmatyar's side.

Masood and Ismael Khan decided that, on their own, they would organize the broad-based jirga promised in the UN settlement plan and the Peshawar Accords. They sent out invitations to hundreds of Afghans representing all Afghan groups to attend a July 20, 1994, jirga in Herat, far from Hekmatyar's artillery range. Rabbani agreed to accept the jirga's verdict to either renominate him or select another Afghan leader. Over 500 Afghans representing all ethnicities, regions, and religions came to Herat to participate. Former prime minister Mohammed Yousuf and other prominent officials in Zahir Shah's cabinets, then exiled in Europe and America, were in attendance. Rabbani assured Masood that he would announce his resignation when inaugurating the jirga on July 20. To the disappointment of his large audience, Rabbani did not follow through with that promise.[36] Instead he delivered a long speech urging the crowd to unify behind his government. The Herat Shura disbanded three days later, leaving Afghanistan no closer to a legitimate Afghan leadership.

ॐ

At the same time that Rabbani was sabotaging Masood's and Ismael Khan's jirga in Herat, in Quetta the ISI was putting its finishing touches on Pakistan's next ludicrous proxy to subdue unruly Afghanistan—the Taliban. The ISI's twenty-one-year campaign to install Hekmatyar in Kabul had failed. The Islamabad Accords had not achieved politically what Hekmatyar could not accomplish militarily. Masood had routed all of Hekmatyar's ISI-supported offensives. Sayyaf and Rabbani, two of Zia's chosen Afghan party leaders, were now aligned with Masood against Hekmatyar. Most of the Pashtun commanders in eastern Afghanistan detested Hekmatyar. Afghans ridiculed Hekmatyar's unparalleled record of changing sides. Not long ago, he had vehemently denounced Dostum, Wahdat, and Mojaddedi on religious, ethnic, or ideological grounds; now he embraced them. His wanton slaughter of Kabul's citizenry appalled ordinary Afghans.[37]

The ISI chose Mullah Mohammad Omar, a former low-level Mujahidin commander, to lead the Taliban. A Hotak Ghilzai Pashtun, Omar was born in 1960 of a religious family of modest means in Dehrawad District, Uruzgan Province, near the border with Kandahar. He joined the anticommunist jihad and went through the Mujahidin training camps in Pakistan in about 1985. Omar fought under Commander Mohammad Rabbani* in the Panjwai and Maiwand districts west of Kandahar city. He was wounded three times and lost an eye. When the Najib regime collapsed, he resumed his religious studies at a village mosque on the Kandahar-Herat road in Maiwand, patronized by a local businessman and narcotics trafficker, Haji Bashir Noorzai.[38]

---

* Mullah Mohammad Rabbani, a Pashtun Ghilzai Kakar, is not related to Burhanuddin Rabbani, the Tajik head of the Kabul regime when Pakistan created the Taliban.

Pakistani and Taliban myth-makers worked overtime to spin stories of the obscure mullah's miraculous rise to become the Taliban's supreme emir. One of the more popular versions depicted him as handing in his weapon after Najib's overthrow to become the prayer leader and religious teacher at the village mosque in Maiwand. As the story goes, on September 4, 1994,[39] one of the local warlords controlling a checkpoint near Omar's village seized a family traveling from Herat to Kandahar. They raped the daughters and sons, and then killed the entire family, throwing their bodies into a fire pit. Omar was one of the first to happen on the grisly scene. He gathered some *talibs* (religious students) and buried the badly burnt bodies with full Islamic religious rites. One of the students dreamed that night that angels from heaven had hovered above the burial party, blessing the group as it worked.

The story continues that Omar and his talibs decided to cleanse Kandahar of all the petty warlords persecuting the population. They named their movement the Taliban (the plural of "talib"). The local merchant, Haji Bashir,[40] recognized Omar's religious purity and God-given mission. He donated money and weapons to Omar's rapidly growing band of mullahs and their religious students. Omar and his acolytes set out to destroy the warlord culture in Afghanistan and create an Islamic Afghan state ruled by Sharia. They did not stop until they conquered Kabul and most of Afghanistan and drove Masood into the northeastern corner of the country.

The true narrative of the Taliban's origins is not so simple. It begins in late 1988 on the heels of the Soviet pullout from southern Afghanistan, not in Afghanistan but in Colonel Sultan Imam's ISI office in Quetta. Imam and Colonel Faizan, then head of the Quetta ISI branch, assembled, armed, and supervised the Argestan Shura. They chose ultraconservative Pakistani and Afghan mullahs to lead it. The mullahs had proven their fighting mettle during the Soviet jihad. After the Soviets left, Imam and Faizan had used them to block restoration of the secular Durrani tribal aristocracy that had dominated Kandahar for over two hundred years. The ISI now had more ambitious plans for this band of semiliterate mullah-warriors.

Colonel Imam and the ISI's Quetta office had been remolding the Argestan Shura into the Taliban for over a year before the apocryphal scene on the road to Kandahar took place. The ancient vendetta between Afghanistan's two largest tribal confederations, the Durrani and the Ghilzai, played an important role in Imam's shrewd construction of the Taliban hierarchy. He gave overriding preference to anti-Durrani Ghilzais, as Zia had in selecting the seven party leaders. And he placed Ghilzai Hotaks, such as Mullah Omar, in strategic control of the movement. Over two centuries had passed since Popalzai Durrani Ahmad Shah Durrani and his Barakzai allies had fought alongside Persian King Nadir Shah to crush the Mirwais Hotak dynasty and expel the Hotak tribe from their lands around Kandahar. That humiliation was still fresh in the minds of Hotaks. So was the imperative for *badal*, retribution.

Colonel Imam mobilized that anti-Durrani sentiment. Hotaks were put in charge of military operations and later occupied key positions in the Taliban government. The Taliban leaders were nearly all Ghilzai Pashtuns from poorer families with only a rudimentary religious education, followed by studies at madrassas in Pakistan run by the Pakistani religious party Jamiat-i Ulema-i Islam or one of its offshoots. In addition to Mullah Omar and Mullah Rabbani, the top-tier Taliban leaders included Mullah Noorudin Turabi, who later became Taliban minister of justice. Mullah Abdul Razak and his Achakzai tribe were at home on both sides of the border. Close to ISI and the Jamiat-i Ulema-i Islam leadership, Razak would become the feared and brutal Taliban interior minister. He functioned as a reliable ISI collaborator inside the Taliban cabinet in Pakistan and in Afghanistan.

The ISI also detached Shahnawaz Tanai, the former PDPA defense minister, from Hekmatyar and sent him to Quetta to join the Taliban. He grew a beard and declared himself a devout Muslim. He commanded several battalions made up of former Khalqi Pashtun officers and soldiers who had defected to Pakistan since the first failed Hekmatyar-Tanai coup in March 1990. The Pakistani Army retrained and reequipped these units, whose Pashtuness coincided with the Pashtun nationalist character of the Taliban movement. They, and not the Taliban's former Mujahidin fighters, became the spearhead for the devastating 1994–1998 Taliban offensives across Afghanistan.

The first language of the Taliban leaders was Pashto, the second Urdu, not the Dari version of Persian spoken by the great majority of Afghans. They were educated at the Saudi-financed, Wahhabi-influenced Deobandi madrassas in Pakistan, where Afghan and Pakistani youth studied side by side. The madrassas were sponsored by JUI clerics, most notably Fazlur Rahman. Rahman traveled frequently to Saudi Arabia to raise funds. JUI curricula closely followed Wahhabi customs and teachings, imparting a rigid, militant version of the Deobandi and Wahhabi ideologies. Only boys attended; girls were denied education.[41]

I was struck by the strong religiosity and simplicity of some future Taliban I encountered during my visits as special envoy to Quetta in 1991 and 1992. I twice met with Mullah Turabi. He had lost an eye and a leg in the war against the Soviets. Turabi seemed oblivious to the world beyond the Frontier. In a 1991 conversation, he told me he would be prepared to move in either of two directions after Najib was gone. He could support Zahir Shah's "return" and a peaceful settlement of the war—or he could fight. The ISI, he told me, had just given him seven truckloads of weapons.

In 1990, three Talibs visited me in the USAID office in Quetta. An overwhelming plainness characterized their personality, clothing, and manners. One, Abdul Hakim, asked for Saudi religious material. I referred him to the Saudi embassy and gave him its telephone number. A few minutes later, my deputy, Tom Greene, and I noticed that an Afghan USAID employee was instructing Hakim on how to use a telephone. Hakim became assistant foreign minister after the Taliban came to power.

The Taliban, its JUI mentor Fazlur Rahman, and the predominantly Pashtun JUI religious party benefited from a political crisis that erupted in Islamabad in late 1993. Prime Minister Sharif attempted to take away President Ghulam Ishak Khan's constitutional authority to remove him and his cabinet. Khan retaliated by dismissing Sharif. Sharif took his case to the Supreme Court and won. Army Chief General Abdul Waheed Kakar privately asked both to resign, and they did. Benazir Bhutto was returned to office in the October 6, 1993, elections. Fazlur Rahman was Bhutto's political ally.

Bhutto appointed Nasrullah Babar, a retired general, Pakistani Pashtun, and longtime Bhutto family confidant, to be interior minister. Together they backed the ISI's launching of the Taliban. Bhutto made Fazlur Rahman, known as the "Taliban's Godfather," chair of the parliament's Foreign Affairs Committee. Rahman's governmental rank added to his stature. It gave him direct access to the Saudi royal family and senior Wahhabi clergy in the kingdom, which he used to lobby for religious, political, and financial support for the Taliban.[42]

The Taliban war machine that conquered most of Afghanistan in the mid- to late 1990s combined the Afghan, Pakistani, and Arab parts of the ISI's unholy alliance. The Taliban mullahs were the junior partner, the Afghan front through which Pakistan's generals, and later Osama bin Laden, pursued their own agendas inside Afghanistan and globally. The Taliban deferred to the ISI's command and control of military operations—as they had done during the Soviet war and in the Argestan Shura after the Soviets withdrew.

ψ

In April 1994, the ISI assembled a diverse collection of unholy alliance fighters in Quetta. It included Taliban mullahs, Tanai's Khalqis, Pakistanis, Afghan JUI madrassa students, and Arab jihadis. The two-hundred-man armed horde crossed the border at Chaman and attacked the Afghan town of Spin Boldak, where the Quetta-Kandahar road enters Afghanistan. The Taliban force easily drove off Hekmatyar's Hezb defenders at Spin Boldak. A secret April 22, 1994, telegram cabled by the American embassy in Islamabad to Washington, citing "an extremely well informed and reliable source," reported that the Taliban's Spin Boldak attack "was preceded by artillery shelling of the base from Pakistani Frontier Corps positions" inside Pakistan. The message noted "coordination provided by Pakistani officers on the scene." It concluded, "The Taliban's military competence . . . and their use of tanks and helicopters strongly suggested Pakistani tutelage or direct control."[43]

After the Spin Boldak victory, inside Pakistan the ISI and General Babar rolled Afghan, Pakistani, and Arab jihadi elements into the Taliban army. They prepared the battle plans for three more military offensives to be launched from Pakistani soil over the next six years. ISI officers coordinated the military operations and handled logistics. Fazlur Rahman, Masood Azhar, and other JUI religious leaders roused thousands of students in JUI madrassas to leave their studies and join each offensive.[44] Fanatical groups of Arabs added more firepower. Thousands of shiny new Japanese pickup trucks purchased by the Saudis were offloaded at Karachi and equipped with machine guns, antiaircraft weapons, and rocket launchers. Their mobility played critical roles in the Taliban's battlefield successes. Tanai and about three hundred Khalqi officers operated the Taliban's small air force, artillery, and communications networks. The two most effective Taliban field commanders were ex-Khalqi generals who tacked "mullah" before their names to certify their jihadi competency.

On November 3, 1994, a month after the Spin Boldak attack, the ISI launched its second major Taliban offensive into Afghanistan from Pakistani territory. It targeted Kandahar, the largest and most important city in southern Afghanistan. The ISI cover for the offensive was a thirty-truck convoy that departed from Quetta and crossed into Afghanistan, ostensibly to go to Herat. The stated purpose was to deliver humanitarian supplies to Herat and continue on to Central Asia. The real objective was to install Mullah Omar in Kandahar. A large Taliban force was positioned in Quetta to reinforce the convoy when, as expected, its passage was blocked by one of the many warlord roadblocks on the road to Kandahar and Herat. ISI colonels Imam and Gul and Mullah Turabi were in the convoy. When protracted negotiations at the first roadblock failed to result in the convoy's release, they summoned the Taliban force left behind in Quetta. It entered Afghanistan and broke the blockade. Instead of continuing to Herat, the convoy and its armed escort drove straight into the center of Kandahar city. Droves of Afghan Taliban fighters joined them on the way. Gul Agha, the Rabbani government's Kandahar governor and a longtime ISI operative, hastily left the city for Pakistan. The Kabul government's military commander, Mullah Naqib, chose not to resist.

A wave of popular enthusiasm carried the Taliban juggernaut across Afghanistan after the fall of Kandahar on November 5, 1994. The Taliban's religious fervor and Pashtun ethnocentrism appealed to rural Pashtuns on both sides of the Durand Line. Many moderate Pashtuns and Tajiks were willing to give the Taliban a try. They hoped that the movement would end the warlord banditry and criminality tormenting the country.

The Taliban quickly overran Helmand in December 1994 and January 1995. Another Taliban column, moving east, occupied Ghazni and Wardak in January. On February 13, Pul-i-Alam, Logar's capital, fell to the Taliban. Hekmatyar abandoned his nearby base of Charasiab and fled east to Sarobi on the Jalalabad-Kabul road. On March 8, 1995, Wahdat leader Mazari reached an agreement with the Khalqi general leading the Taliban force, Mullah Borjan. He invited Borjan to pass through his lines and enter Wahdat-occupied southwest Kabul. Hoping the Taliban would vanquish Masood, Mazari also agreed to give up his heavy weapons to the Taliban commander. But Masood's intelligence detected Mazari's collusion with Borjan. Masood struck first, with an all-out ground, air, and artillery assault on Mazari. He demanded that Mullah Borjan pull out of Kabul. When Borjan refused, Masood attacked the

MAP 20.1   ISI-ORGANIZED TALIBAN OFFENSIVES FROM PAKISTANI
SANCTUARIES, 1994–2000

Taliban. A wing of Mazari's Shia defected to Masood and struck the Taliban flank. Caught in the withering crossfire and suffering hundreds of casualties, the Taliban abandoned Charasiab and the Rishkor military base to Masood and retreated back to Wardak. Borjan invited his erstwhile ally, Mazari, to a meeting. Disregarding the important Pashtunwali tenet of *melamisti* (hospitality), the Taliban commander seized the Shia leader and executed him. Masood occupied Charasiab and Rishkor. He now controlled six provinces around the capital.

Masood held that advantage for the next year. The Taliban postponed further attacks on Kabul to concentrate on capturing Herat, where Sultan Imam had taken up the post of Pakistani consul in 1995. After Ismael Khan rejected Imam's advice to negotiate a settlement with the Taliban, the Taliban launched a western offensive from Kandahar led by fast-moving armed pickup trucks, capturing Herat on September 4, 1995.[45] Ismael Khan fled to

Iran. In February 1996, he returned to Ghor Province with Iranian arms and started a guerrilla campaign against the Taliban. Fighting resumed around Kabul and in eastern Afghanistan in the spring of 1996.

Pakistani Foreign Minister Assef Ahmad Ali and ISI Director General Nasim Rana took Pakistan's message on noninterference in Afghanistan to Washington in February 1996, prior to a massive Taliban offensive from Pakistani soil planned for the summer. In a February 9 meeting with Acting Secretary of State Strobe Talbott at the State Department, Foreign Minister Assef "categorically denied" that Pakistan was giving military assistance to the Taliban. When Assef complained about Iranian support for the Kabul regime, Talbott noted that the United States considered the recent increase in foreign support for Kabul "to be a backlash to Pakistani support for the Taliban." ISI Director General Rana asserted that "not one bullet" had been provided to the Taliban by Pakistan. Assef asked for greater U.S. involvement to promote the UN peace process—a path that Pakistan had blocked since the Soviet invasion and had no intention of allowing now that its Taliban proxy had the momentum.[46]

In April, State Department Assistant Secretary of State Raphel visited Islamabad, Kabul, and Kandahar. After meetings with Pakistani Prime Minister Bhutto, Pakistani Interior Minister Babar, the army chief of staff, and Foreign Minister Assef, she optimistically cabled Washington that Pakistan "appears willing to engage more positively in a reinvigorated UN mission." She reported Prime Minister Bhutto's affirmation that "Pakistan was not providing military support to the Taliban, and only minimal non-lethal aid was being delivered," when the opposite was true. Her telegram to Washington "made clear Pakistan's support for the UN mission's primacy as the lead actor in brokering a peace deal."[47]

The Taliban's shelling of Kabul compelled Masood to meet Raphel at Zahir Shah's former royal guesthouse in the picturesque village of Istalef, nestled in the mountains north of the capital. Their meeting did not go well. Raphel's advice to both Masood and Rabbani to reconcile with the Taliban upheld the State Department's disengaged-neutrality line but also smacked of ISI Colonel Sultan Imam's suggestion to Ismael Khan to collaborate with the Taliban before they attacked Herat. Masood and Rabbani told Raphel they were ready for talks with the Taliban but held firm to the position that the Kabul regime differed from other Afghan factions. It was the internationally recognized, legitimate government of Afghanistan and had the right to acquire arms and defend itself. In her reporting cable to Washington, Raphel dismissed their claims to legitimacy as "highly questionable" and "self-righteous." After her departure, Masood immediately convened a meeting of his most trusted commanders. He announced that the United States was not going to help Afghanistan. They stood alone against Pakistan and the Taliban.[48]

In Kandahar, Raphel heard the rigid Taliban position that it would be necessary to disarm the Kabul regime and the nation before peace could be restored. During her Kandahar stopover, she promoted the Houston oil company Unocal's unrealistic plans to build a pipeline from Turkmenistan through western and southern Afghanistan to Pakistan.[49]

On June 26, spurning Masood's objections and hastening the fall of the Kabul regime, Rabbani invited Hekmatyar to Kabul to take up his position of prime minister and help defend the city against the Taliban. The Hezb leader and 1,000 of his troops entered the capital. Hekmatyar moved into the prime minister's office. Rabbani's invitation to Hekmatyar proved disastrous. Hekmatyar outranked his old nemesis, Masood. They argued about Masood's military plans to defend Kabul against the next Taliban offensives. Hekmatyar insisted that Masood stretch his defense perimeter eastward to include his Sarobi base. Masood was compelled to send a large force to Sarobi, weakening Kabul's defense perimeter.

The ISI inaugurated its third offensive into Afghanistan from Pakistani territory on September 11, 1996. The two-week, massive, well-coordinated armor, air, and infantry attack across the Durand Line could not have been planned and executed by the Taliban's barefoot mullahs. Within the unholy alliance, only Pakistan's own military had the capability to organize the powerful assault on Kabul's defensive perimeter. The armored column and thousands of Afghan, Pakistani, and Arab fighters rushed up the Grand Trunk Road from Peshawar, captured Jalalabad, and closed in on Kabul. A Hekmatyar commander and his men at Sarobi joined the Taliban columns. Masood's troops were forced to fall back toward Kabul. At 3:00 p.m. on September 26, Masood issued orders to evacuate the capital and retreat to the Panshir Valley. Hekmatyar had little choice but to accept Masood's invitation to join him and Rabbani on a helicopter flight to Masood's Panshiri base.

Najib, still languishing at the UN compound, turned Masood's invitation down. He thereby sealed his fate. The former Afghan president gambled that the Pashtun Taliban would honor the Pashtun tradition of *nanawati* (asylum). He lost the gamble. The decision to execute him may have been reached weeks beforehand in Pakistan. Murdering Najib buried forever the possibility that he and his Parcham faction would survive to challenge Pakistan another day—separately or in combination with other Afghan factions.

After Hekmatyar's humiliating escape to the Panshir with Masood, his heretofore sworn enemy, the Hezb leader decamped to Iran via Tajikistan. He carried with him several American Stingers to bestow on his Iranian hosts, whom he had forsaken for the Saudis and Saddam Hussein in the mid-1980s. In VOA and BBC broadcasts from Tehran, Hekmatyar stridently condemned his former Pakistani sponsors for "interference in Afghanistan's affairs." Many Afghan politicians and commanders saw the Taliban capture of Kabul as an opportune time to go with the prevailing winds. Two days after Kabul fell, Mojaddedi tried to resuscitate his lapsed political career. He issued a statement offering his complete support to the Taliban. Khalis announced his switch to the Taliban on October 1.[50]

The combined armies of Masood and Dostum, joined by Wahdat fighters, could have blunted Taliban penetration north of the Hindu Kush. But the animosities dividing the non-Pashtuns were too deep after three years of internecine conflict. Pakistan's ISI consuls in Herat and Mazar reportedly mediated a secret agreement between the Taliban and one of Dostum's Uzbek deputies, General Abdul Malik.[51] Malik switched sides to the Taliban. He then invited Ismael Khan to dinner, captured the famous Mujahidin commander, and turned him over to the Taliban. Malik next attacked Dostum's base in Mazar from the west while the Taliban attacked from the south. Dostum fled to Uzbekistan and moved onward to Turkey.

Pakistani officials could not hide their glee. On May 25, 1997, Pakistani Foreign Minister Assef, who had previously compared the Taliban movement to the French Revolution, announced Pakistan's diplomatic recognition of the Taliban. Saudi Arabia recognized the Taliban on May 26, and the UAE followed suit on May 27.

The Taliban's good fortunes abruptly reversed days later when Malik changed his mind and savagely turned on the Taliban forces attempting to consolidate their control of Mazar. Hazara Shia in the city eagerly participated in the carnage. Estimates of Taliban dead ranged up to 3,000. In August 1998, the Taliban fought their way back into Mazar and sought revenge. They and their Pakistani and Arab allies massacred an estimated 2,000 civilians in Mazar, most of them Hazara Shia. As 1999 began, the Taliban were in control of 80 percent of Afghanistan. A stalemate existed in the northeast, where Masood continued to hold out against overwhelming odds.

A *New York Times* correspondent, David Frantz, later reported that "Western intelligence officials" gave the credit for the Taliban victory "to Pakistani military advisors who fought alongside the Taliban." Two Western diplomats informed that an intercepted phone call from Colonel Sultan Imam recorded him announcing, "My boys and I are riding into Mazar-i-Sharif."[52]

The Taliban now reigned over most of Afghanistan, but they did not govern. Their mullahs could not administer a province, much less a country. Mullah Omar's interest in government was limited to the imposition of medieval Koranic prescriptions. He gave himself the title of *Emir-i-Mominim* (Commander of the Faithful) and proclaimed Afghanistan an Islamic emirate. A Council of Senior Ulema was convened from time to time to assist him in making significant decisions, such as the 2001 destruction of the Bamian Buddhas; otherwise, he ruled by religious fatwas. There was no governmental structure or foreign policy.

The "inner shura" of Taliban mullahs, chaired by Omar, sat in Kandahar. Mohammad Rabbani led the less important Kabul Shura, aided by Defense Minister Obeidullah Akund, Interior Minister Abdul Razak, and Justice Minister Noorudin Turabi. Rural mullahs walked the halls of government buildings. Pakistani ISI officers were stationed in every ministry. In the provinces, the ISI established about eight bases manned by active duty and retired ISI colonels and brigadiers.[53] They provided oversight to the Taliban's light government presence.

Masood's fortunes ebbed and flowed after the Taliban offensive drove him out of Kabul back to northeastern Afghanistan. He still commanded about 20,000 fiercely loyal fighters. The United Nations refused to recognize the Taliban government and allowed the Rabbani and Masood government to keep the

Afghanistan seat at the United Nations. Masood's adviser and Foreign Minister Dr. Abdullah Abdullah gave the annual UN address for Afghanistan.[54]

The Taliban and their unholy alliance partners generally enjoyed battlefield momentum after their capture of Kabul in September 1996. Dr. Abdullah once told me that "the lowest point" of Masood's many lows came in the spring of 1997.[55] Masood had almost depleted his ammunition reserves. The Iranians were estranged. The Russians refused to supply more weapons and ammunition until they were paid. The Indians had been friendly, but they were weighing their options after the Taliban seized Kabul. The Americans were disengaged and deferring to Pakistan. And the UN peace process was moribund. The summer Taliban offensive was not far away.

In May 1997, Abdullah recalled that he and Masood were standing outside Masood's headquarters at Sareecha in the Panshir gazing northward at the far horizon of the 90-mile-long valley. They searched for a sign, any sign, of a solitary helicopter scheduled to bring 300 million Afghanis fresh off Russian printing presses. "We first saw only a black speck," Abdullah told me. "It was very low, well below the mountaintops, but it slowly grew, slightly bobbing from side to side. Masood and I shouted in celebration. We embraced. However slight, a reprieve had been granted to relieve our anxieties."[56]

There were more reprieves. Duplicating an endless historical pattern, the Great Game drew in more external players, this time to thwart Pakistan's reach for hegemony in Afghanistan. Substantial shipments of Russian and Iranian arms began to flow to Masood's warehouses in Dushanbe in 1998. With Russian permission, unmarked trains transported Iranian weapons and ammunition on Soviet rails to Dushanbe. The Tajikistan government gave Masood a section of the Dushanbe airport to relay shipments to his main base at Khwaja Bahauddin on the Afghan side of the Amu Darya.

Masood survived and, with fresh arms and money from Russia, Iran, and India, shored up his defenses in the north. He distanced himself from Rabbani and appointed his own pro-Western envoys, such as Daoud Mir, to represent him abroad. Staking out a moderate political platform, he sought American and Western support. He organized a multiethnic "Supreme Council for the Defense of the Motherland" and named it the "United Front." Western media called it the "Northern Alliance." The alliance included Pashtun Haji Qadir, who came from exile in Germany; Dostum, who returned to Afghanistan from Turkey to create an anti-Taliban Uzbek base west of Mazar;

and Ismael Khan, who rallied his followers in the mountains of Ghor. Hazara Shia leaders Ustad Khalili, Sayeed Hussain Anwari, and Sayed Mustafa Kazimi also joined Masood's United Front. Masood confidently told a European journalist that the Pakistani Army "should come to the conclusion that the same fate awaits them as the Soviets."[57]

⚜

In May 1996, before the fall of Kabul, the Taliban in Kandahar, Rabbani in Kabul, and Yunus Khalis in Jalalabad had vied with each other to welcome bin Laden back to Afghanistan. Rabbani sent an Ariana airplane to Sudan to pick him up; bin Laden came with his wives, his children, and a large entourage, flying into Jalalabad, the largest city in eastern Afghanistan. During the anti-Soviet jihad he had spent most of his time in eastern Afghanistan, mostly with Haqqani and other Khalis commanders at Zhawar Kili and Tora Bora. After a few months as Khalis' guest in Jalalabad, he accepted Mullah Omar's invitation to relocate to Kandahar.

Following bin Laden's return, the ISI coordinated with him to establish scores of new training camps in Afghanistan. The Saudi multimillionaire's personal fortune helped fund the expanding jihadi infrastructure. Pakistani military officers, assisted by Pakistani and Arab jihadi veterans, ran basic training programs and provided classroom instruction. Estimates of the number of jihadis trained from 1996 up to 9/11 range from 20,000 to 80,000.[58]

Pakistani military advisers converted the division-sized Afghan army base at Rishkor, southwest of Kabul, into a huge training camp for volunteers sent by Pakistan's religious parties. Arab militants, Chechens, Chinese Muslim Uighurs, Burmese and Filipino Muslims, Africans, and jihadis from Western countries also went through the Rishkor facility's six-week course, 1,500 at a time.[59] Al-Qaeda closely monitored trainees to choose candidates for its more advanced terrorist courses at Khost in Paktiya and Duranta near Jalalabad. Other graduates were sent to join the annual Taliban-al-Qaeda offensives against Masood, to Kashmir, or to their home countries to wage holy war.

By 1998, the unholy alliance infrastructure in Afghanistan had become the world's training ground for global Islamic terrorism. Arab jihadis from North Africa, the Middle East, and the Gulf, Uzbek militants from Jama Narnagani's Islamic Movement of Uzbekistan and other foreign holy warriors were housed, fed, indoctrinated, and trained in the use of small arms and explosives.[60] In the late 1990s, al-Qaeda terrorist attacks steadily increased in the Middle East, North Africa, the Northern Caucasus, Asia and the West.

Bin Laden began issuing his first formal warnings about targeting Americans three months after his return to Afghanistan. In August 1996, he released a Declaration of War against the United States. In February 1997, he called on Muslims to kill American soldiers. A year later, in February 1998, he appealed to Muslims to attack Americans and their allies, including civilians, anywhere in the world, and in May 1998, three months before the al-Qaeda bombings of the U.S. embassies in Kenya and Tanzania, he told journalists at a press conference in Afghanistan that they would see the results of his warnings in a few weeks.

Bin Laden's threats against the United States, like the unholy alliance's mass production of holy warriors to fight against Masood in the north and around the world, fell below the radar screen of top U.S. policymakers in Washington. Those in the middle levels of the foreign-policy-making bureaucracy in Washington, and in the Islamabad embassy who were responsible for Afghanistan, accepted Pakistan's plausible denials that it was not involved with al-Qaeda and the Taliban. The 9/11 Commission later concluded that "Bin Laden and terrorist activity in Afghanistan were not significant issues in high level contacts with Pakistan until after the Embassy bombings of August 1998."[61]

The planning, financing, and organization of al-Qaeda's embassy bombings in Africa, and subsequent al-Qaeda attacks on the United States, including on 9/11, all took place in Afghanistan. Inevitably, the close working relationship between the ISI and al-Qaeda in Afghanistan raises questions about whether ISI officers were aware of al-Qaeda's preparations for the attacks. Author Steve Coll cited CIA reports as stating that inside Afghanistan, Pakistani intelligence officers at about the colonel level were meeting with bin Laden or his representatives.[62]

It is reasonable to assume that ISI officers and their al-Qaeda counterparts came in contact with each other when managing their respective training camps in Afghanistan, some adjacent to one another. Certainly ISI officers at the ISI's regional stations inside Afghanistan must have worked with al-Qaeda operatives as well as with local Taliban representatives on common issues, particularly in Kandahar, where the ISI had a large presence and bin Laden and Mullah Omar were headquartered. Moreover, ISI-al-Qaeda coordination was essential when bin Laden's two Arab brigades fought side by side with ISI and regular Pakistani Army personnel in the major offensives launched against Masood in the north every year.

Since 9/11, credible information (including declassified intelligence reports) about continuous trilateral interaction between the ISI, ISI cutouts, and bin Laden during the late 1990s up to September 11, 2001, has been voluminous. "Private-sector" cutouts Hamid Gul, former ISI officer Khalid Kharaja, who also knew bin Laden well, Khalid Sheikh Mohammed, and Ahmed Omar Saeed Sheikh routinely circulated between ISI and al-Qaeda representatives in Afghanistan and Pakistan. Two Pakistani nuclear scientists, one reportedly previously involved in Pakistan's secret nuclear weapons program, visited bin Laden in Kabul two weeks before 9/11. Retired ISI chief Hamid Gul was the "honorary patron" of their NGO, known by its acronym, UTN. An active-duty Pakistani Army brigadier was a UTN director.[63]

It therefore stretches the imagination to believe that no one in the ISI's pervasive intelligence network was aware of Khalid Sheikh Mohammed's and al-Qaeda's operational planning for the 9/11 attacks—or that none of the ISI officers working inside Afghanistan were aware of al-Qaeda's plans for major al-Queda strikes against American targets from 1998 to 2001. To the contrary, it is quite possible that the ISI learned details about one or more of these attacks beforehand. If it did, it neither acted to preempt them nor attempted to inform the United States.

A July 2004 article in the British *Guardian* written by a British member of parliament hints at an even more ominous scenario—some elements in the ISI working with ISI cutouts may have been more than passive observers of al-Qaeda's preparations to carry out major terrorist attacks on the United States, specifically the September 11 World Trade Center and Pentagon strikes.[64]

The exponential growth in numbers and combat capability of all parts of the unholy alliance became a growing problem for the ISI in 1998. The parts had been easier for it to manage when they were based in Pakistan during the wars against the Soviet Union and Najib. Coordinating their activities in Afghanistan, a country the size of Texas, was much more challenging. The Taliban mullahs had obeyed their ISI handlers when they were exiled in Pakistan, and during the ISI-organized Taliban conquest of most of Afghanistan. After settling down in Kandahar and Kabul, they grew less tolerant of ISI instructions. The mullahs believed they knew better how to organize an Islamic state. Bin Laden took pains to show his subservience to Zia ul-Haq and the ISI during the 1980s. He operated more freely after his return. He and Mullah Omar established a symbiotic relationship, personally, spiritually, and politically.

Pakistan faced other growing difficulties after bin Laden's return. His international terrorist strikes were generating mounting pressures from the United States on Pakistan to force the Taliban to hand over bin Laden or to expel him. Russia and Afghanistan's other neighbors (except for Turkmenistan, which declared itself neutral) opposed the Taliban. The Taliban's popularity began to go on the downswing in late 1998. By that time, the majority of Afghan faction leaders, Pashtun and non-Pashtun, including Hekmatyar, Sayyaf, Rabbani, Abdul Haq, and Hamid Karzai, opposed the Taliban. Taliban enforcement of the strict Wahhabi version of Sharia antagonized freedom-loving Afghans. Armed "Vice and Virtue" squads of non-literate rural Pashtuns roamed cities, caning women whose ankles were not covered and men who trimmed their beards.

Poverty remained pervasive. Increasing Taliban corruption, mostly extortion and bribe-taking, raised questions about whether the movement's leaders had abandoned their professed spirituality in order to gain personal wealth and power. The presence of tens of thousands of Pakistanis and Arabs in Kabul and elsewhere, the ubiquitous use of Pakistani rupees in Taliban-controlled provinces near Pakistan, and the growing visibility of Pakistani companies inside Afghanistan irritated ordinary Afghans and fed suspicions of Pakistanization of the country. The Taliban's Pashtun chauvinism thoroughly alienated Afghanistan's non-Pashtuns, who make up more than half of Afghanistan's population. Mullah Omar brooked no compromise with his Afghan enemies, Pashtun or non-Pashtun: "These people have sinned and rebelled against Islamic Sharia. . . . They must be fought to the end."[65]

During the late 1990s, Taliban military units and the Arab Wahhabis with them massacred entire Hazara Shia communities in the Hazarajat. Masood's resistance in northern Afghanistan stiffened. He benefited from new recruits. In 1998 he secretly traveled to New Delhi, Moscow, Tehran, and Mashad in western Iran seeking assistance. A Chinese delegation made an unpublicized visit to meet with Masood in the north. India increased its cash outlays to Masood to buy Russian arms, and Iran sent him both weapons and money.

In 2000, the Taliban seemed to have passed their "high-water mark."[66] Anti-Taliban sentiment in Pashtun eastern and southern Afghanistan began to surface. A large Pashtun village in Helmand violently resisted Taliban attempts to conscript more of its sons. The Taliban used helicopters, rocket launchers, and more than six hundred troops in a two-day battle to crush the uprising. Eastern Pashtuns complained about their minimal representation in the southern-dominated Taliban shuras in Kandahar and Kabul. Four hundred Pashtun tribal leaders in Paktiya, Khost, and Paktika delivered an ultimatum to Taliban authorities, demanding that they give back land they had seized.[67] On March 26, 2000, Ismael Khan escaped from the Taliban's maximum security prison in Kandahar with inside help from Taliban guards, shocking the Taliban leaders in the city. Khan returned to the mountains of Ghor Province northeast of Herat to resume his guerrilla campaign against the Taliban.

Pakistan's army compensated for waning Taliban momentum by deploying more and more regular army officers, special forces, commandos, troops, and madrassa students to the front lines facing Masood. The cost to Pakistan in weapons, food, equipment, and men climbed upward, weighing on Pakistan's weak economy. The 200-mile supply line from Peshawar to the front lines in the mountains of Badakhshan and northern Takhar provinces consumed fuel and other resources needed at home. During the late 1990s, Talibanization and savage Shia-Sunni sectarian violence drifted back into Pakistan, ripping Pakistan's social fabric. Mullahs in Pakistan's tribal areas began to call for Talibanization of Pakistan.

Pakistan's proxy war in Afghanistan isolated Islamabad in the Central-South Asia region and internationally. In July 2000, the Chinese foreign minister asked his Pakistani counterpart to urge the Taliban to end ties with Uighur separatists in Afghanistan.[68] Mullah Omar's official recognition of the Chechen government and acceptance of a Chechen embassy in Kabul offended the Russian government. The United States, China, and Saudi Arabia, Pakistan's close allies during the anti-Soviet war, expressed their disapproval of Islamabad's links to the Taliban and the Taliban's human and gender rights violations. The Saudi government, angry at the Taliban's protection of bin Laden, a sworn enemy of the Saudi royal family, closed its embassy and consulates in Afghanistan. It ordered Taliban representatives in Saudi Arabia to leave the kingdom. The Saudi government's suspension of diplomatic interactions with the Taliban did not, however, interrupt the large flow of private

Saudi money to the religious movement and the unholy alliance infrastructure in Pakistan.

Pakistani Army Chief Pervez Musharraf's overthrow of Prime Minister Nawaz Sharif on October 12, 1999, drew Pakistan deeper into the Afghan quicksand. Musharraf committed additional regular army, Frontier Corps, special forces, artillery, and communications units to Afghanistan to reinforce the 2000 offensive against Masood. The offensive overran Toloqan. A *Jane's Defence Weekly* article in 2000 cited a Western military analyst as estimating that, in one battle with the heavily outnumbered Masood, some 30 percent of the 20,000-man Taliban force opposing him consisted of soldiers from Pakistan's regular army, Pakistan's madrassa students, and two Arab brigades organized, trained, and armed by bin Laden. A senior Russian official charged that "30,000 foreign mercenaries" from "Arab nations, as well as Pakistani military men wearing Pakistani uniforms without concealment, and people from Chechnya,"[69] were part of the attacking force. In late September 2000, Pakistan mounted its fourth attack from Pakistani territory, this one from Chitral into Badakhshan. Masood turned back the offensive.

Pakistan's predicament in Afghanistan in the years before 9/11 was similar to the dilemma the Soviets had struggled with in the 1980s. Pakistan could not "win" on the battlefield in Afghanistan despite committing more men and resources to suppress a growing insurgency. Pakistan's Afghan proxies were increasingly unpopular in Afghanistan and even more so in the outside world. The more manpower and resources Islamabad squandered in Afghanistan, the more it alienated the Afghan population. The Afghan war exacerbated grinding poverty, political instability, and sectarian violence inside Pakistan. Pakistan's generals could not generate the collective will in Pakistan's divided society to implement Zia's vision in Afghanistan. Pakistan was bogged down in Afghanistan's rugged mountains; it was fighting above its weight, bleeding resources and men in an endless war.

In 1999, around the time of Musharraf's coup, the ISI cracked down on anti-Taliban Afghan moderates in Pakistan. ISI officers visited Abdul Haq in Peshawar and Hamid Karzai in Quetta and ordered them to leave the country. Haq went to Dubai, leaving his family behind at his home in Peshawar. Taliban assassins broke into his Peshawar residence during nighttime hours. They found Haq's wife and seven-year-old son in an upstairs bedroom and murdered them. Another son, an eleven-year-old, escaped death by hiding under a blanket in the same room. Karzai managed to delay his departure until 9/11, when the expulsion order was withdrawn.

In July 1999, unidentified men on motorcycles who were armed with automatic assault rifles assassinated Hamid Karzai's father, Abdul Ahad Karzai, in Quetta as he walked home from a mosque after Friday prayers.[70] In the aftermath of the assassination, Qayum Karzai, Hamid Karzai's older brother, was invited to meet the French deputy chief of mission in Islamabad. The French diplomat informed him that he was also speaking on behalf of the U.S. embassy. He showed him two assassination lists signed by Mullah Omar.[71] The "priority" list had eighteen names, including the names of Karzai's father and Hamid Karzai. The French embassy officer asked Qayum to warn his brother of the danger, cautioning him that the lists had been compiled in Taliban intelligence headquarters outside of Kandahar, where ISI instructors taught classes, and conducting assassinations was part of the curricula.[72]

Pakistan never seriously investigated the assassinations of Haq's family members or of Abdul Ahad Karzai, and no arrests were made.

꾸

In March 1994, while the ISI was preparing the Taliban for their September-October attacks across the border into Afghanistan, Abdul Haq made an ominous prediction to an American journalist. His warning was carried in the *New York Times*: "For us, Afghanistan is destroyed," he said. "It is turning to poison, and not only for us but for all others in the world. If you are a terrorist, you can have a shelter here, no matter who you are. Day by day, there is the increase of drugs. Maybe one day they will have to send hundreds of thousands of troops to deal with that. And if they step in, they will be stuck. We have a British grave in Afghanistan. We have a Soviet grave. And then we will have an American grave."[73]

Unfortunately for America, Afghanistan, and ultimately Pakistan, the four restraints on U.S Afghan strategy continued through the 1990s to paralyze Washington's potential to counter the terrorism emanating from Afghanistan and Pakistan: the Grand Delusion about Pakistan's motives in Afghanistan; the outsourcing of America's Afghan policy to Pakistan; disengaged neutrality toward the moderate and radical Afghan factions; and public declarations of lofty foreign policy goals in Afghanistan without a U.S. policy to achieve them. The restraints shackled America's ability to understand the threat emerging in Afghanistan and to mobilize its great power and influence to meet it. The foolish de facto acceptance of Pakistan's sphere of influence in Afghanistan in order to stabilize the region was counterproductive. Pakistan's army and ISI were destabilizing the region and increasingly endangering the security of the United States and its allies globally.

Al-Qaeda's August 1998 bombings of the two U.S. embassies in Kenya and Tanzania did not break American policy out of its self-imposed cage. The attacks stimulated only tactical responses when a basic restructuring of U.S. policy toward Afghanistan and Pakistan was desperately needed. American policymakers initiated a combined diplomatic–covert action campaign to apprehend bin Laden that considered Pakistan as part of the solution, when in reality it was part of the problem.

Washington's ineffectual response to bin Laden's August 7, 1998, embassy bombings in Africa led off with the August 20 launch of about seventy cruise missiles from an American warship in the Indian Ocean into bin Laden's al-Badr training complex near Khost. A 9/11 Commission report later indicated that Hamid Gul gave al-Qaeda advance warning about the impending strike before the missiles were fired.* About twenty-eight individuals, most of them low-level Pakistanis and Arabs, were killed in the attack. If bin Laden and members of his inner circle were at the target site, they were able to make their escape before the missiles exploded.[74]

American attempts to capture or kill bin Laden after the cruise missile launch were unsuccessful. Madeleine Albright, President Clinton's secretary

---

* The United States informed Pakistani officials about the strike shortly before the missiles were launched. A paragraph from the 9/11 Commission investigation about later plans for a missile strike that was cancelled suggested that Hamid Gul tipped off al-Qaeda and the Taliban before the August 20, 1998, cruise missile attack: "The U.S. government had information that the former Pakistani Interservices Intelligence Directorate (ISID) head Hamid Gul, as a private citizen, contacted Taliban leaders in July 1999 and advised them that the United States was not planning to attack Afghanistan. He assured them that, as he had 'last time,' he would provide three or four hours of warning should there be another missile launch." This passage illustrated the deep influence Hamid Gul exercised inside the Pakistani government and the ISI even after his retirement from the agency. Steven Strasser, ed., *The 9/11 Investigations: Staff Reports of the 9/11 Commission* (New York: PublicAffairs, 2004), 105.

of state in his second term, and her assistant secretary for the Asia Bureau, Karl Inderfurth, a former journalist and Democratic Party staffer in Congress, stepped up American pressure on the Taliban to hand over bin Laden and to end their outrageous treatment of women. The Taliban rebuffed the American demands. Inderfurth played a leading role in organizing several "Six-Plus-Two" meetings bringing together the United States, Pakistan, Russia, Iran, Uzbekistan, Tajikistan, representatives of the Taliban, and (after Kabul's fall) Masood. The meetings failed to make headway on a political settlement. Only the United States observed an arms embargo agreement signed by the six outside powers. The embargo was ignored by Pakistan, Iran, Russia, Uzbekistan, and Tajikistan. The United States persisted in breathing life into the moribund Six-Plus-Two talks into 2000, long after all the other parties, plus UN Secretary General Kofi Anan, were deriding them.

Albright and Inderfurth continued to espouse goals without enforcing a long-term, strategic, results-based policy to realize them. In July 2000, Inderfurth told a congressional hearing, "It is time Afghans were allowed to restore equilibrium in their political affairs and tranquility within their borders, without outside interference."[75] He highlighted U.S. encouragement of a political settlement, pointing to a nominal $100,000 State Department grant to Zahir Shah for an emergency loya jirga. The small amount of money, like U.S. declaratory support for UN special envoys, was incapable of advancing the Afghan peace process without strong U.S. pressure on Pakistan.

The National Security Council and the State Department worked with the British and other allies to orchestrate two UN Security Council resolutions in 1999 and 2000 sanctioning the Taliban for not expelling bin Laden. The UN resolutions were not, however, integrated into a broader strategic way ahead in Afghanistan, only another tactical reaction incapable of reversing the malevolent trends building in Afghanistan and Pakistan. They called on the Taliban to stop providing sanctuary to international terrorists, to close down terrorist camps, and to hand over bin Laden. The resolutions imposed an arms embargo on the Taliban, requested member states to "close all Taliban offices overseas, reduce the staff at the limited number of Taliban missions abroad, restrict travel of senior Taliban officials, and close all offices of Afghan Ariana Airlines."[76]

Pakistan's compliance with the UN Security Council resolutions was the single most important aspect of its implementation. The resolutions carried the force of international law and the will of the international community. But direct appeals by President Clinton, other world leaders, and the United Nations to Pakistani leaders for help in apprehending bin Laden proved fruitless. Prime Minister Sharif turned down President Clinton's request. In September 1999, Clinton's foreign policy team invited Pakistan's ISI chief, Lieutenant General Khwaja Ziauddin, and Prime Minister Sharif's brother to Washington. Senior administration officials asked that Islamabad pressure the Taliban to hand over bin Laden. General Ziauddin went through the motions of traveling to Kandahar, meeting with Omar, and conveying the American request. Ziauddin reported back that Omar had refused to comply. Clinton tried again with General Musharraf after Musharraf's October 1999 coup. Musharraf's fatuous advice was to forge a "diplomatic solution on bin Laden." After meeting with Mullah Omar personally, the Pakistani dictator informed Clinton that "Pakistan had only limited influence with the Taliban." On August 4, 2001, President George W. Bush wrote to President Musharraf to reiterate the American request for his help in apprehending bin Laden. The letter failed to elicit his cooperation.[77]

☰

The CIA's three-year (1998–2001) attempt to capture or kill bin Laden through covert action came up empty-handed. Most of the agency's operations were mounted from Pakistan. Some required the ISI's active cooperation, guaranteeing that they would not succeed. As a retired CIA officer belatedly acknowledged in a magazine article published not long before bin Laden's attack on the Twin Towers, "Where the Taliban and Usama bin Laden are concerned, Pakistan and the United States aren't allies." President Clinton met with Prime Minister Sharif and ISI chief Ziauddin in the White House in December 1998, four months after the U.S. cruise missile attack. Afterward, he told aides that Sharif and Ziauddin had agreed to the U.S. financing of a Pakistani commando team to go after bin Laden. The commando team was created and equipped but did not produce the desired results.[78]

In early 1999, the CIA established a bin Laden task force led by Afghan analyst Michael Scheuer. It worked with the CIA's Counterterrorism Center to track down and capture bin Laden. But the CIA's relationship with the ISI continued to frustrate the Islamabad station's ability to find bin Laden. The ISI intelligence network, in tandem with Taliban and bin Laden intelligence operations inside Afghanistan, was well equipped to monitor, penetrate, and disarm the CIA's covert operations.

The British colonial intelligence service in India had made long-term investments in money and personnel necessary to enable its agents to penetrate hostile territory inside Afghanistan. But during its two decades of heavy involvement in Afghanistan and Pakistan, the CIA never established a similar capability. In 2001, a former CIA officer acknowledged that "the DO never developed a team of Afghan experts." Most of the relatively small number of officers in Pakistan were not fluent in Afghan languages and rotated out of the country after two or three years.[79]

Scheuer's task force made at least four attempts to find bin Laden in 1999 and 2000. The Islamabad Station hired a group of Afghan tribals to track him in southern Afghanistan. Twice they reported his presence at locations in Kandahar Province that they recommended be struck by cruise missiles. One was the Tarnak Farm, a 100-acre compound near the Kandahar Airport where bin Laden's wives and children lived. The second was a desert hunting lodge west of Kandahar frequented by United Arab Emirates royals and wealthy Arab sheikhs who hunted the elusive bustard game bird in the desert.

CIA Director George Tenet and White House counterterrorism adviser Richard Clarke refused to authorize the cruise-missile launches, contending that the intelligence was too imprecise and fallible. Tenet later wrote that interagency deliberations "could never get over the critical hurdle of being able to corroborate bin Laden's whereabouts" to activate a second round of cruise missile attacks against him. Some in Washington worried that the tribals whom the CIA hired to corner bin Laden were unreliable. There was no independent CIA asset available inside Afghanistan to verify their reports. Other U.S. officials argued that many civilians could be killed in the missile strikes while bin Laden escaped unhurt. Such an outcome would hand a propaganda bonanza to al-Qaeda. In addition, past CIA targeting mistakes made the White House nervous. A CIA-advocated cruise missile strike on Saddam Hussein in the summer of 1998 had miscarried. Poor CIA map work later resulted in the bombing of the Chinese embassy in Belgrade, causing the deaths of two Chinese officials and considerable embarrassment to the

United States. Clarke agreed with Tenet's decision not to approve missile strikes against the Tarnak Farm and the UAE hunting camp, but CIA Afghan analyst Michael Scheuer did not. His outrage was expressed in a blizzard of emotional e-mails after the CIA and White House vetoed the strikes.[80]

In 1999, Cofer Black, the director of the CIA's Counterterrorism Center, sought a dialogue with the president of Uzbekistan, Islam Karimov, aimed at devising a plan to capture or kill bin Laden from bases in Uzbekistan. Unlike the Pakistani Army and the ISI, Karimov and Uzbek security agencies considered bin Laden an enemy. A bin Laden ally, the Islamic Movement of Uzbekistan, was attempting to overthrow Karimov.

Black concluded agreements with the Uzbek government to train an Uzbek commando team to snatch bin Laden. He arranged for the deployment of a Predator drone to an Uzbek airfield. Black proposed to locate bin Laden by analyzing video transmissions from the Predator. The drone could then be armed to kill the Saudi terrorist with missiles. Predators undertook several experimental flights over southern Afghanistan, including Tarnak Farm. In the end, however, State Department lawyers decided that authorizing armed predator flights from Uzbekistan would violate the 1987 U.S.-Soviet Intermediate Ballistic Missile Treaty. The Uzbek commando team was trained and armed, but never used.

By 2000 and the end of the Clinton administration, the CIA's efforts to capture or kill bin Laden by employing Afghan tribal mercenaries in Pakistan and flying drones from Uzbekistan had run their course. From bin Laden's return to Afghanistan in 1996 until September 2001, Ahmed Shah Masood had led the only real Afghan military force in the country capable of assisting in the hunt for the al-Qaeda leader. There were other sensible reasons to work with Masood to go after bin Laden. He was outside of the ISI's control. He was at war with both the Taliban and bin Laden. Though ISI disinformation during the war had branded him a Muslim Brother and a drug runner, he was neither. First and foremost, Masood was an Afghan nationalist.

In military ability and intelligence gathering, Masood had much to offer. A military genius, he had been the single most effective Afghan commander during the Soviet-Afghan war. His intelligence network extended to all regions of Afghanistan, including Taliban and bin Laden strongholds in southern Afghanistan. Masood's agents in Pakistan clandestinely informed him of Pakistan's plans for the ISI-organized Taliban offensive in northeastern Afghanistan. His political advisers, Dr. Abdullah Abdullah, Daoud Mir, and Mohammed Es Haq, periodically made the rounds in Congress and the executive branch. They knew many Americans and were well informed on regional and world trends.

Masood reached out in a personal "Letter to the People of the United States" in 1998. The letter, in the form of a press release, requested American assistance; reviewed Masood's struggles against the Soviets, Pakistanis, the Taliban, and al-Qaeda over the previous two decades; and discussed past mistakes. "Our shortcomings were as a result of political innocence, inexperience, vulnerability, victimization, bickering and inflated egos," Masood wrote.[81]

Masood's letter described Afghanistan as "entering a new stage of struggle and resistance for its survival as a free nation and independent state." It accused "governmental and non-governmental circles in Pakistan" of sending "28,000 Pakistani citizens" as well as military units to fight alongside the Taliban. Masood claimed to have captured more than 500 Pakistani POWs. "For the second time in one decade," he asserted, Afghanistan was "once again an occupied country." The letter appealed to "the international community and the democracies of the world" to help eliminate "the scourge of intolerance, violence and fanaticism," drug production, and "terrorist activities" plaguing Afghanistan. Masood's political adviser, Daoud Mir, told the French daily *Le Figaro* that "the U.S. should intervene in Afghanistan. . . . Quite simply, they have no choice."[82]

In early 2001, Masood again requested U.S. assistance in a letter to Vice President Dick Cheney, which received no response. In March 2001, just weeks after the Taliban's destruction of the ancient Buddhas in Bamian, Masood carried his message to France and the European Parliament at Strasbourg. In speeches, meetings, and press conferences, he portrayed the continuing Afghan conflict as "not a civil war but the result of external interference." He warned that "if President Bush doesn't help us, these terrorists will damage the U.S. and Europe very soon." "Despite General Musharraf's intent to continue the war against us," he said, "very soon you will witness popular uprisings in several fronts, and the Taliban will lose ground." Masood asked for aid but no foreign forces. "We have not asked for and we don't need foreign troops in Afghanistan to defend our land." He stated his commitment to "a moderate Islamic State," the right of women to vote and run for democratic office, and a loya jirga convened by Zahir Shah.[83]

The idea of enlisting Masood's help against the Taliban and al-Qaeda had been discussed off and on in Washington since 1998, but it had never been seriously pursued. Richard Clarke, among others, raised arguments for exercising the Masood option in the hunt for bin Laden. They could not, however, overcome the CIA's animus against the United Front commander. CIA officers who had cooperated with the ISI during the wars against the Soviets and Najib still bore grudges against Masood for disregarding ISI-CIA instructions even after receiving payments to follow them.[84] A retired CIA officer complained in the summer of 2001 that "no CIA case officer has yet debriefed [Masoods's] soldiers on the front lines or the Pakistani, Afghan, Chinese-Turkoman and Arab holy warriors they've captured."[85]

In March 2000, National Security Council counterterrorism specialist Richard Clarke urged his White House superiors and the CIA to expand their dialogue with Masood. The new deputy chief of the Near East Office in the CIA's Directorate of Operations, Gary Schroen, had traveled to northern Afghanistan to meet Masood in 1997. According to Masood's adviser Dr. Abdullah, Masood found Schroen's presentation to be too focused on bin Laden. Masood suggested a broader political dialogue on Afghanistan, one that the United States was not then willing to conduct. In 1999, Directorate of Operations Near East officers delivered communications equipment and some cash payments to Masood. Dr. Abdullah later described these "non-lethal" supplies as "a few pieces of communications equipment," of negligible value to Masood's United Front.[86]

Clarke kept pushing for U.S. cooperation with Masood after the Bush administration took office in January 2001, but he made little headway. Zalmay Khalilzad, Condoleezza Rice's specialist on Southwest Asian, Near East, and North African Affairs in the National Security Council, objected to Clarke's recommendation. Rice and her deputy, Stephen Hadley, supported Khalilzad's position that any U.S. assistance package should also contain a large outlay for Pashtun opponents of the Taliban. Schroen and CIA headquarters were skeptical that Masood would be a reliable ally in apprehending bin Laden. The CIA believed there was less than a 15 percent chance that Masood would cooperate with the United States against bin Laden.[87]

The State Department's vapid policy of U.S. neutrality toward all Afghan factions did not allow for political and military assistance to Masood. The State Department continued to favor working with Pakistan and the Taliban to go after bin Laden. Two memos from the State Department's South Asian Bureau to the under secretary for political affairs on June 28 and June 29, 2001, urged a less confrontational approach to the Taliban and was cautious about assisting Masood.[88]

For Masood, Washington's reluctance to engage demonstrated that the George W. Bush administration's Afghan policy did not differ from the Clinton administration's policy. Both still seemed to follow Pakistan's lead. In an interview a month before 9/11, Masood was asked if he had "seen any change in policy since the Bush Administration came in." Masood responded with laughter: "No! You say U.S. policy in Afghanistan? Actually, [the] USA does not have any Afghan policy so far." President Bush's deputy secretary of state, Richard Armitage, in his testimony to the 9/11 Commission in 2004, confirmed this impression. He explained: "While U.S. diplomats were becoming more active on Afghanistan through the spring and summer of 2001, it would be wrong for anyone to characterize this as a dramatic shift from the previous administration."[89]

Clarke's desire to enlist Masood's active cooperation against bin Laden collapsed under the pressure of White House, CIA, and State Department objections. In July 2001, however, intelligence alerts about a possible al-Qaeda attack on the United States refocused interagency consideration of an aggressive presidential directive to eliminate bin Laden. Military assistance to Masood was included in a list of options inserted into a three-phase action plan prepared for a September 10, 2001, meeting in the White House.[90] The first phase called for a special envoy from the United States to visit Taliban headquarters to deliver an ultimatum to turn over bin Laden. If the Taliban refused, a covert program was to be inaugurated to assist anti-Taliban Afghan forces, including Masood, to establish a battlefield stalemate. Continued Taliban intransigence would trigger phase three, the overthrow of the Taliban regime. The three-phase plan was never finalized or signed by the president. Al-Qaeda attacked the United States the next day. The strategy, in any case, was too little and a decade too late. It would have taken years to implement. At the very least, inevitable Pakistani opposition—both overt and covert— would have complicated, if not foiled, its execution.

⚜

Washington's misunderstanding of Pakistan's motives in Afghanistan and of the Afghan environment were staggering. This ignorance lay at the root of America's foreign policy failures in Afghanistan through the two Clinton administrations and during the Bush administration up to 9/11. The attempts by American presidents, diplomats, and intelligence officers to convince Pakistan and the Taliban to turn over bin Laden were naive and doomed from the start. Tethering Washington's Afghan policy to Pakistan was a mistake that reaped dire consequences. Even if the United States had captured bin Laden, it would not have eliminated the growing terrorist threat in Afghanistan; the rest of the unholy alliance's infrastructure would have continued to flourish.

The State Department's disengaged-neutrality[91] doctrine also weakened America's natural allies in the fight against Islamic terrorism—the Afghan moderates. Looking back after 9/11, Robin Raphel conceded that "we didn't want to choose for the Afghans. That was the view at the time, which[,] in retrospect, may have been incorrect. . . . We'd have been better off if we had chosen a side." Secretary of State Albright candidly told the 9/11 Commission: "We had to do something," but "in the end it didn't work."[92] Richard Clarke, who straddled the Clinton and George W. Bush administrations, cogently summed up his reasons for America's tragic miscalculations before 9/11: "What is clear is that there were failures in the organizations that we trusted to protect us, failures to get information to the right place at the right time, earlier failures to act boldly to reduce or eliminate the threat."[93]

CHAPTER 21

Between the Lions

The most acute threat to a stable, peaceful, and neutral Afghanistan will continue to come from Pakistan, even though nearly all of Afghanistan's other neighbors also support their own Afghan proxies. Just as the Soviets tried saving their communist asset in Kabul by invading Afghanistan, Islamabad has been funneling more troops and military resources to save its own asset, the Taliban. More than 10,000 Pakistanis (and one "brigade" of radical Muslims from Arab states) now fight alongside Taliban forces in what many Afghans describe as a "creeping" Pakistani invasion of Afghanistan. The ISI, the JUI, Arab extremists such as Osama bin Ladin, and the Taliban leadership all cooperate closely. The ISI has long orchestrated this Islamist coalition; its continuing support for the Taliban is the biggest obstacle to a political settlement in Afghanistan.

. . . American policy today is inadequate to deliver on U.S. interests in Afghanistan. U.S. foreign-policy makers must craft a more forceful, creative, and effective approach to address America's geostrategic concerns, the soaring Afghan opium trade, massive Taliban violations of human rights, and the return of the largest refugee population in the world. . . .

The chief danger to U.S. interests is the rising tide of Islamist militancy and international terrorism emanating from bases in Afghanistan. The Afghan springboard for Islamist militancy endangers other pro-Western governments in the Muslim world, including Saudi Arabia.
—AUTHOR, FOREIGN AFFAIRS, 2000[1]

❦

In early 1997, while serving as U.S. ambassador to the Republic of Armenia, I snatched time to write an informal Afghan strategy paper for the second Clinton administration. My State Department base was no longer the South Asian regional bureau that included Afghanistan. The country had been outside my realm of professional responsibility since the summer of 1992. But the State Department's characterization of the Taliban's capture of Kabul as a "positive" step[2] had troubled me. It demonstrated that Washington still suffered from the Grand Delusion about Pakistan's goals in Afghanistan and that there was no independent U.S. Afghan policy. The United States continued its counterproductive outsourcing to a supposed ally whose radical Islamic proxy war in Afghanistan violated U.S. goals in Afghanistan, the region, and globally. The reelection of Clinton to a second term in November 1996 meant that a new South Asian policymaking team at State would take over in early 1997. Perhaps it would be willing to look at some new policy options.

My paper, classified as secret, began with an alarm bell: "We have long underestimated the geo-political threat of Afghan instability to U.S. interests," I wrote. "Afghanistan is far from the U.S. The continuing conflict there, however, carries ripples of tension, Islamic extremism, narcotics trafficking and terrorism to adjoining regions and beyond. The U.S. and like-minded governments should more actively bolster internal Afghan political configurations favorable to peace, stability and Islamic moderation in Afghanistan."[3]

I warned that Pakistan had moved beyond support for Gulbuddin Hekmatyar and was now promoting the Taliban. I predicted that the Taliban would eventually fail, just as Najib and previous foreign-imposed political groups in Afghanistan had. I foresaw an Afghan backlash against Pakistan that would eventually create tensions and instability inside Pakistan itself. Leaving the field to the Pakistani and Arab groups supporting the Islamic extremists, I wrote, endangered U.S. national security.[4]

I recommended that the United States conduct a major Afghan policy review and implement a more resolute Afghan policy. We should be firm in insisting that Pakistan cease supporting the Afghan Islamic extremists. I stressed that UN settlement efforts would never succeed without more heavy lifting by the United States[5] and concluded that only a representative gathering of Afghans could bring stability to Afghanistan. A State Department colleague hand-delivered my paper back to the South Asia Bureau in Washington. I later dropped off a copy with the department's executive secretary, William Burns, to pass to Under Secretary of State for Political Affairs Thomas Pickering.

My unsolicited personal contribution to Afghan strategy could have been dropped in the middle of a dark forest for all the reaction it elicited. The only response was a letter from Assistant Secretary of State for South Asian Affairs Robin Raphel, who had stayed on in the South Asian Bureau until her successor, Karl Inderfurth, arrived. She rejected the warnings about the Taliban, writing, "For now the Taliban appear to us to be Afghan nationalists rather than radical Islamists with an international agenda."[6]

After my retirement in November 1998, Afghan moderates sought me out to obtain access to State Department and White House officials to plead their case. Abdul Haq, Hamid Karzai, and Dr. Abdullah Abdullah rarely got beyond the low-ranking Afghan desk officer. During one trip, using other contacts, Karzai managed to secure a meeting at the CIA. Over dinner at my home the night before, he expressed hope that the meeting might start a dialogue on Afghanistan. It did not. On another occasion, following the August 1998 bombings of Tanzania and Kenya carried out by al-Qaeda, Karzai landed an appointment with Michael Sheehan, head of the State Department's antiterrorism office. Sheehan was more attentive than other U.S. officials to Karzai's appeals for help to mobilize moderate Afghans against the Taliban. But he also was bound by the State Department's disengaged-neutrality doctrine toward the Afghan factions. The meeting ended up as nothing more than a courtesy call.

The George W. Bush administration continued the Clinton administration's practice of outsourcing U.S. Afghan policy to Pakistan. Only four months before 9/11, a delegation from former Afghan king Zahir Shah in Rome, led by his political and foreign policy adviser, Zalmay Rasoul, arrived in Washington.[7] Rasoul was seeking U.S. assistance for a loya jirga presided over by Zahir Shah. He hoped to brief the new assistant secretary for South Asia, Christina Rocca, about the Taliban's declining position in Afghanistan and the opportunities this offered. He had just returned from Moscow, where the Russian deputy foreign minister had received him.

Rasoul found it was a lot harder to obtain appointments in Washington than in Moscow. The delegation waited for a week before they were informed that the most senior-level appointment they could get was with Acting Assistant Secretary Alan Eastham. The delegation's scheduler in Washington, Afghan American Daoud Yaqub,[8] later wrote that "as the delegation arrived at the State Department and was ushered into Mr. Eastham's office, Mr. Eastham exhibited his 'enthusiasm' towards the group by leaning back in his chair, hands behind his head, legs crossed, and feet resting on his desk. 'So why are you guys here?' he asked. One from the delegation answered 'Oh, we're just here in Washington doing some shopping, we caught a play at the Kennedy Center, then we all decided we'd drop by for a visit with you.'"[9]

Two months before 9/11 and three months before the American military attacked the Taliban, National Security Council terrorism specialist Richard Clarke turned down an appointment request to meet Qayum Karzai, Hamid Karzai's older brother and Baltimore restaurateur. Clarke suggested that Karzai and his escort, Daoud Yaqub, call on Randy Beers, the head of the State Department's narcotics and law-enforcement office. After listening to Karzai's presentation, Beers said: "You're basically asking for the overthrow of the Taliban. . . . I'm not sure the government is prepared to do that."[10]

After retiring, my wife, Kim, and I moved to the friendly city of Omaha, Nebraska. For the next three and a half years I taught at the University of Nebraska, which housed the only Afghanistan study center in the United States. I wrote op-eds and magazine articles on Afghanistan, testified in Congress, and delivered speeches, always appealing for fundamental changes in U.S. policy toward Afghanistan, Pakistan, and the region.

An unexpected phone call from Commander Abdul Haq in May 2001 interrupted my tranquil retirement life. At the time, Kim and I were vacationing in Tuscany with our two daughters and their husbands. Haq told me that he was in Rome for meetings with Zahir Shah to discuss convening a loya jirga. He asked if he could stop by. I encouraged him to come whenever he could break away.

Haq made the four-hour drive from Rome to our rented villa in Panzano, Tuscany, on May 20. He came with his new wife, Homa, and American friends James and Kimberly Ritchie. I greeted Haq's party on their arrival. Haq's foot wound, dating from the Soviet war, impeded his ability to climb the steep steps to the villa. I attributed the considerable weight he had put

on since our last meeting in Washington in 1994 to the immobility his prosthetic foot imposed. He slowly limped up to the terrace, where we gathered
around a wooden table.

James Ritchie was a wealthy businessman. We had previously talked on
the phone but had never met. Tall and angular, he wore a cotton shirt, blue
jeans, and cowboy boots. He had a leathery, sunburned face, blue eyes, a short
sandy beard, and an honest, direct personality. Ritchie and his older brother,
Joseph, had spent four years of their childhood in Afghanistan. They developed a life-long attachment to the Afghan people during those formative
years. According to a *Washington Post* article, during Taliban rule the multimillionaire brothers had been shocked by "what they saw as America's con-
fused and disengaged policy in Afghanistan."[11] The Ritchies met and
befriended Abdul Haq, a leader they judged could steer Afghanistan out of
the throes of war.

At the villa, we talked through the afternoon, through dinner, and long
into the night. Haq pressed me to "get active" on Afghanistan. I said I was already active, writing articles, giving interviews, and speaking around the
United States. He glared at me. "That is not enough," he admonished. I answered that I was retired. He persisted. I asked him what he wanted me to do.
He explained that he was reviving the National Commanders' Shura, which,
with my encouragement, he had organized in the early 1990s. He said that it
was only through nationwide military pressure that the Taliban could be overthrown and Afghan independence restored. Masood was fighting back in the
northeast. But the Taliban were a Pashtun force. They could not be defeated
unless Pashtuns in eastern and southern Afghanistan rose against them.

Haq articulated a forward-looking political strategy to go forward with the
revival of the commanders' shura. He said that I could help by encouraging
Zahir Shah to become more active in organizing a loya jirga. The loya jirga
would parallel the commanders' shura and its military operations. It could
choose a new national Afghan leadership to rally the Afghan population and
the commanders' shura against the Taliban.

Haq, as always, was forceful, passionate, and persuasive. He had an un-
canny ability to look ahead, plan, and then actually execute the plans. He was
dynamic, proactive, and very intelligent. He had taught himself English, read
voraciously, and was always current on world events. He liked to quote from
the Declaration of Independence.

Haq was an Afghan patriot. Since age sixteen he had been fighting to re-store Afghan independence, first from the Soviet-imposed communists, and then from Pakistan. He was popular and respected by Afghans as one who would not knuckle under to foreigners. He knew the Afghan people, their weaknesses and strengths. He had great courage and pride, a rib-breaking sense of humor, persistence, and a leader's ability to motivate others.

Like anyone else, Haq also had his faults. Too often, his emotional outbursts undercut his effectiveness. Like all Afghans, he lacked recurring resources. He could not afford to alienate donors, even when he was right. But he did anyway. His Afghan pride, honor, and patriotism lit up a June 1989 letter Haq wrote to the *New York Times* after the Mujahidin defeat at Jalalabad.

> I am not begging you for any help. Jalalabad or some other area will not fall because of your analysts' expectations. We started our struggle with the full support and determination of our people and will con-tinue regardless of the wishes or commands of others.
>
> We don't want to be an American or Soviet puppet.... I would like you to be with us as a friend, not as somebody pulling the strings.[12]

Haq's public scolding of the CIA and the ISI for financing Hekmatyar and the other unpopular Afghan radicals reflected the views of a great majority of Afghans. It also cost him much-needed resources. The CIA cut him off; the ISI kept him at arm's length and eventually expelled him from Pakistan.

Haq's earnest conviction and his logic moved me. His framework for oust-ing the Taliban overlapped with the ideas I had expressed in my 1997 paper to the State Department. But I wished to know more before making a com-mitment. I suggested to Haq that he bring in Hamid Karzai and his older brother, Qayum Karzai.

Haq and Hamid Karzai were the two most influential Pashtun moderates in Afghanistan's Pashtun belt. They each came from prominent families that had played important roles in the country's late nineteenth-century and twentieth-century modernization reforms. Together, they represented the two wings of the country's dominant Pashtun confederation. Karzai was a Durrani from the south, Haq a Ghilzai from the east. Karzai's father headed the royal Popalzai tribe before his 1999 assassination in Quetta, and Karzai had succeeded his father as tribal chief. Haq was a Jabbar Khel, the *khan khel* (leading clan) of the prestigious Ahmadzai tribe. The Ahmadzai are one of the largest Ghilzai tribes. Ahmadzai tribal communities spread out on both sides of the strategic road from Kabul through Jalalabad to Torkham on the Pakistani border.

Hamid Karzai* fielded some important Popalzai commanders in Kandahar and Uruzgan, including Popalzai Jan Mohammad outside Tarinkot, Uruzgan's capital. Karzai and Jan Mohammad had captured Tarinkot in 1990. Karzai was, however, a tribal leader and politician, not a commander. Haq had won a reputation as a Pashtun commander defending Islam during the anti-Soviet jihad. He had switched to politics after receiving his battlefield injury, but his fame as a commander enlarged his political following outside his tribe and region. Karzai's web of informants was in the south. Haq's network of spies was much larger, reaching into the upper levels of the Taliban. Increasing numbers of Pashtun Taliban were secretly contacting him as Taliban popularity trended downward. In the late 1990s and 2000, Haq's home in Peshawar and the Karzai residence in Quetta became the main gathering sites for tribal elders, commanders, and moderate ulema dissatisfied with the Taliban. Daily, crowds of Afghans milled around their courtyards and on the streets outside, waiting for an audience. That is why the ISI had forced Haq out of Pakistan to Dubai and ordered Hamid Karzai to leave Pakistan.

Haq told me that he was already in touch with the Karzais. They were both part of Zahir Shah's "Rome Group" of Afghans planning a loya jirga to select a new Afghan leadership to stand against the Taliban regime. Karzai had visited Masood in 2000 to coordinate their anti-Taliban activities. Masood had suggested that Karzai establish a base in the mountains of southern Afghanistan modeled on his Panshiri redoubt. He offered to supply Karzai from areas under Northern Alliance control in the Hazarajat bordering Uruzgan Province.

---

* Karzai viewed the Taliban in a positive light when they first emerged. He praised their routing of the warlords tormenting southern Afghanistan. He told me that the Pakistanis had asked him to represent the Taliban at the United Nations after they captured Kabul in 1996. But by that time he had seen enough of Islamabad's links to the Taliban (a Pakistani Foreign Ministry official told him to pick up his airline ticket for New York in the ministry's administrative office) and bin Laden's domination of Mullah Omar. Author's July 20, 2000, conversation with Hamid Karzai, Washington, DC, following their testimony to the Senate Foreign Relations Committee that day.

Haq explained that he was communicating by radio with Masood in the northeast, with Ismael Khan in the west, and with Wahdat leaders Karim Khalili and Sayed Mustafa Kazimi in the Hazarajat. Masood and his Northern Alliance must be included in any nationwide political and military effort to oust the Taliban, he commented. Excluding Masood could cause the resumption of a north-south, Pashtun-non-Pashtun conflict after the Taliban were gone.

Haq had a penchant for making sudden, unpredictable statements. That evening, as we sat together at the kitchen table in the villa where my family and I were vacationing in Tuscany, he proposed that I go with him and Ritchie to meet with Masood. His invitation perplexed me. On the one hand, his desire to reach out to Masood was a good sign. The "Lion of Kabul" and the "Lion of Panshir" would make a formidable anti-Taliban team if they combined forces. Haq, Masood, and Karzai, Afghanistan's three leading moderates, could transcend the Pashtun-non-Pashtun, north-south divide. On the other hand, Haq had criticized Masood during our meetings in Peshawar and Washington in the 1990s. He still placed some of the blame for the collapse of the National Commanders' Shura on Masood. In April 1992, while Najib was collapsing, Masood had brushed off Haq's suggestion to organize an interethnic security force to protect Kabul and prevent looting. Haq's pride had suffered a big blow. I knew he had not forgotten that slight.

My doubts about Haq's long-term commitment to coalition-building could have applied to Masood and to Hamid Karzai as well. Afghan coalition-building, always complicated, involved alliances that were usually personal. They tended to quickly appear, disappear, and reappear based on calculations of personal benefit. Haq, Masood, and Karzai were, however, united in their determination to support traditional Afghan structures, get rid of the Taliban, and rebuild Afghanistan. They were pro-Western moderates and Afghan nationalists. But would they be able to bury their differences, escape Afghanistan's recent history of interethnic violence, and stick together into the post-Taliban phase of democracy they all supported? Or might one of them at some opportune moment attempt to monopolize power, occupy the tribal summit, and push the other two down?

I did not convey these qualms to Haq. Later that night, while our families laughed in the game room, I accepted his invitation to assist him with his peace initiative. American policy on Afghanistan was moribund. Bin Laden was getting stronger, not weaker. Abdul Haq had a plan to defeat the unholy alliance and drive bin Laden from Afghanistan. It was formulated by an Afghan, and it would be implemented by Afghans. It was the only approach that could succeed.

ψ

The sun was setting over the Nebraskan cornfields in early June 2001 as Joe Ritchie's sleek executive jet circled Omaha's Eppley Airfield. Joe was at the controls. Abdul Haq sat behind him in the comfortable four-seat passenger compartment. Only two weeks had passed since we had met in Tuscany. The plane banked toward the runway and cruised downward onto the tarmac for a perfect landing. I squeezed into the passenger compartment with Haq. Within a few minutes we were airborne again, climbing into the darkening sky, chasing the sunset west to Denver's airport for refueling.

It was pitch black outside when Joe Ritchie landed the aircraft on the lighted runway near the tiny mountain town of Meeker, Colorado, where the Ritchies owned a ranch. James Ritchie picked us up in a large SUV. We settled in at the Meeker Hotel, the largest building on Meeker's short Main Street. The Ritchies also owned the hotel, built as a hunting lodge in the nineteenth century. Hamid Karzai's older brother, Qayum Karzai, flew in from Baltimore to participate in the deliberations at the Meeker Hotel conference room. Since the elk hunting season was months away, we had the entire hotel to ourselves for two days of meetings on Abdul Haq's action plan.

The military track of Haq's proposal generally followed the National Commanders' Shura strategy formulated in 1990 at Shah Selim. Military activity by major commanders would be coordinated on a countrywide scale. Commanders would stay in touch with each other by radio and meetings inside Afghanistan—no commander would operate from either Pakistan or Iran. The commanders themselves would form a security regime for Kabul to prevent the recurrence of the chaos in the city that had broken out after Najib's fall.

The plan's political track projected Zahir Shah as the symbol of national unity. It gave him a ceremonial role, not formal authority. The king would preside over a fifteen-member Loya Jirga Council representing all Afghan groups. A Loya Jirga Office in Rome would work under the council to plan and organize the loya jirga, which would convene in Rome. It would choose an interim government to replace the Taliban and organize national elections.[13]

After the Meeker meetings, Haq flew to Rome to present his proposal to Zahir Shah and Abdul Wali. Their reaction was positive. He returned to Dubai and contacted Masood to arrange their meeting in Dushanbe, Tajikistan, near Masood's main base of Khwaja Bahauddin across the Amu Darya in Takhar Province. They decided on June 23–25. Haq phoned me to request that Ritchie, Qayum Karzai, and I come to Dubai on June 20.

On June 19, the day before our departure from Washington, Qayum Karzai withdrew from the trip. He claimed that a fire in one of his restaurants and a sick brother-in-law forced him to drop out. I wondered if the Karzai clan was concerned that Haq's plan was designed to promote his personal interests, not theirs.

That same day, Ritchie and I picked up our visas at the Uzbekistan and Tajikistan embassies in Washington. I phoned South Asia Assistant Secretary Christina Rocca to brief her on the visit. She wished us luck and asked that we take security precautions. I promised to brief her on the results of the trip when I returned to Washington. Since we would be traveling through Central Asia, I also phoned the State Department's acting assistant secretary of state for Russia and the Newly Independent States to inform him about the trip.

On Wednesday, June 20, 2001, Ritchie and I flew through London to Dubai. Abdul Haq and his constant companion and loyal assistant, Sayed Hamid Jaglan, met us at the airport. During the drive to Dubai's Hyatt Hotel, Haq asked me about the status of Washington's interagency policy review on Afghanistan. I responded with a smile that it was still under way. Haq knowingly nodded.

Haq checked us into the hotel. Over dinner, he sarcastically questioned whether Qayum Karzai's last-minute withdrawal was really due to overcooked steaks in his restaurant. At breakfast the next morning, he remonstrated that "Rome" (the collective formula for Zahir Shah and his family entourage) was "not capable of doing anything but wishes to do everything!" He told me that Abdul Wali's niece, Helena Malyikar, had awakened him with a phone call from Rome at 2:00 a.m. that morning. She confirmed that the king and his advisers had accepted Haq's idea to establish a Loya Jirga Office. But, she added, they had also decided that they alone would choose the members of the Loya Jirga Council. Haq saw this as another example of the king's relatives attempting to exploit Zahir Shah's image to take over Afghanistan.

When Ritchie and I tried to check out of the hotel after breakfast, Haq intercepted us at the cashier window. He was host, and the Afghan tradition of hospitality obliged him to pay for our stay. Throughout our wanderings in Central Asia and back to Dubai he paid for everything—transportation, lodging, and meals. During the flight to Tashkent, Haq explained his plans for our talks with Masood. In the process, he took the opportunity to unleash an aggressive critique of Masood's past. When he was alone with Masood, he informed, he intended to upbraid him for occupying Kabul on his own in 1992. He claimed that Masood had broken an agreement they had reached to create a broad-based, five-man committee of commanders to maintain stability in the capital after Najib's overthrow. Masood, he charged, must share the blame for the destruction and chaos that tore Kabul from 1992 to 1996.

I urged Haq not to criticize Masood when they met. I told him that his anti-Masood comments were discouraging. His desire for revenge jeopardized prospects for cooperation between Afghanistan's two most famous commanders. Their coordination would be vital to the success of his peace plan and essential to achieving Afghan stability after the Taliban were overthrown.

In Tashkent, we briefed the American ambassador and the Uzbekistan deputy foreign minister about our plans to meet with Masood. We left for Samarkand, the Uzbek city and Tamerlane's thirteenth-century capital, by car on the morning of June 22, arriving late at night. We were up again at 3:30 a.m. the next morning. The hotel staff passed out small cups of mud-like coffee as we stumbled to our vehicles parked outside. The 500-mile drive to Dushanbe was rough, dusty, and immensely scenic. We passed over three mountain ranges. For most of the trip we traversed the great Central Asian steppe of rolling hills, a treeless landscape of brown and green hues. On the road, Haq promised me that he would set aside his criticism of Masood during the meeting. National unity rose above everything else, he said.

The road condition deteriorated and truck traffic thickened as we approached the Tajikistan border. Large numbers of Uzbek women toiled in the fields. Only a few men could be seen in the distance working the land under the scorching sun. The Uzbek women wore long-sleeved, dark robes reaching down to their ankles. Tajik women could be singled out by their red robes, some faded, some very bright. A stretch of no-man's land separated the Uzbek and Tajik border-control shacks, which were located about 60 miles from Dushanbe. The customs and immigration officials on both sides of the border were still clothed in Soviet-era uniforms. Russian border guards mixed with their Tajik counterparts on the Tajikistan side.[14]

❀

Happily, one of Masood's military aides, not representatives from Rabbani's regime-in-exile, met us on the Tajikistan side of the border when we drove up at 3:00 in the afternoon on June 23, 2001. We learned later that Masood had not even informed Rabbani or Rabbani's ambassador in Dushanbe of our arrival. Late on June 24, the ambassador heard we were in town and asked for a meeting. It was too late to arrange one. Masood appeared to prefer it that way, and so did we. Masood's military assistant, a colonel, took us through Dushanbe's pleasant, tree-lined streets to a hotel. After we checked in, he drove us to Masood's home in a quiet residential area of the city.

The famed Tajik commander greeted us warmly, the familiar *pakool* hat perched on his head. He wore a freshly ironed, crisp tan uniform. It had been nine years since I had last met with Masood at the Defense Ministry in Kabul. Since then, he had been in a state of continuous warfare. His eyes still flashed with intelligence. The crevices in his face were longer and deeper, and broad streaks of white had infiltrated his hair and spade beard.

We sat in Masood's living room. As always, Masood listened patiently while others spoke, absorbing their points of view. His responses were methodical, structured, well-reasoned, and optimistic. Haq did not raise Masood's past mistakes,[15] but Masood did. He volunteered that he would issue a written pledge not to accept a position for himself in the government that replaced the Taliban.[16]

Masood briefed us on the situation in Afghanistan while Amrullah Saleh, his young secretary, interpreted.[17] He dwelled on the subjects he knew best: the planning and execution of military operations. He had flown to Dushanbe straight from the battlefield. For fifty uninterrupted minutes he described the order of battle along his front lines in northeastern Afghanistan and the defeat of a ten-day Taliban offensive, which had ended that morning. Masood stated that he had received detailed information on the Pakistani plans for the offensive from his agents in Pakistan five days before it began. His spies had reported the precise dates of movement of military supply and troop convoys before they crossed the border into Afghanistan. He offered to provide information to the United States and the United Nations on the names of specific Pakistani generals stationed inside Afghanistan, the names of Pakistani officers killed in combat, and the locations where they were buried. It was only Pakistani and Arab glue that kept the Taliban fastened together, Masood declared, his voice rising.

Masood continued that, despite the inflow of more and more Pakistani troops, Arabs, and Pakistani jihadi fighters into Afghanistan, the Taliban offensive that had just ended had been "easier" to repel than the 2000 offensive. He commented that Osama bin Laden's two Arab brigades were well trained and well equipped. Three hundred Islamic Movement of Uzbekistan jihadis were attached to bin Laden's al-Qaeda brigades.

Masood noted that in 1979 Afghanistan had been invaded from the north by the Soviet Union. Now it was being invaded from the south by Pakistan. He estimated the number of Pakistani Army and Pakistani jihadi combatants in Afghanistan at 25,000 and rising. According to Masood, much of Pakistan's 9th Division, plus a heavy artillery unit and special forces, participated in the June Takhar offensive. The Pakistanis, he said, like the Soviets before them, would not be able to keep up with the expanding resistance inside Afghanistan and would eventually be defeated. Masood thought that the influx of tens of thousands of Pakistanis and Arabs into Afghanistan had created an Afghan political backlash. The resistance was now in a better situation than in late 1991 and 1992 before Najib fell. The Taliban's standing in Pashtun as well as non-Pashtun areas was weakening. The Taliban's "playing of the religious card" had become less effective, and now, they were "playing the ethnic card," inciting Pashtuns against non-Pashtuns, he stated.

Abdul Haq spoke next. He presented his two-pronged strategy, featuring a representative loya jirga inaugurated by Zahir Shah and revival of the National Commanders' Shura. Masood complimented Haq's proposals. He offered his readiness for "compromise and flexibility."[18] He agreed with the need to create a national political alternative to the Taliban: "I admit to a vacuum. Our goal should be to fill the vacuum. It is clear that the king will fill this vacuum." Masood commented that he had recently sent Yunis Qanuni, his senior political adviser, to open a dialogue with Zahir Shah in Rome. Qanuni would return to Rome for more talks in two weeks. He expressed concern that Rome might conclude a deal with the Taliban that marginalized non-Pashtuns. He wanted Qanuni to clarify whether Zahir Shah might be tempted to lean toward that option. Masood hoped that Haq's assumption that Zahir Shah was committed to Afghan moderates turned out to be true.

Masood recommended that the interim government selected by the loya jirga reestablish an Afghan army and prepare a democratic constitution. Nationwide elections would follow. "As I see it," he said, "all favor a constitutionally based, democratic central government that will support social justice. . . . Political parties will contest elections and represent their communities at the center. All ethnic groups should have a place in the interim government."

Masood invited us to the dining-room table, piled high with steaming Afghan pilaf, mutton chops, fruit, and vegetables. He asked Haq to sit next to him. Ritchie and I sat facing them. Amrullah Saleh, the only one present dressed in a Western suit and tie, sat at one end of the table. During the dinner, Masood agreed with Haq's proposal to reestablish the National Commanders' Shura and hinted that the shura could be built around his United Front. He noted that his United Front was multiethnic and included important Pashtun commanders. Haq's brother, Haji Qadir, was one of them. More prominent Pashtuns in the east and south, he said, should join the anti-Taliban resistance to enlarge the resistance and to give it a national character.

Masood observed that the United Front's command center already coordinated military operations by commanders in different regions of the country. Turning to recent United Front successes, Masood mentioned that Haji Qadir had recently captured two districts, one in Nuristan and the other in Konar. Ismael Khan was besieging the capital of Ghor Province. The day before, he had repelled a Taliban attempt to reinforce the garrison there. Two other military shura members, Abdul Rashid Dostum in the north and Arif Nurzai in the southwest, were opening new fronts.

Masood suggested that any commander joining the military shura should have bases within Afghanistan. He agreed with Haq that no commander should be accepted if he proposed to operate from a foreign country. Masood was critical of commanders who accepted Arab fighters in their ranks. Afghanistan must not be "host to terrorists, extremists, and narcotics smuggling— no military shura member will be permitted to bring any foreigner, any Arab, onto the soil of Afghanistan."

During the dinner, I complimented the idea of pursuing simultaneous political and military progress, pointing out that it would require close coordination among Masood, Haq, the Karzais, and Rome. I bluntly cautioned

Masood and Haq that great skepticism, even cynicism, existed in Washington and Western governments about the ability of Afghan moderates to discard their differences and create an effective national alternative to the Taliban regime. I asked Masood and Abdul Haq to prove through their actions, not just words, that they were capable of genuine cooperation.

Ritchie recalled the destructive period of warlord battles to control Kabul from 1992 to 1996. He asked Masood if he could be sure that warlords would not begin another internal conflict by attacking each other after the Taliban were defeated. Masood answered, "We have learned our lesson—no military shura commander will create his own fiefdom."

At 11:00 p.m., Ritchie and I bid good night to Masood and returned to the hotel. The two famous commanders continued their discussion one-on-one. Haq arrived back at the hotel after 1:00 a.m., exuberant about his private exchange with Masood. He felt that the larger meeting in the evening had confirmed Masood's general support for the two-pronged action plan. In his conversation with Masood, he had concentrated on the need to prevent Rabbani and his Ikhwani advisers from once again undermining a broad-based settlement process. He asked Masood to support complete dismantlement of Rabbani's government-in-exile. This would allow the interim government chosen by the loya jirga to be recognized internationally as the legitimate government of Afghanistan. Haq said at that point he leaned toward Masood to inquire whether he would align with the Zahir Shah–led strategy or with Rabbani and Sayyaf, both members of the United Front leadership shura. Masood, he recounted, had answered "Zahir Shah," reaching out and shaking his hand. Haq agreed to work with Masood to extend Masood's military shura into Pashtun areas. He told Ritchie and me, "I will trust him fully."

Ritchie and I went back to Masood's residence the next morning at 8:30 a.m. for the final round of talks with Masood, which was to begin at 9:00. Amrullah Saleh greeted us. While waiting for Masood to arrive, I asked Saleh if his commander had gotten some sleep. "Oh no!" he responded, Masood never went to bed before 2:00 in the morning. They had stayed up talking with another aide until 5:00. At 9:00 sharp, Masood strode into his living room. He was dressed in a brilliant white shirt, vest, and camouflage trousers topping shiny black combat boots. General Sayeed Hussain Anwari, the well-known United Front Shia commander and United Front shura member, entered the room with Masood.

Masood reiterated his appeal for more active American attention to Afghanistan. "I hope the U.S. can help us achieve peace; this will help the U.S.," he said. I replied that I was now a private citizen. I could not speak for the American government, but I would convey his ideas to Washington. I suggested that he work closely with Abdul Haq, Hamid Karzai, and other moderates. Pashtuns in Taliban-controlled areas near Pakistan, I said, would be more likely to move against the Taliban if Zahir Shah was associated with their efforts. Masood repeated that Qanuni would soon be in Rome, adding, "We are optimistic that we will reach a good resolution."[19]

۷

After arriving back at the American embassy in Tashkent several days later, I prepared three classified telegrams reporting the details of what had transpired during the meetings with Masood. The messages were transmitted to all national security agencies in Washington, fifteen American diplomatic posts abroad, including Islamabad and Riyadh, and the American UN mission in New York. The CIA was tagged to receive all three messages.

I placed a policy recommendation at the end of the first cable. It seemed to me that, despite the many obstacles the Haq-Masood plan would face, it had a better chance of driving al-Qaeda and the Taliban from Afghanistan than any other strategy I had seen. Cruise missile strikes could not destroy the Taliban or al-Qaeda; neither could CIA payments to Afghan tribal mercenaries, or constant pleas to the Taliban and Pakistan to turn over Osama bin Laden. Strengthening the majority Afghan moderates was the only policy option with a chance of success. I wrote:

> Aside from Masood's progress in building coordination among several
> important commanders, at this point there is not yet tangible evidence
> that he, Abdul Haq and other anti-Taliban Afghans can construct a na-
> tionwide alternative to rally support against the Taliban and, in a tran-
> sition period, avoid the conflict among regional commanders which
> occurred in 1992–1996. Haq and Masood plan to increase consulta-
> tions with other anti-Taliban and Afghan leaders in the weeks ahead.
> The U.S. should encourage this process. While a long shot, the success
> of moderate Afghans in replacing the Taliban regime in Kabul would

be the most effective way to address the terrorist, radical Islamist, and narcotics problems menacing the world from Afghan territory.[20]

Back in Dubai, Haq told Ritchie and me that he would be tied up with commanders' meetings in Dubai. He gave us the dubious privilege of stopping in Rome to brief Zahir Shah about Masood's approval of his strategy. Haq explained that opening the Loya Jirga Office in Rome would be the king's first concrete step toward a loya jirga since the Soviet invasion. Rome had now made a commitment to open the office; if the king temporized, Haq said, the office would be moved to either Dubai or inside Afghanistan, close to the commanders.

Zahir Shah's inactivity during the Afghan war had long discouraged Afghan moderates. Turbulent family quarrels within Zahir Shah's royal household on how the king should use his influence in a peace process continued to dissipate his potential to unite Afghans. Abdul Haq, Ahmed Shah Masood, and Hamid Karzai needed the king's support against the Taliban and al-Qaeda. They had no choice but to engage him. He remained the symbol of the traditional, moderate Hanafi mainstream of Afghan politics. That was why Pakistan's generals, the Taliban, Hekmatyar, and Sayyaf all opposed him.

In Rome, I phoned Abdul Wali and scheduled a two-hour session with Zahir Shah for that evening. To minimize disruptions from other royal family members, I requested that only Zahir Shah and Wali meet with Ritchie and me, "two on two." Wali said that would be difficult. His daughter Homeira and the king's grandson Mustafa were already scheduled to attend. I objected. Wali later phoned back with a compromise: Homeira and Mustafa would sit in for ten minutes at the beginning, after which I could request the more restricted session.

At 6:30 that evening, the eighty-six-year-old former monarch walked into the living room of his Rome residence. Wali, Homeira, Mustafa, and Ritchie and I stood up. The king gave us a warm welcome. Compared to our last meeting in 1992, he looked tired. He was less alert, and he walked slightly bent over. At the same time, for a man of his age, he seemed in reasonably good health.

After Homeira and Mustafa left the room, the king invited me to begin. I commented to him that I spoke as a private American citizen and did not represent the U.S. government. I recounted Masood's positive reaction to the idea of the king having a titular role in a political settlement process ending in a loya jirga and elections. Masood was willing to dissolve the Rabbani regime and accept the Afghan interim government established by the loya jirga. I expressed my personal hope that the Qanuni negotiations in Rome would succeed; suggested that a representative of Masood's Northern Alliance be invited to participate in the Loya Jirga Office in Rome that would organize the loya jirga; and urged the king to act expeditiously to open the office. The window of opportunity for an Afghan political settlement had already opened and closed twice since the Soviet invasion. It was opening again as the Taliban declined. Afghans desiring peace in Afghanistan had to act now. The king would be an important catalyst to secure a political settlement. The office could immediately begin the planning and organizational activities necessary for a successful loya jirga.

I frankly stated that many Afghans and foreigners had been disappointed by the king's inactivity while the war in Afghanistan raged on. His resolute action now would break this pattern of talk and no action. I asked that the king select a professional Afghan staff to manage the office and that it be outside of the control of some in his family. Concluding, I asked Zahir Shah to finally unleash his energy and work to his full capacity to make the loya jirga happen. Zahir Shah thanked me for being candid. He assured me he would be taking the necessary action to open the Loya Jirga Office.

As I left Zahir Shah's villa I suffered a flashback in my mind to 1992 when the king retreated from UN Special Envoy Benon Sevan's peace initiative before Najib's regime collapsed. Would things be different this time around? Unlikely, I thought. Abdul Haq and Masood were wise to take into account his capability to unite Afghans, but not to count on it.

The next day, Ritchie and I met with Abdul Wali to discuss the staffing of the Loya Jirga Office. We were joined by Zalmay Rasoul fresh off the plane from Washington via Moscow. Wali asked for our patience, commenting with a smile that Afghans occasionally act like children who need help; sometimes, he said, you need to scold children. Wali then announced that the Loya Jirga Office was approved. Ritchie offered to make $100,000 available. He suggested that the office be placed in a rented apartment outside Rome where the staff could work and live.

I reiterated my suggestion that Wali consider inviting Masood to nominate one representative to work in the office. Wali and Rasoul's silence signaled, accurately it turned out, that they disagreed with my recommendation. The following month, former USAID employee Ziauddin (Zia) Mojadedi, Daoud Yaqub, and a veteran of humanitarian work during the Soviet war, Yusef Nuristani, arrived in Rome to staff the office. All three were Afghan Americans. Wali appointed Rasoul to head the office. A few weeks later, the Italian government donated $47,000 to the office. Qayum Karzai later pledged another $50,000.[21]

I called on Assistant Secretary for South Asia Christina Rocca in her State Department office in early July to brief her on the results of the Masood–Zahir Shah trip. I suggested that American assistance to Afghan moderates be included in the Afghan policy review weaving its way through Washington's bureaucracy. Rocca did not respond. She ended the conversation after fifteen minutes, saying her next appointment was waiting.

While I was leaving Rocca's office, a harassed-looking bureaucrat darted through the door toward her desk. My assumption that he was from the CIA was confirmed when he announced to Rocca, "We still don't want anything to do with Abdul Haq." Having spent her own career in the CIA, Rocca no doubt knew the background of his demand. Abdul Haq was obviously still in the agency's doghouse, side by side with Masood and Hamid Karzai.

Back in Omaha, I made a final attempt to harvest something from the trip to Dushanbe and Rome. I wrote a letter to Rocca repeating my recommendation for Washington to adopt an effective Afghan policy:

> The United States no longer has the luxury to ignore Afghanistan. Indeed, in the Balkans-to-India arc of crisis, an Afghanistan settlement is perhaps the only area where the Bush administration can score a foreign policy triumph, including on bin Laden. To be frank, it is unfortunate that we still lack a comprehensive foreign policy on Afghanistan, with a clear set of policy goals and implementary tracks to achieve them. I hope you and others in the Bush administration can launch and direct such a policy. Also, hopefully, the fresh policy will not, unrealistically, depend on Pakistan voluntarily changing its approach.

> That just will not happen, and was one of the hang-ups that paralyzed
> the Afghan policy of the two Clinton administrations.[22]

The letter drew no response. I knew officials at higher levels in the State Department and the National Security Council and considered going to them. I concluded, however, that the three cables I had sent from Tashkent had been distributed to their desks as well. Meetings and letters were not going to take American Afghan policy out of the blind alley it was in. I continued to speak out and write op-eds, but I gave up trying to convince Bush administration officials that its Afghan policy was not working.

After 9/11, a lengthy *Time* magazine "Special Report," entitled "The Secret History: They Had a Plan," looked back at our effort to stir the State Department into action after the Abdul Haq–Masood meeting in Dushanbe. The article stated, "Only once did something happen that might have given Massoud hope that the U.S. would help. In late June, he was joined in Dushanbe, Tajikistan, by Abdul Haq, a leading Pashtun, based in Dubai, who was opposed to the Taliban." It noted that James Ritchie and I accompanied Haq, stating that my attempts to brief the State Department after returning to Washington drew only a "muted" response. "The American position was clear," it concluded. "If anything was to be done to change the realities in Afghanistan, it would have to be done not by the U.S. but by Pakistan. Massoud was on his own."[23]

⚘

The two Tunisian human bombs had much in common with the 9/11 hijackers. American and European investigators later concluded that they had been sent by Osama bin Laden to kill Masood. In 2002, the then-Taliban intelligence chief, Mullah Abdul Jamad Khaksar, informed an interviewer that bin Laden personally ordered the Tunisians to assassinate Masood. They dressed in casual Western clothes, blue jeans, and T-shirts, blending in with the five Western journalists waiting for an interview with Masood at his main base, the United Front guest house in Khwaja Bahauddin. They both spoke fluent French; one spoke passable English. They claimed to be Moroccan emigrants living in Belgium. They carried Belgian passports. The older one, thirty-four, was short and pudgy. He wore glasses. He told the others at the guest house that he was a reporter preparing a documentary on Afghanistan. The younger one, twenty-nine, was tall. He posed as a video cameraman.[24]

The al-Qaeda plot to kill Masood took the same multiyear, meticulous planning that went into the 9/11 attacks. Investigators in Europe subsequently discovered that al-Qaeda chose the older Tunisian, Dahmane Abd al-Sattar, to pose as the TV reporter requesting an interview with Masood because of his journalism background. He had studied journalism at the University of Tunis before traveling on a Belgium student visa to Brussels in 1989 to enroll in a Belgian university course on communications. Al-Sattar joined an al-Qaeda-linked Tunisian terror cell, the Tunisian Islamic Fighting Group, in Brussels. He and the younger suicide bomber, Burawi El Wahir, were sent to bin Laden's military training complex at Darunta, north of Jalalabad. After returning to Europe, Adel Taberski, a Tunisian al-Qaeda operative specializing in preparing fraudulent travel documents for recruits performing al-Qaeda missions, provided them with fake passports and airline tickets. One of the passports had been stolen from the Belgian consulate in Strasbourg, France, in August 1999, the other from the Belgian embassy in The Hague that same year.

The pair went to London in early July 2001. They picked up a letter of introduction and phony press credentials from an Arabic news service at the Islamic Observation Center, an al-Qaeda front headed by Yasser al-Siri, an Egyptian associated with Ayman al-Zawahiri. The center called itself a "worldwide organization concerned about human rights issues for Muslims around the world." The Pakistani embassy in London granted the two Tunisians one-year multiple-entry visas.[25]

The Tunisians flew to Islamabad from London on July 25, 2001. They remained there for several days, then entered Afghanistan by car through the Khyber Pass. They traveled for three weeks in Taliban-controlled areas and spent time in Kabul. It was probably there, in an al-Qaeda laboratory, that the booby-trap bomb was inserted into the video camera carried by the younger Tunisian. The older assassin, the "journalist," was fitted with a large battery belt, and explosives were placed in the batteries.

Masood's assassination was clearly timed to precede the attack on the Twin Towers. Bin Laden—and surely others in the inner circles of the unholy alliance—must have foreseen the possibility of an American military

580 THE WARS OF AFGHANISTAN

reaction against al-Qaeda inside Afghanistan. It would probably go beyond repetition of the Clinton administration's ineffective 1998 cruise missile strikes. Killing Masood before the 9/11 strike would impair and might altogether deny Washington the ability to secure a base inside Afghanistan from which to launch ground attacks against al-Qaeda and Taliban-controlled areas of Afghanistan. Pakistan, Iran, and China would not permit their territory to be used for this purpose. Russia would object to an American buildup of ground forces in Central Asia.

The Tunisian suicide bombers were therefore on an important mission to preserve Osama bin Laden's beachhead in Afghanistan. Their success would provide tactical and strategic benefits—tactical in terms of removing the last roadblock to the unholy alliance's total conquest of Afghanistan, strategic in terms of preventing the American army from securing a foothold inside Afghanistan.

The two Tunisians received Taliban and United Front permission to cross through the front lines and enter Masood's areas to film their documentary. Likely on instructions from al-Qaeda, they first proceeded to the Panshir, ostensibly to film a meeting of the United Front's executive committee scheduled for August 30. Masood, Rabbani, Sayyaf, and other members of the leadership council were there.[26] The assassins tried to take a group photo, telling Masood's press attaché, Azam Suhail, that it would portray the council's unity to the outside world. When their requests were rejected, they asked permission to film Masood and Rabbani together. That request was also turned down. The executive committee members were too busy to give interviews.

The Tunisians asked for and were given permission to move on to Masood's main base at Khwaja Bahauddin near the Amu Darya, where Masood was to go after the meetings in the Panshir. On arrival, they were provided accommodations in the guest house, located near Masood's headquarters. The five other journalists at the guest house were also hoping to interview Masood. One of two French reporters thought the two Arabs were acting strangely. The younger Arab protectively clasped his camera to his chest as he walked around, but, day after day, he never took pictures. When the French reporter tried to photograph him, he turned his face. "I wondered if they were who they said they were," she later commented. "They said their journey would be in vain if they didn't get to speak to Masood."[27]

Masood was in Dushanbe with his family on September 6 and 7, supervising the transportation of a fresh shipment of Russian arms into Afghanistan. The battle lines in the northeast were quiet. The increasing tempo of United Front military activity along the fronts held by Abdul Rashid Dostum, Ismael Khan, and Haji Qadir was diverting Taliban military units away from territory that Masood controlled in northeastern Afghanistan.

Masood decided to summon his close friend, Ambassador Masood Khalili, from New Delhi, India, to Dushanbe to discuss an upcoming UN General Assembly debate on Afghanistan. Khalili was the envoy to India for the Northern Alliance's government-in-exile. His father, Khalilullah Khalili, had been a renowned poet in Afghanistan before the war. Masood Khalili had inherited his father's fondness for Persian writers in the Sufi tradition. He began each day by reading passages written by the great Sufi poets.

Masood Khalili was proud that the famous thirteenth-century Sufi philosopher-mystic Jalaluddin Rumi was an Afghan.[28] Rumi, his poetry, and Sufism were all banned by the Taliban. Afghans considered this a repudiation of Afghanistan's cultural legacy, similar to the Taliban's destruction of the Bamian Buddhas. While the Taliban's Vice and Virtue squads forced Muslims to obey their narrow, militant version of imported Sharia, Sufis, in contrast, stressed tolerance and the individual's direct relationship with God. That path led to success in the "greater jihad," achieving peace and serenity within oneself.

Khalili arrived at Masood's house in Dushanbe on September 7, 2001.[29] The two men talked into the night about political issues and Masood's military plans. Masood invited his friend to travel with him on September 8 to Khwaja Bahauddin in his helicopter. The next day he would be tied up in meetings with his military commanders, but Masood hoped that they would be able to steal away in the evening to read some poetry. He had just received a recently published book written by the great fourteenth-century Persian poet Hafez from Tehran.[30]

Masood and Khalili flew to Khwaja Bahauddin on September 8. The Northern Alliance leader conferred with his commanders and advisers until 9:30 that night. Meanwhile, two of the Western journalists waiting for an interview with Masood left for the Panshir, hoping Masood would go there next. Bin Laden's assassins patiently stayed on at the guest house, waiting for an opportunity to trap their prey.

At around 10:00 p.m., Masood and Khalili went to a secluded spot an hour's walk from the fabled Amu Darya. A mild night wind blew from the direction of the river. The two talked politics until 2:00 a.m., when Masood handed Khalili his new Hafez book, suggesting they switch to poetry. In Afghanistan and Iran, it is customary for Hafez devotees to flip through the pages of his poetry. They randomly choose a page of his poems expecting it to hold a message about the readers' future. Masood asked Khalili to select the poems they would discuss.

The two debated at length the meaning of each poem Khalili chanced on. As the night wore on, Khalili became disturbed. An unusual number of the passages effused notions of imminent death. One selection stood out:

> Last night before the dawn, they released me from sorrow.
> And in that darkness of the night, they gave me the water of eternal light.

> Last night I saw that the angels knocked at the door of the tavern.
> They mingled the clay of Adam and placed it in the weighing scale.

Khalili quickly turned over a few more pages, stopped and read:

> Plant the sapling of love to reach the fruit aimed at the heart
> Extract the sapling of hate that causes infinite suffering.

Masood liked the poem. He urged Khalili to read on:

> Appreciate the company in the night because after our days,
> The celestial sphere will make infinite circuits
> And many days and nights will come.

> You must value this night sitting and talking
> Because in the days to come this night will not be repeated.

Masood asked Khalili his opinion of these lines. Khalili gave them an auspicious interpretation: "We both will sit again remembering this night." "No," Masood disagreed, "one of us will sit remembering this night.... Who knows what will happen tomorrow?" Then he repeated aloud this last sentence. The discussion heated up. Khalili argued back. "This night cannot be repeated. Look, the Amu Darya is near. So much that is different has happened on its banks through history." At 3:15 a.m. Masood suggested they end the poetry reading. He asked Khalili to stay in Khwaja Bahauddin for a second reading after lunch later in the day.

Before breakfast, Khalili opened another poetry book to conduct his customary morning poetry reading to himself. It was a biography of Sufi saints and poets who lived over nine hundred years ago and contained some of their poems. Khalili intended to use selections from the book for the second poetry reading with Masood in the afternoon. The first poem he came upon discussed the search for a missing man:

> *The one on the camel litter is in another caravan.*
> *I asked, may I see him from a distance*
> *He said: don't ask me, because*
> *The rein of that caravan is not in my hands anymore.*

Khalili was shocked. He had stumbled on another bad omen. When Masood came for him at 9:00 a.m. he was pondering how he could remove "the evil eye" hovering above the famous commander. Masood informed Khalili that he had to give an interview to two Arabs who had waited to see him for many days. It would not take more than five minutes, he promised. Looking down, he noticed Khalili's leather-bound passport on the table. "Your passport is beautiful," he told Khalili. Masood picked it up. "Here, put it in your pocket," he cheerfully remarked, stuffing it in Khalili's jacket pocket.

The interview took place in a midsized room inside Masood's guest house. Masood's young press attaché, Suhail, arranged the furniture. Masood and Khalili sat on a small couch in front of a coffee table, Khalili on Masood's right. The short, English-speaking Tunisian sat on a chair next to Masood. Suhail sat on Khalili's right. The tall, younger Tunisian with the video camera occupied a chair in front of the coffee table. A young Afghan cameraman, Dashtee, was also in the room, filming the interview.

Masood began by apologizing to the two Arabs for their long wait. Khalili translated. Masood asked the Arabs to state their questions and tell him what was happening "on the side of the Taliban." The older Tunisian curtly answered that the "other side" proclaimed that Masood was a bad Muslim.

The Arab's rudeness startled the Afghans. There was a moment of silence. Khalili broke the silence, requesting that the journalist identify his media organization. The Tunisian snapped back that he was from an Islamic organization with offices in Paris, London, and all over the world.

Masood again asked that they provide all of their questions at once. Khalili noted irritation in the commander's voice. After Khalili's translation, the Arabs presented fifteen questions. Many of them displayed loyalty to bin Laden. "Why don't you consider bin Laden the leader?" "Why did you call him a murderer during your trip to Europe?" they asked. Visibly upset, Masood told the Arabs to set up their camera and begin recording the interview.

The cameraman roughly removed the table in front of the couch. He placed his video camera on a tripod only three feet in front of Masood, level with his face. Khalili remembered that the cameraman emitted a strange laugh and had a poisonous smile on his lips as he turned away. Instead of operating the camera, he stood back from it by several feet. The Tunisian journalist, who was armed with the suicide belt, sitting within a few feet of Masood, asked Masood for his opinion on the situation in Afghanistan.

At that point, before Khalili could translate the question, the al-Qaeda assassins detonated their bombs. Khalili remembered a sheet of blue flame racing toward his face before he lost consciousness. The explosions tore the room apart. The Tunisian journalist was blown to pieces. Suhail died instantly. The Tunisian cameraman stumbled out of the room. He was immediately gunned down outside. Masood was mortally wounded. Khalili, miraculously, lived. Dashtee was wounded but later recovered.

Masood and Khalili were hastily placed in Masood's helicopter. It lifted off immediately and headed toward a hospital in Dushanbe. Masood died of his wounds on the way. The date was September 9, 2001—two days before 9/11.

Khalili survived but lost his right eye and hearing in his right ear in the blast. Doctors in Germany removed hundreds of pieces of shrapnel from his body. His wife Sahaila found eight pieces of shrapnel lodged in his passport, which Masood had placed in the vest pocket of Khalili's jacket, over his heart. The thick leather cover and the first five pages were in tatters.

ψ

Qayum Karzai and I heard the news of Ahmed Shah Masood's assassination while we were in Rome. I felt shock, sadness, and anger all at once. Masood was unique, one of the most remarkable of the many leaders I had met during my thirty-two-year career in the State Department. The Soviets and Pakistanis had tried many times to assassinate him. Osama bin Laden's cunning exceeded theirs—his deceit and wickedness had no bounds.

On September 11, I was returning to Washington on a United Airlines flight out of London. The pilot solemnly announced over the intercom that two airplanes had plowed into the Twin Towers in Manhattan. All airplanes in U.S. airspace had been grounded. Flights from Europe less than halfway to the United States were returning to Europe. Since my flight was more than halfway, it was diverted to Newfoundland, Canada.

A visitor met ISI Colonel Sultan Imam at the Pakistani consulate in Herat when news of the 9/11 attack broke. The visitor expressed horror. Imam retorted, "It's good." The visitor objected. Imam rejoined, "They deserved it."[31]

Five weeks later, on October 7, 2001, the United States attacked the Taliban and al-Qaeda in Afghanistan. On October 26, 2001, Abdul Haq was shot dead near Kabul by the Taliban's interior minister, Abdul Razak.

Within four months of my Dushanbe meeting with Ahmed Shah Masood and Abdul Haq, both had been killed, one at the hands of al-Qaeda, the other by the Taliban.

CHAPTER 22

Yankee Meets Tribesman

If they are bombed, they will close ranks. . . . Don't forget the majority of the population has no access to news from outside. . . . People don't know what the war against terrorism is about. All they know is that when the bombs fall, the Taliban will say, "The Americans are trying to kill us, we must fight." They will fight. Despite everything the Taliban has done to destroy human rights, to destroy care of people's health, education, their livelihoods, they will fight. Afghans will always unite in the face of what they see as a foreign enemy and this will help strengthen the Taliban.
—ABDUL HAQ, OCTOBER 2001[1]

I knew this was an important issue, but since I've been here the last two and a half months, this civilian casualty issue is much more important than I even realized. It is literally how we lose the war or in many ways how we win it.
—GENERAL STANLEY A. McCHRYSTAL,
SEPTEMBER 2009[2]

Osama bin Laden's 9/11 attacks struck Americans like a thunderbolt. The Bush administration counterattacked, launching Operation Enduring Freedom. In record speed, Defense Secretary Donald Rumsfeld and four-star general Tommy Franks, commander of U.S. Central Command (CentCom) forces, put together a wartime coalition of countries to back the war effort. Britain and other close allies sent troops. Over thirty countries provided logistical, financial, diplomatic, and political support. Pakistan, the United Arab Emirates, and Central Asian states allowed access to their air space and gave basing rights.

American military operations commenced on October 7, 2001. Within only seventy-five days, with fewer than 10,000 American and coalition troops on the ground,[3] U.S. Air Force, U.S. naval aircraft, and tens of thousands of anti-Taliban Afghan ground forces defeated 35,000 Taliban and their al-Qaeda allies. Afghanistan's northern capital, Mazar-i-Sharif, fell on November 10, Bamian the next day. Unholy alliance concentrations in the north broke and ran, pursued by northern Tajik and Uzbek militia groups. Afghans in predominantly Pashtun eastern and southern Afghanistan rose against the Taliban. The U.S.-led coalition chased thousands of Taliban, al-Qaeda, and Pakistani fighters down to Kabul and onward into Pakistan. On November 14, Northern Alliance forces and American Special Forces advisers entered Afghanistan's capital. Ismael Khan captured Herat the same day. Haji Qadir claimed Jalalabad on November 19, and Hamid Karzai occupied Kandahar on December 7. Hailing an American victory over terrorism, Vice President Dick Cheney announced, "The Taliban is out of business, permanently."[4]

The Bush administration had achieved a military victory in Afghanistan but was in the middle of a long-term policy failure. As headlines declared Operation Enduring Freedom's dramatic military successes, the United States was stumbling ahead without an understanding of the Afghan tribal environment or an effective long-term policy to stabilize Afghanistan. The Grand Delusion about Pakistan's intentions in Afghanistan persisted. The Taliban and al-Qaeda had been driven from Afghanistan but were back in their protected Pakistani sanctuaries, their leadership still mainly intact. They had lost thousands of fighters but would suffer no shortage of new recruits in Pakistan. Corrupt, unpopular warlords on the U.S. payroll controlled most of the country. The ISI and its unholy alliance allies prepared their counterattacks across the Durand Line. In two years time, they would fight their way back into Afghanistan. The Afghan wars would continue.

Prior to 9/11, the Clinton and Bush administrations concentrated on the narrow objective of eliminating Osama bin Laden; after 9/11 that principal objective was widened to include the Taliban. But al-Qaeda and the Taliban were parts of the ISI's unholy alliance. Even if the U.S. military had been able to trap and destroy bin Laden, al-Qaeda, and the Taliban inside Afghanistan, the Islamist infrastructure in Pakistan would have continued to churn out more Mullah Omars and many thousands of new Afghan Taliban, Pakistani, and foreign jihadi fanatics. Now bin Laden and Omar were in Pakistan. The Pakistani Frontier would shortly become the platform for Pakistan's fourth consecutive Afghan proxy war in Afghanistan,* this one against the Karzai government and the U.S.-led coalition attempting to stabilize and reconstruct the country.

America could only succeed in Afghanistan by convincing Pakistan to dismantle the unholy alliance network and allow Afghans to find their own path to stabilizing their country. Pakistani President Perez Musharraf, however, was not a reliable partner. He and his corps commanders, the de facto board of directors of the Pakistani state, still adhered to Zia ul-Haq's vision in Afghanistan. The touchstones of their policies were the opposite of destroying al-Qaeda and the Taliban. They sought to harness radical Islamic fervor to gain strategic depth against India, liberate Kashmir, and fan the flames of religious holy war in the South Asian region and elsewhere in the world. Inside Afghanistan, the United States should have supported its natural allies, moderate-nationalist Afghans and traditional tribal structures at the village level where most Afghans lived. These Afghans were in the majority. They were implacable enemies of Osama bin Laden, al-Qaeda, the Taliban, and the religious totalitarian state they sought to impose on Afghanistan. They opposed self-seeking warlords. They were thankful for the American intervention. They knew that they needed American help and they wanted it. But they were not willing to surrender their independence to any outside power, including the United States.

ψ

When President Bush and his advisers gathered at Camp David, the presidential retreat in Maryland, to chart America's post-9/11 attack on the Taliban, the advantages of exploiting the moderate-nationalist and traditional

---

* The first Pakistani proxy war against an Afghan regime was in 1975 (Chapter 5 and 10). The second lasted from 1978 to 1988. The third Pakistani proxy war in Afghanistan extended from 1988 to 9/11.

tribal mainstream in Afghanistan did not enter the discussion. Most of the participants were men of military or intelligence backgrounds with little or no knowledge of the Afghan context and the country's tribal society. They did not comment on a long-term post-conflict policy vision for Afghanistan or the region. They stressed direct employment of American military power and CIA covert action.

The Camp David discussion focused on a military and CIA campaign to defeat bin Laden and his Taliban protectors. Secretary of State Colin Powell, a retired four-star general, said, "In the first instance, it's about al-Qaeda and UBL [Osama bin Laden]" and targeting their camps and infrastructure. Bush approved CIA Director Tenet's request for a CIA buildup of case officers, paramilitary forces, and drones in Afghanistan. The deliberations considered the Northern Alliance and other anti-Taliban Afghans to be auxiliaries to help implement the American battle plan.[5] Their role would be to support American military operations against the Taliban and al-Qaeda. U.S. military and CIA teams would provide cash, weapons, and advisers to attack specific targets chosen by the Americans paying them. They were one part of an American-created military offensive, designed also to enlist Pakistan's support and cooperation.

The Camp David meeting set the pattern for the Bush administration's ill-fated engagement with Afghanistan over the next seven and a half years. With the best of intentions, the approach undermined America's ability to succeed in Afghanistan. When Bush relinquished office in January 2009, nearly all indicators of progress in Afghanistan—military, political, and economic—were trending downward. His administration had pumped billions into Afghanistan. Yet, bin Laden and al-Qaeda remained active in Afghan-Pakistani border areas. The Taliban were spreading their wings from their sanctuaries in Pakistan into the Pashtun belt and every other region of the country. U.S. and Afghan security forces stood by helplessly as suicide bombings terrorized Kabul. Afghanistan's share of global opium production rose from 75 percent (3,400 tons) in 2002 to 93 percent (7,700 tons) in 2008, the Bush administration's last full year in office.[6] The Karzai government was dysfunctional, corrupt, and completely dependent on foreign troops and resources to survive. Autonomous warlords were denying security and justice in many areas of Afghanistan and Taliban shadow governments were expanding their presence in the countryside. They vowed to remove the warlords as they had done in the 1990s, defeat the foreign occupiers, and reestablish rule by God's law, Sharia.

ψ

President Ronald Reagan did not have faith in Soviet treaty commitments, spoken or written. He insisted on "trust but verify" guidelines to monitor Soviet compliance. The Bush administration should have applied Reagan's precept to President Musharraf's phony commitments to cooperate with the United States against al-Qaeda and the Taliban after 9/11.

Musharraf had been ruling Pakistan for two years when the 9/11 attacks brought America back to the region. He was a master practitioner of Machiavellianism, whether dealing with foreign governments or Pakistani political parties. Musharraf assured Western leaders that he was a loyal ally in the war on terror. He said he intended to return Pakistan to the democratic path. He praised Ataturk, the general who founded the modern, secular, democratic Turkish state. He kept a photo of Jinnah, Pakistan's thoroughly secular founding father, on his office wall.

After 9/11, when Bush demanded that governments choose one or the other side in the war on terror, Musharraf had no choice but to sign up. Refusing to join Washington would have pushed the United States and its allies closer to India. Musharraf renounced Pakistani support for the Taliban, asking, "Why should we put our national interest on the line for a primitive regime that would be defeated?" CentCom Commander Tommy Franks advised, "I can't see conducting operations inside Afghanistan without basing, staging and overflight support from the Paks."[7] Musharraf selectively agreed to American requests to overfly Pakistan and granted the American military use of some remote airfields in Baluchistan and Sindh. He permitted American trucks to transport fuel and other key commodities through Pakistani territory into Afghanistan. Thousands of al-Qaeda operatives were fleeing to Pakistan during and after Operation Enduring Freedom. Pakistani security forces detained and handed over to American custody more than two hundred mostly lower-level Arab militants crossing the border.[8]

Musharraf drove a hard bargain. In return, the Bush administration agreed to lift three sets of sanctions imposed on Pakistan: the 1990 cutoff in American military and economic aid when Pakistan clandestinely achieved nuclear weapons capability; U.S. economic sanctions levied on India and Pakistan after their 1998 nuclear tests; and sanctions applied when Musharraf's coup in 1999 ended rule by elected government in Pakistan. Bush acquiesced to Musharraf's request to encourage World Bank and International Monetary Fund assistance and debt relief for Pakistan. The administration prepared a huge military and economic assistance package for Pakistan, one that would exceed the Reagan administration's levels.

President Bush, the Pentagon, American military commanders, and the CIA were at the controls of Operation Enduring Freedom. They were pleased with Musharraf's steps to support combat operations inside Afghanistan. Still suffering from the Grand Delusion, CIA Director George Tenet complimented Musharraf for acting "heroically" after 9/11. "Pakistan had done a complete about face and become one of our most valuable allies in the war on terrorism," Tenet wrote. "On October 8, as a final measure of his determination to aid America in rooting out al-Qaida, Musharraf replaced Mahmood Ahmed as head of the ISI. . . . I've always considered Musharraf's reversal to be the most important post-9/11 strategic development after the takedown of the Afghan sanctuary itself."[9]

Musharraf's commitments to help stabilize Afghanistan and join Bush's war on terror were insincere. He and the military collective ruling Pakistan considered the Taliban's survival vital to their proxy war strategy in Afghanistan and Kashmir and to maintaining the military's control of the Pakistani state. Musharraf preserved the three-decade-old ISI-managed holy war infrastructure on the Frontier. The Taliban leadership returned to their old sanctuaries in Pakistan. Bin Laden crossed into Pakistan with his wives, children, and long lines of armed al-Qaeda fighters and disappeared from view. Musharraf and the ISI practiced plausible denial concerning bin Laden's whereabouts. They knew exactly where he was.

Low-level al-Qaeda members were expendable. High-value al-Qaeda leaders like Osama bin Laden and Zawahiri were not: Musharraf considered them bargaining chips held back to attract continued U.S. assistance to Pakistan.[10] Harboring the world's two most notorious terrorists fortified the cooperation of the Pakistani religious right and the other parts of the unholy alliance in Pakistan. By revealing their locations or handing them over to the Americans,

Musharraf risked losing some of his usefulness to Bush in America's war on terror. Ironically, protecting America's most sought-after enemy was an important hook to keep American military and economic assistance flowing and to enhance Pakistan's value to Washington.

Musharraf made a show of placing the Taliban's Pakistani religious allies under house arrest during Operation Enduring Freedom. Jamiat-i Ulema-i Islam (JUI) leader Fazlur Rahman was detained and released the same day. Maulana Masood Azhar of Jaish-i Mohammad (Army of Mohammad) and Mohammad Saeed of Lashkar-i Taiba (Army of the Pure) were freed after several weeks. They resumed working closely with the ISI to reconstitute the Taliban leadership in Quetta. When Lashkar-i Taiba and Jaish-i Mohammad attacked the Indian Parliament in New Delhi in December 2001, Musharraf rearrested Azhar and Saeed, but he released them in the spring of 2002. In 2001 after the September 11 attacks, the State Department designated Saeed's Lashkar-i Taiba and Azhar's Jaish-i Mohammad Foreign Terrorist Organizations (FTOs). Musharraf banned both groups but they continued to operate openly in Pakistan. Under international pressure, Musharraf promised to register the Pakistani madrassas churning out young Islamic zealots perpetrating terrorist acts in Afghanistan, India, and around the world, but he never did. Four years after aligning himself with the United States in the antiterrorism fight, only a few hundred of the country's more than 10,000 madrassas had registered with government authorities.[11]

Musharraf and the ISI's initiation of Pakistan's fourth proxy war in Afghanistan following the retreat of the Taliban and al-Qaeda into Pakistan did not seem to be noticed by American diplomatic and intelligence agencies. The strategy mirrored the ISI's 1992–1996 Taliban campaign to overthrow the Rabbani-Masood regime in Kabul. From about early 2002 into 2003, the ISI organized three fronts to conduct offensive operations into Afghanistan from protected sanctuaries in Pakistan. The new Taliban "Quetta Shura" began launching attacks into southern Afghanistan in early 2003. Taliban leaders and commanders moved openly in the Quetta-Chaman corridor organizing cross-border operations. On several occasions, Western journalists interviewed Taliban commanders at the four-star Serena Hotel in Quetta. Taliban press spokesman

Abdul Latif Hakimi gave press conferences boasting about Taliban victories in Afghanistan, the downing of American helicopters, and assassinations of Afghan government officials in Kabul and the provinces.[12]

Gulbuddin Hekmatyar returned from Iranian exile in early 2002 to lead the eastern wing of Pakistan's new proxy war in Afghanistan. Before leaving Tehran, he declared holy war against the United States.[13] The U.S. Treasury Department put him on its "Specially Designated Global Terrorist" list.[14] When asked at the time if Hekmatyar would return to Pakistan, the Pakistani Foreign Ministry spokesman coyly answered, "I don't think there are any such plans."[15]

By mid-2002, the Pakistani and international media were reporting Hekmatyar's standard anti-U.S. ravings from inside Pakistan. From Peshawar and the Bajaur tribal agency, he repeated his call for holy war against the United States from Pakistan, accusing America of "genocide" against Pashtuns.[16] By 2005, his radio broadcasts from inside Pakistan were taking credit for bombings, ambushes, and assassinations in Konar, Nuristan, Baglan, and Kunduz provinces in Afghanistan.

The ISI's central front for the new proxy war inside Afghanistan was North and South Waziristan. Pakistani Waziri and Mahsud tribesmen allied to Arab, Uzbek, Chechen, and other foreign fighters who had fled the American bombing campaign in Afghanistan re-crossed the border to attack coalition forces and Afghan military and police outposts and assassinate Afghan government officials. A "Waziristan Islamic Emirate" declared holy war on the Afghan government and the U.S.-led coalition across the Durand Line. Old ISI warhorse Jalaluddin Haqqani and his son, Saudi-educated Sirajuddin Haqqani, operated from the Miram Shah area of the central front. Khalis' son and the al-Qaeda representative in Nangarhar Province, Anwar al-Haq Mujahid, based himself in the Khurram tribal agency. Their networks carried out attacks in Paktiya, Khost, and Nangarhar provinces. They also specialized in suicide bombings in Kabul.

There were many signs that the ISI, the Taliban, Hekmatyar, al-Haq Mujahid, and al-Qaeda had started a fresh insurgency in Afghanistan from Pakistan after Operation Enduring Freedom overthrew the Taliban regime. Open-source media coverage of the Taliban's Quetta Shura and its cross-border operations was heavy and continuous in the U.S. and international media. Hekmatyar's return to Pakistan and his bellicose anti-U.S. proclamations were also widely covered. Haqqani and al-Haq Mujahid publicized their murderous activities, especially assassinations of Afghan government officials and raids on coalition bases in Afghanistan.

These developments did not appear to stimulate doubts in Washington about Pakistan's dependability in the war on terror and on stabilizing Afghanistan. The administration should have applied pressure on Pakistan in late 2001 and early 2002 to cease its new proxy war in Afghanistan. The fresh outflow of American military and economic aid to Musharraf's regime should have been conditioned on Musharraf taking action to close down the Taliban sanctuaries; suppress the Quetta Shura; arrest Hekmatyar, Haqqani, and al-Haq Mujahid; and apprehend bin Laden. The Bush administration missed these early opportunities to shut down Pakistan's buildup to its fourth Afghan proxy war. By letting them pass unchallenged, at a stroke Washington reduced the odds for its success in Afghanistan from over 70 to well under 50 percent. And it severely damaged prospects for major breakthroughs in its war against terror, including tracking down bin Laden and Zawahiri.

The most remarkable aspect of Musharraf's hoodwinking of the United States was not that he did it—it was that the U.S. government so easily acquiesced to his duplicity. Bush's personal trust in Musharraf's word must have stayed his hand. The apparent absence of intelligence reporting on Pakistan's clandestine reorganization of the three fronts on the Frontier (roughly analogous to the three fronts the ISI operated during the 1990s against the Masood-Rabbani regime in Kabul) may have contributed to the unjustified American optimism on progress in Pakistan and Afghanistan after the Taliban and al-Qaeda retreat to Pakistan. In a 2004 interview with CBS news correspondent Lesley Stahl, Deputy National Security Adviser Stephen Hadley announced: "Saudi Arabia and Pakistan are now allies in the war on terror." Hadley's unjustified claims of success were repeated by other American officials. NATO Commander General James Jones concluded in 2004 that "both al-Qaeda and the Taliban have been decisively beaten."[17]

ψ

The American-planned and -led military campaign in northern Afghanistan in October and the first half of November 2001 broke the back of the Taliban. U.S. Special Forces, CIA case officers, paramilitary teams, and air force tactical air operators performed superbly in coordinating the bombing of Taliban front lines and fortifications. Policymakers in Washington did not, however, mount a political strategy on the ground to match the impressive military success of Operation Enduring Freedom. In fact, there was no comprehensive political strategy, only a political vacuum. As a result, the United States fell back to what it had done in the late 1980s and the 1990s. The CIA reentered the Afghan political cauldron, joined by U.S. military officers, in dispensing mountains of cash to favored Afghans. In Pakistan, the distributions were often done in coordination with the ISI. Inside Afghanistan the Americans were usually on their own in deciding who merited their payments.

The CIA's old "cash to play by our rules" tactic was back. A U.S. Special Forces officer recalled that he "had been told by higher command that for this war, the spooks were 'tourists and cashiers' there to observe and dole out cash." In his 2002 book *Bush at War*, Bob Woodward wrote, "The CIA calculated that they had spent only $70 million in direct cash outlays on the ground in Afghanistan."[18] More millions were passed out to Afghan commanders and warlords operating from Pakistan.

CIA Director Tenet later emphasized in his memoirs that the CIA was "a policy implementer, not a policy maker."[19] But, as was the case with the agency's championing of Hekmatyar against State Department opposition following the 1989 Soviet withdrawal, CIA cashiers after 9/11 were making policy by deciding which Afghans America would back and which Afghans America would not back. As the respected Pakistani expert on Afghanistan Ahmed Rashid said, "the policy was not something abstract now. The policy was who got the guns and who got the money. And whoever got the guns and the money was going to be in the strongest position."[20]

Defense Secretary Rumsfeld protested at an October 16, 2001, National Security Council meeting that the Pentagon was being forced to follow the CIA's lead in Afghanistan. "This is the CIA's strategy," he objected. "They developed the strategy. We're just executing the strategy." Tenet's deputy, John McLaughlin, rebutted the accusation. Rumsfeld persisted, saying, "You guys are in charge. You guys have the contacts."[21] Rumsfeld was correct. But once U.S. military units were on the ground in Afghanistan, they, too, handed out bags, sometimes jeeps, full of cash to Afghan warlords able to persuade them that they would fight the Taliban and help the new Afghan central government unite the country.

Many, if not most, of the CIA and U.S. military stipends went to the warlords who had been responsible for the 1992–1996 civil war and anarchy in Afghanistan after Najib fell. Popular revulsion against them had fueled the Taliban's rise to power. The warlords were more hated by the general Afghan population than the Taliban. They exploited their U.S. payments to reclaim their personal fiefdoms. Most had little education. Some were non-literate or, like Gul Agha Sherzai and Abdul Rashid Dostum, barely literate. They were not interested in Afghanistan's future, only their own.

Gary Schroen, deputy chief of the Near East Division in the CIA's Directorate of Operations, arrived back in the Panshir in September 26, 2001, in the wake of 9/11 and the assassination of Masood. This time he brought a black suitcase bulging with $4.9 million in cash.[22] The Northern Alliance[23] at the time was the strongest Afghan front opposing the Taliban in Afghanistan. Tajiks were in the majority, but Masood had included all ethnicities within its framework. The new Northern Alliance chief, General Mohammad Fahim, along with Dr. Abdullah Abdullah, and Engineer Sarwari Arif,* the alliance's intelligence chief, asked Schroen to respect the alliance's unity and not provide aid separately to its commanders and political leaders.

Schroen refused. He told Fahim, Arif, and Abdullah that it was U.S. policy to pay individual commanders affiliated with the Northern Alliance but not work through the Northern Alliance structure. By doing so, he and other CIA teams and U.S. military commanders were effectively placing the Northern Alliance under American command. Schroen donated a cardboard box filled with $1.7 million to Fahim, Abdullah, and Arif; promised

---

* After Masood's assassination, a select group of Tajik Panshiris met to choose his successor. Dr. Abdullah Abdullah, from Bazarak in the valley's center, was a candidate. So were Qanuni and his cousin Bismullah Khan, a commander from the lower portion of the Panshir around Rokha—the site of the only high school in the valley. The meeting selected Commander Mohammad Fahim, a veteran commander from the valley's conservative north who had long fought with Masood. Fahim did not possess Masood's charisma, intellectual power, or military brilliance, but he had been a loyal and successful military leader since the Soviet invasion. Bismullah Khan was also a leading candidate. He was more educated than Fahim, but he was forward-deployed on the Shomali facing Taliban-occupied Bagram. He needed to be there, not back at the United Front headquarters at Kwaja Bahauddin or in the Panshir.

$250,000 to Northern Alliance Tajik general Atta Mohammad; and gave a $100,000 bundle to Abdul Rasoul Sayyaf. The U.S. military inaugurated a monthly $5 million payment to Fahim.[24] The direct American payments to individual Northern Alliance commanders in other parts of Afghanistan enfeebled the only indigenous, multiethnic Afghan-created military force in the country. In the media, the Northern Alliance continued to be called by that name, but its Tajik, Uzbek, Hazara, and Pashtun commanders now separately answered to American money and orders.

Masood had resisted CIA and ISI dictation in the past, creating tensions with the agency. He would certainly have rebuffed Schroen's conditions, insisting on a cooperative relationship between two equal partners fighting a common enemy. Masood would have also expressed opposition to the deployment of large numbers of American troops to Afghanistan.[25]

ψ

Abdul Haq was Cassandra-like, a simultaneously brilliant and tragic figure. He possessed a remarkable aptitude to predict the future while constantly lacking the resources to successfully shape it. In the decade leading up to 9/11, he warned me, many other American and Western officials, and the Western media about the dangers that the Taliban and al-Qaeda posed to the world. He bristled with action plans to stamp out Islamic extremism in Afghanistan. Haq was the type of anti-Taliban, anti-al-Qaeda moderate-nationalist the United States should have encouraged. And yet, he did not receive any of the funds that the CIA liberally handed out to warlords, commanders, and politicians on the Pakistani Frontier in the weeks after 9/11.

Immediately after 9/11, ISI officials told one of Abdul Haq's brothers to send word to Haq in Dubai that he must not come back to Pakistan. Nonetheless, Haq returned to his house in Peshawar. James Ritchie joined him there. Once more, hundreds of Afghan tribal chiefs and commanders besieged his compound every day. A UN official reported "caravans" of well-wishers crossing the border from Afghanistan to see Haq.[26]

Haq's slim hopes for CIA money to fight the Taliban and al-Qaeda faded. His revulsion against foreign control did not. A "senior U.S. official" said that Haq turned down a secure satellite phone offered by the CIA.[27] He explained that he had already obtained over fifty satellite phones in Dubai and distributed them to his followers inside Afghanistan. An ISI visitor asked Haq not to identify himself with his agency. Haq told him that he need not worry. The ISI had earned a shameful reputation among Afghans.

Television cameras and reporters waited outside of Haq's home hoping to record some of the pungent sound bites for which he was famous. Haq obliged, promoting his two-pronged peace plan. He announced that his strategy envisioned a popular uprising in Afghanistan assisted by large-scale Taliban defections, estimating that "one-third of 40,000 Taliban fighters are disaffected." If Afghans united behind Zahir Shah and the commanders from all Afghan groups coordinated with each other, Afghans—by themselves, without foreign forces—could overthrow the Taliban, he said. In numerous interviews, Haq appealed for the United States to see the overthrow of the Taliban as "a struggle in which the Afghans took the leading role."[28]

I phoned Haq at his home in Peshawar on October 18 to inquire if he was receiving any support from the United States. "Not a dime," he answered. Haq stated that he was in touch with many Afghans inside the country about implementing his plan. "It's still the only way," he told me. I could tell by his voice that Haq was disappointed by the CIA's refusal to assist him. He looked up to the United States. He believed Afghanistan could not regain its independence without American assistance. Though Afghans needed to do the fighting and dying to free Afghanistan, American power was vital because it could help to balance Pakistani and Iranian attempts to interfere. After the Taliban's defeat, American assistance would be crucial to reconstructing the traditional, democratic Afghan state that had existed before the 1978–2001 wars in Afghanistan.

From Peshawar, Haq warned that the introduction of American ground forces would be a mistake. "It's easy to invade Afghanistan, but it will be difficult to get out," he said. "The problem in each foreign invasion with interference like that [sic] has a very long consequence behind it. It will take several years to fix it back."[29] Haq stated that the civilian casualties incurred by the American bombing were fomenting anger against Americans:

> Whatever they do, just go into Afghanistan, bomb them there and kill them. Why they don't [sic] take a different approach. I think just by firing a few rockets and bombing a few places in Afghanistan, it will not stop any terrorist activity in this country. And it will make people upset and angry, especially if some civilians get hurt and civilians get

killed, their houses destroyed. They will all go support the Taliban, although their system is going down, in that way, they will increase that
support and some kind of popularity for Taliban.[30]

♨

Frustrated and without outside support, Haq decided to enter Afghanistan
and start his anti-Taliban uprising without U.S. assistance.[31] His base would
be the Arsala family's ancestral village in Nangarhar's Hisarak District, near
the Logar-Nangarhar border, a three-day walk into Afghanistan from the
Afghan-Pakistani border. He knew the dangers were great, not only from the
Taliban but also from the ISI. The Pakistani spy agency had long opposed
him. It was riddled with pro-Taliban and pro-al-Qaeda elements. He assumed
ISI agents were among the Afghans calling on him in Peshawar and that his
conversations would be passed on to the Taliban.

Haq was confident that his Jabbar Khel clan would protect him if he could
get to Hisarak. The Taliban district chief in Hisarak had secretly offered his
support. Once there, Haq believed he could mobilize anti-Taliban tribal fighters and activate his network of sympathizers inside the Taliban regime.

Abdul Haq slipped across the border into Afghanistan on October 21. Because of his prosthetic foot, he rode a horse. With him were twenty-two supporters. The group included Mohammad Qasim Arsala, a brother, and
Izatullah Arsala, Haq's nephew and a son of Haji Deen Mohammad. Izatullah
was a budding poet. The faithful Sayed Hamid Jaglan, who had accompanied
Haq on his June 2001 trip to meet Masood, was at his side. So were Commander Shapur, who guided Haq's horse, and Commander Shah Wali Naseri.
The party carried only a few AK-47s and a pistol. The horse walked slowly.
The three-day trip stretched into four days. They encountered villagers along
the way who expressed outrage at the American bombing. On the third day,
near Azra in western Logar Province, Haq heard that about 350 Taliban soldiers were coming from Jalalabad to cut him off before he reached Hisarak.
When the Taliban began to close in, Haq's group was still several hours away
from Hisarak.

Haq realized that he had been betrayed. His situation was hopeless. It was
too late for him to go back. His prosthetic foot ruled out a race to safety. He
and his small party were stuck in hilly terrain, and the Taliban would soon
be upon them. Hamid Jaglan used a satellite phone to call Haq's office in Pe-

shawar to request assistance. The office contacted James Ritchie, also in Peshawar, who in turn asked the CIA for helicopters. There were two fields nearby where they could land. The CIA refused.[32] Ritchie then phoned Robert McFarlane, who had been national security adviser in the Reagan administration, in Washington. McFarlane called the CIA Operations Center. In response, the agency sent a predator drone, which fired a missile at a convoy of Taliban in the distance.[33] But the predator arrived too late to help.

Haq ordered his companions to disperse and trek back to Pakistan. They wouldn't leave him. Haq shouted that they must go immediately. Most began to run toward a nearby mountain ridge in the direction of Pakistan, but Haq's relatives, plus Shapur, Naseri, and Hamid Jaglan, still refused to leave. Jaglan insisted he was in charge of Haq's security.

Around this time, a U.S. Special Forces A team led by Captain Jason Amerine standing by at an American base in Karshi-Khanabad, Uzbekistan, was ordered to prepare to enter Afghanistan to assist Haq.[34] Amerine and his men crowded around a table inside their tent, poring over biographic information and other documents about Abdul Haq and maps of eastern Afghanistan. They gathered their weapons, ammunition, and communications gear in preparation for their helicopter flight into Afghanistan.

Back in the hills of Logar Province, the Taliban came into view, first a few, then dozens. They captured Haq and his companions and took them to the Taliban district governor's compound in Azra. At the moment the governor emerged from his office, one of his guards struck Haq on the head with his rocket launcher. Haq fell unconscious to the ground. The governor berated the Taliban guard for injuring a famous Mujahidin. When Haq recovered consciousness, the governor invited him into the passenger seat of his pickup truck for the drive to Kabul. They set off on the road to the Afghan capital.

As the pickup approached the outskirts of the capital, a black SUV raced toward it, blinking its lights. It was signaling for the pickup to stop. Mullah Abdul Razak, the much-feared Taliban minister of interior, climbed out of the SUV. "He cannot go to Kabul," Razak announced. "He must be executed." The Azra district governor stepped back. Hamid Jaglan appealed for Haq's life. Haq silenced him: "Don't beg from these people," he said. "Live your life with honor."[35]

The group returned to their vehicles. The pickup followed the Taliban interior minister's SUV as it turned off the road onto a dirt track. After a few minutes they stopped in a deserted area. After Haq got out of the pickup truck, Razak ordered his arms tied. Haq loudly declared, "This is the will of Allah, and I accept it."[36] Razak told him to stop talking and walk forward. He raised an AK-47, pointing it at Haq's back. The Taliban guards raised their weapons. After Haq had taken about fifteen paces, Razak yelled to him to stop and turn around. As he did, Razak fired, striking him in the forehead. The other guards riddled his downed body with bullets, blowing off the top of Haq's head. Razak then ordered the Taliban gunmen to execute Hamid Jaglan. After gunning down Jaglan, they allowed Shapur and Naseri to walk away.

Back at the U.S. Special Forces forward operating base in Uzbekistan, a sergeant poked his head inside the tent where Captain Amerine and his A team were still studying their maps. "Bad news," he said. "Abdul Haq is dead."[37]

The date was October 26, 2001. Haq was forty-four years old. A few days later, a delegation of elders from Jalalabad came to the Interior Ministry in Kabul to request permission to retrieve Haq's body. They were given a letter allowing them to pass through Taliban checkpoints. After picking up the body, the elders placed a small pile of rocks and a simple green flag where Haq had fallen.[38]

Abdul Haq's American and Afghan supporters let loose a torrent of criticism of the CIA and the ISI in the wake of his execution by the Taliban. Over the years, journalists and other Americans who knew Haq, and his Afghan followers, who worshipped him, had spoken out about the agency's treatment of Haq. They resented that Afghan moderates like Haq, in his case one celebrated in the West for his resistance to the Soviet occupation, were denied American assistance that instead went to Pakistani-favored anti-American extremists. A retired American diplomat who once served in Kabul complained, "The United States still has no competent intelligence of its own in this war and must depend on Pakistan's secret service." An American newspaper reported: "Vince Cannistraro, a former CIA director of counterterrorism, says there is 'credible information' that the ISI tipped off an Afghan tribal leader about Abdul Haq's whereabouts, and the tribal leader told the Taliban. A senior official of the anti-Taliban Northern Alliance made the same charge, ... as did several congressional aides."[39]

In an op-ed written a week after Abdul Haq's death, former national security adviser Robert McFarlane commented, "The tragedy here is not just the loss of a man of courage and excellence to whom the U.S. owed a great deal, but the dysfunction within the CIA that his loss underscores." McFarlane continued:

> The calamity is the CIA's failure to engage with him—or with any of the dozens of other capable Afghan commanders—a year earlier and to put in place the coordination that could have avoided his loss. Such planning would also have put us in a position today to work with Haq's fellow Pashtun commanders. . . . Moreover, the undoing of the Taliban by Afghans would remove any claim of martyrdom from Osama bin Laden, as well as reduce the risk of losing our Muslim coalition partners.[40]

As McFarlane inferred, the CIA's basic problem was that its officers were ignorant of broader political, cultural, and military dimensions of the Afghan war. They looked at the conflict and moderate and extremist Afghans through the ISI's prism. They mimicked their sister intelligence agency's biased interpretation of events and Afghan personalities.

In his comments on Haq's death, well-known Pakistani journalist Ahmed Rashid lambasted the CIA's and ISI's spurning of Haq while pointing out the seemingly piecemeal elimination of potential Afghan national leaders. Rashid wrote: "Haq received no help from the ISI or the CIA, who considered him unruly and unwilling to be directed. . . . The CIA station chief in Islamabad refused to help Haq for fear it would annoy the ISI. . . . Many mourners openly blamed the ISI for Haq's death, saying the ISI had betrayed his location to the Taliban. With the murder of Masud and now Haq, the Taliban were killing off every Afghan leader with a national standing."[41] The Pakistani embassy in Washington denied the allegations.[42]

After the Taliban fled Kabul on November 14, Afghanistan's eastern provinces fell like a stack of dominoes. Many hoped that a new Afghanistan could rise from the ashes of the Taliban- and communist-era wars. The deaths of Abdul Haq and Ahmed Shah Masood left Hamid Karzai as the only well-known Afghan moderate-nationalist. Karzai, who had survived twenty-three years of war, had long been disparaged by the ISI. Like Haq and Masood, he was a moderate-nationalist. Worse still, he represented the traditional Durrani tribal aristocracy.

For years, in both Washington and Islamabad, CIA officers had passed on the ISI's same write-off of Karzai and Haq, erroneously claiming that they had a negligible following inside Afghanistan. They, therefore, did not qualify for American aid. Under fierce criticism for Haq's death, the CIA reversed its treatment of Karzai. The agency would now support him. An American writer commented that if Karzai had been the first to appeal for CIA assistance, he would have perished, and the CIA and a U.S. Special Forces team would have helped Haq.[43]

When I was an adviser in a district in Vietnam's Mekong Delta from 1969 to 1970, I once asked my South Vietnamese counterpart, a lieutenant colonel, why he always left a back door open for the Viet Cong to escape during military operations. I never received a satisfactory answer. The question occurred to me again during the headlong Taliban and al-Qaeda exodus from Afghanistan into Pakistan in late November and December 2001. Over the next two months, from the fall of Mazar-i-Sharif on November 10 to the evacuation of the last group of al-Qaeda defenders from Tora Bora on December 12, Pakistani, Afghan, Arab, Uzbek, and other Islamic militants in the unholy alliance made three Great Escapes into Pakistani territory. Perhaps, I thought, keeping the back door open for the enemy was also an unwritten canon of Afghan tribal warfare. You maul but do not annihilate the enemy, whose family members may come back some day and annihilate you. This may have been part of the explanation for why there were no major battles for Kabul, Herat, Jalalabad, Ghazni, or Kandahar. As long as the Taliban and al-Qaeda were in retreat, Afghans were content to watch them flow south, dodging occasional American bombs, across the border into Pakistan.

Kunduz was an exception to the norm. A force of some 5,000 unholy alliance combatants was surrounded in the northern city. According to Pakistani author Ahmed Rashid, "hundreds of ISI officers and soldiers from the Frontier Corps aiding the Taliban were trapped there."[44] Kunduz had been the Pakistani Army's headquarters for the annual offensives against Masood.

It was the arms depot, the logistics center, and the forward base for Pakistani generals and ISI intelligence officers to assemble the unholy alliance parts and attack the Northern Alliance.

After America's October 7 intervention, it was too late for Pakistan's unholy alliance commanders at Kunduz to order a retreat from the city. Taliban front lines in the north contracted toward Kunduz. The Amu Darya and hostile Uzbekistan lay to the north. Masood's veteran Tajik commanders, generals Daoud Khan and Atta Mohammad, blocked off roads to the east and south. Dostum's hardened Uzbeks closed the circle on the west. The Taliban army was cornered along with its Pakistani commanders and troops and bin Laden's al-Qaeda fighters.

Musharraf was cornered as well. For twelve years, Washington had passively accepted Pakistan's plausible denials of Islamabad's steadily growing military intervention in Afghanistan. America's spies and diplomats had not connected the dots that the ISI's Taliban front contained al-Qaeda and other rabidly anti-Western elements. All the constituents of the unholy alliance were now trapped at Kunduz: ISI personnel, Pakistani military officers, al-Qaeda, Pakistani fighters from the Pakistani religious parties' paramilitary arms, and an array of foreign Arab, Uzbek, Chinese, and Southeast Asian jihadis.

The exposure in Kunduz of hundreds of captured Pakistani military personnel to the Western film crews and journalists waiting outside the city and anxious to report the Taliban surrender would shatter Islamabad's plausible-denial position regarding its deep involvement in the Afghan war. Television screens around the world would highlight sensational footage of defeated Pakistani officers and soldiers surrendering to American and Afghan generals. Afghan militia would be seen herding rows of Pakistani troops walking alongside Taliban and Arab al-Qaeda prisoners into captivity.

Musharraf's position was precarious. There was only one way out. He needed White House approval for a Pakistani military air evacuation of Pakistan's officers and soldiers trapped in Kunduz. The American military controlled the air space over Afghanistan. Musharraf was aware that Bush, Rumsfeld, General Franks, and CIA Director Tenet were delighted with his offer of Pakistani air space and basing facilities for Operation Enduring Freedom. They believed he was committed to America's war on terror. Musharraf decided to capitalize on his image as a reliable American ally.

Around November 18, 2001, Musharraf phoned President Bush. He requested a pause in the American bombing and immediate permission for Pakistani aircraft to fly to Kunduz and evacuate the Pakistani officers and soldiers trapped there. There is no evidence that either the U.S. military or the CIA at the time understood the circumstances motivating Musharraf's request, or that, if they did, they briefed the president on the composition of the force trapped in Kunduz. Hamid Karzai later commented to Pakistani reporter Ahmed Rashid that "even the Americans did not know who got away."[45] Based on all available evidence, including comments by American officers then at Kunduz, it appears that both the CIA and the U.S. military were clueless about the importance of the al-Qaeda, Taliban, and Pakistani foes on the brink of capture, or the valuable intelligence they could have provided about the principal target of Operation Enduring Freedom—Osama bin Laden, then on the run toward Jalalabad, Tora Bora, and Pakistan.

Northern Alliance leaders did not want their unholy alliance enemies to get away. They frantically informed American reporters covering the Kunduz siege that a Taliban defector had told them that at least three Pakistani Air Force planes had landed and taken off in the nighttime in previous days. Daoud Mir, the Northern Alliance representative in Washington, was awakened by a phone call from a very angry General Daoud Khan. According to Mir, the general told him that the Americans had "ordered him to wait for the Taliban surrender in Kunduz but during the nights some unknown planes were taking out the most important and high ranking Pakistani military officers, Taliban commanders and some al-Qaeda." He asked Mir to intervene with American leaders in Washington to halt the air evacuation immediately.[46]

In his 2008 book *Descent into Chaos*, Ahmed Rashid, quoting a "senior U.S. intelligence analyst," wrote that, though Musharraf made his request to Bush, "Cheney took charge":

> The approval was not shared with anyone at State, including Colin Powell, until well after the event. Musharraf said Pakistan needed to save its dignity and its valued people. Two planes were involved, which made several sorties a night over several nights. They took off from air bases in Chitral and Gilgit in Pakistan's northern areas, and landed in Kunduz, where the evacuees were waiting on the tarmac. Certainly hundreds and perhaps as many as one thousand people escaped. Hun-

dreds of ISI officers, Taliban commanders, and foot soldiers belonging to the IMU [Islamic Movement of Uzbekistan] and al Qaeda personnel boarded the planes. What was sold as a minor extraction turned into a major air bridge. The frustrated U.S. SFO [Special Forces officer] who watched it from the surrounding high ground dubbed it "Operation Evil Airlift."

Another senior U.S. diplomat told me afterward, "Musharraf fooled us because after we gave approval, the ISI may have run a much bigger operation and got out more people. We just don't know."[47]

The Bush administration's ignorance of the situation at Kunduz and the CIA's misreading of Musharraf's motives were all on display during the Kunduz air evacuation. Rumsfeld's subsequent claim to the media that "neither Pakistan nor any other country flew any planes into Afghanistan to evacuate anybody"[48] may have been a cover-up for what he believed at the time was a helicopter evacuation. It may also have been a deliberate misrepresentation of the facts on the ground.

Whatever the answer, the American support for Musharraf's request enabled the first Great Escape. It multiplied the dangers that the ISI, the Taliban, and al-Qaeda would pose to the United States in the coming years. American military and intelligence officers outside of Kunduz told reporters that it had been agreed that the nighttime airlifts would be limited, but they slipped out of control. "Dirt got through the screen," a senior intelligence officer remarked to an American journalist.[49]

If Masood had still been alive and at Kunduz, it is hard to imagine that he would have stood by, as Fahim, Daoud, and Dostum did, and let the Pakistani evacuation go forward. He was, above all, an independent-minded, self-confident Afghan nationalist, one who had been fighting the unholy alliance for almost six years. Masood alone had prevented the unholy alliance from conquering all of Afghanistan, with no American assistance. It is likely that he would have vetoed what eventually turned out to be a very costly mistake in the effort to track down and crush al-Qaeda and the Taliban.

ψ

If "dirt got through the screen" at Kunduz, then lots of dirt, including the FBI's Most Wanted Man, also got through at Tora Bora, during the second Great

Escape. The U.S. military uses a term "situational awareness." Acquiring situational awareness about a military situation before engaging an enemy is the critical first step to defeating him. The CIA and the U.S. military did not have situational awareness at Kunduz. Nor did they enjoy that advantage at Tora Bora. Their adversary, bin Laden, did.

Tora Bora (Black Valley) lies 30 miles southwest of Jalalabad, in the White Mountain range abutting Pakistan. The Tora Bora heights range from 7,000 to 13,000 feet in altitude. Inside are a maze of tunnels and caves. Bin Laden's bulldozers had strengthened Tora Bora's defenses during the Soviet war. The Saudi terrorist had lived in the Tora Bora cave complex for a time after his 1996 return to Afghanistan. Bin Laden was well acquainted with the Suleiman Khel tribal elders in the six villages below Tora Bora—he had hired their men to break rocks and perform other manual-labor chores. Tunnels inside the mountain redoubt offered egress in all directions, to Jalalabad, to Khost, and to Logar. To the south lay the Murga Pass and Parachinar, the administrative center of the Khurram tribal agency in Pakistan. The Murga Pass to safety was only a half day's walk away. Parachinar could be reached in less than a day. Bin Laden had walked these trails many times going to and from Pakistan.

On November 8, 2001, bin Laden and Zawahiri were interviewed by a Pakistani journalist reportedly near or in Kabul. Bin Laden then fell back to Jalalabad, and on November 10, the day after Mazar-i-Sharif fell, he hosted a reception for 1,000 local Afghan notables at the city's Institute for Islamic Studies, which he had founded. Dressed in his standard camouflage jacket, he gave a fiery anti-American speech, promising, "God is with us. . . . We will win this war." After his remarks, bin Laden handed out crisp white envelopes bulging with Pakistani rupees worth between $300 and $1,000. On November 13 he left Jalalabad in a white Toyota Corolla for Tora Bora accompanied by a convoy of several hundred cars, trucks, and APCs that were carrying up to 2,000 al-Qaeda fighters and some women and children. "The Americans can bomb all they want, they'll never catch bin Laden," former Peshawar party leader and Jalalabad patriarch Mawlawi Yunus Khalis told an American reporter.[50]

Khalis was a staunch bin Laden ally. The octogenarian had hosted a celebratory reception for bin Laden in Jalalabad when he returned to Afghanistan in 1996. He had turned his guest house over to bin Laden and his family at that time. Khalis' Saudi-educated oldest son, Anwar al-Haq Mujahid, was a devoted bin Laden disciple. Khalis issued a fatwa, believed to have been written by Mujahid, urging Afghans to "wage jihad against America and its allies because their countries have been invaded by the crusaders and their homes are savagely bombed and hit by rockets."[51]

A ninety-man U.S. Delta Force commando unit was in place at Tora Bora by December 8, joining a handful of CIA officers who had arrived in mid-November. The Delta team called in air strikes on the Tora Bora cave complex, including the dropping of 15,000-pound "Daisy Cutter" bombs. Radio intercepts of bin Laden and his men revealed that the bombing was taking a toll of al-Qaeda fighters and causing considerable damage inside the caves where they were hiding.[52]

A bin Laden underground railroad began to shuttle al-Qaeda fighters and their families into Pakistan after bin Laden's large group of Arabs arrived at Tora Bora on November 13. The short trip into Pakistan, assisted by Afghans and Pakistanis on both sides of the border, did not seem to have been detected by the Americans in Jalalabad and at their base near Tora Bora. Ilyas Khel, a former Khalis commander during the Soviet war and later a Taliban commander, was being paid by the Americans to monitor the southern approaches to Tora Bora from Pakistan. Instead, he managed the flow of al-Qaeda leaders and fighters up to and over the Murga Pass and across the Pakistani border and into Pakistan's Khurram tribal agency. After the Tora Bora battle was over, Ilyas's Afghan superior in Jalalabad explained to a reporter: "I paid him 300,000 Pakistani rupees [about $7,000] and gave him a satellite phone to keep us informed. . . . Our problem was that the Arabs had paid him more, and so Ilyas Khel just showed the Arabs the way out of the country into Pakistan."[53]

Bin Laden could count on other Afghan helping hands. The Suleiman Khel village elders at Tora Bora were well compensated for the horses, mules, and escort assistance they provided for the al-Qaeda retreat into Pakistan. Afridi tribal clans on the other side of the border in the Khurram tribal agency gave the Arabs a warm welcome. They were also well paid. One elder remarked to a *New York Times* correspondent wandering through the Khurram agency in December, "What would I do if someone from al-Qaeda came to me? I'd of course grant him refuge, like I would any other man." He explained, "This is the Pashtun way, to defend a guest to your death."[54]

CentCom Commander Tommy Frank's decision not to insert an American blocking force or even small teams of spotters near the trails from Tora Bora into Pakistan became a controversial issue after bin Laden's escape. There were 4,000 Marines available at Camp Rhino southwest of Kandahar and on ships in the Indian Ocean. British Marines were stationed at Bagram; some were on hand at Tora Bora. A U.S. 10th Mountain Division reserve brigade was standing by in Uzbekistan. CIA Director Tenet later revealed that the CIA had urged Franks to rush American troops to Tora Bora, but Franks disagreed, arguing that it would take weeks to deploy the necessarily large contingent of U.S. military to the region, during which time bin Laden might escape anyway. After his retirement, General James N. Mattis, the Marine commander during Operation Enduring Freedom, said that he had sufficient Marines on hand to seal off Tora Bora. CentCom refused his request to do so. Franks instead turned to Musharraf to do the job. Musharraf sent troops to the borders beginning on December 9.[55]

Relying on Musharraf to help apprehend bin Laden was, of course, a mistake. The objectives of Musharraf and the ISI at Tora Bora contradicted American objectives. The Pakistani military dictator and the ISI knew where bin Laden and his immediate entourage, including family members, were when they were in Afghanistan and after their arrival in Pakistan. Pakistani troops sent to the border area picked up several scores of lower-level Arab fighters in Pakistan and handed them over to the Americans. None were senior al-Qaeda leaders.

On December 3, a trio of minor Afghan warlords hired by the CIA began their "attacks" on the al-Qaeda Arabs still holed up in Tora Bora. An American journalist wrote that one of the warlords, Haji Hazarat Ali, had "just a fourth-grade education" and a reputation as a "bully."[56] A former Khalis commander, Haji Zaman Ghamsharik, also led some of the forays up the mountain. The CIA had lured Zaman back from exile in Dijon, France. Zaman was a bad choice. His background indicated he was unreliable and would be responsive to those most likely to protect bin Laden. During the Soviet war, he had defected to the PDPA, then defected back to the Mujahidin. He was a member of Khalis' Pashtun Khugiani tribe. He had worked closely with the ISI over the years. Zaman's brother had been the Taliban consul in Peshawar. The third commander organizing the assault was Haji Abdul Zahir, who was related to Abdul Haq. Zahir may have been chosen because he was the son of the new governor of Nangarhar, Haji Abdul Qadir, then participating in the UN-organized Bonn Conference to choose the interim Afghan regime that would replace the Taliban. Early in the Tora Bora operation, Khalis sent word to the 2,500-man American-financed Afghan attacking force to allow Osama bin Laden and his followers go into Pakistan.

Zaman's force did not move up the main, north frontal trail of the mountain until December 5, at least a week after the majority of bin Laden's force had escaped.[57] Other columns proceeded up the east and west—but not the south—slopes of the mountain. Tribal differences and wrangling over money distributed by the Americans generated constant bickering among the three warlords. The holy month of Ramadan was under way. Fasting during daylight hours was not conducive to combat. CIA Director Tenet noted that "the Afghan troops we were working with were distinctly reluctant to undertake that risk."[58] The thought of severe retribution to come if the assault force harmed Osama bin Laden must have crossed their minds.

The "battle" of Tora Bora unfolded at a desultory pace. The days began with Afghan militia and a few Soviet-era tanks advancing slowly up the mountain. Arab fighters would fire at the advancing Afghans, who would take cover. A firefight would follow, after which the Arabs would retire into caves at a higher elevation. American bombs rained down on the al-Qaeda positions from the sky.

On December 12, without consulting the Americans, Haji Zaman negotiated a cease-fire agreement by radio with the leader of the al-Qaeda group still remaining at Tora Bora. The Arab agreed to surrender the next morning at 8:00 a.m. Zaman's cease-fire ruse outraged the Special Forces officers at Tora Bora,[59] who rejected it. General Richard Meyers, chairman of the Joint Chiefs of Staff, announced in Washington that the American bombing would continue without let-up. But the temporary confusion that followed Zaman's cease-fire claim facilitated the escape of the last remnant of al-Qaeda fighters. That night, assisted by the local Afghan tribal elders, they took the Parachinar trail into Pakistan.

On December 15 and 16, the attacking force rounded up about twenty unresisting Arab and Taliban fighters scattered in and around Tora Bora. On December 17, Zaman proclaimed victory. Special Forces and CIA officers inspected the caves. They found ammunition boxes filled with antiaircraft and artillery shells but not much else. On December 20, President Bush stated that he did not know where bin Laden was, but predicted he would be found if he "tried to slither out" of Afghan territory.

Capturing or killing bin Laden, the terrorist who perpetrated the 9/11 attack, was the single most important objective of Operation Enduring Freedom. The U.S. government had been attempting to track him down since the 1998 al-Qaeda embassy bombings in Africa. But the Tora Bora military campaign to capture or kill him was a debacle. Its failure was largely due to American ignorance about the local tribal architecture, bin Laden's influence in the area, and Musharraf's duplicitous role. There were never more than one hundred U.S. Special Forces personnel engaged at Tora Bora.[60]

Under harsh criticism, Haji Zaman fled to Pakistan. The American military transported at least one of his militia subcommanders to Kabul for interrogations. Charges and countercharges over who was to blame circulated in the U.S. media for years. Democratic presidential candidate John Kerry accused the Bush administration of outsourcing the hunt for bin Laden to Pakistan. General Franks claimed in an October 19, 2004, *New York Times* op-ed that 100,000 Pakistani troops "provided significant help" by sealing the border. Bin Laden, he contended, may not have been at Tora Bora in December 2001 and was "never within our grasp." Bruce Riedel, a senior CIA official at the time, took issue with Franks's statement on bin Laden in his 2008 book *The Search for al Qaeda*. He tended to believe that the United States "almost had" bin Laden at Tora Bora. A 2007 official Pentagon study confirmed Riedel's view, stating that "all source reporting collaborated his presence on several days from 9–14 December."[61]

⚘

The third and final Taliban-al-Qaeda getaway to Pakistan unfolded in southern Afghanistan, at the Taliban's main headquarters in Kandahar. It was not really an escape, although in the long run it proved more damaging than Kunduz or Tora Bora to ending the Afghan wars. In early December, the Taliban leadership, including Mullah Omar, simply shuttled down the Kandahar road to Pakistan and entered Quetta, Omar on a motorcycle. The commute, at 93 miles a drive of less than two hours, transpired like the daily drives of millions of Americans from Baltimore to Washington, San Jose to San Francisco, or San Antonio to Austin. For the Taliban, Quetta was home and the office was in Kandahar. The Taliban mullahs had passed sixteen years in Quetta, Pakistan, during the wars against the Soviets, Najib, and the Rabbani-Masood Islamic government, all under ISI tutelage. They had spent only seven years in Afghanistan beginning with the successful attack on Kandahar from Pakistan in 1994. They effortlessly reoccupied their offices, homes, and training bases in and around Quetta.

While Mullah Omar and his associates were moving back to Pakistan, President Bush was vowing to track them down in Afghanistan. "They can run but not hide," he told the American people. The United States announced a $10 million reward for Mullah Omar. His face was placed near bin Laden's on the FBI's Ten Most Wanted List. Mullah Omar responded through a Saudi newspaper: "The outcome of what we are in is either victory or death. . . . Both are the making of God."[62] Thereupon, with his four wives and twelve children, the Taliban's supreme mullah receded from view inside a Pakistani military cantonment on the outskirts of Quetta.

Abdul Razak, the Taliban's interior minister and executioner of Abdul Haq, relocated to Quetta.[63] Pakistan sequestered Omar but allowed all other Taliban leaders and commanders to operate freely in the Quetta area. They worked with ISI officers and Pakistani religious parties to revive Quetta's 1994–1996 role as the main springboard for the Taliban insurgency in Afghanistan.

While the Taliban's highest-ranking mullahs were settling down in Quetta, American aircraft dropped hundreds of thousands of leaflets with photos of Omar, Razak, and other leading Taliban figures into populated areas of Kandahar Province. The leaflets announced the $10 million bounty on Omar's head—a million times the average weekly income of Afghans. The photo of Omar on the leaflets, however, was of another man, Mawlawi Hafizullah. Hafizullah was a minor Taliban figure. He had two eyes. Omar only had one. "The CIA are blind and stupid," Hafizullah huffed to a British journalist who managed to find him. "I'm afraid to leave the house," he said. "If I do, soldiers or villagers will tear me to pieces so they can get the money."[64]

☙

Hamid Karzai and three companions entered Afghanistan on motorbikes on October 8, 2001, a day after the American bombing began. Karzai did not tell the media that he planned to enter Afghanistan. He did not tell the Pakistanis either. His discretion probably saved his life. Karzai carried a CIA-donated satellite phone. He was to call the CIA if he managed to gather several hundred anti-Taliban insurgents together.

Karzai made his way past the city of Kandahar into Uruzgan Province where he reunited with a fellow Popalzai, Commander Jan Mohammad. The two had collaborated successfully in 1990 when they used a combination of military pressure and defections to capture Tarinkot. Karzai's intention was to grow an insurgency from the tribal communities around the city of about 20,000 located 70 miles northwest of Kandahar. After Tarinkot's fall, he planned to instigate a broader anti-Taliban tribal insurgency in Uruzgan and Kandahar provinces and march on Kandahar.

Karzai and Jan Mohammad had gathered only fifty men when the Taliban garrison in Tarinkot went after them. Karzai retreated to a valley north of the city and used the CIA phone to request help. The public condemnation of the CIA's failure to assist Abdul Haq's mission to start an anti-Taliban uprising may have influenced the U.S. decision to rescue Karzai, despite the small number of men with him. Blackhawk helicopters exfiltrated him and seven tribal followers to a U.S. base in Pakistan on November 3. Only eight days had elapsed since the Taliban had executed Abdul Haq. Karzai flew back to the Tarinkot area with an eleven-man Special Forces A team commanded by Captain Jason Amerine. They brought along enough arms to equip 300 insurgents. During their discussions, Captain Amerine had informed Karzai that his team was there to learn how they could support him to accomplish what he wanted, and not vice versa. "That is something I have waited a long, long time to hear," Karzai responded.[65]

On November 15 and 16, Tarinkot's population revolted against the Taliban, killing the Taliban governor and his security guards. Tarinkot elders invited Karzai, Jan Mohammad, and Amerine and his Special Forces team to dinner in Tarinkot on November 16. On November 17, Captain Amerine and his men brilliantly orchestrated a devastating U.S. air attack on a Taliban column sent from Kandahar to regain the city. Only ten to twenty Taliban—"most of them were Pakistani," according to Captain Amerine[66]—penetrated Tarinkot's defenses. Karzai's tribal militia drove them out of the city. The commander of the Taliban force surrendered a week later.

The Tarinkot victory opened Karzai's route down to Kandahar. His tribal militia along with Amerine's Special Forces detachment and some CIA officers approached Afghanistan's southern capital from the northeast, capturing Shah Wali Kot, the capital of the Kandahar Province district of the same name, only 20 miles from Kandahar city. Meanwhile, the former warlord and governor of Kandahar, Gul Agha, was closing in on Kandahar from the south. With ISI help, Gul Agha had assembled an armed force in Quetta that was much larger and better equipped than Karzai's tribal militia. A separate U.S. Special Forces team and CIA officers accompanied him.

At the time, with UN and U.S. assistance, a multiethnic group of Afghans in Bonn, Germany, were close to selecting Karzai to be the new interim Afghan leader. Karzai was the only Afghan faction leader with some national standing after al-Qaeda killed Masood and the Taliban killed Abdul Haq. He was a descendant of Ahmad Shah Durrani, the founder of Afghanistan and embodiment of Afghan nationalism. Many of his family members lived in the United States. This must have worried Musharraf and the ISI. They did not control Karzai. He could take Afghanistan on an independent path. He might even develop close ties with India.

Gul Agha, in contrast, had a history of close cooperation with the ISI going back to the Soviet war. Whereas Karzai was an Afghan nationalist, Gul Agha sought power and personal gain. He would later restore his corrupt grid of narcotics trafficking and road checkpoints to rob and abuse travelers that he had operated before the Taliban's appearance. Gul Agha was also determined to reclaim the Kandahar governorship that he was forced to give up when the Taliban took over the city in 1994.

The CIA got to know Agha well during the 1980s and 1990s, as did I. After 9/11, the agency brought him into the American embassy during one of General Tommy Franks's visits to Islamabad. They introduced the Barakzai giant to Franks, describing him as typical of the Afghan commanders they were financing to overthrow the Taliban. The American CIA and Special Forces assigned to Gul Agha's offensive on Kandahar from the south may have heard about his reputation for corruption, repression, and drug trafficking. An Associated Press article examining his time in office before the Taliban reported that "Kandahar was so lawless that people there welcomed the Taliban, whose ruthless ways restored order."[67]

⚜

The Taliban asked Hamid Karzai for permission to come to Shah Wali Kot to discuss surrender terms. Only hours before the Taliban delegation arrived, on the morning of December 5, a "friendly fire" 2,000-pound bomb exploded near Karzai's command post outside Kandahar. The errant bomb killed three

U.S. Special Forces troops and about fifty Afghans, many of them Karzai's tribals who had been with him since the beginning of the Tarinkot campaign. Karzai suffered a flesh wound on his cheek caused by flying glass. Amerine was flown to Germany with a serious ear injury and shrapnel wounds in his leg.

Only fifteen minutes after the bomb detonated, as Afghans and Americans urgently attended to the scores of wounded scattered around the command post, BBC correspondent Lyse Ducet phoned Karzai via satellite phone and told him that the Bonn Conference had selected him to be chairman of Afghanistan's Interim Administration. The UN Security Council had passed a resolution approving the decision. Karzai now enjoyed international legitimacy as Afghanistan's acting head of state.

The Taliban delegation met with Karzai on the afternoon of December 5 and returned the next day with a letter of surrender. During those two days, while American planes were still pounding the Tora Bora heights, Taliban leaders and military units still in Kandahar shifted back to Taliban safe havens in Pakistan.

On December 7, Karzai rode into Kandahar on a motorcycle as part of a convoy of more than two hundred vehicles flying the black, red, and green Afghan flag of the precommunist era. Large crowds greeted him. He established an office at Mullah Omar's bombed-out home[68] and appointed Mullah Naqib, the Alokazai tribal chief and veteran Mujahidin commander, to be Kandahar's next governor. Karzai's Popalzai tribe and the Alokazai had a history of close relations. Naqib's tribal fighters and Karzai's men created checkpoints in Kandahar to maintain security.

The Bonn Conference and UN mandates empowering Karzai to govern Afghanistan did not impress Gul Agha. From Kandahar's airport, with his CIA and U.S. Special Forces advisers, he considered his options. He possessed greater military power than Karzai. That counted more than UN resolutions in fragmented, ungoverned Afghanistan. Karzai phoned Gul Agha at the airport to inform him of Naqib's promotion to governor. Gul Agha was furious. In defiance of Afghanistan's new, internationally blessed interim leader's governing authority, he alleged falsely in a BBC broadcast that Naqib could not be governor because he had close ties with the Taliban and al-Qaeda.[69]

With his American advisers and large armed force, Gul Agha unexpectedly marched on Kandahar and occupied the governor's office on December 9.

The fact that he was accompanied by U.S. Special Forces and CIA officers suggested to Kandahar's horrified citizenry that his power grab was supported by the United States. Shocked and dismayed, Karzai went to the governor's office. There he confronted Gul Agha, who sat at a conference table with his American advisers nearby. Neither Abdul Haq, nor Haji Qadir, nor Ahmed Shah Masood would have tolerated Gul Agha's coup. Karzai did. He was a politician, not a military commander. Karzai backed off, explaining to an American reporter afterward that the Americans were supporting Gul Agha.[70] He accepted Gul Agha's *fait accompli*, formally appointed him governor of Kandahar, and left for Kabul. He visited Masood's tomb in the Panshir, then flew on to Rome to receive King Zahir Shah's formal approval to become Afghanistan's next leader.

Gul Agha's return to power in Kandahar indicated to many Afghans not only that the United States was on his side but that it was still working in tandem with Pakistan. A few weeks after Karzai left Kandahar, U.S. officials were appalled to learn that Gul Agha had privately received Taliban Justice Minister Noorudin Turabi and allowed him to travel to Quetta. At the time, Turabi was the subject of a U.S. manhunt in the Kandahar area. Kandahar's new governor also allowed Mullah Omar's spokesman to go to Pakistan.[71]

Gul Agha's men wasted little time in reestablishing checkpoints on the roads in Afghanistan's four southern provinces of Kandahar, Helmand, Farah, and Nimroz. Travelers were robbed and kidnapped. A ticket collector for the bus line from Kandahar to Herat told a reporter, "The situation is worse than it was before the Taliban came to power. . . . Before they were taking cars and money. But now they are also killing people."[72]

The history of foreigners during the Soviet and Taliban periods putting Afghan proxies out in front while exercising real authority was fresh in Afghan minds. The Soviets and Pakistanis were the "supported" partner. Their Afghan proxies were the "supporting" partner. Captain Amerine's comment to Hamid Karzai before the liberation of Tarinkot that his team was there to support what Karzai wished to do and not vice versa placed the Americans in the appropriate supporting role. Amerine's position reflected the position of the U.S. government and the international community at the Bonn Conference and in UN Security Council resolutions, which gave all the rights of sovereignty to the new post-Taliban transitional government. As messy and frustrating as this process would be, the United States and its allies could only succeed in Afghanistan in the long run by, in actual practice, playing the part of supporting the Afghan government.

The position taken by Gul Agha's CIA and Special Forces advisers on December 9 at the governor's office in Kandahar took no notice of Karzai's legitimacy. At that critical moment, the Americans and their superiors at higher levels appeared to be supporting Gul Agha's power maneuver. This was a monumental political blunder. It resonated beyond Kandahar to politically savvy Afghans in Afghanistan and into Pakistan. It produced destructive long-term consequences for U.S. interests. Afghanistan at the time was at a crossroads: One road was the Bonn Conference vision leading to restoration of the traditional, democratic state existing in the 1960s and early 1970s; the other led back to the chaos, bloodshed, Islamic extremism, and terrorism of the Taliban period. The CIA and U.S. military officers sitting with Gul Agha while he defied Karzai's authority on December 9 choose the second path. Once again two contradictory U.S. Afghan strategies were pulling in opposite directions.

Gul Agha's triumph and Karzai's retreat also demonstrated to Afghans that the Americans would be calling the shots in Afghanistan. The Americans would be the supported party in the bilateral relationship. The Afghan government would be the supporting party. A few days later, a new joke was circulating in Kabul's tea shops and bazaars. It depicted President Bush presenting a new car to President Karzai. Giving the keys to Karzai, Bush assured him that he would be the driver.

Karzai protested, "Yes, but it's a taxi."

CHAPTER 23

From Victory to Stalemate

The stunning American-led military victory in Afghanistan which ousted the Taliban-al-Qaeda regime has not been followed up by an effective, adequately funded reconstruction strategy to help Afghans rebuild their country and restore their self-governing institutions. The initial enthusiasm genuinely felt by the Afghan people that peace was returning has clearly faded. Today, there is a sense among Afghans, foreigners working in Afghanistan, and the media that the U.S.-led coalition and the moderate Hamid Karzai government have lost the initiative in Afghanistan.

Mr. Chairman, this does not mean that the momentum is now with the ragtag bands of fanatics left over from the Taliban-al-Qaeda period presently staging sporadic attacks into Afghanistan from Pakistan. No, instead there is a sort of pall, a paralysis, obfuscating the future of Afghanistan. The overwhelming majority of Afghans oppose the Muslim extremists, the hated warlords, and continuing violence. But, increasingly fearful of the future, many are switching gears back to neutral in the event the U.S. and its allies leave and the fanatics return.

If present trends continue, five years from now [i.e., 2008] Afghanistan is likely to look very much like it does today: reconstruction stagnation, a weak central government starved of resources, unable to extend its influence to the regions where oppressive warlords reign, opium production soars, and guerrilla warfare in Afghan-Pakistani border areas generated by Pakistan-based Muslim extremists continues to inflict casualties on coalition and Afghan forces. A second possible scenario five years from now forecasts an even worse outcome: backsliding to the *externally-fueled chaotic 1992–1996 period of warlord conflict and chaos inside Afghanistan.*

—AUTHOR'S TESTIMONY TO THE
COMMITTEE ON INTERNATIONAL RELATIONS,
UNITED STATES HOUSE OF REPRESENTATIVES, 2003[1]

Tragically, by 2008, the last full year of the Bush administration, the security situation in Afghanistan reflected the first scenario projected by my 2003 testimony to Congress.

The ISI-coordinated insurgency launched from three fronts in Pakistan accelerated in 2005, at a time when U.S. Afghan policy was adrift, minimal reconstruction was under way, and minimal resources had been committed to rebuild an Afghan army to assume responsibility for security. Consequently, that year the United States was compelled to invest substantially more of its own troops and considerably more funds to stem the Taliban tide, which continued into the Obama administration. American ignorance of the Afghan environment, Washington's preoccupation with Iraq, Hamid Karzai's weak leadership, and government corruption also frustrated progress. After 2005, the U.S. and Afghan governments found themselves in a defensive, if not losing, battlefield stalemate in Afghanistan. Incremental U.S.-led coalition troop buildups to handle the expanding insurgency leveled off at 130,000 in September 2010—roughly the size of the Soviet Army in Afghanistan at the height of the Soviet-Afghan war.

The Pakistani Army's decision to conduct a fourth proxy war in Afghanistan has been the main reason why Afghanistan has not yet enjoyed peace and stability. It is difficult to imagine any nation, much less one torn apart by three decades of warfare, defending itself against a much larger, more powerful neighbor supporting and encouraging tens of thousands of well-trained, well-armed insurgents to cross the border, create instability, and topple a fragile government. Pakistan's proxy war in Afghanistan could not be defeated with 130,000 foreign troops, or even half a million foreign troops. The Taliban insurgency could only be defeated if Pakistan clamped down on the Taliban's Quetta Shura, Gulbuddin Hekmatyar's bases in northeastern Pakistan, and the Haqqani terrorist network in North Waziristan.

ψ

The pessimism expressed in my 2003 congressional testimony was based in part on what I learned and personally witnessed during an extended visit to Afghanistan in September 2002. Ahmed Shah Masood's family had invited me to Kabul to speak at the first anniversary memorial service of Masood's death on September 9, 2001—two days before the 9/11 attacks. I arrived eight days beforehand to travel in central and northern Afghanistan. Hamid Karzai, then acting interim president, invited me to stay with him at his residence on the grounds of the presidential palace. On September 5, Karzai and I boarded an American C-130 with his senior advisers and a U.S. Delta Force security team protecting him. Karzai had decided to visit Kandahar, the former Taliban capital in southern Afghanistan. It was his first trip to his hometown since leaving it and his rival Gul Agha behind in December 2001. Governor Gul Agha was in charge of organizing his visit.

Thousands of men, women, and children lined Kandahar's main street for Karzai's homecoming. Veteran BBC reporter Lyse Doucet and her crew were in the motorcade, filming its glacial movement down Kandahar's main street. I sat next to Qayum Karzai in the car trailing Karzai's black sedan. Gul Agha, the huge Barakzai governor whom U.S. soldiers nicknamed Jabba the Hutt, sat next to Karzai. The Delta Force commander assigned to guard Karzai rode shotgun in the front seat of Karzai's vehicle.

The festive crowds got larger as the presidential motorcade approached Kandahar's Mosque of the Cloak, the spiritual and cultural heart of the ancient city. President Karzai opened the latch on the roof of his black sedan, rose through it, and waved back to the crowd. The crowd roared its approval. The long line of vehicles snaked into the compound of the mosque, which also included Ahmad Shah Durrani's mausoleum and the governor's palace. The U.S. Delta team surrounded Karzai as he stepped out of his car and attempted to whisk him into the mosque. But the crowd moved too fast. Hundreds of Afghan men and boys swarmed around the tiny group as hands reached out to touch Karzai.

The crowd stayed behind when he entered the mosque—that was sacred ground. People flooded back onto the street outside the compound to await the motorcade's departure. The delegation toured the mosque and Gul Agha's office, which was located on the second floor of the provincial headquarters standing next to it. Karzai's party then returned to the line of vehicles parked near the compound's front gate. I was assigned to one, located two cars in front of Karzai's black sedan. It had tinted windows, an unusual sight in Afghanistan. The motorcade exited the mosque compound. Gul Agha sat on Karzai's right in the back seat. The Delta Force commander sat next to the driver. Our car slowly moved between the double row of security guards onto the main street. The crowd was smaller than before. Governor Agha's personal security unit formed two protective cordons on the roadway leading out of the compound.

A Taliban assassin wearing the uniform of the governor's security force was among them. His tribe was Barakzai. The young man must have been nervous, because he neglected to switch the lever on his AK-47 from single shot to automatic. The crowd clapped and waved as our vehicle and then Karzai's slowly left the compound and began turning onto the street.

Perhaps in a prearranged ploy to confirm Karzai's place in the motorcade, a small boy suddenly broke free from the crowd. He ran through the security cordon and up to Karzai's window, gesturing for Afghanistan's interim president to roll down the window. Karzai did so, and they exchanged greetings. The boy ran back into the crowd.

At that moment, all hell broke loose. The sharp "pop, pop, pop" of a rifle firing split the air. I had not heard that sound since Vietnam. Vehicles in the convoy slowed to a crawl or stopped. I jumped out of the car, as did several Delta commandos. The assassin stood outside Karzai's window, firing into his car as it inched forward. Sometime between his second and third round, the Delta Force squad went into action. A commando fired right through the front window of his vehicle. One of Karzai's Afghan bodyguards grappled with the assassin. The assassin got off another round just as both of them, assailant and presidential bodyguard, were felled by a furious hail of bullets fired by several Delta commandos. By that time, the crowd was scattering in all directions.

"Let's go!" shouted one of the Delta commandos. I jumped back into my seat and closed the door. Our car hurtled past the German-donated green police van leading the convoy. The speedometer hit 90 miles an hour as we surged forward. Kandahar's main street was now completely deserted—all the shops had closed. We had slowed to 30 when our vehicle screeched to a halt inside the governor's residential compound. I stepped out as Karzai's vehicle pulled up a few feet from ours. I reached for his door. It was still locked. I noticed a single bullet hole in the tinted window next to his head. A series of perfectly symmetrical white lines extended out from the hole in the window. The sight was ghastly. My eyes swept the car for more bullet holes. Another had entered a small window behind the one next to Karzai. A third hole was in the rear window. The would-be assassin's first round had grazed the back of the Delta Force commander's head. The second inflicted a flesh wound on Gul Agha's neck. The assassin's failure to put his weapon on full automatic probably saved the lives of all of the sedan's occupants. They could not have escaped a spray of gunfire fired instantaneously from a full clip of the AK-47.

Karzai's car door gradually opened. The Afghan interim president's traditional gray *karakul* wool hat rose slowly above the door frame, then his face and his familiar green Uzbek robe. He was calm. I knew him to be an observant Muslim. Afghan Muslims believe that God, not man, decides when they will leave this earth. His time had not come. "Are you okay?" I asked. "I'm fine," he matter-of-factly answered.

I immediately used a satellite phone to brief U.S. Ambassador Robert Finn in Kabul and the State Department's Operations Center in Washington. The assassination attempt would be front-page news around the world in a few hours.

Karzai's trip to Kandahar was cut short for obvious security reasons. It was not safe to return to the city. In the middle of the night, the delegation was taken to a nearby stadium for a helicopter ride back to the Kandahar Airport where the C-130 was waiting to take us back to Kabul. Sitting next to Karzai and Gul Agha in a row of stadium seats while waiting for the helicopter, I witnessed Karzai's tongue lashing of the much larger, but now very subdued, Kandahar governor. "I have visited cities all over Afghanistan and I come to Kandahar and got shot at," Karzai scolded. Gul Agha's head was wrapped with an enormous bright white bandage instead of a Barakzai turban. He did not respond. His huge body slumped downward. We boarded the military aircraft and flew off into the darkness. Karzai happily signed autographs for the young servicemen and women in the crew of the C-130 as the plane sped toward the safety of Kabul.

✥

Two bomb attacks in Kabul's main business district occurred at roughly the same time on September 5, 2002, the same day as the assassination attempt

on Karzai's life in Kandahar.[2] Thereafter bombings in the Afghan capital sporadically continued each year. The cross-border Taliban insurgency remained
at a low level, confined to some of the Pashtun provinces abutting Pakistan
and Kabul, until 2005. That year Taliban offensives from Pakistan penetrated
western and central Afghanistan. In 2006, the number of suicide attacks numbered 139, a 400 percent increase over 2005. Taliban-planted improvised-
explosive-device incidents leaped from 783 to 1,677, and the number of
Taliban armed attacks climbed from 1,558 to 4,542. Looking back in 2009 at
the Taliban's progress during the previous eight years, Colonel Sultan Imam,
who was officially retired from the ISI but now part of Hamid Gul's virtual
ISI, predicted to a British reporter in Pakistan that the Taliban were destined
for ultimate victory. "I have worked with these people since the 1970s and I
tell you they will never be defeated," he said. "My students are far ahead of
me now. They are giving a lesson to the world. I am very proud of them." He
declared: "You can never win the war in Afghanistan."[3]

The Western media reported credible accounts of Pakistani military officers supervising Taliban military training facilities inside Pakistan. Although
Pakistani spokesmen routinely denied the accusations and defended the ISI,
the Pakistani military intelligence agency was in fact turning out legions of
Taliban to travel the insurgent highway into Afghanistan. Questioned
whether the ISI was operating on its own at a 2002 news conference in Pakistan, President Musharraf took full responsibility for its activities. "The
government formulates policies and tells the ISI what to do. They do not do
on their own. Hence, if there is anything wrong, the government is to be
blamed, not the ISI," he said.[4]

American soldiers fighting in Afghanistan reported numerous incidents
of Pakistani intelligence and Frontier Corps personnel assisting the Taliban
along the Afghan-Pakistani border. Evidence that Pakistan's army was supporting the increasingly virulent Taliban offensives inside Afghanistan proliferated during the second George W. Bush administration. In 2007, a U.S.
air strike against insurgents on the Pakistani border killed eleven soldiers in
Pakistan's Frontier Corps who had joined Taliban fighters firing at American
and Afghan troops from inside Pakistan. In 2007, a Pakistani Frontier Corps
soldier shot and killed 82nd Airborne Division Major Larry Bauguess during
a Pakistani-U.S.-Afghan trilateral meeting in the Khurram tribal agency in Pakistan that had been called to discuss military coordination. In April 2008,

MAP 23.1   ISI-ORGANIZED INSURGENT COUNTERATTACKS FROM
PAKISTANI SANCTUARIES, 2005–2009

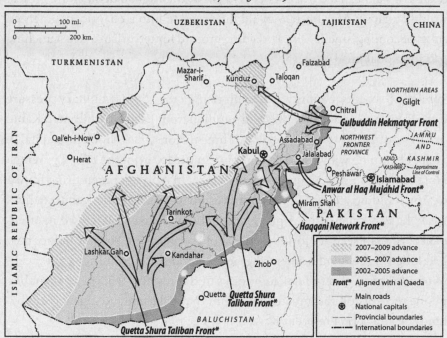

the *Washington Post* quoted a U.S. soldier as saying, "The Frontier Corps might as well be Taliban. . . . They are active facilitators of infiltration." Pakistan's Frontier Corps, the *Post* reporter wrote, "is viewed as nearly an enemy force." The following month in Helmand, British commandos killed a Taliban commander who turned out to be a Pakistani military officer.[5]

The same period witnessed a stream of Afghan government charges, sometimes confirmed by the United States, that Pakistani intelligence organizations were sheltering Osama bin Laden and Mullah Omar in Pakistan. In a 2006 *Frontline* interview, I noted that Musharraf had handed over lower-level al-Qaeda cadre but was withholding information on bin Laden and al-Qaeda elements responsible for the 9/11 attacks. I said that Musharraf considered the al-Qaeda leadership hiding in Pakistani sanctuaries as levers to extract more resources from Washington. Answering questions, I stated there were many reasons why things were not going well in Afghanistan. The violence hemorrhaging out of the ISI's holy war infrastructure on the Pakistani Frontier was the main one. I suggested that the United States stop believing Musharraf's periodic statements of cooperation in stabilizing Afghanistan and insist on results. If Pakistan did not end its proxy war, the Afghan democratic project would collapse. Afghanistan would disintegrate into a chaotic, fragmented state, becoming, once again, a breeding ground for terrorism and a launching pad for global jihad.[6]

While U.S. coalition units coped with rising cross-border military pressure from Pakistan, suicide bombers and gunmen from Pakistan infiltrated Kabul to carry out bloody terrorist attacks. Three major strikes shook the capital in 2008, beginning with a suicide bombing in the lobby of the five-star Serena Hotel, killing six and wounding many more. In April, gunmen firing from a nearby building attempted to shoot President Karzai in the Kabul stadium while he was celebrating Afghan national day with a large crowd in attendance. Afghan security forces fatally shot the gunmen, but not before they had killed three dignitaries sitting near Karzai. After examining their cellphones, Afghan government authorities told the media that they had mobile phone records to substantiate their claim that Pakistani intelligence was behind the attack on President Karzai.[7]

In June, suicide bombers from Pakistan attacked the Indian embassy in Kabul. A *New York Times* article cited "United States government officials" as concluding that "members of Pakistan's powerful spy service helped plan the deadly July 7, [2008,] bombing of India's Embassy in Kabul." The U.S. officials told the reporters that this conclusion "was based on intercepted communications between Pakistani intelligence officers and militants who carried out the attack." A UN study concluded that more than 80 percent of suicide bombers in Afghanistan had been recruited and trained in Pakistan.[8]

Extensive open-source reporting unveiled the operations of the ISI's holy-war infrastructure in Pakistan to train foreign terrorists. The number of European jihadis entering the "terror pipeline" connecting Europe and America to sanctuaries in Pakistan steadily rose through the decade. Denis Blair, U.S. director of national intelligence, warned in February 2009 that "the primary threat from Europe-based extremists stems from al-Qa'ida and Sunni affiliates who return from training in Pakistan to conduct attacks in Europe or the United States."[9]

A remarkable description of Pakistani training camps run by Lashkar-i Taiba and attended by a French jihadi was revealed by a retired French investigating magistrate in November 2009. A French court convicted the French trainee on terrorist charges in 2007 and sentenced him to nine years in prison. The magistrate's book stated that "CIA officers accompanied by Pakistani officials" had made four separate inspection visits to his Lashkar training camp. To prevent the CIA from discovering the presence of the foreign trainees, they were removed from the camp for the duration of the visit. Indications that the camp was associated with Lashkar-i Taiba were also erased. The book's narrative continued:

> But, since most of the officers of Lashkar belonged to the army, these inspections were doomed to draw a blank. The foreign recruits were alerted on the eve of the arrival of the inspection teams by the instructors, military men informed by their hierarchy.
>
> The trainees had to . . . erase any traces of their presence and head to an elevation of more than 13,000 feet while the inspections lasted.[10]

Despite ample evidence that the Pakistani Army was orchestrating Taliban offensives inside Afghanistan, the avalanche of unconditioned American aid to Pakistan continued. From 2002 to 2009, the rising flow of U.S. money to Pakistan paralleled the steady territorial expansion of the Taliban inside Afghanistan. In 2004, the Bush administration named Pakistan a "major non-NATO ally," a position enjoyed only by America's closest democratic allies outside the NATO bloc. The designation gave Pakistan's army access to higher-quality and more sensitive American military equipment, including drones. Presidents Bush and Musharraf kept in close personal touch during this period. Bush was said to wave away intelligence briefings critical of Musharraf.[11] In 2007, the president erroneously told ABC News that "he's been a loyal ally in fighting terrorism. He's also advanced democracy in Pakistan."[12]

After Operation Enduring Freedom drove the Taliban from Afghanistan into Pakistan, the Bush administration transferred a total of $12.4 billion in security and economic assistance to Musharraf's military government, plus several more billions in unpublished covert military and other forms of aid. The huge amounts of unconditioned American assistance to Islamabad indirectly contributed to Taliban military successes against the U.S.-led coalition and Afghan security forces in Afghanistan. Congressman Ed Royce (R-CA) was one of the few on Capitol Hill who consistently objected to providing military and economic aid to Pakistan without a payback in Afghanistan. He wrote in a June 2004 op-ed: "For all the U.S. aid being sent to Islamabad, it is time we got something in return. Pakistan must be held to account if we are going to help Afghanistan succeed."[13]

꙳

Skillful U.S. management of relations with Afghanistan's neighbors, especially Pakistan, was imperative if the United States was going to achieve its goals in Afghanistan after the Taliban's overthrow. So, of course, was effectively working with Afghans to stabilize, secure, and reconstruct their country. Three major U.S. errors inside Afghanistan, however, exacerbated the deteriorating trends primarily caused by Pakistan's renewed proxy war in Afghanistan. The first was Washington's squandering of the initial momentum achieved by the decisive defeat of the Taliban in November and December 2001. The second was the unintended fostering by American and Afghan officials of a ruinous circle of American preeminence and Afghan dependence. The third was the American failure to grasp the importance of the historical equilibrium between Afghanistan's thousands of autonomous microcommunities in the countryside and the Afghan government at the center.

The overthrow of the Taliban regime created an opportunity for the Afghans to carry out the act of self-determination that had been blocked by Pakistan since the Soviet invasion. It was a time for the international community to help Afghans revive their self-governing institutions and to help them succeed by providing resources, training, and advice. The December 2001 Bonn Conference established a roadmap to rebuild the constitutional order that had existed during the 1963–1973 decade of democracy under King Zahir Shah. It tracked with UN special envoy Benon Sevan's 1991–1992 blueprint that Pakistan had publicly supported but covertly sabotaged. Now it could finally be implemented: a loya jirga in 2002 to elect an acting interim president; a second loya jirga to approve a constitution; national presidential elections in 2004, and parliamentary, provincial, and district council elections to follow in 2005.

In 2002 the Afghan people desperately looked to America and the Karzai regime to escape from poverty and war. Their support for Karzai and the U.S. coalition continued unabated up to and past the October 2004 presidential elections, when over 70 percent of eligible voters turned out and gave Karzai

55.4 percent of the vote.[14] The majority of rural voters were non-literate. They did not understand democracy. They were voting for hope—hope that the new system would end their impoverishment and bring back security.

The success of the newly elected Afghan government, however, was critically dependent on results. In 2002, conditions were ripe for progress in most of the country. The Karzai regime announced that its top priority was to improve the population's livelihood. After a quarter century of war, 53 percent of the population lived below the poverty line. One in four children died prior to their first birthday, giving Afghanistan the third-highest infant mortality rate in the world.[15]

The Afghan government required substantial amounts of foreign aid and coalition troops to help Karzai re-create a viable and accountable government and provide security until Afghan security forces were trained and fielded. "There is really no area in which Afghanistan does not require assistance," Karzai stated in December 2001, after his inauguration as interim leader. Only three courthouses were left standing in the country. The Taliban had looted the banks before leaving for Pakistan. Where they existed, government offices lacked such basics as chairs—the Taliban believed in sitting on the floor. The few battered manual typewriters lacked keys. Records were missing, telephones sitting on desks since Najib's rule no longer worked. The deputy minister of irrigation and power apologized to a reporter visiting his bombed-out ministry: "You see, we don't have anything, except our hospitality," he told her.[16]

American assistance to quickly build an Afghan army and police force was vital to preventing a Taliban comeback and ending warlord control of the countryside. In February 2002, the U.S. chairman of the Joint Chiefs of Staff sent a CentCom-led interagency team to Afghanistan to make recommendations on the size and structure of a reconstituted Afghan national army to stabilize the country. Major General Charles "Hondo" Campbell, the U.S. Central Command chief of staff, chaired the delegation. His March 8, 2002, report to the Pentagon painted a gloomy picture of the state of the Afghan Army. The nation's military infrastructure, he informed, had been "substantially destroyed" during the previous two decades of warfare. Karzai's interim government could not afford to uniform, equip, billet, and feed a military force. Afghan Minister of Defense Mohammad Fahim told Campbell that the government could not provide for the most basic needs of an army. Campbell described the eight army corps around the country as a "loose federation of

ill-disciplined armed factions . . . with shifting allegiances." The air force was
"virtually non-existent." The military academy and other military training institutions were not functioning. Campbell advised that the rebuilding of the
Afghan national army begin as "rapidly as possible" to make the Afghan government "capable of controlling its own territory, securing its borders, and
enforcing its laws."[17]

General Campbell's report laid out exactly what was required to rebuild
the Afghan Army. His recommendations should have been implemented, but
they were not. An international donor conference in January 2002 in Tokyo
raised pledges of $4.5 billion for Afghan reconstruction.[18] The meeting, un-
fortunately, did not address rebuilding the Afghan Army and police force.
Those important issues were postponed to a Group of Eight (G-8) meeting
in Geneva in April 2002, where they received haphazard treatment. The
United States assumed the lead responsibility to fund, train, and equip a new
Afghan National Army (ANA). Germany took responsibility for the police,
Italy for the justice sector, Britain counternarcotics, and Japan the disarma-
ment, demobilization, and reintegration of armed groups of militias. Not one
of these efforts was given sufficient resources to succeed, including the U.S.
commitment to the ANA.

Operation Enduring Freedom and the reestablishment of an Afghan government created a momentum that needed to be exploited before the Taliban
came roaring back from Pakistan. For about three years, the Bush administration had a window of opportunity to get Afghanistan back on its feet after
more than two decades of war. President Bush's foreign policy team squandered the opportunity; it would not return during the remaining years of his
presidency.

The president's initial aversion to nation-building may have contributed
to Washington's low levels of economic and military assistance to Afghanistan
after the overthrow of the Taliban. "I think what we need to do is convince
people who live in the lands they live in to build the nation," Bush stated during a 2000 presidential debate. "I mean, we're going to have kind of a nation-
building corps from America? Absolutely not."[19]

In April 2002, President Bush rhetorically reversed his position, pledging
a grandiose plan for Afghanistan in a speech at the Virginia Military Institute.

He did not, however, increase the minuscule portion of the U.S. Agency for International Development's budget earmarked for Afghanistan. The USAID funding appropriated for fiscal year 2003, which began on October 1, 2002, was in fact $35 million *less* than the previous year's budget that overlapped with Taliban rule. In June 2002, USAID "deactivated" its Disaster Assistance Relief Team for Afghanistan, claiming it was no longer necessary. During my September 2002 visit, Afghans and Americans alike complained about the absence of development activity. Only about one hundred small-scale projects by the U.S. military were under way. Missing were the kinds of major efforts USAID could do, from village self-development programs to rural development programs that would stimulate the economy and large road and power projects.[20]

The Bush administration disputed warnings from those who believed that things were going badly in Afghanistan. It projected Afghanistan as a successful American war, a precedent for the coming war with Iraq. Donald Rumsfeld declared in 2003: "We clearly have moved from major combat activity to a period of stability and stabilization and reconstruction activities. . . . The bulk of the country today is permissive, it's secure."[21]

Congress attempted to focus Bush's attention on Afghanistan during the crucial early years of relative stability after the Taliban's defeat. Senator Chuck Hagel (R-NE) and Congressman Henry Hyde (R-IL) sponsored the 2002 Afghanistan Freedom Support Act to raise U.S. humanitarian and economic assistance to $400 million per year. The bill called on the president to formulate a comprehensive Afghan policy, stressed the importance of institution building and Afghan ownership of the reconstruction process. I supported the legislation in congressional hearings, urging Congress to allocate more resources for Afghan reconstruction and particularly to strengthen Afghan self-governing institutions. The legislation passed both houses and was signed by the president in December 2002.[22]

Invited back to Congress to testify on reconstruction progress in October 2003, I told the Senate Committee on Foreign Relations that, so far, most policy and operational elements in the legislation had not been implemented or had been only marginally implemented. In Washington and Afghanistan, drift, policy incoherence, underfunding, and slow and poorly managed execution of reconstruction projects continued to characterize the administration's approach to Afghanistan.[23]

The Bonn Conference and the UN Security Council resolutions gave all the rights of sovereignty and great authority to the Karzai government, mandating that "all Mujahidin, Afghan forces and armed groups in the country shall come under the command and control of the Interim Authority, i.e. the central government."[24] Karzai's government, however, did not have the military or economic capability to exercise these lofty mandates. In the regions, the CIA and the U.S. military subsidized many of the unpopular warlords who had been disarmed, suppressed, or exiled by the Taliban. These warlords offered their services to the Americans, the ISI, Muslim extremists, and sometimes all three simultaneously.[25] They amounted to a militarized wall between the internationally recognized Afghan government and Afghan rural communities desperate for aid and security. Warlords seized customs revenues at points of entry into Afghanistan. Numerous warlords around the country, large and small, ran narcotics and criminal enterprises to sustain their fiefdoms.

Inside Afghanistan, the U.S. embassy, the U.S. military, and the CIA often operated in separate stovepipes and at cross purposes. There was no integrated U.S. policy enforced by the White House to coordinate all U.S. agency efforts. Sometimes one agency backed Afghans who competed with Afghan rivals supported by other agencies, a problem that the Soviet leadership in the 1980s constantly struggled with but never resolved. In 2002, Bacha Khan Zadran, an American-funded warlord in eastern Afghanistan, declared personal dominion over three eastern provinces, Khost, Paktika, and Paktiya. He rejected Karzai's appointment of a new Paktiya governor and issued an ultimatum demanding that Karzai's appointee leave Gardez, Paktiya's provincial capital. When Karzai's governor refused, Zadran shelled and attacked the city with his militia force.

While the CIA and U.S. military were boosting warlords, U.S. Ambassador Robert Finn backed the Karzai government. In 2003, Ambassador Finn ended USAID assistance to warlords Abdul Rashid Dostum and Atta Mohammad when they defied Karzai and started a mini-war against each other in the north. Both were on the payroll of other U.S. agencies. Lacking a national army, Karzai appeased them with official positions, urging them to cooperate; instead, they flouted his authority. While Karzai powerlessly stood by in Kabul, they battled each other with tanks, artillery, and ground forces for control of Mazar-i-Sharif. Over 1,000 died in the fighting.[26]

The Bush administration prepared in 2002 and 2003 to launch the Iraq war, shifting resources and high-level attention from Afghanistan to Iraq. The Pentagon began to pull troops away from Afghanistan in early 2002. That year, Captain Jason Amerine's 5th Special Forces group, which had gained respect among Afghans and familiarity with the Afghan environment, was airlifted out of Afghanistan to the Middle East. Air assets and sophisticated intelligence equipment were moved to the Iraq theater. Even the large U.S. Army generators at the Kandahar Airport were taken out of Afghanistan. A U.S. CentCom official explained why: "We're simply in a world of limited resources, and those resources are in Iraq. . . . Anyone who tells you differently is blowing smoke."[27]

Karzai appointed Haji Qadir, Abdul Haq's brother, to be first vice president. Qadir enthusiastically began to discharge his heavy responsibilities, which also included the Public Works Ministry and the Nangarhar governorship. He was the only Pashtun vice president, a respected veteran Mujahidin commander who had left Pakistan to join Masood's multiethnic Northern Alliance to fight the Taliban. A moderate-nationalist, Qadir was, like his deceased brother Abdul Haq, a member of the prestigious Arsala family of Nangarhar, an Afghan poised to play an important role in Afghan national politics. That was not to be.

In July 2002, a group of assassins cornered Qadir in his car in Kabul at around 11 a.m. in broad daylight. They shot and killed him and made their getaway in a car with a driver parked nearby. Qadir's death delivered a damaging blow to the Afghan stabilization effort. In 2006 Afghan investigators arrested the driver of the assassin's vehicle. An Afghan court sentenced the driver to death. He implicated the ISI-connected warlord of Tora Bora infamy, Haji Zaman Ghamsharik, then still in Pakistan, and his brother Haji Aman Khari. Khari was arrested, jailed, and subsequently freed on a court order.[28]

Reconstructing the Afghan Army was perhaps the single most important project to stabilize Afghanistan. As Abdul Haq and Masood said many times, foreign, especially American, assistance was sorely needed to fight the Taliban, but Afghans should do the fighting and dying. General Campbell's March 2002 recommendations carefully mapped out the ideal path to put Afghans in charge of their own security, to begin standing up an Afghan Army, and to train Afghan trainers to continue that mission over the long run.

"The most pressing need," Campbell stressed in his report, was to establish a "credible and responsive military capability to the Afghan government as rapidly and as effectively as possible."[29] He advised supporting the Karzai government's intention to reestablish the Afghan Army on the precommunist, professional model to be trained by a U.S. training task force for eighteen months:

> This puts 50–60,000 men in the land forces; 45,000 in the border forces; and 45,000 in the transport-oriented aviation force. Additionally, there will be a headquarters layer (MOD and Corps), as well as a robust schooling system. . . . MOD [Ministry of Defense] has agreed to support an ANA training program that will begin a 12-week training cycle for the first three, multi-ethnic, light infantry battalions and a border battalion as early as April 2002. Leader training and a "train the trainer" program will be conducted concurrently with the training of the battalions . . . for approximately eighteen months. At that time, U.S. trained Afghan National Army trainers would assume the training mission.[30]

Campbell estimated the cost of training the necessary sixteen light infantry battalions and ten border battalions over eighteen months at $15.7 million. His report advised that the U.S. reliance on warlord militia was impractical and insufficient.[31]

Because the Bush administration did not implement Campbell's recommendations, there was no Afghan Army to oppose the annual, large scale Taliban offensives that began in 2005. Only unreliable, U.S.-funded warlords filled the security vacuum in the countryside. Washington's sole alternative was to commit increasing numbers of U.S. troops to blunt the Taliban's counterattacks from their bases in Pakistan.

Despite dedicated efforts by National Guard units from Oregon and other states, training programs to build an Afghan National Army and an Afghan National Police (ANP) force from scratch remained at relatively low priority levels during the Bush administration. In June 2008, the U.S. Government Accountability Office (GAO) completed an assessment of the effort. It found, as a Reuters article put it, that "the United States has no comprehensive plan to build Afghanistan's army and police, which remain poorly equipped and significantly unprepared to operate without help."[32] The assessment noted that "less than 2 percent (2 of 105 units) . . . are assessed as fully capable of conducting their primary mission. Thirty-six percent (38 of 105) are assessed as capable of conducting their mission, but require routine international assistance, while the remaining ANA units (65 of 105 units) are either planned, in basic training, or assessed as partially able or unable to conduct their primary mission." The ANP was even worse off: "No Afghan police unit is assessed as fully capable of performing its mission," the report stated.[33]

In addition to squandering the initial momentum after the Taliban's overthrow, the Bush administration also erred in not building the governing capacity of the Afghan government. The Soviet failures in Afghanistan were partially due to the Soviet takeover of civilian and military governing responsibilities normally exercised by the indigenous government. The urge to do it yourself, the Soviet way, did not work in tribal Afghanistan.

In 2006, General David H. Petraeus oversaw a one-year program at the U.S. army base at Ft. Leavenworth, Kansas, to rewrite the army's counterinsurgency (COIN) field manual.[34] Published in 2007, the excellent volume overlapped considerably with the counterinsurgency teachings of British diplomat and civil servant Sir Robert Thompson, one of the architects of Britain's successful campaign against the 1951–1954 Malay insurgency. Both Petraeus and Thompson accented the importance of a "population-centric" strategy, describing the population's loyalty as the center of gravity in counterinsurgencies. General Stanley McChrystal, the U.S. commander in Afghanistan in 2009, called attention to this emphasis when he told an American television audience in September 2009 that, "if the people are against us, we cannot be successful."[35]

Sir Robert Thompson gave relatively more prominence to supporting the host-country government in his COIN philosophy relative to the new U.S. counterinsurgency manual. Thompson stressed that the main task of supporting governments was to increase the ability of the supported government to defeat the insurgency. Thompson urged that the supporting state build the capacity of the government's civilian and military institutions. He highlighted the importance of formulating "an overall plan"[36] integrating military, political, social, economic, administrative, police, and other elements. The plan was important for protecting the population, but it also showed the way for the government to provide the population with social and economic benefits, thereby creating a feeling of "permanence with a promise of further progress and prosperity."[37]

Thompson pinpointed mistakes frequently committed by supporting governments, including permitting various agencies of the supporting states to conduct turf battles with one another. He insisted that all implementing agencies of the supporting state should support the unified plan; otherwise, he cautioned, "a situation will develop in which everyone is fighting his own little war without regard to anyone else." Thompson further advocated that the supporting power's agencies must "resist the temptation to take over" governing functions because "they think they can do them better.... If they give in to the temptation, they will be failing in their main task, which is to build up the administrative machinery of the local government and the experience of the individuals in it so that the local officials themselves perform their duties more effectively."[38]

The 2005 Taliban offensives forced the Bush administration to raise troop levels from 8,000 to over 18,000 in 2006. The United States also raised the level of economic aid and accelerated the Afghan Army's growth from 21,000 in 2006 to 46,000 in 2008. The increased assistance, however, was carried out without regard to Thompson's advice to keep the supported state in the lead. On the ground, Americans and other foreigners directly guided most of the Afghan government's civilian and military functions. Reminiscent of the Soviet period, the Afghans were given assignments to carry out foreign-devised and -funded programs. The American drive to get the job done was well meaning. But that forfeited the greater imperative of building the capacity of the supported state's nascent institutions, however weak, to function when troop drawdowns would eventually begin.

The increased American assistance to Afghanistan after 2005 substantially expanded the Western in-country military and economic presence. That year, the three arms of the U.S.-led coalition, NATO, the International Security Assistance Force (ISAF), and all U.S. military forces in Afghanistan, were consolidated under an American lieutenant general. The influx of foreign aid went toward building schools, waterworks, health clinics, and agricultural projects. New universities opened their doors in regional cities, and USAID sponsored an American University of Kabul. Afghanistan moved past technologies that had bypassed the country during the dark decades of the 1980s and 1990s. Rather than rebuilding the old land-line hard-wired telephone networks, foreign aid supported commercial cellular telephone enterprises to create servers for cellphone users. By 2009, over 30 percent of the population possessed cellphones and had calling plans. Only one television channel was operating in Afghanistan after the Taliban's ouster. By 2010, over a dozen privately owned channels were being broadcast from Kabul alone. Afghanistan also boasted the most progressive press and speech laws in the region. Print media outlets climbed above one hundred. In 2001 there were virtually no paved roads left anywhere in the country. Road construction projects by many foreign countries and multilateral institutions expanded the road network in Afghanistan. By 2009 the national ring road was 90 percent refurbished, and 50 percent of all major roads were paved or otherwise made accessible year-round. The number of students in the classroom leaped to over 10 million, 40 percent of them girls.

All of these initiatives represented widely accepted counterinsurgency measures to attract popular support. But, since the projects were not carried out by the Afghan government, the Afghan population did not give the government credit for bettering their lives—an important COIN goal in the American counterinsurgency manual and Thompson's writings. The average Afghan knew that the projects were conceived, planned, and carried out by foreigners. At best, the Afghan government was in a supporting role. This image of Afghan dependence and American preeminence put more wind in the sails of the insurgency. A frustrated Stanley McChrystal remarked in 2009, "We could do good things in Afghanistan for the next 100 years and fail. Because we're doing a lot of good things and it just doesn't add up to success."[39]

❧

The pattern of American preeminence first appeared during Operation Enduring Freedom in October and November 2001 when the United States subsidized Afghan warlords to perform specific military assignments. This American paymaster–Afghan payee relationship undermined Karzai's authority and that of the central government as well as local governments.

The U.S. military and the CIA assumption that they could buy warlord cooperation to help stabilize the country was flawed. The warlords sought personal power, control over territory, and freedom to undertake criminal activity in their areas unopposed by the U.S. coalition and the Afghan government.

FIGURE 23.1   AMERICAN PREEMINENCE, AFGHAN DEPENDENCE

American Preeminence

Commander of U.S., NATO, coalition
forces in Afghanistan
American ambassador
American military, intelligence,
civilian advisers
Foreign* consultants, contractors,
NGOs

Warlords**

Afghan president (Hamid Karzai)
Afghan cabinet
Tribal chiefs
Ulema
Afghan National Security Forces
Provincial governors and
police chiefs

Afghan Dependence

* Foreign-hired and -paid Afghan diaspora civilians are included among the consultants and contractors.
** Warlords draw on American largesse and also benefit from President Hamid Karzai's appointments.

They viewed the United States as a source of patronage, not an ally. Gul Agha, a major beneficiary of U.S. payments, speaking to a British reporter, once quipped, "Poor Americans scurrying here and there, not knowing who to believe! They think that they can solve everything with dollars."[40]

Early on, Hamid Karzai and the U.S. government equally fell into the pattern of American preeminence and Afghan dependence, prompting many more Afghans to believe he had been chosen by the Americans. American military support had helped Karzai survive at Tarinkot, and the United States had promoted Karzai's selection as interim leader at the Bonn Conference, where no formal vote had been taken. On settling into the presidential palace in January 2002, Karzai found that he exercised no real control over military affairs. Nor did his defense ministers, first the Northern Alliance's Mohammad Fahim and then his successor, Rahim Wardak, the former military adviser to Sayyid Ahmad Gailani. U.S. military commanders decided operational matters. Americans advisers inside the Defense Ministry reported to their in-country ISAF and NATO superiors. The U.S. military still controlled Afghan air space. Under a "dual key" arrangement, both U.S. and Afghan officers had to approve specific deployments of Afghan battalions outside Kabul. U.S. control of military transportation assets further strengthened the coalition's influence over operational decisionmaking. The United States paid the ministry's bills.

To Karzai's annoyance, the U.S. military and the CIA maintained their own prisons inside Afghanistan. In rural areas, U.S. convoys charged down country roads firing warning shots in the air, forcing local civilians into adjoining fields. Civilian casualties caused by bombing and night raids in the tribal hinterland became a major problem. The Pashtunwali imperative of *badal* (retribution) for family members killed, injured, or dishonored, or for property damaged, sowed resentment or outright opposition to the coalition and the Afghan government. The CIA created outposts around the country, and its agents, with Special Forces teams, conducted night raids on homes believed to harbor high-value al-Qaeda and Taliban targets without informing the Afghan government's political or military authorities.

As during the Soviet occupation, foreign advisers in the ministries, foreign embassies, and aid missions made most of the important government decisions; Afghan ministers and President Karzai simply endorsed them. USAID deepened Afghan dependency by directly hiring some nine hundred foreign expatriates[41] to staff senior positions in the Afghan government. These high-ranking bureaucrats were on the USAID payroll and answered to USAID officials, not Afghan ministers or Karzai and his three vice presidents. Most proved disappointing. Many were diaspora Afghans[42] eager to pocket their lucrative salaries, stay glued to Kabul, and return to their families abroad when their contracts expired.[43]

Western NGOs contributed to the ruinous circle by taking over the development reins normally held by national and local governments in aid-receiving nations. A popular joke making the rounds in Afghan government offices boasted that Afghans had defeated the British and the Soviets. Now they faced the most fearsome invader of all: NGOs. Competition among NGOs for grants from foreign governments and international organizations was stiff. Most NGOs are staffed by workers dedicated to helping local populations, but very few look on host-country governments as genuine partners. Generally, they consult with local officials, but only when necessary. Mostly they directly implement projects that they have landed from foreign aid donors; the funds are "theirs," not to be shared with host-country government ministries.

Thousands of NGOs and contractors followed the flow of Washington's aid to countries emerging from conflict, traveling to Bosnia, Kosovo, East Timor, and Afghanistan (and, after 2004, Iraq). Over 10,000 nongovernmental foreign aid workers and contractors flocked to Afghanistan, establishing 341 international NGOs. The Afghan vein they tapped was a thick one. By June 2008, foreign donors had pledged a total of $35 billion for Afghanistan. Foreign NGOs and contractors spent the bulk of the aid in salaries, exorbitant rents in Kabul ($5,000–$6,000 a month), security guards, vehicles, and travel and leave expenses.[44] In the end, less than 15 percent of the original funding was spent on the intended projects. Billions of dollars committed to Afghan reconstruction by the United States and its allies were dissipated through the rampant corruption and enormous waste and misuse of funds on the part of Afghans, NGOs, and private contractors.[45]

The decision to channel the great bulk of foreign assistance for development projects around the Afghan government deprived it of resources to grow. Some of the aid money, about 29 percent, or $4.2 billion out of $14.5 billion, dispersed over the first eight years of Karzai's administration was placed in joint "trust funds" to be managed by foreigners and Afghans. The overall outcome was that the government did not have the funds for its own education, health, and agricultural development programs or for other services the population needed. It could not even pay its employees reasonable wages.[46]

☙

I knew Hamid Karzai to be a very decent and compassionate man. He is a devout Muslim completely dedicated to the Afghan people, an Afghan patriot, and moderate in his politics. I witnessed his bravery under fire during the September 2002 attempt on his life in Kandahar. In the Afghan cultural tradition, he carries his personal honor and that of his country high on his shoulders. President Karzai is ultimately a politician. He uses words; patronage, including appointments; indulgence of vast corruption; and, most notably, his skillful exercise of the Afghan jirga tradition to stay on top of the Afghan tribal summit. Wielding military force does not come naturally to him. This differentiates Karzai from the martyred commanders Abdul Haq, Ahmed Shah Masood, and Haji Abdul Qadir. They each would have been tougher in dealing with the warlords and in rejecting the Afghan dependence syndrome.

Karzai's willingness to defer to the American lead was especially evident from 2002 to 2004, the year when he received his presidential mandate from Afghan voters. Until then his political position was not secure. That vulnerability coincided with the eagerness of some American officials and generals to enter the Afghan political cauldron, thus bolstering American preeminence and Afghan dependence. Afghan dependence consequently flowered at the June 2002 loya jirga in Kabul, convened to choose the Afghan interim president, who would lead the country until the 2004 presidential elections. At the time, Afghan-American Zalmay Khalilzad was the major force behind the Bush administration's decisions on Afghanistan. A leading neoconservative, he enjoyed direct access to Bush and National Security Adviser Condoleezza Rice, according to one reporter.[47] Khalilzad had worked closely with Vice President Dick Cheney, Defense Secretary Donald Rumsfeld, and Deputy Defense Secretary Paul Wolfowitz in previous Republican administrations. He was aggressive where Karzai was passive, sure of himself and confident of White House support.

On June 10, 2002, 900 of the 1,500 delegates banded together near the loya jirga meeting site to support Zahir Shah as transitional president instead of Karzai. The loya jirga was to convene the next day. In a BBC interview, Zahir Shah's chief adviser, Abdul Wali, was asked whether the ex-king would be willing to play the leading role in the country if he was requested to do so. Wali responded that the decision was up to the Afghan people. The king would follow whatever the Afghan people decided. That was a clear sign to most of the BBC audience that the former king—and Abdul Wali behind him—were hoping to regain the Afghan summit. Karzai and Khalilzad thought that Zahir Shah's role should be to legitimize Karzai, not supersede him. He would be the "Father of the Nation" and perform purely ceremonial functions. Wali's indication that Zahir Shah was ready to accept the decision of the loya jirga made Karzai's election no longer a certainty. Indeed, it seemed probable that Zahir Shah would be chosen by the majority of the delegates after the loya jirga commenced the following day, June 11.

On the evening of June 10, the jirga delegates were unexpectedly informed that the schedule had been changed. The June 11 opening had been postponed. According to multiple eyewitness accounts,[48] Khalilzad confronted Abdul Wali at the king's residence. He demanded that Zahir Shah read a statement to the media denying that he was a candidate to lead the transition. Wali acceded to Khalilzad's pressure. Karzai's staff prepared a written statement for the king to read at a hastily convened press conference later that afternoon. During the news conference, with Khalilzad present, Zahir Shah read the statement declaring he would not be a candidate for transitional president of Afghanistan. The news release reporting the king's statement was also written by Karzai's staff. It was distributed to loya jirga delegates and broadcast by the media inside Afghanistan and worldwide. The next day's opening of the conference was uneventful. The delegates formally elected Hamid Karzai a few days later.

By blatantly interfering with the Afghan leadership selection process on behalf of Hamid Karzai, the United States fumbled a rare opportunity to let Afghans themselves choose a leader who would not be seen as imposed by outsiders. The mood during the conference was subdued. Many delegates complained afterward they had not been able to elect the leader they wanted. Once again, outsiders, this time the American government, had intervened to make the decision for them. Three months later in New Delhi, the Afghan ambassador to India, Masood Khalili, commented to me: "Out of 1,500 delegates, 1,000 went back to their villages saying the loya jirga was not fair; the outcome was determined by the Americans." The American interference in the process enlarged Karzai's image as an American puppet.

Khalilzad left the National Security Council and replaced Finn as ambassador in November 2003. During his tenure, he pressed hard for more American economic and military aid for Afghanistan and succeeded in getting it. Overall, however, his invasive style reinforced the pattern of American preeminence and Afghan dependency. According to an American journalist who was reporting extensively on Afghanistan after the Taliban's overthrow:

Khalilzad was far more than an ambassador. U.S. diplomats described his role as the country's chief executive—with Karzai as the figurehead chairman—for the 19 months of his ambassadorship.

By his own account, Khalilzad ate dinner six nights a week at the presidential palace, where he met with Karzai and his advisers into the evening. No significant decision was made by Karzai in that time without Khalilzad's involvement, and sometimes his cajoling and prodding, the diplomats said. . . .

"Khalilzad's approach fundamentally weakened Karzai," said a veteran Western diplomat. "Karzai was seen by many Afghans as a puppet of the Americans. It delegitimized him."[49]

U.S. backing at the 2002 loya jirga strengthened Karzai's political position in the run-up to the 2004 elections. But to survive in the Afghan political arena, he needed to develop a personal patronage network. That lies at the heart of Afghan politics. He did not control the ANA and the ANP. Warlords dominated much of the countryside. To gain their support, Karzai set about co-opting or buying them off with offers of cabinet posts and governorships.[50] He gave power brokers like Rabbani, Sayyaf, and the larger warlords the prerogative to choose cabinet ministers, police chiefs, and members of his presidential staff. He selectively protected their corruption and drug trafficking if they supported him. His brother, Ahmed Wali, became the most powerful warlord in Kandahar. Karzai appointed the American-citizen son of an influential tribal chief in Kandahar to lead the anticorruption office, despite his having spent five years in an American penitentiary for narcotics trafficking. When too many foreign governments complained about the appointment, Karzai made him governor of the drug-infested Farah Province.

Karzai's lack of management capability increased his government's dependency on the United States. He worked extremely long hours each day of the week, conducting meeting after meeting with Afghan government officials, tribal leaders, visiting foreign dignitaries, local ambassadors, and generals. Unreported by the media, he devoted considerable time to mediating tribal disputes and dampening rivalries threatening to erupt into mini-wars. But consistent with Afghan oral traditions and the absence of bureaucratic capacity, his staff kept few written records. Karzai conveyed instructions by word of mouth. There was little follow-up. He approved documents at times without reading their contents. In March 2009 he signed into law the Shiite Personal Status Law, which sanctioned marital rape. After an outburst of Western media criticism, he later admitted that he had not read all of its 240 provisions.[51] The law's most controversial parts were dropped. But no member of his staff suffered for this gross negligence.

Karzai's lax management style was manifested in 2003 when USAID sent him two organizational charts on "The Structure of the Office of the President." He was invited to choose one of the charts to set up his office. The charts each contained forty-three boxes, including positions for the presidential chief of staff and a secretary, three deputies, and a National Security Council overseen by British advisers. A Karzai staffer only slightly adjusted one of the charts and sent it back to USAID for implementation. Karzai's advisers occupying senior positions in his office were paid handsomely, and directly by the U.S. government or the United Nations rather than through the Afghan government's budgetary process. The president's chief of staff and his spokesman each received $6,500 a month.[52]

Karzai dodged demands from donor countries to address corruption. In 2008, Transparency International ranked Afghanistan as number 175 in a survey of 180 countries for its Corruption Perceptions Index. In 2009, Afghanistan fell to second from the bottom, tied with Myanmar and just above Somalia, which was in last place. The booming narcotics trade was insidiously intertwined with the corrupt political system and the insurgency. Senior government ministers, governors, military officers, soldiers, and police shared in the profits.[53]

Foreign governments, including the U.S. embassy and military officers, entered the presidential appointment sweepstakes process, exacerbating the image of Afghan dependence. They made suggestions about whom Karzai should appoint, and in the case of the long-serving defense minister, Rahim Wardak, whom not to fire.[54] In 2009, a young, educated, disillusioned Afghan bureaucrat wrote a critique of government ministers that could easily have applied to the Soviet occupation period. "All are obedient to foreigners," he began. He then noted that Karzai's team "is not really a team, it is chaos, and a ship in chaos usually sinks. Most of the ministers are worried about their dependency on foreign embassies for support; they care more about their standing with ambassadors than they do about Afghan citizens. . . . They care more about having their foreign advisors writing them a speech in English so they can go abroad to a conference than they care about coordinating issues in Kabul."[55]

Karzai's October 2004 election victory offered an opening for him to assert his independence and change his image of dependency on foreigners. He planned to use his May 23, 2005, visit to the White House, his first to Washington after his election victory, to showcase a freely elected Afghan president defending Afghan perspectives. Before departing for the United States, Karzai listed three requests that he intended to present in Washington.

His highest priority was to gain some control over U.S. military operations, particularly regarding American air strikes resulting in Afghan civilian casualties.[56] He had pressed the issue with U.S. generals for four years without results. American military spokespersons usually identified the dead as insurgents. Investigations by the Afghan government and foreign reporters often revealed that they were not. American reluctance to accommodate Karzai partly centered on the essential goal of force protection and the reality that, in any war, civilian casualties were inevitable. In addition to the lives lost, civilian casualties from air strikes and night raids into Afghan homes were turning many Afghans against the United States and Karzai. Karzai was criticized for not stopping them.

The second request Karzai planned to make when meeting with President Bush was that the United States turn custody of Afghan prisoners at American-controlled prison facilities in Afghanistan over to the Afghans. Afghan popular opinion interpreted the existence of American-controlled prisons inside Afghanistan housing hundreds of Afghan prisoners as a blot on the country's honor. The third request was for the United States to take steps to end abuse of Afghan prisoners detained at U.S. military and CIA facilities inside Afghanistan. On May 22, a day before Karzai's meeting with Bush, a front-page *New York Times* article detailed the torture and death of two Afghan prisoners at the American prison at Bagram. Karzai told CNN's televised *Late Edition* that day that this was "simply not acceptable. We are angry about this." Karzai was also upset by the death in CIA custody of an Afghan in Konar. A *Washington Post* article reported that, responding to a request from American officials stationed in Konar, the governor had asked tribal elders to turn the suspect over to the Americans. When they did, a CIA contractor beat him to death.[57]

Karzai failed to move Bush on any of his three requests. He returned to Afghanistan, his position of powerlessness unaltered. The United States retained control over the custody and treatment of Afghan prisoners. The U.S. military's rules of engagement regulating air strikes remained basically unchanged until General Stanley A. McChrystal arrived in 2009.

⚓

The Bush administration's third major misstep in Afghanistan was overlooking the country's historical center-region balance. During the nearly five-decade era of tranquillity (1929–1978), the state structure of a nonintrusive central government and self-governing tribal communities in the regions functioned effectively. The center respected the autonomy of the communities; the communities did not turn against the center. In a January 13, 2011, article, the British Labor Party leader wrote that this historical political model for Afghanistan was the right one.[58]

The model capitalized on some unique features of Afghan society, in particular the autonomy of Afghan rural communities. The communities have never been appendages of the central government. Over half contain only a few hundred inhabitants or less. They have their own governing institutions, notably the jirga, often called by its Arabic-language counterpart, the shura. The communities resist any control from the outside. They are conservative. Islam plays an important role, as do ancient customs and traditions. They welcome government services and aid as long as they do not come with predatory officials, strings attached to compromise local autonomy, or conditions that would destabilize the local tribal and ethnic balances.

To succeed in Afghanistan, the U.S.-led coalition had to avoid upsetting the center-region equilibrium. Washington's reliance on warlords to maintain local security in the countryside inhibited reestablishment of the linkage between the government and communities in the regions. The United States initially did not recognize the value of the traditional village jirga and the influence of tribal elders in Afghanistan's rural communities. Tribal elders were moderate, influential potential allies of the Karzai government. Foreign-assisted, community-focused, bottom-up projects in partnership with the Afghan government could have strengthened the center's linkages to the communities, separating the people from the Taliban. A carefully administered governmental program providing military training, radio equipment, and weapons for community self-defense against the Taliban would have improved local security, denied the Taliban local recruits, and isolated warlords.

The later Bush years (2006–2009) witnessed haphazard attempts to engage local communities. The American and British militaries experimented with a variety of programs to help villages to defend themselves. The World Bank, backed by the United States and other donors, created the National Solidarity Program. Its purpose was to stimulate community-level development through new Community Development Councils tied to the Ministry of Rural Development. The project was a resounding success in many areas of the country. In others, it provoked conflict between traditional village elders chosen by the communities and local competitors attempting to convert the Community Development Councils into a power base from which to weaken the elders. Provincial Reconstruction Teams in the regions did good work in many localities. But their overall impact in the countryside was minimal. For example, only seven civil-action U.S. military officers and two vehicles were assigned to cover Zabul Province, which had a population of over 300,000. Force protection requirements often severely restricted the access that Provincial Reconstruction Teams had to the local population. The Afghan government seldom received credit for the assistance, since the teams usually provided it directly to the communities.

Before the Afghan wars began, the Afghan local policeman was usually the only government representative in the thousands of Afghan rural communities in the hinterland. He offered a government security presence and a communications channel into district or (where they existed) subdistrict offices. Rebuilding an effective ANP force could have made a valuable contribution to reviving the historic center-region equilibrium. From 2002 to 2007, a series of expensive German and American attempts to reestablish the ANP crumbled, one after the other. In 2007, an inspection report written by a retired U.S. general, Barry McCaffrey, concluded that previous American investments of billions of dollars to reform the Afghan police force had failed: "We have no real grasp of what actual ANP presence exists at the 355 District level operations," McCaffrey wrote. "We have trained 60,000 Afghan police—but we have no idea where they are. We do know that 50% more Afghan police were KIA (killed in action) last year than ANA soldiers. Probably there are non-uniformed, untrained, and largely criminal elements in many of the District Capitals. There are no real jails—or prosecutors—or judges—or squad cars."[59]

In 2008, the last year of Bush's presidency, the U.S. military began a major overhaul of the ANP, including its local police and paramilitary arm, the Civil Action Police. "We weren't doing it right," said Lieutenant General William Caldwell, who supervised NATO's police-training program in Afghanistan. "If we don't get the police fixed, we'll never change the dynamics in the country. No matter how well we do clearing and holding, we will never build on that progress and sustain it without a police force."[60]

❦

The bleak outlook in Afghanistan at the end of the Bush administration demanded, more than anything, a sweeping analysis of what had gone wrong during the previous six years. The incoming Obama administration, General Petraeus's appointment as CentCom commander, and General McChrystal's 2009 arrival in Afghanistan offered an opportunity for fresh thinking and initiatives to set a new course.

General Musharraf's fall from power in Pakistan three months before President Obama's election in November 2008 also presented Washington with an opening for a new direction in U.S. policy toward Pakistan. For the first two years after America's intervention in Afghanistan, Musharraf had artfully kept the two pillars of his duplicitous Afghan policy in play. The first pillar was maintaining the flow of billions of dollars of unconditioned American military, economic, and covert aid to Pakistan. The second was controlling the diverse elements of the unholy alliance and mobilizing its Pakistani, Afghan, and Arab Islamist parts to continue Pakistan's proxy war in Afghanistan and Kashmir.

In 2004, cracks appeared in the second pillar, Pakistan's unholy alliance. The loose collection of radical Pakistani tribal Pashtuns and al-Qaeda groupings in North and South Waziristan turned against Musharraf. They coordinated with a smaller group of al-Qaeda-influenced Pakistani extremists holed up in the Bajaur tribal agency on the other side of the Khyber Pass. They exported their defiance of Musharraf to the other five tribal agencies and into adjacent "settled areas" around Peshawar. Soon, a new, militant generation of Pashtun youth influenced by al-Qaeda and Pakistani religious clerics was questioning the Pakistani government's Islamic credentials. They called themselves the *Tehrik-i Taliban* Pakistan, the "Pakistani Taliban." Their criticism of Musharraf and of Pakistan's secular government filtered into the army. Fighters in the mainly Punjabi paramilitary groups that the ISI had covertly created and supported—Lashkar-i Taiba and Jaish-i Mohammad—deserted their units and joined the radicalized anti-Musharraf jihadis in the tribal agencies. They pledged loyalty to Mullah Omar but were ideologically closer to Osama bin Laden.

The Bush administration never appeared to decipher Musharraf's double game. The Pakistani Taliban and al-Qaeda did, and they vehemently rejected it. For them, Musharraf was on the wrong side of the epic battle between Islam and America. Taliban supporter, Jamiat-i Ulema-i Islam (JUI) leader, and member of parliament, Fazlur Rahman, said in a widely reported 2005 press conference in Lahore that "the rulers of Pakistan are not only trying to deceive the United States and the West, but also hoodwinking the entire [Pakistani] nation." An Afghan Taliban sympathizer in Kandahar expressed a similar view while speaking to a Canadian reporter: "The Pakistanis have two faces," he said. "Pakistan gets money from Americans and uses many tricks against the Taliban. They give the Taliban money, training and places to stay. On the other side, they arrest them and sell them."[61]

Mullah Omar and his Quetta Shura, representing the older generation of Taliban, remained supportive of Musharraf. The Afghan Taliban depended on the ISI's logistical cooperation to ship arms, ammunition, and supplies from Pakistan to Taliban forces fighting the American-led coalition in Afghanistan. The ISI kept Mullah Omar, one of America's Most Wanted men, away from the Americans. An order from Musharraf could land the entire Quetta Shura in jail, harm their families, put Omar in American custody, and push thousands of Afghan Taliban fighters across the border into Afghanistan toward the American-led coalition. Gulbuddin Hekmatyar's position in Pakistan was equally tenuous. Antagonizing Musharraf would be suicidal for him.

For over a hundred years the warlike Waziri and Mahsud tribes in North and South Waziristan had alternately pointed the Durand Line's prickly fence thorns north and south. The al-Qaeda presence in their midst sharpened their hostility toward Musharraf as well as the Kabul government and the U.S. coalition. Starting in 2004, Pakistani Taliban raiding parties—joined by criminals looking for plunder and drug traffickers—spreading the Taliban's "pure" brand of Islam penetrated Peshawar and other settled areas outside the tribal agencies. The Pakistani Army launched a desultory attack into South Waziristan, and Pakistani generals engaged the Pakistani Taliban in negotiations. They offered aid and cease-fires if the Pakistani Taliban would agree to turn their thorns back toward Afghanistan. Cease-fire accords were signed in 2006, 2007, and 2008.

The tribals broke each agreement and resumed their raids. Militants associated with al-Qaeda, some in the Pakistani Air Force, twice attempted to assassinate Musharraf. In 2007, Pakistani Taliban elements began to apply the strict Taliban form of Sharia in several areas of the Northwest Frontier Province. Islamabad moved 100,000 troops from the Indian border into the province to deal with the growing violence there. In 2008, an uprising in Islamabad's revered Red Mosque ignited more anti-Musharraf violence. Pakistani Taliban militants occupied the Swat Valley, a popular tourist site east of Peshawar. The Pakistani Army drove them out. Then a wave of kidnapping, murders, and suicide attacks rocked Peshawar. The American USAID officer in Peshawar administering a new $750 million aid program for the tribal agencies was assassinated along with his driver. An Iranian diplomat was kidnapped in Peshawar and his driver executed. In August 2008, three assailants with long beards fired on the American consul's car as she was going to work in Peshawar. The vehicle's armor saved her life.

That same week, a Taliban suicide bomber attacked a bus carrying Pakistani Air Force personnel in Karachi, killing eighteen. [REDACTED] Drone attacks killed dozens of high-value Pakistani Taliban and al-Qaeda operatives who were targeting the Pakistani state and army. At the same time, Musharraf restrained the United States from striking Afghan Taliban bases in the west and Hekmatyar redoubts in the east. They were still waging Pakistan's proxy war in Afghanistan.

Events were not only slipping from Musharraf's control along the Frontier; Pakistan's educated middle class also rose against Musharraf in 2007 after he fired the chief justice, declared emergency rule, and gave himself another presidential term in a sham election. Street demonstrations demanded his resignation. Musharraf relinquished his position as army chief of staff, passing it to his trusted ISI chief, General Ashfaq Parvez Kayani. Kayani quickly distanced himself from his old boss. He issued an order prohibiting military officers from meeting President Musharraf without his personal approval. Few, however, believed Kayani's public announcement that the military would stay out of politics.

Kayani allowed parliamentary elections to take place in February 2008. Benazir Bhutto's assassination during the election campaign made her a national martyr and gave the Pakistan People's Party (PPP) a resounding victory. Pakistani voters decimated the religious parties' representation in legislatures at the center and in the provinces. PPP politician Yousaf Raza Gilani became prime minister.

Pakistani Taliban terrorist violence and political instability continued to roil Pakistan in 2008 and 2009. Civilian fatalities from terrorist incidents rose to 2,155 in 2008 and 2,307 in 2009 (up from 608 in 2006 and 1,523 in 2007). Fatalities among Pakistani security force personnel reached 654 in 2008 and 1,011 in 2009.

Under attack from all sides and to avoid impeachment by the new parliament, Musharraf resigned as president in August 2008 and moved to London. Asif Ali Zardari, husband of the martyred Benazir Bhutto, won the presidency by an indirect vote rather than a popular election. He and Prime Minister Gilani made a half-hearted attempt to break the military's control of the Pakistani state by attempting to transfer the ISI to the Interior Ministry. Kayani forced them to back down. In 2009, the Pakistani Army recovered some control over the Swat Valley and South Waziristan.

Meanwhile, during the 2008 U.S. presidential campaign, Barack Obama took a tougher line against Pakistan. He vowed to place more emphasis than Bush had on winning the Afghan war and tracking down bin Laden. He threatened to act unilaterally if actionable intelligence located Osama bin Laden in Pakistan's tribal areas.

Obama's election victory in November 2008 came two months after Zardari was inaugurated. America's new president would face a profound dilemma, one that Bush had refused to confront, much less resolve: how to expand friendship, security, antiterrorism, and economic ties with Pakistan while convincing Pakistan's generals to stop fueling the insurgency in Afghanistan and to close down Taliban training camps and sanctuaries in Pakistan. However enlightened Obama's Afghan policy might be in the coming years, it could not succeed as long as Pakistan continued to conduct its proxy war in Afghanistan while nurturing the radical Islamic infrastructure on the Frontier producing holy warriors to destabilize the region and carry terrorism to other areas of the world.

President Obama's struggle to resolve the Pakistan dilemma would become one of the signature issues of his presidency.

CHAPTER 24

Needed: Real Change

The future of Afghanistan is inextricably linked to the future of its neighbor, Pakistan. In the nearly eight years since 9/11, al-Qaeda and its extremist allies have moved across the border to the remote areas of the Pakistani frontier. This almost certainly includes al-Qaeda's leadership: Osama bin Laden and Ayman al-Zawahiri. . . .

But this is not simply an American problem—far from it. It is, instead, an international security challenge of the highest order. Terrorist attacks in London and Bali were tied to al-Qaeda and its allies in Pakistan, as were attacks in North Africa and the Middle East, in Islamabad and in Kabul. If there is a major attack on an Asian, European, or African city, it, too, is likely to have ties to al-Qaeda's leadership in Pakistan. The safety of people around the world is at stake. . . .

So I want the American people to understand that we have a clear and focused goal: to disrupt, dismantle and defeat al-Qaeda in Pakistan and Afghanistan, and to prevent their return to either country in the future. That's the goal that must be achieved. That is a cause that could not be more just. And to the terrorists who oppose us, my message is the same: We will defeat you.

—PRESIDENT BARACK OBAMA, MARCH 2009[1]

Tonight, I can report to the American people and to the world that the United States has conducted an operation that killed Osama bin Laden, the leader of al-Qaeda, and a terrorist who's responsible for the murder of thousands of innocent men, women, and children.

> *Today, at my direction, the United States launched a targeted opera-*
> *tion [against bin Laden's] compound in Abbottabad, Pakistan. A small*
> *team of Americans carried out the operation with extraordinary courage*
> *and capability. No Americans were harmed. They took care to avoid civil-*
> *ian casualties. After a firefight, they killed Osama bin Laden and took*
> *custody of his body.*
>
> *For over two decades, bin Laden has been al-Qaeda's leader and sym-*
> *bol, and has continued to plot attacks against our country and our friends*
> *and allies. The death of bin Laden marks the most significant achievement*
> *to date in our nation's effort to defeat al-Qaeda. Yet his death does not*
> *mark the end of our effort. There's no doubt that al-Qaeda will continue*
> *to pursue attacks against us....*
>
> *Over the years, I've repeatedly made clear that we would take action*
> *within Pakistan if we knew where bin Laden was.... But it's important*
> *to note that our counterterrorism cooperation with Pakistan helped lead*
> *us to bin Laden.... Indeed, bin Laden had declared war against Pakistan*
> *as well, and ordered attacks against the Pakistani people.... And going*
> *forward, it is essential that Pakistan continue to join us in the fight against*
> *al-Qaeda and its affiliates.*
>
> —PRESIDENT BARACK OBAMA, MAY 2011

When President Barack Obama took office in January 2009, domestic opinion in the United States, Canada, and the major Western European countries
contributing troops was gradually turning against the Afghan war effort. The
new administration was aware that, within a year, the American public and
media would consider the Afghan war "Obama's war." Obama's strategy
needed to break the Taliban's growing momentum and produce successes by
the end of 2010 and, especially, before the 2012 general elections.

Meanwhile, the United States was grappling with the deepest economic
recession since the 1930s. High unemployment rates and budget cutbacks at
home, coupled with deteriorating security in Afghanistan and Hamid Karzai's
flawed August 2009 reelection, soured Americans on the huge investment
Washington had made in the Afghan war. Over 1,000 American soldiers had
been killed, thousands more wounded, and $120.9 billion had been spent
since 2001.[2] Many questioned whether it was worth sacrificing more lives
and money on the deadlocked eight-year-long conflict. An April 25, 2010,

---

* ABC polling conducted in May 2010 found that 60 percent of young Americans, and
66 percent of those who voted for Obama, felt that the Afghan war was not worth fighting.
Criticism of the war had grown by 8 percent from December 2009. However, President

poll conducted three months after Obama's inauguration showed that only 45 percent of Americans thought the Afghan war was worth fighting.* The disappointing trends in Afghanistan suggested that the percentage of Americans opposing the Afghan war would only grow.

An April 2010 Pentagon analysis reported a staggering 87 percent increase in insurgent violence from February 2009 to March 2010 compared to the year before. The study said the Afghan population's "perceptions of corruption within the Afghan government, the inability of the government to provide essential services, and exploitive behavior of some government officials and ANSF [Afghan National Security Forces] are contributing to the success of the insurgent's campaign."[3] President Karzai's continuing criticism of coalition-caused civilian casualties, along with his own inept governing performance, angered many in the Obama administration and sparked harsh reactions from the U.S. media and Congress.[4]

Some NATO allies began to reconsider their troop commitments in Afghanistan. Perseverance in Afghanistan was the principal campaign issue in the March 3, 2010, Dutch elections that overthrew the sitting government. The new government quickly withdrew the 1,885 Dutch troops[5] serving in Afghanistan. Canada brought home its 2,830 combat troops from Kandahar Province but agreed to provide 950[6] military personnel to help train the Afghan Army. Britain announced that its 9,000 combat troops would be home by 2015 regardless of developments in Afghanistan before that deadline.

⚘

President Obama enunciated his administration's Afghan strategy in speeches delivered on March 27, 2009, from the White House[7] and on December 1, 2009, to West Point cadets.[8] The brief March address, quoted at the beginning of this chapter, concentrated on counterterrorism themes. Obama's West Point speech outlined a wider counterinsurgency strategy and announced a surge of 30,000 troops to be deployed to Afghanistan in 2010. His top priority was to reclaim the military and political initiative that had been lost to the Taliban during the previous six years.

Obama received 56 percent approval on his approach to the Afghan war. The results of the polling were published in Gary Langer, "Ahead of Karzai's Visit, a Division on the War," ABC News, May 9, 2010, http://blogs.abcnews.com/thenumbers/2010/05/ahead-of-karzais -visit-a-division-on-the-war.html.

Obama's counterinsurgency template was patterned on the Iraq model of a U.S. troop surge and withdrawal. It endorsed General David Petraeus's population-centric COIN philosophy. The U.S. military and its coalition partners would coordinate with the Afghan government to clear territory dominated by the Taliban; to hold it; to assist the Afghan government to provide agricultural, education, health, and other services to the population; and to transfer military responsibility to the Afghan Army and police. The resulting stability would permit the U.S.-led coalition to shift from a supported to a supporting role, backing up Afghan security forces, and begin a gradual troop drawdown in July 2011, conditions permitting.

The Iraq surge-withdrawal strategy was still under way in Iraq during Obama's first two years in office. It would face more formidable implementation problems in Afghanistan. Pakistan's cross-border covert support for the Afghan insurgency was of a much greater magnitude than Syria's and Iran's interference in Iraq. Unlike in Afghanistan, the Iraq government's capacity to govern had not been obliterated by thirty-two years of continuous warfare. The American COIN strategy seriously underestimated the infinite complexity of Afghanistan's tribal society and the challenge of influencing the more than 20,000 tribal and clan microcommunities in the countryside where over 80 percent of Afghans lived and ultimate power resided.

The "awakening sheikhs" in Iraq's Anbar Province, who transferred their weight to the side of the American coalition and the Iraqi government in late 2006 to squash al-Qaeda, led larger and, significantly, much more cohesive tribes. Less than ten of the Iraqi tribal leaders in the province dramatically mobilized tens of thousands of their tribal fighters to join the Iraqi military and police forces to expel al-Qaeda from Anbar[9]—a development that changed the course of the Iraq War. The Anbar tribal leaders' ability to muster thousands of fighters in a common effort against al-Qaeda extremists across an entire region of Iraq would be difficult to emulate in Afghanistan's fragmented tribal society. In Afghanistan, the locus of real authority is scattered among innumerable small tribal and clan groupings at the community and subcommunity levels, making mass mobilization across regions much more difficult. The average Afghan tribal leader is an elder with little means of control outside his family and clan. He generally can field less than one hundred fighters, often fewer than fifty. He is ready to join in a unified community approach to resolve problems in the context of the jirga consensus tradition, but unwilling to surrender his autonomy to other individuals or groups. He seeks resources from the outside for his community or clan but insists on a say in their distribution. He is nearly always in a state of competition with local tribal rivals and on guard to protect his position to ensure that the balance of tribal power in the community does not shift against him.

The multiplicity of small power centers in Afghan communities, particularly in the Taliban-threatened Pashtun belt, presented enormous challenges to the U.S. military officers implementing the COIN strategy. At ground level, the U.S. officer was often a young captain commanding a company. The captain needed to understand the local tribal balances to succeed. But accumulating such knowledge is difficult for a Marine on a seven-month tour of duty or an army officer on a one-year tour. Making the right decisions in the distribution of resources to a community would certainly advance the coalition's counterinsurgency goals. However, misunderstanding the local tribal mosaic and entrenched rivalries, different in each community, risked upsetting the local tribal balance, alienating influential tribal elders, and strengthening the insurgency.

The Afghan strategy that the Obama administration framed in 2009 was conceptually and operationally an improvement over the failed Bush strategy. It recognized the importance of rapidly building up Afghan military and governing capacity and strengthening the linkages between the government and local communities whose support was critical to defeating the Taliban. In important aspects, however, the strategy retained several of the major shortcomings of the Bush approach. It lacked a long-term policy—a broad geostrategic overlay to end Pakistan's proxy war in Afghanistan. Essentially the Obama strategy amounted to a collection of tactics that did not capitalize on—and occasionally clashed with—the traditional and moderate pulse of Afghanistan's tribal society. Too much planning and implementation authority was retained by the Pentagon and the CIA from the Bush years. The strategy still overemphasized utilization of U.S. military and intelligence instruments to achieve key political goals. Interagency stovepipe competition continued to impede progress, as did the ruinous preeminence-dependency circle developed during the Bush administration.

ψ

President Obama's Afghan counterinsurgency strategy presented the following core components. A White House assessment was scheduled to take place
at the end of 2010 to review progress.

*A U.S. and coalition troop surge in 2010 coupled with the projected date of July
2011 to begin the withdrawal of combat forces.* Obama tripled the number of
troops in Afghanistan from 32,000 when he took office to 98,000 during his
first two years in office. By September 2010, total coalition manpower, including the 98,000 American troops, peaked at about 130,000.

*The expansion and shifting of security responsibilities to the Afghan Army and
police.* The Obama administration accelerated the buildup in Afghan National
Army (ANA) and Afghan National Police (ANP) forces (collectively labeled
the Afghan National Security Forces, or ANSF) that had begun at the end of
the Bush administration. Obama's strategy called for the ANSF to start assuming lead responsibility for Afghan security in selected provinces in late
2010.[10] ANA numbers, accordingly, increased from approximately 80,000 in
March 2009 to 113,000 in March 2010 and 144,638 in November 2010. ANP
personnel rose from 94,958 in November 2009 to 116,367 in November
2010. The NATO training mission for the Afghan police made literacy classes
mandatory, since 86 percent of the recruits arriving at ANP training centers
were non-literate.[11]

   Total ANSF force levels were scheduled to reach 305,000 by October
2011.[12] General Stanley McChrystal's command also worked to establish a
small Afghan air corps of fixed-wing aircraft and attack and cargo helicopters
designed to support ANSF ground operations. NATO's ramp-up of ANSF
training programs was one of the most expensive line items in the Pentagon's
budget, with total costs of ANSF development leaping from $2.75 billion in
2009 to $9.2 billion in 2010 and a planned price tag of $11.6 billion for 2011.[13]

   The Obama administration's plans to shift the main security burden to
Afghan shoulders coincided with President Karzai's desire for more "Afghanization" in civilian and military affairs. In his second inaugural address on
November 19, 2009, less than a year after Obama assumed office, Karzai announced that the coalition and Afghan government had agreed that Afghan

security forces would assume the lead responsibility for Afghan security within five years.[14] The term "lead" assumed that U.S. and coalition forces would remain in Afghanistan at sufficient levels to perform a supporting role for Afghan troops. In addition, NATO would assign thousands of troops to train new Afghan recruits and embed with Afghan units in the field.

Increased economic and governance assistance and a greater civilian presence. State Department personnel in Afghanistan increased threefold by mid-2010 to about 1,000, and plans called for a further 20 to 30 percent jump before the end of the year.[15] Fresh waves of American diplomats and U.S. Agency for International Development, Agriculture Department, and other U.S. government aid-providers were deployed to Kabul, to American consulates in Herat, Jalalabad, Mazar, and Kandahar, and to the coalition's Provincial Reconstruction Teams (PRTs) in provincial capitals and at NATO military bases. The civilian buildup led to a new scaffolding of the coalition's reconstruction bureaucracy in Afghanistan.

NATO appointed Mark Sedwill, former British ambassador to Afghanistan, to be its senior civilian representative in-country. Sedwill, who in effect reported to NATO commander McChrystal, assembled his own civilian staff in Kabul and at each of the seven military corps headquarters in Afghanistan. The number of U.S. Department of Defense–financed civilian contractors (including Americans, plus thousands of Afghans and third-country national employees) increased by 50 percent in 2009, to 107,000, and was projected to rise to 160,000 by the end of 2010. As a practical matter, most development money and programming responsibility fell under the NATO commander, General McChrystal, until his resignation in June 2010, then to General Petraeus after General McChrystal's departure.[16]

Strengthening U.S. diplomatic capabilities. President Obama appointed a presidential special representative for Afghanistan and Pakistan, veteran diplomat Richard Holbrooke. Holbrooke worked closely with Secretary of State Hillary Clinton. Holbrooke's mission was to give fresh impetus to a political solution of the Afghan war, synchronize U.S. policy toward Afghanistan and Pakistan, integrate the efforts of U.S. government agencies, diplomatically work with the Afghan and Pakistani governments to achieve U.S. goals, and galvanize international support behind achieving peace in Afghanistan.

Holbrooke's mandate was an awesome one. With strong personal backing from Clinton, Holbrooke and his large staff embarked on a diplomatic offensive to focus regional and international attention on ending the long Afghan war. Two large international Afghan assistance conferences in 2010—one in London in January and the second in Kabul in July, and a NATO summit in Lisbon in November—brought together politicians and diplomats from over seventy countries involved in stabilizing Afghanistan. President Karzai delivered speeches endorsing the Obama administration's desire to transfer the combat burden to Afghan shoulders by 2014. President Obama at Lisbon and Secretary Clinton at all three meetings joined numerous other speakers in announcing their countries' commitment to a schedule, conditions permitting, to eventually transfer lead security responsibility for all 34 provinces to ANSF. Speculation focused on Bamian and Parwan provinces in central Afghanistan and Panshir province in the north as the initial candidates. Other provinces in the relatively peaceful north and Nangarhar Province in the east were also under consideration.

The conference participants approved an Afghan government program to engage the Taliban in peace negotiations. International donors pledged $140 million for the implementation of a "Peace and Reintegration Trust Fund" to attract lower-level Taliban with promises of jobs and housing. Only Taliban with no connections to al-Qaeda, who renounced violence and accepted the Afghan Constitution, could participate in the program. Karzai stated: "We must reach out to all our countrymen, especially disenchanted brothers who are not part of al-Qaeda or other terrorist networks who accept the Afghan constitution."[17]

Clinton and Holbrooke energized strategic dialogues with Afghanistan, Pakistan, and India to push the America agenda forward. Holbrooke created an "International Contact Group" of senior diplomats representing countries from China to Saudi Arabia and the West interested in Afghanistan. Afghan officials and Foreign Ministry officials from all of Afghanistan's neighbors, including Pakistan and Iran, participated. General Petraeus traveled to Rome in October 2010 to personally brief Holbrooke's contact group on coalition plans and prospects for Afghanistan.

The "main effort": Taking southern Afghanistan away from the Taliban. The decision to make southern Afghanistan the priority target area in 2010 was a bold one. The insurgency was more powerful in the south than in any other region of Afghanistan. Over 60 percent of all insurgent attacks countrywide took place in the south from October 2009 to March 2010.[18] By 2009, the Taliban had reestablished their sway in Kandahar, Helmand, and adjacent, culturally similar Uruzgan Province. According to NATO and Afghan military assessments, none of the thirty-six districts in these three southern Pashtun-majority provinces supported the Afghan government as of March 18, 2010.*

Kandahar, variously referred to as the Taliban's "spiritual home," its "headquarters," and the "cradle of the Taliban movement," was the top priority. The Taliban were thoroughly ensconced in the local population, especially among the Ghilzai and Panjpai Durrani tribes, which provided most Taliban leaders and fighters. Pakistan's army had made Kandahar the springboard for its successful 1994–2000 Taliban offensives, which overran most of Afghanistan. Pakistani generals returned to that strategy in 2002 after the Taliban were driven from Afghanistan. Taking back Kandahar was the necessary first step in Pakistan's latest proxy war in Afghanistan.

The Taliban domination of the drug trade in southern Afghanistan added to the urgency of breaking its grip on the region.[19] Together, Kandahar and Helmand accounted for over 90 percent of total global opium production. Heroin laboratories in the two provinces were exporting a large and increasing volume of refined heroin to world markets.

ψ

General McChrystal deployed the bulk of the coalition troops arriving in 2010 to southern Afghanistan to participate in the Kandahar campaign. Military operations in other areas of the country were placed in a hold or battlefield "shaping" pattern until 2011. McChrystal's tactics in the southern

---

* A little over one-third of the key districts were in the neutral category. The city of Kandahar was the only area among the key districts in the three provinces that showed a population sympathetic to the Afghan government. U.S. Department of Defense, "Report on Progress Toward Security and Stability in Afghanistan," Report to Congress in accordance with section 1230 of the National Defense Authorization Act for Fiscal Year 2008 (Public Law 110-181), as amended, and United States Plan for Sustaining the Afghanistan National Security Forces, April 2010, www.defense.gov/pubs/pdfs/Report_Final_SecDef_04_26_10.pdf, Figure 6, "Comparison of Overall Assessment of Key Districts, December 24, 2009–March 18, 2010," 36.

campaign were guided by the new counterinsurgency doctrine. A Pentagon report explained that his "campaign design" in the south "focused along five lines of operations," concentrating on "protecting the population, enabling the ANSF, neutralizing malign influences, supporting the extension of government, and supporting socio-economic development."[20]

Ancient tribal alignments and animosities in the south frustrated coalition progress in 2010. ISI and Taliban manipulation of tribal rivalries was a more potent tactic than fanning religious extremism to spread Taliban influence. The ISI and the Taliban tapped into Ghilzai and Panjpai Durrani grievances against the historical Durrani Zirak domination symbolized by Afghan President Hamid Karzai, a Popalzai tribal chief, and his half-brother Ahmed Wali. Wali's marriage to the daughter of an important Panjpai Nurzai tribal leader, Arif Nurzai, gave him some political entry into the Durrani Panjpai tribes.

President Karzai transferred Gul Agha to a Kabul ministry and onward to Jalalabad as governor, facilitating Wali's development of his extensive patronage network in Kandahar. His selection as chairman of the Kandahar Provincial Council further strengthened his position in the province and the south. U.S. and Canadian military commands in Kandahar Province paid Wali millions of dollars for providing security to coalition convoys and bases. Western media reports pointed to Wali's "long-standing ties to the CIA" and reported that he had been "paid by the agency for providing security forces and safe houses in and around Kandahar."[21] Wali coordinated with President Karzai to appoint tribal allies to district police chief and governor positions. According to the Afghan rumor mill, Wali was Hamid Karzai's main go-between for secret negotiations with the Taliban.

The Taliban attempted to drive a wedge between Ahmed Wali and the large number of non-Zirak Kandaharis excluded from his network, mainly poor, rural Ghilzai and Panjpai tribal elders in the region who had backed the Taliban in the 1990s. American commanders in Kandahar pressed the president's half-brother to allow broader tribal representation at the provincial and district levels. "We want to help him be constructive, not destructive," a senior U.S. commander in southern Afghanistan told a reporter. Wali insisted he was being constructive—acting not as a warlord but like a tribal elder honoring jirga values of equality and inclusiveness of all groups. The U.S. intelligence stovepipe defended Wali. One article reported: "A former CIA officer with experience in Afghanistan said the Agency relied heavily on Ahmed Wali

Karzai and often based covert operatives at compounds he owned." In Kabul, President Karzai privately and publicly demanded that U.S. officials produce evidence of accusations against his brother leaked to the press or cease charging him with wrongdoing.[22]

❧

The coalition's 2010 southern campaign at the outset centered on the Taliban-controlled districts of Marja and Nad Ali (hereafter collectively identified as Marja) in central Helmand and the Taliban-infested districts in Kandahar Province. Coalition and ANSF units began "clear, hold, and build" operations in Marja (population: 50,000) in February 2010, just after the London conference. The military offensive was led by U.S. Marines and supported by Afghan, British, and other coalition forces. The 15,000-man assault to reclaim Marja from the Taliban, and the 23,000-man force being assembled for the Kandahar campaign in the summer months, constituted the largest coalition military operations since American military units had entered Afghanistan after 9/11.

Marja stood at the crossroads of a key Taliban infiltration and logistics corridor linking Taliban sanctuaries in Pakistan with the suburbs of Kandahar to the west, Iran to the east, and Helmand's capital of Lashkar Gar to the north. Further north lay the Taliban bastion of Sangin district, which thousands of British troops had tried, unsuccessfully, to pacify for five years. Marja was also a lucrative narcotics trafficking hub and opium-producing region for the Taliban and its drug mafia allies. They trucked opium and heroin to Pakistan and Iran for shipment onward to international markets in the West. In 2009, a four-day, in-and-out coalition strike targeting Marja confiscated 92 tons of stored narcotics products, plus arms and explosive materials.[23]

General McChrystal announced that an Afghan "government in a box" drawing on personnel sent by Afghan ministries in Kabul would be inserted in Marja after coalition "clear" operations were complete. With U.S. funds and coalition assistance, the Afghan officials would carry out quick economic development and good governance programs to win over the population and lure lower-level Taliban fighters and tribal leaders away from the Taliban. The United States budgeted $19 million for road building and agricultural assistance for Marja's residents. McChrystal hoped that counterinsurgency progress in Marja would be a positive precedent for the Kandahar operation scheduled to begin in the summer of 2010 and succeed before the November 19–20 NATO summit in Lisbon and the White House review in December.

The initial phase of the Marja operation went smoothly. Coalition and Afghan troops poured into the area and the adjoining districts (population: 230,000). About 1,000 Taliban offered brief resistance before retreating south toward the Pakistani border or disappearing into the local population. The Marines brought the new Marja district governor, Haji Abdul Zahir Aryan, with them into Marja's main bazaar; he raised the Afghan flag in the town square, then promptly moved into one of the Marine outposts dotting the conquered district. Zahir doled out Marine-provided cash to villagers who had suffered the loss of family members or whose property had been damaged during the offensive.

Some reconstruction activity in Marja was under way when the Taliban struck back in late March, engaging the Marines in almost daily firefights. The Taliban shadow governor returned to Marja and visited homes at night, accompanied by local Taliban, warning residents to cease contact with the Marines and to refuse any cash or material assistance offered. The Taliban's underground intelligence infrastructure informed on residents who ignored the warnings. A series of assassinations, beheadings, and beatings ensued, terrorizing the area. In April, the Taliban shot and killed a twenty-two-year-old Afghan working on a Marine bridge project during daylight hours. The Marines were to rebuild a school but had trouble convincing an Afghan official fearing Taliban reprisals to stand next to them at the contract-signing ceremony.[24]

While reconstruction projects slowly went forward in the heavily occupied central Marja bazaar and adjacent suburbs, families in outlying areas joined refugee caravans traveling to the Helmand capital of Lashkar Gar several miles away. One departing elder told an American reporter, "By day there is government, but by night it's the Taliban." Another farmer who had already fled to Lashkar Gar said, "I am sure if I stay in Marja I will be killed one day either by Taliban or the Americans."[25] The Taliban terror campaign did not halt coalition and Afghan government stabilization efforts. By November, aided by the arrival of additional ANSF personnel, the battlefield momentum in Central Helmand had gone over to coalition and Afghan government forces.

ψ

The Obama administration's substantial progress in Helmand Province, later to be extended to the districts surrounding Kandahar city, did not interrupt Pakistan's proxy war in Afghanistan. Islamabad continued to game the Americans, rejecting foreign charges of Pakistani interference in Afghanistan. "That's rubbish," a Pakistani spokesman responded when asked about a London School of Economics study concluding that it was "official ISI policy" to support the Taliban. A journalist wrote that the spokesman described the accusations as "part of a malicious campaign against the country's military and security agencies." The well-documented paper, reported in a June 13, 2010, BBC broadcast, assessed that, "without a change in Pakistani behavior it will be difficult if not impossible for international forces and the Afghan government to make progress against the insurgency."[26]

Obama hesitated to confront Pakistan on its Afghan policy. Pakistan's generals continued to assume that Pakistan's strategic location, its status as an important middle-level Muslim country on the global chessboard, its nuclear capability, and its episodic cooperation with the CIA and U.S. military in selectively rounding up terrorists in Pakistan would fend off American pressures. Obama's announcement of the July 2011 date to begin withdrawal was interpreted in both Pakistan and Afghanistan as a sure sign that America would again leave the region in a few years' time. In the meantime, the Pakistani Army probably concluded it could hold off the American demands to close down the Taliban sanctuaries in Pakistan. At an opportune time after the United States was gone, the ISI could repackage and install its Islamic extremist proxies back in Kabul.

By the middle of 2010 Pakistan's generals had reason to believe that they once again had the Americans where they wanted them. The flow of unconditioned U.S. military and economic aid to Pakistan indirectly supported Pakistan's hegemonic aspirations in Afghanistan. Pakistan occasionally called for the United States not to withdraw from Afghanistan and leave Pakistan "alone" with the Afghan problem. But these appeals were spurious. Pakistan's military wanted the United States to leave because it would give the ISI a free hand to bring Afghanistan into Islamabad's sphere of influence.

Continued American wishful thinking, more investment of money and sophisticated weaponry in Pakistan, and more jawboning would not change the Pakistani military's strategy in Afghanistan. It would not convince Pakistan to suppress the jihadi bases in Pakistan spawning Islamic terrorism in the world. These were essential tools to maintain the military's grip on domestic Pakistan politics and to pursue its geostrategic goals in the region and globally.

Pakistan's tactics to keep the United States and the West at bay, explained below, dated back to early 1989, when the Soviet Army's withdrawal left Islamabad space to pivot into Afghanistan:

Plausible deniability. Pakistan's military simply rejected evidence exposing Pakistan's duplicitous Afghan policy. Pakistani civilian presidents, prime ministers, and foreign ministers echoed the army's routine denials of covert ISI support for the Taliban and links to radical Islamic groups in Pakistan and their military training bases.

Cultivation of friendly U.S. government military and intelligence constituencies. After 9/11, Musharraf granted basing and transit rights to the U.S. military and limited approval for CIA operations inside Pakistan. He did this very skillfully, in part in order to neutralize disquiet in the White House, Congress, and the U.S. media about Pakistan's support of the Taliban insurgency in Afghanistan. The U.S. military has not wanted to jeopardize its use of Pakistani ports and highways to sustain military operations in Afghanistan. According to one source, "they account for more than 75 percent of all military supplies, and 40 percent of fuel needs, for Western troops in Afghanistan."[27]

The Pakistani Army and the ISI have leveraged the eagerness of Western intelligence agencies for information on terrorists based in Pakistan to enhance Pakistan's value to the United States. Pakistani intelligence reacts to U.S. requests to arrest individual terrorists in Pakistan on a case-by-case basis, usually after the United States provides precise intelligence on their location; but it does not roll up whole groups of terrorists, such as Lashkar-i Taiba, since it created and still supports them. Nor does it move against thousands of other Islamist militants training in and staging from Pakistan.

British intelligence is compelled to turn to the ISI for information on connections between Islamic radicals moving between Britain's large Pakistan immigrant community and terrorist safe havens in Pakistan. With Britain, and other European countries, too, the ISI cooperates on a case-by-case basis, fending off requests for more programmatic collaboration. Islamabad is virtually unresponsive to Indian requests regarding Pakistani-based terrorist attacks in India mounted from within Pakistan. The Pakistani government acknowledged that the Lashkar-i Taiba massacre of over 200 civilians in Mumbai in November 2008 was planned in Pakistan but has not prosecuted those guilty of that horrendous terrorist act.

Attempts to improve Sino-Pakistani relations. Pakistan considers its close relations with China a cushion against another downturn in U.S.-Pakistani relations. There is a history of Pakistan's military transferring American weapons and military technology to the Chinese Army, as it did with American Stingers in the 1980s, to sustain close relations with China.

Claims that America needs to earn Pakistan's trust. Pakistani officials have regularly accused the United States of "betraying" Pakistan during its 1965 and 1971 wars with India. The United States, they said, "abandoned" its Pakistan ally after the Soviet withdrawal, cutting off aid in 1991. These allegations are bogus.[28] Their purpose has been to keep the United States on the defensive, maintain U.S. aid flows, and head off an aggressive U.S. attempt to force a change in Pakistan's Afghan policy. The "We, too, are victims of terrorism" line is a subsidiary of the trust argument. That statement is true. It is also true that Pakistan's full cooperation with the international community in the struggle against terrorism would be the best way to discard its victimhood.

Sporadic assurances that a Pakistani "shift" in policy is under way. This ploy has been regularly manipulated to mislead the United States—in 1988–1989 when the Soviets were leaving, from December 1991 through February 1992 after negative symmetry,[29] and after 9/11, when Musharraf fraudulently declared his support to President Bush's war on terror. A fifty-six-page Pakistani document provided by Pakistan ahead of U.S.-Pakistani "strategic talks" in May 2010 inspired a rash of U.S. backgrounders to the media about "subtle signs of a shift" and an "apparent shift" in Pakistan's policy.[30] But no policy shift on Afghanistan occurred. Given the unrelenting consistency in Pakistan's Afghan policy since Zia's time, it is difficult to believe that a genuine shift will take place unless the United States adopts a more effective Pakistan policy.

ψ

As suggested in the London School of Economics study, General Petraeus was highly unlikely to achieve a breakthrough in his campaign to roll back the Taliban in Afghanistan if Pakistan's military continued its proxy war in Afghanistan. Politically, Army Chief Ashfaq Parvez Kayani and Pakistan's diplomats would seek U.S. acquiescence to Pakistani attempts to force the Kabul government to share power with their extremist proxies in a coalition government, a strategy Pakistan pursued as part of its fight-and-negotiate policy in the early 1990s. Karzai, they calculated, would be jettisoned after the United States withdrew its combat forces from Afghanistan.

Since assuming office in January 2009, President Obama has shown more impatience with Pakistan's duplicity than President George W. Bush did, but he has also indulged it. In 2009, Senate Foreign Relations Committee Chairman John Kerry (D-MA) moved to condition aid to Pakistan, a step Bush rejected during his time in office. The Kerry-Lugar bill, passed by the Senate in June 2009, tripled U.S. nonmilitary aid to Pakistan to $7.5 billion over five years. The original language tied military assistance to Pakistan to Islamabad's actions against the Taliban and al-Qaeda. The final Kerry-Lugar aid legislation, the Enhanced Partnership with Pakistan Act, passed by the House and Senate in September 2009 and signed by President Obama the next month, contained tough wording but only required the administration to certify Pakistani compliance. Vociferous Pakistani objections accepted by the administration led Senators John Kerry and Richard Lugar (R-IN) to issue an "Explanatory Statement." The statement repeated the Bush designation of Pakistan as "a major non-NATO ally of the United States," describing Pakistan as a "valuable partner in the battle against al Qaeda and the Taliban."[31]

On May 1, 2010, a failed attempt by Pakistani American Faisal Shahzad to bomb Times Square in the heart of Manhattan focused Washington's attention on Pakistan's failure to cooperate with the United States on terrorism emanating from Pakistan. Under interrogation Shahzad revealed that he had been trained by the Pakistani Taliban in North Waziristan. In May, U.S. officials began to lay down markers of American disquiet about Islamabad's selective, episodic cooperation on terrorists training or hiding in Pakistan with the Pakistan government's knowledge, if not complicity. Secretary of State

Hillary Clinton went public, telling a CBS *60 Minutes* interviewer on May 9 she believed the Pakistani government was holding back crucial evidence on Osama bin Laden, al-Qaeda, and Mullah Omar. "I'm not saying that they're at the highest levels," she said, but she was convinced that somewhere in the Pakistani government there were officials who knew the whereabouts of Osama bin Laden, Mullah Omar, and other leaders of al-Qaeda and the Afghan Taliban. "We expect more cooperation to help us bring to justice [to], capture, or kill those who attacked us on 9/11." "We cannot tolerate having people encouraged, directed, trained and sent from Pakistan to attack us," she said. "We've made it very clear that, if, heaven forbid, that an attack like this, if we can trace back to Pakistan, were to have been successful, there would be very severe consequences."[32]

On May 17, National Security Adviser James Jones and CIA Director Leon Panetta flew to Pakistan to deliver the same message to Army Chief Kayani and Pakistani President Asif Ali Zardari. A media backgrounder by a "senior administration official" just before their departure expressed "creeping frustration" with Pakistan's hesitation to follow up its operations in Swat and South Waziristan with an offensive in North Waziristan, where Shahzad had been trained. Zardari could do little but absorb the warnings Jones and Panetta delivered about the possibility of U.S. retribution if an individual trained in Pakistan succeeded in killing Americans in a terrorist plot. He wielded no influence over General Kayani.

Kayani was Jones's and Panetta's most important interlocutor in Islamabad. He had been Musharraf's ISI chief from 2005 to 2007, in charge of the reorganization of the Taliban and the first major Taliban offensives back into Afghanistan from Pakistani territory beginning in 2005. Jones and Panetta showed Kayani and his ISI Director, Ahmad Shuja Pasha, photographs and other evidence on Shahzad, the son of a retired general in the Pakistani Air Force. The documents linked Shahzad to the Pakistani Taliban.[33] They failed to budge Kiyani much beyond permitting more drone strikes against the Pakistani Taliban in North Waziristan.[34] Nor did their appeals reduce Taliban attacks against the Afghan government and coalition troops inside Afghanistan.

America's Grand Delusion was apparent during Secretary of State Clinton's July 18–19, 2010, visit to Islamabad for a round of U.S.-Pakistani strategic talks. The American side's negotiating brief was long on "give" and short on "take." Clinton unveiled a $500 million aid package. The funds were the first installment of the Obama administration's plans to triple nonmilitary aid to Pakistan to $7.5 billion over five years. But Clinton's meetings in Islamabad produced no Pakistani movement on three major U.S. priorities. Pakistan did not agree to stop supporting its Afghan proxies operating from Pakistani soil against the American-led coalition and Afghan government in Afghanistan; to help the United States apprehend or kill Osama bin Laden and Mullah Omar, who enjoyed the government's protected sanctuary in Pakistan; or to crack down on the Islamist groups targeting countries around the world.

During media interviews after the negotiating sessions ended, Clinton and Special Representative for Afghanistan and Pakistan Richard Holbrooke had to look outside these core objectives to show results from her visit. They spotlighted a perceived lessening in Pakistani anti-Americanism. Holbrooke explained to journalists that the United States was "producing a change in Pakistani attitudes, first within the government and gradually, more slowly, within the public." An American reporter accompanying Clinton wrote, "She was heartened by the improving dialogue, [while] acknowledging it will take more than financial handouts to shift Pakistan's population firmly into the American camp." Clinton's mild answer to a questioner asking about al-Qaeda leaders—"I believe they are here in Pakistan, and it would be really helpful if we could get them"—was ignored by Pakistan's generals.[35]

Meanwhile, during Clinton's meetings in Islamabad, a NATO general in Kabul publicly informed the media that NATO had captured a letter sent into Afghanistan by Mullah Omar, who was "hiding in Pakistan." In his letter, Omar instructed the Taliban to "fight foreign troops to the death" and assassinate Afghans working for foreign forces, including women "helping or providing information to coalition forces." Clinton's meetings coincided with one of the deadliest months of the nine-year Afghan war for the United States: That same July, more than sixty Americans died.[36]

Clinton announced an additional military aid package for Pakistan when her counterpart, Foreign Minister Shah Mahmood Qureshi, came to Washington for the next round of the U.S.-Pakistani strategic dialogue on October 21–23. The new assistance raised U.S. grants to Pakistan for weapons purchases from $300 million to $400 million and aligned the $2 billion five-year military aid line (2009–2014) with the $7.5 billion economic assistance time frame.[37] President Obama conducted a thirty-five-minute meeting with Qureshi and General Kayani in the White House during their Washington visit. He accepted Qureshi's invitation to visit Pakistan sometime in 2011, balancing off his visit to India planned for the following month. The president asked for more Pakistani cooperation against al-Qaeda and Taliban safe havens in Pakistan, repeating Washington's earlier warning that America would be compelled to respond if terrorist attacks on the United States were launched from Pakistan. But the president's warnings produced no genuine change in Pakistan's policies. In the main, the meeting was evidence that the Bush administration's tradition of doling out great amounts of unconditioned cash and weaponry to a supposed ally whose policies contradicted basic U.S. national security interests had not changed.

The Obama administration and President Karzai got off on the wrong foot in their relationship from the very beginning. During its first fifteen months in office, the administration vacillated in its dealings with Karzai between Special Representative Holbrooke's hard line and the Pentagon's soft stance. The inherent tensions that resulted produced a singularly inconsistent pattern in Washington's relations with Afghanistan's president. Confusion, suspicion, and deep mistrust debilitated the high-level dialogue. American-Afghan relations suffered, as did prospects for stabilizing Afghanistan.

Within the administration, Vice President Joseph Biden shared Holbrooke's view that Karzai's weak leadership was a primary reason why his government was not functioning well. In 2008, a testy exchange between Biden, who was still a senator (D-DE) at the time, and the Afghan president resulted in Biden walking out of a dinner at Karzai's presidential palace. Biden visited Karzai again in the same presidential palace banquet room in January 2009, two and a half weeks before Obama's inauguration, to urge Karzai to improve his performance. Their dialogue quickly spiraled downward. Karzai said that he looked forward to forging the same close personal relations with Obama as he had with Bush. Biden brusquely replied, "You'll probably talk to him or see him a couple of times a year." Biden lectured Karzai on how to improve his leadership capabilities. Karzai reiterated his complaints about U.S. military air strikes, civilian casualties, and nighttime raids, saying they angered the rural population. Biden objected. Karzai insisted that these problems had persisted for too long; the Afghan people should be partners, not victims.[38]

The Obama administration's claims that Karzai lacked leadership skills and a long-term vision and that he tolerated and even facilitated the vast corruption in his government were true. Karzai appeared at times to treat the United States as just one more faction to juggle in his balancing of contending Afghan and outside forces, not as a partner providing essential and enormous support to him and his country. His government consistently failed to fill the governing vacuum in areas where coalition forces had completed the military phase of clear-and-hold operations. Obama's national security team studied Karzai's occasionally erratic behavior. He could be unpredictable, issuing decrees pointing in a specific direction at one moment and then abruptly turning in the opposite direction the next. Some worried that he might, without Washington's knowledge, conduct secret negotiations with Taliban leaders on a reconciliation formula that might not work.

Karzai's former cozy relationship with Bush may have irked Obama's White House advisers. Bush had conducted friendly biweekly video conferences with Karzai. Obama did not continue that practice. During the Bush years, Karzai's excessively optimistic descriptions of progress in Afghanistan had strengthened Bush's position in the public debate leading up to the 2003 American invasion of Iraq.

President Karzai, for his part, found it hard to adjust to President Obama's new team of political advisers. He was an Afghan nationalist sensitive about violations of Afghan sovereignty. He was insecure. He could not count on lasting personal loyalties outside his inner circle and clan. He harbored a suspicion that the United States might again acquiesce to a Pakistani sphere of influence in Afghanistan and leave the region. He was emotionally and politically dedicated to protecting Afghan civilian noncombatants from air bombardment by coalition forces, night raids on private homes, and mistreatment when they were detained at American prison facilities inside Afghanistan. Karzai appreciated the directives General McChrystal issued in an effort to reduce civilian casualties.[39] They represented American responsiveness to his concerns on this issue. But the emphasis on firepower in U.S. military doctrine, the Taliban's infiltration into populated areas, and necessary force protection measures for American soldiers ensured that unintended civilian casualties would continue to rise, and this remained a contentious issue with him.

Karzai and his cabinet pressed the Obama administration for more Afghanization in political, military, and economic areas. Fifteen months into Obama's term, the Afghan finance minister reminded an American audience in Washington that "over 80 percent of all international aid to Afghanistan continues to bypass the Afghan government." He charged that "most of the aid has been wasted or created institutions that have undermined the Afghan government and U.S. initiatives": "We should not be [held] responsible for how 80 percent of the money has been spent," he added. The minister urged that donors attach conditions to their aid in order to promote improvement in the government's performance.[40]

Karzai was pleased when, in early February 2010, General McChrystal sought his permission before launching the combined coalition-Afghan offensive in central Helmand Province. He remarked that McChrystal's request for approval was the first one he had heard since becoming Afghan president.[41] McChrystal's briefing did not change America's de facto control over military and economic decisionmaking in Afghanistan, however. Outside his presidential protection contingent at the palace compound, Karzai exercised no direct authority over the Afghan Army or police.

Most Afghan security and civilian organizations were dependent on their own separate patronage line to different parts of the U.S. coalition or the sprawling foreign civilian apparatus in Afghanistan. Even in his home province of Kandahar, Karzai had no access to coercive mechanisms to compel obedience. He shared common objectives but no direct control over the main powerbrokers in Kandahar, including his brother Ahmed Wali Karzai. Scores of foreign power centers and individuals in Afghanistan, including generals, ambassadors, large contractors, NGOs, and UN office heads, still performed most state sovereignty functions. They provided money, equipment, training, and weapons to Afghans inside and outside the government. Their decisions were rarely certified by Karzai.

ψ

The Obama administration's criticism of Karzai clashed head-on with the Afghan imperative to defend one's honor and pride at all costs. Off and on for fifteen months, from January 2009 to May 2010, Karzai's detractors used a steady drumbeat of White House press leaks and backgrounders to disparage him. Although this kind of campaign is a time-honored technique in Washington politics, the indirect hurling of public condemnation was the wrong method for outsiders to use in Afghanistan's honor-bound environment.

A popular Afghan proverb says: "Through kindness you can even lead an Afghan to hell, but by force you can't even take him to heaven." The widely publicized American accusations humiliated Karzai. In Afghan tradition, the only way he could protect his honor was to retaliate. Karzai, his advisers, and members of the Afghan press counterattacked, faulting Washington for its shabby treatment of Afghanistan's president. Karzai took no effective steps to meet any of the administration's demands. When American visitors pressured him to delegate governing responsibilities to a "chief executive" to manage his government, he did the opposite. He appointed corrupt warlord Mohammad Fahim, whom Washington wanted marginalized, to be his first vice president.

The Afghan president undertook a spate of trips to Iran, China, and India to demonstrate that he possessed strategic alternatives to the United States. On March 10, 2010, standing next to Karzai at a Kabul news conference transmitted to television audiences in the United States, Iranian President Mahmoud Ahmadinejad condemned the United States for creating terrorists. Karzai nodded approvingly at Ahmadinejad's side as the Iranian president spoke. The U.S. administration was outraged. American radio and TV talking heads vied with one another to reprimand the ungrateful Karzai, whose survival depended on American troops and money. Western news headlines highlighted Karzai's "defiance" of Washington.[42]

Holbrooke pushed the administration's line against Karzai at a March 31, 2009, meeting with his European counterparts in The Hague. After the consultations, one unnamed conference participant told reporters, "Karzai is not delivering." Another said, "We need someone next to Karzai, a sort of chief executive, who can get things done, who will be reliable for us and accountable to the Afghan people." When this was reported in the media, Karzai accused foreign governments of undermining the Afghan government. "That is not their job. Afghanistan will never be a puppet state," he said. He and his aides began to refer to a "trust deficit" emerging in U.S.-Afghan relations. His advisers protested to journalists that the Bush administration's early focus on

Iraq and its failure to resource the Afghan government were mainly responsible for the Taliban's comeback.[43]

The Obama administration tried to use the Afghan presidential election campaign leading up to the August 20, 2009, elections as a vehicle to put more pressure on Karzai. Karzai's leading opponent was Dr. Abdullah Abdullah, his former foreign minister. Abdullah obtained endorsements of Afghan faction leaders from all major ethnic groups.[44] He energetically campaigned around the country, speaking to large crowds.

Karzai's former finance minister, Ashraf Ghani, also challenged him. He was known to enjoy close ties to Secretary Clinton as well as to Holbrooke. He was a longtime American resident, was American educated, and had worked for the World Bank. Ghani hired well-known Democratic strategist James Carville to manage his campaign to unseat Karzai. Discussing his campaign strategy, the "Ragin' Cajun" announced: "There is very little confidence in Afghanistan in Karzai as a leader. . . . Our job is to let the people of Afghanistan know that there is an alternative."[45] Carville's political skills could not prevent Ghani's decisive defeat. He received less than 3 percent of the votes cast.

President Obama's new ambassador to Afghanistan, Karl W. Eikenberry, a retired lieutenant general, appeared at press conferences in Kabul for Karzai's principal election opponents, Dr. Abdullah, Ghani, and the deputy speaker of the Afghan parliament, Mirwais Yasini. Eikenberry's claim of strict U.S. neutrality in the elections was greeted with skepticism by conspiracy-minded Afghans. The sight of the American ambassador standing near President Karzai's rivals while they vehemently denounced the Afghan president heightened their suspicions. Karzai's ambassador in Washington complained, "I don't think this is normal protocol anywhere in the world."[46]

Massive fraud, Taliban violence, and voter apathy marked the August elections. The day after the polling, Holbrooke and Eikenberry called on Karzai at his presidential palace before the results were counted. The two American officials urged Karzai to agree to a second round with Abdullah. Karzai angrily refused, insisting that he had won the election. The conversation turned acrimonious. Rebuffed, Holbrooke returned to Washington.

An Election Complaints Commission (ECC) composed of three foreigners designated by the United Nations and two Afghans chosen by Karzai threw out 28 percent of Karzai's votes and 18 percent of Abdullah's votes for suspected election fraud. In October, the commission moved Karzai's vote tally down to just below the 50 percent necessary to avoid a runoff with Abdullah. Abdullah moved up to 31 percent.[47] Secretary of State Clinton, British Prime Minister Gordon Brown, Canadian Prime Minister Stephen Harper, and several leaders of other troop-contributing countries phoned Karzai, advising him to agree to a runoff with Abdullah. Senate Foreign Relations Chairman John Kerry flew to Kabul to reinforce their recommendation. After several hours of talks with Kerry, Karzai agreed to a second round. Abdullah did not, contending that the Afghan election officials appointed by Karzai could not be trusted to run a fair election. After Abdullah's withdrawal, Karzai was declared the victor by default.

The Obama administration and Karzai temporarily cooled down their rhetorical skirmishing when it was clear that Karzai would remain in office after the fraud-ridden election process was complete. Karzai informed Clinton that he wanted the United States to be a "critical partner" during his second term. But the tarnished election had further damaged Karzai's image internationally and domestically. Ambassador Eikenberry sent a classified cable to Washington on November 6, 2009, saying that "President Karzai is not an adequate strategic partner." In January 2010, Eikenberry's evaluation of Karzai was leaked to the *New York Times*. The resulting publicity revived the administration's public jousting match with Karzai. In a January 8 interview, Karzai asked the international community to respect "Afghanistan and its government, and understand that we are a people, we are a country, we have a history, we have interests, we have pride, we have dignity. Our poverty must not become a means of ridicule and insult to us."[48]

Washington's quarrel with Karzai flared again when the Afghan press pounced on a statement Holbrooke made to a Harvard seminar in March 2010: "Almost every Pashtun family has someone involved with the movement," he said, meaning the Taliban. The *Afghanistan Times* scolded, "By making such mindless comments Holbrooke has insulted Pashtuns and has shown disrespect to sacrifices they have made in the fight against terrorism." When Secretary of Defense Robert Gates and Karzai were asked about Holbrooke's comment at a joint press conference a few days later, Gates distanced himself from Holbrooke. First noting that he had a "great deal of respect" for Holbrooke, Gates went on to say: "That doesn't mean I agree with everything he says, including that." Asked for his comment, Karzai coyly answered, "I guess Secretary Gates answered the question for both of us." Republicans in the United States seized on the administration's falling out with Karzai to criticize the Democrats. At a Republican conference in New Orleans, former Alaska governor Sarah Palin said: "This administration alienates our friends. They treated Afghanistan President Hamid Karzai poorly and acted surprised when he reacted in kind."[49]

President Obama's six-hour visit to Kabul on March 28 did not calm the troubled waters. Karzai refused to honor the American request to keep his new vice president, Mohammad Fahim, out of a small meeting that was planned for Obama and only a few officials from each side. In the meeting, Obama raised the corruption issue, but mostly listened to Karzai's comments.

On April 1, tensions soared to an all-time high when Karzai angrily stated to Afghan election workers that in "countries like Afghanistan, where there are more than 100,000 foreign troops, they [foreigners] also pursue their own interests. . . . A very thin curtain distinguishes between cooperation and assistance with the invasion." The media reported that Karzai accused the United Nations, the United States, and the European Union of conducting electoral fraud during the 2009 election and claimed that foreigners were attempting to weaken his regime."[50] In separate comments to parliamentarians, Karzai was alleged to have said that foreign pressures might force him to join the Taliban.

Karzai's accusations ignited another uproar in Washington. The Afghan president phoned Secretary of State Clinton to downplay his allegations. The State Department spokesman nevertheless branded them as "preposterous."[51] The White House expressed "genuine concern" over accusations that the United Nations and foreign countries had perpetrated the election fraud. On April 5, Karzai told a CNN interviewer that "Afghanistan is the home of the Afghans, and we own this place."[52]

Both sides softened their rhetoric during the last week of April. Continuing their food fight in the full glare of the world media was only helping the Taliban. Karzai had refused to bend under American criticism but was ready for a truce with his most important patron. The administration was also prepared for a respite. American criticism of Karzai was stirring anti-American Afghan nationalism at a time when tens of thousands of new American troops were flooding into the country and the Taliban were still expanding. The publicized war of words had improved Karzai's standing in some Afghan quarters but had eviscerated his once positive image in the United States.

ψ

The cease-fire helped make President Karzai's May 10–14, 2010, visit to the United States a success. A White House backgrounder the day before Karzai's arrival noted that President Obama had "bluntly instructed his national security team to treat Afghan President Hamid Karzai with more public respect." Karzai was greeted with smiles and handshakes as well as confidential meetings with President Obama, Secretary of State Clinton, and Secretary of Defense Gates. Vice President Biden hosted a "make-up" dinner at the vice president's mansion on Massachusetts Avenue. Holbrooke informed reporters that his own differences with Karzai had been exaggerated. Karzai was now "working on" the corruption issue.[53]

The administration's campaign against Karzai had created lingering mistrust in both camps. The mistrust could be papered over but would not soon go away. Ironically, Karzai's display of independence from U.S. pressures demonstrated to him that he enjoyed some reverse leverage in Washington. He had stood his ground. He had shown that Afghanistan's president and Afghanistan could not be pushed around. Karzai became more assertive in his dealings with foreigners and Afghans alike.

Obama and his team adjusted to dealing with Afghanistan's unruly leader whom the Americans had hoisted into power. Despite lingering irritation, there were valid grounds to cooperate with Karzai. The West could be comfortable that he was a religious moderate firmly opposed to the extremist ideology espoused by al-Qaeda and the Taliban. Karzai was a committed ally in the international struggle against terrorism. He was driven by Afghan nationalism and determination to forge national unity binding together the country's disparate groups. His cultural and political moorings were tribal, secular, and democratic. A deft politician, he had deep roots in Afghanistan's important Pashtun ethnic group. The administration's "new strategy of making nice with Mr. Karzai," as the *New York Times* called it, motivated Karzai to paint a rosy picture of U.S.-Afghan relations. After his May 10 visit to Washington, he ebul-liently predicted that the U.S. commitment to his country would continue "be-yond the military activity right now" and go on for "generations."

Karzai had pushed hard in Washington for the United States to refrain from using massive firepower in the campaign to pacify Kandahar. Secretary of State Clinton indicated agreement with Karzai's request to emphasize eco-nomic and political over military power during the Kandahar offensive. "We are not calling it an operation," Clinton said. "We talk of a process." Karzai gave Obama assurances about Ahmed Wali's activities in Kandahar. The two presidents agreed to complete "a strengthened U.S.-Afghanistan Strategic Partnership Declaration." The declaration would produce "a reinvigorated U.S.-Afghanistan Strategic Dialogue" featuring a "shared vision and commit-ment to Afghanistan's future." At a joint press conference with Karzai, Obama announced: "I am confident that we're going to be able to reduce our troop strength to Afghanistan starting in July 2011."[54]

The authoritative U.S.-Afghan "Joint Statement" issued on May 12 in Washington outlined long-term U.S.-Afghan bilateral cooperation. The state-ment gave Karzai written assurances about protections for the Afghan pop-ulation. It declared that the two governments undertook "to redouble efforts to prevent civilian casualties"; noted Obama's "desire to see all search, arrest, and detention operations . . . carried out by the Afghan National Security Forces"; and registered both U.S. and Afghan support for Karzai's "pledge of having the Afghan government assume full responsibility over detention op-erations" inside Afghanistan.[55] Obama also acquiesced to Karzai's desire for relaxed coalition combat operations in the Kandahar campaign, now given the less military-sounding nameplate "Cooperation for Kandahar."*

The Joint Statement satisfied important U.S. as well as Afghan objectives. Its positive tone and content dampened the Obama administration's feud with Karzai. It endorsed the goals of "directing at least 50 percent of U.S. as-sistance through the Afghan government" and building Afghan governing capacity. Karzai reiterated his standard, but never honored, promise "to bring to justice those involved in corrupt activities." On his return to Kabul, Karzai announced that military force would only be resorted to in Kandahar

---

* Hamkari Baraye Kandahar.

"if and when and where needed" and "in consultation with the community."
McChrystal adjusted accordingly, noting the Afghan lead and downplaying
conventional military tactics in his statements about the Kandahar operation.
The administration threw another bouquet to Karzai after his departure from
Washington by refusing to meet with his main political rival, Abdullah Ab-
dullah. The presidential election runner-up found the red carpet rolled up in
Washington. "I tried all of them, the White House, the National Security
Council, the State Department, the Pentagon," Abdullah told a reporter.[56]

With his U.S. flank reasonably secure, Karzai activated his peace outreach to
the Taliban with a carefully stage-managed June 2–4 National Peace Jirga in
Kabul. It was attended by 1,600 Afghan notables from around the country
who had been chosen by Karzai and other government officials. Unsuccessful
attempts by the Haqqani Network to rocket the conference site and attack it
with two suicide bombers suggested Pakistan's displeasure that Karzai—and
not ISI—was controlling the Afghan reconciliation process. Some key northern power brokers representing non-Pashtun groups chastised the Peace Jirga.
They rejected the idea of negotiating with the Taliban. Ahmed Shah Masood's
former followers, Abdullah Abdullah, Balkh governor Atta Mohammad, and
Uzbek warlord Abdul Rashim Dostum all stayed away, as did several important Hazaras. The Hazaras, Uzbeks, and Tajiks had suffered the most during
the six-year period of Taliban rule. Their opposition to Karzai's U.S.-backed
outreach to the overwhelmingly Pashtun extremist Taliban raised the specter
of the Pashtun versus non-Pashtun conflict that had ravaged the country in
the 1990s.

Karzai nonetheless pressed ahead with his peace dialogue. He fired two
of his ministers known to oppose his Taliban reconciliation policy. The two
ministers, National Security Director Panshiri Tajik Amrullah Saleh and Pashtun Interior Minister Hanif Atmar, were also the most competent, uncor-
rupted ministers in his government. His stated rationale was their failure to
prevent the Taliban rocket attacks on the Peace Jirga, but few doubted that
the real reason was their opposition to Karzai's outreach to the Taliban. A
Western adviser at the Interior Ministry speculated that Karzai bowed to Pakistani demands.[57] Karzai appointed Rehmat Nabil, one of his closest palace
aides, to take over the powerful National Security position. He somewhat as-

suaged northern resentment at Saleh's dismissal by transferring General Bismullah Khan, like Saleh a former Masood confidant, from his army chief of staff position to the Interior Ministry.

Afghanistan's second parliamentary elections in September 2010 compiled a record of fraud that surpassed even Karzai's 2009 election. Ultimately, over one-quarter of the ballots were invalidated. Countrywide, there were some 1,600 Taliban attacks during the week of the elections, the highest number for any single week since the insurgency began in 2002.[58]

In September, McChrystal's successor, General David Petraeus, discarded the "Cooperation for Kandahar" spirit to launch an all-out anti-Taliban military offensive in Kandahar Province. The campaign, more military-centric than population-centric, sharply increased infantry, Special Forces, and air operations in the districts surrounding Kandahar. Petraeus canceled most of McChrystal's restrictions on the use of firepower, including from the air. Aircraft and drones dropped hundreds of 2,000- and 500-pound bombs and fired rockets at suspected Taliban enclaves. He ordered a sharp upswing in nighttime raids.[59] He also granted the Marine Corps permission to introduce a company of heavy M-1 tanks into the southern theater. U.S. military officers told reporters that 235 insurgent leaders were captured or killed in Petraeus' three-month Kandahar campaign.

Karzai criticized the coalition's military offensive to visiting *Washington Post* reporters in an interview in Kabul. He called on the United States to reduce its military operations in Afghanistan and repeated his demand that the coalition end nighttime raids on Afghan homes. "If a partner means a silent spectator of events conducted by Washington, if that kind of partner you seek, well, I'm not that partner. Nor will be the Afghan people," he stated. His remarks created another spate of public recriminations. Petraeus was reported to have been astonished and disappointed, and Secretary of State Clinton signaled that the United States would not change its tactics.[60]

General Petraeus included the results of his Kandahar offensive in his briefing to the high-level November 19–20 NATO summit in Lisbon. He reported that the coalition had regained the momentum from the Taliban in the south, a theme he repeated during the White House review of progress in December.[61] Skeptics warned that Petraeus's claim was premature. The Taliban still maintained a formidable network of fighters and sympathizers in southern Afghanistan; Taliban safe havens and senior Taliban leaders remained secure in Pakistan; and the Taliban would rapidly replace mid- and lower-level commanders killed or captured in the Kandahar offensive. The movement was expanding its influence in other parts of the country, where coalition forces did not have sufficient troops to launch decisive operations against the enemy.

⚘

As of this writing in early 2011, and as President Obama moves ahead in the second half of his four-year term, there have been a number of significant tactical adjustments and improvements on Afghanistan, some of which can be built upon. But several core flaws of previous administrations remain. If they are not corrected, the outlook is gloomy indeed.

On the positive side, Obama has targeted the beginning of American withdrawal, thus giving the Afghan government and people an incentive to take over ownership of Afghanistan's future. The U.S.-led coalition is growing the size of Afghan forces so they can take over security responsibilities. More rhetorical pressure has been put on Islamabad. The administration has significantly increased the number of drone strikes against Pakistani Taliban and al-Qaeda leaders in the central zone of the Frontier with good results. More attention has been paid to limiting civilian casualties in Afghanistan, and there has been a major increase in economic assistance and a greater civilian presence. The operation to kill bin Laden in Pakistan was a spectacular success.

The negative side of the equation is much heavier, however. Many of the above advances are falling short of their goals and could prove illusory. Fundamental mistakes persist. Despite the new stress on "Afghanization," the "Americanization" of the conflict is clear. The real gains of the military surge seem so far to be incremental and might turn out to be temporary. The military and CIA continue to dominate American planning and decisionmaking on Afghanistan. The administration's see-saw attitude toward Karzai has sowed confusion and mutual distrust between Obama's advisers and Afghan leaders. Washington and Kabul may encounter serious differences on the issue of reconciliation with the Taliban. There is a muddled policy on strengthening the linkage between the capital and the provinces and reviving their historic balance. Corruption and poor governance continue to abound.

The delivery of outside aid remains uncoordinated, poorly managed, and vulnerable to wastage and contractor corruption. Turf battles persist.

Most fundamental of all is a flawed strategic approach to the region and beyond. Obama's Afghan strategy, like Bush's, still resembles a bundle of tactics. It presents no overarching, long-term, comprehensive, geostrategic policy for achieving U.S. goals in Afghanistan and the region. The Obama administration is not effectively addressing the militant Islamic ideology inciting Muslims to violence and terrorism from Kabul to Islamabad to Riyadh to the Horn of Africa to the streets of London and New York.

Once again, the United States is still flinching from taking tough decisions on Pakistan, even while aware of Islamabad's duplicity costing American and coalition lives and treasure over time. The killing of bin Laden hopefully may tilt Pakistan in a positive direction pointing toward ending its proxy war in Afghanistan, permitting an Afghan peace process to go forward without Islamabad's interference, closing down the sanctuaries, apprehending bin Laden's successor, Ayman al-Zawahiri, and neutralizing Mullah Omar.

The United States and its coalition partners, however, cannot realistically count on this. History suggests that Pakistan's army most likely will continue to angle for its own preferred extremist outcome in Afghanistan. Pakistan's generals might even be relieved that bin Laden is dead. After all, it was his global terrorism that brought the American army to Afghanistan and toppled Islamabad's Taliban proxy from power. But fueling the Taliban insurgency will only prolong the Afghan war and incite more global terrorism. Increased levels of U.S. aid to Pakistan, high-level visits, and subdued warnings will not convince Pakistan's army to stop assisting the Afghan Taliban or to close down Taliban sanctuaries on Pakistan's territory.

In short, still another U.S. presidential administration has failed to learn the lessons of Afghan history. It is making the same fundamental mistakes that its predecessors made.

Despite the current troublesome trends, there is still time for U.S. policy changes. There are ways in which the United States can produce an outcome in Afghanistan and the region that is favorable to its interests. It is to this subject that we turn in the final chapter.

CHAPTER 25

The Way Ahead

In a worst-case scenario, when the United States disengages from Afghanistan, the country will slide back into the shatter zone of the 1990s. American delusions about the Pakistani Army's motives in Afghanistan will continue to paralyze U.S. policy after the withdrawal of combat troops scheduled to be completed in 2014. The disastrous results could severely test the constitutional obligation required of all U.S. administrations to protect the United States and its people. Another inning of the long, bloody Afghan wars will commence: Notwithstanding bin Laden's demise, the Islamist infrastructure will expand back into Afghanistan on the heels of a Taliban victory; al-Qaeda, the al-Qaeda-linked Haqqani Network, and ISI-created and -supported Pakistani religious militias will reestablish terrorist bases in Afghanistan; and the unholy alliance will strike the American homeland again and again. America's potent drone missile attacks and firepower from warships and aircraft will be unable to eradicate the terrorist bases in Afghanistan and along Pakistan's Frontier.

Clearly, it is in the interest of the United States and its allies to prevent this worst-case scenario from happening. This chapter offers a comprehensive policy blueprint, a way ahead for safeguarding American interests in Afghanistan and Pakistan over the long term. It seeks to transcend the legacy of failure inherited from previous and current U.S. policies. Given the size and the complexities of the challenges, there can be no assurance that this approach will work. But at least it goes with the flow of Afghan history and culture as presented in the chapters of this book. It offers an opportunity for a limited success—or better. The United States must not stick to its previous failed strategies in Afghanistan and Pakistan. If it does, the consequences for U.S. national security will be dire.

The new U.S. approach would focus on three overarching goals: genuine Afghanization and de-Americanization; a fundamental change in Pakistan's policy; and geostrategic diplomatic reinforcement of global and regional forces to achieve these two outcomes. The relative success or failure of this policy outline will mainly depend on the actions of the three major participants in the long Afghan conflict: the Afghans, the Pakistanis, and the Americans. Saudi policy will also exert heavy influence. The countries in the NATO alliance, Russia, China, India, Iran, the Central Asian states, and non-state movements, principally al-Qaeda, radical Muslim Brotherhood factions, and the array of Taliban groups, will continue to affect the course of the Afghan conflict. But it is the Afghans, the Americans, and the Pakistanis who will remain the most influential players in deciding whether the wars of Afghanistan end during this coming decade. If they do, Eurasia could become a crossroads for transcontinental economic cooperation instead of a hub of conflict.

In this book I have sought to portray how Afghans, the region, and the world reached the current impasse. Past Afghanistan wars ring loud and must be heeded as we chart the way ahead. For the past three decades the United States has consistently failed to learn from the past. The Obama administration needs to reassess the fundamental building blocks of its strategies in Afghanistan and Pakistan. Then it should construct a new, long-term policy architecture to end the long Afghan conflict. Below I describe what I believe are the most important elements of a policy that could yield positive results.

DESTINATION 2020

One should not begin a long journey without knowing the destination. Shaping foreign policy outcomes to realize long-term strategic goals is preferable to reacting to events. Here I outline a destination for 2020. It is an ideal one, unlikely to be achieved in its entirety, if at all. But if such a long-term, comprehensive vision had been established to guide policymakers after 9/11, America would not be mired in Afghanistan today.

The starting point for the roadmap is 2011. Contrary to optimistic pronouncements by U.S. military leaders, security in both Afghanistan and

Pakistan has been deteriorating. The Taliban are in their sixth year of expansion in Afghanistan, and the political and military environment in the country is volatile. Afghanistan could stumble into another north-south, Pashtun-non-Pashtun civil war. Pakistani Islamic radicals and al-Qaeda are hammering the Pakistan government and slaughtering civilians. U.S. delusions about Pakistan's motives in Afghanistan continue to disable U.S. policy in the region.

The new, long-term, geostrategic U.S. policy toward Pakistan and Afghanistan that I lay out here strives for a plainly best-case scenario by 2020.

Afghanistan in 2020

Let us envision the following ideal picture of Afghanistan in 2020:

- The blowback of radical Sunni Islamic terrorism against the Pakistani government and society, plus international pressures and incentives, have convinced the Pakistani military to end its proxy war in Afghanistan. Afghanistan and Pakistan have normalized their relations. They have joined other nations in signing an international agreement re-creating the Afghan buffer in Central Asia.

- Two presidential and two parliamentary elections, perhaps another loya jirga, have moved Afghanistan well beyond the Karzai period. Afghanistan's new leadership and the pullback by Pakistan from internal Afghan politics have encouraged Afghan political and economic growth and reforms. Karzai's successor, elected in 2014 and perhaps reelected in 2019, runs an improved government.

- The Taliban wave has receded. The al-Qaeda threat in Afghan-Pakistani border areas has been all but eliminated. The United States and its coalition partners have withdrawn all of their combat troops and handed over military responsibilities and facilities to the Afghan government.

- The U.S. withdrawal has increased the Afghan government's legitimacy and dignity in the eyes of its population, enhancing stability. The Afghan National Army has been reduced to 80,000 troops.

- The Afghan government is broad-based and inclusive of all major ethnic groups. The historical Afghan equilibrium between the center and the regions has been restored. The center provides resources and training to communities, which direct their own programs. The regions are connected to a central government they deem to be legitimately chosen by Afghans, not foreigners. They look to the government to help mediate their disputes.

- There is a light official U.S. presence in the country and no permanent bases. North Atlantic Treaty Organization advisers continue to help train the Afghan National Security Forces (ANSF). The U.S. civilian presence has fallen from more than 2,500 in 2011 to fewer than 200 diplomats and U.S. Agency for International Development workers at the embassy in Kabul and consulates in Jalalabad, Kandahar, Herat, and Mazar.
- Although the United States remains the largest aid donor, many other countries and the United Nations are also contributing to Afghan reconstruction.
- Strict conditioning of foreign aid and training of a new generation of Afghan civil servants and technocrats have reduced corruption and strengthened government operations.
- Afghan government revenues from foreign investments in Afghan natural resources and pipelines transiting Afghanistan cover all government operating expenses and a portion of the military budget.
- Opium production has plummeted as a result of improved security and counternarcotics programs. The U.S. Department of Agriculture and Japanese aid programs have contributed significantly to the sharp increase in production of wheat and other agricultural commodities. Afghanistan is a net exporter of grain, as it was before the 1978 communist coup.
- Business in Kabul and other Afghan urban areas is booming. Investment by foreign countries and corporations from the large Afghan diaspora in Europe and North America finances the development of Afghanistan's bountiful natural resources of iron ore, copper, lithium, and natural gas.[1] Roads, pipelines, and a growing rail network through Afghanistan connect Pakistan, India, and Iran with Europe, Central Asia, and China, fostering transcontinental trade and commerce.

Pakistan in 2020

Likewise, let us envision the following scenario in Pakistan by 2020:

- Military authoritarianism has diminished in Pakistan. Civilian governments have greater leeway to manage domestic and foreign policy, including Afghan policy.

- Pakistan's military has allowed two elected governments to serve out their terms during the decade.
- Elections, the strengthening of a multiparty system, and economic growth have helped to stabilize Pakistan and improved the government's performance.
- Extremist-generated Sunni-Shia sectarian violence and mosque and other terrorist bombings are rare.
- Pakistani military and ISI officers no longer practice the "just tell us where the terrorists are and we will arrest them" charade with the United States and its coalition partners. Instead, they proactively pursue and arrest wanted terrorists in Pakistan.
- Trilateral U.S.-Afghan-Pakistani counterterrorism cooperation has marginalized the residual al-Qaeda presence on the Frontier.
- The Pakistani Army has dismantled Afghan Taliban sanctuaries and the paramilitary religious groups that the ISI previously fostered, jailing or extraditing their leaders. Hamid Gul and his virtual ISI are no longer active.
- In addition to the 2011 elimination of bin Laden, Ayman al-Zawahiri, Taliban leaders, Jalaluddin and Sirajuddin Haqqani, and Gulbuddin Hekmatyar have either perished or been pushed by the Pakistani military across the border, where they have been apprehended by the Afghan government or the American-led coalition.
- Military operations and foreign-financed development programs have quieted the tribal areas. Improved socioeconomic conditions there bode well for a referendum to merge the tribal agencies into the Northwest Frontier, now renamed Pakhtunkwa Khyber Province.
- Indo-Pakistani negotiations on the difficult Kashmir issue are making progress or have ended in an agreement.
- The regional international trade corridors opening up through Afghanistan have lifted Pakistan's economy. Entrepreneurial Pakistani corporations have joined the global economy. The United States and other countries have resumed investing in Pakistan and are continuing economic aid programs.

The foremost goals of the United States in Afghanistan must be to end Americanization of the Afghan war and to put Afghans in the lead. No foreign army in Afghan history has ever stabilized the country. Only Afghans who are seen by Afghans as running Afghanistan will be able to do that.

There are five main reasons why the United States must reduce its military combat presence in Afghanistan as rapidly as the Afghan National Security Forces can be trained, equipped, and made ready to assume the combat burden. First, the Afghans, from the anti-Taliban, pro-Western urban elite down to tribesmen at the community level, demand it. Second, the withdrawal will negate false Taliban propaganda that the United States is an occupier and anti-Islamic, while sharpening Afghan hostility to the Pakistan-backed Taliban. Third, the departure of U.S. troops will force the Afghans to assume the combat burden. Fourth, it will defuse suspicions among large Eurasian nations, notably China and Russia, that U.S. bases in Afghanistan may become permanent and target them. Finally, withdrawal will allow Washington to give more attention to other security threats around the world.

The sequencing of the troop withdrawals must be part of a long-term policy. It should be a stabilizing, not a destabilizing, process, not a rush for the exits. It should be the bridge to direct control by Afghans of their nation and their destiny.

Afghan nationalism, particularly among urban, educated Afghans, and the country's economic progress since the Taliban were ousted, are forces for national unity. Still, as a nation and a people, Afghans are attempting to overcome differences and to put their multiethnic country back together after over three decades of war. Their "main difficulty," as King Zahir Shah once said to me, is still with themselves. They fiercely resist foreign pressures to unify. At the same time, their internal differences make it very difficult for them to escape their propensity for disunity. Only they can reestablish their unity, the historical center-region equilibrium unique to Afghanistan's tribal society, and the will to think nationally as well as locally.

The United States erred in forcing Hamid Karzai's selection at the 2002 loya jirga. He might have come out on top anyway, but the American intervention cast him as a foreign puppet. More significantly, it discredited the United States as just another in the line of foreign powers attempting to put its surrogate on the Afghan throne. At the time, President Karzai's meek acceptance of the Bush administration's Americanization of the Afghan war impeded prospects for Afghans to restore their traditional intergroup balances at national and local levels and stabilize the country.

During his first term and particularly after the 2009 presidential election, Karzai has exercised the limited authority the American coalition has given him in the same way many Afghan power brokers would: He has stayed on top of the tribal summit by manipulating his personal patronage network and allowing widespread corruption. Karzai's corrupt government is unpopular. Some Afghans speculate that he will attempt to rewrite the constitution to give himself a third term in office. That would block the accession of a new leadership and could drive the country into a much more dangerous phase of instability.

ψ

A combination of a weak, unpopular Afghan government; Pakistani backing of the Pashtun Taliban; Karzai's outreach to the Taliban for peace talks; and anti-Taliban hostility felt by Tajiks, Uzbeks, and Hazaras in the north who suffered the most under Taliban rule is straining Afghan unity. Pashtuns, too, claim discrimination.[2] If not checked, rising interethnic friction could take Afghanistan back to the civil wars of the 1990s. Outside powers again would intervene to support the warring sides, splitting the country into antagonistic ethnic parts. The breakdown of the transregional Afghan linchpin would send dangerous centrifugal forces northward into Central Asia and southward into the subcontinent. Pakistan would suffer the immediate effects of Afghan fragmentation. India could also experience more ethnic, regional, and religious fissiparity. That both of South Asia's two largest states possess nuclear weapons adds to the imperative to stabilize Afghanistan.

ψ

High-level friction in the U.S.-Afghan dialogue has undermined confidence on both sides of the relationship. Many American officials doubt that President Karzai and his corrupt government are good partners to stabilize the country. Afghan political and military leaders worry that the United States might pull out before they are able to defend themselves or again outsource U.S. Afghan policy to Pakistan. Karzai is improving relations with Iran, India, and China, partly to balance relations with the United States and partly as a hedge against a Pakistani decision to intensify Islamabad's proxy war in Afghanistan after the American coalition withdraws.

Public assurances by the United States and NATO have somewhat moderated Afghan fears that the United States will quickly leave. So have NATO programs to train and equip Afghans and pass security responsibilities to the ANSF. But public and congressional support for the Afghan war is draining in America and throughout the NATO coalition.

By the middle of the decade, barring unpredictable leadership developments before or during the 2014 elections, there will be another Afghan leader with his own agenda and style in the presidential palace. It is probable that the Afghan president elected in 2014 will be as moderate, nationalistic, and pro-Western as Karzai, Ahmed Shah Masood, or Abdul Haq. But he will likely be more like Haq and Masood in demanding de-Americanization, particularly in the security sector.

The withdrawal of coalition combat troops will, in any case, be well advanced if not complete by that time. In the best-case scenario, the growth of the ANSF, the residual NATO military training and advisory troops, and a hopeful easing of Pakistani interference by 2014–2015 would give space for the new government to function more effectively and reestablish the center's historical linkages to the regions.

ॐ

The most valuable contribution that America can make to Afghan peace lies not in Afghanistan but in Pakistan. Pakistan's worries about Indian collusion with Afghanistan to catch it in a strategic vice must be addressed in any U.S. policy inducing a Pakistani pullback from Afghanistan. But Washington must protect its own security interests. If Pakistan hews to its fireman and arsonist policy in Afghanistan, the Obama administration will likely make little progress in Afghanistan. U.S. coalition operations and the ANSF will be unable to break the six-year-old stalemate in the Afghan war. The main source of the ongoing conflict will remain at Pakistani military headquarters in Rawalpindi.

Washington and its coalition partners must proceed on the basis that their Afghan strategy and Pakistan's Afghan strategy are in conflict. The coalition and the international community are attempting to stabilize Afghanistan and suppress terrorism. Pakistan's military continues to pursue Zia ul-Haq's vision, conducting its proxy war in Afghanistan and maintaining links to Pakistan-based terrorist groups that stoke regional and global instability and terrorism. Zia's vision contains defensive and offensive dimensions—it is defensive in building strategic depth against India, and offensive in exporting militant Islamism into Afghanistan, Kashmir, and beyond. That offensive thrust increasingly threatens the vital interests of the United States, the West, Saudi Arabia, and most other Muslim countries. The two terrorist incidents in 2009 and 2010 targeting New York were planned and launched from Pakistan's Frontier.[3] After his car bomb failed to explode in Times Square in the 2010 incident, terrorist Faisal Shahzad warned a federal judge, "It's a war. . . . We will be attacking [the] U.S."[4] Faisal Shahzad's warning must be taken seriously.

A NEW U.S. POLICY

During the two Clinton administrations—and the George W. Bush administration up to September 11, 2001—there was no U.S. policy on Afghanistan. The United States outsourced American Afghan policy to Pakistan. This practice, surely one of the greatest diplomatic blunders in American history, continued even after al-Qaeda blew up two U.S. embassies in Africa and attacked an American warship off the Yemeni coast.

The three years from 2002 to 2005 marked the first time in almost a quarter century that Afghanistan enjoyed relative peace. Afghan elites forged a working consensus and with international assistance developed a political structure for Afghanistan's future. It was a period of relative stability offering a window of opportunity for progress. But instead of reinforcing its success in the victory over the Taliban, the United States switched its focus and resources to Iraq. The ISI regrouped and rearmed the Taliban inside Pakistan. In 2005, when Pakistan's current army chief, General Ashfaq Kayani, headed ISI, Pakistan initiated another proxy invasion of Afghanistan. Pakistan has made substantial progress since then in restoring its strategic position in Afghanistan that it lost after 9/11. Its Taliban proxy is inflicting ever-rising casualties on U.S., coalition, and Afghan forces within Afghanistan.

President Obama's strategy has been more enlightened than Bush's. Nonetheless, for most of the same reasons, it, too, is failing. The strategy is narrow. It does not have a long-term geostrategic overlay geared to shaping rather than reacting to developments. Like Bush, Obama has delegated too much strategic planning and implementation authority to military [REDACTED] agencies. Pakistan's generals and the ISI selectively grant tactical military [REDACTED] benefits to prolong the status quo in Afghanistan. They count on Pentagon [REDACTED] domination of U.S. Afghan policy to deter U.S. pressure to force a change in their Afghan policy. The new U.S. policy

should help reduce Indo-Pakistani tensions. Washington can urge Afghanistan not to provoke Pakistani concerns about being caught in an Afghan-
Indian strategic vice.

A new U.S. policy must effectively bind U.S. civilian and military agencies
together in working toward long-term goals under White House direction.
In a departure from current patterns, it should buttress—not displace—the
Afghan lead in stabilizing Afghanistan. And it should, above all, focus on persuading Pakistan's generals that it is in their self-interest to turn away from
Zia's vision. Only a fundamental change in Islamabad's Afghan policy will
end the wars of Afghanistan. And only the United States is in a position to
convince Islamabad's generals to do so. That is why this U.S. policy section
on the way ahead must begin with Pakistan and not Afghanistan.

A Long-Term Pakistan Policy

The following policy recommendations carry risks. The proposals for a
firmer U.S. approach to influence a fundamental change in Pakistan's Afghan
policy could, at least in the near term, provoke deterioration in U.S. relations
with Pakistan—an important, unstable, Muslim, nuclear-armed state in a
strategic location on the world map. The suggested path ahead will encounter
obstacles. But it must be taken.

Washington and its coalition allies have no choice but to end the deadly
pattern of apprehensively waiting to react to the next jihadi bomber trained
in Pakistan to strike their cities. When CIA Director Leon Panetta and National Security Adviser James Jones sought General Kayani's help in May
2010, just after Faisal Shahzad's attempted bombing of Times Square, Kayani
reportedly responded: "I'll be the first to admit, I'm India-centric"—that is,
preoccupied by the threat from India.[5] This response was artfully indirect,
inadequate, and unacceptable. The ISI-linked Jaish-i Mohammad (Army of
Mohammad) terrorists who facilitated Shahzad's training in Pakistan are not
only targeting India. They are operationally connected to al-Qaeda and attacking "infidels" in Muslim Afghanistan, other Muslim countries around the
world, and the United States and its allies. The Obama administration's passive reaction to Pakistani explanations like Kayani's is appallingly misguided,
counterproductive, weak, and bureaucratic. Washington should stop praising
Pakistan's generals for their cooperation on counterterrorism, stop showering
them with unconditioned military aid, and stop embracing them with benign

diplomacy sprinkled with ambiguous warnings that current conditions are not acceptable.

President Obama and the White House need to take full control of Pakistani policy. The broad overlay of the new approach should be long term, political, and geostrategic—not tied down by short-run, tactical military and intelligence objectives. American military power and intelligence operations will be absolutely essential to the policy's long-term success, as they were during the Cold War. The president needs to ensure that U.S. military [REDACTED] agencies no longer dominate policymaking on Afghanistan and Pakistan. They should go back to the policy-implementing, not policy-making, roles they exercised during the Cold War. Each, of course, will provide input to the policymaking process along with the State Department and other agencies. Although still at the level of tactics, President Obama's management of the May 2011 bin Laden operation projected the right decision-making process. The president weighed the options presented, and U.S. military and intelligence agencies flawlessly and courageously implemented his decision.

Within the broader context of U.S.-Pakistani relations, Washington should focus on changing Pakistan's Afghan policy so that Islamabad terminates its proxy wars against Afghanistan; ceases interfering in the Afghan political process; dismantles the Islamist terrorist infrastructure on the Frontier, including the Taliban sanctuaries; and joins the international community in restoring Afghanistan's neutral buffer status at the center of Eurasia.

Through the ups and downs of U.S.-Pakistani relations since Pakistan's independence, the two sides have often been partners. During difficult periods, they have always maintained a dialogue that later provided a foundation for rebuilding ties. At this point in the relationship, the United States can rightly look back at the decade since 9/11 and claim that it has been on the losing end of the partnership. Pakistan's army and the ISI continue Pakistan's proxy wars in Afghanistan from sanctuaries inside Pakistan. Islamic terrorists use Pakistan as a base from which to attack the United States and other countries around the world.

The Obama administration needs to—as a friend—be more candid in using the U.S.-Pakistani dialogue to press Pakistan's leaders, especially the Pakistani Army, to change course in Afghanistan and cooperate with the United States and other nations to clamp down on terrorists conducting their global operations from Pakistan. All of Afghanistan's neighbors and nearly all major world powers outside of South Asia have been victims of terrorist groups in Pakistan. All Muslim countries, except for perhaps Sudan and radical Islamist-controlled areas of Somalia, wish to see the al-Qaeda and Taliban bases in Pakistan dismantled. The international community as a whole is frustrated by Islamabad's reluctance to crack down on indigenous terrorist organizations like the ISI-linked Lashkar-i Taiba and Jaish-i Mohammad and its protection of terrorist training camps preparing international jihidis to launch terrorist operations around the world.

In the South and Central Asian region, Pakistan's export of violent Islamist extremism is fueling trends that are turning the regional correlation of forces against Islamabad. These are natural historical trends, not U.S.-made. As they mature, they will make Pakistan's policy increasingly self-defeating. They are:

A regional shift in the balance of power against Pakistan. Pakistan's fueling of radical Islamism in Afghanistan and Pakistan is indirectly engendering its worst nightmare—a strategic reconfiguration of the regional balance of power threatening its security interests. A similar, momentous turnabout on the global stage took place in the late 1970s when China shifted its geostrategic weight to the anti-Soviet grouping of the United States, Western Europe, and Japan. China's adjustment completed the USSR's isolation among the world's great powers. It marked a turning point in the Cold War.

The closer the radical Taliban and their unholy alliance allies get to Kabul and the Amu Darya, the more the outer ring of countries opposing them will seek common ground against Pakistan. The specter of re-Talibanization of Afghanistan will strengthen unity among Afghan minorities north of the Hindu Kush. These minorities will appeal for weapons and funds from the West, Russia, Iran, and the Central Asian Republics to defend their regions in Afghanistan against the Taliban.

Pakistan may count on Chinese support, but Beijing's interests in a stable, nonextremist Afghanistan could dampen its response. China's worries about Taliban winds blowing into its largely Muslim, Western province of Xinjiang from Afghanistan were evident in a July 2010 comment by a Chinese Foreign Ministry think-tank analyst: "Our interest is clear. We need a peaceful neighbor because we have our own problems in Xinjiang. . . . We want Afghanistan to be successful."[6] The drug traffic from Afghanistan is also a serious problem for Beijing. Finally, an Afghanistan torn by war would deny the voracious Chinese economy's access to the country's vast mineral wealth. China's $3 billion investment in Logar Province's giant copper mine instantly made China Afghanistan's largest investor. A stable Afghanistan would offer opportunity for more multibillion-dollar Chinese investments, giving Beijing a stake in Afghan stability.

Improving Indo-U.S. relations. This trend has been under way since the Clinton administration. The factors powering the deepening Indo-U.S. relationship go well beyond Pakistan's relations with India. India is a major democracy and an economic power whose influence extends into other world regions. The United States should continue to improve relations with India while simultaneously attempting to strengthen ties with Pakistan.

Saudi Arabia's rapprochement with India. Indian Prime Minister Manmohan Singh paid a state visit to Saudi Arabia from February 27 to March 1, 2010. King Abdullah had made an earlier visit to India in 2006. Before that, fifty-one years had elapsed since a Saudi king had last been in New Delhi. In Riyadh, King Abdullah and Prime Minister Singh issued the "Riyadh Declaration" announcing their countries' "strategic partnership" and signed an extradition treaty.[7]

Singh's 2010 state visit to Saudi Arabia spotlighted the warming trend in Saudi-Indian relations. In the zero-sum game of Indo-Pakistani rivalry in the subcontinent, the visit was a gain for India at Pakistan's expense. It contrasted with the tight Saudi-Pakistani relationship of the 1980s and 1990s through the first two and a half years of Taliban rule. The Saudi government was one of only three governments to recognize the Taliban government when it captured Kabul in 1996. But in 1998, the Saudis severed relations with the Taliban regime after Mullah Omar rudely rebuffed Prince Turki's request to arrest Osama bin Laden. From his Afghan base, bin Laden was allegedly linked to several terrorist attacks against Saudi Arabia, including the 2003 and 2008 bombings in Riyadh.

Saudi anger at Pakistan's ongoing promotion of Muslim extremists threatening Saudi Arabia and support for the Taliban has probably influenced the kingdom's coolness toward Pakistan in recent years. Media reports have cited

Pakistani officials complaining that Saudi-promised concessionary oil rates have not been fulfilled and that Riyadh has reduced its annual subsidy to Islamabad.[8]

Saudi Arabia has other reasons to improve ties to India. They include gaining more access to the burgeoning Indian market, Saudi Arabia's sixth largest, and an open door to 8 percent of the world's Muslim population (150 million people). India is an emerging global power, and the Saudis may perceive an advantage in improving Saudi-Indian geopolitical ties.

King Abdullah could not have been happy when an anti-American diatribe taped by bin Laden and sent from Pakistan was broadcast by al-Jazeera television the day President Obama arrived on his first visit to the kingdom in June 2009.[9] Two months later, an al-Qaeda suicide bomber with an explosive in his rectum attempted to assassinate King Abdullah's nephew, the chief of the Saudi antiterrorism office, as he stood in line receiving guests at a reception in Jeddah.[10] Saudi diplomats informed the Taliban that Riyadh would not facilitate Afghan peace talks in Saudi Arabia until the Taliban renounced al-Qaeda—something Mullah Omar has refused to do.

On April 12, 2010, at King Abdullah's request, the Saudi Council of Senior Ulema, chaired by Mohammad al-Sheikh, the al-Sheikh family chief mufti, promulgated an unprecedented antiterrorism fatwa.[11] Citing Koranic passages and authoritative hadiths to justify its conclusions, the fatwa prohibited the financing of terrorism. By criminalizing private Saudi donations to terrorists, the fatwa—if thoroughly implemented—could deal a severe financial blow to the ISI Islamist infrastructure and the terrorism it breeds inside Pakistan.[12]

International exposure of Pakistan's proxy wars in Afghanistan. Clear evidence of Pakistan's covert direction and equipping of the Afghan insurgency dribbled out during the 1980s. For years Pakistan denied such accusations and they were forgotten. Now the steady flow of reports is raising the pressure on Pakistan to change its policy. British Prime Minister David Cameron on July 28, 2010, publicly remonstrated: "We cannot tolerate in any sense the idea that this country [Pakistan] is allowed to look both ways and is able in any way to promote the export of terror, whether to India or whether to Afghanistan or anywhere else in the world. . . . It is not right . . . to have any relationship with groups that are promoting terror. Democratic states that want to be part of the developed world cannot do that."[13]

Surrendering economic advantages. Military-dominated regimes rarely give a high priority to economic issues when formulating national security policy. This was evident in Pakistan during the 1990s. Prime ministers and civilian cabinet ministries optimistically negotiated agreements for pipelines to bring Central Asian gas from Turkmenistan to Pakistan through Afghanistan; Pakistan's military and the ISI made pipeline construction projects impossible by fanning warfare in Afghanistan.

Today, Central Asian governments remain eager to open energy corridors to Pakistan and India. Pakistan's troubled, inflation-saddled economy desperately needs energy, but anti-Western Islamic radical groups have frightened away foreign investment. Only foreign aid infusions maintain some low-level economic growth in the country. Globalization has bypassed Pakistan, and education is a low priority. A demographic bubble in the next few decades will produce tens of millions of unemployable youth.

Pakistan could still become the foundation for a network of east-west, north-south pipelines and roads transiting Afghanistan to the new energy-rich republics in Central Asia and the Caucasus. But for that to happen, Pakistan's military would have to decide to play a constructive role in restoring peace in Afghanistan and stabilizing the Afghan land bridge connecting Pakistan to the economies of Eurasia. By continuing its proxy war in Afghanistan, the Pakistani Army is literally throwing away markets for Pakistan's goods from Central Asia to the Caucasus and the Black Sea.

Sinking back into the Afghan quagmire. Pakistan's proxy war strategy in Afghanistan may, in the short run, promote more Taliban expansion into rural areas. The Taliban could succeed in capturing one or more major Afghan cities for a time. But they cannot subdue Afghanistan. And Pakistan, as in the 1990s, will not be able to muster the required national military strength, resources, and political solidarity to pull Afghanistan into its sphere of influence. A March 2010 Pakistani commentary cogently summed up the danger to Pakistan of Islamabad's futile quest for hegemony in Afghanistan: "The risk of failure and backfiring are much higher in trying to install a friendly government in a foreign country than in attempts to develop friendly relations with an incumbent government. The failure of Pakistan's Afghan policy is a glaring example in this regard."[14]

Snakes biting their trainer. The rising incidence of jihadi attacks on Pakistan's state institutions shows that breeding snakes is easier than controlling them. Since 2004, the radical Sunni Pakistani Taliban, operating from the seven tribal agencies and adjacent districts, have been assaulting the government apparatus and Shia, Sufi, and Ahmedi mosques throughout Pakistan. While there remain high levels of anti-Americanism in Pakistan, the general population— rich and poor alike—is fed up with the rising extremist violence and terrorism tormenting the country, including security forces. The more fanatical members of the ISI-created Lashkar-i Taiba and Jaish-i Mohammad paramilitary groups have joined in the attacks. A Punjabi Taliban splinter group kidnapped and executed two well-known retired ISI colonels in North Waziristan in March 2010, dramatically demonstrating the ISI's deteriorating influence over Pakistani terrorist groups holed up along Pakistan's Frontier. One was Colonel Sultan Imam, "the Father of the Taliban"; the other a Hamid Gul confidant, who was traveling with Imam.

Suggested Elements for a Tougher U.S. Approach

The new U.S. policy needs to truly blend pressures with incentives. It should continue to reach out to Pakistan, through high-level meetings and assistance programs, as a partner. But at the same time, when necessary, it must treat Pakistan as a potential competitor in ending the long Afghan war and fighting global terrorism. Washington can expand relations where there is an overlap in interests, but retaliate in these two areas where Islamabad's double game is endangering the national security interests of the United States and its friends and allies. Thus, the more Pakistan stresses partnership, the more the United States should reciprocate. The more Pakistan supports its proxy war in Afghanistan and terrorist groups in Pakistan, the more the United States should activate appropriate geostrategic, economic, and antiterrorism measures to protect its interests and those of its friends and allies.

The United States, in consultation with its allies, must therefore implement a more results-oriented approach to Pakistan. Below are the measures I recommend to carry out such an approach.

Seek results, not assurances. American political leaders, diplomats, generals, and intelligence officers must privately deliver the identical, firm, and clear message to Army Chief Kayani and the ISI: The United States will no longer submit to the arrangement whereby it handsomely compensates Pakistan's army and the ISI to fight terrorism, even while the ISI maintains active links to terrorist groups on U.S. government terrorist lists. The United States emphatically requests that Pakistan close down sanctuaries and training camps used by terrorists in Pakistan. The United States will implement diplomatic and other actions necessary if Pakistan refuses to address these concerns.

American interlocutors with Kayani should eschew tired formulations about Pakistan's selective cooperation on terrorism. They must insist on concrete results to meet core U.S. Afghan and counterterrorism goals. It will be necessary to apply President Reagan's "trust but verify" guideline, given Pakistan's poor record of matching words with deeds on the issues of Afghanistan and the terrorist groups that the ISI supports in Pakistan.

Condition U.S. assistance. This step is nine years and some $13 billion overdue. The 2009 Kerry-Lugar aid bill's certification language gives the administration an opening to work with Congress to apply actionable conditionality on military aid (but not economic aid) to Pakistan. U.S. support should serve shared interests. Further, the administration should closely examine each facet of American military and covert assistance to Pakistan to confirm that they are all serving and not countermanding U.S. policy goals and interests.

Place or threaten to place Pakistan on the U.S. list of state sponsors of terrorism. This would be a major step by the Obama administration and must be used judiciously. Threatening to place Pakistan on the list would underscore the seriousness of U.S. concerns, but might cause a crisis in ties with Islamabad. Pakistan's leadership may itself downgrade or even sever political and economic relations with the United States. The damage to Pakistan would go beyond termination of American economic and military aid. It would intensify its isolation in the region and globally. American allies would probably follow the U.S. lead and lower or end their aid to Pakistan, citing similar terrorist concerns.

As noted in Chapter 19, the United States activated a diplomatic process pointed toward Pakistan's designation as a terrorist state in early 1993 when U.S. Secretary of State James A. Baker III wrote to Prime Minister Nawaz Sharif to inform him that Pakistan was the subject of an "active continuing review" for inclusion on the list.[15] The Clinton administration withdrew the warning within six months of taking office. The George W. Bush administration did not revive it, nor has the Obama administration to date.

Voluminous information on the ISI's direct support for Afghan and Pakistani terrorist groups based in Pakistan would presumably qualify Pakistan for inclusion on the terrorism list. The United States waited until after 9/11 to place the ISI-connected Lashkar-i Taiba and Jaish-i Mohammad on the State Department's list of Foreign Terrorist Organizations (FTOs). Their continuing operational links to the ISI, an official arm of the Pakistani government, could legally justify identifying Pakistan as a state sponsor of terrorism. Astonishingly, the ISI-assisted Afghan Taliban and the Afghan Haqqani Network have not yet been named FTOs despite their numerous terrorist attacks on the Afghan state and coalition forces inside Afghanistan. They should be so designated. Taking this step would also project American frustration with Islamabad's duplicitous policies and serve as a warning that Pakistan itself may be next.

Pry Pakistan out of the Intra-Afghan peace dialogue. Pakistan, like the United States and other nations in the region, has a legitimate interest in seeing that the intra-Afghan peace dialogue does not damage its own interests. It can, like others, provide its views to Kabul, but it should not expect to decide which Afghans rule in Kabul, as it has been doing for the past thirty-one years.

American diplomats and military commanders should no longer make comments indicating that Pakistan has a legitimate role to play in the intra-Afghan peace dialogue. Each time Pakistan has inserted itself into the Afghan political process, it has been to subvert it. Any Afghan government seen as influenced by Pakistan, such as the Afghan Taliban, will be opposed by the majority of Afghans, including Pashtuns. The outcome would be another cycle of warfare and chaos inside Afghanistan that would eventually spill into Pakistan as well.

Support UN mediation of the Intra-Afghan dialogue. Giving the United Nations lead responsibility to assist in the intra-Afghan peace dialogue remains the only practical way to keep Afghanistan's competing neighbors from undermining the Afghan peace process. During the George H.W. Bush administration, the United States and the Soviet Union stepped back from Cold War regional conflicts to support UN mediation. UN special envoys, supported by the superpowers, succeeded in bringing peace to Cambodia, Namibia, Nicaragua, and Ethiopia. ISI machinations during the 1990s and up to 9/11 prevented UN success in Afghanistan. In today's circumstances, Pakistani President Asif Ali Zardari and General Kayani would probably agree to UN mediation on behalf of all outsiders, a position the United States should support. Whether or not the ISI again sabotages the UN special envoy's negotiations would be a good indicator of their willingness to match words with deeds.

Jointly address terrorism emanating from Pakistan. It is widely believed that U.S. government agencies ignored or did not follow up on a number of leads foreshadowing the 9/11 attack. When those leads were eventually investigated after 9/11, it was, of course, too late to avert the catastrophe. Today, terrorist activities and message traffic around the world are often traced back to terrorist bases in Pakistan. U.S. requests for ISI assistance usually occur after attacks or attempted attacks take place. The ISI generally deals with them on a case-by-case basis, not on a programmatic basis. There is therefore no effective U.S.-Pakistani mechanism to *prevent* future attacks. Terrorists receiving training in Pakistan can strike the United States and its friends and allies at any time. There is virtually no effective coordination mechanism for the Pakistani and U.S. governments to stop them. Clearly this is intolerable.

The United States and other countries that have been victims of terrorism emanating from Pakistan should request Islamabad to cooperate in creating a joint security entity to preempt terrorist attacks while they are still in the planning and preparatory stages on Pakistani soil. Pakistan would chair the new forum. The Pakistani Army and the ISI's positive response to this request, and its constructive follow-up, would be another sign of its intention to proactively cooperate with the international community to fight terrorism.

Maintain a bipartisan consensus on Pakistani policy. The Obama administration will need to work hard to gather and sustain a bipartisan consensus in Congress for its new Pakistani policy. The policy should not change from administration to administration or drift back to the catastrophic passivity of the 1990s.

By the closing months of 2011, before the 2012 American presidential and congressional election campaigns heat up, preparations for a graduated application of aid conditionality and counterterrorist measures could be in place and ready for implementation. Maintaining firm bipartisan unity behind the administration's policy through the 2012 and 2016 U.S. elections, regardless of which party wins at the polls, will be essential to its effectiveness and eventual success.

ॐ

By the end of 2011, American policymakers should have a good grasp of whether or not Pakistan seriously intends to switch to a constructive policy on Afghanistan and international terrorists based in Pakistan. If the trends are truly promising, the United States should respond positively to Pakistani requests on other issues. It is, however, likely that Pakistan's army will continue exercising its familiar, time-tested methods to stave off pressures to change direction. If Pakistan replays past arguments and makes only token gestures, the United States should begin implementing the bilateral measures outlined above and coordinate with its allies to take parallel actions.

Globally and regionally, Washington should also consult with friends and allies to formulate a carefully layered policy structure to contain the export of militant Islamism and terrorism from Pakistan into Afghanistan and other world areas. The first echelon would be Pakistan, which remains the epicenter of world terrorism. The second echelon would be countries in broader South and Central Asia and the Persian Gulf that suffer the most from Pakistan-based terrorism. The third echelon would be China, whose cooperation in a long-term policy to stabilize Afghanistan and persuade Pakistan to crack down on terrorism will be critical to success. The fourth echelon would be the United Nations and the broader international community. At the United Nations, the United States and its allies would begin laying the groundwork for UN Security Council resolutions, first to warn Pakistan, then to sanction it.

The United States should begin consultations with the Afghan government, Saudi Arabia, Russia, China, India, and the Central Asian Republics on a regional counterterrorism regime coordinating defensive collective security efforts to defend against Islamic terrorism from Pakistan. This would include a list of diplomatic and economic actions that the coalition could take directly or through the United Nations to motivate Pakistan to change its policy. Countries in the coalition with good ties to Tehran could enlist Iranian cooperation.

This tougher approach will be controversial in Washington. Previously expressed and plausible arguments will be marshaled against it. They will be the same rationales that have blocked effective counterterrorism steps by previous administrations and the current Obama administration. Opponents will cite fears that the results-based approach will intensify the already high levels of anti-Americanism in Pakistan or that nuclear-armed Pakistan could swing toward Iran, provide nuclear technology to nonnuclear states, perhaps fall apart, or experience a radical Islamic takeover. The argument will also be made that Pakistan's army is the only reliable barrier to Islamic extremism and that it prevents the leakage of nuclear weapons technology to terrorists.

The above concerns, of course, must be taken into account by Washington policymakers. However, they should no longer be allowed to block consideration of the bilateral and geostrategic policy options outlined above. The arguments in favor of introducing a tougher results-based approach line in America's Pakistan policy now demand attention. Whatever the risks of pressuring Pakistan to adjust course, they do not compare to the risks of exposing the American people and U.S. cities to more terrorist attacks launched from bases in Pakistan. Since the late 1940s, the United States had used strong measures to successfully deal with other nuclear-armed nations posing existential threats to its survival. The menace of Pakistan-based Islamic terrorists armed with weapons of mass destruction targeting American cities had reached a similar juncture at the end of the first decade of the twenty-first century. America does not have the luxury of permitting this growing threat to drift further into the second decade.

The consequences of escalating bilateral, regional, and global steps by the international community would be severe for Pakistan. Islamabad may not change its policy. It may appeal to China and other nations for support. Or, it may change its policy. If it does, the United States, the West, Saudi Arabia, and the international community generally should be prepared to offer it extensive economic, military, and counterterrorism assistance.

Whatever the degree of Pakistan's cooperation—or noncooperation— the United States and its allies should immediately begin laying the groundwork for an international conference to reestablish Afghanistan's buffer role in Central Asia. It would be scheduled for the middle of the decade, in 2014 or 2015. By that time, Afghanistan will have taken responsibility for its own security.

The conference organizers could study several historical models of buffer states between larger powers. Some of these are useful—if not fully comparable—precedents. The creation of the Belgian buffer at the 1815 Congress of Vienna ending the Napoleonic wars helped keep the peace in Europe for a century. In the mid-1950s, Cold War negotiators made Austria a buffer between East and West in Central Europe. And, of course, Afghanistan was a neutral buffer between Great Powers in Central Asia from 1881 to 1973.

An international conference sponsored by the United Nations, perhaps with the Organization of the Islamic Countries (OIC) as a cosponsor, could bring together all regional states as well as other countries with an interest in resolving the Afghan war. The final document signed by delegates and ratified by their governments would reestablish Afghanistan's buffer status at the heart of Eurasia. If Pakistan fully cooperates, the conference treaty, like previous international agreements establishing buffer states, would be a historic watershed, ending the wars of Afghanistan. For the first time since the 1917 Bolshevik Revolution, inner Eurasia would be opened up for north-south and east-west trade corridors connecting South Asia, the Persian Gulf, the Middle East, Russia, Central Asia, and China. Countries in Eurasia and beyond would benefit from the upsurge in commerce through Afghanistan. Pakistan, along with Afghanistan, would benefit the most.

A Long-Term Afghan Policy

Two points bear emphasizing. First, Afghanistan is very unpredictable. It is difficult for any foreigner to fathom the many thousands of moving parts always rotating inside its borders. The United States and its coalition partners must expect the unexpected—and be ready to adjust to it. The country could hold together and stabilize during the coming years—or it could fragment, spreading chaos and violence into adjoining countries. Second, no amount of American money and troops can defeat the ISI-stoked insurgency in Afghanistan. Pakistan cannot succeed in implanting an Afghan proxy regime in Kabul. But it has the manpower (population: 184 million) and resources to keep war-wracked, fragmented Afghanistan (population: 29–32 million) in a state of conflict for years to come. Under these conditions, no government in Kabul will be able to consolidate peace and reconstruct Afghanistan until Pakistan concludes that it is in its interest to end its proxy war and seek friendly relations with Afghanistan.

Below are the building blocks for a new long-term American policy toward Afghanistan that takes account of these two factors. In its Afghan policy, the United States should:

Conduct a balancing act. In December 2009, when President Obama announced that the United States would begin withdrawing its troops in Afghanistan in July 2011, many Afghans, Pakistanis, and others in the region interpreted it as a sign that America would effectively leave the region by the end of 2011. Subsequent assurances by the president, other senior U.S. officials, and NATO that the United States was not planning to abandon Afghanistan have somewhat moderated Afghan concerns. It is vital that the United States continue to demonstrate its resolve by maintaining economic, diplomatic, and political support. The new U.S.-Afghan strategic partnership agreement signed in 2011, and the opening of American consulates in Mazar, Herat, Jalalabad, and Kandahar, have projected American determination to assist Afghanistan after American and coalition troops leave by the middle of the decade.

It is equally vital, however, to de-Americanize the Afghan war across the board as rapidly as possible. Top U.S. policymakers in Washington should establish benchmarks for each U.S. government agency to carry out de-Americanization on an urgent basis, with U.S. government inspectors on the ground to examine agency operations and ensure that the policy is being executed. In the process of phasing out the ruinous circle of American preeminence and Afghan dependency, coalition members should not support individuals, but rather institutions, such as government ministries or community jirgas rooted in the local population. When individual Afghans request American and coalition support, the answer should be: "We will agree to anything you Afghans agree to."

The new U.S. approach must thus be a balancing act, one performed simultaneously and in a unified manner by all U.S. government agencies. Its dual thrust—America will still help and America is withdrawing—will satisfy the Afghan government's and Afghan population's desire for genuine Afghanization of the war *as well as* their hope that America will remain to assist Afghans to defend and reconstruct their country. Afghans will not see a contradiction between the coalition's gradual troop reduction and eventual withdrawal, on the one hand, and reassurances that the United States and its friends and allies will remain supportive in their country, on the other. In sum, the majority of Afghans want the heavy American presence to end. They also want the U.S. policy reset to support them in global and regional diplomacy, particularly regarding Pakistani interference, and they want the United

States to continue to provide economic and military aid and to continue training the ANSF.

Implement a conditions-based drawdown of the total American presence in Afghanistan. There are too many U.S. troops and civilians in Afghanistan. As part of its new Afghan policy, the United States should review the need for every U.S. military and civilian position in-country. Where justifications for positions are not convincing, or in cases where Afghans can perform the functions in question (even at lower standards), positions should be eliminated. The survey should establish specific deadlines for Afghans to take over responsibilities from foreign advisers. Ministries at the center and government offices at the provincial and district levels that perform well in executing their responsibilities should be recognized and appropriately rewarded.

Construction of permanent and expensive facilities for U.S. military and intelligence organizations in Afghanistan must be terminated. The Afghan and U.S. governments should begin negotiations on mutually acceptable arrangements for U.S. counterterrorism operations with Afghan counterparts. The United States must *not* request permanent military bases in Afghanistan. This idea is untenable, destabilizing, and conflicts with broader U.S. interests in Eurasia. The Afghan government and people would oppose permanent U.S. bases. Just as important, China, Russia, Iran, and Pakistan would be hostile to permanent American bases so close to their borders.

The U.S.-led coalition must begin, as scheduled, to withdraw combat units (not only cooks, barbers, and PowerPoint specialists) in July 2011. The size and tempo of the three-year reduction process should be linked to the number of Afghans trained and deployed and, as possible, front-loaded with combat forces. Noncombat Afghan engineering, logistics, communications, transportation, and intelligence units have been deemphasized in the buildup of the ANSF combat arms. They will be critical to ensuring ANSF success after the transfer of combat responsibility is completed. U.S. and coalition specialists in these categories should remain in-country, partnered with Afghan units, to support ANSF and American combat forces while the latter depart Afghanistan.

Continue the drone strikes against al-Qaeda and other terrorist training bases on the lawless Frontier. These bases are training terrorists to attack the United

States and other countries. The drone operations have been highly effective in degrading al-Qaeda's leadership and that of its allies and their capabilities to hit the United States and its friends and allies. They should continue. Steps must be taken to negate or minimize civilian casualties.

Enable Afghan governing institutions to do their jobs. The United States should immediately begin reducing the American civilian presence in Afghanistan, including both U.S. government and contractor personnel. The phasing down of huge U.S. and other Western contracting organizations will usefully release thousands of young Afghans with management and technical skill into the private sector and the Afghan government.

The U.S.-led coalition should shift (not increase) funding previously earmarked for U.S. government civilian officials and contractors to the training of Afghan bureaucrats, paralleling the massive training effort under way in the military sector. There should be more targeted investment in the development of Afghan specialists in administrative, budgeting, oversight, human resources, and other areas key to attacking corruption and bad governance at the center and in the provinces. For the first time, the coalition and the United Nations must give Afghan line ministries equal input in the hiring of foreign experts, mentors, and trainers assigned to their ministries. The Provincial Reconstruction Teams (PRTs) in the provinces should follow mutually agreed upon, coalition-Afghan, time-bound plans to transfer their bases and responsibilities to Afghan provincial and district governing units, and fall back to advisory and monitoring roles.

Issue no blank checks. Helping Afghans to rebuild their civilian and military institutions is an important step toward encouraging stability in Afghanistan and the region. But this does not entail writing blank checks. U.S. assistance should be strictly conditioned on honest and effective government and military performance. Pervasive government corruption is a leading cause of the Taliban's advance. International donors should form a united front in conditioning their assistance on the creation of well-trained anticorruption units staffed by Afghan certifying officers and auditors occupying offices in every Afghan government ministry receiving assistance. The Afghan auditors would need to make their agencies' books available to inspection by internationally certified auditors or forfeit foreign assistance for their ministry. The rate at which President Obama's pledge in the May 2010 U.S.-Afghan joint statement to transfer funds directly to the Afghan government should be linked to these anticorruption steps, including in the Finance Ministry and the Central Bank.

Leave the Afghan political cauldron and stay out. Foreigners do not fare well in the Afghan political cauldron. Out of ignorance or through manipulation by Afghans, they usually end up favoring Afghan individuals or factions over their competitors. The CIA promotion of Gulbuddin Hekmatyar's fortunes after the Soviet withdrawal badly damaged U.S. interests. So did the funding of rapacious warlords after 9/11 by both the CIA and the U.S. military. American policymakers should know by now that foreign cash outlays to Afghans cannot buy their loyalty, induce them to support the government, or unify the country.

Stop choosing Afghan leaders. This practice was rampant during the Bush administration, boosting the image of Afghanistan as, once again, a foreign-occupied country. The outside pressures to hire and fire senior Afghan officials diminished after the feud President Karzai conducted with Washington during President Obama's first fifteen months in office. Now, as the U.S.-led coalition reduces its presence in Afghanistan, its diplomats and generals should privately convey their opinions on personnel matters to the Afghan leadership, President Karzai and his successors, then honor their legitimate authority to make the final decision.

It will also, however, be necessary and appropriate to condition aid on the appointments the Afghan leadership makes. It is common knowledge that too many of those President Karzai has appointed are outrageously corrupt. The coalition, the United Nations, and important donors should collectively insist that no resources will be provided to government institutions or offices led by officials known to be corrupt or involved in the drug trade.

Leave the Taliban negotiations to the Afghan government's political leadership. American diplomats, generals, and CIA officers must let the top Afghan leadership conduct the Afghan peace dialogue with the Taliban. Karzai is a moderate-nationalist Afghan who will not give Afghanistan away to the Taliban. A native Kandahari, he is more familiar with the Taliban leaders and their network than any westerner could possibly be. In November 2010, NATO's transportation of a Pakistani shopkeeper in Quetta posing as Akhtar Mohammad Mansoor, Mullah Omar's deputy, to Kabul and into the presidential palace was an embarrassing mistake. It did not produce any lasting problems in the reconciliation process, but another misadventure of this kind could. In the intra-Afghan dialogue, Afghan sovereignty needs to be rigorously respected by the U.S.-led coalition. No member of the coalition should attempt to negotiate either directly or indirectly with the Taliban.

Control disruptive stovepipe competition. The much-publicized exposure of intra-agency feuding surrounding General Stanley A. McChrystal's resignation in June 2010 forced President Obama to insist on unity of purpose within his Afghan team. But the pattern of multiple U.S. Afghan strategies operating at cross-purposes remains a major problem. In the absence of a comprehensive long-term policy architecture integrating interagency efforts, stovepipe competition will continue to frustrate progress inside Afghanistan.

The interagency battles over Afghan turf are symptoms of a larger government-wide dilemma impeding U.S. foreign policy successes. Policy coordination and creation of a unified chain of command from the White House down through the bureaucracy to the field begins with the president. Effective policy planning and coherent interagency implementation are simply not possible if mini–power centers continue to go their own way in Washington. While the president should of course encourage in-house debate, he must be relentless in practicing what he has preached in demanding a united, disciplined execution of settled policy.

⚘

By learning from the past wars of Afghanistan, the Obama administration still has a chance to shape a conclusion to the current one that serves the interests of the United States and its friends, uplifts the people of war-torn Afghanistan, removes Afghanistan as an arena of competition among outside powers, and taps the vast economic potential of middle Eurasia.

The policy proposals suggested in this chapter, if tenaciously implemented by successive administrations during this decade, could turn around the deteriorating trends in Afghanistan and Pakistan. As mentioned earlier, this way ahead cannot guarantee success. But it complies with Afghan history and the cultural setting of Afghanistan's tribal society. To ignore those fundamental realities guarantees failure.

President Obama's Afghanization drive is the right direction for U.S. policy. But if three embedded barriers to peace are not addressed, the wars of Afghanistan will continue. First, it is in U.S. interests, and that of its friends and allies, not to fall victim to the seductive lure of again abandoning Afghanistan to terrorism-soaked anarchy. Second, Pakistan's army continues unabated to have a free hand to pump thousands of insurgents across the border from protected sanctuaries inside Pakistan. And third, chronically divided moderate Afghan ethnic and tribal groups are yet to unite behind a popularly supported leadership committed to reform and good governance.

The international community must encourage and assist Islamabad to dismantle the terrorist sanctuaries inside Pakistan threatening the region and many countries around the world, Muslim and non-Muslim, including Pakistan itself. Moreover, they could play a spoiler role in undermining the hopeful but volatile democratic awakening under way in the Arab world. Constituencies in Pakistan upholding the Muslim Brotherhood and al-Qaeda dogmas, such as the two politico-religious parties, elements in the Pakistani officer corps, and the ISI, may ally with Middle East extremists in pushing the revolutionary wave in a radical Islamist direction.

The hour is late, but the path advised in this chapter—a fundamental change in Pakistan's policy; genuine Afghan custody of the war; and diplomatic regional and global reinforcement—could salvage some long-term success in Afghanistan.

The recommended conceptual umbrella of shifting the lead from America to the host country also applies to other countries where messianic terrorists have struck ideological and operational roots—most notably in Pakistan, Yemen, and the Horn of Africa. The multidecade struggle against the scourge of radical Islamist terrorism will, most of all, be a battle for Muslim minds. The outcome will be decided by many millions of Muslims in their own countries guided by their own history, culture, and aspirations. And how things turn out in Afghanistan will have a major influence on this moderate-extremist competition under way in other parts of the Muslim world.

America and the West should render support to the majority moderates in this struggle, but it is—in the end—a struggle that only they can win.

ACKNOWLEDGMENTS

It took eight years to research, organize, and then write this book. After signing the contract with my publisher, PublicAffairs, in 2008, my wife Kim and I devoted full time to the manuscript. *The Wars of Afghanistan*, however, would never have moved from concept to reality without numerous people who helped and advised me. Words cannot properly acknowledge the invaluable assistance and inspiration they provided. But I shall try.

First and foremost, I would like to pay tribute to Lindsay Jones, my editor at PublicAffairs. In life everyone gets lucky now and then. I got incredibly lucky when Lindsay decided to accept my book project. Thereafter, her commitment to the book was unrelenting. During the ensuing three years, she spent much more time on my book than it deserved, teaching me about maintaining the narrative flow, battling redundancy, and not introducing events until they fit into the timeline. In 2010 she shifted gears to editing, and thankfully it was heavy editing because she possesses brilliant writing skills. She substantially upgraded the manuscript. In addition, Lindsay patiently supported me when I missed all my deadlines, agreed to my request to add the last two chapters, worked with the designer to produce a beautiful cover for the book, and helped me select the final photographs and maps.

Twice during my Foreign Service career I had the privilege of serving under Ambassador Winston Lord. I witnessed firsthand his great integrity, accomplished diplomatic skills, wisdom, steadiness under pressure, and dedication to the national interest. In the early formative stage of the manuscript, I sent him the first chapter and asked for his comments. He must have seen some merit in the book. Thereafter, his contribution was priceless and beyond compare. He devoted countless hours to editing every chapter and rendering invaluable advice. He questioned my concepts, threw out wounded prose, and suggested organizational changes. He was my harshest critic but always urged me on during moments of despair and mental dead ends. He played a crucial role in the development of this book. I cannot thank him enough.

I am deeply indebted to Peter Osnos, PublicAffairs founder and editor-at-large, and Susan Weinberg, PublicAffairs publisher. They and their publishing house, a branch of Perseus Books Group, are a beacon of light for first-time authors seeking a publisher for their nonfiction efforts. Peter and Susan's commitment never flagged. They patiently bore with me as the book slowly evolved and encouraged me with their dedication and enthusiasm. I would also like to thank PublicAffairs's managing editor Melissa Raymond for her assistance in the closing stage of the book, and senior publicist Emily Lavelle for her sagacious advice and unwavering support.

I am grateful to the Perseus Books Group's Kay Mariea, who supervised the final assembly of the book, for her wise counsel, experience, and guidance. My profound appreciation goes out to copyeditor Kathy Streckfus, who significantly improved the quality of the manuscript and made many helpful suggestions for changes that I embraced; to fact checker Nicholas Jahr whose discerning eye ferreted out an embarrassing number of errors; to the designer Timm Bryson, whose splendid artwork graces the book; and to the superb proofreaders Lisa Zales and Meredith Smith. Cartographer Larry Bowring of Bowring Cartographic did a fabulous job in preparing the maps for the book. Photo researcher Melissa Totten of M + Co tenaciously tracked down key photographs important to its story line.

I am also grateful to three outstanding editors at Perseus and PublicAffairs whose professionalism, hard work, encouragement, and advice brought to fruition the paperback edition of *The Wars of Afghanistan*: Michelle Welsh-Horst, Jeff Williams, and Maria Goldverg.

Several institutions were decisive in facilitating the research and writing of *The Wars of Afghanistan*. In this regard, I wish to single out the Potomac Foundation in Vienna, Virginia, for its financial support. I extend my thanks to the Potomac Foundation's president, Dr. Daniel McDonald, and Brenda Hunter, his executive assistant, for their friendship and perseverance.

Numerous staff members of research institutions in the United States gave me a warm welcome and generously offered their time and attention to assist me, despite their busy schedules. In Washington DC, I found the Woodrow Wilson Center's Cold War International History Project a national treasure of original documents from the archives of the communist parties, spy agencies, and the defense and foreign ministries of the Soviet Union and Soviet allies dating from the Cold War era. Its voluminous collection of translated, declassified documents available online support scholars in America and around the world. In Washington, I also benefited from the National Security Archives at George Washington University, especially the trove of primary source documents gathered by the great Russian soldier-scholar, Major General Alexander Antonovich Lyakovsky, a Soviet veteran of the Soviet-Afghan War.

The professional staffs of other research institutions around the country were equally helpful in assisting me in my research and answering my questions. In this connection, I wish to thank the University of Nebraska's unique Center of Afghanistan Studies and the Arthur Paul Afghanistan Collection of books and media reports on Afghanistan; the Hoover Institution at Stanford University; the Naval Post-Graduate School in Monterey, California; the President George H.W. Bush presidential library at College Station, Texas; and not least, the Dolley Madison branch of the Fairfax County, Virginia, Public Library system. I also want to express my appreciation to the following scholars for their research assistance: Svetlana Savranskaya, Jeremy Tigan, Dr. Jeffrey Becker, Katherine A. Spillenkothen, and Haroun Mir. Charles Daris and Mark Ramee, two State Department Freedom of Information Act (FOIA) officers were especially helpful in advising me on the clearance process required of retired ambassadors at the State Department, the CIA, and the National Security Council.

It took a village of family and friends to write a large and challenging book like *The Wars of Afghanistan*. Some devoted time to reading and advising on a chapter or more. Others provided important information and encouragement. John "Jay" Taylor, political counselor at the American embassy in Beijing in the early 1980s, renowned author and friend, read several chapters and offered extremely helpful suggestions that were incorporated in the manuscript. Steve Coll, author, scholar, journalist, and President of the New America Foundation, gave me wise advice on structuring and writing the book. In his off-hours, Daniel Teet of the University of Nebraska at Omaha assisted me in the earliest period of research and writing.

I also thank Leila Poullada for lending me many books, documents, and family letters focusing on Afghanistan in the 1960s and 1970s; Philip Poullada for his meticulous research and advice; and Daoud Mir for his very helpful written and oral accounts of his years with Afghan Commander Ahmed Shah Masood, his diplomatic assignments on behalf of Masood, his translation of important documents, and his photos that appear in this book. My old and dear friend Ambassador Ziauddin Mojadedi's sagacious counsel and his encyclopedic knowledge of Afghanistan's tribal society and the Taliban period were of inestimable value in writing the book. Afghan Media Resource Director Haji Daoud provided key photographs and interviews about the Soviet invasion and occupation of Afghanistan. Khushal Arsala, Abdul Haq's nephew, gave me his valuable insights into Afghan tribal dynamics and politics; and retired Afghan diplomat Omar Malikyar.

My thanks go out to Lawrence and Audrey Sheppard of Lewisporte, Newfoundland, Canada, the Canadian Red Cross, and the numerous citizens of Lewisporte and adjoining towns, who took in hundreds of mostly American passengers when their aircraft were diverted to Gander Airport on 9/11. The Sheppards and local Canadian communities opened their schools and churches to house and fed us until we were allowed to continue our trip home. In my case it was the Lewisporte Academy to shower, the Salvation Army church to sleep, and the Sheppards' warm hospitality to feel at home.

Many other friends also contributed to the development of this book:

Thomas Eighmy, a retired USAID foreign service officer and the world's leading specialist on Afghanistan's demography; Hal Lucius, my high school world history teacher in Blue Ash, Ohio, also a retired Foreign Service officer, and his wife, Mary; longtime friends Qayum and Patricia Karzai, with whom my wife and I spent many hours discussing Afghanistan and world affairs; Ed Burgess, my Peace Corps roommate in Pokhara, Nepal; Ambassadors Harry Barnes, Michael Malinowski, David Dunford, and Kent Weidemann; and Leon J. Weil and his wife, Mabel; the Rev. Mark Lowell Sargent, Diocese of London; Dr. Max Gross; and author journalist Roy Gutman. Also retired foreign service officers James Hall and his wife Huong, Jon Gibney, Bruce Flatin; Afghan Ambassadors Masood Khalili and Wali Masood; well-known Afghan journalist Es Haq; the highly respected scholar and author, Dr. Rizwan Hussain; journalist John Needham; Michael and Brian Epley; my former colleague at the American embassy in Yerevan, Haik Gugarats; Asian scholar Mike Keefe; Dr. Derek Hodgson, former Dean of Faculty at the University of Nebraska at Omaha; Said Issaq Said; Yvette Mimieux; young scholar Nicholas Getka; and Annette Woodward.

Family members shared my moments of exhilaration and despair over the past eight years as I wrote the manuscript. I mostly have my wife, Kim, to thank for getting me to the end. She prodded me forward during difficult times and worked side by side with me to roll out the chapters. She regularly reminded me that I must not hold back from writing what I personally witnessed, interpreted, and believed to be the truth, notwithstanding that others might see things differently from their point of view. The reader and those out there in the universe of ideas will have the final say. Kim's American Field Service's parents, Cliff and Claire Craft of Ashland, Oregon, helped us at the very beginning of our undertaking; my parents-in-law urged me to finish the manuscript first before visiting them; and our two daughters and sons-in-law stole time from their families and careers to help out. They, our five grandchildren, my sister, and Kim's brothers and their families were most forbearing in accepting our long absence. My cousin called me the lost cousin. During visits to our home, our three-year-old granddaughter would silently slip into my study periodically to ask gently, "Grandpa, what chapter are you on?" Now, I can tell her the book is done, thanks to her and everyone else who helped along the way.

APPENDICES

APPENDIX I   CENTRAL ASIAN MIGRATIONS AND INVASIONS OF AFGHANISTAN, 330 B.C.–A.D. 1380

Who	Began Date of Conquest	Origins and Ethnicity	Destinations
Alexander The Great	4th century B.C.	Macedonia, Greek	Persia, Afghanistan, Central Asia, India
Parthians	2nd century B.C.	Central Asia, Persian	Afghanistan, Persia
Sakas	1st century B.C.	Central Asia, Persian	Afghanistan, India
Kushans	1st century	Central Asia, Persian	Afghanistan
White Huns (Hephthalites)	5th century	Takla Mekan, Xinjiang (China), Possibly Caucasion-Turkish	Afghanistan, India
Turks	7th century	Central Asia, Turkish	Afghanistan, Persia, Anatolia
Mongols	13th century	Mongolia, Mongol	China, through Central Asia, Afghanistan, and the Middle East to Eastern Europe
Tamerlane	15th century	Central Asia, Turkic/Mongolian	Afghanistan, India, Persia, Caucasus

APPENDIX II   DURRANI AND GHILZAI TRIBAL NETWORKS

Durrani Tribal Networks
descended from
Qais,
through Sharkbun (Qais's son)

ZIRAK
POPALZAI   BARAKZAI
(the royal tribes)
ALOKAZAI   ACHAKZAI

NURZAI

PANJPAI
ALIZAI

ISHAKZAI

Ghilzai Tribal Networks
descended from
Qais,
through Matto (Qais's granddaughter),
through Ghulzoe (Matto's oldest son)

HOTAK   TOKHI   AHMADZAI

TARAKI   SULEIMAN KHEL   KHAROTI

720

APPENDIX III   THE DURRANI ROYAL DYNASTY

Popalzai Saddozai clan	Barakzai Mohammadzai Clan
Ahmad Shah Durrani (1747–1772)	
Timur Shah (1772–1793)	
Zaman Shah (1793–1800)	
Shah Mahmud (1800–1803)	
Shah Shuja (1803–1809)	
Shah Mahmud (1809–1818)	
	Dost Mohammad Khan (1819–1838)
Shah Shuja (1839–1842)	*First Anglo-Afghan War (1838–1842) British Exile Barakzai Dost Mohammad to India, Install Popalzai Shah Shuja*
	Dost Mohammad Returns (1842–1863)
	Sher Ali (1863–1868; 1869–1879)
	Second Anglo-Afghan War (1878–1880)
	Abdur Rahman Khan (1880–1901)
	Habibullah (1901–1919)
	Amanullah (1919–1929)
	Nadir Shah (1929–1933)
	Zahir Shah (1933–1973)
	Mohammad Daoud (1973–1978)*

* Mohammad Daoud overthrew his cousin, Zahir Shah, abolished the monarchy, and declared himself President of Afghanistan.

Below is a timeline summarizing the internecine clashes between the Khalq (Peoples) and Parcham (Flag) wings of the Afghan communist party during the thirteen-year Afghan communist era. Violent rivalries also played out within each of the Khalq and Parcham factions.

PHASE I: KHALQIS PERSECUTE PARCHAMIS, JULY 1978–MARCH 1979

Nur Mohammad Taraki, Khalqi faction leader, PDPA general secretary, president, and prime minister:

- Sends Babrak Karmal, Parcham faction leader, deputy PDPA chief, and deputy prime minister, abroad as ambassador to Prague, Czechoslovakia, in July 1978, essentially exiling him.
- In August, accuses the Parchamis of coup-plotting against him.
- In November, dismisses all remaining Parcham leaders still occupying important cabinet, military, and party positions.
- During the fall months of 1978, with his PDPA deputy, Khalqi Hafizullah Amin, arrests, imprisons, tortures, and executes hundreds of members of the Parcham faction. Two former Parcham ministers in Taraki's cabinet are tortured and sentenced to death.

PHASE II: KHALQIS AGAINST KHALQIS, MARCH 1979–SEPTEMBER 1979

Taraki's Khalqi deputy, Amin, forces Taraki into a figurehead role after gaining control of the levers of power. He replaces Taraki as prime minister, assumes the defense minister portfolio, and appoints relatives and loyalists to key military positions.

PHASE III: AMIN OVERTHROWS TARAKI AND ASSUMES CONTROL, SEPTEMBER 1979–DECEMBER 27, 1979

Amin captures and murders Taraki in September. He then:

- Assumes Taraki's posts of PDPA general secretary and president.
- Purges remaining members of Taraki's Khalq faction in the Afghan military and civil bureaucracies.

Phase III ends with the Soviet invasion and KGB murder of Amin on December 28, 1979.

continues on page 722

PHASE IV: PARCHAMI BABRAK KARMAL, INSTALLED BY THE SOVIET ARMY, RULES, LATE DECEMBER 1979–1986

Karmal annihilates remnants of Amin's Khalq faction in 1980, but contends with unrelenting opposition from Khalqis and dissident Parchamis.

PHASE V: SOVIETS REPLACE KARMAL* WITH ANOTHER PARCHAMI, SECRET POLICE CHIEF AND KGB PROTÉGÉ MOHAMMAD NAJIB, MAY 4, 1986

In March 1990, Khalqi Defense Minister Shahnawaz Tanai stages an unsuccessful coup against Najib. Tanai flees to Pakistan and joins Gulbuddin Hekmatyar and the ISI.

The bloody Afghan communist era closes when Najib's Parchami military commanders and his foreign minister betray him and defect to the Mujahidin in April 1992. He escapes to the UN compound in Kabul but is tortured and killed by the Taliban in September 1996.

---

* Among the four top leaders of the Afghan communist era, Babrak Karmal was the only one to escape a violent death. He died of liver cancer in a Moscow hospital on December 1, 1996.

	Kabul Regime	Opposition	Disengaged
Phase I **1992**			
	Mojaddedi Rabbani Masood Dostum Mazari* Karzai	Hekmatyar	Abdul Haq Khalis
Phase II **1993–1996**			
	Rabbani Masood Sayyaf Karzai	Mojaddedi Hekmatyar Dostum Mazari Taliban (after 1994)	Abdul Haq Khalis
Phase III **1996–9/11/2001**			
	Taliban/al-Qaeda Khalis	Rabbani Sayyaf Masood Karzai Dostum Khalili (Shia Leader) Abdul Haq	Hekmatyar

---

* Abdul Ali Mazari headed the pro-Iranian, Shia Hezb-i-Wahdat. Replaced by Khalili after the Taliban killed Mazari in 1995.

APPENDIX VI   PAKISTANI PARAMILITARY RELIGIOUS MILITIAS

Hezb ul-Mujahidin
Affiliated with Jamaat-i Islami (JI). Close to ISI.

Harakat ul-Ansar, a.k.a. Harakat ul-Mujahidin (1997)
Lashkar-i Taiba (2001)
Jaish-i Mohammad (2001)
Affiliated with Jamiat-i Ulema-i Islam (JUI) and Jamiat splinters. Close to ISI.

Note: Dates denote when the Pakistani paramilitary religious groups were placed on the U.S. State Department's list of Foreign Terrorist Organizations (FTOs).

Sipah-i Sahaba (anti-Shia)
Lashkar-i Jhangvi (2003) (anti-Shia)
Sipah-i Mohammad (defense of Shia)
Pakistani paramilitary sectarian armed groups not affiliated with JI and JUI.

NOTES

1 — PADSHAHGARDI

1. The Hindu Kush extends from central and eastern Afghanistan into north-western Pakistan. About 1,000 miles long and 200 miles wide, its watershed drains into the Amu Darya on Afghanistan's northern and eastern borders and into the Helmand and Kabul river basins to the west and south. *Kush* means "killing" in Persian. The name Hindu Kush, "Killer of Hindus," appears to derive from the first millennium A.D., when Hindu slaves from the Indian plains often perished while being transported by their Central Asian conquerors through the passes of the region.

2. There has never been a credible census of the Afghan population, only estimates taken from samples. The United Nations placed the Pashtun percentage of the population at under 50 percent when it organized the 2002 and 2004 loya jirgas held in Kabul.

3. David Pryce-Jones, *The Closed Circle: An Interpretation of the Arabs* (Chicago: Ivan R. Dee, 2002), 22.

4. This statement is generally attributed to the Confederate general Nathan Bedford Forrest.

5. In 1992, Afghanistan's neighbors were Pakistan, Iran, China, and the former Central Asian Republics of the Soviet Union, Turkmenistan, Uzbekistan, and Tajikistan.

6. Sandy Gall, "An Interview with Commander Ahmed Shah Masud, Former Minister of Defence, at His Base in Jebal Seraj, North of Kabul, on June 28, 1993," *Asian Affairs* 25, no. 2 (1994), 141.

7. Phillip Corwin, *Doomed in Afghanistan: A UN Officer's Memoir of the Fall of Kabul and Najibullah's Failed Escape, 1992* (New Brunswick, NJ: Rutgers University Press, 2003), 77.

8. The account of Najib's failed attempt to depart Afghanistan and his retreat to Sevan's UN headquarters in Kabul draws on my June 20, 1997, and November

21, 2010, interviews with Benon Sevan; Corwin, *Doomed in Afghanistan*, 85–105; and U.S. State Department and UN reports at the time.

9. London 17650, "Afghan Policy—US Strategy," September 29, 1991, telegram transmitted to Washington from London, secret, declassified and released in part, B1, 1.4(D), October 26, 2004; Islamabad 18863, "Afghanistan: Trends for 1992," December 16, 1991, transmitted to Washington, secret, declassified March 23, 2000.

10. Ibid.; Benon Sevan, interviews with author, June 20, 1997, and November 21, 2010; Andrew Gilmore, e-mail exchanges with author.

11. Nabi Misdaq, *Afghanistan, Political Frailty and External Interference* (New York: Routledge, 2006), 323.

12. Ibid.; Corwin, *Doomed in Afghanistan*, 91–92.

13. Gilmore, e-mail exchanges with author.

14. Ibid.

15. Ibid.; Corwin, *Doomed in Afghanistan*, 103.

16. Corwin, *Doomed in Afghanistan*, 102; FBIS-NES-92-075, April 17, 1992. (FBIS stands for the U.S. Foreign Broadcast Information Service.)

17. The Hazaras are concentrated in the central Afghan mountain highland, the Hazarajat.

18. Abdul Haq, letter to author, January 14, 1993.

19. President Reagan's eloquent commitment to Haq was recorded in a video broadcast by the BBC. See *Afghan Warrior: The Life and Death of Abdul Haq*, Torch Productions, London, directed by Malcolm Brinkworth, 2003.

20. President Bush's wish to get out of Afghanistan was passed orally down the foreign policy bureaucratic ladder. There was no doubt that it was authoritative. I received the instruction from several sources, including from a high-ranking official in Secretary of State James A. Baker III's Policy Planning Office. The decision to disseminate the instruction orally within the department appeared to be based on a concern that conservatives in Congress or the media could charge that the administration was about to abandon Afghanistan. The source of the Bush quote is the former CIA station chief in Islamabad, Milt Bearden, who was present when President Bush made this comment at a White House briefing. Bearden recounted the conversation at a June 14, 2004, Brookings Institute seminar on Afghanistan, in which I participated.

21. Like many Afghans, Najib's bodyguard went by only one name.

22. Alex Thier, interview with author, July 7, 2003, McLean, Virginia.

23. Ibid.

24. Boutros Boutros-Ghali, *Unvanquished: A U.S.-U.N. Saga* (New York: Random House, 1999), 301.

25. The description of Najib's final hours is based on information provided by Ahmed Zia, Masood's brother; Hashim Paktianai, Najib's cousin; and a former

member of President Karzai's Afghan government in a position to know who wishes to remain anonymous.

26. The Afghan source knew Hashim Paktianai. They met often in Peshawar. The source does not want his name revealed. After Najib's execution, Paktianai led a tribal delegation from Najib's Ahmadzai Pashtun village in Paktiya to retrieve his body and bury it in the family cemetery in Paktiya Province. In 1997, four days before he was to join his family in Sweden, where he had been granted political asylum, Paktianai was shot and killed by a gunman on a Peshawar street.

27. This account is based on the author's interviews with knowledgeable Afghan sources who do not want their names cited.

28. Ahmed Zia, interview with author, January 13, 2004, McLean, Virginia. The accounts of ISI involvement were confirmed by another Afghan source who is in a position to know but wishes to remain anonymous.

29. "Rice Says U.S. Should Not Have Abandoned Afghanistan," Radio Free Europe, Radio Liberty, March 17, 2005, www.rferl.org/content/article/1058020 .html; U.S. Congress, House Armed Services Committee, Defense Secretary Gates' testimony, December 11, 2007; Thomas E. Ricks, "Gates Warns Against Leaving Iraq in Chaos," *Washington Post*, November 29, 2006.

2—SHATTER ZONE

1. Plutarch, "Crassus," translated by John Dryden, Greece Http Ltd., www.greek-texts.com/library/Plutarch/Crassus/415.html, 13–14.

2. Olaf Caroe, *The Pathans: 550 B.C.–A.D. 195* (Karachi: Oxford University Press, 1975), 71–73.

3. The term "Hellenistic" denotes Greek culture as it existed in the area from the eastern Mediterranean to the Pamir Mountains, which straddle today's Sino-Afghan border. The Hellenistic era lasted roughly from Alexander the Great's conquest of Afghanistan in 330–323 B.C. to Emperor Augustus's defeat of Cleopatra and Anthony in 31 B.C., twenty-two years after Carrhae.

4. Louis Dupree, *Afghanistan* (Princeton, NJ: Princeton University Press, 1980), 288–295.

5. Ibid., 282.

6. *Takla Mekan*, a barren wasteland in far western China's Xinjiang Province, may have been a hospitable living environment before warfare and desertification forced the population to move on.

7. Dupree, *Afghanistan*, 199.

8. The Kushan kings promoted Gandhara Buddhist art, an eclectic mixture of Buddhist, Greek, and Hindu art themes. They simultaneously carried three titles reflecting their religious tolerance: the Sanskrit *rajatiraja* (king of kings), the Greek *basileus* (king), and *kaisara*, from the Latin "caesar."

9. Procopius, translated by H. B. Dewing, Internet Archive, www.archive.org/ stream/procopiuswithengo1procuoft/procopiuswithengo1procuoft_djvu.txt. See also Arnold Fletcher, *Afghanistan: Highway of Conquest* (Ithaca, NY: Cornell University Press, 1965), 33.

10. Because the White Huns were not related to the Black Huns, most historians, including ancient Greek and Roman writers, have referred to them as the Hephthaliti or Ephthalites.

11. The title *khan* gradually morphed into a surname adopted by the khans' descendants, whatever their walk of life, in Pakistan and India as well as Afghanistan. In recent decades, khans have been presidents of Afghanistan and Pakistan and members of the Indian Parliament. One may also find khans as household servants or taxicab drivers in Kabul, Peshawar, Delhi, and Washington.

12. Caroe, *The Pathans*, 86–87, 90.

13. Arab raiders did advance into Afghanistan as far as Kabul but did not remain as occupiers.

14. It took a week for the Mongols to execute all of the population and livestock in Balkh. The economic and cultural center of Central Eurasia for over a millennium, Balkh was not re-inhabited after the Mongol invasions. It remains in ruins today.

15. Vartan Grigorian, *The Emergence of Modern Afghanistan: Politics of Reform and Modernization, 1880–1946* (Palo Alto, CA: Stanford University Press, 1969), 18; Martin Ewans, *Afghanistan: A Short History of Its People and Politics* (New York: HarperCollins, 2002), 17.

16. Tamerlane's name broken down into English is "Timur the Lame." The Central Asian conqueror, based in Samarkand, went on to sack Delhi and leave a trail of destruction through Persia and the Middle East and into the Caucasus. Uzbek president Islam Karimov has elevated Tamerlane into an Uzbek national hero, placing a large statue of him on a horse in the middle of Tashkent.

17. G. Whitney Azoy, *Buzkashi: Game and Power in Afghanistan* (Philadelphia: University of Pennsylvania Press, 1982), 23–24; Grigorian, *Emergence of Modern Afghanistan*, 12.

18. Ali Banuazizi and Myron Weiner, *The State, Religion, and Ethnic Politics: Afghanistan, Iran, and Pakistan*, Contemporary Issues in the Middle East (Syracuse, NY: Syracuse University Press, 1988), 26.

19. *Durr* means "pearl" in Pashto. The Abdali later adopted the name Durrani.

20. When the Koh-i-Noor was found in southern India's Golconda mineral mines, it was said to weigh 293 carats. The huge diamond was later cut back to 190.3 metric carats. Its nearest competitors have been the Orlov diamond, now in the Kremlin, which weighs 189.62 metric carats, and the Darya-i-Noor (Ocean of Light) diamond at 186 metric carats, part of the Iranian Crown Jewels. The Koh-i-Noor is a white, more spherical diamond than the bluish-green Orlov or the flat, rose-tinted Darya-i-Noor.

21. The Peacock Throne was constructed for Mughal emperor Shah Jehan, who also built the Taj Mahal. The throne is made of solid gold and adorned by two carved peacocks loaded down with diamonds, rubies, sapphires, and emeralds.

22. Bamber Gascoigne, *The Great Moghuls: India's Most Flamboyant Rulers* (New Delhi: B. I. Publications, 1971), 245.

23. John C. Griffiths, *Afghanistan: Key to a Continent* (Boulder: Westview Press, 1981), 24.

24. Grigorian, *Emergence of Modern Afghanistan*, 46.

25. Dupree, *Afghanistan*, 333.

26. Asta Olesen, *Islam and Politics in Afghanistan*, Nordic Institute of Asian Studies, no. 67 (Wiltshire, UK: Antony Rowe, 1995), 32.

27. Once they were together, Zaman informed Shuja that the Koh-i-Noor was one of the few items he had taken from the palace during his aborted flight from Kabul to Peshawar. Betrayed and incarcerated in the Ghilzai tribal chief's fort, he had sequestered the Koh-i-Noor in the cracks of a stone wall. Shuja and an armed escort retrieved the gem and executed the Ghilzai tribal leader. Back in the Punjab, however, he was compelled to accept the hospitality of the Sikh king, Ranjit Singh. According to the Sikh chronicles, Shuja voluntarily gave the Koh-i-Noor to Ranjit Singh. The Afghans, however, insist that the Sikh king forced Shuja to surrender it. Whatever the case, the British later removed the diamond from the Sikh kingdom's treasury after winning the Anglo-Sikh wars. The Koh-i-Noor's wanderings ended on July 3, 1850, when it was handed over to Queen Victoria at Buckingham Palace. The Koh-i-Noor remains today the brightest jewel in the British Crown.

28. One of Kamran's contemporaries wrote that Kamran was one "fond of drinking spirits as well as *bhang* (marijuana) and opium and who spent the whole of his life in ornamenting himself." See Fletcher, *Afghanistan*, 69.

29. Connolly went to Bukhara to rescue another British officer, Colonel Charles Stoddart, whom the emir had thrown into his scorpion- and snake-filled torture pit. Stoddart was taken out of the deep hole when a letter from Queen Victoria arrived requesting mercy for him. But the emir correctly calculated that England was too far away to harm his small realm. He ordered Connolly and Stoddart to be beheaded after digging their own graves. Peter Hopkirk, *The Great Game: The Struggle for Empire in Central Asia* (London: John Murray, 1990), 278.

30. Ewans, *Afghanistan*, 43.

31. Sir John William Kaye, *History of the War in Afghanistan*, vol. 2, Elibron Classics (Chestnut Hill, MA: Adamant Media Corporation, 2005 [1890]), 372–374.

32. Ibid., 374.

33. Dupree, *Afghanistan*, 386.

34. Ewans, *Afghanistan*, 68.

35. Sir Arthur Conan Doyle, creator of Sherlock Holmes, was one of the lucky survivors of the Battle of Maiwand.

36. Ewans, *Afghanistan*, 70; Frank L. Holt, *Into the Land of Bones: Alexander the Great in Afghanistan* (Berkeley: University of California Press, 2005), 4–5.

3—TRIBE AND MOSQUE

1. Olaf Caroe, *The Pathans: 550 B.C.–A.D. 195* (Karachi: Oxford University Press, 1975), 237–238.

2. *The Essential Rumi*, translated by Coleman Barks, with John Moyne (New York: HarperOne, 2004), 37–38.

3. Afghan Constitution, Chapter Six, Article 1. The Constitution's Article 3 balances the tension between tribe and mosque by obfuscating it: "No law can be contrary to the sacred religion of Islam and the values of this Constitution."

4. Naseem Stanakzai, Pashtun VOA journalist, e-mail to author, January 23, 2009.

5. Controversy continues on the politically charged question of population estimates for Afghan ethnic groups, particularly the three largest and most politically prominent—the Pashtuns, the Tajiks, and the Hazaras. A United Nations survey in the 1960s and separate work done in the 1970s by American demographer Thomas H. Eighmy estimated Afghanistan's non-nomadic population at 10.8 million. A 1979 Afghan government survey undertaken with assistance from the United States Agency for International Development (USAID) estimated 13 million. In subsequent years, including through twenty-three years of war, UN procedures for estimating annual increases in population lifted the figure to more than 23 million—despite unknown large numbers of war casualties and massive refugee movement abroad. The truth is, as of early 2011 there is as yet no dependable estimate of Afghanistan's total population or breakdown of its ethnic groups. Dr. Thomas H. Eighmy, unpublished paper, "Afghan Population," February 16, 2002. Unicef, "Information by Country and Programme," Afghanistan, 2007, www.unicef .org/infobycountry/.

6. *Kalash* is a Sanskrit word meaning an empty container. It is also a symbol of space.

7. Some Nuristani and Dard villages are scattered on the Pakistani side of the border near Chitral. Dardic settlements continue into the ancient Baltistan region in divided Kashmir, between Kargil and Leh. The Dards in Kashmir adopted Mahayana Buddhism, the religion of their seventeenth-century Tibetan conquerors. The Dardic population in Afghanistan was forcefully converted to Islam at the same time as the Nuristanis.

8. American anthropologist Louis Dupree's research a generation later related that in several areas of Nuristan that he visited, the inhabitants exhibited at least 30 percent blondism (a combination of blue or mixed eyes and blond or red hair). Louis Dupree, *Afghanistan* (Princeton, NJ: Princeton University Press, 1980), 65.

9. Hans F.K. Gunther, *The Racial Elements of European History*, translated by G. C. Wheeler (Port Washington, NY: Kennikat, 1970), 151.

10. Sir Alexander Burnes, *Cabool: Personal Narrative of a Journey to, and Residence in That City, in the Years 1836, 7, and 8* (Karachi: Indus Publications, 1986), 114–115.

11. Afghans may also worry that they would become second-class citizens if they were dispersed into neighboring countries.

12. The Soviets installed Babrak Karmal as Afghan president during their 1979 invasion. Karmal insisted he was a Pashtun, pointing to his father's claim to be a Ghilzai. Many Afghans did not believe him.

13. Unicef, "Information by Country and Programme," Afghanistan, 2007, www.unicef.org/infobycountry/.

14. Larry P. Goodson, *Afghanistan's Endless War: State Failure, Regional Politics, and the Rise of the Taliban* (Seattle: University of Washington Press, 2001), 19, 127.

15. Dupree, *Afghanistan*, 196.

16. An Afghan saying relates: *Dushman daren, Ma awdarzada darun?* (Do you have an enemy? I have a cousin).

17. James W. Spain, *The Way of the Pathans* (Karachi: Oxford University Press, 1972), 46.

18. A Mujahidin leader told me he once came across a bright young Pashtun orphan in a refugee camp in Pakistan. When asked which profession the boy intended to practice after growing up, the boy's answer was straightforward: He planned to hunt down and kill those who killed his mother, father, and sister. Then he would kill those who were supposed to protect his family.

19. For example, there are the Waziri (of Wazir), the Ahmadzai (sons of Ahmad), and the Jabbar Khel (clan of Jabbar).

20. Arnold Fletcher, *Afghanistan: Highway of Conquest* (Ithaca, NY: Cornell University Press, 1965), 302.

21. In 2009 in eastern Afghanistan, U.S. Special Forces paid a local Shinwari elder $250,000 to defend his region against the Taliban. Other Shinwari elders protested that they had been excluded. Intertribal fighting erupted, killing thirteen and wounding thirty-five. The local defense initiative collapsed; Taliban influence increased. Anand Gopal, "U.S. Plan to Arm Afghan Militia Founders on Tribal Rivalries," McClatchy, April 27, 2010, www.mcclatchydc.com/2010/04/27/92976/us-plan-to-arm-afghan-militia.html.

22. Leon Poullada, *Reform and Rebellion in Afghanistan, 1919–1929* (Ithaca, NY: Cornell University Press, 1973), 19.

23. *Essentials of Rumi*, xiv. Rumi's poetry is popular in the United States today. The United Nations celebrated 2007 as the "International Year of Rumi." More than 750,000 books of his poetry have been sold to date. *Washington Post*, "Rumi's Time Has Come, (Again)," August 30, 2007, www.washingtonpost.com/wp-dyn/content/article/2007/08/29/AR2007082902168.html.

24. The word "Sufi" is derived from the Arabic word *suf,* or "robe," denoting the woolen robes worn by Sufi *pirs* (master or teacher). Sufism rose in the Middle East as a form of dissent against the stagnation, rigidity, and materialism that increasingly came to characterize the Islam of the then-dominant Abbasidian Empire. *Essentials of Rumi,* 67.

25. During the nineteenth and twentieth centuries, Sadullah the "Mad Faqir," the Hadda Mullah, and the Pir of Pagoda fanned tribal revolts against the British in the Pashtun belt on both sides of the Durand Line.

4—MODERNIZING MONARCHS

1. Louis Dupree, *Afghanistan* (Princeton, NJ: Princeton University Press, 1980), 178–179, 462.

2. By the sixteenth century, monarchies in France (Charles VII), England (Henry VIII), and Spain (Ferdinand and Isabelle) had consolidated unified nation-states marked by a growing sense of national patriotism. National armies with a formal officer hierarchy replaced the occasional feudal levies raised for specific campaigns. Soldiers were paid, which was befitting to their station, etymologically speaking: The Latin word for soldier, *solidus,* means "piece of money."

3. *Ataturk: The Birth of a Nation,* illustrated by Mehmet Guldiz (Istanbul: Revas Rehber, 1998), 37.

4. In some Muslim countries, garments are used to screen women from men who are not family members. The covering ranges from a *hijab* head scarf to a full-length tent-like cloak known as the *burka* in Afghan Dari and Persian and the *chador* in Arabic.

5. The Russians created the Cossack Brigade. It was initially commanded by Russian officers. They were withdrawn to Russia at the time of the 1917 Bolshevik Revolution and replaced by British officers. Reza Shah, a Persian brigadier general in the brigade, took over command from the British in January 1921.

6. Anthony Hyman, *Afghanistan Under Soviet Domination, 1964–81* (New York: St. Martin's Press, 1982), 7.

7. A popular British adage at the time was "Rule the Punjabis, intimidate the Sindhis, buy the Pashtuns, and honor the Baluch."

8. "Equerry" refers to the officer-in-charge of the royal stables.

9. Hyman, *Afghanistan Under Soviet Domination,* 8.

10. Dupree, *Afghanistan,* 438–439; Leon Poullada, *Reform and Rebellion in Afghanistan, 1919–1929* (Ithaca, NY: Cornell University Press, 1973), 10–11.

11. Ali Banuazizi and Myron Weiner, *The State, Religion, and Ethnic Politics: Afghanistan, Iran, and Pakistan,* Contemporary Issues in the Middle East (Syracuse, NY: Syracuse University Press, 1988), 239.

12. Ludwig W. Adamec, *A Biographical Dictionary of Contemporary Afghanistan* (Graz, Austria: Akademische Druck Verlagsanstalt, 1987), 47.

13. Ibid.

14. The British created six tribal agencies on the Frontier: North and South Waziristan, Kurram, Orakzai, Khyber, and Mohmand (See Map 3.1). After gaining its independence in 1947, Pakistan added the Bajaur Agency and named the region covered by all seven agencies the Federally Administered Tribal Area (FATA). Pakistan largely continued the British practice of allowing the tribes to govern themselves, overseen by political agents and their staffs representing the government.

15. Twenty-three years later, in 1942, the United States opened its first diplomatic mission in Afghanistan.

16. The Istiqlal (Independence) school was originally the Amaniyeh school, named after Amanullah. The name was changed after Amanullah was overthrown. Nejat's name was later changed to Lycée Amani, honoring Amanullah.

17. Richard S. Newell, *The Politics of Afghanistan* (Ithaca, NY: Cornell University Press, 1972), 54.

18. Adamec, *Biographical Dictionary of Contemporary Afghanistan*, 89.

19. Arnold Fletcher, *Afghanistan: Highway of Conquest* (Ithaca, NY: Cornell University Press, 1965), 205.

20. Leon Poullada, *Reform and Rebellion in Afghanistan, 1919–1929* (Ithaca, NY: Cornell University Press, 1973), 168.

21. Bacha Seqao deserted the Afghan Army during the 1924–1925 Mangal rebellion and opened a tea shop in Peshawar. He was arrested there for smuggling, escaped from jail, and was back in his native Kohistan when the 1928 uprising against Amanullah erupted. Ibid., 169–170.

22. Dupree, *Afghanistan*, 120–121.

23. Martin Ewans, *Afghanistan: A Short History of Its People and Politics* (New York: HarperCollins, 2002), 102.

24. Dupree, *Afghanistan*, 469.

25. Asta Olesen, *Islam and Politics in Afghanistan*, Nordic Institute of Asian Studies, no. 67 (Wiltshire, UK: Antony Rowe, 1995), 186.

26. Akbar S. Ahmed and David M. Hart, eds., *Islam in Tribal Societies: From the Atlas to the Indus* (London: Routledge and Kegan Paul, 1984), 201.

27. The Faqir of Ipi fomented anti-British resistance in the two Waziristans until Britain withdrew from the subcontinent in 1947. He was a constant thorn in the side of Pakistan until his death in 1960.

28. The Musahiban regime granted scholarships to trans-Durand Pashtun students to study at two high schools named after the two great seventeenth-century poets who resisted Mughal control, Rahman Baba and Khushal Khan Khattack.

29. Adamec, *Biographical Dictionary of Contemporary Afghanistan*, 250, 252.

30. Ibid., 251.

31. Ibid.; Andrew Roberts, *Eminent Churchillians* (London: Weidenfeld and Nicholson, 1994), 72.

32. Afghan government agents may also have been planted among the Waziri escorts.

33. After Reza Shah's exile, the U.S. military took command of Iran's railroads, managing land lease shipments from Iranian ports to the Soviet border.

5 — RED SUNRISE

1. Annette Woodward, spouse of Donald Woodward, administrative counselor, U.S. embassy, Kabul, interview with author, November 1, 2003.

2. Donald Woodward, administrative counselor, U.S. embassy, Kabul, interview with author, November 1, 2003. Woodward served in Kabul from 1978 to 1981. He is deceased.

3. Sir Kerr Fraser-Tytler, *Afghanistan: A Study of Political Developments in Central Asia* (London: Oxford University Press, 1953), 124.

4. SEATO linked Pakistan to American treaty allies Thailand and the Philippines. Aside from the United States, Britain, France, New Zealand, and Australia also signed the 1954 SEATO treaty. CENTO was concluded in 1955. Its members were Pakistan, Iran, Iraq, Turkey, and Britain.

5. Leon B. Poullada and Leila D.J. Poullada, *The Kingdom of Afghanistan and the United States, 1828–1973* (Omaha: Center for Afghanistan Studies, University of Nebraska, and Lincoln, NE: Dageforde Publishing, 1995), 149.

6. Afghanistan Online, "History: Quotes from Afghan Personalities of Yesterday and Today," quoting Abdur Rahman Khan, 1880–1901," www.afghan-web.com/history/quotes.html.

7. Arnold Fletcher, *Afghanistan: Highway of Conquest* (Ithaca, NY: Cornell University Press, 1965), 270.

8. A number of excellent publications by Soviet scholars and former KGB officials and memoirs by Soviet leaders have portrayed KGB operations in Afghanistan before and after the December 1979 Soviet invasion. In 1992 former KGB colonel Vasili Mitrokhin defected to Britain with a trove of KGB-sourced documents on Afghanistan. He had served as a KGB operations officer, then as a senior archivist of KGB documents. Mitrokhin's revelations about KGB worldwide operations were first published in 2000 in collaboration with British historian Christopher Andrew in *The Sword and the Shield: The Mitrokhin Archive and the Secret History of the KGB* (New York: Basic Books, 2000). In a BBC interview that same year, Mitrokhin stated that he "wanted to show the tremendous efforts of the machine of evil" (*Washington Post*, January 30, 2004). In 2002, Mitrokhin prepared a small book, *The KGB in Afghanistan*, for a Woodrow Wilson Center Conference in which I participated (Working Paper no. 40, Cold War International History Project [Washington, DC: Woodrow Wilson International Center for Scholars, 2002, updated 2009]), www.wilsoncenter.org/topics/pubs/ACFAE9.pdf. This 173-page volume is the single most valuable account of KGB operations in Afghanistan. Vasili Mitrokhin died in Britain in 2004.

9. Bruce J. Amstutz, *Afghanistan: The First Five Years of Soviet Occupation* (Washington, DC: National Defense University Press, 1986), 22.

10. Anthony Arnold, *Afghanistan's Two-Party Communism: Parcham and Khalq* (Palo Alto, CA: Hoover Institution Press, Stanford University, 1983), 17; Michael Malinowski, former consul at the U.S. embassy in Kabul, interview with author, January 9, 2010, Virginia; Mitrokhin, *The KGB in Afghanistan,* 19, 20, 21, 25, 51.

11. Amstutz, *Afghanistan,* 34.

12. Thomas G. Paterson, Garry J. Clifford, and Kenneth J. Hagan, *American Foreign Relations: A History Since 1895,* vol. 2, 4th ed. (Lexington, MA: D. C. Heath, 1995), 300.

13. NSC Declassified Documents Reference System, vol. 5, no. 1, Fiche no. 44B (NSC 5617).

14. The centerpiece of the Helmand Valley project was the Kajaki dam, which was to provide irrigation and power to the region. The project was plagued by problems from the outset and was still under construction when the 1979 Soviet invasion occurred. Much of the Helmand Valley infrastructure was destroyed over the next three decades of war.

15. Kabul's propaganda depicted "occupied" or "independent" Pashtunistan as divided into three provinces, one in the north, one in the south, and a central province. Baluchistan would be in southern Pashtunistan. Louis Dupree, *Afghanistan* (Princeton, NJ: Princeton University Press, 1980), 541.

16. Mir Hekmatullah Sadat, *The Afghan Experience,* doctoral dissertation, Claremont Graduate University, Claremont, California, 2006, 77.

17. A French specialist on constitutional law advised the Afghan committee that drew up the 1964 Afghan Constitution.

18. Dupree, *Afghanistan,* 574.

19. Ibid., 576.

20. The conclusion of the Soviet-Indian Friendship Treaty on the eve of the 1971 Indo-Pakistani War cemented close Indo-Soviet relations that lasted until the 1991 collapse of the USSR.

21. Mitrokhin, *The KGB in Afghanistan,* 18.

22. Ibid., 19.

23. When he was principal of Avensina High School in 1957, Hafizullah Amin received a USAID scholarship for graduate studies at Columbia University. He returned to Afghanistan with a master's degree in education. Amin gained admission to Columbia's PhD program in 1962 but was dismissed for failing grades. Arnold noted, "In March 1979, eight of the eighteen ministries in the Khalq cabinet of Amin were former high school teachers." Arnold, *Afghanistan's Two-Party Communism,* 29.

24. The English translation of the name Jamiat Islami (Society of Islam) precisely matches that of Pakistan's Jamaat-i Islami and Brotherhood parties in some other Muslim countries.

25. Oliver Roy, *Islam and Resistance in Afghanistan* (Cambridge: Cambridge University Press, 1986), 201.

26. Asta Olesen, *Islam and Politics in Afghanistan,* Nordic Institute of Asian Studies, no. 67 (Wiltshire, UK: Antony Rowe, 1995), 249.

27. Ralph H. Magnus and Eden Naby, *Afghanistan: Mullah, Marx, and Mujahid,* revised and updated (Boulder: Westview Press, 2002), 10.

28. Louis Dupree, quoted in Gilles Dorronsoro, *Revolution Unending—Afghanistan: 1979 to the Present,* translated by John King (New York: Columbia University Press, 2005), 67, noted that there were 39 student strikes in 1966, 80 in 1967, and 133 in 1968. In 1969, 15,000 demonstrated after police killed a student demonstrator.

29. Bashir Babar, interview with author, November 17, 1989, Islamabad. Babar confided that, as a young Pakistani diplomat in Kabul, he once had to deliver an ISI payment to Hekmatyar. Also see Kux, *The United States and Afghanistan,* 274.

30. Erika Knabe, *Women in the Social Stratification of Afghanistan* (Leiden: E. J. Brill, 1977), 158–170.

31. John Barron, *KGB: The Secret Work of Soviet Secret Agents* (New York: Reader's Digest Press, 1974), 313.

32. Magnus and Naby, *Afghanistan,* 115.

33. Abdul Samad Ghaus, *The Fall of Afghanistan: An Insider's Account* (Washington, DC: Pergamon-Brassey's International Defense Publishers, 1988), 107.

34. Magnus and Naby, *Afghanistan,* 116.

35. Dr. Nematullah Pazhwak was a Kabuli graduate of Habibya. He went on to Kabul University and Columbia University, where he received his doctorate.

36. Embassy telegram, "Apparent Coup Attempt," July 17, 1973.

37. Embassy Airgram A-33, May 22, 1973.

38. Top-secret cable in Russian from the Soviet Communist Party Central Committee to the KGB Resident in Kabul, signed by R. Ulyanovski, June 21, 1974, Hoover Institution Archives, Stanford University, Palo Alto, California.

39. Central Committee "Decree" in Russian, Hoover Institution Archives, Stanford University, Palo Alto, California, June 26, 1974, also in author's files. A more urgent Soviet Central Committee cable, personally delivered by the KGB Resident to Karmal and Taraki after Daoud's visit, apprised them of the positive talks Soviet party leader Brezhnev and Prime Minister Kosygin had with Daoud in Moscow. The long instruction told the Resident only to "familiarize" the Soviet ambassador with its contents.

40. Arnold, *Afghanistan's Two-Party Communism,* 46; Andrew Roberts, *Eminent Churchillians* (London: Weidenfeld and Nicholson, 1994), 212.

41. Dorronsoro, *Revolution Unending,* 82.

42. Ibid., 83.

43. The Shalimar Gardens were planned and constructed by the first Mughal emperor, Babur, whose tomb is in Kabul.

44. Ghaus, *The Fall of Afghanistan,* 144.

45. Ibid., 171.

46. Ibid., 179.

47. Ibid.

48. Ibid.

49. Ibid.

50. Anthony Hyman, *Afghanistan Under Soviet Domination, 1964–81* (New York: St. Martin's Press, 1982), 75.

51. Angelo Rasanayagam, *Afghanistan: A Modern History: Monarch, Despotism or Democracy? The Problems of Governance in the Muslim Tradition* (London: I. B. Tauris, 2003), 273.

52. Ghaus, *The Fall of Afghanistan*, 197.

53. Western diplomat, interview with author, October 3, 2003.

54. Watanjar, then a captain, was a commander in the tank column that occupied Gul Khanna Palace during Daoud's 1973 coup.

55. This account is taken from a four-hour taped interview given by Captain Khan to veteran journalist and former Afghan diplomat Omar Malikyar on May 16, 1990, in Peshawar, Pakistan.

56. In July 2008, President Hamid Karzai created a commission, headed by the government health minister, to locate former President Daoud's grave. After a month-long investigation, and with the help of Captain Khan, the commission discovered the grave. The commission identified the bodies of Daoud's son, two daughters, grandchildren aged five and three, and his other relatives who had perished on the night of the communist coup.

6—COMMISSAR MEETS TRIBESMAN

1. "CC CPSU Letter on Afghanistan," May 10, 1988, Appendix 8, from A. Lyakhovsky, *Tragedy and Valor of the Afghanistan Veteran* (Moscow: Iskon, 1995), translated by Gary Goldberg in "Toward an International History of the War in Afghanistan, 1979–1989," Conference in Washington, D.C., April 29–30, 2002, Cold War International History Project in cooperation with The Asia Program and The Kennan Institute for Advanced Russian Studies at the Woodrow Wilson Center, the George Washington Cold War Group at the George Washington University, and the National Security Archive, *Conference Reader*, compiled by Christian F. Ostermann and Mircea Munteanu (Washington, DC: Woodrow Wilson Center, 2002), www.wilsoncenter.org/topics/docs/toward_an_international_history_of_the_war_in_afghanistan1979-1989_vol2.pdf, 409–423.

2. Vasiliy Mitrokhin, *The KGB in Afghanistan*, Working Paper no. 40, Cold War International History Project (Washington, DC: Woodrow Wilson International Center for Scholars, 2002, updated 2009), www.wilsoncenter.org/topics/pubs/ACFAE9.pdf, 26; Alexandr Morozov, "Our Man in Kabul," *New Times* (Moscow), no. 41 (1991): 37–38.

3. Mitrokhin, *The KGB in Afghanistan*, 37.

4. Gennady Bocharov, *Russian Roulette: Afghanistan Through Russian Eyes* (London: Hamish Hamilton, 1990), 5.

Notes to Chapter 6

5. Ibid.; Arne Odd Westad, "Prelude to Invasion: The Soviet Union and the Afghan Communists, 1978–1979," *International History Review* 16, no. 1 (1994): 51.

6. Westad, "Prelude to Invasion," 51.

7. Anthony Arnold, *Afghanistan's Two-Party Communism: Parcham and Khalq* (Palo Alto, CA: Hoover Institution Press, Stanford University, 1983), 84; Jack F. Matlock Jr., *Autopsy on an Empire: The American Ambassador's Account of the Collapse of the Soviet Union* (New York: Random House, 1995), 91.

8. Westad, "Prelude to Invasion," 133.

9. Mitrokhin, *The KGB in Afghanistan*, 27.

10. Kryuchkov was a protégé of KGB chief Yuriy Andropov. They served together in Budapest during the 1956 Hungarian uprising; after becoming KGB director in 1967, Andropov gave Kryuchkov important posts in KGB headquarters and in the party.

11. Morozov, "Our Man in Kabul," 38–39.

12. Arnold, *Afghanistan's Two-Party Communism*, 76.

13. Sharda Urga, "They Now Call It International Terrorism. Survivor's Tale: General Khoshal Peroz," *India Today*, October 8, 2001, http://india-today.com/itoday/20011008/cover-afghanistan5.shtml.

14. Mitrokhin, *The KGB in Afghanistan*, 27.

15. The PDPA and Soviet secret police agencies mirrored each other. Both had to periodically change their acronym-laden names to disassociate themselves from the horrors they inflicted on their respective populations. The feared Soviet state security agencies began with the Cheka, which evolved to become the NKVD and then the KGB. The KGB's Afghan apprentice went from AGSA under Taraki to KAM under Amin and to KHAD under Karmal in less than two years.

16. Although Parchamis were in the minority compared to Khalqis, some Parcham officers had actively participated in the coup against Daoud. The first tank from the rebellious 4th Armored Brigade to attack Daoud's palace was commanded by—yes, another—Omar Sharif, a Parcham major whose father had once been a governor. A rocket fired from within the palace grounds incinerated the tank—and Sharif with it.

17. "Soviet Activities in Afghanistan," Briefing Paper, May 16, 1979, National Security Archives, George Washington University. See also United Nations, "Document No. 17976, Treaty of Friendship, Good-Neighborliness, and Cooperation, Signed in Moscow on 5 December 1978," *United Nations—Treaty Series*, vol. 145, I-17976 (1979): 333–335, http://untreaty.un.org/unts/60001_120000/2/16/00002763.pdf.

18. Bruce J. Amstutz, *Afghanistan: The First Five Years of Soviet Occupation* (Washington, DC: National Defense University Press, 1986), 45.

19. In a 1978 conversation with the Soviet Foreign Ministry's Philippines desk officer, I could not suppress a laugh when told that the march of world socialism would eventually absorb the Philippines.

20. Thomas G. Paterson, Garry J. Clifford, and Kenneth J. Hagan, *American Foreign Relations: A History Since 1895*, vol. 2, 4th ed. (Lexington, MA: D. C. Heath, 1995), 408.

21. Cyrus R. Vance, *Hard Choices: Critical Years in America's Foreign Policy* (New York: Simon and Schuster, 1983), 76.

22. U.S. Department of State, Office of Security Assessment, "The Kidnapping and Death of Ambassador Adolph Dubs, February 14, 1979, Kabul, Afghanistan," February 2, 1980, secret, declassified, 16.

23. Bruce Flatin, interview with author, February 15, 2003, and Michael Malinowski, interview with author, August 30, 2009.

24. U.S. Department of State, Office of Security Assessment, "The Kidnapping and Death of Ambassador Adolph Dubs, February 14, 1979, Kabul, Afghanistan."

25. The Afghan government's official report on Dubs's murder listed four types of weapons in the possession of the kidnappers: three firearms, a machine gun, two pistols of higher caliber than a .22 weapon, and a grenade. Ibid., 12.

26. Ibid. The fact that the kidnappers had only been armed with pistols evinced that the machine gun had been placed in the room before the embassy officials entered to demonstrate that the kidnappers had killed Dubs.

27. Mitrokhin, *The KGB in Afghanistan*, 154–155.

28. Westad, "Prelude to Invasion," 54.

29. Mitrokhin, *The KGB in Afghanistan*, 29–31.

30. Ibid., 29–31, 42–43; Westad, "Prelude to Invasion," 55.

31. Mitrokhin, *The KGB in Afghanistan*, 37.

32. Ibid., 30–31.

33. Ibid., 68; "Documents on the Soviet Invasion of Afghanistan," e-Dossier No. 4, November 2001, Cold War International History Project (Washington, DC: Woodrow Wilson International Center for Scholars), 68.

34. Bocharov, *Russian Roulette*, 61.

35. Quoted in "Information About the Visit of the Afghan Party and State Delegation, Headed by the Secretary General of the People's Democratic Party of Afghanistan, Chairman of the Revolutionary Board and Prime Minister of the Democratic Republic of Afghanistan, Nur Mohamed Taraki, to the USSR [December 1978]," Diplomatic Archive, Sofia, Opis 35, File 335, obtained by Jordan Baev and translated by Kalina Bratanova and Baev, in Christian Ostermann, ed., "New Evidence on the War in Afghanistan," Woodrow Wilson International Center for Scholars, *Cold War International History Project Bulletin*, no. 14/15 (2003–2004): 234, www.coldwar.hu/html/en/publications/b%E9k%E9s-afghanistan.pdf.

36. Amstutz, *Afghanistan*, 53.

37. Neamatollah Nojumi, *The Rise of the Taliban in Afghanistan: Mass Mobilization, Civil War, and the Future of the Region* (New York: Palgrave, 2002), 35.

38. Karen Brutents, *Thirty Years on Staraya Square*, translated by Haik Gugarats (Moscow: Mezhdunarodnye Otnoshenia, 1998). Brutents' book covers the thirty

years he worked in the Central Committee of the Communist Party in Moscow, 456.

39. "Information About the Visit of the Afghan Party and State Delegation," in Ostermann, ed., "New Evidence on the War in Afghanistan."

40. Anthony Hyman, *Afghanistan Under Soviet Domination, 1964–81* (New York: St. Martin's Press, 1982), 208.

41. Mark Urban, *War in Afghanistan* (New York: St. Martin's Press, 1988), 149.

42. A. Lyakhovsky, *Tragedy and Valor of the Afghanistan Veteran* (Moscow: Iskon, 1995), 3.

43. Mitrokhin, *The KGB in Afghanistan*, 41.

44. Meeting of Kosygin, Gromyko, Ustinov, and Ponomarev with Taraki in Moscow, 20 March 1979, "The Soviet Union and Afghanistan, 1978–1979. Documents from the Russian and East German Archives," Woodrow Wilson International Center for Scholars, *Cold War International History Project Bulletin* no. 8/9 (1996–1997): 150.

45. Taraki's citation of Soviet brutality has been well documented. Stalin's forced collectivization and bloody purges in the 1930s killed tens of millions. In 1950, at its height, the vast Soviet gulag network of camps held an estimated 2.5 million prisoners.

46. Central Committee, Communist Party of the Soviet Union, Politburo Transcript (excerpt), 13 November 1986, "The Soviet Union and Afghanistan, 1978–1979. Documents from the Russian and East German Archives," 179.

47. "The Cold War in the Third World and the Collapse of Détente in the 1970s," Woodrow Wilson International Center for Scholars, *Cold War International History Project Bulletin*, no. 8/9 (1996–1997); "Record of Conversation Between Soviet Ambassador to Afghanistan A. M. Puzanov and Taraki, July 10, 1979," Cold War International History Project, Virtual Archive, Woodrow Wilson International Center for Scholars, 47–51, www.wilsoncenter.org.

48. "The Cold War in the Third World and the Collapse of Détente in the 1970s," Cold War International History Project.

49. Kabul 4889, "Meeting with Soviet Diplomat: Part II of III, Soviet-Afghan Relations," June 25, 1979, confidential, declassified, retrieved from the National Security Archive, 2.

50. The victorious Nuristan guerrilla front was led by a former civil servant who armed his tribals with weapons captured from local police and military units.

51. Georgi Arbatov, *The System: An Insider's Life in Soviet Politics* (New York: Random House, 1993), 254.

52. *Messengers from Moscow: The Center Collapses*, documentary by Eugene B. Shirley Jr. and Herbert J. Ellison, directed by Daniel Wolf, produced by PACEM Productions, Barraclough Carey Productions, 1995.

53. Mikhail Gorbachev, *Memoirs* (New York: Doubleday, 1996), 114.

54. Ibid., 208.

55. Deputy Foreign Minister and Politburo member Georgi Kornyienko described Andropov as a "hostage of his own KGB apparatus." Georgi Kornyienko, "The Afghan Endeavor: Perplexities of the Military Incursion and Withdrawal," *Journal of South Asian and Middle Eastern Studies* 27, no. 2 (1994).

56. Arbatov, *The System*, 193.

57. Gorbachev, *Memoirs*, 114.

58. Arbatov recalled that, in two televised ceremonies, "the dying Chernyenko, lifted from his deathbed, was supported under the arms and led over to the camera.... These pictures were broadcasted around the world many times, apparently as a symbol of our weakness—indeed, of our death agony." Arbatov, *The System*, 277.

59. Mitrokhin, *The KGB in Afghanistan*, 52.

60. "The Cold War in the Third World and the Collapse of Détente in the 1970s," Cold War International History Project, 136–140.

61. Ibid., 141.

62. Ibid., 96–97, 141.

63. "Documents on the Soviet Invasion of Afghanistan," e-Dossier No. 4, Cold War International History Project, 70.

64. "The Cold War in the Third World and the Collapse of Détente in the 1970s," Cold War International History Project, 141.

65. "Documents on the Soviet Invasion of Afghanistan," e-Dossier No. 4, Cold War International History Project, 73.

66. Alexandr Morozov, "The KGB and the Afghan Leaders," *New Times* (Moscow), no. 24, 1992.

67. The confiscation of a prosperous Afghan-American joint venture, Wooden High textile factory, was one such example. The factory was turned into a government warehouse and 1,500 workers were sent home.

68. "Documents on the Soviet Invasion of Afghanistan," e-Dossier No. 4, Cold War International History Project, 38.

69. The goal of drawing the Soviets into a "Vietnamese quagmire" was voiced by a U.S. Defense Department official, Walter Slocombe, at a Brzezinski-chaired meeting at the White House on March 30, 1979. Todd Anthony Rosa, "Three Key Phases in the U.S. Response to Soviet Involvement in Afghanistan: What Do the Documents Tell Us, and What Is Left to Learn?" Presentation to the conference "Towards an International History of the War in Afghanistan, 1979–1989," conference organized by the Cold War International History Project at the Woodrow Wilson Center, Washington, D.C., April 29–30, 2002, documents compiled by Christian F. Ostermann and Mircea Munteanu.

70. Lyakhovsky, *Tragedy and Valor*, 4.

71. "The Cold War in the Third World and the Collapse of Détente in the 1970s," Cold War International History Project, 153.

72. Message to East German leader Honecker from the Soviet Central Committee, October 1, 1979. Obtained by the Carter-Brezhnev Project from the East

German archives in Berlin, also located in the National Security Archives, George Washington University, Washington, DC, www.wilsoncenter.org.

73. "Documents on the Soviet Invasion of Afghanistan," e-Dossier No. 4, Cold War International History Project, 40.

7—BIG FOX CATCHES LITTLE FOX

1. Karen Brutents, *Thirty Years on Staraya Square* (Moscow: Mezhdunarodnye Otnoshenia, 1998). Translated by Haik Gugarats. The memoir recounts Brutents' thirty years in the Communist Party Central Committee, 169, 471, 480.

2. Thomas G. Paterson, Garry J. Clifford, and Kenneth J. Hagan, *American Foreign Relations: A History Since 1895*, vol. 2, 4th ed. (Lexington, MA: D. C. Heath, 1995), 377–379; Craig A. Daigle, "Why Did Sadat Throw the Soviets Out of Egypt?" *Middle East Review of International Affairs*, March 2004.

3. After the collapse of the Soviet Union in 1991, former Soviet deputy foreign minister Nikolai Vorontsov said that "everything that was said about helping the Afghan people, and all the rest of it, well that wasn't really what it was all about. Perhaps someone did want to help them, but the main reason was to stake out the territory for ourselves and stop the Americans from getting involved." BBC News, "Superpowers' 'Mistakes' in Afghanistan," December 24, 2004.

4. Paterson et al., *American Foreign Relations*, 377–379.

5. Henry S. Bradsher, *Afghan Communism and Soviet Intervention* (Karachi: Oxford University Press, 2000), 52.

6. Kabul 5459, "GDR Ambassador Reports That Soviets Hope to Replace Prime Minister Amin with the Broader-Based Government," secret/EXDIS, July 18, 1979, declassified July 19, 1999. "EXDIS" stands for "Exclusive Distribution Only."

7. Kabul 5470, "Further Comments by East German Ambassador About Soviet Efforts to Alter Afghan Regime," secret/EXDIS, July 19, 1979, declassified July 19, 1999.

8. Ibid.

9. Kabul 6309, "East German Ambassador Departs Kabul Scene," August 20, 1979, declassified August 20, 1999. Schwiesau did not return to Afghanistan. Almost certainly, his abrupt departure was not due to illness. The KGB may have suspected that his briefing of Amstutz had been a mistake—the Americans may have alerted Amin, who was able to rapidly strengthen his personal grasp on the power ministries before the KGB and Taraki could move against him.

10. Vasiliy Mitrokhin, *The KGB in Afghanistan*, Working Paper no. 40, Cold War International History Project (Washington, DC: Woodrow Wilson International Center for Scholars, 2002, updated 2009), www.wilsoncenter.org/topics/pubs/ACFAE9.pdf, 50–51.

11. Ibid., 51.

12. Raja Anwar, *The Tragedy of Afghanistan: A First-Hand Account*, translated from Urdu by Khalid Hasan (London: Verso, 1988), 168. Anwar quoted an Afghan publication, *Foreign Affairs Bulletin*, July 1978, 37.

13. In addition to aiding in the assault on the hotel room where Ambassador Dubs was held by kidnappers, Tarun played a major role in the PDPA slaughter of thousands of Afghan men, women, and children after the April 1978 communist coup. American Consul Mike Malinowski recalled that he was compelled to meet with Tarun when American citizens were caught up in the bloody events ripping Afghanistan in 1979. He knew of Tarun's reputation for shooting down Afghans in his Ministry of Interior office, where Tarun received Malinowski. During their conversations in his office, Tarun kept a machine gun on his desk pointed in the direction of visitors seated in front of his desk. Mike Malinowski, interview with author, January 6, 2010.

14. Christopher Andrew and Vasili Mitrokhin, *The World Was Going Our Way: The KGB and the Battle for the Third World* (New York: Basic Books, 2005), 194.

15. Amin knew well that the three Pashtun military officers were no strangers to overthrowing governments. They were in the tank columns in the 1973 and 1978 coups.

16. Anwar, *Tragedy of Afghanistan*, 168.

17. Alexander Morozov, "Our Man in Kabul," *New Times* (Moscow), no. 38–44 (1991): 32; Anwar, *Tragedy of Afghanistan*, 169.

18. Kabul 5470, "Further comments by Bruce Flatin Meeting East German Ambassador Schwiesau About Soviets' Hope to Replace Prime Minister Amin with the Broader-Based Government."

19. "The Cold War in the Third World and the Collapse of Détente in the 1970s," Woodrow Wilson International Center for Scholars, *Cold War International History Project Bulletin*, no. 8/9 (1996–1997), Extract from Protocol no. 168 of the CPSU CC Politburo Session on 15 September 1979, 154.

20. Anwar, *Tragedy of Afghanistan*, 166–169.

21. "The Cold War in the Third World and the Collapse of Détente in the 1970s," 154.

22. Ibid.

23. Mitrokhin, *The KGB in Afghanistan*, 52.

24. Anwar, *Tragedy in Afghanistan*, 170.

25. Mitrokhin, *The KGB in Afghanistan*, 61.

26. "The Cold War in the Third World and the Collapse of Détente in the 1970s," 154.

27. Morozov, "Our Man in Kabul," 30.

28. Kabul 7392, "The Position of Amin and Afghanistan's Independence," Part 1, confidential, October 9, 1979, declassified April 2, 1989; Brutents, *Thirty Years*, 470.

29. Mitrokhin, *The KGB in Afghanistan*, 59.

30. Ibid., 61.

31. Ibid.; Kabul 7392.

32. Morozov, "Our Man in Kabul," 34.

33. Mitrokhin, *The KGB in Afghanistan*, 61.

34. Kabul 6849, "Tensions in Kabul," September 14, 1979, declassified; Kabul 6851, "Security Tightens in Kabul," September 14, 1979, declassified.

35. Mitrokhin, *The KGB in Afghanistan*, 64.

36. Anthony Hyman, *Afghanistan Under Soviet Domination, 1964–81* (New York: St. Martin's Press, 1982), 155; Kabul 7392. Nawab Ali's birthplace, Lashkar Gah, was rechristened as Nawabshahr ("Nawab city").

37. Mitrokhin, *The KGB in Afghanistan*, 76.

38. Brutents, *Thirty Years*, 453.

39. The account of the KGB exfiltration of the three anti-Amin Khalqi cabinet ministers is taken from Morozov, "Our Man in Kabul," 34; and Mitrokhin, *The KGB in Afghanistan*, 78–80.

40. Morozov, "Our Man in Kabul," 35.

41. Kabul 7392, "The Position of Amin and Afghanistan's Independence," Part 2, confidential/EXDIS, October 9, 1979, declassified May 4, 1987.

42. Mitrokhin, *The KGB in Afghanistan*, 69.

43. Ibid., 66.

44. Soon after the December 1979 Soviet invasion, one of the brothers, Wudood, appeared on Radio Kabul and made a public confession. Before his execution, Wudood identified the location of Taraki's unmarked gravesite. Within days, it was completely destroyed. Possible culprits include Parchamis, Mujahidin sympathizers, or some of the numerous other Afghans who had lost relatives and friends during Taraki's rule.

45. Bradsher, *Afghan Communism and Soviet Intervention*, 59–60.

46. Arne Odd Westad, "Prelude to Invasion: The Soviet Union and the Afghan Communists, 1978–1979," *International History Review* 16, no. 1 (1994): 62.

47. In 1989, Puzanov told a Supreme Soviet Committee that no senior Soviet official asked to debrief him on his return to Moscow, despite his eight years as Soviet ambassador in Kabul spanning Zahir Shah's years, Daoud's second term in office, and Taraki's rule.

48. Ivanov curried favor with Amin by praising him to his face, while secretly orchestrating his demise through KGB back channels. His KGB deputy in Kabul, Alexander Morozov, once overheard Ivanov telling the Afghan dictator, "I'm also a Stalinist, like yourself, Comrade Amin." Morozov, "Our Man in Kabul."

49. Hekmatyar and Amin shared tribal origins. Both were Kharoti Ghilzai.

50. Kabul 7392. On October 27, chargé Amstutz reported to Washington that Amin "made a strong pitch for U.S. 'material assistance' during a meeting in Amin's office." Kabul 7726, "Meeting with President Amin," October 27, 1979, confidential, declassified.

51. Bruce J. Amstutz, *Afghanistan: The First Five Years of Soviet Occupation* (Washington, DC: National Defense University Press, 1986), 180.

52. Kabul 7726, "Meeting with President Amin," October 28, 1979, confidential, declassified August 1, 1984.

53. Hyman, *Afghanistan Under Soviet Domination*, 158.

54. Kabul 8117, "Amin Publicly Acknowledges That Soviet Support Is Essential for the Khalqis' Survival," November 21, 1979, declassified December 23, 1991.

55. Brutents, *Thirty Years*, 472.

56. Anthony Arnold, *Afghanistan's Two-Party Communism: Parcham and Khalq* (Palo Alto, CA: Hoover Institution Press, Stanford University, 1983), 401; Mitrokhin, *The KGB in Afghanistan*, 94; A. Lyakhovsky, *The Tragedy and Valor of the Afghanistan Veteran* (Moscow: Iskon, 1995), 11–12; "Documents on the Soviet Invasion of Afghanistan," e-Dossier No. 4, November 2001, Cold War International History Project (Washington, DC: Woodrow Wilson International Center for Scholars), 153–154, 157–158.

57. Mitrokhin, *The KGB in Afghanistan*, 94.

58. Andrew and Mitrokhin, *The World Was Going Our Way*, 401. KGB agents operating abroad under false identities pose as citizens of the country where they are assigned.

59. "Documents on the Soviet Invasion of Afghanistan," e-Dossier No. 4, Cold War International History Project, 153–154.

60. Kabul 7326, "Some Disturbing Signs Affecting Afghanistan's Independence and the Position on Amin," October 4, 1979, secret, declassified May 4, 1987.

61. Mitrokhin, *The KGB in Afghanistan*, 89–90; Bradsher, *Afghan Communism and Soviet Intervention*, 90.

62. Arnold, *Afghanistan's Two-Party Communism*, 84.

63. Schulman-Vance, secret memorandum, "Possible Conclusions of a Soviet Policy Review," December 14, 1979, declassified; State 313507, "Excerpts from Noon Briefing, Afghanistan," December 5, 1979, unclassified; Special Coordination Committee, secret briefing paper, December 17, 1979, declassified; *Current Foreign Relations* summary, December 19, 1979, secret, declassified; Moscow 27530, "Ambassador's Meeting with Maltsev on Soviet Military Deployments and Iran," December 17, 1979, secret/NODIS, declassified. "NODIS" stands for "No Distribution."

64. Mitrokhin, *The KGB in Afghanistan*, 88–89.

65. Ibid., 89.

66. "Documents on the Soviet Invasion of Afghanistan," e-Dossier No. 4, Cold War International History Project, personal memorandum, Andropov to Brezhnev, n.d. (early December 1979), 159–160. Also cited in Lyakhovsky, *Tragedy and Valor*.

67. Ibid.

68. Lester W. Grau and Michael A. Gress, eds., *The Soviet-Afghan War: How a Superpower Fought and Lost* (Lawrence, University Press of Kansas, 2002), 11. On October 13, a secret Ministry of Defense "operational group" under the deputy

chief of staff, General Sergei Akhromeyev, began contingency planning for the Soviet invasion.

69. Brutents, *Thirty Years*, 483.

70. Andrew and Mitrokhin, *The World Was Going Our Way*, 400. See also Bradsher, *Afghan Communism and Soviet Intervention*, 79. Kosygin does not seem to have attended a Politburo session on Afghanistan until January 17, 1980, almost three weeks after the Soviet invasion. No copy of the decree was made. It was placed in a special safe and allegedly not discovered in Soviet archives until after the 1991 collapse of the Soviet Union. In 1989, a Congress of People's Deputies investigating committee condemned the Soviet invasion of Afghanistan and accused the troika members of engineering it. Georgi Arbatov, *The System: An Insider's Life in Soviet Politics* (New York: Random House, 1993), 192.

71. Lyakhovsky, *Tragedy and Valor*, 18; "The Cold War: Testimony of a Participant," Woodrow Wilson International Center for Scholars, *Cold War International History Project Bulletin* (1994): 193–195.

72. Lyakhovsky, *Tragedy and Valor*, 52; Anwar, *Tragedy of Afghanistan*, 187–188.

73. Bradsher, *Afghan Communism and Soviet Intervention*, 97.

74. Brutents, *Thirty Years*, 472.

75. Mitrokhin, *The KGB in Afghanistan*, 96.

76. DAO Kabul, telegram, six 800–0075 79, "Soviet Airlift to Kabul," December 26, 1979, declassified.

77. Grau and Gress, eds., *The Soviet-Afghan War*, 11.

78. Ibid., 12.

79. Ibid.

80. Lyakhovsky, *Tragedy and Valor*, 78.

81. Anwar, *Tragedy of Afghanistan*, 187–188.

82. Bradsher, *Afghan Communism and Soviet Intervention*, 97.

83. Lyakhovsky, *Tragedy and Valor*, 105.

84. Ibid., 118–119.

85. Ibid., 100, 116.

86. Raymond Garthoff, *Détente and Confrontation: American-Soviet Relations from Nixon to Reagan*, rev. ed. (Washington, DC: Brookings Institution, 1994), 1019. Also Aleksandr A. Lyakhovsky, *New Russian Evidence on the Crisis and War in Afghanistan*, Working Paper no. 51 (Draft), (Washington, DC: Woodrow Wilson International Center for Scholars, 2007), 70–71.

87. Bradsher, *Afghan Communism and Soviet Intervention*, 99.

88. "The Afghan Archive," *Washington Post*, November 15, 1992, A32.

89. Ibid.

90. Anwar, *Tragedy of Afghanistan*, 190.

91. Lyakhovsky, *Tragedy and Valor*, 56.

92. Haji Daoud was an eyewitness to the December 27 Soviet attack on the Radio-Television Center. Much of the description of the attack is taken from my May 22, 2006, interview with Daoud and a paper he provided to me.

93. Garthoff, *Détente and Confrontation*, 1018; Bradsher, *Afghan Communism and Soviet Intervention*, 98.

94. Bradsher, *Afghan Communism and Soviet Intervention*, 99.

95. FBIS-BK-2107085399, Hong Kong AFP, 0732 GMT, July 21, 1991.

8—GREEN DAWN

1. The muezzin calls Muslims to prayer.

2. The Kaaba, "cube" in Arabic, is a 42-foot-high cube-shaped structure set in the courtyard of the Grand Mosque in Mecca. The Koran states that the structure, which is now covered by a black and gold curtain, was built by the Prophet Abraham and his son Ishmael, who is believed to be the common ancestor of Arabs, though one Islamic tradition holds that the Kaaba was built by Adam, the first man. Shia are taught that Ali, the originator of Shiism, the sect's namesake and the Prophet's son-in-law and cousin, was born in the Kaaba. Today, millions of Muslim pilgrims circle the Kaaba counterclockwise during the annual Haj pilgrimage, gazing toward a black stone embedded in one wall of the Kaaba as they pass. Possibly a meteorite fragment, it symbolizes the union between heaven and earth.

3. The sacred Adhan is the Muslim call to prayer, a function traditionally performed by church bells in most Christian churches. It has been a Christian tradition to cast scripture onto the surface of bells. Cast onto the Liberty Bell at Philadelphia is a quote from Leviticus 25:10: "Proclaim liberty throughout all the land unto all the inhabitants thereof," in essence "let freedom ring." Churches and mosques are traditionally oriented toward Jerusalem and Mecca, respectively, thereby encompassing sacred space and dogma in their place of worship. Fr. Mark Sargeant, Diocese of London, Ontario, Canada, National Federation of Presbyteral Councils, interview with author, December 21, 2010.

4. The Muslim holy city of Mecca lies about 2,000 miles southwest of Kabul.

5. The number of estimated insurgents in the Grand Mosque uprising varies from five hundred to several thousand.

6. Yaroslav Trofimov, *The Siege of Mecca: The Forgotten Uprising in Islam's Holiest Shrine and the Birth of Al Qaeda* (New York: Doubleday, 2007), 7, 254.

7. Although Saudis generally believe "Wahhabism" does not accurately identify their religion, the term is widely used by Western writers and others, including some Saudis, in the Muslim world to describe the literalist and fundamentalist interpretation of Islam preached by its founder, Muhammad ibn Abd al-Wahhab, and practiced by most Saudis today.

8. Robert M. Gates, *From the Shadows: The Ultimate Insider's Story of Five Presidents and How They Won the Cold War* (New York: Simon and Schuster, 1996), 349; Nawaf E. Obaid, "The Power of Saudi Arabia's Islamic Leaders," *Middle East Quarterly* 6, no. 3 (1999): 7.

9. By the eighteenth century, the Papal States, ruled by the pope, had expanded to include most of Italy, including Rome. In 1870, Giuseppe Garibaldi, Italy's great

unifier, declared war on the Papal States, captured Rome, and reduced papal sovereignty to the Vatican.

10. Richard S. Dunn, *The Age of Religious Wars, 1559–1715* (New York: W. W. Norton, 1979), 1.

11. Anthony Shahid, "Abdullah Seals His Claim to the Saudi Throne," *Washington Post*, August 4, 2005, A15.

12. Joseph A. Kechichian, "The Role of the Ulama in the Politics of an Islamic State: The Case of Saudi Arabia," *International Journal of Middle East Studies* 18, no. 1 (1986): 69; Noah Feldman, *The Fall and Rise of the Islamic State* (Princeton: Princeton University Press, 2008), 30.

13. The Koran, the foundation of Sharia, presents the Prophet's teachings based on the revelations he received from Allah through the angel Gabriel. The Sunnah (the Path), the second most important source of Sharia, contains the sayings and behavior of the Prophet during his life as recorded by his contemporaries. *Hadith* refers to interpretations of the Koran and the Prophet's sayings by important religious scholars. Although sometimes contradictory, these are regularly used by Muslim judges and scholars to reach decisions.

14. Kechichian, "The Role of the Ulama," 53, 58.

15. "Caliph" literally means a "substitute" for the Prophet.

16. Muslim countries in South and Southeast Asia where various forms of constitutional democracy is practiced include Afghanistan, Pakistan, Bangladesh, Malaysia, and Indonesia.

17. Kechichian, "The Role of the Ulama," 53.

18. Abd al-Wahhab argued that Allah's oneness transcends the universe; Sufis believe God is omnipresent.

19. John L. Esposito, *Islam: The Straight Path* (London: Oxford University Press, 1990).

20. Wahhabi clothes matched those worn in Arabia during the Prophet's life.

21. "Ikhwan (Saudi Arabia)," Hobson's Choice, www.jamesrmaclean.com/mw/index.php/Ikhwan_(Saudi_Arabia).

22. Jacob Goldberg, "The Shi'i Minority in Saudi Arabia," in Juan R.I. Cole and Nikki R. Keddie, eds., *Shi'ism and Social Protest* (New Haven, CT: Yale University Press, 1986), 235.

23. The Saudi Chief Mufti, the supreme religious leader in Saudi Arabia, has remained in the hands of Abd al-Wahhab's al-Sheikh dynasty to this day.

24. King Saud was deposed by his brothers in 1964.

25. Steve Coll, *The Bin Ladens: An Arabian Family in the American Century* (New York: Penguin, 2008), 157.

26. The one rupture in the understanding occurred toward the end of the 1973 Arab-Israeli War. King Faisal joined the Arab oil embargo on the United States to protest American support for Israel. It is said that Faisal quietly transferred $4 billion to the American government to cushion the blow.

27. David Pryce-Jones, *The Closed Circle: An Interpretation of the Arabs* (Chicago: Ivan R. Dee, 2002), 275.

28. While over 50 percent of college graduates in Saudi Arabia are women, they comprise only 7 percent of the workforce. See Craig Smith, "Underneath Saudi Women Keep their Secrets," *New York Times*, December 3, 2002, 4.

29. David B. Ottaway, "Pressure Builds on the Key Pillar of Saudi Rule," *Washington Post*, June 8, 2004.

30. A more liberal interpretation of this hadith limits the forbidden area to the sacred ground of Mecca and Medina, where only Muslims are permitted to go.

31. Pryce-Jones, *The Closed Circle*, 262.

32. Kechichian, "The Role of the Ulama," 62.

33. Quoted in ibid., 67.

34. Ibid.

35. Trofimov, *Siege of Mecca*, 171.

36. This account of the fighting at the Grand Mosque is largely taken from Trofimov's *Siege of Mecca*. Trofimov, like many others, is skeptical of the Saudi government's official death toll of 117 rebels and 127 on the government side. Unofficial estimates range significantly higher than 1,000. Trofimov, *Siege of Mecca*, 225.

37. Estimates of the number of insurgents who attacked the Grand Mosque range from around 500 to some 1,500. *Le Point*, no. 385, February 4, 1980, 53, as quoted in Kechichian, "The Role of the Ulama," 70.

38. Goldberg, "The Shi'i Minority in Saudi Arabia," 243.

39. Vali Nasr, quoted in the *Herald* (Karachi), September 1962.

40. The Koran describes two jihads. *Jihad Akbar* (Greater Jihad) is the inner struggle whereby Muslims strive to overcome sin and lead a religious life. *Jihad bil Saif* (Lesser Jihad) requires Muslims to come together to fight a defensive war when Islam is threatened by an outside force.

41. Qutb's execution by President Nasser in 1966 inspired not only the Muslim Brotherhood to carry forward his teachings but also other Islamic militants around the world.

42. Gilles Keppel, *Jihad: The Trail of Political Islam* (Cambridge, MA: Belknap Press, 2002), 175–176.

43. Bruce Lawrence, ed., *Messages to the World: The Statements of Osama bin Laden*, translated by James Howarth (New York: Verso, 2005), 26.

44. Abdulla Azzam, "Defence of the Muslim Lands—The First Obligation After Imam," English translation from www.religioscope.com/info/doc/jihad/azzam _defence_4_chap2.htm.

45. The Saud royal family hired Mohammad bin Laden to renovate and expand the Grand Mosque in Mecca in the 1950s and 1960s. His construction company's blueprints of the mosque's underground labyrinth of passageways and rooms were used by Saudi security forces to ferret out, capture, and kill Juhaiman and his followers. For further information on bin Laden's early life, see Coll, *The Bin Ladens*,

137–153; and Steve Coll, *Ghost Wars: The Secret History of the CIA, Afghanistan, and bin Laden, from the Soviet Invasion to September 10, 2001* (New York: Penguin, 2004); Lawrence Wright, *The Looming Tower* (New York: Alfred A. Knopf, 2006), 75–81.

46. An acquaintance of Osama bin Laden's recalled that bin Laden had joined the Muslim Brotherhood when in high school. Coll, *The Bin Ladens*, 146–148.

47. The Saudi minister of Islamic affairs held official administrative positions in the IIRO and WAMY.

48. The growing wealth among private Saudis throughout the 1970s and 1980s contributed to the sharp upswing in Wahhabi proselytizing overseas. The Muslim religious tradition of *zakat*, calling on Muslims to make annual payments to those in need, also played an important role in fundraising. Zakat, a tax, is one of the five pillars of Islam. Individuals provide 2.5 percent of their annual earnings, if possible. In another category of giving called *osha*, Muslims donate additional cash to humanitarian and religious causes.

49. Anthony Cordesman, "Saudi Arabia: Opposition, Islamic Extremism, and Terrorism," *Gulfwire Perspectives*, December 1, 2002.

50. Mark Huband, *Warriors of the Prophet: The Struggle for Islam* (Boulder: Westview Press, 1998), 3.

51. Abu Zayd, "Shaykh Bin Baz—'This Man Did Not Belong to This Century,'" August 4, 2008, ibn1brahim.wordpress.com/2008/08/04/shaykh-bin-baz.

52. Warren Richey, "Trouble Goes Abroad: How a Terrorist Haven Was Born," *Christian Science Monitor*, October 4, 2001; Don Van Natta Jr., with Timothy L. O'Brien, "Saudis Promising Action on Terror," *New York Times*, September 14, 2003, 1; Glenn Kessler, "Saudis Tie al-Qaeda Cell to Attacks: At Least 7 Americans Among 27 Dead in Coordinated Bombings," *Washington Post*, May 14, 2003, A22.

53. Faye Bowers, "Why Saudis Take Firmer Stance on Terror," *Christian Science Monitor*, July 31, 2003, 2.

9—INSUBORDINATE PUPPETS

1. Vasili Mitrokhin, *The KGB in Afghanistan*, Working Paper no. 40, Cold War International History Project (Washington, DC: Woodrow Wilson International Center for Scholars, 2002, updated 2009), www.wilsoncenter.org/topics/pubs/ACFAE9.pdf, 107.

2. Reza Sher Mohammadi, "Ismail Khan: Foreign Troops Must Not Stay Long," October 5, 2008, www.afghanistannewscenter.com/news/2008/october/oct5 2008.html#10.

3. John Burns, "U.S. Repeats Soviet Missteps in Afghanistan, Envoy Says," *New York Times*, October 20, 2008, www.nytimes.com/2008/10/20/world/asia/20iht-kabul.1.17101948.html. See also Alastair Leithead, "Is NATO Repeating the USSR's Mistakes?" BBC News, May 15, 2008, http://news.bbc.co.uk/2/hi/7402887.stm. Zamir Kabulov was one of the Soviet Union's, later Russia's, most

experienced Afghan hands from 1983 to the present. Reputed by some to be a KGB officer, he served as a diplomat in Kabul from 1983 to 1987. He was Russian ambassador to Afghanistan from 2004 to 2009. In between Kabul assignments, Kabulov, an ethnic Uzbek, developed impressive regional expertise during his appointments to the Soviet embassies in Tehran (1979–1983) and Islamabad (1992–1996), with the UN mission on Afghanistan (1996–1998), at the Bonn conference (November–December 2001), and as deputy director of the Russian Foreign Affairs Ministry's department handling South Asian affairs.

4. Artemy Kalinovsky, *The Blind Leading the Blind: Soviet Advisors, Counter-Insurgency and Nation-Building in Afghanistan*, Working Paper no. 60, Cold War International History Project (Washington, DC: Woodrow Wilson International Center for Scholars, 2010), 18–19, 25, 27.

5. Georgy M. Korniyenko, "The Afghan Endeavor," *Journal of South Asian and Middle Eastern Studies* 17, no. 2 (1994): 3.

6. "Soviet Foreign Ministry Circular (27 December 1979)," addressed "to all Soviet Ambassadors," Boris Gromov, *Ogranichenny Kontingent* (Limited Contingent), (Moscow: Progress, 1994), 88–89, in Christian Ostermann, ed., "New Evidence on the War in Afghanistan," Woodrow Wilson International Center for Scholars, *Cold War International History Project Bulletin*, no. 14/15 (2003–2004): 239 (1 of 2), www.coldwar.hu/html/en/publications/b%E9k%E9s-afghanistan.pdf.

7. Ibid., 239–240 (Gromov, 91–95), circular 2 of 2. The second circular was issued the same day.

8. Marshall D. Shulman, "Tales of Afghanistan, Moscow Style," *Current Policy*, no. 43 (1980).

9. United Nations General Assembly, Resolution ES-6/2, January 14, 1980, "reaffirms the right of the Afghan people to determine their own form of government." Without mentioning the Soviet Union, it called for the immediate withdrawal of foreign troops from Afghanistan. In contrast, the European Parliament meeting in Strasbourg in early January 1980 passed a resolution condemning the Soviet invasion of Afghanistan. It called for Soviet troops to withdraw. "The European Community Response to the Afghanistan Crisis," *European Community News*, no. 3/1980, January 18, 1980, declassified October 3, 1983.

10. U.S. Department of State, Bureau of Public Affairs, "Afghanistan: U.N. General Assembly Acts on Soviet Invasion," Statement of Ambassador Donald F. McHenry to the United Nations General Assembly, *Current Policy*, no. 128 (1980). Except for 1982, when there was a two-vote drop in the number of nations condemning the Soviet invasion of Afghanistan (from 116 to 114), the UN General Assembly majorities against the invasion steadily climbed upward, from 104 in 1980 to 123 in 1987, the year before the Soviet Union announced its withdrawal timetable.

11. Raymond Garthoff, *Détente and Confrontation: American-Soviet Relations from Nixon to Reagan* (Washington, DC: Brookings Institution, 1985), 972.

12. Doyle McManus, "Soviet Intervention Called 'Hostile Act' Against Iran," *Pittsburgh Press*, December 28, 1979.

13. Jeddah cable 530, "Saudi Committee to Collect Funds for Afghan Muslims," January 26, 1980, unclassified.

14. Todd Anthony Rosa, "Three Key Phases in the U.S. Response to Soviet Involvement in Afghanistan: What Do the Documents Tell Us, and What Is Left to Learn?" Presentation to the conference "Towards an International History of the War in Afghanistan, 1979–1989," conference organized by the Cold War International History Project at the Woodrow Wilson Center, Washington, D.C., April 29–30, 2002, documents compiled by Christian F. Ostermann and Mircea Munteanu.

15. Malcolm Byrne and Vladislav Zubok, "The Intervention in Afghanistan and the Fall of Détente: A Chronology," in author's files; Letter from Brezhnev to Carter, December 29, 1979, Carter Library Archive, Brzezinski Donated Box 18, reply to an appeal of President Carter on the U.S. position regarding the Soviet invasion of Afghanistan, online at Margaret Thatcher Foundation website, www.margaret thatcher.org/document/8490EE61C7B84A018B22B1029DA8CF20.pdf; Marshall Shulman, special adviser on Soviet affairs, to Secretary of State Cyrus Vance, February 15, 1980, secret, declassified March 9, 1995, 6.

16. Anatoly Dobrynin, *In Confidence: Moscow's Ambassador to America's Six Cold War Presidents (1962–1986)* (New York: Random House, 1995), 451.

17. Ibid.; Karen Brutents, *Thirty Years on Staraya Square*, translated by Haik Gugarats (Moscow: Mezhdunarodnye Otnoshenia, 1998), 455.

18. "CPSU CC Politburo Decision on Afghanistan, with Report by Gromyko-Andropov-Ustinov-Zagladin," April 7, 1980, APRF, f.3, op.82, d.176, 11.9-17, translated by Svetlana Savranskaya, Cold War International History Project, Woodrow Wilson International Center for Scholars, Virtual Archive, www.wilsoncenter.org.

19. Dobrynin, *In Confidence*, 450.

20. U.S. Department of State, Intelligence and Research Bureau (INR), "Soviet Motives in Afghanistan," memorandum to Secretary of State Cyrus Vance, March 4, 1980, secret, declassified March 8, 1990.

21. James M. McCormick, *American Foreign Policy & Process*, 3d ed. (Itasca, IL: F. E. Peacock, 1998), 143.

22. Peter Schweizer, *Reagan's War: The Epic Story of His Forty-Year Struggle and Final Triumph over Communism* (New York: Doubleday, 2002), 115.

23. Thomas G. Paterson, Garry J. Clifford, and Kenneth J. Hagan, *American Foreign Relations: A History Since 1895*, vol. 2, 4th ed. (Lexington, MA: D. C. Heath, 1995), 505.

24. Letter from Brezhnev to Carter, December 29, 1979, in author's files.

25. Paterson et al., *American Foreign Relations*, 509.

26. Henry S. Bradsher, *Afghan Communism and Soviet Intervention* (Karachi: Oxford University Press, 2000), 104. In order to maintain balance with India, the

Reagan administration permitted New Delhi to manufacture the GE-404 aircraft engine used in American F-14 combat fighters. An Indo-American technology agreement was signed, opening the way for India to acquire a range of previously denied dual-use technology items.

27. "Andropov Gromyko Ustinov Ponomarev Report on Events in Afghanistan on 27–28 December 1979," Central Committee, Communist Party of the Soviet Union, top secret, online at Cold War International History Project, Virtual Archive, www.wilsoncenter.org.

28. Ibid.

29. Ibid.

30. Bruce J. Amstutz, *Afghanistan: The First Five Years of Soviet Occupation* (Washington, DC: National Defense University Press, 1986), 289.

31. Ibid., 288.

32. Kalinovsky, *The Blind Leading the Blind*, 12, citing Thomas T. Hammond, *Red Flag over Afghanistan: The Communist Coup, the Soviet Invasion, and the Consequences* (Boulder: Westview Press, 1990), 152.

33. Gennady Bocharov, *Russian Roulette: Afghanistan Through Russian Eyes* (London: Hamish Hamilton, 1990), 59–62.

34. Brutents, *Thirty Years*, 123.

35. The KHAD acronym stands for Khedamat-i-Ettelat-i-Daulet (Government Information Agency). KGB advisers made KHAD a KGB clone. Its line directorates mirrored the KGB organizational chart in Moscow, and KGB officers participated in KHAD arrests, interrogations, and torture sessions. Afghan employees of the American embassy who were summoned to KHAD headquarters were first interrogated by English-speaking KGB officers and then handed off to Afghan KHAD interrogators. (Interview with an Afghan employee at the U.S. embassy in the year after the Soviet invasion. He fled Afghanistan and now lives in the United States, where he wishes to remain anonymous.)

36. Bradsher, *Afghan Communism and Soviet Intervention*, 123.

37. Document 12, "Meeting of CC CPSU Politburo, January 17, 1980," in "The September 11th Sourcebooks, vol. 2, Afghanistan: Lessons from the Last War. The Soviet Experience in Afghanistan: Russian Documents and Memoirs," translated by Svetlana Savranskaya, National Security Archive, George Washington University, www.gwu.edu/~nsarchiv/NSAEBB/NSAEBB57/soviet.html. Also found in "Andropov Gromyko Ustinov Ponomarev Report on Events in Afghanistan on 27–28 December 1979."

38. Kabul 2203, "Situation in Afghanistan," July 27, 1980, confidential, declassified August 14, 1989.

39. Amstutz, *Afghanistan*, 78–79.

40. J. N. Dixit, *An Afghan Diary: Zahir Shah to Taliban* (Delhi: Konark, 2000), 415.

41. Mitrokhin, *The KGB in Afghanistan*, 135. A samovar is the equivalent of the teapot but much larger, finely decorated in Russian style, with a spigot at the bottom.

42. Ibid.

43. Ibid.

44. "Andropov Gromyko Ustinov Ponomarev Report on Events in Afghanistan on 27–28 December 1979." See also Aleksandr Lyakhovsky, *Inside the Soviet Invasion of Afghanistan, and the Seizure of Kabul*, Working Paper no. 51, Cold War International History Project (Washington, DC: Woodrow Wilson International Center for Scholars, 1979).

45. Bocharov, *Russian Roulette*, 10–12.

46. Martin Ewans, *Afghanistan: A Short History of Its People and Politics* (New York: HarperCollins, 2002), 158.

47. Bradsher, *Afghan Communism and Soviet Intervention*, 118.

48. Ewans, *Afghanistan*, 158.

49. Christopher Andrew and Vasili Mitrokhin, *The Sword and the Shield: The Mitrokhin Archive and the Secret History of the KGB* (New York: Basic Books, 1999), 123–124.

50. Ibid., 122–123.

51. Lester W. Grau and Michael A. Gress, eds., *The Soviet-Afghan War: How a Superpower Fought and Lost* (Lawrence, University Press of Kansas, 2002), 331.

52. CIA, "The Soviet Invasion of Afghanistan: Five Years After," May 1985, declassified in sanitized form, 1999, 9.

53. A Pittsburgh hospital fit Abdul Haq with a prosthetic foot in 1987.

54. Robert D. Kaplan, *Soldiers of God* (Boston: Houghton Mifflin, 1990), 178.

55. *Afghan Warrior: The Life and Death of Abdul Haq*, BBC documentary, Torch Productions, London, directed by Malcolm Brinkworth, 2003.

56. Masood's father, Dost Mohammad, died in a mysterious car accident in Peshawar.

57. "Ex-Soviet Commander Unveils Masoud's Secret Pact," *News International*, May 17, 2001.

58. Abdullah Azzam, *A Month with Heroes* (Pakistan: Publication Center of Martyr Azzam, 1996), translated from Dari to English by Daoud Mir.

59. Thirty-nine letters Masood sent to Rabbani between August 1, 1981, and June 15, 1988 (in author's files). They are numbered chronologically. This paragraph draws from letter no. 15, June 5, 1983, to Professor B. Rabbani; and letter no. 19, September 18, 1983, to his younger brother Ahmad Zia.

60. Masood, letter no. 15, June 5, 1983, in author's files.

61. Masood, letter no. 29, October 6, 1984, in author's files.

62. Masood, letter no. 1, August 1, 1981; letter no. 30, November 20, 1984, in author's files.

63. Mikhail S. Gorbachev, *Memoirs* (New York: Doubleday, 1996).

64. Sarah E. Mendelson, *Changing Course: Ideas, Politics, and the Soviet Withdrawal from Afghanistan* (Princeton: Princeton University Press, 1998), 73.

65. Conservative Vladimir Shcherbitsky, sixty-seven, the Ukrainian leader, was on an official visit to Washington and was unable to get back to Moscow in time to participate in Gorbachev's hastily convened meeting. The other missing conservative Politburo member was stuck on the steppes of Soviet Central Asia.

66. "Notes from Politburo Meeting, 21–22 January 1987 (Excerpt)," Gorbachev Foundation, Moscow, provided by Anatoly Chernyaev, translated by Gary Goldberg, in Ostermann, ed., "New Evidence on the War in Afghanistan," 145.

67. Ibid.

68. In November 2008, a highly decorated Soviet veteran of the Afghan war, Lieutenant General Ruslan Aushev, recalled that "in 1979, people gave us a very nice welcome. Exactly a year later, 40% of the people began to hate us. Five years later, 60% of the population hated us. And by the time we were to pull out, 90% hated us." Megan K. Stack, "The Other Afghan War," *Los Angeles Times*, November 23, 2008.

69. "Summary Report by the Commanding General," cited in A. Lyakhovsky, *The Tragedy and Valor of the Afghanistan Veteran* (Moscow: Iskon, 1995), 84–85. Contained in Document Reader, vol. 2, Russian and East European Documents, "Towards an International History of the War in Afghanistan. International Conference, 29–30 April 2002," Woodrow Wilson International Center for Scholars, Cold War International History Project, Virtual Archive, www.wilsoncenter.org ("CWIHP, Document Reader" hereafter).

70. "Record of a Conversation of M. S. Gorbachev with the General Secretary of the Central Committee of the People's Democratic Party of Afghanistan, Cde. Najib, 20 July 1987," Gorbachev Foundation, Moscow, provided by Anatoly Chernyaev, translated by Gary Goldberg, in Ostermann, ed., "New Evidence on the War in Afghanistan," 149.

71. Captain Stephen K. Iwicki, U.S. Army, "The United States Decision to Provide Stinger Missiles to Afghanistan," research paper submitted to the National Defense Intelligence College, Washington, D.C., March 1992, p. 3.

72. Steve Coll, *Ghost Wars: The Secret History of the CIA, Afghanistan, and bin Laden, from the Soviet Invasion to September 10, 2001* (New York: Penguin, 2004), 277.

73. Milton Bearden and James Risen, *The Main Enemy: The Inside Story of the CIA's Final Showdown with the KGB* (New York: Random House, 2003), 312.

74. "Notes from Politburo Meeting, 21–22 January 1987 (Excerpt)," in Ostermann, ed., "New Evidence on the War in Afghanistan," 145.

75. Grau and Gress, *The Soviet-Afghan War*, 43.

76. "11 August 1988 Report on Masood and His Panshir Forces: Excerpt from GRU [Chief Intelligence Directorate of the General Staff of USSR Armed Forces]," Alexander Lyakhovsky, *Plamya Afghana* [Flame of the Afghan Veteran] (Moscow:

GPI Iskon, 1999), 483–484, translated for the Cold War International History Project by Gary Goldberg; CWIHP, Document Reader.

77. Korniyenko, "The Afghan Endeavor," 11.

78. Anatoly Chernyaev, *My Six Years with Gorbachev*, translated and edited by Robert English and Elizabeth Tucker (University Park: Pennsylvania State University Press, 2000), 42.

79. Mikhail Gorbachev, message to East German leader Erich Honecker, June 5, 1986, in author's files; Document 18, "Session of CC CPSU Politburo, November 13, 1986," in "The September 11th Sourcebooks, vol. 2."

80. Document 18, "Session of CC CPSU Politburo, November 13, 1986," in "The September 11th Sourcebooks, vol. 2"; Gilles Dorronsoro, *Revolution Unending: Afghanistan, 1979 to the present*, translated from French by John King (New York: Columbia University Press, in association with the Centre d'études et de recherches internationales, Paris, 2005), 192.

81. Korniyenko, "Afghan Endeavor," 11.

82. In the end, Gorbachev's appointments did not gain him personal loyalties, nor did they change antireform rigidity within the entrenched intelligence and military bureaucracies. KGB resistance to his policies continued after he made Kryuchkov KGB chief in 1988. Nor did Gorbachev's replacement of Defense Minister Sokolov with General Dmitry Yazov alter the Soviet military's opposition to his reforms. Kryuchkov, Yazov, Varennikov, and Akhromeyev, his personal military adviser, betrayed Gorbachev when they led the August 1991 coup to overthrow him.

83. Document 18, "Session of CC CPSU Politburo, November 13, 1986," in "The September 11th Sourcebooks, vol. 2."

84. Ibid., 179.

85. "Notes from Politburo Meeting, 21–22 May 1987 (Excerpt)," Gorbachev Foundation, Moscow, provided by Anatoly Chernyaev, translated by Gary Goldberg, in Ostermann, ed., "New Evidence on the War in Afghanistan," 148.

86. "Record of a Conversation of M. S. Gorbachev with President of Afghanistan Najibullah, 23 August 1990," Gorbachev Foundation, Moscow, provided by Anatoly Chernyaev, translated by Gary Goldberg, in Ostermann, ed., "New Evidence on the War in Afghanistan," 189.

87. "Record of a Conversation of M. S. Gorbachev with the General Secretary of the Central Committee of the People's Democratic Party of Afghanistan Cde. Najib, 20 July 1987 (Excerpt)," in Ostermann, ed., "New Evidence on the War in Afghanistan," 160.

88. "Notes from Politburo Meeting, 21–22 May 1987 (Excerpt)," in Ostermann, ed., "New Evidence on the War in Afghanistan," 148.

89. "Analysis by Soviet Military Experts," in Lyakhovsky, *Plamya Afghana*, 327–331, cited in CWIHP, Document Reader.

90. Ibid.

91. Ibid.

92. Gulabzoi remained in the Soviet Union until Najib's regime imploded in April 1992. After 9/11, Gulabzoi returned to Afghanistan and won a seat in Parliament to represent his native province of Paktiya. During his campaign, he assured his mostly Zadran tribal constituency that, when PDPA interior minister, he had never killed a single Zadran. Carlotta Gall, "Return of Former Communists Stirs Up Afghan Elections," *New York Times*, September 5, 2005.

93. "November 1988: Issues for Discussions with Masood," in Lyakhovsky, *Plamya Afghana*, 497–498, cited in CWIHP, Document Reader.

94. "18 December 1988: Letter from Advisor to Ahmad Shah Massoud," in Lyakhovsky, *Plamya Afghana*, 497–498, cited in CWIHP, Document Reader.

95. Ibid.

96. Boris Gromov, *Ogranichenny Kontingent* (Limited Contingent) (Moscow: Progress, 1994), 89.

97. Paul R. Gregory, "Lenin's Brains and Other Tales from the Secret Soviet Archives," *Hoover Digest*, no. 2 (2008): 131–132.

98. Lyakhovsky, *Tragedy and Valor*, 503–504.

99. Ibid.

100. Lyakhovsky, *Plamya Afghana*.

101. Korniyenko, "Afghan Endeavor," 17.

102. Bearden and Risen, *The Main Enemy*, 358–359.

10—THE GENERAL'S VISION

1. State 160223, U.S. Department of State, Bureau of Intelligence and Research, "INR Analysis—Afghanistan: The Man Who Would Be King," May 20, 1992, secret, declassified April 6, 2000.

2. David Rhode, "Can Pakistan Mix Well with Democracy?" *New York Times*, June 17, 2007, 4.

3. *Dawn*, Independence Day Supplement, August 14, 1999, www.pakistani.org/ pakistan/legislation/constituent_address_11aug1947.html.

4. See CIA, "Pakistan: The Next Years," November 8, 1982, www.faqs.org/cia/ docs/31/0001101023/PAKISTAN:-THE-NEXT-YEARS.html. India's democratic development since its independence has been interrupted only once, in 1975–1976 after Prime Minister Indira Gandhi declared a state of emergency and assumed dictatorial power. India has conducted fifteen general elections since 1947. Ruling parties have peacefully transferred power to opposition parties following elections. India's functioning democratic institution and growing middle class have dampened ethnocentric tensions, assisted economic growth, and fostered political stability. The Indian military has remained in the barracks.

5. Maharaja, "Great King," referred to the rulers of more than 500 semiautonomous "princely states" in the British Indian Empire.

6. The Ahmadi sect of Islam was established in 1889 in the Punjab by Mirza Ghulam Ahmad. Ahmad identified himself as a prophet. Anti-Ahmadi Muslims

charge that Ahmad's claim contravened the Islamic premise that Mohammad was the "seal" of the line of prophets going back to Abraham.

7. Uncoordinated Waziri, Mahsud, Afridi, and Mohmand Lashkars penetrated to the outskirts of Srinigar. Instead of occupying the Kashmir's capital, they shifted their attention to looting. India managed to airlift Sikh and Gurkha regiments to Kashmir and occupy Srinigar.

8. Steve Coll, *Ghost Wars: The Secret History of the CIA, Afghanistan, and bin Laden, from the Soviet Invasion to September 10, 2001* (New York: Penguin, 2004), 61; Shahid Javed Burki and Craig Baxter, *Pakistan Under the Military* (Boulder: Westview, 1991), 6–7.

9. Before he was executed, Zulfikar Ali Bhutto told a courtroom audience: "I chose a chief of staff from the Jamaat-i Islami and the result is now before us." S.V.R. Nasr, "Democracy and Islamic Revivalism," *Political Science Quarterly* 110, no. 2 (1995): 269.

10. George P. Shultz, *Turmoil and Triumph* (New York: Charles Scribners Sons, 1993), 1091.

11. Dennis Kux, *The United States and Pakistan, 1947–2000* (Washington, DC: Woodrow Wilson Center Press, and Baltimore: Johns Hopkins University Press, 2001), 272–273, 275–277.

12. Rizwan Hussain, *Pakistan and the Emergence of Islamic Militancy in Afghanistan* (Farnham, Surrey, UK: Ashgate, 2005), 150.

13. Mohammed Yousuf, *Afghanistan the Bear Trap: The Defeat of a Superpower* (Havertown, PA: Casemate, 1992), 67, 105.

14. Hussain, *Pakistan and the Emergence of Islamic Militancy in Afghanistan*, 146; George Arney, *Afghanistan: The Definitive Account of a Country at the Crossroads* (London: Mandarin, 1990), 159.

15. *The Economist*, December 12, 1981, 48.

16. Shuja Nawaz, *Crossed Swords: Pakistan, Its Army, and the Wars Within* (New York: Oxford University Press, 2009), 375. Nawaz, a Pakistani scholar, attributed this passage to "Conversations with various ISI veterans" (407n). Nawaz comes from a distinguished Pakistani military family. His brother, General Asif Nawaz, rose to be chief of army staff in 1991–1993.

17. Hussain, *Pakistan and the Emergence of Islamic Militancy in Afghanistan*, 139–140.

18. The Deobandi school originated in nineteenth-century British India as a reaction to Western modern and Hindu influences on Muslims. It advocated a literalist return to the "pure" Islam followed during the first century of Islam's existence.

19. Hassan Abbas, *Pakistan's Drift Into Extremism* (Armonk, NY: East Gate, 2005), 114.

20. James M. McCormick, *American Foreign Policy and Process* (Itasca, IL: F. E. Peacock, 1998), 169.

21. Islamabad 9475, "The Secretary's Visit to Pakistan: Afghanistan," June 1, 1983, secret, declassified April 2, 1999.

22. *Afghan Warrior: The Life and Death of Abdul Haq*, BBC documentary, Torch Productions, London, directed by Malcolm Brinkworth, 2003.

23. Letter to the author dated November 24, 1991. The embassy officer is still on active duty and wishes to remain anonymous.

24. Yousuf, *Afghanistan the Bear Trap*, 106.

25. *Frontline* television interview of CIA Station Chief Milton Bearden, August 15, 2009, www.pbs.org/wgbh/pages/frontline/interviews/bearden.html.

26. Peter L. Bergen, *Holy War, Inc.* (New York: Touchstone, 2002), 71–72.

27. Coll, *Ghost Wars*, 72.

28. Abdullah Anas, "Epilogue," in Abdullah Azzam, *A Month with Heroes* (Pakistan: Publication Center of Martyr Azzam, 1996), 97, 137, translated from Dari to English by Daoud Mir and Lina Haidari for the author.

29. "Blowback," *Jane's Intelligence Review*, August 2001, 1.

30. Coll, *Ghost Wars*, 87, 88.

31. The Jordanian government sentenced Khalifa to death in abstentia for attempting to overthrow Jordan's King Hussein. Khalifa's plot, uncovered in 1991, also targeted Hussein's son, Abdullah, the current Jordanian king. Abu Musab al Zarqawi, who was later to gain infamy in Iraq, served a prison sentence in Jordan for his involvement in the plot. See Yaroslav Trofimov, *The Siege of Mecca* (New York: Anchor Books, 2007), 250.

32. Punjabis and Pashtuns in the 1980s made up roughly 65 percent and 15 percent, respectively, of Pakistan's army and about 50 percent and 14 percent, respectively, of Pakistan's total population. "Pakistan Army," www.enotes.com/topic/pakistan_army.

33. According to one of the Afghan organizers of the Quetta loya jirga, the ISI, "like our bosses," ordered that the meeting be canceled. The organizers replied that it was too late for a cancellation. The next day, September 18, 1981, Pakistani security forces blocked Afghans from entering the tented area where the loya jirga was to be held. Author's interview with Afghan source who wishes to remain anonymous, June 19, 1999, Omaha, Nebraska.

34. Raja Anwar, *The Tragedy of Afghanistan: A First-Hand Account*, translated from Urdu by Khalid Hasan (London: Verso, 1988), 252–253.

35. U.S. Department of State, "INR Analysis—Afghanistan."

36. Iqbal Akhund, *Trial and Error: The Advent and Eclipse of Benazir Bhutto* (Karachi: Oxford University Press, 2000), 168.

37. The source was an Afghan who knew and worked with Colonel Faizan (pseudonym) at the time. He wishes to remain anonymous.

38. Gul's duplicity surfaced during a 1987 meeting with a respected British writer, Sandy Gall. Gall presented hard evidence that Hekmatyar commanders had

murdered a British photographer in Nuristan. Gall cited Hamid Gul as claiming that: "Your friend was killed by agents of the Kabul government, the KHAD." Gall later wrote, "I knew he was lying, but I also knew that the ISI would never allow Gulbuddin to be implicated." Sandy Gall, *Behind Russian Lines: An Afghan Journal* (New York: St. Martin's Press, 1984), 176. Also see p. 762, n. 27.

39. Milton Bearden and James Risen, *The Main Enemy: The Inside Story of the CIA's Final Showdown with the KGB* (New York: Random House, 2003), 309.

40. Hussain, *Pakistan and the Emergence of Islamic Militancy in Afghanistan*, 201. Gul admitted to organizing the IJI in a January 2001 interview to the Pakistani magazine *Herald*. See Syed Ali Dayan Hasan, "What Is a Prime Minister?" Interview with General (Ret.) Hameed Gul, former director general of the ISI, *Herald* (Pakistan monthly), January 2001, www.ppp.org.pk/issues/partyissues.html. The name means Islamic Democratic Alliance.

41. Owen Bennett Jones, *Pakistan: Eye of the Storm* (New Haven, CT: Yale University Press, 2003), 240.

42. Ibid.

43. Hasan, "What Is a Prime Minister?"

44. The brigadier was an ISI officer at the time. He asked that his name not be cited.

45. In 1987, Zia agreed to a Pakistani-Iranian nonmilitary nuclear cooperation agreement, but he later blocked its implementation until his death. See John Lancaster and Kamran Khan, "Pakistanis Say Nuclear Scientists Aided Iran," *Washington Post*, January 24, 2004, A-1. After Zia's death, Beg secretly sent Pakistani nuclear scientist A. Q. Khan to Tehran to begin cooperation with Iran in nuclear technology, including centrifuges. Centrifuges are one avenue to enriching uranium to a weapon's grade standard. The centrifuges generated a breakthrough in Iran's stalled nuclear project. In 2008, the Pakistani information minister publicly acknowledged to reporters that A. Q. Khan "gave some centrifuges to Iran." "Iran Bought Centrifuges, Pakistan Says," *Washington Post*, March 11, 2005.

46. Akhund, *Trial and Error*, 122.

47. Ibid., 168.

48. Ibid., 172. Akhund was citing remarks by Humayun Asifi, a relative of Zahir Shah.

49. Islamabad 4374, "Afghan Shura: February 23 Vote," February 24, 1989, confidential, declassified February 19, 1990, and September 13, 2005.

50. Ibid.

51. Author's conversation with Prince Turki, January 8, 2007, Saudi embassy, Washington, D.C.

52. Kux, *The United States and Pakistan*, 298.

53. Ibid.

11—MISSION IMPOSSIBLE

1. The term "Mission Impossible" to describe my Afghan special envoy appointment is taken from Roy Gutman's *How We Missed the Story: Osama Bin Laden, the Taliban and the Hijacking of Afghanistan* (Washington, DC: United States Institute of Peace Press, 2008), 30.

2. David B. Ottaway, "Envoy Named to Afghan Resistance," *Washington Post*, April 6, 1989.

3. Kristen Lundberg, "Politics of Covert Action: The U.S., the Mujahidin and the Stinger Missile," Kennedy School of Government, Case Program C15-99-156.0, 57.

4. Chinese policymakers considered that the Soviet withdrawal from Afghanistan had removed one of the three "obstacles" to Sino-Soviet normalization. The two that remained were the massive Soviet troop concentrations on the Sino-Soviet border and Soviet support for Vietnam.

5. "Political/Military Situation," Tab A, Presidential Briefing Memorandum, March 1989, secret/NODIS, declassified April 4, 2000; Beijing 10512, "Hekmatyar Visit to Beijing," April 18, 1989, confidential, declassified April 4, 2000.

6. Steve Coll, *Ghost Wars: The Secret History of the CIA, Afghanistan, and bin Laden, from the Soviet Invasion to September 10, 2001* (New York: Penguin, 2004), 183.

7. Ibid.

8. Richard Mackenzie, "Afghan Games: How Pakistan Runs the War," *Insight on the News*, April 9, 1990, 14.

9. The Appropriations Act of 1989, section 306(c), stated: "(1) There is established in the Department of State the position of special envoy to the Afghan Resistance who shall be appointed by the President; (2) The special envoy shall hold the personal rank of Ambassador and shall coordinate United States policies and programs with the Afghan Resistance."

10. Secretary Baker's written answer to Senator Warren Rudman regarding appointment of an Afghan special envoy, following up on his January 19, 1989, Senate confirmation hearing. Secretary Baker's response was in February (the document is undated).

11. Ottaway, "Envoy Named to Afghan Resistance."

12. James Rupert, "Baker Favors Envoy to Mujahidin," *Washington Post*, March 18, 1989, A1.

13. Ibid.

14. "Bush to Send Special Envoy to Afghan Guerrilla Government," Xinhua News Agency, June 4, 1989.

15. "US appointing Envoy to Mujahideen," *Times of India*, April 7, 1989, 1.

16. "Bush to Send Special Envoy," Xinhua News Agency.

17. Jim Hoagland, "Why Does Baker Distrust His Own Department?" *Washington Post*, March 7, 1989.

18. Memorandum of Conversation, "Meeting with Senator Gordon Humphrey (June 7, 1989)," June 8, 1989, declassified, March 23, 2000. Participants in the Humphrey meeting were Deputy Secretary Lawrence Eagleburger, Deputy Assistant Secretary for Congressional Affairs Richard Mueller, Eagleburger staff aide Robyn Hinson-Jones, Senator Humphrey's senior aide Michael Pillsbury, plus one more staffer.

19. James. Q. Wilson, *Bureaucracy: What Government Agencies Do and Why They Do It* (New York: Basic Books, 1989), 188–189.

20. Statements by Deputy Secretary Eagleburger and the author, June 20, 1989, swearing-in ceremony, in author's files.

21. "Special Envoy to the Afghan Resistance," action memorandum, June 24, 1989, confidential, declassified March 23, 2002.

22. Haji Daoud had been in the Kabul Radio-Television Center when KGB commandos attacked it during the Soviet invasion. He proved a professionally competent, hardworking AMRC manager. By 1988, an average of twelve AMRC teams of cameramen and reporters roamed Afghanistan, sending back footage, photographs, and printed reports on Mujahidin military operations, Soviet atrocities, and the difficulties faced by ordinary Afghans in their war-torn country. At AMRC headquarters in Peshawar, Daoud distributed media products to major American news organizations, the BBC, Independent Television News in London, Agence France-Presse (AFP), and many other international outlets around the globe. Daoud assumed complete management of AMRC operations when the USIA-AMRC Boston University contract ended in 1988.

23. Senator Humphrey's two dynamic staff aides, Michael Pillsbury and Tom Klein, played critical roles in the Senate passage of the American assistance programs for the Mujahidin during the 1980s. Under Humphrey's guidance, they also helped persuade the Reagan administration to provide Stingers to the resistance over initial State Department and CIA objections.

24. *Congressional Record*, June 16, 1989, p. S6819.

25. Central Intelligence Agency, "USSR: Withdrawal from Afghanistan," Special National Intelligence Estimate, March 1988, secret, declassified April 4, 2000.

26. Office of the White House Press Secretary, Statement by President George H.W. Bush, February 16, 1989.

27. Sandy Gall, *News from the Front: A Television Reporter's Life* (London: Heinemann, 1994), 173. According to Gall, Andy Skrzypkowiak's "only crime was his friendship with Masud." His father "was a Polish army officer" and "was murdered by the KGB . . . grew up in Britain and joined the British Parachute Regiment. . . . After leaving the SAS, he became a freelance cameraman" and worked in Afghanistan.

12—POTEMKIN GOVERNMENT

1. Iqbal Akhund, *Trial and Error: The Advent and Eclipse of Benazir Bhutto* (Karachi: Oxford University Press, 2000), 173.

2. "Political/Military Situation," Tab A, Presidential Briefing Memorandum, March 1989, secret/NODIS, declassified April 4, 2000.

3. Howard B. Schaffer, deputy assistant secretary, Near East and South Asian Affairs, U.S. State Department, testimony to the House Subcommittee on Asian and Pacific Affairs, March 8, 1989.

4. Shamsul Hassan Wajid, private secretary to Prime Minister Benazir Bhutto, interview with author, December 15, 1999, Palais Saint Germaine Hotel, Paris.

5. "Benazir Blames ISI, MI for Destabilizing PPP Govts," Afghanistan News Center, May 2000, www.afghanistannewscenter.com/news/2000/may/may2i2000.htm.

6. Dennis Kux, *The United States and Pakistan, 1947–2000* (Washington, DC: Woodrow Wilson Center Press, and Baltimore: Johns Hopkins University Press, 2001), 302.

7. National Security Adviser Scowcroft warned Beg in early 1989 that Pakistan's nuclear program had moved it "very close to the line" triggering the Pressler Amendment aid cutoff, that the Bush administration's "hands are tied on the nuclear issue," and that President Bush would certify as long as he could but could "not lie." Kux, *The United States and Pakistan*, 299.

8. Islamabad 20176, "Public Affairs Positive on New Approach Towards Afghanistan," September 14, 1989, secret, declassified August 1, 2007.

9. To avoid reprisals, the Pakistani senior official requested that his name be withheld. The official went on to head important Pakistani diplomatic missions.

10. "Tomsen's Model of Islamic Government in Afghanistan," *Weekly Shahadat* (Hezb-i Islami), January 24, 1990.

11. *Muslim*, January 11, 1990, 3 (cartoon); *Muslim*, May 31, 1990, quoting the Muslim Brotherhood Arabic daily *Al Jihad*, published in Peshawar.

12. "U.S. Afghan Policy 'State Terrorism,'" Kabul Bakhtar News Agency, January 23, 1990, FBIS London, serial ID 2401075790.

13. TASS, "Afghan General Briefs Press on Upcoming Rebel Offensive," October 13, 1989.

14. James Rupert, "Soviet: U.S. Aids Afghan Rebel Planning," *Washington Post*, July 9, 1989.

15. "Statement by Press Secretary [Martin] Fitzwater on President [George H.W.] Bush's Meeting with Interim President Sibghatullah Mojaddedi of Afghanistan," November 27, 1989, in John T. Woolley and Gerhard Peters, *The American Presidency Project*, Santa Barbara, California, www.presidency.ucsb.edu/ws/?pid =17871.

16. Neither Ahmed Shah Masood nor Ismael Khan came to Pakistan during the eight-year Soviet-Afghan war.

17. Mike Malinowski was one of the Foreign Service's most experienced Afghan specialists. He covered the Afghan situation from Washington as an intelligence analyst in the Department of State's Intelligence and Research Bureau (1983–1985). When stationed at the American embassy in Kabul (1979–1980), he re-

ported on the Soviet invasion of Afghanistan. After six months as my deputy, in 1989 he was promoted to special assistant to Under Secretary Robert Kimmitt. His considerable expertise on South Asia was felt on the seventh floor and in the White House. He was director of the Pakistan, Afghanistan and Bangladesh Office in the State Department (1997–1999), where he became the only American official to talk to Mullah Omar. Omar rejected Malinowski's request to expel Osama bin Laden. Mike went on to serve as American ambassador to Nepal.

18. Ernest Thomas Greene, the former American consul in Tabriz, Iran, and a fluent Dari speaker, replaced Mike Malinowski as my deputy. Dick Hoagland replaced Tom in 1990. Dick later went on to ambassadorial assignments in Tajikistan and Kazakhstan.

19. Ziauddin Mojadedi was a priceless source of wisdom on Afghanistan and a friend and adviser. He later served on President Hamid Karzai's National Security Council. In 2007, President Karzai appointed him Afghan ambassador to Poland.

20. Said Hyder Akbar and Susan Burton, *Come Back to Afghanistan: Trying to Rebuild a Country with My Father, My Brother, My One-Eyed Uncle, Bearded Tribesmen, and President Karzai* (New York: Bloomsbury, 2005), 15.

21. *Afghan Warrior: The Life and Death of Abdul Haq*, BBC documentary, Torch Productions, London, directed by Malcolm Brinkworth, 2003.

22. Jere Van Dyk, "My Friend, the Afghan Warlord," *Baltimore Sun*, September 29, 2006.

23. Mary Ann Weaver, "Lost at Tora Bora," *New York Times*, September 11, 2005.

24. Akhund, *Trial and Error*, 169.

25. Haqqani deserted Hekmatyar's Hezb to join Khalis. Mullah Omar abandoned Nabi's Harakat.

26. In Afghanistan it is common practice for former students in universities to make the name of their academic discipline a title before their name. "Engineer" is the title most frequently used, even though the individual using it may never have earned a degree.

27. The accounts of the execution of the prisoners are taken from a February 10, 2008, interview I conducted with a Mujahidin from Jalalabad involved in the Jalalabad battle who wishes to remain anonymous.

28. Akhund, *Trial and Error*, 165.

29. During his academic career, Rabbani specialized in translating Sayyid Qutb's books calling for violent holy war against the West and pro-Western Muslim governments.

30. Rabbani represented Afghanistan at an October 19–23, 1991, conclave of the Muslim Brotherhood and other radical Islamist organizations in Tehran organized to reject the Madrid Peace Conference compromise for resolving the Palestinian-Israeli conflict.

31. "Afghans Will Support Pakistan in Case of Indian Aggression," *Frontier Post*, January 16, 1992, 1.

32. Exhibiting striking opportunism, Sayyaf later hosted and highly praised Zahir Shah after both had moved back to Kabul at the end of 2001.

33. After Soviet KGB commandos murdered Amin, his surviving wife and children were thrown into Pul-i-Charkhi prison. When they were eventually released, Sayyaf arranged their safe passage to the Khyber Agency, where they were given armed protection by one of Sayyaf's commanders before immigrating to Australia.

34. On January 8, 1998, a federal court in New York sentenced Yousef to 240 years in prison, plus life, for attempting to blow up the World Trade Center in 1993. The judge presiding at his New York trial recommended that he be kept in solitary confinement throughout his life term in prison. Yousef is a cousin of Khalid Sheikh Mohammed, who orchestrated the 9/11 attacks, and was involved in a number of other terrorist plots targeting the United States and its allies.

35. *The 9/11 Commission Report: Final Report of the National Commission on Terrorist Attacks upon the United States,* authorized ed. (New York: W. W. Norton, 2004), 146.

36. Mohammed Yousuf, *Afghanistan the Bear Trap: The Defeat of a Superpower* (Havertown, PA: Casemate, 1992), 105.

37. Ibid., 38.

38. Mojaddedi told me that, altogether, the PDPA regime executed 108 members of his family.

39. Fatima Gailani, like her father, Ahmad Gailani, married a member of the royal family. During the Soviet occupation, she spent much of her time in London, teaming up with Pakistan's future prime minister, Benazir Bhutto, in broadcasts by the BBC and other news organizations to support the Mujahidin and criticize the Soviet Union. She later studied for a master's degree in Islamic studies at London University. Her second marriage was to Dr. Ahmed al-Hadi, the head of the Afghan Millat Party.

40. Peshawar 1287, "Afghan Resistance Leaders Cancel Travel to Rome to Meet Zahir Shah," December 10, 1981, confidential, declassified.

13 — PAKISTAN PIVOTS

1. Peshawar 1523, "Major Mujahidin Internecine Massacre," July 15, 1989, confidential, declassified November 18, 2004. Ahmed Zia's account of the massacre was based on several days of radio communications with his older brother, Ahmed Shah Masood.

2. Neamat Nojumi, commander of Ismael Khan's Mujahidin, a Herati, told me in a January 7, 2008, interview that Khan negotiated the orderly Soviet withdrawal in correspondence with the Soviet 40th Army commander. According to Nojumi, Khan also used his Mujahidin shadow city council in Herat as a second channel of communication with the Soviet military.

3. Barnett R. Rubin, *The Fragmentation of Afghanistan: State Formation and Collapse in the International System* (New Haven, CT: Yale University Press, 1995), 260.

4. Neamat Nojumi, commander of Ismael Khan's Mujahidin, interview with author, January 7, 2008.

5. Daoud Mir, interview with author, February 17, 2008.

6. Ibid.

7. Ibid.

8. "Islamic Court to Try Jamal, His Men for Farkhar Massacre," *Afghan News*, vol 5, no. 16/17, September 1989.

9. Ibid.

10. Abdullah Anas was the nom de guerre of Algerian-born Boujema Baunouar. He first met Abdullah Azzam in 1984 during the Haj in Mecca.

11. In the mid-1980s, the British Secret Intelligence Service (SIS, also known as MI6) hosted Council of the North commanders and political cadres chosen by Masood to undergo training in military and combat arms. Several Masood advisers, including future Afghan foreign minister Dr. Abdullah Abdullah, were sent to study English and translate for the military trainees.

12. The country produced some 720,000 tons of opium in 1989, becoming the number two narcotics-producing nation in the world.

13. "Afghan Rebels Overlooked as Funds Flow to the Gulf," *Washington Times*, February 22, 1991.

14. Mullah Malang, interview with author, July 10, 1989, Quetta.

15. Commander Naqib's full name was Naqibullah.

16. The Soviets imprisoned Sabir during the occupation. Before evacuating Kandahar, they exchanged the respected religious cleric for two Soviet POWs at a brief ceremony 2 kilometers west of Kandahar.

17. As discussed in chapter 20, the Argestan Shura members were graduates of the Deobandi and Wahhabi madrassas managed by the Pakistani Jamiat-i Ulema-i Islam (JUI) and Arab radicals based in Pakistan. They included Abdul Razak, the future Taliban interior minister; Mullah Rabbani, later leader of the Taliban shura in Kabul (future Taliban leader Mullah Mohammad Omar was one of Mullah Rabbani's subcommanders during the Soviet-Afghan war); Sayyaf commander Mullah Turabi, later Taliban minister of justice; and Khalis commander Mullah Hassan, who would become the Taliban governor of Kandahar.

18. *Afghan Information Center Bulletin*, June–July 1991, nos. 123–124.

19. James Rupert, "After Years of Fighting in Afghan City of Kandahar, Armed Truce Sets In," *Washington Post*, July 16, 1989, A-24.

20. Quetta-based knowledgeable Mujahidin, interview with author, January 6, 2008.

21. The interviewer was author-journalist Roy Gutman, who recorded Ambassador Oakley's comment on Afghanistan's inclusion in Pakistan's sphere of influence in a 2007 interview. See Gutman's book *How We Missed the Story: Osama bin Laden, the Taliban and the Hijacking of Afghanistan* (Washington, DC: United States

Institute of Peace Press, 2008), 26. In *Ghost Wars: The Secret History of the CIA, Afghanistan, and bin Laden, from the Soviet Invasion to September 10, 2001* (New York: Penguin, 2004), Steve Coll cited Ed McWilliams as photocopying a high-level Oakley message to Washington urging officials to accept Pakistan's sphere of influence in Afghanistan.

22. "Report by the Soviet Ambassador Y. M. Vorontsov, Concerning the Current Political Situation Inside Afghanistan and the Possibilities of Solving the Afghan Question, Sent to the Heads of the Embassies and Legations of the Countries of the Socialist Commonwealth in Kabul, [3 February, 1989], State Central Archive, Prague, File 02/1, CC CPCz Politburo 1980–1989, 103rd Meeting, 3 February 1989, in Czech, translated by Todd Hammond and Derek Paton, in Christian Ostermann, ed., "New Evidence on the War in Afghanistan," Woodrow Wilson International Center for Scholars, *Cold War International History Project Bulletin*, no. 14/15 (2003–2004): 226–227, www.coldwar.hu/html/en/publications/b%E9k%E9s-afghanistan.pdf.

23. Steve Coll, *The Secret History of the CIA, Afghanistan, and bin Laden, from the Soviet Invasion to September 10, 2001* (New York: Penguin, 2004), 210.

24. Islamabad 15754, "Afghanistan—Internal Situation," July 22, 1989, secret/ NODIS, declassified.

25. Ibid.

26. See "The Fund for Peace: Promoting Sustainable Security. Failed States Index 2009," www.fundforpeace.org/web/index.php?option=com_content&task =view&id=99&Itemid=140; "Pakistan Recovers in Failed States Index," June 29, 2009, www.nation.com.pk/pakistan-news-newpaper-daily-english-online//Politics/ 29-Jun-2009/Pakistan-recovers-in-failed-states-index. By June 2009, Pakistan ranked tenth from the bottom in the Failed States Index, between Guinea and Ivory Coast.

27. U.S. Defense Intelligence Agency, "Mohammad Najib Replaces Babrak Karmal," unclassified, 88-DIA-0435-88-5F.

28. "Record of a Conversation of M. S. Gorbachev with President of Afghanistan, General Secretary of the CC PDPA Najibullah, Tashkent, 7 April 1988," Gorbachev Foundation, Moscow, provided by Anatoly Chernyaev, translated by Gary Goldberg, in Ostermann, ed., "New Evidence on the War in Afghanistan," 178.

29. A. Vasiliev, "Why Do We Not Leave Afghanistan," *Komsomolskaya Pravda*, June 29, 1991, FBIS-SOV-91-134, July 12, 1991.

30. Sandy Gall, "An Interview with Commander Ahmed Shah Masud, Former Minister of Defence, at His Base in Jebal Seraj, North of Kabul, on June 28, 1993," *Asian Affairs* 25, no. 2 (1994): 139–155, available at www.informaworld.com/ smpp/content~db=all~content=a738552617~frm=abslink. Sandy Gall, a respected and well-known correspondent, had interviewed Masood many times. Gall had covered the war in Afghanistan extensively.

14—TILTING AT WINDMILLS

1. Yuriy Tyssovskiy, "USSR: U.S. Policy in Afghanistan Viewed," TASS, November 1, 1990.

2. Dennis Kux, *The United States and Pakistan, 1947–2000* (Washington, DC: Woodrow Wilson Center Press, and Baltimore: Johns Hopkins University Press, 2001), 308.

3. David Rhode, "Nuclear Inquiry Skips Pakistan Army," *New York Times*, January 30, 2004.

4. A senior Pakistani Foreign Ministry official whom I often met is the source of this information. He was in a position to know but does not want his name to be revealed.

5. Kux, *The United States and Pakistan*, 313.

6. Opportunism influenced both sides in Sharif's alliance with the Pakistani Army. When Sharif attempted to expand his authority as prime minister in 1999, the military forced him from office.

7. Interview with Ahmed Rashid by Soutik Biswas, BBC, August 4, 2008.

8. Steve Coll, *Ghost Wars: The Secret History of the CIA, Afghanistan, and bin Laden, from the Soviet Invasion to September 10, 2001* (New York: Penguin, 2004), 208.

9. U.S. State Department, "Special Envoy Tomsen to Return to U.S.," September 1, 1989, secret/EXDIS Khyber, declassified March 23, 2000.

10. The quotations in this paragraph and the ones that follow are taken from Riyadh 6963, September 6, 1989, secret, declassified.

11. Presidential Findings are designed to ensure that every CIA covert action supports U.S. foreign policy goals and conforms to U.S. law.

12. Ambassador Richard Murphy, who served as assistant secretary of state for Near Eastern and South Asian Affairs from 1983 to 1989, stated that "it was the CIA's War, not State's." Kux, *The United States and Pakistan*, 266.

13. Lieutenant Colonel William P. Tangney, U.S. Army, "Trip Report: Pakistan Visit, 5–14 Nov 1989," Memorandum from the Office of the Deputy Assistant Secretary of Defense, Near Eastern and South Asian Affairs, November 20, 1989, secret, no foreign dissemination (NOFORN), declassified October 28, 2010.

14. Ibid.

15. The assassinations of moderate Afghans exiled in Pakistan began in 1988, when the Soviet withdrawal announcement heightened expectations that a regime change was coming in Kabul. That year, a seventy-six-year-old scholar, former Kapisa governor and outspoken Zahir Shah supporter, Sayed Bahauddin Majrooh, was shot dead one evening when answering a knock at his door. Masood's older brother was also abducted and killed in 1988. Assassins murdered two Afghan Millat Party members working for humanitarian aid organizations in Peshawar in 1989.

16. Cited in Henry S. Bradsher, *Afghan Communism and Soviet Intervention* (Karachi: Oxford University Press, 2000), 330.

17. Rahmillah Yusufzai, "Abducted Nurse Believed to Be Killed," *Frontier Times*, June 1, 1989.

18. Later, Chenzaie's widow and children were granted political asylum in the United States.

19. Islamabad 10379, "Afghanistan: Discussions with MFA on Recent Acts of Terrorism," July 16, 1991, confidential, declassified July 9, 2008.

20. A 1991 cable from Islamabad reported to Washington that the Afghan Construction and Logistics Unit (ACLU), the road-building organization, was "perceived as . . . controlled partly by the GOP [Government of Pakistan] and partly by Hekmatyar's party, both of which, it is alleged, have influenced ACLU's project selection." Islamabad 6012, "Afghanistan—Afghan Construction and Logistics Unit (ACLU)," May 2, 1991, unclassified.

21. The message is in author's files.

22. Brigadier Janjua and Colonel Imam's service in the ISI's Afghan Bureau began under Zia. As chief of the Peshawar office, Janjua planned Mujahidin military operations in eastern, central, and northern Afghanistan. He worked closely with Hamid Gul during and after Gul became ISI director general.

23. An Afghan source who wishes to remain anonymous, interview with author, August 2, 2008.

24. Kurt Lohbeck, *Holy War, Unholy Victory: Eyewitness to the CIA's Secret War in Afghanistan* (Washington, DC: Regnery Gateway, 1993), 273.

25. KGB officers saved Watanjar from Amin's clutches in September 1979. Soviet favor later made him one of the few Khalqis to consistently hold high government posts under Parchamis Karmal and Najib from 1980 to 1992. He was made a Politburo member in 1981. Watanjar replaced Khalqi Interior Minister Gulabzoi when he was exiled to Moscow in 1988 for anti-Parchami coup-plotting.

26. Sandy Gall, "An Interview with Commander Ahmed Shah Masud, Former Minister of Defence, at His Base in Jebal Seraj, North of Kabul, on June 28, 1993, *Asian Affairs* 25, no. 2 (1994): 141, available at www.informaworld.com/smpp/content~db=all~content=a738552617~frm=abslink.

27. Mushahid Hussain, "No Sign of Afghan Settlement," *Frontier Post*, September 12, 1989, 1.

28. Joelle Diderich, "EU Assembly Chief Backs Afghan Opposition," Reuters, April 6, 2001.

29. Steve Coll and James Rupert, "Afghan Rebels Reject Offensive; Pakistan, Backed by U.S., Tried to Press Guerrillas into Action," *Washington Post*, March 17, 1990, A19; Islamabad 06050, "Washington Post Article on Tanai Coup," March 20, 1990, confidential, declassified September 14, 2004.

30. Excerpts of testimony from Richard Clarke, former national coordinator for counterterrorism, in Steven Strasser and Craig R. Whitney, eds., *The 9/11 Investigations: Staff Reports of the 9/11 Commission. Excerpts from the House-Senate Joint Inquiry Report on 9/11. Testimony from 14 Key Witnesses, Including Richard Clarke,*

George Tenet, and Condoleezza Rice, PublicAffairs Reports (New York: PublicAffairs, 2004), 187.

15—WAHHABI EMIRATE

1. Coincidentally, Rudyard Kipling's nineteenth-century short story "The Man Who Would Be King" was also set in the Konar-Nuristan region of eastern Afghanistan. The two English aspiring monarchs met the same fate as Rahman.

2. The five pillars of Islam are: (1) making the declaration of faith (*shahada*) by which an individual becomes a Muslim—"There is no deity worthy of worship but God (Allah) and the Prophet Mohammad is his Messenger"; (2) saying prayers five times a day; (3) making payment of alms (*zakat*) once a year; (4) fasting during the holy month of Ramadan; and (5) conducting a pilgrimage (*haj*) to Mecca once in a lifetime.

3. James A. Placke, "CERA Decision Brief," Cambridge Energy Research Institute, September 1996, 1.

4. The upswing in Saudi oil output during the 1980s delivered a major blow to the sagging Soviet economy, which was heavily dependent on oil exports.

5. After the first Gulf War, during which Yemen supported Iraq, the Saudi government expelled the great majority of Yemeni guestworkers.

6. "Population," http://countrystudies.us/saudi-arabia/19.htm. According to the Country Studies' home page at http://countrystudies.us/, the website "contains the on-line versions of books previously published in hard copy by the Federal Research Division of the Library of Congress as part of the Country Studies/ Area Handbook Series sponsored by the U.S. Department of the Army between 1986 and 1998." The source for the information on Saudi Arabia is from Helen Chapin Metz, ed., *Saudi Arabia: A Country Study* (Washington, DC: Government Printing Office, for the Library of Congress, 1992).

7. David E. Long, *The Kingdom of Saudi Arabia* (Gainesville: University Press of Florida, 1997), 120.

8. Noah Feldman, *The Fall and Rise of the Islamic State* (Princeton, NJ: Princeton University Press, 2008), 1–4.

9. Ibid., 6.

10. Sayed A.I. Tomazi, *Profiles of Intelligence,* 2d ed. (Lahore, Pakistan: Combined Printers, 1995), 295–296.

11. Paul McGeough, "The Puppeteer," *Sydney Morning Herald,* October 8, 2002.

12. Long, *Kingdom of Saudi Arabia,* 121.

13. Sadako Ogata, *The Turbulent Decade: Confronting the Refugee Crises of the 1990s* (New York: Norton, 2005), 312.

14. The United States, Japan, and the European Union countries were the principal donors sustaining the refugees in Pakistan.

15. Peter Bergen, *Holy War, Inc.* (New York: Touchstone, 2001), 60.

16. Jamil Ziabi, "The Legal Ideologue of Al Qaeda Leader, Mussa al Qarni, Recalls the Stages of the Rise and Fall of the Islamic State Dream in Afghanistan," *Dar Al Hayat,* March 13, 2006, http://english.daralhayat.com.

17. "Interview: Milton Bearden," www.pbs.org/wgbh/pages/frontline/shows/binladen/interviews/bearden.html; Bergen, *Holy War, Inc.,* 60. According to Bearden, a senior U.S. intelligence official, there were about 2,000 Arabs in Afghanistan at any one time. Some Arabs were involved in combat, "but the people of Afghanistan fought the war, they bled, they died," said Bearden.

18. Wahhabis wave their heads and speak loudly when they pray. They stand, with their feet positioned apart from each other. Afghans pray in the Hanafi tradition, more silently and with their legs kept close together.

19. Barnett R. Rubin, *The Fragmentation of Afghanistan: State Formation and Collapse in the International System* (New Haven, CT: Yale University Press, 1995), 263; Abdullah Azzam, *A Month with Heroes* (Pakistan: Publication Center of Martyr Azzam, 1996), 140, translated from Dari to English by Daoud Mir and Lina Haidari for the author.

20. The source is a high-ranking Saudi official who does not want his name to be divulged.

21. Steve Coll, *The Bin Ladens: An Arabian Family in the American Century* (New York: Penguin, 2008), 340.

22. Ziabi, "The Legal Ideologue of Al Qaeda," 5.

23. U.S. Department of State, "The Attacks on the Usama bin Ladin Terrorist Network," fact sheet, August 20, 1998. Abdel Rahman is serving life imprisonment for his role in the 1993 World Trade Center bombing.

24. Abdullah Anas, "Epilogue," in Azzam, *A Month with Heroes.*

25. Coll, *The Bin Ladens,* 337–338; Bergen, *Holy War, Inc.,* 66.

26. Hekmatyar's media accusations that Masood had relationships with French nurses working in Council of the North medical facilities were picked up and disseminated by the Pakistani and Saudi press during the early 1980s. The nurses returned to France in 1984 and did not go back to Afghanistan.

27. The description of Azzam's trip is taken from Abdullah Azzam, *A Month with Heroes,* which ends with two chapters written after his death. One was added by the translator, the other by Abdullah Anas.

28. Azzam, *A Month with Heroes,* 90–100.

29. The word "all" in front of "directions" implied that Azzam had Pakistan in mind as well as the Soviet Union.

30. Details of Masood's 1989 in absentia "trial" in Peshawar are taken from Ziabi, "The Legal Ideologue of Al Qaeda."

31. Ibid.

32. All quotes from Azzam's public remarks in Saudi Arabia are taken from Abdullah Anas's epilogue to Azzam, *A Month with Heroes.*

33. Ziabi, "The Legal Ideologue of Al Qaeda."

34. Ibid.

35. Azzam, *A Month with Heroes*; Ziabi, "The Legal Ideologue of Al Qaeda."

36. Jamil ur-Rahman, an Afghan, was not related to the Egyptian terrorist Abdel Rahman. "Rahman" is a widely used Muslim name. It is one of the ninety-nine names of God in Muslim tradition. Rahman's birth name before he Arabized it was Mohammad Hussein.

37. *AIC* [Afghan Information Centre] *Monthly Bulletin*, June-July 1991.

38. The description of the Pakistani Army's participation in Hekmatyar's second attack on Rahman's emirate is based on interviews with two Afghan sources, both familiar with the details of the battle, who wish to remain anonymous.

39. The source is a well-informed Afghan Mujahidin who wishes to remain anonymous.

40. Ibid.

41. Associated Press of Pakistan, "King Fahd's Envoy Calls on Akram Zaki," *The Muslim*, September 8, 1991.

16—DESPERATELY SEEKING MODERATES

1. Zahir Shah said this to the author in Rome on June 10, 1990.

2. Peter Tomsen, "Some Trends in Resistance Thinking Concerning a Political Settlement," March 20, 1990, declassified September 14, 2004; Fida Yunis, Pakistani chargé d'affaires, conversation with author, December 1990.

3. Benazir Bhutto's foreign policy adviser, Iqbal Akhund, once asked Hekmatyar about his visits to Baghdad to meet with Iraqi officials. Hekmatyar replied that the discussions were "to arrange for Najib to quit voluntarily." See Iqbal Akhund, *Trial and Error: The Advent and Eclipse of Benazir Bhutto* (Karachi: Oxford University Press, 2000), 170.

4. Steve Coll and James Rupert, "Afghan Rebels Veto Drive for Kabul," *Washington Post*, November 4, 1990.

5. Kenneth Katzman, "Afghanistan: U.S. Policy Options," *CRS Issue Brief*, Congressional Research Service, updated version, June 1, 1992, 3.

6. The two-phased plan of 1989 proposed strengthening local commanders' shuras, such as Haji Qadir's Jalalabad Shura and Masood's Council of the North. The National Commanders' Shura envisioned bringing all major field commanders in Afghanistan together.

7. Riyadh 5252, "Urgent Message from Afghan Professor on Loya Jirga for Special Envoy Tomsen," June 30, 1990, confidential, declassified March 23, 2000.

8. Rome 5708, "Interview with Zahir Shah," March 20, 1990, unclassified; U.S. Department of State, "Possible Call by Special Envoy Tomsen on Former King Zahir Shah," action memorandum, June 9, 1990, secret, declassified April 9, 2000.

9. U.S. Department of State, "Possible Call by Special Envoy Tomsen."

10. My deputy during the July 9–10, 1990, talks in Rome, Foreign Service Officer Tom Greene, spoke Dari and, afterward, helpfully filled in the gaps left out in the Afghan translations.

11. "Afghan Commanders Shura," memorandum, May 1990, confidential, declassified March 23, 2000.

12. Ibid.

13. Peshawar 1067, "Second Afghan Commander Shura Begins," June 24, 1990, confidential, declassified.

14. Peshawar 114, "Abdul Haq Cautious but Pleased at Results of Second Commanders' Shura," July 5, 1990, confidential, declassified March 23, 2000.

15. Pakistan's generals occasionally relied on the MI directorate, or military intelligence, to conduct highly sensitive operations. The much larger number of ISI operatives, and the ISI's use of civilians as well as military personnel, made it more vulnerable to foreign penetration.

16. "Mujahidin Government May Go," *Frontier Post*, September 10, 1990, 1.

17. Pakistan's nuclear weapons program, overseen by the ISI, passed the redline set by the Pressler Amendment mandating a cutoff in U.S. assistance. U.S. intelligence had concluded that Pakistani nuclear scientist A. Q. Khan's team had connected the two cores of a nuclear bomb earlier in 1990, thereby crossing that threshold.

18. The termination of U.S. economic and military aid to Pakistan did not affect U.S. covert aid and USAID assistance through Pakistan to the Mujahidin.

19. See Steve Coll, *Ghost Wars: The Secret History of the CIA, Afghanistan, and bin Laden, from the Soviet Invasion to September 10, 2001* (New York: Penguin, 2004), 219; Coll and Rupert, "Afghan Rebels Veto Drive for Kabul." Coll and Rupert's November 4, 1990, article in the *Washington Post* was based on interviews in Peshawar and Washington. They wrote that "State Department officials and a CIA spokesman" declined to comment on the reports from Pakistan that U.S. diplomats and CIA officers there had been taking opposing positions on the offensive in talks with their Afghan and Pakistani interlocutors. They quoted several officials in Washington as stating that "the State Department and CIA disagreed over basic policy in the Afghan conflict." The officials asked that their names and agencies not be disclosed.

20. Ibid.

21. Ibid.

22. Ibid.

23. Islamabad 20172, "Kabul Offensive," October 8, 1990, secret, declassified April 6, 2000. The text of the letter was redacted when Islamabad 20172 was declassified.

24. Islamabad 20168, "Planned Kabul Offensive," October 8, 1990, secret/NODIS, declassified April 6, 2000.

25. Ibid.

26. The Tarinkot victory on the eve of the Shah Selim meeting was a morale-raising event, but it was also another depressing reminder of the mob violence that unfolded when Mujahidin leaders could not reach a consensus on post-hostility governing arrangements. The intended turnover of a provincial capital in a manner benefiting its inhabitants instead became a catastrophe for them when Mujahidin groups that were not controlled by Karzai arrived later to loot the town. They executed over ninety prisoners. One commander attempted to assassinate Karzai while he led two trucks carrying USAID wheat into the city. Karzai saved himself by leaping from the truck into a roadside ditch.

27. Masood's assistant and the official spokesman of the commanders' shura, Masood Khalili, phoned me from Gharm Chesma to invite me to come and meet with commanders off the Shah Selim meeting site. I declined, saying that only Afghans should be present.

28. "Final Communiqué of the Third National Commanders' Shura," Copy of the October 14, 1990, communiqué, in author's files.

29. Daoud Mir, interview with author, February 9, 2008.

30. Ibid. Daoud Mir was with Masood every day at Shah Selim, the only non-commander to participate in the meeting. Mir was a Masood political adviser and simultaneously Abdul Haq's assistant at the commanders' shura Peshawar headquarters. He accompanied Masood to Islamabad and Peshawar after the meeting. In Peshawar, he arranged for Masood to meet with UN Special Envoy Benon Sevan. Prince Turki flew to Pakistan and asked for a meeting with Masood. Masood's decision not to meet with Turki was a major mistake.

31. Daoud Mir recalled that Hekmatyar seemed offended when he saw Masood's two armed bodyguards in the room, a privilege not accorded to him at Pakistani Army headquarters. Daoud Mir, interview with author, April 16, 2008.

32. Peshawar 159, "Hekmatyar Still Has Plans for Kabul," February 10, 1991, secret, declassified September 14, 2004.

33. At the time, 70 million Pakistani rupees were equivalent to $7 million in U.S. dollars.

34. Daoud Mir, interview with author, April 16, 2008.

35. See Chapter 10.

36. Dr. Abdullah Abdullah, one of Masood's advisers who was present at Masood's debriefing upon his return from Pakistan, provided a readout in a taped interview with the author in Washington, DC, on September 15, 2008. Two other Masood advisers, Masood Khalili and Mohammad Es Haq, gave additional information from Masood's debriefing.

37. Agence France-Presse (AFP), Hong Kong, "Masud Outlines Mujahidin Warfare Plan," October 28, 1990, FBIS-NES-90-209, October 29, 1990.

38. Brigadier (Ret.) Mohammad Yousaf, "Has Afghan Jihad Been Lost?" *The Muslim*, November 21, 1990.

39. Ibid.; Peshawar 159.

40. "Second Rebel Leader Quits Government-in-Exile in Pakistan," Associated Press, May 6, 1991; "Afghan Leaders Disown Mujahidin on Saudi Arabia," *Dawn* (Karachi), February 19, 1991, 6.

41. Lahore 499, "World Islamic Movements Meet, Demand Allies Withdraw First," February 22, 1991, unclassified; Agence France-Presse (AFP), Hong Kong, "Army Chief Calls Gulf War 'Sheer Madness,'" January 20, 1991, FBIS-NES-91-020, 1403 GMT, January 29, 1991.

42. Islamabad 1372, "Afghanistan: Text of AIG President Mojaddedi's Statement on the Gulf War," January 28, 1991, unclassified.

43. For example, "Saudi Arabia May Not Meet Its War Pledge," *Houston Chronicle*, February 15, 1991, 13A, is accompanied by a large Associated Press photo of an American Marine and an Afghan Mujahidin in a discussion south of the Kuwaiti-Saudi border.

17—IRRECONCILABLE POLICIES

1. London 11690, "Afghan Settlement Process: Assessment and Recommendations," from Peter Tomsen, June 25, 1991, secret/NODIS, declassified.

2. Clifford Krass, "In Hot Spots Like Gulf, He's Baker's Cool Hand," *New York Times*, January 3, 1991, A10.

3. A February 27, 1990, U.S. State Department Intelligence and Research Bureau "Information Memorandum," sent to Under Secretary Kimmitt and entitled "Afghanistan: Aspects of Negative Symmetry," predicted that "negative symmetry would have a strong, immediate, negative psychological impact on the resistance, but the Mujahidin would adjust without long-term damage to their position. The Najibullah regime, however, would ultimately be significantly weakened because of its total dependence on Soviet arms and ammunition." The memo was declassified on March 23, 2000.

4. "US Aid Cut to Be Insignificant: HIA," *Frontier Post*, May 17, 1991.

5. During the Soviet occupation period each of the seven parties had shared equally in USAID programs to study in the United States. Some U.S. embassy officials in Islamabad, resistant to deviating from old policies, groused about my "purging" of the Afghan Construction and Logistics Unit. They did not wish to break the decade-old practice of treating the seven parties equally. I felt compelled to send a formal memorandum to the embassy's chargé d'affaires, Elizabeth Jones, explaining how denying scholarships to Hekmatyar's party was consistent with U.S. policy. I pointed out that providing several thousands of dollars to each of the Hezb participants "would run counter to U.S. policy," which mandated that "no further USG resources . . . go to Hekmatyar and Sayyaf and their representatives" (Tomsen to Jones, "USG Scholarships for Four Prominent Hezb-Hekmatyar officials?" memorandum, June 11, 1991, confidential, declassified April 7, 2000). Also at my request, Eugene Pell, director of Radio Free Europe (RFE), investigated the Hezb employees at RFE's Afghan arm in Munich who broadcast pro–Saddam Hussein,

anti-U.S. messages before, during, and after the Gulf War. His investigation uncovered that the Hezb "faction" at Radio Free Afghanistan was the largest and was "not friendly to the U.S." Their comments on the air were "offensive" and "egregious." He assured that "pre-broadcast controls" he had instituted would contain the problem. "Hezb Influence in RFA Under Investigation," April 23, 1991, unclassified.

6. I was told by Mujahidin sources that, as the fighting at Khost ended, Ahmadzai tribals surrendered to Ahmadzai tribals, Zadran to Zadran, and regime officers to Haqqani, who turned them over to the International Committee of the Red Cross. There were unconfirmed reports that an unknown number of Dostum's Uzbek militia were summarily executed on the battlefield.

7. Robert M. Kimmitt, Under Secretary for Political Affairs, "Post-war Gulf Issues," WorldNet broadcast, United States Information Agency (USIA), April 1, 1991, 9:30 AM-EST, transcript.

8. According to British journalist Sandy Gall's interview with Masood on June 28, 1993, Masood said that "after the commanders shura was held, our offensive started from, both from south and north, and it was intended from the West. . . . [The] deadlock [was] broken eventually by the *shura* of Commanders and the decisions they took and put into effect and the victories that followed." Sandy Gall, "An Interview with Commander Ahmed Shah Masud, Former Minister of Defence, at His Base in Jebal Seraj, North of Kabul, on June 28, 1993," *Asian Affairs* 25, no. 2 (1994): 141, available at www.informaworld.com/smpp/content~db=all~content =a738552617~frm=abslink. Masood's interview with *Le Monde* was published on July 6, 1993. Translated from French into English, it was transmitted from the American embassy in Paris to Washington. Masood stated, "We hope to launch new battles and to win victories when we can cross the passes." He was open to negotiations with the Soviets but not with Najib. He stressed that "the efforts of the U.N. will not bear any fruit as long as Najibullah remains in power or even shares part of the power." Paris 21811, "Le Monde Interview with Massoud," August 12, 1991, unclassified.

9. Peshawar 821, "Ahmed Zia Confirms Masood's Discussions with Soviets on Border Modus Vivendi," August 13, 1991, confidential, declassified March 23, 2000. According to this document, the Russian Commissariat and the Mujahidin delegation also agreed that, in the event of border issues, "the white flag should be hoisted" and the two sides should "come to the middle of the Eshkashem bridge" to negotiate the problem.

10. A *Washington Post* article reported that Nawaz Sharif and many in his ruling coalition "were long aligned with the military government that ruled Pakistan for 11 years until 1988." Steve Coll, "Afghan Rebels Veto Drive for Kabul," *Washington Post*, November 4, 1990, A27.

11. Joint Declaration Unanimously Adopted by the Tripartite Meeting Between Iran and Pakistan, and the Pakistan and Iran Mujahidin, Held on July 29–30, 1991.

12. Khalis refused to participate in the Leadership Council.

13. Signed Leadership Council agreement, in author's files. The agreement announced the "formation of a provisional transitional Islamic government" that would "rule for one year, then transfer power to an elected government."

14. After Khost was captured, Hekmatyar invited his Pakistani mentor, Jamaat chief Qazi Hussain Ahmed, into the city where they delivered speeches about the coming Islamic march into Kabul and Central Asia. ISI chief Durrani and scores of Arab jihadis joined in the victory celebrations.

15. Agence France-Presse, Hong Kong, "Resistance Faction Mends Ties with Saudi Arabia," November 5, 1991.

16. "August 22 Afghan Coordinating Committee Meeting," information memorandum, secret/NODIS, declassified March 23, 2000.

17. The walk through the corridors of the Holy See to Monsignor Claudio Celoi's office was fascinating. Tall, helmeted Swiss Guards, dressed in orange and black Middle Age clothing, stood outside of huge open doors. They held out high spears. An article in *USA Today*, May 7, 2008, noted that the elite Swiss Guard, "founded in 1506, consists of 100 volunteers who must be male, Swiss, Catholic, single, at least 5-foot-8 and beardless."

18. The description of the Sciolino-Tomsen telephone conversation in this and the following paragraphs is taken from a May 9, 1991, U.S. Department of State memorandum, "Elaine Sciolino Story on Stoppage of U.S. Aid for the Resistance," that I sent to Under Secretary Kimmitt, secret, declassified March 23, 2000.

19. Elaine Sciolino, "U.S. Appears Ready to End Aid to Afghan Rebels," *New York Times*, May 12, 1991.

20. State 201138, "Pakistani Senate Chairman Sajjad Meeting with Secretary Baker," June 19, 1991, secret/NODIS, declassified April 6, 2000.

21. Yeltsin began calling for the termination of arms shipments to Afghanistan in July 1990. See "Russian Federation to Halt Weapons Supplies to Afghanistan," Reuters, July 14, 1990. He continued his demand for an arms cutoff through 1991, up to the September 13 signing of the U.S.-Soviet negative symmetry agreement. Occasionally he linked it to the Mujahidin release of POWs, more often to Soviet economic problems.

22. Copy of the Soviet version of the negative symmetry agreement given to Al Kamen by the Soviet embassy, secret, declassified March 3, 2001. The Soviet embassy erased the classification lines.

23. Jack F. Matlock, Jr. *Autopsy on an Empire: The American Ambassador's Account of the Collapse of the Soviet Union* (New York: Random House, 1995), 665.

24. Jack Matlock, former U.S. ambassador to the Soviet Union, wrote: "If I were to reply to the question I posed to Russian politicians regarding the person most responsible for the collapse of the Soviet Union, my answer would be Vladimir Kryuchkov." Matlock, *Autopsy on an Empire*.

25. Ibid., 595.

26. Yeltsin won 57.2 percent of the votes in the June 12, 1991, Russian elections. Gorbachev never risked a popular election. The strength and courage Yeltsin demonstrated during the coup attempt lifted his image and deflated Gorbachev's.

27. Alexander Bessmertnykh, former Soviet ambassador in Washington and Under Secretary Kimmitt's partner in the negative symmetry negations, was fired for cooperating with the coup plotters.

28. Anwar Iqbal, "Pakistan Wants Political Settlement in Afghanistan, U.S. Told," *The News* (Pakistan), September 5, 1991, 1.

29. James A. Baker III with Thomas M. DeFrank, *The Politics of Diplomacy: Revolution, War, and Peace, 1989–1992* (New York: Putnam's, 1995), 528.

30. Secretary of State James A. Baker III, letter to Pakistani Minister of State for Foreign Affairs Mohammad Siddiq Khan Kanju, September 13, 1991, in Section 18022, cable transmitted from Secretary Baker in Moscow, "Implementing Agreement on Afghanistan," September 12, 1991, secret/NODIS, NIACT Immediate Precedence, declassified April 6, 2000. "NIACT" stands for "Night Action." (The Operations Center in the State Department is responsible for contacting the recipient or his or her assistant immediately after receipt of these types of messages because of their importance. The communicator in the embassy is responsible for contacting the ambassador when a NIACT message arrives.

18—FROM MARX TO MULLAHS

1. London 17650, "Afghan Policy—U.S. Strategy," from Special Envoy Tomsen, September 26, 1991, secret, EXDIS/Khyber, declassified, with redaction, October 26, 2004.

2. Bruce Riedel, *The Search for al Qaeda: Its Leadership, Ideology, and Future* (Washington, DC: Brookings Institution Press, 2008), 46; Robert M. Gates, *From the Shadows: The Ultimate Insider's Story of Five Presidents and How They Won the Cold War* (New York: Simon and Schuster, 1996), 433.

3. Thomas G. Paterson, Garry J. Clifford, and Kenneth J. Hagan, *American Foreign Relations: A History Since 1895*, vol. 2, 4th ed. (Lexington, MA: D. C. Heath, 1995), 555.

4. Dr. Rizwan Hussain, e-mail to author, June 1, 2009. Dr. Hussain is the author of the book *Pakistan and the Emergence of Islamic Militancy in Afghanistan* (Hampshire, England: Ashgate, 2005).

5. Secretary of State James A. Baker III, letter to Pakistani Minister of State for Foreign Affairs Mohammad Siddiq Khan Kanju, September 13, 1991, in Section 18022, cable transmitted from Secretary Baker in Moscow, "Implementing Agreement on Afghanistan," September 12, 1991, secret/NODIS, NIACT Immediate Precedence, declassified April 6, 2000.

6. Ibid.

7. Shuja Nawaz, *Crossed Swords: Pakistan, Its Army, and the Wars Within* (New York: Oxford University Press, 2009), 444.

8. Brigadier Afzal Janjua, deputy director of the ISI's Afghan cell, was reassigned to an army unit outside the ISI. Other senior ISI officers were given regular army postings.

9. Assistant Secretary Djerejian was a Middle East and Soviet specialist who had just returned from his posting as ambassador in Syria. In 1979, I had served under Ed when he was political counselor in the American embassy in Moscow. Tezi Schaffer spent most of her thirty-year career in South Asian countries—Pakistan, India, Bangladesh, and also Sri Lanka, were she was ambassador from 1992 to 1995. Ed Abbington had recently returned from a tour in the embassy in Islamabad.

10. State 329934, "U.S.-Soviet Experts' Talks on Afghanistan," Memorandum for National Security Adviser Brent Scowcroft, October 4, 1991, secret/EXDIS, declassified October 14, 2004.

11. The USAID Afghan program fell from $70 million in FY 1990 to $60 million in FY 1991 and $50 million in FY 1992. The Clinton administration terminated the USAID Afghan program during its first year in office.

12. Islamabad 18458, "Afghanistan: Afghans Appeal for Continuing U.S. Involvement, Resources," December 9, 1991, confidential, declassified July 9, 2008.

13. United Nations General Assembly, Agenda Item 29, 46th Session, "The Situation in Afghanistan and Its Implications for International Peace and Security," October 17, 1991; "President Najibullah Digs in for Long Term," *Christian Science Monitor*, January 8, 1992; New Delhi 26549, "Najibullah's Letter to President Bush," December 23, 1991, confidential, declassified March 23, 2000. Following standard protocol, the U.S. State Department refused to accept Najib's letter. Najib's embassy in Washington did manage somehow to get the letter into the White House, however. The White House did not reply—opening an American channel to one of the main roadblocks to the UN process was contrary to U.S. policy.

14. Oliver Wates, "Afghan Rebels End Ground-Breaking Talks in Moscow," Reuters, November 15, 1991.

15. To no avail, Soviet President Gorbachev sought to maintain Soviet unity until December 25, 1991, when he formally declared, "The policy prevailed of dismembering this country and disuniting the state." See Edward H. Judge and John W. Langden, *The Cold War: A History Through Documents* (Upper Saddle River, NJ: Prentice Hall, 1998), 262. Shortly thereafter, the Russian tricolor replaced the red hammer and sickle at the top of the Kremlin.

16. Rutskoi's SU-25 was shot down in Konar in 1987. He was handed over to Pakistani authorities after a ransom was paid to his Mujahidin captors. Benon Sevan arranged Rutskoi's transfer to Soviet custody.

17. Rahimullah Yusufzai, "Controversy Surrounds Identity of POW Released by Mujahidin," *Frontier Post*, December 25, 1991, 1.

18. "General Asif's Meeting with Zahir's Aide Confirmed," *Frontier Post*, January 3, 1992.

19. "Jamaat Opposes Zahir's Return," *Frontier Post,* January 11, 1992; "Hekmatyar Opposes Move to Bring Zahir Shah Back," *The Muslim,* January 3, 1992; "Afghan Peace Efforts are Anti-Islamic, Says Sayyaf," *The News* (Pakistan), January 12, 1992; "Resistance Accepts Former King as Interim Head," *The Nation* (Pakistan), January 23, 1992, 12.

20. Statement on Afghanistan by Pakistan Minister of Foreign Affairs Siddiq Khan Kanju, Ministry of Foreign Affairs, Press Conference, Islamabad, January 27, 1992.

21. Statement by Margaret Tutwiler, U.S. Department of State, Office of the Assistant Secretary/Spokesman, "U.S. Response to the Secretary General's January 27, 1992, Statement on Afghanistan," press release, January 29, 1992; "Russia Hails Pak Support to UN Formula," *The Muslim,* February 10, 1992; "Commentary Notes Major Shift in Pakistan's Afghan Policy," FBIS Bangkok, 3012172, January 1992.

22. "Sevan's Optimism," *The Nation* (Pakistan), February 25, 1992.

23. Perhaps forewarned about Durrani's message, Hekmatyar and Sayyaf were absent. Sayyaf was represented by Mohammad Yasir; Hekmatyar was not represented.

24. The ISI's "S" Department is identified by Director of National Intelligence Mike McConnell in author-journalist Bob Woodward's *Obama's Wars* (New York: Simon and Schuster, 2010), 4. Rizwan Hussain's book *Pakistan and the Emergency of Islamic Militancy in Afghanistan* contains an organization chart of the ISI on p. 251 that sets the "Special Wing" apart from the "Afghan Cell." Hussain wrote that the Special Wing "administers the defense services intelligence training facilities and liaises with foreign intelligence agencies" (p. 250).

25. "New Agenda for the New Chief," *Friday Times,* editorial, February 20–26, 1992, 1.

26. "Commentary Notes Major Shift in Pakistan's Afghan Policy," FBIS Bangkok, TH, 3012172, January 1992; "PM's 'Remark' on Afghan Policy," *Frontier Post,* February 19, 1992, 10.

27. Nawaz, *Crossed Swords,* 452.

28. Javed Syed, "IJ Ministers, Leaders Attack Government Policy on Afghanistan, Kashmir," *The Muslim,* February 16, 1992, 4.

29. Saeed Ahmed, "Hekmatyar Outlines His Own Peace 'Formula,'" *The News* (Pakistan), February 25, 1992; "Hekmatyar Condemns Remarks Against Qazi," *The News* (Pakistan), January 29, 1992.

30. Malcolm Davidson, "Rising Ethnic Tensions Make Afghan Accord Urgent—UN Official," Reuters, February 23, 1991.

31. Cambodia's dynamic Prince Sihanouk was the catalyst that brought the opposing Cambodian factions together in a UN-supervised Cambodian peace accord. An interparty Supreme National Council took power in Phnom Penh in November 1991, ending that country's bloody civil war.

32. Dostum's defection deprived Najib of his most effective ground force in Afghanistan. The Uzbek strongman's mercenaries were deployed to twenty-three of Afghanistan's twenty-nine provinces.

33. London 22586, "Afghanistan: Commander Masood's Views of UN Role in Political Settlement," December 13, 1991, confidential, declassified March 23, 2000.

34. Masood reiterated his support for the UN process in the interview with Remi Favret of *Le Figaro* published December 18, 1991, FBIS-NES-91-245.

35. Daoud Mir, interview with author, June 2009.

36. Sandy Gall, "An Interview with Commander Ahmed Shah Masud, Former Minister of Defence, at His Base in Jebal Seraj, North of Kabul, on June 28, 1993," *Asian Affairs* 25, no. 2 (1994): 144–145.

37. "Address to the Nation by Afghan President Najibullah on 18 March," Kabul Radio, March 18, 1992, 1600GMT, FBIS 179Mar18 (See 129, 137 Mar18).

38. Masood described his "third force" initiative in the December 18, 1991, *Le Figaro* interview (p. 4). He proposed that a "third force" of Afghan "neutral figures, whether from Kabul, from refugee camps, from Mujahidin-controlled areas (inside Afghanistan) or in exile" form the transitional government.

39. On March 26, 1992, a VOA correspondent told me that, during the second week of March, the ISI had begun reassembling the Leadership Council into an interim government.

40. Peshawar 358, "A Revitalized AIG," April 14, 1992, confidential, declassified March 23, 2000.

41. "Statement by the Secretary-General on Afghanistan," Geneva, April 10, 1992.

42. One of the chosen council members, Samed Hamed, former deputy prime minister, phoned me at the State Department from his home in Germany to ask if America truly supported Sevan's initiative. He characterized the Pakistani ambassador in Germany as "frantic" to get him on a plane to Islamabad as soon as possible. I responded that the United States supported Sevan's plan. Unfortunately, Sharif and Nasir did not.

43. This account of Benon Sevan's meeting with the Leadership Council at Nawaz Sharif's residence is taken from author's two interviews with Sevan, on June 20, 1997, and October 20, 2010.

44. Ibid.; Peter Tomsen, "Kabul Situation Update: Hekmatyar and Rabbani Press Statements," memorandum to NEA Assistant Secretary Edward Djerejian and other U.S. State Department officials, April 15, 1992, unclassified.

45. "Afghanistan Update," memorandum, April 16, 1992, confidential, declassified April 4, 2000; "UN Plan Overtaken by Events," Agence France-Presse, Hong Kong, 0511 GMT, August 24, 1992.

19—FROM ONE WAR TO THE NEXT

1. From Peter Tomsen, "Central Asia, Afghanistan and U.S. Policy," confidential memorandum to Edward P. Djerejian, assistant secretary for Near Eastern and South Asian Affairs, U.S. State Department, February 2, 1993, excised, declassified March 23, 2000.

2. Peshawar 382, "Military/Security Situation in Afghanistan as of 1700 Local, April 19," April 19, 1992, confidential, declassified March 23, 2000.

3. Peter Tomsen, "King Fahd Message to the Resistance on Peace, Resolution of the Afghan Issue," memorandum to Edward P. Djerejian, April 23, 1992, unclassified.

4. UN Representative Benon Sevan turned down Nawaz Sharif's invitation to attend the ceremony.

5. Es Haq, adviser to Ahmed Shah Masood, interview with author, Omaha, Nebraska, July 19, 1999.

6. Murtaza Malik, "Interim Council Need Not Come: Hekmatyar," *The Muslim*, April 26, 1992.

7. Peshawar 461, "Afghanistan: A Hezb Perspective of Events," May 13, 1992, confidential, declassified April 4, 2000.

8. American scholar Barnett Rubin call to deputy special envoy Richard Hoagland April 30, 1992, after Dr. Rubin received a phone call from Ahmed Rashid the same day.

9. Moscow 12421, "Afghanistan: Russian April 24 Readout," April 25, 1992, secret, declassified March 23, 2000.

10. State 160962, "Russian Briefing on (Andrei) Kozyrev's Visit to Kabul," May 21, 1992, confidential, declassified April 6, 2000.

11. Dennis Kux, *The United States and Pakistan, 1947–2000* (Washington, DC: Woodrow Wilson Center Press, and Baltimore: Johns Hopkins University Press, 2001), 316, 317; Shuja Nawaz, *Crossed Swords: Pakistan, Its Army, and the Wars Within* (Karachi, Pakistan: Oxford University Press, 2008).

12. Kux, *The United States and Pakistan*, 316–317; Nawaz, *Crossed Swords*, 453.

13. Ibid.; Nicholas Platt, interview with Dennis Kux, New York, February 9, 1995.

14. Islamabad 6211, "Afghanistan: Developments as of 1700 Local Time, April 26," confidential, declassified April 4, 2000.

15. Guy Dinmore, "Last Afghan Rebel Stronghold Seized," Reuters, April 29, 1992.

16. Arthur Max, "Kabul's New Defense Chief Brings Troops," Associated Press, in *Fort Worth Star Telegram*, April 30, 1992. American journalist Richard Mackenzie rode in with Masood, arriving in Kabul on Tuesday, April 28, 1992, at 8 p.m.

17. Nawaz, *Crossed Swords*, 452.

18. Islamabad 6491, "Afghanistan: Developments as of 1600 Local Time, April 30," April 30, 1992, unclassified. Pakistani Prime Minister Nawaz Sharif stated that the victory would pave the way for the "liberation of other Muslim occupied territories." Sharif also paid tribute to Zia ul-Haq for laying down his life for Afghanistan. "Sharif—Mojajedin Rule in Kabul 'Success of Islam,'" Islamabad PTV Television Network in English, May 1, 1992, FBIS-NES-02-087, May 5, 1992.

19. Qaiser Butt, "Interim Set-Up for 2 Years, Not Months—Mojaddedi," *Frontier Post*, May 6, 1992; "Mojaddedi Will Stay If Country Needs Me," Agence France-Presse, Hong Kong, May 5, 1992, FBIS-NES-92-087, May 5, 1992, 39.

20. F. P. Report, "Mujaddedi Has No Right to Announce Cabinet: Hekmatyar," *Frontier Post*, May 6, 1992; Anwar Iqbal, "Mujahidin Leaders Condemn Promotion of Generals," *The News* (Pakistan), May 24, 1992; Sibghatullah Mojaddedi, speech at presidential palace, Kabul, June 28, 1992, transcript issued by the Presidential Office, Department of Press Information.

21. "Gunbattles Rage in Kabul, Death Toll over 100," Reuters, June 5, 1992; "Tehran Reportedly Blamed for Split," *The News* (Pakistan), June 5, 1992, FBIS-NES-92-109, June 5, 1992, 30; "Speech of Professor Sibghatullah Mojaddedi, President of the Jehadi Council and Acting President of the Islamic State of Afghanistan on the Occasion of Transfer of Power," delivered at the presidential palace, June 28, 1992, full speech issued by the Press Information Department of the Presidential Office; "National Security Ministry Given to Shiites," Agence France-Presse, Hong Kong, June 12, 1992, FBIS-NES-92-114.

22. "Gunbattles Rage in Kabul."

23. Ustad Khalili became one of Hamid Karzai's three vice presidents in 2002 after the Taliban's ouster.

24. "Gunbattles Rage in Kabul."

25. Barnett R. Rubin, *The Fragmentation of Afghanistan: State Formation and Collapse in the International System* (New Haven, CT: Yale University Press, 1995), 273.

26. Islamabad 4140, "Afghanistan: GOP Staying the Course," May 18, 1992, confidential, declassified April 6, 2000.

27. Ahmed Shah Masood, press conference, May 5, 1992.

28. Sandy Gall, "An Interview with Commander Ahmed Shah Masud, Former Minister of Defence, at His Base in Jebal Seraj, North of Kabul, on June 28, 1993, *Asian Affairs* 25, no. 2 (1994): 144.

29. Islamabad 6820, "Afghanistan: How Strong Is Hekmatyar," confidential, declassified March 23, 2000.

30. Islamabad 7990, "Afghanistan: Mojaddedi's Visit to Pakistan," May 27, 1992, unclassified.

31. "Afghan Rebel Leader Promises Another War for Islamic State," *Baltimore Sun*, May 13, 1992.

32. Richard Ehrlich, "Genteel Guerrillas Mind Envoy's Kabul Home," *Washington Times*, May 29, 1992, A-8.

33. The Soviet POW rationale was repeated in a November 13, 1992, memo to the acting secretary of state arguing for humanitarian aid to Afghanistan. The memo warned that the chances of winning Afghan cooperation on POWs "will be significantly diminished if we cut our aid for program by 60%," as planned in Congress.

Memorandum to the acting secretary from Assistant Secretary Edward Djerejian, "ESF for Afghanistan: The Russian POW Connection," November 13, 1992, confidential, declassified March 23, 2000. Congress reduced the USAID budget by 15 percent instead of 60 percent.

34. Edward Djerejian, assistant secretary for Near Eastern and South Asian Affairs, "Sending an Envoy to Kabul," action memorandum to the secretary of state, May 8, 1992, secret, declassified March 23, 2000.

35. Islamabad 7394, "Afghanistan: Planning for a Trip to Kabul," May 17, 1992, confidential, declassified March 23, 2000.

36. Ibid.

37. Peter Tomsen, "May 15 Meeting at DOD to Discuss Use of Military Aircraft for Trip to Kabul by a U.S. Envoy," memorandum to Edward P. Djerejian, May 15, 1992, secret, declassified March 23, 2000.

38. Ibid.

39. "Kabul Denies Exporting Revolution to Central Asia," Agence France-Presse, Hong Kong, May 21, 1992, FBIS-NES-92-099, May 21, 1992.

40. See Barbara Crossette, "U.S. Helps Russians Search for Missing in Afghanistan," *New York Times International*, June 23, 1992.

41. State 181833, "Delay in Travel of U.S. Delegation to Kabul," June 6, 1992, secret/EXDIS, declassified March 25, 2000.

42. Ibid.

43. General Aushev, an Ingush, later was elected president of the Russian Republic of Ingushetia in the southern Caucasus.

44. Barbara Crossett, "U.S. Helps Russians Search for Missing in Afghanistan," *New York Times*, June 23, 1992.

45. Sharon Herbaugh, "American Delegation Returns to War-Battered Afghan Capital," Associated Press, June 14, 1992.

46. President George H.W. Bush, letter to Afghan Interim President Sibghatullah Mojaddedi, June 2, 1992, unclassified.

47. Hekmatyar's ANA propaganda mouthpiece falsely reported that I held a long meeting with Babrak Karmal, the former Afghan president (1979–1986), and Sultan Ali Keshtmand during my visit to Kabul.

48. *Afghan News*, vol. 8, no. 7, September 1, 1992, 4.

49. Ibid.

50. For six years beginning in 1985, Congress had requested the executive branch to break up the Near Eastern and South Asian Affairs Bureau in order to give more high-level attention to South Asia. Over State Department objections, Congress mandated the creation of the bureau in legislation that President George H. W. Bush signed in late 1991. The department formally established the new bureau in October 1992. John Malott continued as interim head until the Senate confirmed the bureau's first assistant secretary, Robin Raphel, in 1993.

51. State 323604, "Department Statement on Afghanistan," October 3, 1992, unclassified.

52. John Malott, interview with author, January 16, 2011.

53. George H.W. Bush was previously CIA director, 1976–1977.

54. George P. Shultz, *Turmoil and Triumph: My Years as Secretary of State* (New York: Charles Scribner's Sons, 1993), 837–859.

55. Retired Ambassador Robert Oakley's March 30, 2004, interview with Roy Gutman.

56. Peshawar 941, "Hezb-e-Islami Spokesman Responds to U.S. Criticism," October 14, 1992, unclassified.

57. In length, the wars in Afghanistan have surpassed the Thirty Years' War (1618–1648). The Thirty Years' War pitted Europe's kings and emperors of the day against each other. As in Afghanistan, religious differences intensified and prolonged the bloody conflict.

20—UNHOLY ALLIANCE

1. The State Department, by law, administers two terrorist lists. One designates State Sponsors of Terrorism; the other names Foreign Terrorist Organizations. The lists are updated yearly. See U.S. Department of State, "Terrorist Designation Lists," www.state.gov/s/ct/list/; U.S. Department of State, "State Sponsors of Terrorism," www.state.gov/s/ct/c14151.htm.

2. Paul Watson and Sidhata Barua, "Somalia Link Seen to Al Qaeda," *Los Angeles Times*, February 25, 2002.

3. John Lancaster, "U.S. Pressures Pakistan to Cut Ties with Extremist Groups; Indian Airlines Hijacked Linked to Islamabad Intelligence," *Washington Post*, January 26, 2000.

4. Maulana Masood Azhar has continued to promote global jihad from his bases in Pakistan. Ahmed Omar Sheikh is reportedly in jail, having been sentenced to death by a Pakistani court after admitting responsibility for the murder of American journalist Daniel Pearl in Karachi in early 2002. Many doubt that the sentence will be carried out.

5. "Musharraf Defends Pro-Taliban Policy," News Network International (Islamabad), May 26, 2000, reported that General Pervez Musharraf on May 25 stated that Pakistan's support for the Taliban was "in accordance with Paskistan national interest" and, referring to the Pashtuns, added that they were "a national security interest, both demographic and geographic."

6. Christopher Thomas, "Taliban Rout Ends Islamabad's Dream," *The Australian*, June 4, 1997, 4; "Pakistan Not Interfering in Afghan Affairs," editorial, News Network International, August 14, 1999; Sebastian Rotilla, "War on West Shifts Back to Afghanistan," *Los Angeles Times*, October 25, 2006; Jason Straziuso, "Think Tank: Pakistan Gave Info on U.S.," Associated Press, June 9, 2008. An editorial

entitled "Stop Helping Gulbuddin!" *Afghan News,* vol. 8, no. 17, September 1, 1992, 4, also reminded Prime Minister Nawaz Sharif of his statement of support for the legitimate Afghan government and not allowing elements using Pakistani soil to undermine this legitimate government.

7. In March 2002, one of bin Laden's top lieutenants, Abu Zubaydah, was captured at a Lashkar-i Taiba safehouse in Faizalabad in the Punjab.

8. Ramzi Yusuf was twenty-five and an al-Qaeda operative when he bombed the World Trade Center in 1993. He was born and grew up in Kuwait. His parents were Pakistani. Yusuf and Mir Aimal Kansi, a Pakistani Kakar Pashtun from Quetta, both arrived in New York without visas on Pakistani International Airways (PIA) in 1993. They took advantage of lax U.S. immigration procedures allowing non-visaed foreigners claiming political asylum to enter the United States on "parole" status, pending a U.S. court hearing on their asylum request. Yusuf melted into al-Qaeda circles in Brooklyn to stage the 1993 World Trade Center bombing. Kansi went to the entrance to CIA Langley headquarters in Virginia, where he gunned down two CIA employees in their vehicles waiting at a stop light to turn left into the CIA's entrance. After their respective terrorist attacks, both Yusuf and Kansi boarded PIA flights in New York and flew back to Pakistan.

9. Christopher Dickey and Steve Levine, "Making a Symbol of Terror," *Newsweek,* March 1, 1999, 42; Tim Weiner, "Blowback from the Afghan Battlefield," *New York Times,* March 13, 1994; Susan Schmidt, "New Details Revealed on 9/11 Plans," *Washington Post,* July 23, 2004, A19. According to Tim Weiner in his *New York Times* article, Sheikh Abdel Rahman was "a spiritual leader of the Islamic Group, who struck up a personal and ideological friendship with Hekmatyar."

10. Only one of the operations planned by Khalifa's al-Qaeda cell was carried out. On December 11, 1994, a terrorist planted a bomb on a Philippine Airlines flight departing Manila for Tokyo, Japan, with a stop in Cebu in the Philippines. After the plane took off from Cebu, the bomb exploded, killing one Japanese passenger.

11. "The Rediff Interview: Former ISI Chief Hamid Gul," February 12, 2004, www.rediff.com/news/2004/feb/12inter.htm.

12. John West, "Egypt Woos Militants but Militants Seem Unaffected," Reuters, November 21, 1993. The captured jihadi was one of sixty who had just completed a six-week Hekmatyar training course in Logar.

13. James Bruce, "Arab Veterans of the Afghan War," *Jane's Intelligence Review* 7, no. 4 (1995): 175, www.dalitstan.org/mughalstan/mujahid/veterans.html; West, "Egypt Woos Militants"; Judith Miller: "Holy Warriors: Killing for the Glory of God in a Land Far from Home," *New York Times,* January 16, 2001.

14. In the courtroom, Nasir's insistent claims to religious piety were exceeded only by his self-promoting vanity. Ignoring the utter failure of the Peshawar Accords, he congratulated himself for becoming "an instant international figure when in April 1992, through my own powers of persuasion and motivational talks, I

brought all the warring factions of the Afghan Mujahidin to agree to the historically famous Peshawar Accords." Seema Mustafa, "ISI Brags About Role in Punjab, Bosnia," *Asian Age*, December 27, 2002.

15. Ardeshir Corvasjee, "Three Stars," *Dawn*, January 12, 2003.

16. Hassan Abbas, *Pakistan's Drift into Extremism: Allah, Then Army, and America's War Terror* (Armonk, NY: M. E. Sharpe, 2005), 148; Steve LeVine, "Afghan Fighters Aiding Azerbaijan in Civil War," *Washington Post*, November 8, 1993, A14. The oil-rich Azeris eagerly hired Hekmatyar's mercenaries and put them in the front lines of a fresh offensive against the Armenian foe. The Armenians quickly routed the attackers and sent them fleeing back to Baku, the Azeri capital. Not satisfied with the high salaries and brand new weapons provided by Azerbaijan, Hekmatyar's Mujahidin turned to looting and robbery in Baku. The Azeri government transported them back to Pakistan.

17. Steven Strasser, ed., *The 9/11 Investigations: Staff Reports of the 9/11 Commission* (New York: PublicAffairs, 2004), 187.

18. "Issue Brief for Congress, Pakistani-U.S. Relations," *Congressional Research Service*, Library of Congress, updated July 20, 2001, 15.

19. Dennis Kux, *The United States and Pakistan, 1947–2000* (Washington, DC: Woodrow Wilson Center Press, and Baltimore: Johns Hopkins University Press, 2001), 322.

20. R. Jeffrey Smith and Thomas W. Lippman, "Pakistan Avoids U.S. Listing as Nation Supporting Terrorism," *Washington Post*, July 15, 1993, A28.

21. Steve Coll, *Ghost Wars: The Secret History of the CIA, Afghanistan, and bin Laden, from the Soviet Invasion to September 10, 2001* (New York: Penguin, 2004), 309.

22. Dr. Abdullah Abdullah, e-mail to author, June 1, 2009.

23. The four UN envoys after Benon Sevan's 1992 resignation were former Tunisian foreign minister Mahmoud Mestiri (1993–1996); German diplomat Norbert Holl (1996–1997); former Algerian foreign minister Lakhdar Brahimi (1997–1999); and Spanish diplomat Francese Vendrell (1999–2001).

24. The UN Secretary General's Annual Report, *The Situation in Afghanistan*, 52nd session, Agenda Item 43, November 1997.

25. Robin L. Raphel, assistant secretary of state for South Asian Affairs, testimony to the House International Relations Committee, Subcommittee on Asia and Pacific, May 9, 1996; Islamabad 563, "Afghanistan: Moderate Pashtuns Seek U.S. Support for 'National Front' Solution to Afghan Impasse," January 11, 1993, confidential, declassified March 23, 2000.

26. Islamabad 635, "Afghanistan: Hekmatyar Will Not Accept Rabbani as President; Wants to Maintain Contact with U.S.," January 22, 1993, confidential, declassified; former American consul in Peshawar (1992–1996), telephone interview with author, September 2, 2009.

27. Gulbuddin Hekmatyar, "Message of Freedom Clandestine Radio Station in Pakistan," radio broadcast, June 29, 1992, FBIS-NES-92-126, June 30, 1992, 56; "At Least 100 Killed in Kabul Rocket Barrage," Reuters, July 5, 1992.

28. Barnett R. Rubin, *The Fragmentation of Afghanistan: State Formation and Collapse in the International System* (New Haven, CT: Yale University Press, 1995), 273.

29. FBIS 075Jan03, "Rabbani Addresses Resolution Council," January 4, 1993, unclassified.

30. Roy Gutman, *How We Missed the Story* (Washington, DC: United States Institute of Peace, 2008), 53. Gutman, on the same page, cites a Human Rights Watch report of the Afshar massacre as placing responsibility for the massacre on Sayyaf's fanatical jihadis, although Masood commanded the overall operation on that day.

31. Salamat Ali, "Afghanistan: A Peace on Paper," *Far Eastern Economic Review* 156, no. 11 (1993): 22.

32. "Afghan Cabinet Sworn in Outside Kabul," Reuters, June 17, 1993.

33. *Arab News*, September 9, 1993, citing a September 8, 1993, article by Agence France-Presse.

34. Gutman, *How We Missed the Story*, 59.

35. Daoud Mir, interview with author, February 9, 2008.

36. Daoud Mir, unpublished paper, "The Herat Shura, 20–25 July 1994," given to the author February 17, 2008, in author's files. Masood charged Mir with mobilizing prominent Afghan émigrés in Europe and transporting them to Herat at Masood's expense.

37. Amin Saikal, "The Rabbani Government, 1992–1996," in William Maley, ed., *Fundamentalism Reborn? Afghanistan and the Taliban* (New York: New York University Press, 1998).

38. U.S. Department of Defense, "Biographic Data on Mullah (Omar) and Senior Members of the Taliban Council of Ministers," unclassified, DTG 070908Z Nov 01, in author's files.

39. Some versions of the tale date the incident earlier in 1994.

40. In 2005, Haji Bashir Noorzai was lured to the United States, arrested, and tried for his role in an international narcotics trafficking case. A federal district court in Manhattan sentenced him to life in prison. Benjamin Weiser, "Afghan Linked to the Taliban Sentenced to Life in Drug Trafficking Case," *New York Times*, May 1, 2009. A witness in 2004 congressional committee testimony alleged that "Noorzai smuggles 4,400 lbs of heroin out of the Kandahar region to al-Qaeda operatives in Pakistan every eight weeks." Gregg Zoroya and Donna Leinwand, "Rise of Drug Trade Threat to Afghanistan's Security," *USA Today*, October 26, 2004.

41. Nawaf E. Obaid, "The Power of Saudi Arabia's Islamic Leaders," *Middle East Quarterly* 6, no. 3 (1999), 51–58, www.meforum.org/482/?the-power-of-saudi-arabias-islamic-leaders.

42. Ibid.

43. Islamabad 11584, "Redact Believe Pakistan Is Backing Taliban," December 6, 1994, secret/NOFORN, unclassified, released in part April 22, 2003. "NOFORN" means "Not for release to foreign nationals."

44. Ahmed Rashid, Pakistani author and journalist, estimated that 80,000 Pakistani madrassa students fought in Afghanistan during the Taliban rule.

45. Gutman, *How We Missed the Story*, 72.

46. State 34053, "Pak Foreign Minister Asks U.S. Cooperation on Afghanistan," February 21, 1996, confidential, declassified June 9, 2003.

47. Islamabad 3466, "A/S Raphel Discusses Afghanistan," April 22, 1996, confidential, declassified June 4, 2003.

48. Ibid.; Daoud Mir, interview with author, February 9, 2008. Masood adviser Daoud Mir was present at the Raphel-Masood Istalef meeting.

49. Islamabad 3466. Unocal promised the Taliban $50 million to $100 million a year in transit fees if the pipeline was built. The continuing war in Afghanistan, however, prevented construction, and on August 20, 1998, following the U.S. missile strikes against al-Qaeda bases in Paktiya, Unocal ended its involvement in the Afghan pipeline project.

50. Former Hezb political officer who wishes to remain anonymous, interview with author, September 19, 2007; IRNA-ITAR, TASS-ACSNA, "Leader of Islamic Party Calls for Revolting Against Taliban," Tehran, November 7, 1996; "Afghan Chronology," www.afghan-web.com/politics/chronology.html.

51. Maley, *Fundamentalism Reborn?* 133. Also see Neamatollah Nojumi, *The Rise of the Taliban in Afghanistan: Mass Mobilization, Civil War, and the Future of the Region* (New York: Palgrave, 2002), 145–150, regarding the ISI's covert operations to undermine Ismael Khan prior to Herat's fall to the Taliban.

52. Douglas Frantz, "Pakistan Ended Aid to the Taliban Only Hesitantly," part 2 of 2, *New York Times*, December 8, 2001.

53. Coll, *Ghost Wars*, 439.

54. After 9/11, Abdullah Abdullah continued as Afghan minister of foreign affairs until 2005. He was a presidential candidate in 2009.

55. Dr. Abdullah Abdullah, interview with author, Kabul, September 11, 2002.

56. Peter Tomsen, notes on September 2002 trip to Afghanistan, September 11, 2002.

57. Piotr Balcervorwicz, "The Last Interview with Ahmad Shah Masood," August 2001, www.orient.uw.edu.pl/balcerowicz/texts/Ahmad_Shah_Masood_en.htm.

58. These figures are based on comments by Richard Clarke, White House terrorism adviser, in his September 12, 2003, appearance on the PBS *NewsHour with Jim Lehrer*. See "War on Terror," September 12, 2003, www.pbs.org/newshour/bb/terrorism/jul-dec03/war_09-12.html.

59. Frantz, "Pakistan Ended Aid"; Julius Strauss, "Camp Where They Hanged Abdul Haq," *Daily Telegraph*, December 6, 2001.

60. Chechen rebels opened an embassy in Kabul in July 1999.

61. National Commission on Terrorist Attacks upon the United States, "Diplomacy: Staff Statement No. 5," n.d., www.cbsnews.com/htdocs/pdf/staffstatement5.pdf.

62. Coll, *Ghost Wars*, 439.

63. Robert Anson, "The Journalist and the Terrorist," *Vanity Fair*, August 2002.

64. Michael Meacher, "The Pakistan Connection," *The Guardian*, July 22, 2004.

65. Gutman, *How We Missed the Story*, 125.

66. Peter Tomsen, "A Chance for Peace in Afghanistan: The Taliban's Days Are Numbered," *Foreign Affairs* 70, no. 1 (2000): 179–182.

67. Dexter Filkens, "In the Villages, the Taliban Absolute Hold on Power Begins to Slip," *Los Angeles Times*, August 14, 2000; Scott McDonald, "Afghan Tribes Said to Threaten Taliban with Jihad," Reuters, January 25, 2000.

68. Damon Bristow, "China Flirts with an Independent Pro-Active Afghan Policy," *Central Asia and Caucasus Bi-Weekly Briefing*, Johns Hopkins University, School of Advanced International Studies, January 3, 2001.

69. Anthony Davis, "Struggle and Recognition," *Jane's Defence Weekly Bulletin*, October 4, 2000, 1; Ivan Ivanov, Russian Security Council secretary, quoted in "30,000 Foreigners Fighting in Afghanistan—Russian Official," ITAR TASS, October 13, 2000.

70. An official State Department press statement released July 14, 1999, announced, "We deplore the tragic killing of Afghan tribal leader and former Senator Abdul Ahad Karzai on July 14 in Quetta, Pakistan. His killers have not been identified. . . . In recent years, Mr. Karzai was active in trying to find peace in Afghanistan."

71. Amnesty International, International Secretariat, "Human Rights Defenders in Afghanistan," November 1999, AI Index: ASA 11/12/99, Dist:SC/CO/PUBLIC; knowledgeable source, interview with author, August 4, 1999.

72. A well-informed Afghan source I spoke with stated that the Taliban intelligence office was at Manzil Bagh, a town 3 miles west of Kandahar city. The source wished to remain anonymous.

73. Weiner, "Blowback from the Afghan Battlefield."

74. Aimal Khan, "Attack on Afghan Bases Leaves 28 Dead—Arabs, Pakistanis Among Victims," n.d., www.anusha.com/afghan28.htm.

75. Karl F. Inderfurth, assistant secretary of state for South Asian affairs, testimony to the Senate Foreign Relations Committee, Subcommittee on Near Eastern and South Asian Affairs, July 20, 2000.

76. United Nations Security Council Resolution 1267, passed in November 1999, and United Nations Security Council Resolution passed in December 2000.

77. Strasser, ed., *9/11 Investigations*, 75–77, 78.

78. Coll, *Ghost Wars*, 442, 520–546; Reuel Marc Gerecht, "The Counterterrorist Myth," *Atlantic Monthly* 288, no. 1, July/August 2001, 38–42. In his article,

Gerecht, a former CIA operative, described how lightly Osama bin Laden took American intelligence. Gerecht stated that the agency had "very few operatives from Middle East backgrounds." He wrote that the ISI and the Pakistani Army were tough to deal with and that "American intelligence has not gained and will not gain Pakistan's assistance in its pursuit of bin Ladin."

79. Gerecht, "Counterterrorist Myth."

80. Michael F. Scheuer, "Tenet Tries to Shift the Blame: Don't Buy It. Now He Tells Us," *Washington Post*, April 29, 2007; Coll, *Ghost Wars*, 353; George Tenet, *At the Center of the Storm: My Years at the CIA* (New York: HarperCollins, 2007), 109–110. Michael Scheuer was replaced as bin Laden task force unit chief in 1999. After his retirement, he denounced the decisions to call off the cruise missile attacks in emotional terms in two books and in media appearances.

81. Ahmed Shah Masood, "Letter to the People of America," 1998, www.afghan -web.com/documents/let-masood.html.

82. Patrick de Saint Exupery, "The U.S. Envoy Bill Richardson in Kabul: Afghanistan Is at the Heart of the 'Great Game,'" *Le Figaro*, April 17, 1998, 4.

83. Daoud Mir, interview with author, February 9, 2008; Michael Elliott, "Special Report: The Secret History. They Had A Plan," *Time*, August 4, 2003; *Afghanistan News*, April 8, 2001; Omar Samad, an exclusive Azadi Afghan Radio interview with Dr. Olivier Roy, November 4, 2000, Part 1, published November 8, 2000, no. 534; Joelle Diderich, "EU Assembly Chief Backs Afghan Opposition," Reuters, April 6, 2001; Sandy Gall, "An Interview with Commander Ahmed Shah Masud, Former Minister of Defence, at His Base in Jebal Seraj, North of Kabul, on June 28, 1993," *Asian Affairs* 25, no. 2 (1994). One former CIA officer criticized Masood for "being the worst officer among Mujahidin commanders who would agree to do something we wanted done, take the preferred funding and arms, and then do exactly as they pleased." Michael Scheuer, "Clueless in Kabul," *The American Interest* 2, no. 1 (2006): 114.

84. Coll, *Ghost Wars*, 459.

85. Gerecht, "Counterterrorism Myth," 38–42.

86. *The 9/11 Commission Report: Final Report of the National Commission on Terrorist Attacks upon the United States*, authorized ed. (New York: W. W. Norton, 2004), 187–188; Coll, *Ghost Wars*, 458, 459; Dr. Abdullah Abdullah, interview with author, September 11, 2002.

87. *9/11 Commission Report*, 206; Coll, *Ghost Wars*, 346; Tomsen diary, September 2002.

88. U.S. Department of State, memo, Rocca to Grossman, "Your Participation in Deputies Committee Meeting, Friday, June 29, 2001," June 28, 2001; U.S. Department of State, memo, "Pakistan/Afghanistan DC–Covert Action Issue," n.d. (possibly mid-June 2001), in *9/11 Commission Report*, 511, 206n.

89. Balcervorwicz, "Last Interview"; *9/11 Commission Report*, 205.

90. *9/11 Commission Report*, 142, 206.

91. The term "disengaged neutrality" is taken from Gutman's *How We Missed the Story*.

92. Strasser, ed., *9/11 Investigations*, 72.

93. Gutman, *How We Missed the Story*, 78–79; *9/11 Commission Report*, 72; Richard A. Clarke, *Against All Enemies: Inside America's War on Terror* (New York: Free Press, 2004), 236–238.

21—BETWEEN THE LIONS

1. Peter Tomsen, "A Chance for Peace in Afghanistan: The Taliban's Days Are Numbered," *Foreign Affairs* 79, no. 1 (2000), 179–182.

2. Roy Gutman, *How We Missed the Story* (Washington, DC: United States Institute of Peace, 2008), 78.

3. Peter Tomsen, "Afghanistan Settlement—Analysis and Policy Proposals," secret, declassified April 4, 2000.

4. Ibid.

5. Ibid.

6. Robin Raphel, letter to Peter Tomsen, May 1, 1997, confidential, declassified March 23, 2000.

7. Zalmay Rasoul, a member of the royal Mohammadzai clan, was also Zahir Shah's doctor. He would later become the director of President Hamid Karzai's National Security Council. Karzai appointed him Afghan foreign minister in 2010.

8. Daoud Yaqub was an Afghan émigré who had earned a law degree from the University of Pittsburgh. At the time of the State Department meeting, he was managing the Afghanistan Foundation, a lobbying group founded by former Congressman Don Ritter (R-PA). It operated on a shoestring budget with a staff of two. The second staffer left because, unlike Daoud Yaqub, he was unable to work pro bono.

9. Daoud Yaqub, e-mail to author, September 7, 2009.

10. Ibid.

11. Marc Kauffman and Robert E. Pierre, "Chicago Brothers Shape U.S. Policy on Afghanistan," *Washington Post*, November 8, 2001.

12. Abdul Haq, "Afghanistan Won't Be a U.S. or Soviet Puppet," letter to the editor, *New York Times*, June 9, 1989.

13. This and other excerpts are taken from Abdul Haq's 2001 plan, "Working Plan for Peace and Stability," June 17, 2001, Meeker, Colorado. A copy is in the author's files.

14. Some of the states emerging from the former Soviet Union asked Russia to withdraw the KGB border guards from their territory. They included Ukraine, Uzbekistan, Georgia, Azerbaijan, and the three Baltic states. For security and political reasons after their independence, Tajikistan, Armenia, Kyrgyzstan, Kazakhstan, and Moldova requested that Russia not withdraw the border guards.

15. Two months before this, in a discussion with an Afghan visitor near Dushanbe, Masood had listed forty-one mistakes that he had committed after Najib's ouster. Chief among them was tolerating untrustworthy politicians—a clear jab at Rabbani.

16. Masood's comments during our May 23–24, 2001, meetings in Dushanbe are drawn, in part, from three classified cables I sent from the American embassy in Dushanbe to the State Department: Tashkent 2061, "June 23 First Masood-Haq Meeting, Dushanbe," June 29, 2001, confidential, declassified September 14, 2004, 200401516; Tashkent 2059, "Abdul Haq June 23 One-on-One Meeting with Masood," June 29, 2001, confidential, declassified September 14, 2004, 200401516; Tashkent 2060, "AmCit Mediators' June 24 Meeting with Masood," June 29, 2001, confidential, declassified September 14, 2004. I also referred to the diary I kept on the trip.

17. Amrullah Saleh became the director of the powerful Afghan Intelligence Service after 9/11. He was one of the many bright, young, dedicated Afghans Masood attracted during the long Afghan war. He was a Panshiri. Masood assigned him liaison duties with foreign intelligence agencies. Saleh's views on the emancipation of Afghan women—his wife did not practice purdah—did not affect his virtual father-son relationship with Masood. "I told him that the people would not like that," Masood told a reporter, "but he did not change." Piotr Balcervorwicz, "The Last Interview with Ahmad Shah Masood," August 2001, www.orient.uw.edu.pl/balcerowicz/texts/Ahmad_Shah_Masood_en.htm.

18. Tashkent 2061.

19. Tashkent 2060.

20. Ibid.

21. Concerns over accounting for spent funds and bureaucratic snags delayed disbursement of the State Department's $100,000 pledge to support the loya jirga effort. The first tranche did not clear the bank until December 2001, after the Taliban's defeat and two days before the Bonn Accord was signed. Funding was no longer an issue by then. The international community paid for the Bonn Conference and the two loya jirgas that followed in 2002 and 2004.

22. Tomsen to Rocca letter, July 20, 2001.

23. John F. Dickerson, Elaine Shannon, Mark Thompson, Douglas Waller, Michael Weisskopf in Washington; Hannah Bloch and Tim McGirk in Islamabad; Cathy Booth Thomas in Dallas; Wendy Cole and Marguerite Michaels in Chicago; Bruce Crumley in Paris; James Graff in Brussels; David Schwartz in Phoenix; and Michael Ware in Kabul, "Special Report: The Secret History. They Had A Plan," *Time*, August 12, 2002.

24. Craig Pyes, Sebastian Rotella, and David Zucchino, "Fraudulent Passports Key Weapon for Terrorists," *Los Angeles Times*, December 16, 2001; Kathy Gannon, "Afghan Leader Allegedly Slain on bin Ladin's Order," Associated Press, August 16, 2002; Matthew Campbell, "How They Killed the Afghan Lion," *The Times*

(London), September 23, 2001; Edward Girardet, "Was the Masood Killing a Signal to Start Airliner Attacks on America?" *Independent News*, September 19, 2001.

25. Campbell, "How They Killed the Afghan Lion"; Lawrence Wright, *The Looming Tower: Al-Qaeda and the Road to 9/11* (New York: Alfred A. Knopf, 2006), 355; Bruce Crumley, "Terror Probe: Unmasking the Killer of an Anti-Taliban Leader," *Time*, December 17, 2001; Pyes et al., "Fraudulent Passports."

26. William Branigin, "Masood's Assassins Had Wider Target," *Washington Post*, November 6, 2001, A11.

27. Ibid.

28. Afghans and Iranians argue with each other over Rumi's birthplace. Afghans insist on Balkh; Iranians on Mashad.

29. The description of Masood Khalili's last few days with Ahmed Shah Masood are taken from his recollections as conveyed to the author in numerous conversations. They began on September 1–3, 2002, at his ambassadorial residence in New Delhi and continued periodically until January 9, 2010, when he phoned the author from Turkey after he had received the manuscript excerpts. On that occasion, Ambassador Khalili added to and corrected the manuscript excerpts before they were put in final form.

30. Hafez was born in 1315 and died in 1390. Many Afghans memorize entire poems by Hafez, reciting stanzas in their daily lives.

31. The source of Colonel Sultan Imam's reaction to 9/11 must remain anonymous.

22—YANKEE MEETS TRIBESMAN

1. Keith Dovkants, "Rebel Chief Begs: Don't Bomb Now; Taliban Will Be Gone in a Month," *Evening Standard* (London), October 5, 2001.

2. "McChrystal's Frank Talk on Afghanistan," *Sixty Minutes*, September 27, 2009.

3. Tommy Franks, *American Soldier* (New York: HarperCollins, 2004), 322.

4. Vice President Dick Cheney, "Remarks to the Multinational Force of Observers: South Camp—Sharm el-Shekh, Egypt, Wednesday, March 13, 2002," available at U.S. Embassy, Israel, http://telaviv.usembassy.gov/publish/press/visits/march02/cheney3.html.

5. Bob Woodward, *Bush at War* (New York: Simon and Schuster, 2002), 86–87, 101.

6. Ian S. Livingston, Heather L. Messera, and Michael O'Hanlon, "Afghanistan Index: Tracking Variables of Reconstruction and Security in Post-9/11 Afghanistan," Figure 2.10, "Annual Opium Production in Afghanistan (Metric Tons) and Percentage of Global Production, 1990–2009," 24, www.brookings.edu/~/media/Files/Programs/FP/afghanistan%20index/index20100731.pdf.

7. Ahmed Rashid, "Islamabad's Lingering Support for Islamic Extremists Threatens Pakistan-Afghanistan Ties," Eurasianet.org, July 23, 2003, www.eurasianet

.org/departments/insight/articles/eav072303a.shtml; "Musharraf's Memoir Released—Pakistan Leader Spells Out Allegations of U.S. Intimidation After 9/11," Associated Press, September 25, 2006, www.msnbc.msn.com/id/15003128; Franks, *American Soldier*, 256.

8. Syed Saleem Shahzad, "Pakistan Produces the Goods Again," *Asia Times*, August 4, 2004.

9. George Tenet, *At the Center of the Storm: My Years at the CIA* (New York: HarperCollins, 2007), 281, 285.

10. Shahzad, "Pakistan Produces the Goods Again."

11. Amin Tarzi, "Pakistani Islamist Opens Pandora's Box," Radio Free Europe/Radio Liberty, August 18, 2005; Paul McGeough, "U.S. Fury at Wild West Militants Who Flee Back to Pakistan," *Sydney Morning Herald*, August 22, 2005.

12. Husain Haqqani, "Pakistan Is Playing a Cat and Mouse Game," *Gulf News*, October 19, 2005. Under American pressure, Abdul Latif Hakimi was finally arrested in 2005 and turned over to the Afghan government. Several spokesmen replaced him, carrying on his public relations role in Quetta for the Taliban.

13. Raja Asghar, "Pakistan Doesn't Expect Warlord to Return," Reuters, February 11, 2002.

14. The Specially Designated Global Terrorist list is maintained by the U.S. Treasury Department.

15. In February 2002, the Iranian government closed Hekmatyar's office in Tehran, announcing that it was because he "voiced hostility to the presence of foreign peacekeeping troops in Afghanistan and acted against Iranian national security." Asghar, "Pakistan Doesn't Expect Warlord to Return."

16. Janullah Hashimzada, "Renegade Afghan Commander Urges War," Associated Press, September 5, 2002.

17. Rebecca Leung, "Clark's Take on Terror: What Bush's Ex-Advisors Say About Efforts to Stop War on Terror," CBS News, March 21, 2004; Ahto Lobjak, "Afghanistan: NATO's Top General Says Taliban Defeated," Radio Free Europe/Radio Liberty, August 13, 2004. General Jones, after retiring, later changed his assessment, stating in 2008, "Make no mistake, NATO is not winning in Afghanistan." Tim Reid, "General James Jones in Frame to Be Barack Obama's National Security Adviser," *The Sunday Times* (London), November 22, 2008.

18. Eric Blehm, *The Only Thing Worth Dying For* (New York: HarperCollins, 2010), 77; Woodward, *Bush at War*, 317.

19. Tenet, *At the Center of the Storm*, 143. See also "Intelligence Policy, Staff Statement No. 7," National Commission on Terrorist Attacks, www.9-11commission.gov/staff_statements_7.pdf.

20. *Afghan Warrior: The Life and Death of Abdul Haq*, BBC documentary, Torch Productions, London, directed by Malcolm Brinkworth, 2003.

21. Woodward, *Bush at War*, 243.

22. Gary Schroen, *First In: An Insider's Account of How the CIA Spearheaded the War on Terror* (New York: Presidio Press, 2005).

23. After 9/11, the world media universally referred to the Masood-created United Front as the Northern Alliance. The Northern Alliance leaders supporting the American-organized Operation Enduring Freedom campaign included the core Northern Alliance Tajiks; Panshiri military commanders Mohammad Fahim, Bismullah Khan, and intelligence chief Aref Sarwari; northern-tier Uzbek general Rashid Dostum; Tajik generals Mohammad Atta and Daoud Khan; Hazarat leader Ustad Karim Khalili in the Hazarajat; Pashtun Haji Abdul Qadir in the east; and Ismael Khan in the west.

24. Barnett R. Rubin, *Afghanistan Case Study*, Stanford-Brookings/Center on International Cooperation Joint Project, 5; Franks, *American Soldier*, 312; Schroen, *First In*, 207, 125.

25. According to a Masood adviser who wished to remain anonymous, in 2000 and 2001 Masood refused requests by the American and French governments to insert foreign troops into Northern Alliance–controlled areas.

26. Anonymous source, interview with author, November 3, 2007; *Afghan Warrior* (BBC documentary).

27. Barbara Slavin and Jonathan Weisman, "Taliban Foe's Death Sparks Criticism of U.S. Goals," *USA Today*, October 31, 2001.

28. Robert Novak, "The Taliban's nemesis," *Townhall Daily*, October 1, 2001; Dovkants, "Rebel Chief Begs."

29. *Afghan Warrior* (BBC documentary).

30. Ibid.

31. The account of Abdul Haq's October 21–26, 2001, trip into Afghanistan was mostly taken from the 2003 BBC documentary *Afghan Warrior* (cited above) and my own interviews with members of Haq's family, including a February 18, 2007, conversation with Haq's nephew Khushal Arsala. Two survivors from Haq's ill-fated expedition were interviewed in the BBC show.

32. *Afghan Warrior* (BBC documentary).

33. Khushal Arsala, e-mail to author, November 16, 2009.

34. Blehm, *The Only Thing Worth Dying For*, 59.

35. *Afghan Warrior* (BBC documentary); Khushal Arsala, interview with author, November 1, 2009.

36. *Afghan Warrior* (BBC documentary).

37. Blehm, *The Only Thing Worth Dying For*, 59.

38. Except for Izatullah, the rest of Haq's group eluded Taliban capture and made their way back to Pakistan. Izatullah was caught, shot, and thrown into a well. Unsure whether he was dead, one of the Taliban shouted out that Izatullah's father wanted to know if he was still alive. When Izatullah weakly responded that he was, they fired down into the well, finishing him off.

39. Whitney Azoy, "Doubts and Truths About Abdul Haq," *Bangor Daily News*, November 5, 2001; Slavin and Weisman, "Taliban's Foe's Death Sparks Criticism."

40. Robert McFarlane, "The Tragedy of Abdul Haq: How the CIA Betrayed an Afghan Freedom-Fighter," editorial, *Wall Street Journal*, November 2, 2001.

41. Ahmed Rashid, *Descent into Chaos: The United States and the Failure of Nation Building in Pakistan, Afghanistan, and Central Asia* (New York: Penguin, 2008), 88.

42. Slavin and Weisman, "Taliban Foe's Death Sparks Criticism."

43. Blehm, *The Only Thing Worth Dying For*, 80.

44. Rashid, *Descent into Chaos*, 91.

45. Ibid., 92.

46. Daoud Mir, "2001–2004: Hamed Karzai and A. Z. Masood," unpublished paper, October 20, 2009, 2, in author's files; Dexter Filkins and Carlotta Gall, "Pakistanis Again Said to Evacuate Allies of Taliban," *New York Times*, November 24, 2001.

47. Rashid, *Descent into Chaos*, 91–93.

48. Ibid.

49. Philip Smucker, "How Bin Laden Slipped the Net," *Hamilton Spectator*, March 7, 2002.

50. U.S. Senate, Senate Foreign Relations Committee, Majority Staff Report, "Tora Bora Revisited: How We Failed to Get Bin Laden and Why It Matters Today," November 30, 2009, 4; Smucker, "How Bin Laden Slipped the Net"; United States Special Operations Command (USSOCOM), History and Research Office, *United States Special Operations Command History*, 6th ed., March 31, 2008, 91. The Special Operations official history estimated that between 500 and 2,000 al-Qaeda fighters were at Tora Bora.

51. Tarzi, "Pakistani Islamist Opens Pandora's Box."

52. USSOCOM, *United States Special Operations Command History*, 98, 101.

53. Smucker, "How Bin Laden Slipped the Net."

54. Barry Bearak, Hannah Bloch, Matt Forney, and Mark Thompson, "Tribal Area of Pakistan Gives Refuge to al Qaeda Fighters Fleeing Caves," *New York Times*, December 31, 2001, B5.

55. Tenet, *At the Center of the Storm*, 226; Mary Anne Weaver, "Lost at Tora Bora," *New York Times Magazine*, September 11, 2005; Bearak et al., "Tribal Area of Pakistan Gives Refuge."

56. Weaver, "Lost at Tora Bora."

57. Western intelligence agencies and the media were unable to confirm the precise date when bin Laden or his family members departed Tora Bora.

58. Tenet, *At the Center of the Storm*, 226.

59. Josh Tyrangiel, Hannah Bloch, Matthew Forney, and Mark Thompson, "Inside the Tora Bora Caves," *Time*, December 24, 2001.

60. USSOCOM, *United States Special Operations Command History*, 101.

61. Anthony Loyd, "Fear Vendetta and Treachery—How We Let Bin Laden Get Away," *The Times*, December 3, 2002; Tommy Franks, "War of Words," op-ed, *New York Times*, October 14, 2004; USSOCOM, *United States Special Operations Command History*, 101. It was reported that "General Tommy R. Franks anticipated that ... resistance from Taliban and al-Qaeda fighters would collapse. He did not,

however, position a blocking force to meet them as they fled. Some Bush administration officials now acknowledge privately they consider that a mistake." Barton Gellman, "Second-Guessing Actions in Afghanistan," *Washington Post*, October 22, 2004; Bruce Riedel, *The Search for Al Qaeda, Its Leadership, Ideology, and Future* (Washington, DC: Brookings Institution Press; 2008), 87.

62. Murray Campbell, "See Omar Run: For Someone Who Rarely Left the House," *Toronto Globe and Mail*, January 12, 2002.

63. "U.S. Struggles to Find Allies in Anti-Terror Hunt," Dow Jones International News, January 21, 2002.

64. Christina Lamb, "'I'm Not Mullah Omar' Says the Man on CIA Wanted Poster," *Sunday Telegraph* (London), October 13, 2002.

65. Blehm, *The Only Thing Worth Dying For*, 71, 85–87.

66. "Campaign Against Terror. Interview: U.S. Army Captain Jason Amerine," *Frontline*, PBS, July 12, 2002, www.pbs.org/wgbh/pages/frontline/shows/campaign/interviews/amerine.html.

67. "US Struggles to Find Honest Allies in Anti-Terror Hunt."

68. According to Peter Cheney, "Afghans Flock to Omar's Once Palatial Digs," *Toronto Globe and Mail*, December 13, 2001, Omar's bedroom and its attached bathroom were the only structures still in reasonably good shape after the American bombing. The bedroom boasted formica-laminated cabinets not found in normal Afghan homes. The bathroom was painted entirely in pink.

69. Sarah Chayes, *The Punishment of Virtue* (New York: Penguin, 2006), 60–62, 73.

70. Chayes, *Punishment of Virtue*, 79.

71. Scott Johnson, Evan Thomas, et al., "Mullah Omar Off the Record," *Newsweek*, January 21, 2002; "US Struggles to Find Honest Allies in Anti-Terror Hunt."

72. Norimitsu Onishi, "Afghan Warlords and Bandits Are Back in Business," *New York Times*, December 28, 2001, 13.

23—FROM VICTORY TO STALEMATE

1. Peter Tomsen, testimony to the Committee on International Relations, United States House of Representatives, June 19, 2003, from prepared statement.

2. On September 5, 2002, perhaps in a deliberate attempt to overlap with the September 5 attack on Karzai in Kandahar, terrorists in Kabul detonated two bombs in midafternoon: A small bomb on an abandoned bicycle exploded in Kabul and a large one in a car exploded when a crowd gathered at the site, killing and injuring over twenty Afghans. See www.pbs.org/newshour/bb/asia/july-dec02/Afghan_9-5.html. Also see BBC News, "Karzai Survives Attempt on His Life," September 5, 2002, http://news.bbc.co.uk/2/hi/south_asia/2238428.stm. According to a UN report, "While Afghanistan's first suicide attack occurred on 9 September 2001, the tactic remained rare until 2005. Since then, the suicide attack has become

increasingly commonplace in the Afghan theatre. While suicide bombers else-where in the world tend not to be poor and uneducated, Afghan suicide bombers appear to be young, uneducated and drawn from madrassas across the border in Pakistan." See United Nations Assistance Mission in Afghanistan, "Suicide Attacks in Afghanistan (2001–2007)," September 9, 2007, www.reliefweb.int/rw/RW Files2007.nsf/FilesByRWDocUnidFilename/EKOI-76W52H-Full_Report.pdf/ $File/Full_Report.pdf.

3. Thomas Barfield, "The Roots of Failure in Afghanistan," *Current History*, December 2008, 415; Christina Lamb, "The Taliban Will 'Never Be Defeated,'" *Sunday Times* (London), June 7, 2009, www.timesonline.co.uk/tol/news/world/asia/article6445981.ece.

4. *Daily News* (Pakistan), September 7, 2002.

5. Dexter Filkins, "Right at the Edge," *New York Times Magazine*, September 5, 2008; Ann Scott Tyson, "Border Complicates War in Afghanistan: Insurgents Are Straddling Pakistani Line," *Washington Post*, April 4, 2008, A1; Zaheerul Hassan, "NATO's Senseless Aggressiveness in FATA," *Frontier Post*, June 16, 2008; *Pakistani Daily News*, September 7, 2002; Peter Tomsen, testimony to U.S. Senate, Foreign Relations Committee, October 16, 2003; Mark Mazzetti and Eric Schmitt, "Pakistanis Aided Attack in Kabul, U.S. Officials Say," *New York Times*, August 1, 2008; Ed Johnson, "Most Afghan Suicide Bombers Trained in Pakistan," Bloomberg, September 9, 2007; "UN: Most Afghan Suicide Attacks Start in Pakistan," *Washington Post*, September 9, 2007; Fraser Nelson, "Don't Mention the Afghan-Pakistan War," *The Spectator*, July 26, 2008; Christina Lamb, "Taliban Leader Killed by SAS Was Pakistan Officer," *Sunday Times* (London), October 12, 2008.

6. Douglas Jehl, "Afghan Official Says Pakistanis Helped bin Laden Evade Capture," *New York Times*, February 13, 2002; Peter Tomsen, "Return of the Taliban," *Frontline* interview, October 3, 2006, www.pbs.org/wgbh/pages/frontline/taliban/interviews/tomsen.html.

7. Nelson, "Don't Mention the Afghan-Pakistan War." A few days after the stadium attack, Afghan security officials arrested a Ministry of Defense brigadier for facilitating the attempt on Karzai's life on behalf of the Haqqani Network and al-Qaeda in North Waziristan. Further investigation revealed that the gunman's text messages back to Pakistan during the firefight were in Urdu, the common language in Pakistan. The last Urdu-language text message, sent from the terrorists' base in Pakistan to one of the dying terrorists, proclaimed, "Now you can go to Allah."

8. Mazzetti and Schmitt, "Pakistanis Aided Attack in Kabul"; Johnson, "Most Afghan Suicide Bombers Trained in Pakistan"; "UN: Most Afghan Suicide Attacks Start in Pakistan," *Washington Post*, September 9, 2007.

9. Combating Terrorist Center, "The 2008 Belgium Cell and FATA's Terrorist Pipeline," *Sentinel* 2, no. 4 (2009).

10. Sebastian Rotella, "Famed French Judge Bruguiere Tells of a Troubled Pakistan," http://articles.latimes.com/2009/nov/04/world/fg-terror-judge4.

11. The source is a U.S. intelligence official in a position to know.

12. Emily Wax, "In Pakistan, U.S. Envoy Courts No. 2 General," *Washington Post*, November 21, 2007, A12.

13. U.S. Department of State, "Country Reports on Terrorism, 2008," April 30, 2009, Chapter 5; Ed Royce, "Afghanistan Teetering on the Edge," *Orange County Register*, June 23, 2004.

14. "Afghanistan Presidential Election Results—2004," www.iec.org.af/Public _html/Election%20Results%20Website/english/english.htm.

15. Central Intelligence Agency, "World Factbook, South Asia: Afghanistan, 2009 (see https://www.cia.gov/library/publications/the-world-factbook/geos/ af.html); United Nations World Food Program, "Where We Work: Afghanistan," 2009 (see www.wfp.org/countries/afghanistan).

16. Elizabeth Neuffeur, "New Cabinet Finds a State in Stark Disarray," *Boston Globe*, December 24, 2001.

17. Major General Charles Campbell, Memorandum to CentCom Commander General Tommy Franks, secret/NOFORN, March 8, 2002, declassified with redactions April 22, 2010, 5, 6, 7, 12, 13, 15.

18. Rhoda Margesson, "United Nations Assistance Mission in Afghanistan," Congressional Research Service, July 30, 2009, 7.

19. Commission on Presidential Debates, "October 11, 2000; The Second Gore-Bush Presidential Debate," Debate Transcript, www.debates.org/index.php?page =october-11-2000-debate-transcript.

20. Peter Tomsen, "A Rebuilding Plan That Already Needs Repair," *Washington Post*, October 27, 2002, B03.

21. David Rhode and David E. Sanger, "Losing the Advantage: How the Good War in Afghanistan Went Bad," *New York Times*, August 12, 2007.

22. Afghan Freedom Support Act, 2003; Peter Tomsen, "United States Policy in Afghanistan: Current Issues in Reconstruction," statement submitted to the U.S. House of Representatives, Committee on International Relations, for a hearing on June 19, 2003.

23. Peter Tomsen, "Statement on Afghanistan in Pursuit of Security and Democracy," submitted to the Senate Foreign Relations Committee, U.S. House of Representatives, October 16, 2003.

24. United Nations, "Agreement on Provisional Arrangements in Afghanistan Pending the Re-Establishment of Permanent Government Institutions," December 2001, www.un.org/News/dh/latest/afghan/afghan-agree.htm.

25. Peter Tomsen, "A Delicate Balance: Kabul and the Provinces," op-ed, *Los Angeles Times*, February 24, 2002.

26. Kim Sengupta, "Afghan Warlord Agrees to Hand Over His Weapons to British Team," *The Independent*, December 4, 2003; Ahmed Rashid, "Team Approach Spreads in Afghanistan, but Security Worries Remain," *Eurasia Insight*, August 7, 2003, www.eurasianet.org/departments/insight/articles/eavo80703.shtml.

27. Rhode and Sanger, "Losing the Advantage."

28. In mid-2010, Zaman was killed during a trip into Afghanistan. In the Pashtunwali tradition of restorative justice to end vendettas for the sake of tribal harmony, the families of the deceased Haji Qadir and Zaman, with President Hamid Karzai's help, organized a large jirga that restored peace.

29. Campbell, Memorandum to Franks, 17.

30. Ibid., 25–26.

31. Ibid., 20. The report noted that "the ANA would be the instrument by which Afghans would be freed from armed factionalism . . . [and] the instrument by which other military structures are rendered illegal" (p. 4).

32. Kristin Roberts, "U.S. Lacks Detailed Plan for Afghan Forces—Report," Reuters, June 18, 2008.

33. U.S. Government Accountability Office, "Afghan Security: Further Congressional Action May Be Needed to Ensure Completion of a Detailed Plan to Develop and Sustain Capable Afghan National Security Forces," Report to Congressional Committees, June 2008, available at www.gao.gov/new.items/do8661.pdf.

34. *The U.S. Army/Marine Corps Counterinsurgency Field Manual*, with Forewords by General David H. Petraeus, Lieutenant General James F. Amos, and Lieutenant Colonel John A. Nagl, and a new Introduction by Sarah Sewall (Chicago: University of Chicago Press, 2007). The American counterinsurgency manual gives special acknowledgment to Sir Robert Thompson along with French counterinsurgency expert David Galula and American journalist Dan Baeun. Thompson later rose to the position of defense secretary in the British government.

35. See "McChrystal's Frank Talk on Afghanistan," *60 Minutes*, CBS, September 27, 2009, www.cbsnews.com/stories/2009/09/24/60minutes/main5335445 .shtml.

36. Sir Robert Thompson, *Defeating Communist Insurgency* (New York: Praeger, 1966), 81.

37. Ashley Brown, Sam Elder, Adrian Gilbert, and Richard Williams, eds., *War in Peace* (London: Orbis, 1988).

38. Ibid., 161.

39. "McChrystal's Frank Talk on Afghanistan," *60 Minutes*.

40. Christina Lamb, "The Invisible Man," *Sunday Times* (London), March 18, 2002, www.timesonline.co.uk/tol/news/world/asia/article1511700.ece.

41. Andrew Natsios, "The AID Wars," *The American Interest*, October 2008.

42. Aram Roston, "How the US Funds the Taliban," *The Nation*, November 11, 2009; Aram Roston, "The Afghan Lobby Scam," *The Nation*, December 22, 2009.

43. With the fall of the Taliban regime, thousands of members of the Afghan diaspora returned to Afghanistan. Initially they were welcomed by local Afghans, who viewed them as technically qualified to help Afghanistan meet its massive administrative and institutional needs. Their language skills and Western orientation

gave the returning Afghans access to the international community on a far larger scale than the indigenous Afghans could ever hope to achieve. But those who came back for patriotic reasons were the minority; most arrived intending to fatten their bank accounts and leave. The heavy reliance on diaspora Afghans further set back the project of building local capacity and created mistrust between indigenous and diaspora Afghans. (See Roston, "How the US Funds the Taliban" and "The Afghan Lobby Scam," cited above.)

44. A sum of $250,000 would completely rehabitate a large village's infrastructure of roads, irrigation canals, schools, and health clinics—that was the annual cost of financing a full-time expatriate consultant working in Afghanistan. At best, only a small fraction of aid funds eventually benefited Afghans on the ground. Afghans kept asking where the money went. See Ann Jones, "Why It's Not Working in Afghanistan," *Asia Times Online*, August 30, 2006, www.atimes.com/atimes/South_Asia/HH30Df02.html.

45. Ben Arnoldy, "UN Retreat After Rigged Elections Leaves Afghans Jittery," *Christian Science Monitor*, November 9, 2009; Ashraf Haidari, "For Afghanistan's Secure Future," *Korea Times*, June 11, 2008.

46. Rajiv Chandrasekaran, "Obama, Karzai: Not So Chummy," *Washington Post*, May 6, 2009; Haidari, "For Afghanistan's Secure Future"; Rajiv Chandrasekaran, "Administration Is Keeping Ally at Arms Length," *Washington Post*, May 6, 2009.

47. Rhode and Sanger, "Losing the Advantage."

48. This account of the 2002 loya jirga is based on my interviews with loya jirga delegates and other eyewitnesses present at the events being described.

49. Chandrasekaran, "Obama, Karzai: Not so Chummy."

50. Some Afghans jokingly referred to their president as "Khaki Shah Madart," a reference to a cunning magician in Afghan history famous for manipulating others by promising them lucrative positions.

51. Jessica Leeder, "Didn't Read New Rape Law, Karzai Admits," *Globe and Mail*, April 26, 2009.

52. USAID, e-mail to the presidential palace, May 8, 2003.

53. Transparency International, Corruption Perceptions Index, 2008 and 2009. See www.transparency.org/policy_research/surveys_indices/cpi/2010; Jon Lee Anderson, "Letter from Afghanistan: The Taliban's Opium War," *New Yorker*, July 9, 2007, www.newyorker.com/reporting/2007/07/09/070709fa_fact_anderson.

54. A senior British official working in the Afghan Ministry of Defense once circulated a memo to selected members of the diplomatic and military community on the eve of a postelection cabinet reshuffle. The memo effusively praised Minister of Defense Rahim Wardak and warned of "dire consequences" if he were removed. The defense minister kept his cabinet seat. Richard Berthon, "Influence of Defense Leadership on MOD Reform, the Afghan National Army and Enduring Stability," memo to selected members of the diplomatic and military community, November 28, 2004.

55. Afghan government official who wishes to remain anonymous.

56. Daniel Cooney, "Karzai Seeks More Say Over U.S. Troops in Afghanistan; Also Wants U.S. to Hand Over All Afghan Prisoners," *Chicago Sun-Times*, May 22, 2005.

57. Paul Richter, "Bush Refuses Karzai on Troops, Captives," *Los Angeles Times*, May 24, 2005; Tim Golden, "In U.S. Report: Brutal Details of Two Afghan Inmates' Death," *New York Times*, May 20, 2005; Michael A. Fletcher, "Bush Rejects Afghan Leader's Bid for More Military Control," *Washington Post*, May 24, 2005. President Hamid Karzai had asked President Bush about having a say in U.S. military operations conducted in Afghanistan. Bush had denied the request, which angered Karzai. In an interview with CNN's *Late Edition*, Karzai said that "this is simply, simply not acceptable. We are angry about this." See "Afghan Turmoil," NewsHour with Jim Lehrer Transcript, May 23, 2005, www.pbs.org/newshour/ bb/asia/jan-june05/afghanistan_5-23.html. The Afghan president's reaction was widely reported. See, for example, "Angry Karzai Visits Bush," *Calgary Herald*, May 24, 2005.

58. David Miliband, "Richard Holbrooke's True Memorial Would Be a Lasting Peace in Afghanistan," *The Telegraph* (London), January 13, 2011.

59. "After Action Report—General Barry R. McCaffrey USA (Ret) Visit Afghanistan and Pakistan, 16–23 February 2007," USMA, West Point, New York, February 26, 2007, www.mccaffreyassociates.com/pages/documents/AAR-022 607USMA.pdf.

60. Greg Jaffe, "Effort Aims to Overhaul Afghanistan Police Force," *Washington Post*, March 12, 2010, A10.

61. "Government Trying to Hoodwink US: Fazl," *Daily Times*, August 8, 2005; Graeme Smith, "The Afghan Mission: Talking to the Taliban: Tribal Diplomacy— Pakistan's Brutal Beneficiaries Betray Their Refuge," *Globe and Mail* (Toronto), March 26, 2008, 19.

24—NEEDED: REAL CHANGE

1. For the full text of President Obama's speech, see White House, Office of the Press Secretary, "Remarks by the President on a New Strategy for Afghanistan and Pakistan," press release, March 27, 2009, www.whitehouse.gov/the_press_office/ Remarks-by-the-President-on-a-New-Strategy-for-Afghanistan-and-Pakistan/ ("White House, March 27, 2009, press release," hereafter).

2. The Pentagon stated that the "United States has committed . . . $120.9 billion to the fighting in Afghanistan since 2001," according to a Reuters article on January 29, 2009 ("U.S. Stimulus to Cost More Than Iraq, Afghan War So Far," http://blogs .reuters.com/frontrow/2009/01/29/us-stimulus-to-cost-more-than-iraq-afghan- war-so-far/). On September 28, 2009, Congressional Research Service reported that "As of July 2009, DOD's average monthly obligations for contracts and pay were about $3.6 billion for Afghanistan." The Congressional Budget Office projected that

additional war costs for the fiscal years beginning in 2010 and ending in 2019 could range from $388 billion, if troop levels were at 30,000 by 2011, to $867 billion, if troop levels were at 75,000 by about 2013 (Amy Belasco, "The Cost of Iraq, Afghanistan, and Other Global War on Terror Operations Since 9/11," Congressional Research Service, September 28, 2009, 22, 45). *Forbes* quoted OMB Director Peter Orszag as saying, "It costs about $1 million per year per soldier in the field" (Bruce Barlett, "The Cost of War," *Forbes*, November 26, 2009).

3. U.S. Department of Defense, "Report on Progress Toward Security and Stability in Afghanistan," Report to Congress in accordance with section 1230 of the National Defense Authorization Act for Fiscal Year 2008 (Public Law 110-181), as amended, and United States Plan for Sustaining the Afghanistan National Security Forces, April 2010, www.defense.gov/pubs/pdfs/Report_Final_SecDef_04 _26_10.pdf, 5, 24.

4. According to the *Washington Post*, President Obama responded to President Karzai's criticism of "some U.S. military actions in Afghanistan" and stated that partnership was a "two-way street." President Obama was quoted as saying that "we have to listen and learn. But he's [Karzai's] got to listen to us, as well." Karen DeYoung, "NATO Adopts Transition Plan for Afghanistan," *Washington Post*, November 21, 2010.

5. "ISAF Troops Placemat," NATO-ISAF, www.nato.int/isaf/docu/epub/pdf/ placemat.html.

6. DeYoung, "NATO Adopts Transition Plan." See also Andrew Winning, "Britain Confirms Afghan Combat Mission to End 2015," Star Online, August 31, 2010.

7. White House, March 27, 2009, press release.

8. White House, Office of the Press Secretary, "Remarks by the President in Address to the Nation on the Way Forward in Afghanistan and Pakistan," press release, December 1, 2009, www.whitehouse.gov/the-press-office/remarks-president -address-nation-way-forward-afghanistan-and-pakistan ("White House, December 1, 2009, press release," hereafter).

9. Andrew England, "Dramatic Shift in Iraq's Anbar Province," *Financial Times*, March 4, 2010.

10. The transfer of lead responsibility to the Afghan government was first carried out, at Karzai's insistence, in the Kabul capital region in 2009. In mid-2010, the timeline for shifting security responsibilities for specific Afghan provinces to the ANSF was postponed to the spring of 2011.

11. Institute for the Study of War, "Afghan National Army," www.understand ingwar.org/themenote/afghanistan-national-army-ana; Joshua Partlow, "Milestone in Training Afghan Forces," *Washington Post*, November 9, 2010, A6.

12. U.S. Department of Defense, "Report on Progress."

13. Kate Brannan, "U.S. Adds Staff as Afghan Security Forces Grow," *Defense News*, May 25, 2010.

14. President Karzai's Inauguration Speech, November 19, 2009, released by the Afghan Mission at the United Nations, New York. The transition to an Afghan security lead was also announced at the International Conference on Afghanistan, known as the "London Conference." See Government of the United Kingdom, "London Conference Sets Roadmap for Afghanistan," press release, January 28, 2010.

15. White House, December 1, 2009, press release; "Testimony by Arnold Fields, Special Inspector General for Afghanistan Reconstruction, Before the Sub-committee on International Organizations, Human Rights & Oversight, House Foreign Affairs Committee: Oversight Issues in Afghanistan," May 20, 2010, http://foreignaffairs.house.gov/111/fie052010.pdf.

. 16. Matt Kelley, "Afghanistan Becomes More Dangerous for Contractors," *USA Today*, April 22, 2010; Christine Spolar, "As Afghanistan Contracting Surges, Who's Following the Money?" *Huffington Post*, March 3, 2010.

17. Government of the United Kingdom, "London Conference Sets Roadmap."

18. U.S. Department of Defense, "Report on Progress," 39–40.

19. The United Nations Office on Drugs and Crime (UNODC) found a "strong correlation between insurgency and [opium] cultivation," reporting that "almost 80 per cent of villages with very poor security conditions grew poppy, while opium grows in only 7 per cent of villages unaffected by violence." United Nations Office on Drugs and Crime, "UNODC Predicts Stable Opium Crop in Afghanistan," February 10, 2010, www.unodc.org/unodc/en/frontpage/2010/February/unodc-predicts-stable-opium-crop-in-afghanistan.html. The UNODC's "Afghanistan Opium Survey 2010: Winter Rapid Assessment" found that opium cultivation dropped "one-third over the past two years. . . . The majority of the 20 Afghan provinces that were poppy-free in 2009 will remain so this year." Bad weather contributed to lower opium yields. In more security-stable provinces in northwestern Afghanistan, "60% (of farmers) refrained from growing opium in 2010 'because it is illegal.'" Only 39% of farmers do not cultivate poppies in less secure areas in the southwest. President Karzai stated at the London Conference in 2010 that eradication of opiates must be shown through Afghan leadership. UNODC, "Afghanistan Opium Survey 2010: Winter Rapid Assessment," February 2010, www.unodc.org/documents/frontpage/Afghanistan_Opium_Survey_2010_Final.pdf. See also Stephen Jones, U.K. Parliament, House of Commons, "Afghanistan and Narcotics: Opium Poppy Cultivation Trends, 2001–2009," March 24, 2009, SN/ IA/ 05025. Jones wrote: "Afghanistan is the world's largest producer of opiates, accounting for 93% of global opium production and over 90% of the heroin trafficked into the UK" (p. 1).

20. U.S. Department of Defense, "Report on Progress," 13.

21. Joshua Partlow, "The Brother Karzai—Powerbroker with Grip on Kandahar Is Both an Ally and Obstacle to U.S. Strategy," *Washington Post*, June 13, 2010, A1, A12.

22. Ibid.; Dexter Filkins, Mark Mazzetti, and James Risen, "Brother of Afghan Leader Said to Be Paid by C.I.A.," *New York Times*, October 27, 2009.

23. BBC News, "Record Afghanistan Drugs Bust," May 23, 2009, http://news .bbc.co.uk/2/hi/8065545.stm.

24. Richard A. Oppel Jr., "Violence Helps Taliban Undo Afghan Gains," *New York Times*, April 3, 2010; Mandy Clark, "Marines Work to Gain Trust of Afghan Locals," CBS News, May 27, 2010.

25. Dion Nissenbaum, "McChrystal Calls Marjah a 'Bleeding Ulcer' in Afghan Campaign," *McClatchy*, May 24, 2010; Carlotta Gall, "Taliban Hold Sway in Area Taken by U.S., Farmer Says," *New York Times*, May 16, 2010.

26. "Pakistani Agents Funding and Training Afghan Taliban," BBC News, June 13, 2010.

27. Liam Stack, "Militants Torch NATO Supply Trucks en Route from Pakistan to Afghanistan," *Christian Science Monitor*, June 9, 2010.

28. The U.S. security treaties with Pakistan during the Cold War were directed at Soviet expansionism, not India. When India and Pakistan went to war against each other, the United States cut military aid to both countries and warned Pakistan that it would apply sanctions if it developed nuclear weapons. Pakistan's manufacture of nuclear warheads triggered a congressionally mandated aid cutoff in 1990.

29. As recounted in Chapter 17, in late 1991 Pakistani Army Chief Asif Nawaz Janjua briefly attempted to shift Pakistan toward supporting a UN-led political solution of the Afghan war, but Prime Minister Nawaz Sharif and elements in the military forced him to change his position. Asif Nawaz died under mysterious circumstances before completing his tenure as chief of army staff. See Shuja Nawaz, *Crossed Swords: Pakistan, Its Army, and the Wars Within* (New York: Oxford University Press, 2009), 599–606.

30. Matthew Rosenberg and Peter Spiegel, "U.S. Sees Hope in Pakistani Request for Help," *Wall Street Journal*, March 22, 2010. The paper contained a detailed list of Pakistani requests, ranging from military hardware (including drones) to economic aid, U.S. support for Pakistan's involvement in the Afghan peace negotiations, and U.S. assistance in the Indo-Pakistani dialogue.

31. "Senate Unanimously Passes the Kerry-Lugar Pakistan Aid Package," *California Chronicle*, June 25, 2009; Spencer Ackerman, "Kerry, Lugar, Berman 'Clarify' Pakistan Aid Bill's Intent," *Washington Independent*, October 14, 2009. The Kerry-Lugar bill's Section 302 (10) "requires an evaluation of efforts undertaken by the Government of Pakistan to (A) disrupt, dismantle, and defeat al Qaeda, the Taliban, and other extremist and terrorist groups in the FATA and settled area; (B) eliminate the safe havens of such forces in Pakistan; (C) close terrorist camps, including those of Lashkar-e-Taiba and Jaish-e-Mohammed; (D) cease all support for extremist and terrorist groups; (E) prevent attacks into neighboring countries; (F) increase oversight over curriculum in madrassas, including closing madrassas

with direct links to the Taliban or other extremist and terrorist groups; and (G) improve counterterrorism financing and anti–money laundering laws, apply for observer status for the Financial Action Task Force, and take steps to adhere to the United Nations International Convention for the Suppression of Financing of Terrorism."

32. Scott Pelley, with U.S. Secretary of State Hillary Clinton, on "America's Foreign Policy Challenges, the War on Terror, and Being the Country's Top Diplomat," *60 Minutes*, CBS, May 9, 2010. See also Rob Crilly, "Pakistani Officials Know Where Osama bin Laden Hiding: Hillary Clinton," *The Telegraph* (London), May 11, 2010.

33. Crilly, "Pakistani Officials Know Where Osama bin Laden Hiding." Pakistani officials initially ruled out Pakistani Taliban connections to the bombing, and Petraeus echoed this view. After the Panetta-Jones visit, they acknowledged Pakistani Taliban links to Shahzad.

34. Bob Woodward's *Obama's Wars* (New York: Simon and Schuster, 2010), 366.

35. Matthew Lee, "Clinton Requests Cooperation," Associated Press, published in the *Washington Times*, July 18, 2010; Jay Solomon, "Clinton Offers Aid to Doubtful Pakistanis," *Wall Street Journal*, July 19, 2010; Mark Landler, "In a Visit to Pakistan Clinton Encounters a Less Hostile Reception," *New York Times*, July 19, 2010. During her July visit Clinton witnessed the signing of a transit agreement by the Afghan and Pakistani commerce ministers. The Obama administration had urged the two countries to conclude the agreement.

36. Jonathan Burch, "Taliban Chief Orders Fighters to Kill Civilians: NATO," Reuters, July 18, 2010; Ayaz Gul, "Clinton Reaffirms US Commitment to Pakistan," Voice of America (VOA) News, July 19, 2010.

37. Karen DeYoung, "Administration to Ask for More Pakistani Aid," *Washington Post*, October 23, 2010.

38. James Bone, "U.S. Envoy Richard Holbrooke Should Tread Carefully in Afghanistan," Times Online, January 23, 2009; Woodward, *Obama's War*, 67–69.

39. According to Joe Klein, "A Captain's Story," *Time*, April 26, 2010, General McChrystal issued a series of tactical directives and rules of engagement that placed restrictions on air support to avoid civilian casualties. He allowed his soldiers to use discretion in "a matter of self-defense." U.S. troops on the ground were not happy with these new rules.

40. Elizabeth Ganshert, "The 64,000 Plus Question for Afghanistan," Radio Free Europe/Radio Liberty, April 30, 2010.

41. Matthew Rosenberg and Peter Spiegel, "U.S. Bets Best Ally in Surge Is Old One," *Wall Street Journal*, February 19, 2010.

42. BBC News reported that President Karzai did not say much to rebut the Iranian president's attacks on the United States. See "Iran Attacks US over Afghanistan," BBC News, March 10, 2010, news.bbc.co.uk/2/hi/south_asia/8559084.stm;

Rosenberg and Spiegel, "U.S. Bets Ally in Surge Is Old One"; Lyse Doucet, "Mistrust Imperils Fight Against Taliban," BBC, April 3, 2010.

43. Julian Borger and Ewen MacAskill, "US Will Appoint Afghan 'Prime Minister' to Bypass Hamid Karzai: White House Plans New Executive Role to Challenge Corrupt Government in Kabul," *The Guardian* (London), March 22, 2009; Steve Kroft, interviewing President Barack Obama on *60 Minutes*, December 7, 2009, transcript entitled "President Barack Obama, Part 1," CBS News, www.cbs news.com/stories/2009/12/12/60minutes/main5975421_page3.shtml?tag =contentMain:contentBody; Sue Pleming, "U.S. Raises Hackles with Karzai, Looks to Change," Reuters, February 13, 2009; Indira A.R. Lakshmanan, "Karzai Draws Criticism After Meeting U.S. Senators on War Plans," Bloomberg, May 7, 2009.

44. Dr. Abdullah Abdullah's father is a Pashtun, his mother a Panshiri Tajik.

45. Obaid Karki, "Carville Aids Rival of Afghanistan's Karzai," Associated Press, July 6, 2009. James Carville managed Bill Clinton's presidential election's campaign in 1992.

46. Kenneth P. Vogel, "Will Afghanistan's Elections Be Fair?" Politico, June 23, 2009. Karzai's former interior minister and presidential candidate for a few months, Ali Jalali, groused to a reporter, "Each thought they were America's favorite." See Rajiv Chandrasekaran, "A Softer Approach to Karzai," *Washington Post*, November 20, 2009.

47. Afghan Election Complaints Commission, "October 18, 2009, ECC Decision," www.ecc.org.af/en/index.php?option=com_content&view=artic;e&id=50&Itemid=56.

48. Chandrasekaran, "A Softer Approach to Karzai"; Eric Schmitt, "U.S. Envoy's Cables Show Worries on Afghan Plans," *New York Times*, January 20, 2010; Peter Gaff, "Karzai: Afghan Corruption Blown Out of Proportion," Reuters, January 8, 2010.

49. Dion Nissenbaum, "Holbrooke's Harvard Comments Slammed in Afghanistan," *McClatchy*, March 8, 2010; David Corn, "A Neocon Split on Afghanistan?" Mother Jones Blog, April 9, 2010.

50. Doucet, "Mistrust Imperils Fight"; Joshua Partlow, "Karzai Clarifies Remarks That Sparked White House 'Concern' in Call to Clinton," *Washington Post*, April 3, 2010.

51. Ibid.

52. Atia Abawi, "We Run This Country, Karzai Says of the Afghan People," CNN.com, April 23, 2010.

53. Scott Wilson and Rajiv Chandrasekaran, "Obama Makes Personal Diplomacy Part of Afghan Strategy," *Washington Post*, May 9, 2010; Karen DeYoung, "U.S. Envoy Says Relations with Afghan President Hamid Karzai Are Good," *Washington Post*, April 20, 2010.

54. Helene Cooper and Mark Landler, "U.S. Rolls Up Red Carpet for Karzai Rival," *New York Times*, May 20, 2010; Ramzy Baroud, "Karzai Kiss a Prelude to

Kandahar Storm," *Asia Times*, May 17, 2010; Howard LaFranchi, "How Hamid Karzai Resuscitated His Image," *Christian Science Monitor*, May 17, 2010; White House, Office of the Press Secretary, "Joint Statement from the President and President Karzai of Afghanistan," May 12, 2010; Nissenbaum, "McChrystal Calls Marjah a 'Bleeding Ulcer' in Afghan Campaign."

55. Nissenbaum, "McChrystal Calls Marjah a 'Bleeding Ulcer' in Afghan Campaign."

56. White House, "Joint Statement"; Karen DeYoung, "Results of Kandahar Offensive May Affect Future U.S. Moves," *Washington Post*, May 23, 2010; "Top NATO Commander Addresses Recent Taliban Gains, Vows Commitment to Security," Radio Free Europe/Radio Liberty Broadcast, May 31, 2010; Cooper and Landler, "U.S. Rolls Up Red Carpet."

57. Daniel Schuhman, "Why Did Karzai Fire Washington's Favorite?" *Mother Jones*, June 8, 2010.

58. Joshua Partlow, "Top U.S. Military, Civilian Officials Assess Gains in Afghan War," *Washington Post*, October 17, 2010, A15.

59. Greg Miller, "U.S. Military Campaign to Topple Resilient Taliban Hasn't Succeeded," *Washington Post*, October 27, 2010.

60. Joshua Partlow, "Karzai Calls on U.S. to Lighten Troop Presence," *Washington Post*, November 14, 2010, 1; David Nakamura, "Afghan Officials Play Down Karzai's Comments," *Washington Post*, November 16, 2010, A14.

61. DeYoung, "NATO Adopts Transition Plan."

25 — THE WAY AHEAD

1. A June 2010 newspaper article estimated that Afghanistan possessed nearly "$1 trillion in untapped mineral deposits." The reporter wrote "the Pentagon predicted that Afghanistan in the future could be the 'Saudi Arabia of lithium,' a raw material used to make batteries for laptops and Blackberrys." See James Risen, "U.S. Identifies Vast Mineral Riches in Afghanistan," *New York Times*, June 13, 2010.

2. The Taliban offensive to disrupt the September 2010 parliamentary elections reduced voter turnout and facilitated fraud, especially in the Pashtun belt along the Pakistani border. The net result was the Pashtun loss of over thirty seats in the Afghan parliament. In Pashtun-majority Ghazni, Hazaras won all of the eleven parliamentary seats.

3. A suicide-bombing operation against the London subway system in 2005 killed 52 people. The Laskhar-i Taiba massacre in Mumbai on November 26, 2008, killed nearly 170 people, including 6 Americans.

4. Jerry Makkon, "Guilty Plea in Failed Times Square Bombing," *Washington Post*, June 22, 2010, 2.

5. Bob Woodward, *Obama Wars* (New York: Simon and Schuster, 2010), 366.

6. Tini Tran, "As U.S. Fights, China Spends to Gain Afghan Foothold," Associated Press, July 4, 2010.

7. Saudi-Indian relations froze during the Cold War. The Indian government drifted toward the Soviet Union. It did not condemn the 1979 Soviet invasion of Afghanistan and abstained on the UN General Assembly vote condemning the Soviet invasion of Afghanistan. During an April 2010 visit to India by Prince Salman, third in line to the Saudi throne, Saudi Arabia stated its intention to nearly double oil shipments to India. In a veiled reference to Pakistan, he declared, "We condemn the plague of terrorism and we'll not accept it from any party, whoever it may be" (Mohammed Rasooldeen, "No Tolerance for Terrorism: Prince Salman Stresses Saudi Stance," *Arab News*, April 14, 2010, arabnews.com/ saudiarabia/article42942.ece). Saudi Foreign Minister Saud al-Faisal was more direct. Without elaboration, the Pakistani newspaper *Dawn* quoted Saud telling Indian journalists: "Pakistan is a friendly country. Anytime one sees a dangerous trend in a friendly country, one is not only sorry but worried" (Syed Rashid Husain, "Saudi Arabia Urges Unity Among Pak Leaders," *Dawn*, March 1, 2010). The *Dawn* article reported Saud saying, "It was the duty of all political leaders in Pakistan to unite to ensure that extremists did not achieve their objectives." India is the fourth-largest recipient of oil from Saudi Arabia after China, the United States, and Japan (Harsh V. Pant, "Saudi Arabia Woos China and India," *Middle East Quarterly* (Fall 2006): 45–52, www.mefirym.org/1019/saudi-arabia-woos-china-and -india; "India, Saudi Arabia to Sign About Ten Agreements," *Hindustantimes*, February 28, 2010, www.hindustantimes.com/restofasia/India-Saudi-Arabia-to-sign -about-ten-agreements/.

8. Declan Walsh, "Saudi Arabia Wants Military Rule in Pakistan," *The Guardian*, December 1, 2010.

9. Scott Wilson, "Abdullah Greets Obama in Saudi Arabia," *Washington Post*, June 3, 2009.

10. Margaret Coker, "Assassination Attempt Targets Saudi Prince," *Wall Street Journal*, August 29, 2009; Sheila MacVicar, "Al Qaeda Bombers Learn from Drug Smugglers: New Technique of Storing Bomb Materials Inside Body Cavity Nearly Kills a Saudi Prince," CBS News, September 28, 2009, www.cbsnews.com/stories/ 2009/09/28/eveningnews/main5347847.shtml. King Abdullah's nephew, Prince Muhammad bin Nayef, who is also son of the Saudi interior minister, was lightly injured in the attack. Only the suicide bomber, whose approach to the prince was blocked by Saudi security guards, died in the blast.

11. "Council of Senior Ulema Fatwa on Terror-Financing," May 7, 2010, circulated in a press release by the Saudi embassy in Washington on May 7, 2010.

12. Anthony Lloyd, "Terror Link Alleged as Saudi Millions Flow into Afghanistan War Zone," *The Times* (London), May 31, 2010.

13. Nicholas Watt and Vikram Dodd, "Cameron Sparks Diplomatic Row with Pakistan After 'Export of Terror' Remarks," *The Guardian*, July 28, 2010. Elaborating, the British prime minister added, "It is unacceptable for any support to be given from within Pakistan for any terrorist organizations that export terror. It is

well-documented that that has been the case in the past." The BBC noted that "what Mr. Cameron did not say was that Pakistan seems to have realized that it too is now vulnerable to the Taliban." BBC, "Cameron's New Diplomacy Brings Problems with Pakistan," August 1, 2010, www.bbc.co.uk/news/uk-10831580.

14. Shahid Ilyas, "A Friendly Afghanistan," *Daily Times*, March 2, 2010.

15. Countries currently on the State Department's list of state terrorism sponsors are Iran, Syria, Sudan, and Cuba.

INDEX

Peter Tomsen was President George H.W. Bush's special envoy to the Afghan resistance with the rank of ambassador from 1989 to 1992. In this capacity, he met many Afghan tribal leaders, commanders, and ulema who remain active today. Tomsen entered the Foreign Service in 1967 with an assignment in Thailand. He was posted to Vietnam's Mekong Delta in 1969 as a district senior advisor to a South Vietnamese lieutenant colonel. He subsequently served in India for five years, between 1971 and 1976, and in China for five years. He served in Moscow as first secretary in political section from 1977 to 1979. Between 1983 and 1985 he was the director of the State Department's Office of India, Nepal, Sri Lanka, and Maldives Affairs. He was United States deputy chief of mission in China from 1986 to 1989 and was the principal deputy assistant secretary of state for East Asian Pacific Affairs from 1993 to 1995. He was also American ambassador to Armenia from 1995 to 1998. Among the awards Ambassador Tomsen has received: three Presidential Meritorious Service Awards, two State Department Presidential Awards, one State Department Superior and two Meritorious Honor awards. He speaks Russian, Vietnamese, and Hindi-Urdu. He lives in Virginia with his wife, Kim.

PublicAffairs is a publishing house founded in 1997. It is a tribute to the standards, values, and flair of three persons who have served as mentors to countless reporters, writers, editors, and book people of all kinds, including me.

I. F. STONE, proprietor of *I. F. Stone's Weekly*, combined a commitment to the First Amendment with entrepreneurial zeal and reporting skill and became one of the great independent journalists in American history. At the age of eighty, Izzy published *The Trial of Socrates*, which was a national bestseller. He wrote the book after he taught himself ancient Greek.

BENJAMIN C. BRADLEE was for nearly thirty years the charismatic editorial leader of *The Washington Post*. It was Ben who gave the *Post* the range and courage to pursue such historic issues as Watergate. He supported his reporters with a tenacity that made them fearless and it is no accident that so many became authors of influential, best-selling books.

ROBERT L. BERNSTEIN, the chief executive of Random House for more than a quarter century, guided one of the nation's premier publishing houses. Bob was personally responsible for many books of political dissent and argument that challenged tyranny around the globe. He is also the founder and longtime chair of Human Rights Watch, one of the most respected human rights organizations in the world.

• • •

For fifty years, the banner of Public Affairs Press was carried by its owner Morris B. Schnapper, who published Gandhi, Nasser, Toynbee, Truman, and about 1,500 other authors. In 1983, Schnapper was described by *The Washington Post* as "a redoubtable gadfly." His legacy will endure in the books to come.

Peter Osnos, *Founder and Editor-at-Large*